SOCIAL SECURITY LEGISLATION 2009/10

VOLUME IV: TAX CREDITS AND HMRC-ADMINISTERED SOCIAL SECURITY BENEFITS

SOCIAL SECURITY LEGISLATION 2009/10

General Editor
David Bonner, LL.B, LL.M

VOLUME IV:
TAX CREDITS AND HMRC-ADMINISTERED SOCIAL SECURITY BENEFITS

Commentary By

Nick Wikeley, M.A. (Cantab)
Judge of the Upper Tribunal,
Emeritus Professor of Law, University of Southampton

David W. Williams, LL.M., Ph.D., C.T.A.
Judge of the Upper Tribunal,
Honorary Professor of Tax Law, Queen Mary College, London

Ian Hooker, LL.B.
Formerly Lecturer in Law, University of Nottingham,
Formerly Chairman, Social Security Tribunals

Consultant Editor
Child Poverty Action Group

SWEET & MAXWELL  THOMSON REUTERS

Published in 2009 by
Thomson Reuters (Legal) Limited (Registered in England and Wales,
Company No 1679046. Registered office and address for service:
100 Avenue Road, Swiss Cottage,
London NW3 3PF, trading as Sweet & Maxwell)

For further information on our products and services, visit
http://www.sweetandmaxwell.co.uk

Typeset by Servis Filmsetting Ltd, Stockport, Cheshire
Printed and bound in Great Britain
by Ashford Colour Press, Gosport, Hants

ISBN 978-0-414-04115-8

No natural forests were destroyed to make this product;
only farmed timber was used and replanted.

A CIP catalogue record for this book is
available from the British Library

CHILD POVERTY ACTION GROUP

The Child Poverty Action Group (CPAG) is a charity, founded in 1965, which campaigns for the relief of poverty in the United Kingdom. It has a particular reputation in the field of welfare benefits law derived from its legal work, publications, training and parliamentary and policy work, and is widely recognised as the leading organisation for taking test cases on social security law.

CPAG is therefore ideally placed to act as Consultant Editor to this 4-volume work—**Social Security Legislation 2009/10**. CPAG is not responsible for the detail of what is contained in each volume, and the authors' views are not necessarily those of CPAG. The Consultant Editor's role is to act in an advisory capacity on the overall structure, focus and direction of the work.

For more information about CPAG, its rights and policy publications or training courses, its address is 94 White Lion Street, London, N1 9PF (telephone: 020 7837 7979—website: *http://www.cpag.org.uk*).

PREFACE

Tax Credits and HMRC-administered Social Security Benefits is Volume IV of what is now a four volume series: *Social Security Legislation 2009/10.* The companion volumes are Bonner, Hooker, Poynter, White, Wikeley and Wood, *Volume I: Non Means Tested Benefits and Employment and Support Allowance,* Wood, Poynter, Wikeley and Bonner, *Volume II: Income Support, Jobseeker's Allowance, State Pension Credit and the Social Fund,* Rowland and White, *Volume III: Administration, Adjudication and the European Dimension.*

Each of the volumes in the series provides a legislative text, clearly showing the form and date of amendments, and commentary up to date to April 13, 2009.

The Tax Credits Act 2002, introducing Child Tax Credit (CTC) and Working Tax Credit (WTC) from April 2003, represented a radical shift for the benefits system and provided the initial impetus for this fourth volume in the series. Tax credits require tribunals, advisers and other practitioners to get to grips with concepts, in many ways drawn from the income tax system, which are radically different from traditional welfare state principles and which have also been substantially re-written in recent years as part of the Tax Law Rewrite Project. This volume, designed in the same format as its established companion volumes, covers CTC and WTC along with social security benefits administered by Her Majesty's Revenue and Customs (HMRC, formerly the Inland Revenue) but paid by employers: statutory sick pay (SSP), statutory maternity pay (SMP), statutory paternity pay (SPP) and statutory adoption pay (SAP). This year, following a review of the coverage of the series, we have incorporated the legislation governing Child Benefit and Guardian's Allowance into this volume, along with the expert commentary on these provisions by Ian Hooker. This volume also includes the statutory provisions relating to the child trust funds, in place since April 2005.

The tax credits scheme has yet to generate a significant body of case law. However, we have taken the opportunity in this year's seventh edition of *Volume IV* to bring the statutory text up to date, reflecting the various amendments made by regulations to the scope of WTC and CTC (as well as ironing out some wrinkles identified by some eagle-eyed readers and editing the more historical material). We have also added further commentary on key provisions such as overpayments and reporting changes. As previously, given that there continues to be considerable public interest in the issue of overpayments of tax credits, we have included the text of leaflet WTC7 on Tax Credits penalties and HMRC's revised Code of Practice 26 on the recovery of overpayments.

As well as the usual full menu of miscellaneous amendments over the past year to both the primary and the secondary legislation governing tax credits and HMRC-administered social security benefits, this year's volume also picks up changes in the rules for tax credits and allied social security benefits which are consequential upon the introduction of Employment and Support Allowance (ESA, the substantive provisions for which are covered in Volume I). In addition, the tribunal reforms brought in by the Tribunals, Courts and Enforcement Act 2007, and effective from November 3, 2008, have permitted the deletion of some redundant material. Readers are reminded that the legislation and authoritative commentary on the decision-making and appeals legislation and on the new tribunal procedural rules are to be found in Volume III of this series.

Users of the original three volumes in this series, and their predecessors, have over the years provided valuable comments which have invariably been helpful to the editors in ensuring that the selection of legislative material for inclusion and the commentary upon it reflect the sorts of difficulties encountered in practice. In doing so, readers have thus helped to shape the content of each of the volumes in the current series. We hope that readers will maintain that tradition. Please write to the General Editor of the series, Professor David Bonner, School of Law, University of Leicester, University Road, Leicester, LE1 7RH, who will pass on any comments received to the appropriate commentator.

Our gratitude also goes to the Chamber President of the Social Entitlement Chamber of the First-tier Tribunal and his staff for continuing the tradition of help and encouragement.

July, 2009

Nick Wikeley
David Williams

CONTENTS

PART I
HM REVENUE AND CUSTOMS
TAX CREDITS AND SOCIAL SECURITY

PART II
TAX CREDITS

Contents

PART III
CHILDREN AND GUARDIANS

PART IV
STATUTORY SICK PAY

Contents

PART V
STATUTORY MATERNITY PAY

PART VI
STATUTORY PATERNITY PAY
AND STATUTORY ADOPTION PAY

Contents

USING THIS BOOK: AN INTRODUCTION TO LEGISLATION AND CASE LAW

Introduction

This book is not a general introduction to, or general textbook on, the law relating to social security but it is nonetheless concerned with both of the principal sources of social security law–*legislation* (both primary and secondary) and *case law*. It sets out the text of the most important legislation, as currently in force, and then there is added commentary that refers to the relevant case law. Lawyers will be familiar with this style of publication, which inevitably follows the structure of the legislation.

This note is designed primarily to assist readers who are not lawyers to find their way around the legislation and to understand the references to case law, but information it contains about how to find social security case law is intended to be of assistance to lawyers too.

Primary legislation

Primary legislation of the United Kingdom Parliament consists of *Acts of Parliament* (also known as *statutes*). They will have been introduced to Parliament as *Bills*. There are opportunities for Members of Parliament and peers to debate individual clauses and to vote on amendments before a Bill is passed and becomes an Act (at which point the clauses become sections). No tribunal or court has the power to disapply, or hold to be invalid, an Act of Parliament unless it is inconsistent with European Community law.

An Act is known by its "short title", which incorporates the year in which it was passed (e.g. the Social Security Contributions and Benefits Act 1992), and is given a chapter number (abbreviated as, for instance, "c.4" indicating that the Act was the fourth passed in that year). It is seldom necessary to refer to the chapter number but it appears in the running heads in this book.

Each *section* (abbreviated as "s." or, in the plural, "ss.") of an Act is numbered and may be divided into *subsections* (abbreviated as "subs." and represented by a number in brackets), which in turn may be divided into *paragraphs* (abbreviated as "para." and represented by a lower case letter in brackets) and *subparagraphs* (abbreviated as "subpara." and represented by a small roman numeral in brackets). Subparagraph (ii) of para.(a) of subs.(1) of s.72 will usually be referred to simply as "s.72(1)(a)(ii)". Upper case letters may be used where additional sections or subsections are inserted by amendment and additional lower case letters may be used where new paragraphs and subparagraphs are inserted. This accounts for the rather ungainly s.171ZS of the Social Security Contributions and Benefits Act 1992 (in Vol.IV).

Sections of a large Act may be grouped into a numbered *Part*, which may even be divided into *Chapters*. It is not usual to refer to a Part or a Chapter unless referring to the whole Part or Chapter.

Where a section would otherwise become unwieldy because it is necessary to include a list or complicated technical provisions, the section may simply refer to a *Schedule* at the end of the Act. A Schedule (abbreviated as "Sch.") may be divided into paragraphs and subparagraphs and further divided into heads and subheads. Again, it is usual to refer simply to, say, "para.23(3)(b)(ii) of Schedule 3". Whereas it is conventional to speak of a section *of* an Act, it is usual to speak of a Schedule *to* an Act.

When Parliament wishes to change the law, it may do so by passing a new Act that amends a previous Act or it may do so by passing a freestanding Act, although even then consequential amendments to other legislation are usually required. Thus, for instance, when incapacity benefit was introduced by the Social Security (Incapacity for Work) Act 1994, the changes were largely made by inserting sections 30A to 30E and Part XIIA into the Social Security Contributions and Benefits Act 1992 and repealing the provisions in that Act dealing with sickness and invalidity benefit. In contrast, when jobseeker's allowance was introduced by the Jobseekers Act 1995, it was decided that the main provisions relating to the new benefit would be found in the 1995 Act itself and the 1992 Act was amended only so as to repeal, or amend, the provisions dealing with, or referring to, unemployment benefit.

When there has been a proliferation of Acts or Acts have been very substantially amended, the legislation may be consolidated in a new Act, for which there is a fast track procedure in Parliament. Only limited amendments may be made by a consolidation Act but such an Act reorganises and tidies up the legislation. Because social security law is so frequently amended, it tends to be consolidated every decade or two. The last consolidation Acts relevant to this book were the Social Security Contributions and Benefits Act 1992 (in Vols I and II) and the Social Security Administration Act 1992 (in Vol.III).

Secondary legislation

Secondary legislation (also known as *subordinate legislation* or *delegated legislation*) is made by *statutory instrument* in the form of a set of *Regulations* or a set of *Rules* or an *Order*. The power to make such legislation is conferred on ministers and other persons or bodies by Acts of Parliament. To the extent that a statutory instrument is made beyond the powers (in Latin, ultra vires) conferred by primary legislation, it may be held by a tribunal or court to be invalid and ineffective. Secondary legislation must be laid before Parliament. However, most secondary legislation is not debated in Parliament and, even when it is, it cannot be amended although an entire statutory instrument may be rejected.

A set of Regulations or Rules or an Order has a name indicating its scope and the year it was made and also a number, as in the Social Security (Disability Living Allowance) Regulations 1991 (SI 1991/2890) (the 2890th statutory instrument issued in 1991). Because there are over 3,000 statutory instruments each year, the number of a particular statutory instrument is important as a means of identification and it should usually be cited the first time reference is made to that statutory instrument.

Sets of Regulations or Rules are made up of individual *regulations* (abbreviated as "reg.") or *rules* (abbreviated as "r." or, in the plural, "rr."). An Order is made up of *articles* (abbreviated as "art."). Regulations, rules and articles may be divided into paragraphs, subparagraphs and heads. As in Acts, a set of Regulations or Rules or an Order may have one or more Schedules attached to it. The style of numbering used in statutory instruments is the same as in sections of, and Schedules to, Acts of Parliament. As in Acts, a large statutory instrument may have regulations or rules grouped into Parts and, occasionally, Chapters. Statutory instruments may be amended in the same sort of way as Acts.

Northern Ireland legislation

Most of the legislation set out in this book applies only in Great Britain, social security not generally being an excepted or reserved matter in relation to Northern Ireland. However, Orders in Council, which are statutory instruments but have the effect of primary legislation in Northern Ireland, largely replicate the primary legislation in Great Britain and enable subordinate legislation to be made that, again, largely replicates the subordinate legislation in Great Britain. Much of the commentary in this book will therefore be relevant to the equivalent provision in Northern Ireland legislation.

European Community legislation

The United Kingdom being a Member State of the European Union, European Community legislation has effect within the United Kingdom. The primary legislation is in the form of the *Treaties* agreed by the Member States. Relevant subordinate legislation is in the form of *Regulations*, adopted to give effect to provisions of the Treaties, and *Directives*, addressed to Member States and requiring them to incorporate certain provisions into their domestic laws. Directives are relevant because, where a citizen brings proceedings against an organ of the state, as is invariably the case where social security is concerned, the citizen may rely on the Directive as having direct effect if the Member State has failed to comply with it. European Community Treaties, Regulations and Directives are divided into *Articles* (abbreviated as "Art."). United Kingdom legislation that is inconsistent with European Community legislation may be disapplied. The most relevant provisions of European Community legislation are set out in Part III of *Vol.III: Administration, Appeals and the European Dimension*.

Finding legislation in this book

If you know the name of the piece of legislation for which you are looking, use the list of contents at the beginning of each volume of this book which lists the pieces of legislation contained in the volume. That will give you the paragraph reference to enable you to find the beginning of the piece of legislation. Then, it is easy to find the relevant section, regulation, rule, article or Schedule by using the running heads on the right hand pages. If you do not know the name of the piece of legislation, you will probably need to use the index at the end of the volume in order to find the relevant paragraph number but will then be taken straight to a particular provision.

    The legislation is set out as amended, the amendments being indicated by numbered sets of square brackets. The numbers refer to the numbered entries under the heading "AMENDMENTS" at the end of the relevant section, regulation, rule, article or Schedule, which identify the amending statute or statutory instrument. Where an Act has been consolidated, there is a list of "DERIVATIONS" identifying the provisions of earlier legislation from which the section or Schedule has been derived.

Finding other legislation

Legislation in its unamended form may be found on *http://www.opsi.gov.uk/ legislation/*. Obscure provisions of Great Britain social security legislation not included in this book may be found, as amended, but without a commentary, at *http://www.dwp.gov.uk/publications/specialist-guides/law-volumes/*. Northern Ireland social security legislation may be found at *http://www. dsdni.gov.uk/law_relating_to_social_security*. European Community legislation may be found at *http://eur-lex.europa.eu/en/index.htm*.

Interpreting legislation

Legislation is written in English and generally means what it says. However, more than one interpretation is often possible. Most legislation itself contains definitions. Sometimes these are in the particular provision in which a word occurs but, where a word is used in more than one place, any definition will appear with others. In an Act, an interpretation section is usually to be found towards the end of the Act or of the relevant Part of the Act. In a statutory instrument, an interpretation provision usually appears near the beginning of the statutory instrument or the relevant Part of it. In the more important pieces of legislation in this book, there is included after every section, regulation, rule, article or Schedule a list of "DEFINITIONS", showing where definitions of words used in the provision are to be found.

However, not all words are statutorily defined and there is in any event more to interpreting legislation than merely defining its terms. Decision-makers and tribunals need to know how to apply the law in different types of situations. That is where case law comes in.

Case law and the commentary in this book

In deciding individual cases, courts and tribunals interpret the relevant law and incidentally establish legal principles. Decisions on questions of legal principle of the superior courts and appellate tribunals are said to be binding on decision-makers and the First-tier Tribunal, which means that decision-makers and the First-tier Tribunal must apply those principles. Thus the judicial decisions of the superior courts and appellate tribunals form part of the law. The commentary to the legislation in this book, under the heading "GENERAL NOTE" after a section, regulation, rule, article or Schedule, refers to this *case law*.

The commentary itself in this book is not binding on any decision-maker or tribunal because it is merely the opinion of the author. It is what is actually said in the legislation or in the judicial decision that is important. The legislation is set out in this book, but it will generally be necessary to look elsewhere for the precise words used in judicial decisions. The commentary refers to decisions in a way that enables that to be done.

The largest part of the case law regarding social security benefits is still in the form of decisions of the former Social Security Commissioners and former Child Support Commissioners, who heard appeals from decisions of appeal tribunals. However, on November 3, 2008, when the functions of appeal tribunals were transferred to the First-tier Tribunal, the functions of the Social Security Commissioners and Child Support Commissioners in Great Britain were transferred to the Upper Tribunal and allocated to the Administrative Appeals Chamber of that tribunal. In Northern Ireland, which has a largely separate judiciary and tribunal system, there continue to be Commissioners.

The reporting of decisions of the Upper Tribunal and Commissioners

About 50 of the most important social entitlement decisions of the Administrative Appeals Chamber of the Upper Tribunal are selected to be "reported" each year, using the same criteria as were formerly used for reporting Commissioners' decisions in Great Britain. The selection is made by an editorial board of judges and decisions are selected for reporting only if they are of general importance and command the assent of at least a majority of the relevant judges (i.e. currently, the former Commissioners). The term "reported" simply means that they are published in printed form and on the internet (see *Finding case law*, below) with headnotes (i.e. summaries) and an index, but there are two other important consequences of a decision being reported. Reported decisions are available in all tribunal venues and can be consulted in local social security offices and some main libraries. They also have a greater precedential status than ordinary decisions (see *Judicial precedent* below).

A handful of Northern Ireland Commissioners' decisions are also selected for reporting each year, the selection being made by the Chief Social Security Commissioner in Northern Ireland.

Citing case law

Unreported decisions of the Commissioners in Great Britain were known simply by their file number, which began with a "C", as in *CIS/2287/2008*. The letters following the "C" indicated the type of benefit in issue in the case (e.g. "IS" is income support, "P" is retirement pension, and so on). Scottish and, at one time, Welsh cases were indicated by a "S" or "W" immediately after the "C", as in *CSIS/467/2007*. The last four digits indicated the calendar year in which the case was registered, rather than the year it was decided. A similar system still operates in Northern Ireland, save that the letters indicating the type of benefit appear in brackets after the numbers and, in recent years, the financial year, rather the calendar year, has been identified, as in *C 10/06-07 (IS)*.

Reported decisions of Commissioners were then given a different number, beginning with an "R". The type of benefit in issue was indicated by letters in brackets and the year in which the decision was selected for reporting or, since 2000, the year in which it was published as a reported decision, was indicated just by two digits, as in *R(IS) 2/08*. Scottish and Welsh reported decisions were not distinguished in any way. Again, in Northern Ireland there is a similar system, save that the type of benefit is identified by letters in brackets after the number, as in *R 1/07 (DLA)*.

When they are first registered, Upper Tribunal social security cases are given the same sort of file number as Commissioners' cases were but, once a case is decided, it ceases to be known by that number. Instead, the case is known by the names of the appellant and respondent (or one of each if there was more than one), with the names of individuals anonymised through the use of letters, and it is given a *neutral citation number*, indicating the year and the tribunal that made the decision. "UKUT" stands for the Upper Tribunal and "(AAC)" stands for the Administrative Appeals Chamber. In this book, the names of official bodies are also abbreviated (e.g. SSWP (for Secretary of State for Work and Pensions), HMRC (for Her Majesty's Revenue and Customs) and CMEC (for the Child Maintenance and Enforcement Commission). Thus, one case is *SSWP v JJ* [2009] UKUT 2 (AAC). For the 2009 volume of reported decisions, the same style of number is used for Upper Tribunal decisions as was used for Commissioners' decisions and, when a reported decision is being cited, this should be added after the neutral citation number. *NT v SSWP* [2009] UKUT 37 (AAC); R(DLA) 1/09 is one example.

Decisions of courts are also known by the parties' names (not usually anonymised) and, since 2001, a neutral citation number ("EWCA Civ" for the Civil Division of the Court of Appeal in England and Wales, "NICA" for the Court of Appeal in Northern Ireland, "CSIH" for the Inner House of the Court of Session (in Scotland), "UKHL" for the House of Lords, and so on). If the case is reported, a reference to the relevant set of law reports usually follows. Conventionally, this includes either the year the case was decided (in round brackets) or the year in which it was reported (in square brackets), followed by the volume number (if any), the name of the series of reports (in abbreviated form, so see the Table of Abbreviations at the beginning of each volume of this book) and the page number. *Abdirahman v Secretary of State for Work and Pensions* [2007] EWCA Civ 657; [2008] 1 W.L.R. 254 (also reported as *R(IS) 8/07*) was a Court of Appeal decision, decided in 2007 but reported in 2008 in volume 1 of the Weekly Law Reports at page 254 (and also in the 2007 volume of reported Commissioners' decisions).

It is only necessary to include the neutral citation number or a reference to a series of reports the first time a decision is cited. After that, the name of the case is usually sufficient.

All decisions on the Tribunals Service website have neutral citation numbers. If you wish to refer a tribunal or decision-maker to a decision of the Upper Tribunal that does not have a neutral citation number, contact the office of the Administrative Appeals Chamber (*adminappeals@tribunals. gsi.gov.uk*) who will provide a number and add the decision to the website.

Decision-makers and claimants are entitled to assume that judges and other members of both the First-tier Tribunal and the Upper Tribunal have immediate access to reported decisions of Commissioners or the Upper Tribunal and they need not provide copies, although it may sometimes be helpful to do so. However, where either a decision-maker or a claimant intends to rely on an unreported decision, it will be necessary to provide a copy of the decision to the judge and any other members of the tribunal. A copy of the decision should also be provided to the other party before the hearing because otherwise it may be necessary for there to be an adjournment to enable that party to take advice on the significance of the decision.

Finding case law

The extensive references described above are used so as to enable people easily to find the full text of a decision. Most decisions of any significance since the late 1990s can be found on the internet.

Decisions of the Commissioners in Great Britain and of the Upper Tribunal may be found on the Tribunals Service website at *http://www. administrativeappeals.tribunals.gov.uk/Decisions/decisions.htm*. This includes reported decisions since 1991 and other decisions considered likely to be of interest to tribunals and tribunal users since about 2000. Decisions of Commissioners in Northern Ireland may be found on *http://www.dsdni.gov. uk/index/law_and_legislation.htm*.

In addition, reported decisions of Commissioners in Great Britain were published in bound volumes by The Stationery Office and in looseleaf form by Corporate Document Services, 7 Eastgate, Leeds LS2 7LY (CDS Orderline: tel 0113 3994040) on behalf of the Department for Work and Pensions. The Department reproduce the looseleaf version on the internet (*http://www.dwp.gov.uk/publications/specialist-guides/decisions-of-the-commissioners/*), so reported decisions may be found both there and on the Tribunals Service website. Decisions of the Upper Tribunal are being included in the 2009 bound and looseleaf volumes.

Reported decisions of the Northern Ireland Commissioners are published by The Stationery Office, in the same bound volumes as Great Britain decisions since 2000 and in separate volumes before then. The Stationery Office also publishes individual Northern Ireland decisions in looseleaf form.

Copies of decisions of Commissioners or of the Administrative Appeals Chamber of the Upper Tribunal that are otherwise unavailable may be obtained from the offices of the Upper Tribunal (Administrative Appeals Chamber) or, in Northern Ireland, from the Office of the Social Security and Child Support Commissioners.

Decisions of courts in the United Kingdom may be found on, or through links from, the free website of the British and Irish Legal Information Institute, *http://www.bailii.org/*, which also carries several Northern Ireland Commissioners' decisions. It provides fairly comprehensive coverage of decisions of the House of Lords (through a link to *http://www.publications. parliament.uk/pa/ld/ldjudgmt.htm*) and most of the higher courts in England and Wales since about 1996, decisions of the Court of Session since 1998 and decisions of the Court of Appeal in Northern Ireland since 2000 (although some earlier decisions have been included, so it is always worth looking).

Decisions of the European Court of Justice (concerned with the law of the European Community) are all to be found on *http://www.curia.europa. eu*.

Decisions of the European Court of Human Rights are available at *http:// www.echr.coe.int*, using the HUDOC database.

Most decisions of the courts in social security cases, including decisions of the European Court of Justice on cases referred by United Kingdom courts and tribunals, are reported with the decisions of the Commissioners and Upper Tribunal and may therefore be found on the same websites and in the same printed series of reported decisions. So, for example, *R(I) 1/00* contains Commissioner's decisions *CSI/12/1998*, the decision of the Court of Session upholding the Commissioner's decision and the decision of the House of Lords in *Chief Adjudication Officer v Faulds* reversing the decision of the Court of Session. The most important decisions of the courts can also be found in the various series of law reports familiar to lawyers (in particular, in the *Law Reports*, the *Weekly Law Reports*, the *All England Law*

Reports, the *Public and Third Sector Law Reports*, the *Industrial Cases Reports* and the *Family Law Reports*) but these are not widely available outside academic or other law libraries, although the *All England Law Reports* are occasionally to be found in the larger public libraries. See the Table of Cases at the beginning of each volume of this book for all the places where a decision mentioned in that volume is reported.

If you know the name or number of a decision and wish to know where in a volume of this book there is a reference to it, use the Table of Cases, the Table of Upper Tribunal Decisions or the Table of Social Security Commissioners' Decisions at the beginning of the relevant volume to find the paragraph(s) where the decision is mentioned.

Judicial precedent

As already mentioned, decisions of the Upper Tribunal, the Commissioners and the higher courts in Great Britain become *case law* because they set binding precedents and which must be followed by decision-makers and the First-tier Tribunal in Great Britain. This means that, where the Upper Tribunal, Commissioner or court has decided a point of legal principle, decision-makers and appeal tribunals must make their decisions in conformity with the decision of the Upper Tribunal, Commissioner or court, applying the same principle and accepting the interpretation of the law contained in the decision. So a decision of the Upper Tribunal, a Commissioner or a superior court explaining what a term in a particular regulation means, lays down the definition of that term in much the same way as if the term had been defined in the regulations themselves. The decision may also help in deciding what the same term means when it is used in a different set of regulations, provided that the term appears to have been used in a similar context.

Only decisions on points of law set precedents that are binding and, strictly speaking, only decisions on points of law that were necessary to the overall conclusion reached by the Upper Tribunal, Commissioner or court are binding. Other parts of a decision (which used to be known as *obiter dicta*) may be regarded as helpful guidance but need not be followed if a decision-maker or the First-tier Tribunal is persuaded that there is a better approach. It is particularly important to bear this in mind in relation to older decisions of Social Security Commissioners because, until 1987, the right of appeal to a Commissioner was not confined to points of law.

Where there is a conflict between precedents, a decision-maker or the First-tier Tribunal is generally free to choose between decisions of equal status. For these purposes, most decisions of the Upper Tribunal and decisions of Commissioners are of equal status. However, a decision-maker or First-tier Tribunal should generally prefer a reported decision to an unreported one unless the unreported decision was the later decision and the Commissioner or Upper Tribunal expressly decided not to follow the earlier reported decision. This is simply because the fact that a decision has been reported shows that at least half of the relevant judges of the Upper Tribunal or the Commissioners agreed with it at the time. A decision of a Tribunal of Commissioners (i.e. three Commissioners sitting together) or a decision of a three-judge panel of the Upper Tribunal must be preferred to a decision of a single Commissioner or a single judge of the Upper Tribunal.

A single judge of the Upper Tribunal will normally follow a decision of a single Commissioner or another judge of the Upper Tribunal, but is not bound to do so. A three-judge panel of the Upper Tribunal will generally follow a decision of another such panel or of a Tribunal of Commissioners, but similarly is not bound to do so, whereas a single judge of the Upper Tribunal will always follow such a decision.

Strictly speaking, the Northern Ireland Commissioners do not set binding precedent that must be followed in Great Britain but their decisions are relevant, due to the similarity of the legislation in Northern Ireland, and are usually regarded as highly persuasive with the result that, in practice, they are generally given as much weight as decisions of the Great Britain Commissioners. The same approach is taken in Northern Ireland to decisions of the Upper Tribunal on social security matters and to decisions of the Great Britain Commissioners.

Decisions of the superior courts in Great Britain and Northern Ireland on questions of legal principle are almost invariably followed by decision-makers, tribunals and the Upper Tribunal, even when they are not strictly binding because the relevant court was in a different part of the United Kingdom or exercised a parallel–but not superior– jurisdiction.

Decisions of the European Court of Justice come in two parts: the Opinion of the Advocate General and the decision of the Court. It is the decision of the Court which is binding. The Court is assisted by hearing the Opinion of the Advocate General before itself coming to a conclusion on the issue before it. The Court does not always follow its Advocate General. Where it does, the Opinion of the Advocate General often elaborates the arguments in greater detail than the single collegiate judgment of the Court. Decision-makers, tribunals and Commissioners must apply decisions of the European Court of Justice, where relevant to cases before them, in preference to other authorities binding on them.

The European Court of Human Rights in Strasbourg is quite separate from the European Court of Justice in Luxembourg and serves a different purpose: interpreting and applying the European Convention on Human Rights, which is incorporated into United Kingdom law by the Human Rights Act 1998. Since October 2, 2000, public authorities in the United Kingdom, including courts, Commissioners, tribunals and decision-makers have been required to act in accordance with the incorporated provisions of the Convention, unless statute prevents this. They must take into account the Strasbourg case law and are required to interpret domestic legislation, so far as it is possible to do so, to give effect to the incorporated Convention rights. Any court or tribunal may declare secondary legislation incompatible with those rights and, in certain circumstances, invalidate it. Only the higher courts can declare a provision of primary legislation to be incompatible with those rights, but no court, tribunal or Upper Tribunal can invalidate primary legislation. The work of the Strasbourg Court and the impact of the Human Rights Act 1998 on social security are discussed in the commentary in Part IV of *Vol.III: Administration, Appeals and the European Dimension*.

See the note to s.3(2) of the Tribunals, Courts and Enforcement Act 2007 in Part V of *Vol.III: Administration, Appeals and the European Dimension*) for a more detailed and technical consideration of the rules of precedent.

Other sources of information and commentary on social security law

For a comprehensive overview of the social security system in Great Britain, CPAG's *Welfare Benefits and Tax Credits Handbook*, published annually each spring, is unrivalled as a practical introduction from the claimant's viewpoint.

From a different perspective, the Department for Work and Pensions publishes a number of guides to the law and to the way it applies the law, available at *http://www.dwp.gov.uk/publications/specialist-guides/*, the most important of which is the fourteen-volume *Decision Makers' Guide*. Similarly, Her Majesty's Revenue and Customs publish manuals relating to tax credits, child benefit and guardian's allowance, which they administer, see *http://www.hmrc.gov.uk/thelibrary/manuals-subjectarea.htm*. (Note that the *Child Benefit Technical Manual* (also dealing with guardian's allowance) is found under the heading "personal taxation".) These guides and manuals are extremely useful but their interpretation of the law is not binding on tribunals and the courts, being merely internal guidance for the use of decision-makers.

There are a number of other sources of valuable information or commentary on social security case law: see in particular publications such as the *Journal of Social Security Law*, CPAG's *Welfare Rights Bulletin*, *Legal Action* and the *Adviser*. As far as online resources go there is little to beat *Rightsnet* (*http://www.rightsnet.org.uk*). This site contains a wealth of resources for people working in the welfare benefits field but of special relevance in this context are Commissioners'/Upper Tribunal Decisions section of the "Toolkit" area and also the "Briefcase" area which contains summaries of the decisions (with links to the full decisions). Sweet and Maxwell's online subscription service *Westlaw* is another valuable source (*http://www.westlaw.co.uk*), as is the Merrill Corporation's *Casetrack* (*http://www.casetrack.com/ct/casetrack.nsf/index?openframeset*) and LexisNexis *Lexis* (*http://www.lexis.com*).

Conclusion

The internet provides a vast resource but a search needs to be focused. Social security schemes are essentially statutory and so in Great Britain the legislation which is set out in this book forms the basic structure of social security law. However, the case law shows how the legislation should be interpreted and applied. The commentary in this book should point the way to the case law relevant to each provision and the internet can then be used to find it where that is necessary.

CHANGE OF NAME FROM DEPARTMENT OF SOCIAL SECURITY TO DEPARTMENT FOR WORK AND PENSIONS

The Secretaries of State for Education and Skills and for Work and Pensions Order 2002 (SI 2002/1397) makes provision for the change of name from the Department of Social Security to Department for Work and Pensions. Article 9(5) provides:

"(5) Subject to article 12 [which makes specific amendments], any enactment or instrument passed or made before the coming into force of this Order shall have effect, so far as may be necessary for the purposes of or in consequence of the entrusting to the Secretary of State for Work and Pensions of the social security functions, as if any reference to the Secretary of State for Social Security, to the Department of Social Security or to an officer of the Secretary of State for Social Security (including any reference which is to be construed as such as reference) were a reference to the Secretary of State for Work and Pensions, to the Department for Work and Pensions or, as the case may be, to an officer of the Secretary of State for Work and Pensions."

TABLE OF CASES

Table of Cases

TABLE OF UPPER TRIBUNAL DECISIONS

TABLE OF SOCIAL SECURITY COMMISSIONERS' DECISIONS

TABLE OF ABBREVIATIONS USED IN THIS SERIES

(No.2) Regulations	Statutory Paternity Pay (Adoption) and Statutory Adoption Pay (Adoptions from Overseas) (No.2) Regulations 2003
1978 Act	Employment Protection (Consolidation) Act 1978
1998 Act	Social Security Act 1998
2002 Act	Tax Credits Act 2002
2004 Act	Child Trust Funds Act 2004
AA	Attendance Allowance
AAC	Administrative Appeal Chamber
AA 1992	Attendance Allowance Act 1992
AA Regulations	Social Security (Attendance Allowance) Regulations 1991
A.C.	Law Reports Appeal Cases
A.C.D.	Administrative Court Digest
ADHD	Attention Deficit Hyperactivity Disorder
Adjudication Regs	Social Security (Adjudication) Regulations 1986
Admin L.R.	Administrative Law Reports
Administration Act	Social Security Administration Act 1992
AIDS	Acquired Immune Deficiency Syndrome
All E.R.	All England Reports
All E.R. (E.C.)	All England Reports (European Cases)
AMA	Adjudicating Medical Authority
AO	Adjudication Officer
AOG	*Adjudication Officers' Guide*
ASPP	Additional Statutory Paternity Pay
A.T.C.	Annotated Tax Cases
Attendance Allowance Regulations	Social Security (Attendance Allowance) Regulations 1991
BAMS	Benefits Agency Medical Service
Benefits Act	Social Security Contributions and Benefits Act 1992
B.H.R.C.	Butterworths Human Rights Cases
B.L.G.R.	Butterworths Local Government Reports
Blue Books	*The Law Relating to Social Security*, Vols 1–11
B.M.L.R.	Butterworths Medico Legal Reports
B.P.I.R.	Bankruptcy and Personal Insolvency Reports

B.T.C.	British Tax Cases
B.W.C.C.	Butterworths Workmen's Compensation Cases
C	Commissioner's decision
C&BA 1992	Social Security Contributions and Benefits Act 1992
CAA 2001	Capital Allowance Act 2001
CAB	Citizens Advice Bureau
CAO	Chief Adjudication Officer
CBJSA	Contribution-Based Jobseeker's Allowance
C.C.L. Rep.	Community Care Law Reports
CCM	Claimant Compliance Manual
CCN	New Tax Credits Claimant Compliance Manual
C.E.C.	European Community Cases
CERA	Cortical Evoked Response Audiogram
CESA	Contributory Employment and Support Allowance
Ch.	Chancery Division Law Reports
Child Benefit Regulations	Child Benefit (General) Regulations 2006
Claims and Payments Regulations	Social Security (Claims and Payments) Regulations 1987
Claims and Payments Regulations 1979	Social Security (Claims and Payments) Regulations 1979
C.M.L.R.	Common Market Law Reports
C.O.D.	Crown Office Digest
Com. L.R.	Commercial Law Reports
Commissioners Procedure Regulations	Social Security Commissioners (Procedure) Regulations 1999
Computation of Earnings Regulations	Social Security Benefit (Computation of Earnings) Regulations 1978
Computation of Earnings Regulations 1999	Social Security Benefit (Computation of Earnings) Regulations 1996
Const. L.J.	Construction Law Journal
Contributions and Benefits Act	Social Security Contributions and Benefits Act 1992
Convention	Human Rights Convention
Council Tax Benefit Regulations	Council Tax Benefit (General) Regulations 1992 (SI 1992/1814)
CP	Carer Premium
CP	Chamber President
CPAG	Child Poverty Action Group
C.P.L.R.	Civil Practice Law Reports
CPR	Civil Procedure Rules
C.P. Rep.	Civil Procedure Reports
Cr. App. R.	Criminal Appeal Reports
Cr. App. R. (S.)	Criminal Appeal Reports (Sentencing)

CRCA 2005	Commissioners for Revenue and Customs Act 2005
Credits Regulations 1974	Social Security (Credits) Regulations 1974
Credits Regulations 1975	Social Security (Credits) Regulations 1975
Crim. L.R.	Criminal Law Review
CRU	Compensation Recovery Unit
CSA 1995	Child Support Act 1995
CS(NI)O	Child Support (Northern Ireland) Order 1995
CSO	Child Support Officer Act 2000
CSPSSA 2000	Child Support, Pensions and Social Security Act 2000
CTC	Child Tax Credit
DAT	Disability Appeal Tribunal
DCP	Disabled Child Premium
Decisions and Appeals Regulations 1999	Social Security Contributions (Decisions and Appeals) Regulations 1999
Dependency Regulations	Social Security Benefit (Dependency) Regulations 1977
DLA	Disability Living Allowance
DLA Regulations	Social Security (Disability Living Allowance) Regulations 1991
DLAAB	Disability Living Allowance Advisory Board
DLAAB Regs	Disability Living Allowance Advisory Board Regulations (SI 1991/1746)
DLADWAA 1991	Disability Living Allowance and Disability Working Allowance Act 1991
DM	Decision Maker
DMA	Decision-making and Appeals
DMG	Decision Makers Guide
DMP	Delegated Medical Practitioner
DPTC	Disabled Person's Tax Credit
DSDNI	Department for Social Development, Northern Ireland
DSS	Department of Social Security
DTI	Department of Trade and Industry
DWA	Disability Working Allowance
DWP	Department of Work and Pensions
DWPMS	Department of Work and Pensions Medical Services
EAA	Extrinsic Allergic Alveolitis
EAT	Employment Appeal Tribunal
ECHR	European Convention on Human Rights
ECHR rights	European Convention on Human Rights rights
EctHR	European Court of Human Rights
ECJ	European Court of Justice
E.C.R.	European Court Report

ECSMA Agreement	European Convention on Social and Medical Assistance
EC Treaty	European Community Treaty
EEA	European Economic Area
E.H.R.R.	European Human Rights Reports
E.L.R.	Education Law Reports
EMA	Education Maintenance Allowance
EMO	Examining Medical Officer
EMP	Examining Medical Practitioner
ERA	Evoked Response Audiometry
ERA 1996	Employment Rights Act 1996
ER(NI)O	Employers Rights (Northern Ireland) Order 1996
ESA	Employment and Support Allowance
ESA Regulations	Employment and Support Allowance Regulations 2008
ESA WCAt	Employment and Support Allowance Work Capability Assessment
Eu.L.R.	European Law Reports
FA 1990	Finance Act 1990
FA 1996	Finance Act 1996
FA 2000	Finance Act 2000
FA 2004	Finance Act 2004
F(No.2) A 2005	Finance (No.2) Act 2005
Family Credit Regulations	Family Credit (General) Regulations 1987
Fam. Law	Family Law
F.C.R.	Family Court Reporter
FIS	Family Income Supplement
Fixing and Adjustment of Rates Regulations 1976	Child Benefit and Social Security (Fixing and Adjustment of Rates) Regulations 1976
F.L.R.	Family Law Report
FTT	First-tier Tribunal
GA	Guardians Allowance
GA Regulations	Social Security (Guardian's Allowance) Regulations 1975
General Benefit Regulations 1982	Social Security (General Benefit) Regulations 1982
General Regulations	Statutory Maternity Pay (General) Regulations 1986
GMP	Guaranteed Minimum Pension
G.P.	General Practitioner
GRA	Gender Recognition Act
GRB	Graduated Retirement Benefit
GRP	Graduated Retirement Pension
G.W.D.	Greens Weekly Digest

HASSASSA	Health and Social Services and Social Security Adjudication Act 1983
HCD	House of Commons Debates
HCV	Hepatitis C Virus
HCWA	House of Commons Written Answer
HESC	Health, Education and Social Care
H.L.R.	Housing Law Reports
HMIT	Her Majesty's Inspector of Taxes
HMRC	Her Majesty's Revenue & Customs
HNCIP	(Housewives') Non-Contributory Invalidity Pension
Hospital In-Patients Regulations 1975	Social Security (Hospital In-Patients) Regulations 1975
Housing Benefit Regulations	Housing Benefit (General) Regulations 1987 (SI 1987/1971)
HPP	Higher Pensioner Premium
HRA 1998	Human Rights Act 1998
H.R.L.R.	Human Rights Law Reports–UK Cases
HSE	Health and Safety Executive
IB	Incapacity Benefit
IB/IS/SDA	Incapacity Benefits' Regime
IBJSA	Income based Jobseekers Allowance
IB PCA	Incapacity Benefit Person Capability Assessment
IB Regs	Social Security (Incapacity Benefit) Regulations 1994
IB Regulations	Social Security (Incapacity Benefit) Regulations 1994
IBS	Irritable Bowel Syndrome
ICA	Invalid Care Allowance
ICA Regulations	Social Security (Invalid Care Allowance) Regulations 1976
ICA Unit	Invalid Care Allowance Unit
I.C.R.	Industrial Cases Reports
ICTA 1988	Income and Corporation Taxes Act 1988
IFW Regs	Incapacity for Work (General) Regulations 1995
IIAC	Industrial Injuries Advisory Council
Imm. A.R.	Immigration Appeal Reports
Incapacity for Work Regulations	Social Security (Incapacity for Work) (General) Regulations 1995
Income Support General Regulations	Income Support (General) Regulations 1987
Increases for Dependants Regulations	Social Security Benefit (Dependency) Regulations 1977
IND	Immigration and Nationality Directorate of the Home Office
I.N.L.R.	Immigration and Nationality Law Reports

IO	Information Officer
I.O.	Insurance Officer
IPPR	Institute of Public Policy Research
IRESA	Income Related Employment and Support Allowance
I.R.L.R.	Industrial Relations Law Reports
IS	Income Support
ISAs	Individual Savings Accounts
IS Regs	Income Support Regulations
ITA 2007	Income Tax Act 2007
ITEPA	Income Tax (Earnings and Pensions) Act
ITEPA 2003	Income Tax (Earnings and Pensions) Act 2003
I.T.L. Rep.	International Tax Law Reports
ITS	Independent Tribunal Service
ITTOIA	Income Tax (Trading and Other Income) Act 2005
IVB	Invalidity Benefit
IWA 1994	Social Security (Incapacity for Work) Act 1994
IW (Dependants) Regs	Social Security (Incapacity for Work) (Dependants) Regulations
IW (General) Regs	Social Security (Incapacity for Work) (General) Regulations 1995
IW (Transitional) Regs	Incapacity for Work (Transitional) Regulations
JHRC	Joint Human Rights Committee
Jobseeker's Regulations 1996	Jobseekers Allowance Regulations 1996
J.P.	Justice of the Peace Reports
JSA	Jobseekers Allowance
JSA 1995	Jobseekers Allowance Act 1995
JSA Regs 1996	Jobseekers Allowance Regulations 1996
JSA Regulations	Jobseekers Allowance Regulations
JSA (Transitional) Regulations	Jobseeker's Allowance (Transitional) Regulations 1996
JS(NI)O 1995	Jobseekers (Northern Ireland) Order 1995
J.S.S.L.	Journal of Social Security Law
J.S.W.F.L.	Journal of Social Welfare and Family Law
J.S.W.L.	Journal of Social Welfare Law
K.I.R.	Knight's Industrial Law Reports
L. & T.R.	Landlord and Tenant Reports
LCWA	Limited Capability for Work Assessment
LEL	Lower Earnings Limit
Lewis	R. Lewis, *Compensation for Industrial Injury* (1987)
L.G.R.	Local Government Law Reports
Ll.L.Rep	Lloyd's List Law Report

Table of Abbreviations used in this Series

Lloyd's Rep.	Lloyd's Law Reports
L.S.G.	Law Society Gazette
LTAHAW	Living Together as Husband and Wife
Luxembourg Court	Court of Justice of the European Communities (also referred to as ECJ)
MA	Maternity Allowance
MAF	Medical Assessment Framework
MAT	Medical Appeal Tribunal
Maternity Allowance Regulations	Social Security (Maternity Allowance) Regulations 1987
Maternity Benefit Regulations	Social Security (Maternity Benefit) Regulations 1975
Medical Evidence Regulations	Social Security (Medical Evidence) Regulations 1976
MS	Medical Services
NCIP	Non-Contributory Invalidity Pension
NDPD	Notes on the Diagnosis of Prescribed Diseases
NI	National Insurance
N.I..	Northern Ireland Law Reports
NICs	National Insurance Contributions
NIRS 2	National Insurance Recording System
N.L.J.	New Law Journal
N.P.C.	New Property Cases
OCD	Obsessive compulsive disorder
Ogus, Barendt and Wikeley	A. Ogus, E. Barendt and N. Wikeley, The Law of Social Security (4th ed., Butterworths, 1995)
OPA	Overseas Pensions Act 1973
OPB	One Parent Benefit
OPSSAT	Office of the President of Social Security Appeal Tribunals
Overlapping Benefits Regulations	Social Security (Overlapping Benefits) Regulations 1979
Overpayments Regulations	Social Security (Payments on account, Overpayments and Recovery) Regulations
P.	Probate, Divorce and Admiralty Law Reports
P. & C.R.	Property and Compensation Reports
PAYE	Pay As You Earn
PCA	Personal Capability Assessment
PD	Prescribed Diseases
P.D.	Practice Direction
Pens. L.R.	Pensions Law Reports
Persons Abroad Regulations	Social Security Benefit (Persons Abroad) Regulations 1975
Persons Residing Together Regulations	Social Security Benefit (Persons Residing Together) Regulations 1977
PIE	Period of Interruption of Employment

PILON	Pay In Lieu of Notice
PIW	Period of Incapacity for Work
P.I.W.R.	Personal Injury and Quantum Reports
P.L.R.	Estates Gazette Planning Law Reports
Polygamous Marriages Regulations	Social Security and Family Allowances (Polygamous Marriages) Regulations 1975
PPF	Pension Protection Fund
Prescribed Diseases Regulations	Social Security (Industrial Injuries) (Prescribed Diseases) Regulations 1985
PSCS	DWP's Pension Service Computer System
PTA	Pure Tone Audiometry
PTSR	Public and Third Sector Law Reports
PVS	Private of Voluntary Sectors
Q.B.	Queens Bench Law Reports
R	Reported Decision
RC	Rules of the Court of Session
REA	Reduced Earnings Allowance
Recoupment Regulations	Social Security (Recoupment) Regulations 1990
RIPA	Regulation of Investigatory Powers Act 2000
RMO	Regional Medical Officer
RSI	Repetitive Strain Injury
R.T.R.	Road Traffic Reports
S	Scottish Decision
SAP	Statutory Adoption Pay
SAYE	Save As You Earn
SB	Supplementary Benefit
SBC	Supplementary Benefits Commission
S.C.	Session Cases
S.C. (H.L.)	Session Cases (House of Lords)
S.C. (P.C.)	Session Cases (Privy Council)
S.C.C.R.	Scottish Criminal Case Reports
S.C.L.R.	Scottish Civil Law Reports
SDA	Severe Disablement Allowance
SDP	Severe Disability Premium
SEC	Social Entitlement Chamber
SERPS	State Earnings Related Pension Scheme
Severe Disablement Allowance Regulations	Social Security (Severe Disablement Regulations Allowance) Regulations 1984
S.J.	Solicitors Journal
S.J.L.B.	Solicitors Journal Law Brief
S.L.T.	Scots Law Times
SMP	Statutory Maternity Pay
SMP (General) Regulations	Statutory Maternity Pay (General) Regulations

SMP (General) Regulations 1986	Statutory Maternity Pay (General) Regulations 1986
SP	Senior President
SPC	State Pension Credit
SPCA	State Pension Credit Act 2002
SPCA(NI)	State Pension Credit Act (Northern Ireland) 2002
SPP	Statutory Paternity Pay
SPP and SAP (Administration) Regs 2002	Statutory Paternity Pay and Statutory Adoption Pay (Administration) Regulations 2002
SPP and SAP (General) Regulations 2002	Statutory Paternity Pay and Statutory Adoption Pay (General) Regulations 2002
SPP and SAP (National Health Service)	Statutory Paternity Pay and Statutory Adoption Pay (National Health Service Employees) Regulations 2002
SPP and SAP (Weekly Rates) Regulations	Statutory Paternity Pay and Statutory Adoption Pay (Weekly Rates) Regulations 2002
SSA	Social Security Agency
SSA 1975	Social Security Act 1975
SSA 1978	Social Security Act 1978
SSA 1979	Social Security Act 1979
SSA 1981	Social Security Act 1981
SSA 1986	Social Security Act 1986
SSA 1989	Social Security Act 1989
SSA 1990	Social Security Act 1990
SSA 1992	Social Security Act 1992
SSA 1998	Social Security Act 1998
SSAA 1992	Social Security Administration Act 1992★
SSAC	Social Security Advisory Committee
SSAT	Social Security Appeal Tribunal
SSCBA 1992	Social Security Contributions and Benefits Act 1992★
SSCB(NI) Act 1992	Social Security Contributions (Northern Ireland) Act 1992
SS(CP)A	Social Security (Consequential Provisions) Act 1992
SSHBA 1982	Social Security and Housing Benefits Act 1982
SS(MP) A 1977	Social Security (Miscellaneous Provisions) Act 1977
SS (No.2) A 1980	Social Security (No.2) Act 1980
SSP	Statutory Sick Pay
SSPA 1975	Social Security Pensions Act 1975
SSP (Gen.) Regulations	Statutory Sick Pay (General) Regulations 1982
SSP (General) Regulations 1982	Statutory Sick Pay (General) Regulations 1982

★ Where the context makes it seem more appropriate, these could also be referred to as Contributions and Benefits Act 1992, Administration Act 1992.

SSPA 1975	Social Security Pensions Act 1975
SSWP	Secretary of State for Work and Pensions
State Pension Credit Regulations	State Pension Credit Regulations 2002
S.T.C.	Simon's Tax Cases
S.T.C. (S.C.D.)	Simon's Tax Cases: Special Commissioners Decisions
S.T.I.	Simon's Tax Intelligence
STIB	Short-Term Incapacity Benefit
Strasbourg Court	European Court of Human Rights
T	Tribunal of Commissioners' Decision
Taxes Act	Income and Corporation Taxes Act 1988
T.C.	Tax Cases
TCA 1999	Tax Credits Act 1999
TCA 2002	Tax Credits Act 2002
TC (Claims and Notifications) Regs 2002	Tax Credits (Claims and Notifications) Regulations 2002
TCGA	Taxation of Chargeable Gains Act 1992
TCTM	Tax Credits Technical Manual
TEU	Treaty on European Union
TMA 1970	Taxes Management Act 1970
T.R.	Taxation Reports
Transfer of Functions Act	Social Security Contributions (Transfer of Functions etc.) Act 1999
Treaty	Rome Treaty
U	Unemployment Benefit
U.K.H.R.R.	United Kingdom Human Rights Reports
UKUT	United Kingdom Upper Tribunal
Unemployment, Sickness and Invalidity Benefit Regs	Social Security (Unemployment, Sickness and Invalidity Benefit) Regulations 1983
USI Regs	Social Security (Unemployment, Sickness and Invalidity Benefit) Regulations 1983
UT	Upper Tribunal
VAMS	Veterans Agency Medical Service
VCM	Vinyl Chloride Monomer-Related
VERA 1992	Vehicle Excise and Registration Act 1992
VWF	Vibration White Finger
W	Welsh Decision
WCA	Work Capability Assessment
WCAt	First Element of Limited Work Capability Assessment
WFHRAt	Work Focused Health Related Assessment
WFTC	Working Families Tax Credit
Widow's Benefit and Retirement Pensions Regs	Social Security (Widow's Benefit and Retirement Pensions) Regulations 1979
Wikeley, Annotations	N. Wikeley, "Annotations to Jobseekers Act 1995

	(c.18)" in *Current Law Statutes Annotated* (1995)
Wikeley, Ogus and Barendt	Wikeley, Ogus and Barendt, *The Law of Social Security* (5th ed., Butterworths, 2002)
W.L.R.	Weekly Law Reports
Workmen's Compensation Acts	Workmen's Compensation Acts 1925 to 1945
WRA 2007	Welfare Reform Act
WRAAt	Work Related Activity Assessment
WRPA 1999	Welfare Reform and Pensions Act 1999
WRP(NI)O 1999	Welfare Reform and Pensions (Northern Ireland) Order
WTC	Working Tax Credit
WTC (Entitlement and Maximum Rate) Regulations 2002	Working Tax Credit (Entitlement and Maximum Rate) Regulations 2002
W.T.L.R.	Wills & Trusts Law Reports

PART I

HM REVENUE AND CUSTOMS
TAX CREDITS AND SOCIAL SECURITY

Taxes Management Act 1970

(1970 C.9)

ARRANGEMENT OF SELECTED SECTIONS

PART I

ADMINISTRATION

PART II

RETURNS OF INCOME AND GAINS

Income tax

Records

PART IV

ASSESSMENTS AND CLAIMS

Relief for excessive assessments

Time-limits

PART V

APPEALS AND OTHER PROCEEDINGS

Proceedings before Commissioners

PART X

PENALTIES, ETC.

PART XI

MISCELLANEOUS AND SUPPLEMENTAL

Documents

Interpretation

INTRODUCTION AND GENERAL NOTE

1.2   The TMA 1970 was a consolidation measure, but it has been extensively and repeatedly amended since 1970. Only two sections apply directly to tax credits: s.1 (read to include tax credits) and s.54. For the express application of s.54, see Tax Credits (Appeals) Regulations 2002, reg.3. But TCA 2002 refers to several other sections. Set out below are the key sections of the TMA 1970 that apply for the purposes of the income tax assessments, alongside which tax credit calculations will be made in most cases.

In addition, the selection includes other provisions setting out the power of HMRC to investigate and deal with income tax assessments, the scope for a taxpayer to amend a self-assessment or request an amendment of an assessment, and formal sections dealing with evidence and documentation.

As s.1 indicates, this Act also deals with assessments and administration of capital gains tax and corporation tax, but all provisions relating only to those taxes have been excluded from this selection, as have provisions dealing with other taxes or past taxes.

PART I

ADMINISTRATION

Responsibility for certain taxes

1. The Commissioners for Her Majesty's Revenue and Customs shall be responsible for the collection and management of— **1.3**
  (a) income tax,
  (b) corporation tax, and
  (c) capital gains tax.

PART II

RETURNS OF INCOME AND GAINS

Income tax

Personal return

8.—(1) For the purpose of establishing the amounts in which a person is chargeable to income tax and capital gains tax for a year of assessment, . . . he may be required by a notice given to him by an officer of the Board— **1.4**
  (a) to make and deliver to the officer, a return containing such information as may reasonably be required in pursuance of the notice, and
  (b) to deliver with the return such accounts, statements and documents, relating to information contained in the return, as may reasonably be so required.
(1A) The day referred to in subsection (1) above is—
  (a) the 31st January next following the year of assessment, or
  (b) where the notice under this section is given after the 31st October next following the year, the last day of the period of three months beginning with the day on which the notice is given.
(1AA) For the purposes of subsection (1) above—
  (a) the amounts in which a person is chargeable to income tax and capital gains tax are net amounts, that is to say, amounts which take into account any relief or allowance a claim for which is included in the return; and

(b) the amount payable by a person by way of income tax is the difference between the amount in which he is chargeable to income tax and the aggregate amount of any income tax deducted at source and any tax credits to which section 231 of the principal Act applies.

(1B) In the case of a person who carries on a trade, profession, or business in partnership with one or more other persons, a return under this section shall include each amount which, in any relevant statement, is stated to be equal to his share of any income, loss, tax, credit or charge for the period in respect of which the statement is made.

(1C) In subsection (1B) above "relevant statement" means a statement which, as respects the partnership, falls to be made under section 12AB of this Act for a period which includes, or includes any part of, the year of assessment or its basis period.

(1D) A return under this section for a year of assessment (Year 1) must be delivered—
(a) in the case of a non-electronic return, on or before 31st October in Year 2, and
(b) in the case of an electronic return, on or before 31st January in Year 2.

(1E) But subsection (1D) is subject to the following two exceptions.

(1F) Exception 1 is that if a notice in respect of Year 1 is given after 31st July in Year 2 (but on or before 31st October), a return must be delivered—
(a) during the period of 3 months beginning with the date of the notice (for a non-electronic return), or
(b) on or before 31st January (for an electronic return).

(1G) Exception 2 is that if a notice in respect of Year 1 is given after 31st October in Year 2, a return (whether electronic or not) must be delivered during the period of 3 months beginning with the date of the notice.

(1H) The Commissioners—
(a) shall prescribe what constitutes an electronic return, and
(b) may make different provision for different cases or circumstances.

(2) Every return under this section shall include a declaration by the person making the return to the effect that the return is to the best of his knowledge correct and complete.

(3) A notice under this section may require different information, accounts and statements for different periods or in relation to different descriptions of source of income.

(4) Notices under this section may require different information, accounts and statements in relation to different descriptions of person.

(5) In this section and sections 8A, 9 and 12AA of this Act, any reference to income tax deducted at source is a reference to income tax deducted or treated as deducted from any income or treated as paid on any income.

Returns to include self-assessment

1.5

9.—(1) Subject to subsections (1A) and (2) below, every return under section 8 or 8A of this Act shall include a self-assessment, that is to say—
(a) an assessment of the amounts in which, on the basis of the information contained in the return and taking into account any relief or allowance a claim for which is included in the return, the person making the return is chargeable to income tax and capital gains tax for the year of assessment; and

(b) an assessment of the amount payable by him by way of income tax, that is to say, the difference between the amount in which he is assessedto income tax under paragraph (a) above and the aggregate amount of any income tax deducted at source and any tax credits to which section 7 of ITTOIA 2005 applies

but nothing in this subsection shall enable a self-assessment to show as repayable any income tax treated as deducted or paid by virtue of section 246D(1) of the principal Act or section 626 of ITEPA.

(1A) The tax to be assessed on a person by a self-assessment shall not include any tax which, under Chapter I or IV of Part XIV of the principal Act or under section 394(2) of ITEPA 2003, is charged on the administrator of a scheme (within the meaning of section 658A of that Act) and is assessable by the Board in accordance with that section.

(2) A person shall not be required to comply with subsection (1) above if he makes and delivers his return for a year of assessment—

(a) on or before the 31st October next following the year; or

(b) where the notice under section 8 or 8A of this Act is given after the 31st August next following the year, within the period of two months beginning with the day on which the notice is given.

(3) Where, in making and delivering a return, a person does not comply with subsection (1) above, an officer of the Board shall, if subsection (2) above applies, and may in any other case—

(a) make the assessment on his behalf on the basis of the information contained in the return; and

(b) send him a copy of the assessment so made;

and references in this Act to a person's self-assessment include references to an assessment made on a person's behalf under this subsection.

(3A) An assessment under subsection (3) above is treated for the purposes of this Act as a self-assessment and as included in the return.

(4) Subject to subsection (5) below—

(a) at any time before the end of the period of nine months beginning with the day on which a person's return is delivered, an officer of the Board may by notice to that person so amend that person's self-assessment as to correct any obvious errors or mistakes in the return (whether errors of principle, arithmetical mistakes or otherwise); and

(b) at any time before the end of the period of twelve months beginning with the filing date, a person may by notice to an officer of the Board so amend his self-assessment as to give effect to any amendments to his return which he has notified to such an officer.

(5) No amendment of a self-assessment may be made under subsection (4) above at any time during the period—

(a) beginning with the day on which an officer of the Board gives notice of his intention to enquire into the return; and

(b) ending with the day on which the officer's enquiries into the return are completed.

(6) In this section and section 9A of this Act "the filing date" means the day mentioned in section 8(1A) or, as the case may be, section 8A(1A) of this Act.

Amendment of personal or trustee return by taxpayer

9ZA.—(1) A person may amend his return under section 8 or 8A of this Act by notice to an officer of the Board.

1.6

(2) An amendment may not be made more than 12 months after the filing date.

(3) In this section "the filing date", in respect of a return for a year of assessment (Year 1), means—

    (a) 31st January of Year 2, or

    (b) if the notice under section 8 or 8A is given after 31st October of Year 2, the last day of the period of three months beginning with the date of the notice.

Correction of personal or trustee return by Revenue

1.7   **9ZB.**—(1) An officer of the Board may amend a return under section 8 or 8A of this Act so as to correct —

    (a) obvious errors or omissions in the return (whether errors of principle, arithmetical mistakes or otherwise), and

    (b) anything else in the return that the officer has reason to believe is incorrect in the light of information available to the office.

(2) A correction under this section is made by notice to the person whose return it is.

(3) No such correction may be made more than nine months after—

    (a) the day on which the return was delivered, or

    (b) if the correction is required in consequence of an amendment of the return under section 9ZA of this Act, the day on which that amendment was made.

(4) A correction under this section is of no effect if the person whose return it is gives notice rejecting the correction.

(5) Notice of rejection under subsection (4) above must be given—

    (a) to the officer of the Board by whom the notice of correction was given,

    (b) before the end of the period of 30 days beginning with the date of issue of the notice of correction.

Notice of enquiry

1.8   **9A.**—(1) An officer of the Boardmay enquire into a return under section 8 or 8A of this Act if he gives notice of his intention to do so ("notice of enquiry")—

    (a) to the person whose return it is ("the taxpayer"),

    (b) within the time allowed.

(2) The time allowed is—

    (a) if the return was delivered on or before the filing date, up to the end of the period of twelve months after the filing date;

    (b) if the return was delivered after the filing date, up to and including the quarter day next following the first anniversary of the day on which the return was delivered;

    (c) if the return is amended under section 9ZA of this Act, up to and including the quarter day next following the first anniversary of the day on which the amendment was made.

For this purpose, the quarter days are 31st January, 30th April, 31st July and 31st October.

(3) A return which has been the subject of one notice of enquiry may not be the subject of another, except one given in consequence of an amendment (or another amendment) of the return under section 9ZA of this Act.

(4) An enquiry extends to anything contained in the return, or required to be contained in the return, including any claim or election included in the return, subject to the following limitation.

Amendment of return by taxpayer during enquiry

9B.—(1) This section applies if a return is amended under section 9ZA of this Act (amendment of personal or trustee return by taxpayer) at a time when an enquiry is in progress into the return.

(2) The amendment does not restrict the scope of the enquiry but may be taken into account (together with any matters arising) in the enquiry.

(3) So far as the amendment affects the amount stated in the self-assessment included in the return as the amount of tax payable, it does not take effect while the enquiry is in progress and—

(a) if the officer states in the closure notice that he has taken the amendment into account and that—
  (i) the amendment has been taken into account in formulating the amendments contained in the notice, or
  (ii) his conclusion is that the amendment is incorrect, the amendment shall not take effect;

(b) otherwise, the amendment takes effect when the closure notice is issued.

(4) For the purposes of this section the period during which an enquiry is in progress is the whole of the period—

(a) beginning with the day on which notice of enquiry is given; and
(b) ending with the day on which the enquiry is completed.

Amendment of self-assessment during enquiry to prevent loss of tax

9C.—(1) This section applies where an enquiry is in progress into a return as a result of notice of enquiry by an officer of the Board under section 9A(1) of this Act.

(2) If the officer forms the opinion—

(a) that the amount stated in the self-assessment contained in the return as the amount of tax payable is insufficient; and
(b) that unless the assessment is immediately amended there is likely to be a loss of tax to the Crown,

he may by notice to the taxpayer amend the assessment to make good the deficiency.

(3) In the case of an enquiry which under section 9A(5) of this Act is limited to matters arising from an amendment of the return, subsection (2) above only applies so far as the deficiency is attributable to the amendment.

(4) For the purposes of this section the period during which an enquiry is in progress is the whole of the period—

(a) beginning with the day on which notice of enquiry is given, and
(b) ending with the day on which the enquiry is completed.

Records

Records to be kept for purposes of returns

12B.—(1) Any person who may be required by a notice under section 8, 8A, or 12AA of this Act (or under any of those sections as extended by

1.9

1.10

1.11

section 12 of this Act) to make and deliver a return for a year of assessment or other period shall—

   (a) keep all such records as may be requisite for the purpose of enabling him to make and deliver a correct and complete return for the year or period; and

   (b) preserve those records until the end of the relevant day, that is to say, the day mentioned in subsection (2) below or, where a return is required by a notice given on or before that day, whichever of that day and the following is the latest, namely—

      (i) where enquiries into the return or any amendment of the return are made by an officer of the Board, the day on which, by virtue of section 28A(1) or 28B(1) of this Act, those enquiries are treated as completed; and

      (ii) where no enquiries into the return or any amendment of the return are so made, the day on which such an officer no longer has power to make such enquiries.

(2) The day referred to in subsection (1) above is—

   (a) in the case of a person carrying on a trade, profession or business alone or in partnership or a company, the fifth anniversary of the 31st January next following the year of assessment or (as the case may be) the sixth anniversary of the endof the period;

   (b) [otherwise], the first anniversary of 31st January next following the year of assessment . . .

or (in either case) such earlier day as may be specified in writing by the Commissioners for Her Majesty's Revenue and Customs (and different days may be specified for different cases).

(2A) Any person who—

   (a) is required, by such a notice as is mentioned in subsection (1) above given at any time after the end of the day mentioned in subsection (2) above, to make and deliver a return for a year of assessment or other period; and

   (b) has in his possession at that time any records which may be requisite for the purpose of enabling him to make and deliver a correct and complete return for the year or period,

shall preserve those records until the end of the relevant day, that is to say, the day which, if the notice had been given on or before the day mentioned in subsection (2) above, would have been the relevant day for the purposes of subsection (1) above.

(3) In the case of a person carrying on a trade, profession or business alone or in partnership—

   (a) the records required to be kept and preserved under subsection (1) or (2A) above shall include records of the following, namely—

      (i) all amounts received and expended in the course of the trade, profession or business and the matters in respect of which the receipts and expenditure take place, and

      (ii) in the case of a trade involving dealing in goods, all sales and purchases of goods made in the course of the trade . . .

(3A) The Commissioners for Her Majesty's Revenue and Customs may by regulations—

   (a) provide that the records required to be kept and preserved under this section include, or do not include, records specified in the regulations, and

(b) provide that those records include supporting documents so specified.

(4) The duty under subsection (1) or (2A) to preserve records may be discharged—

(a) by preserving them in any form and by any means, or

(b) by preserving the information contained in them in any form and by any means, subject to subsection (4A) and any conditions or further exceptions specified in writing by the Commissioners for Her Majesty's Revenue and Customs.

(4A) Subsection (4)(b) does not apply in the case of the following kinds of records

(a) any statement in writing such as is mentioned in—

(i) subsection (1) of section 234 of the principal Act (amount of qualifying distribution and tax credit); or

(ii) section 495(1) or 975(2) or (4) of ITA 2007 (statements about deduction of income tax), which is furnished by the company or person there mentioned, whether after the making of a request or otherwise;

(b) any certificate or other record (however described) which is required by regulations under section 566(1) of the principal Act to be given to a sub-contractor (within the meaning of Chapter IV of Part XIII of that Act) on the making of a payment to which section 559 of that Act (deductions on account of tax) applies;

(c) any such record as may be requisite for making a correct and complete claim in respect of, or otherwise requisite for making a correct and complete return so far as relating to, an amount of tax—

(i) which has been paid under the laws of a territory outside the United Kingdom, or

(ii) which would have been payable under the law of such a territory but for a relief to which section 788(5) of the principal Act (relief for promoting development and relief contemplated by double taxation arrangements) applies.

(5) Subject to subsections (5A) and (5B) below any person who fails to comply with subsection (1) or (2A) above in relation to a year of assessment or accounting period shall be liable to a penalty not exceeding £3,000.

(5A) Subsection (5) above does not apply where the records which the person fails to keep or preserve are records which might have been requisite only for the purposes of claims, elections or notices which are not included in the return.

(5B) Subsection (5) above also does not apply where—

(a) the records which the person fails to keep or preserve are records falling within paragraph (a) of subsection (4A) above; and

(b) an officer of the Board is satisfied that any facts which he reasonably requires to be proved, and which would have been proved by the records, are proved by other documentary evidence furnished to him.

(6) For the purposes of this section—

(a) a person engaged in the letting of property shall be treated as carrying on a trade; and

(b) "supporting documents" includes accounts, books, deeds, contracts, vouchers and receipts.

(5C) Regulations under this section may—
(a) make different provision for different cases, and
(b) make provision by reference to things specified in a notice published by the Commissioners for Her Majesty's Revenue and Customs in accordance with the regulations (and not withdrawn by a subsequent notice).

PART IV

ASSESSMENT AND CLAIMS

Completion of enquiry into personal or trustee return

1.12   **28A.**—(1) An enquiry under section 9A(1) of this Act is completed when an officer of the Boardby notice (a "closure notice") informs the taxpayer that he has completed his enquiries and states his conclusions. In this section "the taxpayer" means the person to whom notice of enquiry was given.

(2) A closure notice must either—
(a) state that in the officer's opinion no amendment of the return is required; or
(b) make the amendments of the return required to give effect to his conclusions.

(3) A closure notice takes effect when it is issued.

(4) The taxpayer may apply to the tribunal for a direction requiring an officer of the Board to issue a closure notice within a specified period.

(5) Any such application is to be subject to the relevant provisions of Part 5 of this Act (see, in particular, section 48(2)(b)).

(6) The tribunal shall give the direction applied for unless . . . satisfied that there are reasonable grounds for not issuing a closure notice within a specified period.

Assessment where loss of tax discovered

1.13   **29.**—(1) If an officer of the Board or the Board discover, as regards any person (the taxpayer) and a year of assessment—
(a) that income which ought to have been assessed to income tax, or chargeable gains which ought to have been assessed to capital gains tax, have not been assessed, or
(b) that an assessment to tax is or has become insufficient, or
(c) that any relief which has been given is or has become excessive,
the officer or, as the case may be, the Board may, subject to subsections (2) and (3) below, make an assessment in the amount, or the further amount, which ought in his or their opinion to be charged in order to make good to the Crown the loss of tax.

(2) Where—
(a) the taxpayer has made and delivered a return under section 8 or 8A of this Act in respect of the relevant chargeable period, and
(b) the situation mentioned in subsection (1) above is attributable to an error or mistake in the return as to the basis on which his liability ought to have been computed,

the taxpayer shall not be assessed under that subsection in respect of the year of assessment there mentioned if the return was in fact made on the basis or in accordance with the practice generally prevailing at the time when it was made.

(3) Where the taxpayer has made and delivered a return under section 8 or 8A of this Act in respect of the relevant year of assessment, he shall not be assessed under subsection (1) above—

(a) in respect of the year of assessment mentioned in that subsection; and

(b) in the case of a return under section 8 or 8A, in the same capacity as that in which he made and delivered the return,

unless one of the two conditions mentioned below is fulfilled.

(4) The first condition is that the situation mentioned in subsection (1) above was brought about carelessly or deliberately by the taxpayer or a person acting on his behalf.

(5) The second condition is that at the time when an officer of the Board—

(a) ceased to be entitled to give notice of his intention to enquire into the taxpayer's return under section 8 or 8A of this Act in respect of the relevant year of assessment; or

(b) informed the taxpayer that he had completed his enquiries into that return,

the officer could not have been reasonably expected, on the basis of the information made available to him before that time, to be aware of the situation mentioned in subsection (1) above.

(6) For the purposes of subsection (5) above, information is made available to an officer of the Board if—

(a) it is contained in the taxpayer's return under section 8 or 8A of this Act in respect of the relevant year of assessment (the return), or in any accounts, statements or documents accompanying the return;

(b) it is contained in any claim made as regards the relevant year of assessment by the taxpayer acting in the same capacity as that in which he made the return, or in any accounts, statements or documents accompanying any such claim;

(c) it is contained in any documents, accounts or particulars which, for the purposes of any enquiries into the return or any such claim by an officer of the Board, are produced or furnished by the taxpayer to the officer . . .; or

(d) it is information the existence of which, and the relevance of which as regards the situation mentioned in subsection (1) above—

(i) could reasonably be expected to be inferred by an officer of the Board from information falling within paragraphs (a)–(c) above; or

(ii) are notified in writing by the taxpayer to an officer of the Board.

(7) In subsection (6) above—

(a) any reference to the taxpayer's return under section 8 or 8A of this Act in respect of the relevant year of assessment includes—

(i) a reference to any return of his under that section for either of the two immediately preceding year of assessment; and

(ii) where the return is under section 8 and the taxpayer carries

13

on a trade, profession or business in partnership, a reference
to any partnership return with respect to the partnership for
the relevant year of assessment or either of those periods;
and

(b) any reference in paragraphs (b) to (d) to the taxpayer includes a reference to a person acting on his behalf.

(8) An objection to the making of an assessment under this section on the
ground that neither of the two conditions mentioned above is fulfilled shall
not be made otherwise than on an appeal against the assessment.

(9) Any reference in this section to the relevant year of assessment is a
reference to—

(a) in the case of the situation mentioned in paragraph (a) or (b) of subsection (1) above, the chargeable period mentioned in that subsection; and

(b) in the case of the situation mentioned in paragraph (c) of that
subsection, the year of assessment in respect of which the claim
was made.

(10) In this section "profits"—

(a) in relation to income tax, means income,

(b) in relation to capital gains tax, means chargeable gains, and

(c) in relation to corporation tax, means profits as computed for the purposes of that tax.

Relief for excessive assessments

Double assessment

1.14   **32.**—(1) If on a claim made to the Board it appears to their satisfaction
that a person has been assessed to tax more than once for the same cause
and for the same chargeable period, they shall direct the whole, or such part
of any assessment as appears to be an overcharge, to be vacated, and thereupon the same shall be vacated accordingly.

(2) An appeal may be brought against the refusal of a claim under this
section.

(3) Notice of appeal under subsection (2) must be given—

(a) in writing;

(b) within 30 days after the day on which notice of the refusal is given;

(c) to the officer of Revenue and Customs by whom that notice was
given.

Error or mistake

1.15   **33.**—(1) If a person who has paid income tax or capital gains tax under
an assessment (whether a self assessment or otherwise) alleges that the
assessment was excessive by reason of some error or mistake in a return,
he may by notice in writing at any time not more than 4 years after the end
of the year of assessment to which the return relates, make a claim to the
Board for relief.

(2) On receiving the claim the Board shall inquire into the matter and
shall, subject to the provisions of this section, give by way of repayment
such relief . . . in respect of the error or mistake as is reasonable and just:

Provided that no relief shall be given under this section in respect of an error or mistake as to the basis on which the liability of the claimant ought to have been computed where the return was in fact made on the basis or in accordance with the practice generally prevailing at the time when the return was made.

(2A) No relief shall be given under this section in respect of—

(a) an error or mistake as to the basis on which the liability of the claimant ought to have been computed where the return was in fact made on the basis or in accordance with the practice generally prevailing at the time when it was made; or

(b) an error or mistake in a claim which is included in the return.

(3) In determining the claim the Board shall have regard to all the relevant circumstances of the case, and in particular shall consider whether the granting of relief would result in the exclusion from charge to tax of any part of the profits of the claimant, and for this purpose the Board may take into consideration the liability of the claimant and assessments made on him in respect of chargeable periods other than that to which the claim relates.

(4) If any appeal is brought from the decision of the Board on the claim, the tribunal shall determine the appeal in accordance with the principles to be followed by the Board in determining claims under this section.

(4A) The determination of the tribunal of an appeal under subsection (4) shall be final and conclusive (notwithstanding the provisions of sections 11 and 13 of the TCEA 2007) except on a point of law arising in connection with the computation of profits.

(5) In this section, "profits"—

(a) in relation to income tax, means income; and

(b) in relation to capital gains tax, means chargeable gains; and

(c) in relation to corporation tax, means profits as computed for the purposes of that tax.

Time limits

Ordinary time-limit of four years

34.—(1) Subject to the following provisions of this Act, and to any other provisions of the Taxes Acts allowing a longer period in any particular class of case, an assessment to income tax or capital gains tax may be made at any time not more than 4 years after the end of the year of assessment to which it relates.   1.16

(2) An objection to the making of any assessment on the ground that the time-limit for making it has expired shall only be made on an appeal against the assessment.

Time limit: income received after year for which they are assessable

35.—(1) Where income to which this section applies is received in a year of assessment subsequent to that for which it is assessable, an assessment to   1.17

income tax as respects that income may be made at any time not more than 4 years after the end of the year of assessment in which it is received.

(2) This section applies to—

(a) employment income

(b) pension income, and

(c) social security income.

Loss of tax brought about carelessly or deliberately etc.

1.18   **36.**—(1) An assessment on a person in a case involving a loss of income tax or capital gains tax brought about carelessly by the person may be made at any time not more than 6 years after the end of the year of assessment to which it relates (subject to subsection (1A) and any other provision of the Taxes Acts allowing a longer period).

(1A) An assessment on a person in a case involving a loss of income tax or capital gains tax —

(a) brought about deliberately by the person,

(b) attributable to a failure by the person to comply with an obligation under section 7, or

(c) attributable to arrangements in respect of which the person has failed to comply with an obligation under section 309, 310 or 313 of the Finance Act 2004 (obligation of parties to tax avoidance schemes to provide information to Her Majesty's Revenue and Customs),

may be made at any time not more than 20 years after the end of the year of assessment to which it relates (subject to any provision of the Taxes Acts allowing a longer period).

(1B) In subsections (1) and (1A) references to a loss brought about by the person who is the subject of the assessment include a loss brought about by another person acting on behalf of that person.

(2) Where the person mentioned in subsection (1) or (1A) ("the person in default") carried on a trade, profession or business with one or more other persons at any time in the period for which the assessment is made, an assessment in respect of the profits or gains of the trade, profession or business for the purpose mentioned in subsection (1A) or (1B) may be made not only on the person in default but also on his partner or any of his partners.

(3) If the person on whom the assessment is made so requires, in determining the amount of the tax to be charged for any chargeable period in any assessment made for the purpose mentioned in subsection (1) or (1A) above, effect shall be given to any relief or allowance to which he would have been entitled for that chargeable period on a claim or application made within the time allowed by the Taxes Acts.

(3A) In subsection (3) above, "claim or application" does not include an election under section 257BA of the principal Act (elections as to transfer of married couple's allowance).

(4) Any act or omission such as is mentioned in section 98B below on the part of a grouping (as defined in that section) or member of a grouping shall be deemed for the purposes of subsections (1) and (1A) to be the act or omission of each member of the grouping.

PART V

APPEALS AND OTHER PROCEEDINGS

Proceedings before the Commissioners

Setting of appeals by agreement

54.—(1) Subject to the provisions of this section, where a person gives
notice of appeal and, before the appeal is determined by the tribunal, the
inspector or other proper officer of the Crown and the appellant come to an
agreement, whether in writing or otherwise, that the [1. . .] decision under
appeal should be treated as upheld without variation, or as varied in a particular manner or as discharged or cancelled, the like consequences shall
ensue for all purposes as would have ensued if, at the time when the agreement was come to, the tribunal had determined the appeal and had upheld
the assessment or decision without variation, had varied it in that manner or
had discharged or cancelled it, as the case may be.

1.19

(2) Subsection (1) of this section shall not apply where, within thirty days
from the date when the agreement was come to, the appellant gives notice
in writing to the [1 officer of the Board] that he desires to repudiate or resile
from the agreement.

[2(3) Where an agreement is not in writing—
  (a) the preceding provisions of this section shall not apply unless the
      Board give notice, in such form and manner as they consider appro-
      priate, to the appellant of the terms agreed between the officer of the
      Board and the appellant; and
  (b) the references in those preceding provisions to the time when the
      agreement was come to shall be construed as references to the date
      of that notice.]

(3) Where an agreement is not in writing—
  *(a) the preceding provisions of this section shall not apply unless the fact that
      an agreement was come to, and the terms agreed, are confirmed by notice
      in writing given by the [3officer of the Board] to the appellant or by the
      appellant to the [3officer of the Board]; and*
  *(b) the references in the said preceding provisions to the time when the agree-
      ment was come to shall be construed as references to the time of the giving
      of the said notice of confirmation.*

(4) Where—
  (a) a person who has given a notice of appeal notifies the [1officer of the
      Board], whether orally or in writing, that he desires not to proceed
      with the appeal; and
  (b) thirty days have elapsed since the giving of the notification without
      the [1officer of the Board] giving to the appellant notice in writing
      indicating that he is unwilling that the appeal should be treated as
      withdrawn,

the preceding provisions of this section shall have effect as if, at the date of
the appellant's notification, the appellant and the [1officer of the Board] had
come to an agreement, orally or in writing, as the case may be, that the [1. . .]
decision under appeal should be upheld without variation.

(5) The references in this section to an agreement being come to with an appellant and the giving of notice or notification to or by an appellant include references to an agreement being come to with, and the giving of notice or notification to or by, a person acting on behalf of the appellant in relation to the appeal.

[¹(6) In subsection (1) "appeal tribunal" means an appeal tribunal constituted—

(a) in Great Britain, under Chapter 1 of Part 1 of the Social Security Act 1998 (social security appeals: Great Britain), and

(b) in Northern Ireland, under Chapter 1 of Part 2 of the Social Security (Northern Ireland) Order 1998 (social security appeals: Northern Ireland).]

MODIFICATIONS

1. Modifications applying to both tax credit cases and child trust fund cases by virtue of reg.3 of the Tax Credits (Appeals) Regulations 2002 (SI 2002/2926) and reg.4 of the Child Trust Funds (Non-tax Appeals) Regulations 2005 (SI 2005/191).

2. Modifications applying only to tax credit cases by virtue of reg.3 of the Tax Credits (Appeals) Regulations 2002 (SI 2002/2926).

3. Modifications applying only to child trust fund cases by virtue of reg.4 of the Child Trust Funds (Non-tax Appeals) Regulations 2005 (SI 2005/191).

DEFINITIONS

"appeal tribunal"—see subs.(6).

"the Board"—see s.67 of the Tax Credits Act 2002 but note that the functions of the Board have now been transferred to the Commissioners for Her Majesty's Revenue and Customs (Commissioners for Revenue and Customs Act 2005, s.5(2)).

GENERAL NOTE

1.20   By virtue of reg.3 of the Tax Credits (Appeals) Regulations 2002, this section is applied in this modified form to those tax credit appeals which, by virtue of s.63 of the Tax Credits Act 2002, lie to the Social Entitlement Chamber of the First-tier Tribunal. Regulation 4 of the Child Trust Funds (Non-tax Appeals) Regulations 2005 applies the section to child trust fund appeals with the same modifications, save in subs.(3) where the amendments have the effect that notice is to be given by an officer of the Board (now an officer of Revenue and Customs) rather than the Board. The regulation-making power for the Tax Credits (Appeals) Regulations 2002, in s.63(8) of the Tax Credits Act 2002, was amended from April 1, 2009 by SI 2008/2833, Sch.3, para.191(6) and further by SI 2009/56, Sch.1, para.316(8) so as to restrict the power to Northern Ireland. As a result, presumably these regulations have lapsed for tax credits appeals in Great Britain. If so, then this section does not apply to those appeals. While that will not stop settlement of appeals, it will remove the specific section 54 procedure for, and status of, a settlement. See further the note to s.63 at para.1.349 below.

This section is central to the way that HMRC deals with tax and tax credit appeals. It is also widely used in settling disputes about underpayments and penalties. In February 2005, this was emphasised by Treasury Ministers in a House of Commons Written Answer: "Where possible the Department aims to settle an appeal by agreement with the appellant." (HCWA, HCD, February 8, 2005, col.1400W).

For application to tax credit penalties, see the note to s.31. For the HMRC published practices in dealing with tax credits settlements see the Codes of Practice published at the end of this work.

Subs. (1)

1.21   This allows the parties to compromise an appeal and reach an agreement that is as final as a decision of a tribunal. Indeed, it is more final because, not actually being a decision of a tribunal, there can be no appeal to the Upper Tribunal. Note that the agreement must be reached before the appeal tribunal determines the appeal. Therefore, this sort of agreement cannot put an end to an appeal to the Upper Tribunal, notwithstanding the definition of "tax credit appeal" in reg.2 of the Tax Credits (Appeals) Regulations 2002, although a Judge or registrar would no doubt have regard to any agreement when deciding whether or not to allow an appeal to be withdrawn under rule 17 of the Tribunal Procedure (Upper Tribunal) Rules 2008. If a Judge sets aside a decision of an appeal tribunal and refers the case to another tribunal, it again becomes possible for an agreement to be made.

The effect of an agreement is to prevent an officer of Revenue and Customs from making any further decision in respect of the same issue and the same period (*Cenlon Finance Co Ltd v Ellwood* [1961] Ch.50). However, an officer is not barred from making a new decision if it is discovered that the agreement was based on incorrect information supplied by the appellant (*Gray v Matheson* [1993] 1 W.L.R. 1130). It is suggested that an officer is also not barred from making a decision under s.18 of the Tax Credits Act 2000 if the agreement related to a s.14 decision and it may also not be inappropriate to revise, under, says s.15 or s.16, an agreed award, depending on what exactly had been the scope of the agreement. In the context of tax credit cases there will not often be any doubt as to the scope of the agreement but where there was more than one issue between the parties—perhaps where the amount of earnings from self-employment is in dispute—the test is whether, looking objectively at all the relevant circumstances (including, in particular, the issues raised by the appellant and all the material known to have been in the possession of Her Majesty's Revenue and Customs), a reasonable man would conclude that the officer had accepted all the appellant's contentions (*Scorer v Olin Energy Systems Ltd* [1984] 1 W.L.R. 675). If the agreement is not in writing, see subs.(3).

Subs.(2)

This provides a 30-day cooling-off period for an appellant (but not an officer of Revenue and Customs) and may be particularly relevant in the light of subs.(5). It could give rise to delay if a hearing date is cancelled in the light of an agreement from which an appellant later resiles. On the other hand, the delay is no greater than can arise in a social security case where the Secretary of State makes a new decision, causing an appeal to lapse under s.9(6) of the Social Security Act 1998 but generating a new right of appeal.

1.22

Subs.(3)

If an agreement is not in writing, Her Majesty's Revenue and Customs must set out in writing their understanding of the agreement and give the appellant 30 days to object. This ensures a reasonable degree of certainty as to the terms of the agreement. The appellant is not required expressly to accept the written version.

1.23

Subs.(4)

There is no provision in the Tax Credits (Appeals) (No.2) Regulations 2002 allowing an appellant to withdraw an appeal by giving notice to the clerk to the tribunal (compare rule 17 of the Tribunal Procedure (First-tier Tribunal)(Social Entitlement Chamber) Rules 2008. Instead, an appellant may give notice of his desire to abandon the appeal to the officer of Revenue and Customs and the officer has 30 days in which to object. If the officer signifies agreement within the 30 days, subss.(1)–(3) will be brought into operation, as will be the case if the officer does nothing for 30 days. If the officer objects within the 30 days, the appeal proceeds. Presumably that means that any attempt to withdraw an appeal is ineffective for 30 days unless the officer consents. This provision applies only to appeals. The 2008 Rules permit the unilateral withdrawal of an application for a direction or penalty proceedings where a tribunal has a first instance jurisdiction.

1.24

Subs. (5)

1.25   By virtue of this subsection, an agreement under subs.(1) may be entered into by an appellant's representative. However, such an agreement may be repudiated by the appellant under subs.(2).

PART X

PENALTIES, ETC.

Evidence in cases of fraud or wilful default

1.26   **105.**—(1) Statements made or documents produced by or on behalf of a person shall not be inadmissible in any such proceedings as are mentioned in subsection (2) below by reason only that it has been drawn to his attention that—

(a) pecuniary settlements may be accepted instead of a penalty being determined, or proceedings being instituted, in relation to any tax, and

(b) though no undertaking can be given as to whether or not the Board will accept such a settlement in the case of any particular person, it is the practice of the Board to be influenced by the fact that a person has made a full confession of any fraudulent conduct to which he had been a party and has given full facilities for investigation,

and that he was or may have been induced thereby to make the statements or produce the documents.

(2) The proceedings mentioned in subsection (1) above are—

(a) any criminal proceedings against the person in question for any form of fraudulent conduct in connection with or in relation to tax; and

(b) any proceedings against him for the recovery of any tax due from him and

(c) any proceedings for a penalty or on appeal against the determination of a penalty.

PART XI

MISCELLANEOUS AND SUPPLEMENTAL

Documents

Loss, destruction or damage to assessments, returns, etc.

1.27   **112.**—(1) Where any assessment to tax, or any duplicate of assessment to tax, or any return or other document relating to tax, has been lost or destroyed, or been so defaced or damaged as to be illegible or otherwise useless, HMRC may, notwithstanding anything in any enactment to the contrary, do all such acts and things as they might have done, and all acts and things done under or in pursuance of this section shall be as valid and effectual for all purposes as they would have been, if the assessment or duplicate of assessment had not been made, or the return or other document had not been made or furnished or required to be made or furnished.

Provided that, where any person who is charged with tax in consequence or by virtue of any act or thing done under or in pursuance of this section proves to the satisfaction of the tribunal that he has already paid any tax for the same chargeable period in respect of the subject matter and on the account in respect of and on which he is so charged, relief shall be given to the extent to which the liability of that person has been discharged by the payment so made either by abatement from the charge or by repayment, as the case may require.

. . .

(3) The references in subsection (1) above to assessments to tax include references to determinations of penalties; and in its application to such determinations the proviso to that subsection shall have effect with the appropriate modifications.

Want of form or errors not to invalidate assessments, etc.

114.—(1) An assessment or determination, warrant or other proceeding which purports to be made in pursuance of any provision of the Taxes Acts shall not be quashed, or deemed to be void or voidable, for want of form, or be affected by reason of a mistake, defect or omission therein, if the same is in substance and effect in conformity with or according to the intent and meaning of the Taxes Acts, and if the person or property charged or intended to be charged or affected thereby is designated therein according to common intent and understanding. 1.28

(2) An assessment or determination shall not be impeached or affected—
 (a) by reason of a mistake therein as to—
  (i) the name or surname of a person liable, or
  (ii) the description of any profits or property, or
  (iii) the amount of the tax charged, or
 (b) by reason of any variance between the notice and the assessment or determination.

Interpretation

Interpretation

118.—(1) In this Act, unless the context otherwise requires— 1.29
"Act" includes an Act of the Parliament of Northern Ireland; and "enactment" shall be construed accordingly;
"the Board" means the Commissioners of Inland Revenue;
"body of persons" means any body politic, corporate or collegiate, and any company, fraternity, fellowship and society of persons, whether corporate or not corporate;
"chargeable gain" has the same meaning as in the 1992 Act;
"chargeable period" means a year of assessment or a company's accounting period;
"collector" means any collector of taxes;
"company" has the meaning given by section 992(1) of ITA 2007;

. . .

"HMRC" means Her Majesty's Revenue and Customs;

"incapacitated person" means any infant, person of unsound mind, lunatic, idiot or insane person;

"infant", in relation to Scotland, except in section 73 of this Act, means a person under legal disability by reason of nonage, and, in the saidsection 73, means a person under the age of 18 years;

"inspector" means any inspector of taxes;

"ITEPA 2003" means the Income Tax (Earnings and Pensions) Act 2003;

"ITTOIA 2005" means the Income Tax (Trading and Other Income) Act 2005;

"ITA 2007" means the Income Tax Act 2007;

"partnership return" has the meaning given by section 12AA(10A) of this Act;

"the principal Act" means the Income and Corporation Taxes Act 1988;

"the relevant trustees", in relation to a settlement, shall be construed in accordance with section 7(9) of this Act;

"return" includes any statement or declaration under the Taxes Acts;

. . .

"successor", in relation to a person who is required to make and deliver, or has made and delivered, a partnership return, and "predecessor" and "successor", in relation to the successor of such a person, shall be construed in accordance with section 12AA(11) of this Act;

"tax", where neither income tax nor capital gains tax nor corporation tax is specified, means any of those taxes except that in sections 20, 20A, 20B and 20D it does not include development land tax;

"the Taxes Acts" means this Act and—

(a) the Tax Acts; and

(b) the Taxation of Chargeable Gains Act 1992 and all other enactments relating to capital gains tax;

"the TCEA 2007" means the Tribunals, Courts and Enforcement Act 2007;

"the 1992 Act" means the Taxation of Chargeable Gains Act 1992;

"trade" includes every trade, manufacture, adventure or concern in the nature of trade.

"the tribunal" is to be read in accordance with section 47C;

(2) For the purposes of this Act, a person shall be deemed not to have failed to do anything required to be done within a limited time if he did it within such further time, if any, as the Board or the tribunal or officer concerned may have allowed; and where a person had a reasonable excuse for not doing anything required to be done he shall be deemed not to have failed to do it unless the excuse ceased and, after the excuse ceased, he shall be deemed not to have failed to do it if he did it without unreasonable delay after the excuse had ceased.

. . .

(4) For the purposes of this Act, the amount of tax covered by any assessment shall not be deemed to be finally determined until that assessment can no longer be varied, whether by the tribunal on an appeal notified to it or by the order of any court.

(5) For the purposes of this Act a loss of tax or a situation is brought about carelessly by a person if the person fails to take reasonable care to avoid bringing about that loss or situation.

(6) Where—
(a) information is provided to Her Majesty's Revenue and Customs,
(b) the person who provided the information, or the person on whose behalf the information was provided, discovers some time later that the information was inaccurate, and
(c) that person fails to take reasonable steps to inform Her Majesty's Revenue and Customs,

any loss of tax or situation brought about by the inaccuracy shall be treated for the purposes of this Act as having been brought about carelessly by that person.

(7) In this Act references to a loss of tax or a situation brought about deliberately by a person include a loss of tax or a situation that arises as a result of a deliberate inaccuracy in a document given to Her Majesty's Revenue and Customs by or on behalf of that person.

Social Security Contributions and Benefits Act 1992

(1992 c.4)

SECTIONS REPRODUCED

PART III

NON-CONTRIBUTORY BENEFITS

PART 8A

HEALTH IN PREGNANCY GRANT

PART IX

CHILD BENEFIT

PART XI

STATUTORY SICK PAY

Employer's liability

PART XII

STATUTORY MATERNITY PAY

PART XIIZA

STATUTORY PATERNITY PAY

PART XIIZB

STATUTORY ADOPTION PAY

PART XIII

GENERAL

Interpretation

SCHEDULES

Guardian's allowance

Guardian's allowance

77.—(1) A person shall be entitled to a guardian's allowance in respect of   1.31
a child [³ or qualifying young person] if—

25

(a) he is entitled to child benefit in respect of that child [³ or qualifying young person], and

(b) the circumstances are any of those specified in subsection (2) below; [¹ . . .]

(2) The circumstances referred to in subsection (1)(b) above are—

(a) that both of the [³ parents of the child or qualifying young person] are dead; or

(b) that one of the [³ parents of the child or qualifying young person] is dead and the person claiming a guardian's allowance shows that he was at the date of the death unaware of, and has failed after all reasonable efforts to discover, the whereabouts of the other parent; or

(c) that one of the [³ parents of the child or qualifying young person] is dead and the other is in prison.

(3) There shall be no entitlement to a guardian's allowance in respect of a child [³ or qualifying young person] unless at least one of the [³ parents of the child or qualifying young person] satisfies, or immediately before his death satisfied, such conditions as may be prescribed as to nationality, residence, place of birth or other matters.

(4) Where, apart from this subsection, a person is entitled to receive, in respect of a particular child [³ or qualifying young person], payment of an amount by way of a guardian's allowance, that amount shall not be payable unless one of the conditions specified in subsection (5) below is satisfied.

(5) Those conditions are—

(a) that the beneficiary would be treated for the purposes of Part IX of this Act as having the child [³ or qualifying young person] living with him; or

(b) that the requisite contributions are being made to the cost of providing for the child [³ or qualifying young person].

(6) The condition specified in subsection (5)(b) above is to be treated as satisfied if, but only if—

(a) such contributions are being made at a weekly rate not less than the amount referred to in subsection (4) above—
   (i) by the beneficiary; or
   (ii) where the beneficiary is one of two spouses [² or civil partners] residing together, by them together; and

(b) except in prescribed cases, the contributions are over and above those required for the purpose of satisfying section 143(1)(b) below.

(7) A guardian's allowance in respect of a child [³ or qualifying young person] shall be payable at the weekly rate specified in Schedule 4, Part III, paragraph 5.

(8) Regulations—

(a) may modify subsection (2) or (3) above in relation to cases in which a child [³ or qualifying young person] has been adopted or is illegitimate, or the marriage of [³ the parents of a child or qualifying young person] has been terminated by divorce [² or the civil partnership of the child's parents has been dissolved];

(b) shall prescribe the circumstances in which a person is to be treated for the purposes of this section as being in prison (by reference to his undergoing a sentence of imprisonment for life or of a prescribed minimum duration, or to his being in legal custody in prescribed circumstances); and

(c) may, for cases where entitlement to a guardian's allowance is established by reference to a person being in prison, provide—
  (i) for requiring him to pay to the National Insurance Fund sums paid by way of a guardian's allowance;
  (ii) for suspending payment of an allowance where a conviction, sentence or order of a court is subject to appeal, and for matters arising from the decision of an appeal;
  (iii) for reducing the rate of an allowance in cases where the person in prison contributes to the cost of providing for the child [³ or qualifying young person].

(9) Where a husband and wife are residing together and, apart from this subsection, they would each be entitled to a guardian's allowance in respect of the same child [³ or qualifying young person], only the wife shall be entitled, but payment may be made either to her or to him unless she elects in the prescribed manner that payment is not to be made to him.

(10) Subject to subsection (11) below, no person shall be entitled to a guardian's allowance in respect of a child [³ or qualifying young person] of which he or she is the parent.

(11) Where a person—
(a) has adopted a child [³ or qualifying young person]; and
(b) was entitled to guardian's allowance in respect of the child [³ or qualifying young person] immediately before the adoption,
subsection (10) above shall not terminate his entitlement.

AMENDMENTS

1. Tax Credits Act 2002, s.60 and Sch.6 (April 6, 2003).
2. Civil Partnership Act 2004, s.254 and Sch.24, para.34 (December 5, 2005).
3. Child Benefit Act 2005, s.1 and Sch.1, para.4 (April 10, 2006).

DEFINITIONS

"child": s.122.
"entitled": *ibid.*
"Great Britain": by art.1 of the Union with Scotland Act 1706, this means England, Scotland and Wales.
"United Kingdom": by Sch.1 of the Interpretation Act 1978, this means Great Britain and Northern Ireland.
"week": s.122.

GENERAL NOTE

Since April 2003 responsibility for the administration of Guardian's Allowance has lain with HMRC. Arrangements for claims, payments, decisions and appeals are now to be found in the Child Benefit and Guardian's Allowance (Administration) Regulations (SI 2003/492), the Child Benefit and Guardian's Allowance (Administrative Arrangements) Regulations (SI 2003/494), and the Child Benefit and Guardian's Allowance (Decisions and Appeals) Regulations (SI 2003/916). These regulations may be found in Volume III of this work.   1.32

Subs.(1)

Guardian's Allowance is a benefit paid to those caring for children who are, or are in effect, orphans. The claimant does not have to be in any legal sense the guardian of the child (e.g. under the Children Act 1989), but they must be entitled to child benefit in respect of the child (whether or not they actually receive it) or be treated as if they are entitled.   1.33

Subs. (2)

1.34   A claim for Guardian's Allowance can only succeed if it is shown that either

(a) both of the child's parents are dead, or

(b) that one of them is dead and the whereabouts of the other is and has been unknown since the date of that death or

(c) that one of them is dead and the other is in prison.

Proof of death will normally be supplied by production of a death certificate though death might be presumed in circumstances similar to those for bereavement benefits.

In showing that the whereabouts of a surviving parent are unknown it is necessary for the claimant to show that this has always been the situation since the death of the other, and remains the situation despite having made all reasonable efforts of discovery.

In considering whether the whereabouts of a surviving parent can reasonably be discovered under (b) above, a tribunal may take into account information which came to light after the claim had been made but before the decision maker had come to a decision, even where the whereabouts of the surviving parent became known otherwise than through the efforts of the claimant. The operative date is the date of decision by the DM. The tribunal must consider the case on the basis of the facts known as at the date of the decision (*R(G) 3/68*). Once the whereabouts of the parent have become known, the claim to the allowance cannot be resurrected on the subsequent disappearance of that parent (*R(G)2/83*). This was a case where the surviving parent attended the funeral of the dead parent but then disappeared and his whereabouts could not be ascertained. The claim to the allowance failed. In the same case the Commissioner said that "all reasonable efforts" means the efforts someone could reasonably be expected to make if they wished to find the person for whom they were searching. "Whereabouts" is not the same as residence, so knowing the town but not the address where the missing parent lives may be enough to defeat the claim to benefit. It should be noted that Commissioners in Northern Ireland have taken a different view, saying that in an urban environment "whereabouts" must mean a place identifiable with "some particularity" (*R3/74(P)*). Indeed, Commissioners in Northern Ireland have taken an altogether more generous view of the conditions to be satisfied, holding that knowledge that a parent is alive does not defeat a claim if the whereabouts of the living parent cannot be ascertained after reasonable efforts (*R3/74/(P)* and *R3/75/(P)*, a decision of a Tribunal of Commissioners). In *R3/75/(P)*, the Tribunal of Commissioners suggested that the Commissioners in Great Britain appeared to be regarding the inquiries as being directed to whether the other parent was alive rather than where that parent was living. In an *obiter* statement in *R(G) 2/83* the Commissioner appears to share this view, suggesting that mere evidence that the second parent is alive will not amount to knowledge of whereabouts so as to defeat a claim, but this does not, of course, overrule the earlier decisions noted above. It seems that the Northern Ireland Commissioners have viewed the benefit as one payable in the absence of a parent able to assume financial responsibility for the child, whereas the British Commissioners see it as concerned primarily with those rendered orphans.

Two unreported Commissoners' decisions demonstrate just how difficult it has become to interpret this subsection where the underlying philosophy of the provisions is unclear.

In the first of them (*CG/60/92*), the claimant grandmother had custody of a child whose mother had died. The father was known and had visited the child at the grandmother's house on four occassions since the death of the mother. As well, he had been served notice of custody proceedings either at, or through, his parents' address, though subsequently they denied knowledge of his whereabouts. The Commissioner held that the claimant must be taken to have known of the father's whereabouts when she had him in her house and could talk to him. An argument was pressed that knowing the where- abouts of someone must mean knowing an address of residence, or of employment, or at any rate of regular attendance, at which something like service of process could be accomplished. If the reason behind GA has indeed shifted to the idea of a resource for maintenance of the child then there would be something to be said for this argument, but the Commissioner thought that the essence of knowing the whereabouts of a person meant no more than being able in some way to communicate with him, and that was clearly achieved here on the four occasions of his visits. The Commissioner relied in this case on the view expressed in *R(G) 2/83* (where the claimant was visited once, and knew of an address that was valid for a week) which also seems to accept that an ability to communicate with the parent is the touchstone.

In the other case (*CSG/8/92*), the claimant, again a grandmother with the custody of her deceased daughter's child, had had no contact with the child's father, but she had provided an address for service in custody proceedings, she had said that she knew where the other parent was living at the time of her daughter's death, and that she had been told that he was at the funeral, though she had not seen him herself. There was no suggestion that the custody address had been effective and it would appear that at a subsequent SSAT appeal the claimant must have given evidence suggesting that the other matters were based only on rumour. The Commissioner allowed an appeal by the adjudication officer on the ground that the SSAT had failed to explain adequately why they were rejecting the original statements and preferring her later accounts, and he sent the matter back for consideration by another tribunal. In doing so he gave further attention to the meaning of reasonable steps to discover the whereabouts of a parent. First, he seems to accept that actual contact with the other parent, or even a chance to communicate, is a conclusive block to the claimant; she cannot in those circumstances say that at all times since the death she has been unaware of the whereabouts of the other parent. Seeing the other parent at the funeral is probably enough to preclude her claim because she could have taken the opportunity to establish contact. It is not enough for the claimant to say that she had no wish to speak to the other (probably estranged) parent, because the test suggested in *R(G) 2/83*, and adopted in these cases, is that reasonable efforts to discover the whereabouts of another person mean the steps that would be reasonable for a person who *wanted* to find that other person. (Though, *quaere*, it might be possible to argue that one could want to find another person and yet reasonably refrain from making inquiries upon an occasion of particular emotion and distress such as the funeral.)

Both cases (and *R(G) 2/83*), therefore, agree that where actual contact has been made, even though transitory, the claimant knows (or rather has known) the whereabouts of the other parent and the claim must fail. The Commissioner goes on to consider, however, the question of how much knowledge of the other parent's location will suffice if no contact is made. Put another way, the question is what is meant by "whereabouts" when someone is being sought, and how much do you have to know in order to say you have found him? Knowing that the parent is somewhere in the world cannot be sufficient because, as has been pointed out, this equates to knowing that he is alive, whereas the statute requires knowledge of his whereabouts. There seems much good sense in the observation of the Northern Ireland Commissioner that while the name of a village may suffice to locate someone living there, something more must be known of someone in an urban environment. *R(G) 3/68* held that knowing an address (in Russia) from which letters had purported to have been sent, but from which no reply was obtained, did amount to knowing the whereabouts of that person. *CG/60/92* rejects the argument that "whereabouts" should be equated with address for service, but only in the context of a claimant who had actual, if transitory, contact. In *CSG/8/92*, the Commissioner seemed ready to accept that "whereabouts" should now be taken to mean knowledge of the person's residence, of employment, or place of attendance by habit (such as a public house) by which he could be located without undue further difficulty. An unresponsive address in Russia would fail this test. This seems a workable and common sense approach and is one step towards rationalising GA, at least in part, as a benefit for the replacement of parental maintenance.

The circumstances in which a child is regarded as "orphaned" by the surviving parent being in prison are defined in reg.7 of the Guardian's Allowance (General) Regulations 2003.

Where a child has been adopted the adopted parents are put for all purposes in the place of the child's parents. Where a child has been adopted by only one parent a claim may be made in respect of that child when only that parent has died. (see reg. 4 of the Guardian's Allowance (General) Regulations 2003.)

Where a child's parents are not married to each other a claim may be made following the death of the mother if paternity of the child has not been established by a court and is not regarded as having been established by the determining authority. (reg.4, Guardian's Allowance (General) Regulations 2003.)

Where a child's parents have been divorced a claim may be made following the death of the parent with whom the child was living if there is no residence order in favour of the surviving parent and no liability for that parent to maintain the child either under a court order or a decision in force under the Child Support Act 1991. (reg.6 Guardian's Allowance (General) Regulations 2003).

Subs. (3)

1.35   Conditions as to residence of the child's parents are to be found in reg.9 of Guardian's Allowance (General) Regulations 2003.

Subss. (4), (5) and (6)

1.36   A claim for Guardian's Allowance can only succeed if the claimant is either:

(a) treated as having the child living with them for the purpose of a claim for Child Benefit or

(b) is contributing (or if living with their spouse, the spouse is contributing) to the cost of maintaining the child to an extent equal to the amount of Guardian's Allowance that is payable. This contribution must be in addition to any contribution necessary to qualify for the payment of child benefit.

Subs. (9)

1.37   This is a curiously worded provision. Where husband and wife are living together and, but for this provision, they would each be entitled to claim Guardian's Allowance, only the wife is to be entitled. Nevertheless HMRC could make payment to the husband unless his wife has elected in the proper way to deny payment to her husband.

Subs. (10)

1.38   This prevents a claim for Guardian's Allowance by a parent of the child. But for this purpose a step-parent is not regarded as a parent and such a claim could also succeed if it is made by the natural parent of a child whose adoptive parents have died—the effect of the adoption is to substitute the adoptive parents as the child's "parents" for this purpose. *(R(G)4/83(T)*—and see reg.4 Guardian's Allowance (General) Regulations 2003.)

[¹ PART 8A

HEALTH IN PREGNANCY GRANT

Entitlement

1.39   **140A.**— (1) A woman who satisfies prescribed conditions in relation to a pregnancy of hers is entitled to payment of a lump sum (to be known as "health in pregnancy grant").

(2) A condition prescribed under subsection (1) may, in particular, require a woman to have reached a specified stage of her pregnancy.

(3) A woman is not entitled to health in pregnancy grant unless—

(a) she has received advice on matters relating to maternal health from a health professional;

(b) she is in Great Britain at the time she makes a claim for the grant in accordance with the Administration Act.

(4) Circumstances may be prescribed in which a woman is to be treated for the purposes of subsection (3)(b) as being, or as not being, in Great Britain.

(5) In this section—

"health professional" has such meaning as may be prescribed,

"prescribed" means prescribed by regulations, and

"woman" means a female of any age.

(6) The power to make regulations under this section is exercisable by the Treasury.]

AMENDMENT

1. Health and Social Care Act 2008, s.131 (January 1, 2009).

GENERAL NOTE

Part 4 of the Health and Social Care Act 2008 inserted the new Part 8A of the   **1.40**
Social Security Contributions and Benefits Act 1992 and made provision for a new lump sum payment, the health in pregnancy grant. The grant, currently set at £190, is a non-contributory, non-means tested and non-taxable benefit, payable to all expectant mothers from the twenty-fifth week of their pregnancy who are ordinarily resident in the UK, providing that they receive maternal health advice from a health professional. HMRC are responsible for the payment and management of the health in pregnancy grant (Health and Social Care Act 2008, s.138(1)).

The origins of the health in pregnancy grant lie in the Chancellor of the Exchequer's December 2006 *Pre-Budget Report,* which announced that child benefit would be extended to all expectant mothers from week 29 of their pregnancy, in view of the importance of good nutrition during the final stages of pregnancy. The Secretary of State for Health subsequently announced (in September 2007) that the additional support would be provided by way of a one-off payment, rather than an extension of child benefit. The detailed entitlement rules are contained in the Health in Pregnancy Grant (Entitlement and Amount) Regulations 2009 (SI 2008/3108). The health in pregnancy grant is paid in addition to the sure start maternity grant and healthy start vouchers for pregnant mothers on low incomes.

[¹Amount

140B.— (1) Health in pregnancy grant is to be of an amount prescribed   **1.41**
by regulations made by the Treasury.

(2) Different amounts may be prescribed in relation to different cases.]

AMENDMENT

1. Health and Social Care Act 2008, s.131 (January 1, 2009).

GENERAL NOTE

The value of the health in pregnancy grant is set at a lump sum of £190 (Health in   **1.42**
Pregnancy Grant Entitlement and Amount) Regulations 2008 (SI 2008/3108), reg. 10). The payment is made on a per pregnancy basis, not a per child basis, and so the same single payment is made for twins or other multiple births. The purpose of the grant is to provide additional financial support to women in the final stages of preg-

nancy, and particularly towards ensuring that they have a healthy diet. However, there are no post-payment checks on the use to which the payment is put: according to the Secretary of State for Health, "we won't send round the broccoli police if someone spends part of their grant on other items they may need in pregnancy" (Rt Hon A. Johnson MP, Toynbee Hall speech, September 12, 2007).

PART IX

CHILD BENEFIT

Child benefit

1.43   **141.**—A person who is responsible for one or more children [¹ or qualifying young persons] in any week shall be entitled, subject to the provisions of this Part of this Act, to a benefit (to be known as "child benefit") for that week in respect of the [¹ child or qualifying young person, or each of the children or qualifying young persons] for whom he is responsible.

AMENDMENT

1. Child Benefit Act 2005, s.1 (April 10, 2006).

GENERAL NOTE

1.44   Since April 2003 administration of Child Benefit has lain with HMRC, but the structure of the benefit remains substantially unchanged.

The administrative arrangements for claims, payments, decisions and appeals are now to be found in Child Benefit and Guardians Allowance (Administration) Regulations, (SI 2003/492), the Child Benefit and Guardians Allowance (Administrative Arrangements) Regulations, (SI 2003/494), and the Child Benefit and Guardians Allowance (Decisions and Appeals) Regulations 2003, (SI 2003/916). All of these are to be found in Volume III of this work.

Child Benefit is a benefit paid to those responsible for a child or qualifying young person. Under the new definitions adopted from 2006 a "child" is a person under the age of 16 (whether or not they are in education) and a "qualifying young person" will be defined by regulation generally as a young person who remains in non advanced education or in certain forms of training up to the age of 20 (see s.142 below). Those responsible for a child include not only those with whom the child is living, but also those contributing sufficiently to the cost of maintaining that child.

Child Benefit is paid at a higher rate in respect of the first or only child and at a lower rate for all other children in the family.

Until July 1998 a supplement (commonly known as one parent benefit) was paid to single parents in respect of the first child—some claimants may still qualify for this rate on the basis of a continuous claim.

Claimants for Child Benefit are also subject to conditions as to residence and presence (including the presence of the child) and are disqualified while they are subject to immigration control—see s.146A.

[¹ 142 "Child" and "qualifying young person"

1.45   (1) For the purposes of this Part of this Act a person is a child if he has not attained the age of 16.

(2) In this Part of the Act "qualifying young person" means a person, other than a child, who—

(a) Has not attained such age (greater than 16) as is prescribed by regulations made by the Treasury, and

(b) satisfies conditions so prescribed.]

AMENDMENT

1. Child Benefit Act 2005, s.1 (April 10, 2006).

Meaning of "person responsible for [³ child or qualifying young person]"

143.—(1) For the purposes of this Part of this Act a person shall be treated as responsible for a child [³ or qualifying young person] in any week if—   1.46

(a) he has the child [³ or qualifying young person] living with him in that week; or

(b) he is contributing to the cost of providing for the child [³ or qualifying young person] at a weekly rate which is not less than the weekly rate of child benefit payable in respect of the child [³ or qualifying young person] for that week.

(2) Where a person has had a child [⁴ or qualifying young person] living with him at some time before a particular week he shall be treated for the purposes of this section as having the child [⁴ or qualifying young person] living with him in that week notwithstanding their absence from one another unless, in the 16 weeks preceding that week, they were absent from one another for more than 56 days not counting any day which is to be disregarded under subsection (3) below.

(3) Subject to subsection (4) below, a day of absence shall be disregarded for the purposes of subsection (2) above if it is due solely to the [⁴ the fact that the child or qualifying young person is]—

(a) receiving [⁴ education or training of a description prescribed by regulations made by the Treasury];

(b) undergoing medical or other treatment as an in-patient in a hospital or similar institution; or

(c) [⁴ . . .], in such circumstances as may be prescribed, in residential accommodation pursuant to arrangements made under—

    [¹[⁵(i) paragraph 2 of Schedule 20 to the National Health Service Act 2006 or paragraph 2 of Schedule 15 to the National Health Service (Wales) Act 2006]

    (ii) the Children Act 1989;]

    [²(iii) the Social Work (Scotland) Act 1968;

    (iv) the National Health Service (Scotland) Act 1978;

    (v) the Education (Scotland) Act 1980;

    (vi) the Mental Health (Scotland) Act 1984; or

    (vii) the Children (Scotland) Act 1995.]

(4) The number of days that may be disregarded by virtue of subsection (3)(b) or (c) above in the case of any child [⁴ or qualifying young person] shall not exceed such number as may be prescribed unless the person claiming to be responsible for the child [⁴ or qualifying young person] regularly incurs expenditure in respect [⁴ of him].

(5) Regulations may prescribe the circumstances in which a person is or is not to be treated—

(a) as contributing to the cost of providing for a child [⁴ or qualifying young person] as required by subsection (1)(b) above; or

(b) as regularly incurring expenditure in respect of a child [⁴ or qualifying young person] as required by subsection (4) above;
and such regulations may in particular make provision whereby a contribution made or expenditure incurred by two or more persons is to be treated as made or incurred by one of them or whereby a contribution made or expenditure incurred by one of two spouses [³ or civil partners] residing together is to be treated as made or incurred by the other.

AMENDMENTS

1. Social Security (Consequential Provisions) Act 1992, s.6 and Sch.4, para.5 (April 1, 1993).
2. Child Support Pensions and Social Security Act 2000, s.72 (October 9, 2000).
3. Civil Partnership Act 2004, s.254 and Sch.24, para.47 (December 5, 2005).
4. Child Benefit Act 2005, s.1 and Sch.1 para.9 (April 10, 2006).
5. National Health Service (Consequential Provisions) Act 2006, Sch.1, para.146 (March 1, 2007).

GENERAL NOTE

Subs. (1)

1.47   A person is regarded as being "responsible for a child or qualifying young person" if they either have the child living with them, or if they are contributing to the upkeep of that child a weekly sum not less that the amount of Child Benefit payable for that week. See Regulation 11 of the Child Benefit (General) Regulations 2006. To be "living with" the claimant in this context requires that the child resides in the same house in a "settled course of daily living". In *R(F) 2/81* the claimant failed because his daughter spent only the day time hours each weekend in his home. Mere residence on its own may be insufficient if the child is normally living elsewhere (as for example where a child spends its holidays living away from home). But where the child is living with a parent who has rights of care and control it may be regarded as living with that parent even though at other times it may be living with the other parent *(R(F) 2/79)*.
The interaction of subss (1) and (2) together with s.144(3) and Sch.10 referred to there is applied in *CF/3348/2002*. There the child remained with the wife when her husband, who had been in receipt of Child Benefit, left her. In accordance with s.144(3) and Sch.10, he nevertheless remained entitled to receive the benefit for the next three weeks.

Subs. (2)

1.48   A child may continue to live with the claimant even though one or other of them may be absent provided that the absence is not more than 56 days in a period of 16 weeks. Where the absence is continuous, therefore, entitlement will cease after 8 weeks.

Subs. (3)

1.49   In counting days of absence certain days are disregarded. These include days away at boarding school, days in hospital or otherwise undergoing medical treatment, or days in local authority care on disability or health grounds—Reg.9 Child Benefit (General) Regulations 2006.

Subs. (4)

1.50   Where the child is absent for medical treatment or in care on grounds of disability or health the period of permitted absence is extended to 12 weeks— Regulation 10 Child Benefit (General) Regulations 2006.

But entitlement may be continued further provide that the claimant can show that they are regularly incurring expenditure in respect of the child.

Subs. (5)

Regulation 11 of the Child Benefit (General) Regulations 2006 provides for the aggregation of amounts where two or more persons are contributing to the cost of maintaining a child and for either agreement between them or, failing that, a determination by the Board as to which of them will be treated as entitled to benefit. Where spouses are residing together a contribution made by one of them may be treated as having been made by the other.

1.51

Exclusions and priority

144.—(1) [¹ . . .]

(2) Schedule 9 to this Act shall have effect for excluding entitlement to child benefit [¹ . . .].

(3) Where, apart from this subsection, two or more persons would be entitled to child benefit in respect of the same child [¹ or qualifying young person] for the same week, one of them only shall be entitled; and the question which of them is entitled shall be determined in accordance with Schedule 10 to this Act.

1.52

AMENDMENT

1. Child Benefit Act 2005, s.1 and Sch.1, para.10 (April 10, 2006).

GENERAL NOTE

Note that recourse to Sch.10 is appropriate only where two or more people are entitled to Child Benefit in respect of the same child for the same week. If, therefore, only one of them remains entitled under s.143 there is no recourse to Sch.10. But where, for example, a child has ceased to reside with one parent (s.143(1)) that parent may remain entitled for a period by the application of the other provisions of s.143 and by the effect of s.13(2) of the SSAA 1992. See *CF/2826/2008* and the notes following Sch.10.

1.53

Rate of child benefit

145.—(1) Child benefit shall be payable at such weekly rate as may be prescribed.

(2) Different rates may be prescribed in relation to different cases, whether by reference to the age of the child [² or qualifying young person] in respect of whom the benefit is payable or otherwise.

(3) The power to prescribe different rates under subsection (2) above shall be exercised so as to bring different rates into force on such day as the Secretary of State may by order specify.

(4) No rate prescribed in place of a rate previously in force shall be lower than the rate that it replaces.

(5) [¹ . . .]

(6) An order under subsection (3) above may be varied or revoked at any time before the date specified thereby.

(7) An order under that subsection shall be laid before Parliament after being made.

1.54

AMENDMENTS

1. Tax Credits Act 2002, s.60 and Sch.6 (April 1, 2003).
2. Child Benefit Act 2005, s.1 and Sch.1, para.11 (April 10, 2006).

[¹ Entitlement after death of child [³ or qualifying young person]

1.55

145A.—(1) If a child [³ or qualifying young person] dies and a person is entitled to child benefit in respect of him for the week in which his death occurs, that person shall be entitled to child benefit in respect of the child [³ or qualifying young person] for a prescribed period following that week.

(2) If the person entitled to child benefit under subsection (1) dies before the end of that prescribed period and, at the time of his death, was—

(a) a member of a married couple [² or civil partnership] and living with the person to whom he was married [² or who was his civil partner], or

(b) a member of an unmarried couple [² or a cohabiting same sex couple],

that other member of the [² couple or partnership] shall be entitled to child benefit for the period for which the dead person would have been entitled to child benefit under subsection (1) above but for his death.

(3) If a child [³ or qualifying young person] dies before the end of the week in which he is born, subsections (1) and (2) apply in his case as if references to the person entitled to child benefit in respect of a child [³ or qualifying young person] for the week in which his death occurs were to the person who would have been so entitled if the child had been alive at the beginning of that week (and if any conditions which were satisfied, and any facts which existed, at the time of his death were satisifed or existed then).

(4) Where a person is entitled to child benefit in respect of a child under this section, section 77 applies with the omission of subsections (4) to (6).

(5) In this section—

[² "civil partnership" means two people of the same sex who are civil partners of each other and are neither—

(a) separated under a court order, nor

(b) separated in circumstances in which the separation is likely to be permanent,

"cohabiting same-sex couple" means two people of the same sex who are not civil partners of each other but are living together as if they were civil partners.]

"married couple" means a man and a woman who are married to each other and are neither—

(a) separated under a court order, nor

(b) separated in circumstances in which the separation is likely to be permanent, and

"unmarried couple" means a man and a woman who are not a married couple but are living together as husband and wife.]

[² (6) For the purposes of this section, two people of the same sex are to be regarded as living together as if they were civil partners if, but only if, they would be regarded as living together as husband and wife were they instead two people of the opposite sex.]

AMENDMENTS

1. Tax Credits Act 2002, s.56 (April 1, 2003).
2. Civil Partnership Act 2004, s.254 and Sch.24, para.48 (December 5, 2005).
3. Child Benefit Act 2005, s.1 and Sch.1, para.12 (April 10, 2006).

[¹Presence in Great Britain

146.—(1) No child benefit shall be payable in respect of a child [² or quali-   1.56
fying young person] for a week unless he is in Great Britain in that week.

(2) No person shall be entitled to child benefit for a week unless he is in
Great Britain in that week.

(3) Circumstances may be prescribed in which [² any] person is to be
treated for the purposes of [² subsection (1) or (2) above] as being, or as
not being, in Great Britain.]

AMENDMENTS

1. Tax Credits Act 2002, s.56 (April 1, 2003).
2. Child Benefit Act 2005, s.1 and Sch.1, para.13 (April 10, 2006).

GENERAL NOTE

This section was inserted with effect from April 2003. It replaces an earlier   1.57
version, but the effect of this section when combined with the Child Benefit
(General) Regulations is largely the same. See the notes to those Regulations.

Persons subject to immigration control

[¹ **146A.**—[² . . .]]   1.58

AMENDMENTS

1. Asylum and Immigration Act 1996, s.10 (August 19, 1996).
2. Immigration and Asylum Act 1999, s.169(3) and Sch.16 (April 3, 2000).

Interpretation of Part IX and supplementary provisions

147.—(1) In this Part of this Act—   1.59
"prescribed" means prescribed by regulations;
"recognised educational establishment" [² omitted]
"voluntary organisation" means a body, other than a public or local
    authority, the activities of which are carried on otherwise than for
    profit; and
"week" means a period of 7 days beginning with a Monday.

(2) Subject to any provision made by regulations, references in this Part
of this Act to any condition being satisfied or any facts existing in a week
shall be construed as references to the condition being satisfied or the facts
existing at the beginning of that week.

(3) References in this Part of this Act to a parent, father or mother of a
child [² or qualifying young person] shall be construed as including references to a step-parent, step-father or step-mother.

(4) Regulations may prescribe the circumstances in which persons are
or are not to be treated for the purposes of this Part of this Act as residing
together.

(5) Regulations may make provision as to the circumstances in which [¹ a
marriage during the subsistence of which a party to it is at any time married to
more than one person is to be treated for the purposes of this Part of this Act
as having, or not having, the same consequences as any other marriage.]

(6) Nothing in this Part of this Act shall be construed as conferring a
right to child benefit on any body corporate; but regulations may confer
such a right on voluntary organisations and for that purpose may make such
modifications as the Secretary of State thinks fit—

(a) of any provision of this Part of this Act; or

(b) of any provision of the Administration Act relating to child benefit.

AMENDMENTS

1. Private International Law (Miscellaneous Provisions) Act 1995, the Schedule, para.4(3) (January 8, 1996).

2. Child Benefit Act 2005, s.1 and Sch.1, para.14 (April 10, 2006).

GENERAL NOTE

"week"

1.60   A week is defined as a period of seven days beginning on a Monday. Falling short of a full week by a few hours can be ignored: *R(F) 1/82(S)*. The provision in subs.(2) is a trap for the unwary. It means that, subject to provisions in regulations imposing a different rule, a condition to be satisfied or circumstances existing on a Monday (which, of course, begins at midnight on Sunday) are taken as subsisting for the whole week.

The meaning of parent is also extended by the effect of the Children Act 1989, to include any person in whose favour a residence order has been made. This is because the "parental responsibility" conferred by the order made under that Act is defined to include all the rights which, by law, a parent has in relation to that child. For the purposes of the Contributions and Benefits Act, the word parent is to be construed as the "legal parent" of the child. (See *Secretary of State for Social Services v Smith* [1983] 1 W.L.R. 1110, where the effect of an order made under equivalent legislation then in force, was to include an adoptive parent of the child and at the same time to exclude the natural parent.) The same reasoning was applied by Commissioner Howell in *R(F) 1/08* where a lesbian couple had two children with the assistance of artificial insemination and after they had separated a residence order had been made in favour of both of them. The Commissioner held that both must be regarded as parents, not just the biological mother, and consequently it became necessary for HMRC to exercise the discretion provided for in para.5.

PART XI

STATUTORY SICK PAY

GENERAL NOTE

1.61   Statutory sick pay (SSP) was originally introduced in April 1983 by the Social Security and Housing Benefits Act 1982. The main primary legislation is now to be found in Pt XI, annotated here; there are also various sets of regulations, principally the SSP (General) Regulations 1982 (SI 1982/894), which are contained in Pt III of this volume. Section 151(1) of the SSCBA 1992 provides that an employer is liable to pay to an employee for any day of incapacity for work in relation to the employee's contract of service with that employer, where the day in question is a qualifying day (see s.154) which forms part of a period of incapacity to work (see s.152) and falls within a period of entitlement as between that employer and that employee (s.153 and Sch.11). Incapacity must be duly notified to the employer, and SSP may be withheld in the event of non-existent or late notification (see s.156). Those who are self-employed (who by definition lack an employer) and those who are unemployed are excluded from entitlement to SSP. Some employees are also excluded from SSP. Section 153(3) and Sch.11 prevent the requisite period of entitlement arising as between employer and employees in various types of case (e.g. low earners, women at a certain stage of pregnancy, some persons affected by trade disputes).

SSP is payable at a weekly rate. The daily rate will depend on the number of qualifying days in the week (see s.157). SSP is not payable in respect of the first three
qualifying days (or "waiting days") in any period of entitlement (see s.155(1)). SSP
cannot be paid in kind or by the provision of board and lodging or other services
or facilities (SSP (General) Regulations 1982 (SI 1982/894), reg.8). Any day of
incapacity for work in relation to a contract of service which falls within a period of
entitlement to SSP precludes concurrent entitlement to incapacity benefit (Sch.12,
para.1). Employees reach their maximum entitlement to SSP as against any one
employer in any one period of entitlement when they have been entitled in that
period to 28 times the appropriate weekly rate of SSP (see s.155(4)). This is typically after 28 weeks of continuous incapacity. If the person remains incapacitated
after that, he or she must look to incapacity benefit or, failing that, a means-tested
benefit.

At the start of the SSP scheme in 1983, employers were able to recoup the entire
amount paid from the National Insurance contributions and the PAYE tax that they
were required to collect and account for to the Inland Revenue. The initial effect of
SSP was thus to transfer the cost of administration from the State to the employer.
The Statutory Sick Pay Act 1991 limited employers to recouping 80 per cent of
the cost of SSP payments, but "small employers" were still able to claim full reimbursement. This was followed by the Statutory Sick Pay Act 1994, which abolished
employers' general right to recover (some of) the costs of SSP. The special rules
for reimbursing small employers were then repealed (although they remain for the
purposes of SMP). Instead, in principle any employer—not just small employers—
can recover the costs of SSP payments under the Percentage Threshold Scheme.
However, this reimbursement is only available where the employer's expenditure on
SSP exceeds 13 per cent of their gross National Insurance contributions liability—in
other words, only where there is an epidemic of illness in the workforce (see further
Statutory Sick Pay Threshold Order 1995 (SI 1995/512)).

In certain circumstances, where an employer does not, or because of insolvency,
cannot, discharge their statutory liability to pay SSP, that liability became that of the
Board of Inland Revenue (s.151(6), SSP (General) Regulations 1982 (SI 1982/894),
regs 9A–9C). This liability was transferred from the Secretary of State to the Board
of the Inland Revenue with effect from April 1, 1999, under the Social Security
Contributions (Transfer of Functions, etc.) Act 1999, s.1(2) and Sch.2, along with
those functions under SSP (General) Regulations 1982, regs 10 and 14.

The arrangements for resolving disputes about entitlement to SSP were changed
with effect from April 1, 1999. Before that date, certain questions could be referred
to an AO, thus opening up the usual channels of appeal to SSATs, Commissioners
and ultimately the courts. Since that date the Social Security Contributions
(Transfer of Functions, etc.) Act 1999 and the Statutory Sick Pay and Statutory
Maternity Pay (Decisions) Regulations 1999 (SI 1999/776) have replaced the
AO with an officer of Revenue and Customs. Consequently, decision-making and
appeals are now governed by Pt II of the 1999 Act, with the right of appeal lying to
the tax chamber of the First-tier Tribunal. An employment tribunal has no jurisdiction under the Employment Rights Act 1996 to entertain an employee's complaint
that SSP has not been paid: (per Mr Recorder Luba Q.C. in *Taylor Gordon & Co
Ltd v Timmons* ([2004] I.R.L.R. 180, at para.43)).

Employer's liability

Employer's liability

151.—(1) Where an employee has a day of incapacity for work in relation   1.62
to his contract of service with an employer, that employer shall, if the conditions set out in sections 152 to 154 below are satisfied, be liable to make

him, in accordance with the following provisions of this Part of this Act, a payment (to be known as "statutory sick pay") in respect of that day.

(2) Any agreement shall be void to the extent that it purports—

(a) to exclude, limit or otherwise modify any provision of this Part of this Act; or

(b) to require an employee to contribute (whether directly or indirectly) towards any costs incurred by his employer under this Part of this Act.

(3) For the avoidance of doubt, any agreement between an employer and an employee authorising any deductions from statutory sick pay which the employer is liable to pay to the employee in respect of any period shall not be void by virtue of subsection (2)(a) above if the employer—

(a) is authorised by that or another agreement to make the same deductions from any contractual remuneration which he is liable to pay in respect of the same period, or

(b) would be so authorised if he were liable to pay contractual remuneration in respect of that period.

(4) For the purposes of this Part of this Act [¹a day of incapacity for work in relation to a contract of service means a day on which] the employee concerned is, or is deemed in accordance with regulations to be, incapable by reason of some specific disease or bodily or mental disablement of doing work which he can reasonably be expected to do under that contract.

(5) In any case where an employee has more than one contract of service with the same employer the provisions of this Part of this Act shall, except in such cases as may be prescribed and subject to the following provisions of this Part of this Act, have effect as if the employer were a different employer in relation to each contract of service.

(6) Circumstances may be prescribed in which, notwithstanding the provisions of subsections (1) to (5) above, the liability to make payments of statutory sick pay is to be a liability of the [²Commissioners of Inland Revenue].

[²(7) Regulations under subsection (6) above must be made with the concurrence of the Commissioners of Inland Revenue.]

AMENDMENTS

1. Social Security (Incapacity for Work) Act 1994, s.11(1) and Sch.1, para.34 (April 13, 1995).

2. Social Security Contributions (Transfer of Functions, etc.) Act 1999, s.1(1) and Sch.1, para.9 (April 1, 1999).

DEFINITIONS

"contract of service"—see s.163(1).
"employee"—*ibid.* and SSP (General) Regulations 1982, reg.16.
"employer"—see s.163(1).
"prescribed"—*ibid.*

GENERAL NOTE

Subss. (1)–(3)

1.63   The general liability on employers to pay SSP—where the qualifying conditions are fulfilled by the employee—is set out in subs.(1). Employers cannot contract out of this liability (subs.(2), but note the qualification in subs.(3)).

Subs. (4)

For the purposes of SSP, a day of incapacity for work in relation to any contract of service may arise in either of two ways. The first is where the employee is actually incapable by reason of some specific disease or bodily or mental disablement of doing work which he or she can reasonably be expected to do under that contract. On "incapable of work" and "by reason of some specific disease or bodily or mental disablement", see the annotations to SSCBA 1992, s.171B(2) in Vol.I to this series. The second, and alternative, possibility is where the employee, although not actually incapable, falls within the protection of regulations which deem a day to be one of incapacity for work. On deemed incapacity, see SSP (General) Regulations 1982 (SI 1982/894), reg.2.

1.64

Subs. (5)

This contemplates that an employee who has more than one contract of service with the same employer could get SSP in respect of each contract of service, where the eligibility conditions were satisfied with respect to each contract. This provision is modified by SSP (General) Regulations 1982 (SI 1982/894), reg.21.

1.65

Subs. (6)

See SSP (General) Regulations 1982 (SI 1982/894), regs 9A–9C and see also General Note to Pt XI of this Act, above.

1.66

The qualifying conditions

Period of incapacity for work

152.—(1) The first condition is that the day in question forms part of a period of incapacity for work.

1.67

(2) In this Part of this Act "period of incapacity for work" means any period of four or more consecutive days, each of which is a day of incapacity for work in relation to the contract of service in question.

(3) Any two periods of incapacity for work which are separated by a period of not more than 8 weeks shall be treated as a single period of incapacity for work.

(4) The Secretary of State may by regulations direct that a larger number of weeks specified in the regulations shall be substituted for the number of weeks for the time being specified in subsection (3) above.

(5) No day of the week shall be disregarded in calculating any period of consecutive days for the purposes of this section.

(6) A day may be a day of incapacity for work in relation to a contract of service, and so form part of a period of incapacity for work, notwithstanding that—

(a) it falls before the making of the contract or after the contract expires or is brought to an end; or

(b) it is not a day on which the employee concerned would be required by that contract to be available for work.

DEFINITIONS

"contract of service"—see s.163(1).
"employee"—*ibid.* and SSP (General) Regulations 1982, reg.16.
"period of incapacity for work"—see subs.(2).
"week"—see s.163(1).

GENERAL NOTE

1.68   Liability to pay SSP can only arise if the qualifying day which is one of incapacity for work also forms part of a period of incapacity for work (subs.(1)). A period of incapacity for work is formed by any period of four or more consecutive days of incapacity for work in relation to the contract of service in question (subs.(2)). Every day of the week counts for determining periods of consecutive days (subs.(4)). Any two periods of incapacity "link" to form a single period where they are not separated by more than eight weeks, counting the separation period from the end of the "first" period. Note that under subs.(5), a day can still be one of incapacity for work in relation to the contract of service and thus be part of a period of incapacity for work where it is not one on which the contract would require the employee to be available for work, or where it falls before the contract was made or after it expires or is otherwise brought to an end.

Period of entitlement

1.69   **153.**—(1) The second condition is that the day in question falls within a period which is, as between the employee and his employer, a period of entitlement.

(2) For the purposes of this Part of this Act a period of entitlement, as between an employee and his employer, is a period beginning with the commencement of a period of incapacity for work and ending with whichever of the following first occurs—

(a) the termination of that period of incapacity for work;

(b) the day on which the employee reaches, as against the employer concerned, his maximum entitlement to statutory sick pay (determined in accordance with section 155 below);

(c) the day on which the employee's contract of service with the employer concerned expires or is brought to an end;

(d) in the case of an employee who is, or has been, pregnant, the day immediately preceding the beginning of the disqualifying period.

(3) Schedule 11 to this Act has effect for the purpose of specifying circumstances in which a period of entitlement does not arise in relation to a particular period of incapacity for work.

(4) A period of entitlement as between an employee and an employer of his may also be, or form part of, a period of entitlement as between him and another employer of his.

(5) The Secretary of State may by regulations—

(a) specify circumstances in which, for the purpose of determining whether an employee's maximum entitlement to statutory sick pay has been reached in a period of entitlement as between him and an employer of his, days falling within a previous period of entitlement as between the employee and any person who is or has in the past been an employer of his are to be counted; and

(b) direct that in prescribed circumstances an employer shall provide a person who is about to leave his employment, or who has been employed by him in the past, with a statement in the prescribed form containing such information as may be prescribed in relation to any entitlement of the employee to statutory sick pay.

(6) Regulations may provide, in relation to prescribed cases, for a period of entitlement to end otherwise than in accordance with subsection (2) above.

(7) In a case where the employee's contract of service first takes effect

on a day which falls within a period of incapacity for work, the period of entitlement begins with that day.

(8) In a case where the employee's contract of service first takes effect between two periods of incapacity for work which by virtue of section 152(3) above are treated as one, the period of entitlement begins with the first day of the second of those periods.

(9) In any case where, otherwise than by virtue of section 6(1)(b) above, an employee's earnings under a contract of service in respect of the day on which the contract takes effect do not attract a liability to pay secondary Class 1 contributions, subsections (7) and (8) above shall have effect as if for any reference to the contract first taking effect there were substituted a reference to the first day in respect of which the employee's earnings attract such a liability.

(10) Regulations shall make provision as to an employer's liability under this Part of this Act to pay statutory sick pay to an employee in any case where the employer's contract of service with that employee has been brought to an end by the employer solely, or mainly, for the purpose of avoiding liability for statutory sick pay.

(11) Subsection (2)(d) above does not apply in relation to an employee who has been pregnant if her pregnancy terminated, before the beginning of the disqualifying period, otherwise than by confinement.

(12) In this section—

"confinement" is to be construed in accordance with section 171(1) below;

"disqualifying period" means—

(a) in relation to a woman entitled to statutory maternity pay, the maternity pay period; and

(b) in relation to a woman entitled to maternity allowance, the maternity allowance period;

"maternity allowance period" has the meaning assigned to it by section 35(2) above; and

"maternity pay period" has the meaning assigned to it by section 165(1) below.

DEFINITIONS

"confinement"—see subs.(12).
"contract of service"—see s.163(1).
"disqualifying period"—see subs.(12).
"employee"—see s.163(1) and SSP (General) Regulations 1982, reg.16.
"employer"—*ibid*.
"maternity allowance"—*ibid*.
"maternity allowance period"—subs.(12).
"maternity pay period"—*ibid*.
"period of incapacity for work"—see s.163(1).
"prescribed"—see *ibid*.
"week"—see *ibid*.

GENERAL NOTE

Subss.(1) and (2)

There can be no liability to pay SSP unless the qualifying day, being one of incapacity for work forming part of a period of incapacity for work, also falls within a period of entitlement as between the employee and his employer (subs.(1)). Such a period of

1.70

entitlement generally begins on the first day of a period of incapacity for work (subs. (2)), but note the modifications effected by subss.(7), (8), and (9). A period of entitlement ends with whichever of the circumstances set out in subs.(2)(a)–(d) first occurs. Note that subs.2(d) does not apply in the circumstances set out in subs.(11).

The position of "regular casual" workers was dealt with by the Court of Appeal in *Brown v Chief Adjudication Officer* [1997] I.R.L.R. 110. So long as such workers have worked continuously for a period of three months, or for a series of periods totalling three months in aggregate and not separated by more than eight weeks, they become entitled to the minimum periods of notice provided for by s.86 of Employment Rights Act 1996, and their contract of employment will not terminate unless it is frustrated or is terminated by their employer. See further the commentary to Sch.11, para.2 below.

Subs.(3)

1.71   In the circumstances set out in Sch.11 below, no period of entitlement arises with respect to the particular period of incapacity for work there referred to, thus excluding certain employees from SSP in respect of that period of incapacity for work.

Subs.(4)

1.72   An employee may have a period of entitlement with more than one employer at the same time, albeit that the length of the period with each is not coterminous.

Subs.(5)

1.73   See SSP (General) Regulations 1982 (SI 1982/894), reg.3A.

Subs.(6)

1.74   See SSP (General) Regulations 1982 (SI 1982/894), reg.3 dealing with prisoners, pregnant women entitled neither to SMP nor to maternity allowance, and setting a maximum three-year limit on any one period of entitlement.

Subs.(10)

1.75   See SSP (General) Regulations 1982 (SI 1982/894), reg.4.

Qualifying days

1.76   **154.**—(1) The third condition is that the day in question is a qualifying day.

(2) The days which are for the purposes of this Part of this Act to be qualifying days as between an employee and an employer of his (that is to say, those days of the week on which he is required by his contract of service with that employer to be available for work or which are chosen to reflect the terms of that contract) shall be such day or days as may, subject to regulations, be agreed between the employee and his employer or, failing such agreement, determined in accordance with regulations.

(3) In any case where qualifying days are determined by agreement between an employee and his employer there shall, in each week (beginning with Sunday), be at least one qualifying day.

(4) A day which is a qualifying day as between an employee and an employer of his may also be a qualifying day as between him and another employer of his.

DEFINITIONS

"contract of service"—see s.163(1).
"employee"—*ibid.* and SSP (General) Regulations 1982, reg.16.
"employer"—see s.163(1).
"week"—*ibid.*

1.77

GENERAL NOTE

In order to attract SSP liability, the day of incapacity which forms part of a period of incapacity for work and falls within a period of entitlement must also be a qualifying day (subs.(1)). Under subs.(2) an employer and employee are permitted a degree of freedom to determine by agreement which days of the week will for them rank as such, although subs.(3) stipulates that such agreements must specify at least one qualifying day per week. Furthermore SSP (General) Regulations 1982 (SI 1982/894), reg.5(3) renders ineffective an agreement treating as qualifying days any day identified expressly or otherwise by reference to it being a day of incapacity for work in relation to the employee's contract of service with an employer, or by reference to a period of incapacity for work or to a period of entitlement. Where there is no agreement on qualifying days or the only agreement is one rendered ineffective by reg.5(3), qualifying days are determined in accordance with SSP (General) Regulations 1982, reg.5(2).

Limitations on entitlement, etc.

Limitations on entitlement

155.—(1) Statutory sick pay shall not be payable for the first three qualifying days in any period of entitlement.

(2) An employee shall not be entitled, as against any one employer, to an aggregate amount of statutory sick pay in respect of any one period of entitlement which exceeds his maximum entitlement.

(3) The maximum entitlement as against any one employer is reached on the day on which the amount to which the employee has become entitled by way of statutory sick pay during the period of entitlement in question first reaches or passes the entitlement limit.

(4) The entitlement limit is an amount equal to 28 times [[1]the weekly rate applicable in accordance with] section 157 below.

(5) Regulations may make provision for calculating the entitlement limit in any case where an employee's entitlement to statutory sick pay is calculated by reference to different weekly rates in the same period of entitlement.

1.78

AMENDMENT

1. Social Security (Incapacity for Work) Act 1994, s.8 (April 6, 1995).

DEFINITIONS

"employee"—see s.163(1) and SSP (General) Regulations 1982, reg.16.
"employer"—see s.163(1).
"period of entitlement"—*ibid.*
"qualifying day"—*ibid.*

Notification of incapacity for work

156.—(1) Regulations shall prescribe the manner in which, and the time within which, notice of any day of incapacity for work is to be given by or on behalf of an employee to his employer.

(2) An employer who would, apart from this section, be liable to pay an amount of statutory sick pay to an employee in respect of a qualifying day (the "day in question") shall be entitled to withhold payment of that amount if—

1.79

(a) the day in question is one in respect of which he has not been duly notified in accordance with regulations under subsection (1) above; or

(b) he has not been so notified in respect of any of the first three qualifying days in a period of entitlement (a "waiting day") and the day in question is the first qualifying day in that period of entitlement in respect of which the employer is not entitled to withhold payment—

    (i) by virtue of paragraph (a) above; or

    (ii) in respect of an earlier waiting day by virtue of this paragraph.

(3) Where an employer withholds any amount of statutory sick pay under this section—

(a) the period of entitlement in question shall not be affected; and

(b) for the purposes of calculating his maximum entitlement in accordance with section 155 above the employee shall not be taken to have become entitled to the amount so withheld.

Rates of payment, etc.

Rates of payment

1.80   **157.**—(1) Statutory sick pay shall be payable by an employer at the weekly rate of [²£79.15].

(2) The Secretary of State may by order—

[¹(a) amend subsection (1) above so as to substitute different provision as to the weekly rate or rates of statutory sick pay; and]

(b) make such consequential amendments as appear to him to be required of any provision contained in this Part of this Act.

(3) The amount of statutory sick pay payable by any one employer in respect of any day shall be the weekly rate applicable on that day divided by the number of days which are, in the week (beginning with Sunday) in which that day falls, qualifying days as between that employer and the employee concerned.

AMENDMENTS

1. Social Security (Incapacity for Work) Act 1994, s.8 (April 6, 1995).

2. Social Security Benefits Up-rating Order 2009 (SI 2009/497), art.9 (April 6, 2009).

Recovery by employers of amounts paid by way of statutory sick pay

1.81   **158.** [¹ . . .]

AMENDMENT

1. Statutory Sick Pay Percentage Threshold Order 1995 (SI 1995/512), reg.5(a) (April 6, 1995).

Power to substitute provisions for section 158(2)

1.82   **159.** [¹ . . .]

AMENDMENT

1. Statutory Sick Pay Percentage Threshold Order 1995 (SI 1995/512), reg.5(a) (April 6, 1995).

[¹Power to provide for recovery by employers of sums paid by way of statutory sick pay

159A.—(1) The Secretary of State may by order provide for the recovery by employers, in accordance with the order, of the amount (if any) by which their payments of, or liability incurred for, statutory sick pay in any period exceeds the specified percentage of the amount of their liability for contributions payments in respect of the corresponding period.

(2) An order under subsection (1) above may include provision—

(a) as to the periods by reference to which the calculation referred to above is to be made;

(b) for amounts which would otherwise be recoverable but which do not exceed the specified minimum for recovery not to be recoverable;

(c) for the rounding up or down of any fraction of a pound which would otherwise result from a calculation made in accordance with the order; and

(d) for any deduction from contributions payments made in accordance with the order to be disregarded for such purposes as may be specified,

and may repeal sections 158 and 159 above and make any amendments of other enactments which are consequential on the repeal of those sections.

(3) In this section—

"contributions payments" means payments which a person is required by or under any enactment to make in discharge of any liability of his as an employer in respect of primary or secondary Class 1 contributions; and

"specified" means specified in or determined in accordance with an order under subsection (1).

(4) The Secretary of State may by regulations make such transitional and consequential provision, and such savings, as he considers necessary or expedient for or in connection with the coming into force of any order under subsection (1) above.]

1.83

AMENDMENT

1. Statutory Sick Pay Act 1994, s.3 (February 10, 1994).

Miscellaneous

Relationship with benefits and other payments, etc.

160. Schedule 12 to this Act has effect with respect to the relationship between statutory sick pay and certain benefits and payments.

1.84

Crown employment—Part XI

161.—(1) Subject to subsection (2) below, the provisions of this Part of this Act apply in relation to persons employed by or under the Crown as they apply in relation to persons employed otherwise than by or under the Crown.

1.85

(2) The provisions of this Part of this Act do not apply in relation to persons serving as members of Her Majesty's forces, in their capacity as such.

(3) For the purposes of this section Her Majesty's forces shall be taken to consist of such establishments and organisations as may be prescribed [¹by regulations made by the Secretary of State with the concurrence of the

Treasury], being establishments and organisations in which persons serve under the control of the Defence Council.

AMENDMENT

1. Social Security Contributions (Transfer of Functions, etc.) Act 1999, s.1(1) and Sch.1, para.10 (April 1, 1999).

Special classes of persons

1.86   **162.**—(1) The Secretary of State [¹may with the concurrence of the Treasury] make regulations modifying this Part of this Act in such manner as he thinks proper in their application to any person who is, has been or is to be—

    (a) employed on board any ship, vessel, hovercraft or aircraft;

    (b) outside Great Britain at any prescribed time or in any prescribed circumstances; or

    (c) in prescribed employment in connection with continental shelf opeations, as defined in section 120(2) above.

    (2) Regulations under subsection (1) above may in particular provide—

    (a) for any provision of this Part of this Act to apply to any such person, notwithstanding that it would not otherwise apply;

    (b) for any such provision not to apply to any such person, notwithstanding that it would otherwise apply;

    (c) for excepting any such person from the application of any such provision where he neither is domiciled nor has a place of residence in any part of Great Britain;

    (d) for the taking of evidence, for the purposes of the determination of any question arising under any such provision, in a country or territory outside Great Britain, by a British consular official or such other person as may be determined in accordance with the regulations.

AMENDMENT

1. Social Security Contributions (Transfer of Functions, etc.) Act 1999, s.1(1) and Sch.1, para.11 (April 1, 1999).

Interpretation of Part XI and supplementary provisions

1.87   **163.**—(1) In this Part of this Act—

"contract of service" (except in paragraph (a) of the definition below of "employee") includes any arrangement providing for the terms of appointment of an employee;

"employee" means a person who is—

    (a) gainfully employed in Great Britain either under a contract of service or in an office (including elective office) with [⁴ general earnings (as defined by section 7 of the Income Tax (Earnings and Pensions) Act 2003)];

[⁵. . .]

but subject to regulations, which may provide for cases where any such person is not to be treated as an employee for the purposes of this Part of this Act and for cases where any person who would not otherwise be an employee for those purposes is to be treated as an employee for those purposes;

[⁵"employer", in relation to an employee and a contract of service of his, means a person who—

(a) under section 6 above is liable to pay secondary Class 1 contributions in relation to any earnings of the employee under the contract, or

(b) would be liable to pay such contributions but for—

> (i) the condition in section 6(1)(b), or
>
> (ii) the employee being under the age of 16:]

"period of entitlement" has the meaning given by section 153 above;

"period of incapacity for work" has the meaning given by section 152 above;

[¹. . .]

"prescribed" means prescribed by regulations;

"qualifying day" has the meaning given by section 154 above;

"week" means any period of seven days.

(2) For the purposes of this Part of this Act an employee's normal weekly earnings shall, subject to subsection (4) below, be taken to be the average weekly earnings which in the relevant period have been paid to him or paid for his benefit under his contract of service with the employer in question.

(3) For the purposes of subsection (2) above, the expressions "earnings" and "relevant period" shall have the meaning given to them by regulations.

(4) In such cases as may be prescribed an employee's normal weekly earnings shall be calculated in accordance with regulations.

(5) Without prejudice to any other power to make regulations under this Part of this Act, regulations may specify cases in which, for the purposes of this Part of this Act or such of its provisions as may be prescribed—

(a) two or more employers are to be treated as one;

(b) two or more contracts of service in respect of which the same person is an employee are to be treated as one.

(6) Where, in consequence of the establishment of one or more National Health Service trusts under [⁶the National Health Service Act 2006, the National Health Service (Wales) Act 2006] or the National Health Service (Scotland) Act 1978, a person's contract of employment is treated by a scheme under [⁶any of those Acts] as divided so as to constitute two or more contracts, [³or where an order [⁶paragraph 26(1) of Schedule 3 to the National Health Service Act 2006] provides that a person's contract of employment is so divided,] regulations may make provision enabling him to elect for all of those contracts to be treated as one contract for the purposes of this Part of this Act or of such provisions of this Part of this Act as may be prescribed; and any such regulations may prescribe—

(a) the conditions that must be satisfied if a person is to be entitled to make such an election;

(b) the manner in which, and the time within which, such an election is to be made;

(c) the persons to whom, and the manner in which, notice of such an election is to be given;

(d) the information which a person who makes such an election is to provide, and the persons to whom, and the time within which, he is to provide it;

(e) the time for which such an election is to have effect;

(f) which one of the person's employers under the two or more contracts is to be regarded for the purposes of statutory sick pay as his employer under the one contract;

and the powers conferred by this subsection are without prejudice to any other power to make regulations under this Part of this Act.

(7) Regulations may provide for periods of work which begin on one day and finish on the following day to be treated, for the purposes of this Part of this Act, as falling solely within one or other of those days.

AMENDMENTS

1. Jobseekers Act 1995, s.41(5) and Sch.3 (April 1, 1996).
2. Social Security Act 1998, s.86 and Sch.7, para.74 (April 6, 1999).
3. Health Act 1999 (Supplementary, Consequential etc. Provisions) Order 2000 (SI 2000/90), art.3(1) and Sch.1, para.27 (February 8, 2000).
4. Income Tax (Earnings and Pensions) Act 2003, s.722 and Sch.6, para.181 (April 6, 2003).
5. Employment Equality (Age) Regulations 2006 (SI 2006/1031), reg.49(1) and Sch.8, para.9 (October 1, 2006).
6. National Health Service (Consequential Provisions) Act 2006, s.2 and Sch.1, para.147 (March 1, 2007).

PART XII

STATUTORY MATERNITY PAY

Statutory maternity pay—entitlement and liability to pay

1.88   **164.**—(1) Where a woman who is or has been an employee satisfies the conditions set out in this section, she shall be entitled, in accordance with the following provisions of this Part of this Act, to payments to be known as "statutory maternity pay".

(2) The conditions mentioned in subsection (1) above are—

(a) that she has been in employed earner's employment with an employer for a continuous period of at least 26 weeks ending with the week immediately preceding the 14th week before the expected-week of confinement but has ceased to work for him, [³ . . .];

(b) that her normal weekly earnings for the period of eight weeks ending with the week immediately preceding the 14th week before the expected week of confinement are not less than the lower earnings limit in force under section 5(1)(a) above immediately before the commencement of the 14th week before the expected week of confinement; and

(c) that she has become pregnant and has reached, or been confined before reaching, the commencement of the 11th week before the expected week of confinement.

(3) The liability to make payments of statutory maternity pay to a woman is a liability of any person of whom she has been an employee as mentioned in subsection (2)(a) above.

[³(4) A woman shall be entitled to payments of statutory maternity pay only if—

(a) she gives the person who will be liable to pay it notice of the date from which she expects his liability to pay her statutory maternity pay to begin; and

(b) the notice is given at least 28 days before that date or, if that is not reasonably practicable, as soon as is reasonably practicable.]

(5) The notice shall be in writing if the person who is liable to pay the woman statutory maternity pay so requests.

(6) Any agreement shall be void to the extent that it purports—

(a) to exclude, limit or otherwise modify any provision of this Part of this Act; or

(b) to require an employee or former employee to contribute (whether directly or indirectly) towards any costs incurred by her employer or former employer under this Part of this Act.

(7) For the avoidance of doubt, any agreement between an employer and an employee authorising any deductions from statutory maternity pay which the employer is liable to pay to the employee in respect of any period shall not be void by virtue of subsection (6)(a) above if the employer—

(a) is authorised by that or another agreement to make the same deductions from any contractual remuneration which he is liable to pay in respect of the same period; or

(b) would be so authorised if he were liable to pay contractual remuneration in respect of that period.

(8) Regulations shall make provision as to a former employer's liability to pay statutory maternity pay to a woman in any case where the former employer's contract of service with her has been brought to an end by the former employer solely, or mainly, for the purpose of avoiding liability for statutory maternity pay.

(9) The Secretary of State may by regulations—

(a) specify circumstances in which, notwithstanding subsections (1) to (8) above, there is to be no liability to pay statutory maternity pay in respect of a week;

(b) specify circumstances in which, notwithstanding subsections (1) to (8) above, the liability to make payments of statutory maternity pay is to be a liability [²of the Commissioners of Inland Revenue];

(c) specify in what circumstances employment is to be treated as continuous for the purposes of this Part of this Act;

(d) provide that a woman is to be treated as being employed for a continuous period of at least 26 weeks where—

(i) she has been employed by the same employer for at least 26 weeks under two or more separate contracts of service; and

(ii) those contracts were not continuous;

(e) provide that any of the provisions specified in subsection (10) below shall have effect subject to prescribed modifications [³in such cases as may be prescribed]

[³(ea) provide that subsection (4) above shall not have effect, or shall have effect subject to prescribed modifications, in such cases as may be prescribed;]

(f) provide for amounts earned by a woman under separate contracts of service with the same employer to be aggregated for the purposes of this Part of this Act; and

(g) provide that—

(i) the amount of a woman's earnings for any period; or

(ii) the amount of her earnings to be treated as comprised in any payment made to her or for her benefit, shall be calculated or estimated in such manner and on such basis as may be prescribed and that for that purpose payments of a particular class or description made or falling to be made to or by a woman shall, to such extent as may be prescribed, be disregarded or, as the case may be, be deducted from the amount of her earnings.

(10) The provisions mentioned in subsection (9)(e) above are—

(a) subsection (2)(a) and (b) above; and

(b) [⁴section 166(1) and (2)], [¹. . .] below.

[²(11) Any regulations under subsection (9) above which are made by virtue of paragraph (b) of that subsection must be made with the concurence of the Commissioners of Inland Revenue.]

AMENDMENTS

1. Maternity Allowance and Statutory Maternity Pay Regulations 1994 (SI 1994/1230), reg.6 (October 16, 1994).

2. Social Security Contributions (Transfer of Functions, etc.) Act 1999, s.1(1) and Sch.1, para.12 (April 1, 1999).

3. Employment Act 2002, s.20 (April 6, 2003).

4. Employment Act 2002, s.53 and Sch.7, para.6 (April 6, 2003).

DEFINITIONS

"confined"—see s.171(1).

"confinement"—see *ibid.*

"earnings"—see *ibid.* and reg.20 of the Statutory Maternity Pay (General) Regulations 1986.

"employee"—see s.171 and reg.17 of the Statutory Maternity Pay (General) Regulations 1986.

"employed earner"—see s.2.

"employer"—see s.171(1).

"modifications"—see *ibid.*

"normal weekly earnings"—see s.171(4).

"prescribed"—see s.171(1).

"week"—see *ibid.*

GENERAL NOTE

1.89   Statutory Maternity Pay (SMP) provides an income for employees and former employees during a period of maternity leave. In order to qualify for SMP a woman must have worked for an employer for 26 weeks continuously into the week (known as the qualifying week) preceding the 14th week before the expected date of her confinement (subs.(2)(a)). Part III of the SMP (General) Regulations 1986 (SI 1986/1960) defines the concept of continuous employment. The woman must also have been earning during the last eight weeks of her employment an amount at least equal to the lower earnings limit for contribution purposes (subs.(2)(b)). She must, moreover, have become pregnant and have reached (or given birth before reaching) the start of the 11th week before the expected week of confinement (subs.(2)(c)). The further requirement that she must actually have left that employment because of her pregnancy or confinement was repealed by the Employment Act 2002. This repeal itself effectively supersedes reg.2 of the Statutory Maternity Pay (General) (Modification and Amendment) Regulations 2000 (SI 2000/2883), which modified the original version of subs.(2)(a) of the Act in relation to pregnant women who were dismissed or whose employment was otherwise terminated without consent.

Where a woman leaves her employment earlier than 11 weeks before the expected week of confinement she loses her entitlement to SMP (unless she has given birth), but if her employer has dismissed her solely or mainly for the purpose of avoiding the liability to pay SMP she will remain entitled. This applies even if she has been working for that employer for only a short period, so long as it is at least eight continuous weeks (see reg.3 of the SMP (General) Regulations 1986 (SI 1986/1960)). If a woman qualifies for SMP from more than one employer she is entitled to receive it from each of them (*ibid.*, reg.18).

It is a precondition of entitlement to SMP that the woman has given notice of her intention to leave by reason of pregnancy or confinement at least 28 days (21 days before the Employment Act 2002) before leaving, unless it is not reasonably practicable to do so and she gives it thereafter as soon as it is reasonably practicable to do so (subs.(4); see further SMP (General) Regulations 1986 (SI 1986/1960), reg.23). This would be so if the baby arrives unexpectedly early, but may also extend to a woman who did not know of the notice requirement and had not been put on inquiry about it. (That was the position taken by the Employment Appeal Tribunal in *Nu-Swift International Ltd v Mallinson* [1979] I.C.R. 157 in relation to maternity pay.) The notice must be in writing if the employer so requests (subs.(5)).

A woman is not entitled to SMP if at any time during the maternity pay period (on which see s.165) she is imprisoned or sentenced to imprisonment (other than suspended). SMP is lost for the remainder of the period whether or not she is imprisoned for the whole period (see reg.9 of the SMP (General) Regulations 1986 (SI 1986/1960)).

The liability to pay SMP rests with the employer (subs.(3)). In certain circumstances, where an employer does not, or because of insolvency, cannot discharge his liability to pay SMP, that liability is discharged by the Board, now HMRC (at least since April 1, 1999; see subs.(9)(b), SMP (General) Regulations 1986 (SI 1986/1960), reg.7 and Social Security Contributions (Transfer of Functions, etc.) Act 1999, s.1(2) and Sch.2.; the same applies to the Secretary of State's functions under SMP (General) Regulations, regs 25, 30 and 31).

SMP, therefore, like SSP, is administered by the employer whilst HMRC is responsible for the resolution of certain disputes about entitlement. Until April 1, 1999, this was achieved by enabling the reference of certain questions to an AO, thereby opening up the usual channels of appeal to SSATs, Commissioners and the courts. With effect from April 1, 1999, the Social Security Contributions (Transfer of Functions, etc.) Act 1999, and the Statutory Sick Pay and Statutory Maternity Pay (Decisions) Regulations 1999 (SI 1999/776) replaced the role of AO with that of an officer of the Board of Inland Revenue (now HMRC). Consequently decision-making and appeals relating to SMP are governed by Pt II of the 1999 Act, with the right of appeal lying to the tax appeal Commissioners.

The maternity pay period

165.—(1) Statutory maternity pay shall be payable, subject to the provisions of this Part of this Act, in respect of each week during a prescribed period ("the maternity pay period") of a duration not exceeding [²52 weeks].

[³(2) Subject to subsections (3) and (7), the maternity pay period shall begin with the 11th week before the expected week of confinement.

(3) Cases may be prescribed in which the first day of the period is to be a prescribed day after the beginning of the 11th week before the expected week of confinement, but not later than the day immediately following the day on which she is confined.]

(4) [³Except in such cases as may be prescribed,] statutory maternity pay shall not be payable to a woman by a person in respect of any week during any part of which she works under a contract of service with him.

(5) It is immaterial for the purposes of subsection (4) above whether the work referred to in that subsection is work under a contract of service which existed immediately before the maternity pay period or a contract of service which did not so exist.

(6) Except in such cases as may be prescribed, statutory maternity pay

1.90

shall not be payable to a woman in respect of any week after she has been confined and during any part of which she works for any employer who is not liable to pay her statutory maternity pay.

(7) Regulations may provide that this section shall have effect subject to prescribed modifications in relation—

(a) to cases in which a woman has been confined before the 11th week before the expected week of confinement; and

(b) to cases in which—

(i) a woman is confined[¹ at any time after the end of the week immediately preceding the 11th week] before the expected week of confinement; and

(ii) the maternity pay period has not then commenced for her.

[³(8) In subsections (1), (4) and (6) "week" means a period of seven days beginning with the day of the week on which the maternity pay period begins.]

AMENDMENTS

1. Maternity Allowance and Statutory Maternity Pay Regulations 1994 (SI 1994/1230), reg.3 (October 16, 1994).
2. Employment Act 2002, s.18 (April 6, 2003).
3. Work and Families Act 2006, s.1 (October 1, 2006).
4. Work and Families Act 2006, s.11 and Sch.1, para.7 (October 1, 2006).

DEFINITIONS

"confined"—see s.171(1).
"confinement"—*ibid.*
"employer"—*ibid.*
"maternity pay period"—*ibid.*
"modifications"—*ibid.*
"prescribed"—*ibid.*
"week"—*ibid.*

GENERAL NOTE

1.91   SMP is now payable for a period of 39 weeks (previously 26 weeks as a result of the Employment Act 2002, in force in April 2003, before which the maximum period was 18 weeks). As a general rule, the maternity pay period begins with the 11th week before the expected week of confinement (subs.(2)). Regulations provide for this period to be varied when the woman gives birth early (see SMP (General) Regulations 1986 (SI 1986/1960), reg.2).

The normal rule under subs.(4) that a woman is not entitled to receive SMP for any week in which she works for the employer who is liable to pay her SMP has now been relaxed. A woman may now work for her employer for a maximum of 10 days without losing entitlement to SMP (see reg.9A of the SMP (General) Regulations 1986 (SI 1986/1960)). A woman is not entitled to SMP if she works for another employer after her confinement (subs.(6)) unless she had worked for two or more employers up to her qualifying week, one of whom was not liable to pay her SMP, and it is now that employer for whom she is working after confinement (see reg.8 of the SMP (General) Regulations 1986 (SI 1986/1960)). But where she works for a new employer after her confinement, even if she works only briefly, she loses her entitlement for the remainder of the maternity pay period. Apparently there is no restriction on working for another employer before confinement.

[¹Rate of statutory maternity pay

1.92   **166.**—(1) Statutory maternity pay shall be payable to a woman—

(a) at the earnings-related rate, in respect of the first six weeks in respect of which it is payable; and

(b) at whichever is the lower of the earnings-related rate and such weekly rate as may be prescribed, in respect of the remaining portion of the maternity pay period.

[²(1A) In subsection (1) "week" means any period of seven days.]

(2) The earnings-related rate is a weekly rate equivalent to 90 per cent of a woman's normal weekly earnings for the period of eight weeks immediately preceding the 14th week before the expected week of confinement.

(3) The weekly rate prescribed under subsection (1)(b) above must not be less than the weekly rate of statutory sick pay for the time being specifiedin section 157(1) above or, if two or more such rates are for the time being so specified, the higher or highest of those rates.]

[²(4) Where for any purpose of this Part of this Act or of regulations it is necessary to calculate the daily rate of statutory maternity pay, the amount payable by way of statutory maternity pay for any day shall be taken as one seventh of the weekly rate.]

AMENDMENTS

1. Employment Act 2002, s.19 (April 6, 2003).
2. Work and Families Act 2006, s.11 and Sch.1, para.8 (October 1, 2006).

DEFINITIONS

"confinement"—see s.171(1).
"maternity pay period"—*ibid.*
"normal weekly earnings"—*ibid.*
"prescribed"—*ibid.*
"week—*ibid.*

GENERAL NOTE

A new s.166 was substituted by s.19 of the Employment Act 2002. This pre- **1.93** served the pre-existing position so far as the rate of payment for the first six weeks of the maternity pay period is concerned. During this initial period SMP is paid at the earnings-related rate of 90 per cent of the woman's average weekly earnings in the eight weeks preceding the qualifying week (subss.(1)(a) and (2)). Thereafter, SMP is paid at either the standard prescribed rate (£112.75 per week in 2007/08) or the earnings-related rate, whichever is the lower (subs.(1)(b)), for the balance of 20 weeks. Previously the balance of the maternity pay period was just 12 weeks, but the then lower rate was always payable, irrespective of whether the earnings-related rate was lower.

There remains an important issue relating to the SMP earnings calculation and the extent to which this takes into account pay rises. As a result of the decision of the European Court of Justice in *Gillespie v Northern Health and Social Services Board* [1996] I.R.L.R. 214, the earnings calculation for SMP purposes must take into account any pay rise which is backdated into the "relevant period" (on the meaning of which see SSCBA 1992, s.171(4) and (5) and SMP (General) Regulations 1986 (SI 1986/1960, reg.21)). The *Gillespie* decision led to a limited amendment to the relevant regulations (SMP (General) Regulations 1986, reg.21(7), inserted by the SMP (General) Amendment Regulations 1996 (SI 1996/1335)). The question remains whether a woman on maternity leave should receive the benefit of any pay rise which has been implemented after the qualifying week and before the end of paid maternity leave. The original reg.21(7), it was argued, failed to give full effect to the ruling in *Gillespie* by limiting it to cases in which the pay increase is backdated into the relevant period. The Court of Appeal referred a series of questions on this point to the European Court of Justice in *Alabaster v Woolwich Plc* [2002] EWCA Civ. 211; [2002] 1 C.M.L.R. 56; [2002] I.R.L.R. 420. On the request for a preliminary ruling, the ECJ ruled as follows:

"Article 119 of the Treaty must be interpreted as requiring that, in so far as the pay received by the worker during her maternity leave is determined, at least in part, on the basis of the pay she earned before her maternity leave began, any pay rise awarded between the beginning of the period covered by the reference pay and the end of the maternity leave must be included in the elements of pay taken into account in calculating the amount of such pay. This requirement is not limited to cases where the pay rise is back-dated to the period covered by the reference pay."

Alabaster v Woolwich plc and Secretary of State for Social Security Case C-147/02 [2004] I.R.L.R. 486, para.50.

A new reg.21(7) was subsequently inserted with effect from April 6, 2005, to ensure that a woman's entitlement (or potential entitlement) to statutory maternity pay reflects any pay rise that the woman would have received, but for her maternity leave, and which is effective at any time between the start of the period used to calculate her entitlement and the end of her maternity leave. See further Statutory Maternity Pay (General) (Amendment) Regulations 2005 (SI 2005/729), reg.3. A month later (May 3, 2005), the Court of Appeal delivered its judgment following the decision of the ECJ: see *Alabaster v Barclays Bank Plc and the Secretary of State for Social Security* [2005] EWCA Civ 508. The Court of Appeal held that in order to give effect to the appellant's rights under EU law it was necessary to disapply those parts of Equal Pay Act 1970 s.1 which imposed the requirement for a male comparator.

[¹Funding of employers' liabilities in respect of statutory maternity pay

1.94   **167.**—(1) Regulations shall make provision for the payment by employers of statutory maternity pay to be funded by the Commissioners of Inland Revenue to such extent as may be prescribed.

(2) Regulations under subsection (1) shall—

(a) make provision for a person who has made a payment of statutory maternity pay to be entitled, except in prescribed circumstances, to recover an amount equal to the sum of—

  (i) the aggregate of such of those payments as qualify for small employers' relief; and

  (ii) an amount equal to 92 per cent of the aggregate of such of those payments as do not so qualify; and

(b) include provision for a person who has made a payment of statutory maternity pay qualifying for small employers' relief to be entitled, except in prescribed circumstances, to recover an additional amount, determined in such manner as may be prescribed—

  (i) by reference to secondary Class 1 contributions paid in respect of statutory maternity pay;

  (ii) by reference to secondary Class 1 contributions paid in respect of statutory sick pay; or

  (iii) by reference to the aggregate of secondary Class 1 contributions paid in respect of statutory maternity pay and secondary Class 1 contributions paid in respect of statutory sick pay.

(3) For the purposes of this section a payment of statutory maternity pay which a person is liable to make to a woman qualifies for small employers' relief if, in relation to that woman's maternity pay period, the person liable to make the payment is a small employer.

(4) For the purposes of this section "small employer", in relation to a woman's maternity pay period, shall have the meaning assigned to it by regulations, and, without prejudice to the generality of the foregoing, any such regulations—

(a) may define that expression by reference to the amount of a person's contributions payments for any prescribed period; and

(b) if they do so, may in that connection make provision for the amount of those payments for that prescribed period—

    (i) to be determined without regard to any deductions that may be made from them under this section or under any other enactment or instrument; and

    (ii) in prescribed circumstances, to be adjusted, estimated or otherwise attributed to him by reference to their amount in any other prescribed period.

(5) Regulations under subsection (1) may, in particular, make provision—

(a) for funding in advance as well as in arrear;

(b) for funding, or the recovery of amounts due under provision made by virtue of subsection (2)(b), by means of deductions from such amounts for which employers are accountable to the Commissioners of Inland Revenue as may be prescribed, or otherwise;

(c) for the recovery by the Commissioners of Inland Revenue of any sums overpaid to employers under the regulations.

(6) Where in accordance with any provision of regulations under subsection (1) an amount has been deducted from an employer's contributions payments, the amount so deducted shall (except in such cases as may be prescribed) be treated for the purposes of any provision made by or under any enactment in relation to primary or secondary Class 1 contributions—

(a) as having been paid (on such date as may be determined in accordance with the regulations); and

(b) as having been received by the Commissioners of Inland Revenue, towards discharging the employer's liability in respect of such contributions.

(7) Regulations under this section must be made with the concurrence of the Commissioners of Inland Revenue.

(8) In this section, "contributions payments", in relation to an employer, means any payments which the employer is required, by or under any enactment, to make in discharge of any liability in respect of primary or secondary Class 1 contributions.]

AMENDMENT

1. Employment Act 2002, s.21 (April 6, 2003).

DEFINITIONS

"contributions payments"—see subs.(8).
"employer"—see s.171(1).
"maternity pay period"—*ibid.*
"prescribed"—*ibid.*

GENERAL NOTE

The new s.167, substituted by s.21 of the Employment Act 2002, is different from its predecessor in two main respects. First, it allows regulations to be made which

1.95

enable employers to recover SMP from tax and other payments due to HMRC (see subs.(5)(b) and now Statutory Maternity Pay (Compensation of Employers) and Miscellaneous Amendment Regulations 1994 (SI 1994/1882), reg.6), and not just from payments of national insurance contributions, as was previously the case. Secondly, as with the tax credits regime, it provides for regulations to be made enabling employers to apply to HMRC for advance funding (*ibid.*, reg.5). Formerly employers could only deduct, in arrears, the amount of SMP payments from contributions payments due to the Revenue.

Relationship with benefits and other payments, etc.

1.96   **168.** Schedule 13 to this Act has effect with respect to the relationship between statutory maternity pay and certain benefits and payments.

GENERAL NOTE

1.97   As a general rule, entitlement to SMP precludes any entitlement to maternity allowance, SSP or incapacity benefit for the same period. Where SMP is paid, it is treated as going towards the employer's contractual obligation (if any) to pay maternity pay for the same period. If a woman receives maternity allowance because she does not earn enough to qualify for SMP, but then receives a backdated pay increase, making her then entitled to SMP, the employer is required to meet the difference between the maternity allowance paid and the SMP due (SMP (General) Regulations 1986 (SI 1986/1960), reg.21B).

Crown employment—Part XII

1.98   **169.** The provisions of this Part of this Act apply in relation to women employed by or under the Crown as they apply in relation to women employed otherwise than by or under the Crown.

Special classes of persons

1.99   **170.**—(1) The Secretary of State may [¹with the concurrence of the Treasury] make regulations modifying this Part of this Act in such manner as he thinks proper in their application to any person who is, has been or is to be—

 (a) employed on board any ship, vessel, hovercraft or aircraft;
 (b) outside Great Britain at any prescribed time or in any prescribed circumstances; or
 (c) in prescribed employment in connection with continental shelf operations, as defined in section 120(2) above.

 (2) Regulations under subsection (1) above may in particular provide—

 (a) for any provision of this Part of this Act to apply to any such person, notwithstanding that it would not otherwise apply;
 (b) for any such provision not to apply to any such person, notwithstanding that it would otherwise apply;
 (c) for excepting any such person from the application of any such provision where he neither is domiciled nor has a place of residence in any part of Great Britain;
 (d) for the taking of evidence, for the purposes of the determination of any question arising under any such provision, in a country or territory outside Great Britain, by a British consular official or such other person as may be determined in accordance with the regulations.

AMENDMENT

1. Social Security Contributions (Transfer of Functions, etc.) Act 1999, s.1(1) and Sch.1, para.14 (April 1, 1999).

DEFINITIONS

"Great Britain"—see s.172(a).
"prescribed"—see s.171(1).

Interpretation of Part XII and supplementary provisions

171.—(1) In this Part of this Act—   1.100
"confinement" means—

  (a) labour resulting in the issue of a living child; or
  (b) labour after [¹24 weeks] of pregnancy resulting in the issue of a child whether alive or dead;

and "confined" shall be construed accordingly; and where a woman's labour begun on one day results in the issue of a child on another day she shall be taken to be confined on the day of the issue of the childor, if labour results in the issue of twins or a greater number of children, she shall be taken to be confined on the day of the issue of the last of them;

"dismissed" is to be construed in accordance with [³Part X of the Employment Rights Act 1996];

"employee" means a woman who is—

  (a) gainfully employed in Great Britain either under a contract of service or in an office (including elective office) with [⁵ general earnings (as defined by section 7 of the Income Tax (Earnings and Pensions) Act 2003)]

[⁷. . .]

but subject to regulations [⁴made with the concurrence of [⁵Her Majesty's Revenue and Customs] which may provide for cases where any such woman is not to be treated as an employee for the purposes of this Part of this Act and for cases where a woman who would not otherwise be an employee for those purposes is to be treated as an employee for those purposes;

[⁷"employer", in relation to a woman who is an employee, means a person who—

  (a) under section 6 above is liable to pay secondary Class 1 contributions in relation to any of her earnings; or
  (b) would be liable to pay such contributions but for—
       (i)   the condition in section 6(1)(b), or
       (ii) the employee being under the age of 16;]

"maternity pay period" has the meaning assigned to it by section 165(1) above;

"modifications" includes additions, omissions and amendments, and related expressions shall be construed accordingly;

"prescribed" means specified in or determined in accordance with regulations;

[⁸. . .]

[⁸(1A) In this Part, except section 165(1), (4) and (6), section 166(1) and paragraph 3(2) of Schedule 13, "week" means a period of 7 days beginning with Sunday or such other period as may be prescribed in relation to any particular case or class of case.]

(2) Without prejudice to any other power to make regulations under this Part of this Act, regulations may specify cases in which, for the purposes of this Part of this Act or of such provisions of this Part of this Act as may be prescribed—

(a) two or more employers are to be treated as one;

(b) two or more contracts of service in respect of which the same woman is an employee are to be treated as one.

(3) Where, in consequence of the establishment of one or more National Health Service trusts [⁹the National Health Service Act 2006, the National Health Service (Wales) Act 2006] or the National Health Service (Scotland) Act 1978, a woman's contract of employment is treated by a scheme under [⁹any of those Acts] as divided so as to constitute two or more contracts, [²or where an order under [⁹paragraph 26(1) of Schedule 3 to the National Health Service Act 2006] provides that a woman's contract of employment is so divided,] regulations may make provision enabling her to elect for all of those contracts to be treated as one contract for the purposes of this Part of this Act or of such provisions of this Part of this Act as may be prescribed; and any such regulations may prescribe—

(a) the conditions that must be satisfied if a woman is to be entitled to make such an election;

(b) the manner in which, and the time within which, such an election is to be made;

(c) the persons to whom, and the manner in which, notice of such an election is to be given;

(d) the information which a woman who makes such an election is to provide, and the persons to whom, and the time within which, she is to provide it;

(e) the time for which such an election is to have effect;

(f) which one of the woman's employers under the two or more contracts is to be regarded for the purposes of statutory maternity pay as her employer under the one contract;

and the powers conferred by this subsection are without prejudice to any other power to make regulations under this Part of this Act.

(4) For the purposes of this Part of this Act a woman's normal weekly earnings shall, subject to subsection (6) below, be taken to be the average weekly earnings which in the relevant period have been paid to her or paid for her benefit under the contract of service with the employer in question.

(5) For the purposes of subsection (4) above "earnings" and "relevant period" shall have the meanings given to them by regulations.

(6) In such cases as may be prescribed a woman's normal weekly earnings shall be calculated in accordance with regulations.

[⁴(7) Regulations under any of subsections (2) to (6) above must be made with the concurrence of the Commissioners of Inland Revenue.]

AMENDMENTS

1. Still-Birth (Definition) Act 1992, s.2 (October 1, 1992).

2. Health Act 1999 (Supplementary, Consequential etc. Provisions) Order 2000, art.3, Sch.1, para.27 (SI 2000/90) (February 8, 2000).

3. Employment Rights Act 1996, s.240 and Sch.1, para.51(5) (August 23, 1996).

4. Social Security Contributions (Transfer of Functions, etc.) Act 1999, s.1(1) and Sch.1, para.15 (April 1, 1999).

5. Income Tax (Earnings and Pensions) Act 2003, s.722 and Sch.6, para.182 (April 6, 2003).

6. Commissioners for Revenue and Customs Act 2005, s.50 and Sch.4, para.43 (April 18, 2005).

7. Employment Equality (Age) Regulations 2006 (SI 2006/1031), reg.49(1) and Sch.8, para.10 (October 1, 2006).

8. Work and Families Act 2006, s.11 and Sch.1, para.9 (October 1, 2006).

9. National Health Service (Consequential Provisions) Act 2006, s.2 and Sch.1, para.148 (March 1, 2007).

[¹PART XIIZA

STATUTORY PATERNITY PAY

AMENDMENT

1. Part XIIZA was inserted by the Employment Act 2002, s.2 (December 8, 2002).

GENERAL NOTE

Part XIIZA of the SSCBA 1992 was inserted by the Employment Act 2002. The **1.101** 2002 Act followed the Employment Relations Act 1999, which itself included a number of "family friendly" employment measures (e.g. new rights to 13 weeks' unpaid parental leave and to unpaid time off to deal with family crises). The ordinary period of maternity leave was also increased in 1999 from 14 to 18 weeks (this period was extended to 26 weeks in April 2003 by other provisions in the Employment Act 2002), along with several other reforms designed to simplify the notoriously complex rules governing maternity leave and pay. A further review was announced in the 2000 Budget statement, which led to the publication of a Green Paper, *Work and Parents: Competitiveness and Choice* (DTI, December 2000). The Government's decisions on that review were announced at or around the time of the 2001 Budget statement, and were followed by the issue of three further consultation documents on the frameworks for maternity, paternity and adoption leave and pay. In November 2001 the DTI published a summary of responses to these various papers in the *Government's Response on Simplification of Maternity Leave, Paternity Leave and Adoption Leave*.

The Government's proposals were then brought forward in the Bill which became the Employment Act 2002. Part I of the 2002 Act dealt with statutory leave and pay. Thus, s.1 introduced a right to paternity leave in the Employment Rights Act 1996 (inserting ss.80A–80E), while s.2 inserted this Pt XIIZA into the SSCBA 1992 to make provision for statutory paternity pay (SPP). Sections 3 and 4 dealt with adoption leave and statutory adoption pay (SAP) respectively (on the latter see SSCBA 1992, Pt XIIZB). The procedural provisions relating to SPP and SAP were contained in ss.5–16 of the 2002 Act. (The 2002 Act also included measures to establish statutory minimum dismissal, disciplinary and grievance procedures and changes to employment tribunal procedures.)

The amendments made by c.1 of Pt I of the Employment Act 2002 relating to paternity and adoption, including the insertion of Pt XIIZA into the SSCBA 1992, came into force on December 8, 2002 (Employment Act 2002 (Commencement No.3 and Transitional and Saving Provisions) Order 2002, art.2(2) and Sch.1, Pt II). However, art.3 and Sch.3, para.1 of the same Order provide that Pt XIIZA shall have effect only in relation to a person who satisfies the prescribed conditions of entitlement in respect of a child who is either (a) born on or after April 6, 2003 (or whose expected week of birth begins on or after that date); or (b) matched for the purposes of adoption with a person who is notified of having been matched on or after April 6, 2003 (or placed for adoption on or after that date).

SPP is payable for a two week period only (SSCBA 1992, s.171ZE(2)). Such paid paternity leave must be taken in a single block within the first eight weeks after the child's birth (SSCBA 1992, s.171ZE(3)). There are, in fact, two forms of SPP, known in the regulations (the Statutory Paternity Pay and Statutory Adoption Pay (General) Regulations 2002 (SI 2002/2822)) as SPP (birth) and SPP (adoption), although these terms do not appear in the primary legislation. The principal eligibility criteria for SPP (birth) are set out in SSCBA 1992, s.171ZA and for SPP (adoption) in s.171ZB. Entitlement to SPP (birth) arises in respect of children born on or after April 6, 2003, or whose expected week of birth begins on or after that date (SPP and SAP (General) Regulations 2002, reg.3(1)(a); see also (Employment Act 2002 (Commencement No.3 and Transitional and Saving Provisions) Order 2002, art.3 and Sch.3). Similarly, entitlement to SPP (adoption) arises where the adoptive parent is notified of having been matched on or after April 6, 2003 or the child is placed for adoption on or after that date (SPP and SAP (General) Regulations 2002, reg.3(1)(b)). Section 171ZC contains general conditions of entitlement (e.g. as to giving the requisite notice to the employer). Section 171ZD places the liability to make payments of SPP on employers (the recovery mechanisms are the same as for SMP), while s.17ZE, with the associated regulations, deals with matters such as the rate and period of pay. Although paid for a shorter period than SMP, SPP is paid at the same rate as SMP. Sections 171ZF–171ZK make provision for various types of special cases and matters of interpretation, etc.

Entitlement: birth

1.102   **171ZA.**—(1) Where a person satisfies the conditions in subsection (2) below, he shall be entitled in accordance with the following provisions of this Part to payments to be known as "statutory paternity pay".

(2) The conditions are—

(a) that he satisfies prescribed conditions—
 (i) as to relationship with a newborn child; and
 (ii) as to relationship with the child's mother;

(b) that he has been in employed earner's employment with an employer for a continuous period of at least 26 weeks ending with the relevant week;

(c) that his normal weekly earnings for the period of eight weeks ending with the relevant week are not less than the lower earnings limit in force under section 5(1)(a) above at the end of the relevant week; and

(d) that he has been in employed earner's employment with the employer by reference to whom the condition in para.(b) above is satisfied for a continuous period beginning with the end of the relevant week and ending with the day on which the child is born.

(3) The references in subsection (2) above to the relevant week are to the week immediately preceding the 14th week before the expected week of the child's birth.

(4) A person's entitlement to statutory paternity pay under this section shall not be affected by the birth, or expected birth, of more than one child as a result of the same pregnancy.

(5) In this section, "newborn child" includes a child stillborn after 24 weeks of pregnancy.

DEFINITIONS

"employer"—see s.171ZJ(1).
"newborn child"—see subs.(5).

62

"prescribed"—see s.171ZJ(1).
"the relevant week"—see subs.(3).
"week"—see s.171ZJ(5).

GENERAL NOTE

Subs.(2)(a)

The entitlement conditions referred to in subs.(2)(a) are those prescribed in   1.103
regs 4(2)(b) and (c) of the Paternity and Adoption Leave Regulations 2002 (SI
2002/2788), which are incorporated by the cross-reference in reg.4 of the SPP and
SAP (General) Regulations 2002 (SI 2002/2822). These requirements are that the
employee is, first, either (i) the father of the child, or (ii) married to or the partner
of the child's mother, but not the child's father (reg.4(2)(b)); and, secondly, has, or
expects to have (i) responsibility for the upbringing of the child (if he is the child's
father); or (ii) the main responsibility (apart from any responsibility of the mother)
for the upbringing of the child (if he is the mother's husband or partner but not the
child's father) (reg.4(2)(c)).

Subs.(2)(b)

On the extended meaning of continuous employment, see SPP and SAP   1.104
(General) Regulations 2002, regs 33–37.

Subs.(2)(c)

The minimum threshold requirement that the claimant's earnings are not less   1.105
than the National Insurance lower earnings limit necessarily excludes those fathers
on very low incomes, and typically in part-time work, from SPP. Arguably this is
the group of men whose families are most at risk of social exclusion and thus most
in need of support such as SPP. The problem is exacerbated by the fact that the
National Insurance scheme, unlike the income tax system, does not aggregate earnings from e.g. two part-time jobs with different employers. (But note the special case
of associated employers: see SPP and SAP (General) Regulations 2002, reg.38.)
Women who do not meet the lower earnings limit requirement do not qualify for
SMP (SSCBA 1992, s.164(2)(b)) but may qualify for maternity allowance (SSCBA
1992, s.35—see Vol.I of this series). There is, at present, no such alternative form
of income maintenance for fathers in a similar position. This was the one aspect in
relation to this part of the Employment Act 2002 which caused considerable dis-
quiet amongst Government back-benchers during the Standing Committee debates
on the Bill (Standing Committee F, January 10, 2002, cols 333–360). The minister
promised members that the DWP and Department of Health were actively considering how to provide support for low-wage adoptive parents with some form of
support equivalent to maternity allowance.

Subs.(2)(b)–(d)

The entitlement conditions are modified if a person fails to meet the conditions   1.106
set out in subs.(2)(b)–(d) because the child's birth occurred earlier than the 14th
week before the expected week of the birth: see SPP and SAP (General) Regulations
2002, reg.5. This modification is in exercise of the regulation-making powers under
s.171ZC(3)(a).

Subs.(4)

Thus, SPP is not paid for twice as long in the case of a father of twins.   1.107

Entitlement: adoption

171ZB.—(1) Where a person satisfies the conditions in subsection (2)   1.108
below, he shall be entitled in accordance with the following provisions of
this Part to payments to be known as "statutory paternity pay".

(2) The conditions are—

(a) that he satisfies prescribed conditions—

    (i) as to relationship with a child who is placed for adoption under the law of any part of the United Kingdom, and

    (ii) as to relationship with a person with whom the child is so placed for adoption;

(b) that he has been in employed earner's employment with an employer for a continuous period of at least 26 weeks ending with the relevant week;

(c) that his normal weekly earnings for the period of 8 weeks ending with the relevant week are not less than the lower earnings limit in force under section 5(1)(a) at the end of the relevant week;

(d) that he has been in employed earner's employment with the employer by reference to whom the condition in paragraph (b) above is satisfied for a continuous period beginning with the end of the relevant week and ending with the day on which the child is placed for adoption; and

(e) where he is a person with whom the child is placed for adoption, that he has elected to receive statutory paternity pay.

(3) The references in subsection (2) to the relevant week are to the week in which the adopter is notified of being matched with the child for the purposes of adoption.

(4) A person may not elect to receive statutory paternity pay if he has elected in accordance with section 171ZL below to receive statutory adoption pay.

(5) Regulations may make provision about elections for the purposes of subsection (2)(e) above.

(6) A person's entitlement to statutory paternity pay under this section shall not be affected by the placement for adoption of more than one child as part of the same arrangement.

(7) In this section, "adopter", in relation to a person who satisfies the condition under subsection (2)(a)(ii) above, means the person by reference to whom he satisfies that condition.

DEFINITIONS

    "adopter"—see subs.(7).
    "employer"—see s.171ZJ(1).
    "normal weekly earnings"—see s.171ZJ(6).
    "prescribed"—see s.171ZJ(1).
    "the relevant week"—see subs.(3).
    "week"—see s.171ZJ(5).

GENERAL NOTE

1.109   The conditions prescribed under subs.(2)(a) are, first, that the claimant is married to or the partner of a child's adopter (or in a case where there are two adopters, married to or the partner of the other adopter) and, secondly, has, or expects to have, the main responsibility for the upbringing of the child (apart from the responsibility of the child's adopter, or in a case where there two adopters, together with the other adopter): SPP and SAP (General) Regulations 2002 (SI 2002/ 2822), reg.11. Note that, unusually, reg.11 specifically includes same-sex partners. "Partner" is defined by reg.11(2) as meaning a person (excluding certain defined relatives) "who lives with the adopter and the child in an enduring family relationship", irrespective of whether the relationship between the adults is heterosexual or same-sex in nature.

Entitlement: general

171ZC.—(1) A person shall be entitled to payments of statutory paternity pay in respect of any period only if— 1.110

(a) he gives the person who will be liable to pay it notice of the date from which he expects the liability to pay him statutory paternity pay to begin; and

(b) the notice is given at least 28 days before that date or, if that is not reasonably practicable, as soon as is reasonably practicable.

(2) The notice shall be in writing if the person who is liable to pay the statutory paternity pay so requests.

(3) The Secretary of State may by regulations—

(a) provide that subsection (2)(b), (c) or (d) of section 171ZA or 171ZB above shall have effect subject to prescribed modifications in such cases as may be prescribed;

(b) provide that subsection (1) above shall not have effect, or shall have effect subject to prescribed modifications, in such cases as may be prescribed;

(c) impose requirements about evidence of entitlement;

(d) specify in what circumstances employment is to be treated as continuous for the purposes of section 171ZA or 171ZB above;

(e) provide that a person is to be treated for the purposes of section 171ZA or 171ZB above as being employed for a continuous period of at least 26 weeks where—

   (i) he has been employed by the same employer for at least 26 weeks under two or more separate contracts of service; and

   (ii) those contracts were not continuous;

(f) provide for amounts earned by a person under separate contracts of service with the same employer to be aggregated for the purposes of section 171ZA or 171ZB above;

(g) provide that—

   (i) the amount of a person's earnings for any period; or

   (ii) the amount of his earnings to be treated as comprised in any payment made to him or for his benefit,

shall be calculated or estimated for the purposes of section 171ZA or 171ZB above in such manner and on such basis as may be prescribed and that for that purpose payments of a particular class or description made or falling to be made to or by a person shall, to such extent as may be prescribed, be disregarded or, as the case may be, be deducted from the amount of his earnings.

DEFINITIONS

"employer"—see s.171ZJ(1).
"modifications"—see *ibid.*
"prescribed"—see *ibid.*
"week"—see s.171ZJ(5).

GENERAL NOTE

See further regs 6 and 7 of the SPP and SAP (General) Regulations 2002 (SI 1.111 2002/2822) on the period of payment and notice requirements for SPP (birth). The requirements relating to evidence of entitlement are in reg.9. The equivalent provisions for SPP (adoption) are in regs 12, 13 and 15.

Liability to make payments

1.112   **171ZD.**—(1) The liability to make payments of statutory paternity pay under section 171ZA or 171ZB above is a liability of any person of whom the person entitled to the payments has been an employee as mentioned in subsection (2)(b) and (d) of that section.

(2) Regulations shall make provision as to a former employer's liability to pay statutory paternity pay to a person in any case where the former employee's contract of service with him has been brought to an end by the former employer solely, or mainly, for the purpose of avoiding liability for statutory paternity pay.

(3) The Secretary of State may, with the concurrence of the Board, by regulations specify circumstances in which, notwithstanding this section, liability to make payments of statutory paternity pay is to be a liability of the Board.

DEFINITIONS

"the Board"—see s.171ZJ(1).
"employer"—see *ibid.*

GENERAL NOTE

1.113   This section, placing the liability to make payments of SPP on employers, follows the same approach as the provisions governing SMP (ss.164(3) and (8)). Note that there is no liability to pay SPP in respect of any week during which the claimant either is entitled to SSP or is detained in custody (or sentenced to imprisonment): SPP and SAP (General) Regulations 2002 (SI 2002/2822), reg.18. Similarly, there is no liability to pay SPP in the week that the person entitled dies.

The rules governing the funding of SPP and employers' responsibilities in connection with SPP payments are contained in the SPP and SAP (Administration) Regulations 2002 (SI 2002/2820). The special circumstances in which the Board is liable to pay SPP under subs.(3) are set out in SPP and SAP (General) Regulations 2002, reg.43.

Rate and period of pay

1.114   **171ZE.**—(1) Statutory paternity pay shall be payable at such fixed or earnings-related weekly rate as may be prescribed by regulations, which may prescribe different kinds of rate for different cases.

(2) Statutory paternity pay shall be payable in respect of—

(a) a period of two consecutive weeks within the qualifying period beginning on such date within that period as the person entitled may choose in accordance with regulations; or

(b) if regulations permit the person entitled to choose to receive statutory paternity pay in respect of—
    (i) a period of a week, or
    (ii) two non-consecutive periods of a week,
such week or weeks within the qualifying period as he may choose in accordance with regulations.

(3) For the purposes of subsection (2) above, the qualifying period shall be determined in accordance with regulations, which shall secure that it is a period of at least 56 days beginning—

(a) in the case of a person to whom the conditions in section 171ZA(2) above apply, with the date of the child's birth, and

(b) in the case of a person to whom the conditions in section 171ZB(2) above apply, with the date of the child's placement for adoption.

(4) Statutory paternity pay shall not be payable to a person in respect of a statutory pay week if it is not his purpose at the beginning of the week—

(a) to care for the child by reference to whom he satisfies the condition in sub-paragraph (i) of section 171ZA(2)(a) or 171ZB(2)(a) above; or

(b) to support the person by reference to whom he satisfies the condition in sub-paragraph (ii) of that provision.

(5) A person shall not be liable to pay statutory paternity pay to another in respect of a statutory pay week during any part of which the other works under a contract of service with him.

(6) It is immaterial for the purposes of subsection (5) above whether the work referred to in that subsection is work under a contract of service which existed immediately before the statutory pay week or a contract of service which did not so exist.

(7) Except in such cases as may be prescribed, statutory paternity pay shall not be payable to a person in respect of a statutory pay week during any part of which he works for any employer who is not liable to pay him statutory paternity pay.

(8) The Secretary of State may by regulations specify circumstances in which there is to be no liability to pay statutory paternity pay in respect of a statutory pay week.

(9) Where more than one child is born as a result of the same pregnancy, the reference in subsection (3)(a) to the date of the child's birth shall be read as a reference to the date of birth of the first child born as a result of the pregnancy.

(10) Where more than one child is placed for adoption as part of the same arrangement, the reference in subsection (3)(b) to the date of the child's placement shall be read as a reference to the date of placement of the first child to be placed as part of the arrangement.

[[1](10A) Where for any purpose of this Part of this Act or of regulations it is necessary to calculate the daily rate of ordinary statutory paternity pay, the amount payable by way of ordinary statutory paternity pay for any day shall be taken as one seventh of the weekly rate.]

(11) In this section—

"statutory pay week", in relation to a person entitled to statutory paternity pay, means a week chosen by him as a week in respect of which statutory paternity pay shall be payable;

"week" means any period of seven days.

AMENDMENT

1. Work and Families Act 2006 s.11 and Sch.1, para.16(1) and (3) (October 1, 2006).

DEFINITIONS

"employer"—see s.171ZJ(1).
"statutory pay week"—see subs.(11).
"week"—see *ibid.*

GENERAL NOTE

The weekly rate of SPP for 2009–10 is the lesser of £123.06 and 90 per cent of normal weekly earnings (on which see SPP and SAP (General) Regulations

1.115

2002 (SI 2002/2822), reg.40): SPP and SAP (Weekly Rates) Regulations 2002 (SI 2002/2818), reg.2.

The qualifying period for SPP (birth), i.e. the period within which the SPP period must occur, is the period of 56 days from the date of the child's birth (SPP and SAP (General) Regulations 2002, reg.8). For SPP (adoption), the 56 days runs from the date of the child's placement for adoption: see reg.14.

Regulation 18 of the SPP and SAP (General) Regulations 2002, made under para.(8), sets out the circumstances in which there is no liability to pay SPP (where SSP is payable, or the person has died or is in legal custody).

The rules governing the time for paying SPP are set out in reg.42 of the SPP and SAP (General) Regulations 2002. SPP may be paid in the same way as ordinary remuneration but must not include payment in kind or by way of board and lodging: reg.41.

Restrictions on contracting out

1.116   **171ZF.**—(1) Any agreement shall be void to the extent that it purports—

(a) to exclude, limit or otherwise modify any provision of this Part of this Act; or

(b) to require an employee or former employee to contribute (whether directly or indirectly) towards any costs incurred by his employer or former employer under this Part of this Act.

(2) For the avoidance of doubt, any agreement between an employer and an employee authorising any deductions from statutory paternity pay which the employer is liable to pay to the employee in respect of any period shall not be void by virtue of subsection (1)(a) above if the employer—

(a) is authorised by that or another agreement to make the same deductions from any contractual remuneration which he is liable to pay in respect of the same period; or

(b) would be so authorised if he were liable to pay contractual remuneration in respect of that period.

DEFINITION

"employer"—see s.171ZJ(1).

GENERAL NOTE

1.117   These restrictions on contracting out follow the equivalent provisions for SSP (s.151(2)–(3)) and SMP (s.164(6)–(7)).

Relationship with contractual remuneration

1.118   **171ZG.**—(1) Subject to subsections (2) and (3) below, any entitlement to statutory paternity pay shall not affect any right of a person in relation to remuneration under any contract of service ("contractual remuneration").

(2) Subject to subsection (3) below—

(a) any contractual remuneration paid to a person by an employer of his in respect of any period shall go towards discharging any liability of that employer to pay statutory paternity pay to him in respect of that period; and

(b) any statutory paternity pay paid by an employer to a person who is an employee of his in respect of any period shall go towards discharging any liability of that employer to pay contractual remuneration to him in respect of that period.

(3) Regulations may make provision as to payments which are, and those which are not, to be treated as contractual remuneration for the purposes of subsections (1) and (2) above.

DEFINITIONS

"contractual remuneration"—see subs.(1).
"employer"—see s.171ZJ(1).

GENERAL NOTE

This section mirrors Sch.12, para.2, the equivalent provision in relation to SSP, and Sch.13, para.3, which governs SMP to the same effect. The basic principle is that entitlement to SPP does not affect a claimant's rights to any contractual remuneration (subs.(1)), subject to the significant exception that any payment of contractual remuneration can be regarded as the discharge of SPP liability and vice versa (subs.(2)). Regulations made under subs.(3) provide that the payments to be treated as contractual remuneration are sums payable under a contract of service (a) by way of remuneration, (b) for incapacity for work due to sickness or injury, or (c) by reason of the birth or adoption of a child (SPP and SAP (General) Regulations 2002 (SI 2002/2822), reg.19).

1.119

Crown employment—Part XIIZA

171ZH. The provisions of this Part of this Act apply in relation to persons employed by or under the Crown as they apply in relation to persons employed otherwise than by or under the Crown.

1.120

GENERAL NOTE

This mirrors s.169, the equivalent provision for SMP.

1.121

Special classes of person

171ZI.—(1) The Secretary of State may with the concurrence of the Treasury make regulations modifying any provision of this Part of this Act in such manner as he thinks proper in its application to any person who is, has been or is to be—

1.122

(a) employed on board any ship, vessel, hovercraft or aircraft;
(b) outside Great Britain at any prescribed time or in any prescribed circumstances; or
(c) in prescribed employment in connection with continental shelf operations, as defined in section 120(2) above.

(2) Regulations under subsection (1) above may, in particular, provide—

(a) for any provision of this Part of this Act to apply to any such person, notwithstanding that it would not otherwise apply;
(b) for any such provision not to apply to any such person, notwithstanding that it would otherwise apply;
(c) for excepting any such person from the application of any such provision where he neither is domiciled nor has a place of residence in any part of Great Britain;
(d) for the taking of evidence, for the purposes of the determination of any question arising under any such provision, in a country or territory outside Great Britain, by a British consular official or such other person as may be determined in accordance with the regulations.

DEFINITIONS

"Great Britain"—see s.172(a).
"prescribed"—see s.171ZJ(1).

GENERAL NOTE

1.123   This enabling provision is in the same terms as s.162, which applies to SSP. See further the Statutory Paternity Pay and Statutory Adoption Pay (Persons Abroad and Mariners) Regulations 2002 (SI 2002/2821).

Part XIIZA: supplementary

1.124   **171ZJ.**—(1) In this Part of this Act—
"the Board" means the Commissioners of Inland Revenue;
[²"employer", in relation to a person who is an employee, means a person who—
(a) under section 6 above is, liable to pay secondary Class 1 contributions in relation to any of the earnings of the person who is an employee; or
(b) would be liable to pay such contributions but for—
(i) the condition in section 6(1)(b), or
(ii) the employee being under the age of 16;]
"modifications" includes additions, omissions and amendments, and related expressions are to be read accordingly;
"prescribed" means prescribed by regulations.
(2) In this Part of this Act, "employee" means a person who is—
(a) gainfully employed in Great Britain either under a contract of service or in an office (including elective office) with [¹general earnings (as defined by section 7 of the Income Tax (Earnings and Pensions) Act 2003)]
[². . .]
(3) Regulations may provide—
(a) for cases where a person who falls within the definition in subsection (2) above is not to be treated as an employee for the purposes of this Part of this Act; and
(b) for cases where a person who would not otherwise be an employee for the purposes of this Part of this Act is to be treated as an employee for those purposes.
(4) Without prejudice to any other power to make regulations under this Part of this Act, regulations may specify cases in which, for the purposes of this Part of this Act or of such provisions of this Part of this Act as may be prescribed—
(a) two or more employers are to be treated as one;
(b) two or more contracts of service in respect of which the same person is an employee are to be treated as one.
(5) In this Part, except section 171ZE, "week" means a period of seven days beginning with Sunday or such other period as may be prescribed in relation to any particular case or class of cases.
(6) For the purposes of this Part of this Act, a person's normal weekly earnings shall, subject to subsection (8) below, be taken to be the average weekly earnings which in the relevant period have been paid to him or paid for his benefit under the contract of service with the employer in question.

(7) For the purposes of subsection (6) above, "earnings" and "relevant period" shall have the meanings given to them by regulations.

(8) In such cases as may be prescribed, a person's normal weekly earnings shall be calculated in accordance with regulations.

(9) Where—

(a) in consequence of the establishment of one or more National Health Service trusts under [³the National Health Service Act 2006, the National Health Service (Wales) Act 2006], or the National Health Service (Scotland) Act 1978 a person's contract of employment is treated by a scheme under [³any of those Acts] as divided so as to constitute two or more contracts; or

(b) an order under [³paragraph 26(1) of Schedule 3 to the National Health Service Act 2006] provides that a person's contract of employment is so divided;

regulations may make provision enabling the person to elect for all of those contracts to be treated as one contract for the purposes of this Part of this Act or such provisions of this Part of this Act as may be prescribed.

(10) Regulations under subsection (9) above may prescribe—

(a) the conditions that must be satisfied if a person is to be entitled to make such an election;

(b) the manner in which, and the time within which, such an election is to be made;

(c) the persons to whom, and the manner in which, notice of such an election is to be given;

(d) the information which a person who makes such an election is to provide, and the persons to whom, and the time within which, he is to provide it;

(e) the time for which such an election is to have effect;

(f) which one of the person's employers under two or more contracts is to be regarded for the purposes of statutory paternity pay as his employer under the contract.

(11) The powers under subsections (9) and (10) are without prejudice to any other power to make regulations under this Part of this Act.

(12) Regulations under any of subsections (4) to (10) above must be made with the concurrence of the Board.

AMENDMENTS

1. Income Tax (Earnings and Pensions) Act 2003, s.722 and Sch.6, para.183 (April 6, 2003).

2. Employment Equality (Age) Regulations 2006 (SI 2006/1031) reg.49(1) and Sch.8, Pt 1, para.11(2) (October 1, 2006).

3. National Health Service (Consequential Provisions) Act 2006, s.2 and Sch.1, para.149 (March 1, 2007).

GENERAL NOTE

"*Earnings*": The definition and enabling power under subss.(6) and (7) should be read with reg.39 of the SPP and SAP (General) Regulations 2002 (SI 2002/2822), which defines this term.

"*Employee*": The definition under subs.(2) is modified by regulations made under subs.(3). Thus those who are treated as employed earners under the Social Security (Categorisation of Earners) Regulations 1978 (SI 1978/1689) are also treated as employees for the purpose of SPP: SPP and SAP (General) Regulations 2002, reg.32(1). Apprentices are also covered (reg.32(2)). Employed earners who

1.125

71

do not meet the residence or presence requirements under the rules governing National Insurance contributions are excluded from the definition of employee for these purposes (reg.32(3)). Continuous employment is dealt with by regs 33–37. Employment with more than one employer (subs.(4)) is covered by reg.38.

"*National Health Service trusts*": The special position of NHS employees with more than one contract of employment (e.g. with different NHS trusts) is dealt with by the SPP and SAP (National Health Service Employees) Regulations 2002 (SI 2002/2819). These regulations enable such employees to elect to treat two or more such contracts as one contract of employment.

"*Normal weekly earnings*": The definition and enabling power under subss.(6) and (7) should be read with reg.40 of the SPP and SAP (General) Regulations 2002, which defines this term.

Power to apply Part XIIZA to adoption cases not involving placement

1.126   **171ZK.**—The Secretary of State may by regulations provide for this Part to have effect in relation to cases which involve adoption, but not the placement of a child for adoption under the law of any part of the United Kingdom, with such modifications as the regulations may prescribe.

DEFINITIONS

"modifications"—see s.171ZJ(1).
"United Kingdom"—see s.172(b).

GENERAL NOTE

1.127   See further the Social Security Contributions and Benefits Act 1992 (Application of Pts 12ZA and 12ZB to Adoptions from Overseas) Regulations 2003 (SI 2003/499) and the Statutory Paternity Pay (Adoption) and Statutory Adoption Pay (Adoptions from Overseas) (No.2) Regulations 2003 (SI 2003/1194).

[¹PART XIIZB

STATUTORY ADOPTION PAY

AMENDMENT

1. Part XIIZB was inserted by the Employment Act 2002, s.4 (December 8, 2002).

GENERAL NOTE

1.128   Part XIIZB of the SSCBA 1992 was inserted by the Employment Act 2002. On the background to the introduction of statutory adoption pay (SAP), see the General Note to Pt XIIZA on statutory paternity pay (SPP), introduced at the same time. The amendments made by c.1 of Pt I of the Employment Act 2002 relating to paternity and adoption, including the insertion of Pt XIIZB into the SSCBA 1992, came into force on December 8, 2002 (Employment Act 2002 (Commencement No.3 and Transitional and Saving Provisions) Order 2002, art.2(2) and Sch.1, Pt 2). However, art.3 and Sch.3, para.2 of the same Order provide that Pt XIIZB shall have effect only in relation to a person with whom a child is, or is expected to be placed for adoption on or after April 6, 2003.

Adoptive parents have a right under employment legislation to 26 weeks' ordinary adoption leave with the option of 26 weeks' additional adoption leave, mirroring the arrangements now in place for maternity leave. SAP is payable for 26 weeks (SSCBA 1992, s.171ZN(2)), as with SMP (but unlike the mere two weeks for SPP). The rules governing entitlement to SAP are set out in SSCBA 1992, s.171ZL: employees must have completed 26 weeks' service with their employer by the time they are matched with the child to be adopted and their earnings, on average, must be at least equal to the lower earnings limit for the purpose of National Insurance contributions. The liability to make payments of SAP is placed on employers (SSCBA 1992, s.171ZM), with the recovery arrangements being as for SMP. Provision for various types of special cases and for matters of interpretation is to be found in SSCBA 1992, ss.171ZO–171ZT.

Entitlement

171ZL.—(1) Where a person who is, or has been, an employee satisfies the conditions in subsection (2) below, he shall be entitled in accordance with the following provisions of this Part to payments to be known as "statutory adoption pay".

1.129

(2) The conditions are—

(a) that he is a person with whom a child is, or is expected to be, placed for adoption under the law of any part of the United Kingdom;

(b) that he has been in employed earner's employment with an employer for a continuous period of at least 26 weeks ending with the relevant week;

(c) that he has ceased to work for the employer;

(d) that his normal weekly earnings for the period of 8 weeks ending with the relevant week are not less than the lower earnings limit in force under section 5(1)(a) at the end of the relevant week; and

(e) that he has elected to receive statutory adoption pay.

(3) The references in subsection (2)(b) and (d) above to the relevant week are to the week in which the person is notified that he has been matched with the child for the purposes of adoption.

(4) A person may not elect to receive statutory adoption pay if—

(a) he has elected in accordance with section 171ZB above to receive statutory paternity pay, or

[¹(b) he falls within subsection (4A);

(4A) A person falls within this subsection if—

(a) the child is, or is expected to be, placed for adoption with him as a member of a couple;

(b) the other member of the couple is a person to whom the conditions in subsection (2) above apply; and

(c) the other member of the couple has elected to receive statutory adoption pay.

(4B) For the purposes of subsection (4A), a person is a member of a couple if—

(a) in the case of an adoption or expected adoption under the law of England and Wales, he is a member of a couple within the meaning of section 144(4) of the Adoption and Children Act 2002;

(b) in the case of an adoption or an expected adoption under the law of Scotland or of Northern Ireland, he is a member of a married couple.]

(5) A person's entitlement to statutory adoption pay shall not be affectedby the placement, or expected placement, for adoption of more than one childas part of the same arrangement.

(6) A person shall be entitled to payments of statutory adoption pay only if—

    (a) he gives the person who will be liable to pay it notice of the date from which he expects the liability to pay him statutory adoption pay to begin; and

    (b) the notice is given at least 28 days before that date or, if that is not reasonably practicable, as soon as is reasonably practicable.

(7) The notice shall be in writing if the person who is liable to pay the statutory adoption pay so requests.

(8) The Secretary of State may by regulations—

    (a) provide that subsection (2)(b), (c) or (d) above shall have effect subject to prescribed modifications in such cases as may be prescribed;

    (b) provide that subsection (6) above shall not have effect, or shall have effect subject to prescribed modifications, in such cases as may be prescribed;

    (c) impose requirements about evidence of entitlement;

    (d) specify in what circumstances employment is to be treated as continuous for the purposes of this section;

    (e) provide that a person is to be treated for the purposes of this section as being employed for a continuous period of at least 26 weeks where—

        (i) he has been employed by the same employer for at least 26 weeks under two or more separate contracts of service; and

        (ii) those contracts were not continuous;

    (f) provide for amounts earned by a person under separate contracts of service with the same employer to be aggregated for the purposes of this section;

    (g) provide that—

        (i) the amount of a person's earnings for any period; or

        (ii) the amount of his earnings to be treated as comprised in any payment made to him or for his benefit;

shall be calculated or estimated for the purposes of this section in such manner and on such basis as may be prescribed and that for that purpose payments of a particular class or description made or falling to be made to or by a person shall, to such extent as may be prescribed, be disregarded or, as the case may be, be deducted from the amount of his earnings;

    (h) make provision about elections for statutory adoption pay.

AMENDMENT

1. Adoption and Children Act 2002 (Consequential Amendment to Statutory Adoption Pay) Order 2006 (SI 2006/2012), art.3 (October 1, 2006).

DEFINITIONS

    "employee"—see s.171ZS(2).
    "employer"—see s.171ZS(1).
    "modifications"—see *ibid.*
    "normal weekly earnings"—see s.171ZS(6).
    "prescribed"—see s.171ZS(1).
    "relevant week"—see subs.(3).
    "United Kingdom"—see s.172(b).
    "week"—see s.171ZS(5).

GENERAL NOTE

This section sets out the qualifying conditions for receipt of SAP. A person
is entitled to SAP if he or she meets each of five conditions (subs.(2)). First, the
claimant must have an approved match with the child. Secondly, the person must
be an employee who has satisfied the service qualification of continuous service
with the same employer for at least 26 weeks by the week in which the approved
match is made. Thirdly, the person must have actually stopped working for that
employer (see also s.171ZN(3) (and (4)). Fourthly, the employee's average weekly
earnings must be not less than the lower earnings limit for National Insurance contributions. Finally, the person must have elected to receive SAP, which requires
that he or she provide the employer with an appropriate notification (see subss.
(6) and (7); see also reg.23 of the SPP and SAP (General) Regulations 2002 (SI
2002/2822)) and evidence of entitlement (SPP and SAP (General) Regs 2002,
reg.24).

1.130

SAP is available to an adoptive parent of a child newly placed for adoption,
whether the child is being adopted within the United Kingdom or from overseas.
There are, however, some slight differences in the provisions for SAP for domestic
and overseas adoptions respectively: see further SSCBA 1992, s.171ZT. It is also
important to note that entitlement to SAP arises only for children who are newly
placed for adoption. It is therefore not possible to receive SAP for a step-family
adoption or where the child is adopted by his or her existing foster carers.

Liability to make payments

171ZM.—(1) The liability to make payments of statutory adoption pay
is a liability of any person of whom the person entitled to the payments has
been an employee as mentioned in section 171ZL(2)(b) above.

1.131

(2) Regulations shall make provision as to a former employer's liability
to pay statutory adoption pay to a person in any case where the former
employee's contract of service with him has been brought to an end by the
former employer solely, or mainly, for the purpose of avoiding liability for
statutory adoption pay.

(3) The Secretary of State may, with the concurrence of the Board, by
regulations specify circumstances in which, notwithstanding this section,
liability to make payments of statutory adoption pay is to be a liability of
the Board.

DEFINITIONS

"the Board"—see s.171ZS(1).
"employee"—see s.171ZS(2).
"employer"—see s.171ZS(1).

GENERAL NOTE

This section, placing the liability to make payments of SAP on employers, follows
the same approach as the provisions governing SMP (ss.164(3) and (8)) and SPP
(s.171ZD). Note that there is no liability to pay SAP in respect of any week during
which the claimant either is entitled to SSP or is detained in custody (or sentenced to imprisonment): SPP and SAP (General) Regulations 2002 (SI 2002/2822),
reg.27 (but note that, unlike with SPP, there are exceptions to the latter preclusionary rule: reg.27(2)). As with SPP, however, there is no liability to pay SAP in the
week that the person entitled dies.

1.132

The rules governing the funding of SAP and employers' responsibilities in connection with SAP payments are contained in the SPP and SAP (Administration)
Regulations 2002 (SI 2002/2820). The special circumstances in which HMRC is

liable to pay SAP under subs.(3) are set out in SPP and SAP (General) Regulations 2002, regs 43 and 44 (the latter applying solely to SAP and not SPP).

Rate and period of pay

1.133

171ZN.—(1) Statutory adoption pay shall be payable at such fixed or earnings-related weekly rate as the Secretary of State may prescribe by regulations, which may prescribe different kinds of rate for different cases.

(2) Statutory adoption pay shall be payable, subject to the provisions of this Part of this Act, in respect of each week during a prescribed period ("the adoption pay period") of a duration not exceeding [¹52 weeks].

(3) [¹Except in such cases as may be prescribed,] a person shall not be liable to pay statutory adoption pay to another in respect of any week during any part of which the other works under a contract of service with him.

(4) It is immaterial for the purposes of subsection (3) above whether the work referred to in that subsection is work under a contract of service which existed immediately before the adoption pay period or a contract of service which did not so exist.

(5) Except in such cases as may be prescribed, statutory adoption pay shall not be payable to a person in respect of any week during any part of which he works for any employer who is not liable to pay him statutiory adoption pay.

(6) The Secretary of State may by regulations specify circumstances in which there is to be no liability to pay statutory adoption pay in respect of a week.

[²(6A) Where for any purpose of this Part of this Act or of regulations it is necessary to calculate the daily rate of statutory adoption pay, the amount payable by way of statutory adoption pay for any day shall be taken as one seventh of the weekly rate.]

(7) In subsection (2) above, "week" means any period of seven days.

(8) In subsection (3), (5) and (6) above, "week" means a period of seven days beginning with the day of the week on which the adoption pay period begins.

Amendments

1. Work and Families Act 2006, s.2 (October 1, 2006).
2. Work and Families Act 2006, s.11 and Sch.1, para.21 (October 1, 2006).

Definitions

"adoption pay period"—see subs.(2).
"employer"—see s.171ZS(1).
"prescribed"—see *ibid.*
"week"—see subss.(7) and (8).

General Note

1.134

This section provides that SAP is payable for a period of up to 52 weeks (the "adoption pay period" under subs.(2)). The rate of SAP is the same as that for SMP, namely (from April 2008) the lesser of £123.06 a week or 90 per cent of the employee's average weekly earnings: SPP and SAP (Weekly Rates) Regulations 2002 (SI 2002/2818), reg.3. More detailed rules relating to the adoption pay period are set out in regs 21 and 22 of the SPP and SAP (General) Regulations 2002 (SI 2002/2822).

Restrictions on contracting out

171ZO.—(1) Any agreement shall be void to the extent that it   1.135
purports—

(a) to exclude, limit or otherwise modify any provision of this Part of this
Act; or

(b) to require an employee or former employee to contribute (whether
directly or indirectly) towards any costs incurred by his employer or
former employer under this Part of this Act.

(2) For the avoidance of doubt, any agreement between an employer and
an employee authorising any deductions from statutory adoption pay which
the employer is liable to pay to the employee in respect of any period shall
not be void by virtue of subsection (1)(a) above if the employer—

(a) is authorised by that or another agreement to make the same deductions from any contractual remuneration which he is liable to pay in
respect of the same period; or

(b) would be so authorised if he were liable to pay contractual remuneration in respect of that period.

DEFINITIONS

"employee"—see s.171ZS(2).
"employer"—see s.171ZS(1).

GENERAL NOTE

These restrictions on contracting out are in the same terms as the equivalent pro-   1.136
visions for SSP (s.151(2)–(3)), SMP (s.164(6)–(7)) and SPP (s.171ZF). See also
SPP and SAP (General) Regulations 2002 (SI 2002/2822), reg.30.

Relationship with benefits and other payments etc.

171ZP.—(1) Except as may be prescribed, a day which falls within the   1.137
adoption pay period shall not be treated as a day of incapacity for work for
the purposes of determining, for this Act, whether it forms part of a period
of incapacity for work for the purposes of incapacity benefit.

(2) Regulations may provide that in prescribed circumstances a day
which falls within the adoption pay period shall be treated as a day of incapacity for work for the purposes of determining entitlement to the higher
rate of short-term incapacity benefit or to long-term incapacity benefit.

(3) Regulations may provide that an amount equal to a person's statutory
adoption pay for a period shall be deducted from any such benefit in respect
of the same period and a person shall be entitled to such benefit only if there
is a balance after the deduction and, if there is such a balance, at a weekly
rate equal to it.

(4) Subject to subsections (5) and (6) below, any entitlement to statutory
adoption pay shall not affect any right of a person in relation to remuneration under any contract of service ("contractual remuneration").

(5) Subject to subsection (6) below—

(a) any contractual remuneration paid to a person by an employer of
his in respect of a week in the adoption pay period shall go towards
discharging any liability of that employer to pay statutory adoption
pay to him in respect of that week; and

(b) any statutory adoption pay paid by an employer to a person who is an
employee of his in respect of a week in the adoption pay period shall

go towards discharging any liability of that employer to pay contractual remuneration to him in respect of that week.

(6) Regulations may make provision as to payments which are, and those which are not, to be treated as contractual remuneration for the purposes of subsections (4) and (5) above.

(7) In subsection (5) above, "week" means a period of seven days beginning with the day of the week on which the adoption pay period begins.

DEFINITIONS

"adoption pay period"—see s.171ZN(2).
"contractual remuneration"—see subs.(4).
"employee"—see s.171ZS(2).
"employer"—see s.171ZS(1).
"prescribed"—see *ibid.*
"week"—see subs.(7).

GENERAL NOTE

1.138   The basic principle is that entitlement to SAP does not affect a claimant's rights to any contractual remuneration (subs.(4)), subject to the significant exception that any payment of contractual remuneration can be regarded as the discharge of SAP liability and vice versa (subs.(5)). Regulations made under subs.(6) provide that the payments to be treated as contractual remuneration are sums payable under a contract of service (a) by way of remuneration, (b) for incapacity for work due to sickness or injury or (c) by reason of the adoption of a child (SPP and SAP (General) Regulations 2002 (SI 2002/2822), reg.28).

Crown employment—Part XIIZB

1.139   **171ZQ.** The provisions of this Part of this Act apply in relation to persons employed by or under the Crown as they apply in relation to persons employed otherwise than by or under the Crown.

GENERAL NOTE

1.140   This mirrors s.169, the equivalent provision for SMP, and s.171ZH, which deals with SPP.

Special classes of person

1.141   **171ZR.**—(1) The Secretary of State may with the concurrence of the Treasury make regulations modifying any provision of this Part of this Act in such manner as he thinks proper in its application to any person who is, has been or is to be—

(a) employed on board any ship, vessel, hovercraft or aircraft;

(b) outside Great Britain at any prescribed time or in any prescribed circumstances; or

(c) in prescribed employment in connection with continental shelf operations, as defined in section 120(2) above.

(2) Regulations under subsection (1) above may, in particular, provide—

(a) for any provision of this Part of this Act to apply to any such person, notwithstanding that it would not otherwise apply;

(b) for any such provision not to apply to any such person, notwithstanding that it would otherwise apply;

(c) for excepting any such person from the application of any such provision where he neither is domiciled nor has a place of residence in any part of Great Britain;

(d) for the taking of evidence, for the purposes of the determination of any question arising under any such provision, in a country or territory outside Great Britain, by a British consular official or such other person as may be determined in accordance with the regulations.

DEFINITIONS

"Great Britain"—see s.172(a).
"prescribed"—see s.171ZS(1).

GENERAL NOTE

This enabling provision is in the same terms as s.162, which applies to SSP, and s.17ZI, which deals with SPP. See further the Statutory Paternity Pay and Statutory Adoption Pay (Persons Abroad and Mariners) Regulations 2002 (SI 2002/2821).

1.142

Part XIIZB: supplementary

171ZS.—(1) In this Part of this Act—
"adoption pay period" has the meaning given by section 171ZN(2) above;
"the Board" means the Commissioners of Inland Revenue;
[²"employer", in relation to a person who is an employee, means a person who—

(a) under section 6 above is liable to pay secondary Class 1 contributions in relation to any of the earnings of the person who is an employee; or

(b) would be liable to pay such contributions but for—
  (i) the condition in section 6(1)(b), or
  (ii) the employee being under the age of 16;]

"modifications" includes additions, omissions and amendments, and related expressions are to be read accordingly;
"prescribed" means prescribed by regulations.

(2) In this Part of this Act, "employee" means a person who is—

(a) gainfully employed in Great Britain either under a contract of service or in an office (including elective office) with [¹general earnings (as defined by section 7 of the Income Tax (Earnings and Pensions) Act 2003)]

[². . .]

(3) Regulations may provide—

(a) for cases where a person who falls within the definition in sub-section (2) above is not to be treated as an employee for the purposes of this Part of this Act; and

(b) for cases where a person who would not otherwise be an employee for the purposes of this Part of this Act is to be treated as an employee for those purposes.

(4) Without prejudice to any other power to make regulations under this Part of this Act, regulations may specify cases in which, for the purposes of this Part of this Act or of such provisions of this Part of this Act as may be prescribed—

(a) two or more employers are to be treated as one;

1.143

(b) two or more contracts of service in respect of which the same person is an employee are to be treated as one.

(5) In this Part, except sections 171ZN and 171ZP, "week" means a period of seven days beginning with Sunday or such other period as may be prescribed in relation to any particular case or class of cases.

(6) For the purposes of this Part of this Act, a person's normal weekly earnings shall, subject to subsection (8) below, be taken to be the average weekly earnings which in the relevant period have been paid to him or paid for his benefit under the contract of service with the employer in question.

(7) For the purposes of subsection (6) above, "earnings" and "relevant period" shall have the meanings given to them by regulations.

(8) In such cases as may be prescribed, a person's normal weekly earnings shall be calculated in accordance with regulations.

(9) Where—

(a) in consequence of the establishment of one or more National Health Service trusts under [³the National Health Service Act 2006, the National Health Service (Wales) Act 2006] or the National Health Service (Scotland) Act 1978, a person's contract of employment is treated by a scheme under [³any of those Acts] as divided so as to constitute two or more contracts; or

(b) an order under [³paragraph 26(1) of Schedule 3 to the National Health Service Act 2006] provides that a person's contract of employment is so divided;

regulations may make provision enabling the person to elect for all of those contracts to be treated as one contract for the purposes of this Part of this Act or such provisions of this Part of this Act as may be prescribed.

(10) Regulations under subsection (9) above may prescribe—

(a) the conditions that must be satisfied if a person is to be entitled to make such an election;

(b) the manner in which, and the time within which, such an election is to be made;

(c) the persons to whom, and the manner in which, notice of such an election is to be given;

(d) the information which a person who makes such an election is to provide, and the persons to whom, and the time within which, he is to provide it;

(e) the time for which such an election is to have effect;

(f) which one of the person's employers under two or more contracts is to be regarded for the purposes of statutory adoption pay as his employer under the contract.

(11) The powers under subsections (9) and (10) are without prejudice to any other power to make regulations under this Part of this Act.

(12) Regulations under any of subsections (4) to (10) above must be made with the concurrence of the Board.

AMENDMENTS

1. Income Tax (Earnings and Pensions) Act 2003, s.722 and Sch.6, para.184 (April 6, 2003).

2. Employment Equality (Age) Regulations 2006 (SI 2006/1031) , reg.49(1) and Sch.8, Pt 1, para.12 (October 1, 2006).

3. National Health Service (Consequential Provisions) Act 2006, s.2 and Sch.1, para.150 (March 1, 2007).

DEFINITIONS

"Earnings": see General Note to s.171ZJ.
"Employee": see General Note to s.171ZJ.
"National Health Service trusts": see General Note to s.171ZJ.
"Normal weekly earnings": see General Note to s.171ZJ.

Power to apply Part XIIZB to adoption cases not involving placement

171ZT. The Secretary of State may by regulations provide for this Part   1.144
to have effect in relation to cases which involve adoption, but not the
placement of a child for adoption under the law of any part of the United
Kingdom, with such modifications as the regulations may prescribe.

GENERAL NOTE

See further the Social Security Contributions and Benefits Act 1992 (Application   1.145
of Pts 12ZA and 12ZB to Adoptions from Overseas) Regulations 2003 (SI 2003/499)
and the Statutory Paternity Pay (Adoption) and Statutory Adoption Pay (Adoptions
from Overseas) (No.2) Regulations 2003 (SI 2003/1194).

PART XIII

GENERAL

Interpretation

Application of Act in relation to territorial waters

172. In this Act—   1.146
(a) any reference to Great Britain includes a reference to the territorial
waters of the United Kingdom adjacent to Great Britain;
(b) any reference to the United Kingdom includes a reference to the territorial waters of the United Kingdom.

Age

173. For the purposes of this Act a person—   1.147
(a) is over or under a particular age if he has or, as the case may be, has
not attained that age; and
(b) is between two particular ages if he has attained the first but not the
second;
and in Scotland (as in England and Wales) the time at which a person
attains a particular age expressed in years is the commencement of the relevant anniversary of the date of his birth.

References to Acts

174. In this Act—   1.148
"the 1975 Act" means the Social Security Act 1975;
"the 1986 Act" means the Social Security Act 1986;
"the Administration Act" means the Social Security Administration Act
1992;

"the Consequential Provisions Act" means the Social Security (Consequential Provisions) Act 1992;

"the Northern Ireland Contributions and Benefits Act" means the Social Security Contributions and Benefits (Northern Ireland) Act 1992;

"the Old Cases Act" means the Industrial Injuries and Diseases (Old Cases) Act 1975; and

"the Pensions Act" means the [¹ Pensions Schemes Act 1993].

AMENDMENT

1. Pension Schemes Act 1993, s.190 and Sch.8, para.41 (February 7, 1994).

SCHEDULE 9

EXCLUSIONS FROM ENTITLEMENT TO CHILD BENEFIT

Children [³ and qualifying young persons] in detention, care, etc.

1.149   **1.**—Except where regulations otherwise provide, no person shall be entitled to child benefit in respect of a child [³ or qualifying young person] for any week if in that week the child [³ or qualifying young person]—

(a) is undergoing imprisonment or detention in legal custody;

(b) is subject to a supervision requirement made under section 44 of the Social Work (Scotland) Act 1968 and is residing in a residential establishment within the meaning of that section; or

(c) is in the care of a local authority in such circumstances as may be prescribed.

[³ . . .]

Married children [³ and qualifying young persons]

3.—Except where regulations otherwise provide, no person shall be entitled to child benefit in respect of a child [³ or qualifying young person] who is married.

Persons exempt from tax

4.—[² . . .].

Children entitled to severe disablement allowance

5.—[¹ . . .].

DEFINITIONS

1.150   "child": s.142.

"week": s.147.

AMENDMENTS

1. Welfare Reform and Pensions Act 1999. Sch.13, part IV (April 6,2001)

2. Tax Credits Act 2002. s.57, Sch.6 (April 7, 2003).

3. Child Benefit Act 2005, s.1 and Sch.1, para.17 (April 10, 2006).

SCHEDULE 10

PRIORITY BETWEEN PERSONS ENTITLED TO CHILD BENEFIT

Person with prior award

1.151   **1.**—(1) Subject to sub-paragraph (2) below, as between a person claiming child benefit in respect of a child [¹ or qualifying young person] for any week and a person to whom child benefit in respect of that child [¹ or qualifying young person] for that week has already been awarded when the claim is made, the latter shall be entitled.

(2) Sub-paragraph (1) above shall not confer any priority where the week to which the claim relates is later than the third week following that in which the claim is made.

Person having child [¹ and qualifying young person] living with him

2.—Subject to paragraph 1 above, as between a person entitled for any week by virtue of paragraph (a) of subsection (1) of section 143 above and a person entitled by virtue of paragraph (b) of that subsection the former shall be entitled.

Husband and wife

3.—Subject to paragraphs 1 and 2 above, as between a husband and wife residing together the wife shall be entitled.

Parents

4.—(1) Subject to paragraphs 1 to 3 above, as between a person who is and one who is not a parent of the child [¹ or qualifying young person] the parent shall be entitled.

(2) Subject as aforesaid, as between two persons residing together who are parents of the child [¹ or qualifying young person] but not husband and wife, the mother shall be entitled.

Other cases

5.—As between persons not falling within paragraphs 1 to 4 above, such one of them shall be entitled as they may jointly elect or, in default of election, as the Secretary of State may in his discretion determine.

Supplementary

6.—(1) Any election under this Schedule shall be made in the prescribed manner.

(2) Regulations may provide for exceptions from the modifications of the provisions of paragraphs 1 to 5 above in relation to such cases as may be prescribed.

AMENDMENT

1. Child Benefit Act 2005, s.1 and Sch.7, para.18 (April 10, 2006).

DEFINITIONS

"child": s.142.
"parent, father or mother": s.147(3).
"week": s.147.

1.152

GENERAL NOTE

Under s.143 it is possible for more than one person to be entitled to claim Child Benefit. For example, the child may live with one parent while being maintained to the requisite extent by the other; or the child may live with a parent in the home of a grandparent. In such cases only one award of Child Benefit can be made and Sch.10 determines the order of priority between multiple claimants. Note that s.144 and Sch. 10 apply only where more than one person is entitled to benefit for the same child in respect of that week. Where the child has ceased to live with one parent as provided for in s.143, and a claim is not precluded by the effect of s.13(2) of SSAA 1992 (which prevents a claim being made where payment of benefit has been made already to another claimant, and the decision to make such payment has not been revised, nor has the payment been repaid voluntarily) then Sch. 10 does not apply. In that case the DM should decide the case on the basis of s.143 alone. For an explanation of these provisions and their interaction see *CF/2826/2008*.

In the first place no payment will be made unless there has been a claim, so that if only one claim is made, even by a person of lower priority, that claim will be met. Where, however, there are multiple claims priority will be given in the following order.

(1) the person with whom the child is living.

(2) the wife, as between a husband and wife who are residing together.

1.153

(3) a parent, as between a person who is a parent and one who is not.

(4) the mother, as between parents who are residing together but are not married.

(5) the person agreed by them, as between any other persons.

(6) the person determined by a decision maker of HMRC, where such other persons cannot agree.

Where there is an existing award of Child Benefit in payment at the time a rival claim is made, the existing award will continue to be paid for a period of three weeks (provided the claimant continues to satisfy the other conditions of entitlement), even though the new claimant may be entitled thereafter by priority. The reservation of entitlement to the current claimant for a period of three weeks was applied in *CF/3348/2002*.

The meaning of "residing together" for the purposes of Child Benefit is dealt with largely by reg.34 of the Child Benefit (General) Regulations, and is not the same as in other benefit contexts. Spouses and parents who are not married to each other are treated as residing together if their separation is not likely to be permanent and, in the case of spouses only, if it is for the purposes of medical treatment. In *R(F) 4/85* it was held that a couple who married while the husband was in prison, and who had never lived together, had to be treated under this regulation as if they were residing together because their separation was not likely to be permanent—they could be expected to commence cohabitation when the husband was released from prison. (The effect in this case was to deprive the claimant of the increase for one parent benefit.) It has also been accepted in this context that parties may not be residing together if they maintain separate households under the same roof (*R(F) 3/81*).

Where the parents of a child are residing together (whether married or not) and the mother of the child obtains a certificate of gender recognition as a man he will continue to be regarded as the mother of their child for this purpose because s.12 of the Gender Recognition Act 2004, provides that the acquired status does not affect the status of a person as the mother or father of a child.

A "parent" for the purposes of Child Benefit is given an extended meaning by s.147(3) to include a step parent. The meaning of parent is also extended by the effect of the Children Act 1989, to include any person in whose favour a residence order has been made. This is because the parental responsibility conferred by the order made under that Act is defined to include all the rights which, by law, a parent has in relation to that child. For the purposes of the Contributions & Benefits Act, the word parent is to be construed as the "legal parent" of the child. (See *Secretary of State v Smith* [1983] 1 W.L.R. 1110, where the effect of an order made under equivalent legislation then in force, was to include an adoptive parent of the child and at the same time to exclude the natural parent.) The same reasoning was applied by Commissioner Howell in *R(F), 1/08* where a lesbian couple had two children with the assistance of artificial insemmination and after they had separated a residence order had been made in favour of both of them. The Commissioner held that both must be regarded as parents, not just the biological mother and, consequently it became necessary for HMRC to exercise the discretion provided for in para.5.

The particular problem that arises when the parents of a child have separated and the care of the child is then shared between them (e.g. in holidays and at weekends) is referred to by Judge Wikeley in *CIS/2457/2008*. The issue arose only indirectly in that case, which was a determination of the claimant's entitlement to Income Support, but that entitlement depended, in turn, on her right to receive Child Benefit, and the judge added an appendix to his decision that covers earlier cases (*Chester v Secretary of State for Social Security* [2001] EWHC Admin 119, *Barber v Secretary of State for Social Security* [2002] EWHC 1915 (Admin) and *R on the relation of Ford v Board of Inland Revenue* [2005] EWHC 1109 (Admin)) where decisions awarding all of the Child Benefit to one parent had been quashed on review.

A decision by HMRC in default of agreement is not appealable but an application for revision or review may be made. In *Chester v Sec of State for Social Security* [2001] EWHC Admin 1119, (approved in *Barber* [2002] EWHC 1915) it was held that such a default decision engaged the right to private and family life in Art.8 ECHR though in that case there was no need for the claimant to rely upon it. Note too, that it is now possible for an application for judicial review to be transferred to the Upper Tribunal.

The procedure for making an election as to priority, and for waiving priority, is provided for in regulations 14 and 15 of the Child Benefit (General) Regulations 2006.

Section 153(3)   SCHEDULE 11

CIRCUMSTANCES IN WHICH PERIODS OF ENTITLEMENT TO
STATUTORY SICK PAY DO NOT ARISE

1. A period of entitlement does not arise in relation to a particular period of incapacity for work in any of the circumstances set out in para.2 below or in such other circumstances as may be prescribed.

1.154

[⁴**1A.** Regulations made under paragraph 1 must be made with the concurrence of the Treasury.]

2. The circumstances are that—
   (a) [⁶. . .]
   (b) [⁵. . .];
   (c) at the relevant date the employee's normal weekly earnings are less than the lower earnings limit then in force under section 5(1)(a) above;
  [¹(d) in the period of 57 days ending immediately before the relevant date the employee had at least one day on which—
      (i) he was entitled to incapacity benefit (or would have been so entitled had he satisfied the contribution conditions mentioned in section 30A(2)(a) above); or
      (ii) [³. . .]
      (iii) he was entitled to a severe disablement allowance;]
 [⁸(dd) in the period of 85 days ending immediately before the relevant date the employee had at least one day on which he was entitled to an employment and support allowance (or would have been so entitled had he satisfied the requirements in section 1(2) of the Welfare Reform Act 2007.]
   (e) [¹. . .]
   (f) the employee has done no work for his employer under his contract of service;
   (g) on the relevant date there is [². . .] a stoppage of work due to a trade dispute at the employee's place of employment;
   (h) the employee is, or has been, pregnant and the relevant date falls within the disqualifying period (within the meaning of section 153(12) above).

3. In this Schedule, "relevant date" means the date on which a period of entitlement would begin in accordance with section 153 above if this Schedule did not prevent it arising.

4. [⁵. . .]

5. [¹. . .]

[⁷**5A.** —(1) Paragraph 2(d)(i) above does not apply if, at the relevant date, the employee is over pensionable age and is not entitled to incapacity benefit.

(2) Paragraph 2(d)(i) above ceases to apply if, at any time after the relevant date, the employee is over pensionable age and is not entitled to incapacity benefit.

(3) In this paragraph "pensionable age" has the meaning given by the rules in paragraph 1 of Schedule 4 to the Pensions Act 1995.]

6. For the purposes of paragraph 2(f) above, if an employee enters into a contract of service which is to take effect not more than eight weeks after the date on which a previous contract of service entered into by him with the same employer ceased to have effect, the two contracts shall be treated as one.

7. Paragraph 2(g) above does not apply in the case of an employee who proves that at no time on or before the relevant date did he have a direct interest in the trade dispute in question.

8. Paragraph 2(h) above does not apply in relation to an employee who has been pregnant if her pregnancy terminated, before the beginning of the disqualifying period, otherwise than by confinement (as defined for the purposes of statutory maternity pay in section 171(1) above).

AMENDMENTS

1. Social Security (Incapacity for Work) Act 1994, s.11(1) and Sch.1, para.43 (April 6, 1995).
2. Jobseekers Act 1995, s.41(5) and Sch.3 (October 7, 1996).
3. Social Security Act 1998, s.73 (April 6, 1999).
4. Social Security Contributions (Transfer of Functions, etc.) Act 1999, s.1(1) and Sch.1, para.20 (April 1, 1999).
5. Fixed-term Employees (Prevention of Less Favourable Treatment) Regulations 2002 (SI 2002/2034), reg.11 and Sch.2, para.1 (October 1, 2002).
6. Employment Equality (Age) Regulations 2006 (SI 2006/1031), reg.49(1) and Sch.8, Pt 1, para.13(1) (October 1, 2006).
7. Employment Equality (Age) (Consequential Amendments) Regulations 2007 (SI 2007/825), reg.2 (April 6, 2007).
8. Employment and Support Allowance (Consequential Provisions) (No.2) Regulations 2008 (SI 2008/1554), reg.44 (October 27, 2008).

DEFINITIONS

"contract of service"—see s.163(1).
"disqualifying period"—see s.153(12).
"employee"—see s.163(1) and SSP (General) Regulations 1982, reg.16.
"employer"—see s.163(1).
"period of entitlement"—see *ibid.*
"period of incapacity for work"—see s.163(1).
"prescribed"—see *ibid.*
"relevant date"—see para.(3).

GENERAL NOTE

Para. 1

1.155   The general rule, stated here, is that no period of entitlement to SSP can arise in any of the circumstances set out in para.2 or in such circumstances as are prescribed by regulations. The relevant regulation is reg.3 of the SSP (General) Regulations 1982 (SI 1982/894), which excludes prisoners and women entitled neither to SMP nor to maternity allowance who have reached a particular stage in their pregnancy or have been confined before reaching that stage.

Para. 2

1.156   This sets out the categories of persons for whom a period of entitlement does not arise for the purposes of para.1, and so who are excluded from the scope of SSP. The "relevant date" is the date on which a period of entitlement would otherwise begin were it not for the provisions of this Schedule (para.3). Thus the relevant date will usually be the first day of incapacity for work in the period of incapacity for work in question (s.153(2), but note the modifying provisions in (7), (8) and (9)). Those persons who are excluded from SSP by virtue of this paragraph may be able to claim incapacity benefit or, in the case of pregnant women, SMP or maternity allowance. The particular exclusions are:

(1) employees whose earnings are below the National Insurance lower earnings limit (sub-para.2(c));

(2) claimants whose day of incapacity links back to a recent entitlement to incapacity benefit (sub-para.2(d)). But note also para.5A, which ensures that employees who cannot return to incapacity benefit as they are now over pensionable age, but who would have returned to IB rather than becoming entitled to SSP had they been under pensionable age, are now entitled to SSP;

(3) employees who have yet to start work under the contract of service (sub-para.2(f), but note the linking rule in para.6);

(4) employees who are subject to a stoppage of work due to a trade dispute at their place of employment (sub-para.2(g), but note the exception in para.7);

(5) employees who are or have been pregnant and where the relevant date falls within the disqualifying period for persons entitled to SMP or maternity allowance (sub-para.2(h), but note the exception in para.8).

In addition, under the original para.(2)(b), employees with a contract of service for a specified period of not more than 3 months were excluded from entitlement to SSP. This exclusion was repealed by the Fixed-term Employees (Prevention of Less Favourable Treatment) Regulations 2002 (SI 2002/2034) as from October 1, 2002. The effect of this amendment was considered by Lewison J in *Commissioners for HMRC v Thorn Baker Ltd* [2006] EWHC 2190 (Ch), who held that the 2002 Regulations had no impact on employees working under fixed-term contracts who were agency workers. The effect of that decision is that SSP is not payable to agency workers whose contract with the agency is for a specified period of 3 months or less. The Court of Appeal has dismissed HMRC's appeal ([2007] EWCA Civ 626).

Para.7

The effect of the wording of this exception is that if the employee has at some time before the relevant date had a direct interest in the trade dispute, he or she cannot take advantage of this provision and so is caught by the exclusion in sub-para.2(g): see *R(SSP)1/86*.

1.157

Section 160   SCHEDULE 12

RELATIONSHIP OF STATUTORY SICK PAY WITH BENEFITS
AND OTHER PAYMENTS, ETC.

The general principle

1. Any day which—
   (a) is a day of incapacity for work in relation to any contract of service; and
   (b) falls within a period of entitlement (whether or not it is also a qualifying day);
shall not be treated for the purposes of this Act as a day of incapacity for work for the purposes of determining whether a period is [¹ . . .] [² a period of incapacity for work for the purposes of incapacity benefit].

1.158

Contractual remuneration

2.—(1) Subject to sub-paragraphs (2) and (3) below, any entitlement to statutory sick pay shall not affect any right of an employee in relation to remuneration under any contract of service ("contractual remuneration").

1.159

(2) Subject to sub-para.(3) below—
   (a) any contractual remuneration paid to an employee by an employer of his in respect of a day of incapacity for work shall go towards discharging any liability of that employer to pay statutory sick pay to that employee in respect of that day; and
   (b) any statutory sick pay paid by an employer to an employee of his in respect of a day of incapacity for work shall go towards discharging any liability of that employer to pay contractual remuneration to that employee in respect of that day.

(3) Regulations may make provision as to payments which are, and those which are not, to be treated as contractual remuneration for the purposes of sub-paragraph (1) or (2) above.

[²*Incapacity ¡benefit*

3.—(1) This paragraph and paragraph 4 below have effect to exclude, where a period of entitlement as between an employee and an employer of his comes to an end, the provisions by virtue of which short-term incapacity benefit is not paid for the first three days.

1.160

(2) If the first day immediately following the day on which the period of entitlement came to an end—

    (a) is a day of incapacity for work in relation to that employee; and

    (b) is not a day in relation to which paragraph 1 above applies by reason of any entitle-
          ment as between the employee and another employer,

that day shall, except in prescribed cases, be or form part of a period of incapacity for work
notwithstanding section 30C(1)(b) above (by virtue of which a period of incapacity for work
must be at least 4 days long).

    (3) Where each of the first two consecutive days, or the first three consecutive days, follow-
ing the day on which the period of entitlement came to an end is a day to which paragraph
(a) and (b) of sub-paragraph (2) above apply, that sub-paragraph has effect in relation to the
second day or, as the case may be, in relation to the second and third days, as it has effect in
relation to the first.

    4.—(1) Where a period of entitlement as between an employee and an employer of his
comes to an end, section 30A(3) above (exclusion of benefit for first three days of period) does
not apply in relation to any day which—

    (a) is or forms part of a period of incapacity for work (whether by virtue of paragraph 3
          above or otherwise); and

    (b) falls within the period of 57 days immediately following the day on which the period
          of entitlement came to an end.

    (2) Where sub-paragraph (1) above applies in relation to a day, section 30A(3) above does
not apply in relation to any later day in the same period of incapacity for work.]

[²*Incapacity benefit for widows and widowers*

1.161   **5.** Paragraph 1 above does not apply for the purpose of determining whether the conditions
specified in section 40(3) or (4) or section 41(2) or (3) above are satisfied.]

Unemployability supplement

1.162   **6.** Paragraph 1 above does not apply in relation to paragraph 3 of Schedule 7 to this Act
and accordingly the references in paragraph 3 of that Schedule to a period of interruption of
employment shall be construed as if the provisions re-enacted in this Part of this Act had not
been enacted.

AMENDMENTS

    1. Jobseekers Act 1995, s.41(5) and Sch.3, para.1 (October 7, 1996).

    2. Social Security (Incapacity for Work) Act 1994, s.11(1) and Sch.1, para.44
(April 13, 1995).

GENERAL NOTE

Para. 1

1.163   No day which falls within a period of entitlement for the purposes of SSP
(whether or not it is a qualifying day) can count as a day of incapacity for the purposes of establishing entitlement to incapacity benefit.

Paras 3 and 4

1.164   These paragraphs assist certain persons, not caught by para.1, who have days of
incapacity subsequent to the end of a period of entitlement, to qualify for incapacity benefit by not applying the normal rules, e.g. on waiting days. See further SSP
(General) Regulations 1982 (SI 1982/894), reg.12.

Section 168	SCHEDULE 13

RELATIONSHIP OF STATUTORY MATERNITY PAY WITH BENEFITS AND OTHER PAYMENTS, ETC.

The general principle

1.165   [²**1.** Except as may be prescribed, a day which falls within the maternity pay period
shall not be treated as a day of incapacity for work for the purposes of determining, for this
Act, whether it forms part of a period of incapacity for work for the purposes of incapacity
benefit.]

[¹*Incapacity benefit*

2.—(1) Regulations may provide that in prescribed circumstances a day which falls within the maternity pay period shall be treated as a day of incapacity for work for the purpose of determining entitlement to the higher rate of short-term incapacity benefit or to long-term incapacity benefit.

(2) Regulations may provide that an amount equal to a woman's statutory maternity pay for a period shall be deducted from any such benefit in respect of the same period and a woman shall be entitled to such benefit only if there is a balance after the deduction and, if there is such a balance, at a weekly rate equal to it.]

1.166

Contractual remuneration

3.—(1) Subject to sub-paragraphs (2) and (3) below, any entitlement to statutory maternity pay shall not affect any right of a woman in relation to remuneration under any contract of service ("contractual remuneration").

1.167

(2) Subject to sub-paragraph (3) below—
  (a) any contractual remuneration paid to a woman by an employer of hers in respect of a week in the maternity pay period shall go towards discharging any liability of that employer to pay statutory maternity pay to her in respect of that week; and
  (b) any statutory maternity pay paid by an employer to a woman who is an employee of his in respect of a week in the maternity pay period shall go towards discharging any liability of that employer to pay contractual remuneration to her in respect of that week.

[³(2A) In sub-paragraph (2) "week" means a period of seven days beginning with the day of the week on which the maternity pay period begins.]

(3) Regulations may make provision as to payments which are, and those which are not, to be treated as contractual remuneration for the purposes of sub-paragraphs (1) and (2) above.

AMENDMENTS

1. Social Security (Incapacity for Work) Act 1994, s.11(1) and Sch.1, para.45(3) (April 6, 1995).
2. Jobseekers Act 1995, s.41(4) and Sch.2, para.37 (October 7, 1996).
3. Work and Families Act 2006, s.11 and Sch.1, para.23 (October 1, 2006).

Social Security Administration Act 1992

(1992 c.5)

SECTIONS REPRODUCED

PART I

CLAIMS FOR PAYMENTS AND GENERAL ADMINISTRATION OF BENEFIT

Statutory sick pay

14. Duties of employees, etc. in relation to statutory sick pay

1.168

Statutory maternity pay

15. Duties of women etc. in relation to statutory maternity pay

PART I

CLAIMS FOR AND PAYMENTS AND GENERAL ADMINISTRATION OF BENEFIT

Statutory Sick Pay

Duties of employees etc. in relation to statutory sick pay

1.169

14.—(1) Any employee who claims to be entitled to statutory sick pay from his employer shall, if so required by his employer, provide such information as may reasonably be required for the purpose of determining the duration of the period of entitlement in question or whether a period of entitlement exists as between them.

(2) The Secretary of State may by regulations direct—

(a) that medical information required under subsection (1) above shall, in such cases as may be prescribed, be provided in a prescribed form;

(b) that an employee shall not be required under subsection (1) above to provide medical information in respect of such days as may be prescribed in a period of incapacity for work.

(3) Where an employee asks an employer of his to provide him with a

written statement, in respect of a period before the request is made, of one
or more of the following—
  (a) the days within that period which the employer regards as days in
      respect of which he is liable to pay statutory sick pay to that employee;
  (b) the reasons why the employer does not so regard the other days in
      that period;
  (c) the employer's opinion as to the amount of statutory sick pay to
      which the employee is entitled in respect of each of those days,
the employer shall, to the extent to which the request was reasonable,
comply with it within a reasonable time.

Statutory maternity pay

Duties of women etc. in relation to statutory maternity pay

15.—(1) A woman shall provide the person who is liable to pay her statu-   1.170
tory maternity pay—
  (a) with evidence as to her pregnancy and the expected date of confine-
      ment in such form and at such time as may be prescribed; and
  (b) where she commences work after her confinement but within the mater-
      nity pay period, with such additional information as may be prescribed.
[¹(1A) Any regulations for the purposes of subsection (1) above must be
made with the concurrence of the Inland Revenue.]
  (2) Where a woman asks an employer or former employer of hers to
provide her with a written statement, in respect of a period before the
request is made, of one or more of the following—
  (a) the weeks within that period which he regards as weeks in respect of
      which he is liable to pay statutory maternity pay to the woman;
  (b) the reasons why he does not so regard the other weeks in that period; and
  (c) his opinion as to the amount of statutory maternity pay to which the
      woman is entitled in respect of each of the weeks in respect of which
      he regards himself as liable to make a payment;
the employer or former employer shall, to the extent to which the request
was reasonable, comply with it within a reasonable time.

AMENDMENT

1. Social Security Contributions (Transfer of Functions, etc.) Act 1999, s.2 and
Sch.3, para.43.

PART VI

ENFORCEMENT

[¹Statutory sick pay and statutory maternity pay: breach of regulations

113A.—(1) Where a person fails to produce any document or record, or   1.171
provide any information, in accordance with—
  (a) regulations under section 5(1)(i) and (5), so far as relating to statu-
      tory sick pay or statutory maternity pay,
  (b) regulations under section 130 or 132, or
  (c) regulations under section 153(5)(b) of the Contributions and
      Benefits Act,

that person is liable to the penalties mentioned in subsection (2).

(2) The penalties are—

    (a) a penalty not exceeding £300, and

    (b) if the failure continues after a penalty is imposed under paragraph (a), a further penalty or penalties not exceeding £60 for each day on which the failure continues after the day on which the penalty under that paragraph was imposed (but excluding any day for which a penalty under this paragraph has already been imposed).

(3) Where a person fails to maintain a record in accordance with regulations under section 130 or 132, he is liable to a penalty not exceeding £3,000.

(4) No penalty may be imposed under subsection (1) at any time after the failure concerned has been remedied.

(5) But subsection (4) does not apply to the imposition of a penalty under subsection (2)(a) in respect of a failure to produce any document or record in accordance with regulations under section 130(5) or 132(4).

(6) Where, in the case of any employee, an employer refuses or repeatedly fails to make payments of statutory sick pay or statutory maternity pay in accordance with any regulations under section 5, the employer is liable to a penalty not exceeding £3,000.

(7) Section 118(2) of the Taxes Management Act 1970 (extra time for compliance etc) applies for the purposes of subsections (1), (3) and (6) as it applies for the purposes of that Act.

(8) Schedule 1 to the Employment Act 2002 (penalties relating to statutory paternity pay and statutory adoption pay: procedures and appeals) applies in relation to penalties imposed under this section (with the modifications set out in subsection (9)).

(9) That Schedule applies as if—

    (a) references to a penalty under section 11 or 12 of that Act were to a penalty under this section,

    (b) in paragraph 1(2), the reference to section 11(2)(a) of that Act were to subsection (2)(a) of this section, and

    (c) the provisions of the Taxes Management Act 1970 having effect in relation to an appeal mentioned in paragraph 3(2) of that Schedule did not include section 50(9) of that Act.]

AMENDMENT

1. National Insurance Contributions and Statutory Payments Act 2004, s.9(5) (April 6, 2005).

GENERAL NOTE

1.172   This provision brings in a compliance regime based on civil penalties, as with the administration of tax. Section 113A provides for civil penalties for failures to keep records, to produce records, to provide information or to pay either statutory sick pay or statutory maternity pay. The appeals procedures for such penalties are governed by Sch.1 to the Employment Act 2002 (see ss.113A(8) and (9)). Section 113B below is concerned with breaches by commission, and provides for penalties in cases of fraud or negligence which involve employers making incorrect statements or declarations, producing incorrect documents or records, making incorrect payments of statutory sick pay and statutory maternity pay and receiving incorrect advances of statutory maternity pay. HMRC has stated that penalties will be reserved for "serious situations such as where there has been a deliberate manipulation of the schemes, where a failure has continued after we have put the employer right and where the employer has failed to pay after the appeal period against a formal decision on liability" (*Regulatory Impact Assessment*, Annex E, para.7).

[¹Statutory sick pay and statutory maternity pay: fraud and negligence

113B.—(1) Where a person fraudulently or negligently— 1.173

(a) makes any incorrect statement or declaration in connection with establishing entitlement to statutory sick pay or statutory maternity pay, or

(b) produces any incorrect document or record or provides any incorrect information of a kind mentioned in—

    (i) regulations under section 5(1)(i) and (5), so far as relating to statutory sick pay or statutory maternity pay,

    (ii) regulations under section 130 or 132, or

    (iii) regulations under section 153(5)(b) of the Contributions and Benefits Act,

he is liable to a penalty not exceeding £3,000.

(2) Where an employer fraudulently or negligently makes an incorrect payment of statutory sick pay or statutory maternity pay, he is liable to a penalty not exceeding £3,000.

(3) Where an employer fraudulently or negligently receives an overpayment in pursuance of regulations under section 167 of the Contributions and Benefits Act (statutory maternity pay: advance payments to employers), he is liable to a penalty not exceeding £3,000.

(4) Schedule 1 to the Employment Act 2002 (penalties relating to statutory paternity pay and statutory adoption pay: procedures and appeals) applies in relation to penalties imposed under this section (with the modifications set out in subsection (5)).

(5) That Schedule applies as if—

(a) references to a penalty under section 11 or 12 of that Act were to a penalty under this section, and

(b) the provisions of the Taxes Management Act 1970 having effect in relation to an appeal mentioned in paragraph 3(2) of that Schedule did not include section 50(9) of that Act.]

AMENDMENT

1. National Insurance Contributions and Statutory Payments Act 2004, s.9(5) (April 6, 2005).

PART VII

[¹INFORMATION

Information held by tax authorities

Supply of information held by tax authorities for fraud prevention and verification

122.—[¹(1) This section applies— 1.174

(a) to information which is held—

    (i) by the Inland Revenue, or

(ii) by a person providing services to the Inland Revenue, in connection with the provision of those services,
but is not information to which section 121E above applies, and

(b) to information which is held—

(i) by the Commissioners of Customs and Excise, or

(ii) by a person providing services to the Commissioners of Customs
and Excise, in connection with the provision of those services.]

(2) Information to which this section applies may, with the authority of
the Commissioners concerned, be supplied to, or to a person providing services to, the Secretary of State or the Northern Ireland Department—

(a) for use in the prevention, detection, investigation or prosecution of
offences relating to social security; or

(b) for use in checking the accuracy of information relating to benefits,
contributions or national insurance numbers or to any other matter
relating to social security and (where appropriate) amending or supplementing such information.

(3) Information supplied under subsection (2) above shall not be supplied by the recipient to any other person or body unless—

(a) it could be supplied to that person or body under that subsection;

(b) it is supplied for the purposes of any civil or criminal proceedings
relating to the Contributions and Benefits Act, the Jobseekers Act
1995 or this Act or to any provision of Northern Ireland legislation
corresponding to any of them; or

(c) it is supplied under section 122C below;
and shall not be so supplied in those circumstances without the authority of
the Commissioners concerned.

(4) But where information supplied under subsection (2) above has been
used (in accordance with paragraph (b) of that subsection) in amending or
supplementing other information, it is lawful for it to be—

(a) supplied to any person or body to whom that other information
could be supplied; or

(b) used for any purpose for which that other information could be used.

(5) This section does not limit the circumstances in which information
may be supplied apart from this section.]

AMENDMENTS

1. Social Security Administration (Fraud) Act 1997, s.1 (July 1, 1997).
2. Social Security Contributions (Transfer of Functions, etc.) Act 1999, s.6 and
Sch.6, para.2 (April 1, 1999).

GENERAL NOTE

1.175   This and subsequent sections must now be read with CRCA 2005, combining the
Commissioners of Inland Revenue with the Commissioners of Customs and Excise to
form HRMC. Accordingly, the information flows are now between HMRC as a whole
and DWP or other public authorities. These flows are now facilitated electronically by
the Generalised Matching Service and similar programmes. These use the National
Insurance number and other details to check if, for example, any bank or building
society has deducted income tax from interest payable by it to any benefit recipient.

[¹Disclosure of contributions etc. information by [² Her Majesty's Revenue and Customs]

1.176   **122AA.** —(1) No obligation as to secrecy imposed by statute or otherwise
on [³ Revenue and Customs officials (within the meaning of section 18 of

the Commissioners for Revenue and Customs Act 2005 (confidentiality)] shall prevent information held for the purposes of the functions of [³ Her Majesty's Revenue and Customs] in relation to contributions, statutory sick pay or statutory maternity pay from being disclosed—

(a) to any of the authorities to which this paragraph applies, or any person authorised to exercise any function of that authority, for the purposes of the functions of that authority, or

(b) in a case where the disclosure is necessary for the purpose of giving effect to any agreement to which an order under section 179(1) below relates.

(2) The authorities to which subsection(1)(a) above applies are—

(a) the Health and Safety Executive,

(b) the Government Actuary's Department,

(c) the [⁴ Statistics Board], and

(d) the [² Pensions Regulator.]

AMENDMENTS

1. Social Security Contributions (Transfer of Functions, etc.) Act 1999, s.6 and Sch.6, para.3 (April 1, 1999).

2. Pensions Act 2004, s.319 and Sch.12, para.7 (April 6, 2005).

3. Commissioners for Revenue and Customs Act 2005, s.50(4) and Sch.4, para.46 (April 18, 2005).

4. Statistics and Registration Service Act 2007, s.46 and Sch.2, para.5 (April 1, 2008).

Statutory sick pay and other benefits

Disclosure by Secretary of State for purpose of determination of period of entitlement to statutory sick pay

129. Where the Secretary of State considers that it is reasonable for information held by him to be disclosed to an employer, for the purpose of enabling that employer to determine the duration of a period of entitlement under Part XI of the Contributions and Benefits Act in respect of an employee, or whether such a period exists, he may disclose the information to that employer.

1.177

Duties of employers—statutory sick pay and claims for other benefits

130.—(1) Regulations may make provision requiring an employer, in a case falling within subsection (3) below to furnish information in connection with the making, by a person who is, or has been, an employee of that employer, of a claim for—

[¹(a) short-term incapacity benefit;]

(b) a maternity allowance;

[¹(c) long-term incapacity benefit;]

(d) industrial injuries benefit; [³ . . .]

(e) [³ . . .].

(2) Regulations under this section shall prescribe—

(a) the kind of information to be furnished in accordance with the regulations;

1.178

(b) the person to whom information of the prescribed kind is to be furnished; and

(c) the manner in which, and period within which, it is to be furnished.

(3) The cases are—

(a) where, by virtue of paragraph 2 of Schedule 11 to the Contributions and Benefits Act or of regulations made under paragraph 1 of that Schedule, a period of entitlement does not arise in relation to a period of incapacity for work;

(b) where a period of entitlement has come to an end but the period of incapacity for work which was running immediately before the period of entitlement came to an end continues; and

(c) where a period of entitlement has not come to an end but, on the assumption that—

(i) the period of incapacity for work in question continues to run for a prescribed period; and

(ii) there is no material change in circumstances;

the period of entitlement will have ended on or before the end of the prescribed period.

(4) Regulations [²made with the concurrence of the Inland Revenue]—

(a) may require employers to maintain such records in connection with statutory sick pay as may be prescribed;

(b) may provide for—

(i) any person claiming to be entitled to statutory sick pay; or

(ii) any other person who is a party to proceedings arising under Part XI of the Contributions and Benefits Act;

to furnish to the Secretary of State [² or the Inland Revenue (as the regulations may require)], within a prescribed period, any information required for the determination of any question arising in connection there with; and

(c) may require employers who have made payments of statutory sick pay to furnish to the Secretary of State [² or the Inland Revenue (as the regulations may require)] such documents and information, at such times, as may be prescribed.

[⁴(5) Regulations made with the concurrence of the Inland Revenue may require employers to produce wages sheets and other documents and records to officers of the Inland Revenue, within a prescribed period, for the purpose of enabling them to satisfy themselves that statutory sick pay has been paid, and is being paid, in accordance with regulations under section 5 above, to employees or former employees who are entitled to it.]

AMENDMENTS

1. Social Security (Incapacity for Work) Act 1994, s.11(1) and Sch.1, para.49 (April 6, 1995).

2. Social Security Contributions (Transfer of Functions, etc.) Act 1999, s.6 and Sch.6, para.3 (April 1, 1999).

3. Welfare Reform and Pensions Act 1999, s.88 and Sch.13, Pt IV (April 6, 2001).

4. National Insurance Contributions and Statutory Payments Act 2004, s.9(2) (January 1, 2005).

Statutory maternity pay and other benefits

Disclosure by Secretary of State for purpose of determination of period of entitlement to statutory maternity pay

131. Where the Secretary of State considers that it is reasonable for infor-   1.179
mation held by him to be disclosed to a person liable to make payments
of statutory maternity pay for the purpose of enabling that person to determine—

   (a) whether a maternity pay period exists in relation to a woman who is
       or has been an employee of his; and

   (b) if it does, the date of its commencement and the weeks in it in
       respect of which he may be liable to pay statutory maternity pay,

he may disclose the information to that person.

Duties of employers—statutory maternity pay and claims for other benefits

132.—(1) Regulations may make provision requiring an employer in   1.180
prescribed circumstances to furnish information in connection with the
making of a claim by a woman who is or has been his employee for—

   (a) a maternity allowance;

   (b) [[1]short-term incapacity benefit;]

   (c) [[1]long-term incapacity benefit under section 30A], 40 or 41 of the
       Contributions and Benefits Act; [[3]. . .]

   (d) [[3]. . .].

(2) Regulations under this section shall prescribe—

   (a) the kind of information to be furnished in accordance with the
       regulations;

   (b) the person to whom information of the prescribed kind is to be fur-
       nished; and

   (c) the manner in which, and period within which, it is to be fur-
       nished.

(3) Regulations [[2]made with the concurrence of the Inland Revenue]—

   (a) may require employers to maintain such records in connection with
       statutory maternity pay as may be prescribed;

   (b) may provide for—

      (i) any woman claiming to be entitled to statutory maternity
          pay; or

      (ii) any other person who is a party to proceedings arising under
          Part XII of the Contributions and Benefits Act,

       to furnish to the Secretary of State [[2]or the Inland Revenue (as the
       regulations may require)], within a prescribed period, any informa-
       tion required for the determination of any question arising in con-
       nection there with; and

   (c) may require persons who have made payments of statutory maternity
       pay to furnish to the Secretary of State [[2]or the Inland Revenue (as
       the regulations may require)] such documents and information, at
       such time, as may be prescribed.

[[4](4) Regulations made with the concurrence of the Inland Revenue
may require employers to produce wages sheets and other documents and
records to officers of the Inland Revenue, within a prescribed period, for the

purpose of enabling them to satisfy themselves that statutory maternity pay has been paid, and is being paid, in accordance with regulations under section 5 above, to employees or former employees who are entitled to it.]

AMENDMENTS

1. Social Security (Incapacity for Work) Act 1994, s.11(1) and Sch.1, para.50 (April 6, 1995).
2. Social Security Contributions (Transfer of Functions, etc.) Act 1999, s.6 and Sch.1, para.27 (April 1, 1999).
3. Welfare Reform and Pensions Act 1999, s.88 and Sch.13, Pt IV (April 6, 2001).
4. National Insurance Contributions and Statutory Payments Act 2004, s.9(3) (January 1, 2005).

Social Security Contributions (Transfer of Functions, etc.) Act 1999

(1999 C.2)

1.181   An Act to transfer from the Secretary of State to the Commissioners of Inland Revenue or the Treasury certain functions relating to national insurance contributions, the National Insurance Fund, statutory sick pay, statutory maternity pay or pension schemes and certain associated functions relating to benefits; to enable functions relating to any of those matters in respect of Northern Ireland to be transferred to the Secretary of State, the Commissioners of Inland Revenue or the Treasury; to make further provision, in connection with the functions transferred, as to the powers of the Commissioners of Inland Revenue, the making of decisions and appeals; to provide that rebates payable in respect of members of money purchase contracted-out pension schemes are to be payable out of the National Insurance Fund; and for connected purposes.

ARRANGEMENT OF SECTIONS

PART II

DECISIONS AND APPEALS

PART III

MISCELLANEOUS AND SUPPLEMENTAL

27.   Interpretation

PART II

DECISIONS AND APPEALS

Decisions by officers of Board

8.—(1) Subject to the provisions of this Part, it shall be for an officer of   1.183
the Board—
  (a) to decide whether for the purposes of Parts I to V of the Social
      Security Contributions and Benefits Act 1992 a person is or was an
      earner and, if so, the category of earners in which he is or was to be
      included;
  (b) to decide whether a person is or was employed in employed earner's
      employment for the purposes of Part V of the Social Security Con-
      tributions and Benefits Act 1992 (industrial injuries);
  (c) to decide whether a person is or was liable to pay contributions of
      any particular class and, if so, the amount that he is or was liable
      to pay,
  (d) to decide whether a person is or was entitled to pay contributions of
      any particular class that he is or was not liable to pay and, if so, the
      amount that he is or was entitled to pay,
  (e) to decide whether contributions of a particular class have been paid
      in respect of any period,
  (f) subject to and in accordance with regulations made for the purposes
      of this paragraph by the Secretary of State with the concurrence of
      the Board, to decide any issue arising as to, or in connection with,
      entitlement to statutory sick pay, [⁴, statutory maternity pay, statu-
      tory paternity pay or statutory adoption pay],
  (g) to make any other decision that falls to be made [⁴under Parts XI to
      XIIZB of the Social Security Contributions and Benefits Act 1992
      (statutory sick pay, statutory maternity pay, statutory paternity pay
      and statutory adoption pay)],
  [⁴(ga) to make any decision that falls to be made under regulations under
      section 7 of the Employment Act 2002 (funding of employers'
      liabilities to make payments of statutory paternity or adoption
      pay),];
  (h) to decide any question as to the issue and content of a notice under
      subsection (2) of section 121C of the Social Security Administration
      Act 1992 (liability of directors etc. for company's contributions);
  (i) to decide any issue arising under section 27 of the Jobseekers
      Act 1995 (employment of long-term unemployed: deductions by
      employers), or under any provision of regulations under that section,
      as to—

(i) whether a person is or was an employee or employer of another;

(ii) whether an employer is or was entitled to make any deduction from his contributions payments in accordance with regulations under section 27 of that Act;

(iii) whether a payment falls to be made to an employer in accordance with those regulations;

(iv) the amount that falls to be so deducted or paid; or

(v) whether two or more employers are, by virtue of regulations under section 27 of that Act, to be treated as one,

[³(ia) to decide whether to give or withdraw an approval for the purposes of para.3B(1)(b) of Sch.1 to the Social Security Contributions and Benefits Act 1992,];

(j) [² . . .];

(k) to decide whether a person is liable to a penalty under—

(i) paragraph 7A(2) or 7B(2)(h) of Schedule 1 to the Social Security Contributions and Benefits Act 1992; or

(ii) section 113(1)(a) of the Social Security Administration Act 1992;

(l) to decide the [² . . .] penalty payable under any of the provisions mentioned in [²paragraph (k)] above; and

(m) to decide such issues relating to contributions, other than the issues specified in paragraphs (a) to (l) above or in paragraphs 16 and 17 of Schedule 3 to the Social Security Act 1998, as may be prescribed by regulations made by the Board.

(2) Subsection (1)(c) and (e) above do not include any decision relating to Class 4 contributions other than a decision falling to be made—

(a) under subsection (1) of section 17 of the Social Security Contributions and Benefits Act 1992 as to whether by regulations under that subsection a person is or was excepted from liability for Class 4 contributions, or his liability is or was deferred; or

(b) under regulations made by virtue of subsection (3) or (4) of that section or section 18 of that Act.

(3) Subsection (1)(g) above does not include—

(a) any decision as to the making of subordinate legislation; or

(b) any decision as to whether the liability to pay statutory sick pay [⁴, statutory maternity pay, statutory paternity pay or statutory adoption pay] is a liability of the Board rather than the employer.

(4) [¹ . . .].

AMENDMENTS

1. Welfare Reform and Pensions Act 1999, s.88 and Sch.13, Pt VI (April 6, 2000).

2. Child Support, Pensions and Social Security Act 2000, ss.76(6), 85 and Sch.9, Pt VIII (July 28, 2000).

3. Child Support, Pensions and Social Security Act 2000, ss.77(5) (July 28, 2000).

4. Employment Act 2002, ss.9(2) and (3) (December 8, 2002).

DEFINITIONS

"Board"—see s.27.

"contributions"—*ibid.*

"employed earner"—see SSCBA 1992, s.2(1)(a).
"employment"—see SSCBA 1992, s.122.

GENERAL NOTE

This section provides for HMRC to take decisions on a range of specified questions   1.184
in relation to SMP, SSP, NICs, employment status and related matters. The extensive list of such decisions, set out in subs.(1), covers much of the former jurisdiction of
the Secretary of State for Social Security under SSAA 1992, s.17(1), with the addition
of some further matters. For example, the function of making decisions as to entitlement to SMP or SSP (subs.(1)(f)) was traditionally a function of an adjudication
officer (SSAA 1992, s.20(3)) but was then transferred to the Secretary of State (SSA
1998, s.8(1)(d)) before now moving to an officer of the Board (now HMRC). This is
one of the areas in which the power to make regulations still rests with the Secretary
of State (albeit with the agreement of HMRC), as the policy responsibility for these
benefits is retained by the DWP (see General Note to s.2). However, in terms of decision making on matters of entitlement to SSP (and, by analogy, to SMP, SPP and
SAP), HMRC has an "exclusive and exhaustive jurisdiction" (per Mr Recorder Luba
QC in *Taylor Gordon & Co Ltd v Timmons* ([2004] I.R.L.R. 180, at para.43). Thus an
employment tribunal has no jurisdiction under the Employment Rights Act 1996 to
entertain an employee's complaint that SSP has not been paid.

For the relevant regulation-making powers, see s.9 and for provision for variation
and supersession of decisions made under s.8, see s.10. From April 6, 2009 appeals
go to the First-tier Tribunal Tax Chamber. One result of the tribunal reforms
introduced then is that a number of judges now sit both to hear tax appeals and
appeals under this section as well as appeals on social security matters in the Social
Entitlement Chamber.

Regulations with respect to decisions

9.—(1) Subject to the provisions of this Part and of the Social Security   1.185
Administration Act 1992, provision may be made by the Board by regulations as to the making by their officer of any decision under or in connection with the Social Security Contributions and Benefits Act 1992, the
Social Security Administration Act 1992 or the Jobseekers Act 1995 which
falls to be made by such an officer.

(2) Where it appears to an officer of the Board that a matter before him
involves a question of fact requiring special expertise, he may direct that in
dealing with that matter he shall have the assistance of one or more experts.

(3) In subsection (2) above "expert" means a person appearing to the
officer of the Board to have knowledge or experience which would be relevant in determining the question of fact requiring special expertise.

DEFINITIONS

"Board"—see s.27.
"expert"—see subs.(3).

GENERAL NOTE

Subsection (1), modelled on SSA 1998, s.11, provides for HMRC to make reg-   1.186
ulations governing procedural matters relating to decisions made by HMRC staff
under s.8.

Subsections (2) and (3) enable HMRC to seek specialist advice before making
a decision (e.g. as to medical evidence relevant to a claim for SSP). In the first
instance SMP or SSP decisions are made by the employer, and only referred for
a formal decision where the parties are unable to reach agreement. There are only

about 500 referrals each year concerning SMP or SSP; most of these cases concern the linking or employment rules, with perhaps no more than 50 involving a medical issue (*per* Baroness Hollis of Heigham, Parliamentary Under-Secretary of State for Social Security, *Hansard*, H.L. Debs. Vol.596, col.322 (January 14, 1999)).

Decisions varying or superseding earlier decisions

1.187   **10.**—(1) [[1] Subject to subsection (2A) below,] the Board may by regulations make provision—

(a) for any decision of an officer of the Board under section 8 of this Act (including a decision superseding an earlier decision) to be varied either within the prescribed period or in prescribed cases or circumstances;

(b) for any such decision to be superseded, in prescribed circumstances, by a subsequent decision made by an officer of the Board; and

(c) for any such decision as confirmed or varied by the [[2] First-tier Tribunal or Upper Tribunal] on appeal to be superseded, in the event of a material change of circumstances since the decision was made, by a subsequent decision made by an officer of the Board.

(2) The date as from which—

(a) any variation of a decision, or

(b) any decision superseding an earlier decision,

is to take effect shall be determined in accordance with the regulations.

[[1](2A) The decisions in relation to which provision may be made by regulations under this section shall not include decisions falling within section 8(1)(ia) above.]

(3) In this section "prescribed" means prescribed by regulations under this section.

AMENDMENTS

1. Child Support, Pensions and Social Security Act 2000, s.77(6) (July 28, 2000).
2. Transfer of Tribunal Functions and Revenue and Customs Appeals Order 2009 (SI 2009/56), art.3 and Sch.1 (April 1, 2009).

DEFINITIONS

"Board": s.27.
"prescribed": subs.(3).

GENERAL NOTE

1.188   This enabling provision reflects similar powers, governing Secretary of State decisions, contained in SSA 1998, ss.9 (revision) and 10 (supersession).

Appeals against decisions of Board

1.189   **11.**—(1) This section applies to any decision of an officer of the Board under section 8 of this Act or under regulations made by virtue of section 10(1)(b) or (c) of this Act (whether as originally made or as varied under regulations made by virtue of section 10(1)(a) of this Act).

(2) In the case of a decision to which this section applies—

(a) if it relates to a person's entitlement to statutory sick pay [[1], statutory maternity pay, statutory paternity pay or statutory adoption pay], the employee and employer concerned shall each have a right to appeal to the [[2] tribunal], and

(b) in any other case, the person in respect of whom the decision is made and such other person as may be prescribed shall have a right to appeal to the [² tribunal].

(3) In subsection (2)(b) above "prescribed" means prescribed by the Board by regulations.

(4) This section has effect subject to section 121D of the Social Security Administration Act 1992 (appeals in relation to personal liability notices).

AMENDMENTS

1. Employment Act 2002, s.9(4) (December 8, 2002).
2. Transfer of Tribunal Functions and Revenue and Customs Appeals Order 2009 (SI 2009/56), art.3 and Sch.1 (April 1, 2009).

DEFINITIONS

"Board"—see s.27.
"prescribed"—see subs.(3)
[² tribunal]

GENERAL NOTE

This provides a right of appeal to the First-tier Tribunal. It will normally go to 1.190 the Tax Chamber (but see First-tier Tribunal and Upper Tribunal (Chambers) (Amendment No.3) Order 2009 (SI 2009/1590) with effect from September 1, 2009). Tribunal reforms allow this to be dealt with by a judge familiar with both tax law and social security law, so allowing consideration to be given to the problem that a s.8 appeal may be considered while removed from its social security context. Both employees and employers have a right of appeal in relation to decisions on SMP and SSP entitlement (subs.(2)(a)). Note also that subs.(2)(b) contains a broader regulation-making power to give interested parties in other decisions a right of appeal. This provision only provides for additional rights of appeal; unlike SSA 1998, s.12(2), there is no power to prescribe in regulations for cases in which there is to be no right of appeal.

Exercise of right of appeal

12.—(1) Any appeal against a decision must be brought by a notice of 1.191 appeal in writing given within 30 days after the date on which notice of the decision was issued.

(2) The notice of appeal shall be given to the officer of the Board by whom notice of the decision was given.

[¹ (3) The notice of appeal shall specify the grounds of appeal.]

(4) [¹. . .]

(5) [¹. . .]

AMENDMENT

1. Transfer of Tribunal Functions and Revenue and Customs Appeals Order 2009 (SI 2009/56), art.3 and Sch.1 (April 1, 2009).

DEFINITIONS

"Board"—see s.27.

GENERAL NOTE

This section, governing rights of appeal, is modelled on the provisions governing 1.192 tax appeals (Taxes Management Act 1970, s.31) rather than those for social security matters (SSA 1998, s.12).

Subs. (1)

1.193   This provision adopts the standard 30-day appeal deadline in s.31(1) of the Taxes Management Act 1970.

Subs. (2)

1.194   This requirement mirrors s.31(2) of the Taxes Management Act 1970.

Regulations with respect to appeals

1.195   **13.**—(1) The Board may, by regulations made with the concurrence of the Lord Chancellor and the Lord Advocate, make provision with respect to appeals to the [¹tribunal] under this Part.

(2) Regulations under subsection (1) above may, in particular—

(a) make provision with respect to any of the matters dealt with in the following provisions of the Taxes Management Act 1970—

(i) [¹. . .]

(ii) sections 48 to 54 (appeals to the [¹tribunal] under the Taxes Acts); and

(iii) [¹ section 56 (payment of tax where there is a further appeal)] or

(b) provide for any of those provisions of that Act to apply, with such modifications as may be specified in the regulations, in relation to an appeal to the [¹tribunal] under this Part.

[¹. . .]

Amendment

1. Transfer of Tribunal Functions and Revenue and Customs Appeals Order 2009 (SI 2009/56), art.3 and Sch.1 (April 1, 2009).

Definition

"Board"—see s.27.

General Note

1.196   This section enables HMRC to make regulations about the procedures to apply for appeals to the tax appeal Commissioners against decisions under s.8. Such regulations can only be made with the concurrence of the Lord Chancellor and the Lord Advocate, who are responsible for funding the tax appeal Commissioners. In general terms, most of the provisions about appeals in Pt V of the Taxes Management Act 1970 are adopted for the purposes of such appeals. However, given that there are material differences between tax and matters such as SSP and SMP, subs.(2)(b) provides for appropriate modifications to be made to these appellate procedures. This reflects the existing arrangements for appeals to the tax appeal Commissioners in relation to Class 4 NICs, under SSCBA 1992, Sch.2, para.8.

Matters arising as respects decisions

1.197   **14.**—(1) The Board may by regulations make provision as respects matters arising—

(a) pending any decision of an officer of the Board under section 8 of this Act which relates to—

(i) statutory sick pay [¹, statutory maternity pay, statutory paternity pay or statutory adoption pay], or

(ii) any person's liability for contributions;

(b) pending the determination by the [²tribunal] of an appeal against any such decision,

(c) out of the variation, under regulations made under section 10 of this Act or on appeal, of any such decision, or

(d) out of the making of a decision which, under regulations made under that section, supersedes an earlier decision.

(2) Regulations under this section may, in particular—

(a) make provision making a person liable to pay contributions pending the determination by the [²tribunal] of an appeal against a decision of an officer of the Board; and

(b) make provision as to the repayment in prescribed circumstances of contributions paid by virtue of the regulations.

(3) Regulations under this section must be made with the concurrence of the Secretary of State in so far as they relate to statutory sick pay [¹, statutory maternity pay, statutory paternity pay or statutory adoption pay].

AMENDMENTS

1. Employment Act 2002, s.9(5) (December 8, 2002).
2. Transfer of Tribunal Functions and Revenue and Customs Appeals Order 2009 (SI 2009/56), art.3 and Sch.1 (April 1, 2009).

DEFINITIONS

"Board"—see s.27.
"contributions"—*ibid.*

GENERAL NOTE

This section is modelled on SSA 1998, s.18. It vests HMRC with a parallel regulation-making power to deal with matters arising before a decision is made or an appeal is heard (subss.(1)(a) and (b)), or concerning the consequences of varying or superseding a previous decision (including a variation following an appeal) (subss.(1)(c) and (d)). As such regulations may have implications for benefit rights in relation to SMP and SSP, in those instances the power can only be exercised with the agreement of the Secretary of State for Work and Pensions (subs.(3)). **1.198**

Arrangements for discharge of decision-making functions

17.—(1) The Secretary of State may make arrangements with the Board for any of his functions under Chapter II of Part I of the Social Security Act 1998 in relation to— **1.199**

(a) a decision whether a person was (within the meaning of regulations) precluded from regular employment by responsibilities at home; or

(b) a decision whether a person is entitled to be credited with earnings or contributions in accordance with regulations made under section 22(5) of the Social Security Contributions and Benefits Act 1992;

to be discharged by the Board or by officers of the Board.

(2) No such arrangements shall affect the responsibility of the Secretary of State or the application of Chapter II of Part I of the Social Security Act 1998 in relation to any decision.

(3) Until the commencement of Chapter II of Part I of the Social Security Act 1998, the references to that chapter in subsections (1) and

(2) above shall have effect as references to Part II of the Social Security Administration Act 1992.

DEFINITION

"Board"—see s.27.

GENERAL NOTE

1.200   This section enables decisions on home responsibilities protection or credits to be performed by HMRC as agents for the Secretary of State for Work and Pensions. This arrangement is appropriate as such decisions primarily impact upon entitlement to social security benefits.

Amendments relating to decisions and appeals

1.201   **18.** Schedule 7 to this Act (which contains amendments relating to decisions and appeals) shall have effect.

GENERAL NOTE

1.202   Schedule 7 provides for the detailed responsibilities of existing legislation relating to decision-making and appeals (Taxes Management Act 1970, SSCBA 1992, SSAA 1992, Pensions Schemes Act 1993, Employment Rights Act 1996 and SSA 1998).

[¹ Interpretation of Part II

1.203   **19.** In this Part—
"tribunal" means the First-tier Tribunal or, where determined by or under Tribunal Procedure Rules, the Upper Tribunal.]

AMENDMENT

1. Transfer of Tribunal Functions and Revenue and Customs Appeals Order 2009 (SI 2009/56), art.3 and Sch.1 (April 1, 2009).

PART III

MISCELLANEOUS AND SUPPLEMENTAL

1.204   **20.–26.** [*Omitted.*]

Interpretation

1.205   **27.** In this Act, unless a contrary intention appears—
"the Board" means the Commissioners of Inland Revenue;
"contributions" means contributions under Part I of the Social Security Contributions and Benefits Act 1992.
28. [*Omitted.*]

GENERAL NOTE

1.206   The provisions in Pt III (with the exception of s.27) fall outside the scope of this volume and so are omitted. Section 20 provides that rebates in respect of money purchase contracted-out pension schemes should be funded from the National Insurance Fund. Sections 21 and 22 deal with the transfer of contracts and property from the former DSS to the Inland Revenue. Section 23 provides for the transfer of functions by Order in Council. Section 24 enables provision to be made for Northern Ireland by Order in Council while s.25 concerns regulation and Order making powers generally; s.26 introduces Schs 8 (savings and transitional provisions), 9 (consequential amendments) and 10 (repeals and revocations). Section 28 governs the short title, commencement and extent of the Act.

Tax Credits Act 2002

(2002 c.21)

ARRANGEMENT OF SECTIONS

PART I

TAX CREDITS

General

1.207

Child tax credit

Working tax credit

Rate

Decisions

PART II

CHILD BENEFIT AND GUARDIAN'S ALLOWANCE

49.–57. (*Omitted*)

PART III

SUPPLEMENTARY

Information etc.

58.   Administrative arrangements
59.   Use and disclosure of information

Other supplementary provisions

60.   Repeals
61.   Commencement
62.   Transitional provisions and savings
63.   Tax credits appeals etc.: temporary modifications
64.   Northern Ireland
65.   Regulations, orders and schemes
66.   Parliamentary etc. control of instruments
67.   Interpretation
68.   Financial provision (*omitted*)
69.   Extent (*omitted*)
70.   Short title (*omitted*)

Schedule 1—Rights of employees (*omitted*)
Schedule 2—Penalties: supplementary
Schedule 3—Tax credits: consequential amendments (*omitted*)
Schedule 4—Transfer of functions: consequential amendments (*omitted*)
Schedule 5—Use and disclosure of information (*omitted*)
Schedule 6—Repeals and revocations (*omitted*)

GENERAL NOTE

Scope and scheme of the Act

  The Tax Credits Bill 2001 was introduced to the House of Commons as a **1.208** Treasury measure. It was subject to minimal amendment as it went through its parliamentary proceedings in the House of Commons. The Speaker ruled that it was not a Money Bill (possibly because of Pt II of the Act). It was subject to rigorous challenge in the House of Lords. The criticisms ranged from normal political confrontations about tax and social security measures to a challenge to the fundamental approach, even the title, of the Bill itself. It was at that stage also (after strong protests from the opposition parties and an apology from the minister piloting the Bill through the House) that important government technical and drafting amendments were tabled. The main focus of opposition criticism was on the issue whether tax credits counted as public expenditure or as tax uncollected. In fact, that issue did not feature in the Bill at all as it does not require legislation. The answer (after a disagreement about the right approach, recorded in the note) was published in the Red Book (the Financial Statement) published by the Treasury to accompany the Chancellor 2002 Budget (See *2002 Financial Statement*, Box C2, p.216). It is that tax credits count as public expenditure in so far as they exceed the income tax due from the claimant, and as negative taxation in so far as they do not. Tax credits under the Tax Credits Act 1999 are classified as public expenditure. During Parliamentary debates, it was said that as a ball-park figure, 90 per cent of the amount was public expenditure and 10 per cent tax foregone.

The Tax Credits Act 2002 ("this Act") repeals and replaces the Tax Credits Act 1999 ("TCA 1999") in its entirety and carries further the reforms started by that Act. The Act is structured in three Parts. Part I (Tax credits) provides the necessary primary legislative framework to introduce the child tax credit and working tax credit. It also provides a common procedure for those tax credits. Schedules 1–3 to the Act are associated with this Part. Part II (Child benefit and guardian's allowance) makes provision for the transfer of functions concerning child benefit and guardian's allowance to the Treasury and HMRC, and the associated minor amendments to entitlement. Schedule 4 is associated with this Part. Part III (Supplementary) makes additional provision for both other Parts. Schedules 5 and 6 are associated with this Part.

Tax credits

1.209   The introduction of a programme of tax credits has been a major aspect of the approach to reform of the tax and benefit systems by the Treasury since the Labour government took office in 1997. But neither the TCA 1999 nor this Act were opposed in principle on this issue by the other main political parties. The substantive policy and the detail have been criticised, but not the general approach. The main thrust of Pt I of this Act, introducing the child tax credit (CTC) and the working tax credit (WTC), is to extend the tax credits introduced by the TCA 1999 and consolidate those reforms.

Tax credits under the Tax Credits Act 2002

1.210   The introduction of the current reforms was announced by the Chancellor of the Exchequer, Gordon Brown, in his 1999 Budget and confirmed in his 2000 Budget. The detailed shape of the proposals was first announced in an HMRC consultation paper published in July 2001: *New Tax Credits: Supporting families, making work pay and tackling poverty.* This received significant comment from many sources and the HMRC published its *Response* in November 2001.

Child tax credit

1.211   CTC is a means-tested social security benefit for all those responsible for children and qualifying young persons, although it is presented as a tax credit. Government policy for the support of children appears to be motivated by two interacting pressures. The first is that the Government's target is to halve child poverty by 2010 and to abolish it altogether by 2020. The second is the profound demographic shift occurring in Britain, as in the rest of Europe, because of the reduction in the number of children being born, due to a sharp drop in the female fertility rate. The government's response is the CTC, which provides a single tax credit payable to any person who is responsible for one or more children or qualifying young persons (s.8(1)). The Act provides only minimal detail about how CTC works, but the intended figures were published in the 2002 Budget and draft regulations were published before the Bill was given royal assent. Details are set out in the note to ss.8 and 9 below.

Support for children through the tax and social security systems was previously provided in several ways. The first and most important provision was child benefit. The second line of support for children in poorer families was by way of an addition or increase to individual means-tested benefits (or tax credits). Thirdly, and separately from the income-related benefits, contributory and other social security benefits also made provision for dependent children (e.g. the child dependency increases under SSCBA 1992, ss.80 and 85 and the child increase for carer's allowance under SSCBA 1992, s.90). There were further provisions in the Social

Security (Dependency) Regulations 1977 (SI 1977/343). Moreover, a few individuals looking after children as their guardians can claim guardian's allowance, under SSCBA 1992, s.77. Finally, and separately again from these sources of assistance for those bringing up children, the Finance Act 2000 introduced the children's tax credit as s.257AA of the ICTA 1988, supported by Sch.13B to that Act. Despite its name, this was not a tax credit, but an income tax reduction. It only overlapped with the social security benefits in so far as the claimants of those benefits were also income tax payers. This Act sweeps away all mention of SSCBA 1992, ss.80 and 90 (but *not* s.85, which allows for increases for retirement pensioners for an adult caring for children for whom the pensioner is receiving child credit). With them go the relevant regulations. Section 257AA of ICTA 1988 also goes. So also, by regulation, does the overlap between child benefit and CTC. Any overlap with WTC is also avoided by regulation. Further regulations under s.1 were intended to transfer all child elements from all income-related benefits to CTC. That proved far harder than was anticipated. The provisions originally intended to be in place in 2004 were repeatedly postponed, and are now being phased in for new claims from 2009 as detailed in the note to s.1.

Working tax credit

WTC is not a social security benefit. It is aimed at assisting the low paid as a replacement in part of the former WFTC and also as a replacement to the New Deal 50 Plus payable to older workers returning to work. New Deal 50 Plus was the name given to a variant of the employment credits payable under the Employment and Training Act 1973. As its name suggests, it was a new form of employment assistance brought in to encourage the older claimant back into work. It was not a social security benefit and was never within the scope of the former DSS, being run instead by the former separate Department for Education and Employment and its predecessors.

WTC is designed as a general provision for all in "qualifying remunerative work", though tantalisingly this Act does not define that central term. Rather, regulations specify that work will qualify (if paid or in the expectation of payment) if it is over 16 hours a week for those with children, those who are disadvantaged by disability, and those over 50. Anyone else over 25 will qualify if working 30 hours a week (Working Tax Credit (Entitlement and Maximum Rate) Regulations 2002 (SI 2002/2005), reg.4). Those under 25 who are not in the specific groups are excluded. The definition is designed to integrate with the national minimum wage to provide a minimum level of take-home pay for all those entitled to claim. HMRC now also has responsibility for enforcement of the national minimum wage.

While WTC and CTC replace benefits, grants and allowances, they are aimed at operating separately for claimants. Originally, this was to be emphasised by paying WTC to earners through their pay packets and by paying CTC to carers directly. But both are now paid in most cases through bank accounts. The practical effect is to make the two benefits largely indistinguishable for couples receiving the sums through joint bank accounts. Some commentators suggest that the blurring is exacerbated by making childcare credit part of WTC rather than CTC or a free-standing credit.

Development of the credits

The tax credits system has evolved in a number of ways since its introduction. It is in essence a redistributive system. As it has developed from initial plans to first introduction to a maturing system, its focus has been sharpened on to its main beneficiaries—"mainstream" couples or lone parents who have children at home or school and who are in work and stay in work.

The most generous real increases in the value of tax credits go to those who can claim the childcare element of WTC. For those with two or more children being looked after, the weekly maximum amount that can be claimed against childcare expenses has risen from 70 per cent of £200 a week to 80 per cent of £300. At the

1.212

1.213

same time, the range of those who may be employed as a childcare provider has been increased, so removing whole categories of cases of those who could not receive the credit for practical reasons. The background to this is that the Chancellor gave a commitment to raise the CTC credits in line with earnings rather than the cost of living. Only one element of CTC has not been altered. The £50,000 floor for the family element has not changed in the opening years, and the level of the credit (£545) has also not been altered, so is slowly declining in real value. By contrast, the levels of WTC—apart from the childcare element—have been altered by reference to rises in the cost of living, and so are relatively less generous.

The administration and delivery of tax credits during introduction was a disaster that does not need retelling. This led to a large number of overpayments—some apparently generated by computers paying out more than they were told, while others arose from a rush to deliver initial payments. Things are running more smoothly now, though in part only because—as several expert agencies have protested—the Revenue (now HMRC) has smoothed the administrative process, and reports suggest that it does not always comply fully with its own rules about making decisions. But the rules themselves assist that smoothness. For example, it is very easy to claim, and to have a claim backdated, as compared with the old rules applied by the then DSS to claims and in particular late claims. Partly, one suspects, because of this, partly because there is a power and commitment to settle disputes rather than fight them, and partly because of a more proactive approach to claimants than was the practice of the old DSS, there have been to date few appeals.

Commencement

1.214   Section 61 (Commencement) and subsequent sections came into effect on Royal Assent (8 July 2002). Pt I (ss.1–48) is brought into effect under the Tax Credits Act 2002 (Commencement No.1) Order 2002 (SI 2002/1727) made that day. The balance of the Act was brought in by the Tax Credits Act 2002 (Commencement No.2) Order 2003 (SI 2003/392) (Pt II), the Tax Credits Act 2002 (Commencement No.3 and Transitional Provisions and Savings) Order 2003 (SI 2003/938) (the abolition of the child additions and benefits under s.1(3) of the Act) and Tax Credits Act 2002 (Commencement No.4, Transitional Provisions and Savings) Order 2003 (SI 2003/962) (the remainder).

The pattern of introduction of tax credits is as follows:

General:
July 9, 2002   regulation-making powers

For all claimants except those on income support and jobseeker's allowance:
August 1, 2002   making claims and relevant provisions
January 1, 2003   making decisions on claims
April 6, 2003   entitlements to payment of awards and abolition of child additions from all benefits save as below.

For claimants over 60 transferring to or qualifying for state pension credit:
October 1, 2003   making claims and awards.

For other claimants of income support or jobseeker's allowance:
December 31, 2008   phased introduction of CTC to all claimants.

General problems with the 2002 Act

1.215   The first two years of the operation of the Tax Credits Act 2002 cannot, by any stretch of imagination, be called an outstanding success. Overall, it proved far harder to start the system than anticipated. But the Government was proved right on one aspect of the new tax credits. Some claimed that the take-up rates for the credits would be low. This was a longstanding problem with family credit. But the estimated take-up for child tax credit in its first year was 80 per cent, compared to 65 per cent and 57 per cent in the first years of working families' tax credit and family credit respectively. In addition, no less than 480,000 claimants claimed nil credits (i.e. they put in protective claims in 2004–5 but did not receive anything).

General administration of tax credits proved far more complex than planned. Indeed, the government was forced to abandon its intentions of having the credits paid through people's pay packets. This was an aim of government as long ago as 1973 when family income supplement was turned into family credit. It was a firm aim of government in 2002, following the approach of s.6 of the Tax Credits Act 1999. But the 2002 Act contained a more limited measure than the original proposals. Section 25 provides for payment of working tax credit, or prescribed elements, by employers. This was never used to pay the full credit, as the childcare element was paid direct to the family. In 2004 the Chancellor announced that even the partial payment was to cease. And by April 2006 all payments by employers ceased. From then, payment is made only by HMRC.

The system is also suffering from the consequences of a combination of intended and unintended short-term generosity. The unintended generosity appears to have come from significant overpayments made by error by the computer systems to many thousands of households. These overpayments are errors in many cases where they were in excess of both the amounts claimed and the amounts authorised. Indeed, in the terms of the 2002 Act, they are arguably not "overpayments" at all because they exceeded the amounts awarded under the Act.

The intended generosity comes from the approach taken to administering the credits. The HMRC approach is to accept a claim as it stands, then to investigate it later for accuracy. In the first year of the new scheme, a claimant's income was assumed initially to be that of two years before, whereas the normal rule is to base that assessment on the previous year's income. This was compounded by what several expert observers have reported to be a high error rate in decision making, including serial failure to make a correct decision for many claimants, and serial failures in accepting notifications of changes of circumstances. The combined weight of evidence in the reports of the Parliamentary Ombudsman and the National Association of Citizens Advice Bureaux show serious repeated maladministration and other errors.

Not all overpayments may be the result of official error. Some claimants deliberately refrain from informing HMRC of changes of circumstances that they are not required to report. They then receive a current overpayment to be set off only later by a repayment.

Unusually, the fact that tax credits are authorised in two stages means that the statistics of these errors are cruelly accurate. All credits are paid on an award at the start of the in year payment, and are then checked by the entitlement decision at the end of the year. These showed a level of inaccuracy in awards that was itself likely to be very accurate. The total sums paid inaccurately totalled £2.395 billion in 2004–2005. The headline figures appear less than that because a total of overpayments approaching £2 billion were offset by underpayments approaching £0.5 billion. There were about 6.1 million tax creditors in 2004–2005. Of those nearly 500,000 were entitled to, and received, nothing (see above). Another 1 million were benefit claimants who would have been receiving child tax credit but for delays in bringing in that measure. That leaves some 4.5 million creditors subject to these errors. Dividing total errors by that number suggests that the average award was wrong by about £530 in the year.

The full story appears worse. The figures compare entitlement decisions after the year with the award paid by the end of the year. Other information shows that many claimants received regularly changed awards—arriving for many every two months or so according to figures in the reports noted above. But the effect of trying to correct the errors of a previous decision through another decision itself also likely either to be incorrect or to be replaced in a matter of weeks by a third decision has led to payments becoming almost erratic and certainly unpredictable for their recipients. Large overpayments were followed by demands for full repayment.

Further, errors spilled over from one tax year to the next as the government decided to recover the overpayments in stages. Complaints systems received large numbers of complaints from claimants experiencing the swings of the system.

Changes since enactment

1.216   Five aspects of the original scheme have been delayed, watered-down or abandoned: (1) All payments are made direct by HMRC and none through the pay packet; (2) CTC is yet to be made payable to all claimants of income related benefits under s.1 of the 2002 Act; (3) the power to make shared awards of CTC where there is shared responsibility for a child has not been used; (4) despite the terms of s.7, awards are based almost entirely on income of the previous year; (5) year-on-year increases are taken into account only when over £25,000.

Two underlying aims have been achieved. There is a significantly greater take-up of child tax credit than of its predecessors. The HMRC central estimate of take-up for 2005/06 was 82 per cent of maximum caseload and 91 per cent of maximum value. There is a lower rate of take-up of working tax credit (61 per cent and 82 per cent respectively). At least part of the failure to take up tax credits is a failure to claim small amounts of credit in the more marginal cases. Behind this there is therefore a more successful regime to redistribute help to low paid families in particular than the previous systems.

Several years of problems with handling overpayments have yet to be resolved. It still remains to be seen whether all income-related child benefits can be paid to low income families through the annual cycle of tax credits without endemic problems of overpayment.

Is credits advice tax advice?

1.217   The hybrid nature of tax credits as part tax, part benefits, part employment subsidies leads to a number of anomalies. One is the question whether advice on tax credits is tax advice. If it is then advisers may need to ensure that they comply with all relevant European and UK regulations about money laundering. This was raised at the Tax Credits Consultative Group Meeting in November 2006. In a note issued after the meeting HMRC advised that, having consulted policy experts at the Treasury (though not, according to the note, lawyers) HMRC does not think that advisers are caught by the rules. In part this is because they do not advertise themselves as offering tax advice. And in part "it seems they give advice on government benefits rather than tax advice". If so, why are they called tax credits?

PART I

TAX CREDITS

General

Introductory

1.218   **1.**—(1) This Act makes provision for—

(a) a tax credit to be known as child tax credit, and

(b) a tax credit to be known as working tax credit.

(2) In this Act references to a tax credit are to either of those tax credits and references to tax credits are to both of them.

(3) The following (which are superseded by tax credits) are abolished—

(a) children's tax credit under section 257AA of the Income and Corporation Taxes Act 1988 (Chapter 1),

(b) working families' tax credit,

(c) disabled person's tax credit,

(d) the amounts which, in relation to income support and income-based jobseeker's allowance, are prescribed as part of the applicable amount in respect of a child or young person, the family premium, the enhanced disability premium in respect of a child or young person and the disabled child premium,

(e) increases in benefits in respect of children under sections 80 and 90 of the Social Security Contributions and Benefits Act 1992 (Chapter 4) and sections 80 and 90 of the Social Security Contributions and Benefits (Northern Ireland) Act 1992 (Chapter 7), and

(f) the employment credit under the schemes under section 2(2) of the Employment and Training Act 1973 (Chapter 50) and section 1 of the Employment and Training Act (Northern Ireland) 1950 (Chapter 29 (NI)) known as "New Deal 50 Plus".

DEFINITIONS

"child tax credit"—see s.8.
"tax credit"—see subs.2.
"working tax credit"—see s.10.

GENERAL NOTE

Section 1 is, as its title states, purely an introductory section. Strictly it adds nothing to the enacting provisions of Pt I, but it flags up the two kinds of tax credit payable under the Act and also the benefits repealed (by s.60 and Sch.6). Subsection (1) lists the two tax credits introduced by the Act, but (as with the rest of Pt I) is drafted so that other tax credits could be added to the list in the subsection, and the machinery sections of the Act (which apply to "tax credits" as defined in subs.(2)) would then apply to the new tax credits also. At the date of writing, no specific further tax credits have been suggested. The abolition of the child premiums to income support and JSA were deferred to December 31, 2008.

1.219

Indeed, it has proved harder than anticipated to introduce child tax credits for those on income support and jobseeker's allowance. It is understood that there are many cases where one parent of a child is claiming one of these benefits with child addition while the other parent is claiming child tax credit for the same child or children. In *CSTC/326/2003* Commissioner Parker considered an argument that the measures taken to postpone the introduction of s.1(3)(d) discriminated against those receiving income support as against those who received the tax credits direct. The appellant's wife received income support. Entitlement to child tax credit was higher than to income support. But under the transitional legislation the appellant could claim CTC only from the date of his claim. No backdating was allowed. The appellant argued that either this was ultra vires the TCA 2002 or it was discriminatory under the European Convention on Human Rights. The Commissioner rejected both arguments. In dealing with somewhat unfocussed arguments about the European Convention on Human Rights, the Commissioner took the view that CTC is a means-tested social security benefit but assumed for the purposes of argument that both art.8 of, and art.1, Protocol 1 to, the Convention were engaged. She then considered if there was discrimination within the meaning of art.14 but found none. Her decision reveals that the process of suspending s.1(3)(d) while benefit claimants are "migrated" to it as being in some confusion. Of the relevant subordinate legislation (in particular SI 2005/773, SI 2005/776 and SI 2005/1106), she comments (at para.16):

"the last minute nature of the amendment order, the curiosity of two substantially overlapping measures produced on the same day (the transitional provisions order 2005 and the second transitional provisions order), a draft order which was never laid, and the failure to enact a consistent statutory scheme of backdating to prevent double recovery, indicate a history of some haste and confusion by the legislators. There has been a complex web of measures, note always successful, necessitated because the prospects for the completion of intended migration seem ever to recede."

[¹Function of Commissioners

1.220   **2.** The Commissioners for Her Majesty's Revenue and Customs shall be responsible for the payment and management of tax credits.]

AMENDMENT

1. Commissioners for Revenue and Customs Act 2005, Sch.4, para.88 (April 6, 2005).

DEFINITIONS

"tax credits"—see s.1(2).
"the Commissioners for Revenue and Customs"—see CRCA 2005 s.4.

GENERAL NOTE

1.221   This short section replaced its lengthy predecessor as CRCA 2005 came into effect. That Act repealed and replaced the Inland Revenue Regulation Act 1890 to which this section previously referred. All necessary provisions for both the payment of tax credits (and repayment) and management and administration are now either in the CRCA 2005 or this Act. The wording of this section reflects the similar wording in CRCA 2005 applying also to taxes, duties and benefits.

Claims

1.222   **3.**—(1) Entitlement to a tax credit for the whole or part of a tax year is dependent on the making of a claim for it.
(2) Where the Board—
(a) decide under section 14 not to make an award of a tax credit on a claim, or
(b) decide under section 16 to terminate an award of a tax credit made on a claim,
(subject to any appeal) any entitlement, or subsequent entitlement, to the tax credit for any part of the same tax year is dependent on the making of a new claim.
(3) A claim for a tax credit may be made—
(a) jointly by the members of a [²couple] both of whom are aged at least sixteen and are in the United Kingdom [(and neither of whom are members of a polygamous unit)]¹; or
[(aa) jointly by the members of a polygamous unit all of whom are aged at least sixteen and are in the United Kingdom, or]¹;
(b) by a person who is aged at least sixteen and is in the United Kingdom but is not entitled to make a claim under paragraph (a) (jointly with another).
(4) Entitlement to a tax credit pursuant to a claim ceases—

(a) in the case of a joint claim, if the persons by whom it was made could no longer jointly make a joint claim; and

[(aa) in the case of a joint claim under subsection (3)(a), if a member of the [²couple] becomes a member of a polygamous unit, and

(ab) in the case of a joint claim under subsection (3)(aa), if there is any change in the persons who comprise the polygamous unit, and]¹

(b) in the case of a single claim, if the person by whom it was made could no longer make a single claim.

(5) [² . . .

(5A) In this Part "couple" means—

(a) a man and woman who are married to each other and are neither—
  (i) separated under a court order, nor
  (ii) separated in circumstances in which the separation is likely to be permanent,

(b) a man and woman who are not married to each other but are living together as husband and wife,

(c) two people of the same sex who are civil partners of each other and are neither—
  (i) separated under a court order, nor
  (ii) separated in circumstances in which the separation is likely to be permanent, or

(d) two people of the same sex who are not civil partners of each other but are living together as if they were civil partners.]

(6) [² . . .]

[(6A) In this Part, "polygamous unit" has the meaning given by regulation 2 of the Tax Credits (Polygamous Marriages) Regulations 2003.]¹

(7) Circumstances may be prescribed in which a person is to be treated for the purposes of this Part as being, or as not being, in the United Kingdom.

(8) In this Part—

"joint claim" means a claim under paragraph (a) [or (aa)]¹ of subsection (3), and

"single claim" means a claim under paragraph (b) of that subsection.

AMENDMENTS

1. Modifications for the purposes of application to polygamous units by Tax Credits (Polygamous Marriages) Regulations 2003 (SI 2003/742), reg.4 (April 6, 2003).

2. Civil Partnership Act 2004, s.254 and Sch.24, para.144 (December 5, 2005).

DEFINITIONS

"award"—see s.14(1).
"the Board"—see s.67.
"claim"—see subs.(1), s.4.
"couple"—see subs.(5A).
"entitlement"—see s.18(1).
"joint claim"—see subs.(8).
"prescribed"—see s.67.
"single claim"—see subs.(8).
"tax credit"—see s.1(2).
"tax year"—see s.47.

GENERAL NOTE

1.223   This is the first of the sections in the Act that create the necessary compromise for tax credits between the general approach of income tax administration and the general approach of social security administration. Subsection (1) adopts and adapts the requirement from SSAA 1992, s.1(1), that there can be no entitlement to a tax credit without a claim. Subsection (2) reinforces this. Subsections (3) and following set out both the main conditions for making a claim and the requirement that both (or all) those who are partners to a marriage (or equivalent) join in making the claim. Subsection (8) adopts appropriate definitions for joint and single claims. There is also a definition of "claimant" in s.9(8), which would be better placed here in subs.(8).

    Determining when a claim is made is important because of the operation of the "three month" rule for a new claim following some changes of circumstances. The ability to make claims by telephone or email in addition to the traditional posted claim means that this may be a matter to be determined on appeal in the light of conflicting evidence from the claimants and HMRC. See *CSIS/48/1992* for the presumption that a document that can be served by post is delivered in ordinary course of post. HMRC treat the rule with a little generosity because it directs staff to assume that for these purposes three months is always 91 days and a single month always has 31 days.

Subs. (1)

1.224   The standard claim form is TC600 for new claims. In practice claims can be made over the telephone. See TC(Claims and Notifications) Regs 2002, reg.5 and *CIS/995/2004* discussed at para.2.276 below. Further, although renewal claims are needed each year, a renewal claim may be treated as being made as the procedure for checking a past claim takes place at the end of that year of claim.

    HMRC have accepted that it is appropriate in some cases to make protective claims where a claim will lead to a nil award on the then current information about income, but where a claimant may later in the tax year be entitled to tax credits. In such cases, nil awards will be made. See *Tax Adviser*, June 2003, p.13. HMRC statistics show that in December 2006 there were about 0.8 million claimants with zero awards. This suggests that these claims have become standard practice for many advisers, as the total number of recipients of credit had not risen in the previous two years while the number of zero awards doubled. Another explanation is that 0.6 million lower paid individuals (perhaps self-employed) without children now receive zero awards, and the number of such claimants also doubled in that period. Another reason is that HMRC may revise an award to zero rather than cancel it when a claimant is no longer entitled to receive a positive award.

Subs. (2)

1.225   This adopts in part a policy of SSA 1998, s.8, that a claim ceases to have effect when a decision has been made on it. A new claim is required if the Board refuses or ends a tax credit award for a tax year and for any reason the claimant wants that decision revisited. In practice, however, the Board may choose to make a "nil" award, so leaving the matter open to review if circumstances change, rather than a reclaim.

Subs. (3)

1.226   This is the primary provision entitling a claim to be made. It imposes a series of conditions on all claimants:

    (a) if a claimant is one of a married or unmarried couple (or of a polygamous unit) then the claim can only be made in the names of both (or all) of them;

    (b) the claimant or claimants must be over 16; and

118

(c) the claimant or claimants (and if more than one, all) must be "in the UK".

The following subsections make provisions for those conditions. But s.42 excludes those subject to immigration control from entitlement except in specified cases. The approach of requiring joint claims is also reinforced by s.4(1)(g), which enables regulations to treat a single claim as a joint claim. This has been extended by regulations under s.43 to cover polygamous units, the policy again being that all the members of a polygamous unit must be linked to the claim.

Following the enactment of the Gender Recognition Act 2004, HMRC have issued guidance that if an individual has gender recognition certificate issues under the Act, then this will or affect the status of the individual as a single or joint claimant: see TCTM 06100. However, there will be a potential interaction with the new definition of "couple" following the enactment of the Civil Partnership Act 2004. See below.

In *CSTC/724/2006* the Commissioner considered the application of subs.(3) (a) and (b) to an entitlement decision under s.19. The Commissioner followed the comments of the deputy Commissioner in *CTC/3864/2004* (an appeal about a s.16 decision) in confirming that the paragraphs are mutually exclusive. An individual cannot acquire entitlement to a tax credit if he or she did not claim it. The Commissioner rejected a decision of a tribunal that took the view that HMRC had the power to amend an award to take into account that the claimant became one of a couple. The appropriate single and joint claims must remain exclusive. Therefore a member of a couple who made a claim as a single claimant could have no entitlement to tax credits in either capacity. The other member of the couple could not be made liable for any overpayment in respect of any such decision if he or she was not a claimant.

Subs.(4)

This is designed to stop the claim under subs.(3) continuing if the identity of the claimant(s) changes because an individual gains a partner, a couple breaks up, or a polygamous unit changes membership. But it deals with *entitlement* not *award*, and its inclusion at this point in this section is a little obscure. It links with the provisions on joint claims (or deemed joint claims) to withdraw *entitlement* where joint claimants are no longer *entitled to make* a joint claim, thus stopping both joint claims and claims deemed to be joint. Nonetheless its interaction with ss.17 and 18 and with a continuing *award* is not clear. It appears to suggest that an award can continue without underlying entitlement. However, under the Tax Credits (Claims and Notifications) Regulations 2002 (SI 2002/2014), reg.21, notification must be given whenever a joint claim should become a single claim, or the reverse. In practice, this applies to awards as much as to entitlement.

1.227

Subss.(5A), (6A)

The original subs.(5) defined "married couple" and subs.(6) defined "unmarried couple". Both definitions have been replaced under the Civil Partnership Act 2004, but the new subsections reflect the former compromise between the income tax definition of a married couple (see ICTA s.282) and the social security definition (*see* Vol.II of this work for SSCBA 1992, s.137).

1.228

Decisions by HMRC that two individuals are a couple and should be making a joint claim continue to cause disputes. Commissioners have commented in several decisions on the approach to be taken. In *CTC/3059/2004* a deputy Commissioner decided that an appellant and her husband-to-be were not, on the facts, living together as wife and husband before their marriage although both HMRC and the tribunal had found that they were. (HMRC later supported the appeal to the Commissioner on the basis that the tribunal's findings of fact had gone beyond the evidence). Deputy Commissioner White held:

"12. Though the term "unmarried couple" is defined in the Tax Credits Act 2002, the concept of "living together as husband and wife" is not defined in the legislation. There appears to be no dispute that it is appropriate to use the guidance provided in Commissioners' decisions in relation to other benefits in considering such questions when they arise in relation to tax credits. I agree that the framework established in relation to other benefits is helpful.

13. That framework (*the Commissioner referred to Volume II*) indicates that a number of factors should be considered as a whole in deciding whether, on the balance of probabilities, a man and a woman are living together as husband and wife."

The deputy Commissioner then examined the facts by reference to: where the husband-to-be lived; financial support; sexual relationship; stability of relationship; care of the children of the wife-to-be; and public acknowledgement. He accepted that there were difficulties in using the latter three factors with regard to an engaged couple. But he concluded on the evidence that the engaged couple were not living together.

In *CTC/3864/2004* deputy Commissioner Green held that HMRC and another tribunal had erred on the same question, and again HMRC supported the claimant's appeal. It is to be noted that one ground on which HMRC supported the appeal was that the tribunal failed to provide an explanation why they did not find all the claimant's evidence reliable. The deputy Commissioner agreed, commenting that the tribunal had on one point rejected the claimant's evidence although that was the only evidence before the tribunal on that point. It may be that the HMRC support on this point reflects an HMRC expectation that it might expect to have to meet more exacting standards of evidence as to truth and credibility when appearing before the tax tribunals. More generally, deputy Commissioner Green took the same approach as in *CTC/3059/2004* (although without reference to it) in adopting the decisions of social security commissioners on the question of living together and referring to the guidance formerly in the *Supplementary Benefits Handbook* and in *R(SB) 17/81*.

In *CTC/1629/2005* a deputy Commissioner considered the importance in what has become subs.(5A) of the test of "separated in circumstances in which the separation is likely to be permanent." The context was a claim by a wife whose marriage to her husband was in difficulties. Divorce proceedings had been put on hold after they were started. HMRC decided that the claim she made should have been a joint claim. The tribunal agreed, but that decision was set aside. The deputy Commissioner emphasised the importance in cases such as this of making proper decisions about the credibility of a claimant. In this case the tribunal failed to deal adequately with the claimant's oral evidence and also with correspondence produced by her from others about the status of the marriage. But he does not deal with the question of obtaining evidence from the husband.

In *CTC/2090/2004* Commissioner Bano dealt with some of the consequences of competing claims for child tax credit. He resisted an argument put by HMRC that the appeal tribunal should have summonsed the mother to give evidence before finding for the father on a claim made by him. He also raised issues about the duty on HMRC itself in such a situation. In *CTC/3543/2004* Commissioner Jacobs considered who are the parties to proceedings in cases where there are joint claims. In his view where there is a joint claim both the claimants must be parties to any proceedings against one of them. The Commissioner referred to both SSA 1998 s.14(3)(d) and the Social Security and Child Support (Decisions and Appeals) Regulations 1999, reg.1(2) to decide that if there is an overpayment relating to a joint claim then both the claimants must be parties to the proceedings even if only one has appealed. Conversely it would follow that where a claim should be a joint claim but is not, the non-claimant is not automatically subject to a decision against the claimant.

See the note to s.6 for the effect of the introduction of the potential change of status of couples who become civil partners after December 5, 2005 while one or both of them is receiving tax credits, or who are to be treated as if they are living together as civil partners from that date while one or both is claiming tax credits. Anyone making a new claim after that date must disclose if she or he has a civil partner or is living together with another person as civil partners.

HMRC issues extensive guidance about identifying couples and related questions. See *Tax Credits Claims Compliance Manual* paragraphs CCM 15000—CCM 15350. This guidance is of course not binding on tribunals. CCM15040 follows the standard DWP approach to identifying who are a couple, save that the reference to sexual relationships is omitted. CCM15120 confirms the policy and gives officials the following guidance:

"Appeal tribunals sometimes ask claimants about their sexual relationships, however, it remains our policy that you must not ask such questions. If a tribunal asks you why you have not established the position you should say that our internal policy, in common with that in DWP, is not to ask about this side of the relationship."

CCM15045 stresses the nature of "modern-day relationships":

"By 2004, 70% of first domestic partnerships involved unmarried couples and it is now common for each party in a couple to work full-time, keep their own incomes and bank accounts and perhaps only pay money into a joint account for items of joint responsibility. Often because of demands on time both parties share childcare and domestic tasks."

Subs. (7)

This allows jurisdictional limits to be placed on entitlement to tax credit. Again, this breaks away from social security practice (which deals with Great Britain and Northern Ireland separately) to adopt income tax practice. It is supplemented by s.42 (persons subject to immigration control) and regulations made under that section. The main regulations under this subsection are the Tax Credits (Residence) Regulations 2003 (SI 2003/642). These impose a test of "ordinary residence" on most claimants.

1.229

Claims: supplementary

4.—(1) Regulations may—

1.230

(a) require a claim for a tax credit to be made in a prescribed manner and within a prescribed time,

(b) provide for a claim for a tax credit made in prescribed circumstances to be treated as having been made on a prescribed date earlier or later than that on which it is made,

(c) provide that, in prescribed circumstances, a claim for a tax credit may be made for a period wholly or partly after the date on which it is made,

(d) provide that, in prescribed circumstances, an award on a claim for a tax credit may be made subject to the condition that the requirements for entitlement are satisfied at a prescribed time,

(e) provide for a claim for a tax credit to be made or proceeded with in the name of a person who has died,

(f) provide that, in prescribed circumstances, one person may act for another in making a claim for a tax credit,

(g) provide that, in prescribed circumstances, a claim for a tax credit made by one member of a [2. . .] couple is to be treated as also made by the other member of [2 the couple]1, and

(h) provide that a claim for a tax credit is to be treated as made by a person or persons in such other circumstances as may be prescribed.

(2) The Board may supply to a person who has made a claim for a tax credit (whether or not jointly with another)—

    (a) any information relating to the claim, to an award made on the claim or to any change of circumstances relevant to the claim or such an award,

    (b) any communication made or received relating to such an award or any such change of circumstances, and

    (c) any other information which is relevant to any entitlement to tax credits pursuant to the claim or any such change of circumstances or which appeared to be so relevant at the time the information was supplied.

AMENDMENTS

1. Tax Credits (Polygamous Marriages) Regulations 2003 (SI 2003/742) amends s.4(1)(g) as follows for the purposes of polygamous marriages:
"In section 4(1)(g)—

    (a) for "member of a married couple or an unmarried couple" substitute "or more members of a polygamous unit";

    (b) for "of the married couple or unmarried couple" substitute "or members".

2. Civil Partnership Act 2004, s.254 and Sch.24, para.145 (December 5, 2005).

DEFINITIONS

"award"—see s.14(1).
"the Board"—see s.67.
"claim"—see s.3(1).
"couple"—see s.3(5A).
"entitlement"—see s.18(1).
"joint claim"—see s.3(8).
"prescribed"—see s.67.
"single claim"—see s.3(8).
"tax credit"—see s.1(2).
"tax year"—see s.47.

GENERAL NOTE

1.231   Regulations for the purposes of subs.(1) are made by HMRC by negative procedure: ss.65(2), 66(3). The main regulations made are the Tax Credits (Claims and Notifications) Regulations 2002 (SI 2002/2014). References to "the Board" are now references to the Commissioners for Revenue and Customs: CRCA 2005, s.4.

The most important point relevant to this section is that those Regulations require a claim to be made not later than three months after the date from which it can operate. For a claim to be effective from the beginning of a tax year, it must be made (that is, received by an appropriate office) before July 6 in that year. If made later than that, it will not operate for more than three months before the date on which the claim was actually made. But, unlike backdated claims for social security benefits, the three months backdating is automatic and is not dependent on grounds being shown for a "late claim". Nor is there any discretion to extent the three months' backdating of a claim in any circumstances. See reg.7 of those regulations. The only exception, under reg.8, applies to claimants claiming a disability element of WTC as part of the claim.

Subsection (2) gives HMRC power that it would otherwise not have to inform a claimant of information of which it knows that is relevant to a claim, or to an award or entitlement continuing. This will ensure that either member of a joint claiming couple can be informed of anything that the other member of the couple tells HMRC. This cuts across the privacy as between members of a couple that was respected by HMRC following the introduction of individual self-assessment for income tax.

Period of awards

5.—(1) Where a tax credit is claimed for a tax year by making a claim before the tax year begins, any award of the tax credit on the claim is for the whole of the tax year.

(2) An award on any other claim for a tax credit is for the period beginning with the date on which the claim is made and ending at the end of the tax year in which that date falls.

(3) Subsections (1) and (2) are subject to any decision by the Board under section 16 to terminate an award.

1.232

DEFINITIONS

    "award"—see s.14(1).
    "the Board"—see s.67.
    "claim"—see s.3(1).
    "tax credit"—see s.1(2).
    "tax year"—see s.47.

GENERAL NOTE

This section applies to both CTC and WTC. It confirms the import of s.3(1), namely that a claim is for one tax year at a time, and provides that any award is for that tax year (or, if made during the year, for what is left of it). This is subject to the power in s.16 to end an award, after which a new claim must be made (s.3(2)). Effect is given to these provisions by the Tax Credits (Claims and Notifications) Regulations 2002 (SI 2002/2014), regs 4–11. Regulations 11 and 12 of those regulations provide a mechanism whereby a reply to a notice relating to one year of claim under s.17 of this Act can be treated as a claim for the following year.

1.233

Subsection (2), on its face, prevents retrospective claims, but it must be read with regs 4 and following of the Tax Credits (Claims and Notifications) Regulations 2002. These make provision for the "date on which a claim is made". Under reg.7, the general rule is that a claim is treated as made for the purposes of this subsection up to three months before the date on which the claim is received by an appropriate office, if *entitlement* extends that far back. This, like other issues about *award* and *entitlement*, seems to conflate the making of an award with entitlement (see the note to s.6). It will only be known that a person is entitled once a final decision is made under s.17 of this Act after the end of the year, while the award operates on the basis that the person is probably entitled.

See also Tax Credits Act 2002 (Transitional Provisions) Order 2005 (SI 2005/773), art.6.

Notifications of changes of circumstances

6.—(1) Regulations may provide that any change of circumstances of a prescribed description which may increase the maximum rate at which a person or persons may be entitled to a tax credit is to do so only if notification of it has been given.

(2) Regulations under subsection (1) may—

    (a) provide for notification of a change of circumstances given in prescribed circumstances to be treated as having been given on a prescribed date earlier or later than that on which it is given,

1.234

(b) provide that, in prescribed circumstances, a notification of a change of circumstances may be given for a period wholly or partly after the date on which it is given, and

(c) provide that, in prescribed circumstances, an amendment of an award of a tax credit in consequence of a notification of a change of circumstances may be made subject to the condition that the requirements for entitlement to the amended amount of the tax credit are satisfied at a prescribed time.

(3) Regulations may require that, where a person has or persons have claimed a tax credit, notification is to be given if there is a change of circumstances of a prescribed description which may decrease the rate at which he is or they are entitled to the tax credit or mean that he ceases or they cease to be entitled to the tax credit.

[[1](3A) For the purposes of this section, a change of circumstances shall be treated as having occurred where by virtue of the coming into force of Part 14 of Schedule 24 to the Civil Partnership Act 2004 (amendments of the Tax Credits Act 2002) two people of the same sex are treated as a couple.

(3B) In subsection (3A), "couple" has the meaning given in paragraph 144(3) of Part 14 of Schedule 24 to the Civil Partnership Act 2004.]

(4) Regulations under this section may—

(a) require a notification to be given in a prescribed manner and within a prescribed time,

(b) specify the person or persons by whom a notification may be, or is to be, given, and

(c) provide that, in prescribed circumstances, one person may act for another in giving a notification.

AMENDMENT

1. Tax Credits Notification of Changes of Circumstances (Civil Partnership) (Transitional Provisions) Order 2005 (SI 2005/828), art.2 (April 8, 2005). Note that these provisions have effect only for the tax year 2005/06.

DEFINITIONS

"award"—see s.14(1).
"claim"—see s.3(1).
"entitlement"—see s.18(1).
"maximum rate"—see ss.9 and 11.
"prescribed"—see s.67.
"tax credit"—see s.1(2).

GENERAL NOTE

1.235   The Bill on which this Act was based was tabled in, and passed through, the House of Commons without a clear distinction being drawn between the measures relating to *award* of a tax credit on a claim and the later issue of *entitlement* to that credit. As a result, there is no clear progression in the sections of the Act from claims to award to entitlement. This section might from context appear to be about awards, but subs.(1) is drafted to cover only entitlement issues. The link is provided partly under subs.(2) and partly by s.15, which links changes in awards to the rate at which someone *may be* entitled to a tax credit.

"Change of circumstances" is, of course, a familiar social security concept on which the SSA 1998 relies heavily for powers to change decisions after they are made but where they have continuing effect. There is also a general duty on claimants to report changes of circumstances of relevance to benefit awards. This section allows a similar duty to be imposed on tax credit claimants. The section is purely empowering. Regulations may be made by the Revenue by negative procedure: ss.65(2) and 66(3). The relevant regulations are the Tax Credits (Claims and Notifications) Regulations 2002 (SI 2002/2014), regs 19–29. Those regulations, however, take a substantially different approach to changes of circumstances to those operated for social security benefits.

The nature of a "change of circumstances" and the treatment adopted for making and dealing with changes of circumstance requires some further explanation because of the differences in the ways in which the rules operate compared with those for income support or jobseeker's allowance. The main differences are—

- (a) not all changes of circumstances during a year will result in a change of circumstances affecting the award or entitlement;
- (b) the duty to notify changes of circumstances is limited in scope and applies only to some changes;
- (c) failure to notify when there is a duty to do so may make the person failing to notify liable to penalties and penalty proceedings under ss.31(1) and 32(3).

Relevant changes of circumstances

Because the income test under s.7 is applied to the tax year (or period of award) as a whole, a change in income levels during a year may be irrelevant to award or entitlement levels, and so not constitute a change of circumstances. This will be particularly so towards the end of a tax year. Further, because of the "buffer" built into the income test by s.7(3), any increase of income over the year as a whole of less than £25,000 is irrelevant in any event. Changes in capital are also immaterial, as it is only the (taxable) income from capital that affects the level of award and entitlement. For similar reasons, a change of job (with a gap of under seven days between jobs) will also not affect an award or entitlement unless either it changes the income level significantly over the year as a whole or it decreases the hours worked below 16, or—for WTC only—it increases or decreases the hours above or below 30.

The changes that are relevant are significant income changes, as noted above, and other changes that will stop entitlement or cause its overall level to be changed. This may apply differently to CTC and WTC. But not all those changes must be reported.

Changes that must be reported

There is no general duty to report all changes of circumstances, although it may be in a claimant's interest to do so. See Code of Practice 26 at the end of this volume.

HMRC handle the issue of changes by requiring some changes to be reported within one month of the change. The list of items that must be reported within one month is in regulation 21 of the Tax Credits (Claims and Notifications) Regulations 2002. See para.2.307 below.

Changes that may be reported

Under regs 20 and 25 of the Tax Credits (Claims and Notifications) Regulations 2002, a change of circumstances that may increase an award or entitlement to either WTC or CTC will only do so if notification of the change has been given to HMRC within three months of the date when the change occurred. Later notice will be backdated not more than three months. This time limit is, however, extended under reg.26 for those claiming the disability or severe disability elements of WTC. In all other cases, notification of any change of circumstances that will or may benefit the claimant should be made within the three months' limit to prevent both loss of award and loss of entitlement.

Current HMRC guidance on voluntary reporting is:

"You do not have to tell us about the following changes, but it is in your interest to do so because they may increase the amount of tax credits you are due.

1.236

1.237

1.238

"Please tell us if:

- A young person over 16 continues in full time education, registers with a careers service, Connexions, or equivalent, or joins an approved Government training scheme. If you do not tell us, their Child Tax Credit will stop on 1st September after their 16th birthday.
- Your income goes down.
- Your income goes up. This may not affect your current tax credits, but it will affect how much we should pay you for next year. If we pay you too much because you delay telling us about any changes, you will be asked to pay back any tax credits overpaid.
- Your child care costs go up by £10 a week or more.
- Your usual working hours change from less than 16 hours a week to 16 or more.
- Your usual working hours change from less than 30 hours a week to 30 or more. For couples with children, it is your joint working hours that count towards the 30 hours.
- To report a change please call the tax credits Helpline on 0845 300 3900. The lines are open from 8.00am–8.00pm seven days a week."

Where changes are reported, HMRC practice is to issue a new award notice based on the details reported. Claimants are asked to check the award notice and report any errors. They are also asked to enquire if they do not receive a new award notice within one month of notifying the changes. See s.15 and COP 26 below.

Automatic notification?

1.239   Part II of this Act transfers responsibility for child benefit to HMRC. The decision of the House of Lords in *Hinchy v Secretary of State for Work and Pensions* [2005] UKHL 16 confirms the traditional view that a claimant must tell the relevant office about changes of circumstances. It is therefore not enough that, for example, a claimant tells the HMRC Child Benefit Office but not the tax credits office or the local social security office or housing benefit authority of the changed position of one of the claimant's children. However, the growth of public computer-based records and the interlinking of records between departments under the Generalised Matching Service increasingly notifies one department of information known to another. That is no defence under the tax credit scheme to liability to repay any overpaid tax credit. It will be for consideration whether this is relevant to any penalty proceedings under ss.31 or 32. It is understood that HMRC is notified automatically about decisions of the termination of disability living allowance awards.

Failure to report

1.240   Leaving aside fraudulent or other cases of deliberate non-disclosure, if a change of circumstances is not reported when it happens it will be picked up directly or indirectly when the claimant replies to HMRC's final notice issued under s.17. This is because of the declaration necessary under s.17. If it is a relevant change, then the entitlement to WTC and/or CTC will be confirmed at a different rate to that of the award. This will result in an overpayment (see s.28) if the level of award is, as a result, higher than the level of entitlement. It could also result in an underpayment (see s.30), but only to the extent that the notification is regarded as in time for any part of the relevant tax year. In most cases, if the notification is more than three months after the end of the tax year then the right to an increased entitlement will have been lost.

HMRC has announced that it will not seek penalties from a taxpayer who has a nil award following a claim and who then fails to make a mandatory notification of a change of circumstances. See *Tax Adviser*, June 2003, p.13.

Both the Parliamentary Ombudsman and the Citizens Advice Bureaux published further reports about tax credits in October 2007. *Tax Credits: Getting it wrong?* was published as the 5th Report of the Parliamentary Ombudsman (HC 1010, Session 2006–07). The report contains detailed case studies about, in particular, overpayments and their recovery, and notes that complaints about tax credits continue to form a growing part of the workload of the Ombudsman. In the year starting on April 1, 2007 to the end of August, tax credits complaints formed 26 per cent of the Ombudsman's workload, and three quarters of those complaints were upheld either in whole or in part. It also comments on the complaints and appeals procedures. Nearly all current complaints are about overpayments.

The National Association of Citizens Advice Bureaux published a report at the same time entitled *Tax Credits: the current picture*. This summarises the comments of 1,500 respondents to a survey on their experiences of tax credits—drawn from 186,000 people helped by CABs in handling their tax credits in the last year. The report notes as worrying the number of respondents who stopped claiming tax credits because of the problems involved.

Income test

7.—(1) The entitlement of a person or persons of any description to a tax credit is dependent on the relevant income—

1.241

   (a) not exceeding the amount determined in the manner prescribed for the purposes of this paragraph in relation to the tax credit and a person or persons of that description (referred to in this Part as the income threshold), or

   (b) exceeding the income threshold by only so much that a determination in accordance with regulations under section 13(2) provides a rate of the tax credit in his or their case.

(2) Subsection (1) does not apply in relation to the entitlement of a person or persons to a tax credit for so long as the person, or either of the persons, is entitled to any social security benefit prescribed for the purposes of this subsection in relation to the tax credit.

(3) In this Part "the relevant income" means—

   (a) if an amount is prescribed for the purposes of this paragraph and the current year income exceeds the previous year income by not more than that amount, the previous year income,

   (b) if an amount is prescribed for the purposes of this paragraph and the current year income exceeds the previous year income by more than that amount, the current year income reduced by that amount,

   (c) if an amount is prescribed for the purposes of this paragraph and the previous year income exceeds the current year income by not more than that amount, the previous year income,

   (d) if an amount is prescribed for the purposes of this paragraph and the previous year income exceeds the current year income by more than that amount, the current year income increased by that amount, and

   (e) otherwise, the current year income.

(4) In this Part "the current year income" means—

   (a) in relation to persons by whom a joint claim for a tax credit is made, the aggregate income of the persons for the tax year to which the claim relates, and

   (b) in relation to a person by whom a single claim for a tax credit is made, the income of the person for that tax year.

(5) In this Part "the previous year income" means—

(a) in relation to persons by whom a joint claim for a tax credit is made, the aggregate income of the persons for the tax year preceding that to which the claim relates, and

(b) in relation to a person by whom a single claim for a tax credit is made, the income of the person for that preceding tax year.

(6) Regulations may provide that, for the purposes of this Part, income of a prescribed description is to be treated as being, or as not being, income for a particular tax year.

(7) In particular, regulations may provide that income of a prescribed description of a person for the tax year immediately before the preceding tax year referred to in subsection (5) is to be treated as being income of that preceding tax year (instead of any actual income of that description of the person for that preceding tax year).

(8) Regulations may for the purposes of this Part make provision—

(a) as to what is, or is not, income, and

(b) as to the calculation of income.

(9) Regulations may provide that, for the purposes of this Part, a person is to be treated—

(a) as having income which he does not in fact have, or

(b) as not having income which he does in fact have.

(10) The Board may estimate the amount of the income of a person, or the aggregate income of persons, for any tax year for the purpose of making, amending or terminating an award of a tax credit; but such an estimate does not affect the rate at which he is, or they are, entitled to the tax credit for that or any other tax year.

AMENDMENTS

1. Subsection (2) is amended as it applies to polygamous units by Tax Credits (Polygamous Marriages) Regulations 2003 (SI 2003/742), reg.6.

2. References to "the Board" are now references to the Commissioners for Revenue and Customs: CRCA 2005, s.4.

DEFINITIONS

"award"—see s.14(1).
"the Board"—see s.67.
"claim"—see s.3(1).
"couple"—see s.3(5A).
"entitlement"—see s.18(1).
"joint claim"—see s.3(8).
"prescribed"—see s.67.
"single claim"—see s.3(8).
"tax credit"—see s.1(2).
"tax year"—see s.47.

GENERAL NOTE

1.242   This is a framework and empowering section making provision for the imposition of an income test on all claimants for both CTC and WTC. The relevant regulations are the Tax Credits (Definition of Calculation of Income) Regulations 2002 (SI 2002/2006) and the Tax Credits (Income Thresholds and Determination of Rates) Regulations 2002 (SI 2002/2008). The powers to make regulations are Treasury powers requiring affirmative procedures. Further, the regulations link the income test closely to income tax rules, thus breaking away from the separate social security means tests.

Subs.(1)

This is worded to refer "a tax credit" so that different amounts may be pre- **1.243** scribed for different tax credits. Regulation 3 of the Tax Credits (Income Thresholds and Determination of Rates) Regulations 2002 sets a threshold for WTC of £6,420, and for CTC of £16,040 with a further higher threshold for the family element only of CTC of £50,000 in reg.8 of those Regulations. See para.2.251.

Although this section defines the amounts of income above which tax credits are reduced by reference to income as "income threshold", HMRC literature, includ-ing formal papers, refers to them instead as "taper start points". A Commissioner criticised this change of language, without any accompanying explanation, in *CTC/2113/2006*. In that case, which concerned the operation of these start points or threshold, the Commissioner criticised the failure of HMRC to explain how its language fitted in with the statutory language. This left a claimant unable to under-stand the HMRC submissions and the appeal tribunal's decision agreeing with the submission (but using the statutory language also without explanation).

Subs.(2)

This disapplies the income test, so allowing payment of a tax credit without refer- **1.244** ence to separate means-testing, where the prescribed benefits are in payment. The benefits are prescribed by Tax Credits (Income Thresholds and Determination of Rates) Regulations 2002, reg.4 as covering only some claimants for income support, state pension credit and jobseeker's allowance.

Subss. (3)–(5)

This is another part of the Act that operates in a substantially different way to the **1.245** original intent. Subsection (3)(c) and (d) have never been brought into effect. From April 6, 2006, subss.(a) and (b) also have limited effect as the prescribed amount is £25,000. In other words, awards of tax credits for a year are based on the income of the previous year unless either the current year income exceeds that of the previous year by at least £25,000 or, under paragraph (e), there was no previous year income. For the regulations and an example see para.2.233.

Subs.(4)

CTC/2270/2007 confirmed HMRC's interpretation on an important aspect of **1.246** subs.(7)(a). Where two individuals become a couple during a year and make a joint claim, this requires that the aggregate income for the year is the income for the entire year of both of the couple. The deputy Commissioner rejected the argument of a man whose partner, and later wife, moved in with him during the year that her income before she moved in was irrelevant to the joint claim made after she moved in. The plain language of Parliament required that the full income for the year of both of them was to be calculated, and then apportioned to the part of the year during which they made the joint claim. It followed that part of the wife's income was to be taken into account in respect of the joint income even though she had earned nothing since she moved in with her husband. The deputy Commissioner reasoned that:

> ". . . the position is that Parliament in passing the Act and the Treasury in making the Regulations have chosen a method of determining income that may be criticised as somewhat rough and ready and as such producing anomalous outcomes in cases like the present, but is nevertheless relatively simple to operate compared with the alternative of enquiring into the actual income of each single and joint claimant in respect of claim periods of less than a year."

The result of this interpretation is that in every case the full year income of any individual must be taken into account under subs. (4)(b), with the amount relevant to any claim being apportioned. The subsection as a whole is anomalous. The result where A and B became partners during a year and then split up again during that year is that the incomes of both A and B are to be taken into account from the beginning of the year to the time they split up, but then apportioned to the period of the joint claim. But after the couple split up their incomes must be disaggregated and any claim by either A or B is then to be based only on her or his income for that year.

Subss. (6)–(9)

1.247   See the Tax Credits (Definition and Calculation of Income) Regulations 2002, as amended.

Subs. (10)

1.248   This is a wide power to deal with awards. It allows HMRC to make, change or stop an award during the tax year on the basis of an estimate only. That estimate will be the decision made under ss.14(1), 15(1) or 16(1). Any of these decisions are subject to appeal and, on appeal, it will be for the appeal tribunal to make the estimate (subject to any settlement of the appeal under s.54 of the TMA 1970). See further the note to s.39 below. It is understood that the standard practice of HMRC is to make all initial decisions on the basis of the previous year's income using this power. Where a claim form indicates that the current year's income should be used, HMRC then makes an immediate revision under s.15.

Child tax credit

Entitlement

1.249   **8.**—(1) The entitlement of the person or persons by whom a claim for child tax credit has been made is dependent on him, or either of them, being responsible for one or more children or qualifying young persons.

(2) Regulations may make provision for the purposes of child tax credit as to the circumstances in which a person is or is not responsible for a child or qualifying young person.

(3) For the purposes of this Part a person is a child if he has not attained the age of sixteen; but regulations may make provision for a person who has attained that age to remain a child for the purposes of this Part after attaining that age for a prescribed period or until a prescribed date.

(4) In this Part "qualifying young person" means a person, other than a child, who—

(a) has not attained such age (greater than 16) as is prescribed, and

(b) satisfies prescribed conditions.

(5) Circumstances may be prescribed in which a person is to be entitled to child tax credit for a prescribed period in respect of a child or qualifying young person who has died.

AMENDMENT

1. Subsection (1) is amended as it applies to polygamous units by Tax Credits (Polygamous Marriages) Regulations 2003 (SI 2003/742), reg.7.

DEFINITIONS

"child"—see subs.(3).
"prescribed"—see s.67.
"qualifying young person"—see subs.(4).

GENERAL NOTE

This section sets the central tests for claiming child tax credits, namely that there be   **1.250**
a child or young person for whom the claimant is, or joint claimants are, responsible.
Subsection (1) provides that entitlement to child tax credit is dependent on these
tests. It is deliberately parallel to SSCBA 1992, s.141, the section entitling claimants
to child benefit for each of the children for whom a claimant is responsible. Subsection
(2) makes provision for regulations defining responsibility for a child. This is covered
by SSCBA 1992, s.143 and supporting regulations. The regulations also deal with
competing claims for child tax credit for the same child. See paras 2.187 and ff.
Subsection (3) defines a child as someone who has not reached the age of 16, but also
allows the age to be extended by regulation. Child benefit is payable for all children
who have not reached 16 (SSCBA 1992, s.142(1)). Child benefit is also payable for
certain children over 16, but for child tax credit purposes they are known as "qualifying young persons". Subsection (4) allows regulations to define that category. The
intention is, as with child benefit, to include certain young persons over 16 but not
over 19, depending on ongoing education (but not covering students undergoing
higher education). The effect confirms a general policy to exclude those over 16 from
being "children" for state benefit purposes, but to include them, along with students,
in a separate category. This is because those over 16 can claim some benefits in their
own right. See further the Child Tax Credit Regulations 2002 (SI 2002/2007).

Subs. (5)

This makes identical provision as that in s.54 of this Act, ensuring that both child   **1.251**
benefit and child tax credit remain payable for a period (set by regulations at eight
weeks) after the death of a child or, in the case of child tax credit, qualifying young
person.

Maximum rate

9.—(1) The maximum rate at which a person or persons may be entitled   **1.252**
to child tax credit is to be determined in the prescribed manner.

(2) The prescribed manner of determination must involve the inclusion of—

    (a) an element which is to be included in the case of all persons entitled
to child tax credit, and

    (b) an element in respect of each child or qualifying young person for
whom the person is, or either of them is or are, responsible.

(3) The element specified in paragraph (a) of subsection (2) is to be
known as the family element of child tax credit and that specified in paragraph (b) of that subsection is to be known as the individual element of
child tax credit.

(4) The prescribed manner of determination may involve the inclusion of
such other elements as may be prescribed.

(5) The prescribed manner of determination—

    (a) may include provision for the amount of the family element of child
tax credit to vary according to the age of any of the children or qualifying young persons or according to any such other factors as may
be prescribed,

    (b) may include provision for the amount of the individual element of
child tax credit to vary according to the age of the child or qualifying
young person or according to any such other factors as may be prescribed, and

    (c) must include provision for the amount of the individual element of child
tax credit to be increased in the case of a child or qualifying young

131

person who is disabled and to be further increased in the case of a child or qualifying young person who is severely disabled.

(6) A child or qualifying young person is disabled, or severely disabled, for the purposes of this section only if—

(a) he satisfies prescribed conditions, or

(b) prescribed conditions exist in relation to him.

(7) If, in accordance with regulations under section 8(2), more than one claimant may be entitled to child tax credit in respect of the same child or qualifying young person, the prescribed manner of determination may include provision for the amount of any element of child tax credit included in the case of any one or more of them to be less than it would be if only one claimant were so entitled.

(8) "Claimant" means—

(a) in the case of a single claim, the person who makes the claim; and

(b) in the case of a joint claim, the persons who make the claim.

AMENDMENT

1. Subsection (2) is amended as it applies to polygamous units by Tax Credits (Polygamous Marriages) Regulations 2003 (SI 2003/742), reg.8.

DEFINITIONS

"child"—see s.8(3).
"child tax credit"—see s.8.
"claimant"—see subs.(8).
"disabled"—see subs.(6).
"prescribed"—see s.67.
"qualifying young person"—see s.8(4).
"severely disabled"—see subs.(6).

GENERAL NOTE

1.253   This section is again a mixture of defining provisions and empowering provisions. Subsection (1) provides that the way in which entitlement to CTC is to be calculated is to be set out in regulations. The regulations for this purpose are the Child Tax Credit Regulations 2002 (SI 2002/2007). Subsections (2) and (3) provide that in every case an award of CTC must involve both a "family element" for the claimant and an "individual element" for each child or young person. The amount of the individual element must be higher for children or young persons who are disabled, and higher again if they are seriously disabled, but definition of those conditions is left to regulations: subss.(5)(c) and (6). The other provisions in the section are permissive.

Subs.(7)

1.254   As with child benefit, both HMRC and the appeal tribunals are regularly faced with disputes between two estranged parents or others both claiming child tax credit for the same child or children. The rules giving HMRC a discretion to decide to whom to pay child benefit do not apply to child tax credits. And the power to divide a single award in this subsection has not been used. In some cases the optimal approach where there is more than one child is for the parents (or other carers) to agree to split the award, or to have it paid to the claimant who can claim most. For the rules that apply where they cannot agree see Child Tax Credit Regulations, reg.3.

In *HMRC v DH* [2009] UKUT 24 (AAC) Judge Jacobs found that any breach of the human rights of a claimant for CTC who had a substantial minority responsibility for the shared care of a child because HMRC declined to share an award was justified by HMRC's evidence. This is set out at length in the decision. The decision is under appeal to the Court of Appeal as *Humphreys v HMRC*.

Working tax credit

Entitlement

10.—(1) The entitlement of the person or persons by whom a claim for working tax credit has been made is dependent on him, or either of them, being engaged in qualifying remunerative work.

(2) Regulations may for the purposes of this Part make provision—

(a) as to what is, or is not, qualifying remunerative work, and

(b) as to the circumstances in which a person is, or is not, engaged in it.

(3) The circumstances prescribed under subsection (2)(b) may differ by reference to—

(a) the age of the person or either of the persons,

(b) whether the person, or either of the persons, is disabled,

(c) whether the person, or either of the persons, is responsible for one or more children or qualifying young persons, or

(d) any other factors.

(4) Regulations may make provision for the purposes of working tax credit as to the circumstances in which a person is or is not responsible for a child or qualifying young person.

1.255

<small>AMENDMENT</small>

1. Subsections (1) and (3) are amended as they apply to polygamous units by Tax Credits (Polygamous Marriages) Regulations 2003 (SI 2003/742), reg.9.

<small>DEFINITIONS</small>

"child"—see s.8(3).
"disabled"—see s.11(7).
"engaged"—see subs.(2).
"qualifying remunerative work"—see subs.(2).
"qualifying young person"—see s.8(4).
"responsible for a child"—see subs.(4).

<small>GENERAL NOTE</small>

This section is the parallel to s.8, laying down the central test for claiming WTC by single or joint claimants, and defining or providing for definition of the key terms.

1.256

Subs. (1)

This makes the central test for WTC "being engaged in qualifying remunerative work". It is used in the regulations defining entitlement to income support and jobseeker's allowance. See the notes to Income Support (General) Regulations 1987, reg.4, and Jobseeker's Allowance Regulations 1996, reg.51, in Vol.II of this work. The test of "work" has been held by Commissioners to be wider than "employment" *(R(FC) 2/90)*, although the requirement that it be "remunerative"—defined as work done for payment or in expectation of payment—excludes volunteers *(R(IS) 12/92)*.

Although the test is the same both for tax credits and for income support and JSA, experience has shown that gaps can occur between one award ending and the

1.257

other starting, particularly where work ends near the end of a tax year for example because of ill health or disablement. HMRC has no powers to assist someone who stops being a credit claimant in these circumstances and is under no duty to forward a claim to the Department for Work and Pensions. Nor can an appeal assist such a claimant.

Subs. (2)

1.258   This provides for further definition of what is "qualifying" work, and also when someone is "engaged" in work. This is used to set the number of hours that must be worked in order to count for WTC purposes, but it also allows the start and finish of a period of work to be defined and intermittent work patterns to be subject to regulation.

See the WTC (Entitlement and Maximum Rate) Regulations 2002 (SI 2002/2005), reg.4.

Subs. (3)

1.259   This permits the qualifying conditions for WTC to be varied between different claimants. Regulation 4 of the Working Tax Credit (Entitlement and Maximum Rate) Regulations 2002 provides that the minimum work level is 16 hours a week for those with children, those over 50, and those suffering disabilities (carrying forward the tests from WFTC, New Deal 50 Plus, and DPTC) but 30 hours a week for other claimants aged 25 or over. No WTC is to be payable to those aged under 25 unless one of the "16-hour" tests applies to them.

Subs. (4)

1.260   This provides that responsibility for a child or qualifying young person may be defined differently for WTC purposes to the definition under s.8 for CTC purposes. This links with s.12, the childcare element of WTC. However, the regulations have not to date adopted any distinction.

Maximum rate

1.261   **11.**—(1) The maximum rate at which a person or persons may be entitled to working tax credit is to be determined in the prescribed manner.

(2) The prescribed manner of determination must involve the inclusion of an element which is to be included in the case of all persons entitled to working tax credit.

(3) The prescribed manner of determination must also involve the inclusion of an element in respect of the person, or either or both of the persons, engaged in qualifying remunerative work—

   (a) having a physical or mental disability which puts him at a disadvantage in getting a job, and

   (b) satisfying such other conditions as may be prescribed.

(4) The element specified in subsection (2) is to be known as the basic element of working tax credit and the element specifiedin subsection (3) is to be known as the disability element of working tax credit.

(5) The prescribed manner of determination may involve the inclusion of such other elements as may be prescribed.

(6) The other elements may (in particular) include—

   (a) an element in respect of the person, or either of the persons or the two taken together, being engaged in qualifying remunerative work to an extent prescribed for the purposes of this paragraph;

   (b) an element in respect of the persons being the members of [¹ a couple],

   (c) an element in respect of the person not being a member of [¹ a couple] but being responsible for a child or qualifying young person;

(d) an element in respect of the person, or either or both of the persons, being severely disabled; and

(e) an element in respect of the person, or either or both of the persons, being over a prescribed age, satisfying prescribed conditions and having been engaged in qualifying remunerative work for not longer than a prescribed period.

(7) A person has a physical or mental disability which puts him at a disadvantage in getting a job, or is severely disabled, for the purposes of this section only if—

(a) he satisfies prescribed conditions, or

(b) prescribed conditions exist in relation to him.

AMENDMENTS

1. For the purposes of applying this section to polygamous units, Tax Credits (Polygamous Marriages) Regulations 2003 (SI 2003/742), reg.10 omits subs.(6)(c) and introduces alternative wording to subss.(3) and (6).

2. Civil Partnership Act 2004, s.254 and Sch.24, para.145 (December 5, 2005).

DEFINITIONS

"child"—see s.8(3).
"couple"—see s.3(5A).
"physical or mental disability"—see subs.(7).
"prescribed"—see s.67.
"qualifying young person"—see s.8(4).
"severely disabled"—see subs.(7).

GENERAL NOTE

This parallels s.9 for WTC. Subsection (1) allows the determination of WTC rates to be set by regulations, but subss.(2) and (4) require that anyone entitled to WTC must receive a basic element of credit. There must also be an additional disability element in appropriate cases (carrying forward the policy of DPTC): subss. (3) and (4). Subsection (7) sets the test for the disability element. There may also be a childcare element, but this is provided for in s.12. Subsections (5) and (6) are purely permissive. Effect is given to these provisions by the WTC (Entitlement and Maximum Rate) Regulations 2002 (SI 2002/2005).

1.262

Childcare element

12.—(1) The prescribed manner of determination of the maximum rate at which a person or persons may be entitled to working tax credit may involve the inclusion, in prescribed circumstances, of a childcare element.

1.263

(2) A childcare element is an element in respect of a prescribed proportion of so much of any relevant childcare charges as does not exceed a prescribed amount.

(3) "Childcare charges" are charges of a prescribed description incurred in respect of childcare by the person, or either or both of the persons, by whom a claim for working tax credit is made.

(4) "Childcare", in relation to a person or persons, means care provided—

(a) for a child of a prescribed description for whom the person is responsible, or for whom either or both of the persons is or are responsible, and

(b) by a person of a prescribed description.

(5) The descriptions of persons prescribed under subsection (4)(b) may include descriptions of persons approved in accordance with a scheme made by the appropriate national authority under this subsection.

(6) "The appropriate national authority" means—

(a) in relation to care provided in England, the Secretary of State,

(b) in relation to care provided in Scotland, the Scottish Ministers,

(c) in relation to care provided in Wales, the National Assembly for Wales, and

(d) in relation to care provided in Northern Ireland, the Department of Health, Social Services and Public Safety.

(7) The provision made by a scheme under subsection (5) must involve the giving of approvals, in accordance with criteria determined by or under the scheme, by such of the following as the scheme specifies—

(a) the appropriate national authority making the scheme;

(b) one or more specified persons or bodies or persons or bodies of a specified description, and

(c) persons or bodies accredited under the scheme in accordance with criteria determined by or under it.

(8) A scheme under subsection (5) may authorise—

(a) the making of grants or loans to, and

(b) the charging of reasonable fees by, persons and bodies giving approvals.

AMENDMENT

1. Subsections (3) and (4) are modified, as they apply to polygamous units, by Tax Credits (Polygamous Marriages) Regulations 2003 (SI 2003/742), reg.11.

DEFINITIONS

"appropriate national authority"—see subs.(6).
"child"—see s.8(3).
"childcare"—see subs.(4).
"childcare charges"—see subs.(3).
"maximum rate"—see s.11(1).
"prescribed"—see s.67.
"tax credit"—see s.1(2).

GENERAL NOTE

1.264   The childcare element was introduced to family credit in response to a successful discrimination challenge to the previous law before the European Court of Justice in *Meyers v Adjudication Officer*, Case C-116/94 [1995] All E.R. (EC) 705. Successive governments have made it more generous, and it is now given further prominence by its own section in this Act. However, the section is in form entirely permissive, even if the failure to implement it at all might invite a further challenge to the European Court. Subsections (2)–(4) provide that the element is a credit for a part of the charges incurred by a claimant for "childcare" provided for prescribed children by prescribed persons. Regulation 7 of the Tax Credits (Income Thresholds and Determination of Rates) Regulations 2002 (SI 2002/2008) specifies the proportion as 80 per cent from April 2006. The important issue here is the identity of those who may provide the childcare. Government policy is that childcare providers should be licensed or supervised. But the way in which that is to be done is a devolved matter for the separate governments of England, Scotland, Wales and

Northern Ireland. This reflects the fact that both education and social welfare functions are now functions of the separate national authorities. Subsections (5)–(8) give effect to this. Responsibility for both policy and operation of the childcare registration rules is therefore outside the responsibilities of HMRC and outside the jurisdiction of the appeal tribunals.

Parents are often able to secure free or subsidised childcare through their employers or from national or local schemes. In these cases, the childcare element is only paid for costs not met by the other scheme. For example if a nursery place is free for the child but the parent has to meet costs such as food, then those costs alone may be claimed.

Employers can provide employees with free childcare places or vouchers for childcare, often in exchange for a salary sacrifice. See sections 318–381C of ITEPA (set out below). Where there are such schemes, parents may be able to choose between receiving employer vouchers or the childcare element of working tax credit, but they cannot receive both. It is a matter for individual calculation as to which is better. Current HMRC guidance is as follows:

"You cannot claim tax credits help for childcare costs met by your employer or with childcare vouchers. . . ."

Your family will generally be better off accepting childcare vouchers in return for a salary sacrifice if you can answer "yes" to one or more of the following:

- Your eligible childcare costs are more than £175 per week if you have one child or £300 per week if you have two or more children. In this case you will always be better off accepting childcare vouchers to cover your childcare costs above these limits.
- You are receiving tax credits at the family element (£545 per year, or £1090 per year if you have a baby aged under one) or less and you are claiming for your childcare costs.
- You pay tax on your earnings at the higher rate of 40 per cent.

Your family will generally be worse off or, at best, no better off accepting childcare vouchers in return for a salary sacrifice if you can answer "yes" to all of the following:

- You are receiving tax credits of more than £545 per year (or £1090 per year if you have a baby aged under one) and you are claiming for your childcare costs.
- You do not pay tax on your earnings at the higher rate of 40 per cent.
- Your eligible childcare costs are no more than £175 per week if you have one child or £300 per week if you have two or more children."

Rate

Rate

13.—(1) Where, in the case of a person or persons entitled to a tax credit, the relevant income does not exceed the income threshold (or his or their entitlement arises by virtue of section 7(2)), the rate at which he is or they are entitled to the tax credit is the maximum rate for his or their case.

(2) Regulations shall make provision as to the manner of determining the rate (if any) at which a person is, or persons are, entitled to a tax credit in any other case.

1.265

(3) The manner of determination prescribed under subsection (2)—

(a) may involve the making of adjustments so as to avoid fractional amounts, and

(b) may include provision for securing that, where the rate at which a person or persons would be entitled to a tax credit would be less than a prescribed rate, there is no rate in his or their case.

DEFINITIONS

"the income threshold"—see s.7(1)(a).
"maximum rate"—see ss.9(1) and 11(1).
"prescribed"—see s.67.
"relevant income"—see s.7(3).
"tax credit"—see s.1(2).

GENERAL NOTE

1.266   This short section supplements s.7 in defining the maximum rate of WTC for a claimant, and a minimum level of payment, and provides for regulations to determine these. See the Tax Credits (Income Thresholds and Determination of Rates) Regulations 2002 (SI 2002/2008), which set out a multi-stage formula.

Decisions

Initial decisions

1.267   **14.**—(1) On a claim for a tax credit the Board must decide—
(a) whether to make an award of the tax credit, and
(b) if so, the rate at which to award it.
(2) Before making their decision the Board may by notice—
(a) require the person, or [either or both][any or all][1] of the persons, by whom the claim is made to provide any information or evidence which the Board consider they may need for making their decision, or
(b) require any person of a prescribed description to provide any information or evidence of a prescribed description which the Board consider they may need for that purpose, by the date specified in the notice.
(3) The Board's power to decide the rate at which to award a tax credit includes power to decide to award it at a nil rate.

AMENDMENTS

1. Subsection (2) is modified in its application to polygamous units by Tax Credits (Polygamous Marriages) Regulations 2003 (SI 2003/742), reg.12.
2. References to "the Board" are now references to the Commissioners for Revenue and Customs: CRCA 2005, s.4.
3. The section is disapplied for claimants subject to immigration control. See Tax Credits (Immigration) Regulations 2003 (SI 2003/623) regs 3, 4.

DEFINITIONS

"claim"—see s.3(8).
"the Board"—see s.67.
"tax credit"—see s.1(2).

GENERAL NOTE

This section imposes a duty on HMRC to decide a claim properly made under **1.268**
s.3 by making an award (or not), but it sets no time limit on that decision. An award
is a decision to pay the tax credit. It is not a decision on entitlement. That is made
later, under s.18. This explains the section title "initial decisions" (in the first draft
of the Bill it was "provisional decisions"). Section 7(10) provides that HMRC may
make this decision on the basis of an estimate. A decision under subs.(1) can be
appealed (s.38). HMRC terms these notices "award notices".

This imposes the formal duty to deal with a claim by making or refusing an
award. HMRC may use the power to estimate the income of claimants under
s.7(10) rather than wait for information from an examination of the claim. Or it
may make an award and examine the claim more thoroughly afterwards. A decision
to award or refuse under this subsection is subject to appeal: s.38(1). However,
HMRC practice is to attempt to deal with any such appeal by a settlement under the
terms of s.54 of the Taxes Managements Act 1970. See the note to s.39 below.

HMRC has now automated most of the process. There is no "ownership" of a tax
credits decision. One team run the computers that make the initial award decisions,
then other teams take over to deal with other aspects of the case. There is also no
"local office" culture in HMRC tax credit administration. That being so, it would
appear to be arguable that the recognition of that aspect of DWP administration by
the House of Lords in *Hinchy* would have no application to HMRC.

For judicial criticism of the practice of HMRC issuing informal decisions
and then, sometimes after several months, later issuing formal decisions see
CTC/244/2008, para.3. In *CTC/3692/2008* a social security commissioner applied
R(IB) 2/04, a decision of a Tribunal of three Commissioners, to HMRC tax credit
decisions in the same way as to social security decisions. He decided that an HMRC
decision was so faulty that the only proper course was to allow the appeal and send
the issue back to HMRC to take the decision properly.

Subs.(2)

This empowers HMRC to require further information before making the deci- **1.269**
sion by notice (see s.45 as to the notice). Penalties attach to failure to reply to a
notice or to wrong replies (ss.31 and 32). The subsection also permits information
to be required from others. This has been applied by the Tax Credits (Claims and
Notifications) Regulations 2002 (SI 2002/2014), regs 30–32 to employers and those
providing childcare.

HMRC practice appears not to be using this section and those that follow as
drafted. Subsection (2) gives the Revenue powers to seek information "before
making their decision". There are separate powers once an award is made. HMRC
practice is to examine claims both before and during the award in the same way. In
other words, the award is often made and then examined. This is possible for tax
credits, as they are based on a full year's claim at a time, in a way that is not possible
for most social security benefits, to which individuals have entitlements on a daily or
weekly basis. Rather, it follows the approach long used by HMRC under the PAYE
system for taxing employment income.

In decision *CIS/995/2004* Commissioner Mesher confirmed the view stated
above that the power in this section is available to deal with enquiries only *before*
a decision is made. The Commissioner also criticises the standard letter TC602
used by HMRC in connection with these enquiries. It follows that HMRC have
no power to impose a penalty under s.32 for failure to answer an enquiry that is
purportedly made under this section but not in accordance with its terms. However,
the power cited by HMRC in its notices to claimants about both enquiries and
examinations cite s.19 powers, not s.14 powers (see WTC/FS1 and WTC/FS2
issued in 2007). But the power under s.19 is available only after a s.18 decision has
been taken. If *CIS/995/2004* is correct, it would seem there is no power to impose
a penalty for a failure to respond to a check made between the issue of the initial

award under this section and the final decision under s.18 save where HMRC can show reasonable grounds for using its s.16 powers. This provides a limit on HMRC checking powers that may not have been intended but nonetheless removes liability to penalties.

Subs. (3)

1.270   This allows the award of a nil rate, so awarding a tax credit without payment. This "has the effect of keeping an entitlement going even though no money is in payment or in process. It makes it easier for the claimant and it makes it easier for us" (Baroness Hollis, House of Lords Grand Committee, May 23, 2002, CWH 146). This again reflects the fact that at this stage the decision is an initial decision only. It also means that a claimant with a nil award can ask for a review to deal with a change of circumstances rather than having to make a new claim. This gives a practical solution to a recurring problem under the SSAA 1992 and the SSA 1998 of reviews, revisions and supersessions. The adoption of this practice will, in particular, avoid some of the more awkward aspects of supersession.

Revised decisions after notifications

1.271   **15.**—(1) Where notification of a change of circumstances increasing the maximum rate at which a person or persons may be entitled to a tax credit is given in accordance with regulations under section 6(1), the Board must decide whether (and, if so, how) to amend the award of the tax credit made to him or them.

(2) Before making their decision the Board may by notice—

    (a) require the person by whom the notification is given to provide any information or evidence which the Board consider they may need for making their decision; or

    (b) require any person of a prescribed description to provide any information or evidence of a prescribed description which the Board consider they may need for that purpose,

by the date specified in the notice.

AMENDMENT

1. The section is disapplied for claimants subject to immigration control. See Tax Credits (Immigration) Regulations 2003 (SI 2003/623) regs 3, 4.

DEFINITIONS

"the Board"—see s.67.
"maximum rate"—see ss.9(1) and 11(1).
"prescribed"—see s.67.
"tax credit"—see s.1(2).

GENERAL NOTE

1.272   Section 6 makes provision for a claimant to tell HMRC of a change of circumstances that should or may increase the tax credit to be awarded. This section imposes a duty on HMRC to consider if the award made under s.14 should be amended if such a notification is given (subs.(1)). The decision, including a decision not to amend, is appealable (s.38). Subsection (2) gives HMRC the same powers to enquire as s.14(2). The same provisions about notice (s.45) and penalties (ss.31 and 32) apply. Following the comment in s.14, it may be noted that although the heading of the section refers to revision, the text of the section does not. The power in this section is to "amend". That is the term used in the TMA 1970 when either the taxpayer or HMRC changes a tax return (see ss.9ZA and 9ZB of the TMA 1970).

Other revised decisions

16.—(1) Where, at any time during the period for which an award of a tax credit is made to a person or persons, the Board have reasonable grounds for believing—

    (a) that the rate at which the tax credit has been awarded to him or them for the period differs from the rate at which he is, or they are, entitled to the tax credit for the period; or

    (b) that he has, or they have, ceased to be, or never been, entitled to the tax credit for the period,

the Board may decide to amend or terminate the award.

(2) Where, at any time during the period for which an award of a tax credit is made to a person or persons, the Board believe—

    (a) that the rate at which a tax credit has been awarded to him or them for the period may differ from the rate at which he is, or they are, entitled to it for the period, or

    (b) that he or they may have ceased to be, or never been, entitled to the tax credit for the period,

the Board may give a notice under subsection (3).

(3) A notice under this subsection may—

    (a) require the person, or either or both of the persons, to whom the tax credit was awarded to provide any information or evidence which the Board consider they may need for considering whether to amend or terminate the award under subsection (1); or

    (b) require any person of a prescribed description to provide any information or evidence of a prescribed description which the Board consider they may need for that purpose,

by the date specified in the notice.

1.273

AMENDMENTS

1. Subsection (3) is modified as it appplies to polygamous units by Tax Credits (Polygamous Marriages) Regulations 2003 (SI 2003/742), reg.13.
2. The section is disapplied for claimants subject to immigration control. See Tax Credits (Immigration) Regulations 2003 (SI 2003/623) regs 3, 4.

DEFINITIONS

"the Board"—see s.67.
"tax credit"—see s.1(2).

GENERAL NOTE

The procedure laid down in this section gives the Board flexibility to alter a decision at any time because HMRC has "reasonable grounds to believe" that a change is appropriate (subs.(1)). These general terms reflect the flexibility given to the Secretary of State under the SSA 1998, and transferred to the Board by the TCA 1999. But it is clear that, unlike that under the TCA 1999, the procedure is not a mirror of the 1998 Act procedure. As noted in s.15, the drafter has deliberately avoided the revision and supersession language of both the SSAA 1992 and the SSA 1998. Despite the heading of the section, the operative power is to "amend" or "terminate" an award. Both this section and s.15 also avoid introducing the troublesome distinction between revisions and supersessions under the SSA 1998.

1.274

Again in contrast to the 1998 procedures, this section provides a power, not a duty. In *CTC/4390/2004* the Commissioner noted that on an appeal against a s.16 decision the tribunal also had a power, not a duty, to act. The express right to appeal a s.16 decision is granted in s.38(1). In such cases it is for the tribunal to decide for itself if there are reasonable grounds to make the decision, and if so it whether a decision is to be made.

The Board has power to give notice if it "believes" that the award of a tax credit may be wrong (subs.(2)). As might be expected, this is wider than the power to amend or terminate. The notice may require information or evidence from claimants and others, as defined in regulations (subs.(3)). Current regulations empower HMRC to seek information from employers and childcare providers (see note to s.14). Penalties attach to the failure to respond or to a false response (ss.31 and 32).

A standard HMRC use of the section is, somewhat obscurely, announced as a footnote to the regular series of official statistics on tax credits. They explain by way of a note to the table of total awards why, every year, there has been a reduction in the total number of awards made for both forms of tax credit in December as compared with the previous April as follows:

"Note: between each April and December families' awards are stopped at (a) 31 August if their only qualifying child falls out of entitlement at that date, or (b) in the autumn if they fail to return their Annual Declaration for the previous year. This introduces some seasonality into the figures."

In *CTC/2576/2004* the Commissioner set aside a decision of a tribunal confirming a decision of HMRC under s.16. The Commissioner also set aside the s.16 decision and referred the matter back to HMRC. HMRC could not produce the actual decision made, and had contradicted itself in letters to the claimant. The tribunal considered this in the same way as a revision or supersession under the SSA 1998. The Commissioner found that the tribunal erred in this approach and should have relied on the TCA 2002 procedures. In addition, HMRC had erred in both its versions of its original decision. The Commissioner commented that "the decision of the Board was not properly articulated in that the intimations of it to the claimant were contradictory". It is not clear from the decision whether s.23 of this Act was also considered, as HMRC conceded that its decisions were in error.

In *CTC/3981/2006* the Commissioner analysed both the s.16 procedure and the effectiveness of appeals against s.16 decisions.

Final notice

1.275   **17.**—(1) Where a tax credit has been awarded for the whole or part of a tax year—

(a) for awards made on single claims, the Board must give a notice relating to the tax year to the person to whom the tax credit was awarded, and

(b) for awards made on joint claims, the Board must give such a notice to the persons to whom the tax credit was awarded (with separate copies of the notice for each of them if the Board consider appropriate).

(2) The notice must either—

(a) require that the person or persons must, by the date specified for the purposes of this subsection, declare that the relevant circumstances were as specified or state any respects in which they were not, or

(b) inform the person or persons that he or they will be treated as having declared in response to the notice that the relevant circumstances were as specified unless, by that date, he states or they state any respects in which they were not.

(3) "Relevant circumstances" means circumstances (other than income) affecting—

(a) the entitlement of the person, or joint entitlement of the persons, to the tax credit, or

(b) the amount of the tax credit to which he was entitled, or they were jointly entitled, for the tax year.

(4) The notice must either—

(a) require that the person or persons must, by the date specified for the purposes of this subsection, declare that the amount of the current year income or estimated current year income (depending on which is specified) was the amount, or fell within the range, specified or comply with subsection (5), or

(b) inform the person or persons that he or they will be treated as having declared in response to the notice that the amount of the current year income or estimated current year income (depending on which is specified) was the amount, or fell within the range, specified unless, by that date, he complies or they comply with subsection (5).

(5) To comply with this subsection the person or persons must either—

(a) state the current year income or his or their estimate of the current year income (making clear which); or

(b) declare that, throughout the period to which the award related, subsection (1) of section 7 did not apply to him or them by virtue of subsection (2) of that section.

(6) The notice may—

(a) require that the person or persons must, by the date specified for the purposes of subsection (4), declare that the amount of the previous year income was the amount, or fell within the range, specified or comply with subsection (7), or

(b) inform the person or persons that he or they will be treated as having declared in response to the notice that the amount of the previous year income was the amount, or fell within the range, specified unless, by that date, he complies or they comply with subsection (7).

(7) To comply with this subsection the person or persons must either—

(a) state the previous year income, or

(b) make the declaration specified in subsection (5)(b).

(8) The notice must inform the person or persons that if he or they—

(a) makes or make a declaration under paragraph (a) of subsection (4), or is or are treated as making a declaration under paragraph (b) of that subsection, in relation to estimated current year income (or the range within which estimated current year income fell); or

(b) states or state under subsection (5)(a) his or their estimate of the current year income;

he or they will be treated as having declared in response to the notice that the amount of the (actual) current year income was as estimated unless, by the date specified for the purposes of this subsection, he states or they state the current year income.

(9) "Specified", in relation to a notice, means specified in the notice.

(10) Regulations may—

(a) provide that, in prescribed circumstances, one person may act for another in response to a notice under this section, and

(b) provide that, in prescribed circumstances, anything done by one member of a [²couple] in response to a notice given under this section is to be treated as also done by the other member of [²the couple].

AMENDMENTS

1. Subsection (10) is modified as it applies to polygamous units by Tax Credits (Polygamous Marriages) Regulations 2003 (SI 2003/742), reg.14.

2. Civil Partnership Act 2004, s.254 and Sch.24, para.145 (December 5, 2005).

3. The section is disapplied for claimants subject to immigration control. See Tax Credits (Immigration) Regulations 2003 (SI 2003/623) regs 3, 4.

DEFINITIONS

"the Board"—see s.67.
"couple"—see s.3(5A).
"current year income"—see s.7(4).
"joint claims"—see s.3(8).
"prescribed"—see s.67.
"previous year income"—see s.7(5).
"relevant circumstances"—see subs.(3).
"specified"—see subs.(9).
"tax credit"—see s.1(2).
"tax year"—see s.47.

GENERAL NOTE

1.276   What are now ss.17 and 18 were originally drafted as one clause. It was divided by amendments in the House of Lords into the notice provisions (s.17) and the decision provisions (s.18), to avoid it being overlong. Together the two sections provide the regime for checking the s.14 initial decision on an award before turning it into an entitlement, and then for making the entitlement decision. The underlying pattern is that the award decision must be made in response to a claim. Payment is then made under the award decision for a tax year. At the end of the tax year, HMRC uses the s.17 powers to check whether the claimant is, or remains, entitled to the tax credit awarded, or to some higher or lower rate of tax credit. After checking, a "final decision" is made on entitlement.

The effect of subs.(1) is that all awards of tax credit must be checked. In every case a notice must be sent to a claimant (or joint claimants). Notices must take one of two forms. One is a demand for a declaration that there has been no change of relevant circumstances (subs.(2)(a)). It can also demand details (or an estimate) of the current year's income (subs.(4)(a)). The other is a notice telling people that it will be assumed that there is no change of circumstances unless any changes are reported by a given date (subs.(2)(b)). It can also tell people that it is assumed that their income is of an assumed level or range unless a declaration is made stating otherwise (subs.(4)(b)). The notice may also take either of those approaches about the previous year's income (subs.(6)). Further provisions are laid down in the Tax Credits (Claims and Notifications) Regulations 2002 (SI 2002/2014). The section also states the ways in which people must comply with these notices. Penalties may be imposed on failures to reply and wrong replies (ss.31 and 32).

HMRC calls the notices issued under this section "Annual Declarations". The annual declarations may also constitute claims under s.3. The point may arise as to which years the declaration and claim relate to. In *CTC/1594/2006* the Commissioner accepted HMRC's argument that it was for HMRC to decide this, subject to judicial review rather than appeal, but also suggested it might depend on the wording used.

Decisions after final notice

1.277   **18.**—(1) After giving a notice under section 17, the Board must decide —

(a) whether the person was entitled, or the persons were jointly entitled, to the tax credit, and

(b) if so, the amount of the tax credit to which he was entitled, or they were jointly entitled, for the tax year.

(2) But, subject to subsection (3), that decision must not be made before a declaration or statement has been made in response to the relevant provisions of the notice.

(3) If a declaration or statement has not been made in response to the relevant provisions of the notice on or before the date specified for the purposes of section 17(4), that decision may be made after that date.

(4) In subsections (2) and (3) "the relevant provisions of the notice" means—

(a) the provision included in the notice by virtue of subsection (2) of section 17,

(b) the provision included in the notice by virtue of subsection (4) of that section, and

(c) any provision included in the notice by virtue of subsection (6) of that section.

(5) Where the Board make a decision under subsection (1) on or before the date referred to in subsection (3), they may revise it if a new declaration or statement is made on or before that date.

(6) If the person or persons to whom a notice under section 17 is given is or are within paragraph (a) or (b) of subsection (8) of that section, the Board must decide again—

(a) whether the person was entitled, or the persons were jointly entitled, to the tax credit, and

(b) if so, the amount of the tax credit to which he was entitled, or they were jointly entitled, for the tax year.

(7) But, subject to subsection (8), that decision must not be made before a statement has been made in response to the provision included in the notice by virtue of subsection (8) of section 17.

(8) If a statement has not been made in response to the provision included in the notice by virtue of that subsection on or before the date specified for the purposes of that subsection, that decision may be made after that date.

(9) Where the Board make a decision under subsection (6) on or before the date referred to in subsection (8), they may revise it if a new statement is made on or before that date.

(10) Before exercising a function imposed or conferred on them by subsection (1), (5), (6) or (9), the Board may by notice require the person, or either or both of the persons, to whom the notice under section 17 was given to provide any further information or evidence which the Board consider they may need for exercising the function by the date specified in the notice.

(11) Subject to sections 19 and 20 and regulations under section 21 (and to any revision under subsection (5) or (9) and any appeal)—

(a) in a case in which a decision is made under subsection (6) in relation to a person or persons and a tax credit for a tax year, that decision, and

(b) in any other case, the decision under subsection (1) in relation to a person or persons and a tax credit for a tax year,

is conclusive as to the entitlement of the person, or the joint entitlement of the persons, to the tax credit for the tax year and the amount of the tax credit to which he was entitled, or they were jointly entitled, for the tax year.

AMENDMENTS

1. Subsection (10) is modified as it applies to polygamous units by Tax Credits (Polygamous Marriages) Regulations 2003 (SI 2003/742), reg.15.
2. The section is modified for claimants subject to immigration control. See Tax Credits (Immigration) Regulations 2003 (SI 2003/623) regs 3, 4.

DEFINITIONS

"the Board"—see s.67.
"prescribed"—see s.67.
"relevant provisions of the notice"—see subs.(4).
"tax credit"—see s.1(2).
"tax year"—see s.47.

GENERAL NOTE

1.278   HMRC calls these notices "finalised awards". In *CTC/2113/2006* a Commissioner criticised this use of language, and a more general failure to distinguish between awards and entitlements, in HMRC notices and literature in the case papers.

See the note to s.17 for the general scheme of which this is part. Subsection (1) of this section imposes the duty on HMRC to make a decision on entitlement in every case, but only after the s.17 notice procedure has been followed (subs.(2)) or the full time to comply has been allowed (subs.(3)). Subsection (4) links the procedures under this section with the relevant notice provisions in s.17. Subsection (5) allows an entitlement decision under subs.(1) to be revised if there is a reply or further reply from a claimant after a decision has been made. The use of "revise" was avoided in earlier sections in favour of "amend" (despite their headings: see ss.15 and 16), but is here applied to changes to a final decision. Such revisions can be of the whole or only part of the decision. The language avoids attaching formalities or threshold conditions to the process. Subsections (6)–(9) repeat the substance of subss.(1)–(5) for claimants who estimated their current year income in their claims or initial responses to the s.17 notice. In either case, HMRC may require further information (subs.(10)). The standard penalty regime applies to subs.(10). Subsection (11) makes a subs.(1) or subs.(6) decision conclusive unless it is revised under subss.(5) or (9), or it is appealed under s.38, or it is altered under any of the powers in ss.19–21. The Claimant Compliance Manual (CCM) (on the CCM, see note to TCA 2002, s.31 below) emphasises that a decision under subs.(6) should be taken by an officer as a "best judgment" decision, not just a guess. "You can use some guess-work but it must be honest guess-work" (at para.10270).

For an analysis of the procedure under s.18, see CTC/2662/2005.

Power to enquire

1.279   **19.**—(1) The Board may enquire into—
    (a) the entitlement of a person, or the joint entitlement of persons, to a tax credit for a tax year, and
    (b) the amount of the tax credit to which he was entitled, or they were jointly entitled, for the tax year,
if they give notice to the person, or each of the persons, during the period allowed for the initiation of an enquiry.
    (2) As part of the enquiry the Board may by notice—
    (a) require the person, or either or both of the persons, to provide any

146

information or evidence which the Board consider they may need for the purposes of the enquiry, or

(b) require any person of a prescribed description to provide any information or evidence of a prescribed description which the Board consider they may need for those purposes, by the date specified in the notice.

(3) On an enquiry the Board must decide—

(a) whether the person was entitled, or the persons were jointly entitled, to the tax credit, and

(b) if so, the amount of the tax credit to which he was entitled, or they were jointly entitled,

for the tax year.

(4) The period allowed for the initiation of an enquiry is the period beginning immediately after the relevant section 18 decision and ending—

(a) if the person, or either of the persons, to whom the enquiry relates is required by section 8 of the Taxes Management Act 1970 (c.9) to make a return, with the day on which the return becomes final (or, if both of the persons are so required and their returns become final on different days, with the later of those days), or

(b) in any other case, one year after the beginning of the relevant section 17 date.

(5) "The relevant section 18 decision" means—

(a) in a case in which a decision must be made under subsection (6) of section 18 in relation to the person or persons and the tax year to which the enquiry relates, that decision; and

(b) in any other case, the decision under subsection (1) of that section in relation to the person or persons and that tax year.

(6) "The relevant section 17 date" means—

(a) in a case in which a statement may be made by the person or persons in response to provision included by virtue of subsection (8) of section 17 in the notice given to him or them under that section in relation to the tax year, the date specified in the notice for the purposes of that subsection, and

(b) in any other case, the date specified for the purposes of subsection (4) of that section in the notice given to him or them under that section in relation to the tax year.

(7) A return becomes final—

(a) if it is enquired into under section 9A of the Taxes Management Act 1970 (c.9), when the enquiries are completed (within the meaning of section 28A of that Act), or

(b) otherwise, at the end of the period specified in subsection (2) of that section in relation to the return.

(8) An enquiry is completed at the time when the Board give notice to the person or persons of their decision under subsection (3); but if the Board give notice to the persons at different times the enquiry is completed at the later of those times.

(9) The person, or either of the persons, to whom the enquiry relates may at any time before such notice is given apply for a direction that the Board must give such a notice.

[⁴ (10) Any such application is to be subject to the relevant provisions of Part 5 of the Taxes Management Act 1970 (see, in particular, section 48(2) (b) of that Act), and the tribunal must give the direction applied for unless satisfied that the Board have reasonable grounds for not making the decision or giving the notice.]

(11) Where the entitlement of a person, or the joint entitlement of persons, to a tax credit for a tax year has been enquired into under this section, it is not to be the subject of a further notice under subsection (1).

(12) Subject to section 20 and regulations under section 21 (and to any appeal), a decision under subsection (3) in relation to a person or persons and a tax credit for a tax year is conclusive as to the entitlement of the person, or the joint entitlement of the persons, to the tax credit for the tax year and the amount of the tax credit to which he was entitled, or they were jointly entitled, for the tax year.

AMENDMENTS

1. Subsections (2), (4) and (9) are modified for polygamous units by Tax Credits (Polygamous Marriages) Regulations 2003 (SI 2003/742), reg.16.
2. Subsection (10) is modified by TCA 2002, s.63(5)(a), the modification being indicated by square brackets.
3. The section is modified for claimants subject to immigration control. See Tax Credits (Immigration) Regulations 2003 (SI 2003/623) regs 3, 4.
4. Transfer of Tribunal Functions and Revenue and Customs Appeals Order 2009 (SI 2009/56), art.3(1), Sch.1, para.313 (April 1, 2009).

DEFINITIONS

"the Board"—see s.67.
"General Commissioners"—see s.47.
"prescribed"—see s.67.
"Special Commissioners"—see s.47.
"the relevant section 17 date"—see subs.(6).
"the relevant section 18 decision"—see subs.(5).
"tax credit"—see s.1(2).

GENERAL NOTE

1.280   This provision gives HMRC a broad general power similar to that in s.9A of the TMA 1970 (power to enquire into self-assessment returns) to enquire into the correctness of a s.18 entitlement decision. An enquiry under this section can be opened at any time after the s.18 decision is made until a year after the final date for replying to a s.17 notice, unless HMRC uses its power to issue a demand for a personal tax return under s.8 of the TMA 1970 on the claimant. A return for a year must be made by January 31 next after the tax year ends (each April) or, if demanded later, three months after it is required. Section 9A (which entitles HMRC to issue a notice of enquiry into a return under s.8) allows about a year (the period is defined precisely) for a HMRC enquiry to follow a personal return.

An individual who is the subject of an enquiry has the same power to apply to a tribunal to stop the enquiry as exists for the equivalent income tax provisions, save that the application goes to the appeal tribunal (see s.63), not a tax tribunal.

Subss. (9) and (10) allow an individual to ask a tribunal to close an HMRC enquiry. This power has been created because there is otherwise no time limit to end an enquiry provided that it is started by HMRC within the correct time limits. The practice of tax tribunals, approved by the courts, is to deal with many applications by setting a time limit on HMRC rather than closing the enquiry immediately. It is also clear that rejection by a tribunal of one application to close an enquiry does not prevent an individual later making another application if the enquiry continues. The amended version of subs. (10) aligns the procedure with the new procedure for reviewing all tax decisions introduced by the Finance Act

2008 by way of amendments now in the Taxes Management Act 1970 from s.48. HMRC is given the right to review any decision before it goes forward to a tribunal, unless the appellant directly notifies the tribunal of the decision that is subject to appeal.

The power to look into a decision about entitlement to tax credits is referred to both in this section and in practice as an enquiry. This is to be distinguished from an investigation into a claim for, or award of, a tax credit, which is referred to by HMRC as an examination. The key difference is that an award is provisional, while an enquiry relates to an award that has been or is being finalised to give rise to entitlement.

HMRC have issued a short series of factsheets about its powers and practices for claimants: WTC/FS1 on enquiries; WTC/FS2 on examinations; WTC/FS3 on formal requests for information; and WTC/FS4 on meetings with an officer of Revenue and Customs.

Decisions on discovery

20.—(1) Where in consequence of a person's income tax liability being revised the Board have reasonable grounds for believing that a conclusive decision relating to his entitlement to a tax credit for a tax year (whether or not jointly with another person) is not correct, the Board may decide to revise that decision.   1.281

(2) A person's income tax liability is revised—

(a) on the taking effect of an amendment of a return of his under section 9ZA(1) of the Taxes Management Act 1970,

(b) on the issue of a notice of correction under section 9ZB of that Act amending a return of his (provided that he does not give a notice of rejection before the end of the period of thirty days beginning with the date of issue of the notice of correction),

(c) on the amendment of an assessment of his by notice under section 9C of that Act,

(d) on the amendment of a return of his under section 12ABA(3)(a) of that Act,

(e) on the amendment of a return of his under subsection (6)(a) of section 12ABB of that Act after the correction of a partnership return under that section (provided that the amendment does not cease to have effect by reason of the rejection of the correction under subsection (4) of that section),

(f) on the issue of a closure notice under section 28A of that Act making amendments of a return of his;

(g) on the amendment of a return of his under section 28B(4)(a) of that Act,

(h) on the making of an assessment as regards him under section 29(1) of that Act,

(i) on the vacation of the whole or part of an assessment of his under section 32 of that Act,

(j) on giving him relief under section 33 of that Act, or

(k) on the determination (or settlement) of an appeal against the making, amendment or vacation of an assessment or return, or a decision on a claim for relief, under any of the provisions mentioned in paragraphs (c), (f) and (h) to (j).

(3) But no decision may be made under subsection (1)—

(a) unless it is too late to enquire into the person's entitlement under section 19, or

(b) after the period of one year beginning when the person's income tax liability is revised.

(4) Where the Board have reasonable grounds for believing that—

(a) a conclusive decision relating to the entitlement of a person, or the joint entitlement of persons, to a tax credit for a tax year is not correct, and

(b) that is attributable to fraud or neglect on the part of the person, or of either of the persons, or on the part of any person acting for him, or either of them,

the Board may decide to revise that decision.

(5) But no decision may be made under subsection (4)—

(a) unless it is too late to enquire into the entitlement, or joint entitlement, under section 19, or

(b) after the period of five years beginning with the end of the tax year to which the conclusive decision relates.

(6) "Conclusive decision", in relation to the entitlement of a person, or joint entitlement of persons, to a tax credit for a tax year, means—

(a) a decision in relation to it under section 18(1), (5), (6) or (9) or 19(3) or a previous decision under this section, or

(b) a decision under regulations under section 21 relating to a decision within paragraph (a),

including a decision made on an appeal against such a decision.

(7) Subject to any subsequent decision under this section and to regulations under section 21 (and to any appeal), a decision under subsection (1) or (4) in relation to a person or persons and a tax credit for a tax year is conclusive as to the entitlement of the person, or the joint entitlement of the persons, to the tax credit for the tax year and the amount of the tax credit to which he was entitled, or they were jointly entitled, for the tax year.

AMENDMENT

1. Subsection (4) is modified as it applies to polygamous units by Tax Credits (Polygamous Marriages) Regulations 2003 (SI 2003/742), reg.17.

CROSS-REFERENCES

1.282 TMA 1970:

s.9ZA	Amendment of personal or trustee return by taxpayer
s.9ZB	Correction of personal return by taxpayer
s.9C	Amendment of self-assessment during enquiry to prevent loss of tax
s.12ABA	Amendment of partnership return by taxpayer
s.12ABB	Correction of partnership return by Revenue
s.28A	Completion of enquiry into personal or trustee return
s.28B	Completion of enquiry into partnership return
s.29	Assessment where loss of tax discovered
s.32	Double assessment
s.33	Error or mistake

DEFINITIONS

"conclusive decision"—see subs.(6).
"income tax"—see ICTA 1988, s.1.
"prescribed"—see: s.67.
"tax credit"—see s.1(2).

GENERAL NOTE

Discovery is the traditional term used for finding out or taking informed guesses about undisclosed income for income tax purposes. The power to make assessments where loss of tax is discovered is in s.29 of the TMA 1970. This section is wider than that, although in part it flows from it. Section 29 allows an officer who discovers unassessed tax or excessive relief to make an assessment of the amount which, in the officer's opinion, ought to be charged to tax, and also imposes other conditions before the power can be used. This section, by contrast, allows action by HMRC in two sets of circumstances.

The first is if HMRC has reasonable grounds for believing an otherwise conclusive decision about tax credit (defined in subs.(6)) is not correct because of a revision of income tax liability (subs.(1)). HMRC may act if one of the TMA 1970 powers listed in subs.(2) has been used for a revision. These include s.29 and also the powers to revisit personal and partnership tax returns and decisions made by settlement or on appeal. Revisions under this power can be made only if it is too late to use s.19. And they cannot be made unless the revision is made within a year of the income tax revision (subs.(3)).

The second power (in subs.(4)) arises where HMRC has reasonable grounds to believe that an otherwise conclusive decision is wrong because of "fraud or neglect". "Fraud or neglect" are not defined in the Act. They are based on the version of s.29(4) of the Taxes Management Act 1970 in force when this Act was enacted. From April 6, 2009 s.29(4) is amended to refer to "carelessly or deliberately" and those terms are given definitions. The new terms apply to all tax penalties but have not been applied to tax credits. There has been mininal use by HMRC of, and no case law relating to, this penalty provision.

A decision made under this section is itself conclusive, subject only to further decisions under this section or on appeal or because of official error (subs.(7)).

Decisions subject to official error

21. Regulations may make provision for a decision under section 14(1), 15(1), 16(1), 18(1), (5), (6) or (9), 19(3) or 20(1) or (4) to be revised in favour of the person or persons to whom it relates if it is incorrect by reason of official error (as defined by the regulations).

GENERAL NOTE

"Official error" is defined by the Tax Credits (Official Error) Regulations 2003 (SI 2003/692). See the note on those regulations. The provision is significantly narrower than the equivalent provision for income tax in s.33 of the TMA 1970 (error or mistake), which applies to any error or mistake.

Information etc. requirements: supplementary

22.—(1) Regulations may make provision as to the manner and form in which—
(a) information or evidence is to be provided in compliance with a requirement imposed by a notice under section 14(2), 15(2), 16(3), 18(10) or 19(2), or
(b) a declaration or statement is to be made in response to a notice under section 17.

(2) Regulations may make provision as to the dates which may be specified in a notice under section 14(2), 15(2), 16(3), 17, 18(10) or 19(2).

GENERAL NOTE

These regulation-making powers are necessary because the standard regulations applying to social security decision-making (the Social Security and Child

1.283

1.284

1.285

1.286

1.287

Support (Decisions and Appeals) Regulations 1999 (SI 1999/991)) do not apply and there are no equivalents in the TMA 1970. The regulations made under these powers are the Tax Credits (Claims and Notifications) Regulations 2002 (SI 2002/2014).

Notice of decisions

1.288   **23.**—(1) When a decision is made under section 14(1), 15(1), 16(1), 18(1), (5), (6) or (9), 19(3) or 20(1) or (4) or regulations under section 21, the Board must give notice of the decision to the person, or each of the persons, to whom it relates.

(2) Notice of a decision must state the date on which it is given and include details of any right to appeal against the decision under section 38.

(3) Notice need not be given of a decision made under section 14(1) or 18(1) or (6) on the basis of declarations made or treated as made by the person or persons in response to the notice given to him or them under section 17 if—

(a) that notice, or

(b) in the case of a decision under subsection (6) of section 18, that notice or the notice of the decision under subsection (1) of that section,

stated what the decision would be and the date on which it would be made.

DEFINITION

"the Board"—see s.67.

GENERAL NOTE

1.289   This section requires HMRC to adopt the same approach as for social security decisions of giving formal notice of every decision (save in limited cases where notice has already been given). The notice must set out any appeal rights. Section 45 makes provision for the form of a notice. Further details are laid down in the Tax Credits (Claims and Notifications) Regulations 2002 (SI 2002/2014). However, it may be viewed as significant that this provision is in primary legislation, while the equivalent for social security purposes (Social Security and Child Support (Decisions and Appeals) Regulations 1999 (SI 1999/991), reg.28) is made by regulation only. It is suggested therefore that the mandatory terms of subs.(1) (the Board *must* give notice) and subs.(2) (the notice *must* state) are not amenable to the somewhat relaxed approach to formalities applied to the social security equivalent (see the note to reg.28 of those Regulations). In particular, if no notice is given, it is arguable that no effective decision has been made, or alternatively that the decision is not final and the appeal period cannot start running.

The resulting effect on appeal rights is compounded by HMRC practice to give informal decisions before giving decisions to which this provision applies. See for example the criticism in *CTC/244/2008* para.3.

Payment

Payments

1.290   **24.**—(1) Where the Board have made an award of a tax credit, the amount of the tax credit awarded must be paid to the person to whom the award is made, subject to subsections (2) and (3).

(2) Where an award of a tax credit is made to the members of [²a couple], payments of the tax credit, or of any element of the tax credit, are to be made to whichever of them is prescribed.

(3) Where an award of a tax credit is made on a claim which was made by one person on behalf of another, payments of the tax credit, or of any element of the tax credit, are to be made to whichever of those persons is prescribed.

(4) Where an award of a tax credit has been made to a person or persons for the whole or part of a tax year, payments may, in prescribed circumstances, continue to be made for any period, after the tax year, within which he is or they are entitled to make a claim for the tax credit for the next tax year.

(5) Payments made under subsection (4) are to be treated for the purposes of this section and the following provisions of this Part as if they were payments of the tax credit for the next tax year.

(6) Subject to section 25, payments of a tax credit must be made by the Board.

(7) Regulations may make provision about the time when and the manner in which a tax credit, or any element of a tax credit, is to be paid by the Board.

(8) If the regulations make provision for payments of a tax credit, or any element of a tax credit, to be made by the Board by way of a credit to a bank account or other account notifiedto the Board, the regulations may provide that entitlement to the tax credit or element is dependent on an account having been notifiedto the Board in accordance with the regulations.

AMENDMENTS

1. Subsection (2) is modified as it applies to polygamous units by Tax Credits (Polygamous Marriages) Regulations 2003 (SI 2003/742), reg.18.
2. Civil Partnership Act 2004, s.254 and Sch.24, para.145 (December 5, 2005).

DEFINITIONS

"claim"—see s.3(8).
"couple"—see s.3(5A).
"the Board"—see s.67.
"prescribed"—see s.67.
"tax credit"—see s.1(2).
"tax year"—see s.47.

GENERAL NOTE

From April 2006 HMRC makes all WTC and CTC payments. Payment by employers has been discontinued. Sections 25 (Payment by employers), 26 (liability of officers for sums paid to employers) and 33 (failure by employers to make correct payments) and the related regulations therefore have no current relevance and are not set out in this volume. For the texts see the volume for previous years.

1.291

Rights of employees

27. Schedule 1 (rights of employees not to suffer unfair dismissal or other detriment) has effect.

1.292

"employee"—see s.25(5).

GENERAL NOTE

1.293   This section introduces Sch.1. Both this section and the Schedule are based on s.7 of, and Sch.3 to, the TCA 1999. The aim is to provide employees with direct rights to ensure that employers do not discriminate against them because of WTC. The underlying fear is that employers would rather get rid of employees than implement the WTC process. Schedule 1 makes the necessary amendments to the Employment Rights Act (GB) and Order (NI) to give employees a right not to suffer detriment and a right not to be unfairly dismissed because of tax credits. The text of Sch.1 is not included here as it is a matter of employment law.

Overpayments

1.294   **28.**—(1) Where the amount of a tax credit paid for a tax year to a person or persons exceeds the amount of the tax credit to which he is entitled, or they are jointly entitled, for the tax year (as determined in accordance with the provision made by and by virtue of sections 18 to 21), the Board may decide that the excess, or any part of it, is to be repaid to the Board.

(2) In this Part such an excess is referred to as an overpayment.

(3) For overpayments made under awards on single claims, the person to whom the tax credit was awarded is liable to repay the amount which the Board decide is to be repaid.

(4) For overpayments made under awards on joint claims, the persons to whom the tax credit was awarded are jointly and severally liable to repay the amount which the Board decide is to be repaid unless the Board decide that each is to repay a specified part of that amount.

(5) Where it appears to the Board that there is likely to be an overpayment of a tax credit for a tax year under an award made to a person or persons, the Board may, with a view to reducing or eliminating the overpayment, amend the award or any other award of any tax credit made to the person or persons; but this subsection does not apply once a decision is taken in relation to the person or persons for the tax year under section 18(1).

(6) Where the Board decide under section 16 to terminate an award of a tax credit made to a person or persons on the ground that at no time during the period to which the award related did the person or persons satisfy—

(a) section 8(1) (if the award related to child tax credit), or

(b) section 10(1) (if it related to working tax credit),

the Board may decide that the amount paid under the award, or any part of it, is to be treated for the purposes of this Part (apart from subsection (5)) as an overpayment.

DEFINITIONS

"the Board"—see s.67.
"joint claim"—see s.3(8).
"overpayment"—see subs.(2).
"single claim"—see s.3(8).
"tax credit"—see s.1(2).
"tax year"—see s.47.

An overpayment is an excess of a tax credit awarded and paid as against the amount   **1.295**
of tax credit to which a claimant is entitled under a final decision about entitlement
(subs.(2)). This will usually arise where the final decision on entitlement is for a lesser
amount than the amount awarded. It may also arise under a later revision under
ss.19 or 20, or when an award was made that should not have been made (subs.(6)).
Subsection (1) gives a power to (but does not impose a duty on) HMRC to collect
overpayments. The decision of HMRC whether or not to collect an overpayment is
not subject to appeal, and is not conditional on the fulfilment of any test by the claimant. This is a different approach from that taken for social security purposes, and by
the previous tax credits regime, where it had to be shown in most cases that the claimant had caused the overpayment by a failure to disclose, or a misrepresentation of,
a material fact. In addition, the decision on recoverability for social security purposes
is subject to appeal.

The government has consistently failed to act on the recommendations of the
Parliamentary Ombudsman and others that there be a right of appeal against
overpayment decisions. Dispute about the underlying entitlement to tax credits
are appealable, though such disputes do not often reach tribunals. Disputes about
the amount of overpayments are dealt with as recovery questions. See further
s.29.

Recovery of overpayments

29.—(1) Where an amount is liable to be repaid by a person or persons   **1.296**
under section 28, the Board must give him, or each of them, a notice specifying the amount.

(2) The notice must state which of subsections (3) to (5) is to apply in
relation to the amount or any specified part of the amount; and a notice may
at any time be replaced by another notice containing a different statement.

(3) Where a notice states that this subsection applies in relation to an
amount (or part of an amount), it is to be treated for the purposes of Part
6 of the Taxes Management Act 1970 (c.9) (collection and recovery) as if
it were tax charged in an assessment and due and payable by the person or
persons to whom the notice was given at the end of the period of 30 days
beginning with the day on which the notice is given.

(4) Where a notice states that this subsection applies in relation to an
amount (or part of an amount), it may, subject to provision made by regulations, be recovered by deduction from payments of any tax credit under an
award made for any period to the person, or either or both of the persons,
to whom the notice was given.

(5) Where a notice states that this subsection applies in relation to an
amount (or part of an amount), [PAYE regulations][1] apply to it as if it were
an underpayment of tax for a previous year of assessment by the person or
persons to whom the notice was given.

1. Words amended by ITEPA 2003, Sch.6, para.266 (April 6, 2003). Subs.
(4) is modified by the Tax Credits (Polygamous Marriages) Regulations 2003 (SI
2003/742), reg.12 as it applies to polygamous units.

"the Board"—see s.67.
"overpayment"—see s.28(2).

GENERAL NOTE

1.297   There is no appeal against a decision about either recovery or recoverability under this Act. The absence of a right of appeal has been consistently confirmed by Commissioners. See *CTC/2662/2005*, *CTC/3981/2006* and *CTC/2270/2007*. As that last decision emphasises, the approach is not the same as that applied to the former WFTC (as illustrated by *CTC/1907/2007*). The decision that can be appealed is the entitlement decision under which the overpayment arises. That decision must be notified to the claimant under s.23, save where one of the exceptions in s.23(3) applies. It may be anticipated that, following equivalent experience in social security cases, some recipients will only object, and attempt to appeal, when they receive notice of an overpayment under this section rather than notice of the decision that gives rise to the overpayment. Whether this can amount to an effective and timely appeal against the entitlement decision will depend on part on how and when the required notices are given, and is for decision under s.39.

This section is the equivalent of s.30 of the TMA 1970. HMRC may give a formal notice to someone whom it has decided has been overpaid tax credit. The notice may activate all or any of three alternative methods of recovering the overpaid tax credit. The first, under subs.(3), is by using ss.60–70A of the TMA 1970. These empower HMRC's collection and recovery powers for unpaid income tax demands. These allow distraint and action in both civil courts and magistrates' courts. Subsection (4) entitles HMRC to collect the overpayment by deducting it from other payments of tax credit: see further Tax Credits (Payments by the Board) Regulations 2002 (SI 2002/2173), reg.12A, inserted by the Tax Credits (Miscellaneous Amendments) Regulations 2004 (SI 2004/762), reg.18. Subsection (5) allows overpayments of tax credits to be collected with income tax and NI contributions but this power is not used.

The way in which HMRC decides which overpayments will be recovered, and how they will be recovered, have been matters of continuing controversy since the start of the tax credits scheme. They have also been subject to repeated critical review by the Parliamentary Ombudsman, parliamentary committees and other organisations. The current result, after extended consultation, is the further revised version of the Code of Practice 26, *What happens if we have paid you too much tax credit?* published in 2008. It is set out in full at the end of the volume.

That code emphasises the importance of individuals both reporting changes of circumstances and checking the details of award notices and other notices sent to them by HMRC.

HMRC are running pilot schemes to allow repayments of overpaid tax credit to be made by lump sum or by deduction under the PAYE system from pay in place of the standard process of deducting overpayments of past credits from current payments of credits.

Someone wishing to dispute recovery of an overpayment should send a copy of form TC846 (available on the HMRC website) to the Overpayments Dispute Team, Tax Credits Office, Preston PR1 0SB (or Belfast BT2 7WF).

Underpayments

1.298   **30.**—(1) Where it has been determined in accordance with the provision made by and by virtue of sections 18 to 21 that a person was entitled, or persons were jointly entitled, to a tax credit for a tax year and either—

(a) the amount of the tax credit paid to him or them for that tax year was less than the amount of the tax credit to which it was so determined that he is entitledor they are jointly entitled, or

(b) no payment of the tax credit was made to him or them for that tax year,

the amount of the difference, or of his entitlement or their joint entitlement, must be paid to him or to whichever of them is prescribed.

(2) Where the claim for the tax credit was made by one person on behalf of another, the payment is to be made to whichever of those persons is prescribed.

DEFINITIONS

"prescribed"—see s.67.
"tax credit"—see s.1(2).
"tax year"—see s.47.

GENERAL NOTE

This provision is the converse of s.28. However, the procedure that triggers it is not a mirror of the provisions giving rise to an overpayment. In particular, see the note to s.6 on notifications of changes of circumstances. If there is an underpayment, this section requires HMRC to make it good. But underpayments, unlike repayments of income tax, or overpayments of tax credit, do not carry interest. Nor does the section impose any time-limit on the payment.

1.299

Penalties

Incorrect statements etc.

31.—(1) Where a person fraudulently or negligently—

1.300

(a) makes an incorrect statement or declaration in or in connection with a claim for a tax credit or a notification of a change of circumstances given in accordance with regulations under section 6 or in response to a notice under section 17, or

(b) gives incorrect information or evidence in response to a requirement imposed on him by virtue of section 14(2), 15(2), 16(3), 18(10) or 19(2) or regulations under section 25,

a penalty not exceeding £3,000 may be imposed on him.

(2) Where a person liable to a penalty under subsection (1) is a person making, or who has made, a claim for a tax credit for a period jointly with another and the penalty is imposed—

(a) under paragraph (a) of that subsection in respect of the claim, a notification relating to the tax credit claimed or a notice relating to the tax credit awarded on the claim, or

(b) under paragraph (b) of that subsection in respect of a requirement imposed on him with respect to the tax credit for the period,

a penalty of an amount not exceeding £3,000 may be imposed on the other person unless subsection (3) applies.

(3) This subsection applies if the other person was not, and could not reasonably have been expected to have been, aware that the person liable to the penalty under subsection (1) had fraudulently or negligently made the incorrect statement or declaration or given the incorrect information or evidence.

(4) Where penalties are imposed under subsections (1) and (2) in respect of the same statement, declaration, information or evidence, their aggregate amount must not exceed £3,000.

(5) Where a person acts for another—

(a) in or in connection with a claim or notification referred to in subsection (1), or

(b) in response to a notice so referred to,

subsection (1) applies to him (as well as to any person to whom it applies apart from this subsection).

AMENDMENT

1. Subsection (2) is modified as it applies to polygamous units by Tax Credits (Polygamous Marriages) Regulations 2003 (SI 2003/742), reg.20.

DEFINITIONS

"change of circumstances"—see s.6(1).
"claim"—see s.3(8).
"joint claim"—*ibid.*
"tax credit"—see s.1(2).

GENERAL NOTE

1.301   This Act reflects a concern about potential fraud with regard to claims and payments. There were originally several sources of concern. One – abuse by employers in payments through the wage packet – no longer applies. All payments are made by HMRC. Concern about the payment process itself is dealt with in part by ensuring that most payments are made direct to bank accounts. The remaining original concern was fraud by claimants. Events showed that another, unanticipated, source of fraud proved a big problem. This was the fraudulent use by third parties of the facility to make claims online. This resulted in the online facility being closed down some years ago. It has yet to be reinstated. The focus of ss. 31-34 and Sch.2 is now mainly claimants. The powers are wide enough to catch anyone else involved, such as someone providing childcare on the basis of false information.

Sections 31–34 draw on the then regime applying for income tax. This was in Part X of the TMA 1970. After full consultation, HMRC secured a complete rewrite of tax penalty powers in the Finance Act 2008. This came into effect on April 1, 2009. It applies to all direct and indirect taxes. It does not apply to tax credits. There have been no changes to these sections equivalent to the changes for tax purposes, so the "old" law continues to apply here.

This section deals with the problem where anyone required to make a declaration, statement or notification or to give information or evidence does so "incorrectly" and where the person does so "fraudulently or negligently". It applies both to the person making the declaration, etc., and to anyone acting for that person (subs. (5)), and both could be subject to penalty proceedings in connection with the same matter.

HMRC have published two leaflets of guidance about the exercise of their penalty powers: WTC3, *Tax Credit Penalties, How tax credit examinations are settled,* and WTC4, *Tax Credit penalties, How tax credit enquiries are settled.* They apply to penalties under both this section and s.32. These reflect the differences between examinations (taking place about current claims or awards) and enquiries (taking place when an award is finalised or after entitlement has been established). They are now combined with WTC7, which is set out at the end of this volume. The leaflets set out the procedure for dealing with the imposition of penalties and the basis on which HMRC decide at what level a penalty will be set. HMRC's practice follows that applying for similar income tax examinations and enquiries. Discounts to the maximum penalty will be applied to reflect: the extent to which the error was disclosed voluntarily by the claimant; the extent to which the claimant has cooperated with HMRC in the examination or enquiry; the seriousness of the errors or omissions; and whether this is a first or subsequent occasion on which there has been an error or omission. All penalty decisions are open to appeal. Appeals go to the First-tier Tribunal and then the Upper Tribunal. Since the introduction of the new appeal system an appellant must obtain leave to appeal to take the appeal to the Upper Tribunal. Under the original system no leave was needed to appeal against a penalty to the social security commssioners. No such appeal was considered by them, and few were considered by the social security tribunals. This is in part because HMRC were reluctant at first to use the penalty provisions. It is also because HMRC usually offer to settle a penalty with the individual under the terms of s.54 of the TMA 1970.

Fraudulently or negligently

The former penalty provisions in TMA 1970 had been subject to consideration in the courts on a number of occasions, and it is to be expected that the common phraseology of those sections and these (such as "fraudulently or negligently") will receive a similar interpretation. On this basis, the fraud or neglect of an agent will be regarded as the fraud or neglect of the claimant: *Clixby v Pountney* (1968) 44 T.C. 575. It is clearly established in income tax law that the onus of proving fraud or neglect is on HMRC. *Hillenbrand v IRC* (1966) 42 T.C. 617 established that there is no presumption of fraud or neglect because of an omission, although the omission might give a factual basis for a decision on this point. However, if HMRC establish the fraud or neglect, then the burden shifts to the taxpayer to show that any assessment made by HMRC as a result is incorrect. It is also established that HMRC does not have to show the precise nature of discovered income: *Hudson v Humbles* (1965) 42 T.C. 380. That is part of the process of making and appealing an assessment. It is suggested that the same approaches would be appropriate here, save that in addition HMRC and appeal tribunal will be able to take account of evidence gathered for income tax purposes in deciding the outcome of a s.20 review.

1.302

Additionally, since the Human Rights Act 1998 came into effect, it is arguable that this section imposes a "criminal" liability under Art.6(3) of the European Convention on Human Rights. (For the text, see Vol.III of this work). Courts have applied the criminal standard to equivalent provisions in income tax and VAT legislation. If art.6(3) applies then close consideration needs to be given to the burden of proof under this section, the evidence available for establishing or resisting the application of the section and the availability of legal aid.

A penalty under this section bears interest under s.37. It is treated as unpaid tax for the purposes of recovery and collection (Sch.2, para.7). Appeals against penalty decisions are dealt with in Sch.2 (see s.34).

Subsections (2) and (3) deal with a problem that is no longer relevant to income tax, namely the case where one of a couple making a joint claim has failed fully to co-operate with the other, so that the declaration is wrong but one of the joint claimants is not aware that this is so. In such cases responsibility remains joint and several unless one of the claimants can show that the defence in subs.(3) applies. This imposes a double test of both fact and reasonableness.

The conduct of penalty cases

Appeals under s.31 are "criminal" in the sense that arts 6(2) and (3) of the European Convention on Human Rights apply in addition to art.6(1). This is clear from the decision of the European Court of Human Rights in *King v United Kingdom (No.2)*, Application 13881/02, of February 17, 2004, [2004] S.T.C. 911. See Vol.3 of this work for the text of the Article and commentary. That approach will be strengthened by the decision of that court in *PM v United Kingdom*, Application 6638/03, [2005] S.T.C. 1566. In that case a taxpayer was held entitled to invoke the scope of art.1, Protocol 1 (rights of property) in alleging discrimination about the terms of entitlement to a deduction for maintenance payments under s.347 of the Income and Corporation Taxes Act 1988. As there was no internal remedy for discrimination caused by primary legislation, the European Court awarded damages to the appellant.

1.303

The HMRC Claimant Compliance Manual (CCM) refers to s.31 as being a power to punish. But this does not apply to s.32. See the detailed analysis of the equivalent income tax provisions in *Gladders v Prior* [2003] S.T.C. (S.C.D.) 245

(decision of Special Commissioner of Income Tax, not appealed). A notice requiring information does not breach the rule on self-incrimination. See *Sharkey v De Croos* [2005] S.T.C. (S.C.D.) 336 citing *R. v Allen* [2002] A.C. 509 on a similar income tax provision.

There is authority that receipt of a relevant notice is crucial to the activation of the sections, and that the Interpretation Act presumptions do not apply: Macpherson J. in *CEC v Medway Draughting and Technical Service Ltd* [1989] S.T.C. 346 dealing with a similar VAT provision.

The burden of proof rests with HMRC, who should open any appeal. The degree of proof remains the civil burden, namely that something is "more likely than not". Removal of the unused open power to appeal against the decision of the first tribunal leaves questions of fact entirely in the control, now, of the judges of the First-tier Tribunal. This will include issues about setting the specific level of any penalty.

The level of penalties

1.304   The procedure to be followed by HMRC officers when imposing or applying for tax credits penalties are set out in the *New Tax Credits Claimant Compliance Manual* (abbreviated as CCN). This is available on the HMRC website at *http://www.hmrc.gov.uk/ manuals/ccmmanual/Index.htm*. However, some parts of CCM have been withheld from publication under the Freedom of Information Act 2000. See, for example CCM10070 (even the number of that paragraph is withheld, but it is referred to in cross-references not withheld as covering "Penalties: calculation of penalties in incorrect claims"). The main issue withheld in that paragraph is the calculation of the amount of a penalty to be imposed under subs.(4) of this section. CCM 10080 on the calculation of a percentage of an overpaid claim is not withheld, although it makes little sense in the absence of CCM 10070. This is in contrast to the approach adopted by HMRC with regard to penalties under the income tax penalty regime, and in which percentages play a major role. See now the recently published *Code of Practice 9 (2005)* on civil investigation into cases of suspected serious fraud. This specifically details reductions of maximum penalties by the following percentages:

— up to 20 per cent for voluntary disclosure (or 30 per cent for full disclosure with no risk of discovery);

— up to 40 per cent for cooperation with an investigation, including full disclosures of information requested;

— up to 40 per cent for seriousness of errors and omissions.

Withholding information under the 2000 Act does not apply when HMRC must explain to an appeal tribunal how it reaches the level of penalty it has selected. As a result, various parts of the withheld information have come to the attention of individual appeal tribunals. That is not a satisfactory situation.

It would seem that the approach broadly follows the income tax penalty approach save that in the case of tax penalties the maximum amount of the penalty is a set figure and not a percentage of the income tax under-declared. For example, CCM 10080 shows that an officer should look at the percentage of the overclaimed credits as compared with total credits originally claimed. CCM10090 refers to "the relatively small amount of penalties for first offences". CCM 10100 refers to an abatement of a maximum of 50 per cent for full and prompt cooperation with an enquiry or examination. These statements, and the examples at CCM10110, all point to the same broad approach as that used for income tax. CCM also emphasises that penalties for second and subsequent incorrect statements are likely to be significantly higher than initial penalties. Officers are required to notify claimants of this when imposing an initial penalty.

That aside, CCM sets out in considerable detail the procedures to be used by individual HMRC officers in the process of imposing or requesting penalties.

CCM 10040 emphasises that the penalty power related to s.17 notifications applies only once although the information applies to two years. However, if there are incorrect s.17 notices at both ends of a year, HMRC may levy two penalties. In addition, there may be separate penalties up to the maximum where there is an incorrect s.17 notification and some other "offence" as the CCM terms it.

Failure to comply with requirements

32.—(1) Where a person fails—   1.305
- (a) to provide any information or evidence which he is required to provide by virtue of section 14(2), 15(2), 16(3), 18(10) or 19(2) or regulations under section 25, or
- (b) to comply with a requirement imposed on him by a notice under section 17 by virtue of subsection (2)(a), (4)(a) or (6)(a) of that section,

the penalties specified in subsection (2) may be imposed on him.

(2) The penalties are—
- (a) a penalty not exceeding £300, and
- (b) if the failure continues after a penalty is imposed under paragraph (a), a further penalty or penalties not exceeding £60 for each day on which the failure continues after the day on which the penalty under that paragraph was imposed (but excluding any day for which a penalty under this paragraph has already been imposed).

(3) Where a person fails to give a notification required by regulations under section 6(3), a penalty not exceeding £300 may be imposed on him.

(4) No penalty under subsection (2) may be imposed on a person in respect of a failure after the failure has been remedied.

(5) For the purposes of this section a person is to be taken not to have failed to provide information or evidence, comply with a requirement or give a notification which must be provided, complied with or given by a particular time—
- (a) if he provided, complied with or gave it within such further time (if any) as the Board may have allowed,
- (b) if he had a reasonable excuse for not providing, complying with or giving it by that time, or
- (c) if, after having had such an excuse, he provided, complied with or gave it without unreasonable delay.

(6) Where the members of [¹ a couple] both fail as mentioned in sub-section (1)(b), the aggregate amount of any penalties under subsection (2) imposed on them in relation to their failures must not exceed the amounts specified in that subsection; and where the members of [¹ a couple] both fail as mentioned in subsection (3), the aggregate amount of any penalties imposed on them in relation to their failures must not exceed £300.

AMENDMENT

1. Civil Partnership Act 2004, s.254 and Sch.24, para.145 (December 5, 2005).

DEFINITIONS

"the Board"—see s.67.
"couple"—see s.3(5A).

GENERAL NOTE

1.306   See the note to s.31 on the penalty regime as a whole. This section imposes penalties on those who fail to comply with any notices under s.17, who fail to provide information or evidence under any of the powers to require this, or who fail to give notification of a change of circumstances under s.6. It imposes a potential penalty on all failures, regardless of the reason for the failure. There is no test of fraud or negligence. The policy of all these measures is to impose a relatively low initial maximum penalty (£300 in all cases), but then to provide a cumulatively daily penalty as a strong deterrent to those who choose to ignore not only the notices and requirements but also the initial penalty. In each case, the maximum daily rate is £60. But the daily rate stops when the failure is remedied.

A penalty under this section bears interest under s.37. It is treated as unpaid tax for the purposes of recovery and collection (Sch.2, para.7). Appeals against penalty decisions are dealt with in Sch.2 (see s.34). By contrast with s.31, this section does not demand proof of fraud or negligence, and may therefore impose a civil penalty rather than a criminal penalty for the purposes of the European Convention on Human Rights.

For details of HMRC's practice in setting and dealing with penalties, see the note to s.31 and HMRC. The full text of WTC7 is set out at the end of the volume. HMRC has announced that it will, on a concessionary basis, not seek penalties from those who fail to comply with the mandatory provisions in this section when the award made to the individual is a nil award.

Subsection (1) lists the powers under which HMRC can demand information within the penalty regime. It is important to note that those powers are not all-embracing but are subject to clear time limits laid down in primary legislation. See further the notes to ss.14 and 19 above.

The CCM (Claimant Compliance Manual—see note to p.160 above) states that:

> "Penalties under s.32(1) are not intended to punish a person who will not provide information. The penalties are intended to encourage the person to comply with the notice and if you do not think the penalties will achieve this result you should not normally begin penalty action" (CCM 10230).

The guidance also states that s.32 penalties will not normally be needed for s.14(2) or s.15(2) failures. In-year challenges will normally only be those under s.16 (CCM 10235, 10240). Similarly, CCM discourages s.32 penalties for s.17 notices.

CCM 10300 provides that submissions to appeal tribunals for s.32 penalties must be transferred to and made by a single office of HMRC, the Cross-Cutting Policy (Stockport Technical Unit).

CCM 10170 gives internal guidance on the meaning of "reasonable excuse". The examples of reasonable excuses include notifications lost or delayed in the post because of an unforeseen event, serious illness of the claimant or a close relative, or death of a relative. The examples are somewhat similar to those applying to a social security claim under reg.19 of the Social Security (Claims and Payments) Regulations 1987, on which see Vol.III leaflet WTC7, *Tax Credit Penalties: what happens at the end of a check.* of this work, but a statutory formulation has been avoided. "Too busy" and "did not understand what was required" are said not to be reasonable excuses. CCM 10620 accepts that there is no negligence if a claimant has acted on official guidance, but warns officers to check official telephone logs and any contemporary notes kept by claimants. CCM 10640 accepts that acting on advice of "a legitimate source" such as a CAB or Jobcentre Plus may be a reasonable excuse.

The Treasury and HMRC have announced that HMRC will pilot recovery of overpayments through the PAYE system from April 2009, and a wider opportunity for overpayments to be repaid in a lumps sum rather than by deduction against later payments.

Supplementary

34. Schedule 2 (penalties: supplementary) has effect.

Fraud

Offence of fraud

35.—(1) A person commits an offence if he is knowingly concerned in any fraudulent activity undertaken with a view to obtaining payments of a tax credit by him or any other person.

(2) A person who commits an offence under subsection (1) is liable—

(a) on summary conviction, to imprisonment for a term not exceeding six months, or a fine not exceeding the statutory maximum, or both, or

(b) on conviction on indictment, to imprisonment for a term not exceeding seven years, or a fine, or both.

DEFINITION

"tax credit"—see s.1(2).

GENERAL NOTE

Like the penalties provisions, this section reflects the fear of fraud by claimants and others abusing the tax credits system. There is no equivalent of this section in the TCA 1999. The new offence is briefly stated and is clearly intended to have a wide reach. It is not confined to claimants or employers and could be applied, for example, to a childcare provider.

Powers in relation to documents

36.—(1) Section 20BA of the Taxes Management Act 1970 (c.9) (orders for delivery of documents) applies (with Schedule 1AA and section 20BB) in relation to offences involving fraud in connection with, or in relation to, tax credits as in relation to offences involving serious fraud in connection with, or in relation to, tax.

(2) [¹ . . .]

(3) [¹ . . .]

(4) Any regulations under Schedule 1AA to the Taxes Management Act 1970 which are in force immediately before the commencement of subsection (1) apply, subject to any necessary modifications, for the purposes of that Schedule as they apply by virtue of that subsection (until amended or revoked).

AMENDMENT

1. Finance Act 2007, s.84(4) and Sch.22, para.14 (December 1, 2007).

DEFINITION

"tax credit"—see s.1(2).

GENERAL NOTE

This applies specific powers available to HMRC for dealing with tax fraud to tax credit fraud. Sections 20BA and 20BB of the TMA 1970 deal with orders for delivery of documents and offences of fraud respectively. The statutory instrument currently made under Sch.1AA is the Orders for the Delivery of Documents (Procedure) Regulations 2000 (SI 2000/2875).

Interest

Interest

1.312   **37.**—(1) If an overpayment of a tax credit for a period is attributable to fraud or neglect on the part of the person, or either or both of the persons, to whom the award of the tax credit was made (or a person acting for him, or for either or both of them, in making the claim for the tax credit), the Board may decide that the whole or any part of the overpayment is to carry interest.

(2) Where the Board so decide the overpayment (or part of the overpayment) carries interest at a prescribed rate from the date 30 days after the appropriate date.

(3) "The appropriate date" is—

(a) in the case of an amount treated as an overpayment by virtue of section 28(6), the date of the decision under section 16 to terminate the award; and

(b) in any other case, the date specified for the purposes of subsection (4) of section 17 in the notice given to the person or persons under that section in relation to the tax credit.

(4) The Board must give notice of a decision under subsection (1) to the person, or each of the persons, to whom it relates; and the notice must state the date on which it is given and include details of the right to appeal against the decision under section 38.

(5) A penalty under any of sections 31 to 33 carries interest at the prescribed rate from the date on which it becomes due and payable; but the Board may in their discretion mitigate any interest or entirely remit any interest which would otherwise be carried by a penalty.

(6) Any interest carried under this section by an overpayment or penalty is to be regarded for the purposes of section 29(3) to (5) or paragraph 7 of Schedule 2 as if it were part of the overpayment or penalty.

AMENDMENT

Subsection (1) is modified as it applies to polygamous units by Tax Credits (Polygamous Marriages) Regulations 2003 (SI 2003/742), reg.21.

DEFINITIONS

"the Board"—see s.67.
"prescribed"—*ibid.*
"overpayment"—see s.28.
"tax credit"—see s.1(2).

GENERAL NOTE

1.313   Interest has long been imposed on taxpayers who do not make timely payments of income tax. This includes an underpayment (or repayment) of tax reliefs and deductions (see TMA 1970, s.86). By contrast, interest is not imposed on those required to repay an overpayment of social security benefits. Interest was not imposed on overpayments under the TCA 1999, although penalties under s.9 of that Act carried interest (Sch.4, para.8 to that Act).

This section adopts a compromise in imposing interest payments on overpayments caused by fraud or neglect, but not generally. It also imposes again an interest charge on payments of penalties. Interest does not run unless a decision is made to impose it, and that cannot start until either the date on which the award of tax credit was terminated under s.16 or the closing date of a notice issued under s.17.

The "prescribed rate" is set out in the Tax Credits (Interest Rate) Regulations 2003 (SI 2003/123).

Appeals

Appeals

38.—(1) An appeal may be brought against—   1.314
  (a) a decision under section 14(1), 15(1), 16(1), 19(3) or 20(1) or (4) or regulations under section 21,
  (b) the relevant section 18 decision in relation to a person or persons and a tax credit for a tax year and any revision of that decision under that section,
  (c) a determination of a penalty under paragraph 1 of Schedule 2, and
  (d) a decision under section 37(1).
(2) "The relevant section 18 decision" means—
  (a) in a case in which a decision must be made under subsection (6) of section 18 in relation to the person or persons and the tax credit for the tax year, that decision, and
  (b) in any other case, the decision under subsection (1) of that section in relation to the person or persons and the tax credit for the tax year.

DEFINITIONS

"tax credit"—see s.1(2).
"tax year"—see s.47.

GENERAL NOTE

This section creates a series of specific rights of appeal. The following decisions   1.315
or actions of HMRC are subject to the appeal process:

  (a) an initial decision to award or refuse tax credits under s.14(1);

  (b) a decision whether (and if so, how) to amend a s.14 decision under s.15(1);

  (c) a decision amending or terminating a s.14 decision under s.16(1);

  (d) a decision on entitlement made under s.18(1) or (6);

  (e) a decision after an enquiry under s.19(3);

  (f) a decision revising a previous decision on entitlement under s.20(1);

  (g) a decision revising a previous decision on entitlement on the grounds of fraud or neglect under s.20(4);

  (h) a decision to revise a decision on entitlement because of official error under s.21;

  (i) a determination of a penalty under Sch.2 para.1;

  (j) a decision to impose interest under s.37(1).

In *CTC/31/2006* the Commissioner rejected as outside his jurisdiction an attempt to appeal a decision of HMRC that a claim was not properly made. The claim had been made on an income tax return, and HMRC had refused to accept it. The Commissioner held that this was not within the terms of s.38. He also held that it could not be read into the section by reference to the European Convention on Human Rights. In the view of the Commissioner judicial review was an adequate means of challenging a decision to refuse a claim that was alleged to be unlawful. *CTC/1594/2006* illustrates the importance of checking for which year or years an appeal is made. This is potentially more of a problem for tax credits than most benefits because of the effect of having an award decision during the same year as the entitlement decision for the previous year. The Commissioner accepted the arguments for HMRC in that case that a claimant could not use an appeal to challenge more than the specific decisions challenged. As Commissioners have observed on more than one occasion, this means that challenges against award decisions may be of limited value. HMRC is no more debarred from altering a tribunal decision about an award at the end of the year than any other award decision. This issue is not always easy to clarify as HMRC uses terminology in its literature that conflates awards and entitlement decisions. See para.1.287.

It is to be emphasised that this section gives the right of appeal, and s.39 as amended by s.63 is concerned only with how the appeal is made. It is often said that the appeal is to HMRC and not an appeal tribunal. That is not correct. The appeal is to the tribunal ,while notification is to HMRC. The importance of this used to be that it was for HMRC to deal with passing a tribunal a case for listing. There was a major change of approach adopted for all tax cases when the Special and General Commissioners were abolished and replaced by the Tax Chamber of the First-tier Tribunal. It was agreed that listing was no longer for HMRC but is now a function of the Tribunals Service, operating through its Tax Chamber offices. The trigger in direct tax cases is notification of the appeal directly to the Tribunals Service by the appellant. The same should therefore apply to all tax credit appeals. These should therefore be listed by the Tribunals Service for hearing or decision as it considers appropriate when an appellant notifies the tribunal of the appeal. This change may deal with some of the recurring complaints that appeals about tax credits entitlement (as against unappealable decisions about overpayments) do not reach the tribunals.

The absence of appeals undoubtedly reflects the power of the Inland Revenue and now the HMRC to settle cases under s.54 of the TMA 1970. This is a power not possessed by the Department for Work and Pensions or local authorities (or the former Customs and Excise Commissioners). That power is particularly useful in dealing with questions of disputed income and with penalty cases, although it is of limited use in cases such as whether two individuals should be making a joint claim. But on one view HMRC is making too wide a use of that power. In *Tax Credits Agenda for Improvement*, published in September 2004 jointly by the Chartered Institute of Taxation, Citizens Advice, CPAG, The Institute of Chartered Accountants of England and Wales, the Low Income Tax Reform Group, and One Parent Families, the approach of HMRC to settlement was criticised. The bodies jointly asked for:

> "adherence to proper procedures when the IR decide to settle an appeal, rather than 'cancelling' the appeal and issuing revised decisions outside the appeal process."

While HMRC have, as noted, a power to settle under s.54 of the TMA it is a process with its own safeguards (see para.1.19 above). Similarly, once an appeal has been made it cannot be "cancelled" otherwise than by a properly reached settlement or as part of the appeal process. Any attempt to interfere with the appeal process outside those protective limits is an interference by one party in the appeal process and as such is likely to be in breach of the "equality of arms" principle laid down by the European Court of Human Rights. That principle demands that all parties have equal access to a court or tribunal as part of the fundamental principle of fair hearings laid down in art.6 of the European Convention on Human Rights. (See Volume III of this series for that provision and the Human Rights Act 1998 that introduces it into United Kingdom law.)

This section clearly gives separate appeal rights against s.14 decisions as against s.18 decisions. The automated process, followed by checks, that is used for awards (see the notes to s.14) would suggest that the administrative approach adopted by HMRC, while undoubtedly efficient in many cases, may be the reason why the joint protest has arisen.

Separately from these, the appellate authorities can be invoked in two other situations. HMRC cannot itself make a determination of daily penalties under s.32(2) and must instead start proceedings for such penalties before the appellate authorities. This is not technically an appeal (see Sch.2, para.3). An individual subject to an enquiry under s.19 can, under s.19(8), apply to the appellate authorities to direct the enquiry to end. Such an application is to be treated as if it was an appeal (s.19(10)).

The 2007 special report of the Parliamentary Ombudsman noted above continues to recommend that appeal rights should be given to an independent tribunal in connection with overpayments. It also sets out the government response to that recommendation, which is an enhanced complaints procedure. This procedure is now applied by both HMRC and the Ombudsman to all tax credits complaints, including appeals. In effect, a complaint only gets to the Ombudsman or an appeal to a tribunal as a fourth level of review.

[¹Exercise of right of appeal

39.—(1) Notice of an appeal under section 38 against a decision must be given to the Board in the prescribed manner within the period of thirty days after the date on which notice of the decision was given (or, in the case of a decision to which section 23(3) applies, the date of the decision).

(2) Notice of such an appeal must specify the grounds of appeal.

(5) . . .

1.316

AMENDMENT

1. Text of section amended as provided in s.63.

DEFINITIONS

"the Board"—see s.67.
"General Commissioners"—see s.47.
"modifications"—see s.67.
"prescribed"—*ibid.*
"Special Commissioners"—see s.47.

GENERAL NOTE

The text of the section set out here is that as amended by s.63. Subss.(3), (4), (6) and (7) of the original wording of the section were repealed by the Transfer of Tribunal Functions and Revenue and Customs Order 2009 (SI 2009/56), Sch. 1 from April 1, 2009. The unamended section originally applied to employer appeals, but there is no basis on which these can arise after the abolition of payment by employers after April 6, 2006. The section is the compromise that resulted when the original plan to route all appeals to the General and Special Commissioners proved impossible to implement. From April 2009, the former tax tribunals have been absorbed into the First-tier Tribunal as its Tax Chamber, alongside the Social Entitlement Chamber. There is now little to distinguish the two tribunal chambers, not least as there are now several judges and members of the Social Entitlement Chamber also appointed to act as judges and members of the Tax Chamber.

1.317

Subs. (1)

1.318   This gives a 30-day time-limit on appeals (the usual HMRC time-limit), compared with a normal time-limit of one month from social security decisions to those
tribunals. For the prescribed manner of notice of appeal see Tax Credits (Notice of
Appeal) Regulations 2002 (SI 2002/3119), reg.2, and for late appeals see reg.5 of
those Regulations.

One problem behind this provision is how it deals with appeals about joint claims,
and in particular the case where an individual states that he or she is not a joint
claimant with another person and that other person has no interest in the appeal
proceedings. If the two individuals have both made separate claims (or one has
claimed a social security benefit and the other a tax credit) it is open to question
whether the ordinary appeal processes would bring the appeals to be heard together,
although robust tribunals clearly achieve this.

Subs. (2)

1.319   This requires the grounds of appeal to be specified. The equivalent social security
requirement is that particulars of the grounds be stated.

The notice of appeal should also indicate clearly which tax year is under appeal.
As accepted in *CTC/1594/2006*, an appellant cannot challenge both the entitlement
decision for one year and the award decision for the next year unless both those
decisions are challenged expressly.

Supplementary

Annual reports

1.320   **40.**—(1) The Board must make to the Treasury an annual report
about—

(a) [¹ . . .]
(b) the number of awards of child tax credit and of working tax credit,
(c) the number of enquiries conducted under section 19,
(d) the number of penalties imposed under this Part, and
(e) the number of prosecutions and convictions for offences connected
with tax credits.

(2) The Treasury must publish each annual report made to it under subsection (1) and lay a copy before each House of Parliament.

AMENDMENTS

1. Commissioners for Revenue and Customs Act 2005, s.50 and Sch.4, para.89
(April 18, 2005).
2. References to "the Board" are now references to the Commissioners for
Revenue and Customs: CRCA 2005, s.4.

DEFINITIONS

"the Board"—see s.67.
"child tax credit"—see s.8.
"tax credits"—see s.1(2).
"working tax credit"—see s.10.

GENERAL NOTE

1.321   This section derives from a clause adopted by the House of Lords against the
wishes of government, and represents the one major amendment in the Act not

moved by the Government itself. The aim is to ensure a specific report that would be put before Parliament each year about both the scale of the tax credits system and the extent of fraud within it. The wording of the section comes from a government amendment moved to replace the Lords clause in the House of Commons. It was recognised that to some extent it duplicates figures already published by HMRC in its more general reports.

The first such report to be published under s.40 is exceedingly brief (just 2 sides of A4). It is to be found at *http://hmrc.gov.uk/si/s40-tax-credits.pdf*.

Annual review

41.—(1) The Treasury must, in each tax year, review the amounts specified in subsection (2) in order to determine whether they have retained their value in relation to the general level of prices in the United Kingdom as estimated by the Treasury in such manner as it considers appropriate.   **1.322**

(2) The amounts are monetary amounts prescribed—

(a) under subsection (1)(a) of section 7;

(b) for the purposes of any of paragraphs (a) to (d) of subsection (3) of that section;

(c) under section 9;

(d) under section 11, otherwise than by virtue of section 12, or

(e) under subsection (2) of section 13, otherwise than by virtue of subsection (3) of that section.

(3) The Treasury must prepare a report of each review.

(4) The report must include a statement of what each amount would be if it had fully retained its value.

(5) The Treasury must publish the report and lay a copy of it before each House of Parliament.

DEFINITION

"prescribed"—see s.67.

GENERAL NOTE

This provides for the annual uprating review of the monetary amounts used in awarding tax credits.   **1.323**

Persons subject to immigration control

42.—(1) Regulations may make provision in relation to persons subject to immigration control or in relation to prescribed descriptions of such persons—   **1.324**

(a) for excluding entitlement to, or to a prescribed element of, child tax credit or working tax credit (or both), or

(b) for this Part to apply subject to other prescribed modifications.

(2) "Person subject to immigration control" has the same meaning as in section 115 of the Immigration and Asylum Act 1999 (c.33).

DEFINITIONS

"child tax credit"—see s.8.

"modifications"—see s.67.

"persons subject to immigration control"—see Immigration and Asylum Act 1999, s.115.

"prescribed"—see s.67.
"working tax credit"—see s.10.

GENERAL NOTE

1.325   Although listed in the "supplementary" part of Pt I of the Act, this makes provision for excluding anyone from entitlement to tax credits if he or she is "subject to immigration control", a phrase derived from the Immigration and Asylum Act 1999. The definition covers those who are not nationals of an EEA state and who require leave to enter the United Kingdom or have certain forms of conditional leave. For the detailed application of this section, see the Tax Credits (Immigration) Regulations 2003 (SI 2003/653). An attempt to challenge the regulations made under this section as discriminatory by reference to the Human Rights Act 1999 failed in *CTC/3692/2008*.

Polygamous marriages

1.326   **43.**—(1) Regulations may make provision for this Part to apply in relation to persons who are parties to polygamous marriages subject to prescribed modifications.

(2) A person is a party to a polygamous marriage if—
(a) he is a party to a marriage entered into under a law which permits polygamy, and
(b) either party to the marriage has a spouse additional to the other party.

DEFINITION

"modifications"—see s.67.

GENERAL NOTE

1.327   This is another of the necessary compromises between the general approach to income tax and the general approach to social security. Social security benefits have long contained special provisions dealing with polygamous marriages, if only to prevent more than two of the marriage partners benefiting for a particular benefit as a married couple. In contrast, the point is not so significant in the context of income tax as there is now individual assessment. The standard treatment of monogamous marriages is set out in s.3.

Effect is given to this section by the Tax Credits (Polygamous Marriages) Regulations 2003 (SI 2003/742). Where those regulations provide for a modification of the sections of this Act, that is noted in this volume as an amendment to the section.

Crown employment

1.328   **44.** This Part applies in relation to persons employed by or under the Crown (as in relation to other employees).

DEFINITIONS

"Crown"—see Interpretation Act 1978, Sch.1.
"employed"—see s.25(5).

GENERAL NOTE

1.329   This section avoids any unintended exclusion of civil and other public servants by reason of the Crown Proceedings Act 1947 or otherwise. The Tax Credits (Residence) Regulations 2003 (SI 2003/642) extend this further by applying the

Act to Crown Servants working overseas and their partners. The main concern of both this section and those regulations is that Crown servants receive full entitlement to CTC.

Inalienability

45.—(1) Every assignment of or charge on a tax credit, and every agreement to assign or charge a tax credit, is void; and, on the bankruptcy of a person entitled to a tax credit, the entitlement to the tax credit does not pass to any trustee or other person acting on behalf of his creditors.

(2) In the application of subsection (1) to Scotland—

(a) the reference to assignment is to assignation ("assign" being construed accordingly), and

(b) the reference to the bankruptcy of a person is to the sequestration of his estate or the appointment on his estate of a judicial factor under section 41 of the Solicitors (Scotland) Act 1980 (c.46).

1.330

DEFINITION

"tax credit"—see s.1(2).

GENERAL NOTE

This mirrors (and repeats much of the wording of) SSAA 1992, s.187. While informal pledges of both benefit and benefit books occur, that section renders any such arrangement unenforceable in the courts or as against government departments. This section ensures that this also applies to tax credits.

1.331

Giving of notices by Board

46. The Board may give any notice which they are required or permitted to give under this Part in any manner and form which the Board consider appropriate in the circumstances.

1.332

DEFINITION

"the Board"—see s.67.

GENERAL NOTE

No provision is made in this section for regulations or for deemed notice. There is no equivalent of TMA 1970, s.114 (want of form not to invalidate assessments) or 115 (delivery and service of documents) provided for in the Act. However, it is suggested that this does not discharge HMRC from the duty of complying with specific provisions as to content in this Act, in the Tax Credits (Claims and Notifications) Regulations 2002 (SI 2002/2014), or elsewhere. HMRC is also required, by reason of the art.6 of the European Convention on Human Rights and the Human Rights Act 1998 (see Vol.III in this series), to ensure that proper notice is given of any appeal to the appeal tribunals or the appellant as the case may be.

1.333

Consequential amendments

47. Schedule 3 (consequential amendments) has effect.

1.334

GENERAL NOTE

This section gives effect to Sch.3 (not included in this volume). Section 68(1) ensures that those provisions are co-extensive with the provisions they affect. Most

1.335

of the provisions are concerned to replace WFTC with WTC and to substitute a reference to CTC in place of references to the various previous child benefits and credits. Paragraph 25 amends s.30C of the SSCBA 1992, and para.30 amends s.42 of that Act. Both deal with transfers between benefit and tax credit.

Interpretation

1.336

48.—[¹(1)] In this Part—

"child" has the meaning given by section 8(3),

[¹"couple" has the meaning given by section 3(5A)],

"the current year income" has the meaning given by section 7(4),

"employee" and "employer" have the meaning given by section 25(5),

[² . . .]

"the income threshold" has the meaning given by section 7(1)(a),

"joint claim" has the meaning given by section 3(8),

[¹ . . .],

"overpayment" has the meaning given by section 28(2) and (6),

"the previous year income" has the meaning given by section 7(5),

"qualifying remunerative work", and being engaged in it, have the meaning given by regulations under section 10(2),

"qualifying young person" has the meaning given by section 8(4),

"the relevant income" has the meaning given by section 7(3),

"responsible", in relation to a child or qualifying young person, has the meaning given by regulations under section 8(2) (for the purposes of child tax credit) or by regulations under section 10(4) (for the purposes of working tax credit),

"single claim" has the meaning given by section 3(8),

[² . . .]

"tax year" means a period beginning with 6th April in one year and ending with 5th April in the next, and

[¹ . . .].

[¹(2) For the purposes of this Part, two people of the same sex are to be regarded as living together as if they were civil partners if, but only if, they would be regarded as living together as husband and wife were they instead two people of the opposite sex.]

Amendments

1. Civil Partnership Act 2004, ss.254 and 261(4) and Sch.24, para.147 and Sch.30 (December 5, 2005).

2. Transfer of Tribunal Functions and Revenue and Customs Appeals Order 2009 (SI 2009/56), art.3(1), Sch.1, para.315 (April 1, 2009).

General Note

1.337

See also s.67 for further definitions.

Part II

Child Benefit and Guardian's Allowance

49.–57. (*Omitted*)

PART III

SUPPLEMENTARY

Information etc.

Administrative arrangements

58.—(1) This section applies where regulations under—   1.338
(a) section 4 or 6 of this Act,
(b) section 5 of the Social Security Administration Act 1992 (c.5), or
(c) section 5 of the Social Security Administration (Northern Ireland) Act 1992 (c.8),
permit or require a claim or notification relating to a tax credit, child benefit or guardian's allowance to be made or given to a relevant authority.
(2) Where this section applies, regulations may make provision—
(a) for information or evidence relating to tax credits, child benefit or guardian's allowance to be provided to the relevant authority (whether by persons by whom such claims and notifications are or have been made or given, by the Board or by other persons),
(b) for the giving of information or advice by a relevant authority to persons by whom such claims or notifications are or have been made or given, and
(c) for the recording, verification and holding, and the forwarding to the Board or a person providing services to the Board, of claims and notifications received by virtue of the regulations referred to in sub-section (1) and information or evidence received by virtue of paragraph (a).
(3) "Relevant authority" means—
(a) the Secretary of State,
(b) the Northern Ireland Department, or
(c) a person providing services to the Secretary of State or the Northern Ireland Department.

DEFINITIONS

"child benefit"—see SSCBA 1992, s.141.
"claim"—see s.3(8).
"guardian's allowance"—see SSCBA 1992, s.77.
"relevant authority"—see subs.(3).
"tax credit"—see s.1(2).

GENERAL NOTE

Section 5 of the SSAA 1992 and its Northern Ireland equivalent provide the   1.339
authority for the Social Security (Claims and Payments) Regulations 1987 (SI 1987/1968) under which regulations for all aspects of claiming benefits are detailed. This section enables claims and notifications for tax credits and child benefit being validly given to both HMRC and the social security authorities, and to anyone acting under contract to the social security authorities. It will, for example, allow claims for child benefit and CTC to be made together to one authority. See also the Tax Credits (Administrative Arrangements) Regulations 2002 (SI 2002/3036).
CRCA 2005 contains a wide general power for HMRC to use for all its statutory purposes all the information that comes into its possession for any purpose. This is

subject to limits in Sch.2 of that Act. There are no limits in the Schedule relevant to the management and payment of tax credits.

Use and disclosure of information

1.340   **59.** Schedule 5 (use and disclosure of information) has effect.

GENERAL NOTE

1.341   This section incorporates Sch.5 into the Act. The Schedule adds further provisions to the statutory authority already available so that tax authorities, social security authorities, other government departments, and local authorities can exchange information. The widest power is the power to give information to anyone for the purposes of the Learning and Skills Act 2000 (para.10). This wide power is linked to a new criminal offence if it is misused (para.10(4)). Paragraph 11 includes disclosures about tax credits in the general offence of disclosing information held by a person in connection with tax, tax credit and social security functions unless the information is disclosed with lawful authority or certain other conditions are met. This replaces the inclusion of tax credits within that section under s.12 of the TCA 1999. Paragraph 9 of the Schedule has given effect by the Tax Credits (Provision of Information) (Functions Relating to Health) Regulations 2003 (SI 2003/731) and the Tax Credits (Provision of Information) (Functions Relating to Health) (No.2) Regulations 2003 (SI 2003/1650) and a series of other short specific provisions.

Other supplementary provisions

Repeals

1.342   **60.** Schedule 6 (repeals) has effect.

GENERAL NOTE

1.343   This section incorporates the standard repeals Schedule into the Act. It provides the authority for the abolitions flagged up in s.1(3). It confirms that this Act replaces the whole of the TCA 1999.

Commencement

1.344   **61.** Apart from section 54(1) and (2), the preceding provisions of this Act come into force in accordance with orders made by the Treasury.

GENERAL NOTE

1.345   See end of the introductory General Note to the Act as a whole.

Transitional provisions and savings

1.346   **62.**—(1) The Secretary of State may by order make as respects England and Wales and Scotland, and the Northern Ireland Department may by order make as respects Northern Ireland, any transitional provisions or savings which appear appropriate in connection with the commencement of the abolition of the increases referred to in section 1(3)(e).

(2) Subject to any provision made by virtue of subsection (1), the Treasury may by order make any transitional provisions or savings which appear appropriate in connection with the commencement of any provision of this Act.

See the note to the previous section.   1.347

Tax credits appeals etc.: temporary modifications

63.—(1) Until such day as the Treasury may by order appoint, Part I of   1.348
this Act has effect subject to the modifications specified in this section; and
an order under this subsection may include any transitional provisions or
savings which appear appropriate.

[² (2) Except in the case of an appeal against an employer penalty, an
appeal under section 38 is to—
  (a) in Great Britain, the First-tier Tribunal; or
  (b) in Northern Ireland, the appeal tribunal;
and in either case section 39(6) shall not apply.]

[² (3) The function of giving a direction under section 19(10) is a function of—
  (a) in Great Britain, the First-tier Tribunal; or
  (b) in Northern Ireland, the appeal tribunal;
and in either case the relevant provisions of Part 5 of the Taxes
Management Act 1970 shall not apply.]

[² (4) In Northern Ireland, except in the case of an employer information
penalty, proceedings under paragraph 3 of Schedule 2 are by way of information in writing, made to the appeal tribunal (rather than to the tribunal),
and upon summons issued by them to the defendant to appear before them
at a time and place stated in the summons; and they must hear and decide
each case in a summary way.]

(5) So far as is appropriate in consequence of subsections (2) to (4)—
  (a) the references to the [² tribunal in section 19(10)] and paragraphs 2
       and 3(2) of Schedule 2 are to the [² appeal tribunal], [² . . .]
  (b) [² . . .]

[² (6) In Northern Ireland, an appeal under paragraph 2(2) or 4(1) of
Schedule 2 from a decision of, or against the determination of a penalty
by, the appeal tribunal lies to the Northern Ireland Social Security
Commissioner (rather than to the Upper Tribunal).]

(7) So far as is appropriate in consequence of subsection (6), the references in paragraphs 2(2) and 4 of Schedule 2 [² to the Upper Tribunal are
to the Northern Ireland Social Security Commissioner].

(8) Regulations may apply any provision contained in—
  (a) Chapter 2 of Part I of the Social Security Act 1998 (c.14) (social
       security appeals: Great Britain),
  (b) Chapter 2 of Part II of the Social Security (Northern Ireland) Order
       1998 (SI 1998/1506 (N.I. 10)) (social security appeals: Northern
       Ireland), or
  (c) section 54 of the Taxes Management Act 1970 (c.9) (settling of
       appeals by agreement),
in relation to appeals which, by virtue of this section, are to [¹ the appeal
tribunal or lie to] [[¹a]Northern Ireland Social Security Commissioner],
but subject to such modifications as are prescribed.
[² . . .]

([¹ (10) "Appeal tribunal" means an appeal tribunal constituted under
Chapter 1 of Part 2 of the Social Security (Northern Ireland) Order
1998.]

(11) "Employer penalty" means—

(a) a penalty under section 31 or 32 relating to a requirement imposed by virtue of regulations under section 25, or

(b) a penalty under section 33.

(12) "Employer information penalty" means a penalty under section 32(2)(a) relating to a requirement imposed by virtue of regulations under section 25.

(13) ["Northern Ireland Social Security Commissioner" means] the Chief Social Security Commissioner or any other Social Security Commissioner appointed under the Social Security Administration (Northern Ireland) Act 1992 (c.8) or a tribunal of two or more Commissioners constituted under Article 16(7) of the Social Security (Northern Ireland) Order 1998 (SI 1998/1506 (N.I. 10)).

[¹ (14) "tribunal" (other than in the expression "appeal tribunal") shall have the meaning in section 47C of the Taxes Management Act 1970.]

AMENDMENTS

1. Transfer of Tribunals Functions Order 2008 (SI 2008/2833), art.9(1), Sch.3, para.191 (November 3, 2008).
2. Transfer of Tribunal Functions and Revenue and Customs Appeals Order 2009 (SI 2009/56), art.3(1), Sch.1, para.316 (April 1, 2009).

DEFINITIONS

"appeal tribunal"—see subs.(10).
"employer information penalty"—see subs.(12).
"employer penalty"—see subs.(11).
"General Commissioners"—see s.47.
"modifications"—see s.67.
"Social Security Commissioner"—see subs.(13).
"Special Commissioners"—see s.47.

GENERAL NOTE

1.349   The original aim of this section was to introduce what was said to be a temporary transfer of tax credits from the General and Special Commissioners to the social security tribunals. No such transfer took place, and events have been overtaken by the more general reforms of both tribunals. The choice is now between the Social Entitlement Chamber of the First-tier Tribunal, where appeals are now heard, and the Tax Chamber of the same tribunal, where it is still the policy intention to have the appeals heard. In practice, the distinction matters little as the rules and practices are now substantially the same and there are, in any event, few tax credits appeals. A major focus of difficulty in the appeals now heard are on the issue of whether a claim should have been a joint claim (that is, the claimant is living with a partner). That is a kind of appeal in which the social entitlement tribunals have considerable experience and the tax tribunals have none.

As part of those reforms, the procedure on appeals is now the standard First-tier Tribunal procedure. See Volume III of this work. Again as part of those reforms, appeals from the tax tribunals no longer go to the High Court or Court of Session, but now go to the Upper Tribunal, as do all social entitlement appeals.

There was no equivalent reform of the Northern Ireland system. The section therefore provides that appeals go to the "old" tribunals and Commissioners there.

Subsection (8), together with s.65, empowered making the Tax Credits (Appeals) Regulations 2002 (SI 2002/3196). It was amended as shown above by SI 2008/2833, Sch.3, para.191(6) and further by SI 2009/56, Sch.1, para.316(8) from

April 1, 2009. The effect of the amendments is to restrict the authority in subs.(8) to Northern Ireland. Presumably, therefore, those regulations have lapsed for Great Britain. It would appear that the effect is to lapse the application in Great Britain for tax credits purposes of the Social Security Act 1998 and of s.54 of the Taxes Management Act 1970.

Northern Ireland

64.—(1) The Northern Ireland Act 1998 (c.47) has effect subject to the amendments in subsections (2) and (3).

1.350

(2) In Schedule 2 (excepted matters), after paragraph 10 insert—

"**10A.** Tax credits under Part 1 of the Tax Credits Act 2002.
10B. Childbenefit and guardian's allowance."

(3) In section 87 (consultation and co-ordination on social security matters), after subsection (6) insert—

"(6A) But this section does not apply to the legislation referred to in subsection (6) to the extent that it relates to child benefit or guardian's allowance."

(4) For the purposes of that Act, a provision of—

(a) an Act of the Northern Ireland Assembly; or
(b) a Bill for such an Act,

which amends or repeals any of the provisions of the Employment Rights (Northern Ireland) Order 1996 (SI 1996/1919 (N.I. 16)) dealt with in Schedule 1 shall not be treated as dealing with tax credits if the Act or Bill deals with employment rights conferred otherwise than by that Schedule in the same way.

DEFINITION

"tax credits"—see s.1(2).

GENERAL NOTE

The provisions on Northern Ireland are necessary because of the transfer of the administration of child benefit and guardian's allowance from the Northern Ireland authorities to the Home Civil Service. The amendments also confirm the effect of s.16 of the Tax Credits Act 1999 in reserving tax credits as excepted matters.

1.351

Regulations, orders and schemes

65.—(1) Any power to make regulations under sections 3, 7 to 13, 42 and 43, and any power to make regulations under this Act prescribing a rate of interest, is exercisable by the Treasury.

1.352

(2) Any other power to make regulations under this Act is exercisable by the Board.

(3) Subject to subsection (4), any power to make regulations, orders or schemes under this Act is exercisable by statutory instrument.

(4) The power—

(a) of the Department of Health, Social Services and Public Safety to make schemes under section 12(5), and
(b) of the Northern Ireland Department to make orders under section 62(1),

is exercisable by statutory rule for the purposes of the Statutory Rules

(Northern Ireland) Order 1979 (S.I. 1979/1573 (N.I. 12)).

(5) Regulations may not be made under section 25 or 26 in relation to appeals in Scotland without the consent of the Scottish Ministers.

(6) Regulations may not be made under section 39(6) or 63(8) without the consent of the Lord Chancellor and the Scottish Ministers.

(7) Any power to make regulations under this Act may be exercised—

(a) in relation to all cases to which it extends, to all those cases with pre-scribed exceptions or to prescribed cases or classes of case,

(b) so as to make as respects the cases in relation to which it is exercised the full provision to which it extends or any less provision (whether by way of exception or otherwise),

(c) so as to make the same provision for all cases in relation to which it is exercised or different provision for different cases or classes of case or different provision as respects the same case or class of case for different purposes,

(d) so as to make provision unconditionally or subject to any prescribed condition,

(e) so as to provide for a person to exercise a discretion in dealing with any matter.

(8) Any regulations made under a power under this Act to prescribe a rate of interest may—

(a) either themselves specify a rate of interest or make provision for any such rate to be determined by reference to such rate or the average of such rates as may be referred to in the regulations,

(b) provide for rates to be reduced below, or increased above, what they otherwise would be by specified amounts or by reference to specified formulae,

(c) provide for rates arrived at by reference to averages to be rounded up or down,

(d) provide for circumstances in which alteration of a rate of interest is or is not to take place, and

(e) provide that alterations of rates are to have effect for periods begin-ning on or after a day determined in accordance with the regulations in relation to interest running from before that day as well as from or from after that day.

(9) Any power to make regulations or a scheme under this Act includes power to make any incidental, supplementary, consequential or transitional provision which appears appropriate for the purposes of, or in connection with, the regulations or scheme.

DEFINITIONS

"the Board"—see s.67, but note that the functions of the Board have been trans-ferred to Her Majesty's Revenue and Customs by the Commissioners for Revenue and Customs Act 2005.

"prescribe"—see s.67.

Parliamentary etc. control of instruments

1.353   **66.**—(1) No regulations to which this subsection applies may be made unless a draft of the instrument containing them (whether or not together with other provisions) has been laid before, and approved by a resolution of, each House of Parliament.

(2) Subsection (1) applies to—

(a) regulations prescribing monetary amounts that are required to be reviewed under section 41,

(b) regulations made by virtue of subsection (2) of section 12 prescribing the amount in excess of which charges are not taken into account for the purposes of that subsection, and

(c) the first regulations made under sections 7(8) and (9), 9, 11, 12 and 13(2).

(3) A statutory instrument containing—

(a) regulations under this Act,

(b) a scheme made by the Secretary of State under section 12(5), or

(c) an Order in Council under section 52(7),

is (unless a draft of the instrument has been laid before, and approved by a resolution of, each House of Parliament) subject to annulment in pursuance of a resolution of either House of Parliament.

(4) A statutory instrument containing a scheme made by the Scottish Ministers under section 12(5) is subject to annulment in pursuance of a resolution of the Scottish Parliament.

(5) A statutory rule containing a scheme made by the Department of Health, Social Services and Public Safety under section 12(5) is subject to negative resolution within the meaning of section 41(6) of the Interpretation Act (Northern Ireland) 1954 (c. 33 (N.I.)).

Interpretation

67. In this Act—   1.354

"the Board" means the Commissioners of Inland Revenue,

"modifications" includes alterations, additions and omissions, and "modifies" is to be construed accordingly,

"the Northern Ireland Department" means the Department for Social Development in Northern Ireland,

"prescribed" means prescribed by regulations, and

"tax credit" and "tax credits" have the meanings given by section 1(2).

GENERAL NOTE

For references to "the Board" see now s.2 above and CRCA 2005, s.1.   1.355

68.—70. *Omitted.*

Sch.1. *Omitted.*

SCHEDULE 2

PENALTIES: SUPPLEMENTARY

Determination of penalties by Board

1.—(1) The Board may make a determination—   1.356

(a) imposing a penalty under section 31, 32(2)(b) or (3) or 33; and

(b) setting it at such amount as, in their opinion, is appropriate.

(2) The Board must give notice of a determination of a penalty under this paragraph to the person on whom the penalty is imposed.

(3) The notice must state the date on which it is given and give details of the right to appeal against the determination under section 38.

(4) After the notice of a determination under this paragraph has been given the determination must not be altered except on appeal.

(5) A penalty determined under this paragraph becomes payable at the end of the period of 30 days beginning with the date on which the notice of determination is given.

2.—(1) On an appeal [· . . .] under section 38 against the determination of a penalty under [¹ paragraph 1 that is notified to the First-tier Tribunal, the tribunal] may—

    (a) if it appears that no penalty has been incurred, set the determination aside,

    (b) if the amount determined appears to be appropriate, confirm the determination,

    (c) if the amount determined appears to be excessive, reduce it to such other amount (including nil) as [¹ the First-tier Tribunal considers] appropriate, or

    (d) if the amount determined appears to be insufficient, increase it to such amount not exceeding the permitted maximum [¹ the First-tier Tribunal considers] consider appropriate.

[¹ (2) In addition to any right of appeal on a point of law under section 11(2) of the Tribunals, Courts and Enforcement Act 2007, the person liable to the penalty may appeal to the Upper Tribunal against the amount of the penalty which has been determined under sub-paragraph (1), but not against any decision which falls under section 11(5)(d) or (e) of that Act and was made in connection with the determination of the amount of the penalty.

(2A) Section 11(3) and (4) of the Tribunals, Courts and Enforcement Act 2007 applies to the right of appeal under sub-paragraph (2) as it applies to the right of appeal under section 11(2) of that Act.

(2B) On an appeal under this paragraph the Upper Tribunal has the same powers as are conferred on the First-tier Tribunal by virtue of this paragraph.]

Penalty proceedings before [¹ tribunal]

1.357   **3.**—(1) The Board may commence proceedings for a penalty under section 32(2)(a) [¹ before the tribunal].

[¹ (2) The person liable to the penalty shall be a party to the proceedings.

(3) "tribunal" is to be read in accordance with section 47C of the Taxes Management Act 1970.]

4.—[¹ (1) In addition to any right of appeal on a point of law under section 11(2) of the Tribunals, Courts and Enforcement Act 2007, the person liable to the penalty may appeal to the Upper Tribunal against the determination of a penalty in proceedings under paragraph 2(1), but not against any decision which falls under section 11(5)(d) or (e) of that Act and was made in connection with the determination of the amount of the penalty.

(1A) Section 11(3) and (4) of the Tribunals, Courts and Enforcement Act 2007 applies to the right of appeal under sub-paragraph (1) as it applies to the right of appeal under section 11(2) of that Act.]

(2) On any such appeal the [¹Upper Tribunal] may—

    (a) if it appears that no penalty has been incurred, set the determination aside,

    (b) if the amount determined appears to be appropriate, confirm the determination,

    (c) if the amount determined appears to be excessive, reduce it to such other amount (including nil) as the [¹Upper Tribunal] considers appropriate, or

    (d) if the amount determined appears to be insufficient, increase it to such amount not exceeding the permitted maximum as the [¹Upper Tribunal] considers appropriate.

Mitigation of penalties

1.358   **5.** The Board may in their discretion mitigate any penalty under this Part or stay or compound any proceedings for any such penalty and may also, after judgment, further mitigate or entirely remit any such penalty.

Time limits for penalties

1.359   **6.**—(1) In the case of a penalty under s.31 relating to a tax credit for a person or persons for the whole or part of a tax year (other than a penalty to which sub-paragraph (3) applies), the Board may determine the penalty at any time before the latest of—

    (a) the end of the period of one year beginning with the expiry of the period for initiating an enquiry under section 19 into the entitlement of the person, or the joint entitlement of the persons, for the tax year,

(b) if such an enquiry is made, the end of the period of one year beginning with the day on which the enquiry is completed, and

(c) if a decision relating to the entitlement of the person, or the joint entitlement of the persons, for the tax year is made under section 20(1) or (4), the end of the period of one year beginning with the day on which the decision is made.

(2) In the case of a penalty under section 32 relating to a tax credit for a person or persons for the whole or part of a tax year (other than a penalty to which sub-paragraph (3) applies), the Board may determine the penalty, or commence proceedings for it, at any time before—

(a) if an enquiry into the entitlement of the person, or the joint entitlement of the persons, for the tax year is made under section 19, the end of the period of one year beginning with the day on which the enquiry is completed, and

(b) otherwise, the end of the period of one year beginning with the expiry of the period for initiating such an enquiry.

(3) In the case of—

(a) a penalty under section 31 or 32 relating to a requirement imposed by virtue of regulations under section 25; or

(b) a penalty under section 33,

the Board may determine the penalty, or commence proceedings for it, at any time before the end of the period of six years after the date on which the penalty was incurred or began to be incurred.

Recovery of penalties

7.—(1) A penalty payable under this Part is to be treated for the purposes of Part VI of the Taxes Management Act 1970 (c.9) (collection and recovery) as if it were tax charged in an assessment and due and payable.   **1.360**

(2) Regulations under section 203(2)(a) of the Income and Corporation Taxes Act 1988 (c.1) (PAYE) apply to a penalty payable under this Part as if it were an underpayment of tax for a previous year of assessment.

AMENDMENTS

1. Transfer of Tribunal Functions and Revenue and Customs Order 2009 (SI 2009/56), Sch.1, paras. 312, 317 and 318 (April 1, 2009).

DEFINITIONS

"appeal tribunal"—s.63(10).
"the Board"—s.57 but note that the functions of the Board have been transferred to HMRC by CRCA 2005.
"Social Security Commissioner"—s.63(13).
"tax credit"—by virtue of s.67, see s.1(2).
"tax year"—s.47.

GENERAL NOTE

This Schedule is set out as modified by s.63, which has the effect that, except in   **1.361** cases involving employer penalties or employer information penalties (neither of which can arise since payment by employers was abolished from April 6, 2006), the jurisdiction of the General Commissioners and Special Commissioners was exercised by appeal tribunals and the jurisdiction of the High Court and the Court of Session as the Court of Exchequer in Scotland was exercised by Social Security Commissioners. Since April 2009 all appeals now go to the First-tier Tribunal and then the Upper Tribunal. For more general information, see the note to s.39.

Para.2

Initial penalty determinations are by HMRC under para.1 except where the   **1.362** penalty is an initial penalty for failing to provide information to be imposed under s.32(2)(a). Section 38 provides a right of appeal against determinations under para.1 and s.39 provides for its exercise. Paragraph 2 makes provision for the

powers of the tribunal and, as modified by ss.63(6) and (7) for an appeal to the
Upper Tribunal on issues of quantum. In other words, the appeal is not confined to
points of law. But the power to appeal without first obtaining permission to appeal
has been removed.

Paras 3 and 4

1.363   Paragraph 3 provides for HMRC to bring proceedings before a tribunal for an
initial information penalty under s.32(2)(a). See para.6(2) for the time limit for
bringing such proceedings. Paragraph 4 provides a right of appeal to the Upper
Tribunal. It is similar to that provided in para.2 but see the note to s.63(8).

Para.5

1.364   Section 54 of the Taxes Management Act 1970 would enable an appeal to a tribunal under para.2 to be compromised but this provision also allows proceedings
under para.3 to be abandoned and for an appeal to the Upper Tribunal to be compromised. Note that HMRC may reduce a penalty imposed by a tribunal but may
not increase it. There is no provision for an appeal by HMRC against the amount
of any reduction in a penalty.

Sch.3–Sch.6. *Omitted.*

Employment Act 2002

(2002 c.22)

ARRANGEMENT OF SECTIONS

PART I

STATUTORY LEAVE AND PAY

CHAPTER 1

PATERNITY AND ADOPTION

Rights to leave and pay

CHAPTER 2

MATERNITY

PART II

TRIBUNAL REFORM

PART III

DISPUTE RESOLUTION, ETC.

PART IV

MISCELLANEOUS AND GENERAL

★These sections make amendments to SSCBA 1992 which are incorporated in the text of that legislation elsewhere in this volume.

GENERAL NOTE

On the background to the Employment Act 2002, see the General Note to SSCBA 2002, Pt 12ZA.   **1.366**

PART I

STATUTORY LEAVE AND PAY

CHAPTER 1

PATERNITY AND ADOPTION

Administration and enforcement: pay

Financial arrangements

6. [*Omitted.*]

GENERAL NOTE

1.367   This section amends SSAA 1992 and SSCBA 1992 to ensure that SPP and SAP are treated in the same was as SPP and SMP in terms of their administration.

Funding of employers' liabilities

1.368   **7.**—(1) The Secretary of State shall by regulations make provision for the payment by employers of statutory paternity pay and statutory adoption pay to be funded by the Board to such extent as the regulations may specify.

(2) Regulations under subsection (1) shall—

(a) make provision for a person who has made a payment of statutory paternity pay or statutory adoption pay to be entitled, except in such circumstances as the regulations may provide, to recover an amount equal to the sum of—

   (i) the aggregate of such of those payments as qualify for small employers' relief; and

   (ii) an amount equal to 92 per cent of the aggregate of such of those payments as do not so qualify; and

(b) include provision for a person who has made a payment of statutory paternity pay or statutory adoption pay qualifying for small employers' relief to be entitled, except in such circumstances as the regulations may provide, to recover an additional amount equal to the amount to which the person would have been entitled under section 167(2)(b) of the Social Security Contributions and Benefits Act 1992 (corresponding provision for statutory maternity pay) had the payment been a payment of statutory maternity pay.

(3) For the purposes of subsection (2), a payment of statutory paternity pay or statutory adoption pay qualifies for small employers' relief if it would have so qualified were it a payment of statutory maternity pay, treating the period for which the payment is made, in the case of statutory paternity pay, or the payee's adoption pay period, in the case of statutory adoption pay, as the maternity pay period.

(4) Regulations under subsection (1) may, in particular—

(a) make provision for funding in advance as well as in arrear;

(b) make provision for funding, or the recovery of amounts due under provision made by virtue of subsection (2)(b), by means of deductions from such amounts for which employers are accountable to the Board as the regulations may provide, or otherwise;

(c) make provision for the recovery by the Board of any sums overpaid to employers under the regulations.

(5) Where in accordance with any provision of regulations under subsection (1) an amount has been deducted from an employer's contributions payments, the amount so deducted shall (except in such cases as the Secretary of State may by regulations provide) be treated for the purposes of any provision made by or under any enactment in relation to primary or secondary Class 1 contributions—

(a) as having been paid (on such date as may be determined in accordance with the regulations), and

(b) as having been received by the Board, towards discharging the employer's liability in respect of such contributions.

(6) Regulations under this section must be made with the concurrence of the Board.

(7) In this section, "contributions payments", in relation to an employer, means any payments which the employer is required, by or under any enactment, to make in discharge of any liability in respect of primary or secondary Class 1 contributions.

DEFINITIONS

"the Board"—see s.16.
"contributions payments"—see subs.(7).
"employer"—see *ibid.*

GENERAL NOTE

See further the SPP and SAP (Administration) Regs 2002, especially regs 3–8.   1.369

Regulations about payment

8.—(1) The Secretary of State may make regulations with respect to the   1.370
payment by employers of statutory paternity pay and statutory adoption pay.

(2) Regulations under subsection (1) may, in particular, include provision—

(a) about the records to be kept by employers in relation to payments of statutory paternity pay and statutory adoption pay, including the length of time for which they are to be retained;

(b) for the production of wages sheets and other documents and records to officers of the Board for the purpose of enabling them to satisfy themselves that statutory paternity pay and statutory adoption pay have been paid and are being paid, in accordance with the regulations, to employees who are entitled to them;

(c) for requiring employers to provide information to employees (in their itemised pay statements or otherwise);

(d) for requiring employers to make returns to the Board containing such particulars with respect to payments of statutory paternity pay and statutory adoption pay as the regulations may provide.

(3) Regulations under subsection (1) must be made with the concurrence of the Board.

185

DEFINITIONS

"the Board"—see s.16.
"employer"—see *ibid.*

GENERAL NOTE

1.371   See further the SPP and SAP (Administration) Regs 2002, regs 9 and 10.

Decisions and appeals

9. [*Omitted.*]

GENERAL NOTE

1.372   This section amends ss.8, 11 and 14 of the Social Security Contributions (Transfer of Functions, etc.) Act 1999; the relevant amendments are incorporated elsewhere in this volume.

Powers to require information

1.373   **10.**—(1) The Secretary of State may by regulations make provision enabling an officer of the Board authorised by the Board for the purposes of this section to require persons of a description specified in the regulations to provide, or produce for inspection, within such period as the regulations may require, such information or documents as the officer may reasonably require for the purpose of ascertaining whether statutory paternity pay or statutory adoption pay is or was payable to or in respect of any person.

(2) The descriptions of person which may be specified by regulations under subsection (1) include, in particular—

(a) any person claiming to be entitled to statutory paternity pay or statutory adoption pay,

(b) any person who is, or has been, the spouse or partner of such a person as is mentioned in paragraph (a),

(c) any person who is, or has been, an employer of such a person as is mentioned in paragraph (a),

(d) any person carrying on an agency or other business for the introduction or supply to persons requiring them of persons available to do work or to perform services, and

(e) any person who is a servant or agent of any such person as is specified in paragraphs (a) to (d).

(3) Regulations under subsection (1) must be made with the concurrence of the Board.

DEFINITIONS

"the Board"—see s.16.
"employer"—see *ibid.*

GENERAL NOTE

1.374   See further the SPP and SAP (Administration) Regs 2002, especially regs 11–14.

Penalties: failures to comply

1.375   **11.**—(1) Where a person—

(a) fails to produce any document or record, provide any information or make any return, in accordance with regulations under section 8, or

(b) fails to provide any information or document in accordance with regulations under section 10,

he shall be liable to the penalties mentioned in subsection (2) below (subject to subsection (4)).

(2) The penalties are—

(a) a penalty not exceeding £300, and

(b) if the failure continues after a penalty is imposed under paragraph (a), a further penalty or penalties not exceeding £60 for each day on which the failure continues after the day on which the penalty under that paragraph was imposed (but excluding any day for which a penalty under this paragraph has already been imposed).

(3) Where a person fails to keep records in accordance with regulations under section 8, he shall be liable to a penalty not exceeding £3,000.

(4) Subject to subsection (5), no penalty shall be imposed under subsection (2) or (3) at any time after the failure concerned has been remedied.

(5) Subsection (4) does not apply to the imposition of a penalty under subsection (2)(a) in respect of a failure within subsection (1)(a).

(6) Where, in the case of any employee, an employer refuses or repeatedly fails to make payments of statutory paternity pay or statutory adoption pay in accordance with any regulations under section 8, the employer shall be liable to a penalty not exceeding £3,000.

(7) Section 118(2) of the Taxes Management Act 1970 (c.9) (extra time for compliance, etc.) shall apply for the purposes of subsections (1), (3) and (6) as it applies for the purposes of that Act.

(8) Schedule 1 to this Act (penalties: procedure and appeals) has effect in relation to penalties under this section.

DEFINITIONS

"the Board"—see s.16.
"employer"—see *ibid.*

GENERAL NOTE

This provision, imposing penalties on employers who fail to comply with the requirements of the SPP and SAP schemes, is modelled on the equivalent provision for tax credits: TCA 2002, s.32.

1.376

Penalties: fraud etc.

12.—(1) Where a person fraudulently or negligently—

1.377

(a) makes any incorrect statement or declaration in connection with establishing entitlement to statutory paternity pay, or

(b) provides any incorrect information or document of a kind mentioned in regulations under section 10(1) so far as relating to statutory paternity pay,

he shall be liable to a penalty not exceeding £300.

(2) Where a person fraudulently or negligently—

(a) makes any incorrect statement or declaration in connection with establishing entitlement to statutory adoption pay, or

(b) provides any incorrect information or document of a kind mentioned in regulations under section 10(1) so far as relating to statutory adoption pay, he shall be liable to a penalty not exceeding £3,000.

(3) Where an employer fraudulently or negligently makes incorrect payments of statutory paternity pay, he shall be liable to a penalty not exceeding £300.

(4) Where an employer fraudulently or negligently makes incorrect payments of statutory adoption pay, he shall be liable to a penalty not exceeding £3,000.

(5) Where an employer fraudulently or negligently—

(a) produces any incorrect document or record, provides any incorrect information or makes any incorrect return, of a kind mentioned in regulations under section 8; or

(b) receives incorrect payments in pursuance of regulations under section 7;

he shall be liable to a penalty not exceeding £3,000 or, if the offence relates only to statutory paternity pay, £300.

(6) Schedule 1 (penalties: procedure and appeals) has effect in relation to penalties under this section.

DEFINITIONS

"the Board"—see s.16.
"employer"—see *ibid.*

GENERAL NOTE

1.378   This provision, imposing penalties on employers who act fraudulently in connection with the SPP and SAP schemes, is modelled on the equivalent provision for tax credits: TCA 2002, s.31.

Supply of information held by the Board

1.379   **13.**—(1) This section applies to information which is held for the purposes of functions relating to statutory paternity pay or statutory adoption pay—

(a) by the Board, or

(b) by a person providing services to the Board, in connection with the provision of those services.

(2) Information to which this section applies may be supplied—

(a) to the Secretary of State or the Department; or

(b) to a person providing services to the Secretary of State or the Department;

for use for the purposes of functions relating to social security, child support or war pensions.

DEFINITIONS

"the Board"—see s.16.
"the Department"—see *ibid.*

Supply of information held by the Secretary of State

1.380   **14.**—(1) This section applies to information which is held for the purposes of functions relating to statutory paternity pay or statutory adoption pay—

(a) by the Secretary of State or the Department, or

(b) by a person providing services to the Secretary of State or the Department, in connection with the provision of those services.

(2) Information to which this section applies may be supplied—

   (a) to the Board, or

   (b) to a person providing services to the Board,

for use for the purposes of functions relating to statutory paternity pay or statutory adoption pay.

DEFINITIONS

   "the Board"—see s.16.

   "the Department"—see *ibid.*

Use of information by the Board

15.—(1) Information which is held—   **1.381**

   (a) by the Board, or

   (b) by a person providing services to the Board, in connection with the provision of those services,

for the purposes of any functions specified in any paragraph of subsection (2) below may be used for the purposes of, or for any purposes connected with, the exercise of any functions specified in any other paragraph of that subsection, and may be supplied to any person providing services to the Board for those purposes.

   (2) The functions referred to in subsection (1) above are—

   (a) the functions of the Board in relation to statutory paternity pay;

   (b) their functions in relation to statutory adoption pay, and

   (c) their functions in relation to tax, contributions, statutory sick pay, statutory maternity pay or tax credits, or functions under Part III of the Pension Schemes Act 1993 (c.48) (certification of pension scheme, etc.) or Part III of the Pension Schemes (Northern Ireland) Act 1993 (c.49) (corresponding provisions for Northern Ireland).

   (3) In subsection (2)(c) above, "contributions" means contributions under Part I of the Social Security Contributions and Benefits Act 1992 (c.4) or Part I of the Social Security Contributions and Benefits (Northern Ireland) Act 1992 (c.7).

DEFINITION

   "the Board"—see s.16.

Interpretation

16. In sections 5 to 15—   **1.382**

"the Board" means the Commissioners of Inland Revenue;

"the Department" means the Department for Social Development or the Department for Employment and Learning;

"employer" and "employee" have the same meanings as in Parts 12ZA and 12ZB of the Social Security Contributions and Benefits Act 1992.

CHAPTER 2

MATERNITY

17.–21. [*Omitted.*]

1.383   Section 17 amends the provisions governing the right to maternity leave under the Employment Rights Act 1996. Sections 18–20 amend ss.164 and 165 of the SSCBA 1992, and substitutes a new s.166 of that Act, while s.21 substitutes a new s.167 of the same Act. These amendments are incorporated elsewhere in this volume.

SCHEDULE 1

PENALTIES: PROCEDURE AND APPEALS

Determination of penalties by officer of Board

1.384   **1.**—(1) Subject to sub-paragraph (2) and except where proceedings have been instituted under paragraph 5, an officer of the Board authorised by the Board for the purposes of this paragraph may make a determination—
   (a)   imposing a penalty under section 11 or 12, and
   (b)   setting it at such amount as, in his opinion, is correct or appropriate.
   (2) Sub-paragraph (1) does not apply to the imposition of such a penalty as is mentioned in section 11(2)(a).
   (3) Notice of a determination of a penalty under this paragraph shall be served on the person liable to the penalty and shall state the date on which it is issued and the time within which an appeal against the determination may be made.
   (4) After the notice of a determination under this paragraph has been served the determination shall not be altered except in accordance with this paragraph or on appeal.
   (5) If it is discovered by an officer of the Board authorised by the Board for the purposes of this paragraph that the amount of a penalty determined under this paragraph is or has become insufficient, the officer may make a determination in a further amount so that the penalty is set at the amount which, in his opinion, is correct or appropriate.

Provisions supplementary to paragraph 1

1.385   **2.**—(1) A penalty determined under paragraph 1 above shall be due and payable at the end of the period of thirty days beginning with the date of the issue of the notice of determination.
   (2) Part 6 of the Taxes Management Act 1970 (c.9) shall apply in relation to a penalty determined under para.1 as if it were tax charged in an assessment and due and payable.

Appeals against penalty determinations

1.386   **3.**—(1) An appeal may be brought against the determination of a penalty under paragraph 1.
   (2) The provisions of the Taxes Management Act 1970 relating to appeals, except section 50(6) to (8), shall have effect in relation to an appeal against such a determination as they have effect in relation to an appeal against an assessment to tax [1 except that references to the tribunal shall be taken to be references to the First-tier Tribunal].
   (3) On an appeal by virtue of sub-paragraph (2) against the determination of a penalty under paragraph 1, the [1 First-tier Tribunal] may—
   (a)   if it appears [1 . . .] that no penalty has been incurred, set the determination aside,
   (b)   if the amount determined appears [1. . .] to be appropriate, confirm the determination,
   (c)   if the amount determined appears [1 . . .] to be excessive, reduce it to such other amount (including nil) as [1 the tribunal considers] appropriate,
   (d)   if the amount determined appears [1 . . .] to be insufficient, increase it to such amount not exceeding the permitted maximum as [1 the tribunal considers] appropriate.
   [1(4) In addition to any right of appeal on a point of law under section 11(2) of the Tribunals, Courts and Enforcement Act 2007, the person liable to the penalty may appeal to the Upper Tribunal against the amount of the penalty which had been determined under sub-paragraph (3), but not against any decision which falls under section 11(5)(d) or (e) of that Act and was made in connection with the determination of the amount of the penalty.
   (4A) Section 11(3) and (4) of the Tribunals, Courts and Enforcement Act 2007 applies to the right of appeal under sub-paragraph (4) as it applies to the right of appeal under section 11(2) of that Act.

(4B) On an appeal under this paragraph the Upper Tribunal has the like jurisdiction as is conferred on the First-tier Tribunal by virtue of this paragraph.]

Penalty proceedings before [¹ First-tier Tribunal]

4.—(1) An officer of the Board authorised by the Board for the purposes of this paragraph may commence proceedings for any penalty to which sub-paragraph (1) of paragraph 1 does not apply by virtue of sub-paragraph (2) of that paragraph.

[¹ (2) The person liable to the penalty shall be a party to the proceedings.]

(3) Part 6 of the Taxes Management Act 1970 (c.9) shall apply in relation to a penalty determined in proceedings under this paragraph as if it were tax charged in an assessment and due and payable.

[¹ (4) In addition to any right of appeal on a point of law under section 11(2) of the Tribunals, Courts and Enforcement Act 2007, the person liable to the penalty may appeal to the Upper Tribunal against the determination of a penalty in proceedings under sub-paragraph (1), but not against any decision which falls under section 11(5)(d) or (e) of that Act and was made in connection with the determination of the amount of the penalty.

(4A) Section 11(3) and (4) of the Tribunals, Courts and Enforcement Act 2007 applies to the right of appeal under sub-paragraph (4) as it applies to the right of appeal under section 11(2) of that Act.]

(5) On any such appeal the [¹Upper Tribunal] may—
    (a) if it appears that no penalty has been incurred, set the determination aside;
    (b) if the amount determined appears to be appropriate, confirm the determination;
    (c) if the amount determined appears to be excessive, reduce it to such other amount (including nil) as the [¹Upper Tribunal] considers appropriate;
    (d) if the amount determined appears to be insufficient, increase it to such amount not exceeding the permitted maximum as the [¹Upper Tribunal] considers appropriate.

1.387

Penalty proceedings before court

5.—(1) Where in the opinion of the Board the liability of any person for a penalty under section 11 or 12 arises by reason of the fraud of that or any other person, proceedings for the penalty may be instituted before the High Court or, in Scotland, the Court of Session as the Court of Exchequer in Scotland.

(2) Subject to sub-paragraph (3), proceedings under this paragraph shall be instituted—
    (a) in England and Wales, in the name of the Attorney General; and
    (b) in Scotland, in the name of the Advocate General for Scotland.

(3) Sub-paragraph (2) shall not prevent proceedings under this paragraph being instituted in England and Wales under the Crown Proceedings Act 1947 (c.44) by and in the name of the Board as an authorised department for the purposes of that Act.

(4) Any proceedings under this paragraph instituted in England and Wales shall be deemed to be civil proceedings by the Crown within the meaning of Part II of the Crown Proceedings Act 1947.

(5) If in proceedings under this paragraph the court does not find that fraud is proved but considers that the person concerned is nevertheless liable to a penalty, the court may determine a penalty notwithstanding that, but for the opinion of the Board as to fraud, the penalty would not have been a matter for the court.

1.388

Mitigation of penalties

6. The Board may in their discretion mitigate any penalty under section 11 or 12, or stay or compound any proceedings for a penalty, and may also, after judgment, further mitigate or entirely remit the penalty.

1.389

Time-limits for penalties

7. A penalty under section 11 or 12 may be determined by an officer of the Board, or proceedings for the penalty may be commenced before the [¹Tribunal] or the court, at any time within six years after the date on which the penalty was incurred or began to be incurred.

1.390

Interest on penalties

8.—(1) After paragraph (p) of section 178(2) of the Finance Act 1989 (c.26) (setting rates of interest) there shall be inserted—

"(q) paragraph 8 of Schedule 1 to the Employment Act 2002."

1.391

(2) A penalty under section 11 or 12 shall carry interest at the rate applicable under section 178 of the Finance Act 1989 from the date on which it becomes due and payable until payment.

Interpretation

1.392

9. In this Schedule—
"the Board" means the Commissioners of Inland Revenue;
[¹. . .]

AMENDMENTS

1. Transfer of Tribunal Functions and Revenue and Customs Order 2009 (SI 2009/56), Sch. 1, paras. 322–325 (April 1, 2009).

Income Tax (Earnings and Pensions) Act 2003

(2003 c.1)

ARRANGEMENT OF SELECTED SECTIONS

PART 1

OVERVIEW

PART 2

EMPLOYMENT INCOME: CHARGE TO TAX

CHAPTER 1

INTRODUCTION

CHAPTER 2

TAX ON EMPLOYMENT INCOME

PART 4

EMPLOYMENT INCOME: EXEMPTIONS

CHAPTER 11

MISCELLANEOUS EXEMPTIONS

PART 5

EMPLOYMENT INCOME: DEDUCTIONS ALLOWED FROM EARNINGS

CHAPTER 1

DEDUCTIONS ALLOWED FROM EARNINGS: GENERAL RULES

Introduction

General rules

CHAPTER 2

DEDUCTIONS FOR EMPLOYEE'S EXPENSES

Introduction

PART 10

SOCIAL SECURITY INCOME

CHAPTER 1

INTRODUCTION

CHAPTER 2

TAX ON SOCIAL SECURITY INCOME

CHAPTER 3

TAXABLE UK SOCIAL SECURITY BENEFITS

CHAPTER 4

TAXABLE UK SOCIAL SECURITY BENEFITS: EXEMPTIONS

Incapacity benefit

Income support

Jobseeker's allowance

Increases in respect of children

CHAPTER 5

UK SOCIAL SECURITY BENEFITS WHOLLY EXEMPT FROM INCOME TAX

CHAPTER 6

TAXABLE FOREIGN BENEFITS

PART 13

SUPPLEMENTARY PROVISIONS

Interpretation

INTRODUCTION AND GENERAL NOTE

This Act (destined to be known as ITEPA or ITEPA 2003) is the second of the   **1.394**
major income tax Acts produced by the Tax Law Rewrite Project. (The first was
the Capital Allowances Act 2001.) It took effect from and including the start of the
2003–04 income tax year, April 6, 2003, the same day that the TCA 2002 came
fully into effect. It is of considerable importance to tax credits because it entirely
rewrites the income tax rules dealing with earnings from employments and offices,
pension income, and social security income. The time-hallowed "Schedule E" and
its charge to tax on "offices and employments on emoluments therefrom" has at
last been relegated to history and a codified set of provisions taxing employment
income, pension income and social security income put in its place. The approach

of TCA 2002 is to rely on income tax rules for the calculation of income for tax credits purposes. The provisions of ITEPA are therefore the rules that will apply to the great majority of claimants for tax credits.

ITEPA is of considerable length and detail, running to 725 sections and 8 Schedules on enactment. It has been drafted in the form of a code, and therefore includes signposting provisions and a far stronger internal structure than the previous legislation.

ITEPA also uses, where possible, plain English. Its language is therefore updated from the "old" language of "Sch.E" and "emoluments".

The Tax Credits (Definition and Calculation of Income) Regulations 2002, as amended to take into account ITEPA, refer to a considerable number of provisions of ITEPA. This selection of sections from ITEPA includes the more important of those sections, together with the sections that set out the internal signposting of ITEPA and its definitions. It is not a complete reproduction of all ITEPA sections, as some of the anti-avoidance provisions that are applied to tax credits are highly technical and, in practice, sometimes quite controversial in application, while others will, it is anticipated, rarely be directly relevant to tax credits claims. In particular, the following parts are entirely omitted:

Part 4: Employment income: Exemptions

Part 6: Employment Income: Income which is not earnings or share-related

Part 7: Employment income: Share-related income and exemptions

Part 8: Former employees: Deductions for liabilities

Part 9: Pay As You Earn

Schs 2–8

Part 2, Chapter 8 of ITEPA (ss.48–61) deal with the so-called IR35 provisions, namely the provisions under which income of a "pocket book" company could be treated as the employment income of the individual who owned the company so that income was not diverted so as to be excluded from income tax. It was understood that these sections would apply to tax credits and they were therefore included in the 2003–04 edition of this volume. However, amendments to the Working Tax Credit (Entitlement and Maximum Rate) Regulations 2002 were made by the Tax Credits (Miscellaneous Amendments No.2) Regulations 2003 (SI 2003/2815) to clarify the intended policy that these provisions do not apply to tax credits. They are therefore no longer of relevance to this volume.

Part 7 of ITEPA was repealed completely and replaced by new provisions by the Finance Act 2003, s.140 and Sch.22 with effect from April 15, 2003. The original Pt 7 was outside the scope of tax credits income calculations. The new Pt 7 is not, by reason of amendment of the Tax Credits (Definition and Calculation of Income) Regulations 2002 (SI 2002/2006), reg.4. See the note to that regulation. The text of the new Pt 7 is not reproduced in this volume.

But particular attention has been paid to sections making special provision for those who are sick or disabled, and to the taxation of state pensions and social security benefits.

ITEPA and the Commissioners for Revenue and Customs Act 2005

1.395   The merger of the Inland Revenue and HM Customs and Excise, and the creation of the new joint HMRC (the new Commissioners and its officers under the new title "officer of Revenue and Customs"), requires textual amendment to most sections in ITEPA. The approach taken by the Rewrite team was to replace previous references—in many forms to "the Commissioners", "the Board", or "an inspector" or "an officer" with either "the Board" (if the function was unlikely to be delegated) or "an officer of the Board" in all other cases. CRCA 2005 adopts a different approach not entirely consistent with this. This is of limited importance in ITEPA. But, for example, the reference to the Board of Inland Revenue in s.343 should now be read as a reference to "the Commissioners", but probably "the Inland Revenue" in s.344 should now be "an officer of Revenue and Customs"—although that is not clear. This lack of clarity is emphasised by the repeal of the definition of those terms as part of the repeal of the definitions in s.720 (which formerly defined "the Inland Revenue" as meaning any officer of the Board. The old text—save for s.720—has not been amended by CRCA 2005 expressly and has been left in this edition.

PART 1

OVERVIEW

Overview of contents of this Act

1.—(1) This Act imposes charges to income tax on—   1.396

(a) employment income (see Parts 2 to 7),

(b) pension income (see Part 9), and

(c) social security income (see Part 10).

(2) *Repealed*

(3) This Act also—

(a) confers certain reliefs in respect of liabilities of former employees (see Part 8);

(b) provides for the assessment, collection and recovery of income tax in respect of employment, pension or social security income that is PAYE income (see Part 2); and

(c) allows deductions to be made from such income in respect of payroll giving (see Part 12).

Abbreviations and general index in Schedule 1

2.—(1) Schedule 1 (abbreviations and defined expressions) applies for   1.397
the purposes of this Act.

(2) In Schedule 1—

(a) Part 1 gives the meaning of the abbreviated references to Acts and instruments used in this Act; and

(b) Part 2 lists the places where expressions used in this Act are defined or otherwise explained.

(3) *Omitted.*

PART 2

EMPLOYMENT INCOME: CHARGE TO TAX

CHAPTER 1

INTRODUCTION

Structure of employment income Parts

3.—(1) The structure of the employment income Parts is as follows—   1.398
This Part imposes the charge to tax on employment income, and sets out—

(a) how the amount charged to tax for a tax year is to be calculated; and

(b) who is liable for the tax charged;

Part 3 sets out what are earnings and provides for amounts to be treated as earnings;

Part 4 deals with exemptions from the charge to tax under this Part (and, in some cases, from other charges to tax);

Part 5 deals with deductions from taxable earnings;

Part 6 deals with employment income other than earnings or share-related income; and

Part 7 deals with share-related income and exemptions.

(2) In this Act "the employment income Parts" means this Part and Parts 3 to 7.

GENERAL NOTE

1.399   Part 4 (Employment income: Exemptions)—ss.227–326—is entirely omitted from this work. It comprises a codified list of all exemptions from the charge to income tax otherwise imposed by ITEPA on various earnings and benefits, under the following chapter heads: mileage allowances and passenger payments; transport travel and subsistence; education and training; recreational benefits; non-cash vouchers and credit-tokens; removal benefits and expenses; special kinds of employee; pension provision; termination of employment; and miscellaneous. The general rule of income tax law is that it is for a claimant to claim for, and show that he or she is entitled to, the benefit of an exemption.

Part 6 is also entirely omitted. It comprises ss.386–416, and deals with payments to, and benefits from, non-approved pension schemes, and payments on termination of employment.

Part 7 is also entirely omitted. It is a lengthy part—ss.417–564 and Schs 2–5. They deal with the detail of the various kinds of tax charge on, and exemption of, share-related income including all forms of benefits obtained by shares or interests in shares.

"Employment" for the purposes of the employment income Parts

1.400   **4.**—(1) In the employment income Parts "employment" includes in particular—

(a) any employment under a contract of service,

(b) any employment under a contract of apprenticeship, and

(c) any employment in the service of the Crown.

(2) In those Parts, "employed", "employee" and "employer" have corresponding meanings.

GENERAL NOTE

1.401   There are no general income tax (or, more generally, tax) rules defining whether an individual is an employee or self-employed, or whether a relationship is an employment relationship. That is a matter to be decided by general law. There is considerable case law on the subject, some of it deriving from income tax and some from social security cases. Under the Social Security Contributions (Transfer of Functions) Act 1999, s.8, decisions about the same question for the purposes of the Social Security Contributions and Benefits Act 1992 were transferred to the Inland Revenue and, on appeal, to the tax appeal tribunals. There is, however, no equivalent provision in the TCA 2002. It would seem, therefore, that appeals about Revenue decisions about employment for tax credit purposes go to appeal tribunals, not tax appeal tribunals.

Application to offices and office-holders

5.—(1) The provisions of the employment income Parts that are   1.402
expressed to apply to employments apply equally to offices, unless otherwise indicated.

(2) In those provisions as they apply to an office—

(a) references to being employed are to being the holder of the office;

(b) "employee" means the office-holder;

(c) "employer" means the person under whom the office-holder holds
office.

(3) In the employment income Parts "office" includes in particular any
position which has an existence independent of the person who holds it and
may be filled by successive holders.

CHAPTER 2

TAX ON EMPLOYMENT INCOME

Nature of charge to tax on employment income

6.—(1) The charge to tax on employment income under this Part is a   1.403
charge to tax on—

(a) general earnings; and

(b) specific employment income.

The meaning of "employment income", "general earnings" and "specific
employment income" is given in section 7.

(2) The amount of general earnings or specific employment income
which is charged to tax in a particular tax year is set out in section 9.

(3) The rules in Chapters 4 and 5 of this Part, which are concerned
with—

(a) the residence and domicile of an employee in a tax year; and

(b) the tax year in which amounts are received or remitted to the United
Kingdom;

apply for the purposes of the charge to tax on general earnings but not that
on specific employment income.

(4) The person who is liable for any tax charged on employment income
is set out in section 13.

(5) Employment income is not charged to tax under this Part if it is
within the charge to tax under Part 2 of ITTOIA by virtue of section 15 of
that Act (divers and diving supervisors).

Meaning of "employment income", "general earnings" and "specific employment income"

7.—(1) This section gives the meaning for the purposes of the Tax Acts   1.404
of "employment income", "general earnings" and "specific employment
income".

(2) "Employment income" means—

(a) earnings within Chapter 1 of Part 3;

(b) any amount treated as earnings (see subsection (5)); or

(c) any amount which counts as employment income (see subsection (6)).

(3) "General earnings" means—

(a) earnings within Chapter 1 of Part 3; or

(b) any amount treated as earnings (see subsection (5));

excluding in each case any exempt income.

(4) "Specific employment income" means any amount which counts as employment income (see subsection (6)), excluding any exempt income.

(5) Subsection (2)(b) or (3)(b) refers to any amount treated as earnings under—

(a) Chapters 7 and 8 of this Part (application of provisions to agency workers and workers under arrangements made by intermediaries),

(b) Chapters 2 to 11 of Part 3 (the benefits code),

(c) Chapters 12 of Part 3 (payments treated as earnings), or

(d) section 262 of CAA 2001 (balancing charges to be given effect by treating them as earnings).

(6) Subsection (2)(c) or (4) refers to any amount which counts as employment income by virtue of—

(a) Part 6 (income which is not earnings or share-related),

(b) Part 7 (share-related income and exemptions), or

(c) any other enactment.

Meaning of "exempt income"

1.405   **8.** For the purposes of the employment income Parts, an amount of employment income within paragraph (a), (b) or (c) of section 7(2) is "exempt income" if, as a result of any exemption in Part 4 or elsewhere, no liability to income tax arises in respect of it as such an amount.

CHAPTER 3

OPERATION OF TAX CHARGE

Amount of employment income charged to tax

1.406   **9.**—(1) The amount of employment income which is charged to tax under this Part for a particular tax year is as follows.

(2) In the case of general earnings, the amount charged is the net taxable earnings from an employment in the year.

(3) That amount is calculated under section 11 by reference to any taxable earnings from the employment in the year (see section 10(2)).

(4) In the case of specific employment income, the amount charged is the net taxable specific income from an employment for the year.

(5) That amount is calculated under section 12 by reference to any taxable specific income from the employment for the year (see section 10(3)).

(6) Accordingly, no amount of employment income is charged to tax under this Part for a particular tax year unless—

(a) in the case of general earnings, they are taxable earnings from an employment in that year; or

(b) in the case of specific employment income, it is taxable specific income from an employment for that year.

Meaning of "taxable earnings" and "taxable specific income"

10.—(1) This section explains what is meant by "taxable earnings" and "taxable specific income" in the employment income Parts.

(2) "Taxable earnings" from an employment in a tax year are to be determined in accordance with—

(a) Chapter 4 of this Part (rules applying to employees resident, ordinarily resident and domiciled in the UK); or

(b) Chapter 5 of this Part (rules applying to employees resident, ordinarily resident or domiciled outside the UK).

(3) "Taxable specific income" from an employment for a tax year means the full amount of any specific employment income which, by virtue of Part 6 or 7 or any other enactment, counts as employment income for that year in respect of the employment.

1.407

Calculation of "net taxable earnings"

11.—(1) For the purposes of this Part, the "net taxable earnings" from an employment in a tax year are given by the formula—

$$TE - DE,$$

where—

TE means the total amount of any taxable earnings from the employment in the tax year; and

DE means the total amount of any deductions allowed from those earnings under provisions listed in sections 327(3) to (5) (deductions from earnings: general).

(2) If the amount calculated under subsection (1) is negative, the net taxable earnings from the employment in the year are to be taken to be nil instead.

(3) Relief may be available under section 128 of ITA 2007 (set-off against general income)—

(a) where TE is negative; or

(b) in certain exceptional cases where the amount calculated under subsection (1) is negative.

(4) If a person has more than one employment in a tax year, the calculation under subsection (1) must be carried out in relation to each of the employments.

1.408

Calculation of "net taxable specific income"

12.—(1) For the purposes of this Part the "net taxable specific income" from an employment for a tax year is given by the formula—

$$TSI - DSI,$$

where—

TSI means the amount of any taxable specific income from the employment for the tax year; and

1.409

DSI means the total amount of any deductions allowed from that income under provisions of the Tax Acts not included in the lists in section 327(3) and (4) (deductions from earnings: general).

(2) If the amount calculated under subsection (1) is negative, the net taxable specific income from the employment for the year is to be taken to be nil instead.

(3) If a person has more than one kind of specific employment income from an employment for a tax year, the calculation under subsection (1) must be carried out in relation to each of those kinds of specific employment income; and in such a case the "net taxable specific income" from the employment for that year is the total of all the amounts so calculated.

Person liable for tax

1.410   **13.**—(1) The person liable for any tax on employment income under this Part is the taxable person mentioned in subsection (2) or (3). This is subject to subsection (4).

(2) If the tax is on general earnings, "the taxable person" is the person to whose employment the earnings relate.

(3) If the tax is on specific employment income, "the taxable person" is the person in relation to whom the income is, by virtue of Part 6 or 7 or any other enactment, to count as employment income.

(4) If the tax is on general earnings received, or remitted to the United Kingdom, after the death of the person to whose employment the earnings relate, the person's personal representatives are liable for the tax.

(5) In that event the tax is accordingly to be assessed on the personal representatives and is a debt due from and payable out of the estate.

CHAPTER 7

APPLICATION OF PROVISIONS TO AGENCY WORKERS

Agency workers

Treatment of workers supplied by agencies

1.411   **44.**—(1) This section applies if—
  (a) an individual ("the worker") personally provides, or is under an obligation personally to provide, services (which are not excluded services) to another person ("the client");
  (b) the services are supplied by or through a third person ("the agency") under the terms of an agency contract;
  (c) the worker is subject to (or to the right of) supervision, direction or control as to the manner in which the services are provided; and
  (d) remuneration receivable under or in consequence of the agency contract does not constitute employment income of the worker apart from this chapter.

(2) If this section applies—
  (a) the services which the worker provides, or is obliged to provide, to

the client under the agency contract are to be treated for income tax purposes as duties of an employment held by the worker with the agency; and

(b) all remuneration receivable under or in consequence of the agency contract (including remuneration which the client pays or provides in relation to the services) is to be treated for income tax purposes as earnings from that employment.

PART 3

EMPLOYMENT INCOME: EARNINGS AND BENEFITS, ETC. TREATED AS EARNINGS

CHAPTER 1

EARNINGS

Earnings

62.—(1) This section explains what is meant by "earnings" in the employment income Parts.   1.412

(2) In those Parts, "earnings", in relation to an employment, means—

(a) any salary, wages or fee;

(b) any gratuity or other profit or incidental benefit of any kind obtained by the employee if it is money or money's worth; or

(c) anything else that constitutes an emolument of the employment.

(3) For the purposes of subsection (2), "money's worth" means something that is—

(a) of direct monetary value to the employee; or

(b) capable of being converted into money or something of direct monetary value to the employee.

(4) Subsection (1) does not affect the operation of statutory provisions that provide for amounts to be treated as earnings (and see section 721(7)).

CHAPTER 2

TAXABLE BENEFITS: THE BENEFITS CODE

The benefits code

The benefits code

63.—(1) In the employment income Parts "the benefits code" means—   1.413
this chapter,

Chapter 3 (expenses payments),

Chapter 4 (vouchers and credit-tokens),
Chapter 5 (living accommodation),
Chapter 6 (cars, vans and related benefits),
Chapter 7 (loans),
Chapter 10 (residual liability to charge), and
Chapter 11 (exclusion of lower-paid employments from parts of benefits code).

(2) If an employment is an excluded employment, the general effect of section 216(1) (provisions not applicable to lower-paidemployments) is that only the following chapters apply to the employment—
this chapter,

Chapter 4 (vouchers and credit-tokens),
Chapter 5 (living accommodation), and
Chapter 11 (exclusion of lower-paidemployments from parts of benefits code).

(3) Section 216(5) and (6) explain and restrict the effect of section 216(1).

(4) In the benefits code, "excluded employment" means an employment to which the exclusion in section 216(1) applies.

Relationship between earnings and benefits code

1.414   **64.**—(1) This section applies if, apart from this section, the same benefit would give rise to two amounts ("A" and "B")—

(a) A being an amount of earnings as defined in Chapter 1 of this Part; and

(b) B being an amount to be treated as earnings under the benefits code.

(2) In such a case—

(a) A constitutes earnings as defined in Chapter 1 of this Part; and

(b) the amount (if any) by which B exceeds A is to be treated as earnings under the benefits code.

(3) This section does not apply in connection with living accommodation to which Chapter 5 of this Part applies.

(4) In that case section 109 applies to determine the relationship between that chapter and Chapter 1 of this Part.

Dispensations relating to benefits within provisions not applicable to lower-paid employment

1.415   **65.**—(1) This section applies for the purposes of the listed provisions where a person ("P") supplies the Inland Revenue with a statement of the cases and circumstances in which—

(a) payments of a particular character are made to or for any employees; or

(b) benefits or facilities of a particular kind are provided for any employees,

whether they are employees of P or some other person.

(2) The "listed provisions" are the provisions listed in section 216(4) (provisions of the benefits code which do not apply to lower-paid employments).

(3) If the Inland Revenue are satisfied that no additional tax is payable by virtue of the listed provisions by reference to the payments, benefits or facilities mentioned in the statement, they must give P a dispensation under this section.

(4) A "dispensation" is a notice stating that an officer of Revenue and Customs agrees that no additional tax is payable by virtue of the listed provisions by reference to the payments, benefits or facilities mentioned in the statement supplied by P.

(5) If a dispensation is given under this section, nothing in the listed provisions applies to the payments, or the provision of the benefits or facilities, covered by the dispensation or otherwise has the effect of imposing any additional liability to tax in respect of them.

(6) If in their opinion there is reason to do so, the Inland Revenue may revoke a dispensation by giving a further notice to P.

(7) That notice may revoke the dispensation from—

(a) the date when the dispensation was given; or

(b) a later date specified in the notice.

(8) If the notice revokes the dispensation from the date when the dispensation was given—

(a) any liability to tax that would have arisen if the dispensation had never been given is to be treated as having arisen; and

(b) P and the employees in question must make all the returns which they would have had to make if the dispensation had never been given.

(9) If the notice revokes the dispensation from a later date—

(a) any liability to tax that would have arisen if the dispensation had ceased to have effect on that date is to be treated as having arisen; and

(b) P and the employees in question must make all the returns which they would have had to make if the dispensation had ceased to have effect on that date.

General definitions for benefits code

Meaning of "employment" and related expressions

66.—(1) In the benefits code—   1.416

(a) "employment" means a taxable employment under Part 2; and

(b) "employed", "employee" and "employer" have corresponding meanings.

(2) Where a chapter of the benefits code applies in relation to an employee—

(a) references in that chapter to "the employment" are to the employment of that employee; and

(b) references in that chapter to "the employer" are to the employer in respect of that employment.

(3) For the purposes of the benefits code an employment is a "taxable employment under Part 2" in a tax year if the earnings from the employment for that year are (or would be if there were any) general earnings to which the charging provisions of Chapter 4 or 5 of Part 2 apply.

(4) In subsection (3)—

(a) the reference to an employment includes employment as a director of a company; and

(b) "earnings" means earnings as defined in Chapter of this Part.

CHAPTER 3

TAXABLE BENEFITS: EXPENSES PAYMENTS

Sums in respect of expenses

1.417

70.—(1) This chapter applies to a sum paid to an employee in a tax year if the sum—

(a) is paid to the employee in respect of expenses; and

(b) is so paid by reason of the employment.

(2) This chapter applies to a sum paid away by an employee in a tax year if the sum—

(a) was put at the employee's disposal in respect of expenses;

(b) was so put by reason of the employment; and

(c) is paid away by the employee in respect of expenses.

(3) For the purposes of this chapter it does not matter whether the employment is held at the time when the sum is paid or paidaway so long as it is held at some point in the tax year in which the sum is paid or paidaway.

(4) References in this chapter to an employee accordingly include a prospective or former employee.

(5) This chapter does not apply to the extent that the sum constitutes earnings from the employment by virtue of any other provision.

Meaning of paid or put at disposal by reason of the employment

1.418

71.—(1) If an employer pays a sum in respect of expenses to an employee it is to be treated as paid by reason of the employment unless—

(a) the employer is an individual, and

(b) the payment is made in the normal course of the employer's domestic, family or personal relationships.

(2) If an employer puts a sum at an employee's disposal in respect of expenses it is to be treated as put at the employee's disposal by reason of the employment unless—

(a) the employer is an individual, and

(b) the sum is put at the employee's disposal in the normal course of the employer's domestic, family or personal relationships.

Sums in respect of expenses treated as earnings

1.419

72.—(1) If this chapter applies to a sum, the sum is to be treated as earnings from the employment for the tax year in which it is paid or paidaway.

(2) Subsection (1) does not prevent the making of a deduction allowed under any of the provisions listed in subsection (3).

(3) The provisions are—

section 336 (deductions for expenses: the general rule);

section 337 (travel in performance of duties);

section 338 (travel for necessary attendance);

section 340 (travel between group employments);

section 341 (travel at start or finish of overseas employment);

section 342 (travel between employments where duties performed abroad);

section 343 (deduction for professional membership fees);
section 344 (deduction for annual subscriptions);
section 346 (deduction for employee liabilities);
section 353 (deductions from earnings charged on remittance).

CHAPTER 4

TAXABLE BENEFITS: VOUCHERS AND CREDIT-TOKENS

Cash vouchers: introduction

Cash vouchers to which this chapter applies

73.—(1) This chapter applies to a cash voucher provided for an employee   1.420
by reason of the employment which is received by the employee.

(2) A cash voucher provided for an employee by the employer is to be
regarded as provided by reason of the employment unless—
  (a) the employer is an individual; and
  (b) the provision is made in the normal course of the employer's domes-
       tic, family or personal relationships.

(3) A cash voucher provided for an employee and appropriated to the
employee—
  (a) by attaching it to a card held for the employee; or
  (b) in any other way;
is to be treated for the purposes of this chapter as having been received by
the employee at the time when it is appropriated.

Provision for, or receipt by, member of employee's family

74.—For the purposes of this chapter any reference to a cash voucher   1.421
being provided for or received by an employee includes a reference to it
being provided for or received by a member of the employee's family.

Meaning of "cash voucher"

Meaning of "cash voucher"

75.—(1) In this chapter "cash voucher" means a voucher, stamp or similar   1.422
document capable of being exchanged for a sum of money which is—
  (a) greater than;
  (b) equal to; or
  (c) not substantially less than,
the expense incurred by the person at whose cost the voucher, stamp or
similar document is provided.

(2) For the purposes of subsection (1) it does not matter whether the
document—
  (a) is also capable of being exchanged for goods or services;
  (b) is capable of being exchanged singly or together with other vouchers,
       stamps, or documents;

(c) is capable of being exchanged immediately or only after a time.

(3) Subsection (1) is subject to section 76 (sickness benefits-related voucher).

Sickness benefits-related voucher

1.423 **76.**—(1) This section applies where—

(a) the expense incurred by the person at whose cost a voucher, stamp or similar document is provided ("the provision expense") includes costs to that person of providing sickness benefits ("sickness benefits costs"),

(b) the voucher, stamp or document would be a cash voucher (apart from this section) but for the fact that the sum of money for which it is capable of being exchanged ("the exchange sum") is substantially less than the provision expense, and

(c) the whole or part of the difference between the exchange sum and the provision expense represents the sickness benefits costs.

(2) The voucher, stamp or document is a cash voucher within the meaning of this chapter if—

$$E = \frac{PE}{D}$$

or

$$E \text{ is not substantially less than } \frac{PE}{D},$$

where—

E is the exchange sum;

PE is the provision expense; and

D is the amount of the difference between E and PE which represents the sickness benefits costs.

(3) In this section "sickness benefits" mean benefits in connection with sickness, personal injury or death.

Benefit of cash voucher treated as earnings

Benefit of cash voucher treated as earnings

1.424 **81.**—(1) The cash equivalent of the benefit of a cash voucher to which this chapter applies is to be treated as earnings from the employment for the tax year in which the voucher is received by the employee.

(2) The cash equivalent is the sum of money for which the voucher is capable of being exchanged.

Non-cash vouchers: introduction

Non-cash vouchers to which this chapter applies

1.425 **82.**—(1) This chapter applies to a non-cash voucher provided for an employee by reason of the employment which is received by the employee.

(2) A non-cash voucher provided for an employee by the employer is to be regarded as provided by reason of the employment unless—
(a) the employer is an individual; and
(b) the provision is made in the normal course of the employer's domestic, family or personal relationships.

(3) A non-cash voucher provided for an employee and appropriated to the employee—
(a) by attaching it to a card held for the employee; or
(b) in any other way,

is to be treated for the purposes of this chapter as having been received by the employee at the time when it is appropriated.

Meaning of "non-cash voucher"

Meaning of "non-cash voucher"

84.—(1) In this chapter "non-cash voucher" means—   1.426
(a) a voucher, stamp or similar document or token which is capable of being exchanged for money, goods or services;
(ab) a childcare voucher
(b) a transport voucher, or
(c) a cheque voucher,
but does not include a cash voucher.

(2) For the purposes of subsection (1)(a) it does not matter whether the document or token is capable of being exchanged—
(a) singly or together with other vouchers, stamps, documents or tokens;
(b) immediately or only after a time.

(2A) In this chapter "childcare voucher" means a voucher, stamp or similar document or token intended to enable a person to obtain the provision of case for a child (whether or not in exchange for it).

(3) In this chapter "transport voucher" means a ticket, pass or other document or token intended to enable a person to obtain passenger transport services (whether or not in exchange for it).

(4) In this chapter "cheque voucher" means a cheque—
(a) provided for an employee; and
(b) intended for use by the employee wholly or mainly for payment for—
(i) particular goods or services; or
(ii) goods or services of one or more particular classes;
and, in relation to a cheque voucher, references to a voucher being exchanged for goods or services are to be read accordingly.

Benefit of non-cash voucher treated as earnings

Benefit of non-cash voucher treated as earnings

87.—(1) The cash equivalent of the benefit of a non-cash voucher to which   1.427
this chapter applies is to be treated as earnings from the employment for the tax year in which the voucher is received by the employee.

(2) The cash equivalent is the difference between—

(a) the cost of provision; and

(b) any part of that cost made good by the employee to the person incurring it.

(3) In this chapter the "cost of provision" means, in relation to a non-cash voucher, the expense incurred in or in connection with the provision of—

(a) the voucher, and

(b) the money, goods or services for which it is capable of being exchanged,

by the person at whose cost they are provided.

(3A) In the case of a childcare voucher, the reference in subsection (3)(b) to the services for which the voucher is capable of being exchanged is to the provision of care for a child which may be obtained by using it.

(4) In the case of a transport voucher, the reference in subsection (3)(b) to the services for which the voucher is capable of being exchanged is to the passenger transport services which may be obtained by using it.

(5) If a person incurs expense in or in connection with the provision of non-cash vouchers for two or more employees as members of a group or class, the expense incurred in respect of one of them is to be such part of that expense as is just and reasonable.

(6) This section is subject to section 89 (reduction for meal vouchers).

Credit-tokens: introduction

Credit-tokens to which this chapter applies

1.428 **90.**—(1) This chapter applies to a credit-token provided for an employee by reason of the employment which is used by the employee to obtain money, goods or services.

(2) A credit-token provided for an employee by the employer is to be regarded as provided by reason of the employment unless—

(a) the employer is an individual; and

(b) the provision is made in the normal course of the employer's domestic, family or personal relationships.

Meaning of "credit-token"

Meaning of "credit-token"

1.429 **92.**—(1) In this chapter "credit-token" means a credit card, debit card or other card, a token, a document or other object given to a person by another person ("X") who undertakes—

(a) on the production of it, to supply money, goods or services on credit; or

(b) if a third party ("Y") supplies money, goods or services on its production, to pay Y for what is supplied.

(2) A card, token, document or other object can be a credit-token even if—

214

(a) some other action is required in addition to its production in order for the money, goods or services to be supplied;

(b) X in paying Y may take a discount or commission.

(3) For the purposes of this section—

(a) the use of an object given by X to operate a machine provided by X is to be treated as its production to X, and

(b) the use of an object given by X to operate a machine provided by Y is to be treated as its production to Y.

(4) A "credit-token" does not include a cash voucher or a non-cash voucher.

Benefit of credit-token treated as earnings

Benefit of credit-token treated as earnings

94.—(1) On each occasion on which a credit-token to which this chapter applies is used by the employee in a tax year to obtain money, goods or services, the cash equivalent of the benefit of the token is to be treated as earnings from the employment for that year.

(2) The cash equivalent is the difference between—

(a) the cost of provision; and

(b) any part of that cost made good by the employee to the person incurring it.

(3) In this section the "cost of provision" means the expense incurred—

(a) in or in connection with the provision of the money, goods or services obtained on the occasion in question; and

(b) by the person at whose cost they are provided.

(4) If a person incurs expense in or in connection with the provision of credit-tokens for two or more employees as members of a group or class, the expense incurred in respect of one of them is to be such part of that expense as is just and reasonable.

1.430

General supplementary provisions

Disregard for money, goods or services obtained

95.—(1) This section applies if the cash equivalent of the benefit of a cash voucher, a non-cash voucher or a credit-token—

(a) is to be treated as earnings from an employee's employment under this chapter; or

(b) would be so treated but for a dispensation given under section 96.

(2) Money, goods or services obtained—

(a) by the employee or another person in exchange for the cash voucher or non-cash voucher; or

(b) by the employee or a member of the employee's family by use of the credit-token,

are to be disregarded for the purposes of the Income Tax Acts.

(3) But the goods or services are not to be disregarded for the purposes of applying sections 362 and 363 (deductions where non-cash voucher or credit-token provided).

1.431

(3A) In the case of a childcare voucher, the reference in subsection (2) (a) to the services obtained in exchange for the voucher is to the provision of care for a child which may be obtained by using it.

(4) In the case of a transport voucher, the reference in subsection (2) (a) to the services obtained in exchange for the voucher is to the passenger transport services obtained by using it.

CHAPTER 10

TAXABLE BENEFITS: RESIDUAL LIABILITY TO CHARGE

Introduction

Employment-related benefits

1.432   **201.**—(1) This chapter applies to employment-related benefits.
(2) In this chapter—
"benefit" means a benefit or facility of any kind;
"employment-related benefit" means a benefit, other than an excluded benefit, which is provided in a tax year—
  (a) for an employee; or
  (b) for a member of an employee's family or household;
    by reason of the employment.
For the definition of "excluded benefit" see section 202.
(3) A benefit provided by an employer is to be regarded as provided by reason of the employment unless—
  (a) the employer is an individual; and
  (b) the provision is made in the normal course of the employer's domestic, family or personal relationships.
(4) For the purposes of this chapter it does not matter whether the employment is held at the time when the benefit is provided so long as it is held at some point in the tax year in which the benefit is provided.
(5) References in this chapter to an employee accordingly include a prospective or former employee.

Excluded benefits

1.433   **202.**—(1) A benefit is an "excluded benefit" for the purposes of this chapter if—
  (a) any of Chapters 3 to 9 of the benefits code applies to the benefit;
  (b) any of those chapters would apply to the benefit but for an exception; or
  (c) the benefit consists in the right to receive, or the prospect of receiving, sums treated as earnings under section 221 (payments where employee absent because of sickness or disability).
(2) In this section, "exception", in relation to the application of a

chapter of the benefits code to a benefit, means any enactment in the chapter which provides that the chapter does not apply to the benefit. But for this purpose section 86 (transport vouchers under pre-26th March 1982 arrangements) is not an exception.

Cash equivalent of benefit treated as earnings

Cash equivalent of benefit treated as earnings

203.—(1) The cash equivalent of an employment-related benefit is to be treated as earnings from the employment for the tax year in which it is provided.

(2) The cash equivalent of an employment-related benefit is the cost of the benefit less any part of that cost made good by the employee to the persons providing the benefit.

(3) The cost of an employment-related benefit is determined in accordance with section 204 unless—

(a) section 205 provides that the cost is to be determined in accordance with that section; or

(b) section 206 provides that the cost is to be determined in accordance with that section.

1.434

Determination of the cost of the benefit

Cost of the benefit: basic rule

204. The cost of an employment-related benefit is the expense incurred in or in connection with provision of the benefit (including a proper proportion of any expense relating partly to provision of the benefit and partly to other matters).

1.435

Exemption of minor benefits

210.—(1) The Treasury may make provision by regulations for exempting from the application of this Chapter such minor benefits as may be specified by regulation.

(2) An exemption conferred by such regulations is conditional on the benefit being made available to the employer's employees generally on similar terms.

1.436

GENERAL NOTE

For regulations made under this section see the Income Tax (Exemption of Minor Benefits) Regulations 2002 (SI 2002/205) as amended by the Income Tax (Exemption of Minor Benefits)(Amendment) Regulations 2003 (SI 2003/1434). These regulations are not included in this volume. They remove taxation from minor benefits, such as free meals, provided by employers that would otherwise be liable to taxation.

1.437

CHAPTER 11

TAXABLE BENEFITS: EXCLUSION OF LOWER-PAID EMPLOYMENT FROM
PARTS OF BENEFITS CODE

Introduction

Provisions not applicable to lower-paid employments

1.438   **216.**—(1) The chapters of the benefits code listed in subsection (4) do
not apply to an employment in relation to a tax year if—
  (a) it is lower-paid employment in relation to that year (see section 217);
       and
  (b) condition A or B is met.
  (2) Condition A is that the employee is not employed as a director of a
company.
  (3) Condition B is that the employee is employed as a director of a
company but has no material interest in the company and either—
  (a) the employment is as a full-time working director; or
  (b) the company is non-profit-making or is established for charitable
       purposes only.
"Non-profit-making" means that the company does not carry on a trade
and its functions do not consist wholly or mainly in the holding of investments or other property.
  (4) The chapters referred to in subsection (1) are—
Chapter 3 (taxable benefits: expenses payments);
Chapter 6 (taxable benefits: cars, vans and related benefits);
Chapter 7 (taxable benefits: loans);
Chapter 10 (taxable benefits: residual liability to charge).
  (5) Subsection (1)—
  (a) means that in any of those chapters a reference to an employee does
       not include an employee whose employment is within the exclusion
       in that subsection, if the context is such that the reference is to an
       employee in relation to whom the chapter applies; but
  (b) does not restrict the meaning of references to employees in other con-
       texts.
  (6) Subsection (1) has effect subject to—
section 188(2) (discharge of loan: where employment becomes lower-
paid);
  and
section 220 (employment in two or more related employments).

What is lower-paid employment?

Meaning of "lower-paid employment"

1.439   **217.**—(1) For the purposes of this chapter an employment is "lower-
paid employment" in relation to a tax year if the earnings rate for the

employment for the year (calculated under section 218) is less than £8,500.

(2) Subsection (1) is subject to section 220 (employment in two or more related employments).

Calculation of earnings rate for a tax year

218.—(1) For any tax year the earnings rate for an employment is to be calculated as follows— 1.440

Step 1

Find the total of the following amounts—
  (a) the total amount of the earnings from the employment for the year within Chapter 1 of this Part;
  (b) the total of any amounts that are treated as earnings from the employment for the year under the benefits code (see subsections (2) and (3));
  (c) the total of any amounts that are treated as earnings from the employment for the year under Chapter 12 of this Part (payments treated as earnings); and
  (d) in the case of an employment within section 56(2) (deemed employment of worker by intermediary), the amount of the deemed employment payment for the year (see section 54), excluding any exempt income.

Step 2

Add to that total any extra amount required to be added for the year by section 219 (extra amounts to be added in connection with a car).

Step 3

Subtract the total amount of any authorised deductions (see subsection (4)) from the result of step 2.

Step 4

The earnings rate for the employment for the year is given by the formula—

$$\frac{Y}{R \times E}$$

where—
  R is the result of step 3;
  Y is the number of days in the year; and
  E is the number of days in the year when the employment is held.

(2) Section 216(1) (provisions not applicable to lower-paid employment) is to be disregarded for the purpose of determining any amount under step 1.

(3) If the benefit of living accommodation is to be taken into account under step 1, the cash equivalent is to be calculated in accordance with section 105 (even if the cost of providing the accommodation exceeds £75,000).

(4) For the purposes of step 3, "authorised deduction" means any deduction that would (assuming it was an amount of taxable earnings) be allowed from any amount within step 1 under—

section 346 (employee liabilities);

section 352 (agency fees paid by entertainers);

section 355 (corresponding payments by non-domiciled employees with foreign employers);

section 368 (fixed sum deductions from earnings payable out of public revenue);

section 370 (travel costs and expenses where duties performed abroad: employee's travel);

section 371 (travel costs and expenses where duties performed abroad: visiting spouse's, civil partner's or child's travel);

section 373 (non-domiciled employee's travel costs and expenses where duties performed in United Kingdom);

section 374 (non-domiciled employee's spouse's, civil partner's or child's travel costs and expenses where duties performed in United Kingdom);

section 376 (foreign accommodation and subsistence costs and expenses (overseas employments));

section 377 (costs and expenses in respect of personal security assets and services);

section 713 (payroll giving to charities); section 592(7) of ICTA (contributions to exempt approved schemes); section 594 of ICTA (contributions to exempt statutory schemes); or section 262 of CAA 2001 (capital allowances to be given effect by treating them as deductions).

Extra amounts to be added in connection with a car

1.441   **219.**—(1) The provisions of this section apply for the purposes of section 218(1) in the case of a tax year in which a car is made available as mentioned in section 114(1) (cars, vans and related benefits) by reason of the employment.

(2) Subsection (3) applies if in the tax year—

(a) an alternative to the benefit of the car is offered; and

(b) the amount that would be earnings within Chapter 1 of this Part if the benefit of the car were to be determined by reference to the alternative offered exceeds the benefit code earnings (see subsection (4)).

(3) The amount of the excess is an extra amount to be added under step 2 in section 218(1).

(4) For the purposes of subsection (2) "the benefit code earnings" is the total for the year of—

(a) the cash equivalent of the benefit of the car (calculated in accordance with Chapter 6 of this Part); and

(b) the cash equivalent (calculated in accordance with that chapter) of the benefit of any fuel provided for the car by reason of the employment.

(7) Section 216(1) (provisions not applicable to lower-paid employment) is to be disregarded for the purpose of determining any amount under this section.

Part 4

Employment Income: Exemptions

Chapter 11

Miscellaneous Exemptions

Childcare: exemption for employer-provided care

318.—(1) No liability to income tax arises in respect of the provision   1.442
for an employee of care for a child if conditions A to D are met. For the
meaning of "care" and "child", see section 318B.

(2) If those conditions are met only as respects part of the provision, no
such liability arises in respect of that part.

(3) Condition A is that the child—

(a) is a child or stepchild of the employee and is maintained (wholly or
partly) at the employee's expense,

(b) is resident with the employee, or

(c) is a person in respect of whom the employee has parental
responsibility.

For the meaning of "parental responsibility", see section 318B.

(4) Condition B is that—

(a) the premises on which the care is provided are not used wholly or
mainly as a private dwelling, and

(b) any applicable registration requirement is met.

(5) The registration requirements are—

(za) in England, that under Part 10A of the Children Act 1989 or Part 3
of the Childcare Act 2006;

(a) in . . .Wales, that under Part 10A of the Children Act 1989;

(b) in Scotland, that under Part 1 or 2 of the Regulation of Care
(Scotland) Act 2001;

(c) in Northern Ireland, that under Part XI of the Children (Northern
Ireland) Order 1995.

(6) Condition C is that—

(a) the premises on which the care is provided are made available by the
scheme employer alone, or

(b) the partnership requirements are met.

In this section "scheme employer" means the employer operating the
scheme under which the care is provided (who need not be the employer
of the employee).

(7) The partnership requirements are—

(a) that the care is provided under arrangements made by persons who
include the scheme employer,

(b) that the premises on which it is provided are made available by one
or more of those persons, and

(c) that under the arrangements the scheme employer is wholly or partly
responsible for financing and managing the provision of the care.

(8) Condition D is that the care is provided under a scheme that is open—

(a) to the scheme employer's employees generally, or

(b) generally to those of the scheme employer's employees at a particular location,

and that the employee to whom it is provided is either an employee of the scheme employer or is an employee working at the same location as employees of the scheme employer to whom the scheme is open.

GENERAL NOTE

1.443   This and the following sections are inserted into ITEPA by Finance Act 2004, s.78 and Sch.13 from April 6, 2005. They are set out here as they are seen by some as alternatives to the provision of childcare in return for payment by an individual using the childcare element of WTC.

Section 318C was amended from April 6, 2007 for England by the Income Tax (Qualifying Child Care) Regulations 2007 (SI 2007/849). The formal introduction to the regulations makes clear that these changes were made in coordination with changes to the equivalent regulations for the childcare element of tax credits.

Childcare: limited exemption for other care

1.444   **318A.**—(1) If conditions A to C are met in relation to the provision for an employee of care for a child—

(a) no liability to income tax arises under section 62 (general definition of earnings), and

(b) liability to income tax by virtue of Chapter 10 of Part 3 (taxable benefits: residual liability to charge) arises only in respect of so much of the cash equivalent of the benefit as exceeds the exempt amount.

For the meaning of "care" and "child", see section 318B.

(2) If those conditions are met only as respects part of the provision, subsection (1) applies in respect of that part.

(3) Condition A is that the child—

(a) is a child or stepchild of the employee and is maintained (wholly or partly) at the employee's expense, or

(b) is resident with the employee and is a person in respect of whom the employee has parental responsibility.

For the meaning of "parental responsibility", see section 318B.

(4) Condition B is that the care is qualifying child care.

For the meaning of "qualifying child care", see section 318C.

(5) Condition C is that the care is provided under a scheme that is open—

(a) to the employer's employees generally, or

(b) generally to those at a particular location.

(6) For the purposes of this section the "exempt amount", in any tax year, is £55 for each qualifying week in that year.

(7) A "qualifying week" means a tax week in which care is provided for a child in circumstances in which conditions A to C are met. "tax week" means one of the successive periods in a tax year beginning with the first day of that year and every seventh day after that (so that the last day of a tax year or, in the case of a tax year ending in a leap year, the last two days is treated as a separate week).

(8) An employee is only entitled to one exempt amount even if care is pro-

vided for more than one child. It does not matter that another person may also be entitled to an exempt amount in respect of the same child.

(9) An employee is not entitled to an exempt amount under this section and under section 270A (limited exemption for childcare vouchers) in respect of the same tax week.

Childcare: meaning of "care", "child" and "parental responsibility"

318B.—(1) For the purposes of sections 318 and 318A (exemptions for employer-provided or employer-contracted childcare) "care" means any form of care or supervised activity that is not provided in the course of the child's compulsory education.

(2) For the purposes of those sections a person is a "child" until the last day of the week in which falls the 1st September following the child's fifteenth birthday (or sixteenth birthday if the child is disabled).

(3) For the purposes of subsection (2) a child is disabled if—

(a) a disability living allowance is payable in respect of him, has ceased to be payable solely because he is a patient,

(b) he—

    (i) is registered as blind in a register compiled by a local authority under section 29 of the National Assistance Act 1948 (welfare services),

    (ii) has been certified as blind in Scotland and in consequence is registered as blind in a register maintained by or on behalf of a local authority in Scotland, or

    (iii) has been certified as blind in Northern Ireland and in consequence is registered as blind in a register maintained by or on behalf of a Health and Social Services Board, or

(c) he ceased to be so registered as blind within the previous 28 weeks.

(4) In subsection (3)(a) "patient" means a person (other than a person who is serving a sentence imposed by a court in a prison or custody institution or, in Scotland, a young offenders' institution) who is regarded as receiving free in-patient treatment within the meaning of the Social Security (Hospital In-Patients) Regulations 1975 or the Social Security (Hospital In-Patients) Regulations (Northern Ireland) 1975.

(5) For the purposes of sections 318 and 318A "parental responsibility" means all the rights, duties, powers, and authority which by law a parent of a child has in relation to the child and the child's property.

(6) In this section and section 318C "local authority" means—

(a) in relation to England, the council of a county or district, a metropolitan district, a London Borough, the Common Council of the City of London or the Council of the Isles of Scilly;

(b) in relation to Wales, the council of a county or county borough;

(c) in relation to Scotland, a council constituted under section 2 of the Local Government etc. (Scotland) Act 1994.

Childcare: meaning of "qualifying child care"

318C.—(1) For the purposes of section 318A "qualifying child care" means registered or approved care within any of subsections (2) to (6) below that is not excluded by subsection (7) below.

1.445

1.446

(2) Care provided for a child in England is registered or approved care if it is provided—

(a) by a person registered under Part 10A of the Children Act 1989,

(b) . . .

(ba) by a person registered under Part 3 of the Childcare Act 2006,

(c) by or under the direction of the proprietor of a school on the school premises (subject to subsection (2B)),

(d) by a child care provider approved by an organisation accredited under the Tax Credit (New Category of Child Care Provider) Regulations 1999,

(ea) by a child care provider approved in accordance with the Tax Credits (Approval of Child Care Providers) Scheme 2005,

(eb) . . .

(f) by a domiciliary care worker under the Domiciliary Care Agencies Regulations 2002, or

(g) by a foster parent under the Fostering Services Regulations 2002 in relation to a child other than one whom the foster parent is fostering.

(2A) In subsection (2)(c)—

"proprietor", in relation to a school, means—

(a) the governing body incorporated under section 19 of the Education Act 2002, or

(b) if there is no such body, the person or body of persons responsible for the management of the school;

"school" means a school that Her Majesty's Chief Inspector of Education, Children's Services and Skills (the "Chief Inspector") is or may be required to inspect;

"school premises" means premises that may be inspected as part of an inspection of the school by the Chief Inspector.

(2B) Care provided for a child in England is not registered or approved care under subsection (2)(c) if—

(a) it is provided during school hours for a child who has reached compulsory school age, or

(b) it is provided in breach of a requirement to register under Part 3 of the Childcare Act 2006.

(3) Care provided for a child in Wales is registered or approved care if it is provided—

(a) by a person registered under Part 10A of the Children Act 1989,

(b) by a school or establishment that does not need to be registered under that Part to provide the care because of an exemption under paragraph 1 or 2 of Schedule 9A to that Act,

(c) in the case of care provided for a child out of school hours, by a school on school premises or by a local authority,

(d) by a child care provider approved by an organisation accredited under the Tax Credit (New Category of Child Care Provider) Regulations 1999,

(e) by a domiciliary care worker under the Domiciliary Care Agencies (Wales) Regulations 2004,

(f) by a child care provider approved under the Tax Credits (Approval of Child Care Providers) (Wales) Scheme 2007, or

(g) by a foster parent under the Fostering Services (Wales) Regulations 2003 in relation to a child other than one whom the foster parent is fostering.

(4) Care provided for a child in Scotland is registered or approved care if it is provided—

(a) by a person in circumstances where the care service provided by him—

    (i) consists of child minding or of day care of children within the meaning of section 2 of the Regulation of Care (Scotland) Act 2001, and

    (ii) is registered under Part 1 of that Act, or

(b) by a local authority in circumstances where the care service provided by the local authority—

    (i) consists of child minding or of day care of children within the meaning of section 2 of the Regulation of Care (Scotland) 2001, and

    (ii) is registered under Part 2 of that Act.

(5) Care provided for a child in Northern Ireland is registered approved care if it is provided—

(a) by a person registered under Part XI of the Children (Northern Ireland) Order 1995, or

(b) by an institution or establishment that does not need to be registered under that Part to provide the care because of an exemption under Article 121 of that Order, or

(c) in the case of care provided for a child out of school hours, by a school on school premises or by an education and library board or an HSS trust.

(6) Care provided for a child outside the United Kingdom is registered or approved child care if it is provided by a child care provider approved by an organisation accredited under the Tax Credit (New Category of Child Care Provider) Regulations 2002.

(7) Child care is excluded from section 318A—

(a) if it is provided by the partner of the employee in question,

(b) if it is provided by a relative of the child wholly or mainly in the child's home or (if different) the home of a person having parental responsibility for the child, or

(c) in the case of care falling within subsection (2)(ea) or (3)(f) if—

    (i) it is provided wholly or mainly in the home of a relative of the child, and

    (ii) the provider usually provides care there solely in respect of one or more children to whom the provider is a relative.

(8) In subsection (7)—

"partner" means one of a couple (within the meaning given by section 137(1) of Social Security Contributions and Benefits Act 1992 or section 133(1) of SSCB(NI)A 1992); and

"relative" means parent, grandparent, aunt, uncle, brother or sister, whether by blood, half blood or marriage or civil partnership.

(9) In subsection (7)(c), "relative in relation to a child, also includes—

(a) a local authority foster parent in relation to the child,

(b) a foster parent with whom the child has been placed by a voluntary organisation,

(c) a person who fosters the child privately (within the meaning of section 66 of the Children Act 1989, or

(d) a step-parent of the child.

PART 5

EMPLOYMENT INCOME: DEDUCTIONS ALLOWED FROM EARNINGS

CHAPTER 1

DEDUCTIONS ALLOWED FROM EARNINGS: GENERAL RULES

Introduction

Deductions from earnings: general

1.447   **327.**—(1) This Part provides for deductions that are allowed from the taxable earnings from an employment in a tax year in calculating the net taxable earnings from the employment in the tax year for the purposes of Part II (see section 11(1)).

(2) In this Part, unless otherwise indicated by the context—

(a) references to the earnings from which deductions are allowed are references to the taxable earnings mentioned in subsection (1); and

(b) references to the tax year are references to the tax year mentioned there.

(3) The deductions for which this Part provides are those allowed under—

Chapter 2 (deductions for employee's expenses);

Chapter 3 (deductions from benefits code earnings);

Chapter 4 (fixed allowances for employee's expenses);

Chapter 5 (deductions for earnings representing benefits or reimbursed expenses); and

Chapter 6 (deductions from seafarers' earnings).

(4) Further provision about deductions from earnings is made in—

section 232 (giving effect to mileage allowance relief);

section 619 of ICTA (contributions under retirement annuity contracts); and

section 262 of CAA 2001 (capital allowances to be given effect by treating them as deductions from earnings).

(5) Further provision about deductions from income including earnings is made in—

Part 12 (payroll giving);

section 592(7) of ICTA (contributions to exempt approved schemes); and

section 594(1) of ICTA (contributions to exempt statutory schemes).

General rules

The income from which deductions may be made

1.448   **328.**—(1) The general rule is that deductions under this Part are allowed—

(a) from any earnings from the employment in question; and

(b) not from earnings from any other employment. This is subject to subsections (2) to (4).

(2) Deductions under section 351 (expenses of ministers of religion) are allowed from earnings from any employment as a minister of a religious denomination.

(3) Deductions under section 368 (fixed sum deductions from earnings payable out of public revenue) are allowed only from earnings payable out of the public revenue.

(4) Deductions limited to specified earnings (see subsection (5)) are allowed—

(a) only from earnings from the employment that are taxable earnings under certain of the charging provisions of Chapters 4 and 5 of Part 2; and

(b) not from other earnings from it.

(5) "Deductions limited to specified earnings" are deductions under—

sections 336 to 342 (deductions from earnings charged on receipt: see sections 335(2) and 354);

section 353 (deductions from earnings charged on remittance);

sections 370 to 374 (travel deductions from earnings charged on receipt), and Chapter 6 of this Part (deductions from seafarers' earnings: see section 378(1)(a)).

Deductions from earnings not to exceed earnings

329.—(1) The amount of a deduction allowed under this Part may not exceed the earnings from which it is deductible.

1.449

If two or more deductions allowed under this Part are deductible from the same earnings, the amounts deductible may not in aggregate exceed those earnings.

(3) If deductions allowed otherwise than under this Part fall to be allowed from the same earnings as amounts deductible under this Part, the amounts deductible under this Part may not exceed the earnings remaining after the other deductions.

(4) Subsections (1) and (2) do not apply to a deduction under section 351 (expenses of ministers of religion), and subsection (3) applies as if such a deduction were allowed otherwise than under this Part.

(5) This section is to be disregarded for the purposes of the deductibility provisions (see section 332).

(6) See also section 380 of ICTA (which provides that where a loss in an employment is sustained, relief may be given against other income).

Prevention of double deductions

330.—(1) A deduction from earnings under this Part is not allowed more than once in respect of the same costs or expenses.

1.450

(2) If apart from this subsection—

(a) a deduction would be allowed under Chapter 4 of this Part (fixed allowances for employee's expenses) for a sum fixed by reference to any kind of expenses; and

(b) the employee would be entitled under another provision to a deduction for an amount paid in respect of the same kind of expenses;

only one of those deductions is allowed.

Order for making deductions

1.451 **331.**—(1) This Part needs to be read with section 835(3) and (4) of ICTA (general rule that deductions are to be allowed in the order resulting in the greatest reduction of liability to income tax).

In the case of deductions under this Part, the general rule in that section is subject to—

(a) section 23(3) (which requires certain deductions to be made in order to establish "chargeable overseas earnings"); and

(b) section 381 (which requires deductions under other provisions to be taken into account before deductions under Chapter 6 of this Part (seafarers)).

Meaning of "the deductibility provisions"

1.452 **332.** For the purposes of this Part, "the deductibility provisions" means the following provisions (which refer to amounts or expenses that would be deductible if they were incurred and paid by an employee)—

the definition of "business travel" in section 171(1) (definitions for Chapter 6 of Part 3),

section 179(6) (exception for certain advances for necessary expenses), the definition of "business travel" in section 236(1) (definitions for Chapter 2 of Part 4),

section 240(1)(c) and (5) (exemption of incidental overnight expenses and benefits),

section 252(3) (exception from exemption of work-related training provision for non-deductible travel expenses),

section 257(3) (exception from exemption for individual learning account training provision for non-deductible travel expenses),

section 305(5) (offshore oil and gas workers: mainland transfers),

section 310(6)(b) (counselling and other outplacement services),

section 311(5)(b) (retraining courses),

section 361(b) (scope of Chapter 3 of this Part: cost of benefits deductible as if paid by employee),

section 362(1)(c) and (2)(b) (deductions where non-cash voucher provided),

section 363(1)(b) and (2)(b) (deductions where credit-token provided),

section 364(1)(b) and (2) (deductions where living accommodation provided),

section 365(1)(b) and (2) (deductions where employment-related benefit provided).

CHAPTER 2

DEDUCTIONS FOR EMPLOYEE'S EXPENSES

Introduction

Scope of this chapter: expenses paid by the employee

1.453 **333.**—(1) A deduction from a person's earnings for an amount is allowed under the following provisions of this chapter only if the amount—

(a) is paid by the person; or

(b) is paid on the person's behalf by someone else and is included in the earnings.

(2) In the following provisions of this chapter, in relation to a deduction from a person's earnings, references to the person paying an amount include references to the amount being paid on the person's behalf by someone else if or to the extent that the amount is included in the earnings.

(3) Subsection (1)(b) does not apply to the deductions under—

(a) section 351(2) and (3) (expenses of ministers of religion); and

(b) section 355 (deductions for corresponding payments by non-domiciled employees with foreign employers),

and subsection (2) does not apply in the case of those deductions.

(4) Chapter 3 of this Part provides for deductions where—

(a) a person's earnings include an amount treated as earnings under Chapter 4, 5 or 10 of Part 3 (taxable benefits: vouchers, etc., living accommodation and residual liability to charge); and

(b) an amount in respect of the benefit in question would be deductible under this chapter if the person had incurred and paid it.

Effect of reimbursement, etc.

334.—(1) For the purposes of this chapter, a person may be regarded as paying an amount despite—   1.454

(a) its reimbursement; or

(b) any other payment from another person in respect of the amount.

(2) But where a reimbursement or such other payment is made in respect of an amount, a deduction for the amount is allowed under the following provisions of this chapter only if or to the extent that—

(a) the reimbursement; or

(b) so much of the other payment as relates to the amount; is included in the person's earnings.

(3) *Omitted.*

General rule for deduction of employee's expenses

Deductions for expenses: the general rule

336.—(1) The general rule is that a deduction from earnings is allowed for an amount if—   1.455

(a) the employee is obliged to incur and pay it as holder of the employment; and

(b) the amount is incurred wholly, exclusively and necessarily in the performance of the duties of the employment.

(2) The following provisions of this chapter contain additional rules allowing deductions for particular kinds of expenses and rules preventing particular kinds of deductions.

(3) No deduction is allowed under this section for an amount that is deductible under sections 337 to 342 (travel expenses).

Travel expenses

Travel in performance of duties

1.456   **337.**—(1) A deduction from earnings is allowed for travel expenses if—
     (a) the employee is obliged to incur and pay them as holder of the employment; and
     (b) the expenses are necessarily incurred on travelling in the performance of the duties of the employment.

     (2) This section needs to be read with section 359 (disallowance of travel expenses: mileage allowances and reliefs).

Travel for necessary attendance

1.457   **338.**—(1) A deduction from earnings is allowed for travel expenses if—
     (a) the employee is obliged to incur and pay them as holder of the employment; and
     (b) the expenses are attributable to the employee's necessary attendance at any place in the performance of the duties of the employment.

     (2) Subsection (1) does not apply to the expenses of ordinary commuting or travel between any two places that is for practical purposes substantially ordinary commuting.

     (3) In this section, "ordinary commuting" means travel between—
     (a) the employee's home and a permanent workplace; or
     (b) a place that is not a workplace and a permanent workplace.

     (4) Subsection (1) does not apply to the expenses of private travel or travel between any two places that is for practical purposes substantially private travel.

     (5) In subsection (4), "private travel" means travel between—
     (a) the employee's home and a place that is not a workplace; or
     (b) two places neither of which is a workplace.

     (6) This section needs to be read with section 359 (disallowance of travel expenses: mileage allowances and reliefs).

Meaning of "workplace" and "permanent workplace"

1.458   **339.**—(1) In this Part, "workplace", in relation to an employment, means a place at which the employee's attendance is necessary in the performance of the duties of the employment.

     (2) In this Part "permanent workplace", in relation to an employment, means a place which—
     (a) the employee regularly attends in the performance of the duties of the employment; and
     (b) is not a temporary workplace.
This is subject to subsections (4) and (8).

     (3) In subsection (2), "temporary workplace", in relation to an employment, means a place which the employee attends in the performance of the duties of the employment—
     (a) for the purpose of performing a task of limited duration; or
     (b) for some other temporary purpose.
This is subject to subsections (4) and (5).

(4) A place which the employee regularly attends in the performance of the duties of the employment is treated as a permanent workplace and not a temporary workplace if—

   (a) it forms the base from which those duties are performed; or

   (b) the tasks to be carried out in the performance of those duties are allocated there.

(5) A place is not regarded as a temporary workplace if the employee's attendance is—

   (a) in the course of a period of continuous work at that place—

      (i) lasting more than 24 months, or

      (ii) comprising all or almost all of the period for which the employee is likely to hold the employment; or

   (b) at a time when it is reasonable to assume that it will be in the course of such a period.

(6) For the purposes of subsection (5), a period is a period of continuous work at a place if over the period the duties of the employment are performed to a significant extent at the place.

(7) An actual or contemplated modification of the place at which duties are performed is to be disregarded for the purposes of subsections (5) and (6) if it does not, or would not, have any substantial effect on the employee's journey, or expenses of travelling, to and from the place where they are performed.

(8) An employee is treated as having a permanent workplace consisting of an area if—

   (a) the duties of the employment are defined by reference to an area (whether or not they also require attendance at places outside it);

   (b) in the performance of those duties the employee attends different places within the area;

   (c) none of the places the employee attends in the performance of those duties is a permanent workplace; and

   (d) the area would be a permanent workplace if subsections (2), (3), (5), (6) and (7) referred to the area where they refer to a place.

PART 9

PENSION INCOME

CHAPTER 1

INTRODUCTION

Structure of Part 9

565. The structure of this Part is as follows—

Chapter 2—

   (a) imposes the charge to tax on pension income; and

   (b) provides for deductions to be made from the amount of income chargeable;

Chapters 3 to 15 set out the types of income which are charged to tax under this Part and, for each type of income, identify—

   (a) the amount of income chargeable to tax for a tax year; and

1.459

(b) the person liable to pay any tax charged;

Chapter 15A makes provision about exemptions and charges in relation to lump sums under registered pension schemes; Chapters 17 and 18 deal with other exemptions from the charge to tax (whether under this Part or any other provision).

GENERAL NOTE

1.460   In the ICTA, most forms of pension income were taxed in the same way as emoluments under Schedule E. One of the main changes undertaken as part of the Tax Law Rewrite Project was to extract all the various provisions relating to the taxation of pensions of employees and office holders (both in the United Kingdom and overseas) and put them together in a single code. That code now forms Pt 9 of ITEPA 2003. It contains all the primary legislation from the ICTA 1988 and successive Finance Acts on the taxation of state pensions (including social security pensions), occupational pensions payable to officeholders and employees, and personal pensions. It recognises the division between earnings and pensions, but prevails over the separate provisions in Pt 10, dealing with social security income. It includes provisions in separate chapters dealing with foreign pension income.

The Tax Credits (Definition and Calculation of Income) Regulations 2002 rely on that code for defining pension income for the purposes of the tax credits income test. This selection of sections sets out the key provisions from that code. Foreign pensions, are not, however, included as pension income for tax credits purposes, so no reference is made to those chapters of Pt 9 of ITEPA. Foreign pensions should therefore be considered as foreign income, not pension income, for tax credits purposes. The Finance Act 2004, Pt 4 and associated Schedules, completely replaced the taxation rules applying to pensions and pension funds (though not the taxation of ordinary social security pension income) with a fundamentally new regime. As part of that, much of Pt 9 of this Act was repealed and replaced. But the new provisions are beyond the scope of this volume and are omitted, and only the general rules and social security pension rules are included.

CHAPTER 2

TAX ON PENSION INCOME

Nature of charge to tax on pension income and relevant definitions

1.461   **566.**—(1) The charge to tax on pension income under this Part is a charge to tax on that income excluding any exempt income.

(2) "Pension income" means the pensions, annuities and income of other types to which the provisions listed in subsection (4) apply.

This definition applies for the purposes of the Tax Acts.

(3) "Exempt income" means pension income on which no liability to income tax arises as a result of any provision of Chapters 16 to 18 of this Part.

This definition applies for the purposes of this Part.

(4) These are the provisions referred to in subsection (2)—

Provision	Income	Chapter (of this Part)
Section 569	United Kingdom pensions	Chapter 3
Section 573	Foreign pensions	Chapter 4
Section 577	United Kingdom social security pensions	Chapter 5

Provision	Income	Chapter (of this Part)
Section 579A	Pensions under registered pension schemes	Chapter 5A
Section 609	Annuities for the benefit of dependants	Chapter 10
Section 610	Annuities under sponsored superannuation schemes	Chapter 10
Section 611	Annuities in recognition of another's services	Chapter 10
Section 615	Certain overseas government pensions paid in the United Kingdom	Chapter 11
Section 619	The House of Commons Members' Fund	Chapter 12
Section 629	Pre-1973 pensions paid under OPA 1973	Chapter 14
Section 633	Voluntary annual payments	Chapter 15
Section 636B	Pensions treated as arising from payment of trivial commutation lump sums and winding-up lump sums under registered pension schemes	Chapter 15A
Section 636C	Pensions treated as arising from payment of trivial commutation lump sum death benefits and winding-up lump sum death benefits under registered pension schemes	Chapter 15A

Amount charged to tax

567.—(1) The amount of pension income which is charged to tax under this Part for a particular tax year is as follows.

1.462

(2) In relation to each pension, annuity or other item of pension income, the amount charged to tax is the "net taxable pension income" for the tax year.

(3) The net taxable pension income for a pension, annuity or other item of pension income for a tax year is given by the formula—

$$\frac{\text{TPI}}{\text{DPI}}$$

where—
 TPI means the amount of taxable pension income for that pension, annuity or item of pension income for that year (see subsection (4)); and
 DPI means the total amount of any deductions allowed from the pension, annuity or item of pension income (see subsection (5)).

(4) For the purposes of this Act—
 (a) the amount of taxable pension income for a pension, annuity or other item of pension income for a tax year is determined in accordance with Chapters 13 to 15A of this Part (which contain provisions relating to this amount for each type of pension income); and

233

(b) in determining the amount of taxable pension income for a pension, annuity or other item of pension income, any exempt income is to be excluded.

(5) The deductions allowed from a pension, annuity or other item of pension income are those under—

section 617 (10% deduction from an overseas government pension to which section 615 applies);

Part 22 (payroll giving).

Person liable for tax

1.463   **568.** For the provision identifying which person is liable for any tax charged under this Part on a pension, annuity or other item of pension income, see Chapters 3 to 15.

CHAPTER 3

UNITED KINGDOM PENSIONS: GENERAL RULES

United Kingdom pensions

1.464   **569.**—(1) This section applies to any pension paid by or on behalf of a person who is in the United Kingdom.

(2) But this section does not apply to a pension if any provision of Chapters 5 to 14 of this Part applies to it.

(3) For pensions paid by or on behalf of a person who is outside the United Kingdom, see Chapter 4 of this Part.

GENERAL NOTE

1.465   Most UK pensions will be caught under the new Chapter 5A, ss.579A–D, taxing pensions under registered pension schemes on the same basis as ss.571 and 572 below, subject to the exceptions for some lump sums and other payments detailed in the FA 2004 provisions. The detailed new provisions are omitted as they will be of limited importance to most tax credit claimants.

"Pension": interpretation

1.466   **570.** In this chapter, "pension" includes a pension which is paid voluntarily or is capable of being discontinued.

Taxable pension income

1.467   **571.** If section 569 applies, the taxable pension income for a tax year is the full amount of the pension accruing in that year, irrespective of when any amount is actually paid.

Person liable for tax

1.468   **572.** If section 569 applies, the person liable for any tax charged under this Part is the person receiving or entitled to the pension.

CHAPTER 5

UNITED KINGDOM SOCIAL SECURITY PENSIONS

United Kingdom social security pensions

577.—(1) This section applies to—
the state pension;
graduated retirement benefit;
industrial death benefit;
widowed mother's allowance;
widowed parent's allowance; and
widow's pension.

(1A) But this section does not apply to any social security pension lump sum (within the meaning of section 7 of F(No.2)A 2005).

(2) In this section—
"state pension" means any pension payable under—
  (a) section 44, 48A, 48B, 48BB, 51 or 78 of SSCBA 1992; or
  (b) section 44, 48, 48B, 48BB, 51 or 78 of SSCB(NI)A 1992;
"graduated retirement benefit" means any benefit payable under—
  (a) section 36 or 37 of the National Insurance Act 1965 (Chapter 51); or
  (b) section 35 or 36 of the National Insurance Act (Northern Ireland) 1966 (Chapter 6 (NI));
"industrial death benefit" means any benefit payable under—
  (a) section 94 of, and Part 6 of Schedule 7 to SSCBA 1992; or
  (b) section 94 of, and Part 6 of Schedule 7 to SSCB(NI)A 1992;
"widowed mother's allowance" means any allowance payable under—
  (a) section 37 of SSCBA 1992; or
  (b) section 37 of SSCB(NI)A 1992;
"widowed parent's allowance" means any allowance payable under—
  (a) section 39A of SSCBA 1992; or
  (b) section 39A of SSCB(NI)A 1992;
"widow's pension" means any pension payable under—
  (a) section 38 of SSCBA 1992; or
  (b) section 38 of SSCB(NI)A 1992.

(3) In subsection (2), in paragraph (b) of the definition of state pension, the reference to section 48 of SSCB(NI)A 1992 is a reference to the section 48 inserted by paragraph 3(1) of Schedule 2 to the Pensions (Northern Ireland) Order 1995 (SI 1995/3213 (NI 22)).

(4) Chapter 17 of this Part provides a partial exemption for a pension to which this section applies in respect of any part of the pension which is attributable to an increase in respect of a child (see section 645).

1.469

GENERAL NOTE

This section lists forms of state pension to be brought within the charge to tax in s.578. The exclusion of social security lump sums is because separate provision is made to tax those sums in ss.7 and 8 of F(No.2)A 2005. Lump sums are treated as income for income tax purposes but are given special treatment to prevent the recipients losing their age-related personal allowances. They are also to be taxed regardless of the residence or domicile of the recipients. Section 8 sets the date on which the tax charge is to apply. It is usually in the tax year in which the right to the pension starts.

1.470

Taxable pension income

1.471   **578.** If section 577 applies, the taxable pension income for a tax year is the full amount of the pension, benefit or allowance accruing in that year, irrespective of when any amount is actually paid.

Person liable for tax

1.472   **579.** If section 577 applies, the person liable for any tax charged under this Part is the person receiving or entitled to the pension, benefit or allowance.

PART 10

SOCIAL SECURITY INCOME

CHAPTER 1

INTRODUCTION

Structure of Part 10

1.473   **655.**—(1) The structure of this Part is as follows—
Chapter 2—
    (a) imposes the charge to tax on social security income; and
    (b) provides for deductions to be made from the amount of income chargeable;
Chapter 3 sets out the United Kingdom social security benefits which are charged to tax under this Part and identifies—
    (a) the amount of income chargeable to tax for a tax year; and
    (b) the person liable to pay any tax charged;
Chapters 4 and 5 deal with exemptions from the charge to tax on United Kingdom social security benefits (whether under this Part or any other provision);
Chapters 6 and 7 make provisions about foreign benefits.
(2) For other provisions about the taxation of social security benefits see—
    section 151 of FA 1996 (power for the Treasury to make orders about the taxation of benefits payable under Government pilot schemes);
    section 781 of ITA 2007 (exemption of payments under New Deal 50plus);
    section 782 of ITA 2007 (exemption of payments under Employment Zones programme).
(3) For the charge to tax on social security pensions see Part 9.

GENERAL NOTE

1.474   "Social security income" is another head of charge created from the Tax Law Rewrite Project. Previously, all forms of social security income were fitted, sometimes somewhat uncomfortably, in Schedule E. Part 10 of ITEPA is now used to codify the charge to income tax on all forms of social security benefit and allowance other than pensions. As this section records, Pt 9 deals with pensions. The opportunity has also been taken to set out the various provisions in a systematic way, and dealing with both United Kingdom and other benefits.

Because of the general importance of these provisions for social security purposes, the Part has been included more extensively than other Parts of ITEPA for social security purposes, and not restricted to those relevant only for tax credits purposes.

Subsection (1) is a signposting provision.

Subsection (2) lists the three sections (not included in this volume) under which limited exemptions from income tax may be made for social security benefits. The power under s.151 of FA 1996 is used to exempt payments made to claimants under pilot schemes. For current exemptions under this provision, see: the Taxation of Benefits under Government Pilot Schemes (Return to Work Credit and Employment Retention and Advancements Schemes) Order 2003 (SI 2003/2339) (not reproduced in this volume), in effect from October 1, 2003; and the Taxation of Benefits under government Pilot Schemes (Working Neighbourhoods Pilot and In Work Credit) Order 2004 (SI 2004/575), in effect from April 6, 2004. Both orders fully exempt payments under those schemes form income tax. The reference to s.84 of FA 2000 is superseded from the start of working tax credit as New Deal payments have now been incorporated into the credit.

Subsection (3) is a signpost to s.577 (United Kingdom social security pensions).

CHAPTER 2

TAX ON SOCIAL SECURITY INCOME

Nature of charge to tax on social security income

656.—(1) The charge to tax on social security income is a charge to tax on that income excluding any exempt income.

(2) "Exempt income" is social security income on which no liability to income tax arises as a result of any provision of Chapters 4, 5 or 7 of this Part.

This definition applies for the purposes of this Part.

1.475

DEFINITIONS

"social security income"—see s.657(2).
"tax"—see ICTA, s.832(3).

GENERAL NOTE

This section is extremely important because it emphasises that the exemption provisions in the Part override the charges to tax. In practice, very few forms of UK social security income are chargeable to tax under this Part. Remember that pensions are chargeable under Pt 9. In most cases statutory sick pay and the other statutory payments are chargeable to tax under Pt 2. Any such payments that are not caught by Pt 3 are caught by a "safety net" provision in this Part.

Provisions in this part exempt child benefit, guardian's allowance and child tax credit and so exclude all child-related benefit. Other provisions exempt all disablement related benefits payable to the disabled or incapacitated individual.

Tax credits under the TCA 2002 are themselves exempted from tax under this Part. So are the local government benefits of housing benefit and council tax benefit. Benefits received from the national health service, in kind or in cash, are not income for any income tax purpose, and are not affected by this Part. Welfare benefits in kind, such as welfare foods and publicly provided accommodation, are not within the definition of "social security income" in s.657 and so are excluded from the charge to tax under this Part. They do not fall to be charged under any other part of ITEPA 2003.

1.476

This leaves income tax payable only on some parts of some payments of income support, jobseeker's allowance and incapacity benefit, and also on bereavement allowance (in practice linked with pension entitlements but not a form of pension income) and carer's allowance (formerly known as invalid care allowance).

The equivalent approach is adopted for foreign social security payments.

Meaning of "social security income", "taxable benefits", etc.

1.477   **657.**—(1) This section defines—

"social security income" for the purposes of the Tax Acts; and

"taxable benefits", "Table A" and "Table B" for the purposes of this Part.

(2) "Social security income" means—

(a) the United Kingdom social security benefits listed in Table A;

(b) the United Kingdom social security benefits listed in Table B;

(c) the foreign benefits to which section 678 applies; and

(d) the foreign benefits to which section 681(2) applies.

(3) "Taxable benefits" means—

(a) the United Kingdom social security benefits listed in Table A; and

(b) the foreign benefits to which section 678 applies.

(4) Subsections (2) and (3) are subject to section 660(2).

(5) "Table A" means Table A in section 660.

(6) "Table B" means Table B in section 677.

GENERAL NOTE

1.478   This section defines the term "social security income" used in s.656, which is the charging section. Unless a form of income is within the scope of the definition in subs.(2), it is not liable to income tax under this Part. Nor will it be liable to income tax under any other general provision in the Taxes Act. However, the interpretation of the scope of this section must take into account the very wide provisions dealing with benefits provided by employers in Pt 2, which in practice covers some forms of payments that are in principle social security payments (such as statutory maternity pay). Further, anything that is a "pension" is taxable under Pt 9 and is removed from this Part by s.655(3).

Amount charged to tax

1.479   **658.**—(1) The amount of social security income which is charged to tax under this Part for a particular tax year is as follows.

(2) In relation to a taxable benefit, the amount charged to tax is the net taxable social security income for the tax year.

(3) The net taxable social security income for a taxable benefit for a tax year is given by the formula—

$$TSSI - PGD$$

where—

TSSI means the amount of taxable social security income for that benefit for that year (see subsections (4) to (7)); and

PGD means the amount of the deduction (if any) allowed from the benefit under Part 12 (payroll giving).

(4) In relation to bereavement allowance, carer's allowance, contributory employment and support allowance, incapacity benefit and income support (which are listed in Table A), the amount of taxable social security income is determined in accordance with section 661.

(5) In relation to any other benefit listed in Table A, the amount of

taxable social security income is the amount of the benefit that falls to be charged to tax.

(6) In relation to foreign benefits to which section 678 applies, the amount of taxable social security income is determined in accordance with section 679.

(7) In determining for the purposes of this Act the amount of taxable social security income, any exempt income is to be excluded.

DEFINITIONS

"exempt income"—see s.656(2).
"social security income"—see s.657(2).
"tax year"—see s.721(1).
"taxable benefit"—see s.657(3).

Person liable for tax

659. The person liable for any tax charged under this Part is identified in—   1.480

  (a) section 662 (United Kingdom benefits); or
  (b) section 680 (foreign benefits).

CHAPTER 3

TAXABLE UNITED KINGDOM SOCIAL SECURITY BENEFITS

Taxable benefits: United Kingdom benefits—Table A

660. (1) This is Table A: 1.481

TABLE A   1.482

TAXABLE UK BENEFITS

Social security benefit	Payable under	
Bereavement allowance	SSCBA 1992	Section 39B
	SSCB(NI)A 1992	Section 39B
Carer's allowance	SSCBA 1992	Section 70
	SSCB(NI)A 1992	Section 70
Contributory employment and support allowance	WRA 2007	Section 1(2) (a)
	Any provision made for Northern Ireland which corresponds to section 1(2)(a) of WRA 2007	
Incapacity benefit	SSCBA 1992	Section 30A(1) or (5), 40 or 41
	SSCB(NI)A 1992	Section 30A(1) or (5), 40 or 41

Social security benefit	Payable under	
Income support	SSCBA 1992	Section 123
	SSCB(NI)A 1992	Section 124
Jobseeker's allowance	JSA 1995	Section 1
	JS(NI)O 1995	Article 3
Statutory adoption pay	SSCBA 1992	Section 171ZL
	Any provision made for Northern Ireland which corresponds to section 171ZL of SSCBA 1992	
Statutory maternity pay	SSCBA 1992	Section 164
	SSCB(NI)A 1992	Section 160
Statutory paternity pay	SSCBA 1992	Section 171ZA or 171ZB
	Any provision made for Northern Ireland which corresponds to section 171ZA or section 171ZB of SSCBA 1992	
Statutory sick pay	SSCBA 1992	Section 151
	SSCB(NI)A 1992	Section 147.

(2) A benefit listed below is not "social security income" or a "taxable benefit" if it is charged to tax under another Part of this Act—

statutory adoption pay;
statutory maternity pay;
statutory paternity pay;
statutory sick pay.

DEFINITIONS

"social security income"—see s.657(2).
"taxable benefit"—see s.657(3).

GENERAL NOTE

1.483   For the full forms of the abbreviations in Table A see Sch.1, Pt 1 to the Act. Subsection (2) provides that a charge to tax under Pt 2 of the Act takes priority over this Part, but the section ensures that all statutory payments are taxable.

Taxable social security income

1.484   **661.**—(1) This section applies in relation to each of the following taxable benefits listed in Table A—

bereavement allowance;
carer's allowance;
contributory employment and support allowance.
incapacity benefit; and
income support.

(2) The amount of taxable social security income for a taxable benefit for a tax year is the full amount of the benefit accruing in the tax year irrespective of when any amount is actually paid.

DEFINITIONS

"tax year"—see s.721(1).
"taxable benefit"—see s.675(3).

This is a new rule under ITEPA introduced to replace both inconsistent previous   **1.485**
legislation and a lack of legislation, the rules apparently varying from one benefit to
another for no good reason. "Accrued" is standard income tax language not normally used for social security purposes. In social security terms, as the section makes
clear, it means payable not paid.

Person liable for tax

662.—The person liable for any tax charged under this Part on a taxable   **1.486**
benefit listed in Table A is the person receiving or entitled to the benefit.

GENERAL NOTE

"Received or entitled" is familiar income tax language applied to social security   **1.487**
income by ITEPA in place of a lack of any clear previous rule. As the wording indicates it covers both the person for whom the benefit is payable and the person who
actually receives it. The wording will make joint claimants for jobseeker's allowance
both liable for any income tax on the allowance. It is, however, not clear how this is
applied to appointees appointed to receive income support for a claimant.

CHAPTER 4

TAXABLE UK SOCIAL SECURITY BENEFITS: EXEMPTIONS

Incapacity benefit

Long-term incapacity benefit: previous entitlement to invalidity benefit

663.—(1) No liability to income tax arises on long-term incapacity   **1.488**
benefit if—
   (a) a person is entitled to the benefit for a day of incapacity for work
       which falls in a period of incapacity for work which is treated for the
       purposes of that benefit as having begun before April 13, 1995; and
   (b) the part of that period which is treated as having fallen before that
       date includes a day for which that person was entitled to invalidity
       benefit.
(2) In this section—
"invalidity benefit" means invalidity benefit under—
   (a) Part 2 of SSCBA 1992; or
   (b) Part 2 of SSCB(NI)A 1992;
"long-term incapacity benefit" means incapacity benefit payable
under—
   (a) section 30A(5), 40 or 41 of SSCBA 1992; or
   (b) section 30A(5), 40 or 41 of SSCB(NI)A 1992.

Short-term incapacity benefit not payable at the higher rate

664.—(1) No liability to income tax arises on short-term incapacity   **1.489**
benefit unless it is payable at the higher rate.

(2) In this section—
  (a) "short-term incapacity benefit" means incapacity benefit payable under—
    (i) section 30A(1) of SSCBA 1992; or
    (ii) section 30A(1) of SSCB(NI)A 1992;
  (b) the reference to short-term incapacity benefit payable at the higher rate is to be construed in accordance with—
    (i) section 30B of SSCBA 1992; or
    (ii) section 30B of SSCB(NI)A 1992.

Income support

Exempt unless payable to member of couple involved in trade dispute

1.490   **665.**—(1) No liability to income tax arises on income support unless—
  (a) the income support is payable to one member of a couple ("the claimant"); and
  (b) section 126 of SSCBA 1992 or section 125 of SSCB(NI)A 1992 (trade disputes) applies to the claimant but not to the other member of the couple.

(2) In this section, couple has the same meaning as in section 137(1) of SSCBA 1992 or section 133(1) of SSCB(NI)A 1992.

Child maintenance bonus

1.491   **666.** No liability to income tax arises on a part of income support which is attributable to a child maintenance bonus (within the meaning of section 10 of CSA 1995 or Article 4 of CS(NI)O 1995).

Amounts in excess of taxable maximum

1.492   **667.**—(1) If the amount of income support paid to a person ("the claimant") for a week or a part of a week exceeds the claimant's taxable maximum for that period, no liability to income tax arises on the excess.

(2) The claimant's taxable maximum for a period is determined under section 668.

Taxable maximum

1.493   **668.**—(1) A claimant's taxable maximum for a week is determined under this subsection if the applicable amount for the purpose of calculating the income support consists only of an amount in respect of the relevant couple.

The taxable maximum is equal to one half of the applicable amount.

(2) A claimant's taxable maximum for a week is determined under this subsection if the applicable amount includes amounts that are not in respect of the relevant couple.

The taxable maximum is equal to one half of the amount which is included in the applicable amount in respect of the relevant couple.

(3) A claimant's taxable maximum for a part of a week is determined as follows—

Step 1

Assume that the income support is paid to the claimant for the whole of, rather than part of, the week.

Step 2

Determine under subsection (1) or (2) what the claimant's taxable maximum for that week would be on that assumption.

Step 3

Determine the claimant's taxable maximum for the part of the week using this formula—

$$\frac{N}{7} \times TMW$$

where—
   N is the number of days in the part of the week for which the claimant is actually paid the income support; and
   TMW is the taxable maximum for the whole week determined under step 2.

Interpretation

669.—(1) In section 668, except in relation to Northern Ireland—   1.494
   "applicable amount" means the amount prescribed in relation to income support in regulations made under section 135 of SSCBA 1992;
   "couple" has the same meaning as in section 137(1) of Social Security Contributions and Benefits Act 1992;
   (2) In section 668, in relation to Northern Ireland—
   "applicable amount" means the amount prescribed in relation to income support in regulations made under section 131 of SSCB(NI)A 1992;
   "couple" has the same meaning as in section 133(1) of Social Security Contributions and Benefits (Northern Ireland) Act 1992;
   (3) In section 668, "relevant couple", in relation to a claimant, means the couple of which the claimant is a member.

GENERAL NOTE

This section applies the definition of "couple" adopted for social security pur-   1.495
poses following the replacement by the Civil Partnership Act 2004 of all references
to "married couples" and "unmarried couples" for the purposes of ITEPA. The
effect is to impose the social security meaning of "couple" on the income tax treatment of social security income, and not the income tax definition.

Jobseeker's allowance

Child maintenance bonus

670. No liability to income tax arises on a part of a jobseeker's allowance   1.496
which is attributable to a child maintenance bonus (within the meaning of
section 10 of CSA 1995 or Article 4 of CS(NI)O 1995).

Amounts in excess of taxable maximum

1.497   **671.**—(1) If the amount of jobseeker's allowance paid to a person ("the claimant") for a week or a part of a week exceeds the claimant's taxable maximum for that period, no liability to income tax arises on the excess.

(2) The claimant's taxable maximum for a period is determined under sections 672 to 674.

Taxable maximum: general

1.498   **672.**—(1) A claimant's taxable maximum for a week is determined—
   (a) under section 673, if the claimant is paid an income-based jobseeker's allowance for that week; or
   (b) under section 674, if the claimant is paid a contribution-based jobseeker's allowance for that week.

(2) A claimant's taxable maximum for a part of a week is determined as follows—

Step 1

Assume that the jobseeker's allowance is paid to the claimant for the whole of, rather than part of, the week.

Step 2

Determine under section 673 or 674 what the claimant's taxable maximum for that week would be on that assumption.

Step 3

Determine the claimant's taxable maximum for the part of the week using this formula—

$$\frac{N}{7} \times TMW$$

where—
   N is the number of days in the part of the week for which the claimant is actually paidthe jobseeker's allowance; and
   TMW is the taxable maximum for the whole week determined under step 2.

Taxable maximum: income-based jobseeker's allowance

1.499   **673.**—(1) A claimant's taxable maximum for a week is determined under this section if—
   (a) the claimant is paid an income-based jobseeker's allowance for that week, or
   (b) the claimant is assumed under section 672(2) to be paid an income-based jobseeker's allowance for that week.

(2) If the claimant is not a member of a couple, the claimant's taxable maximum for the week is equal to the age-related amount which would be applicable to the claimant if a contribution based jobseeker's allowance were payable to the claimant for that week.

(3) If the claimant is a member of a couple, the claimant's taxable maximum for the week is equal to the portion of the applicable amount which is included in the jobseeker's allowance in respect of the couple for that week.

(4) But if—
   (a) the claimant is a member of a couple; and
   (b) the other member of that couple is prevented by section 14 of JSA

1995 or Article 16 of JS(NI)O 1995 (trade disputes) from being entitled to a jobseeker's allowance;
the claimant's taxable maximum for that week is equal to half the portion
of the applicable amount which is included in the jobseeker's allowance in
respect of the couple for that week.

Taxable maximum: contribution-based jobseeker's allowance

674.—(1) A claimant's taxable maximum for a week is determined under
this section if—

(a) the claimant is paid a contribution-based jobseeker's allowance for
that week; or

(b) the claimant is assumed under section 672(2) to be paid a contribution-based jobseeker's allowance for that week.

(2) If the claimant is not a member of a couple, the claimant's taxable
maximum for the week is equal to the age-related amount which is applicable to the claimant for that week.

(3) If the claimant is a member of a couple, the claimant's taxable
maximum for the week is equal to the portion of the applicable amount
which would be included in the jobseeker's allowance in respect of the
couple if an income-based jobseeker's allowance were payable to the claimant for that week.

1.500

Interpretation

675.—(1) In sections 671 to 674, except in relation to Northern
Ireland—

"age-related amount" and "applicable amount" mean the amounts
determined as such in accordance with regulations made under section
4 of JSA 1995;

"contribution-based jobseeker's allowance" and "income-based job-seeker's allowance" have the same meaning as in section 1(4) of JSA 1995;

"married couple" and "unmarried couple" have the same meaning as in
section 35(1) of JSA 1995.

(2) In sections 671 to 674, in relation to Northern Ireland—

"age-related amount" and "applicable amount" mean the amounts
determined as such in accordance with regulations made under Article
6 of JS(NI)O 1995;

"contribution-based jobseeker's allowance" and "income-based jobseeker's allowance" have the same meaning as in Article 3(4) of JS(NI)
O 1995;

"couple" has the same meaning as in s.351(1) of JSA 1995.

1.501

Increases in respect of children

Increases in respect of children

676. No liability to income tax arises on a part of a taxable benefit listed
in Table A which is attributable to an increase in respect of a child.

1.502

GENERAL NOTE

This is superseded from 2003–04 for incapacity benefit and carer's allowance, by
the introduction of child tax credit, which is exempt from tax.

1.503

CHAPTER 5

UK SOCIAL SECURITY BENEFITS WHOLLY EXEMPT FROM
INCOME TAX

UK social security benefits wholly exempt from tax: Table B

1.504   **677.**—(1) No liability to income tax arises on the United Kingdom social
security benefits listed in Table B.

TABLE B—PART I

1.505   BENEFITS PAYABLE UNDER PRIMARY LEGISLATION

Social security benefit	*Payable under*
Attendance allowance	SSCBA 1992, s.64
	SSCB(NI)A 1992, s.64
Back to work bonus	JSA 1995, s.26
	JS(NI)O 1995, Article 28
Bereavement payment	SSCBA 1992, s.36
	SSCB(NI)A 1992, s.36
Child benefit	SSCBA 1992, s.141
	SSCB(NI)A 1992, s.137
Child's special allowance	SSCBA 1992, s.56
	SSCB(NI)A 1992, s.56
Child tax credit	TCA 2002, Part 1
Council tax benefit	SSCBA 1992, s.131
Disability living allowance	SSCBA 1992, s.71
	SSCB(NI)A 1992, s.71
Guardian's allowance	SSCBA 1992, s.77
	SSCB(NI)A 1992, s.77
Health in Pregnancy Grant	SSCBA 1992, s.140A
	SSCB(NI)A 1992, s.136A
Housing benefit	SSCBA 1992, s.130
	SSCB(NI)A 1992, s.129
Income-related employment and support allowance	WRA 2007 s.1(2)(b)
	Any provision made for Northern Ireland which corresponds to section 1(2)(b) of WRA 2007
In-work credit	ETA 1973, S.2
	ETA(NI) 1950, s.1
In-work emergency discretion fund payment	ETA 1973, s.2
In-work emergency fund payment	ETA(NI) 1950, s.1
Industrial injuries benefit (apart from industrial death benefit)	SSCBA 1992, s.94
	SSCB(NI)A 1992, s.94

Social security benefit	Payable under
Pensioner's Christmas bonus	SSCBA 1992, s.148
	SSCB(NI)A 1992, s.144
Payments out of the social fund	SSCBA 1992, s.138
	SSCB(NI)A 1992, s.134
Return to work credit	ETA 1973, s.2
	ETA(NI) 1950, s.1
Severe disablement allowance	SSCBA 1992, s.68
	SSCB(NI)A 1992, s.68
State maternity allowance	SSCBA 1992, s.35
	SSCB(NI)A 1992, s.35
State pension credit	SPCA 2002, s.1
	SPCA(NI) 2002, s.1
Working tax credit	TCA 2002, Part 1

TABLE B—PART 2

BENEFITS PAYABLE UNDER REGULATIONS   1.506

Social security benefit	Payable under regulations made under
Payments to reduce under-occupation by housing benefit claimants	WRPA 1999, s.79 WRP(NI)O 1999, Article 70

(2) Industrial death benefit is charged to tax under Part 9 (see section 577).

(3) In this section "industrial death benefit" means any benefit payable under—

(a) section 94 of, and Part 6 of Schedule 7 to, SSCBA 1992; or

(b) section 94 of, and Part 6 of Schedule 7 to, SSCB(NI)A 1992.

CHAPTER 6

TAXABLE FOREIGN BENEFITS

Taxable benefits: foreign benefits

678.—(1) This section applies to any benefit which is payable under the   1.507
law of a country or territory outside the United Kingdom if—

(a) it is substantially similar in character to a benefit listed in Table A, and

(b) it is payable to a person resident in the United Kingdom.

(2) But this section does not apply to a benefit which is charged to tax under Pt 9 (pension income).

247

1.508   This is a new statutory provision in ITEPA. Until its enactment, the Inland Revenue refrained from taxing foreign social security benefits on the basis of an extra-statutory concession. The only real problem area is the divide between social security income, exempt under this provision, and pension income, taxed under Pt 9.

Taxable social security income

1.509   **679.**—(1) If section 678 applies, the taxable social security income for a taxable benefit for a tax year is the amount on which tax would be chargeable if the benefit were chargeable to tax under Case V of Schedule D (see in particular the provisions of ICTA listed in subsection (2)).

(2) Those provisions of ICTA are—

(a) sections 65 and 68 (calculation of the amount of the income on which tax is to be charged in the tax year);

(b) section 584 (relief for unremittable overseas income);

(c) section 585 (relief on delayed remittances).

Person liable for tax

1.510   **680.**—The person liable for any tax charged under this Part on a benefit to which section 678 applies is the person receiving or entitled to the benefit.

PART 13

SUPPLEMENTARY PROVISIONS

Interpretation

Other definitions

1.511   **721.**—(1) In this Act—

"cash voucher" has the same meaning as in Chapter 4 of Part 3 (see section 75);

"credit-token" has the same meaning as in Chapter 4 of Part 3 (see section 92);

"foreign employer" means—

(a) in the case of an employee resident in the United Kingdom, an individual, partnership or body of persons resident outside the United Kingdom and not resident in the United Kingdom or the Republic of Ireland, and

(b) in the case of an employee not resident in the United Kingdom, an individual, partnership or body of persons resident outside and not resident in the United Kingdom;

"non-cash voucher" has the same meaning as in Chapter 4 of Part 3 (see section 84);

(3) Any reference in this Act to being domiciled in the United Kingdom is to be read as a reference to being domiciled in any part of the United Kingdom.

(4) For the purposes of this Act the following are members of a person's family—

(a) the person's spouse [¹or civil partner],

(b) the person's children and their spouses [¹or civil partners],

(c) the person's parents, and

(d) the person's dependants.

(5) For the purposes of this Act the following are members of a person's family or household—

(a) members of the person's family,

(b) the person's domestic staff, and

(c) the person's guests.

(6) The following provisions (which relate to the legal equality of illegitimate children) are to be disregarded in interpreting references in this Act to a child or children—

(a) section 1 of the Family Law Reform Act 1987 (Chapter 42),

(b) the paragraph inserted in Schedule 1 to the Interpretation Act 1978 (Chapter 30) by paragraph 73 of Schedule 2 to the 1987 Act,

(c) section 1(2) of the Law Reform (Parent and Child) (Scotland) Act 1986 (Chapter 9),

(d) Article 155 of the Children (Northern Ireland) Order 1995 (SI 1995 No.755 (NI 2)).

(7) In the employment income Parts any reference to earnings which is not limited by the context—

(a) to earnings within Chapter 1 of Part 3, or

(b) to any other particular description of earnings; includes a reference to any amount treated as earnings by any of the provisions mentioned in section 7(5) (meaning of "employment income" etc.).

GENERAL NOTE

See further for definitions ITA 2007, Sch.4 of which (not included in this work) includes an index of terms defined for the Income Tax Acts.   **1.512**

Child Trust Funds Act 2004

(2004 c.6)

ARRANGEMENT OF SECTIONS

Introductory

Child Trust Funds Act 2004

An Act to make provision about child trust funds and for connected purposes.

INTRODUCTION AND GENERAL NOTE

The basic scheme of the Child Trust Fund Act 2004 is that all children in the   1.514
United Kingdom born after August 31, 2002 will have a "child trust fund account",
which will in effect be a universal savings policy. Building societies and other financial institutions will have to seek HMRC approval to be an "account provider"
under this Act. It is a condition of approval that account providers offer equity-based
stakeholder accounts (although cash accounts may also be offered). The Treasury
provides an initial endowment of £250 for each child at the point when the account
is opened, or £500 in the case of children in low income families or those who are
being looked after by a local authority. The Government subsequently approved a
further endowment (of £250, or £500 for children in low income families) when
every child reaches the age of seven. Parents, relatives and family friends are able
to make further contributions to the child trust fund account at any time. The
minimum such investment is £10 (unless the account provider permits smaller
deposits) and the maximum annual aggregate contribution by family and friends is
£1,200. Subject to some very narrow exceptions, no withdrawals will be permitted
until the child is 18, so that the child reaches adulthood with a "nest-egg" which can
then be re-invested, spent on education or setting up in business, etc. The cost of
the scheme is estimated to be in the order of £4 billion over 18 years.

The Government has set out four objectives for child trust fund accounts. These
are "to help people understand the benefits of saving and investing; to encourage
parents and children to develop the savings habit; to ensure that all children have a
financial asset at the start of their adult life; and to build on financial education and
help people make better financial choices throughout their lives" (Lord McIntosh of
Haringey, Parliamentary Under-Secretary of State, *Hansard* HL Debates Vol.658,
col.351, February 26, 2004). The Child Trust Fund Act may thus be seen as
an example of the Government's commitment to the principles of "asset-based
welfare" and "progressive universalism". It will, of course, take some time to assess
whether the scheme fulfils its goals.

The idea of child trust funds emerged through the work of the Institute of Public
Policy Research (IPPR) in 2000 and was canvassed by the Treasury in its consultation paper *Savings and Assets for All*, The Modernisation of Britain's Tax and
benefit System, Number 8 (April 2001). The proposal also appeared in the Labour
Party's 2001 general election manifesto. The Government set out its proposals
more fully in the Treasury papers *Delivering Saving and Assets* (November 2001)
and especially in *Detailed proposals for the Child Trust Fund* (October 2003). The
House of Commons Treasury Committee has issued a report supporting the initiative, although making some further recommendations: *Child Trusts Funds* (Second
Report of Session 2003–04, HC 86), and see further *Government Response to the
Committee's Second Report on Child Trust Funds* (HC 86) (First Special Report of
Session 2003–04, HC 387). In the 2003 Budget the Chancellor of the Exchequer
announced the Government's intention that the scheme should commence opera-
tions in April 2005 (but confirming that it would also apply to all children born after
August 31, 2002). For a full analysis of the scheme, see N. Wikeley, "Child Trust
Funds—asset-based welfare or a recipe for increased inequality?" (2004) 11 *Journal
of Social Security Law* 189.

Section 1 of the Act explains what is meant by a child trust fund, whilst s.2 defines
the crucial qualifying category of "eligible children". The nature and management
of child trust fund accounts is governed by s.3. Funds in such accounts are inal-
ienable (s.4). The expectation is that accounts will be opened by a "responsible
person", typically a parent, or by the child (in the case of a child aged 16 or over,
who, for example, has just arrived in the country); see s.5, which makes the award
of child benefit the trigger for entitlement to a child trust fund account. The fall-
back position is that HMRC will open an account (s.6) for any child lacking a child

trust fund. Accounts may be transferred to another financial institution (s.7). The initial and supplementary Treasury contributions to be made at the opening of the account are governed by ss.8 and 9. All children receive the initial contribution under s.8 (children being looked after by local authorities receive a higher rate) and children in low income families qualify for the supplementary contribution under s.9. Section 10 makes provision for further Treasury contributions to be made at some late date (or dates). Where Treasury contributions have been credited in error, they can be recovered by virtue of s.11. Section 12 deals with contributions by parents and others to child trust fund accounts. The tax position is covered by ss.13 and 14 while ss.15–18 make provision for the disclosure and exchange of information relating to accounts. Section 19 makes special provision for the situation where a payment is due after a child beneficiary has died. Sections 20 and 21 concern penalties and ss.22–24 set out appeal rights. The remaining sections of the Act are supplementary in nature (ss.25–31). The first regulations under the Act are the Child Trust Funds Regulations 2004 (SI 2004/1450).

Commencement and extent

1.515   The supplementary provisions in this Act (ss.25–31) came into force on Royal Assent (May 13, 2004): see s.27. Various procedural provisions came into force on January 1, 2005: Child Trust Funds Act 2004 (Commencement No.1) Order 2004 (SI 2004/2422, C.103). The remainder of the Act was brought into force by the Child Trust Funds Act 2004 (Commencement No.2) Order 200 (SI 2004/3369, C.158). The Child Trust Funds Regulations 2004 (SI 2004/1450) came into force for various purposes on January 1, 2005 and for remaining purposes on "the appointed day", namely April 6, 2005. The Act extends to the whole of the United Kingdom (see further ss.25 and 30).

Introductory

Child trust funds

1.516   **1.**—(1) This Act makes provision about child trust funds and related matters.

(2) In this Act "child trust fund" means an account which—

(a) is held by a child who is or has been an eligible child (see section 2),

(b) satisfies the requirements imposed by and by virtue of this Act (see section 3), and

(c) has been opened in accordance with this Act (see sections 5 and 6).

(3) The matters dealt with by and under this Act are to be under the care and management of the Inland Revenue.

DEFINITIONS

"child": s.29.
"child trust fund": subs.(2) and s.29.
"eligible child": ss.2 and 29.
"Inland Revenue": s.29.

GENERAL NOTE

1.517   This is a genuinely introductory section.

Subs. (1)

1.518   This provision is no more illuminating than the long title to the Act.

Subs.(2)
This is more helpful than subs.(1) in that it stipulates the three defining charac-   **1.519**
teristics of a child trust fund—that it be held by an "eligible child" (see s.2), that it
meet the statutory requirements (see s.3) and that it has been opened in the appropriate manner (either by a "responsible person" (typically a parent) under s.5 or by
HMRC under s.6).

Subs.(3)
This reflects a standard principle of revenue law (see e.g. Taxes Management Act   **1.520**
1970, s.1(1)), namely that such matters are "under the care and management of the
Inland Revenue". The only difference is one of nomenclature in the reference to
"the Inland Revenue", rather than the more usual statutory formula of "the Board".
This principle enables the Revenue to apply the law with a degree of administrative
flexibility in appropriate cases. For example, in the context of taxation, this is the
basis upon which the Revenue has traditionally promulgated extra-statutory conces-
sions and reached settlements in disputes with taxpayers.

Eligible children

2.—(1) For the purposes of this Act a child is an "eligible child" if the   **1.521**
child was born after 31st August 2002 and either—
  (a) a person is entitled to child benefit in respect of the child, or
  (b) entitlement to child benefit in respect of the child is excluded by the
       provisions specified in subsection (2)(a) or (b) (children in care of
       authority),
but subject as follows.
(2) The provisions referred to in subsection (1)(b) are—
  (a) paragraph 1(c) of Schedule 9 to the Social Security Contributions
       and Benefits Act 1992 (c. 4) and regulations made under it, and
  (b) paragraph 1(1)(f) of Schedule 9 to the Social Security Contributions
       and Benefits (Northern Ireland) Act 1992 (c. 7) and regulations
       made under it.
(3) Where entitlement to child benefit in respect of a child is excluded
because of a directly applicable Community provision or an international
agreement, subsection (1) applies as if that exclusion did not apply.
(4) Where a person is entitled to child benefit in respect of a child only
because of a directly applicable Community provision or an international
agreement, subsection (1) applies as if the person were not so entitled.
(5) A child who—
  (a) does not have the right of abode in the United Kingdom within the
       meaning given by section 2 of the Immigration Act 1971 (c.77),
  (b) is not a qualified person, or a family member of a qualified person,
       within the meaning of the Immigration (European Economic Area)
       Regulations 2000 (SI 2000/2326), and
  (c) is not settled in the United Kingdom within the meaning given by
       section 33(2A) of the Immigration Act 1971,
is not an eligible child.
(6) A person is not to be regarded for the purposes of subsection (1)(a)
as entitled to child benefit in respect of a child (otherwise than by virtue of
subsection (3)) unless it has been decided in accordance with—
  (a) Chapter 2 of Part 1 of the Social Security Act 1998 (c.14), or
  (b) Chapter 2 of Part 2 of the Social Security (Northern Ireland) Order
       1998 (SI 1998/1506 (N.I. 10)),
that the person is so entitled (and that decision has not been overturned).

(7) Regulations may amend subsection (1) by substituting for the reference to 31st August 2002 a reference to an earlier date.

DEFINITIONS

"child": s.29.
"eligible child": subs.(1) and s.29.

GENERAL NOTE

1.522   This section defines the concept of an "eligible child", the first of the three fundamental features of a child trust fund. The basic definition is to be found in subs.(1), as expanded by subs.(2) to deal with the special case of children being looked after by a local authority. Cases that have an international dimension are covered by subss.(3)–(5). Subsection (6) acts as a definition provision for subs.(1). Subsection (7) provides the potential for the scope of the child trust fund scheme to be expanded to include children born before the cut-off date for eligibility for a child trust fund.

Subs.(1)
1.523   This is the core definition of who is an "eligible child". There are two basic rules. First, the child must have been born *after* August 31, 2002. This date was chosen to align entitlement with the school year (at least in England and Wales), so that all pupils in any given school year (after that date) would be equally entitled. There will, however, be cases involving siblings born either side of the eligibility date: for the position of children who were born *before* September 1, 2002, see further the annotation to subs.(7) below. Secondly, *either* someone must be entitled to child benefit for that child (subs.(1)(a); see further subs.(6)) *or* that person's entitlement is excluded because the child is being looked after by a local authority (subss.(1)(b) and (2)). Thus in general terms, and subject to that special case, entitlement to child benefit is employed as a gateway to eligibility for a child trust fund. Subsections (3)–(5) make special provision for cases with an international dimension.

Subs.(2)
1.524   The case of a child being looked after by a local authority is the only situation in which the rule requiring that a person be entitled to child benefit in respect of the child is waived. It must follow that in the other situations set out in SSCBA 1992, Sch.9 in which there is no entitlement to child benefit, there is also no entitlement to a child trust fund. These situations include children in detention (but see s.10(4)) and married children. These exclusions, and particularly the latter, may eventually affect a handful of children who are recent immigrants to the country.

Subs.(3)
1.525   There will be some children who live in the United Kingdom but in respect of whom child benefit is not payable because of EU law or an international agreement. This provision ensures that such children remain eligible for a child trust fund, notwithstanding that there is no child benefit entitlement. In practice this will apply most commonly to some children who live in Northern Ireland but whose parent works in the Republic of Ireland. In such circumstances, under the EU rules governing the benefit entitlement of migrant workers in Reg.1408/71, child benefit is payable by the benefit authorities in the Republic. As a result of subs.(3) such children are eligible for a child trust fund account.

Subs.(4)
1.526   This deals with the converse position to that in subs.(3). In some cases there is entitlement to child benefit in the United Kingdom solely because of provisions in EU law or under an international agreement. This would apply where a citizen and resident of the Republic of Ireland (or any other EU country) works in the United

Kingdom but his or her child lives in the Republic (or other Member State). Again, EU Reg.1408/71 provides that child benefit is payable by the UK authorities. This subsection provides, in effect, that children in this type of case will not be eligible for a child trust fund, unless and until they come to live in the United Kingdom. This will affect fewer than 500 children, according to official estimates. The Government's view is that "there is no case for the UK Government to pay endowments to encourage saving for and by children whose ties are not within the UK" (Ruth Kelly, Financial Secretary to the Treasury, Standing Committee A, col.37, January 6, 2004). This exclusion will not affect the special position of the children of Crown servants, such as army personnel, who are entitled to child benefit when stationed overseas by virtue of a provision in purely domestic law (Child Benefit (General) Regulations 2003 (SI 2003/493), reg.30).

However, it is by no means certain that the exclusion of EU workers (and their children) who reside outside but work in the United Kingdom from eligibility for child trust funds will necessarily survive legal scrutiny. There are a number of different avenues that might be used to challenge the validity of this provision under EU law. First, art.7(2) of EU Reg.1612/68 requires migrant workers to "enjoy the same social and tax advantages as national workers". Of course, one of the fundamental purposes of the child trust fund scheme is to benefit the child, rather than the worker. Indeed, case law demonstrates that the social or tax advantage must be of some direct or indirect benefit to the worker, and not just to a family member (*Centre Public d'Aide Sociale de Courcelles v Lebon*, Case 316/85 [1987] E.C.R. 2811). But a broad view of the child trust fund scheme might meet this requirement. See also *Reina v Landeskredit Bank Baden-Württemberg* Case 65/81 [1982] E.C.R. 33, in which it was held that an interest-free childbirth loan granted only to German nationals was a social advantage within art.7(2), and so could not be denied to an Italian couple. Although one of the fundamental objectives of the child trust fund scheme is to benefit *children* by providing them with a valuable asset on attaining their majority, it does not require too much imagination to see that the scheme might be construed as being of indirect benefit to the parent-worker. Yet the other purposes of the 2004 Act are framed in terms of domestic policy imperatives, such as encouraging savings, which have no obvious linkage with the free movement of labour. Moreover, the ECJ jurisprudence on art.7(2) has typically concerned the migrant worker who goes both to work and *live* in another Member State, and not merely to work there; the problem identified in this note is strictly more to do with 'frontier workers' than 'migrant workers'. On that basis, therefore, it may be that s.2(4) is not inconsistent with art.7(2) of Reg.1612/68.

Even if this is the case, it does not necessarily follow that s.2(4) is EU-compliant. A second or parallel type of challenge might be made on the basis that the child trust fund scheme confers a "family benefit" within the scope of Reg.1408/71, so bringing into play Ch.7 of that Regulation. Given the linkage between entitlement to child benefit and eligibility for a child trust fund payment, this point is at least arguable. Finally, there remains the broader argument that this provision in the 2004 Act is in breach of art.12 of the Treaty itself, which prohibits "within the scope of the application" of the Treaty "any discrimination on grounds of nationality". Section 2(4) makes no express reference to parents' nationality, but may be viewed as indirectly discriminatory in that its operation in practice is more likely to affect (for example) Irish nationals than British nationals. In recent years the ECJ has demonstrated greater willingness to invoke art.12 for the benefit of citizens of other Member States (see e.g. *Martínez Sala* [1998] E.C.R. I-2691 and Case C-184/99 *Grzelczyk* [2001] E.C.R. I-6193; Case C-209/03 *R. (Bidar) v Ealing London Borough Council* [2005] 2 W.L.R. 1078; and see further R.C.A. White, 'Residence, Benefit Entitlement and Community Law' [2005] 12 *Journal of Social Security Law* 10).

Subs.(5)

A child who lacks a proper immigration status cannot be an "eligible child". This covers children who, under the Immigration Act 1971, have no right of abode or

1.527

are not settled in the United Kingdom. However, subs.(5)(c) may give rise to problems in the context of citizenship of the Union: see further the Advocate General's Opinion of November 11, 2004 in Case C-209/03 *Bidar*. Children who have no entitlement to reside in the United Kingdom under EEA law are likewise excluded from access to the child trust fund scheme.

Subs. (6)

1.528   This provides that a person is not entitled to child benefit until a decision has been taken to that effect (and has not been overturned) in accordance with the SSA Act 1998 (or its Northern Ireland equivalent). Thus HMRC decision to award child benefit acts as the trigger for eligibility for a child trust fund account.

Subs. (7)

1.529   For the purposes of this Act a child is only an "eligible child" if born after August 31, 2002 (subs.(1)). This provision allows the Government to use secondary legislation to substitute an earlier date for the purpose of this definition, thus bringing older children into the scope of eligibility for a child trust fund account. Any such regulations will be subject to the affirmative procedure (see ss.28(5) and (6)(a)). There are obvious arguments in favour of such an extension in the scheme's remit, not least the fact that under the present arrangements older siblings are potentially disadvantaged, and parents and other relatives may naturally wish to make equal financial provision for children in the same family, irrespective of the accident of their date of birth. This problem will be particularly acute in the case of twins, and doubtless there are some, where one twin was born in the last minutes of August 31, 2002 and the younger twin arrived after the stroke of midnight. The House of Commons Treasury Committee recommended that consideration be given to extending the scope of the children to include older children, but without government endowments (*Second Report*, Session 2003–04, HC 86, para.34). The Government has not, to date, demonstrated any significant enthusiasm for extending the remit of the scheme even in this limited way, noting the potential burden on providers.

Requirements to be satisfied

1.530   **3.**—(1) A child trust fund may be held only with a person (referred to in this Act as an "account provider") who has been approved by the Inland Revenue in accordance with regulations.

(2) An account is not a child trust fund unless it is an account of one of the descriptions prescribed by regulations.

(3) The provision which may be made by regulations under subsection (1) includes making approval of an account provider dependent on the person undertaking to provide accounts of such of the descriptions for which provision is made by regulations under subsection (2) as is prescribed by the regulations.

(4) The terms of a child trust fund must—

(a) secure that it is held in the name of a child,

(b) secure that the child is beneficially entitled to the investments under it,

(c) secure that all income and gains arising on investments under it constitute investments under it,

(d) prevent withdrawals from it except as permitted by regulations, and

(e) provide that instructions may be given to the account provider with respect to its management only by the person who has the authority to manage it.

(5) Regulations may impose other requirements which must be satisfied in relation to child trust funds.

(6) The person who has the authority to manage a child trust fund held by a child—

    (a) if the child is 16 or over, is the child, and

    (b) if the child is under 16, is the person who has that authority by virtue of subsection (7) (but subject to subsection (10)).

(7) If there is one person who is a responsible person in relation to the child, that person has that authority; and if there is more than one person who is such a person, which of them has that authority is to be determined in accordance with regulations.

(8) For the purposes of this Act a person is a responsible person in relation to a child under 16 if the person has parental responsibility in relation to the child and is not—

    (a) a local authority or, in Northern Ireland, an authority within the meaning of the Children (Northern Ireland) Order 1995 (S.I. 1995/755 (N.I. 2)), or

    (b) a person under 16.

(9) "Parental responsibility" means—

    (a) parental responsibility within the meaning of the Children Act 1989 (c.41) or the Children (Northern Ireland) Order 1995, or

    (b) parental responsibilities within the meaning of the Children (Scotland) Act 1995 (c.36).

(10) Regulations may provide that, in circumstances prescribed by the regulations, the person who has the authority to manage a child trust fund held by a child under 16 is to be the Official Solicitor (in England and Wales or Northern Ireland) or the Accountant of Court (in Scotland).

(11) A person who has the authority to manage a child trust fund by virtue of subsection (10) is entitled to give any instructions to the account provider with respect to its management which appear to the person who has that authority to be for the benefit of the child.

(12) Where a contract is entered into by or on behalf of a child who is 16 or over in connection with a child trust fund—

    (a) held by the child, or

    (b) held by another child in relation to whom the child has parental responsibility,

the contract has effect as if the child had been 18 or over when it was entered into.

DEFINITIONS

"account provider": subs.(1) and s.29.
"child": s.29.
"child trust fund": *ibid.*
"Inland Revenue": *ibid.*
"parental responsibility": subs.(9).
"responsible person": subs.(8).

GENERAL NOTE

This section sets out various administrative and procedural requirements which must be satisfied in order for a child trust fund account to come into existence. Only authorised financial institutions may offer child trust fund accounts (subs.(1)) and such accounts must meet a number of criteria (subss.(2)–(5)). This section also defines who has the authority to manage the child's account. This will usually be

    1.531

a person with parental responsibility or, in the case of a child aged at least 16, the child him or herself (subss.(6)–(12)).

Subs. (1)

1.532   Financial institutions, known as "account providers" in this Act, must be approved by HMRC before they can offer child trust fund accounts. The details of the approval process, which are set out in regulations, are modelled on those that apply to Individual Savings Accounts (ISAs) (see Child Trust Funds Regulations 2004, regs 14–17 and 19–20). Institutions denied approval have a right of appeal (see s.22(1)).

Subs. (2)

1.533   Approval operates at two levels. First, the account provider itself must be approved by HMRC under subs.(1). Secondly, by virtue of this subsection, only certain types of accounts may qualify as child trust fund accounts. In order to qualify an account must meet the criteria which are set out in regulations and are based on the arrangements governing ISAs (see Child Trust Funds Regulations 2004, reg.8).

Subs. (3)

1.534   This provision means that the regulations governing the approval of financial institutions may require account providers to provide particular types of account as a condition of such approval. The general rule is that, in order to be authorised as an account provider for the purposes of the child trust fund scheme, institutions must offer stakeholder accounts to the general public (see Child Trust Funds Regulations 2004, reg.14(2)(b)(i)). The characteristics of a stakeholder account are defined in the Schedule to the Regulations. The policy justification for this requirement is that it will enable beneficiaries to gain from the potentially higher returns from equities as a long-term investment. Further, the risk of a fall in the value of equities is reduced by the requirement to spread the investment over a number of companies (*ibid.*, para.2(2)(c)) and to transfer the investment to other assets (e.g. cash or gilts) as the maturity date nears.

Subs. (4)

1.535   This provision sets out the core requirements which must be met in order for an account to qualify for the purposes of the child trust fund scheme. For further details, see Child Trust Funds Regulations 2004, reg.8.

The general rule is that no withdrawals are permitted from a child trust fund account before the child attains 18 (subs.(4)(d)). The Government's argument is that this restriction is essential if such accounts are to achieve their long-term goals. The only exceptions to this principle in the regulations as originally drafted related to withdrawals on closure in the event of the child's death and to deductions for management charges due (Child Trust Funds Regulations 2004, reg.18; there is a cap of 1.5 per cent on administration fees: *ibid.*, Sch., para.3(2)). However, following sustained pressure in Parliament, the Government conceded that a further exception should be made in the case of children suffering from a terminal illness. See now Child Trust Funds Regulations 2004, reg.18A. In contrast to the tight restrictions on withdrawals before the age of 18, there are no controls whatsoever on how young adults apply their child trust fund account holdings on reaching that age.

Subs. (5)

1.536   For further details, see Child Trust Funds Regulations 2004, reg.8.

Subs. (6)

1.537   The effect of this provision, taken together with the definitions and qualifications in the following subsections, is that the child trust fund account is managed by the child, if he or she is 16 or over, and otherwise by the person with parental responsibility in respect of that child. This provision was inserted as a government amendment to the original Bill, which had given 16 and 17 year olds in Scotland the right to manage their accounts, but not their peers south of the border (reflecting the special rules in Scots law relating to the age of majority). Following debate, the Government accepted that it was difficult to sustain this distinction in the context of the child trust fund, and so brought forward this provision to ensure that all 16 and 17 year olds in the United Kingdom have the right to manage their child trust fund account. Such individuals are deemed to have full contractual authority to manage their accounts by virtue of subs.(12). They will not be able to withdraw funds until they reach the age of 18 (see subs.(4)(d)).

Subss. (7)–(9)

In the case of children under the age of 16, the "responsible person" is designated **1.538** as the individual with the authority to manage the child trust fund account (subs. (7)). The basic rule is that the "responsible person" in respect of a child under 16 is the person with parental responsibility for that child under the Children Act 1989 (or the relevant legislation for other parts of the United Kingdom: see subs. (9)). There are two exceptions to this rule (subs.(8))—first, a local authority (which may have parental responsibility by virtue of a care order) cannot be a "responsible person"; secondly, a young parent under the age of 16 cannot assume that role. It follows, for example, that the child trust fund accounts of both a 15-year-old mother and her baby will have to be managed by a third party.

It is common, of course, for two individuals to share parental responsibility for a child, as in the case of a married couple (Children Act 1989, s.2(1)). In such cases voucher will be sent to the holder of the child benefit award (see s.5 and Child Trust Funds Regulations 2004, reg.3(2)). Moreover, there can be only one person with authority to manage the child trust fund account, known as the "registered contact" (*ibid.*, reg.8(1)(d)). Typically this will be a "single responsible person", i.e. a person with parental responsibility (see further *ibid.*, reg.13).

Subs. (10)

This was another government amendment to the original Bill. It is designed to **1.539** deal with the problem created by the lack of a "responsible person" for some children in local authority care. A local authority cannot be a responsible person (subs. (8)(a)). In the case of most children being looked after by a local authority, this will not matter, as the child's parent will retain parental responsibility and so be a responsible person. However, there will be a minority of cases in which no individual person holds parental responsibility (e.g. some orphans in care). The Government has announced that the Official Solicitor (in England, Wales and Northern Ireland) or the Accountant of Court (in Scotland) will undertake the function of managing the accounts of children in care for whom there is no one with parental responsibility. See now Child Trust Funds Regulations 2004, reg.33A.

Inalienability

4.—(1) Any assignment of, or agreement to assign, investments under a **1.540** child trust fund, and any charge on or agreement to charge any such investments, is void.

(2) On the bankruptcy of a child by whom a child trust fund is held, the entitlement to investments under it does not pass to any trustee or other person acting on behalf of the child's creditors.

(3) "Assignment" includes assignation; and "assign" is to be construed accordingly.

(4) "Charge on or agreement to charge" includes a right in security over or an agreement to create a right in security over.

(5) "Bankruptcy", in relation to a child, includes the sequestration of the child's estate.

DEFINITIONS

"assign": subs.(3).
"assignment": *ibid.*
"bankruptcy": subs.(5)
"charge on or agreement to charge": subs.(4).
"child trust fund": s.29.

GENERAL NOTE

1.541   The principle of the inalienability of social security benefits is enshrined in SSAA 1992, s.187 (see also Tax Credits Act 2002, s.45). This section provides, in similar fashion, for the inalienability of investments held under a child trust fund. The parallel provision in SSAA 1992, s.187 was applied (in the Scottish context) in *Mulvey v Secretary of State for Social Security*, 1997 S.C. (HL) 105, where the House of Lords held that the bankrupt's right to income support could not be owed to the permanent trustee (the Scottish equivalent of a trustee in bankruptcy). However, the House of Lords held that deductions could lawfully be made from income support to pay a social fund debt incurred prior to sequestration.

Opening and transfers

Opening by responsible person or child

1.542   **5.**—(1) In the case of each child who is first an eligible child by virtue of section 2(1)(a) the Inland Revenue must issue, in a manner prescribed by regulations, a voucher in such form as is so prescribed.

(2) The voucher must be issued to the person who is entitled to child benefit in respect of the child (or, in the case of a child who is such an eligible child because of section 2(3), to a responsible person).

(3) An application may be made—

(a) if the child is 16 or over, by the child, or

(b) otherwise, by a responsible person,

to open for the child with an account provider a child trust fund of any description provided by the account provider.

(4) The application is to be made—

(a) within such period beginning with the day on which the voucher is issued as is prescribed by regulations, and

(b) in accordance with regulations.

(5) When the application has been made the account provider must—

(a) open, in accordance with regulations, a child trust fund of that description for the child, and

(b) inform the Inland Revenue in accordance with regulations.

DEFINITIONS

"account provider": s.29.
"child": *ibid.*
"child trust fund": *ibid.*
"eligible child": s.2(1) and s.29.
"Inland Revenue": s.29.
"responsible person": ss.3(8) and 29.

GENERAL NOTE

This section sets out the framework within which child trust fund accounts are to be opened, typically by the "responsible person" (as defined by s.3(8)) and in exceptional cases by the child (assuming he or she is 16 or over). The default position is that an account must be opened by HMRC (see further s.6).

1.543

Subs. (1)

This places a duty on HMRC to issue a voucher in respect of any eligible child (within the normal definition in s.2(1)(a)). The issue of the voucher will be triggered by the award of child benefit (which, as a result of the Tax Credits Act 2002, is now administered by HMRC rather than the Department for Work and Pensions). See further Child Trust Funds Regulations 2004, reg.3.

1.544

Subs. (2)

The voucher must be issued to the individual who is entitled to child benefit. The voucher is in the amount of the initial Treasury contribution to be paid to all eligible children (£250). It should be noted that the process of issuing vouchers is designed to be an automatic process—there is no requirement in the legislation for the parent or other responsible person to make an independent claim for a child trust fund account voucher. In the special cross-border situation where the child lives in the United Kingdom but the parent works in another EU Member State (e.g. the Republic of Ireland) there will be no child benefit recipient in this jurisdiction (see annotation to s.2(3)). Accordingly in such cases the voucher must be issued to a responsible person for that child.

1.545

Subs. (3)

This enables the "responsible person" to apply to open a child trust fund account with an approved account provider (see further subs.(4)). As originally drafted, the Bill would have required the responsible person physically to present the voucher to the account provider. As a result of a government amendment, the details of this procedure are now left to regulations. The Child Trust Funds Regulations 2004 still envisage a physical transfer of the voucher (reg.5(1), condition 1), but may in the future make provision for an entirely on-line application process. The "responsible person" is not, as such, under a statutory duty to make such an application. If he or she fails to do so, the default position is that ultimately HMRC will step in (see further s.6). In exceptional cases a child aged 16 or 17 may make an application to open a child trust fund account in his or her own name. The most likely circumstance in which this will arise is in the future where a child (born after August 31, 2002) moves to the United Kingdom at the age of 16 having never previously had an entitlement to a child trust fund account.

1.546

Subs. (4)

The application procedure is set out in regulations (see Child Trust Funds Regulations 2004, regs 5 and 13). The responsible person can select both the account provider and the type of account for the child trust fund. The voucher issued by HMRC will be valid for one year from the date of issue (*ibid.*, reg.3(2)), so applicants have a year in which to make the application. If they fail to do so, HMRC's default duty under s.6 arises.

1.547

Subs. (5)

Once a valid application has been made, an account provider is required to open a child trust fund account for the child in question and to inform the Revenue that it has done so. The Child Trust Funds Regulations 2004 require institutions to make both fortnightly and annual returns of such information to the Revenue (regs 30 and 32).

1.548

Opening by Inland Revenue

1.549   **6.**—(1) In the case of each child to whom this section applies, the Inland Revenue must apply to open for the child with an account provider selected in accordance with regulations a child trust fund of a description so selected.

(2) The application is to be made in accordance with regulations.

(3) The account provider must—

(a) open, in accordance with regulations, a child trust fund of that description for the child, and

(b) inform the Inland Revenue in accordance with regulations.

(4) This section applies—

(a) to a child in respect of whom a voucher is issued under section 5(1) but in whose case subsection (5) is satisfied, and

(b) to a child who is first an eligible child by virtue of section 2(1)(b).

(5) This subsection is satisfied in the case of a child if—

(a) the period prescribed under section 5(4) expires without a child trust fund having been opened for the child, or

(b) the child is under 16 and it appears to the Inland Revenue that there is no-one who is a responsible person in relation to the child.

(6) No liability is to arise in respect of the selection of an account provider, or a description of child trust fund, in accordance with regulations under this section.

DEFINITIONS

"account provider": s.29.
"child": *ibid.*
"child trust fund": *ibid.*
"eligible child": s.2(1) and s.29.
"Inland Revenue": s.29.
"responsible person": ss.3(8) and 29.

GENERAL NOTE

1.550   Normally a child's parent (or other adult who is the child benefit recipient), as a "responsible person", will make an application for a child trust fund account in accordance with s.5. There will inevitably be cases where no such application is made. This section therefore performs a 'mop-up' function, placing the onus on HMRC to ensure that accounts are opened for such children who would otherwise miss out. HMRC's obligation under subs.(1) to open a child trust fund account arises in two types of case. The first is where either, following an award of child benefit, a voucher has been issued to the "responsible person" but no application has been made to open a child trust fund account for that child within the required period (12 months) or there appears to be no "responsible person" for that child (subss.(4)(a) and (5)). The second is where the child is being looked after by a local authority and so there is no individual entitled to child benefit (subs.(4)(b)).

Subs.(1)

1.551   In cases to which this section applies (see subss.(4) and (5) and the General Note), HMRC *must* take the initiative and apply to open a child trust fund account for the child in question. The details of the procedure to be adopted are set out in the Child Trust Funds Regulations 2004, reg.6. Account providers are not required to offer these default HMRC-allocated accounts under this arrangement. However, *if* institutions do agree to offer such accounts, they must then accept any HMRC application to open such an account (see subs.(3) and Child Trust Funds Regulations 2004, reg.6(2)). HMRC will maintain a list of account providers willing to offer such accounts, and select account holders in rotation to ensure parity of treatment (*ibid.*, reg.6(3)). If account holders offer more than one type of stakeholder account, the account will likewise be chosen in rotation (*ibid.*, reg.6(4)). The legislation expressly exempts HMRC from any liability in respect of such decisions (subs.(6)). In these cases HMRC's role is furthermore limited to *opening* the account; it will have no role in *managing* the account in such a case. It will always be open to parents to transfer the account to another provider (s.7).

Subs. (2)
See further Child Trust Funds Regulations 2004, reg.6.   1.552

Subs. (3)
This is in parallel terms to the obligation imposed on account providers by   1.553
s.5(5).

Subss. (4) and (5)
See the General Note to this section.   1.554

Subs. (6)
See the annotation to subs.(1).   1.555

Transfers

7. Regulations may make provision about the circumstances in which—   1.556
  (a) a child trust fund which is an account of one of the descriptions pre-
      scribed by regulations may become an account of another of those
      descriptions, and
  (b) a child trust fund held with one account provider may be transferred
      to another.

DEFINITIONS

"account provider": s.29.
"child trust fund": *ibid.*

GENERAL NOTE

This allows regulations to be made which permit the responsible person to change   1.557
the type of child trust fund account (e.g. from a cash to a stakeholder account)
and to move from one provider to another. The procedural rules for transfers are
similar to those relating to transfers of ISA accounts, but require transfers to be free
of charge (save for share dealing costs); see further Child Trust Funds Regulations
2004, reg.21.

Contributions and subscriptions

Initial contribution by Inland Revenue

8.—(1) The Inland Revenue must pay to an account provider such   1.558
amount as is prescribed by regulations if the account provider has—
  (a) informed the Inland Revenue under section 5(5) or 6(3) that a child
      trust fund has been opened, and
  (b) made a claim to the Inland Revenue in accordance with regula-
      tions.

(2) On receipt of the payment the account provider must credit the child trust fund with the amount of the payment.

"account provider": s.29.
"child trust fund": *ibid.*
"Inland Revenue": *ibid.*

GENERAL NOTE

1.559 This section explains how the initial Treasury contribution of £250 stated on the voucher issued to the child benefit recipient is actually converted, albeit indirectly, into cash (the voucher itself cannot be exchanged for money: see Child Trust Funds Regulations 2004, reg.3(1)). Once a child trust fund account has been opened, either in the normal way (s.5) or through the process of HMRC allocation (s.6), the account provider is required to notify HMRC. Account providers then make a claim to HMRC (these are to be made on a fortnightly basis—see Child Trust Funds Regulations 2004, reg.30. HMRC must in turn pay the account holder "such amount as is prescribed by regulations" by way of an initial contribution (subs.(1)), which the account holder must credit to the relevant account (subs.(2)). Children born into the poorest families may also qualify for a "supplementary contribution" under s.9. There is, moreover, a further Treasury contribution for all eligible children when they reach the age of seven (see s.10).

The regulations describe the "initial" and "supplementary" contributions as "Government contributions" (Child Trust Funds Regulations 2004, reg.7). The basic rule for children born on or after the appointed day (April 6, 2005) is that the initial contribution will be £250, or £500 for those in local authority care (*ibid.*, reg.7(4)). Slightly higher amounts have been prescribed for those born on or after September 1, 2002 (the first date on which a child could qualify as an eligible child under s.2(1)) but before the appointed day. These higher amounts are designed to reflect the fact that these children have not had the benefit of interest on their investments to date. The rates are £277 for children born after August 31, 2002 but before the end of the 2002/03 tax year, £268 for those born in the 2003/04 tax year, and £256 for those born between April 6, 2004 and the appointed day (*ibid.*, reg.7(2)). For children in care, the equivalent figures are £553, £536 and £512.

Supplementary contribution by Inland Revenue

1.560 **9.**—(1) If this section applies to a child the Inland Revenue must inform the account provider with whom a child trust fund is held by the child that this section applies to the child.

(2) If the account provider makes a claim to the Inland Revenue in accordance with regulations, the Inland Revenue must pay to the account provider such amount as is prescribed by regulations.

(3) On receipt of the payment the account provider must credit the child trust fund with the amount of the payment.

(4) This section applies to a child if—

(a) a child trust fund is held by the child,
(b) the child was first an eligible child by virtue of section 2(1)(a), and
(c) the condition in subsection (5) is satisfied in relation to the child.

(5) That condition is that it has been determined in accordance with the provision made by and by virtue of sections 18 to 21 of the Tax Credits Act 2002 (c. 21)—

(a) that a person was, or persons were, entitled to child tax credit in respect of the child for the child benefit commencement date, and

(b) that either the relevant income of the person or persons for the tax year in which that date fell does not exceed the income threshold or the person, or either of the persons, was entitled to a relevant social security benefit for that date,

and that determination has not been overturned.

(6) In subsection (5)(b)—

"the income threshold" has the meaning given by section 7(1)(a) of the Tax Credits Act 2002,

"the relevant income", in relation to a person or persons and a tax year, has the meaning given by section 7(3) of that Act in relation to a claim by the person or persons for a tax credit for the tax year,

"relevant social security benefit" means any social security benefit prescribed for the purposes of section 7(2) of that Act, and

"tax year" means a period beginning with 6th April in one year and ending with 5th April in the next.

(7) If the child benefit commencement date is earlier than 6th April 2005, this section applies in relation to the child even if the condition in subsection (5) is not satisfied in relation to the child provided that the condition in subsection (8) is so satisfied.

(8) That condition is that—

(a) income support, or income-based jobseeker's allowance, was paid for the child benefit commencement date to a person whose applicable amount included an amount in respect of the child, or

(b) working families' tax credit, or disabled person's tax credit, was paid for that date to a person whose appropriate maximum working families' tax credit, or appropriate maximum disabled person's tax credit, included a credit in respect of the child.

(9) If the child benefit commencement date is earlier than 6th April 2003, subsection (5) has effect as if—

(a) the reference in paragraph (a) to the child benefit commencement date were to any date in the tax year beginning with 6th April 2003,

(b) the reference in paragraph (b) to the tax year in which the child benefit commencement date fell were to the tax year beginning with 6th April 2003, and

(c) the reference in paragraph (b) to being entitled to a relevant social security benefit for the child benefit commencement date were to being so entitled for any date in that tax year for which the person was, or the persons were, entitled to child tax credit in respect of the child.

(10) "Child benefit commencement date", in relation to a child, means—

(a) the first day for which child benefit was paid in respect of the child (otherwise than because of a directly applicable Community provision or an international agreement), or

(b) in the case of a child to whom section 2(3) applies or section 2(5) has applied, such day as is prescribed by regulations.

DEFINITIONS

"account provider": s.29.
"child": *ibid*.
"child benefit commencement date": subs.(10).

"child trust fund": s.29.
"eligible child": ss.2(1) and 29.
"income threshold": subs.(6)
"Inland Revenue": s.29.
"relevant income": subs.(6).
"relevant social security benefit": *ibid.*
"tax year": *ibid.*

GENERAL NOTE

1.561   In addition to the initial contribution under s.8, children born into families on low incomes will be eligible for a "supplementary contribution" to boost their child trust fund account investment at the outset. This section sets out the rules governing the award of the supplementary contribution. Subss.(1)–(3) specify the procedure to be followed. Subsection (4) spells out the criteria for receipt of the supplementary condition. Children being looked after in local authority care will *not* qualify for this extra amount (see subs.(4)(b)), but they will in any event qualify for an equivalent amount under s.8 by virtue of their status. The means-test is explained in subs.(5), with various terms defined by subss.(6) and (10). Subsections (7)–(9) deal with various awkward transitional cases.

Subs. (1)

1.562   There is no need for parents on low incomes to claim the supplementary contribution; indeed, there is no facility for them to do so. Instead, the legislation requires HMRC to inform the account provider if a child is eligible for the supplementary contribution. HMRC will have this information as it is responsible for administering child tax credit under the Tax Credits Act 2002, which acts as the trigger for entitlement to the extra Treasury contribution (see subss.(4)(c) and (5)).

Subss. (2) and (3)

1.563   Having been informed that the child in question is eligible for the supplementary contribution, the account provider may then make a claim for that extra amount (subs.(2); see Child Trust Funds Regulations 2004, reg.30(6)(b)). This section then requires HMRC to pay the account provider the appropriate amount by way of a supplementary contribution. In the case of children born after the appointed day, this is a further £250 (*ibid.*, reg.7(7)), making £500 in total. The amounts are increased for those born on or after September 1, 2002 but before the appointed day (*ibid.*, reg.7(6)). The account provider must then credit the extra amount to the child's account (subs.(3)). Subsequent regulations amending the amount of the supplementary contribution under subs.(2) will be subject to the affirmative procedure (see ss.28(5) and (6)(b)).

Subs. (4)

1.564   This sets out the criteria for the award of the supplementary contribution. The child must have a child trust fund account, have qualified on the basis of an award of child benefit and meet the child tax credit means-test set out in subs.(5). The second of these requirements has the effect of excluding children who initially qualified for an account because they were in care (see s.2(1)(b)), as they will, in any event, receive the higher initial contribution (see annotation to s.8).

Subs. (5)

1.565   This provision sets out the means-test which determines whether a child is eligible to receive the supplementary as well as the initial Treasury contribution. Two separate conditions must each be satisfied. In the case of both these requirements, the determination of entitlement must have been a final one in accordance with ss.18–21 of the Tax Credits Act 2002 and must not have been overturned.

The first condition is that someone was entitled to child tax credit for the child in question at the date when child benefit was first paid (known as the "child benefit commencement date": see subs.(10)). The second requirement is that *either* their income does not exceed the child tax credit income threshold for the tax year in issue *or* that person is entitled to a "relevant social security benefit". The statutory authority for the child tax credit income threshold is Tax Credits Act 2002, s.7(1)(a) (see subs.(6)). The annual amount of this threshold is prescribed in regulations, and for the 2009/10 tax year is £16,040 (Tax Credits (Income Threshold and Determination of Rates) Regulations 2002 (SI 2002/2008), reg.3(3), as amended by Tax Credits Up-rating Regulations 2005 (SI 2005/681), reg.4). The expression "relevant social security benefit" is defined by reference to Tax Credits Act 2002, s.7(2)) (see subs.(6)), and so includes only income support, income-based jobseeker's allowance and pension credit (Tax Credits (Income Threshold and Determination of Rates) Regulations 2002 (SI 2002/2008), reg.4, as amended by Tax Credits (Miscellaneous Amendments No.2) Regulations 2003 (SI 2003/2815), reg.18).

These tests require some modification so that they operate in the desired fashion for eligible children born in the transitional period between August 31, 2002 and April 6, 2005. There are two sets of special transitional rules contained in subss. (7)–(9).

Subss.(7) and (8)

The first transitional problem relates to the phasing in of child tax credit for families in receipt of income support or income-based jobseeker's allowance. Child tax credit, payable under the Tax Credits Act 2002, came into force on April 6, 2003, at least so far as new claimants and those claiming working tax credit (the successor to working families' tax credit) were concerned. Originally it was anticipated that families already in receipt of income support or income-based jobseeker's allowance would move over to child tax credit a year later on April 6, 2004. In fact, only new claimants of these benefits have received child tax credit from that date. The revised plan was that the process of 'migration' for existing benefits cases would then start in October 2004, with a view to such transfers being completed by the end of the 2004/05 tax year. (In the meantime all such families have received the cash equivalent of child tax credit through their existing benefits). Some families have therefore not meet the strict terms of subs.(5) because, although they were getting income support or income-based jobseeker's allowance at the material time, they were not yet, as a result of this phasing process, receiving child tax credit. Subsections (7) and (8) deal with this by disapplying the means-test based on entitlement to child tax credit in subs.(5). Instead, they provide alternatively that it is sufficient that a child born before April 6, 2005 was in a household which received one of the means-tested benefits or tax credits listed in subs.(8) in respect of that child.

As matters have transpired, this process of migration has been further delayed and had not been commenced, let alone completed, by the end of the 2004/05 tax year. The current plan is to have this process completed by December 31, 2011: see Tax Credits Act 2002 (Commencement No.4, Transitional Provisions and Savings) Order 2003 (SI 2003/962 (c. 51)) as amended.

Subs.(9)

This deals with a separate transitional problem relating to children born between September 1, 2002 and April 5, 2003. The first condition in the means-test (subs. (5)(a)) is that a person was entitled to child tax credit in respect of the child when child benefit was first paid. However, child tax credit did not come into operation until April 6, 2003, and so subs.(5)(a) cannot be satisfied if child benefit was payable *before* that date. There are also knock-on problems in terms of complying with subs.(5)(b) in such cases. This sub-section resolves these problems by deeming the child benefit commencement date (and hence the entitlement to child tax credit) as having been in the 2003/04 tax year.

1.566

1.567

Further contributions by Inland Revenue

1.568   **10.**—(1) Regulations may make provision for the making by the Inland Revenue in the circumstances mentioned in subsection (2) of payments to account providers of child trust funds held by—

(a) eligible children, or

(b) any description of eligible children,

of amounts prescribed by, or determined in accordance with, regulations.

(2) The circumstances referred to in subsection (1) are—

(a) the children attaining such age as may be prescribed by the regulations, or

(b) such other circumstances as may be so prescribed.

(3) The regulations must include provision—

(a) for making account providers aware that such amounts are payable,

(b) about the claiming of such payments by account providers, and

(c) about the crediting of child trust funds by account providers with the amount of such payments.

(4) For the purposes of this section, a child is to be treated as being an eligible child if entitlement to child benefit in respect of the child is excluded by—

(a) paragraph 1(a) of Schedule 9 to the Social Security Contributions and Benefits Act 1992 (c. 4) (children in custody), or

(b) paragraph 1(1)(a) to (d) of Schedule 9 to the Social Security Contributions and Benefits (Northern Ireland) Act 1992 (c. 7) (corresponding provision for Northern Ireland).

DEFINITIONS

"account provider": s.29.

"child": *ibid.*

"child trust fund": *ibid.*

"eligible child": ss.2(1) and 29.

"Inland Revenue": s.29.

GENERAL NOTE

1.569   This is an enabling measure, allowing regulations to be made which may provide for a further Treasury contribution to be credited to the child's account at a later date. Any regulations made under subs.(1) or (2) will be subject to the affirmative procedure (see s.28(5) and (6)(a)).

Subss. (1) and (2)

1.570   The powers enshrined in the section are expressed in broad terms—thus regulations may provide that further contributions are made to all eligible children, or just to a subset of them (subs.(1)). The trigger for a further contribution may be when the child attains a particular age, as set out in regulations, or some other factor (subs.(2)). The Government's stated intention is that there will be one further contribution which will be payable to all eligible children at the age of seven (rather than three payments at ages 5, 11 and 16, as suggested in *Savings and Assets for All*). It follows that the first such payments will not become due until 2009 (see now Child Trust Funds Regulations 2004, reg.7A). In its 2004 Pre-Budget Report the Government announced a consultation process on the appropriate levels for such further contributions. The consultation paper suggested that there be a further universal payment of £250 at age seven, with an extra £250 for children in low-income families (Treasury Press Notice 5, December 2, 2004). A further consultation was initiated by the 2005 Budget, with a view to seeing whether there is support for a further contribution to children of secondary school age and, if so, at what age and in what amounts. In both consultations the Government has invited views on the appropriate ratio of progressivity (currently 1:2, i.e. £250 universal and £500 means-tested). The rationale for further contributions is that they will enable additional endowment funds to be targeted on those most in need. It will also help to keep the accounts 'live' by reminding both children and their parents of the existence and growth of such funds. Note also that account providers will have to issue annual account statements (Child Trust Funds Regulations 2004, reg.10).

Subs. (3)

As well as specifying matters such as the amount of the further contribution and the age at which it becomes payable, the regulations which are to be made nearer the time must also address the various procedural matters referred to in this sub-section.

1.571

Subs. (4)

A child will remain an eligible child for these purposes even if there is no child benefit entitlement at the date when the further contribution becomes payable because he or she is detained in custody. Clearly children aged seven are not going to be in custody. However, a future government might decide to make further Treasury contributions to children at the age of 12 or over, when this could become an issue. The Government's view, as a matter of principle, was that it was not justifiable "to disadvantage such children on the grounds that they were in custody on a particular birthday". Such an exclusion from the further contribution might also result in anomalies depending on the length of time the child was in custody and when their birthday fell.

1.572

Recouping Inland Revenue contributions

11.—(1) Regulations may make provision requiring that, in circumstances prescribed by the regulations, a person of a description so prescribed is to account to the Inland Revenue for amounts credited to a child trust fund in respect of Inland Revenue contributions (together with any income and gains arising in consequence of the crediting of those amounts).

(2) "Inland Revenue contributions" means payments made by the Inland Revenue which were required to be made under or by virtue of sections 8 to 10 or which the Inland Revenue considered were required to be so made.

1.573

DEFINITIONS

"child trust fund": s.29.
"Inland Revenue": *ibid.*
"Inland Revenue contributions": subs.(2).

GENERAL NOTE

In some cases payments will be made under ss.8, 9 or 10 which should not have been so credited; in social security parlance these would be described as overpayments. This section allows the Treasury to make regulations governing the recovery of such payments, e.g. where more than one account has been opened or where the child in question was never an eligible child within s.2. The intention is that recovery will be possible from the account provider, the child, the registered contact (typically the parent) and anyone into whose hands the funds have come.

1.574

Subscription limits

1.575   **12.**—(1) No subscription may be made to a child trust fund otherwise than by way of a monetary payment.

(2) Regulations may prescribe the maximum amount that may be subscribed to a child trust fund in each year (otherwise than by way of credits made under or by virtue of this Act or income or gains arising on investments under the child trust fund).

(3) "Year", in relation to a child trust fund held by a child, means—

(a)   the period beginning with the day on which the child trust fund is opened and ending immediately before the child's next birthday, and

(b)   each succeeding period of twelve months.

DEFINITIONS

"child trust fund": s.29.
"year": subs.(3).

GENERAL NOTE

1.576   Whereas ss.8–11 are all concerned with Treasury contributions to a child trust fund account, this section deals with contributions to such accounts by others, for example a child's family and friends. Such non-governmental contributions may only be in money terms (subs.(1)), and so shares cannot be transferred to a child trust fund account. There will also be an annual aggregate limit on such non-governmental contributions, prescribed by regulations made under subs. (2). This cap is to be £1,200 a year at the outset (Child Trust Fund Regulations 2004, reg.9(2); there is no facility to carry over any unused allowance to a following year (*ibid.*, reg.9(3)). A year, in this context, means each year from the date of the individual child's birthday (subs.(3)), not each calendar year or each tax year. The minimum contribution on any one transaction is £10, unless the account provider permits a smaller amount (Child Trust Fund Regulations 2004, Sch., para.2(4)).

There is no provision in the Act for automatic indexation of the annual aggregate limit; the Government intends to treat the cap in the same way as the ISA limit, so any uprating will be announced in the Budget or simply through regulations.

Tax

Relief from income tax and capital gains tax

1.577   **13.**—(1) Regulations may make provision for and in connection with giving relief from—

(a)   income tax, and

(b)   capital gains tax,

in respect of investments under child trust funds.

(2) The regulations may, in particular, include—

(a)   provision for securing that losses are disregarded for the purposes of capital gains tax where they accrue on the disposal of investments under child trust funds, and

(b)   provision dealing with anything which, apart from the regulations, would have been regarded for those purposes as an indistinguishable part of the same asset.

(3) The regulations may specify how tax relief is to be claimed by persons entitled to it or by account providers on their behalf.

(4) The regulations may include provision requiring that, in circumstances prescribed by the regulations, the person prescribed by the regulations is to account to the Inland Revenue for—

(a) tax from which relief has been given under the regulations, and

(b) income or gains arising in consequence of the giving of relief under the regulations,

or for an amount determined in accordance with the regulations in respect of such tax.

(5) Provision made by virtue of this section may disapply, or modify the effect of, any enactment relating to income tax or capital gains tax.

DEFINITIONS

"account provider": s.29.
"child trust fund": *ibid.*
"Inland Revenue": *ibid.*

GENERAL NOTE

This section is concerned with the tax treatment of investments held in child trust funds. It allows regulations to make provision for relief in respect of income tax and capital gains tax (subs.(1)), and how such tax relief should be claimed (subs. (3)). Such regulations may effectively ring-fence child trust fund investments from any other investments held by the child concerned; this will mean that any capital losses arising on the disposal of child trust fund investments will not be deductible from any capital gains outside the child trust fund (subs.(2)(a)). Regulations will also provide for the separate identification of disposals of shares within and outside a child trust fund (subs.(2)(b)). Regulations may provide for the repayment of tax relief that is given in circumstances where it should not have been (subs.(4)). Subsection (5) is a general power that enables regulations to modify income tax and capital gains tax legislation for child trust fund accounts (see generally Child Trust Funds Regulations 2004, Pt 3 and especially regs 24 and 36).

1.578

Insurance companies and friendly societies

14.—[¹ . . .]

1.579

AMENDMENT

1. Finance Act 2007, s.114 and Sch.27, Part 2 (July 19, 2007).

Information etc.

Information from account providers etc.

15.—(1) Regulations may require, or authorise officers of the Inland Revenue to require, any relevant person—

(a) to make documents available for inspection on behalf of the Inland Revenue, or

(b) to provide to the Inland Revenue any information,

relating to, or to investments which are or have been held under, a child trust fund.

1.580

(2) The following are relevant persons—

(a) anyone who is or has been the account provider in relation to the child trust fund,

(b) the person by whom the child trust fund is or was held,

(c) the person (if any) to whom a voucher was issued under section 5(1) in respect of the child by whom the child trust fund is or was held,

(d) the person who applied to open the child trust fund (unless it was opened by the Inland Revenue),

(e) anyone who has given instructions with respect to the management of the child trust fund, and

(f) anyone entitled to child benefit in respect of the child.

(3) The regulations may include provision requiring documents to be made available or information to be provided—

(a) in the manner and form, and

(b) by the time and at the place,

prescribed by or under the regulations.

DEFINITIONS

"account provider": s.29.
"child": *ibid*.
"child trust fund": *ibid*.
"Inland Revenue": *ibid*.
"relevant person": subs.(2).

GENERAL NOTE

1.581   This section enables the Treasury to make regulations requiring account providers and other "relevant persons" (as defined by subs.(2)) to supply information or make documents available for inspection (and subject to requirements stipulated under subs.(3)). The Child Trust Funds Regulations 2004 require account holders to supply HMRC with both fortnightly and annual returns (regs 30 and 32). The fortnightly returns will both act as a claim for payment of the government contributions and enable HMRC to identify children for whom accounts have not been opened.

Information about children in care of authority

1.582   **16.**—(1) Regulations may require, or authorise officers of the Inland Revenue to require, an authority—

(a) to make documents available for inspection on behalf of the Inland Revenue, or

(b) to provide to the Inland Revenue any information,

which the Inland Revenue may require for the discharge of any function relating to child trust funds and which is information to which subsection (2) applies.

(2) This subsection applies to information relating to a child who falls or has fallen within—

(a) paragraph 1(c) of Schedule 9 to the Social Security Contributions and Benefits Act 1992 (c. 4), or

(b) paragraph 1(1)(f) of Schedule 9 to the Social Security Contributions and Benefits (Northern Ireland) Act 1992 (c. 7),

by reason of being, or having been, in the care of the authority in circumstances prescribed by regulations under that provision.

(3) The regulations may include provision requiring documents to be made available or information to be provided—
(a) in the manner and form, and
(b) by the time and at the place,
prescribed by or under the regulations.

DEFINITIONS

"child": s.29.
"child trust fund": *ibid.*
"Inland Revenue": *ibid.*

GENERAL NOTE

The normal rule is that a child is an "eligible child" if child benefit is payable in respect of him or her (s.2(1)(a)). Receipt of child benefit thus acts as a passport to entitlement to the child trust fund. HMRC is also responsible for administering child benefit and accordingly has access to all the relevant information in such cases. However, child benefit cannot be claimed for children in local authority care, for whom special provision has to be made to make them "eligible children" (ss.2(1)(b) and 2(2)). As these children will not appear in the records of current child benefit payments, HMRC will have to obtain the necessary information direct from local authorities. This section accordingly enables the Treasury to make regulations requiring local authorities to provide the information necessary to arrange for a child trust fund account to be opened or for further contributions to be made. Local authorities are required to make monthly returns (Child Trust Funds Regulations 2004, reg.33).

1.583

Use of information

17.—(1) Information held for the purposes of any function relating to child trust funds—
(a) by the Inland Revenue, or
(b) by a person providing services to the Inland Revenue, in connection with the provision of those services,
may be used, or supplied to any person providing services to the Inland Revenue, for the purposes of, or for any purposes connected with, the exercise of any such function.

1.584

(2) Information held for the purposes of any function relating to child trust funds—
(a) by the Inland Revenue, or
(b) by a person providing services to the Inland Revenue, in connection with the provision of those services,
may be used, or supplied to any person providing services to the Inland Revenue, for the purposes of, or for any purposes connected with, the exercise of any other function of the Inland Revenue.

(3) Information held for the purposes of any function other than those relating to child trust funds—
(a) by the Inland Revenue, or
(b) by a person providing services to the Inland Revenue, in connection with the provision of those services,
may be used, or supplied to any person providing services to the Inland Revenue, for the purposes of, or for any purposes connected with, the exercise of any function of the Inland Revenue relating to child trust funds.

(4) Information held by the Secretary of State or the Department for Social Development in Northern Ireland, or any person providing services to the Secretary of State or that Department, may be supplied to—

(a) the Inland Revenue, or

(b) a person providing services to the Inland Revenue, in connection with the provision of those services,

for use for the purposes of, or for any purposes connected with, the exercise of any function of the Inland Revenue relating to child trust funds.

DEFINITIONS

"child trust fund": s.29.
"Inland Revenue": *ibid.*

GENERAL NOTE

1.585   This section allows information relating to child trust funds to be shared both within government and between government departments and their contractors (typically their IT providers). Subsection (1) allows information relating to child trust funds to be used for purposes relating to such funds. Subsection (2), on the other hand, enables such information to be used for other (non-child trust fund) purposes by HMRC (e.g. official evaluations of savings policies). Subsection (3) permits information held by HMRC in connection with other purposes to be used for child trust fund purposes. This allows HMRC to access information about a person's child tax credit status in order to determine eligibility for the supplementary contribution (see s.9(5)). Finally, subs.(4) allows other government departments to provide information to HMRC (or its contractors) for reasons connected with child trust funds. In particular, this will enable HMRC to obtain information from the Department for Work and Pensions about a person's benefit status. This will be relevant to determining entitlement to the supplementary condition in respect of children born on or after September 1, 2002 but before child tax credit became payable to the household in question.

Disclosure of information

1.586   **18.** [*Section omitted.*]

GENERAL NOTE

1.587   This section amends the Finance Act 1989, s.182 and so brings the child trust fund scheme within the existing statutory provisions which deal with the confidentiality of personal information held by HMRC, and the exceptions to that principle.

Payments after death

Payments after death of child

1.588   **19.**—(1) Where a relevant child dies, the Inland Revenue may make a payment to the personal representatives of the child if any one or more of the conditions specified in subsection (3) is satisfied.

(2) "Relevant child" means a child who is or has been an eligible child (or would have been had this Act come into force on the date referred to in section 2(1)).

(3) The conditions are—

(a) that either no payment had been made under section 8 by the Inland Revenue or, if one had, the amount of the payment had not been credited to the child trust fund held by the child,

(b) that section 9 applied to the child (or would have had this Act come into force on the date referred to in section 2(1)) but either no payment had been made under that section by the Inland Revenue or, if one had, the amount of the payment had not been credited to the child trust fund held by the child, and

(c) that the Inland Revenue was required by regulations under section 10 to make a payment in respect of the child but either the payment had not been made or, if it had, the amount of the payment had not been credited to the child trust fund held by the child.

(4) The amount of the payment is to be equal to the amount of the payment or payments which had not been made or credited.

DEFINITIONS

"child": s.29.
"child trust fund": *ibid.*
"eligible child": *ibid.*
"Inland Revenue": *ibid.*
"relevant child": subs.(2).

GENERAL NOTE

This section gives HMRC the power to make child trust fund payments in respect of children born after August 31, 2002 but who have died before such payments have been credited to an account. Any one (or more) of three requirements must be satisfied. These are (1) that no initial contribution has been paid under s.8 (or it has not been credited to the account); (2) that the child was entitled to a supplementary contribution under s.9 but this had not been paid or credited to the account; or (3) that a further contribution was due under s.10 but again had not been paid or credited (subs.(3)). The amount payable is a sum equal to the amount of the outstanding payment(s) (subs.(4)) and is payable to the child's personal representatives (subs.(1)). Note that there is no absolute right to such a payment; HMRC *may* make such a payment. The element of discretion has been inserted to allow HMRC to refuse to make payments in cases where the child has been unlawfully killed by the parent. The personal representatives have a right of appeal in the event of a dispute about payment (s.22(5)).

1.589

Penalties

Penalties

20.—(1) A penalty of £300 may be imposed on any person who fraudulently—

(a) applies to open a child trust fund,

(b) makes a withdrawal from a child trust fund otherwise than as permitted by regulations under section 3(4)(d), or

(c) secures the opening of a child trust fund by the Inland Revenue.

(2) A penalty not exceeding £3,000 may be imposed on—

(a) an account provider who fraudulently or negligently makes an

1.590

incorrect statement or declaration in connection with a claim under section 8 or 9 or regulations under section 10 or 13, and

(b) any person who fraudulently or negligently provides incorrect information in response to a requirement imposed by or under regulations under section 15.

(3) Penalties may be imposed on—

(a) an account provider who fails to make a claim under section 8 or 9 or regulations under section 10 by the time required by regulations under the section concerned, and

(b) any person who fails to make a document available, or provide information, in accordance with regulations under section 15.

(4) The penalties which may be imposed under subsection (3) are—

(a) a penalty not exceeding £300, and

(b) if the failure continues after a penalty under paragraph (a) is imposed, a further penalty or penalties not exceeding £60 for each day on which the failure continues after the day on which the penalty under that paragraph was imposed (but excluding any day for which a penalty under this paragraph has already been imposed).

(5) No penalty under subsection (3) may be imposed on a person in respect of a failure after the failure has been remedied.

(6) For the purposes of subsection (3) a person is to be taken not to have failed to make a claim, make available a document or provide information which must be made, made available or provided by a particular time—

(a) if the person made it, made it available or provided it within such further time (if any) as the Inland Revenue may have allowed,

(b) if the person had a reasonable excuse for not making it, making it available or providing it by that time, or

(c) if, after having had such an excuse, the person made it, made it available or provided it without unreasonable delay.

(7) A penalty may be imposed on an account provider in respect of—

(a) the provision by the account provider, as a child trust fund, of an account which does not meet the condition in subsection (8),

(b) a failure by the account provider to comply with section 8(2) or 9(3) or with a requirement imposed on the account provider by regulations under section 5(5), 6(3), 7 or 10(3), or

(c) a breach of section 12(1), or regulations under section 12(2), in relation to a child trust fund held with the account provider.

(8) An account meets the condition referred to in subsection (7)(a) if—

(a) it is of one of the descriptions prescribed by regulations under section 3(2),

(b) section 3(4) is complied with in relation to it, and

(c) the requirements imposed by regulations under section 3(5) are satisfied in relation to it.

(9) The penalty which may be imposed under subsection (7) on the account provider is a penalty not exceeding—

(a) £300, or

(b) £1 in respect of each account affected by the matter, or any of the matters, in respect of which the penalty is imposed,

whichever is greater.

DEFINITIONS

"account provider": s.29.

276

"child trust fund": *ibid.*
"Inland Revenue": *ibid.*

GENERAL NOTE

This section makes provision for penalties to be imposed in connection with child trust fund applications and related matters. Individuals who fraudulently apply to open or secure the opening of an account, or make an account withdrawal, are subject to a penalty of £300 (subs.(1)). Account providers and others who make fraudulent or negligent statements or declarations are liable to a penalty not exceeding £3,000 (subs.(2)). Account providers and others are also liable to a £300 penalty (and £60 per day thereafter for continued non-compliance) for failing to make claims in respect of reimbursements or for failing to provide information or produce documentation (subss.(3) and (4); see further subss.(5) and (6)). Subsections (7)–(9) make further provision for penalties to be imposed on account providers in respect of non-compliance with various statutory requirements.

Any penalties under this section are imposed by HMRC (s.21(1)), subject to the various procedural requirements in s.21. There is a right of appeal against any decision to impose a penalty, or its amount (s.22(6)).

1.591

Decisions, appeals, mitigation and recovery

21.—(1) It is for the Inland Revenue to impose a penalty under section 20.

1.592

(2) If the Inland Revenue decide to impose such a penalty the decision must (subject to the permitted maximum) set it at such amount as, in their opinion, is appropriate.

(3) A decision to impose such a penalty may not be made after the end of the period of six years beginning with the date on which the penalty was incurred or began to be incurred.

(4) The Inland Revenue must give notice of such a decision to the person on whom the penalty is imposed.

(5) The notice must state the date on which it is given and give details of the right to appeal against the decision under section 22.

(6) After the notice has been given, the decision must not be altered except on appeal.

(7) But the Inland Revenue may, in their discretion, mitigate any penalty under section 20.

(8) A penalty under section 20 becomes payable at the end of the period of 30 days beginning with the date on which notice of the decision is given.

(9) On an appeal under section 22 against a decision under this section, the [¹ appropriate tribunal] may—

(a) if it appears that no penalty has been incurred, set the decision aside,

(b) if the amount set appears to be appropriate, confirm the decision,

(c) if the amount set appears to be excessive, reduce it to such other amount (including nil) as [¹ the tribunal considers] appropriate, or

(d) if the amount set appears to be insufficient, increase it to such amount not exceeding the permitted maximum as [¹ the tribunal considers] appropriate.

[¹(10) In addition to any right of appeal on a point of law under section 11(2) of the Tribunals, Courts and Enforcement Act 2007, the person liable to the penalty may appeal to the Upper Tribunal against the amount of a penalty which has been determined under subsection (9), but not against any decision which falls under section 11(5)(d) and (e) of that Act and was made in connection with the determination of the amount of the penalty.

(10A) Section 11(3) and (4) of the Tribunals, Courts and Enforcement Act 2007 applies to the right of appeal under subsection (10) as it applies to the right of appeal under section 11(2) of that Act.

(10B) On an appeal under this section the Upper Tribunal has a similar jurisdiction to that conferred on the First-tier Tribunal by virtue of this section.

(10C) In Northern Ireland, an appeal from a decision of the appropriate tribunal lies, at the instance of the person on whom the penalty was imposed to a Northern Ireland Social Security Commissioner, who shall have a similar jurisdiction on such an appeal to that conferred on the appeal tribunal by subsection (9).]

(11) A penalty is to be treated for the purposes of Part 6 of the Taxes Management Act 1970 (c. 9) (collection and recovery) as if it were tax charged in an assessment and due and payable.

AMENDMENT

1. Transfer of Tribunal Functions and Revenue and Customs Appeals Order 2009 (SI 2009/56), art.3(1), Sch.1, para.415 (April 1, 2009).

DEFINITIONS

"appeal tribunal"—s.24(6).
"the Inland Revenue"—s.29 but note that the functions of the Inland Revenue have been transferred to HMRC by CRCA 2005.

Appeals

Rights of appeal

1.593   **22.**—(1) A person may appeal against—
(a) a decision by the Inland Revenue not to approve the person as an account provider, or
(b) a decision by the Inland Revenue to withdraw the person's approval as an account provider.

(2) A person who is a relevant person in relation to a child may appeal against a decision by the Inland Revenue—
(a) not to issue a voucher under section 5 in relation to the child,
(b) not to open a child trust fund for the child under section 6,
(c) not to make a payment under section 8 or 9 in respect of the child, or
(d) not to make a payment under regulations under section 10 in respect of the child.

(3) "Relevant person", in relation to a child, means—
(a) the person (if any) entitled to child benefit in respect of the child,
(b) anyone who applied to open a child trust fund for the child, and
(c) anyone who has, at any time, given instructions with respect to the management of the child trust fund held by the child.

(4) A person who is required by the Inland Revenue to account for an

amount under regulations under section 11 or 13 may appeal against the decision to impose the requirement.

(5) The personal representatives of a child who has died may appeal against a decision by the Inland Revenue not to make a payment to them under section 19.

(6) A person on whom a penalty under section 20 is imposed may appeal against the decision to impose the penalty or its amount.

DEFINITIONS

"account provider": s.29.
"child": *ibid.*
"child trust fund": *ibid.*
"Inland Revenue": *ibid.*
"relevant person": subs.(3).

GENERAL NOTE

This section sets out the categories of person who can appeal against a decision relating to the child trust fund. In so far as there are any appeals, most appeals will presumably be brought by individuals and will concern the entitlement to child trust fund payments in individual cases (subs.(2)). However, companies who are refused permission by HMRC to act as account providers also have a right of appeal (subs. (1)). Subsections (4)–(6) ensure that various other persons have a right of appeal as appropriate. In particular, subs.(6) provides that any person on whom a penalty is imposed has a right of appeal against both the decision to levy the penalty and also the amount. The tribunal's powers on hearing appeals under this section are set out in s.21(9). In the short to medium term, child trust fund appeals will be heard by the First-tier Tribunal and, on further appeal, by the Upper Tribunal (s.24, temporarily modifying s.23: see General Note to s.21). 1.594

Exercise of rights of appeal

23.—(1) Notice of an appeal under section 22 against a decision must be given to the Inland Revenue in the manner prescribed by regulations within the period of thirty days after the date on which notice of the decision was given. 1.595

(2) Notice of such an appeal must specify the grounds of appeal.

[[1] (3) An appeal under section 22 is to the appropriate tribunal.]

(4) [[1]. . .]

(5) On the hearing of an appeal under section 22 the [[1]appeal tribunal] may allow the appellant to put forward grounds not specified in the notice, and take them into consideration if satisfied that the omission was not wilful or unreasonable.

[[1] (6) Regulations may apply (with or without modifications) any provision contained in—

(a) the Social Security Act 1998 (c. 14) (social security appeals: Great Britain),

(b) the Social Security (Northern Ireland) Order 1998 (SI 1998/1506 (NI 10))(social security appeals: Northern Ireland), or

(c) section 54 of the Taxes Management Act 1970 (settling of appeals by agreement),

in relation to appeals which by virtue of this section are to the appropriate tribunal or in relation to appeals under this Act which lie to a Social Security Commissioner.]

(7) [[1]. . .]

AMENDMENT

1. Transfer of Tribunal Functions and Revenue and Customs Appeals Order 2009 (SI 2009/56), art.3(1), Sch.1, para.416 (April 1, 2009).

DEFINITIONS

"the Inland Revenue"—s.29 but note that the functions of the Inland Revenue have been transferred to HMRC by CRCA 2005.

Temporary modifications

1.596   **24.**—[¹. . .]

AMENDMENT

1. Transfer of Tribunal Functions and Revenue and Customs Appeals Order 2009 (SI 2009/56), art. 3(1), Sch. 1, para. 417 (April 1, 2009).

Supplementary

Northern Ireland

1.597   **25.** In Schedule 2 to the Northern Ireland Act 1998 (c. 47) (excepted matters), after paragraph 9 insert—
"9A Child Trust Funds."

GENERAL NOTE

The child trust fund scheme is added to the Schedule of excepted matters in the Northern Ireland Act 1998, so ensuring that the Fund is governed by legislation common to the whole of the United Kingdom (see also s.30).

1.598   **26.** [*Omitted.*]

1.599   **27.** [*Omitted.*]

1.600   **28.** [*Omitted.*]

Interpretation

1.601   **29.** — In this Act—
"account provider" is to be construed in accordance with section 3(1),
[¹ "appropriate tribunal" means
(a) the First-tier Tribunal, or
(b) in Northern Ireland, an appeal tribunal constituted under Chapter 1 of Part 2 of the Social Security (Northern Ireland) Order 1998,]
"child" means a person under the age of 18,
"child trust fund" has the meaning given by section 1(2),
"eligible child" is to be construed in accordance with section 2,
[¹ ...]
"the Inland Revenue" means the Commissioners of Inland Revenue,
[¹ "Northern Ireland Social Security Commissioner" means the Chief Social Security Commissioner or any other Social Security Commissioner appointed under the Social Security Administration (Northern Ireland) Act 1992 (c. 8) or a tribunal of three or more Commissioners constituted under article 16(7) of the Social Security (Northern Ireland) Order 1998,]
"responsible person" has the meaning given by section 3(8), and
[¹ . . .]

AMENDMENT

1. Transfer of Tribunal Functions and Revenue and Customs Appeals Order 2009 (SI 2009/56), art. 3(1), Sch. 1, para. 418 (April 1, 2009).

Income Tax (Trading and Other Income) Act 2005

(2005 c.5)

CONTENTS

PART 1

OVERVIEW

PART 2

TRADING INCOME

CHAPTER 1

INTRODUCTION

CHAPTER 2

INCOME TAXED AS TRADE PROFITS

Charge to tax on trade profits

Trades and trade profits

Social security contributions

CHAPTER 2

INTEREST

Charge to tax on interest

Other income taxed as interest

CHAPTER 3

DIVIDENDS ETC. FROM UK RESIDENT COMPANIES ETC.

Introduction

Charge to tax on dividends and other distributions

CHAPTER 4

DIVIDENDS FROM NON-UK RESIDENT COMPANIES

Charge to tax on dividends from non-UK resident companies

CHAPTER 7

PURCHASED LIFE ANNUITY PAYMENTS

PART 5

MISCELLANEOUS INCOME

CHAPTER 1

INTRODUCTION

CHAPTER 5

SETTLEMENTS: AMOUNTS TREATED AS INCOME OF SETTLOR

Charge to tax under Chapter 5

Income charged and person liable

CHAPTER 8

INCOME NOT OTHERWISE CHARGED

PART 6

EXEMPT INCOME

CHAPTER 1

INTRODUCTION

CHAPTER 2

NATIONAL SAVINGS INCOME

CHAPTER 8

OTHER ANNUAL PAYMENTS

Certain annual payments by individuals

Periodical payments of personal injury damages etc.

Health and employment insurance payments

Payments to adopters

CHAPTER 9

OTHER INCOME

CHAPTER 10

GENERAL

PART 7

INCOME CHARGED UNDER THIS ACT: RENT-A-ROOM AND FOSTER-CARE RELIEF

CHAPTER 1

RENT-A-ROOM RELIEF

Introduction

Basic definitions

Individual's limit

CHAPTER 2

FOSTER-CARE RELIEF

Introduction

Basic definitions

PART 10

GENERAL PROVISIONS

CHAPTER 1

INTRODUCTION

864.   Overview of Part 10

CHAPTER 2

GENERAL CALCULATON RULES ETC.

868.   Social security contributions: non-trades etc.

INTRODUCTION AND GENERAL NOTE

ITTOIA is the third of the series of Acts produced under the Tax Law Rewrite   **1.605**
Project. It came into effect on April 6, 2005. Together with ITEPA it has rewritten
all the main charging provisions of income tax as they apply to individuals, partnerships and trusts. Provisions applying to companies have not been rewritten, but they
are not relevant to tax credits.

ITTOIA completes the abolition of all the former income tax schedules as its provisions replace the old Sch.A (taxation of income from land in the United Kingdom)
and Sch.D, Cases I to VI (trading and professional income, investment income, and
foreign source income). Following the approach adopted in ITEPA it also merges
provisions about the taxation of UK-source income with the taxation of foreign
source income. The relevance here is that assessment of income for tax credits purposes includes worldwide income. With effect from the tax year 2006–07 no reference therefore need be made to the old law for tax credits purposes.

The pattern adopted by ITTOIA is as follows. The charges to tax under the
various Schedules and other separate charging sections have been converted
into charges on different classes of income, and the rules relating to each kind
of income are set out in separate Parts of the Act. These are then followed by
general exemptions and other provisions. Each part has "signposts" in it, including an initial overview and provisions dealing with priorities between charging
provisions.

The most important difference between kinds or classes of income is the one that
lies between ITEPA and ITTOIA: is an individual employed or self-employed?
ITTOIA operates if ITEPA does not, but the decision whether someone is employed
or not in that narrower sense is left outside both Acts and for the ordinary law—and
in the social security context is usually to be determined under the provisions of s.8
of the Social Security (Transfer of Functions) Act 1999.

The new charges to tax, exemptions and reliefs are:

Part 2 Trading income (including professions and vocations)

Part 3 Property income (including both UK and foreign land)

Part 4 Savings and investment income (including interest and dividends)

Part 5 Miscellaneous income (the "sweeper")

Part 6 Exempt income

Part 7 Rent-a-room and foster care reliefs

Trading income replaces the old Sch.D Cases I and II and part of Case VI. Property income replaces the old Sch.A and part of Sch.D Case V. Savings and investment income replaces the old Sch.D Case III and Case IV, part of Case V and part of Case VI. It also replaces Sch.F. (It also includes the former Sch.C, which was repealed and replaced by provisions included in Sch.D some years ago). As the former Sch.B was repealed many years ago, this completes the repeal for income tax (and therefore tax credits) purposes of all the old 1803 income tax schedules.

A consistent pattern within each part is to place the most important provisions at the start of the Part. For example, in the savings and investment income part the charge on interest comes first, then dividends, with less commonly used provisions following in decreasing order of importance. The Act also seeks to put all the important measures in the main text of the Act, rather than in schedules. This explains the need for a lengthy Pt 7, dealing with the important but inevitably detailed provisions that exempt small incomes from income tax if drawn from renting rooms in the individual's only or main residence or from foster care payments (or both).

The sections selected for inclusion

1.606   The sections set out in this work are selected for two reasons: first, they are the main sections of the Act and the ones to which reference is most likely to be made, directly or indirectly, in straightforward tax credits cases involving either the self-employed or forms of savings and investment income. Second, sections are included where they deal expressly with social security income or the kinds of income received in particular by those with disabilities. Provisions providing exemption from two specific kinds of income widely received by those with entitlement to tax credits are also included: tax relief under the rent-a-room scheme exempting income where a resident owner lets part of his or her house to a lodger; and the exemption of income paid to foster parents under foster-care relief.

The law is as applied for 2008–09 after any amendments in the Finance Acts. No history of amendments is set out. However, the full history of the original ITTOIA provisions (to which as yet little amendment has been made) are in the full explanatory notes to ITTOIA issued by the Tax Law Rewrite Project.

PART 1

OVERVIEW

Overview of Act

1.607   **1.**—(1) This Act imposes charges to income tax under—
(a) Part 2 (trading income),
(b) Part 3 (property income),
(c) Part 4 (savings and investment income), and
(d) Part 5 (certain miscellaneous income).

(2) *Repealed.*

(3) Exemptions from those charges are dealt with in Part 6 (exempt income) but any Part 6 exemptions which are most obviously relevant to particular types of income are also mentioned in the provisions about those types of income.

(4) What is or is not mentioned in those provisions does not limit the effect of Part 6.

(5) This Act also contains—

(a) provision about rent-a-room relief and foster-care relief (see Part 7),

(b) special rules for foreign income (see Part 8),

(c) special rules for partnerships (see Part 9), and

(d) certain calculation rules and general provisions (see Part 10).

(6) For abbreviations and defined expressions used in this Act, see 885 and Sch.4.

Overview of priority rules

2.—(1) This Act contains some rules establishing an order of priority in respect of certain amounts which would otherwise— 1.608

(a) fall within a charge to income tax under two or more Chapters or Parts of this Act, or

(b) fall within a charge to income tax under a Chapter or Part of this Act and ITEPA 2003.

(2) See, in particular—

section 4 (provisions which must be given priority over Part 2),

section 261 (provisions which must be given priority over Part 3),

section 262 (priority between Chapters within Part 3),

section 366 (provisions which must be given priority over Part 4),

section 367 (priority between Chapters within Part 4),

section 575 (provisions which must be given priority over Part 5), and

section 576 (priority between Chapters within Part 5).

(3) But the rules in those sections need to be read with other rules law (whether in this Act or otherwise) about the scope of particular provisions or the order of priority to be given to them.

(4) Section 171(2) of FA 1993 (profits of Lloyd's underwriters charged only under Chapter 2 of Part 2 of this Act) is one example of another rule of law.

PART 2

TRADING INCOME

CHAPTER 1

Overview of Part 2

3.—(1) This Part imposes charges to income tax under— 1.609

(a) Chapter 2 (the profits of a trade, profession or vocation which meet the territorial conditions mentioned in section 6),

 (b) Chapter 17 (amounts treated as adjustment income under section 228), and

 (c) Chapter 18 (post-cessation receipts that are chargeable under this Part).

(2) Part 6 deals with exemptions from the charges under this Part.

(3) See, in particular, the exemptions under sections 777 (VAT repayment supplements) and 778 (incentives to use electronic communications).

(4) The charges under this Part apply to non-UK residents as well as UK residents but this is subject to sections 6(2) and (3) and 243(3) and (4) (charges on non-UK residents only on UK income).

(5) The rest of this Part contains rules relevant to the charges to tax under this Part.

(6) This section needs to be read with the relevant priority rules (see sections 2 and 4).

GENERAL NOTE

1.610 Part 2 rewrites (and to some extent also codifies) the previous provisions in Sch.D Case I (income from trade wholly or partly in the UK) and Case II (income from professions and vocations) and aspects of Case IV (other income) previously in ICTA 1988 and subsequent Finance Acts. But the definition of "trade" remains in ICTA 1988 s.832. The charges under this Part on non-UK residents are not covered in this work.

Provisions which must be given priority over Part 2

1.611 **4.**—(1) Any receipt or other credit item, so far as it falls within—

 (a) Chapter 2 of this Part (receipts of trade, profession or vocation), and

 (b) Chapter 3 of Part 3 so far as it relates to a UK property business,

is dealt with under Part 3.

(2) Any receipt or other credit item, so far as it falls within—

 (a) this Part, and

 (b) Part 2, 9 or 10 of ITEPA 2003 (employment income, pension income or social security income),

is dealt with under the relevant Part of ITEPA 2003.

CHAPTER 2

INCOME TAXED AS TRADE PROFITS

Charge to tax on trade profits

Charge to tax on trade profits

1.612 **5.** Income tax is charged on the profits of a trade, profession or vocation.

Territorial scope of charge to tax

1.613 **6.**—(1) Profits of a trade arising to a UK resident are chargeable to tax under this Chapter wherever the trade is carried on.

(2) Profits of a trade arising to a non-UK resident are chargeable to tax under this Chapter only if they arise—

(a) from a trade carried on wholly in the United Kingdom, or

(b) in the case of a trade carried on partly in the United Kingdom and partly elsewhere, from the part of the trade carried on in the United Kingdom.

(3) This section applies to professions and vocations as it applies to trades.

Income charged

7.—(1) Tax is charged under this Chapter on the full amount of the profits of the tax year.　　　　1.614

(2) For this purpose the profits of a tax year are the profits of the basis period for the tax year.

(3) For the rules identifying the basis period for a tax year, see Chapter 15.

(4) This section is subject to Part 8 (foreign income: special rules).

(5) And, for the purposes of section 830 (meaning of "relevant foreign income"), the profits of a trade, profession or vocation arise from a source outside the United Kingdom only if the trade, profession or vocation is carried on wholly outside the United Kingdom.

Person liable

8. The person liable for any tax charged under this Chapter is the person receiving or entitled to the profits.　　　　1.615

Trades and trade profits

Farming and market gardening

9.—(1) Farming or market gardening in the United Kingdom is treated for income tax purposes as the carrying on of a trade or part of a trade (whether or not the land is managed on a commercial basis and with a view to the realisation of profits).　　　　1.616

(2) All farming in the United Kingdom carried on by a person, other than farming carried on as part of another trade, is treated for income tax purposes as one trade.

(3) In the case of farming carried on by a firm, this rule is explained by section 859(1).

Starting and ceasing to trade

Effect of becoming or ceasing to be a UK resident

17.—(1) This section applies if—　　　　1.617

(a) an individual carries on a trade wholly or partly outside the United Kingdom otherwise than in partnership, and

(b) the individual becomes or ceases to be UK resident.

(2) The individual is treated for income tax purposes—

   (a) as permanently ceasing to carry on the trade at the time of the change of residence, and

   (b) so far as the individual continues to carry on the trade, as starting to carry on a new trade immediately afterwards.

(3) But subsection (2) does not prevent a loss made before the change of residence from being deducted under section 831 of ITA 2007 against profits arising after the change.

(4) This section applies to professions and vocations as it applies to trades.

(5) In the case of a trade carried on by a firm, see sections 852(6) (7) and 854(5).

Rent-a-room and foster-care relief

Rent-a-room and foster-care relief

1.618   **23.**—(1) The rules for calculating the profits of a trade carried on by an individual are subject to Chapter 1 of Part 7 (rent-a-room relief).

(2) That Chapter provides relief on income from the use of furnished accommodation in the individual's only or main residence (see, in particular, sections 792 and 796).

(3) The rules for calculating the profits of a trade, profession or vocation carried on by an individual are subject to Chapter 2 of Part 7 (foster-care relief).

(4) That Chapter provides relief on income from the provision by the individual of foster care (see, in particular, sections 813, 816, 822 and 823).

CHAPTER 3

TRADE PROFITS: BASIC RULES

Professions and vocations

1.619   **24.** Apart from section 30 (animals kept for trade purposes), the provisions of this Chapter apply to professions and vocations as they apply to trades.

Generally accepted accounting practice

1.620   **25.**—(1) The profits of a trade must be calculated in accordance with generally accepted accounting practice, subject to any adjustment required or authorised by law in calculating profits for income tax purposes.

(2) This does not—

   (a) require a person to comply with the requirements of the Companies Act 1985 (c. 6) or the Companies (Northern Ireland) Order 1986 (S.I. 1986/1032 (N.I. 6)) except as to the basis of calculation, or

   (b) impose any requirements as to audit or disclosure.

(3) This section is subject to section 160 (barristers and advocates in early years of practice).

(4) This section does not affect provisions of the Income Tax Acts relating to the calculation of the profits of Lloyd's underwriters.

Losses calculated on same basis as profits

26.—(1) The same rules apply for income tax purposes in calculating losses of a trade as apply in calculating profits.

(2) This is subject to any express provision to the contrary.

1.621

Receipts and expenses

27.—(1) In the Income Tax Acts, in the context of the calculation of the profits of a trade, references to receipts and expenses are to any items brought into account as credits or debits in calculating the profits.

(2) There is no implication that an amount has been actually received or paid.

(3) This section is subject to any express provision to the contrary.

1.622

Items treated under CAA 2001 as receipts and expenses

28. The rules for calculating the profits of a trade need to be read with—
  (a) the provisions of CAA 2001 which treat charges as receipts of a trade, and
  (b) the provisions of CAA 2001 which treat allowances as expenses of a trade.

1.623

Interest

29. For the purpose of calculating the profits of a trade, interest is an item of a revenue nature, whatever the nature of the loan.

1.624

Relationship between rules prohibiting and allowing deductions

31.—(1) Any relevant permissive rule in this Part—
  (a) has priority over any relevant prohibitive rule in this Part, but
  (b) is subject to sections 48 (car or motor cycle hire) and 55 (crime-related payments).

(2) In this section "any relevant permissive rule in this Part" means any provision of—
  (a) Chapter 5 (apart from sections 60 to 67),
  (b) Chapter 11, or
  (c) Chapter 13,
which allows a deduction in calculating the profits of a trade.

(3) In this section "any relevant prohibitive rule in this Part", in relation to any deduction, means any provision of this Part (apart from sections 48 and 55) which might otherwise be read as—
  (a) prohibiting the deduction, or
  (b) restricting the amount of the deduction.

1.625

CHAPTER 4

TRADE PROFITS: RULES RESTRICTING DEDUCTIONS

Introduction

Professions and vocations

32. The provisions of this Chapter apply to professions and vocations as they apply to trades.

1.626

Capital expenditure

Capital expenditure

1.627   **33.** In calculating the profits of a trade, no deduction is allowed for items of a capital nature.

Wholly and exclusively and losses rules

Expenses not wholly and exclusively for trade and unconnected losses

1.628   **34.**—(1) In calculating the profits of a trade, no deduction is allowed for—

(a) expenses not incurred wholly and exclusively for the purposes of the trade, or

(b) losses not connected with or arising out of the trade.

(2) If an expense is incurred for more than one purpose, this section does not prohibit a deduction for any identifiable part or identifiable proportion of the expense which is incurred wholly and exclusively for the purposes of the trade.

Bad and doubtful debts

Bad and doubtful debts

1.629   **35.**—(1) In calculating the profits of a trade, no deduction is allowed for a debt owed to the person carrying on the trade, except so far as—

(a) the debt is bad,

(b) the debt is estimated to be bad, or

(c) the debt is released wholly and exclusively for the purposes of the trade as part of a statutory insolvency arrangement.

(2) If the debtor is bankrupt or insolvent, the whole of the debt is estimated to be bad for the purposes of subsection (1)(b), except so far as any amount may reasonably be expected to be received on the debt.

Unpaid remuneration

Unpaid remuneration

1.630   **36.**—(1) This section applies if, in calculating the profits of a trade of a period of account—

(a) an amount is charged in the accounts for the period in respect of employees' remuneration, and

(b) a deduction for the remuneration would otherwise be allowable for the period.

(2) No deduction is allowed for the remuneration for the period of account unless it is paid before the end of the period of 9 months immediately following the end of the period of account.

(3) If the remuneration is paid after the end of that 9 month period, deduction for it is allowed for the period of account in which it is paid.

Business entertainment and gifts

Business entertainment and gifts: general rule

45.—(1) The general rule is that no deduction is allowed in calculating   1.631
the profits of a trade for expenses incurred in providing entertainment or gifts in connection with the trade.

(2) A deduction for expenses which are incurred—

(a) in paying sums to or on behalf of an employee of the person carrying on the trade ("the trader"), or

(b) in putting sums at the disposal of an employee of the trader,

is prohibited by the general rule if (and only if) the sums are paid, or put at the employee's disposal, exclusively for meeting expenses incurred or to be incurred by the employee in providing the entertainment or gift.

(3) The general rule is subject to exceptions—

for entertainment (see section 46), and

for gifts (see section 47).

(4) For the purposes of this section and those two sections—

(a) "employee", in relation to a company, includes a director of the company and a person engaged in the management of the company,

(b) "entertainment" includes hospitality of any kind, and

(c) the expenses incurred in providing entertainment or a gift include expenses incurred in providing anything incidental to the provision of entertainment or a gift.

Social security contributions

Social security contributions

53.—(1) In calculating the profits of a trade, no deduction is allowed for   1.632
any contribution paid by any person under—

(a) Part 1 of the Social Security Contributions and Benefits Act 1992 (c. 4), or

(b) Part 1 of the Social Security Contributions and Benefits (Northern Ireland) Act 1992 (c. 7).

(2) But this prohibition does not apply to an employer's contribution.

(3) For this purpose "an employer's contribution" means—

(a) a secondary Class 1 contribution;

(b) a Class 1A contribution, or

(c) a Class 1B contribution,

within the meaning of Part 1 of the Social Security Contributions and Benefits Act 1992 or of the Social Security Contributions and Benefits (Northern Ireland) Act 1992.

CHAPTER 6

TRADE PROFITS: RECEIPTS

Introduction

Professions and vocations

1.633

95. Apart from section 105 (industrial development grants), the provisions of this Chapter apply to professions and vocations as they apply to trades.

Capital receipts

Capital receipts

1.634

96.—(1) Items of a capital nature must not be brought into account as receipts in calculating the profits of a trade.

(2) But this does not apply to items which, as a result of any provision of this Part, are brought into account as receipts in calculating the profits of the trade.

Debts released

Debts incurred and later released

1.635

97.—(1) This section applies if—
(a) in calculating the profits of a trade, a deduction is allowed for the expense giving rise to a debt owed by the person carrying on the trade,
(b) all or part of the debt is released, and
(c) the release is not part of a statutory insolvency arrangement.

(2) The amount released—
(a) is brought into account as a receipt in calculating the profits of the trade, and
(b) is treated as arising on the date of the release.

CHAPTER 15

BASIS PERIODS

Introduction

Professions and vocations

1.636

196. The provisions of this Chapter apply to professions and vocations as they apply to trades.

Accounting date

Meaning of "accounting date"

197.—(1) In this Chapter "accounting date", in relation to a tax year,   **1.637**
means—
  (a) the date in the tax year to which accounts are drawn up, or
  (b) if there are two or more such dates, the latest of them.
(2) This is subject to—
  (a) section 211(2) (middle date treated as accounting date), and
  (b) section 214(3) (date treated as accounting date if date changed in tax
       year in which there is no accounting date).

The normal rules

General rule

198.—(1) The general rule is that the basis period for a tax year is the   **1.638**
period of 12 months ending with the accounting date in that tax year.
(2) This applies unless a different basis period is given by one of the following sections—
    section 199 (first tax year),
    section 200 (second tax year),
    section 201 (tax year in which there is no accounting date),
    section 202 (final tax year),
    section 209 or 210 (first accounting date shortly before end of tax year),
    section 212 (tax year in which middle date treated as accounting date),
    section 215 (change of accounting date in third tax year), and
    section 216 (change of accounting date in later tax year).

PART 3

PROPERTY INCOME

CHAPTER 1

INTRODUCTION

Overview of Part 3

260.—(1) This Part imposes charges to income tax under—   **1.639**
  (a) Chapter 3 (the profits of a UK property business or an overseas
       property business),
  (b) Chapter 7 (amounts treated as adjustment income under section 330),
  (c) Chapter 8 (rent receivable in connection with a UK section 12(4)
       concern),
  (d) Chapter 9 (rent receivable for UK electric-line wayleaves),
  (e) Chapter 10 (post-cessation receipts arising from a UK property busi-
       ness), and

    (f) Chapter 11 (overseas property income of a person to whom the remittance basis applies).

    (2) Part 6 deals with exemptions from the charges under this Part.

    (3) See, in particular, the exemptions under sections 769 (housing grants), 777 (VAT repayment supplements) and 778 (incentives to use electronic communications).

    (4) The charges under Chapters 3, 7, 8, 9 and 10 apply to non-UK residents as well as UK residents but this is subject to section 269 (charges on non-UK residents only on UK source income).

    (5) This section needs to be read with the relevant priority rules (see sections 2 and 261).

GENERAL NOTE

1.640   Part 3 brings together and rewrites the income tax rules formerly in Sch.A (applying to income from UK land) and Sch.D Case V (applying to income from overseas land) formerly in ICTA 1988 as amended. The way in which income from land has been taxed has varied over the years. The most recent approach, adopted here, is to align the income of landlords and others receiving income from the exploitation of land closely to the taxation of income from trade, and therefore to the rules now set out in Pt 2.

Provisions which must be given priority over Part 3

1.641   **261.** Any receipt or other credit item, so far as it falls within—
    (a) Chapter 3 of this Part so far as it relates to an overseas property business or Chapter 8 or 9 of this Part (rent receivable in connection with a UK section 12(4) concern or for UK electric-line wayleaves), and
    (b) Chapter 2 of Part 2 (receipts of a trade, profession or vocation),
is dealt with under Part 2.

Priority between Chapters within Part 3

1.642   **262.**—(1) Any receipt, so far as it falls within—
    (a) Chapter 3 so far as it relates to a UK property business, and
    (b) Chapter 8 (rent receivable in connection with a UK section 12(4) concern),
is dealt with under Chapter 8.

    (2) Any receipt, so far as it falls within—
    (a) Chapter 3 so far as it relates to a UK property business, and
    (b) Chapter 9 (rent receivable for UK electric-line wayleaves),
is dealt with under Chapter 9.

    (3) Any receipt, so far as it falls within Chapter 8 (rent receivable in connection with a UK section 12(4) concern) and Chapter 9 (rent receivable for UK electric-line wayleaves), is dealt with under Chapter 9.

CHAPTER 2

PROPERTY BUSINESSES

Introduction

Introduction

1.643   **263.**—(1) This Chapter explains for the purposes of this Act what is meant by—

(a) a person's UK property business (see section 264), and

(b) a person's overseas property business (see section 265).

(2) Both those sections need to be read with—

(a) section 266 (which explains what is meant by generating income from land), and

(b) section 267 (which provides that certain activities do not count as activities for generating income from land).

(3) In the case of the property business of a firm, the basic rules in sections 264 and 265 are explained in section 859(2) and (3).

(4) References in this Act to an overseas property business are to an overseas property business so far as any profits of the business are chargeable to tax under Chapter 3 (as to which see, in particular, section 269).

(5) Accordingly, nothing in Chapter 4 or 5 is to be read as treating an amount as a receipt of an overseas property business if the profits concerned would not be chargeable to tax under Chapter 3.

(6) In this Act "property business" means a UK property business or an overseas property business.

Basic meaning of UK and overseas property business

UK property business

264. A person's UK property business consists of—   1.644

(a) every business which the person carries on for generating income from land in the United Kingdom, and

(b) every transaction which the person enters into for that purpose otherwise than in the course of such a business.

Overseas property business

265. A person's overseas property business consists of—   1.645

(a) every business which the person carries on for generating income from land outside the United Kingdom, and

(b) every transaction which the person enters into for that purpose otherwise than in the course of such a business.

Generating income from land

Meaning of "generating income from land"

266.—(1) In this Chapter "generating income from land" means exploit-   1.646
ing an estate, interest or right in or over land as a source of rents or other receipts.

(2) "Rents" includes payments by a tenant for work to maintain or repair leased premises which the lease does not require the tenant to carry out.

(3) "Other receipts" includes—

(a) payments in respect of a licence to occupy or otherwise use land,

(b) payments in respect of the exercise of any other right over land, and

(c) rentcharges and other annual payments reserved in respect of, or charged on or issuing out of, land.

(4) For the purposes of this section a right to use a caravan or houseboat at only one location is treated as a right deriving from an estate or interest in land.

CHAPTER 3

PROFITS OF PROPERTY BUSINESSES: BASIC RULES

Charge to tax on profits of a property business

Charge to tax on profits of a property business

1.647   **268.** Income tax is charged on the profits of a property business.

Territorial scope of charge to tax

1.648   **269.**—(1) Profits of a UK property business are chargeable to tax under this Chapter whether the business is carried on by a UK resident or a non-UK resident.

(2) Profits of an overseas property business are chargeable to tax under this Chapter only if the business is carried on by a UK resident.

(3) But, in the case of an overseas property business carried on by a UK resident to whom the remittance basis applies, the only profits of the business chargeable to tax under this Chapter are those in respect of land in the Republic of Ireland.

(4) For a UK resident to whom the remittance basis applies, see also Chapter 11 (charge to tax on overseas property income other than income arising in Republic of Ireland).

Income charged

1.649   **270.**—(1) Tax is charged under this Chapter on the full amount of the profits arising in the tax year.

(2) Subsection (1) is subject to Part 8 (foreign income: special rules).

Person liable

1.650   **271.** The person liable for any tax charged under this Chapter is the person receiving or entitled to the profits.

Calculation of profits

Profits of a property business: application of trading income rules

1.651   **272.**—(1) The profits of a property business are calculated in the same way as the profits of a trade.

(2) *Omitted.*

(3) *Omitted.*

PART 4

SAVINGS AND INVESTMENT INCOME

CHAPTER 1

INTRODUCTION

Overview of Part 4

365.—(1) This Part imposes charges to income tax under—
(a) Chapter 2 (interest),
(b) Chapter 3 (dividends etc. from UK resident companies etc.),
(c) Chapter 4 (dividends from non-UK resident companies),
(d) Chapter 5 (stock dividends from UK resident companies),
(e) Chapter 6 (release of loan to participator in close company),
(f) Chapter 7 (purchased life annuity payments),
(g) Chapter 8 (profits from deeply discounted securities),
(h) Chapter 9 (gains from contracts for life insurance etc.),
(i) Chapter 10 (distributions from unauthorised unit trusts),
(j) Chapter 11 (transactions in deposits),
(k) Chapter 12 (disposals of futures and options involving guaranteed returns), and
(l) Chapter 13 (sales of foreign dividend coupons).

(2) Part 6 deals with exemptions from the charges under this Part.

(3) See, in particular, any exemptions mentioned in the particular Chapters.

(4) The charges under this Part apply to non-UK residents as well as UK residents but this is subject to section 368(2) (charges on non-UK residents only on UK source income).

(5) This section needs to be read with the relevant priority rules (see sections 2 and 366).

1.652

GENERAL NOTE

Part 4 brings together a number of separate charges to income tax on what used to be termed unearned income: interest and similar income from the former Sch.D Cases III (UK source) and IV (foreign securities) and V (foreign possessions), with dividends from the former Sch.F (distributions from UK companies) and again Sch.D Case V (dividends from foreign companies), and other payments such as annuities and income gains from life assurance policies and other forms of investment. Originally to be called investment income, it was given a wider flavour by adding "savings" to the heading. But it is not all-encompassing because other forms of unearned income are included in Pt 5. In practice, wide use is made of tax-exempt forms of saving and investment. The details of the exemptions are in Pt 6 of the Act, which—along with pension savings under Pt 9 of ITEPA and the treatment of capital gains under the separate regime under the Taxation of Chargeable Gains Act 1992—mean that many people pay only limited income tax on their savings income. Most of these exemptions also apply for tax credits. Tax credits also take no account of capital gains. As a result, claimants can protect their savings from tax credits as well as income tax.

1.653

Provisions which must be given priority over Part 4

1.654   **366.**—(1) Any income, so far as it falls within—
(a) any Chapter of this Part, and
(b) Chapter 2 of Part 2 (receipts of a trade, profession or vocation),
is dealt with under Part 2.
(2) Any income, so far as it falls within—
(a) any Chapter of this Part, and
(b) Chapter 3 of Part 3 so far as the Chapter relates to a UK property business,
is dealt with under Part 3.
(3) Any income, so far as it falls within—
(a) any Chapter of this Part other than Chapter 3 or 6, and
(b) Part 2, 9 or 10 of ITEPA 2003 (employment income, pension income or social security income),
is dealt with under the relevant Part of ITEPA 2003.
(4) Nothing in this section prevents amounts both—
(a) being counted as income for the purposes of Chapter 9 of this Part (gains from contracts for life insurance etc.), and
(b) being taken into account in calculating income, or counting as income, for the purposes of other Parts of this Act,
but see section 527 (reduction for sums taken into account otherwise than under Chapter 9).

Priority between Chapters within Part 4

1.655   **367.**—(1) Any income, so far as it falls within Chapter 2 (interest) and Chapter 8 (profits from deeply securities), is dealt with under Chapter 8.
(2) Any income, so far as it falls within Chapter 3 (dividends etc. UK resident companies etc.) and another Chapter, is dealt with under Chapter 3 (but this is subject to subsection (3)).
(3) Any income, so far as it falls within—
(a) Chapter 2 (interest) as a result of section 372 (building society dividends) or 379 (industrial and provident society payments), and
(b) Chapter 3,
is dealt with under Chapter 2.

Territorial scope of Part 4 charges

1.656   **368.**—(1) Income arising to a UK resident is chargeable to tax under this Part whether or not it is from a source in the United Kingdom.
(2) Income arising to a non-UK resident is chargeable to tax under this Part only if it is from a source in the United Kingdom.
(3) References in this section to income which is from a source in the United Kingdom include, in the case of any income which does not have a source, references to income which has a comparable connection to the United Kingdom.
(4) This section is subject to any express or implied provision to the contrary in this Part (or elsewhere in the Income Tax Acts).

CHAPTER 2

INTEREST

Charge to tax on interest

Charge to tax on interest

369.—(1) Income tax is charged on interest.

(2) The following sections extend what is treated as interest for certain purposes—

section 372 (building society dividends),
section 373 (open-ended investment company interest distributions),
section 376 (authorised unit trust interest distributions),
section 379 (industrial and provident society payments),
section 380 (funding bonds), and
section 381 (discounts).

(3) For exemptions, see in particular—

(a) Chapter 2 of Part 6 (national savings income),
(b) Chapter 3 of Part 6 (income from individual investment plans),
(c) Chapter 4 of Part 6 (SAYE interest),
(d) Chapter 6 of Part 6 (income from FOTRA securities),
(e) sections 749 to 756 (interest arising from repayment supplements, reserve certificates, damages for personal injury, employees' share schemes, repayments of student loans, the redemption of funding bonds and interest on certain foreign currency securities), and
(f) sections 757 to 767 (interest and royalty payments).

(4) Subsection (1) is also subject to Chapter 3 of Part 12 of ITA 2007 (exemptions for interest on securities to which Chapter 2 of that Part applies).

1.657

Income charged

370.—(1) Tax is charged under this Chapter on the full amount of the interest arising in the tax year.

(2) Subsection (1) is subject to Part 8 (foreign income: special rules).

1.658

Person liable

371. The person liable for any tax charged under this Chapter is the person receiving or entitled to the interest.

1.659

Other income taxed as interest

Building society dividends

372.—(1) Any dividend paid by a building society is treated as interest for the purposes of this Act.

(2) In this section "dividend" includes any distribution (whether or not described as a dividend).

1.660

CHAPTER 3

DIVIDENDS ETC. FROM UK RESIDENT COMPANIES ETC.

Introduction

Contents of Chapter

1.661   **382.**—(1) This Chapter—

(a) imposes a charge to income tax on dividends and other distributions of UK resident companies (see section 383),

(b) treats dividends as paid in some circumstances (see sections 386 to 391), and

(c) makes special provision where the charge is in respect of shares awarded under an approved share incentive plan (see sections 392 to 396).

(2) This Chapter also makes provision about tax credits, tax being treated as paid and reliefs available in respect of certain distributions which applies whether or not the distributions are otherwise dealt with under this Chapter (see sections 397 to 401).

(3) For exemptions from the charge under this Chapter, see in particular—

Chapter 3 of Part 6 (income from individual investment plans),

Chapter 5 of that Part (venture capital trust dividends),

section 770 (amounts applied by SIP trustees acquiring dividend shares or retained for reinvestment), and

section 498 of ITEPA 2003 (no charge on shares ceasing to be subject to SIP in certain circumstances).

(4) In this Chapter "dividends" does not include income treated as arising under section 410 (stock dividends).

Charge to tax on dividends and other distributions

Charge to tax on dividends and other distributions

1.662   **383.**—(1) Income tax is charged on dividends and other distributions of a UK resident company.

(2) For income tax purposes such dividends and other distributions are to be treated as income.

(3) For the purposes of subsection (2), it does not matter that those dividends and other distributions are capital apart from that subsection.

Income charged

1.663   **384.**—(1) Tax is charged under this Chapter on the amount or value of the dividends paid and other distributions made in the tax year.

(2) Subsection (1) is subject to—
>   section 393(2) and (3) (later charge where cash dividends retained in SIPs are paid over), and
>   section 394(3) (distribution when dividend shares cease to be subject to SIP).

(3) See also section 398 (under which the amount or value of the dividends or other distributions is treated as increased if any person is entitled to a tax credit in respect of them).

Person liable

385.—(1) The person liable for any tax charged under this Chapter is—   1.664
   (a) the person to whom the distribution is made or is treated as made (see Part 6 of ICTA and sections 386(3) and 389(3)), or
   (b) the person receiving or entitled to the distribution.
(2) Subsection (1) is subject to—
>   section 393(4) (later charge where cash dividends retained in SIPs are paid over), and
>   section 394(4) (distribution when dividend shares cease to be subject to SIP).

CHAPTER 4

DIVIDENDS FROM NON-UK RESIDENT COMPANIES

Charge to tax on dividends from non-UK resident companies

Charge to tax on dividends from non-UK resident companies

402.—(1) Income tax is charged on dividends of a non-UK resident company.   1.665

(2) For exemptions, see in particular section 770 (amounts applied by SIP trustees acquiring dividend shares or retained for reinvestment).

(3) Subsection (1) is also subject to section 498 of ITEPA 2003 (no charge on shares ceasing to be subject to SIP in certain circumstances).

(4) In this Chapter "dividends" does not include dividends of a capital nature.

Income charged

403.—(1) Tax is charged under this Chapter on the full amount of the dividends arising in the tax year.   1.666

(2) Subsection (1) is subject to—
>   section 406(2) and (3) (later charge where cash dividends retained in SIPs are paid over),
>   section 407(3) (dividend payment when dividend shares cease to be subject to SIP), and
>   Part 8 (foreign income: special rules).

Person liable

1.667   **404.**—(1) The person liable for any tax charged under this Chapter is the person receiving or entitled to the dividends.

(2) Subsection (1) is subject to—

section 406(4) (later charge where cash dividends retained in SIPs are paid over), and

section 407(4) (dividend payment when dividend shares cease to be subject to SIP).

CHAPTER 7

PURCHASED LIFE ANNUITY PAYMENTS

Charge to tax on purchased life annuity payments

1.668   **422.**—(1) Income tax is charged on annuity payments made under a purchased life annuity.

(2) For exemptions, see in particular—

(a) section 717 (exemption for part of purchased life annuity payments),

(b) section 725 (annual payments under immediate needs annuities),

(c) section 731 (periodical payments of personal injury damages), and

(d) section 732 (compensation awards).

Meaning of "purchased life annuity"

1.669   **423.**—(1) In this Chapter "purchased life annuity" means an annuity—

(a) granted for consideration in money or money's worth in the ordinary course of a business of granting annuities on human life, and

(b) payable for a term ending at a time ascertainable only by reference to the end of a human life.

(2) For this purpose it does not matter that the annuity may in some circumstances end before or after the life.

Income charged

1.670   **424.**—(1) Tax is charged under this Chapter on the full amount of the annuity payments arising in the tax year.

(2) Subsection (1) is subject to Part 8 (foreign income: special rules).

Person liable

1.671   **425.** The person liable for any tax charged under this Chapter is the person receiving or entitled to the annuity payments.

308

PART 5

MISCELLANEOUS INCOME

CHAPTER 1

INTRODUCTION

Overview of Part 5

574.—(1) This Part imposes charges to income tax under—   1.672
(a) Chapter 2 (receipts from intellectual property),
(b) Chapter 3 (films and sound recordings: non-trade businesses),
(c) Chapter 4 (certain telecommunication rights: non-trading income),
(d) Chapter 5 (settlements: amounts treated as income of settlor),
(e) Chapter 6 (beneficiaries' income from estates in administration),
(f) Chapter 7 (annual payments not otherwise charged), and
(g) Chapter 8 (income not otherwise charged).

(2) Part 6 deals with exemptions from the charges under this Part.

(3) See, in particular, any exemptions mentioned in the Chapters of this Part.

(4) The charges under this Part apply to non-UK residents as well as UK residents but this is subject to section 577(2) (charges on non-UK residents only on UK source income).

(5) This section needs to be read with the relevant priority rules (see sections 2, 575 and 576).

Provisions which must be given priority over Part 5

575.—(1) Any income, so far as it falls within—   1.673
(a) any Chapter of this Part, and
(b) Chapter 2 of Part 2 (receipts of a trade, profession or vocation),
is dealt with under Part 2.

(2) Any income, so far as it falls within—
(a) any Chapter of this Part, and
(b) Chapter 3 of Part 3 so far as the Chapter relates to a UK property business,
is dealt with under Part 3.

(3) Any income, so far as it falls within—
(a) any Chapter of this Part, and
(b) Chapter 2 or 3 of Part 4 (interest and dividends etc. from UK resident companies etc.),
is dealt with under the relevant Chapter of Part 4.

(4) Any income, so far as it falls within—
(a) any Chapter of this Part, and
(b) Part 2, 9 or 10 of ITEPA 2003 (employment income, pension income or social security income),
is dealt with under the relevant Part of ITEPA 2003.

Priority between Chapters within Part 5

1.674 **576.** Any income, so far as it falls within Chapter 2 (receipts from intellectual property) and Chapter 3 (films and sound recordings: non-trade businesses), is dealt with under Chapter 3.

CHAPTER 5

SETTLEMENTS: AMOUNTS TREATED AS INCOME OF SETTLOR

Charge to tax under Chapter 5

Charge to tax under Chapter 5

1.675 **619.**—(1) Income tax is charged on—

(a) income which is treated as income of a settlor as a result of section 624 (income where settlor retains an interest),

(b) income which is treated as income of a settlor as a result of section 629 (income paid to unmarried minor children of settlor),

(c) capital sums which are treated as income of a settlor as a result of section 633 (capital sums paid to settlor by trustees of settlement), and

(d) capital sums which are treated as income of a settlor as a result of section 641 (capital sums paid to settlor by body connected with settlement).

(2) The charge on the settlor under subsection (1)(a) or (b) above operates on distribution income by treating the income as if it were income to which Chapter 2 of Part 2 of ITA 2007 (rates at which income tax is charged) applies as a result of subsection (2)(b) that section (income chargeable under Chapter 3, 5 or 6 of Part 4: etc. from UK resident companies etc. and release of loan to participator in close company).

(3) In subsection (2) "distribution income" means income which represents income received by the trustees of the settlement, or any other person to whom it is payable, which is—

(a) income chargeable under Chapter 3 of Part 4 (dividends etc. from UK resident companies etc.),

(b) income chargeable under Chapter 4 of Part 4 (dividends from non-UK resident companies),

(c) income chargeable under Chapter 5 of Part 4 (stock dividends from UK resident companies),

(d) income chargeable under Chapter 6 of Part 4 (release of loan to participator in close company), or

(e) a relevant foreign distribution chargeable under Chapter 8 of this Part (income not otherwise charged).

(4) In subsection (3) "relevant foreign distribution" means any distribution of a non-UK resident company which—

(a) is not chargeable under Chapter 4 of Part 4, but

(b) would be chargeable under Chapter 3 of that Part if the company were UK resident.

310

The provisions in this chapter are complex but important as they include very   1.676
wide anti-avoidance provisions that can affect income earners at all levels. They are
all applied to the calculation of income for tax credit purposes, and therefore now
have a double effect on many middle range income earners who seek to use trusts to
cut their incomes. Sections 624–628 contain provisions designed to stop tax avoidance by putting money into a form of trust where the settlor has an interest in the
trust, unless it is a trust between spouses or partners, or it is to a charity. Section
629 is a very widely drawn provision that has the effect of transferring back to a
settlor any income given by the settlor to an unmarried minor child of the settlor (for
example, by putting money in a building society account in the name of the child,
or buying National Savings Certificates in the child's name). But see now the tax
provisions designed to assist child trust funds, which allow all these provisions to be
sidestepped to a limited extent if a child trust fund is used.

Meaning of "settlement" and "settlor"

620.—(1) In this Chapter—   1.677
"settlement" includes any disposition, trust, covenant, agreement, or
    transfer of assets (except that it does not include a charitable loan
    arrangement), and
"settlor", in relation to a settlement, means any person by whom the
    settlement was made.
(2) A person is treated for the purposes of this Chapter as having made
a settlement if the person has made or entered into the settlement directly
or indirectly.
(3) A person is, in particular, treated as having made a settlement if the
person—
(a) has provided funds directly or indirectly for the purpose of the
    settlement,
(b) has undertaken to provide funds directly or indirectly for the purpose
    of the settlement, or
(c) has made a reciprocal arrangement with another person for the other
    person to make or enter into the settlement.
(4) This Chapter applies to settlements wherever made.
(5) In this section—
"charitable loan arrangement" means any arrangement so far as it
    consists of a loan of money made by an individual to a charity
    either—
(a) for no consideration, or
(b) for a consideration which consists only of interest, and
"charity" includes—
(a) trustees of the National Heritage Memorial Fund
(b) Historical Buildings and Monuments Commission for England
(c) National Endowment for Science, Technology and the Arts.

Income charged and person liable

Income charged

621. Tax is charged under this Chapter on all income and capital sums to   1.678
which section 619(1) applies.

Person liable

1.679   **622.** The person liable for any tax charged under this Chapter is the settlor.

CHAPTER 8

INCOME NOT OTHERWISE CHARGED

Charge to tax on income not otherwise charged

1.680   **687.**—(1) Income tax is charged under this Chapter on income from any source that is not charged to income tax under or as a result of any other provision of this Act or any other Act.

(2) Subsection (1) does not apply to annual payments.

(3) Subsection (1) does not apply to income that would be charged to income tax under or as a result of another provision but for an exemption.

(4) The definition of "income" in section 878(1) does not apply for the purposes of this section.

(5) For exemptions from the charge under this Chapter, see in particular—

section 768 (commercial occupation of woodlands), and

section 779 (gains on commodity and financial futures).

Income charged

1.681   **688.**—(1) Tax is charged under this Chapter on the full amount of the income arising in the tax year.

(2) Subsection (1) is subject to—

(a) Chapter 1 of Part 7 (which provides relief on income from the use of furnished accommodation in an individual's only or main residence: see, in particular, sections 794 and 798),

(b) Chapter 2 of that Part (which provides relief on income from the provision by an individual of foster care: see, in particular, sections 814 and 817), and

(c) Part 8 (foreign income: special rules).

Person liable

1.682   **689.** The person liable for any tax charged under this Chapter is the person receiving or entitled to the income.

PART 6

EXEMPT INCOME

CHAPTER 1

INTRODUCTION

Overview of Part 6

1.683   **690.**—(1) This Part provides for certain exemptions from charges to income tax under this Act.

(2) The exemptions are dealt with in—
(a) Chapter 2 (national savings income),
(b) Chapter 3 (income from individual investment plans),
(c) Chapter 4 (SAYE interest),
(d) Chapter 5 (venture capital trust dividends),
(e) Chapter 6 (income from FOTRA securities),
(f) Chapter 7 (purchased life annuity payments),
(g) Chapter 8 (other annual payments), and
(h) Chapter 9 (other income).

(3) Chapter 10 explains that, in general, the effect of the exemptions is that the exempt amounts are ignored for other income tax purposes.

(4) Other exemptions, such as exemptions relating to particular categories of persons, may also be relevant to the charges to income tax under this Act.

(5) And the exemptions dealt with in this Part may themselves be relevant to charges to income tax outside this Act.

CHAPTER 8

OTHER ANNUAL PAYMENTS

Certain annual payments by individuals

Foreign maintenance payments

730.—(1) No liability to income tax arises under Part 5 in respect of an annual payment if— 1.684
(a) it is a maintenance payment,
(b) it arises outside the United Kingdom, and
(c) had it arisen in the United Kingdom it would be exempt from income tax under section 727 (certain annual payments by individuals).

(2) In subsection (1) "maintenance payment" means a periodical payment which meets conditions A and B.

(3) Condition A is that the payment is made under a court order or a written or oral agreement.

(4) Condition B is that the payment is made by a person—
(a) as one of the parties to a marriage [¹ or civil partnership] to, or for the benefit of, and for the maintenance of, the other party,
(b) to any person under 21 for that person's own benefit, maintenance or education, or
(c) to any person for the benefit, maintenance or education of a person under 21.

(5) In subsection (4) "marriage" includes a marriage that has been dissolved or annulled, and "civil partnership" includes a civil partnership that has been dissolved or annulled.

(6) Subsection (1) also applies to a payment made by an individual's personal representatives if—
(a) the individual would have been liable to make it, and
(b) that subsection would have applied if the individual had made it.

Periodical payments of personal injury damages

1.685   **731.**—(1) No liability to income tax arises for the persons specified in section 733 in respect of periodical payments to which subsection (2) or annuity payments to which subsection (3) applies.

(2) This subsection applies to periodical payments made pursuant to—

(a) an order of the court, so far as it is made in reliance on section 2 of the Damages Act 1996 (c. 48) (periodical payments) (including an order as varied),

(b) an order of a court outside the United Kingdom which is similar to an order made in reliance on that section (including an order as varied),

(c) an agreement, so far as it settles a claim or action for damages in respect of personal injury (including an agreement as varied),

(d) an agreement, so far as it relates to making payments on account of damages that may be awarded in such a claim or action (including an agreement as varied), or

(e) a Motor Insurers' Bureau undertaking in relation to a claim or action in respect of personal injury (including an undertaking as varied).

(3) This subsection applies to annuity payments made under an annuity purchased or provided—

(a) by the person by whom payments to which subsection (2) applies would otherwise fall to be made, and

(b) in accordance with such an order, agreement or undertaking as is mentioned in subsection (2) or a varying order, agreement or undertaking.

(4) In this section "damages in respect of personal injury" includes in respect of a person's death from personal injury.

(5) In this section "personal injury" includes disease and impairment of physical or mental condition.

(6) In this section "a Motor Insurers' Bureau undertaking" means an undertaking given by—

(a) the Motor Insurers' Bureau (being the company of that name incorporated on 14th June 1946 under the Companies Act 1929 (c. 23)), or

(b) an Article 75 insurer under the Bureau's Articles of Association.

Compensation awards

1.686   **732.**—(1) No liability to income tax arises for the persons specified in section 733 in respect of annuity payments if they are made under an annuity purchased or provided under an award of compensation made under the Criminal Injuries Compensation Scheme.

(2) The Treasury may by order provide for sections 731, 733 and 734 to apply, with such modifications as they consider necessary, to periodical payments by way of compensation for personal injury for which provision is made under a scheme or arrangement other than the Criminal Injuries Compensation Scheme.

(3) In this section—
"the Criminal Injuries Compensation Scheme" means—
(a) the schemes established by arrangements made under the Criminal Injuries Compensation Act 1995 (c. 53),
(b) arrangements made by the Secretary of State for compensation for criminal injuries in operation before the commencement of those schemes, or
(c) the scheme established under the Criminal Injuries (Northern Ireland) Order 2002 (S.I. 2002/796) (N.I.1), and
"personal injury" includes disease and impairment of physical or mental condition.

Persons entitled to exemptions for personal injury payments etc.

733. The persons entitled to the exemptions given by sections 731(1) and 732(1) for payments are—
(a) the person entitled to the damages under the order, agreement, or to the compensation under the award in question ("A"),
(b) a person who receives the payment in question on behalf of A, and
(c) a trustee who receives the payment in question on trust for the benefit of A under a trust under which A is, while alive, the only person who may benefit.

1.687

Payments from trusts for injured persons

734.—(1) No liability to income tax arises for the persons specified in subsection (2) in respect of sums paid under a lifetime trust—
(a) to the person ("A") who is entitled to—
  (i) a payment under an order, agreement or undertaking within section 731(2) or an annuity purchased or provided as mentioned in section 731(3), or
  (ii) compensation under an award within section 732(1), or
(b) for the benefit of A.
(2) The persons are—
(a) A, and
(b) if subsection (1)(b) applies, a person who receives the sum on behalf of A.
(3) For the purposes of subsection (1), sums are paid under a lifetime trust if they are paid—
(a) by the trustees of a trust under which A is, while alive, the only person who may benefit, and
(b) out of payments within section 731(2) or (3) or 732(1) which are received by them on trust for A.

1.688

Health and employment insurance payments

Health and employment insurance payments

735.—(1) No liability to income tax arises under this Act in respect of an annual payment under an insurance policy if—

1.689

315

(a) the payment is a benefit provided under so much of the policy as insures against a health or employment risk (see section 736),

(b) no part of any premiums under the policy has been deductible in calculating the income of the insured for income tax purposes, and

(c) the conditions in sections 737 and 738 and, so far as applicable, in sections 739 and 740 are met in relation to the policy.

(2) Subsection (1)(b) is subject to section 743.

(3) For the meaning of "the insured", see sections 742 and 743(2).

Health and employment risks and benefits

1.690   **736.**—(1) For the purposes of sections 735 and 737 to 743, a policy insures against a health risk if it insures against the insured becoming, or becoming in any specified way, subject—

(a) to any physical or mental illness, disability, infirmity or defect, or

(b) to any deterioration in a condition resulting from any such illness, disability, infirmity or defect.

(2) For the purposes of sections 735 and 737 to 743, a policy insures against an employment risk if it insures against circumstances arising as a result of which the insured ceases—

(a) to be employed or hold office, or

(b) to carry on any trade, profession or vocation.

(3) For the purposes of section 735, this section and sections 737 to 743, references to insurance against a risk include insurance providing for benefits payable otherwise than by way of indemnity if the circumstances insured against occur.

Payments to adopters

Payments to adopters: England and Wales

1.691   **744.** No liability to income tax arises in respect of the following payments —

(a) any payment or reward falling within section 57(3) of the Adoption Act 1976 (c. 36) (payments authorised by the court) which is made to a person who has adopted or intends to adopt a child,

(b) payments under section 57(3A)(a) of that Act (payments by adoption agencies of legal or medical expenses of persons seeking to adopt),

(c) payments of allowances under regulations under section 57A of that Act (permitted allowances to persons who have adopted or intend to adopt children),

(d) payments of financial support made in the course of providing adoption support services within the meaning of the Adoption and Children Act 2002 (c. 38) (see section 2(6) and (7) of that Act), and

(e) payments made under regulations under paragraph 3(1) of Schedule 4 to that Act (transitional and transitory provisions: adoption support services).

CHAPTER 9

OTHER INCOME

Interest on damages for personal injury

751.—(1) No liability to income tax arises in respect of interest on damages for personal injury or death if—   **1.692**
  (a) it is included in a sum awarded by a court,
  (b) it does not relate to the period between the making and satisfaction of the award, and
  (c) in the case of an award by a court in a country outside the United Kingdom, it is exempt from any charge to tax in that place.
(2) No liability to income tax arises in respect of interest if—
  (a) it is included in a payment in satisfaction of a cause of action (including a payment into court), and
  (b) it would fall within subsection (1) if it were included in a sum awarded by a court in respect of a cause of action.
(3) In subsection (1)—
"damages" in Scotland includes solatium, and
"personal injury" includes disease and impairment of physical or mental condition.

Interest on repayment of student loan

753.—(1) No liability to income tax arises in respect of interest if—   **1.693**
  (a) it is paid to a person to whom a student loan has been made, and
  (b) it relates to an amount repaid to the person after being recovered from the person in respect of the loan.
(2) In this section "student loan" means a loan made under—
section 22 of the Teaching and Higher Education Act 1998 (c. 30),
section 73(f) of the Education (Scotland) Act 1980 (c. 44), or
Article 3 of the Education (Student Support) (Northern Ireland) Order 1998 (S.I. 1998/1760 (N.I. 14)).

Scholarship income

776.—(1) No liability to income tax arises in respect of income from a scholarship held by an individual in full-time education at a university, college, school or other educational establishment.   **1.694**
(2) This exemption is subject to section 215 of ITEPA 2003 (under which only the scholarship holder is entitled to the exemption if the scholarship is provided by reason of another person's employment).
(3) In this section "scholarship" includes a bursary, exhibition or other similar educational endowment.

Disabled person's vehicle maintenance grant

780.—(1) No liability to income tax arises in respect of a disabled person's vehicle maintenance grant.   **1.695**
(2) For this purpose a "disabled person's vehicle maintenance grant" means a grant to any person owning a vehicle that is made under—

(a) paragraph 2 of Schedule 2 to the National Health Service Act 1977 (c. 49),

(b) section 46(3) of the National Health Service (Scotland) Act 1978 (c. 29), or

(c) Article 30 of the Health and Personal Social Services (Northern Ireland) Order 1972 (S.I. 1972/1265 (N.I. 14)), and Training Act (Northern Ireland) 1950 (c. 29 (N.I.)).

CHAPTER 10

GENERAL

General disregard of exempt income for income tax purposes

1.696   **783.**—(1) Amounts of income which are exempt from income tax as a result of this Part (whether because the type of income concerned is exempt from every charge to income tax or because it is exempt from every charge that is relevant to those particular amounts) are accordingly to be ignored for all other income tax purposes.

(2) An exception to this is that interest on deposits in ordinary accounts with the National Savings Bank which is exempt under this Part from every charge to income tax is not to be ignored for the purpose of providing information.

(3) This express exception to subsection (1) is without prejudice to the existence of any other implied or express exception to that subsection (whether in connection with the provision of information or otherwise).

PART 7

INCOME CHARGED UNDER THIS ACT: RENT-A-ROOM AND FOSTER-CARE RELIEF

CHAPTER 1

RENT-A-ROOM RELIEF

Introduction

Overview of Chapter 1

1.697   **784.**—(1) This Chapter provides relief on income from the use of furnished accommodation in an individual's only or main residence. The relief is referred to in this Chapter as "rent-a-room relief".

(2) The form of relief depends on whether the individual's total rent-a-room amount exceeds the individual's limit (see sections 788 to 790).

(3) If it does not, the income is not charged to income tax unless the individual elects otherwise (see sections 791 to 794).

(4) If it does, the individual may elect for alternative methods of calculating the income (see sections 795 to 798).

Person who qualifies for relief

785.—(1) An individual qualifies for rent-a-room relief for a tax year if the individual—   **1.698**
   (a) has rent-a-room receipts for the tax year (see section 786), and
   (b) does not derive any taxable income other than rent-a-room receipts from a relevant trade, letting or agreement.

(2) "Taxable income" means receipts or other income in respect of which the individual is liable to income tax for the tax year.

(3) A relevant trade, letting or agreement is one from which the individual derives rent-a-room receipts for the tax year.

Basic definitions

Meaning of "rent-a-room receipts"

786.—(1) For the purposes of this Chapter an individual has rent-a-room   **1.699**
receipts for a tax year if—
   (a) the receipts are in respect of the use of furnished accommodation in a residence in the United Kingdom or in respect of goods or services supplied in connection with that use,
   (b) they accrue to the individual during the income period for those receipts (see subsections (3) and (4)),
   (c) for some or all of that period the residence is the individual's only or main residence, and
   (d) the receipts would otherwise be brought into account in calculating the profits of a trade or UK property business or chargeable to income tax under Chapter 8 of Part 5 (income not otherwise charged).

(2) Meals, cleaning and laundry are examples of goods or services supplied in connection with the use of furnished accommodation in a residence.

(3) If the receipts would otherwise be brought into account in calculating the profits of a trade, the income period is the basis period for the tax year (see Chapter 15 of Part 2).

(4) Otherwise the income period is the period which—
   (a) begins at the beginning of the tax year or, if later, the beginning of the letting in respect of which the receipts arise, and
   (b) ends at the end of the tax year or, if earlier, the end of that letting.

Meaning of "residence"

787.—(1) In this Chapter "residence" means—   **1.700**
   (a) a building, or part of a building, occupied or intended to be occupied as a separate residence, or
   (b) a caravan or houseboat.

(2) If a building, or part of a building, designed for permanent use as a single residence is temporarily divided into two or more separate residences, it is still treated as a single residence.

319

Meaning of "total rent-a-room amount"

1.701   **788.**—(1) For the purposes of this Chapter an individual's "total rent-a-room amount" for a tax year is the total of—

(a) the individual's rent-a-room receipts for the tax year, and

(b) any relevant balancing charges for the tax year (see section 802).

(2) In calculating the total rent-a-room amount, no deduction is allowed for expenses or any other matter.

Individual's limit

The individual's limit

1.702   **789.**—(1) For the purposes of this Chapter an individual's limit for a tax year depends on whether the individual meets the exclusive receipts condition for the tax year (see section 790).

(2) If the individual does, the individual's limit for the tax year is the basic amount for the tax year.

(3) If the individual does not, the individual's limit for the tax year is half that amount.

(4) The basic amount for a tax year is £4250.

(5) The Treasury may by order amend the sum for the time being specified in subsection (4).

CHAPTER 2

FOSTER-CARE RELIEF

Introduction

Overview of Chapter 2

1.703   **803.**—(1) This Chapter provides relief on income from the provision by an individual of foster care.

The relief is referred to in this Chapter as "foster-care relief".

(2) The form of relief depends on whether the individual's total foster-care receipts exceed the individual's limit (see sections 807 to 811).

(3) If they do not, the income is not charged to income tax (see sections 812 to 814).

(4) If they do, the individual may elect for an alternative method of calculating the income (see sections 815 to 819).

(5) If the foster-care receipts are the receipts of a trade, special rules apply—

(a) if the period of account of the trade does not end on 5th April (see sections 820 to 823), and

(b) in relation to capital allowances (see sections 824 to 827).

(6) The provisions of this Chapter which are expressed to apply in relation to trades also apply in relation to professions and vocations.

Person who qualifies for relief

804.—(1) An individual qualifies for foster-care relief for a tax year if the individual—

   (a) has foster-care receipts for the tax year (see section 805), and

   (b) does not derive any taxable income other than foster-care receipts from a relevant trade or arrangement.

(2) "Taxable income" means receipts or other income in respect of which the individual is liable to income tax for the tax year.

(3) A relevant trade or arrangement is one from which the individual derives foster-care receipts for the tax year.

1.704

Basic definitions

Meaning of "foster-care receipts"

805.—(1) For the purposes of this Chapter an individual has foster-care receipts for a tax year if—

   (a) the receipts are in respect of the provision of foster care,

   (b) they accrue to the individual during the income period for those receipts (see subsections (2) and (3)), and

   (c) the receipts would otherwise be brought into account in calculating the profits of a trade or chargeable to income tax under Chapter 8 of Part 5 (income not otherwise charged).

(2) If the receipts would otherwise be brought into account in calculating the profits of a trade, the income period is the basis period for the tax year (see Chapter 15 of Part 2).

(3) Otherwise the income period is the tax year.

1.705

Meaning of providing foster care

806.—(1) For the purposes of this Chapter foster care is provided if an individual—

   (a) provides accommodation and maintenance for a child, and

   (b) does so as a foster carer.

(2) An individual is a foster carer if the child is placed with the individual under any of the following enactments, unless the individual is excluded by subsection (5).

(3) The enactments are—

   (a) section 23(2)(a) or 59(1)(a) of the Children Act 1989 (c. 41) (provision of accommodation for children by local authorities or voluntary organisations),

   (b) regulations under section 5 of the Social Work (Scotland) Act 1968 (c. 49),

   (c) section 70 of the Children (Scotland) Act 1995 (c. 36), and

   (d) Article 27(2)(a) or 75(1)(a) of the Children (Northern Ireland) 1995 (S.I. 1995/755 (N.I. 2)) (provision of accommodation for children by authorities or voluntary organisations).

(4) An individual is also a foster carer if—

   (a) the individual is approved as a foster carer by a local authority or a voluntary organisation in accordance with regulations under section 5 of the Social Work (Scotland) Act 1968 (c. 49), and

1.706

(b) the child in respect of whom the accommodation is provided is being "looked after" by a local authority within the meaning of section 17(6) of the Children (Scotland) Act 1995 (c. 36), unless the individual is excluded by subsection (5).

(5) The following are excluded individuals—

(a) a parent of the child,

(b) an individual who is not a parent of the child but who has parental responsibility (or, in Scotland, parental responsibilities) in relation to the child,

(c) if the child is in care and there was a residence order in force with respect to the child immediately before the care order was made, an individual in whose favour the residence order was made, and

(d) (in Scotland) if the child is in care and there was a residence order or contact order in force with respect to the child immediately before the child was placed in care, an individual in whose favour the residence order or contact order was made.

PART 10

GENERAL PROVISIONS

CHAPTER 1

INTRODUCTION

Overview of Part 10

1.707   **864.** This Part—

(a) contains general rules which are of wider application than to a particular Part of this Act including certain calculation rules (see Chapter 2), and

(b) deals with supplementary matters including general definitions (see Chapter 3).

Social security contributions

Social security contributions: non-trades etc.

1.708   **868.**—(1) This section applies for the purpose of calculating profits or other income charged to income tax.

(2) For this purpose "profits or other income" does not include—

(a) the profits of a trade, profession, or vocation,

(b) the profits of a property business, or

(c) employment income,

but see subsection (6).

(3) No deduction is allowed for any contribution paid by any person under—

(a) Part 1 of the Social Security Contributions and Benefits Act 1992 (c.4), or

(b) Part 1 of the Social Security Contributions and Benefits (Northern Ireland) Act 1992 (c.7).

(4) But this prohibition does not apply to an employer's contribution.

(5) For this purpose "an employer's contribution" means—

(a) a secondary Class 1 contribution,

(b) a Class 1A contribution, or

(c) a Class 1B contribution,

within the meaning of Part 1 of the Social Security Contributions and Benefits Act 1992 (c.4) or of the Social Security Contributions and Benefits (Northern Ireland) Act 1992 (c.7).

(6) Provision corresponding to that made by this section is made by—

(a) section 53 (in relation to trades, professions and vocations),

(b) section 272 (in relation to property businesses), and

(c) section 360A of ITEPA 2003 (in relation to employment income).

Commissioners for Revenue and Customs Act 2005

(2005 c.11)

Arrangement of Sections

Introduction and General Note

1.710   This Act provides the necessary statutory machinery to bring about a major restructuring of the policy formation and administration of all United Kingdom taxes and of the tax credits, benefits and other matters formerly administered by the Commissioners (or Board) of Inland Revenue and the Commissioners of HM Customs and Excise. Although this may seem a major reform in the British context as it abolishes the oldest British government department, it is perhaps a catching-up exercise with others. The United Kingdom is the last of the European Union states to bring together the collection of its direct and indirect taxes. The process was not simply a merger. The central policy teams of both the Inland Revenue and Customs and Excise were transferred to the Treasury, uniting the previously divided fiscal policy teams. Law enforcement has also been transferred elsewhere. The Act creates a separate Revenue and Customs Prosecution Office (under provisions not set out in this book), while some enforcement officers were transferred to the new Serious Crimes agency.

The opportunity was also taken to start the process of rationalising the powers of the previous two Departments, reflecting a process of integration that started some time before the formal merger took place in April 2005. The Inland Revenue Regulation Act 1890, set out in previous editions of this volume, has been repealed in entirety as have other administrative provisions dealing with the two Departments. Like its predecessors, the new Department, formally known as Her Majesty's Revenue and Customs (or HMRC), is headed by a body of Commissioners and not Ministers of the Crown. But for legal purposes the Commissioners for Revenue and Customs (as they are known) together are deemed to be a Minister of the Crown. As part of the merger, the hallowed (if not revered) status of Her Majesty's Inspector of Taxes has gone, as have other separate roles for individual officers of the two Departments. Instead, they now become "officers of Revenue and Customs"—though we doubt that the old practice of using initials (HMIT) will be used for the new name! One result is that the past custom of having the names of individual inspectors of tax on the names of court and tribunal cases has ended. All new tax, duty, tax credit and benefit cases will be taken in the name of HM Revenue and Customs.

The Act provides the relevant authority for HMRC to take over all existing responsibilities from the previous Boards and officers and for all necessary changes to be read into Acts of Parliament and subordinate legislation. We have adopted those revisions in this volume. References to "the Board" (meaning the Board of Inland Revenue) are therefore replaced by references to "the Commissioners", and references to "an officer of the Board" or similar by references to "an officer of Revenue and Customs". This will have the incidental effect of standardising widely variant language in past Acts. Further, wide powers of delegation are contained in this Act. In practice powers will be given to "the Commissioners" or "an officer of Revenue and Customs". But the former has authority to delegate almost all its functions to officers. An example of this delegation being standard practice is the delegation under the Tax Credits Act 2002. This Act replaces s.2 of that Act and, in effect, reads this Act into the administrative provisions relevant to that Act.

The Act was intended to come into effect on April 1, 2005, the beginning of the financial and tax year. The start was delayed a few days by the process leading up to the general election in May, but in effect HMRC may be regarded as being established with effect from the beginning of the 2005 tax year.

Commissioners and officers

The Commissioners

1.—(1) Her Majesty may by Letters Patent appoint Commissioners for Her Majesty's Revenue and Customs.   **1.711**

(2) The Welsh title of the Commissioners shall be Comisynwyr Cyllid a Thollau Ei Mawrhydi.

(3) A Commissioner—

(a) may resign by notice in writing to the Treasury, and

(b) otherwise, shall hold office in accordance with the terms and conditions of his appointment (which may include provision for dismissal).

(4) In exercising their functions, the Commissioners act on behalf of the Crown.

(5) Service as a Commissioner is service in the civil service of the State.

Officers of Revenue and Customs

2.—(1) The Commissioners may appoint staff, to be known as officers of Revenue and Customs.   **1.712**

(2) A person shall hold and vacate office as an officer of Revenue and Customs in accordance with the terms of his appointment (which may include provision for dismissal).

(3) An officer of Revenue and Customs shall comply with directions of the Commissioners (whether he is exercising a function conferred on officers of Revenue and Customs or exercising a function on behalf of the Commissioners).

(4) Anything (including anything in relation to legal proceedings) by or in relation to one officer of Revenue and Customs may be continued by or in relation to another.

(5) Appointments under subsection (1) may be made only with the approval of the Minister for the Civil Service as to terms and conditions of service.

(6) Service in the employment of the Commissioners is service in the civil service of the State.

(7) In Schedule 1 to the Interpretation Act 1978 (c. 30) (defined expressions) at the appropriate place insert—

"'Officer of Revenue and Customs' has the meaning given by section 2(1) of the Commissioners for Revenue and Customs Act 2005."

Declaration of confidentiality

3.—(1) Each person who is appointed under this Act as a Commissioner or officer of Revenue and Customs shall make a declaration acknowledging his obligation of confidentiality under section 18.   **1.713**

(2) A declaration under subsection (1) shall be made—

(a) as soon as is reasonably practicable following the person's appointment, and

(b) in such form, and before such a person, as the Commissioners may direct.

(3) For the purposes of this section, the renewal of a fixed term appointment shall not be treated as an appointment.

"Her Majesty's Revenue and Customs"

1.714   **4.**—(1) The Commissioners and the officers of Revenue and Customs may together be referred to as Her Majesty's Revenue and Customs.

(2) The Welsh title of the Commissioners and the officers of Revenue and Customs together shall be Cyllid a Thollau Ei Mawrhydi.

(3) In Schedule 1 to the Interpretation Act 1978 (defined expressions) at the appropriate place insert—

     " 'Her Majesty's Revenue and Customs' has the meaning given by section 4 of the Commissioners for Revenue and Customs Act 2005."

Functions

Commissioners' initial functions

1.715   **5.**—(1) The Commissioners shall be responsible for—

  (a) the collection and management of revenue for which the Commissioners of Inland Revenue were responsible before the commencement of this section,

  (b) the collection and management of revenue for which the Commissioners of Customs and Excise were responsible before the commencement of this section, and

  (c) the payment and management of tax credits for which the Commissioners of Inland Revenue were responsible before the commencement of this section.

(2) The Commissioners shall also have all the other functions which before the commencement of this section vested in—

  (a) the Commissioners of Inland Revenue (or in a Commissioner), or

  (b) the Commissioners of Customs and Excise (or in a Commissioner).

(3) This section is subject to section 35.

(4) In this Act "revenue" includes taxes, duties and national insurance contributions.

Former Inland Revenue matters

1.716   **7.**—(1) This section applies to the matters listed in Schedule 1.

(2) A function conferred by an enactment (in whatever terms) on any of the persons specified in subsection (3) shall by virtue of this subsection vest in an officer of Revenue and Customs—

  (a) if or in so far as it relates to a matter to which this section applies, and

  (b) in so far as the officer is exercising a function (whether or not by virtue of paragraph (a)) which relates to a matter to which this section applies.

(3) Those persons are—

  (a) an officer of the Commissioners of Inland Revenue,

  (b) an officer of the Board of Inland Revenue,

  (c) an officer of inland revenue,

  (d) a collector of Inland Revenue,

  (e) an inspector of taxes,

  (f) a collector of taxes,

(g) a person authorised to act as an inspector of taxes or collector of
taxes for specific purposes,
(h) an officer having powers in relation to tax,
(i) a revenue official,
(j) a person employed in relation to Inland Revenue (or "the Inland
Revenue"), and
(k) an Inland Revenue official.

(4) In so far as an officer of Revenue and Customs is exercising a function
which relates to a matter to which this section applies, section 6(1) shall
not apply.

(5) This section is subject to section 35.

Ancillary powers

9.—(1) The Commissioners may do anything which they think—   1.717
(a) necessary or expedient in connection with the exercise of their functions, or
(b) incidental or conducive to the exercise of their functions.

(2) This section is subject to section 35.

Commissioners' arrangements

12.—(1) The Commissioners shall make arrangements for—   1.718
(a) the conduct of their proceedings, and
(b) the conduct of the proceedings of any committee established by
them.

(2) Arrangements under subsection (1) may, in particular—
(a) make provision for a quorum at meetings;
(b) provide that a function of the Commissioners—
(i) may be exercised by two Commissioners, or
(ii) may be exercised by a specified number of Commissioners
(greater than two).

(3) A decision to make arrangements under subsection (1) must be taken
with the agreement of more than half of the Commissioners holding office
at the time.

Exercise of Commissioners' functions by officers

13.—(1) An officer of Revenue and Customs may exercise any function   1.719
of the Commissioners.

(2) But subsection (1)—
(a) does not apply to the functions specified in subsection (3), and
(b) is subject to directions under section 2(3) and arrangements under
section 12.

(3) The non-delegable functions mentioned in subsection (2)(a) are—
(a) making, by statutory instrument, regulations, rules or an order,
(b) approving an application for a warrant to search premises under
section 20 C of the Taxes Management Act 1970 (c. 9),
(c) approving an application for a warrant to enter premises under
Part 7 of Schedule 13 to the Finance Act 2003 (c. 14), and
(d) giving instructions for the disclosure of information under section
20(1)(a), except that an officer of Revenue and Customs may give an
instruction under section 20(1)(a) authorising disclosure of specified
information relating to—

>>> (i) one or more specified persons,
>>> (ii) one or more specified transactions, or
>>> (iii) specified goods.

GENERAL NOTE

1.720   Subss.(3)(b) and (c) are to be repealed with effect from a date to be ordered by HM Treasury (Finance Act 2007 s.84 and Sch.27, Pt 5).

Information

Use of information

1.721   **17.**—(1) Information acquired by the Revenue and Customs in connection with a function may be used by them in connection with any other function.

(2) Subsection (1) is subject to any provision which restricts or prohibits the use of information and which is contained in—

(a) this Act,

(b) any other enactment, or

(c) an international or other agreement to which the United Kingdom or Her Majesty's Government is party.

(3) In subsection (1) "the Revenue and Customs" means—

(a) the Commissioners,

(b) an officer of Revenue and Customs,

(c) a person acting on behalf of the Commissioners or an officer of Revenue and Customs,

(d) a committee established by the Commissioners,

(e) a member of a committee established by the Commissioners,

 (f) the Commissioners of Inland Revenue (or any committee or staff of theirs or anyone acting on their behalf),

(g) the Commissioners of Customs and Excise (or any committee or staff of theirs or anyone acting on their behalf), and

(h) a person specified in section 6(2) or 7(3).

(4) In subsection (1) "function" means a function of any of the persons listed in subsection (3).

(5) In subsection (2) the reference to an enactment does not include—

(a) an Act of the Scottish Parliament or an instrument made under such an Act, or

(b) an Act of the Northern Ireland Assembly or an instrument made under such an Act.

(6) Part 2 of Schedule 2 (which makes provision about the supply and other use of information in specified circumstances) shall have effect.

Confidentiality

1.722   **18.**—(1) Revenue and Customs officials may not disclose information which is held by the Revenue and Customs in connection with a function of the Revenue and Customs.

(2) But subsection (1) does not apply to a disclosure—

(a) which—

>> (i) is made for the purposes of a function of the Revenue and Customs, and

  (ii) does not contravene any restriction imposed by the Commissioners,
(b) which is made in accordance with section 20 or 21,
(c) which is made for the purposes of civil proceedings (whether or not within the United Kingdom) relating to a matter in respect of which the Revenue and Customs have functions,
(d) which is made for the purposes of a criminal investigation or criminal proceedings (whether or not within the United Kingdom) relating to a matter in respect of which the Revenue and Customs have functions,
(e) which is made in pursuance of an order of a court,
(f) which is made to Her Majesty's Inspectors of Constabulary, the Scottish inspectors or the Northern Ireland inspectors for the purpose of an inspection by virtue of section 27,
(g) which is made to the Independent Police Complaints Commission, or a person acting on its behalf, for the purpose of the exercise of a function by virtue of section 28, or
(h) which is made with the consent of each person to whom the information relates.

(3) Subsection (1) is subject to any other enactment permitting disclosure.

(4) In this section—
(a) a reference to Revenue and Customs officials is a reference to any person who is or was—
  (i) a Commissioner,
  (ii) an officer of Revenue and Customs,
  (iii) a person acting on behalf of the Commissioners or an officer of Revenue and Customs, or
  (iv) a member of a committee established by the Commissioners,
(b) a reference to the Revenue and Customs has the same meaning as in section 17,
(c) a reference to a function of the Revenue and Customs is a reference to a function of—
  (i) the Commissioners, or
  (ii) an officer of Revenue and Customs,
(d) a reference to the Scottish inspectors or the Northern Ireland inspectors has the same meaning as in section 27, and
(e) a reference to an enactment does not include—
  (i) an Act of the Scottish Parliament or an instrument made under such an Act, or
  (ii) an Act of the Northern Ireland Assembly or an instrument made under such an Act.

Freedom of information

23.—(1) Revenue and customs information relating to a person, the disclosure of which is prohibited by section 18(1), is exempt information by virtue of section 44(1)(a) of the Freedom of Information Act 2000 (c. 36) (prohibitions on disclosure) if its disclosure—   1.723
(a) would specify the identity of the person to whom the information relates, or
(b) would enable the identity of such a person to be deduced.

(2) Except as specified in subsection (1), information the disclosure of which is prohibited by section 18(1) is not exempt information for the purposes of section 44(1)(a) of the Freedom of Information Act 2000.

(3) In subsection (1) "revenue and customs information relating to a person" has the same meaning as in section 19.

Obstruction

1.724   **31.**—(1) A person commits an offence if without reasonable excuse he obstructs—

(a) an officer of Revenue and Customs,

(b) a person acting on behalf of the Commissioners or an officer of Revenue and Customs, or

(c) a person assisting an officer of Revenue and Customs.

(2) A person guilty of an offence under this section shall be liable on summary conviction to—

(a) imprisonment for a period not exceeding 51 weeks,

(b) a fine not exceeding level 3 on the standard scale, or

(c) both.

(3) In the application of this section to Scotland or Northern Ireland the reference in subsection (2)(a) to 51 weeks shall be taken as a reference to six months.

Assault

1.725   **32.**—(1) A person commits an offence if he assaults an officer of Revenue and Customs.

(2) A person guilty of an offence under this section shall be liable on summary conviction to—

(a) imprisonment for a period not exceeding 51 weeks,

(b) a fine not exceeding level 5 on the standard scale, or

(c) both.

(3) In the application of this section to Scotland or Northern Ireland the reference in subsection (2)(a) to 51 weeks shall be taken as a reference to six months.

Power of arrest

1.726   **33.**—(1) An authorised officer of Revenue and Customs may arrest a person without warrant if the officer reasonably suspects that the person—

(a) has committed an offence under section 30, 31 or 32,

(b) is committing an offence under any of those sections, or

(c) is about to commit an offence under any of those sections.

(2) In subsection (1) "authorised" means authorised by the Commissioners.

(3) Authorisation for the purposes of this section may be specific or general.

(4) In Scotland or Northern Ireland, a constable may arrest a person without warrant if the constable reasonably suspects that the person—

(a) has committed an offence under this Act,

(b) is committing an offence under this Act, or

(c) is about to commit an offence under this Act.

General

Consequential amendments, &c.

50.—(1) In so far as is appropriate in consequence of section 5 a reference
in an enactment, instrument or other document to the Commissioners of
Customs and Excise, to customs and excise or to the Commissioners of
Inland Revenue (however expressed) shall be taken as a reference to the
Commissioners for Her Majesty's Revenue and Customs.

(2) In so far as is appropriate in consequence of sections 6 and 7 a reference in an enactment, instrument or other document to any of the persons
specified in section 6(2) or 7(3) (however expressed) shall be taken as a
reference to an officer of Revenue and Customs.

1.727

SCHEDULE 1

FORMER INLAND REVENUE MATTERS

1   Capital gains tax.
2   Charities.
3   Child benefit.
4   Child tax credit.
5   Child trust funds.
6   Corporation tax (and amounts assessable or chargeable as if they were
   corporation tax).
7   Guardian's allowance.
8   Income tax.
9   Inheritance tax.
10 The issue of bank notes.
11 National insurance contributions.
12 The National Insurance Fund.
13 The national minimum wage.
14 Oil and gas royalties.
15 Payment of or in lieu of rates.
16 Payment in lieu of tax reliefs, in so far as the Commissioners of
   Inland Revenue were responsible before the commencement of section
   5.
17 Pension schemes.
18 Petroleum revenue tax.
19 Rating lists.
20 Recovery of taxes due in other member States, in relation to
   matters corresponding to those for which the Commissioners of
   Inland Revenue were responsible before the commencement of
   section 5.
21 Stamp duty.
22 Stamp duty land tax.
23 Stamp duty reserve tax.
24 Statutory adoption pay.
25 Statutory maternity pay.
26 Statutory paternity pay.
27 Statutory sick pay.

1.728

Income Tax Act 2007

(2007 c.3)

ARRANGEMENT OF SELECTED SECTIONS

PART 1

OVERVIEW

PART 2

BASIC PROVISIONS

CHAPTER 1

CHARGES TO INCOME TAX

PART 14

INCOME TAX LIABILITY: MISCELLANEOUS RULES

CHAPTER 2

RESIDENCE

INTRODUCTION AND GENERAL NOTE

This Act came into effect on April 6, 2007. It is the fourth of the Acts produced as part of the Tax Law Rewrite Project. It brings to a close the complete rewrite of all primary legislation dealing with income tax save only for the areas (not relevant to this work) listed in s.1 below. As s.1 signposts, it is to be read with ITEPA and ITTOIA. Save as mentioned in that section, all the parts of the Income and Corporation Taxes Act 1988 that referred to income tax have now been repealed and replaced. The extracts from that Act previously in this volume have therefore been deleted. Only a few sections from this Act are relevant to this work, but section 2 is included to show the full and extensive contents of the Act. As with the other Tax Law Rewrite Acts, an extensive explanatory note (running for this Act to three volumes) was published with the Act. Anyone wishing to consider any reference to the Act further should look at that note as a starting point.

1.730

PART 1

OVERVIEW

Overview of Income Tax Acts

1.731   **1.**—(1) The following Acts make provision about income tax—
   (a) ITEPA 2003 (which is about charges to tax on employment income, pension income and social security income),
   (b) ITTOIA 2005 (which is about charges to tax on trading income, property income, savings and investment income and some other miscellaneous income), and
   (c) this Act (which contains the other main provisions about income tax).

   (2) There are also provisions about income tax elsewhere: see in particular—
   (a) Part 18 of ICTA (double taxation relief),
   (b) CAA 2001 (allowances for capital expenditure), and
   (c) Part 4 of FA 2004 (pension schemes etc).

   (3) Schedule 1 to the Interpretation Act 1978 (c.30) defines "the Income Tax Acts" (as all enactments relating to income tax).

Overview of Act

1.732   **2.**— (1) This Act has 17 Parts.
   (2) Part 2 contains basic provisions about income tax including-
   (a) provision about the annual nature of income tax (Chapter 1),
   (b) the rates at which income tax is charged (Chapter 2), and
   (c) the calculation of income tax liability (Chapter 3).
   (3) Part 3 is about taxpayers' personal reliefs including—
   (a) personal allowances (Chapter 2),
   (b) blind persons' allowances (Chapter 2), and
   (c) tax reductions for married couples and civil partners (Chapter 3).
   (4) Part 4 is about loss relief including relief for—
   (a) trade losses (Chapters 2 and 3),
   (b) losses from property businesses (Chapter 4),
   (c) losses in an employment or office (Chapter 5),
   (d) losses on disposal of shares (Chapter 6), and
   (e) losses from miscellaneous transactions (Chapter 7).
   (5) Part 5 is about relief under the enterprise investment scheme.
   (6) Part 6 is about—
   (a) relief for investment in venture capital trusts, and
   (b) other matters relating to venture capital trusts.
   (7) Part 7 is about community investment tax relief.
   (8) Part 8 is about a variety of reliefs including relief for—
   (a) interest payments (Chapter 1),
   (b) gifts to charity including gift aid (Chapters 2 and 3),
   (c) annual payments and patent royalties (Chapter 4), and
   (d) maintenance payments (Chapter 5).
   (9) Part 9 contains special rules about settlements and trustees including—

(a) general provision about settlements and trustees (Chapter 2),

(b) special income tax rates for trusts (Chapters 3, 4, 5 and 6),

(c) rules about trustees' expenses (Chapters 4 and 8),

(d) rules about trustees' discretionary payments (Chapter 7),

(e) rules about unauthorised unit trusts (Chapter 9), and

(f) rules about heritage maintenance settlements (Chapter 10).

(10) Part 10 contains special rules about charitable trusts etc.

(11) Part 11 is about manufactured payments and repos.

(12) Part 12 is about accrued income profits.

(13) Part 13 is about tax avoidance in relation to—

(a) transactions in securities (Chapter 1),

(b) transfers of assets abroad (Chapter 2),

(c) transactions in land (Chapter 3),

(d) sales of occupation income (Chapter 4), and

(e) trade losses (Chapter 5).

(14) Part 14 deals with some miscellaneous rules about income tax liability, including—

(a) limits on liability to income tax for non-UK residents (Chapter 1),

(b) special rules about residence (Chapter 2), and

(c) rules about jointly held property (Chapter 3).

(15) Part 15 is about the deduction of income tax at source.

(16) Part 16 contains definitions which apply for the purposes of the Income Tax Acts and other general provisions which apply for the purposes of those Acts.

(17) Part 17—

(a) contains provisions to be used in interpreting this Act,

(b) introduces Schedule 1 (minor and consequential amendments),

(c) introduces Schedule 2 (transitional provisions and savings),

(d) introduces Schedule 3 (repeals and revocations, including of spent enactments),

(e) introduces Schedule 4 (index of defined expressions that apply for the purposes of this Act),

(f) confers powers on the Treasury to make orders, and

(g) makes provision about the coming into force of this Act.

PART 2

BASIC PROVISIONS

CHAPTER 1

CHARGES TO INCOME TAX

Overview of charges to income tax

3.—(1) Income tax is charged under—   1.733

(a) Part 2 of ITEPA 2003 (employment income),

(b) Part 9 of ITEPA 2003 (pension income),

(c) Part 10 of ITEPA 2003 (social security income),

(d) Part 2 of ITTOIA 2005 (trading income),
(e) Part 3 of ITTOIA 2005 (property income),
(f) Part 4 of ITTOIA 2005 (savings and investment income), and
(g) Part 5 of ITTOIA 2005 (miscellaneous income).
(2) Income tax is also charged under other provisions, including—
(a) Chapter 5 of Part 4 of FA 2004 (registered pension schemes: tax charges),
(b) section 7 of F(No.2)A 2005 (social security pension lump sums),
(c) Part 10 of this Act (special rules about charitable trusts etc),
(d) Chapter 2 of Part 12 of this Act (accrued income profits), and
(e) Part 13 of this Act (tax avoidance).

Income tax an annual tax

1.734   **4.**—(1) Income tax is charged for a year only if an Act so provides.
(2) A year for which income tax is charged is called a "tax year".
(3) A tax year begins on 6 April and ends on the following 5 April.
(4) "The tax year 2007–08" means the tax year beginning on 6 April 2007 (and any corresponding expression in which two years are similarly mentioned is to be read in the same way).
(5) Every assessment to income tax must be made for a tax year.
(6) Subsection (5) is subject to Chapter 15 of Part 15 (by virtue of which an assessment may relate to a return period).

GENERAL NOTE

1.735   The Rewrite Acts retain the long-standing approach of providing framework legislation for income tax. It is the relevant section in each year's Finance Act that actually imposes the tax for the year. That section triggers s.4 and thence the charging sections in s.3 and in ITEPA and ITTOIA. The list of charging sections here may be compared with the similar—but not identical—list of chapters to the Tax Credits (Definition and Calculation of Income) Regulations 2002 below.

PART 14

INCOME TAX LIABILITY: MISCELLANEOUS RULES

CHAPTER 2

RESIDENCE

Residence of individuals temporarily abroad

1.736   **829.**—(1) This section applies if—
(a) an individual has left the United Kingdom for the purpose only of occasional residence abroad, and
(b) at the time of leaving the individual was both UK resident and ordinarily UK resident.
(2) Treat the individual as UK resident for the purpose of determining the individual's liability for income tax for any tax year during the whole or

a part of which the individual remains outside the United Kingdom for the purpose only of occasional residence abroad.

GENERAL NOTE

This section and those that follow rewrite the former ss.334–336 of ICTA. They set out the only legislative meanings given to "resident" for income tax purposes. The detailed view of how HMRC assesses residence and ordinary residence in the light of these provisions and the relevant case law is set out in HMRC booklet IR20.

1.737

Residence of individuals working abroad

830.—(1) This section applies for income tax purposes if an individual works full-time in one or both of—

(a) a foreign trade, and

(b) a foreign employment.

(2) In determining whether the individual is UK resident ignore any living accommodation available in the United Kingdom for the individual's use.

(3) A trade is foreign if no part of it is carried on in the United Kingdom.

(4) An employment is foreign if all of its duties are performed outside the United Kingdom.

(5) An employment is also foreign if in the tax year in question—

(a) the duties of the employment are in substance performed outside the United Kingdom, and

(b) the only duties of the employment performed in the United Kingdom are duties which are merely incidental to the duties of the employment performed outside the United Kingdom in the year.

(6) In this section—

"employment" includes an office, and

"trade" includes profession and vocation.

1.738

Foreign income of individuals in the United Kingdom for temporary purpose

831.—(1) Subsection (2) applies in relation to an individual if—

(a) the individual is in the United Kingdom for some temporary purpose only and with no view to establishing the individual's residence in the United Kingdom, and

(b) during the tax year in question the individual spends (in total) less than 183 days in the United Kingdom.

In determining whether an individual is within paragraph (a) ignore any living accommodation available in the United Kingdom for the individual's use.

(1A) In determining whether an individual is within subsection (1)(b) treat a day as a day spent by the individual in the United Kingdom if (and only if) the individual is present in the United Kingdom at the end of the day.

(1B) But in determining that issue do not treat as a day spent by the individual in the United Kingdom any day on which the individual arrives in the United Kingdom as a passenger if—

(a) the individual departs from the United Kingdom on the next day, and

1.739

    (b) during the time between arrival and departure the individual does not engage in activities that are to a substantial extent unrelated to the individual's passage through the United Kingdom.

(2) Apply the following rules in determining the individual's liability for income tax.

Rule 1

In relation to pension or social security income arising from a source outside the United Kingdom, treat the individual as non-UK resident for the purposes of the following—

    (a) Chapter 4 of Part 9 of ITEPA 2003 (tax on foreign pensions),

    (b) Chapter 5A of that Part (tax on pensions under registered pension schemes) but only if the income is an annuity under a registered pension scheme within paragraph 1(1)(f) of Schedule 36 to FA 2004,

    (c) Chapter 10 of that Part (tax on employment-related annuities),

    (d) Chapter 15 of that Part (tax on voluntary annual payments),

    (e) section 647 of ITEPA 2003 (meaning of "foreign residence condition") but only in its application for the purposes of section 651 of that Act (which provides an exemption for tax under Chapter 14 of Part 9 of that Act), and

    (f) Chapter 6 of Part 10 of ITEPA 2003 (taxable foreign benefits).

See sections 566 and 657 of ITEPA 2003 for the definitions of "pension income" and "social security income".

Rule 2

In relation to income arising from a source outside the United Kingdom, treat the individual as non-UK resident for the purposes of any charge under a provision mentioned in section 830(2) of ITTOIA 2005 (which contains a list of provisions under which relevant foreign income is charged).

In this rule "income" does not include income chargeable as a result of section 844 of ITTOIA 2005 (unremittable income: income charged on withdrawal of relief after source ceases).

(3) Paragraph (e) of Rule 1 in subsection (2) applies only if—

    (a) the individual makes a claim as mentioned in section 647(3)(a) of ITEPA 2003, and

    (b) the Commissioners are satisfied that subsection (2) of this section applies in relation to the individual.

(4) Subsection (5) applies in relation to an individual if subsection (2) would have applied in relation to the individual but for subsection (1)(b).

(5) Apply the rules set out in subsection (2) in determining the individual's liability for income tax.

But—

    (a) instead of treating the individual as non-UK resident in relation to the income and for the purposes mentioned in those rules, treat the individual as UK resident, and

    (b) ignore subsection (3).

Employment income of individuals in the United Kingdom for temporary purpose

1.740   **832.**—(1) Subsection (2) applies in relation to an individual if—

    (a) the individual is in the United Kingdom for some temporary purpose only and with no intention of establishing the individual's residence in the United Kingdom, and

(b) during the tax year in question the individual spends (in total) less than 183 days in the United Kingdom.

In determining whether an individual is within paragraph (a) ignore any living accommodation available in the United Kingdom for the individual's use.

(1A) In determining whether an individual is within subsection (1)(b) treat a day as a day spent by the individual in the United Kingdom if (and only if) the individual is present in the United Kingdom at the end of the day.

(1B) But in determining that issue do not treat as a day spent by the individual in the United Kingdom any day on which the individual arrives in the United Kingdom as a passenger if—

(a) the individual departs from the United Kingdom on the next day, and

(b) during the time between arrival and departure the individual does not engage in activities that are to a substantial extent unrelated to the individual's passage through the United Kingdom.

(2) Treat the individual as non-UK resident for the purposes of Chapters 4 and 5 of Part 2 of ITEPA 2003 (which set out rules for determining taxable earnings from employment).

(3) Subsection (4) applies in relation to an individual if subsection (2) would have applied in relation to the individual but for subsection (1)(b).

(4) Treat the individual as UK resident for the purposes of the provisions mentioned in subsection (2).

CHAPTER 3

JOINTLY HELD PROPERTY

Jointly held property

836.—(1) This section applies if income arises from property held in the names of individuals—

(a) who are married to, or are civil partners of, each other, and

(b) who live together.

(2) The individuals are treated for income tax purposes as beneficially entitled to the income in equal shares.

(3) But this treatment does not apply in relation to any income within any of the following exceptions.

Exception A

Income to which neither of the individuals is beneficially entitled.

Exception B

Income in relation to which a declaration by the individuals under section 837 has effect (unequal beneficial interests).

Exception C

Income to which Part 9 of ITTOIA 2005 applies (partnerships).

Exception D

Income arising from a UK property business which consists of, or so far

1.741

as it includes, the commercial letting of furnished holiday accommodation (within the meaning of Chapter 6 of Part 3 of ITTOIA 2005).

Exception E

Income consisting of a distribution arising from property consisting of—

(a) shares in or securities of a close company to which one of the individuals is beneficially entitled to the exclusion of the other, or

(b) such shares or securities to which the individuals are beneficially entitled in equal or unequal shares.

"Shares" and "securities" have the same meaning as in section 254 of ICTA.

Exception F

Income to which one of the individuals is beneficially entitled so far as it is treated as a result of any other provision of the Income Tax Acts as—

(a) the income of the other individual, or

(b) the income of a third party.

GENERAL NOTE

1.742   This section and the machinery section that follows should be read with s.1011 below. It sets out the general rule that couples living together are assumed to own any property, and therefore to receive any income from that property, in equal shares. Section 837 allows the couple to alter that position. However, that will make little difference to tax credits claims as entitlement is assessed on the total incomes of both members of the couple. Note that this rule does not apply to unmarried or unregistered couples, but again that does not affect tax credit entitlement. It does however affect income tax liability where the two members of the couple are liable to income tax at different rates at the margin.

Jointly held property: declarations of unequal beneficial interests

1.743   **837.**—(1) The individuals may make a joint declaration under this section if—

(a) one of them is beneficially entitled to the income to the exclusion of the other, or

(b) they are beneficially entitled to the income in unequal shares, and their beneficial interests in the income correspond to their beneficial interests in the property from which it arises.

(2) The declaration must state the beneficial interests of the individuals in—

(a) the income to which the declaration relates, and

(b) the property from which that income arises.

(3) The declaration has effect only if notice of it is given to an officer of Revenue and Customs—

(a) in such form and manner as the Commissioners for Her Majesty's Revenue and Customs may prescribe, and

(b) within the period of 60 days beginning with the date of the declaration.

(4) The declaration has effect in relation to income arising on or after the date of the declaration.

(5) The declaration continues to have effect until such time (if any) as there is a change in the beneficial interests of the individuals in either—

(a) the income to which the declaration relates, or

(b) the property from which that income arises.

PART 16

INCOME TAX ACTS DEFINITIONS ETC

CHAPTER 1

DEFINITIONS

Overview of Chapter

988.—(1) This Chapter contains definitions which apply for the purposes of the Income Tax Acts, except where, in those Acts, the context otherwise requires.

(2) To find a definition go first to section 989, which sets out some of the definitions in full.

(3) If a definition is not set out in full in section 989, the section indicates where it is set out in full.

(4) In some cases it is stated that a definition does not apply for the purposes of specified provisions of the Income Tax Acts (see, for example, sections 990(2), 992(3) and 1007(4)).

(5) And in some cases it is stated that a definition has effect only for the purposes of specific provisions of the Income Tax Acts (see, for example, sections 991, 993, 995 and 1006).

The definitions

989.—The following definitions apply for the purposes of the Income Tax Acts—

"Act" has the meaning given by section 990,

. . .

"bank" is to be read in accordance with section 991,

. . .

"body of persons" means any body politic, corporate or collegiate and any company, fraternity, fellowship or society of persons whether corporate or not corporate,

. . .

"capital allowance" means any allowance under CAA 2001,

"the Capital Allowances Act" means CAA 2001,

"chargeable gain" has the same meaning as in TCGA 1992,

"chargeable period" means an accounting period of a company or a tax year,

"charity" means a body of persons or trust established for charitable purposes only,

. . .

"company" has the meaning given by section 992,

. . .

"dividend income" has the meaning given by section 19

. . .

"farming" has the meaning given by section 996,

"for accounting purposes" has the meaning given by section 997(4),

1.744

1.745

. . .

"generally accepted accounting practice" has the meaning given by section 997(1) and (3),

"grossing up" is to be read in accordance with section 998,

. . .

"international accounting standards" has the meaning given by section 997(5),

. . .

"non-UK resident" means not resident in the United Kingdom (and references to a non-UK resident or a non-UK resident person are to a person who is not resident there),

"normal self-assessment filing date", in relation to a tax year, means the 31 January following the tax year,

"notice" means notice in writing or in a form authorised (in relation to the case in question) by directions under section 118 of FA 1998,

. . .

"overseas property business" has the meaning given by Chapter 2 of Part 3 of ITTOIA 2005,

"period of account"—

(a) in relation to a person, means any period for which the person draws up accounts, and

(b) in relation to a trade, profession, vocation or other business, means any period for which the accounts of the business are drawn up,

. . .

"personal representatives" in relation to a person who has died, means—

(a) in the United Kingdom, persons responsible for administering the estate of the deceased, and

(b) in a territory outside the United Kingdom, those persons having functions under its law equivalent to those of administering the estate of the deceased,

"profits or gains" does not include chargeable gains,

. . .

"relevant foreign income" has the meaning given by section 830(1) to

(3) of ITTOIA 2005 but also includes, for any purpose mentioned in any provision listed in section 830(4) of that Act, income treated as relevant foreign income for that purpose by that provision,

"research and development" is to be read in accordance with section 1006,

"retail prices index" means—

(a) the general index of retail prices (for all items) published by the Office for National Statistics, or

(b) if that index is not published for a relevant month, any substituted index or index figures published by that Office,

. . .

"Schedule A business" means any business the profits of which are chargeable to corporation tax under Schedule A, including the business in the course of which any transaction is (as a result of paragraph 1(2) of that Schedule) to be treated as entered into,

. . .

"settled property" (together with references to property comprised in a settlement) is to be read in accordance with section 466, "settlor" is to be read in accordance with sections 467 to 473,

. . .

"stepchild", in relation to a civil partner, is to be read in accordance with section 246 of the Civil Partnership Act 2004 (c.33),

. . .

"tax" is to be read in accordance with section 832(3) of ICTA,

"tax credit" means a tax credit under section 397(1) of ITTOIA 2005,

"tax year" has the meaning given by section 4(2),

"the tax year 2007–08" (and any corresponding expression in which two years are similarly mentioned) has the meaning given by section 4(4),

"total income" has the meaning given by section 23 (see Step 1 in that section and also section 31),

"trade" includes any venture in the nature of trade,

"tribunal" means the First-tier Tribunal or, where determined by or under Tribunal Procedure Rules, the Upper Tribunal,

. . .

"UK generally accepted accounting practice" has the meaning given by section 997(2),

"UK property business" has the meaning given by Chapter 2 of Part 3 of ITTOIA 2005,

"UK resident" means resident in the United Kingdom (and references to a UK resident or a UK resident person are to a person who is resident there),

. . .

"year of assessment" means a tax year, and

"the year 1988–1989" means the tax year 1988–1989 (and any corresponding expression in which two years are similarly mentioned is to be read in the same way).

Meaning of "company"

992.—(1) In the Income Tax Acts "company" means any body corporate or unincorporated association, but does not include a partnership, a local authority or a local authority association.   1.746

(2) Subsection (1) needs to be with read with section 468 of ICTA (authorised unit trusts).

. . .

References to married persons, or civil partners, living together

1011.—Individuals who are married to, or are civil partners of, each other are treated for the purposes of the Income Tax Acts as living together unless—   1.747

(a) they are separated under an order of a court of competent jurisdiction,

(b) they are separated by deed of separation, or

(c) they are in fact separated in circumstances in which the separation is likely to be permanent.

HEALTH AND SOCIAL CARE ACT 2008

PART 4

HEALTH IN PREGNANCY GRANT

ENGLAND, WALES AND SCOTLAND

GENERAL AND SUPPLEMENTARY

General and supplementary

1.748   **138** (1) The Commissioners for Her Majesty's Revenue and Customs are responsible for the payment and management of health in pregnancy grant.

(2) In section 115 of the Immigration and Asylum Act 1999 (c. 33) (exclusion from entitlement to benefits), in subsection (1), after paragraph (h), insert—

"(ha) health in pregnancy grant,".

(3) In subsections (5) and (6) of that section, before "child benefit" insert "health in pregnancy grant or".

PART II

TAX CREDITS

Tax Credits Act 2002 (Commencement No.3 and Transitional Provisions and Savings) Order 2003

(SI 2003/938)

The Treasury, in relation to articles 1 and 2, in exercise of the powers conferred upon them by section 61 of the Tax Credits Act 2002 and the Secretary of State for Work and Pensions, in relation to articles 1 and 3 to 5 in exercise of the powers conferred on him by s.62(1) of that Act and of all other powers enabling each of them in that behalf, hereby make the following Order:

ARRANGEMENT OF ARTICLES

1. Citation and interpretation.   2.1
2. Appointed day.
3. Saving provision.
4. Transitional application of sections 37 and 39A of the Contributions and Benefits Act.
5. Transitional application of section 154 of the Administration Act.

Schedule—Repeals specified in Schedule 6 to the 2002 Act which are commenced by this order.

Citation and interpretation

1.—(1) This Order may be cited as the Tax Credits Act 2002 (Com-   2.2
mencement No.3 and Transitional Provisions and Savings) Order 2003.

(2) In this Order—

"the 2002 Act" means the Tax Credits Act 2002;

"the Administration Act" means the Social Security Administration Act 1992;

"the Contributions and Benefits Act" means the Social Security Contributions and Benefits Act 1992.

Appointed day

2. The day appointed for the coming into force of—   2.3

(a) section 1(3)(e) of the 2002 Act (abolition of increases in benefits in respect of children under sections 80 and 90 of the Contributions and Benefits Act);

(b) section 60 of, and Schedule 6, to, the 2002 Act, in so far as they repeal the provisions specified in the Schedule to this Order, is 6th April 2003.

Saving provision

3.—(1) Notwithstanding the coming into force of the specified provi-   2.4
sions, the Contributions and Benefits Act and the Administration Act shall, in cases to which paragraph (2) applies, subject to paragraph (3), continue to have effect from the commencement date as if those provisions had not come into force.

347

(2) This paragraph applies where a person—

(a) is entitled to a relevant increase on the day before the commencement date; or

(b) claims a relevant increase on or after the commencement date and it is subsequently determined that he is entitled to a relevant increase in respect of a period which includes the day before the commencement date.

(3) The provisions saved by paragraph (1) shall continue to have effect until—

(a) subject to sub-paragraph (c), where a relevant increase ceases to be payable to a person to whom paragraph (2) applies for a period greater than 58 days beginning with the day on which it was last payable, on the day 59 days after the day on which it was last payable; or

(b) in any other case, subject to sub-paragraph (c), on the date on which entitlement to a relevant increase ceases;

(c) where regulation 6(19) or (23) of the Social Security (Claims and Payments) Regulations 1987 applies to a further claim for a relevant increase, on the date on which entitlement to that relevant increase ceases.

(4) In this article—

"the commencement date" means 6th April 2003;

"a relevant increase" means an increase under section 80 or 90 of the Contributions and Benefits Act;

"the specified provisions" means the provisions of the 2002 Act which are brought into force by article 2.

Transitional application of sections 37 and 39A of the Contributions and Benefits Act

2.5   **4.** For the purposes of the continuing application of sections 37 (widowed mother's allowance) and 39A (widowed parent's allowance) of the Contributions and Benefits Act in cases to which article 3(2) applies, those sections shall apply as if the amendments specified in paragraphs 26 and 28 of Schedule 3 to the 2002 Act had not come into force.

Transitional application of section 154 of the Administration Act

2.6   **5.** For the purposes of the continuing application of section 154(2)(c) of the Administration Act in cases to which article 3(2) applies, that section shall apply as if it had not been repealed in Schedule 6 to the 2002 Act and the reference to child benefit in that section shall be treated as including a reference to child tax credit under section 8 of the 2002 Act.

Article 2 SCHEDULE

REPEALS SPECIFIED IN SCHEDULE 6 TO THE 2002 ACT WHICH ARE COMMENCED BY THIS ORDER

Act	*Provision*
Contributions and Benefits Act	In section 20(1), the words "(with increase for child dependants)" (in each place) and in paragraph (f)(i), the words "and child". In section 30B(3), the word "80,". In section 56(1), the words "(and in particular to those of section 81 below)". Section 60(6). In sections 61(1) and (2), the words "on account of a child or an adult". In section 63(c) and (f)(i), the words "and child". In section 77(1), the words following paragraph (b). In section 78(4)(d), the word "80". Sections 80 and 81. In section 89(1), the words "section 80 and" and in the heading the words "child or". In section 90, the words "child or". In section 91(1)(b), the words "for an adult dependant". In Schedule 4, in Part IV, in column (1), the entries relating to widowed mother's allowance, widowed parent's allowance and child's special allowance and col.(2). In Schedule 5, in paragraph 2(5)(b) the word "80".
Administration Act	In section 3(3), the words "(together with any increase under section 80(5) of the Contributions and Benefits Act)". Section 150(1)(f).

Tax Credits Act 2002 (Commencement No.4, Transitional Provisions and Savings) Order 2003

(SI 2003/962 (C.51)) (AS AMENDED)

The Treasury, in exercise of the powers conferred upon them by sections 61 and 62(2) of the Tax Credits Act 2002, hereby make the following Order:

ARRANGEMENT OF ARTICLES

Schedule 2—Provisions of Sch.6 to the Act coming into force on 8th April 2003

Citation and interpretation

2.9 **1.**—(1) This Order may be cited as the Tax Credits Act 2002 (Commencement No.4, Transitional Provisions and Savings) Order 2003.

(2) In this Order—

"the Act" means the Tax Credits Act 2002;

"the 1999 Act" means the Tax Credits Act 1999; and

"the superseded tax credits" means working families' tax credit and disabled person's tax credit.

Commencement of provisions of the Act

2.10 **2.**—(1) [. . .]

(2) [. . .]

(3) [. . .]

(4) [. . .]

(5) Section 1(3)(d) of the Act (child premia in respect of income support and income-based jobseeker's allowance) shall come into force on [¹31st December 2011].

AMENDMENT

1. Tax Credits Act 2002 (Transitional Provisions) Order 2008 (SI 2008/3151), art.3(2).

GENERAL NOTE

2.11 Section 1(3)(d) is the only major part of the 2002 Act not yet in force. Its introduction has been postponed by a series of provisions, and the latest postponement puts off the introduction until 2012. For a discussion of the problems leading to this postponement see para.1.219 above.

Tax Credits Act 2002 (Transitional Provisions) Order 2005

(SI 2005/773) (AS AMENDED)

The Treasury in exercise of the powers conferred upon them by section 62(2) of the Tax Credits Act 2002 make the following Order:

Citation and interpretation

2.12 **1.** This Order may be cited as the Tax Credits Act 2002 (Transitional Provisions) Order 2005.

2.13 **2.** In this Order—

"the Board" means the Commissioners of Inland Revenue;

"benefit week" has the meaning given in regulation 2(1) of the Income Support Regulations in relation to the child premia in respect of income support and regulation 1(3) of the Jobseeker's Allowance Regulations in relation to the child premia in respect of income based jobseeker's allowance;

"the child premia in respect of income support or income based jobseeker's allowance" means the amounts referred to in section 1(3)(d) of the Tax Credits Act 2002;

"polygamous unit" has the meaning given in the Tax Credits (Polygamous Marriages) Regulations 2003.

Claims and entitlement

3.—(1) A claim for a child tax credit is treated as made by the person specified in article 4 ("the specified person") on the date specified in article 5 ("the specified date") for the period specified in article 6.

2.14

(2) If the specified person is a member of a married couple or an unmarried couple or a polygamous unit, the specified person and the other member of the couple or member or members of polygamous unit are treated as making a joint claim.

(3) The specified person is treated as being responsible for the child or children or qualifying young person or persons to whom his entitlement to the child premia in respect of income support or income based jobseeker's allowance relates.

Specified person

4.—(1) For the purposes of article 3 a specified person is a person who—

2.15

 (a) until the specified date was receiving the child premia in respect of income support or income support jobseeker's allowance, and

 (b) has not made a claim for a child tax credit.

This is subject to paragraph (2).

(2) A person claiming income support in accordance with regulation 6(2) of the Income Support (General) Regulations 1987 or regulation 6(2) of the Income Support (General) Regulations (Northern Ireland) 1987 (lone parent returning to work) is not a specified person.

Specified date

5. For the purposes of this Order the specified date is the day following the date notified to an officer of the Board—

2.16

 (a) by the Department for Work and Pensions if the specified person is claiming in Great Britain, or

 (b) by the Department for Social Development if the specified person is claiming in Northern Ireland,

as the proposed final day of the last benefit week for which the child premia in respect of income support or income based jobseeker's allowance is to be paid to the specified person.

Period of award

6. Notwithstanding section 5(2) of the Tax Credits Act 2002, an award on a claim under article 3 is for the period beginning with the later of—

2.17

 (a) the specified date, and

 (b) the date on which the Board notify the Department for Work and Pensions or the Department for Social Development, as appropriate, of an award of child tax credit, and

ending at the end of the tax year in which that date falls.

Transitional provision

7. Notwithstanding regulation 7 of the Tax Credits (Claims and Notifications) Regulations 2002, a person shall not be entitled to a tax credit in

2.18

respect of any day prior to the day on which he makes a claim for it ("the earlier day") if—

(a) the earlier day falls before [¹31st December 2008], and

on the earlier day the claimant is entitled, or in the case of a joint claim, either of the claimants is entitled, to the child premia in respect of income support or income based jobseeker's allowance.

AMENDMENT

1. Tax Credits Act 2002 (Commencement and Transitional Provisions) Order 2006 (SI 2006/3369 (C.124)), art.4 (December 14, 2006).

Tax Credits Act 2002 (Transitional Provisions) Order 2008

(SI 2008/3151)

The Treasury, in exercise of the powers conferred by section 62(2) of the Tax Credits Act 2002 make the following Order:

Citation

2.19   **1.** This Order may be cited as the Tax Credits Act 2002 (Transitional Provisions) Order 2008.

Deemed claims for tax credits

2.20   **2.**—(1) A claim shall be deemed to be made under section 3(1) of the Tax Credits Act 2002 where—

(a) Her Majesty's Revenue and Customs receive a claim for tax credits from the Department for Work and Pensions;

(b) the claim is in respect of a person whose entitlement to income support is due to end as a result of the Social Security (Lone Parents and Miscellaneous Amendments) Regulations 2008;

(c) the claim complies with regulation 5(2), and contains the information required in regulation 5(3) to (5) of the Tax Credits (Claims and Notifications) Regulations 2002;

(2) The claim shall be deemed to be made by the person in respect of whom it is made.

(3) The claim shall be deemed to be made on the date when it is recorded on a computer system of Her Majesty's Revenue and Customs. This is subject to the effect of Article 3(3).

Amendments to the Tax Credits Act 2002 (Commencement No. 4, Transitional Provisions and Savings) Order 2003

2.21   **3.**—(1) The Tax Credits Act 2002 (Commencement No. 4, Transitional Provisions and Savings) Order 2003 shall be amended as follows:

(2) In Article 2(5) for "31ˢᵗ December 2008" substitute "31ˢᵗ December 2011".

(3) In Article 5(4) for paragraph (a) substitute—

"(a) the earlier day falls before 31st December 2011; and".

Working Tax Credit (Entitlement and Maximum Rate) Regulations 2002

(SI 2002/2005) (AS AMENDED)

Whereas a draft of this instrument, which prescribes the amount in excess of which, by virtue of subsection (2) of section 12 of the Tax Credits Act 2002, charges are not to be taken into account for the purposes of that subsection, and which also contains the first regulations made under sections 11 and 12 of that Act, has been laid before, and approved by resolution of, each House of Parliament:

Now, therefore, the Treasury, in exercise of the powers conferred upon them by sections 10, 11, 12, 65(1) and (7) and 67 of the Tax Credits Act 2002, hereby make the following Regulations:

REGULATIONS

PART 1

GENERAL

2.22

PART II

CONDITIONS OF ENTITLEMENT

BASIC ELEMENT

PART III

MAXIMUM RATE

PART I

GENERAL

Citation, commencement and effect

1. These Regulations may be cited as the Working Tax Credit (Entitlement   **2.23**
and Maximum Rate) Regulations 2002 and shall come into force—
  (a) for the purpose of enabling claims to be made, on 1st August 2002;
  (b) for the purpose of enabling decisions on claims to be made, on
      1st January 2003; and
  (c) for all other purposes, on April 6, 2003;
and shall have effect for the tax year beginning on 6th April 2003 and subsequent tax years.

DEFINITIONS

  "claim"—see TCA 2002, s.3(8).
  "tax year"—see TCA 2002, s.47.

GENERAL NOTE

  These regulations give substance to ss.10 (entitlement) and 11 (maximum rate)   **2.24**
of the TCA 2002. These are the only sections in the Act that apply specifically to
the award and entitlement to working tax credit. Most of the provisions in those
sections are enabling only. These are the regulations giving substance to working
tax credit.

Interpretation

  2.—(1) In these Regulations, except where the context otherwise requ-   **2.25**
ires—
    "the Act" means the Tax Credits Act 2002, and a reference without
       more to a numbered section is a reference to the section of the Act
       bearing that number;
    "the Board" means the Commissioners of Inland Revenue;
    "the Contributions and Benefits Act" means the Social Security Contri-
       butions and Benefits Act 1992;
    "child" has the same meaning as it has in the Child Tax Credit Regu-
       lations 2002;
    "claim" means a claim for working tax credit and "joint claim" and
       "single claim" have the meanings respectively assigned in [1section
       3(8)];
    "claimant" means the person making a claim and, in the case of a joint
       claim, means either of the claimants;
    [6 "contributory employment and support allowance" means a contribu-
       tory allowance under Part 1 of the Welfare Reform Act;]
    [3"couple" has the meaning given by section 3(5A) of the Act;]
    "the determination of the maximum rate" means the determination of
       the maximum rate of working tax credit;
    [1"employed", except in the expression "self-employed" means employed
       under a contract of service or apprenticeship where the earnings under
       the contract are chargeable to income tax as employment income under

Parts II–VII of the Income Tax (Earnings and Pensions) Act 2003 [² otherwise than by reason of Chapter 8 of Part 2 of that Act (deemed employment in respect of arrangements made by intermediaries)];]

[⁴"employment zone" means an area within Great Britain—

(a) subject to a designation for the purposes of the Employment Zones Regulations 2003 by the Secretary of State, or

[⁵(b) listed in the Schedule to the Employment Zones (Allocation to Contractors) Pilot Regulations 2006],

pursuant to section 60 of the Welfare Reform and Pensions Act 1999.]

"employment zone programme" means a programme which is—

(a) established for one or more employment zones; and

(b) designed to assist claimants for a jobseeker's allowance to obtain sustainable employment;

[¹"initial claim" shall be construed in accordance with regulation 9A;]

"local authority" means—

(a) in relation to England, the council of a county or district, a metropolitan district, a London Borough, the Common Council of the City of London or the Council of the Isles of Scilly;

(b) in relation to Wales, the council of a county or county borough; or;

(c) in relation to Scotland, a council constituted under section 2 of the Local Government, etc. (Scotland) Act 1994;

[¹"partner" means a member of a [³. . .] couple making a joint claim;]

"patient" means a person (other than a person who is serving a sentence, imposed by a court, in a prison or youth custody institution or, in Scotland, a young offenders' institution) who is regarded as receiving free in-patient treatment within the meaning of the Social Security (Hospital In-Patients) Regulations 1975;

"period of award" shall be construed in accordance with [¹section 5];

"qualifying young person" means a person who satisfies regulation 5 of the Child Tax Credit Regulations 2002;

"relevant childcare charges" has the meaning given by regulation 14;

[¹. . .]

"self-employed" means engaged in the carrying on of a trade profession or vocation;

"sports award" means an award made by one of the Sports Councils named in section 23(2) of the National Lottery etc. Act 1993 out of sums allocated to it for distribution under that section;

"surrogate child" means a child in respect of whom an order has been made under section 30 of the Human Fertilisation and Embryology Act 1990;

[¹. . .]

"training allowance" means an allowance (whether by way of periodical grants or otherwise) payable—

(a) out of public funds by a Government department or by or on behalf of the Secretary of State, Scottish Enterprise or Highlands and Islands Enterprise or the Department for Employment and Learning ("the relevant paying authority");

(b) to a person in respect of his maintenance or in respect of a member of his family; and

(c) for the period, or part of the period, during which he is following a course of training or instruction—

    (i) provided by, or in pursuance of arrangements made with, the relevant paying authority; or

   (ii) approved by the relevant paying authority in relation to him, but does not include an allowance, paid by a Government department, Northern Ireland department or the Scottish Executive to or in respect of a person by reason of the fact that he is training as a teacher, or is following a course of full-time education, other than under arrangements made under section 2 of the Employment and Training Act 1973, section 2 or 3 of the Disabled Persons (Employment) Act (Northern Ireland) 1945, or section 1(1) of the Employment and Training Act (Northern Ireland) 1950;

[¹"training for work" shall be construed in accordance with regulation 9B;]
"week" means a period of seven days beginning with midnight between Saturday and Sunday.

[⁶ "the Welfare Reform Act" means the Welfare Reform Act 2007.]

(2) For the purposes of these Regulations a person is responsible for a child or qualifying young person if he is treated as being responsible for that child or qualifying young person in accordance with the rules contained in regulation 3 of the Child Tax Credit Regulations 2002.

(3) A reference in these Regulations to an enactment applying to Great Britain but not to Northern Ireland shall, unless the context otherwise requires, include a reference to the corresponding enactment applying in Northern Ireland.

[¹(4) In these Regulations as they apply to an office a reference to being employed includes a reference to being the holder of an office.]

[⁶ (5) For the purpose of these Regulations—

  (a) two or more periods of entitlement to employment and support allowance are linked together if they satisfy the conditions in regulation 145 of the Employment and Support Allowance Regulations 2008; and

  (b) a period of entitlement to employment and support allowance is linked together with a period of entitlement to statutory sick pay if it follows that period within 12 weeks.]

AMENDMENTS

1. Working Tax Credit (Entitlement and Maximum Rate) (Amendment) Regulations 2003 (SI 2003/701), reg.3 (April 6, 2003).

2. Tax Credits (Miscellaneous Amendments No.2) Regulations 2003 (SI 2003/2815), reg.13 (November 26, 2003).

3. Civil Partnership Act 2004 (Tax Credits, etc.) (Consequential Amendments) Order 2005 (SI 2005/2919), art.2(2) (December 5, 2005).

4. Tax Credits (Miscellaneous Amendments) Regulations 2006 (SI 2006/766), reg.20(2) (April 6, 2006).

5. Tax Credits (Miscellaneous Amendments) Regulations 2007 (SI 2007/824), reg.3 (April 6, 2007).

6. Employment and Support Allowance (Consequential Provisions) (No.3) Regulations 2008 (SI 2009/1879), reg.20(2) (October 27, 2008).

DEFINITIONS

See also TCA 2002, s.47. For definitions of terms used in income tax legislation see ITEPA 2003, Sch.1, and the index of definitions in ITA 2007, Sch.4 (not included in this work).

Other elements of working tax credit

2.26   **3.**—(1) For the purposes of determining the maximum rate of working tax credit, in addition to the basic element and the disability element, the following elements are prescribed—

(a) a 30 hour element;
(b) a second adult element;
(c) a lone parent element;
(d) a childcare element;
(e) a severe disability element; and
(f) a 50 Plus element.

(2) It is a condition of entitlement to the other elements of working tax credit that the person making the claim for working tax credit is entitled to the basic element.

(3) If the claim for working tax credit is a joint claim, and both members of the couple satisfy the conditions of entitlement for—

(a) the disability element;
(b) the severe disability element; or
(c) the 50 Plus element,

the award must include two such elements.

DEFINITIONS

"basic element"—see TCA 2002, s.11(4).
"claim"—see reg.2.
"joint claim"—see reg.2.

GENERAL NOTE

2.27   Section 11(2) of the TCA 2002 requires that all awards of working tax credit must contain a common element (known as the basic element—see s.11(4)). Section 11(3) requires that there be an element related to those with disabilities putting them at a disadvantage in getting a job. The list of other elements in s.11(6) is, however, permissive only. This regulation sets out the other elements to which claimants may for the time being be entitled as part of their working tax credit award, save one: the childcare element is not included because it is dealt with separately under s.12 of the TCA 2002.

The structure adopted is to require all claimants to show that they are entitled to the basic element in accordance with reg.4. Unless a claimant establishes that entitlement, he or she does not qualify for working tax credit at all. Once entitlement to the basic element is shown, a claimant may claim any or all of the other elements—subject, of course, to showing additional separate entitlement to each of them.

PART II

CONDITIONS OF ENTITLEMENT

Basic element

Entitlement to basic element of working tax credit: qualifying remunerative work

2.28   **4.**—(1) Subject to the qualification in paragraph (2), a person shall be treated as engaged in qualifying remunerative work if, and only if, he satisfies all of the following conditions.

First condition

The person—   2.29
(a) is working at the date of the claim; or
(b) has an offer of work which he has accepted at the date of the claim
     and the work is expected to commence within 7 days of the making
     of the claim.

In relation to a case falling within sub-paragraph (b) of this condition,
references in the second third and fourth conditions below to work which
the person undertakes are to be construed as references to the work which
the person will undertake when it commences.

In such a case the person is only to be treated as being in qualifying
remunerative work when he begins the work referred to in that subparagraph.

Second condition

The person—   2.30
[¹(a) is aged at least 16 and—
          (i)   undertakes work for not less than 16 hours per week,
          (ii) either he or his partner is responsible for a child or qualifying
                young person, or he has a physical or mental disability which
                puts him at a disadvantage in getting a job and satisfies regula-
                tion 9(1)(c),]
(b) satisfies the conditions in regulation 18, or
(c) is aged at least 25 and undertakes not less than 30 hours work per
     week in any other case.

Third condition

The work which the person undertakes is expected to continue for at   2.31
least 4 weeks after the making of the claim or, in a case falling within sub-
paragraph (b) of the first condition, after the work starts.

Fourth condition

The work is done for payment or in expectation of payment. Paragraphs   2.32
(3) and (4) provide the method of determining the number of hours of
qualifying remunerative work that a person undertakes.

Regulations 5 to 8 apply in relation to periods of absence from work connected with childbirth or adoption, sickness, seasonal absence from work in
relation to which there is a recognised yearly cycle of employment and those
who have a gap between periods of work.

Regulation 9 prescribes the conditions which must be satisfied by, or exist
in relation to, a person so that he is to be treated as having a physical or
mental disability which puts him at a disadvantage in getting a job.

[⁵ A social security benefit is not payment for the purposes of satisfying
this condition.]

(2) A person who would otherwise satisfy the conditions in paragraph
(1) shall not be regarded as engaged in qualifying remunerative work to the
extent that he is—
(a) engaged by a charitable or voluntary organisation, or is a volunteer,
     if the only payment received by him or due to be paid to him is a
     payment by way of expenses which falls to be disregarded under

item 1 in Table 7 in regulation 19 of the Tax Credits (Definition and Calculation of Income) Regulations 2002;

(b) engaged in caring for a person who is not a member of his household but is temporarily residing with him if the only payment made to him for providing that care is disregarded income by virtue of item 3 or 4 in Table 8 in regulation 19 of the Tax Credits (Definition and Calculation of Income) Regulations 2002;

(c) engaged on a scheme for which a training allowance is being paid;

(d) participating in the Intensive Activity Period specified in regulation 75(1)(a)(iv) of the Jobseeker's Allowance Regulations 1996 or the Preparation for Employment Programme specified in regulation 75(1)(a)(v) of the Jobseeker's Allowance Regulations (Northern Ireland) 1996;

(e) engaged in an activity in respect of which—

    (i) a sports award has been made, or is to be made, to him, and

    (ii) no other payment is made, or is expected to be made, to him; or

(f) participating in an employment zone programme, that is to say a programme established for one or more areas designated pursuant to section 60 of the Welfare Reform and Pensions Act 1999, and subject to the [³ Employment Zones 2003 and the Employment Zones (Allocation to Contractors) Pilot Regulations 2005] if he receives no payments under that programme other than—

    (i) discretionary payments disregarded in the calculation of a claimant's income under item 6(b) in [¹Table 6] in regulation 19 of the Tax Credits (Definition and Calculation of Income) Regulations 2002; or

    (ii) training premiums.

[⁴(g) a person who—

    (i) is serving a custodial sentence or has been remanded in custody awaiting trial or sentence, and

    (ii) is engaged in work (whether inside or outside a prison) while he is serving the sentence or remanded in custody.]

[²This is subject to the following qualification.

(2A) Neither sub-paragraph (c) nor sub-paragraph (d) of paragraph (2) applies if—

(a) in a case falling within sub-paragraph (c), the training allowance, or

(b) in a case falling within sub-paragraph (d), any payment made by the Secretary of State, or, in Northern Ireland, by the Department for Social Development, in connection with the Intensive Activity Period,

is chargeable to income tax as the profits of a trade, profession or vocation.]

(3) The number of hours for which a person undertakes qualifying remunerative work is—

(a) in the case of an apprentice, employee or officeholder, the number of hours of such work which he normally performs—

    (i) under the contract of service or of apprenticeship under which he is employed, or

    (ii) in the office in which he is employed;

(b) in the case of an agency worker, the number of hours in respect of which remuneration is normally paid to him by an employment agency with whom he has a contract of employment; or

(c) in the case of a person who is self-employed, the number of hours he normally performs for payment or in expectation of payment.

This is subject to the following qualification.

(4) In reckoning the number of hours of qualifying remunerative work which a person normally undertakes—

(a) any period of customary or paid holiday; and

(b) any time allowed for meals or refreshment, unless the person is, or expects to be paid earnings in respect of that time, shall be disregarded.

[[1](5) In reckoning the number of hours of qualifying remunerative work which a person normally undertakes, any time allowed for visits to a hospital, clinic or other establishment for the purpose only of treating or monitoring the person's disability shall be included; but only if the person is, or expects to be, paid in respect of that time.]

AMENDMENTS

1. Working Tax Credit (Entitlement and Maximum Rate) (Amendment) Regulations 2003 (SI 2003/701), reg.4 (April 6, 2003).

2. Tax Credits (Miscellaneous Amendments) Regulations 2004 (SI 2004/762), reg.5 (April 6, 2004).

3. Tax Credits (Miscellaneous Amendments) Regulations 2006 (SI 2006/766), reg.20(3) (April 6, 2006).

4. Tax Credits (Miscellaneous Amendments) Regulations 2007 (SI 2007/824), reg.4 (April 6, 2007).

5. Tax Credits (Miscellaneous Amendments) Regulations 2009 (SI 2009/697), reg.3 (April 6, 2009).

DEFINITIONS

"agency worker"—see ITEPA 2003, s.44.
"child"—see reg.2.
"claim"—see reg.2.
"employed"—see reg.2.
"Employment Zone programme"—see reg.2.
"office-holder"—see ITEPA 2003, s.5.
"partner"—see reg.2.
"qualifying young person"—see reg.2.
"responsible for a child"—see TCA 2002, s.48.
"self-employed"—see reg.2.
"sports award"—see reg.2.
"training allowance"—see reg.2.
"week"—see reg.2.

GENERAL NOTE

The structure of this key regulation is somewhat misleading. It suggests that there are four conditions for qualifying for entitlement to the basic element of working tax credit. This somewhat disguises the fact that there are four different and alternative bases for claiming working tax credit, all of which are wrapped up together in the "second condition", while the other three conditions are common to all groups of claimant. **2.33**

First condition

Section 10(1) requires that all claimants for working tax credit must be in "qualifying remunerative work". This condition defines the scope of being "in" work. A claimant cannot receive working tax credit until he or she has started work (or, **2.34** in the case of joint claimants or members of a polygamous unit, one of them has started work), or the work is to start within seven days.

Second condition

2.35   As noted above, this creates four alternative conditions, or routes to entitlement:

Route 1 is for a claimant working 16 or more hours a week and who, or whose partner, is responsible for a child or qualifying young person. The requirement of responsibility for a child or qualifying young person is the same test as for child tax credit purposes, and the regulations adopt the relevant definitions from the Child Tax Credit Regulations. In practical terms, they are the same tests as those for claiming child benefit for a child. The 16-hour test and the reference to remunerative work reflect the similar test in reg.5 of the Income Support (General) Regulations 1987 (SI 1987/1967).

Route 2 is for a disabled claimant suffering prejudice in the job market. The full conditions for this route are in reg.9. It again uses the 16-hour test.

Route 3 is for those over 50 who would, before these tax credits were introduced, have been entitled to a grant from the "New Deal 50 Plus" scheme of the former Department for Education and Employment. The conditions are set out in reg.18.

Route 4 is the safety net basis of claim for anyone over 25 who is working full time (defined as 30 hours a week) but receiving only minimal earnings. The assumption behind working tax credit is that all employees are receiving the national minimum wage (and it is the task of HMRC to enforce the national minimum wage legislation). But this will not take a claimant who is working substantially less than the national maximum working week of 48 hours above the income threshold for working tax credit. And there will be many self-employed (for example, subsistence farmers) who will meet the 30-hour work test but also have an income below the working tax credit threshold. This route, like Route 3 to the working tax credit, is not a social security benefit of any kind. It is a subsidy to the low paid without reference to any social circumstances, and its effect is, as noted, to link with the national minimum wage to provide a national minimum take-home pay for all workers, whether employed or self-employed, over 25.

Third condition

2.36   This imposes a minimum level of continuity before working tax credit can be claimed. It is separate from, but to be read with, the 16 and 30-hour requirements of the second condition. In other words, it would seem that it has in cases of doubt to be shown that the work will be at a level of 16 or 30 hours a week for those four weeks. That will be a question of fact in all cases. The self-employed may have to show that they are, in that sense, "ordinarily self employed", which is the test for payment of Class 2 NI contributions. In the modern context of flexible employment and allegedly zero-hours contracts, close attention may have to be paid not only to the terms of agreement between the two parties to the work relationship but also to whether there is "an irreducible minimum of obligation on each side to create a contract of service": Stephenson L.J. in *Nethermere (St Neots) Ltd v Gardiner* [1984] I.C.R. 612, CA. If there is, the question is then whether on the facts it is shown that it will (or, at the end of the year, did) last for four weeks at the required level. But there is a possible practical problem of timing for a claimant in this sort of work because of the interaction of this requirement with the terms of the first condition—requiring that the work start within seven days of the offer of work—and the backdating rule that prevents a claim being made more than three months after entitlement starts.

Fourth condition

2.37   This echoes the well known test from income support (reg.5 of the Income Support (General) Regulations 1987 (SI 1987/1967)). The test is that the work is done either for payment or in the expectation of it. There is considerable case law from the Courts and Commissioners on whether work is, in this sense, remunerative. The same test will apply to tax credits also. For the question whether work is remunerative, see in particular *R(IS) 22/95* and the decision of the Court of Appeal in *Chief Adjudication Officer v Ellis* (reported as the appendix to that decision). In *R(FIS) 1/86* it was established that the remuneration did not come from the work. That may cause other problems for tax credits, as it may not be clear whether money received in this way from work is "employment income". However, the courts have found, for example, that tips paid to a taxi driver are earnings from the driver's employment even though paid by third parties: see *Shilton v Wilmshurst* [1991] S.T.C. 88, HL. But the question whether the work is remunerative, and the question of the level of earnings from the work, are for separate determination.

Para. (2)

This paragraph lists seven specific activities that are excepted from "work" for working tax credit purposes. The addition of condition (g) in 2007 avoids claims that arose in individual cases from prisoners working in the community on day release. 2.38

The number of hours worked

Paragraphs (3)–(5), together with regs 5–8, help define the number of hours worked by a claimant or partner. Subject to the specific provisions, it is essentially a question of fact to be determined over the claim period which will (unlike for the previous benefits replaced by working tax credit) normally be a full year. The practical approach of *R(FC) 1/92* was to look at the hours actually worked, rather than the contractual requirements. The wording of this form of the rule would suggest that this is the proper approach to be taken. 2.39

Paragraph (3) provides the starting point for deciding the number of hours, but each category of work is tested against what is "normal". The main previous test was by reference to the hours worked in the week of claim, or either of the two previous weeks, or the following week, or the week next following any current holiday. Anyone meeting those tests was then assumed to be "normally" employed at the relevant level. This makes it clearer that the issue is one of fact, and is for most claimants a significant simplification of the rules. Paragraph (4) repeats the previous disregard of paid holidays and unpaid breaks, and para. (5) extends this to allow the inclusion of paid medical visits.

In *CTC/2103/2006*, a deputy Commissioner decided that it was not correct to calculate the number of hours worked in a fluctuating situation by averaging hours across a month from a monthly pay slip. There was also no requirement in the legislation that 16 hours be worked every week. There was no set, or hard and fast, rule for deciding the number of hours worked. It is a question of fact in each case. However, it is one that causes repeated problems in administering tax credits. For this reason claimants are now required to notify HMRC within one month if their work hours change so that they stop working for 30, or 16, hours a week, as the case may be. See para. 2.307 below. It will not always be easy to establish when that duty arises in cases of uncertainty such as that in *CTC/2103/2006*. But reg. 7D below will provide a one-month period that deals with most cases.

[¹ Time off in connection with [²childbirth] and adoption]

5.—(1) This regulation applies for any period during which a person— 2.40
(a) is paid maternity allowance,
(b) is paid statutory maternity pay,
(c) is absent from work during an ordinary maternity leave period under section 71 of the Employment Rights Act 1996 or Article 103 of the Employment Rights (Northern Ireland) Order 1996;

[³(ca) is absent from work during the first 13 weeks of an additional maternity leave period under section 73 of the Employment Rights Act 1996 or article 105 of the Employment Rights (Northern Ireland) Order 1996,]

(d) is paid statutory paternity pay,

(e) is absent from work during a paternity leave period under s.80A of the Employment Rights Act 1996 or Article 112A of the Employment Rights (Northern Ireland) Order 1996,

(f) is paid statutory adoption pay, [³. . .]

(g) is absent from work during an ordinary adoption leave period under section 75A of the Employment Rights Act 1996 or Article 107A of the Employment Rights (Northern Ireland) Order 1996. [³,or

(ga) is absent from work during the first 13 weeks of an additional adoption leave period under section 75B of the Employment Rights Act 1996 or article 107B of the Employment Rights (Northern Ireland) Order 1996.]

(2) For the purposes of the conditions in regulation 4(1), the person is treated as being engaged in qualifying remunerative work during the period. This is subject to paragraph (3).

(3) The person must have been engaged in qualifying remunerative work immediately before the beginning of the period.

(4) A person who is self-employed is treated as engaged in qualifying remunerative work for the requisite number of hours during any period for which paragraph (1) would have applied in his case but for the fact that the work he performed in the week immediately before the period began, although done for payment or in the expectation of payment, was not performed under a contract of service or apprenticeship.]

AMENDMENTS

1. Working Tax Credit (Entitlement and Maximum Rate) (Amendment) Regulations 2003 (SI 2003/701), reg.5 (April 6, 2003).

2. Tax Credits (Miscellaneous Amendments) Regulations 2004 (SI 2004/762), reg.6 (April 6, 2004).

3. Tax Credits (Miscellaneous Amendments) Regulations 2007 (SI 2007/824), reg.5 (April 6, 2007).

DEFINITIONS

"qualifying remunerative employment"—see reg.4.
"self-employed"—see reg.2.
"week"—see reg.2.

GENERAL NOTE

2.41   This regulation was rewritten to take account of the extended rights of mothers and fathers, including adoptive parents, to parental leave as from 2003. It is designed to stop an award of working tax credit being terminated by such leave. See also reg.5A.

[¹ **Time off in connection with childbirth and placement for adoption: further provisions**

2.42   **5A.**—(1) This regulation applies to a person for any period—

(a) which falls within a period to which regulation 5 applies; and

(b) which follows the birth or the placement for adoption of the child in connection with whose birth or placement entitlement to the allowance, pay or leave mentioned in regulation 5(1) arises.

(2) A person who was undertaking qualifying remunerative work for at least 16 hours per week, immediately before the beginning of a period to which regulation 5 applies, shall be treated as satisfying the requirements of regulation 4(1) during the period mentioned in paragraph (1) above.

(3) Paragraph (4) of regulation 5 applies for the purpose of this regulation as it applies for the purpose of that regulation.]

AMENDMENT

1. Tax Credits (Miscellaneous Amendments) Regulations 2004 (SI 2004/762), reg.7 (April 6, 2004).

GENERAL NOTE

This regulation reduces the number of hours, for which a person must have been engaged in qualifying remunerative work immediately before beginning a period of statutory leave in connection with the birth or placement for adoption of a child, in order to qualify for tax credit for so much of that period as follows the birth or placement for adoption of the relevant child.

2.43

[¹Periods of illness [², incapacity for work or limited capability for work]

6.—(1) This regulation applies for any period during which a person—

2.44

(a) is paid statutory sick pay;

(b) is paid short-term incapacity benefit at the lower rate under sections 30A–30E of the Contributions and Benefits Act;

(c) is paid income support on the grounds of incapacity for work under paragraphs 7 and 14 of Schedule 1B to the Income Support (General) Regulations 1987,

[²(cc) is paid an employment and support allowance under Part 1 of the Welfare Reform Act, or]

(d) receives national insurance credits on the grounds of incapacity for work [² or limited capability for work] under reg.8B of the Social Security (Credits) Regulations 1975.

(2) For the purposes of the conditions in regulation 4(1), the person is treated as being engaged in qualifying remunerative work during the period.

This is subject to paragraphs (3) and (4).

(3) The person must have been engaged in qualifying remunerative work immediately before the beginning of the period.

(4) If the person is paid income support as specified in paragraph (1) (c) [² or employment and support allowance as specified in paragraph (1) (cc)] or receives national insurance credits as specified in paragraph (1)(d) he is treated as being engaged in qualifying remunerative work for a period of 28 weeks only, beginning with the day on which he is first paid income support [² or employment and support allowance] or receives national insurance credits (as the case may be).

(5) A person who is self-employed is treated as engaged in qualifying remunerative work for the requisite number of hours during any period for which paragraph (1) would have applied in his case but for the fact that

the work he performed in the week immediately before the period began, although done for payment or in the expectation of payment, was not performed under a contract of service or apprenticeship.]

AMENDMENTS

1. Working Tax Credit (Entitlement and Maximum Rate) (Amendment) Regulations 2003 (SI 2003/701), reg.6 (April 6, 2003).
2. Employment and Support Allowance (Consequential Provisions) (No.3) Regulations 2008 (SI 2009/1879), reg.20(3) (October 27, 2008).

DEFINITIONS

"incapacity for work"—see Social Security Contributions and Benefits Act 1992, s.171A.
"qualifying remunerative employment"—see reg.4.
"self-employed"—see reg.2.
"week"—see reg.2.

GENERAL NOTE

2.45   This paragraph allows continuity of a claim for working tax credit into a period of sickness or disability, provided that one of the alternative forms of benefit is received for the period. Paragraph 7 of Sch.1B to the Income Support (General) Regulations 1987 (SI 1987/1967) deal with those treated as incapable of work under the SSCBA 1992 and those entitled to statutory sick pay. Paragraph 14 deals with pregnant women who are incapable of work by reason of the pregnancy or are within 11 weeks before the expected date of confinement or seven weeks after the pregnancy ends. There is a 28-week limit on the overlap between working tax credit and either income support or contribution credits.

Term time and other seasonal workers

2.46   7.—(1) For the purposes of the conditions in regulation 4(1), paragraph (2) applies if a person—
    (a) works at a school, other educational establishment or other place of employment;
    (b) there is a recognisable cycle to his employment there; and
    (c) the length of that recognisable cycle is one year and includes periods of school holidays or similar vacations during which he does not work.
    (2) If this paragraph applies, the periods mentioned in paragraph (1)(c) are disregarded in determining whether the conditions in regulation 4(1) are satisfied.

GENERAL NOTE

2.47   This regulation deals with cyclical and "term time only" employment. To claim working tax credit the claimant must establish normal work of 16 hours a week. The income test is by reference to actual earnings over the entire year. As a consequence, this rule will operate to the advantage of those such as supply teachers, school learning support assistants and seasonal staff. They will continue to get their working tax credit throughout the year if the conditions of this regulation are met, while their earnings will be established without reference to assumed earnings during assumed hours of work. For example, someone working 20 hours a week for 40 weeks a year at, say, £125 a week, will meet the hours test for every week of the year if the conditions of this regulation are met, but will earn from that source only £5,000 so will be below the minimum figure of earnings for claiming working tax credit in full. This means also a continuing entitlement to claim childcare charges when appropriate. In addition, because child tax credit is now separated from working tax credit and will be separated from all other benefits, there will be no adverse effect on any child tax credit entitlement from fluctuating work patterns.

[¹Strike periods

7A.—(1) This regulation applies for any period during which a person is on strike.

(2) For the purposes of the conditions in regulation 4(1), the person is treated as being engaged in qualifying remunerative work during the period.

This is subject to paragraph (3).

(3) The person—

(a) must have been engaged in qualifying remunerative work immediately before the beginning of the period, and

(b) must not be on strike for longer than a period of 10 consecutive days on which he should have been working.]

2.48

AMENDMENT

1. Working Tax Credit (Entitlement and Maximum Rate) (Amendment) Regulations 2003 (SI 2003/701), reg.7 (April 6, 2003).

DEFINITION

"qualifying remunerative employment"—see reg.4.

GENERAL NOTE

This rule is a relaxation from the strict set of rules preventing workers benefiting during a strike. The effect of this regulation is to stop a break in entitlement occurring for a strike of 10 consecutive days or less.

2.49

[¹Persons suspended from work

7B.—(1) This regulation applies for any period during which a person is suspended from work while complaints or allegations against him are investigated.

(2) For the purposes of the conditions in regulation 4(1), the person is treated as being engaged in qualifying remunerative work during the period.

This is subject to paragraph (3).

(3) The person must have been engaged in qualifying remunerative work immediately before the beginning of the period.]

2.50

AMENDMENT

1. Working Tax Credit (Entitlement and Maximum Rate) (Amendment) Regulations 2003 (SI 2003/701), reg.7 (April 6, 2003).

DEFINITIONS

"qualifying remunerative employment"—see reg.4.

GENERAL NOTE

This deals with a practical problem similar in part to that behind reg.7A. However, in the case of someone is suspended from work, for example while a complaint is investigated, the period of suspension will often not be known.

2.51

[¹Pay in lieu of notice

2.52   **7C.**—(1) This regulation applies if a person stops work and receives pay in lieu of notice.

(2) For the purposes of the conditions in regulation 4(1), the person shall not be treated as being engaged in qualifying remunerative work during the period for which he receives the pay.]

[² (3) This regulation is subject to regulation 7D.]

AMENDMENTS

1. Working Tax Credit (Entitlement and Maximum Rate) (Amendment) Regulations 2003 (SI 2003/701), reg.7 (April 6, 2003).

2. Working Tax Credit (Entitlement and Maximum Rate) (Amendment) Regulations 2007 (SI 2007/968), reg.2 (April 6, 2007).

DEFINITION

"qualifying remunerative employment"—see reg.4.

GENERAL NOTE

2.53   This deals in a pragmatic way with the problem caused when someone stops work before a period of notice has ended, but who receives pay in lieu of notice (often abbreviated to PILON). This regulation excludes the claimant from entitlement to working tax credit. But a problem may arise if the employee does not find other work during that period (and he or she may be prevented from doing so). The provisions about calculating earnings from employment for jobseeker's allowance purposes allow sums to be spread over the period for which they are paid, unless they are excluded from earnings for that purpose, and so may exclude entitlement to JSA. See regs 94 and 98 of the Jobseeker's Allowance Regulations 1996 (SI 1996/207) and the notes to them in Vol.II of this work. So the individual may be excluded from both working tax credit and jobseeker's allowance.

[¹Ceasing to undertake work or working for less than 16 hours per week

2.54   **7D.**—(1) This regulation applies for the four-week period immediately after—

(a) a person who has been undertaking qualifying remunerative work for not less than 16 hours per week ceases to work or starts to work less than 16 hours per week, or

(b) a person who has been undertaking qualifying remunerative work for not less than 30 hours per week ceases to work or starts to work less than 16 hours per week.

(2) For the purposes of the conditions in regulation 4(1), the person is treated as being engaged in qualifying remunerative work during that period.

This is subject to paragraph (3).

(3) The person must have been engaged in qualifying remunerative work immediately before the beginning of that period.]

AMENDMENT

2.55   1. Working Tax Credit (Entitlement and Maximum Rate) (Amendment) Regulations 2007 (SI 2007/968, reg.2(3) (April 6, 2007).

GENERAL NOTE

This regulation provides for a four week run-on of WTC to those claimants whose hours fall below 16 hours a week. Where entitled, claimants will be eligible to claim income support or JSA whilst in receipt of WTC for the four week period (although the WTC will be treated as income for assessing entitlement to those benefits). The purpose of this rule is to reduce overpayments of tax credits and to ease the transition from tax credits to benefits. It is consistent with the shift from April 2007 of a mandatory reporting requirement on tax credits claimants to inform HMRC within a month of ceasing work.

Note that where the four week run-on applies, the claimant's child remains entitled to free school lunches by virtue of s.512ZB of the Education Act 1996 (see Education (Free School Lunches) (Working Tax Credit) (England) Order 2009 (SI 2009/830), art.2).

Gaps between jobs

8. For the purposes of the conditions in regulation 4(1), a person shall be treated as being engaged in qualifying remunerative work for the requisite number of hours if he has been so engaged within the past seven days. | 2.56

DEFINITION

"qualifying remunerative employment"—see reg. 4. | 2.57

GENERAL NOTE

Regulation 4 allows someone to make a claim for working tax credit if he or she has an offer of a job starting within seven days of the claim (see the first condition in reg.4). However, if there is a gap of not more than that period between jobs, this regulation allows the gap to be bridged so as to avoid the need to make a new claim. This is also consistent with the provisions of the Tax Credits (Claims and Notifications) Regulations 2002 (SI 2002/2014), reg.10, allowing claims for working tax credit seven days in advance.

Disability element

[¹Disability element and workers who are to be treated as at a disadvantage in getting a job

9.—(1) The determination of the maximum rate must include the disability element if the claimant, or, in the case of a joint claim, one of the claimants— | 2.58

    (a) undertakes qualifying remunerative work for at least 16 hours per week;

    (b) has any of the disabilities listed in Part I of Schedule 1, or in the case of an initial claim, satisfies the conditions in Part II of Schedule 1; and

    (c) is a person who satisfies any of Cases A to G on a day for which the maximum rate is determined in accordance with these Regulations.

[⁴ (2) Case A is where the person has, for at least one day in the preceding 182 days ("the qualifying day"), been in receipt of—

    (a) higher rate short-term incapacity benefit;

    (b) long-term incapacity benefit;

    (c) severe disablement allowance; or

(d) employment and support allowance where entitlement to employment and support allowance or statutory sick pay has existed for a
period of 28 weeks immediately preceding the qualifying day comprising one continuous period or two or more periods which are
linked together.]

(3) Case B is where, for at least one day in the preceding 182 days, the
person has been a person [² for whom at least one of the following benefits
has been payable and for whom the applicable amount] included a higher
pensioner or disability premium [²in respect of him] determined—

(a) in the case of income support, in accordance with [² paragraphs
10(1)(b) or (2)(b) or 11, and where applicable 12,] of Part III of
Schedule 2 to the Income Support (General) Regulations 1987;

(b) in the case of income-based jobseeker's allowance, in accordance
with [² paragraphs 12(1)(a), or (b)(ii), or (c), or 13, and where
applicable 14 of Part 3 of] Schedule 1 to the Jobseeker's Allowance
Regulations 1996;

(c) in the case of housing benefit, in accordance with [² [³paragraphs
11(1)(b) or 11(2)(b) or 12, and where applicable, 13 of Part 3
Schedule 3 of the Housing Benefit Regulations 2006];

(d) in the case of Council Tax Benefit, in accordance with [² [³paragraphs
11(1)(b) or 11(2)(b) or 12, and where applicable, 13 of Part 3 of
Schedule 1 of the Council Tax Benefit Regulations 2006].

For the purposes of this Case "the applicable amount" has the meaning
given by section 135 of the Contributions and Benefits Act.

(4) Case C is where the person is a person to whom at least one of the
following is payable—

(a) a disability living allowance;

(b) an attendance allowance;

(c) a mobility supplement or a constant attendance allowance which is
paid, in either case, in conjunction with a war pension or industrial
injuries disablement benefit.

(5) Case D is where the person has an invalid carriage or other vehicle
provided under—

(a) section 5(2)(a) of, and Schedule 2 to, the National Health Service
Act 1977,

(b) section 46 of the National Health Service (Scotland) Act 1978; or

(c) Article 30(1) of the Health and Personal Social Services (Northern
Ireland) Order 1972.

(6) Case E is where the person—

[⁴ (a) has received—

(i) on account of his incapacity for work, statutory sick pay, occupational sick pay, short-term incapacity benefit payable at the
lower rate or income support, for a period of 140 qualifying
days, or has been credited with Class 1 or Class 2 contributions
under the Contributions and Benefits Act for a period of 20
weeks on account of incapacity for work, and where the last of
those days or weeks (as the case may be) fell within the preceding 56 days; or

(ii) on account of his having limited capability for work, an employment and support allowance for a period of 140 qualifying days,
or has been credited with Class 1 or Class 2 contributions under
the Contributions and Benefits Act for a period of 20 weeks on

account of having limited capability for work, and where the last of those days or weeks (as the case may be) fell within the preceding 56 days;]
  (b) has a disability which is likely to last for at least six months, or for the rest of his life if his death is expected within that time; and
  (c) has gross earnings which are less than they were before the disability began by at least the greater of 20 per cent and £15 per week.

For the purpose of this Case "qualifying days" are days which form part of a single period of incapacity for work within the meaning of Part XI of the Contributions and Benefits Act [⁴ or a period of limited capability for work within the meaning of regulation 2(1) of the Employment and Support Allowance Regulations 2008].

  (7) Case F is where the person—
  (a) has undertaken training for work for at least one day in the preceding 56 days; and
[⁴ (b) has, within 56 days before the first day of that period of training for work, received—
      (i) higher rate short-term incapacity benefit;
      (ii) long-term incapacity benefit;
      (iii) severe disablement allowance; or
      (iv) contributory employment and support allowance where entitlement to that allowance or statutory sick pay has existed for a period of 28 weeks comprising one continuous period or two or more periods which are linked together provided that, if the person received statutory sick pay, the person satisfied the first and second contribution conditions set out in paragraphs 1 and 2 of Schedule 1 to the Welfare Reform Act.]

  (8) Case G is where the person was entitled, [² for at least one day in the preceding 56 days], to the disability element of working tax credit or to disabled person's tax credit by virtue of his having satisfied the requirements of Case A, B, E or F at some earlier time.

For the purposes of this Case a person is treated as having an entitlement to the disability element of working tax credit if that element is taken into account in determining the rate at which the person is entitled to a tax credit.

  (9) For the purposes of the Act, a person who satisfies paragraph (1)(b) is to be treated as having a physical or mental disability which puts him at a disadvantage in getting a job.]

AMENDMENTS

  1. Working Tax Credit (Entitlement and Maximum Rate) (Amendment) Regulations 2003 (SI 2003/701), reg.8 (April 6, 2003).
  2. Tax Credits (Miscellaneous Amendments No.2) Regulations 2003 (SI 2003/2815), reg.14 (November 26, 2003).
  3. Housing Benefit and Council Tax Benefit (Consequential Provisions) Regulations 2006 (SI 2006/217), reg.22(2) (March 6, 2006).
  4. Employment and Support Allowance (Consequential Provisions) (No.3) Regulations 2008 (SI 2009/1879), reg.20(4) (October 27, 2008).

DEFINITIONS

  "claim"—see reg.2.
  "initial claim"—see reg.9A.
  "joint claim"—see reg.2.

"qualifying remunerative employment"—see reg.4.
"training for work"—see reg.9B.
"week"—see reg.2.

GENERAL NOTE

2.59   This regulation, read with Schedule 1, provides the tests for claiming working tax credit by Route 2, the route for those with disabilities. It imposes three separate sets of conditions, all of which must be met to meet the second condition in reg.4 of these Regulations. The first of the three conditions is the requirement that the claimant work 16 or more hours a week in qualifying remunerative work. This restates one of the requirements of the second condition, but with the specific addition of the reference to "qualifying remunerative" work. The other two conditions may be termed the "disability conditions".

In *CTC/643/2005* a Commissioner decided that entitlement under reg.9(1) arises only during the period when a claimant is also entitled under one of the cases A to G. This follows from the reference in reg.9(1)(c) to the claimant satisfying any of Cases A to G "on a day for which the maximum rate is determined . . .". A claimant could not claim the disability element throughout a year unless he or she met the requirements of one of the cases throughout the year.

In *CSTC/76/2006* the Commissioner considered how the conditions are to be applied to joint claimants. She confirmed the view of HMRC that all the disablement conditions are to be met by the same individual and that individual must also undertake work for at least 16 hours a week. She rejected an attempt to argue a claim under this regulation where one of the joint claimants worked to the required extent and the other was disabled. This reflects the origin of this provision in the former disabled person's tax credit and disability working allowance. It is also consistent with the entitlement of a working partner to claim carer's allowance if caring for a disabled partner to the required level.

First disability condition

2.60   To come within this condition, the claimant must have one or more of the disabilities listed in Pt 1 of Sch.1 to these Regulations (see below). Paragraph (5) emphasises that a person meeting this condition is to be treated as being put at a disadvantage by reason of the disability.

Second disability condition

2.61   To come within this condition, the claimant must meet the conditions of one or more of seven separate "cases" labelled Case A to Case G. Briefly these link with other benefits or activities as follows:

Case A: entitlement to long-term incapacity benefit, the higher rate of short-term incapacity benefit, severe disablement allowance or employment and support allowance;

Case B: entitlement to a higher pensioner or disability premium of income support, income-based jobseeker's allowance, housing benefit and/or council tax benefit;

Case C: entitlement to disability living allowance, attendance allowance, mobility supplement or constant attendance allowance;

Case D: membership of the Motability scheme;

Case E: entitlement to occupational or statutory sick pay, short-term incapacity benefit, income support, employment and support allowance or "disability credits"; a continuing disability; and earnings that have reduced since the disability started by 20 per cent or £15 a week;

Case F: training for work linked with payment of the benefits in Case A;

Case G: immediate previous entitlement to the disability element ofWTC or DPTC under Cases A, B, E or F.

There are special rules that apply to initial claims, noted under reg.9A below.

[¹Initial claims

9A.—(1) In regulation 9(1)(b) an "initial claim" means a claim which— 2.62
- (a) is made for the disability element of working tax credit, and
- (b) relates to a person who has not had an entitlement to that element or to disabled person's tax credit during the two years immediately preceding the making of the claim.

(2) In paragraph (1) any reference to the making of a claim includes the giving of notification, in accordance with regulation 20 of the Tax Credits (Claims and Notifications) Regulations 2002, of a change of circumstances falling within that regulation.

(3) For the purposes of paragraph (1)(b), a person is treated as having an entitlement to the disability element of working tax credit if, by virtue of the person being a person who satisfies regulation 9, that element is taken into account in determining the rate at which the person is entitled to a tax credit.]

AMENDMENT

1. Working Tax Credit (Entitlement and Maximum Rate) (Amendment) Regulations 2003 (SI 2003/701), reg.8 (April 6, 2003).

DEFINITIONS

"claim"—see reg.2.
"claimant"—see reg.2.
"disability element"—see reg.9.

GENERAL NOTE

This regulation makes clear that an "initial claim" for the purposes of reg.9 is a 2.63
first claim involving disability, or a notification that may involve the addition of a disability element to an award already made on other grounds. This clarifies the scope of reg.9(1), which extends the test of disability under the second disability condition for a first claim. An initial claim will have an extended relevance for working tax credit as compared with its predecessors as the claim will, in normal course of events, last for the balance of the tax year from the effective date of claim.

[¹Training for work, etc.

9B.—(1) In [²regulation 9], "training for work" means training for work 2.64
received—
- (a) in pursuance of arrangements made under—
  - (i) section 2(1) of the Employment and Training Act 1973,
  - (ii) section 2(3) of the Enterprise and New Towns (Scotland) Act 1990, or
  - (iii) section 1(1) of the Employment and Training Act 1950, or
- (b) on a course whose primary purpose is the teaching of occupational or vocational skills, and which the person attends for 16 hours or more a week.

(2) For the purposes of regulation 9(7), a period of training for work means a series of consecutive days of training for work, there being disregarded any day specified in paragraph (3).

(3) Those days are any day on which the claimant was—

(a) on holiday;

(b) attending court as a justice of the peace, a party to any proceedings, a witness or a juror;

(c) suffering from some disease or bodily or mental disablement as a result of which he was unable to attend training for work, or his attendance would have put at risk the health of other persons;

(d) unable to participate in training for work because—

   (i) he was looking after a child because the person who usually looked after that child was unable to do so;

   (ii) he was looking after a member of his family who was ill;

   (iii) he was required to deal with some domestic emergency; or

   (iv) he was arranging or attending the funeral of his partner or a relative; or

(e) authorised by the training provider to be absent from training for work.

(4) For the purposes of paragraph (3)(d)(iv) "relative" means close relative, grandparent, grandchild, uncle, aunt, nephew or niece; and in this paragraph "close relative" means parent, parent-in-law, son, son-in-law, daughter, daughter-in-law, step-parent, step-son, step-daughter, brother, sister, or the spouse of any of the preceding persons or, if that person is one of an unmarried couple, the other member of that couple.]

AMENDMENTS

1. Working Tax Credit (Entitlement and Maximum Rate) (Amendment) Regulations 2003 (SI 2003/701), reg.8 (April 6, 2003).

2. Tax Credits (Miscellaneous Amendments) Regulations 2004 (SI 2004/762), reg.8 (April 6, 2004).

DEFINITIONS

"claim"—see reg.2.
"claimant"—see reg.2.
"week"—see reg.2.

GENERAL NOTE

2.65   This definition is necessary to clarify the scope of Case F in reg.9(7).

30 hour element

30 hour element

2.66   **10.**—(1) The determination of the maximum rate must include a 30 hour element if the claimant, or in the case of a joint claim, at least one of the claimants, is engaged in qualifying remunerative work for at least 30 hours per week.

(2) The determination of the maximum rate must also include the 30-hour element if—

(a) the claim is a joint claim,

(b) at least one of the claimants is responsible for one or more children or qualifying young people,

(c) the aggregate number of hours for which the couple engage in qualifying remunerative work is at least 30 hours per week, and

(d) at least one member of the couple engages in qualifying remunerative work for at least 16 hours per week.

[[1](3) For the purposes of determining whether the condition in paragraph (2)(c) is met, the words "for not less than 16 hours per week" in paragraph (a) of the second condition in regulation 4(1) are omitted.]

AMENDMENT

1. Working Tax Credit (Entitlement and Maximum Rate) (Amendment) Regulations 2003 (SI 2003/701), reg.9 (April 6, 2003).

DEFINITION

"child"—see reg.2.
"claim"—see reg.2.
"claimant"—see reg.2.
"couple"—see reg.2.
"joint claim"—see TCA 2002, s.3.
"qualifying remunerative work"—see reg.4.
"qualifying young person"—see reg.2.
"responsible"—see TCA 2002, s.48.
"week"—see reg.2.

GENERAL NOTE

An additional element of £775 a year is payable if the claimant or couple work 30 hours a week. Paragraphs (1) and (2) together ensure that the total of 30 hours can be worked by either of the couple or by both together if one or both of them are responsible for a child or qualifying young person. Paragraph (3) deals with a drafting problem in applying the second condition in reg.4 for establishing that a claimant is engaged in qualifying remunerative work to both members of a couple jointly working 30 hours a week but where only one is working over 16 hours.

2.67

Second adult element

[[1]**Second adult element**

11.—(1) The determination of the maximum rate must include the second adult element if the claim is a joint claim.

2.68

This is subject to the following provisions of this regulation.

(2) The determination of the maximum rate shall not include the second adult element if—

(a) one of the claimants is aged 50 or over;
(b) the 50 plus element is payable, and
(c) neither of the claimants is engaged in qualifying remunerative work for at least 30 hours per week.

(3) But subsection (2) does not apply if at least one of the claimants—

(a) is responsible for a child or a qualifying young person, or
(b) satisfies regulation 9(1).

[[2] (4) The determination of the maximum rate shall also not include the second adult element if neither claimant has responsibility for a child or qualifying young person, and

(a) one claimant is serving a custodial sentence of more than twelve months, or
(b) one claimant is subject to immigration control within the meaning of section 115(9)(a) of the Immigration and Asylum Act 1999.]

AMENDMENTS

1. Working Tax Credit (Entitlement and Maximum Rate) (Amendment) Regulations 2003 (SI 2003/701), reg.10 (April 6, 2003).
2. Tax Credits (Miscellaneous Amendments) Regulations 2009 (SI 2009/697), reg.4 (April 6, 2009).

DEFINITIONS

"50 Plus element"—see reg.18.
"child"—see reg.2.
"claimant"—see reg.2.
"joint claim"—see reg.2.
"qualifying remunerative work"—see reg.4.
"qualifying young person"—see reg.2.
"responsible"—see TCA 2002, s.48.
"week"—see reg.2.

GENERAL NOTE

2.69   The value of the second adult element is a little below that of the basic element. The effect of para.2 is that it limits entitlements of those within it where they work less than 30 hours a week. The effect is that both this element and the increased 30-hour element for those over 50 can be claimed only if one of the claimants works over 30 hours a week. Para.4 was added to clarify these exceptions.

Lone parent element

Lone parent element

2.70   **12.** The determination of the maximum rate must include the lone parent element if—
    (a) the claim is a single claim; and
    (b) the claimant is responsible for [¹a child or qualifying young person].

AMENDMENT

1. Working Tax Credit (Entitlement and Maximum Rate) (Amendment) Regulations 2003 (SI 2003/701), reg.11 (April 6, 2003).

DEFINITION

"child"—see reg.2.
"claim"—see reg.2.
"qualifying young person"—see reg.2.
"responsible"—see TCA 2002, s.48.

GENERAL NOTE

2.71   The value of the lone parent element is the same as that of the second adult element.

Childcare element

Entitlement to childcare element of working tax credit

2.72   **13.**—(1) The determination of the maximum rate must include a childcare element where that person, or in the case of a joint claim at least one of those persons, is incurring relevant childcare charges and—

(a) is a person, not being a member of a [³. . .] couple, engaged in [¹qualifying remunerative work];

[¹(b) is a member or are members of a [³. . .] couple where both are engaged in qualifying remunerative work; or

(c) is a member or are members of a [³. . .] couple where one is engaged in qualifying remunerative work and the other—

    (i) is incapacitated;

    (ii) is an in-patient in hospital; or

    (iii) is in prison (whether serving a custodial sentence or remanded in custody awaiting trial or sentence).]

(2) For the purposes of paragraph (1), a person is not treated as incurring relevant childcare charges where the average weekly charge calculated in accordance with regulation 15 is nil or where an agreement within regulation 15(4) has not yet commenced.

[¹(3) [². . .]]

(4) For the purposes of para.(1)(c)(i), the other member of a couple is incapacitated in any of the circumstances specified in paragraphs (5) to (8).]

(5) The circumstances specified in this paragraph are where either council tax benefit or housing benefit is payable under Part VII of the Contributions and Benefits Act to the other member or his partner and the applicable amount of the person entitled to the benefit includes—

(a) a disability premium; or

(b) a higher pensioner premium by virtue of the satisfaction of—

    (i) in the case of housing benefit, [⁴ paragraph 11(2)(b) of Schedule 1 to the Counsil Tax Benefit Regulations 2006];

    (ii) in the case of housing benefit, [⁴ paragraph 11(2)(b) of Schedule 3 to the Housing Benefit Regulations 2006],

on account of the other member's incapacity or [⁴ regulation 18(1)(c) of the Council Tax Benefit Regulations 2006] (treatment of childcare charges) or, as the case may be, [⁴ regulation 28(1)(c) of the Housing Benefit Regulations 2006] (treatment of childcare charges) applies in that person's case;

(6) The circumstances specified in this paragraph are where there is payable in respect of him one or more of the following pensions or allowances—

(a) short-term incapacity benefit [¹payable at the higher rate] under section 30A of the Contributions and Benefits Act;

(b) long-term incapacity benefit under section 40 or 41 of the Contributions and Benefits Act;

(c) attendance allowance under section 64 of that Act;

(d) severe disablement allowance under section 68 of that Act;

(e) disability living allowance under section 71 of that Act;

(f) increase of disablement pension under section 104 of that Act;

(g) a pension increase under a war pension scheme or an industrial injuries scheme which is analogous to an allowance or increase of disablement pension under sub-paragraph (b), (d) or (e) above;

[⁵ (h) contributory employment and support allowance where entitlement to that allowance or statutory sick pay has existed for a period of 28 weeks comprising one continuous period or two or more periods which are linked together provided that, if the person received statutory sick pay, the person satisfied the first and second contribution conditions set out in paragraphs 1 and 2 of Schedule 1 to the Welfare Reform Act.]

(7) The circumstances specified in this paragraph are where a pension or allowance to which sub-paragraph [¹(c)], (d), (e) or (f) of paragraph (6) refers, was payable on account of his incapacity but has ceased to be payable only in consequence of his becoming a patient.

(8) The circumstances specified in this paragraph are where he has an invalid carriage or other vehicle provided to him under section 5(2)(a) of and Schedule 2 to the National Health Service Act 1977, section 46 of the National Health Service (Scotland) Act 1978; or Article 30(1) of the Health and Personal Social Services (Northern Ireland) Order 1972.

AMENDMENTS

1. Working Tax Credit (Entitlement and Maximum Rate) (Amendment) Regulations 2003 (SI 2003/701), reg.12 (April 6, 2003).
2. Tax Credits (Miscellaneous Amendments) Regulations 2004 (SI 2004/762), reg.9 (April 6, 2004).
3. Civil Partnership Act 2004 (Tax Credits, etc.) (Consequential Amendments) Order 2005 (SI 2005/2919), art.2(3) (December 5, 2005).
4. Housing Benefit and Council Tax Benefit (Consequential Provisions) Regulations 2006 (SI 2006/217), reg.22(3) (March 6, 2006).
5. Employment and Support Allowance (Consequential Provisions) (No.3) Regulations 2008 (SI 2009/1879), reg.20(5) (October 27, 2008).

DEFINITIONS

"child"—see reg.2.
"childcare"—see reg.14.
"couple"—see TCA 2002, s.3.
"claimant"—see reg.2.
"joint claim"—see reg.2.
"partner"—see reg.2.
"patient"—see reg.2.
"qualifying remunerative work"—see reg.4.
"relevant childcare charges"—see reg.14.

GENERAL NOTE

2.73   Specific provision is made for the childcare element in TCA 2002, s.12. The element may be claimed by those entitled to working tax credit and incurring relevant childcare charges for a child for whom a claimant is responsible in three circumstances:
(a)   a lone parent working 16 hours a week;
(b)   a couple both of whom are working 16 hours a week; or
(c)   a couple, one of whom is working 16 hours a week and the other of whom is incapacitated, in hospital or in prison.

Incapacitated

2.74   The test of incapacity is set out in paras (4)–(8). Each of these tests refers to entitlement to a form of benefit to which only the disabled or incapacitated are entitled. This follows the policy of the tax credits legislation in relying on the determination by others of disability or incapacity in most cases. Paragraph (5) is by reference to housing benefit and council tax benefit, paras (6) and (7) by reference to benefits awarded by the Department for Work and Pensions, and para.(8) by reference to the Motability scheme.

Entitlement to childcare element of working tax credit

14.—(1) [¹Subject to paragraph (1A),] for the purposes of section 12 of   2.75
the Act charges incurred for childcare are charges paid by the person, or
in the case of a joint claim, by either or both of the persons, for childcare
provided for any child for whom the person, or at least one of the persons,
is responsible [² within the meaning of regulation 3 of the Child Tax Credit
Regulations 2002].

In these Regulations, such charges are called "relevant childcare
charges".

[¹(1A) Childcare charges do not include charges in respect of care
provided by [⁴—

(a) a relative of the child, wholly or mainly in the child's home, or
(b) a provider mentioned in regulation 14(2)(e)(ia), in circumstances
where the care is excluded from being qualifying child care by
Article 5(2)(c) of the Tax Credits (Approval of Child Care Providers)
Scheme 2005.]
[⁷(c) a provider mentioned in regulation 14(2)(c), in circumstances where
the care is excluded from being qualifying chid care by article 4(2)
(c) of the Tax Credits (Approval of Home Child Care Providers)
Scheme (Northern Ireland) 2006.]
[⁸(d) a provider mentioned in regulation 14(2)(f)(ii), in circumstances
where the care is excluded from being qualifying child care by Article
5(3)(d) of the Tax Credits (Approval of Child Care Providers)
(Wales) Scheme 2007.]
(1B) For the purposes of this regulation—
(a) "relative" means parent, grandparent, aunt, uncle, brother or sister
whether by blood, half blood, marriage [⁵, civil patnership] or
affinity;
(b) "the child's home" means the home of the person, or in the case
of a joint claim of either or both of the persons, responsible for the
child.]
(2) "Child care" means care provided for a child—
(a) in England [¹⁰ . . .]—
     (i) [¹² . . .]
    (ii) [¹¹ . . .]
[¹¹ (iia) by a person registered under Part 3 of the Childcare Act
          2006;]
[¹¹ (iii) in respect of any period on or before the last day the child
          is treated as a child for the purpose of this regulation by or
          under the direction of the proprietor of a school on the school
          premises [¹² (subject to paragraph 2(B))]]
    (iv) [⁹ . . .] [¹⁰ . . .]
[³(v) by a foster parent under the Fostering Services Regulations
      2002 [¹⁰ . . .] in relation to a child other than one whom he is
      fostering;]
[¹⁰(vi) by a child care provider approved in accordance with the Tax
        Credits (Approval of Child Care Providers) Scheme 2005;
 (vii) by a domiciliary care worker under the Domiciliary Care Agencies
        Regulations 2002; or
(viii) by a child care provider registered under the Childcare
        (Voluntary Registration) Regulations 2007;]

    (b) in Scotland—

        (i) by a person in circumstances where the care service provided by him consists of child minding or of day care of children within the meaning of section 2 of the Regulation of Care (Scotland) Act 2001 and is registered under Part I of that Act; [[2]. . .]

      [[7](ia) by a child care agency where the service consists of or includes supplying, or introducing to persons who use the service, child carers within the meaning of sections 2(7) and (8) of the Regulation of Care (Scotland) Act 2001;]

      (ii) by a local authority in circumstances where the care service provided by the local authority consists of child minding or of day care of children within the meaning of section 2 of the Regulation of Care (Scotland) Act 2001 and is registered under Part II of that Act; [[2]or]

    [[3](iii) by a foster carer under the Fostering of Children (Scotland) Regulations 1996 in relation to a child other than one whom he is fostering;]

    (c) in Northern Ireland—

        (i) by persons registered under Part XI of the Children (Northern Ireland) Order 1995; [[2]. . .]

      (ii) by institutions and establishments exempt from registration under that Part by virtue of Article 121 of that Order; or

    [[3](iii) in respect of any period ending on or before the day on which he ceases to be a child for the purposes of this regulation, where the care is provided out of school hours by a school on school premises or by an Education and Library Board or a Health and Social Services Trust; or

    (iv) by a foster parent under the Foster Placement (Children) Regulations (Northern Ireland) 1996 in relation to a child other than one whom he is fostering; or]

    [[7](v) by a child care provider approved in accordance with the Tax Credits (approval of Home Child Care Providers) Scheme (Northern Ireland) 2006.]

    (d) [[1]anywhere outside the United Kingdom]—

        (i) by a childcare provider approved by an accredited organisation within the meaning given by regulation 4 of the Tax Credit (New Category of Child Care Provider) Regulations 2002; or

      (ii) [[1]. . .]

[[10] . . .]

[[10] (f) in Wales—

        (i) by persons registered under Part 10A of the Children Act 1989;

      (ii) in schools or establishments which are exempted from registration under Part 10A of the Children Act 1989 by virtue of paragraph 1 or 2 of Schedule 9A to that Act;

    (iii) in respect of any period on or before the last day he is treated as a child for the purposes of this regulation, where the care is provided out of school hours, by a school on school premises or by a local authority;

    (iv) by a child care provider approved by an accredited organisation within the meaning given by regulation 4 of the Tax Credit (New Category of Child Care Provider) Regulations 1999;

(v) by a foster parent under the Fostering Services (Wales) Regulations 2003 in relation to a child other than one whom he is fostering;

(vi) by a domiciliary care worker under the Domiciliary Care Agencies (Wales) Regulations 2004; or

(vii) by a child care provider approved under the Tax Credits (Approval of Child Care Providers) (Wales) Scheme 2007.]

[[11] (2A) In paragraph (2)(a)(iii)—

"proprietor", in relation to a school, means –

(a) the governing body incorporated under section 19 of the Education Act 2002, or

(b) if there is no such body, the person or body of persons responsible for the management of the school;

"school" means a school that Her Majesty's Chief Inspector of Education, Children's Services and Skills (the "Chief Inspector") is or may be required to inspect;

"school premises" means premises that may be inspected as part of an inspection of the school by the Chief Inspector.

(2B) Care provided for a child in England is not [[12] child care] under paragraph (2)(a)(iii) if—

(a) it is provided during school hours for a child who has reached compulsory school age, or

(b) it is provided in breach of a requirement to register under Part 3 of the Childcare Act 2006.]

(3) For the purposes of this regulation a person is a child until the last day of the week in which falls 1st September following that child's 15th birthday (or 16th birthday if the child is disabled).

(4) For the purposes of paragraph (3), a child is disabled where—

(a) a disability living allowance is payable in respect of that child, or has ceased to be payable solely because he is a patient;

(b) the child is registered as blind in a register compiled by a local authority under section 29 of the National Assistance Act 1948 (welfare services) or, in Scotland, has been certified as blind and in consequence is registered as blind in a register maintained by or on behalf of a local authority in Scotland, or, in Northern Ireland has been certified as blind and in consequence is registered as blind in a register maintained by or on behalf of a Health and Social Services Board; or

(c) the child ceased to be registered as blind in such a register within the 28 weeks immediately preceding the date of claim.

(5) Charges paid in respect of the child's compulsory education or charges paid by a person to a partner or by a partner to the person in respect of any child for whom either or any of them is responsible are not relevant childcare charges.

(6) Where regulation 15(4) (agreement for the provision of future childcare) applies—

(a) the words "charges paid" in paragraph (1) include charges which will be incurred; and

(b) the words "childcare provided" in paragraph (1) include care which will be provided.

(7) [[2]. . .]

(8) Relevant childcare charges are calculated on a weekly basis in accordance with regulation 15.

AMENDMENTS

1. Working Tax Credit (Entitlement and Maximum Rate) (Amendment) Regulations 2003 (SI 2003/701), reg.13 (April 6, 2003).

2. Tax Credits (Miscellaneous Amendments) Regulations 2004 (SI 2004/762), reg.10 (April 6, 2004).

3. Working Tax Credit (Entitlement and Maximum Rate) (Amendment) Regulations 2004 (SI 2004/1276), reg.2 (June 1, 2004).

4. Working Tax Credit (Entitlement and Maximum Rate) (Amendment) Regulations 2005 (SI 2005/769), reg.4(b) (April 6, 2005).

5. Civil Partnership Act 2004 (Tax Credits, etc.) (Consequential Amendments) Order 2005 (SI 2005/2919), art.2(4) (December 5, 2005).

6. Working Tax Credit (Entitlement and Maximum Rate) (Amendment) Regulations 2005 (SI 2005/769), reg.4(a) (January 1, 2006).

7. Tax Credits (Miscellaneous Amendments) Regulations 2006 (SI 2006/766), reg.20(4) (April 6, 2006).

8. Tax Credits (Miscellaneous Amendments) Regulations 2007 (SI 2007/824), reg.6 (April 6, 2007).

9. Working Tax Credit (Entitlement and Maximum Rate) (Amendment No.2) Regulations 2007 (SI 2007/2479), reg.2 (October 1, 2007).

10. Tax Credits (Miscellaneous Amendments) Regulations 2008 (SI 2008/604), reg.3 (April 6, 2008).

11. Tax Credits (Miscellaneous Amendments) (No.2) Regulations 2008 (SI 2008/2169), reg.2 (September 1, 2008).

12. Tax Credits (Miscellaneous Amendments) Regulations 2009 (SI 2009/697), reg.5 (April 6, 2009).

DEFINITIONS

"child"—see reg.2.
"claim"—see reg.2.
"partner"—see reg.2.
"patient"—see reg.2.

GENERAL NOTE

2.76   The main content of this regulation is the definition of the main phrases on which reg.13 relies. "Child" receives a slightly limited definition compared with the standard approach for child tax credit and working tax credit, as para.(3) puts an upper limit on the relevant age of a child. The provision does not apply at all to those over 16, who are known as "qualifying young persons" for working tax credit and child tax credit purposes. There is an upwards extension of the age limit for disabled children in paras (3) and (4). This is by reference to payment of any level of disability living allowance or by blindness. There is also a limit applying to the youngest children. Paragraph (7) links with reg.13(3) to exclude a claim by someone on maternity, paternity or adoption leave by reference only to the child in respect of whom the leave is granted.

"Child care" is given an extensive definition. This is necessary because responsibility for childcare legislation is part of the devolved responsibilities of the Scottish and Northern Irish parliaments and the Welsh assembly. In addition, the definition has been extended to childcare outside the United Kingdom. This links with the provisions in the Tax Credits (Residence) Regulations 2003 (SI 2003/642) under which Crown servants outside the United Kingdom, and their partners, are regarded as being in the United Kingdom for tax credits purposes. Accordingly, staff provided with approved childcare facilities by, for example, defence establishments, can qualify for the childcare element of working tax credit. Any dispute about whether someone is providing "childcare" is for the authorities responsible for that particular set of registration rules.

"Relevant childcare charges" is defined by reference to charges for "childcare", with the important exception in para.(1A) of childcare provided by a (registered) relative in the child's home. It can, however, be provided in the carer's home even though the carer is, say, a grandparent. The condition ensures that both the carer, and the carer's premises, are open to inspection. Paragraph (5) excludes charges for education as against care, and payments made by one of a married or unmarried couple to the other (although the one to whom the payments are made may not be responsible for the child).

The scope of reg.14(5) was discussed by the deputy Commissioner in *CTC/3646/2007*, where the deputy Commissioner upheld a tribunal's decision to refuse to take account of apportioned fees for a "waiting class". Regulation 15(3) could not therefore be applied on the facts. The issue is further clarified by the addition of a definition of "full time education" to the Child Tax Credit Regulations by SI 2008/2169, reg.7(3) with effect from September 1, 2008.

Calculation of relevant childcare charges

15.—(1) Relevant childcare charges are calculated by aggregating the average weekly charge paid for childcare for each child in respect of whom charges are incurred [¹and rounding up the total to the nearest whole pound]. This is subject to [¹paragraphs (1A) and (2)].

[¹(1A) In any case in which the charges in respect of childcare are paid weekly, the average weekly charge for the purposes of paragraph (1) is established—

  (a) where the charges are for a fixed weekly amount, by aggregating the average weekly charge paid for childcare for each child in respect of whom charges are incurred in the most recent four complete weeks; or

  (b) where the charges are for variable weekly amounts, by aggregating the charges for the previous 52 weeks and dividing the total by 52.]

(2) In any case in which the charges in respect of childcare are paid monthly, the average weekly charge for the purposes of paragraph (1) is established—

  (a) where the charges are for a fixed monthly amount, by multiplying that amount by 12 and dividing the product by 52; or

  (b) where the charges are for variable monthly amounts, by aggregating the charges for the previous 12 months and dividing the total by 52.

(3) In a case where there is insufficient information for establishing the average weekly charge paid for childcare in accordance with paragraphs (1) and (2), an officer of the Board shall estimate the charge—

  (a) in accordance with information provided by the person or persons incurring the charges; and

  (b) by any method which in the officer's opinion is reasonable.

(4) If a person—

  (a) has entered into an agreement for the provision of childcare; and

  (b) will incur under that agreement relevant childcare charges in respect of childcare during the period of the award, the average weekly charge for childcare is based upon a written estimate of the future weekly charges provided by that person.

2.77

AMENDMENT

1. Working Tax Credit (Entitlement and Maximum Rate) (Amendment) Regulations 2003 (SI 2003/701), reg.14 (April 6, 2003).

DEFINITIONS

"child"—see reg.14(3).
"childcare"—see reg.14(2).
"relevant childcare charges"—see reg.14(1).

GENERAL NOTE

2.78   This regulation sets out the methods to be used in calculating the amount of childcare charges on which the childcare element is to be based. The regulation was amended just before it came into effect because the previous form of the regulation was accepted as being seriously flawed. This created potential unfairness as between those who pay monthly for their childcare on an annualised basis and those who pay weekly on an actual basis. While the monthly payers usually have a steady pattern of payments, the weekly payers often pay more during school terms than during school holidays.

The rules deal with monthly payments by either using the fixed monthly charge, or the average of the last 12 monthly charges, to determine the weekly figure. Varying weekly charges are calculated by reference to the last 52 weeks, while fixed weekly charges are calculated by reference to the last four weeks. Presumably, however, regard must be had to more than four past weeks in applying this rule to avoid the problem of assessing the charges for the wrong four weeks.

There are two important provisos to these rules. The first is that HMRC may rely on estimates based on "any method . . . which is reasonable". This should allow a solution to the problem of increases in the charges that should be reflected in increases in the childcare element. The second proviso, in para.(4), allows an estimate of the future charges to be taken into account provided that the claimant has entered into a written agreement for the provision of childcare.

Change of circumstances

2.79   **16.**—(1) There is a relevant change in circumstances if—
   (a) [¹. . .]
   (b) [¹during the period of an award, the weekly relevant childcare charges, rounded up to the nearest whole pound]—
      (i)   exceed the average weekly charge calculated in accordance with regulation 15 by £10 a week or more;
      (ii) are less than the average weekly charge calculated in accordance with regulation 15 by £10 a week or more; or
      (iii) are nil.
   If there is a relevant change in circumstances, the amount of the childcare element of working tax credit shall be recalculated with effect from the specified date.

[¹(2) For the purposes of paragraph (1), the weekly relevant childcare charge—
   (a) where the childcare charges are for a fixed weekly amount, is the aggregate of the weekly charge paid for childcare for each child in respect of whom charges are incurred in each of the four consecutive weeks in which the change occurred; or
   (b) where the childcare charges are for variable weekly amounts, is established by aggregating the anticipated weekly charge paid for childcare for each child in respect of whom charges will be incurred for the following 52 weeks and dividing the total by 52.]

(3) If in any case the charges in respect of childcare are paid monthly, the weekly relevant childcare charge for the purposes of paragraph (1) is established—

(a) where the charges are for a fixed monthly amount, by multiplying that amount by 12 and dividing the product by 52; or

(b) where the charges are for variable monthly amounts, by aggregating the [¹anticipated] charges for the [¹next] 12 months and dividing the total by 52.

(4) In a case where there is insufficient information for establishing the weekly relevant childcare charge paid for childcare in accordance with paragraphs (2) and (3), an officer of the Board shall estimate the charge—

(a) in accordance with information provided by the person or persons incurring the charges; and

(b) by any method which in the officer's opinion is reasonable.

(5) For the purpose of paragraph (1) the specified date is—

(a) where the childcare charges are increased, the later of—

   (i) the first day of the week in which the change occurred, and

   (ii) the first day of the week in which falls the day which is three months prior to the date notification of the change is given,

(b) where the childcare charges are decreased, the first day of the week following

the four consecutive weeks in which the change occurred.

AMENDMENT

1. Working Tax Credit (Entitlement and Maximum Rate) (Amendment) Regulations 2003 (SI 2003/701), reg.15 (April 6, 2003).

DEFINITIONS

"award"—see TCA 2002, s.14.
"change of circumstances"—see TCA 2002, s.6.

GENERAL NOTE

This regulation brings into play the mechanisms for amending or terminating an award of working tax credit. Section 6(3) of the TCA 2002 makes provision for regulations to impose a duty on a claimant to report a change of circumstances that may decrease the rate of entitlement to a tax credit. Regulation 21 of the Tax Credits (Claims and Notifications) Regulations 2002 (SI 2002/2014) imposes the requirement that notification of a change of circumstances as defined in this regulation must be given within one month of the change occurring. Regulations 22–24 of those Regulations set out how and by whom this is to be done.

    2.80

Failure to notify may make the claimant liable to a penalty of £300 under s.32(3) of the TCA 2002.

Severe disability element

Severe disability element

17.—(1) The determination of the maximum rate must include the severe disability element if the claimant, or, in the case of a joint claim, one of the claimants satisfies paragraph (2).

    2.81

(2) A person satisfies this paragraph if a disability living allowance, attributable to the care component payable at the highest rate prescribed under section 72(3) of the Contributions and Benefits Act or an attendance allowance at the higher rate prescribed under section 65(3) of that Act—

(a) is payable in respect of him; or

(b) would be so payable but for a suspension of benefit by virtue of regulations under section 113(2) of the Contributions and Benefits Act (suspension during hospitalisation), or an abatement as a consequence of hospitalisation.

DEFINITIONS

"claimant"—see reg.2.
"joint claim"—see reg.2.

GENERAL NOTE

2.82　　This is separate from the disability element provided for in reg.9. It adds a further £1075 to the entitlement of the claimant or claimants. But it is restricted to the case where the disabled individual is receiving the highest rate of the care component of disability living allowance (or the attendance allowance equivalent), which means that both day and night attention or supervision are needed.

There is no express provision dealing with interaction with the disability element. *CST/76/2006* makes it clear that the language of reg.9 requires that, in the case of a joint claim, the person who is disabled must also be the same person who is working 16 hours a week: see para.2.56. But this regulation does not repeat that language. Nor is this element dependent on the receipt of the disability element under reg.9. The mandatory language of reg.17 suggests that all joint claimants are entitled to the severe disability element if either of them meets the general conditions to claim WTC and either is in receipt of the highest rate of the care component of disability living allowance (or the higher rate of attendance allowance). It would follow that this element may be claimed by claimants following any of the four Routes noted at para.2.32 and not merely Route 2.

50 Plus element

50 Plus element

2.83　　**18.**—(1) The determination of the maximum rate must include the 50 plus element if—

(a) in the case of a single claim, the claimant satisfies paragraph(3); or

(b) in the case of a joint claim, at least one of the claimants satisfies that paragraph.

This is subject to the qualification in paragraph (2).

(2) The 50 plus element shall not be payable in respect of a claimant—

(a) for a continuous period of longer than 12 months; or

(b) for periods amounting in aggregate to more than 12 months if the gap between any consecutive pair of those periods is not more than 26 weeks.

(3) A claimant satisfies this paragraph if—

[1(a) he is aged at least 50; and

(b) he starts qualifying remunerative work; and]

(c) he undertakes qualifying remunerative work for at least 16 hours per week; and

(d) he satisfies the condition in paragraphs (4), (6), (7), (8) or (9).

(4) The condition is that—

(a) for a period of at least six months immediately before his starting [¹qualifying remunerative] work as mentioned in paragraph (3)(b); or

(b) for consecutive periods, amounting in the aggregate to at least six months, the last of which ends immediately before his starting [¹ qualifying remunerative] work as mentioned in paragraph (3)(b), paragraph (5) is satisfied.

[²(4A) For the purposes of paragraph (4)(b) "consecutive periods" are periods, any pair of which is separated by a gap of not more than 12 weeks.]

(5) This paragraph is satisfied while the claimant is receiving—

(a) income support;

(b) a jobseeker's allowance;

(c) incapacity benefit;

(d) severe disablement allowance; [². . .]

(e) both a state retirement pension and [²state pension credit within the meaning of the State Pension Credit Act 2002; [³ . . .]]

[²(f) a training allowance paid by the Secretary of State under section 2(1) of the Employment and Training Act 1973 to a person in his capacity as a participant in either of the schemes provided by, or under arrangements made with, the Secretary of State and known as "Work-Based Learning for Adults" and "Training for Work";] [³ or

(g) an employment and support allowance.]

(6) The condition is that for at least six months immediately prior to his starting [¹qualifying remunerative] work—

(a) another person was receiving—

(i) the payment mentioned in sub-paragraphs (a) to (d) of paragraph (5); or

(ii) both the payments mentioned in paragraph (5)(e); and

(b) an increase in respect of the claimant, as a dependant of the other person—

(i) in a case falling within sub-paragraph (a)(i) was payable with that payment; or

(ii) in a case falling within sub-paragraph (a)(ii) was payable with that pension.

(7) The condition is that for at least six months immediately prior to his starting [¹qualifying remunerative] work as mentioned in paragraph (3)(b) he satisfied the conditions entitling him to be credited with contributions or earnings in accordance with the Social Security (Credits) Regulations 1975.

(8) The condition is that—

(a) the condition in paragraph (4)(a), (6) or (7) would have been satisfied if the reference to six months were omitted;

(b) immediately prior to the period during which that condition, as modified by sub-paragraph (a), is satisfied there is a period during which the condition in paragraph (9) is satisfied; and

(c) the total of the periods during which—

(i) the condition in paragraph (4)(a), (6) or (7), as modified by sub-para.(a), is satisfied; and

(ii) the condition in para.(9) is satisfied, equals or exceeds six months.

(9) The condition is that the claimant, or, in the case of a joint claim, one of the claimants, is receiving—

(a) [¹carer's] allowance;

(b) bereavement allowance; or

(c) widowed parent's allowance.

DEFINITIONS

"claimant"—see reg.2.

"joint claim"—see reg.2.

"qualifying remunerative work"—see reg.4.

AMENDMENTS

1. Tax Credits (Miscellaneous Amendments No.2) Regulations 2003 (SI 2003/2815), reg.16 (November 26, 2003).

2. Tax Credits (Miscellaneous Amendments) Regulations 2004 (SI 2004/762), reg.11 (April 6, 2004).

3. Employment and Support Allowance (Consequential Provisions) (No.3) Regulations 2008 (SI 2009/1879), reg.20(6) (October 27, 2008).

GENERAL NOTE

2.84   Unlike all the other elements of working tax credit, this is limited in time. It is payable only for a maximum of 12 months in total (though not necessarily in one period): para.(2). This is one of the routes to working tax credit that does not involve a social security element. It is instead the replacement of the former "New Deal 50 Plus" payable by the former Department for Employment under employment legislation. Its aim is to give an encouragement for those over 50 and on benefit to get back to work. The regulation lays down two sets of requirements for the element to be paid: first, the claimant must now have qualifying remunerative work for 16 hours a week, and secondly, he or she must have been claiming benefits or incapacity credits before the work, or someone else was claiming benefits for him or her, for a period of at least six months. Part of the period of six months may be counted, under paras (8) and (9), by reference to the award of invalid care allowance (now carer's allowance) or an award to a widow or widower.

Death of a child or qualifying young person for whom the claimant is responsible

Entitlement after death of a child or qualifying young person for whom the claimant is responsible

2.85   **19.**—(1) Paragraph (2) applies if—

(a) the death occurs of a child or qualifying young person;

(b) working tax credit is payable to a person who was, or to a couple at least one of whom was, immediately before the death responsible for that child or qualifying young person;

(c) the prescribed conditions for an element of working tax credit were satisfied because the claimant, or at least one of the claimants, was responsible for that child or qualifying person, but would not have been satisfied but for that responsibility; and

(d) the prescribed conditions would have continued to be satisfied but for the death.

(2) If this paragraph applies, working tax credit shall continue to be

payable, as if the child or qualifying young person had not died, for the period for which child tax credit continues to be payable in accordance with regulation 6 of the Child Tax Credit Regulations 2002.

DEFINITIONS

"child"—see reg.2.
"qualifying young person"—see reg.2.

GENERAL NOTE

Section 55 of the TCA 2002 provides an extension of the payment of child benefit **2.86** for a period of eight weeks after the death of a child for whom the benefit is paid. Section 5(5) makes similar provision for child tax credit, and effect is given to this by reg.6 of the Child Tax Credit Regulations 2002 (SI 2002/2007). This regulation matches those extensions for working tax credit also, s.10(3)(d) of the TCA 2002 providing authority for this.

Claimants are required, from November 2006, to report the death of a child or qualifying young person for whom they are receiving additional credit within one month of the death. See para.2.310.

PART III

MAXIMUM RATE

Maximum rates of elements of Working Tax Credit

20.—(1) The maximum annual rate of working tax credit (excluding the **2.87** childcare element) payable to a single claimant or to a couple making a joint claim is the sum of whichever of the following elements are applicable—

(a) the basic element specified in column.(2) of the table in Schedule 2 at paragraph 1;

(b) in respect of a claimant who satisfies regulation 9(1), the disability element specified in column (2) of the table in Schedule 2 at paragraph 2;

(c) the 30-hour element specified in column (2) of the table in Schedule 2 at paragraph 3 in respect of—

 (i) a single claimant who works for not less than 30 hours per week;

 (ii) a couple either or both of whom work for not less than 30 hours per week; or

 (iii) a couple, at least one of whom is responsible for a child or a qualifying young person and at least one of whom works for 16 hours per week if their hours of work when aggregated amount to at least 30 hours per week;

(d) the second-adult element specified in column (2) of the table in Schedule 2 at paragraph 4 where regulation 11 so provides;

(e) the lone-parent element specified in column (2) of the table in Schedule 2 at paragraph 5 where regulation 12 applies;

(f) the severe disability element specified in column (2) of the table in Schedule 2 at paragraph 6—

 (i) in respect of a single claimant who satisfies regulation 17; or

(ii) in respect of a member of a couple making a joint claim who satisfies regulation 17; and

(g) the 50 Plus element in respect of a person who satisfies regulation 18(2) at whichever of the rates specified in column 2 of the Table in Schedule 2 at paragraph 7 applies in his case.

(2) The maximum rate of the childcare element of a working tax credit is [³80] per cent of the maxima specified in paragraph (3).

(3) The maxima are—

(a) [²£175] per week, where the [¹claimant or, in the case of a joint claim, at least one of the claimants, is responsible for] only one child in respect of whom relevant childcare charges are paid; and

(b) [²£300] per week where the [¹claimant or, in the case of a joint claim, at least one of the claimants, is responsible for] more than one child in respect of whom relevant childcare charges are paid.

AMENDMENTS

1. Working Tax Credit (Entitlement and Maximum Rate) (Amendment) Regulations 2003 (SI 2003/701), reg.16 (April 6, 2003).

2. Tax Credits Up-rating Regulations 2005 (SI 2005/681), reg.3(1) (April 6, 2005).

3. Tax Credits Up-rating Regulations 2006 (SI 2006/963), reg.3(1) (April 6, 2006).

DEFINITIONS

"claimant"—see reg.2.
"joint claim"—see reg.2.

GENERAL NOTE

2.88

This regulation emphasises that the entitlement of a claimant or claimants to working tax credit is made up of each of the elements to which there is entitlement. It is "the sum of whichever of the . . . elements are applicable". However, as noted above, there must be entitlement under reg.4. to the basic element in all cases. Paragraph (1) provides the necessary drafting provision to tie each of the other elements (save for the childcare element), the conditions for which have been defined above, into the rate of award and entitlement to working tax credit to the claimant or claimants under s.11 of the TCA 2002.

Paragraphs (2) and (3) then provide the effective rate of the childcare element. They set the maximum weekly childcare element at £300 for care for two or more children, and £175 for care for a single child.

The current figures for the maximum rates of all elements other than the childcare element are in Sch.2.

The varying levels of working tax credit by reference to these differing elements and the different routes by which, under reg.4, claims can be made for working tax credit can be illustrated by some short examples. The examples show the maximum entitlement to working tax credit in each case. They do not take into account the income or benefit entitlements of the claimant(s).

Route 1: Lone-parent with three children, working 32 hours a week, and incurring childcare costs of £350 a week.

Her entitlement is:

Basic element	*£ 1,890*
30-hour element	*£ 775*
Lone parent element	*£ 1,860*
Childcare element	*£ 12,480 (limited to 80 per cent of £300 a week)*
Maximum entitlement	*£ 17,005*

In addition, the lone parent will be entitled to child benefit, and child tax credit for herself and the three children.

Route 2: Couple with no children, one of whom is working for 16 hours a week despite also being entitled to disability living allowance, and the other of whom is working for over 30 hours a week.

Basic element	*£1,890*
30-hour element	*£775*
Second adult element	*£1,860*
Disability element	*£2,530*
Maximum entitlement	*£7,055*

Under this Route, the person receiving the disability living allowance (or otherwise disabled) must be working for 16 hours a week: reg.9(1)(a).

Route 3: Couple, both over 70. One has just started work for 20 hours a week. The couple are receiving their state retirement pension and state pension credit. They have no serious disabilities.

Basic element	*£1,890*
50 plus element	*£1,300 (lower rate)*
Maximum entitlement	*£3,190*

There is no entitlement to the second adult element in this case: reg.11(2).

Route 4: Unmarried couple. He is 26 and working 32 hours a week. She is 18, expecting their child soon, and is not and has not been working.
Their entitlement is:

Basic entitlement	*£1,890*
30-hour element	*£775*
Second adult element	*£1,860*
Maximum entitlement	*£4,505*

The couple will be entitled to child benefit, child tax credit (including the additional element for the first year) and perhaps also working tax credit with the childcare element, maternity benefits and statutory paternity pay when the child is born.

SCHEDULE 1   **Regulation 9(1)**

DISABILITY WHICH PUTS A PERSON AT A DISADVANTAGE IN GETTING A JOB

PART I

1. When standing he cannot keep his balance unless he continually holds onto something.   **2.89**
2. Using any crutches, walking frame, walking stick, prosthesis or similar walking aid which he habitually uses, he cannot walk a continuous distance of 100 metres along level ground without stopping or without suffering severe pain.
3. He can use neither of his hands behind his back as in the process of putting on a jacket or of tucking a shirt into trousers.
4. He can extend neither of his arms in front of him so as to shake hands with another person without difficulty.
5. He can put neither of his hands up to his head without difficulty so as to put on a hat.
6. Due to lack of manual dexterity he cannot, with one hand, pick up a coin which is not more than $2^{1}/_{2}$ centimetres in diameter.
7. He is not able to use his hands or arms to pick up a full jug of 1 litre capacity and pour from it into a cup, without difficulty.
8. He can turn neither of his hands sideways through 180 degrees.

9. He—

    (a)   is registered as blind or registered as partially sighted in a register compiled by a local authority under section 24(9)(g) of the National Assistance Act 1948;

    (b)   has been certified as blind or as partially sighted and, in consequence, registered as blind or partially sighted in a register maintained by or on behalf of a council constituted under the Local Government (Scotland) Act 1994; or

    (c)   has been certified as blind and in consequence is registered as blind in a register maintained by or on behalf of a Health and Social Services Board in Northern Ireland.

10. He cannot see to read 16 point print at a distance greater than 20 centimetres, if appropriate, wearing the glasses he normally uses.

11. He cannot hear a telephone ring when he is in the same room as the telephone, if appropriate, using a hearing aid he normally uses.

12. In a quiet room he has difficulty in hearing what someone talking in a loud voice at a distance of 2 metres says, if appropriate, using a hearing aid he normally uses.

13. People who know him well have difficulty in understanding what he says.

14. When a person he knows well speaks to him, he has difficulty in understanding what that person says.

15. At least once a year during waking hours he is in a coma or has a fit in which he loses consciousness.

16. He has a mental illness for which he receives regular treatment under the supervision of a medically qualified person.

17. Due to mental disability he is often confused or forgetful.

18. He cannot do the simplest addition and subtraction.

19. Due to mental disability he strikes people or damages property or is unable to form normal social relationships.

20. He cannot normally sustain an 8-hour working day or a 5-day working week due to a medical condition or intermittent or continuous severe pain.

PART II

2.90   **21.** As a result of an illness or accident he is undergoing a period of habilitation or rehabilitation.

GENERAL NOTE

2.91   Under reg.9 of these Regulations, a person is treated as having a disability which puts him or her at a disadvantage in getting a job only if one of the paragraphs of this Schedule applies to him or her. If a paragraph does apply, reg.9 deems the claimant to be at a disadvantage in getting a job, whether or not the disability actually has that effect. See the notes to regs 9 and 9A for the application of these tests to initial and repeat claims.

The Schedule requires the exercise of a considerable amount of judgement. For instance, the words "without difficulty" frequently appear. The difficulty need not be severe and plainly a person may have difficulty with an action without necessarily suffering pain when performing it. Slowness may well be sufficient.

Attention is drawn to the final condition in para.20 before detailed comment is made on the specific disabilities. This is the overarching condition that a person cannot sustain a full working day or a full working week due either to a medical condition (of any nature, physical or mental) or intermittent or continuous severe pain. *R(S) 11/51* emphasised that this has to be determined by what a claimant can reasonably be expected to do with regard to his or her age, education, training and other personal factors. It is suggested that this should be the starting point for consideration of the application of this Schedule, with reference being made to the specific disabilities in that context.

Para. 2

2.92   Note that this test is not the same as the test prescribed in reg.12(1)(a)(ii) of the Social Security (Disability Living Allowance) Regulations 1991 (SI 1991/2890) in respect of the mobility component of disability living allowance. Not only is the distance of 100 metres prescribed, but the question is whether that distance can be walked "without stopping" or without "severe pain" (rather than "severe discomfort"). It should also be noted that only artificial aids which are habitually used are to be taken into account, so there is no need to consider whether an aid which is not used might be suitable. In *R(M) 2/89*, the Commissioner held that a person walks only when putting one foot in front of the other, so that a person who has to swing through crutches, rather than using them to help him or her move both legs separately, cannot walk.

Para. 6

2.93

Two-and-a-half centimetres (1 inch) is the diameter of a 50 pence coin. Since their reduction in size, other coins, apart from the £2 coin, are smaller. Note that the claimant satisfies the test (and so may qualify for benefit) if he or she can pick up a large coin in one hand but not the other. In *CDWA 3123/1997* the claimant had no thumb on his left hand and the terminal joint of his right thumb was missing. He maintained that he was only able to pick up a coin of 2.5 centimetres in diameter by pushing it across a surface and catching it in his hand. The Commissioner holds that the tests in Sch. 1 were to be performed in the normal way and not by employing some unusual or awkward manoeuvre. The normal way of picking up coins with one hand was to use the pinch grip between the thumb and fingers. An ability to pick up with the fingers alone was irrelevant because that ability did not demonstrate the presence or absence of the pinch grip. The Commissioner also confirmed that para. 6 would be satisfied if the claimant could not pick up a coin of the prescribed size with one hand even if he could with the other.

Para. 7

2.94

This is a test of both steadiness and strength, using both hands or arms at once if necessary. The Commissioner in *CDWA 3123/1997* confirmed that the position was different under para. 7 (as compared with para. 6) since, here, the question was whether the claimant could perform the pouring task using both hands and arms together. An inability to do so with either hand alone is immaterial if he or she can manage the task with both hands. But any realistic difficulty, however slight, in carrying out that task would satisfy the test in para. 7. Arguably, an ability to pick up and pour with one hand alone, where the claimant has no use of the other arm at all, would mean that the claimant would not qualify under this paragraph, although that question did not arise in that case.

Para. 8

2.95

Presumably, this is a test of wrist movements and is intended to be performed with the elbows kept still.

Para. 10

2.96

16 point print is 4 mm high. It is this size.

Paras 12–14

2.97

If hearing or understanding is possible, but only with difficulty (perhaps after repetition), the claimant still qualifies. The precise relationship between paras 12 and 14 is unclear. Difficulty in understanding may arise for reasons other than loss of hearing and, indeed, a person without hearing may be able to understand through lip-reading. Can a person who can hear a loud voice, but not an ordinary conversational voice, at a distance of 2 metres qualify under para. 14 if he or she cannot lip-read? In principle, the answer would seem to be "yes". That would not mean that para. 12 had no effect because the person would only be able to qualify under para. 14 if he or she was further disadvantaged by an inability to make use of other methods of comprehending speech.

Para. 16

2.98

Medication taken on prescription will be enough, provided that it is regular. Mental illness is not defined, but, if a person is receiving treatment there is likely to be a diagnosis of an illness and if it is an illness of the mind it will be mental illness.

Para.17

2.99   Mental disability is not defined and neither is the extent of confusion or forgetfulness required. On one view, any confusion or forgetfulness suggests some disability of the mind and the question is whether the degree of confusion or forgetfulness is sufficient to warrant the view that the legislator intended such a claimant to qualify (see the approach of the Court Appeal in *W v L* [1974] Q.B. 711). On the other hand, in *R(A) 2/92*, a Commissioner considered that a specific diagnosis was required and that suggests that the first question is whether there is such a diagnosis. Only after that has been answered does one go on to consider whether there is any resulting confusion or forgetfulness.

Para.19

2.100   See the note to para.17. The approach taken in *R(A) 2/92* would create real difficulties here given the view expressed there that "personality disorder" can be distinguished from "mental disability".

Para.21

2.101   This applies only on an initial claim.

SCHEDULE 2   **Regulation 20(1)**

MAXIMUM RATES OF THE ELEMENTS OF A WORKING TAX CREDIT

2.102

[¹*Relevant element of Working Tax Credit*	*Maximum annual rate*
1. Basic element	£1,890
2. Disability element	£2,530
3. 30 hour element	£775
4. Second adult element	£1,860
5. Lone parent element	£1,860
6. Severe disability element	£1,075
7. 50 plus element— (a) in the case of a person who normally undertakes qualifying remunerative work for at least 16 hours but less than 30 hours per week; and	£1,300
(b) in the case of a person who normally undertakes qualifying remunerative work for at least 30 hours per week	£1,935]

AMENDMENT

1. Tax Credits Up-rating Regulations 2009 (SI 2009/800), reg.3 and Sch. (April 6, 2009).

Tax Credits (Definition and Calculation of Income) Regulations 2002

(SI 2002/2006) (AS AMENDED)

Whereas a draft of this instrument, which contains the first regulations made under section 7(8) and (9) of the Tax Credits Act 2002, has been laid before, and approved by resolution of, each House of Parliament:

Now, therefore, the Treasury, in exercise of the powers conferred upon them by sections 7(8) and (9), 65(1), (7) and (9) and 67 of the Tax Credits Act 2002, hereby make the following Regulations:

PART I

General provisions

1.   Citation, commencement and effect.   **2.103**
2.   Interpretation.

PART II

INCOME FOR THE PURPOSES OF TAX CREDITS

General

3.   Calculation of income of claimant.

CHAPTER 2

Employment income

4.   Employment income.

CHAPTER 3

Pension income

5.   Pension income.

CHAPTER 4

Trading income

6.   Trading income.

13.   Introduction.
14.   Claimants treated for any purpose as having income by virtue of the Income
          Tax Acts.
15.   Claimants depriving themselves of income in order to secure entitlement.
16.   Claimants to whom income becomes available upon the making of a claim.
17.   Claimants providing services to other persons for less than full earnings.

CHAPTER 11

Miscellaneous income

18. Miscellaneous income.

PART III

Sums disregarded in the calculation of income

General disregards in the calculation of income

19. General disregards in the calculation of income.

INTRODUCTION AND GENERAL NOTE

Section 7 of TCA 2002 provides that entitlement to a tax credit is subject to an   2.104
income test. These regulations provide the detail of that test. They do so by adopting, with some important modifications, the rules for deciding on the income of an
individual in the rewritten income tax legislation adopted over the last few years by
Parliament from the draft bills produced by the Tax Law Rewrite Project. The Acts
produced by the Rewrite Project have modernised the language and presentation of
income tax law, and parallel changes in annual Finance Acts have also rationalised
parts of it. This has made it easier to abandon the previous approach of having
a different set of defining rules of income for benefit purposes and to adopt the
income tax rules into the benefit system.

The rewritten income tax law

With effect from April 6, 2007 all the former primary legislation dating back to   2.105
the 1840s under which income tax was imposed and collected has been repealed
and replaced by the new rewritten legislation. This is contained in three major Acts,
the Income Tax (Earnings and Pensions) Act 2003, the Income Tax (Trading and
Other Income) Act 2005 and the Income Tax Act 2007. In practice these contain
all the income rules necessary for any tax credits calculation save for the rules about
capital allowances in the Capital Allowances Act 2000, another rewrite measure.

A fundamental change in approach

The income test used for tax credits is fundamentally different to that used for the   2.106
income-related benefits such as income support, jobseeker's allowance and housing
benefit. The main differences are as follows:

(1) *There is no capital rule.* There has never been a wealth tax in the United Kingdom, save for that, in effect, imposed on those claiming means-tested benefits. The approach is to tax income from capital as (and if) it arises. This is the approach now adopted for tax credits.

(2) *Capital gains are irrelevant.* Income tax is supplemented for individuals by a separate capital gains tax, e.g. on the capital gain made on selling an asset. Capital gains are also ignored for tax credits purposes.

(3) *There are no rules deeming income from capital held.* The rules treating capital as income, and attributing tariff income to capital, have been abolished and not replaced.

(4) *There is no all-inclusive definition of income.* The previous approach was to base the calculation of non-earned income on "gross income and any capital treated as income". The income tax based approach is to calculate income from each named source and to then aggregate the totals to establish the relevant income. If income arises from a source that is not one of the named sources, it is excluded from the calculation.

(5) *Claimants may choose forms of income that avoid the calculation.* The rules generally follow the approach of income tax in looking at actual income from capital, if any. They no longer follow the approach of the rules for the income-related benefits (perhaps more correctly the income and capital related benefits) of assuming income from capital at set rates while ignoring actual income from capital. They also leave any capital gains out of account. However, there remain some important anti-avoidance provisions based on the former family credit rules that take some account of capital and notional income. See regs 13–17 below.

Differences between tax credits income calculations and income tax assessments

2.107   The calculation of income for tax credits is based closely on the income tax approach. This allows HMRC to base its tax credits calculations on its income tax assessments or, in most cases, on the self-assessments of those individuals to income tax or the assessment and collection of income tax from employees by employers and agencies through the PAYE (Pay As You Earn) system. There are, however, some important differences from income tax assessments and these should also be noted:

(1) *Couples are assessed jointly, not separately.* The income tax system was transferred from a system in which married couples were assessed on their joint incomes in the name of the husband to a system of separate assessment of each partner in 1990. One reason for this was the growing concern about discrimination against couples who were married, and assessed jointly, as against those who were unmarried and separately assessed. The new rules require both married and unmarried couples to make joint applications for working tax credit and child tax credit. This is the first time that HMRC has been concerned to calculate the joint income of unmarried couples, and it will bring sharply into focus the need to look carefully at when two individuals are required to make a joint claim. The starting point in any calculation of income for tax credits purposes is therefore to establish who the claimant is or claimants are. If two people become a couple, or a couple breaks up, then that fact must be reported to HMRC and a new claim made.

(2) *The income tax personal allowances do not apply to tax credits.* Instead, claimants are entitled to the appropriate "elements". One important effect of this, combined with the first point, is that the widespread practice of transferring income from the working partner of a couple to the non-working partner, so as to claim the maximum value from personal allowances and to minimise higher-rate tax, and so to reduce income tax, will not work to reduce income for tax credits purposes.

(3) *The taxable forms of income are not identical to those used for income tax.* They are similar, but include some additional items, including rules dealing with income foregone and income of which a person has deprived himself or herself.

(4) *Claimants are taxed on worldwide income.* This is linked to (3). Tax credits may only be claimed by those who are ordinarily resident in the United Kingdom, but they are subject to the obligation to declare their full incomes, regardless of any reliefs by way of double taxation or exemption that they might receive under the Income Tax Acts or double taxation agreements.

(5) *Claimants are usually assessed on last year's income.* The income tax rules now use the current year's income for almost all income tax assessments. Since 2007, calculations of income for tax credits purposes will, with rare exceptions, be based on the income of the previous year. Note will only be taken of the income of the current year if there was no income in the previous year, or the current year's income exceeds that of the previous year by at least £25,000.

(6) *The thresholds for income tax and each tax credit are different.* There is now a single personal allowance for income tax and NI contributions for all those under 65, with a higher figure for those over 65. But there are separate thresholds for working tax credit and child tax credit, and these are not linked to income tax.

(7) *Deductions and exclusions are not identical.* Nor are specific inclusions, so the assessment of income from employment for income tax purposes will not be identical, and nor will the total income.

The drafting techniques used in these Regulations are also those of the Rewrite Project, for example in the use of signposting provisions and the use of the "command" tense of verbs in taking the user step by step through a calculation. Following this approach, reg.3 lays down in clear terms how income is to be calculated. But it is, in practice, the fifth of five questions that need to be answered to establish the relevant income of a claimant or claimants.

The questions to be decided:

(1) Who is claiming?   **2.108**

(2) IS or JSA . . . or SPC?

(3) Which tax year?

(4) Are there any income changes during the tax year?

(5) What income?

The questions are as follows:

(1) Who is claiming?
Is the claim a single claim, a joint claim or a claim by a polygamous unit? The   **2.109**
income of each claimant must be calculated.

(2) IS, JSA, SPC?
Automatic entitlement to child tax credit has yet to be introduced for those   **2.110**
on income support and jobseeker's allowance, although it now exists for those of
pensionable age receiving state pension credit instead. The 16 hour rule effectively
prevents those on these benefits claiming working tax credit as well.

(3) Which tax year?
As noted above, in most cases the relevant income for tax credits is the income of   **2.111**
the previous year not the current year income used for most income tax purposes. But

attention must be paid to current income where there is a sharp increase in income between one year and the next. (This does not apply to capital gains, so will most often catch employees, as sums received from employment are seldom regarded as capital).

(4) Are there any changes during the year?

2.112   The award of tax credit under ss.5 and 14 of the Act are by reference initially to the income of the previous year. But there may be relevant changes of circumstances that lead to a revision of the award if there is a notified change of circumstances under reg.6. The decision on entitlement is made only after the end of the tax year under s.19.

(5) What kinds of income?

2.113   This is determined by the current regulations.

CROSS-REFERENCES

2.114   The notes to each paragraph set out in full the Parts, Chapters and section titles to all Chapters and Sections of the Taxes Act, ITEPA and Finance Acts referred to in these regulations. The regulations include cross references to a considerable number of income tax provisions, only some of which will be of more than occasional importance to tax credits assessments. In addition, as explained below, major parts of both Acts are of no relevance to tax credits. The volume contains a selection of the more important provisions from both Acts, and the cross references supplement that by noting the full title of each Chapter and section referred to in these Regulations.

PART I

General provisions

Citation, commencement and effect

2.115   **1.** These Regulations may be cited as the Tax Credits (Definition and Calculation of Income) Regulations 2002 and shall come into force—
   (a) for the purpose of enabling claims to be made, on 1st August 2002;
   (b) for the purpose of enabling awards to be made, on 1st January 2003; and
   (c) for all other purposes, on 6th April 2003;
and shall have effect for the tax year beginning on 6th April 2003 and subsequent tax years.

DEFINITIONS

"award"—see TCA 2002, s.5.
"claim"—see TCA 2002, s.3.
"tax year"—see reg.2.

Interpretation

2.116   **2.**—(1) In these Regulations, unless the context otherwise requires—
"the Act" means the Tax Credits Act 2002;
"the Contributions and Benefits Act" means the Social Security Contributions and Benefits Act 1992; [³. . .]
"the Employment Act" means the Employment and Training Act 1973 [³; and
"the Northern Ireland Contributions and Benefits Act" means the Social Security Contributions and Benefits (Northern Ireland) Act 1992.]

(2) In these Regulations except where the context otherwise requires—
"the 1992 Fund" means moneys made available from time to time
   by the Secretary of State for Social Security for the benefit of persons
   eligible for payment in accordance with the provisions of a scheme
   established by him on 24th April 1992 as respects England and Wales
   and Northern Ireland and on 10th April 1992 as respects Scotland;
[⁶"the Board" means the Commissioners for Her Majesty's Revenue and
   Customs";]
"child" has the meaning given in the Child Tax Credit Regulations
   2002;
"claim" means a claim for child tax credit or working tax credit and "joint
   claim" and "single claim" shall be construed in accordance with [²sec-
   tion 3(8)] of the Act and "claimant" shall be construed accordingly;
[⁴"couple" has the meaning given by section 3(5A) of the Act;]
[¹"earnings" shall be construed in accordance with section 62 of the
   ITEPA;]
"the Eileen Trust" means the charitable trust of that name established on
   29th March 1993 out of funds provided by the Secretary of State for
   Social Security for the benefit of persons eligible in accordance with
   its provisions;
[¹. . .];
[⁵"employment zone" means an area within Great Britain—
 (i) subject to a designation for the purposes of the Employment Zones
     Regulations 2003 by the Secretary of State, or
[⁷(ii) listed in the Schedule to the Employment Zones (Allocation to
     Contractors) Pilot Regulations 2006,]
   pursuant to section 60 of the Welfare Reform and Pensions Act 1999;]
"employment zone programme" means a programme which is—
 (a) established for one or more employment zones; and
 (b) designed to assist claimants for a Jobseeker's Allowance to obtain
     sustainable employment;
"family" means—
 (a) in the case of a joint claim, the [⁴. . .] couple by whom the claim is
     made and any child or qualifying young person for whom at least
     one of them is responsible, in accordance with regulation 3 of the
     Child Tax Credit Regulations 2002; and
 (b) in the case of a single claim, the claimant and any child or qualify-
     ing young person for whom he is responsible in accordance with
     regulation 3 of the Child Tax Credit Regulations 2002;
"the Independent Living Fund" means the charitable trust of that name
   established out of funds provided by the Secretary of State for Social
   Services for the purpose of providing financial assistance to those persons
   incapacitated by or otherwise suffering from very severe disablement who
   are in need of such assistance to enable them to live independently;
[⁹ "the Independent Living Fund (2006)" means the Trust of that name
   established by a deed dated 10th April 2006 and made between the
   Secretary of State for Work and Pensions of the one part and Margaret
   Rosemary Cooper, Michael Beresford Boyall and Marie Theresa
   Martin of the other part;]
"the Independent Living Funds" means the Independent Living Fund,
   [⁹ the Independent Living (Extension) Fund, the Independent Living
   (1993) Fund and the Independent Living Fund (2006)]

"the Independent Living (Extension) Fund" means the trust of that name established on 25th February 1993 by the Secretary of State for Social Security and Robin Glover Wendt and John Fletcher Shepherd;

"the Independent Living (1993) Fund" means the trust of that name established on 25th February 1993 by the Secretary of State for Social Security and Robin Glover Wendt and John Fletcher Shepherd;

[8 "ITA" means the Income Tax Act 2007]

[1"ITEPA" means the Income Tax (Earnings and Pensions) Act 2003;]

[6"ITTOIA" means the Income Tax (Trading and Other Income) Act 2005;]

"the Macfarlane (Special Payments) Trust" means the trust of that name established on 29th January 1990 partly out of funds provided by the Secretary of State for Health for the benefit of certain persons suffering from haemophilia;

"the Macfarlane (Special Payments) (No.2) Trust" means the trust of that name established on 3rd May 1991 partly out of funds provided by the Secretary of State for Health for the benefit of certain persons suffering from haemophilia and other beneficiaries;

"the Macfarlane Trust" means the charitable trust established partly out of funds provided by the Secretary of State for Health to the Haemophilia Society for the relief of poverty or distress among those suffering from haemophilia;

"the Macfarlane Trusts" means the Macfarlane Trust, the Macfarlane (Special Payments) Trust and the Macfarlane (Special Payments) (No.2) Trust;

"pensionable age" has the meaning given by the rules in paragraph 1 of Schedule 4 to the Pensions Act 1995;

"pension fund holder", in relation to a [5registered pension scheme], means the trustees, managers or scheme administrators of the scheme [5. . .];

"qualifying young person" has the meaning given in the Child Tax Credit Regulations 2002;

[5"registered pension scheme" has the meaning given by section 150(2) of the Finance Act 2004;]

[5. . .]

[5. . .]

[6. . .];

[1. . .];

"the Service Pensions Order" means the Naval, Military and Air Forces, etc. (Disablement and Death) Service Pensions Order 1983;

"tax year" means a period beginning with the 6th April in one year and ending with 5th April in the next;

"the Taxes Act" means the Income and Corporation Taxes Act 1988;

"voluntary organisation" means a body, other than a public or local authority, the activities of which are carried on otherwise than for profit;

"war pension" has the meaning given in section 25(4) of the Social Security Act 1989.

(3) For the purposes of these Regulations, whether a person is responsible for a child or a qualifying young person is determined in accordance with regulaton 3 of the Child Tax Credit Regulations 2002.

(4) In these Regulations—

(a) a reference to a claimant's partner is a reference to a claimant's spouse [⁴or civil partner] or a person with whom the claimant lives as a spouse [⁴or civil partner]; and

(b) a reference to a claimant's former partner is a reference to a claimant's former spouse [⁴or civil partner] or a person with whom the claimant has lived as a spouse [⁴or civil partner]; and

(c) a reference in these Regulations to an Extra Statutory Concession is a reference to that Concession as published by the Inland Revenue on 1st July 2002.

AMENDMENTS

1. Tax Credits (Definition and Calculation of Income) (Amendment) Regulations 2003 (SI 2003 No.732), reg.4 (April 6, 2003).

2. Tax Credits (Miscellaneous Amendments No.2) Regulations 2003 (SI 2003/2815), reg.3 (November 26, 2003).

3. Tax Credits (Miscellaneous Amendments) Regulations 2004 (SI 2004/762), reg.13 (April 6, 2004).

4. Civil Partnership Act 2004 (Tax Credits, etc.) (Consequential Amendments) Order 2005 (SI 2005/2919), art.3(2) (December 5, 2005).

5. Taxation of Pension Schemes (Consequential Amendments) Order 2006 (SI 2006/745), art.26(2) (April 6, 2006).

6. Tax Credits (Miscellaneous Amendments) Regulations 2006 (SI 2006/766), reg.7 (April 6, 2006).

7. Tax Credits (Miscellaneous Amendments) Regulations 2007 (SI 2007/824), reg.8 (April 6, 2007).

8. Tax Credits (Definition and Calculation of Income) (Amendment) Regulations 2007 (SI 2007/1305), reg.3 (May 16, 2007).

9. Independent Living Fund (2006) Order 2007 (SI 2007/2538), art.7 (October 1, 2007).

GENERAL NOTE

See also the definitions in TCA 2002, ss.48 and 65 (above) and ITA 2007 Sch.4 (not included in this work).   2.117

PART II

INCOME FOR THE PURPOSES OF TAX CREDITS

CHAPTER 1

General

Calculation of income of claimant

3.—(1) The manner in which income of a claimant, or, in the case of a joint claim, the aggregate income of the claimants, is to be calculated for a tax year for the purposes of Part I of the Act is as follows.   2.118

Step 1

Calculate and then add together—   2.119
  (a) the pension income (as defined in regulation 5(1));
  (b) the investment income (as defined in regulation 10);
  (c) the property income (as defined in regulation 11);

(d) the foreign income (as defined in regulation 12); and

(e) the notional income (as defined in regulation 13),

of the claimant, or, in the case of a joint claim, of the claimants.

If the result of this step is £300 or less, it is treated as nil.

If the result of this step is more than £300, only the excess is taken into account in the following steps.

Step 2

2.120 Calculate and then add together—

(a) the employment income (as defined in regulation 4);

(b) the social security income (as defined in regulation 7);

(c) the student income (as defined in regulation 8); and

(d) the miscellaneous income (as defined in regulation 18), of the claimant, or in the case of a joint claim, of the claimants.

Step 3

2.121 Add together the results of steps 1 and 2.

Step 4

2.122 Calculate the trading income (as defined in regulation 6) of the claimant, or in the case of a joint claim, of the claimants.

Add the result of this step to that produced by step 3 [¹ . . .] in the year.

If there has been a trading loss in the year, [¹ subtract] the amount of that loss from the result of step 3.

[⁴A loss shall not be available for tax credit purposes, unless the trade was being carried on upon a commercial basis and with a view to the realisation of profits in the trade or, where the carrying on of the trade formed part of a larger undertaking, in the undertaking as a whole.]

[²Any trading loss in the year not set off as a result of the calculations in Steps One to Four above due to an insufficiency of income may be carried forward and set off against trading income (if any) of the same trade, profession or vocation in subsequent years (taking earlier years first) for the purposes of calculation of income under this regulation.]

(2) Subject to the qualifications in the following paragraphs of this regulation, and the provisions of Part III, the result of step 4 in paragraph (1) is the income of the claimant, or, in the case of a joint claim, of the claimants, for the purposes of the Act.

(3) Income which—

(a) arises in a territory outside the United Kingdom; and

(b) is, for the time being, unremittable for the purposes of [⁴Chapter 4 of Part 8 of ITTOIA],

is disregarded in calculating the income of the claimant or, in the case of a joint claim, of the claimants.

(4) Paragraph (5) applies in the case of a claimant who is [¹, for income tax purposes]

(a) resident [¹and domiciled but not ordinarily resident] in the United Kingdom; [². . .]

(b) resident and ordinarily resident but not domiciled in the United Kingdom [²or]

[²(c) resident but neither ordinarily resident nor domiciled in the United Kingdom.]

(5) In the case of a person to whom this paragraph applies—

[¹(a) any income arising outside the United Kingdom is to be taken into account, subject to any specific provision of these Regulations, regardless of the domicile or residence of the claimant; and;]

(b) references to a sum being [¹taken into account] are to be construed as including a sum which would be taxable if he were resident, ordinarily resident and domiciled in the United Kingdom.

[¹(5A) Any income is to be taken into account, subject to any specific provision of these Regulations, notwithstanding the provision of any Order in Council under section 788 of the Taxes Act (double taxation agreements).]

(6) In the case of a claimant who would be chargeable to income tax but for some special exemption or immunity from income tax, income shall be calculated on the basis of the amounts which would be so chargeable but for that exemption or immunity.

[¹(6A) Income paid to a claimant in a currency other than sterling shall be converted into sterling at the average of the exchange rates applicable for the conversion of that currency into sterling in the period of 12 months [⁵ending on 31st March] in the tax year in which the income arises.]

(7) In calculating income under this Part there shall be deducted [¹. . .]—

(a) [¹the amount of] any banking charge or commission payable in converting to sterling a payment of income which is made in a currency other than sterling;

(b) [¹the grossed up amount of] any qualifying donation (within the meaning of [⁶ Chapter 2 of Part 8 of ITA (gift aid)]), made by the claimant or, in the case of a joint claim, by either or both of the claimants; [². . .] [⁴. . .]

[³(c) the amount of any contribution made by the claimant, or in the case of a joint claim, by either or both of the claimants to a registered pension scheme together with the amount of any tax relief due on those contributions.]

[³. . .]

[²(8) If—

(a) a claimant has sustained a loss in relation to a [⁴ UK property business] or an overseas property business; and

(b) the relief to which he is entitled in accordance with [⁶ section 120 of ITA (deduction of property losses from general income)] exceeds the amount of his property income or foreign income for tax credits purposes, for the year in question;

the amount of his total income for tax credit purposes, computed in accordance with the preceding provisions of this regulation, shall be reduced by the amount of the excess.

[⁴In this paragraph "UK property business" and "overseas property business" have the same meaning as the have in the Taxes Act.]

AMENDMENTS

1. Tax Credits (Definition and Calculation of Income) (Amendment) Regulations 2003 (SI 2003/732), reg.5 (April 6, 2003).

2. Tax Credits (Miscellaneous Amendments No.2) Regulations 2003 (SI 2003/2815), reg.4 (November 26, 2003).

3. Taxation of Pension Schemes (Consequential Amendments) Order 2006 (SI 2006/745), art.26(3) (April 6, 2006).

4. Tax Credits (Miscellaneous Amendments) Regulations 2006 (SI 2006/766), reg.8 (April 6, 2006).

5. Tax Credits (Miscellaneous Amendments) Regulations 2007 (SI 2007/824), reg.9 (April 6, 2007).

6. Tax Credits (Definition and Calculation of Income) (Amendment) Regulations 2007 (SI 2007/1305), reg.4 (May 16, 2007).

GENERAL NOTE

2.123   Regulation 3(1) and (2) state that there are four steps to calculating the aggregate income of a claimant or joint claimants for a tax year, but it is suggested that this would be better presented as five steps. The four steps are:

(1) Add the totals of income from sources subject to the £300 discount and deduct that discount.

(2) Add the totals from all other sources, apart from trading income.

(3) Add the totals of (1) and (2).

(4) Add to, or subtract from, the total from (3) the net income (or net loss) from trading income.

The "fifth step" is then to deduct from that sum the various general deductions, exclusions, exemptions and disregards in these regulations. These are set out in reg.3(3) (unremittable income), reg.3(7) (other general deductions), reg.9 (exempt scholarship income) and the Tables 6, 7 and 8 in reg.19 (general disregards).

Paragraph (7) is part of the "fifth step", along with para.(3). It provides for two important deductions commonly made against income for income tax purposes. The first is to allow the deduction from income for tax credits purposes of any sums given to charities within the terms of the FA 1990, s.25. That is the provision authorising the tax deduction for "gift aid" payments for all non-refundable gifts of money to charities made otherwise than by covenant, the charity being treated as receiving the sum under deduction of tax at the basic rate. The other allows deductions from total income for contributions to registered pension schemes under the FA 2004 and related provisions.

Paragraphs (3) to (6) are a motley of provisions dealing with foreign elements. The combined effect of paras (4), (5), and (5A) includes all foreign income in the income to be used to calculate tax credits notwithstanding that for income tax purposes the income is excluded from a charge to income tax in the United Kingdom either because of the domicile of the taxpayer or because of a double tax agreement. It seems that para.(6) has, in part, the same aim, but it is not clear how it can override the tax exemptions applicable to diplomats and consuls under general international law and, in the United Kingdom, the Diplomatic Privileges Act 1964 and the Consular Relations Act 1968.

CHAPTER 2

Employment income

Employment income

2.124   **4.**—(1) In these Regulations, "employment income" means—

(a) any [1earnings] from an office or employment received in the tax year;

(b) so much of any payment made to a claimant in that year in respect of expenses as is chargeable to income tax [¹by virtue of section 62 or section 72 of ITEPA];

(c) [¹the cash equivalent of] any non-cash voucher received by the claimant in that year and chargeable to income tax under [¹section 87 of ITEPA];

(d) [¹the cash equivalent of] any credit-token received by the claimant in that year and chargeable to income tax under [¹section 94 of ITEPA];

(e) [¹the cash equivalent of] any cash voucher received by the claimant in that year and chargeable to income tax under [¹section 81 of ITEPA];

[¹(f) any amount chargeable to tax under Chapter 3 of Part VI of ITEPA;]

(g) so much of a payment of statutory sick pay, received by the claimant during the year, as is subject to income tax [¹by virtue of section 660 of ITEPA;]

(h) the amount (if any) by which a payment of [¹statutory maternity pay, statutory paternity pay or statutory adoption pay] exceeds £100 per week;

(i) any amount charged to income tax for that year [¹under section 120 or section 149 of ITEPA;]

[¹(j) any sum to which section 225 of ITEPA applies;]

(k) any amount paid in that year by way of strike pay to the claimant as a member of a trade union;

[²(l) any amount charged to income tax for that year under Part 7 of ITEPA.]

[⁶(m) any amount paid to a person serving a custodial sentence or remanded in custody awaiting trial or sentence, for work done while serving the sentence or remanded in custody.]

For the purposes of this paragraph, references to the receipt of a payment of any description are references to its receipt by or on behalf of the claimant, or in the case of a joint claim of either of the claimants, in any part of the world.

This paragraph is subject to the following qualifications.

(2) Employment income does not include pension income.

[³(2A) [⁵ . . .]

(2B) [⁵ . . .]

[²(3) This paragraph applies if (apart from section 64 of ITEPA) the same benefit would give rise to two amounts ("A" and "B")—

(a) "A" being an amount of earnings from a claimant's employment as defined in section 62 of ITEPA, and

(b) "B" being an amount to be treated as earnings under any provision of Chapter 10 of Part 3 of ITEPA.

In such a case, the amount to be taken into account in computing the claimant's employment income is the greater of A and B, and the lesser amount shall be disregarded.]

(4) In calculating employment income, the payments and benefits listed in Table 1 shall be disregarded.

Table 1. Payments [¹and benefits] disregarded in the calculation of employment income

2.125

1. Any payment in respect of qualifying removal expenses, or the provision of any qualifying removal benefit, within the meaning of [¹Chapter 7 of Part 4 of ITEPA].

[¹**2A.** The payment or reimbursement of expenses incurred in the provision of transport to a disabled employee (as defined in section 246(4) of ITEPA) by his employer, if no liability to income tax arises in respect of that payment or reimbursement (as the case may be) by virtue of section 246 of ITEPA.

2B. The provision to a disabled employee (as defined in section 246(4) of ITEPA) by his employer of a car, the provision of fuel for the car, or the reimbursement of expenses incurred in connection with the car, if no liability to income tax arises in respect of that provision or reimbursement (as the case may be) by virtue of section 247 of ITEPA.

2C. The payment or reimbursement of expenses incurred on transport, if no liability to income tax arises in respect of that payment or reimbursement (as the case may be) by virtue of section 248 of ITEPA.]

3. Travel facilities provided for the claimant as a member of the naval, military or air forces of the Crown for the purpose of going on, or returning from, leave.

[⁶**3A.** The payment by the Secretary of State for Defence of an operational allowance to a member of Her Majesty's forces in respect of service in an operational area specified by the Secretary of State for Defence.]

[⁷**3B.** A payment designated by the Secretary of State for Defence as Council Tax Relief and made by the Secretary of State for Defence to a member of Her Majesty's forces.]

4. Payment or reimbursement of expenses in connection with the provision for, or use by, the claimant as a person holding an office or employment of a car-parking space at or near his place of work.

5. Any benefit or non-cash voucher provided to the claimant, or to any member of his family or household, [¹in respect of which no liability to income tax arises by virtue of Chapter 5 of Part 4 of ITEPA.]

6. Any payment of incidental overnight expenses [¹in respect of which no liability to income tax arises by virtue of section 240 of ITEPA.]

[¹**7.** Food, drink and mess allowances for the armed forces and training allowances payable to members of the reserve forces in respect of which no liability to income tax arises by virtue of section 297 or 298 of ITEPA.]

8. The value of meal vouchers issued to the claimant as an employee [¹if section 89 of ITEPA applies to the vouchers.]

9. Any cash payment received by the claimant as a miner in lieu of free coal, or the provision of the coal itself, [¹in respect of which no liability to income tax arises by virtue of section 306 of ITEPA.]

10. An award made to the claimant as a director or employee by way of a testimonial to mark long service [¹if, or to the extent that, no liability to income tax arises in respect of it by virtue of section 323 of ITEPA.]

11. Payment of a daily subsistence allowance [¹in respect of which no liability to income tax arises by virtue of section 304 of ITEPA.].

[¹**11A.** The payment or reimbursement of reasonable expenses incurred by an employee who has a permanent workplace at an offshore installation, on transfer transport, related accommodation and subsistence or local transport, if no liability to income tax arises in respect of that payment or reimbursement (as the case may be) by virtue of section 305 of ITEPA.

For the purposes of this item, expressions which are defined in section 305 of ITEPA have the same meaning here as they do there.

11B. Payment of an allowance to a person in employment under the Crown in respect of which no liability to income tax arises by virtue of section 299 of ITEPA.

11C. The payment or reimbursement to an employee of any sum in connection with work-related training, or individual learning account training (as respectively defined in sections 251 and 256 of ITEPA) if no liability to income tax arises in respect of that payment or reimbursement (as the case may be) by virtue of any provision of Chapter 4 of Part 4 of ITEPA.

11D. The provision for an employee of a non-cash voucher or a credit-token, to the extent that liability to income tax does not arise in respect of that voucher or credit-token (as the case may be), under Chapter 4 of [²Part 3 of ITEPA, by virtue of any provision of Chapter 6 of Part 4 of ITEPA.]

11E. The provision for an employee of free or subsidised meal vouchers or tokens (within the meaning of section 317(5) of ITEPA), if no liability to income tax arises in respect of that provision by virtue of section 317 of ITEPA.]

[⁶ **11F.** The provision of one mobile telephone for an employee in respect of which no liability to income tax arises by virtue of section 319 of ITEPA.]

12. An award made to the claimant under a Staff Suggestion Scheme, if the conditions specified in [¹sections 321 and 322 of ITEPA [³are satisfied].]

13. Travelling and subsistence allowances paid to or on behalf of the claimant by his employer [¹in respect of which no liability to income tax arises by virtue of section 245 of ITEPA.]

14. Any gift consisting of goods, or a voucher or token to obtain goods, [¹in respect of which no liability to income tax arises by virtue of section 270 or 324 of ITEPA.]

[¹**14A.** Any payment or reimbursement of expenses incurred in connection with an employment-related asset transfer (as defined in section 326(2) of ITEPA), if no liability to income tax arises in respect of that payment or reimbursement (as the case may be) by virtue of section 326 of ITEPA.

14B. Any payment of expenses incurred by an employee in connection with a taxable car if no liability to income tax arises in respect of the payment by virtue of section 239(2) of ITEPA.]

[²**14C.** The discharge of any liability of an employee in connection with a taxable car if no liability to income tax arises by virtue of section 239(1) of ITEPA.

14D. A benefit connected with a taxable car if no liability to income tax arises by virtue of section 239(4) of ITEPA.]

15. A cash voucher, non-cash voucher or credit-token to the extent that it is used by the recipient for the provision of childcare, the costs of which if borne by the recipient would be relevant childcare charges within the meaning of regulation 14 of the Working Tax Credit (Entitlement and Maximum Rate) Regulations 2002.

[³16. A payment made by the Department for Work and Pensions under section 2 of the Employment Act—

(a) by way of In-Work Credit [⁸, Better Off In-Work Credit], Job Grant or Return to Work Credit, [⁸ . . .]

(b) under the Employment Retention and Advancement Scheme or the Working Neighbourhoods Pilot.]

[⁸ (c) under the City Strategy Pathfinder Pilots,

(d) by way of an In-Work Emergency Discretion Fund payment pursuant to arrangements made by the Secretary of State, or

(e) by way of an Up-front Childcare Fund payment pursuant to arrangements made by the Secretary of State.]

[⁵16A. A payment made by the Department for Employment and Learning in Northern Ireland under section 1 of the Employment and Training Act (Northern Ireland) 1950 by way of Return to Work Credit.]

[⁸ 16B. Any In-Work Emergency Fund payment made to a person pursuant to arrangements made by the Department of Economic Development under section 1 of the Employment and Training Act (Northern Ireland) 1950.]

[²17. The payment or reimbursement of reasonable additional household expenses incurred by an employee who works from home, within the meaning of section 316A of ITEPA.

18. The payment or reimbursement of retraining course expenses within the meaning of the section 311 of ITEPA.]

[⁴19. Provision of computer equipment in respect of which no liability to income tax arises by virtue of section 320 of ITEPA.]

[⁸ 20. Pay As You Earn (PAYE) settlement agreements made under Part 6 of the Income Tax (PAYE) Regulations ("the PAYE Regulations") 2003.

For the purposes of this item the special arrangements under regulation 141 of the PAYE Regulations also apply.]

---

(5) From the amount of employment income, calculated in accordance with the preceding provisions of this regulation, there shall be deducted the amount of any deduction permitted in calculating [¹calculating earnings by virtue of any provision of sections [²231 to 232,] 336–344, or s.346, 347, 351, 352, 362, 363, 367, 368, 370, 371, 373, 374, 376, 377 or 713 of ITEPA].

AMENDMENTS

1. Tax Credits (Definition and Calculation of Income) (Amendment) Regulations 2003 (SI 2003/732), reg.6 (April 6, 2003).

2. Tax Credits (Miscellaneous Amendments No.2) Regulations 2003 (SI 2003/2815), reg.5 (November 26, 2003).

3. Tax Credits (Miscellaneous Amendments) Regulations 2004 (SI 2004/762), reg.14 (April 6, 2004).

4. Tax Credits (Miscellaneous Amendments No.3) Regulations 2004 (SI 2004/2663) reg.2 (November 3, 2004).

5. Tax Credits (Miscellaneous Amendments) Regulations 2006 (SI 2006/766), reg.9 (April 6, 2006).

6. Tax Credits (Miscellaneous Amendments) Regulations 2007 (SI 2007/824), reg.10 (April 6, 2007).

7. Tax Credits (Miscellaneous Amendments) Regulations 2008 (SI 2008/604), reg.2(2) (April 1, 2008).

8. Tax Credits (Miscellaneous Amendments) (No.2) Regulations 2008 (SI 2008/2169), reg.4 (September 1, 2008).

CROSS-REFERENCES

The regulation adopts for tax credits purposes the following chapters and sections of ITEPA, all relating to employment income:

Pt 3: Employment income: Earnings and benefits etc treated as earnings

s.62	Earnings

Pt 3, Ch.4 Taxable benefit: vouchers and credit-tokens

s.72	Sums in respect of expenses treated as earnings
s.81	Benefit of cash voucher treated as earnings
s.87	Benefit of non-cash voucher treated as earnings
s.89	Reduction for meal vouchers
s.94	Benefit of credit-token treated as earnings

Pt 3, Ch.6 Taxable benefits: cars, vans and related vehicles

s.120	Benefit of car treated as earnings
s.149	Benefit of car fuel treated as earnings

Pt 3, Ch.10 Taxable benefits: residual liability to charge

s.201	Employment-related benefits
s.211	Special rules for scholarships: introduction

Pt 3, Ch.11 Taxable benefits: exclusion of lower-paid employments

Pt 3, Ch.12 Payments treated as earnings

s.225	Payments for restrictive covenants

Pt 4: Employment income: exemptions

s.239	Payments and benefits connected with taxable cars and vans and exempt heavy goods vehicles
s.240	Incidental overnight expenses and benefits
s.245	Travelling and subsistence during public transport strikes
s.246	Transport between work and home for disabled employees
s.247	Provision of cars for disabled employees
s.248	Transport home: late-night working and failure of car-sharing arrangements

Pt 4, Ch.4 Exemptions: education and training

s.251	Meaning of "work-related training"
s.256	Meaning of "individual learning account training"

Pt 4, Ch.5 Exemptions; recreational benefits

Pt 4, Ch.6 Exemptions: non-cash vouchers and credit-tokens

s.270	Exemptions of small gifts of vouchers and tokens from third parties

Pt 4, Ch.7 Exemptions: removal benefits and expenses

s.297	Armed forces' food, drink and mess allowances
s.298	Reserve and auxiliary forces' training allowances
s.299	Crown employees' foreign service allowances
s.304	Experts seconded to the European Commission
s.305	Offshore oil and gas workers: mainland transfers
s.306	Miners, etc.: coal and allowances in lieu of coal
s.317	Subsidised meals
s.321	Suggestion awards
s.322	Suggestion awards: "the permitted maximum"
s.323	Long service awards
s.324	Small gifts from third parties
s.326	Expenses incidental to transfer of a kind not normally met by transferor

GENERAL NOTE

2.126   This regulation defines "employment income" for the purposes of reg.3. Although the result may be obvious in most cases, four questions have to be asked to set the context of a tax credits calculation of employment income when regard is had to a particular source of income:

What income is relevant?
What exemptions and deductions apply?
Whose income is it?
When is the income brought into calculation?

These are discussed in turn. The same pattern is followed in the notes on other regulations.

What income is relevant? The scope of ITEPA and regulation 4

2.127   In marginal cases it is always necessary to ask both if an income-generating activity is employment, self-employment or something else, and what earnings come from any employment, as against any other source.

Employment and self-employment

2.128   The common context of a dispute about whether an activity is or is not an employment is the contention by the individual concerned that he or she is self-employed. This issue is discussed in the general note to reg. 6 below. "Office" used to be a separate provision in the old Sch.E, reflecting the antiquity of the phraseology used. ITEPA, s.5 now relegates the status of office-holders (rightly in terms of relative importance) to a secondary status in the legislation. It also codifies the common law definition of "office". For all tax credits purposes, as for all ITEPA purposes, "employee" is to be read as including office holders, and "being employed" includes holding an office. "Office" is now defined (in words adopted from the income tax case of *GWR v Bater* [1920] 3 K.B. 266) as including "any position which has an existence independent of the person who holds it and may be filled by successive holders". For a discussion of that in the context of the borderline between holding an office and being self-employed see *Edwards v Clinch* [1982] A.C. 845.

Employment income

ITEPA deals with the income taxation of employment income in Pts 1–8 of the Act. For the structure of those Parts, see s.3 of ITEPA, and for the main charge to tax, see s.6. As can be seen from the list of cross-references, the policy and drafting approaches taken for the purposes of calculating employment income for tax credits purposes are to select from the provisions of those parts (ss.1–564), rather than simply to adopt the whole code, or those parts of the code felt appropriate. TCTM04101 directs HMRC officers to "Note that, although based on income tax law, not all of the additional rules for income chargeable to tax as employment income have been included in the tax credit employment income rules", and "not all of the general exemptions and reliefs from inclusion as income chargeable as employment income have been included . . .". This will also apply to ITEPA. The only major part of the code omitted as a whole is Pt 7 (Employment income: share-related income and exemptions—ss.417–554), although Pt 8 (relating to former employees) is also excluded. Elsewhere, close attention has to be paid to those charges and exemptions that are included (as listed in the cross-reference list derived from reg. 3) and those that are excluded.

So, for example, while most sections in Pt 3 (Employment Income: earnings and benefits etc treated as earnings) are adopted, Ch. 5 (taxable benefits: living accommodation) is not, nor is Ch. 7 (taxable benefits: loans). Similarly, while most of the sections in Pt 4 (Employment income: exemptions) are allowed also as exemptions for tax credits purposes, again the approach has been to select those that are applied and those that are not. The same is true of Pt 5 (Employment income: deductions allowed from earnings). This reflects in part an assessment of the provisions that are not relevant (e.g. Pt 4, Ch. 10 (exemptions on termination of employment)) are excluded as not relevant either to working tax credit or to child tax credit, but that does not always appear to explain the omission. For example, the exemption for subsidised meals in s.317 is applied, but not the exemption for care for children in s.318.

The resulting picture is one of some complexity, because one cannot simply adopt the income tax assessment of all employees for tax credits without looking through at least some of them to see on which sections of ITEPA the charge to tax is based or the exemption or deduction is claimed. In any case, other than the most straightforward, it may therefore be necessary to look at the breakdown of any charge to tax not based simply on earnings and the usual expenses and deductions. That also means that the approach of adopting a figure from the P45 or P60 supplied to an employee at the end of an employment or the end of a tax year may not be enough in those cases. While this might sound an over-exact approach to the calculation of income, it has to be borne in mind that the effective value of any charge or exemption for tax credit purposes is, at the margin, 39 per cent of the amount charged or claimed. So, a failure to allow a deduction for a £150 expense (which, if deductible at the basic rate of income tax, will have in effect cost the employee not £150 but £117) will "cost" the employee £59 in lost tax credits, or nearly half the actual cost to the employee of the amount for which the deduction is claimed.

To follow that point with a relevant example, it would seem from the exclusion of s.317 that a claimant for WTC may claim for childcare charges if paid by the

2.129

employee, but is liable to have the value of the advantage of employer-provided childcare taken into account as income for tax credits purposes although, of course, the employee will not be paying for, and therefore not able to claim for, that provision. However, this depends how the employer provides the advantage. If the employer provides childcare through the mechanism of providing the employee with a cash voucher, non-cash voucher or credit-token, the exclusion from calculation of that value by Table 1, Item 15, is broader than the income tax exclusion. As the working tax credit childcare element is not itself taxable to income tax (Taxes Act, s.617A), the justification for this mismatch is not clear.

Differences between income tax assessments and tax credit calculations of employment income

2.130   The only full way of noting the differences between total net (i.e. after deductions) employment income for income tax purposes and for tax credits purposes is by precise reference to individual provisions in ITEPA. This must cover the ITEPA sections included in, and excluded from, reg.4 together with those provisions that are included in reg.4 but not by reference to specific provisions in ITEPA. Cross-references from reg.4 are not assisted by the reenactment of the employment income provisions since the regulation was drafted, as the previous drafting order of the regulation has been lost. As ITEPA is an immediately contemporary codification of employment income taxation, no reference for 2003–04 need be made to any other provision. In future years, it may be assumed that changes will, where appropriate, be made in parallel.

The full list of sections of ITEPA included by cross reference is set out above, and from that the obvious gaps can be identified. There are no differences with regard to cash earnings or equivalent (see ss.62 and 72 of ITEPA). But only some parts of the Pt 3 provisions on taxable benefits apply. Chapter 3 (expense payments), Ch.4 (vouchers and credit-tokens), Ch.6 (cars, vans and related benefits) and Ch.10 (residual liability) apply, but no part of Ch.5 (living accommodation), Ch.7 (loans), Ch.8 (notional loans in respect of acquisition of shares), or Ch.9 (disposals of shares for more than market value) apply. And of the six specific payments treated as earnings by ch.12, only one (restrictive covenants under s.225) is expressly brought into the calculation.

Three kinds of income only are mentioned in reg.4 that are not related directly to specific provisions in ITEPA. Regulation 4(1)(h) requires inclusion of only the excess of statutory maternity pay over £100. For income tax purposes the sum is fully taxable. Regulation 4(1)(k) requires the inclusion of strike pay, whether or not that is otherwise taxable under this or any other head of income. These both reflect social security rules rather than income tax rules. Regulation 4(1)(m) adds prisoners' earnings.

What exemptions and deductions apply?

2.131   The exclusions from para.(4) are far harder to summarise. Part 4 deals with exemptions. Chapter 1 deals with general exemptions rules. Of the specific rules, Ch.2 (mileage allowances and passenger payments) is not within the scope of tax credits, and nor are many of the specific exemptions related to transport, travel and subsistence in Ch.3. Of ss.237–248 in that Chapter, only ss.239, 240 and 245–8 are permitted exclusions for tax credits calculations. Chapter 4 (education and training) exemptions are allowed, as are Ch.5 (recreational benefits) and Ch.7 (removal expenses). But the exemptions in Ch.8 (special kinds of employees) and Ch.11 (miscellaneous exemptions) are included on a selected basis only. In part, this selection excludes exemptions related to foreign elements, and to living accommodation (the benefit of which is excluded from the calculation of income), and so reflects the broader policy of the definition of relevant income. But there is no substitute in this Part of the Act for a detailed comparison of individual provisions.

There are only four groups of exemptions mentioned in reg.4 without express reference to ITEPA provisions. In the Table, Items 3, 3A and 3B (forces' payments) are defined broadly rather than in terms of s.296 of ITEPA, which is to the same effect. Item 4 (parking) is also broader than the equivalent s.237. Likewise, Item 15 (cash vouchers, etc.) is broader than ss.266–267. Items 16, 16A and 16B are tax-free public–funded payments.

By comparison, the deductions rules incorporated in para.(5) by section number follow closely the equivalent rules in Pt 5 of ITEPA, with only minor omissions. The differences are restricted largely to foreign issues or irrelevant categories of deduction, such as those related to (non-included) living accommodation.

TCTM confirms the HMRC view that most of the provisions in this regulation "mirror" or "are identical with" the equivalent ITEPA provisions. The guidance is to apply the same considerations for tax credits calculations in those cases as for income tax on employment income (and there are specific cross-references to the Inspectors Manual on employment income). It may in general be thought that the tax credits appeal authorities and tax appeal authorities would also strive to a common approach, as it may be predicted that that is the approach that superior courts would take if asked to consider the same rules in the different contexts.

In practice, HMRC relies on the information given by claimants to decide on any exemptions or deductions. If a claimant does not claim any expenses, then they will not usually be considered. And it will usually be too late to ask for them to be taken into account on an appeal, as the three month rule applies to these changes as it does to all other aspects of a claim. See *CTC/2113/2006*.

Whose income is it?

This is rarely in issue in a tax credits context. One of the few practical problems arises where income is shared between husband and wife, but the joint claimant rules render that irrelevant here. The identity of the income tax payer, applying here also, is set out in ITEPA, s.13. The taxable person, and therefore the person whose income it is for tax credits purposes, is the person to whose employment the earnings relate.

2.132

When is the income brought into calculation?

The employment income to be calculated for tax credits is the income "received by the claimant . . . in" or "paid to" the claimant in the tax year in question: para. (1). That tax year will either be the current year or the previous year, as determined under s.7(3) of the TCA 2002. The income for a tax year is therefore the income, in that sense, of the year. This is consistent with the general income tax rules for assessment on a current year basis. ITEPA, s.19 provides for taxation to be based on the "net taxable earnings from an employment in the year". It is calculated when received, not when earned. That is a question of fact. This may be important for bonuses and other non-regular payments. In practice, that is also how the PAYE system operates.

2.133

CHAPTER 3

Pension income

Pension income

5.—[¹(1) In these Regulations, except where the context otherwise require, "pension income" means—

(a) any pension to which section 577 or 629 of ITEPA applies;

(b) any pension to which section 569 of ITEPA applies;

(c) any voluntary annual payment to which section 633 of ITEPA applies;

2.134

[²(d) any pension, annuity or income withdrawal to which section 579A of ITEPA applies;

(e) any unauthorised member payments to which section 208(2)(a) or (b) of the Finance Act 2004 applies;]

(f) any periodical payment to which section 619 of ITEPA applies;

[²...]

[²...]

[²...]

[²...]

[²(k) any annuity paid under a retirement annuity contract to which Chapter 9 of Part 9 of ITEPA applies;]

(l) any annuity to which section 609, 610 or 611 of ITEPA applies;

[⁴...]

[³(n) any social security lump sum to which section 7 of the Finance Act 2005 applies; and

(o) any lump sum to which section 636B or 636C of ITEPA applies.]

(2) In calculating the amount of a person's pension income there shall be disregarded any [¹payment or benefit mentioned] in Column 1 of Table 2 to the extent specified in the corresponding entry in Column 2.

Table 2. [¹Pensions, other payments and benefits] disregarded in the calculation of pension income

2.135

1. Payment	2. Extent of disregard
1. A wounds pension or disability pension to which [¹section 641 of ITEPA] applies.	So much of the payment as is disregarded by virtue of [¹section 641 of ITEPA].
2. An annuity or additional pension payable to a holder of the Victoria Cross, George Cross or any other decoration mentioned in [¹section 638 of ITEPA].	The whole of the annuity or additional pension and, if both are payable, the whole of both such annuity and additional pension.
3. A pension or allowance to which [¹section 639 of ITEPA] applies.	[¹The amount of the pension or allowance.]
4. A pension or allowance by reason of payment of which a pension or allowance specified in [¹section 639 of ITEPA] is withheld or abated.	[¹The amount treated as falling within section 639 of ITEPA by virtue of section 640(2) of that Act.]
5. In the case of a claimant in receipt of a pension under the Service Pensions Order, any increase in the rate of that pension in respect of a dependant who is not a member of the claimant's family.	The amount of the increase.
6. A mobility supplement, or a payment in respect of attendance, paid in conjunction with a war pension.	The amount of the supplement or payment.

416

1. Payment	2. Extent of disregard
7. Any supplementary pension under Article 29(1A) of the Service Pensions Order.	The amount of the supplementary pension.
8. A pension awarded at the supplementary rate under article 27(3) of the Personal Injuries (Civilians) Scheme 1983.	The amount for the time being specified in paragraph 1(c) of Schedule 4 to the Scheme.
9. A pension awarded on retirement through disability caused by injury on duty or by a work-related illness.	[¹The exempt amount of the pension calculated in accordance with section 644(3) of ITEPA.]
[¹**10.** A lump sum on which no liability to income tax arises by virtue of [² section 636A of ITEPA].	The amount of the lump sum.
11. Coal or smokeless fuel provided as mentioned in section 646(1) of ITEPA, or an allowance in lieu of such provision.	The amount on which no liability to income tax arises by virtue of that section.]

[¹(3) From the amount of pension income, calculated in accordance with the preceding provisions of this regulation, there shall be deducted any amount deductible for income tax purposes in computing pension income (as defined in ITEPA) under section 713 of that Act.]

AMENDMENTS

1. Tax Credits (Definition and Calculation of Income) (Amendment) Regulations 2003 (SI 2003/732), reg.7 (April 6, 2003).
2. Taxation of Pension Schemes (Consequential Amendments) Order 2006 (SI 2006/745), art.26(4) (April 6, 2006).
3. Tax Credits (Miscellaneous Amendments) Regulations 2006 (SI 2006/766), reg.10 (April 6, 2006).
4. Tax Credits (Miscellaneous Amendments) Regulations 2008 (SI 2008/604), reg.2(2) (April 6, 2008).

GENERAL NOTE

2.136
This regulation defines "pension income" for the purposes of reg.3. "Pension income" is a new concept evolved by the Tax Law Rewrite Project and launched in ITEPA. Previously, taxation of pensions has mainly been as if pensions were emoluments, and therefore subject to Sch.E, with other rules bringing certain kinds of pension into various cases of Sch.D. The pension income provisions in ITEPA bring together most of the various charges to tax on different kinds of pensions, including some pensions payable to the former self-employed, and also pensions payable without reference to work of any kind. It also includes social security provisions by way of pension.

What income is relevant?

2.137
ITEPA Pt 9 rewrote the whole of the relevant provisions of the then income tax legislation dealing with income tax on pensions. However, no sooner had it been rewritten than much of it was rewritten again—by the Finance Act 2004.

The provisions of FA 2004 came into effect on April 6, 2006. The amended Pt 9 applies to all pension income (including social security pensions from the UK and abroad, voluntary pensions, and pensions payable for ill-health retirements). The aim behind reg.5 is to include all pensions as income under this regulation for tax credits purposes.

What exemptions and deductions apply?

2.138   Again, the pattern is to adopt all relevant provisions in ITEPA, Pt 9. Of the three chapters dealing with exemptions, Ch.16 (exemption for certain lump sums) applies fully. Ch.17 (exemptions: any taxpayer) applies in large part. The sections not applied relate for the most part to foreign pensions, and are dealt with under the foreign income provision in reg.12. This also applies to Ch.18 (exemptions: non-United Kingdom resident taxpayers). The only other section not applied is ITEPA, s.645 (social security pensions: increases for children), which does not apply by reason of the repeal of those provisions and their replacement by child tax credit by TCA 2002 (save for the oversight of the rare payments under s.85 of the SSCBA 1992 not being repealed by the Act).

Whose income is it?

2.139   ITEPA, s.572 provides that the person liable for any tax charged is the person receiving or entitled to the pension. This is therefore the operative rule for inclusion of pension income for the calculation of tax credits income. It is the alternative to deal with those who are not entitled to a pension being received (as with voluntary pensions), but will rarely present problems. There is no significance for tax credits purposes in most cases about pensions to couples. If it is significant then, of course, entitlement is a question of law and receipt a question of fact.

When is the income brought into the calculation?

2.140   This also follows from s.572. As a result, pension income is to be included when entitlement arises. If there is no entitlement, as with voluntary pensions, then it is when the pension is received. That should follow the income tax treatment.

CHAPTER 4

Trading income

Trading income

2.141   **6.** The claimant's trading income is—
  (a) the amount of his taxable profits for the tax year from—
     (i) any trade carried on in the United Kingdom or elsewhere;
     (ii) any profession or vocation the income from which does not fall under any other provisions of these Regulations; or
  (b) if the claimant is a partner in the trade, profession or vocation, his taxable profit for the year arising from his share of the partnership's trading or professional income.
[¹ Here "taxable profits" has the same meaning as it has in Part 2 of ITTOIA but disregarding Chapter 16 of that Part (averaging profits of farmers and creative artists.]

AMENDMENT

1. Tax Credits (Miscellaneous Amendments) Regulations 2006 (SI 2006/766), reg.11 (April 6, 2006).

GENERAL NOTE

This regulation defines "trading income" for the purposes of reg. 3. It does so, since 2006, by reference to the newly codified rules for taxing trading income set out in ITTOIA 2005. This now includes all income from trades, professions and vocations and some related forms of income. It covers income both sourced in the United Kingdom and sourced abroad.

2.142

Employment and self-employment

The critical distinction in the case of many of those with smaller incomes who claim to be traders or self-employed is whether that is a true description in both law and fact of the individual's status. This is directly relevant for the calculation of tax credits because it must be decided if regs 4 or 6 applies. Following from that decision are subsidiary questions about the exemptions and deductions that must be calculated in finding the net income; the question of which period of income is to be taken into account; and the provision in Step 4 of reg. 3 allowing trading losses to be deducted from other income. The rules assume that there cannot be a net loss by way of employment income, and do not allow for it. But this is an important overall change in the tax credit rules because previously no income losses were allowed.

2.143

The status of employee or self-employed is important for several reasons besides the current context:

Income tax: employment income or trading income?

NI contributions: Class 1 or Class 2 contributions?

VAT: is the person carrying on registerable activities?

Benefits: is the individual entitled to benefits available only to employees?

In addition, there are other issues that arise from the employment status, such as the minimum wage, holiday entitlements, and employer liability, that are again to be decided separately.

Drawing a line between employment and self-employment has always been difficult. It is also wide open to abuse, for example to reduce NI contributions but to increase benefit entitlement. This has led to people claiming to be an employee for some purposes and self-employed for others, and to different government agencies in the past adopting different answers to an individual's status in different contexts.

One result has been a series of initiatives to concentrate the decision-making on this issue so as to avoid inconsistent official decisions. Another is a series of legislative initiatives to define more clearly where the borderline is and to deal with abusive situations.

As a result of various initiatives, HMRC are now the effective deciders, subject to appeal, of employment status. The Social Security (Transfer of Functions, etc.) Act 1999 transferred NI contribution administration to the Inland Revenue. In addition, s. 8 of that Act transferred to the Inland Revenue the decision whether someone is employed or self-employed for most social security benefit purposes. Appeals from a HMRC decision under s. 8, about contributions, and about income tax liability, all go to the tax appeal commissioners. In the case of the s. 8 decisions, most of these were previously dealt with on appeal by social security appeal tribunals, so this was a transfer of appeal jurisdiction. HMRC has also inherited responsibility for the national minimum wage legislation.

There are several provisions that now provide that someone is, or is to be treated as, an employee rather than self-employed. Two of these deserve emphasis. The first is the category of workers who in practical terms are somewhere between the two main groups—agency workers. ITEPA, Pt 1, Ch. 7 deals with agency workers. Section 44 provides that in most such cases the worker is regarded as the employee of the agency even if that is not the formal status adopted. The second concerns Ch. 8 of that Part, which codifies the controversial "IR35" rules for what are sometimes known as "pocket book companies". These rules provide that in stated situations an individual who is under an obligation to provide services to a third party via an intermediary in circumstances where the worker is not paid as an employee by the intermediary can be treated as being an employee of the intermediary with a deemed employment income from that intermediary. This is used, for example, where someone works for a genuine third party, but where the contractual relationship with the third party is, typically, through a company of which the individual is the only shareholder. The company then pays the individual in some indirect way—benefits, loans, dividends—which the individual claims (if asked) to be either not income at all or not employment income.

What income is relevant? What exemptions and deductions apply?

2.144   "Trade" is defined in the Taxes Act, s.832 as "every trade, manufacture, adventure or concern in the nature of trade". There is considerable case law on this meaning, of which reference might be made in the marginal case to the decisions of the House of Lords in *Ransom v Higgs* [1974] 1 W.L.R. 1594 and *Ensign Tankers v Stokes* [1992] 1 A.C. 655. In *Ransom*, the House of Lords made clear the wide factual scope of "trade", in the light of the extending definition. The fact, for example, that no particular name could be given to the activity did not stop it being a trading activity if it was an economic or commercial activity aimed at generating profit (even if it did not do so). The converse of this is that activities that appear to be commercial but are not aimed at making a profit may be regarded in some cases as tax avoidance manoeuvres and not as trading (*Ensign Tankers*). Reference in marginal cases is usually made to the so-called "badges of trade". The badges were first identified by the Royal Commission on the Taxation of Income in 1952 as:

    (a) the subject-matter of the sale or realisation;
    (b) the length of the period of ownership of assets realised;
    (c) the frequency or number of similar transactions by that person;
    (d) whether there was supplementary work on or in connection with the assets realised or the realisation;
    (e) the reasons for the realisation of the assets;
    (f) motive.

Two other points should be emphasised. First, there is a need to distinguish activities generating capital from those generating income. For the calculation of tax credits income, all activities generating capital should be ignored. (This introduces into the tax credits context a much fought-over income tax borderline removed in part for income tax purposes by the introduction of capital gains tax.) Secondly, and seemingly by contrast to the first, a "one off" activity generating profit may be a trading activity. The statutory definition indicates that a single activity may be caught as an "adventure" or a "concern in the nature of trade". From these follow a third point: a payment is either a trading payment or it is capital. There is no middle ground. If a receipt is not a trading receipt, it cannot be brought into charge to income tax (and it is therefore suggested to tax credits either) under other income charging provisions. See *Jones v Leeming* [1930] A.C. 415.

As reg.6 reflects, the charge to income tax on the self-employed is based on the accounts of the business. Increasingly, both the legislative provision for, and the HMRC practice relating to, the taxation of commercial activity is accounts-based. The concern in calculating income for tax credits is therefore with the claimant's business accounts for any trade.

In practice, in the simplest cases, the accounts will be "three-liners". HMRC will accept these for income tax purposes and presumably also for tax credits purposes. The three lines are:

    (a) income;
    (b) deductions (including capital allowances if any);
    (c) net income.

It is assumed that the net income is the difference between the other two! Three-line accounts in this form are accepted where the gross income (turnover) of the trading activity is less than £15,000 a year. If turnover is over that limit, then full accounts itemising income and expenditure will need to be provided, or at least the individual will have to provide all the details required in the standard self-employment pages to the self-assessment form for income tax. In the more complex cases, there should be two sets of accounts: the ordinary working accounts produced for the business (be it company, partnership or individual) and the tax computations or adjustments necessary to change the accounts from the approach adopted for the business to the approach necessary for income tax purposes. For example, the standard item "depreciation" on capital assets held for the business must be removed and replaced by a claim for any specific capital allowances to which the taxpayer is entitled. A second and further set of such computations may be necessary for tax credits purposes—or at least points may need following up. It is common for a business run by a husband to make a payment to an otherwise-non-earning wife. That is a deduction for trading purposes, but must be added back in for the joint claim they should be making for tax credits purposes as earnings of the wife. The business may be paying rent for the accommodation to the owners of the premises used. If that is the jointly owned (or owned in common) home of the joint claimants, again the rental income needs to go back into the tax credits calculation as property income.

Whose income is it?

2.145

It is the income of the individual or partner running the business. The tax credits rules are silent as to partners' shares, so it will be the same share of the trading income as for income tax. That is based on the proposition that for English law purposes (but not Scottish law) a partnership is not a separate entity, so the trading income of the partnership is directly the trading income of the partners, divided as they decide or, by default, under the general rules of the Partnership Act 1890.

When is the income to be brought into the calculation?

2.146

The standard rule for income tax, and therefore tax credits, is that the tax payable in any one tax year (April 6 to April 5) is the income of that year. But for ongoing trades the tax is charged instead on the income of the "basis period" for that year. The basis period for a year is defined as the 12 months immediately following the basis period of the previous year. This is designed to prevent gaps occurring between tax years. In practice, this will be the 12 months accounts period for the business ending in that tax year. Many businesses end their accounting years on April 30. This creates the maximum convenient (for the business) gap between the accounts year and the tax year. Where a business using this practice ends its accounts, for example, on April 30, 2005, that will be the basis period for the tax year 2005–2006.

There are special rules for the opening and closing years of a business, and anti-avoidance rules where a business changes its accounting year.

CHAPTER 5

Social security income

Social security income

7.—(1) The claimant's social security income is the total amount payable—

2.147

  (a) under any provision of the Social Security Act 1988, the Contributions and Benefits Act [³, the Jobseekers Act 1995 or Part 1 of the Welfare Reform Act 2007] or under section 69 of the Child Support, Pensions and Social Security Act 2000;

  (b) [¹. . .];

  (c) by the Secretary of State in respect of the non-payment of a payment which ought to have been made under a provision mentioned in sub-paragraph (a); and

  (d) by way of an ex-gratia payment made by the Secretary of State, or in

Northern Ireland by the Department for Social Development, in connection with a benefit, pension or allowance under the Contributions and Benefits Act.

This is subject to the following provisions of this regulation.

(2) Pensions under the Contributions and Benefits Act which are pension income by virtue of regulation 5(1)(a) are not social security income.

(3) In calculating the claimant's social security income the payments in Table 3 shall be disregarded.

Table 3. Payments under, or in connection with, the Act, the Social Security Act 1988, the Contributions and Benefits Act [³ the Jobseekers Act 1995 or Part 1 of the Welfare Reform Act 2007] disregarded in calculation of social security income

2.148

1. An attendance allowance under section 64 of the Contributions and Benefits Act.
2. A back to work bonus under section 26 of the Jobseekers Act 1995.
3. A bereavement payment under section 36 of the Contributions and Benefits Act.
4. Child benefit under Part II of the Act.
5. A Christmas bonus under section 148 of the Contributions and Benefits Act.
6. Council tax benefit under section 131 of the Contributions and Benefits Act.
7. A disability living allowance under section 71 of the Contributions and Benefits Act.
8. Disabled person's tax credit under section 129 of the Contributions and Benefits Act.
9. Any discretionary housing payment pursuant to regulation 2(1) of the Discretionary Financial Assistance Regulations 2001.
10. An ex-gratia payment by the Secretary of State or, in Northern Ireland, the Department for Social Development, to a person over pensionable age by way of supplement to incapacity benefit.
11. A guardian's allowance under section 77 of the Contributions and Benefits Act.
12. Housing benefit under section 130 of the Contributions and Benefits Act.
13. Income support under section 124 of the Contributions and Benefits Act, unless it is chargeable to tax under [¹section 665 of ITEPA.].
14. Incapacity benefit which is— (a) short term incapacity benefit payable at the lower rate; or

(b) payable to a person who had received invalidity benefit before 13th April 1995 if the period of incapacity for work is treated, by virtue of regulation 2 of the Social Security (Incapacity Benefit) (Transitional) Regulations 1995 (days to be treated as days of incapacity for work) as having begun before that date.

15. Industrial injuries benefit [¹(except industrial death benefit)] under section 94 of the Contributions and Benefits Act.

16. A contribution-based jobseeker's allowance under the Jobseekers Act 1995, to the extent that it exceeds the maximum contained in [¹section 674 of ITEPA.].

17. An income-based jobseeker's allowance under the Jobseekers Act 1995.

18. A maternity allowance under section 35 of the Contributions and Benefits Act.

19. A severe disablement allowance under section 68 or 69 of the Contributions and Benefits Act

20. A social fund payment under Part VIII of the Contributions and Benefits Act.

[¹**20A.** Statutory adoption pay under Part XIIZB of the Contributions and Benefits Act.

21A. Statutory paternity pay under Part XIIZA of the Contributions and Benefits Act.]

21. Statutory maternity pay under Part XII of the Contributions and Benefits Act.

22. Statutory sick pay under Part IX of the Contributions and Benefits Act.

23. Working families' tax credit under section 128 of the Contributions and Benefits Act.

24. A payment by way of compensation for the non-payment of, or in respect of loss of entitlement (whether wholly or partly) of, income support, jobseeker's allowance, [²or housing benefit].

25. A payment in lieu of milk tokens or the supply of vitamins under the Welfare Food Regulations 1996.

[³ **26.** An income-related employment and support allowance payable under Part 1 of the Welfare Reform Act 2007.]

[⁴ **27.** A payment by way of health in pregnancy grant made pursuant to Part 8A of the Contributions and Benefits Act.]

(4) If an increase in respect of a child dependant is payable with an allowance, benefit, pension or other payment ("the main payment") listed

in Table 3, the increase shall also be wholly disregarded in calculating the income of the recipient of the main payment.

(5) [¹. . .]

[¹(5A) From the amount of social security income, calculated in accordance with the preceding provisions of this regulation, there shall be deducted any amount deductible for income tax purposes in computing social security income (as defined in ITEPA) under section 713 of ITEPA.]

(6) A reference in this regulation to an enactment applying only in Great Britain includes a reference to a corresponding enactment applying in Northern Ireland.

AMENDMENTS

1. Tax Credits (Definition and Calculation of Income) (Amendment) Regulations 2003 (SI 2003/732), reg.8 (April 6, 2003).

2. Tax Credits (Miscellaneous Amendments No.2) Regulations 2003 (SI 2003/2815), reg.6 (November 26, 2003).

3. Employment and Support Allowance (Consequential Provisions) (No.3) Regulations 2008 (SI 2009/1879), reg.21 (October 27, 2008).

4. Tax Credits (Miscellaneous Amendments) Regulations 2009 (SI 2009/697), reg.7 (April 6, 2009).

CROSS-REFERENCE

ITEPA, s.713   Donations to charity: payroll giving scheme

GENERAL NOTE

2.149   This regulation defines "social security income" for the purposes of reg.3. "Social security income" is another creation of the Tax Law Rewrite Project. Like pension income, it forms a separate code in Pt 10 of ITEPA (ss.655–681). But, unlike the employment income and pensions income regulations, this regulation adopts the approach of parallel legislation to Pt 10 of ITEPA rather than adopting ITEPA provisions themselves. Nonetheless, the relevant ITEPA provisions are included in this volume both for cross-reference and for more general reference in handling social security benefits.

Part 10 of ITEPA is in the following pattern. Chapter 1 sets out the structure of the Part. Chapter 2 deals with general points on tax on social security income, including a definition of the terms used. Chapter 3 lists the taxable United Kingdom social security benefits. This is in the form of Table A to s.660. Chapter 4 lists exemptions from the ch.3 charge to specific benefits. Chapter 5 lists benefits wholly exempt from tax, in the form of Table B to s.677. Chapter 6 lists taxable foreign benefits, and ch.7 lists exemptions from the benefits brought in under ch.6. Of those chapters, chs 6 and 7 are irrelevant to the head of the tax credits income calculation as it is limited to United Kingdom benefits only.

What income is relevant?

2.150   As just noted, reg.7 is expressly limited to benefits to which a claimant is entitled under United Kingdom legislation only. Foreign social security benefits are to be included under foreign income. There are two other limitations on social security income. The first, deriving from a parallel with ITEPA, is that state retirement benefits are treated as pension income not as social security income. The second, not deriving from that source, is the treatment of the statutory payments (sick, maternity, adoption, paternal) as employment income. ITEPA treats these as social security income (although this is a default rule—if they are taxed as employment income then they are excluded here: ITEPA s.660(2)).

With those exclusions, the other benefits that are taxable under Table A in ITEPA, and also relevant for calculating tax credit income, are:
Widowed mother's/parent's allowance
Carer's allowance
Incapacity benefit (some)
Income support (some)
Jobseeker's allowance (some)
In each case there are provisions about how much of the income is taxed. In practice, much of that tax is collected under the PAYE scheme.

What exclusions and deductions apply?
The list in Table 3 parallels the list in Table B to s.677 of ITEPA (payments 2.151
wholly exempt), along with the provisions, in particular, for jobseeker's allowance and incapacity benefit, save for the statutory payments (noted above) and the treatment of present and past tax credits. CTC and WTC are not taxable. The list is very extensive, and it leaves relevant to tax credits only the short list of benefits noted in the previous paragraph.

There is no specific provision in the regulations dealing with overpayments of benefit. In practice, this may not be a major problem because of the limited extent to which account is taken of benefits. But the position might arise where, say, a widowed parent's allowance was overpaid (perhaps because of the living together rule) so that income previously paid was required to be repaid. For income tax purposes, late account can be taken of this for up to five years after the event. For tax credits purposes, the reduction in income for the relevant period will be relevant only in so far as there can be a recalculation of the income for tax credits, and there is a timely claim made. As the main time-limit is three months, there will only be a limited extent to which such adjustments can be requested, even with the benefit of a rapid notification of the change of circumstances. The two benefits administered by HMRC, child benefit and guardian's allowance, are exempt in any event.

Social security beneficiaries may also set charitable giving against their income.

Whose income is it?
The regulation is silent on this point, which therefore falls to be decided by refer- 2.152
ence to the social security rules. ITEPA, s.662 imposes the income tax on the person receiving or entitled to the benefit, so covering appointees as well as claimants.

When is the income brought into the calculation?
The calculation is based on the amount actually received in the year, regardless of 2.153
the period for which it is received.

CHAPTER 6

Student income

[¹Student Income

8. "Student income" means, in relation to a student— 2.154
[³ (a) in England, any adult dependant's grant payable—
   (i) under regulation 41 of the Education (Student Support) Regulations 2006 in relation to an academic year which begins on or after 1st September 2006 but before 1st September 2007;
   (ii) under regulation 43 of the Education (Student Support) Regulations 2007 in relation to an academic year which begins on or after 1st September 2007 but before 1st September 2008;

    (iii) under regulation 42 of the Education (Student Support) Regulations 2008 in relation to an academic year which begins on or after 1st September 2008 but before 1st September 2009; or

    (iv) under regulation 44 of the Education (Student Support) (No. 2) Regulations 2008 in relation to an academic year which begins on or after 1st September 2009;]

  (b) in Scotland, any dependant's grant payable under regulation 4(1)(c) of the Students' Allowances (Scotland) Regulations 1999; [²...]

  (c) in Northern Ireland, any grant which corresponds to income treated as student income in England and Wales by virtue of paragraph (a);] [² and

[³ (d) in Wales, any adult dependant's grant payable—

    (i) under regulation 22 of the Assembly Learning Grants and Loans (Higher Education) (Wales) Regulations 2006 in relation to an academic year which begins on or after 1st September 2006 but before 1st September 2007;

    (ii) under regulation 26 of the Assembly Learning Grants and Loans (Higher Education) (Wales) Regulations 2007 in relation to an academic year which begins on or after 1st September 2007 but before 1st September 2008; or

    (iii) under regulation 26 of the Assembly Learning Grants and Loans (Higher Education) (Wales) Regulations 2008 in relation to an academic year which begins on or after 1st September 2008.]

AMENDMENTS

1. Tax Credits (Miscellaneous Amendments No.2) Regulations 2003 (SI 2003/2815), reg.7 (November 26, 2003).
2. Tax Credits (Miscellaneous Amendments) Regulations 2006 (SI 2006/766), reg.12 (April 6, 2006).
3. Tax Credits (Miscellaneous Amendments) (No.2) Regulations 2008 (SI 2008/2169), reg.5 (September 1, 2008).

GENERAL NOTE

2.155   This regulation defines "student income" for the purposes of reg.3. "Student income" is not a head of taxation under the Taxes Act or under the scheme used by the Tax Law Rewrite Project. Instead, this is taken from social security law. It must be read with the exemptions in regs 9 and 19, and the general principles of income tax.

The effect of the narrow point in reg.8 with the various exemptions is to exclude most forms of income that students receive (other than earnings).

The award of student grants is now a devolved function, and differing rules now apply in the four countries of the UK. Only parts of the various forms of grant are included as student income, and most students' grants will be excluded. The equivalent income tax rules (in s.776 of ITTOIA) exempt most forms of scholarship income, subject to anti-avoidance provisions, on the principle that such income is a gift or grant, not taxable income. Interest on the reimbursement of student loan income is also exempt (s.753 of ITTOIA). (HMRC monitor this as it is the authority responsible for collecting repayments of student grants through earnings.) Reg.9 applies these provisions to tax credit calculations.

Two other sources of student "income", in the widest sense, are or may be exempt from inclusion under general principles: loans and gifts. The extent to which this is so illustrates the difference between the means-tested benefits approach to assessing a claimant's income, and the rules for calculating tax credits income.

The question of the status of loans was discussed by the Court of Appeal at some length in *Morrell v Secretary of State for Work and Pensions* [2003] EWCA Civ 526. A claimant for income support had been receiving regular monthly sums from her mother by way of loan. Some of the money was paid by the mother to the claimant's landlord. The question was whether the sums were income for the purposes of income support. The Court of Appeal followed the recent decision of that Court in *Leeves v Chief Adjudication Officer* [1999] 1 E.L.R. 90. In that case the question was whether a student grant was to be treated as income for income support purposes. Potter L.J. adopted the submission for the claimant that "income" should be given its ordinary and natural meaning, and that money accruing in respect of which there was an obligation of immediate and equivalent repayment was not income. On the facts, the student grant for maintenance was income but immediately repayable debts were not. The grant was income until the demand for repayment was made, when it ceased to be income.

But a further question arises for tax credits purposes. The payments must not only have the quality of income, but must fall under one of the kinds of income being taken into account. The definition of "student income" in reg.8 does not cover these loans, nor gifts, even if they are recurring. The question is whether such loans or gifts are income within any of the other kinds of income in the regulations. We shall return to that at para.2.207.

Further sources of income linked to education and training are exempt under the specific provisions listed in Table 6 of reg.19—items 4, 5, 6 and 7 are all relevant.

[1Payments of income in connection with students to be disregarded for the purposes of regulation 3

9. Income which is exempt from income tax by virtue of section 753 or 776 of ITTOIA (which deal respectively with interest on the repayment of student loans and scholarship income) is disregarded in calculating a claimant's income under regulation 3.]

2.156

AMENDMENT

1. Tax Credits (Miscellaneous Amendments) Regulations 2006 (SI 2006/766), reg.13 (April 6, 2006).

GENERAL NOTE

This regulation is an exempting regulation only. See note to reg.8.

2.157

CHAPTER 7

Investment income

Investment income

10.—(1) In these Regulations, "investment income" means the gross amount of—

    (a) any interest of money whether yearly or otherwise, or any annuity or other annual payment, whether such payment is payable within or out of the United Kingdom, either as a charge on any property of the person paying it by virtue of any deed or will or otherwise, or as

2.158

a reservation out of it, or as a personal debt or obligation by virtue of any contract, or whether the payment is received and payable half-yearly or at any shorter or longer periods, but not including property income;

(b) any discounts on securities;

(c) any income from securities payable out of the public revenues of the United Kingdom or Northern Ireland;

(d) dividends and other distributions of a company resident in the United Kingdom and any tax credit associated with that payment; and

(e) any amount treated as forming part of the individual's income for the year for income tax purposes by virtue of [³Chapter 9 of Part 4 of ITTOIA disregarding section 535 (top slicing relief)].

This is subject to the following qualification.

(2) In calculating investment income, there shall be disregarded—

(a) any amount listed in column 1 of Table 4 to the extent shown in the corresponding entry in column 2;

(b) any amount listed in column 1 of Table 5 during the period shown in the corresponding entry in column 2;

(c) any income arising from savings certificates, and interest on tax reserve certificates, exempted from tax by [³section 692, 693 or 750 of ITTOIA] (savings certificates and tax reserve certificates);

(d) the first £70 in any tax year of interest on deposits with National Savings and Investments, exempted from income tax by [³section 691 of ITTOIA (National Savings Bank ordinary account interest)];

(e) any payment to a claimant which does not form part of his income for the purposes of income tax by virtue of [³section 727 of ITTOIA (certain annual payments by individuals).]

Table 4. Payments disregarded in the calculation of investment income

1. Description of income to be disregarded	2. Extent of disregard
1. Any interest, dividends, distributions, profits or gains in respect of investments under— (a) a Personal Equity Plan; or (b) an Individual Savings Account; in respect of which the claimant is entitled to relief from income tax under [³Chapter 3 of Part 6 of ITTOIA] or which is taxed only in accordance with regulation 23 of the Individual Savings Account Regulations 1998.	The whole amount, unless it is interest under a personal equity plan to which regulation 17A(2) of the Personal Equity Plan Regulations 1989 applies. Interest to which that paragraph applies is disregarded only to the extent that it does not exceed the annual limit of £180 mentioned in that regulation.

2.159

1. Description of income to be disregarded	2. Extent of disregard
2. [³. . .]	[³. . .]
[³3. Any interest payable under a certified SAYE savings arrangement for the purposes of Chapter 4 of Part 6 of ITTOIA.]	The whole amount.
4. Any winnings from betting, including pool betting, or lotteries or games with prizes.	The whole amount.
5. Any interest on a payment of £10,000 made by the Secretary of State to a person who was held prisoner by the Japanese during the Second World War or to the spouse of such a person, if the payment is held in a distinct account and no payment (other than interest) has been added to the account.	The whole amount of the interest.
6. Any interest on a payment made to the claimant by, or on behalf, of a government of country outside the United Kingdom, either from its own resources or with contributions from any other organisation, by way of compensation for a victim of National Socialism if the payment is held in a distinct account and no payment (other than interest) has been added to the account. Here a reference to a victim of National Socialism is a reference to a person who was required to work as a slave or a forced labourer for National Socialists or their sympathisers during the Second World War, or suffered property loss, or suffered injury or is the parent of a child who died, at the hands of National Socialists or their sympathisers during the Second World War.	The whole amount of the interest.

1. Description of income to be disregarded	2. Extent of disregard
7. Any monies paid to the claimant by a bank or building society as compensation in respect of an unclaimed account held by a Holocaust victim and which vested in the Custodian of Enemy Property under section 7 of the Trading with the Enemy Act 1939 and treated as exempt from income tax by [4section 756A of ITTOIA]	The amount [4of interest exempted from income tax under section 756A of ITTOIA.]

8. Any interest, or payment [3. . .], which is disregarded for income tax purposes by virtue of—
     [3(a) section 751 of ITTOIA (interest on damages for personal injury),or]
     (b) [3section 731 of ITTOIA (periodical payments of personal injury damages)] (personal injury damages in the form of periodical payments).
	The amount so disregarded.

[19]. Annuity payments under an award of compensation made under the Criminal Injuries Compensation Scheme (within the meaning of [3section 732(3) of ITTOIA].	The amount of any payment which is treated as not being income of the claimant or his partner by virtue of [3section 731 of ITTOIA.]
[110]. A payment under a life annuity.	The amount of interest eligible for relief under section 353 of the Taxes Act by virtue of section 365 of that Act.
[111]. Any interest, or payment in respect of interest, which is compensation to a person who is under the age of 18 years for the death of one or both of his parents.	The whole of the interest or payment.
12. A purchased life annuity to which [3Chapter 7 of Part 4 of ITTOIA] applies.	[3The amount exempted under section 717 of ITTOIA as calculated under section 719 of that Act.]

1. Description of income to be disregarded	2. Extent of disregard

[³ **13.** Any payments which are exempt from Income tax by virtue of—
   (a) section 725 of ITTOIA (annual payments under immediate needs annuities), or
   (b) section 735 of ITTOIA (health and employment insurance payments).]
	The whole amount.

Table 5. Payments in connection with very severe disablement, Creutzfeldt–Jakob disease and haemophilia

1. Description of income to be disregarded	2. Applicable period	

1. A trust payment made to —
   (a) a diagnosed person;
   (b) the diagnosed person's partner; or
   (c) the person who was his partner at the date of his death.
	The period beginning on the date on which the trust payment is made and ending with the death of the person to whom the payment is made.	**2.160**

2. A trust payment made to a parent of a deceased diagnosed person, or a person acting in the place of his parent.	The period beginning on the date on which the trust payment is made and ending two years after that date.	
3. The amount of any payment out of the estate of a person to whom a trust payment has been made, which is made to the person who was the diagnosed person's partner at the date of his death.	The period beginning on the date on which the payment is made and ending on the date on which that person dies.	
4. The amount of any payment out of the estate of a person to whom a trust payment has been made, which is made to a parent of a deceased diagnosed person, or a person acting in the place of his parent.	The period beginning on the date on which the payment is made and ending two years after that date.	

(3) The amounts disregarded under Items 3 and 4 in Table 5 shall not exceed the total amount of any trust payments made to the person to whom the trust payment had been made.

(4) In this regulation, "diagnosed person" means—

(a) a person who has been diagnosed as suffering from, or who after his death has been diagnosed has having suffered from, variant Creutzfeldt–Jakob disease;

(b) a person who is suffering or has suffered from haemophilia; or

(c) a person in respect of whom a payment has been made from the 1992 Fund, the Eileen Trust or the Independent Living Funds; and a reference to a person being a member of the diagnosed person's household at the date of the diagnosed person's death includes a person who would have been a member of his household but for the diagnosed person being in residential accommodation, a residential care home or a nursing home on that date.

(5) In this regulation—

"relevant trust" means—

(a) a trust established out of funds provided by the Secretary of State in respect of persons who suffered, or who are suffering, from variant Creutzfeldt–Jakob disease for the benefit of persons eligible for payments in accordance with its provisions;

(b) the Macfarlane Trusts; or

(c) the 1992 Fund, the Eileen Trust or the Independent Living Funds.

"residential accommodation", "residential care home" and "nursing home" have the meanings given by regulation 2(1) of the Income Support (General) Regulations 1987; and

"trust payment" means a payment under a relevant trust.

AMENDMENTS

1. Tax Credits (Definition and Calculation of Income) (Amendment) Regulations 2003 (SI 2003/732), reg.9 (April 6, 2003).

2. Tax Credits (Miscellaneous Amendments No.2) Regulations 2003 (SI 2003/2815), reg.8 (November 26, 2003).

3. Tax Credits (Miscellaneous Amendments) Regulations 2006 (SI 2006/766), reg.14 (April 6, 2006).

4. Tax Credits (Miscellaneous Amendments) Regulations 2007 (SI 2007/824), reg.12 (April 6, 2007).

GENERAL NOTE

2.161   This regulation was drafted ahead of, and anticipated, the relevant provisions of ITTOIA. But there were some changes to the Rewrite Bill after this regulation was brought into force, including the retitling of the relevant part of ITTOIA to cover "Savings and investment income". That accurately reflects the scope of this regulation. It completely reshapes the relevant provisions in the previous income tax legislation and, more than any other part of the Rewrite Acts, should be considered in the new form and not as a continuation of old history.

The relevant provisions in ITTOIA are in Pt 4, which has the following structure:

Chapter 1   Introduction
Chapter 2   Interest
Chapter 3   Dividends from UK resident companies
Chapter 4   Dividends from non-UK resident companies

Chapter 5	Stock dividends from UK resident companies
Chapter 6	Release of loan to participator in close company
Chapter 7	Purchased life annuity payments
Chapter 8	Profits from deeply discounted securities
Chapter 9	Gains from contracts for life assurance
Chapter 10	Distributions from unauthorised unit trusts
Chapter 11	Transactions in deposits
Chapter 12	Disposals of futures and options involving guaranteed Returns
Chapter 13	Sales of foreign dividend coupons.

Most of these chapters contain provisions designed to prevent avoidance, in particular by turning income into capital by one means or another. But by bringing them all together the overall picture is now far clearer than it was before ITTOIA in that the full pattern of the scope of the income tax charges on forms of income from savings and investments can be seen from this list.

But reg.10 retains, at least for the time being, much of the flavour of the previous law, its wording still coming from the former s.18 of the Income and Corporation Taxes Act 1988.

Income from savings and investments is included in the calculation of income for tax credits purposes no account is taken of capital when someone claims a tax credit under the 2002 Act. In practice, however, some of the most popular forms of savings are shielded from an income tax charge, and assessment to tax credits, by the very important disregards listed out in Table 4. Interest and dividends received from saving held within an ISA (individual savings account) are protected not only from income tax but also tax credits assessment by item 1. Interest and bonuses paid under SAYE schemes (save as you earn) are protected by item 3. But interest on ordinary deposits with banks or building societies is taxable (subject to deduction of income tax at source).

Because reg.10 follows the former law, and not the present income tax law, express provision has been made to remove winnings from betting and lotteries. This is not an exemption but rather a limitation set by case law on the previous legislation. [Winnings were excluded to stop losses being claimed.]

CHAPTER 8

Property income

Property income

11.—(1) In these Regulations, "property income" means the annual taxable profits arising from a business carried on for the exploitation, as a source of rents or other receipts, of any estate, interest or rights in or over land in the United Kingdom.

2.162

Expressions which are used in this paragraph which are defined in [² Part 3 of ITTOIA] for the purposes of [² that Part] bear the same meaning here as they bear in [² that Part].

This paragraph is subject to the following [¹qualifications].

[² (2) In calculating property income there shall be disregarded any profits—

(a) treated as nil by section 791 to 794 of ITTOIA (full rent-a-room relief); or

(b) excluded from profits by section 795 to 798 of ITTOIA (alternative calculation of profits if amount exceeds limit).]

[¹(3) [² Where a property business (as defined in Part 3 of ITTOIA] makes a loss to which the relief provisions [³ contained in sections 118 (carry forward against subsequent property business profits) and 119 (how relief works) of ITA] apply, then such relief as may arise under [³ those sections] shall be applied in calculating property income for the purposes of this regulation.]

AMENDMENTS

1. Tax Credits (Miscellaneous Amendments No.2) Regulations 2003 (SI 2003/2815), reg.9 (November 26, 2003).
2. Tax Credits (Miscellaneous Amendments) Regulations 2006 (SI 2006/766), reg.15 (April 6, 2006).
3. Tax Credits (Definition and Calculation of Income) (Amendment) Regulations 2007 (SI 2007/1305), reg.6 (May 16, 2007).

GENERAL NOTE

2.163   This regulation reflects Pt 3 of ITTOIA under the same heading. However, the label is perhaps the least helpful of the new titles created by the Tax Law Rewrite Project. Part 3 and this regulation are limited to real property, and do not apply to any other kind of property. But it was thought better to avoid referring to income from land because the drafters wished to use popular terms and avoid legal complications.

The rules in Pt 3 remove another distinction in the former income tax law. Because taxation of income from land is usually sourced-based—that is, taxed where the land it—different rules used to apply to income from land in the UK and income received in the UK from land elsewhere. That distinction has now largely been removed in ITTOIA. But it has not been removed for tax credits purposes. Following the pattern of the old law, income from foreign land is foreign income within reg.12. In income tax practice, double taxation agreements normally reserve the taxation of income from land to the state where the land is, exempting it—or providing relief—elsewhere. But that does not apply for tax credits purposes. So someone who has, say, an apartment in Spain which is let for part of the year may not pay any UK income tax on the rent, but should have it taken into account for tax credits purposes under reg.12 alongside any income from UK land brought within reg.11.

CHAPTER 9

Foreign income

2.164   **12.**—(1) In these Regulations, "foreign income" means income arising, in the year in question, from [³a source outside the United Kingdom or from foreign holdings] which are not—
(a) employment income;
(b) trading income; or
(c) investment income falling within regulation 10(1)(e).
This is subject to the following provisions of this regulation.

[³(2) The reference in paragraph (1) to "foreign holdings" shall be construed in accordance with section 571 of ITTOIA.]

(3) In calculating the claimant's foreign income there shall be disregarded—

(a) any payment by way of an annuity or pension payable under any special provision for victims of National Socialist persecution which is made by the law of the Federal Republic of Germany, or any part of it, or of Austria;

[⁴(aa) any monies paid by a bank or building society which are exempted from income tax under section 756A of ITTOIA (interest on certain deposits of victims of National-Socialist persecution).]

[³(b) the amount authorised to be deducted by the relevant provision if the claimant's foreign income comprises or includes a pension to which the following provisions of ITEPA apply—

    (i) sections 567(5) and 617 (deduction allowed for taxable pension income);

    (ii) section 575(2) (taxable pension income: foreign pensions);

    (iii) section 613(3) (taxable pension income: foreign annuities); and

    (iv) section 635(3) (taxable pension income: foreign voluntary annual payments); and]

(c) any amount which would be disregarded for the purposes of income tax by virtue of—

    (i) Extra Statutory Concession A10 (lumps sums paid by overseas pension schemes);

    (ii) [¹s.681 of ITEPA];

    (iii) [³section 751(1)(c) of ITTOIA] (interest on damages for personal injuries awarded by a foreign court); or

    (iv) Extra Statutory Concession A44 (education allowances payable to public officials of overseas territories); [³or

    (v) section 730 of ITTOIA (foreign maintenance payments)].

[²(4) Where an overseas property business ;[³(within the meaning of Part 3 of ITTOIA)] makes a loss to which the relief provisions [⁵ contained in sections 118 (carry forward against subsequent property business profits) and 119 (how relief works) of ITA apply], then such relief as may arise under [⁵ those sections] shall be applied in calculating foreign income for the purposes of this regulation.]

AMENDMENTS

1. Tax Credits (Definition and Calculation of Income) (Amendment) Regulations 2003 (SI 2003/732), reg.10 (April 6, 2003).

2. Tax Credits (Miscellaneous Amendments No.2) Regulations 2003 (SI 2003/2815), reg.10 (November 26, 2003).

3. Tax Credits (Miscellaneous Amendments) Regulations 2006 (SI 2006/766), reg.16 (April 6, 2006).

4. Tax Credits (Miscellaneous Amendments) Regulations 2007 (SI 2007/824), reg.13 (April 6, 2007).

5. Tax Credits (Definition and Calculation of Income) (Amendment) Regulations 2007 (SI 2007/1305), reg.7 (May 16, 2007).

GENERAL NOTE

The provisions in reg.3 above ensure that all forms of the foreign income of a tax credits claimant are potentially relevant to the calculation of income for tax credits purposes even if they would be exempt from income tax in the United Kingdom. "Foreign income" is not a specific head of charge for income tax purposes. And in practice most problems are dealt with not under the United Kingdom legislation

2.165

but under the terms of the relevant double tax agreements. That approach and those agreements do not apply for tax credits purposes, so there is need to make express provision instead.

This regulation, as amended from 2006, provides for all foreign income charged to income tax to be relevant for tax credits save for specific exemptions. It also provides for the priorities between competing charges that arise, for example, where income is both foreign income and employment income, to prevent a double charge. The combination of exemptions and rules giving priority to other heads of assessment result in this head of charge still being of limited importance. But note that this provision will apply to some kinds of foreign pension and foreign savings or investment income.

"Foreign holdings" is defined in s.571 of ITTOIA as meaning shares and other securities outside the UK that are issued by a government or public authority of another country or by or on behalf of a body of persons not resident in the UK.

CHAPTER 10

Notional Income

Introduction

2.166   **13.** In these Regulations, "notional income" means income which, by virtue of regulations 14 to 17 a claimant is treated as having, but which he does not in fact have.

GENERAL NOTE

2.167   This regulation emphasises that the provisions of regs 14–17 are not parallels to income tax in the ordinary sense, in that the income is not in fact income of the claimant (or any of the joint claimants). It may, as the notes to the following regulations show, be the income of someone else.

Claimants treated for any purpose as having income by virtue of the Income Tax Acts

2.168   **14.**—(1) If an amount is treated for any purpose as the claimant's income under any provision mentioned in paragraph (2), he is to be treated as having that amount of income.

(2) The provisions mentioned in paragraph (1) are—

(a) the following provisions of the Taxes Act—

[1. . .];

(ix) section 714 (transfers of securities: treatment of deemed sums and reliefs) or 716 (transfer of unrealised interest);

(x) section 730 (transfer of income arising from securities);

[2 . . .]

(xiv) section 761 (charge to income tax of offshore income gain); and

[2 . . .]

[1(b) the following provisions of ITTOIA—

(i) sections 277 to 283 (amounts treated as receipts: leases);

(ii) Chapter 5 of Part 4 (stock dividends from UK resident companies);

    (iii) Chapter 6 of Part 4 (release of loan to participator in close company);

    (iv) section 427 (charge to tax on profits from deeply discounted securities);

    (v) Chapter 11 of Part 4 (transactions in securities);

    (vi) sections 624 to 628 (income treated as income of settlor: retained interests);

    (vii) sections 629 to 632 (income treated as income of settlor: unmarried children);

    (viii) section 633 (capital sums paid to settlor by trustees of settlement);

    (ix) section 641 (capital sums paid to settlor by body connected with settlement);

    (x) section 652 (estate income: absolute interests in residue); and

    (xi) sections 654 to 655 (estate income: interests in residue);

[² (ba) the following provisions of ITA—

    (i) Chapter 5 of Part 11 (price differences under repos);

    (ii) Chapter 2 of Part 13 (transfer of assets abroad); and

    (iii) Chapter 3 of Part 13 (transactions in land).]

  (c) section 84 and Schedule 15 to the Finance Act 2004 (charge to income tax by reference to enjoyment of property previously owned).]

AMENDMENTS

1. Tax Credits (Miscellaneous Amendments) Regulations 2006 (SI 2006/766), reg.17 (April 6, 2006).

2. Tax Credits (Definition and Calculation of Income) (Amendment) Regulations 2007 (SI 2007/1305), reg.8 (May 16, 2007).

GENERAL NOTE

This regulation has been rewritten substantially with effect from the 2006–07 income tax year, but its contents remains broadly the same. It collects together a series of important income tax anti-avoidance provisions and includes them together as providing "notional income" for step 1 of the calculation of income for tax credits purposes under reg.3(1).   **2.169**

Note that this regulation is worded so that the assessment for tax credit purposes depends on self-assessment or an assessment for income tax purposes. A claimant who is treated as having an amount of any of these kinds of income for income tax purposes is treated as having that amount of income for the purposes of this regulation. It may therefore be assumed, it is suggested, that the issue will not arise for tax credits purposes unless it has already been identified for income tax purposes.

The regulation collects together both well-known and less well-known anti-avoidance provisions. The newest, in para.(2)(c), attracted considerable attention when enacted. It is the provision that deems someone who has given her or his property away (usually for inheritance tax purposes) but who continues to have a right to reside in the property to be in receipt of income and so liable to income tax on (broadly) the rent that could have been received from the property. That also applies for a tax credit assessment.

Claimants depriving themselves of income in order to secure entitlement

15. If a claimant has deprived himself of income for the purpose of securing entitlement to, or increasing the amount of, a tax credit, he is treated as having that income.   **2.170**

2.171   This is equivalent to Income Support (General) Regulations 1987 (SI 1987/1967), reg.42(1), and the note on that in Vol.II in this series should be consulted. Note, however, that this provision is defined by reference to deprivation for the purposes of securing or increasing entitlement to tax credits (and not, for example, income support). TCTM04920 gives the example of someone who transfers entitlement to an occupational pension to someone else by deed of gift. Without reference to authority, it emphasises that securing or increasing entitlement to tax credit may not be a claimant's main motive but it must be a significant one. That is a question of fact.

Claimants to whom income becomes available upon the making of a claim

2.172   **16.**—(1) If income would become available to a claimant upon the making of an application for that income, he is treated as having that income.

This is subject to the following qualification.

(2) Paragraph (1) does not apply in relation to income—

(a) under a trust derived from a payment made in consequence of a personal injury;

(b) under a personal pension scheme or retirement annuity contract;

(c) consisting in a sum to which Item 8 of Table 4 in regulation 10 refers (compensation for personal injuries which is administered by the Court); or

(d) consisting in a rehabilitation allowance made under section 2 of the Employment Act.

[¹(3) Paragraph (1) also does not apply to income by way of—

(a) a Category A or Category B retirement pension,

(b) a graduated retirement benefit, or

(c) a shared additional pension,

payment of which has been deferred.

Here—

"Category A retirement pension" means a pension to which a person is entitled by virtue of section 44 of the Contributions and Benefits Act or the Northern Ireland Contributions and Benefits Act;

"Category B retirement pension" means a pension to which a person is entitled by virtue of any of sections 48A to 48C of the Contributions and Benefits Act or sections 48A to 48C of the Northern Ireland Contributions and Benefits Act;

"graduated retirement benefit" means a pension payable under—

(a) sections 36 and 37 of the National Insurance Act 1965; or

(b) sections 35 and 36 of the National Insurance Act (Northern Ireland) 1966; and

"shared additional pension" means a pension to which a person is entitled by virtue of section 55A of the Contributions and Benefits Act or section 55A of the Northern Ireland Contributions and Benefits Act.]

AMENDMENT

1. Tax Credits (Miscellaneous Amendments) Regulations 2004 (SI 2004/762), reg.15 (April 6, 2004).

DEFINITIONS

"Category A retirement pension"—see para.(3).

"Category B retirement pension"—see *ibid.*

"graduated retirement benefit"—see *ibid*.
"shared additional pension"—see *ibid*.

GENERAL NOTE

See the note to the similar provision in Income Support (General) Regulations 2.173
1987 (SI 1987/1967), reg.42(2)–(4). The precise operative scope of this provision
is not clear. For income support, sums not received may not count as earnings or
other income. But most of the charges to income tax, as noted above, are on those
"receiving or entitled to". So entitlement is enough to bring the sums in both for
income tax purposes and tax credit purposes, even if they are not received. This
regulation could, however, extend that to cover sums to which entitlement had
not arisen, for example because no demand had been made for the sum under a
contractual entitlement operative on such demand.

Claimants providing services to other persons for less than full earnings

17.—(1) If a claimant provides a service for another person and— 2.174
  (a) the other person makes no payment of earnings or pays less than those
       paid for a comparable employment (including self-employment) in
       the area; and
  (b) the Board are satisfied that the means of the other person are suffi-
       cient for him to pay for, or to pay more for, the service,
the claimant is to be treated as having such an amount of employment
income, or in the case of a service provided in the course of a trade or business, such an amount of trading income as is reasonable for the employment of the claimant to provide the service.
  This is subject to the following qualification.
  (2) Paragraph (1) does not apply where—
  (a) the claimant is a volunteer or is engaged to provide the service by a
       charitable or voluntary organisation and the Board are satisfied that
       it is reasonable for the claimant to provide the service free of charge;
       or
  (b) the service is provided in connection with the claimant's participa-
       tion in an employment or training programme—
     (i) in Great Britain in accordance with regulation 19(1)(q) of the
          Jobseeker's Allowance Regulations 1996 other than where it is
          provided in connection with the claimant's participation in the
          Intensive Activity period specified in regulation 75(1)(a)(iv) of
          those Regulations; or
     (ii) in Northern Ireland in accordance with regulation 19(1)(p)
          of the Jobseeker's Allowance Regulations (Northern Ireland)
          1996 other than where it is provided in connection with the
          claimant's participation in the Preparation for Employment
          Programme specified in regulation 75(1)(a)(v) of those
          Regulations.

GENERAL NOTE

See the note in Vol.II in this series to the similar (though differently drafted) 2.175
provision in Income Support (General) Regulations 1987 (SI 1987/1967),
reg.42(6).

CHAPTER 11

Miscellaneous income

Miscellaneous income

2.176   **18.** In these Regulations, "miscellaneous income" means income which does not fall within any other provision of these Regulations and which is subject to income tax under [¹ Part 5 of ITTOIA].

AMENDMENT

1. Tax Credits (Miscellaneous Amendments) Regulations 2006 (SI 2006/766), reg.18 (April 6, 2006).

GENERAL NOTE

2.177   Part 5 of ITTOIA contains the "sweeper" provisions to bring within liability to income tax any forms of income that fall outside the specific charges to income tax. If, therefore, something can properly be regarded as employment income, trading income, savings and investment income, pension income, social security income or some other more specific form of income, then this provision does not apply. But it is not a "catch-all", and there is no global definition of "income" in United Kingdom income tax legislation.

Part 5 applies to "annual profits or gains" not otherwise charged to tax. It does not catch gifts or loans, nor does it catch single "one-off" payments unless they are of a trading or business nature. Nor does it catch receipts of capital sums, which in tax terms fall to be taxed under the Taxation of Chargeable Gains Act 2001, if at all. See the note to reg.6.

PART III

Sums disregarded in the calculation of income

General disregards in the calculation of income

2.178   **19.**—(1) For the purposes of regulation 3—
(a) the sums specified in Table 6 are disregarded in the calculation of income;
(b) the sums specified in column 1 of Table 7 are disregarded in the calculation of income if the condition in the corresponding entry in column 2 of that Table is satisfied; and
(c) the sums specified in column 1 of Table 8 are disregarded in the calculation of income to the extent specified in the corresponding entry in column 2 of that Table.

(2) In this regulation—
"the JSA Regulations" means the Jobseeker's Allowance Regulations 1996; and
"the JSA (NI) Regulations" means the Jobseeker's Allowance (Northern Ireland) Regulations 1996.

Table 6. Sums disregarded in the calculation of income

1. Any payment of an employment credit under a scheme under section 2(2) of the Employment Act known as "New Deal 50 Plus" or the corresponding scheme under section 1 of the Employment and Training Act (Northern Ireland) 1950.

2. Any payment made—
  (a) under section 15 of the Disabled Persons (Employment Act) 1944 or section 15 of the Disabled Persons (Employment) Act (Northern Ireland) 1945; or
  (b) in accordance with arrangements made under section 2 of the Employment Act or section 1 of the Employment and Training Act (Northern Ireland) 1950
to assist disabled persons to obtain or retain employment despite their disability.

3. Any mandatory top-up payment made pursuant to—
  (a) section 2 of the Employment Act [³ or section 1 of the Employment and Training Act (Northern Ireland) 1950] in respect of the claimant's participation in—
    (i) an employment programme specified in regulation 75(1)(a)(ii)(bb) of the JSA Regulations or regulation 75(1)(a)(ii) of the JSA (NI) Regulations (Voluntary Sector Option of the New Deal);
    (ii) an employment programme specified in regulation 75(1)(a)(ii)(cc) of the JSA Regulations (Environmental Task Force Option of the New Deal) or regulation 75(1)(a)(iii) of the JSA (NI) Regulations; or
    (iii) the Intensive Activity Period of the New Deal Pilots for 25 Plus specified in regulation 75(1)(a)(iv) of the JSA Regulations or, in Northern Ireland, the Preparation for Employment Programme specified in regulation 75(1)(a)(v) of the JSA (NI) Regulations; or
  (b) a written arrangement entered into between—
    (i) the Secretary of State and the person who has arranged for the claimant's participation in the Intensive Activity Period of the New Deal for 25 Plus and which is made in respect of his participation in that Period; or
    (ii) the Department for Employment and Learning and the person who has arranged for the claimant's participation in the Preparation for Employment Programme and which is made in respect of the claimant's participation in the Programme.
[³This item applies only to the extent that the payment is not taxable as a profit of a trade, profession or vocation.]

4. Any discretionary payment pursuant to section 2 of the Employment Act, or, in Northern Ireland, section 1(1) of the Employment and Training Act (Northern Ireland) 1950 to meet, or help to meet, special needs in respect of the claimant's participation in the Full-Time Education and Training Option of the New Deal as specified in regulation 75(1)(b)(ii) of the JSA Regulations or of the JSA (NI) Regulations.

2.179

5. Any—
  (a) education maintenance allowance in accordance with regulations made under section 518 of the Education Act 1996 (payment of school expenses; grant of scholarships, etc.); or
  (b) payment (not within sub-paragraph (a)) in respect of a course of study attended by a child or qualifying young person payable—
    (i) in accordance with regulations made under section 518 of the Education (Scotland) Act 1980 (power to assist persons to take advantage of educational facilities) or section 12(2) (c) of the Further and Higher Education (Scotland) Act 1992 (provision of financial assistance to students); or
    (ii) by virtue of regulations made in Article 50, 51 or 55(1) of the Education and Libraries (Northern Ireland) Order 1986 (provisions to assist persons to take advantage of educational facilities).

6. Any payment made by an employment zone contractor payable in respect of the claimant's participation in the employment zone programme by way of—
  (a) a training premium;
  (b) a discretionary payment, being a fee, grant, loan or otherwise; or
  (c) any arrears of subsistence allowance paid as a lump sum.

7. [³. . .]

8. An amount of income equal to any qualifying maintenance payment within section 347B of the Taxes Act.

[²**9.** Any payment by way of foster care receipts to the extent that those receipts qualify for relief under [⁴ Chapter 2 of Part 7 to ITTOIA].]

10. Any payment of maintenance, whether under a court order or not, which is made or due to be made by—
  (a) the claimant's former partner, or the claimant's partner's former partner; or
  (b) the parent of a child or qualifying young person where that child or qualifying young person is a member of the claimant's household except where that parent is the claimant or the claimant's partner.

11. Any payment in respect of a child or qualifying young person who is a member of the claimant's household made—
  [²(a) to adopters which is exempt from income tax by virtue of [⁴ sections 744 to 746 of ITTOIA];]
  (b) by a local authority in pursuance of paragraph 15(1) of Schedule 1 to the Children Act 1989 (local authority contribution to child's maintenance);
  [³(bb) by a local authority by way of special guardianship support services pursuant to regulations under section 14F(1)(b) of the Children Act 1989; or]
  (c) by an authority, as defined in Article 2 of the Children (Northern Ireland) Order 1995, in pursuance of Article 15 of, and paragraph 17 of Schedule 1 to, that Order (contribution by an authority to child's maintenance).

12. Any payment in respect of travelling expenses—
  (a) in relation to England and Wales, under regulation 3, 5 or 8 of the National Health Service (Travelling Expenses and Remission of Charges) Regulations 1988;
  (b) in relation to Scotland, under regulation 3, 5 or 8 of the National Health Service (Travelling Expenses and Remission of Charges) (Scotland) Regulations 1988;
  (c) in relation to Northern Ireland under regulation 3, 5 or 8 of the Travelling Expenses and Remission of Charges Regulations (Northern Ireland) 1989; or
  (d) made by the Secretary of State for Health, the Scottish Ministers, the Secretary of State for Wales, or the Department of Health, Personal Social Services and Public Safety and which is analogous to a payment specified in paragraph (a), (b) or (c).

13. Any payment made by the Secretary of State or the Scottish Ministers under a scheme established to assist relatives and other persons to visit persons in custody.

[²**14.** Any payment under the Community Care (Direct Payments) Act 1996, section 57 of the Health and Social Care Act 2001, section 12B of the Social Work (Scotland) Act 1968, Article 15A of the Health and Personal Social Services (Direct Payments) (Northern Ireland) Order 1996 or section 8 of the Carers and Direct Payments Act (Northern Ireland) 2002.]

[¹**14A.** Any payment made under the "Supporting People" programme—
  (a) in England and Wales, under section 93 of the Local Government Act 2000;
  (b) in Scotland, under section 91 of the Housing (Scotland) Act 2001; or
  (c) in Northern Ireland, under Article 4 of the Housing Support Services (Northern Ireland) Order 2002.]

15. [¹Any payment or a voucher] provided under section 95 or 98 of the Immigration and Asylum Act 1999 for any former asylum-seeker or his dependants.

16. Any payment of a provident benefit by a trade union.
  Here—
  "provident benefit" has the meaning given in section 467(2) of the Taxes Act; and
  "trade union" has the meaning given in section 467(4) of the Taxes Act.

Table 7. Sums disregarded in calculating income if conditions are satisfied

2.180

1. Description of payment	2. [³Conditions] that must be satisfied
1. Any payment in respect of any expenses incurred by a claimant who is engaged by a charitable or voluntary organisation or is a volunteer.	The claimant does not receive remuneration or profit from the engagement and is not treatedas possessing any employment income under regulation 17 in respect of that engagement.
2. A payment by way of— (a) travelling expenses reimbursed to the claimant; (b) a living away from home allowance under section 2(2)(d) of the Employment Act, section 2(4)(c) of the Enterprise and New Towns (Scotland) Act 1990 or section 1 of the Employment and Training Act (Northern Ireland) 1950; (c) training grant; or (d) childcare expenses reimbursed to the claimant in respect of his participation in— (i) a New Deal option; (ii) the Intensive Activity Period of the New Deal Pilots for 25 Plus; or (iii) the Preparation for Employment Programme.	The claimant— (a) participates in arrangements for training made under— (i) section 2 of the Employment Act; (ii) section 2 of the Enterprise and New Towns (Scotland) Act 1990; or (iii) section 1 of the Employment and Training Act (Northern Ireland) 1950; or (b) attends a course at an employment rehabilitation centre established under section 2 of the Employment Act. [³The payment is not taxable as a profit of a trade, profession or vocation.]

Table 8. Sums partly disregarded in the calculation of income

2.181

Type of payment to be disregarded	Limit on, or exception to, the extent of disregard
1. Any discretionary payment made pursuant to section 2 of the Employment Act, or,	A payment is not within this item to the extent that it relates to travel expenses

Type of payment to be disregarded	Limit on, or exception to, the extent of disregard
in Northern Ireland, section 1(1) of the Employment and Training Act (Northern Ireland) 1950 to meet, or help meet, the claimant's special needs in undertaking a qualifying course within the meaning of regulation 17A(7) of the JSA Regulations or regulation 17A(7) of the JSA (NI) Regulations.	incurred as a result of the claimant's attendance on the course if an amount in respect of those expenses has already been disregarded pursuant to regulation 8.
2. Any payment made in respect of a career development loan paid pursuant to section 2 of the Employment Act.	A payment is not within this item to the extent that the loan has been applied for or paid in respect of living expenses for the period of education and training supported by the loan.
3. Any payment made to the claimant or his partner in respect of a person who is not normally a member of the claimant's household but is temporarily in his care, by— (a) a health authority; (b) a local authority; (c) a voluntary (c) organisation; (d) that person pursuant to section 26(3A) of the National Assistance Act 1948; (e) a primary care trust established under section 16A of the National Health Service Act 1977.	A payment is only to be disregarded by virtue of this item if [¹(a)] any profits[⁴. . .] arising from the payment mentioned in col.1 are treated as nil by [⁴ section 791 to 794 of ITTOIA (full rent-a-room relief)]; or [¹(b)] excluded from profits [⁴by section 795 to 798 of ITTOIA (alternative calculation of profits if amount exceeds limit).]
4. Any payment made in Northern Ireland to the claimant or his partner in respect of a person who is not normally a member of the claimant's household but is temporarily in his care— (a) pursuant to Article 36(7) of the Health and Personal Social Services (Northern	A payment is only to be disregarded by virtue of this item if— [¹(a)] any profits [⁴. . .] arising from the payment mentioned in column 1 are treated as nil by [⁴ section 791 to 794 of ITTOIA (full rent-a-room relief)]; or

Type of payment to be disregarded	Limit on, or exception to, the extent of disregard
Ireland) Order 1972 by an authority; a voluntary organisation; or the person concerned; or (b) by a training school within the meaning of section 137 of the Children and Young Persons Act (Northern Ireland) 1968. In this item "an authority" has the meaning given by Article 2 of the Children (Northern Ireland) Order 1995.	[¹(b) excluded from profits [⁴by section 795 to 798 of ITTOIA (alternative calculation of profits if amount exceeds limit).]
5. Any payment under an insurance policy taken out to insure against the risk of being unable to maintain the repayments— (a) on a loan which is secured on the dwelling house which the claimant occupies as his home; or (b) under a regulated agreement or under a hire-purchase agreement or a conditional sale agreement. For the purposes of paragraph (b)— "regulated agreement" has the meaning given in the Consumer Credit Act 1974; and "hire-purchase agreement" and "conditional sale agreement" have the meanings given in Part 3 of the Hire-Purchase Act 1964.	A payment is only to be disregarded by virtue of this item to the extent that it is used to— (a) maintain the repayments referred to in col.(1); and (b) meet any amount due by way of premiums on— (i) that policy; or (ii) in a case to which paragraph (a) of this item applies, an insurance policy taken out to insure against loss or damage to any building or part of a building which is occupied by the claimant as his home and which is required as a condition of the loan referred to in column (1).
[¹6]. Any payment in respect of the claimant's attendance at court as a juror or witness.	This item applies only to the extent that the payment is not compensation for loss of

Type of payment to be disregarded	Limit on, or exception to, the extent of disregard
	earnings or for the loss of payment of social security income.
[¹7]. Any payment of a sports award except to the extent that it has been made in respect of living expenses.	For the purposes of this item "living expenses" does not include— (a) the cost of vitamins, minerals or other special dietary supplements intended to enhance the performance of the claimant in the sport in respect of which the award was made; or (b) accommodation costs incurred as a consequence of living away from home whilst training for, or competing in, the sport in respect of which the award was made.

AMENDMENTS

1. Tax Credits (Definition and Calculation of Income) (Amendment) Regulations 2003 (SI 2003/732), reg.11 (April 6, 2003).

2. Tax Credits (Miscellaneous Amendments No.2) Regulations 2003 (SI 2003/2815), reg.11 (November 26, 2003).

3. Tax Credits (Miscellaneous Amendments) Regulations 2004 (SI 2004/762), reg.16 (April 6, 2004).

4. Tax Credits (Miscellaneous Amendments) Regulations 2006 (SI 2006/766), reg.19 (April 6, 2006).

CROSS-REFERENCES

Taxes Act, s.347B	Qualifying maintenance payments
F(2)A 1992, Sch.10	Furnished Accommodation

GENERAL NOTE

2.182

This regulation adds to the exemptions and exceptions in regs 3 and 9 that apply generally to income. Exceptions, exemptions and deductions that are specific to one or more kinds of income, but not all kinds of income, are detailed under the specific regulations.

Table 6

2.183   This sets out the sums to be disregarded in total. For fuller notes, see the equivalent provisions to the similar items in Income Support (General) Regulations 1987 (SI 1987/1967), Sch.9 (in Vol.II in this series). Several of the provisions are wider than the equivalent provision in the Income Support (General) Regulations 1987 because these provisions also apply to Northern Ireland, while the Income Support (General) Regulations 1987 apply to Great Britain only.

Paragraph 1—see Sch.9, para.63.
Paragraph 2—see Sch.9, para.51.
Paragraph 3—see Sch.9, para.62.
Paragraph 4—see Sch.9, para.13.
Paragraph 5—see Sch.9, para.11.
Paragraph 6—see Sch.9, para.72.
Paragraph 8—this excludes all sums within the scope of ITA 2007, ss.453–456. (certain periodic payments made by one party to a marriage or former marriage to the other party for the maintenance of the other party or their children under a court order or agreement).
Paragraph 9—see Sch.9, para.26.
Paragraph 10—this widens out the scope of para.8.
Paragraph 11—see Sch.9, para.25.
Paragraph 12—see Sch.9, para.48.
Paragraph 13—see Sch.9, para.50.
Paragraph 14—see Sch.9, para.58.
Paragraph 14A—this is a new provision.
Paragraph 15—this is specifically focussed on former asylum-seekers or dependants.
Paragraph 16—s.467 of the Taxes Act provides exemption from tax to trade unions that provide provident benefits to their members not exceeding £4,000 as a capital sum or £825 a year as an annuity during sickness, incapacity or old age, or after an accident, theft or death. The excludes the annuities from counting as income of claimants.

However, there are some differences between the tax credit provisions and the income support provisions listed. For example, the disregard in para.11 in Table 6 omits to mention local authority payments in Scotland under ss.34(6) or 50 of the Children Act 1975, whereas these payments are included in the equivalent income support rule: see Income Support (General) Regulations 1987 (SI 1987/1967), Sch.9, para.25(1)(b)). This would suggest that such payments in Scotland are disregarded for income support purposes but not for tax credits assessments. Note that, so far as England and Wales is concerned, the Children Act 1975 was repealed by the Children Act 1989, but this did not extend to Scotland: Children Act 1989, s.108(11).

Table 7

2.184   For item 1 see also the Income Support (General) Regulations 1987 (SI 1987/1967), Sch.9 para.2. For Item 2, see Sch.9, para.13.

Table 8

2.185   The final table lists those disregards that apply to part only of a payment. Item 1 is to the same effect as Income Support (General) Regulations 1987 (SI 1987/1967), Sch.9, para.65. Item 2 is based on Sch.9, para.59. Item 3 is similar to Sch.9, para.27, but excepts from it any payments that are or would be protected from income tax under the rent-a-room provisions (see reg.11). Item 4 is the equivalent provision for Northern Ireland. Item 5 parallels Sch.9, paras 29 and 30ZA. Item 6 is the same as Sch.9, para.43. Item 7 is based on Sch.9, para.69.

(SI 2002/2007) (as amended)

Child Tax Credit Regulations 2002

(SI 2002/2007) (AS AMENDED)

Whereas a draft of this instrument, which contains the first regulations made under section 9 of the Tax Credits Act 2002 has been laid before, and approved by resolution of, each House of Parliament:

Now, therefore, the Treasury, in exercise of the powers conferred on them by sections 8, 9, 65 and 67 of the Tax Credits Act 2002, hereby make the following Regulations:

Citation, commencement and effect

1. These Regulations may be cited as the Child Tax Credit Regulations   2.187
2002 and shall come into force—
  (a) for the purpose of enabling claims to be made, on 1st August 2002;
  (b) for the purpose of enabling awards to be made, on 1st January 2003; and
  (c) for all other purposes on 6th April 2003; and shall have effect for the tax year beginning on 6th April 2003 and subsequent tax years.

Interpretation

2.—(1) In these Regulations, unless the context otherwise requires—   2.188
"the Act" means the Tax Credits Act 2002;
"advanced education" means full-time education for the purposes of—
  (a) a course in preparation for a degree, a diploma of higher education, a higher national diploma, a higher national diploma or higher national certificate of Edexcel or the Scottish Qualifications Authority, or a teaching qualification; or
  (b) any other course which is of a standard above ordinary national diploma, a national diploma or national certificate of Edexcel [2. . .], a general certificate of education (advanced level), [2or Scottish national qualifications at higher or advanced higher level];

449

[4"approved training" has the meaning given by regulation 1(3) of the Child Benefit (General) Regulations 2006;]

[1"the Board" means the Commissioners [4for Her Majesty's Revenue and Customs];]

"the Careers Service" means—

    (a) in England and Wales, a person with whom the Secretary of State or the National Assembly of Wales has made arrangements under s.10(1) of the Employment Act, and a local education authority to whom the Secretary of State or the National Assembly of Wales has given a direction under section 10(2) of that Act;

    (b) in Scotland, a person with whom the Scottish Ministers have made arrangements under section 10(1) of the Employment Act and any education authority to which a direction has been given by the Scottish Ministers under section 10(2) of that Act; and

    (c) [1. . .];

"child" means a person who has not attained the age of sixteen [5 . . .];

"claimant" has the meaning in section 9(8) of the Act, except in regulation 7, where that expression and "joint claimants" have the meanings given in regulation 7(1);

"the Connexions Service" means a person of any description with whom the Secretary of State has made an arrangement under section 114(2)(a) of the Learning and Skills Act 2000 and section 10(1) of the Employment Act, and any person to whom he has given a direction under section 114(2)(b) of the former Act and section 10(2) of the latter Act;

"the Contributions and Benefits Act" means the Social Security Contributions and Benefits Act 1992;

[3"couple" has the meaning given by section 3(5A) of the Act];

"custodial sentence"—

    (a) in England and Wales, has the meaning in section 76 of the Powers of Criminal Courts (Sentencing) Act 2000;

    (b) in Scotland, means detention under a sentence imposed by a court under section 44, 205, 207 or 208 of the Criminal Procedure (Scotland) Act 1995; and

    (c) in Northern Ireland, means a custodial sentence under the Criminal Justice (Children) (Northern Ireland) Order 1998;

"disability living allowance" means a disability living allowance under section 71 of the Contributions and Benefits Act;

"the Employment Act" means the Employment and Training Act 1973;

"the family element of child tax credit" and "the individual element of child tax credit" shall be construed in accordance with section 9(3) of the Act;

[5 "full-time education" means education received by a person attending a course of education where, in pursuit of that course, the time spent receiving instruction or tuition, undertaking supervised study, examination or practical work or taking part in any exercise, experiment or project for which provision is made in the curriculum of the course, exceeds or exceeds on average 12 hours a week in normal term-time, and shall include gaps between the ending of one course and the commencement of another, where the person is enrolled on and commences the latter course;]

"joint claim" and "single claim" shall be construed in accordance with section 3(8) of the Act;

"looked after by a local authority" has the meaning in section 22 of the Children Act 1989, section 17(6) of the Children (Scotland) Act 1995 or (in Northern Ireland) Article 25 of the Children (Northern Ireland) Order 1995 (with the modification that for the reference to a local authority there is substituted a reference to an authority within the meaning in Article 2 of that Order);

the "main responsibility test" has the meaning given in rule 2.2. of regulation 3;

the "normally living with test" has the meaning given in rule 1.1. of regulation 3;

"Part I" means Part I of the Act;

"patient" means a person (other than a person who is serving a custodial sentence) who is regarded as receiving free in-patient treatment within the meaning of the Social Security (Hospital In-patients) Regulations 1975, or the Social Security (Hospital In-patients) Regulations (Northern Ireland) 1975;

"placing for adoption" means placing for adoption in accordance with the Adoption Agencies Regulations 1983, the Adoption Agencies (Scotland) Regulations 1984 or the Adoption Agencies Regulations (Northern Ireland) 1989;

[5 "qualifying body" means–
  (a) the Careers Service or Connexions Service;
  (b) the Ministry of Defence;
  (c) in Northern Ireland, the Department for Employment and Learning or an Education and Library Board established under Article 3 of the Education and Libraries (Northern Ireland) Order 1986; or
  (d) for the purposes of applying Council Regulation (EEC) No. 1408/71, any corresponding body in another member state;]

"qualifying young person" means a person, other than a child, who—
  (a) has not attained the age of [4twenty]; and
  (b) satisfies the conditions in regulation 5(3) and (4);

[5 . . .]

"remunerative work" means work which is—
  (a) done for payment or in expectation of payment;
  (b) undertaken for not less than 24 hours a week, calculated in accordance with regulation 4(3) of the Working Tax Credit (Entitlement and Maximum Rate) Regulations 2002; and
  (c) not excluded from the meaning of engagement in remunerative work by regulation 4(2) of those Regulations;

and other expressions have the same meanings as defined in the Act.

(2) In the application of these Regulations to Northern Ireland, a reference to a provision of an enactment which applies only to Great Britain or England and Wales, shall be construed, so far as necessary, as including a reference to the corresponding enactment applying to Northern Ireland.

AMENDMENTS

1. Child Tax Credit (Amendment) Regulations 2003 (SI 2003/738), reg.3 (April 6, 2003).

2. Tax Credits (Miscellaneous Amendments No.2) Regulations 2003 (SI 2003/2815), reg.17 (November 26, 2003).

3. Civil Partnership Act 2004 (Tax Credits, etc.) (Consequential Amendments) Order 2005 (SI 2005/2919), art.4(2) (December 5, 2005).

2.189

4. Child Tax Credit (Amendment) Regulations 2006 (SI 2006/222), reg.3 (April 6, 2006).

5. Tax Credits (Miscellaneous Amendments) (No.2) Regulations 2008 (SI 2008/2169), reg.7 (September 1, 2008).

Circumstances in which a person is or is not responsible for a child or qualifying young person

2.190   **3.**—(1) For the purposes of child tax credit the circumstances in which a person is or is not responsible for a child or qualifying young person shall be determined in accordance with the following Rules.

Rule 1

2.191   **1.1.** A person shall be treated as responsible for a child or qualifying young person who is normally living with him (the "normally living with test").

     1.2. This Rule is subject to rules 2 to 4.

Rule 2 (Competing claims)

2.192   **2.1.** This Rule applies where—

     (a) a child or qualifying young person normally lives with two or more persons in—
         (i) different households; or
         (ii) the same household, where those persons are not limited to the members of a [² ...] couple; or
         (iii) a combination of (i) and (ii); and

     (b) two or more of those persons make separate claims (that is, not a single joint claim made by a [² ...] couple) for child tax credit in respect of the child or qualifying young person.

     2.2. The child or qualifying young person shall be treated as the responsibility of—

     (a) only one of those persons making such claims; and
     (b) whichever of them has (comparing between them) the main responsibility for him (the "main responsibility test");

subject to rules 3 and 4.

Rule 3

2.193   **3.1.** The persons mentioned in rule 2.2. (other than the child or qualifying young person) may jointly elect as to which of them satisfies the main responsibility test for the child or qualifying young person, and in default of agreement the Board may determine that question on the information available to them at the time of their determination.

Rule 4

2.194   **4.1.** A child or qualifying young person shall be treated as not being the responsibility of any person during any period in which any of the following Cases applies.

[⁴ **4.2.** Where a child or qualifying young person is in residential accommodation referred to in regulation 9 of the Child Benefit (General) Regulations 2006 and in the circumstances prescribed in paragraphs (a) or (b) of that regulation, he shall be treated as being the responsibility of any person who was treated as being responsible for him immediately before he entered that accommodation.]

Case A	The child or qualifying young person is provided with, or placed in, accommodation under Part III of the Children Act 1989, Part II of the Children (Scotland) Act 1995 or Part IV of the Children (Northern Ireland) Order 1995, and the cost of that child's or qualifying young person's accommodation or maintenance is borne wholly or partly— (i) out of local authority funds under section 23 of the Children Act 1989 or section 26 of the Children (Scotland) Act 1995; (ii) in Northern Ireland, by an authority, within the meaning in Article 2, and under Article 27, of that Order; or (iii) out of other public funds. [4 . . .]
Case B	The child or qualifying young person— (i) is being looked after by a local authority; and (ii) has been placed for adoption by that authority in the home of a person proposing to adopt him, and a local authority is making a payment in respect of the child's or qualifying young person's accommodation or maintenance, or both, under section 23 of the Children Act 1989, section 26 of the Children (Scotland) Act 1995 or Article 27 of the Children (Northern Ireland) Order 1995. This Case applies in Northern Ireland with the modification that for references to a local authority there are substituted references to an authority (within the meaning in Article 2 of that Order).
Case C	A custodial sentence— (a) for life; (b) without limit of time; (c) of detention during Her Majesty's pleasure; (d) in Northern Ireland, of detention during the pleasure of the Secretary of State; or (e) for a term or period of more than four months, has been passed on the child or qualifying young person.
Case D	The [5 . . .] qualifying young person claims and is awarded child tax credit in his or her own right, in respect of a child for whom he or she is responsible, for that period.
[1Case E	[5 . . .] The qualifying young person, claims incapacity benefit [6 or contributory employment and support allowance payable under Part 1 of the Welfare Reform

	Act 2007] in his or her own right and that benefit is paid to or in respect of him or her for that period.
	
	This Case does not apply at any time ("the later time") during a period of incapacity for work which began before 6th April 2004 in the case of a person in respect of whom, at a time—
	    (a) during that period of incapacity, and
	    (b) before that date,
	both incapacity benefit and child tax credit were payable, if child tax credit has been payable in respect of him or her continuously since 5th April 2004 until that later time. For the purposes of this Case "period of incapacity" shall be construed in accordance with section 30C of the 1992 Act (incapacity benefit: days and periods of incapacity for work) but disregarding subsections (5) and (5A) of that section.]

[³Case F	[⁵ . . .] The qualifying young person claims and receives working tax credit in his or her own right (whether alone or on a joint claim). [⁵ . . .]
[⁵ Case G	The qualifying young person has a spouse, civil partner or partner with whom they are living and the spouse, civil partner or partner is not in full-time education or approved training as provided for under regulation 5(3).
Case H	The responsible person is the spouse, civil partner or partner of a qualifying young person with whom they are living. [⁷ Cases G and H do] not apply to persons in receipt of child tax credit for a qualifying young person who is living with a partner on the day before 1st September 2008.]

(2) Where—
    (a) a claimant is treated as responsible for a child or qualifying young person by virtue of the preceding Rules, and
    (b) the child or qualifying young person has a child of his or her own, normally living with him or her,
the claimant shall also be treated as responsible for, and as having made a claim for child tax credit in respect of, the child of the child or qualifying young person (but without prejudice to the facts as to which of them is mainly responsible for that child).

AMENDMENTS

1. Tax Credits (Miscellaneous Amendments) Regulations 2004 (SI 2004/762), reg.2 (April 6, 2004).

2. Civil Partnership Act 2004 (Tax Credits, etc.) (Consequential Amendments) Order 2005 (SI 2005/2919), art.4(3) (December 5, 2005).

3. Child Tax Credit (Amendment No. 2) Regulations 2006 (SI 2006/1163), reg.2 (May 24, 2006).

4. Child Tax Credit (Amendment) Regulations 2007 (SI 2007/2151), reg.3 (August 16, 2007).

5. Tax Credits (Miscellaneous Amendments) (No.2) Regulations 2008 (SI 2008/2169), reg.8 (September 1, 2008).

6. Employment and Support Allowance (Consequential Provisions) (No.3) Regulations 2008 (SI 2009/1879), reg 22(2) (October 27, 2008).

7. Tax Credits (Miscellaneous Amendments) Regulations 2009 (SI 2009/697), reg.10 (April 6, 2009).

DEFINITIONS

"child"—see reg.2(1).
"claimant"—see *ibid*.
"custodial sentence"—see *ibid*.
"joint claim"—see *ibid*.
"looked after by a local authority"—see *ibid*.
"main responsibility test"—see *ibid*.
"normally living with test"—see *ibid*.
"placing for adoption"—see *ibid*.
"qualifying young person"—see *ibid*.

GENERAL NOTE

Section 8(1) of the TCA 2002 provides that entitlement to child tax credit is 2.195 dependent upon the claimant (and/or his or her partner in the case of a joint claim) "being responsible for one or more children or qualifying young persons". The 2002 Act then provides that this expression may be defined further by regulations (s.8(2)). This regulation accordingly sets out a number of rules for determining whether a person is or is not responsible for a child or young person. The starting point is in r.1, namely that as a general rule, a person is responsible for a child or young person normally living with him or her. This presumption is then subject to r.2, which deals with competing claims, as well as r.3 (election by the parties or determination by HMRC in default of such agreement) and r.4 (special cases, principally involving children or young persons being accommodated at public expense and so not to be the subject of a child tax credit award). The Upper Tribunal rejected an attempt to challenge these rules as discriminatory against men in *HMRC v DH* UKUT [2009] 24 (AAC).

Para. (1) 2.196

Rule 1: The presumption is that a person is responsible for a child or qualifying 2.197 young person "who is normally living with him" (r.1, para.1.1). This "normally living with test" has been inherited from WFTC (and, before that, family credit: see Family Credit (General) Regulations 1987 (SI 1987/1973, reg.7(1)). The "normally living with test" was new to family credit, although the phrase "living with" the claimant was (and still is) used in the child benefit legislation (SSCBA 1992, s.143 and see, in particular *R(F) 2/79* and *R(F) 2/81*).

In the context of family credit (and later WFTC), *CFC 1537/1995* decided that a child "normally lives with" a person for the purposes of reg.7(1) if he or she spent more time with that person than anyone else. This was the construction that made sense of reg.7(2) of the 1987 Regulations, which made provision for cases where a child either spent equal amounts of time in different households or there was doubt as to which household a child was living in. But reg.7(2) only applied in cases of real doubt; if there was simply a factual dispute this was not enough to bring it into play. Where reg.7(2) applied, there was then a series of tests. The first was receipt of child benefit, the rules for which include methods of establishing priorities between claimants. If no one was receiving child benefit then if only one person had claimed child benefit, that person had priority. If there had been no claims (or more than one claim), the final test was who had "primary responsibility".

Rule 2: Rule 2, which applies to competing claims for child tax credit, adopts a 2.198

slightly different approach to the old reg.7(2). Accordingly, it does not necessarily follow that *CFC 1537/1995* applies in precisely the same way. Rule 2 applies where two or more people (not being a couple) make child tax credit claims and the relevant child or qualifying young person "normally lives with two or more persons" *either* in different households *or* in the same household (other than in the case of a couple with a child in the same household) *or* in an arrangement that is a combination of these two first possibilities (r.2, para.2.1). Thus, r.2 only comes into play when the child or young person may, as a matter of fact, already be regarded as "normally" (but separately) living with at least two persons. For example, a child might spend weekdays living with one parent and weekends with the other parent in a different household. Although the child will spend more time living with the weekday parent, it is perfectly proper to say that he or she *also* normally lives with the weekend parent, at least for part of the week. This being so, the definition of "normally living with" applied in *CFC 1537/1995* (i.e. spending more time with one person than anyone else) cannot apply for the purposes of the meaning of "normally lives" in r.2, para.2.1, as that is specifically designed to deal with the situation where a child or young person by definition "normally" lives in more than one place. However, where r.2 does so apply, the general rule is that, as between the competing claimants, the child or young person is treated as the responsibility of the person with "main responsibility" for him or her (r.2, para.2.2). Thus, although *CFC 1537/1995* should be applied with care in this context, ultimately it may be a distinction without a difference.

As we have seen, the former reg.7(2) of the 1987 Regulations resolved problematic cases by reference first to the person in receipt of child benefit and then, in the absence of a child benefit claim, to the person with "primary responsibility" for the child or young person. Rule 2 makes no reference to the child benefit position. Instead, cases of shared care—as these will inevitably be—are to be determined by reference to who has "main responsibility" for the child or young person. This is presumably likely to be determined on a time basis, and so the weekdays parent in the example above is likely to be regarded as the one with such responsibility. As with the former reg.7(2), "responsibility" has no special meaning in the legislation and so must be determined according to the ordinary everyday meaning of the word. It would not seem that there is any material difference between "primary responsibility" (reg.7) and "main responsibility" (r.2). It would also appear that under r.2, as under the former reg.7, responsibility or the normality of living may be judged on an overall basis over a period. This is different from the income support provision, where the test of responsibility still has to be applied week by week (*CIS 49/1991* and *Whelan v Chief Adjudication Officer, The Independent*, November 14, 1994).

It will be evident from the analysis above that there is, under these Rules, no provision for the division of child tax credit between competing parents. The Rules are premised on establishing which claimant (or which couple of joint claimants) is entitled to child tax credit for a given child or young person, not on apportioning child tax credit entitlement between separated individual claimants (e.g. 5/7 to the weekdays parent and 2/7 to the weekend parent). Although the practical and administrative difficulties with such an arrangement are obvious, it did appear from the primary legislation that this might be a possibility (see, e.g. TCA 2002, ss.8(2) and 9(7)). There remains, therefore, the prospect of human rights challenges in this area, as with social security benefits which have elements related to a child or children's presence in a particular household for part-weeks in cases of shared care: see the General Note to Income Support (General) Regulations 1987 (SI 1987/1967), reg.15, in Vol.II in this series). See now *HMRC v DH* [2009] UKUT 24 (AAC) discussed in the commentary to s.9(7) of the Tax Credits Act 2002.

Commissioners have now had to consider competing claims in joint care cases both for child benefit and child tax credit. *CTC/4390/2004* decided that a tribunal must decide between two seemingly equally placed claimants, perhaps by looking at the one who would benefit more from the claim. *CTC/1686/2007* emphasises that the discretion available to the Secretary of State in child benefit cases is not available for child tax credit. On an appeal the tribunal must decide on the facts, and has no discretion. However, the Commissioner endorsed the view of the tribunal that it is better if the two competing claimants can agree between themselves. HMRC has indicated that it will respect such agreements, including where the result is that the competing claimants "divide" the children between them for claim purposes.

The attribution of responsibility for a child or young person to a particular person under r.2 is itself subject to rs 3 and 4. In *CTC/3096/2007* the Commissioner emphasised the need to apply the "main responsibility" test. See also *CTC/1686/2007* where the Commissioner compares these rules with those for child benefit and child support. see also *KN v HMRC* [2009] UKUT 79 (AAC), in which Judge Gamble emphasised that the test is "responsibility" not "care". He put weight on the person responsible when the child was at school.

Rule 3: Where there are competing claims under r.2, the parties may by agreement notify HMRC as to which of them satisfies the main responsibility test for the child or young person in question. If the adults in question fail to agree, HMRC may determine that question on the information then available.
 2.199

Rule 4: Rule 4 sets out a number of specific circumstances (or Cases) in which a child or young person is not to be treated as the responsibility of a tax credit claimant, even though any of rs 1–3 above might otherwise apply. Cases A–C all deal with situations in which a child or young person is being accommodated at public expense in one way or another and so payment of child tax credit is inappropriate. These are similar to the exclusions under the child benefit scheme. Case D covers the special case of a child (aged at least 16) or young person who has herself been awarded child tax credit in respect of her own child (see also para.(2) where child tax credit has not been awarded in such circumstances to the young parent).
 2.200

Case A: This exclusion covers children or young persons who are provided with or placed in accommodation under Pt III of the Children Act 1989 or associated legislation. The exception in reg.3 of the Child Benefit (General) Regulations 1976 (now Child Benefit (General) Regulations 2003 (SI 2003/493), reg.2) deals with children or young persons who are provided with residential accommodation on account of their disability.
 2.201

Case B: This exclusion applies where (i) a child or young person is being looked after by a local authority (in the sense that term is used under the Children Act 1989); (ii) he or she has been placed for adoption, and (iii) a fostering allowance is in payment.
 2.202

Case C: CTC will continue to be paid unless the child or young person has been sentenced to detention for a period of four months or longer. This is more generous than the equivalent rules for income support and income-based jobseeker's allowance, under which benefit for the child or young person ceases immediately he or she is taken into custody (Income Support (General) Regulations 1987 (SI 1987/1967), reg.16(5)(f) and (6); see also reg.15(3) regarding home leave). It is also more generous than the former WFTC and DPTC rules, under which there was no entitlement to the elements of those tax credits relating to children where a custodial sentence had been passed (Family Credit (General) Regulations 1987 (SI 1987/1973), reg.8(2)(e)). The justifications for the change given by ministers are the extra costs associated with contact and the need to enable families to maintain contact with the child or young person for whom they are responsible, and to assist with that person's re-integration in the community. It is difficult to see how these arguments do not apply equally forcefully in the context of income support and income-based jobseeker's allowance.
 2.203

Case D: See also para.(2) below.
 2.204

Case E: The effect of this provision is that a person is not to be treated as responsible for a child or a qualifying young person in respect of whom incapacity benefit is
 2.205

payable. There is transitional protection during a period of incapacity which began before April 6, 2004 for cases where both incapacity benefit and child tax credit were in payment in respect of the child or qualifying young person before that date.

2.206   *Case F:* This exclusion means that a person is not to be treated as responsible for a child or qualifying young person who is receiving WTC in his or her own right, whether alone or as part of a joint claim, with a spouse or partner. It also provides for a period of transitional protection for some CTC recipients.

Cases G and H: These exclusions ensure alignment between the rules for CTC and those for child benefit.

2.207   *Paragraph (2):* This deals with the special case where a person (the claimant) is found to be responsible for a child or young person under rs 1–4 above (and so the exception in Case D of r.4 does not apply) and that child or young person herself has a child. In such circumstances, the claimant is treated as responsible for child tax credit purposes for both his or her child (or young person) and that child's own child.

[¹ Period for which a person who attains the age of sixteen is a qualifying young person

2.208   **4.**—(1) A person who attains the age of sixteen is a qualifying young person from the date on which that person attained that age until 31st August which next follows that date.

(2) Paragraph (1) is subject to regulation 5 but as if there were no requirement to satisfy the first condition specified in paragraph (3) of that regulation.]

AMENDMENT

1. Tax Credits (Miscellaneous Amendments) (No.2) Regulations 2008 (SI 2008/2169), reg.9 (September 1, 2008).

GENERAL NOTE

2.209   Section 8(3) of the TCA 2002 defines a child as a person who "has not attained the age of sixteen", but the same provision enables regulations to be made allowing a person to remain a "child" for tax credit purposes "for a prescribed period or until a prescribed date". This regulation provides that a child remains a child for both child tax credit and working tax credit purposes until August 31 following his or her 16th birthday.

Maximum age and prescribed conditions for a qualifying young person

2.210   **5.**—(1) For the purposes of Part I, a person ceases to be a qualifying young person (unless disqualified earlier under the following paragraphs) on the date on which he attains the age of [³twenty].

(2) A person who is not a child, but has not attained the age of [³twenty] years, is a qualifying young person for any period during which the following conditions are satisfied with regard to him [¹(and once a person falls within the terms of paragraph (3)(b), he shall be treated as having satisfied the first condition from the [⁴relevant leaving date] mentioned in that paragraph)].

(3) The first condition is that he is [³. . .]—
    (a) receiving full-time education, not being—
        (i) advanced education, or

      (ii) education received by that person by virtue of his employment or of any office held by him; [³. . .]

[³(ab) undertaking approved training [⁵, is enrolled or has been accepted to undertake such training,] which is not provided [⁷ by means of a contract of employment]; or]

  (b) under the age of eighteen years and—

    [²[³(i) he ceased to receive full-time education or to undertake approved training (the date of that event being referred to as "the relevant leaving date");]

    (ii) within three months of the [³relevant leaving date], he has notified the Board (in the manner prescribed by regulation 22 of the Tax Credits (Claims and Notifications) Regulations 2002) that he is registered for work or training with [⁷ a qualifying body]; and

    (iii) not more than 20 weeks has elapsed since the [³relevant leaving date.]

[³(3A) A person who has attained the age of nineteen years satisfies paragraph (3)(a) or (ab) only where the course of education or training began before he attained that age [⁵, or he enrolled or was accepted to undertake that course before he attained that age].]

(4) The second condition is that the period in question is not (and does not include)—

  (a) a week in which he (having ceased to receive full-time education [³or approved training]) becomes engaged in remunerative work; [³or]

  (b) [³. . .]

  (c) a period in respect of which that person receives income support [⁸income-related employment and support allowance payable under Part 1 of the Welfare Reform Act 2007] or income-based jobseeker's allowance within the meaning of section 1(4) of the Jobseekers Act 1995.

[⁷ (5) For the purposes of paragraphs (3) and (4) a person shall be treated as being in full-time education if full-time education is received by that person by undertaking a course—

  (a) at a school or college, or

  (b) where that person has been receiving that education prior to attaining the age of sixteen, elsewhere, if approved by the Board,]

where in pursuit of that course, the time spent receiving instruction or tuition, undertaking supervised study, examination or practical work or taking part in any exercise, experiment or project for which provision is made in the curriculum of the course, exceeds or exceeds on average 12 hours a week in normal term-time [⁵ . . .].

(6) In calculating the time spent in pursuit of the course, no account shall be taken of time occupied by meal breaks or spent on unsupervised study.

[³(7) In determining whether a person is undertaking a course of fulltime education or approved training, there shall be disregarded any interruption—

  (a) for a period of up to 6 months, whether beginning before or after the person concerned attains age 16, to the extent that it is reasonable in the opinion of the Board to do so; and

  (b) for any period due to illness or disability of the mind or body of the person concerned provided that it is reasonable in the opinion of the Board to do so.]

AMENDMENTS

1. Child Tax Credit (Amendment) Regulations 2003 (SI 2003/738), reg.4 (April 6, 2003).

2. Child Tax Credit (Amendment) Regulations 2003 (SI 2003/738), reg.5 (April 6, 2003).

3. Child Tax Credit (Amendment) Regulations 2006 (SI 2006/222), reg.4 (April 6, 2006).

4. Tax Credits (Miscellaneous Amendments) Regulations 2006 (SI 2006/766), reg.3 (April 6, 2006).

5. Child Tax Credit (Amendment) Regulations 2007 (SI 2007/2151), reg.4 (August 16, 2007).

6. Tax Credits (Miscellaneous Amendments) (No.2) Regulations 2008 (SI 2008/2169), reg.10 (September 1, 2008).

7. Employment and Support Allowance (Consequential Provisions) (No.3) Regulations 2008 (SI 2009/1879), reg.22(3) (October 27, 2008).

DEFINITIONS

"advanced education"—see reg.2(1).
"Careers Service"—see *ibid*.
"Connexions Service"—see *ibid*.
"child"—see *ibid*.
"full-time education"—see para.(5).
"Pt I"—see reg.2(1).
"qualifying young person"—see *ibid*.
"recognised educational establishment"—see *ibid*.
"relevant training programme"—see *ibid*.
"remunerative work"—see *ibid*.

GENERAL NOTE

2.211
Section 8(4) of the TCA 2002 enables regulations to be made prescribing conditions to be met by a person in order to count as a "qualifying young person" (CTC being payable in respect of children and qualifying young persons (TCA 2002, s.8(1)). This regulation provides that the maximum age for a "qualifying young person" is the date on which he or she reaches the age of 19 (para.(1)). It also spells out the conditions which must be met by a person who is no longer a child (on which note the extended meaning of "child" in reg.4) in order to rank as a "qualifying young person" (paras (2)–(6)). Two conditions must be satisfied in this regard (they are cumulative and not alterna tive). First, the young person must *either* be receiving full-time education, as defined by para.(3)(a) (and see also paras (5) and (6)) *or* be aged under 18, have ceased to receive full-time education, be registered for work or training with one of the relevant official agencies, and have met the latter two criteria for no more than 20 consecutive weeks (para.(3)(b)). Secondly, the period in question must not be or include a week in which the young person becomes engaged in remunerative work (having ceased full-time education), or a period in which he or she received a training allowance under a training programme or received income support or income-based jobseeker's allowance (para.(4)).

These conditions are modelled on those that apply to child benefit, on which see SSCBA 1992, s.142 (and the commentary above). The definition of full-time education likewise is in identical terms to the relevant provision for child benefit purposes (Child Benefit (General) Regulations 2003 (SI 2003/493), reg.5.

Entitlement to child tax credit after death of child or qualifying young person

2.212
6. If—

(a) a child or qualifying young person dies; and

(b) a person is (or would, if a claim had been made, have been) entitled to child tax credit in respect of the child or qualifying young person immediately before the death,

that person shall be entitled to child tax credit in respect of the child or qualifying young person for the period of eight weeks immediately following the death or, in the case of a qualifying young person, until the date on which he or she would have attained the age of [1twenty] if earlier.

AMENDMENT

1. Child Tax Credit (Amendment) Regulations 2006 (SI 2006/222), reg.5 (April 6, 2006).

DEFINITIONS

"child"—see reg.2(1).
"qualifying young person"—see *ibid.*

GENERAL NOTE

Section 8(5) of the TCA 2002 enables regulations to be made allowing entitlement to child tax credit to continue for a prescribed period notwithstanding the death of the relevant child or qualifying young person. This regulation makes provision for the continued payment of child tax credit for a further eight weeks in such a situation. The same concession has been made in relation to child benefit (SSCBA 1992, s.145A, inserted by TCA 2002, s.55).

2.213

Determination of the maximum rate at which a person or persons may be entitled to child tax credit

7.—(1) In the following paragraphs—
   (a) in the case of a single claim (but not a joint claim), the person making the claim is referred to as the "claimant"; and
   (b) in the case of a joint claim, the members of the [1...] couple making the claim are referred to as the "joint claimants".
(2) The maximum rate at which a claimant or joint claimants may be entitled to child tax credit shall be the aggregate of—
   (a) the family element of child tax credit; and
   (b) an individual element of child tax credit, in respect of each child or qualifying young person for whom—
      (i) the claimant; or
      (ii) either or both of the joint claimants;
      as the case may be, is or are responsible.
(3) The family element of child tax credit—
   (a) in a case where any of the children referred to in paragraph (2)(b) above is under the age of one year, is £1,090; and
   (b) in any other case, is £545.
(4) The individual element of child tax credit for any child or qualifying young person referred to in paragraph (2)(b) above—
   (a) where the child is disabled, is [2£4,905];
   (b) where the child is severely disabled, is [2£5,980];
   (c) in the case of any other child, is [2£2,235];
   (d) where the qualifying young person is disabled, is [2£4,905];
   (e) where the qualifying young person is severely disabled, is [2£5,980]; and
   (f) in the case of any other qualifying young person, is [2£2,085].

2.214

AMENDMENTS

1. Civil Partnership Act 2004 (Tax Credits, etc.) (Consequential Amendments) Order 2005 (SI 2005/2919), art.4(4) (December 5, 2005).
2. Tax Credits Up-rating Regulations 2009 (SI 2009/800), reg.2 (April 6, 2009).

DEFINITIONS

"child"—see reg.2(1).
"claimant"—see *ibid.* and para.(1)(a).
"the family element of child tax credit"—see reg.2(1).
"the individual element of child tax credit"—see *ibid.*
"joint claim"—see *ibid.*
"qualifying young person"—see *ibid.*
"single claim"—see *ibid.*

GENERAL NOTE

2.215   Section 9 of the TCA 2002 makes provision for the maximum rate of child tax credit. This regulation provides the detail on how this rate is to be arrived at (para. (2)). It also sets out the actual annual rates for the component elements (paras (3) and (4)). Claimants who are entitled to income support or income-based jobseeker's allowance are automatically entitled to the maximum child tax credit applicable in their circumstances (TCA 2002, s.7(2) and Tax Credits (Income Thresholds and Determination of Rates) Regulations 2002 (SI 2002/ 2008), reg.4). The entitlement of other claimants is dependent upon the operation of the thresholds and withdrawal rates specified in the Income Thresholds and Determination of Rates Regulations.

Prescribed conditions for a disabled or severely disabled child or qualifying young person

2.216   **8.**—(1) For the purposes of section 9 of the Act a child or qualifying young person—
  (a) is disabled if he satisfies the requirements of paragraph (2); and
  (b) is severely disabled if he satisfies the requirements of paragraph (3).
  (2) A person satisfies the requirements of this paragraph if—
  (a) disability living allowance is payable in respect of him, or has ceased to be so payable solely because he is a patient; or
  (b) he is—
      (i) registered as blind in a register compiled by a local authority under section 29 of the National Assistance Act 1948 (welfare services);
      (ii) in Scotland, has been certified as blind in a register maintained by or on behalf of a local government area (as defined in the Local Government etc. (Scotland) Act 1994), or
      (iii) in Northern Ireland, has been certified as blind and in consequence is registered as blind in a register maintained by or on behalf of a Health and Social Services Board; or
  (c) he ceased to be so registered or certified as blind within the 28 weeks immediately preceding the date of claim.
  (3) A person satisfies the requirements of this paragraph if the care component of disability living allowance—
  (a) is payable in respect of him; or
  (b) would be so payable but for either a suspension of benefit in accordance with regulations under section 113(2) of the Contributions and Benefits Act or an abatement as a consequence of hospitalisation,
at the highest rate prescribed under section 72(3) of that Act.

DEFINITIONS

"the Act"—see reg.2(1).
"child"—see *ibid.*
"the Contributions and Benefits Act"—see *ibid.*
"disability living allowance"—see *ibid.*
"patient"—see *ibid.*
"qualifying young person"—see *ibid.*

GENERAL NOTE

Sections 9(5)(d) and (6) of the TCA 2002 make provision for a disabled child   **2.217**
element and a severely disabled child element to be component parts of child tax
credit. This regulation defines those terms. Thus, a child or qualifying young person
is disabled if disability living allowance (DLA) is payable for them (or has ceased
to be payable but only because he or she is now a patient) or if he or she is a registered blind person (or has ceased to be so registered in the immediately preceding
28 weeks) (para.(2)). A child or qualifying young person is severely disabled if they
are entitled to the highest rate of the DLA care component (i.e. they satisfy both the
"day" and "night" conditions in terms of their need for personal care or supervision): para.(3). The rates for these elements are set out in regs 8(4)(a) and (b).

Tax Credits (Income Thresholds and
Determination of Rates) Regulations 2002

(SI 2002/2008) (AS AMENDED)

Whereas a draft of this instrument, which contains the first regulations made   **2.218**
under section 13(2) of the Tax Credits Act 2002, has been laid before, and approved
by resolution of, each House of Parliament:

Now, therefore, the Treasury, in exercise of the powers conferred upon them by
sections 8(1) to (3), 13(2) and (3), 65(1) and (7) and 67 of the Tax Credits Act
2002, hereby make the following Regulations:

Made by the Treasury under ss.8(1)–(3), 13(2) and (3), 65(1) and (7) and 67 of
the Tax Credits Act 2002.

1. Citation, commencement and effect.
2. Interpretation.
3. Manner in which amounts to be determined for the purposes of section 7(1)
   (a) of the Act.
4. Social security benefits prescribed for the purposes of section 7(2) of the Act.
5. Amounts prescribed for the purposes of section 7(3)(a) and (b) of the Act.
6. Manner of determining the rate at which a person is, or persons are, entitled
   to a tax credit.
7. Determination of rate of working tax credit.
8. Determination of rate of child tax credit.
9. Cases in which there is no rate of tax credit.

Citation, commencement and effect

1.—(1) These Regulations may be cited as the Tax Credits (Income   **2.219**
Thresholds and Determination of Rates) Regulations 2002 and shall come
into force—

(a) for the purpose of enabling claims to be made, on August 1, 2002;

(b) for the purpose of enabling decisions on claims to be made, on 1st January 2003; and

(c) for all other purposes, on 6th April 2003.

(2) These Regulations shall have effect for the tax year beginning with 6th April 2003 and subsequent tax years.

DEFINITIONS

"claim"—see TCA 2002, s.3.
"decision on claim"—see TCA 2002, s.14.
"tax year"—see reg.2.

Interpretation

2.220

2. In these Regulations—
"the Act" means the Tax Credits Act 2002;
"the income threshold" has the meaning given by section 7(1)(a) of the Act;
"period of award" shall be construed in accordance with section 5 of the Act;
"the relevant income" has the meaning given by section 7(3) of the Act;
"tax year" means a period beginning with 6th April in one year and ending with 5th April in the next.

Manner in which amounts to be determined for the purposes of section 7(1)(a) of the Act

2.221

3.—(1) This regulation prescribes the manner in which amounts are to be determined for the purposes of section 7(1)(a) of the Act.

(2) In the case of a person or persons entitled to working tax credit, the amount in relation to that tax credit is [¹£6,420].

(3) In the case of a person or persons entitled to child tax credit, the amount in relation to that tax credit is [²£16,040].

AMENDMENTS

1. Tax Credits Up-rating Regulations 2005 (SI 2005/681), reg.4 (April 6, 2005).
2. Tax Credit Up-rating Regulations 2009 (SI 2009/800), reg.4(3) (April 6, 2009).

DEFINITION

"the Act"—see reg.2.

GENERAL NOTE

2.222

This regulation makes the necessary provision to give full operative effect to s.7(1) of the Act (income test).

HMRC does not use the term "income threshold". Instead it describes it in its literature as "taper start point". However, as the Commissioner noted in *CTC/2113/2006*, a failure to explain that this is how HMRC refers to the income thresholds can cause confusion.

Subsection (1)

2.223

Section 7(1) of TCA 2002 imposes an income test on all claimants for tax credits, the test being whether the relevant income of the claimant (or claimants) for the tax year exceeds "the amount" for that tax credit. If the relevant income does exceed the amount, then it must be calculated by how much it does so. This applies to all claimants apart from those within s.7(2) and reg.4 below. In other words, "the amount" is the income threshold for claiming that tax credit. Only those with no incomes or incomes below the threshold can claim the full tax credit for the year. The section allows, and this regulation provides, different thresholds for different tax credits.

The thresholds are reconsidered annually, and have been set at:

Year	CTC (£ pa)	WTC (£ pa)
2003–04	13,230	5,060
2004–05	13,480	5,060
2005–06	13,910	5,220
2006–07	14,155	5,220
2007–08	14,495	5,220
2008–09	15,575	6,420
2009–10	16,040	6,420

The existence of separate thresholds means that in many cases separate calculations have to be made under s.7(1) about entitlement to each tax credit. The current thresholds have the effect that many more people are entitled to the child tax credit than to the working tax credit. Regulations 7 and 8 of these Regulations make provision for dealing with this.

Social security benefits prescribed for the purposes of section 7(2) of the Act

4. The following are social security benefits prescribed for the purposes of section 7(2) of the Act in relation to child tax credit and working tax credit—

2.224

(a) income support under Part VII of the Social Security Contributions and Benefit Act 1992 other than income support to which a person is entitled only by virtue of regulation 6(2) and (3) of the Income Support (General) Regulations 1987;

(b) income support under Part VII of the Social Security Contributions and Benefit (Northern Ireland) Act 1992 other than income support to which a person is entitled only by virtue of regulation 6(2) and (3) of the Income Support (General) Regulations (Northern Ireland) 1987;

(c) an income-based jobseeker's allowance within the meaning of the Jobseekers Act 1995 or the Jobseekers (Northern Ireland) Order 1995.

[1(d) state pension credit within the meaning of the State Pension Credit Act 2002 or the State Pension Credit Act (Northern Ireland) 2002.]

[2(e) an income-related employment and support allowance payable under Part 1 of the Welfare Reform Act 2007 [3 or Part 1 of the Welfare Reform Act (Northern Ireland) 2007].]

DEFINITION

"the Act"—see reg.2.

AMENDMENTS

1. Tax Credits (Miscellaneous Amendments No.2) Regulations 2003 (SI 2003/2815), reg.18 (November 26, 2003).

2. Employment and Support Allowance (Consequential Provisions) (No.3) Regulations 2008 (SI 2009/1879), reg.23 (October 27, 2008).

3. Employment and Support Allowance (Consequential Provisions No.2) Regulations (Northern Ireland) 2008 (SI 2008/412 (NI), reg.10 (October 27, 2008)).

GENERAL NOTE

2.225   Section 7(2) of the TCA 2002 provides that those entitled to any of the social security benefits prescribed for the purposes of that subsection are not to be subject to the income test in s.7(1). This does not apply to exclude the claimant from any other requirements for an award.

Four benefits only have been prescribed by this regulation. They are:

(a) income support payable to any claimant. The exception applies to anyone who is a lone parent treated by regs 6(2) or (3) of the Income Support (General) Regulations 1987 (and its Northern Ireland equivalent) as being entitled to income support for the first 14 days of a period of remunerative work because he or she was a lone parent who was, for at least 26 weeks before the work started, receiving income support or income-based job-seeker's allowance;

(b) income-based jobseeker's allowance;

(c) state pension credit;

(d) income-related employment and support allowance.

Amounts prescribed for the purposes of section 7(3)(a) and (b) of the Act

2.226   **5.** The amount prescribed for the purposes of section 7(3)(a) and (b) of the Act is [¹£25,000].

AMENDMENT

1. Tax Credit Up-rating Regulations 2006 (SI 2006/963), reg.4(2) (April 6, 2006).

DEFINITIONS

"the Act"—see reg.2.

GENERAL NOTE

2.227   The original approach behind s.7 of the TCA 2002 was to base tax credits on both the previous year's income and the current year income. All personal income tax is now based on the current year's income, so that was thought in principle to be the better basis for tax credits. This overlooked the fact that most problems about the income tax payable for a year are sorted out the following year. Given the additional complications of tax credit assessments, events have shown that the only practical basis in most cases is the previous year's income. To achieve this, s.7(3)(c) and (d) have not been activated, while this regulation sets the figures for 7(3)(a) and (b) at a high figure.

Example: Alf's income in 2006–07 is £16,000 and in 2007–08 is £20,000. His partner, Zeta, is not working and has no other income. Their income for tax credits purposes in 2007–08 is his income for the previous year. This means that they are entitled to a more generous level of tax credits than would be the case if his income were assessed on his income for the current year. However, if Zeta starts work in 2007–08, their income in 2007–08 will also include her income for that year because she had no income in the previous year.

Manner of determining the rate at which a person is, or persons are, entitled to a tax credit

2.228   **6.** Regulations 7, 8 and 9 make provision as to the manner of determining the rate (if any) at which a person is, or persons are, entitled to a tax credit in any case where—

(a) the relevant income exceeds the income threshold; and

(b) his or their entitlement does not arise by virtue of section 7(2) of the Act.

DEFINITIONS

"entitlement"—see TCA 2002, ss.8 and 10.
"income threshold"—see reg.2.
"relevant income"—see reg.2.
"the Act"—see reg.2.

GENERAL NOTE

This is, on its face, purely a signposting regulation. It serves to remind the reader   2.229
of the exception from the income test in s.7 of the TCA 2002, and also to tie in
the £26 rule in reg.9 with the two main regulations: reg.7 dealing with working tax
credit, and reg.8 dealing with child tax credit. As will be seen from those regulations,
that order is intentional as entitlement to working tax credit, if any, must be calculated before entitlement to child tax credit.

There is, however, a drafting mismatch between the wording of this regulation
and the approach of regs 7 and 8, which appears to deflect its intention. Regulation
6 states that the other regulations make provision for determining the rate of *entitlement* to tax credits. By contrast, regs 7 and 8 talk about periods of *award*. "Period of
award" is defined in reg.2 of these Regulations by reference to s.5 of the TCA 2002
(entitled "periods of award"). And regs 7 and 8 of these Regulations refer to the elements of the credits to which a claimant "may be entitled" (regs 7(2)(a) and 8(2)).

The purpose of s.5 of TCA 2002 is to determine the period for which an award of
tax credit is made. Awards are made under s.14 of the Act, and are made in advance
of, or at the start of, the year of claim, using s.7(10) of the Act to estimate the
income. At that point, the "period of award" can in most cases only be the whole tax
year, or the balance of that year from the effective starting date of the award. Awards
must ignore uncertain future changes as they are not then known. Regulations 7 and
8 set out in considerable detail how to deal with part-years. But, save for the case of
claims made only part-way through a year, the "relevant period" for an award will
always be the whole year, and the complexities of regs 7 and 8 are not needed.

The full calculations under regs 7 and 8 of these Regulations cannot be made until
the end of the tax year, when the task of HMRC is to make entitlement decisions
under s.18 of the Act. So why refer to periods of award rather than periods of entitlement? It would appear that this mismatch between *award* and *entitlement* is a leftover
of the changes made to the Tax Credits Bill during its passage through Parliament
(as discussed in the notes to those sections). It is suggested that, to make practical
sense of this regulation, the definition of "period of award" as applied to both regs 7
and 8 has to take in periods of entitlement as well.

Determination of rate of working tax credit

7.—(1) In relation to a person or persons entitled to working tax credit,   2.230
the rate shall be determined by finding the rate for each relevant period and,
where necessary, adding together those rates.

(2) "Relevant period" means any part of the period of award throughout
which—

(a) the elements of working tax credit (other than the childcare element)
to which the person or persons may be entitled, remain the same;
and

(b) there is no relevant change of circumstances for the purposes of
the childcare element of working tax credit, within the meaning of

reg.16(1) of the Working Tax Credit (Entitlement and Maximum Rate) Regulations 2002 (change of circumstances for the purposes of childcare element).

(3) The rate for each relevant period shall be found in accordance with the following steps—

Step 1—Finding the daily maximum rate for each element other than the childcare element

2.231   For each element of the tax credit (other than the childcare element) to be included in the case of the person or persons entitled to the tax credit, find the daily maximum rate using the following formula:

$$\frac{MR}{N1}$$

where:

"MR" is the maximum rate in relation to that element for the tax year to which the claim for the tax credit relates;

"N1" is the number of days in that tax year.

Step 2—Finding the maximum rate for the relevant period for each element other than the childcare element

2.232   For each element of the tax credit to be so included, find the amount produced by multiplying the daily maximum rate (found under Step 1 and rounded up to the nearest penny) by the number of days in the relevant period.

Step 3—finding the income for the relevant period

2.233   Find the income for the relevant period by using the following formula:

$$\frac{I}{N1} \times N2$$

where:

"I" is the relevant income for the tax year to which the claim for the tax credit relates;

"N1" is the number of days in that tax year;

"N2" is the number of days in the relevant period.

Step 4—Finding the threshold for the relevant period

2.234   Find the threshold for the relevant period using the following formula:

$$\frac{[^1 £6,420]}{N1} \times N2$$

where:

"N1" is the number of days in that tax year;

"N2" is the number of days in the relevant period.

Step 5—Finding the amount of the reduction

2.235   Find the amount which is [¹ 39] per cent of the amount by which the income for the relevant period (found under Step 3 and rounded down to the nearest penny) exceeds the threshold for the relevant period (found under Step 4 and rounded up to the nearest penny).

Step 6—Reducing the elements of the tax credit (other than any childcare element)

If the amount found under Step 5 (rounded down to the nearest penny) is less than or equal to the total of the amounts found under Step 2 for the elements of the tax credit, deduct the amount found under Step 5 (rounded down to the nearest penny) from the total of those amounts found under Step 2.

2.236

Step 7—Finding the actual weekly childcare costs for the relevant period

Find the relevant childcare charges for the relevant period in accordance with reg.15 of the Working Tax Credit (Entitlement and Maximum Rate) Regulations 2002.

2.237

Step 8—Finding the actual childcare costs for the relevant period

Multiply the result of Step 7 by $\dfrac{52}{N1} \times N2$

2.238

Here, N1 and N2 have the same meanings as in Step 3.
The result of this step is the amount of actual childcare costs for the relevant period.

Step 9—Finding the prescribed maximum childcare costs for the relevant period

Divide whichever of the maxima in reg.20(3) of the Working Tax Credit (Entitlement and Maximum Rate) Regulations 2002 is applicable by seven, round the result up to the nearest penny and multiply the resulting figure by the number of days in the relevant period.

The result of this is the prescribed maximum childcare costs for the relevant period.

2.239

Step 10—Finding the childcare element for the period

Take the lesser of the results of Steps 8 and 9.
Multiply that figure by [²80] per cent and round the result up to the nearest penny.
The result of this step is the maximum rate of the childcare element for the relevant period.

2.240

Step 11—Reducing the elements of the tax credit (including any childcare element)

If the amount found under Step 5 (rounded down to the nearest penny) exceeds the total of the amounts found under Step 2 for the elements of the tax credit—
(a) deduct the excess from the amount found under Step 10 for any childcare element; and
(b) reduce the total of the amounts found under Step 2 for the other elements of the tax credit to nil.

2.241

Step 12—Finding the rate for the relevant period

2.242   Add together—
(a) the total of the amounts found under Step 2 for the elements of the tax credit (other than any childcare element) after reduction in accordance with Step 6 or Step 11; and
(b) the amount found under Step 10 for any childcare element after any reduction in accordance with Step 11.
This is the rate for the relevant period.
(4) "Child care element" has the meaning given by section 12(2) of the Act.

AMENDMENT

1. Tax Credits Up-rating Regulations 2008 (SI 2008/796), reg.4(4) (April 6, 2008).

DEFINITIONS

"childcare element"—see TCA 2002, s.12.
"period of award"—see reg.2.
"rate"—see TCA 2002, s.13.

GENERAL NOTE

2.243   See the general note to reg.6 above. The effect of this regulation and reg.8—both together and separately—is to limit the amount of tax credit that a claimant can have to the relevant daily (or in the case of childcare element of working tax credit only, weekly) amount of the credit, if circumstances of a claimant change during a tax year. This approach is, as a result, less generous than the personal allowances for income tax, including children's tax credit. For example, the main personal allowance of an individual is the same amount for that individual throughout the year as is, for example, a bereaved person's allowance or a blind person's allowance. By contrast, the basis of calculation imposed by this regulation and reg.8 is that the elements of both working tax credit and child tax credit are payable only for the precise periods of the year for which the claimant can meet the requirement for that credit and element. For example, the family element of child tax credit increases from £545 to £1,090 for a family with a child under one in it. But under reg.8 that only increases the total child tax credit from the day when the child is born. Parents will only receive the full £1,090 in the relevant year if the child is actually born on April 6. Equally, however, the additional child tax credit continues to be payable up to the day before the child's first birthday in the following year (subject to the income test and save for marginal cases).

Paras (1) and (2)
2.244   As noted above, "period of award" must be read as including also "period of entitlement" to make sense of this regulation. Likewise, the reference to "may be entitled" in para.(2) should include "is entitled".

Para. (3)
2.245   This paragraph is written in the "step-by-step" style, using the command tense of relevant verbs, that has been adopted as part of the Tax Law Rewrite approach to tax regulations. It is also written so that the rules in the paragraph can be operated in full by a computer.

Relevant periods of a full year
2.246   In most cases, as noted above, the complexities of this rule can be sidestepped because the question of an award of, or entitlement to, a tax credit can be judged

by the full tax year. If the decision relates to a full year, then the steps can be telescoped as follows:

Step 1 with Step 2: Identify the annual amount of each element of working tax credit to which the claimant is entitled, apart from the childcare element, for that tax year.

2.247

Step 3: Identify the relevant income for the tax year (current year income or previous year income).

2.248

Step 4 with Step 5 and Step 6: If the income from Step 3 exceeds the annual amount from Steps 1 and 2, reduce the amount from Steps 1 and 2 by 39 per cent of that excess. The result is the excess income for the tax year. The rate of reduction was increased from 37 per cent to 39 per cent for 2008–09 and forward, at the same time as the basic rate of income tax was reduced from 22 per cent to 20 per cent.

2.249

Step 7 with Step 8: Find the relevant childcare charges for the tax year.

2.250

Step 9 with Step 10: The childcare element is, from 2006, 80 per cent of either £15,600 (for two or more children) or £9,100 (for one child), or, if less, 80 per cent of the total childcare charges for the tax year.

2.251

Steps 11 and 12: If there is excess income for the tax year from Steps 4–6, reduce the annual amount from Steps 1 and 2 by the amount of that excess, if necessary to nil. If the excess is greater than that amount, next reduce the amount from Steps 9 and 10 by the amount by which that excess income exceeds the annual amount from Steps 1 and 2. If the excess income is greater than both amounts, then the amount of working tax credit for the tax year is nil.

2.252

Note from this that the childcare element of working tax credit is to be calculated on a weekly, not daily, basis in the event of any problem, and also is to be left in payment after the other elements have stopped being payable under these rules.

Relevant periods of less than a year

These periods arise only where there is a change of circumstances during a year that brings a relevant period to an end and/or starts a new one. Until 2006 this could cause problems where this happened in circumstances where claimants were not under a duty to report changes. The extension of the duty to report under reg.21 of the Tax Credits (Claims and Notifications) Regulations 2002, together with the reduction of the period in which the changes must be reported to one month, and the extension of award or entitlement by reg.7D of the Working Tax Credit (Entitlement and Maximum Rate) Regulations 2002 for 4 weeks after someone ceases work or works for less than 16 hours a week, have removed many of these problems.

2.253

CTC/2270/2007 confirms that the relevant income of a couple is their income for the year even if they only become a couple during the year. See the note to TCA 2002, s.7(4) above.

Determination of rate of child tax credit

8.—(1) In relation to a person or persons entitled to child tax credit, the rate shall be determined by finding the rate for each relevant period and, where necessary, adding together those rates.

2.254

(2) "Relevant period" means—

(a) in the case of a person or persons entitled to child tax credit only, any part of the period of award throughout which the maximum rate at which he or they may be entitled to the tax credit remains the same;

(b) in the case of a person or persons entitled to both child tax credit and working tax credit, any part of the period of award throughout which the maximum rate of child tax credit to which he or they may be entitled remains the same and both sub-paras (a) and (b) of reg.7(2) are met.

(3) The rate for each relevant period shall be found in accordance with the following steps—

Step 1—Finding the daily maximum rate for each element

2.255   For each element of the tax credit to be included in the case of the person or persons entitled to the tax credit, find the daily maximum rate using the following formula:

$$\frac{MR}{NI}$$

where:

"MR" is the maximum rate in relation to that element for the tax year to which the claim for the tax credit relates;

"NI" is the number of days in that tax year.

Step 2—Finding the maximum rate for the relevant period for each element

2.256   For each element of the tax credit to be so included, find the amount produced by multiplying the maximum rate (found under Step 1 and rounded up to the nearest penny) by the number of days in the relevant period.

Step 3—Finding income for the relevant period

2.257   Find the income for the relevant period by using the following formula:

$$\frac{I}{NI} \times N2$$

where:

"I" is the relevant income for the tax year to which the claim for the tax credit relates;

"NI" is the number of days in that tax year;

"N2" is the number of days in the relevant period.

Step 4—Finding the threshold for the relevant period

2.258   Find the amount produced by the following formula:

$$\frac{[^1 £16,040]}{NI} \times N2$$

where:

"NI" is the number of days in that tax year;

"N2" is the number of days in the relevant period.

The threshold for the relevant period is—

    (a) in the case of a person or persons entitled to child tax credit only, that amount;

    (b) in the case of a person or persons entitled to both child tax credit and working tax credit—

        (i) that amount; or

        (ii) if greater, the lowest amount of income for the relevant period (found under Step 3) which, disregarding reg.9, would result in a determination in accordance with reg.7 providing for no rate of working tax credit in his or their case for that period.

Step 5—Finding the amount of the reduction of the elements of the tax credit (other than the family element)

Find the amount (if any) which is [1 39] per cent of the amount by which the income for the relevant period (found under Step 3 and rounded down to the nearest penny) exceeds the threshold for the relevant period (found under Step 4 and rounded up to the nearest penny).

2.259

Step 6—Reducing the elements of the tax credit (other than the family element)

If the amount found under Step 5 (rounded down to the nearest penny) is less than the total of the amounts found under Step 2 for the elements of the tax credit (other than the family element), deduct the amount found under Step 5 (rounded down to the nearest penny) from the total of those amounts.

2.260

Step 7—Reducing the elements of the tax credit (other than the family element) to nil

If the amount found under Step 5 (rounded down to the nearest penny) is equal to or exceeds the total of the amounts found under Step 2 for the elements of the tax credit (other than the family element), reduce the total of those amounts to nil.

2.261

Step 8—Finding the amount of the reduction of the family element

Find the amount (if any) which is 6.67 per cent of the amount by which the income for the relevant period (found under Step 3 and rounded down to the nearest penny) exceeds—

2.262

(a) in any case where the total of the amounts found under Step 2 for the elements of the tax credit (other than the family element) would be reduced in accordance with Step 7 to nil if the relevant income were £50,000 or less, "X";

(b) in any other case, "Y";

where:

"X" is the amount found in accordance with Step 9 and rounded up to the nearest penny;

"Y" is the lowest amount of income for the relevant period (found under Step 3 and rounded up to the nearest penny) which would result in the total of the amounts of the elements of the tax credit (other than the family element) being reduced to nil in accordance with Step 7.

Step 9—Finding "X" for the purposes of Step 8

Find "X" using the following formula:

2.263

$$\frac{£50,000}{N1} \times N2$$

where:

"N1" is the number of days in that tax year;

"N2" is the number of days in the relevant period.

Step 10—Reducing the family element

2.264   Deduct any amount found under Step 8 (rounded down to the nearest penny) from the amount found under Step 2 for the family element.

Step 11—Finding the rate for the relevant period

2.265   Add together—
(a) the total of the amounts found under Step 2 for the elements of the tax credit (other than the family element) after any reduction in accordance with Step 6 or Step 7; and
(b) the amount found under Step 2 for the family element after any reduction in accordance with Step 10.
This is the rate for the relevant period.
(4) "The family element" means the family element of child tax credit within the meaning given by section 9(3) of the Act.

AMENDMENT

1. Tax Credits Up-rating Regulations 2009 (SI 2009/800), reg.4(3) (April 6, 2009).

DEFINITIONS

"period of award"—see reg.2.
"the Act"—see reg.2.

GENERAL NOTE

2.266   See the general note to reg.6 above and the opening note to reg.7.

Paras (1) and (2)
2.267   The same comments apply as those to paras (1) and (2) of reg.7.

Para. (3)
2.268   This appears to be the equivalent for child tax credit of reg.7, but it has two additional elements. First, the effect of the steps is to remove an award of or entitlement to working tax credit before that of child tax credit. This may be important where one of a couple is receiving one of the credits while the other is receiving the other tax credit. The effect is to take the credit from the earner (and the duty to pay from the employer) before it is taken from the carer.

Secondly, the family element of child tax credit is removed only when a second, higher income threshold of £50,000 is exceeded. Further, the family element (currently £545 a year, increased to £1,090 if any of the children are less than a year old: Child Tax Credit Regulations 2002 (SI 2002/2007), reg.7(3)) is reduced only by 6.67 per cent of the excess of relevant income over £50,000. As the cut-off point for payment of child tax credit is £26 (reg.9 below), this makes the top relevant income to receive any tax credit about £66,000, but only where there is a child aged under one.

Relevant periods of a full year
2.269   In parallel with reg.7, reg.8 is straightforward as applied to a period of award of a full year. Steps 1–6 require that the annual amount of all elements (including the family element) be found, that the income for the year also be found, and that the excess of the income over the £16,040 threshold, if any, be calculated. The maximum amount of child tax credit is found by reducing the annual amount of all elements *excluding* the family element by 39 per cent of the excess of the income over the threshold. The rate of reduction was increased from 37 per cent to 39 per cent for 2008–09 and forward at the same time as the basic rate of income tax was reduced from 22 per cent to 20 per cent.

Relevant periods of less than a year

The changes noted in para.2.250 for the equivalent rule for WTC apply equally to CTC and have also removed most of the potential problems for this provision also.

2.270

Cases in which there is no rate of tax credit

9.—(1) In the case of a person or persons entitled to working tax credit only or child tax credit only, where the rate at which the person or persons would be entitled to the tax credit (as determined in accordance with reg.7 or 8) would be less than £26, there is no rate in his or their case.

2.271

(2) In the case of a person or persons entitled to both working tax credit and child tax credit, where the total of the rates at which the person or persons would be entitled to the tax credits (as determined in accordance with regulations 7 and 8) would be less than £26, there are no rates in his or their case.

GENERAL NOTE

This cut-off provision is authorised by s.13(3)(b) of the Act.

2.272

Tax Credits (Claims and Notifications) Regulations 2002

(SI 2002/2014) (AS AMENDED)

The Commissioners of Inland Revenue, in exercise of the powers conferred upon them by ss.4(1), 6, 14(2), 15(2), 16(3), 17(10), 19(2), 22(1)(b) and (2), 65(1), (2) and (7) and 67 of the Tax Credits Act 2002, hereby make the following Regulations:

ARRANGEMENT OF REGULATIONS

PART I

GENERAL

2.273

PART II

CLAIMS

475

PART III

NOTIFICATIONS OF CHANGES OF CIRCUMSTANCES

PART IV

NOTICES TO PROVIDE INFORMATION OR EVIDENCE

32. Dates to be specified in notices under section 14(2), 15(2), 16(3), 18(10) or 19(2) of the Act.

PART V

FINAL DECISIONS

33. Dates to be specified in notices under section 17 of the Act.
34. Manner in which declaration or statement in response to a notice under section 17 of the Act to be made.
35. Circumstances where one person may act for another in response to a notice under section 17 of the Act—receivers, etc.
36. Circumstances where one person may act for another in response to a notice under section 17 of the Act.

PART I

GENERAL

Citation, commencement and effect

1.—(1) These Regulations may be cited as the Tax Credits (Claims and Notifications) Regulations 2002 and shall come into force on 12th August 2002.

2.274

(2) These Regulations have effect in relation to claims for a tax credit for periods of award beginning on or after 6th April 2003.

Interpretation

2. In these Regulations—
"the Act" means the Tax Credits Act 2002;

2.275

[³ "appropriate office" means Comben House, Farriers Way, Netherton, Merseyside or any other office specified in writing by the Board;]
"the Board" means the Commissioners of Inland Revenue;
[² "couple" has the meaning given by section 3(5A) of the Act;]
"disability element" shall be construed in accordance with section 11(4) of the Act;
"joint claim" has the meaning given by section 3(8) of the Act;
[² . . .]
[¹ "relevant authority" means—
 (a) the Board;
 (b) the Secretary of State or the Department for Social Development in Northern Ireland; or
 (c) a person providing services to the Board, the Secretary of State or that Department in connection with tax credits;]
"severe disability element" has the meaning in regulation 17 of the Working Tax Credit Regulations;

477

"single claim" has the meaning given by section 3(8) of the Act;
"tax year" means a period beginning on 6th April in one year and ending
with 5th April in the next;
[².. .]
"the Working Tax Credit Regulations" means the Working Tax Credit
(Entitlement and Maximum Rate) Regulations 2002.

AMENDMENTS

1. Tax Credits (Claims and Notifications and Payments by the Board)
(Amendment) Regulations 2003 (SI 2003/723), reg.3(1) (April 6, 2003).
2. Civil Partnership Act 2004 (Tax Credits, etc.) (Consequential Amendments)
Order 2005 (SI 2005/2919), art.4(2) (December 5, 2005).
3. Tax Credits (Miscellaneous Amendments) Regulations 2009 (SI 2009/697),
reg.12 (April 6, 2009).

Use of electronic communications to make claims or to give notices or notifications

2.276   **3.**—(1) In these Regulations "writing" includes writing produced by
electronic communications that are approved by directions issued by or on
behalf of the Board.
(2) If a claim which is required by these Regulations to be made to [¹a
relevant authority at an appropriate office] is made in writing produced
by electronic communications, it shall be treated for the purposes of these
Regulations as having been made to, and received by, [¹a relevant authority
at an appropriate office] on the date on which it is recorded on an official
computer system.
(3) If a notice or notification which is required by these Regulations to be
given to [¹a relevant authority at an appropriate office] is given in writing
produced by electronic communications, it shall be treated for the purposes
of these Regulations as having been given to, and received by, [¹a relevant
authority at an appropriate office] on the date on which it is recorded on an
official computer system.
(4) In this regulation—
(a) "electronic communications" has the meaning given by section
132(10) of the Finance Act 1999;
(b) "official computer system" means a computer system maintained by
or on behalf of the Board to—
(i) send or receive information, or
(ii) process or store information.

AMENDMENT

1. Tax Credits (Claims and Notifications and Payments by the Board)
(Amendment) Regulations 2003 (SI 2003/723), reg.3(2) (April 6, 2003).

DEFINITIONS

"appropriate office"—see reg.2.
"the Board"—see *ibid.*
"electronic communications"—see para.(4)(a).
"official computer system"—see para.(4)(b).
"relevant authority"—see reg.2.
"writing"—see para.(1).

See further the decision of Mr Commissioner Mesher in *CIS/995/2004*, discussed   2.277
in the annotations to reg.4 below and Tax Credits Act 2002, s.14(2) above.

This regulation enables use of the internet and an official website for claims. The
HMRC website claim facility was closed down after severe problems with fraud.
The House of Commons Public Accounts Committee has since disclosed that
the website was established outside recommended security procedures. It remains
closed at the time of writing.

PART II

CLAIMS

Interpretation of this Part

4. In this Part (and Part III) "the relevant date", in relation to a claim for   2.278
a tax credit, means—

    (a) in cases where regulation 6 applies, the date on which the claim
        would be treated as being made by that regulation disregarding regu-
        lations 7 and 8;

    (b) in cases where sub-paragraph [²(d)] of regulation 11(3) applies, the
        date on which the claim would be treated as being made by that sub-
        paragraph disregarding regulations 7 and 8;

    (c) in any other case, the date on which the claim is received by [¹ a rel-
        evant authority at an appropriate office].

AMENDMENTS

1. Tax Credits (Claims and Notifications and Payments by the Board)
(Amendment) Regulations 2003 (SI 2003/723), reg.3(2) (April 6, 2003).

2. Tax Credits (Miscellaneous Amendments) Regulations 2009 (SI 2009/697),
reg.13 (April 6, 2009).

DEFINITIONS

    "appropriate office"—see reg.2.
    "relevant authority"—see *ibid.*
    "the relevant date"—see reg.4.

The general rule is that the "relevant date" (or date of claim in social secur-   2.279
ity terms) is the date on which the claim for tax credits is received by "a relevant
authority at an appropriate office" (para.(c)). On the basis of the definition of these
latter terms in reg.2, this will normally, but not always, be an HMRC office. For the
date of receipt of electronic communications, e.g. online claims for tax credits, see
reg.3. There are two modifications to the general rule in para.(c). First, amended
claims are treated as made on the date on which the amended claim is received (see
para.(a) and reg.6(3)). Secondly, where a claimant responds to a final notice under
TCA 2002, s.17 within the specified time, the date of claim is the previous April
6 (reg.11(3)(a)). If the claimant's declaration is submitted beyond that time limit,
then the date of claim is the latest date on which such declaration is received (see
para.(b) and reg.11(3)(b)). Note that there are special rules governing the effective date of claim by refugees who have made a successful application for asylum

and who subsequently make a retrospective claim for tax credits (see Tax Credits (Immigration) Regulations 2003 (SI 2003/653), regs 3 and 4).

Mr Commissioner Mesher's decision in *CIS/995/2004* deals with the complex interaction between tax credits and income support and what constitutes a claim for the former. Early in 2003 the claimant in *CIS/995/2004* claimed income support. On January 10, 2003, he also completed an online application form for child tax credit (CTC) and transmitted it to the Inland Revenue. In March 2003 the claimant received a TC602 letter from the Inland Revenue notifying him of his family's CTC entitlement for the 2003/04 tax year and asking him to sign and return the accompanying declaration. Having made further enquiries, the claimant discovered that he would be better off retaining entitlement to income support. He accordingly did not sign and return the TC602 declaration. However, the Revenue started making CTC payments in April 2003 and notified the DWP of this fact. This led the Secretary of State to decide that the claimant was no longer entitled to income support as his income exceeded his applicable amount.

The claimant appealed to a tribunal which disallowed his appeal, holding that reg.7 of the Social Security (Working Tax Credit and Child Tax Credit) Consequential Amendments Regulations 2003 (SI 2003/455) required the DWP to treat the claimant's income as including an amount equivalent to his CTC entitlement. Although finding error in the tribunal's reasoning in other respects, the Commissioner held that the tribunal had come to the only conclusion open to it as a matter of law and on the evidence before it. In particular, the Commissioner rejected the claimant's argument that he had only made a preliminary application for CTC which could not be completed until he had signed and returned the TC602 declaration. On the contrary, the online completion and transmission of the application form, notwithstanding the absence of any written confirmation at the time or later, amounted to a claim. Mr Commissioner Mesher thus held that the claimant had made a valid claim on January 10, 2003, whether in an approved electronic format (and so under regs 3 and 5(2)(a)—a point which did not have to be resolved) or alternatively under the wide power in reg.5(2)(b). A valid award of CTC had then followed. The Commissioner expressly left open the question whether an appeal tribunal or Commissioner has jurisdiction to go behind the Board's determination that a claim had been made.

The informality with which HMRC will accept renewals claims was emphasised in a public letter to the Institute of Chartered Accountants in England and Wales published on October 1, 2004. Speaking of renewal claims, the Deputy Chairman of the then Inland Revenue said:

"Claimants simply have to confirm or correct the information we hold about their circumstances and report their income for the year just finished. For those not in a position to provide actual income figures at the time they reply, an estimate will be accepted. The information necessary to renew can be accepted by telephone or through our e-portal or by filling in a short paper form."

He added: "I should also make clear, in answer to a concern you raise, that renewals information is logged on receipt, even if it has not yet been processed, to make sure the payments continue."

Manner in which claims to be made

2.280　　**5.**—(1) This regulation prescribes the manner in which a claim for a tax credit is to be made.

(2) A claim must be made to [¹a relevant authority at an appropriate office]—

    (a) in writing on a form approved or authorised by the Board for the purpose of the claim; or

[² (b) in such other manner as the Board may decide having regard to all the circumstances.]

(3) A claim must contain the information requested on the form (or such of that information as the Board may accept as sufficient in the circumstances of the particular case).

(4) In particular, a claim must include in respect of every person by whom the claim is made—

(a) a statement of the person's national insurance number and information or evidence establishing that that number has been allocated to the person; or

(b) information or evidence enabling the national insurance number that has been allocated to the person to be ascertained; or

(c) an application for a national insurance number to be allocated to the person which is accompanied by information or evidence enabling such a number to be so allocated.

This paragraph is subject to [³ paragraphs (6) and (8)].

(5) "National insurance number" means the national insurance number allocated within the meaning of regulation 9 of the Social Security (Crediting and Treatment of Contributions, and National Insurance Numbers) Regulations 2001.

(6) Paragraph (4) does not apply if the Board are satisfied that the person or persons by whom the claim was made had a reasonable excuse for making a claim which did not comply with the requirements of that paragraph.

(7) At any time after a claim has been made but before the Board have given notice of their decision under section 14(1) of the Act in relation to the claim, the person or persons by whom the claim was made may amend the claim by giving notice orally or in writing to [¹a relevant authority at an appropriate office].

[³ (8) Paragraph (4) does not apply to any person who is subject to immigration control within the meaning set out in section 115(9)(a) of the Immigration and Asylum Act 1999 and to whom a national insurance number has not been allocated.]

AMENDMENTS

1. Tax Credits (Claims and Notifications and Payments by the Board) (Amendment) Regulations 2003 (SI 2003/723), reg.3(2) (April 6, 2003).

2. Tax Credits (Miscellaneous Amendments) (No.2) Regulations 2008 (SI 2008/2169), reg.12 (September 1, 2008).

3. Tax Credits (Miscellaneous Amendments) Regulations 2009 (SI 2009/697), reg.14 (April 6, 2009).

DEFINITIONS

"the Act"—see reg.2.
"appropriate office"—see *ibid*.
"the Board"—see *ibid*.
"National insurance number"—see para.(5).
"relevant authority"—see reg.2.
"writing"—see reg.3(1).

GENERAL NOTE

Para. (2)
This rule is similar to, but not identical to, the standard social security provision in reg.4(1) of the Social Security (Claims and Payments) Regulations 1987 (SI 1987/1968). The fundamental difference is that it is not possible to make an

2.281

oral claim for a social security benefit under reg.4(1) of the 1987 Regulations. This appears to be possible in the case of tax credits as the requirement that the claim be in writing appears only in para.(a), which will cover the great majority of cases, and not in the residual category envisaged by para.(b).

Paras (4)–(6)

2.282   The requirement to provide a national insurance number (or the information or evidence specified) mirrors the requirement for social security benefits set out in SSAA 1992, s.1(1B). Note however HMRC discretion not to apply this requirement if satisfied that the claimant had a reasonable excuse for making a claim which failed to comply with it (para.(6)). There is no equivalent discretion to disapply the requirement in the social security scheme.

Para. (7)

2.283   This provision is similar to the social security rule in reg.5(1) of the Social Security (Claims and Payments) Regulations 1987 (SI 1987/1968). However, a tax credits claim can be amended by giving oral notice, whereas the social security rule requires written notice. See further reg.6 on the determination of the date of claim for amended claims for tax credits.

Amended claims

2.284   **6.**—(1) In the circumstances prescribed by paragraph (2) a claim for a tax credit which has been amended shall be treated as having been made as amended and, subject to regulations 7 and 8, as having been made on the date prescribed by paragraph (3).

(2) The circumstances prescribed by this paragraph are where a person has amended or persons have amended the claim in accordance with reg.5(7).

(3) The date prescribed by this paragraph is the date on which the claim being amended was received by [¹ a relevant authority at an appropriate office].

AMENDMENT

1. Tax Credits (Claims and Notifications and Payments by the Board) (Amendment) Regulations 2003 (SI 2003/723), reg.3(2) (April 6, 2003).

DEFINITIONS

"appropriate office"—see reg.2.
"relevant authority"—see *ibid*.

Time-limit for claims (if otherwise entitled to tax credit up to three months earlier)

2.285   **7.**—(1) In the circumstances prescribed by paragraph (2), a claim for a tax credit received by [¹ a relevant authority at an appropriate office] shall be treated as having been made on the date prescribed by paragraph (3).

(2) The circumstances prescribed by this paragraph are those where the person or persons by whom the claim is made would (if a claim had been made) have been entitled to the tax credit either—

(a) on the date falling three months before the relevant date (or on 6th April 2003, if later); or

(b) at any later time in the period beginning on the date in subparagraph (a) and ending on the relevant date.

(3) The date prescribed by this paragraph is the earliest date falling within the terms of paragraph (2)(a) or (b) when the person or the persons by whom the claim is made would (if a claim had been made) have become entitled to the tax credit.

AMENDMENT

1. Tax Credits (Claims and Notifications and Payments by the Board) (Amendment) Regulations 2003 (SI 2003/723), reg.3(2) (April 6, 2003).

DEFINITIONS

"appropriate office"—see reg.2.
"relevant authority"—see *ibid*.

GENERAL NOTE

The standard rule is that tax credits claims can be backdated only three months. This has given rise to a number of appeals, but there are no exceptions or discretions in the rule save for that in reg.8. Regulation 25 imposes a similar time limit on notifying changes of circumstances that may increase awards. This contrasts with the relevant income tax rule that allows corrections to be made (for example because no claim has been made for an allowance or no deduction for an expense) for up to six years after the relevant time. It also contrasts with the powers for HMRC to amend tax credits awards and entitlements to deal with overpayments.

Once a claim has been made, there may be an amendment to deal with corrections when the annual declaration is made ahead of the entitlement decision.

It is therefore better to make a claim if there may be entitlement rather than waiting to see. This has led to the widespread practice, accepted by HMRC, of protective claims, and also to the practice of HMRC reducing awards to nil rather than terminating them during the year where circumstances change. Statistics show that at any one time in recent years there are about ½ million nil or protective claims in the system.

[¹ Date of claims – disability element of working tax credit

8.—(1) In the circumstances prescribed by paragraph (2), the claim referred to in paragraph (2)(a) shall be treated as having been made on the date prescribed by paragraph (3).

(2) The circumstances prescribed by this paragraph are where–

(a) a claim for working tax credit including the disability element ("the tax credits claim") is made by a person or persons ("the claimants") which results in the Board making an award of working tax credit including the disability element;

(b) the claim is made within 3 months of the date that a claim for any of the benefits referred to in regulation 9(2) to (8) of the Working Tax Credit Regulations ("the benefits claim") is determined in favour of the claimants (or one of them); and

(c) the claimants would (subject to making a claim) have been entitled to working tax credit if (and only if) they had satisfied the requirements of regulation 9(1)(c) of the Working Tax Credit Regulations, on any day in the period—

(i) beginning on the date of the benefits claim, and

(ii) ending on the date of the tax credits claim.

(3) The date prescribed by this paragraph is–

(a) the first date in respect of which the benefit claimed is payable; or

2.286

2.287

(b) if later, the date falling 3 months before the claim for the benefit is made; or

(c) if later, the first day identified under paragraph (2)(c).]

AMENDMENT

1. Tax Credits (Miscellaneous Amendments) Regulations 2009 (SI 2009/697), reg.15 (April 6, 2009).

GENERAL NOTE

2.288   The new version of this regulation provides two special rules for claims for the disability element of a tax credit from 2009. In *SP v HMRC* [2009] UKUT (AAC), CTC/2878/2008. The Upper Tribunal upheld a ruling that under the previous rule a claimant for disability living allowance had to inform the Tax Credit Office separately of both the claim for the allowance and the award of the allowance if the claim to a disability element of a tax credit was to operate from the date of award of the allowance. In that case a claim was made, but refused and then awarded on appeal. Because the claimant had not notified the claim, the disability element of the tax credit could only be backdated for three months from notification of the award, not the full year back to the date when the allowance had first been awarded. The 2009 amending regulations recognized and changed the weak drafting of the original version, and so the Commissioner's decision no longer applies. A claimant need only notify an award to have the disability element backdated to start at the same time as the allowance, even if that is more than 3 months in the past.

Advance claims before the year begins

2.289   **9.**—(1) In the circumstances prescribed by paragraph (2) a claim for a tax credit may be made for a period after the relevant date.

(2) The circumstances prescribed by this paragraph are where a tax credit is claimed for a tax year by making a claim before the tax year begins.

(3) This regulation shall cease to have effect in relation to the tax year beginning on 6th April 2004 and subsequent tax years.

DEFINITIONS

   "the relevant date"—see reg.4.
   "tax year"—see reg.2.

GENERAL NOTE

2.290   This regulation provides, at least at the outset of the tax credits scheme, for claims for such credits to be made before the beginning of the tax year to which they relate (see also reg.14). There is further provision in reg.10 for advance claims for working tax credit where a person is about to start work.

Advance claims—working tax credit

2.291   **10.**—(1) In the circumstances prescribed by paragraph (2) a claim for a tax credit may be made for a period after the relevant date.

(2) The circumstances prescribed by this paragraph are where—

(a) the tax credit in question is working tax credit; and

(b) the case falls within sub-paragraph (b) of the First Condition in regulation 4(1) of the Working Tax Credit Regulations (person who has accepted an offer of work which is expected to commence within seven days).

(3) In the circumstances prescribed by paragraph (2)—

(a) an award on a claim for tax credit may be made subject to the condition that the requirements for entitlement are satisfied no later than the date prescribed by paragraph (4); and

(b) if those requirements are satisfied no later than that date, the claim shall be treated as being made on the date on which they are satisfied.

(4) The date prescribed by this paragraph is the date falling 7 days after the relevant date.

DEFINITIONS

"the relevant date"—see reg.4.
"the Working Tax Credit Regulations"—see reg.2.

GENERAL NOTE

This rule allows for working tax credit claims to be made up to seven days in advance where a person has accepted an offer of employment and is expected to commence within that week.

2.292

Circumstances in which claims to be treated as made—notices containing provision under section 17(2)(a), (4)(a) or (6)(a) of the Act

11.—(1) In the circumstances prescribed by paragraph (2), a claim for a tax credit is to be treated as made.

2.293

(2) The circumstances prescribed by this paragraph are where (in the case where there has been a previous single claim) a person has or (in the case where there has been a previous joint claim) both persons have made a declaration in response to provision included in a notice under section 17 of the Act by virtue of—

(a) subsection (2)(a) of that section;
(b) subsection (4)(a) of that section;
(c) subsection (6)(a) of that section; or
(d) any combination of those subsections.

The declaration made shall (subject to regulation 5(3)) be treated as a claim for tax credit by that person or persons for the tax year following that to which the notice relates.

[² (3) The claim shall be treated as made—

(a) in a case where the declaration is made by 31st July next following the end of the tax year to which the claim relates, on 6th April preceding that date;

[³(aa) in a case where the declaration is made by the date specified on the section 17 notice in the tax year following that to which the claim relates, on 6th April preceding that date.]

(b) in a case where the declaration, not having been made by 31st July next following the end of the tax year to which the claim relates, is made within 30 days following the date on the notice to the claimant that payments of tax credit under section 24(4) of the Act have ceased due to the claimant's failure to make the declaration, on 6th April preceding the date on which the declaration is made;

(c) in a case where the declaration, not having been made by 31st July next following the end of the tax year to which the claim relates or within the 30 days specified in sub-paragraph (b), is made before 31st January next following the end of the tax year to which the claim relates, and, in the opinion of the Board, the claimant had good cause for not making the declaration as mentioned in sub-paragraphs (a) or (b),[3 on 6th April next following the end of the tax year to which the claim relates]; or

(d) in any other case, on the latest date on which the declaration is received by a relevant authority at an appropriate office (subject to the application of regulation 7).]

[1(4) Paragraph (3) does not apply—

(a) in the case where there has been a previous single claim (to which the notice referred to in paragraph (2) relates) if the person by whom it was made could no longer make a single claim; or

(b) in the case where there has been a previous joint claim (to which the notice referred to in paragraph (2) relates) if the persons by whom it was made could no longer make a joint claim.]

AMENDMENTS

1. Tax Credits (Miscellaneous Amendments) Regulations 2004 (SI 2004/762), reg.3(2) (April 6, 2004).
2. Tax Credits (Miscellaneous Amendments) Regulations 2008 (SI 2008/604), reg.4(2) (April 6, 2008).
3. Tax Credits (Miscellaneous Amendments) Regulations 2009 (SI 2009/697), reg.16 (April 6, 2009).

DEFINITIONS

"the Act"—see reg.2.
"appropriate office"—see *ibid*.
"the Board"—see *ibid*.
"joint claim"—see *ibid*.
"relevant authority"—see *ibid*.
"single claim"—see *ibid*.
"tax year"—see *ibid*.

GENERAL NOTE

2.294   This allows the claimant's (or claimants') declaration in response to a HMRC final notice under various provisions of the TCA 2002, s.17, to be treated as a claim for tax credits. This effectively eases the process of making renewal claims for subsequent tax years. This assumes that the claimant(s) provide the necessary information as requested on the official form (para.(2) and reg.5(3)). The date of claim is the preceding April 6, i.e. the start of the tax year, assuming the declaration is returned within the designated time (para.(3)). There are further deeming rules under reg.12 in relation to s.17 final notices.

HMRC indicated at the Tax Credits Consultation Group meeting on January 15, 2008, in connection with late renewals after July 31, that: "claims could be renewed after July 31 if customers had good cause for the delay. Most cases are restored without difficulty but, for a small number, technical problems may prevent them being restored—where that happens, manual payments would be set up" (*http:// www.hmrc.gov.uk/taxcredits/minutes150108.htm*). Legislative effect was given to this from April 6, 2008 by the replacement of para.(3). "Good cause" is the standard social security test derived from *R(S) 2/63*.

Circumstances in which claims to be treated as made—notices containing provision under section 17(2)(b), (4)(b) and (6)(b) of the Act

2.295   **12.**—(1) In either of the circumstances prescribed by paragraphs (2) and (4) a claim for a tax credit is to be treated as made.

(2) The circumstances prescribed by this paragraph are where a person is

or persons are treated as having made a declaration in response to provision included in a notice under section 17 of the Act by virtue of—

(a) subsection (2)(b) of that section; and

(b) subsection (4)(b) of that section,

or a combination of those subsections and subsection (6)(b) of that section.

(3) The declaration referred to in paragraph (2) shall (subject to regulation 5(3)) be treated as a claim by that person or persons for tax credit for the tax year following that to which the notice relates.

(4) The circumstances prescribed by this paragraph are where a person or any of the persons has—

(a) made a statement under paragraph (b) of subsection (2) of section 17 of the Act in response to such a notice by the date specified for the purposes of that subsection; or

(b) made a statement under paragraph (b) of subsection (4) of that section in response to such a notice by the date specified for the purposes of that subsection,

or a combination of any of those subsections and subsection (6)(b) of that section.

(5) The notice referred to in paragraph (4), together with (and as corrected by) the statement or statements there referred to, shall (subject to regulation 5(3)) be treated as a claim for tax credit by that person or persons for the tax year following that to which the notice relates.

(6) The claim shall be treated as made on 6th April preceding the dates specified in the notice for the purposes of subsection (2) or (4) of section 17 of the Act.

(7) Paragraph (5) shall not apply—

(a) in the case where there has been a previous single claim (to which the notice relates), the person by whom it was made could no longer make a single claim; or

(b) in the case where there has been a previous joint claim (to which the notice relates), the persons by whom it was made could no longer jointly make a joint claim.

DEFINITIONS

"the Act"—see reg.2.
"joint claim"—see *ibid*.
"single claim"—see *ibid*.
"tax year"—see *ibid*.

GENERAL NOTE

Regulation 11 makes provision for the claimant's declaration in response to an HMRC final notice to be treated as a claim for tax credits for the following tax year. This regulation makes similar provision for those cases in which the claimant is sent a final notice informing them that they will be treated as having declared that their circumstances as are specified in the notice. On the position of couples, see further reg.13.   **2.296**

Circumstances in which claims made by one member of a couple to be treated as also made by the other member of the couple

13.—(1) In the circumstances prescribed by paragraph (2) [² or (3)] a claim for a tax credit made by one member of a [¹. . .] couple is to be treated as also made by the other member of the [¹. . .] couple.   **2.297**

Tax Credits (Claims and Notifications) Regulations 2002

(2) The circumstances prescribed by this paragraph are those where one member of a [1. . . .] couple is treated by regulation 12 as having made a claim for a tax credit in response to a notice under section 17 of the Act given to both members of the couple.

[2 (3) A claim for a tax credit made by one member of a couple is to be treated as also made by the other member of the couple in such manner and in such circumstances as the Board may decide.]

AMENDMENTS

1. Civil Partnership Act 2004 (Tax Credits, etc.) (Consequential Amendments) Order 2005 (SI 2005/2919), art.5(3) (December 5, 2005).
2. Tax Credits (Miscellaneous Amendments) (No.2) Regulations 2008 (SI 2008/2169), reg.13 (September 1, 2008).

DEFINITIONS

"the Act"—see reg.2.
"couple"—see *ibid.*

GENERAL NOTE

2.298   HMRC has indicated that the new provision in para. (3) initially applies to telephone claims only. The effect is to require both partners to fill in the forms confirming the claims while validating the initial claim as a joint claim.

Circumstances in which awards to be conditional and claims treated as made—decisions under section 14(1) of the Act made before 6th April 2003

2.299   **14.**—*(transitional only—spent)*

Persons who die after making a claim

2.300   **15.**—(1) This regulation applies where any person who has made a claim for a tax credit dies—

(a) before the Board have made a decision in relation to that claim under section 14(1) of the Act;

(b) having given a notification of a change of circumstances increasing the maximum rate at which a person or persons may be entitled to the tax credit, before the Board have made a decision whether (and, if so, how) to amend the award of tax credit made to him or them; or

(c) where the tax credit has been awarded for the whole or part of a tax year, after the end of that tax year but before the Board have made a decision in relation to the award under section 18(1), (5), (6) or (9) of the Act.

(2) In the case of a single claim, the personal representatives of the person who has died may proceed with the claim in the name of that person.

(3) In the case of a joint claim where only one of the persons by whom the claim was made has died, the other person with whom the claim was made may proceed with the claim in the name of the person who has died as well as in his own name.

(4) In the case of a joint claim where both the persons by whom the claim was made have died, the personal representatives of the last of them to die may proceed with the claim in the name of both persons who have died.

488

(5) For the purposes of paragraph (4), where persons have died in circumstances rendering it uncertain which of them survived the other—

    (a) their deaths shall be presumed to have occurred in order of seniority; and

    (b) the younger shall be treated as having survived the elder.

DEFINITIONS

    "the Act"—see reg.2.
    "the Board"—see *ibid.*
    "joint claim"—see *ibid.*
    "single claim"—see *ibid.*
    "tax year"—see *ibid.*

GENERAL NOTE

    This regulation makes provision as to how a claim is to proceed after the person or persons die after making it. In short, the personal representatives of the deceased person(s) may proceed with the claim (paras (2) and (4)), although in the case of a couple where only one partner has died the survivor may proceed with the claim in both their names (para.(3); see further reg.16). Paragraph (5) reflects the property law rule on contemporaneous deaths to be found in Law of Property Act 1925, s.184.

2.301

Persons who die before making joint claims

    16.—(1) This regulation applies where one member of a [1. . .] couple dies and the other member of the [1. . .] couple wishes to make a joint claim for a tax credit.

2.302

    (2) The member who wishes to make the claim may make and proceed with the claim in the name of the member who has died as well as in his own name.

    (3) Any claim made in accordance with this regulation shall be for a tax credit for a period ending with—

    (a) the date of the death of the member of the [1. . .] couple who has died; or

    (b) if earlier, 5th April in the tax year to which the claim relates.

AMENDMENT

    1. Civil Partnership Act 2004 (Tax Credits, etc.) (Consequential Amendments) Order 2005 (SI 2005/2919), art.5(4) (December 5, 2005).

DEFINITIONS

    "couple"—see reg.2.
    "joint claim"—see *ibid.*

GENERAL NOTE

    See note to reg.15.

2.303

Circumstances where one person may act for another in making a claim—receivers, etc.

    17.—(1) In the circumstances prescribed by paragraph (2), any receiver or other person mentioned in sub-paragraph (b) of that paragraph may act

2.304

for the person mentioned in sub-paragraph (a) of that paragraph in making a claim for a tax credit.

(2) The circumstances prescribed by this paragraph are where—

(a) a person is, or is alleged to be, entitled to a tax credit but is unable for the time being to make a claim for a tax credit; and

(b) there are any of the following—

  (i) a receiver appointed by the Court of Protection with power to make a claim for a tax credit on behalf of the person;

  (ii) in Scotland, a tutor, curator or other guardian acting or appointed in terms of law who is administering the estate of the person; and

  (iii) in Northern Ireland, a controller appointed by the High Court, with power to make a claim for a tax credit on behalf of the person.

Circumstances where one person may act for another in making a claim—other appointed persons

2.305 **18.**—(1) In the circumstances prescribed by paragraph (2), any person mentioned in sub-paragraph (b) of that paragraph may act for the person mentioned in sub-paragraph (a) of that paragraph in making a claim for a tax credit.

(2) The circumstances prescribed by this paragraph are where—

(a) a person is, or is alleged to be, entitled to a tax credit but is unable for the time being to make a claim for a tax credit; and

(b) in relation to that person, there is a person appointed under—

  (i) regulation 33(1) of the Social Security (Claims and Payments) Regulations 1987;

  (ii) regulation 33(1) of the Social Security (Claims and Payments) Regulations (Northern Ireland) 1987; or

  (iii) paragraph (3).

(3) Where there is no person mentioned in regulation 17(2)(b) in relation to the person who is unable to act, the Board may appoint under this paragraph a person who—

(a) has applied in writing to the Board to be appointed to act on behalf of the person who is unable to act; and

(b) if a natural person, is aged 18 years or more.

(4) An appointment under paragraph (3) shall end if—

(a) the Board terminate it;

(b) the person appointed has resigned from the appointment having given one month's notice in writing to the Board of his resignation; or

(c) the Board are notified that a receiver or other person mentioned in regulation 17(2)(b) has been appointed in relation to the person who is unable to make a claim.

DEFINITIONS

"the Board"—see reg.2.
"writing"—see reg.3(1).

GENERAL NOTE

2.306 HMRC operate this provision by use of form TC 689. This has caused some controversy, for example about the period for which the authority given by the form remains valid. The form and related practices are under review.

PART III

NOTIFICATIONS OF CHANGES OF CIRCUMSTANCES

Interpretation of this Part

19. In this Part "the notification date", in relation to a notification, means—

(a) the date on which the notification is given to [¹a relevant authority at an appropriate office]; or

(b) in cases where regulation 24 applies, the date on which the notification would be treated by that regulation as being given disregarding regulations 25 and 26.

2.307

AMENDMENT

1. Tax Credits (Claims and Notifications and Payments by the Board) (Amendment) Regulations 2003 (SI 2003 No.723), reg.3(2) (April 6, 2003).

DEFINITIONS

"appropriate office"—see reg.2.
"relevant authority"—see *ibid*.

Increases of maximum rate of entitlement to a tax credit as a result of changes of circumstances to be dependent on notification

20.—(1) Any change of circumstances of a description prescribed by para.(2) which may increase the maximum rate at which a person or persons may be entitled to tax credit is to do so only if notification of it has been given in accordance with this Part.

(2) The description of changes of circumstances prescribed by this paragraph are changes of circumstances other than those in consequence of which the Board have given notice of a decision under section 16(1) of the Act in accordance with section 23 of the Act.

2.308

DEFINITIONS

"the Act"—see reg.2.
"the Board"—see *ibid*.

GENERAL NOTE

The effect of this provision is that increases in the maximum rate of entitlement to a tax credit, as a result of some relevant change of circumstances, are dependent upon notification. The normal rule is that changes which have the effect of increasing entitlement are backdated for a maximum of three months from the date of notification (reg.25).

2.309

Requirement to notify changes of circumstances which may decrease the rate at which a person or persons is or are entitled to tax credit or mean that entitlement ceases

21.—(1) [¹Subject to paragraph (1A),] where a person has or persons have claimed a tax credit, notification is to be given within the time prescribed by

2.310

paragraph (3) if there is a change of circumstances of the description prescribed by paragraph (2) which may decrease the rate at which he is or they are entitled to the tax credit or mean that he ceases or they cease to be entitled to the tax credit.

[[1](1A) Paragraph (1) does not apply where advance notification has been given under regulation [[2] 27(2), (2A) or (3)].]

(2) The changes of circumstances described by this paragraph are those where—

(a) entitlement to the tax credit ceases by virtue of section 3(4), or regulations made under section 3(7), of the Act;

(b) there is a change in the relevant child care charges which falls within regulation 16(1)(b) (omitting paragraph (i)) of the Working Tax Credit Regulations;

(c) a person ceases to undertake work for at least 16 hours per week for the purposes of—

   (i) the Second Condition in regulation 4(1) (read with regulations 4(3) to (5) and 5 to 8), or

   (ii) regulation 13(1),

of the Working Tax Credit Regulations;

(d) a person ceases to undertake work for at least 30 hours per week for the purposes of the Second Condition in regulation 4(1) of the Working Tax Credit Regulations (read with regulations 4(3) to (5) and 5 to 8), except in a case where he still falls within the terms of paragraph (a) or (b) of that Condition;

(e) a person ceases to undertake, or engage in, qualifying remunerative work for at least 16 hours per week for the purposes of—

   (i) regulation 9(1)(a) (disability element),

   (ii) regulation 10(2)(d) (30 hour element), or

   (iii) regulation 18(3)(c) (50 plus element),

of the Working Tax Credit Regulations;

(f) a person ceases to engage in qualifying remunerative work for at least 30 hours per week, for the purposes of—

   (i) regulation 10(1) (30 hour element), or

   (ii) regulation 11(2)(c) (second adult element), in a case where the other claimant mentioned in that provision is not so engaged for at least 30 hours per week,

of the Working Tax Credit Regulations;

(g) a couple cease to engage in qualifying remunerative work for at least 30 hours per week, for the purposes of regulation 10(2)(c) (30 hour element) of the Working Tax Credit Regulations;

(h) a person ceases to be treated as responsible for a child or qualifying young person, for the purposes of child tax credit or of the Working Tax Credit Regulations;

(i) in a case where a person has given advance notification under regulation 27(2B) that a child is expected to become a qualifying young person, the child does not become a qualifying young person for the purposes of Part 1 of the Act;

(j) a person ceases to be a qualifying young person for the purposes of Part 1 of the Act, other than by attaining the age of twenty; or

(k) a child or qualifying young person dies.]

(3) The time prescribed by this paragraph is the period of [[3] one] months beginning on the date on which the change of circumstances occurs or

[²(except in the case of paragraph (2)(j))], if later, the period of [³one] months beginning on [² the date on which the person first becomes aware of the change in circumstances].

AMENDMENTS

1. Tax Credits (Claims and Notifications and Payments by the Board) (Amendment) Regulations 2003 (SI 2003/723), reg.4 (April 6, 2003).
2. Tax Credits (Claims and Notifications) (Amendment) Regulations 2006 (SI 2006/2689), regs 4 and 5 (November 1, 2006).
3. Tax Credits (Claims and Notifications) (Amendment) Regulations 2006 (SI 2006/2689), reg.6 (April 6, 2007).

DEFINITIONS

"the Act"—see reg.2.
"Working Tax Credit Regulations"—see *ibid*.

GENERAL NOTE

The amendments to this regulation in 2006 significantly harden the previously   2.311
relaxed regime about reporting changes that may terminate or decrease an award of credits. First, many more changes of circumstances must now be reported. Second, the time limit for reporting is reduced from three months to one month. The duty to notify is imposed by s.6(3) of TCA 2002 read with this regulation. Failure to comply with s.6(3) may incur a penalty not exceeding £300: s.32(3) of the Act. Fraudulently or negligently making an incorrect statement under that section can incur a penalty of up to £3,000: s.31(1)(a) of the Act. HMRC literature draws attention to these penalties.
    In broad terms (and as stated by HMRC in the literature) the changes of circumstances that must now be reported within a month are:
For both tax credits:
  • Getting married or becoming a civil partner
  • Living together with someone else as husband and wife or civil partners
  • Stopping living together with a spouse or civil partner or other partner
  • Leaving the UK for more than 8 weeks
  • Death of child or young person for whom claimant is responsible
  • Child leaves home to live with someone else
For CTC:
  • Child does not become or stops being qualifying young person when 16 (eg leaves college or training) or until 20
  • Young person starts to claim benefits or credits personally
  • Child or young person stops being entitled to support from claimant
For WTC:
  • Claimant or partner stops working for 16 hours a week
  • Claimant or partner stops working for 30 hours a week
  • Claimant or partner stops paying for childcare or bill goes down by £10 a week
  • Being on strike for over 10 days
The duty to report under this regulation also covers any other circumstance in which entitlement to or an award of tax credits should end under s.3(4) or (7) of TCA 2002. This includes changes in a polygamous relationship, ceasing to be entitled by reason of ceasing to be a resident of the UK, or adverse changes in immigration status. It does not include changes in disablement as for instance where disability living allowance stops being paid. This may be because HMRC is informed of this automatically by DWP. There is also no general duty to report changes of income if hours of work are not affected.
    COP26 (set out in Part VII below) indicates that HMRC also has 30 days to deal with notifications of changes of circumstances. After reminding readers of the duty to

report changes as set out above, COP26 adds: "We also recommend that you report any changes in income as soon as possible to reduce the chance of receiving an overpayment." It also advises readers to notify HMRC of any failure to issue a new award notice after a change of circumstances within a month of the notification, or of any error in a new notice. COP26 sets these out as "your responsibilities". If a claimant fails in these responsibilities then COP26 indicates that any overpayment will normally be collected in full. The practical effect is to extend the duty to report beyond those set out in this regulation if recovery of any overpayment is to be avoided or reduced.

CIS/1813/2007 adds an additional reason for claimants ensuring they report changes promptly. In that case deputy Commissioner Mark decided that where a claimant for income support had acted promptly and informed HMRC of a change in circumstances relating to tax credits, she was not to be penalised in connection with her claim for income support by delays on the part of HMRC to act on the information given. In that case the claimant properly notified HMRC that she had stopped work and no longer wished to claim working tax credit. HMRC took many weeks to stop payment. The overpayments were repayable to HMRC. The deputy Commissioner was satisfied that the overpayments were not part of the claimant's income or, if that was incorrect, then that they were voluntary payments. He commented: "For such payments to prevent the award of income support would mean that one branch of government could foist on a claimant money that the claimant does not want and that that branch could later reclaim, and so deprive the claimant of money that she could otherwise legitimately claim from another branch of government. Given that the payments are normally made directly into the claimant's bank account by standing order, it would be impossible for a claimant to prevent such payments being received except by closing the account. I do not consider that she is required to go to such an extreme."

Manner in which notifications to be given

2.312   **22.**—(1) This regulation prescribes the manner in which a notification is to be given.

(2) A notification must be given to [¹a relevant authority at an appropriate office].

(3) A notification may be given orally or in writing.

(4) At any time after a notification has been given but before the Board have made a decision under section 15(1) or 16(1) of the Act in consequence of the notification, the person or persons by whom the notification was given may amend the notification by giving notice orally or in writing to [¹a relevant authority at an appropriate office].

AMENDMENT

1. Tax Credits (Claims and Notifications and Payments by the Board) (Amendment) Regulations 2003 (SI 2003 No.723), reg.3(2) (April 6, 2003).

DEFINITIONS

"the Act"—see reg.2.
"appropriate office"—see *ibid.*
"the Board"—see *ibid.*
"relevant authority"—see *ibid.*
"writing"—reg.3(1).

GENERAL NOTE

2.313   Problems of proof may emerge from the combination of reg.22(2) and (3) when linked in particular to penalty cases under s.32(3). Adequate notification to an "appropriate office" of a "relevant authority" would appear, from reg.2, to include notification given at a Jobcentre Plus office. This can give rise to disputes where an individual maintains that he or she has informed the local social security office and regards that as notification also to HMRC, particularly if the local office does not keep records in the same way as HMRC best practice. It is not clear whether local housing benefit services are regarded as persons providing services to the Secretary of State under the current regime by which investigations for housing benefit also include other benefits. There is a duty on such authorities to pass on information received. See Tax Credits (Administrative Arrangements) Regulations 2002, regs 3, 5.

Person by whom notification may be, or is to be, given

23.—(1) In the case of a single claim, notification is to be given by the person by whom the claim for a tax credit was made.

(2) In the case of a joint claim, notification may be given by either member of the [1. . .] couple by whom the claim for a tax credit was made.

2.314

AMENDMENT

1. Civil Partnership Act 2004 (Tax Credits, etc.) (Consequential Amendments) Order 2005 (SI 2005/2919), art.5(5) (December 5, 2005).

DEFINITIONS

"couple"—see reg.2.
"joint claim"—see *ibid*.
"single claim"—see *ibid*.

Amended notifications

24.—(1) In the circumstances prescribed by paragraph (2) a notification which has been amended shall be treated as having been given as amended and, subject to regulations [²25, 26 and 26A], as having been given on the date prescribed by paragraph(3).

(2) The circumstances prescribed by this paragraph are where the person or persons by whom the notification is given amends or amend the notification in accordance with regulation 22(4).

(3) The date prescribed by this paragraph is the date on which the notification being amended was given to [¹a relevant authority at an appropriate office].

2.315

AMENDMENTS

1. Tax Credits (Claims and Notifications and Payments by the Board) (Amendment) Regulations 2003 (SI 2003 No.723), reg.3(2) (April 6, 2003).
2. Tax Credits (Miscellaneous Amendments) Regulations 2004 (SI 2004/762), reg.3(3) (April 6, 2004).

DEFINITIONS

"appropriate office"—see reg.2.
"relevant authority"—see *ibid*.

Date of notification—cases where change of circumstances which may increase the maximum rate

25.—(1) Where a notification of a change of circumstances which may increase the maximum rate at which a person or persons may be entitled

2.316

to tax credit is given in the circumstances prescribed by paragraph (2), that notification is to be treated as having been given on the date specified by paragraph (3).

(2) The circumstances prescribed by this paragraph are where notification is given to [¹a relevant authority at an appropriate office] of a change of circumstances which has occurred other than in the circumstances prescribed by [² regulations] 26(2) [² and 26A(2)].

(3) The date specified by this paragraph is—

(a) the date falling three months before the notification date; or

(b) if later, the date of the change of circumstances.

AMENDMENTS

1. Tax Credits (Claims and Notifications and Payments by the Board) (Amendment) Regulations 2003 (SI 2003/723), reg.3(2) (April 6, 2003).

2. Tax Credits (Miscellaneous Amendments) Regulations 2009 (SI 2009/697), reg.17 (April 6, 2009).

DEFINITIONS

"appropriate office"—see reg.2.

"the notification date"—see reg.19.

"relevant authority"—see reg.2.

GENERAL NOTE

2.317   Where a change in circumstances leads to an increase in the claimant's entitlement to tax credits, the change can be backdated for up to three months before the date of notification. The requirement for notification itself in such circumstances is contained in reg.20. See also notes on reg.7 (time limit for claims).

[¹ **Date of notification – disability element and severe disability element of working tax credit**

2.318   **26.**—(1) In the circumstances prescribed by paragraph (2), the notification of a change in circumstances is to be treated as having been given on the date prescribed by paragraph (3).

(2) The circumstances prescribed by this paragraph are where–

(a) a notification is given of a change of circumstances in respect of a claim to working tax credit, which results in the Board making an award of the disability element or the severe disability element of working tax credit (or both of them) in favour of a person or persons; and

(b) the notification date is within 3 months of the date that a claim for any of the benefits referred to in regulation 9(2) to (8) or 17(2) of the Working Tax Credit Regulations is determined in favour of those persons (or one of them).

(3) The date prescribed by this paragraph is the latest of the following:

(a) the first date in respect of which the benefit claimed was payable;

(b) the date falling 3 months before the claim for the benefit was made;

(c) the date the claim for working tax credit was made (or treated as made under regulation 7);

(d) (for the purposes of the disability element only), the first date that the person or persons satisfied the conditions of entitlement for the disability element.]

AMENDMENT

1. Tax Credits (Miscellaneous Amendments) Regulations 2009 (SI 2009/697), reg.18 (April 6, 2009).

GENERAL NOTE

This regulation was replaced in 2009 at the same time as reg.8. See the General Note to that regulation.   2.319

[¹ Date of notification – disability element and severe disability element of child tax credit

26A.—(1) In the circumstances prescribed by paragraph (2), the notifi-   2.320
cation of a change in circumstances is to be treated as having been given on the date prescribed by paragraph (3).

(2) The circumstances prescribed by this paragraph are where–

(a) a notification is given of a change of circumstances in respect of a claim to child tax credit which results in the Board making an award of the disability element or the severe disability element of child tax credit (or both of those elements) in favour of a person or persons, in respect of a child; and

(b) the notification date is within 3 months of the date that a claim for a disability living allowance in respect of the child is determined in favour of those persons (or one of them).

(3) The date prescribed by this paragraph is the latest of the following:

(a) the first date in respect of which the disability living allowance was payable;

(b) the date falling 3 months before the claim for the disability living allowance was made;

(c) the date the claim for child tax credit was made (or treated as made under regulation 7).]

AMENDMENT

1. Tax Credits (Miscellaneous Amendments) Regulations 2009 (SI 2009/697), reg.19 (April 6, 2009).

GENERAL NOTE

The replacement of this regulation in 2009 was part of a package with regs 8 and   2.321
26. See the General Note to reg.8.

Advance notification

27.—(1) In [¹any] of the circumstances prescribed by paragraphs (2)   2.322
[¹, 2A] and (3) a notification of a change of circumstances may be given for a period after the date on which it is given.

(2) The circumstances prescribed by this paragraph are those prescribed by regulation 10(2) (working tax credit: person who has accepted an offer of work expected to commence within seven days), the reference to "the claim" being read as a reference to the notification.

[¹(2A) The circumstances prescribed by this paragraph are where either regulation 15(4) (agreement for the provision of future childcare) or regulation 16(1) (relevant change in circumstances) of the Working Tax Credit Regulations applies.]

(3) The circumstances prescribed by this paragraph are where a tax credit has been claimed for the tax year beginning on 6th April 2003 by making a claim before that tax year begins, and the notification relates to that tax year and is given before that date.

(4) In the circumstances prescribed by paragraph (2), an amendment of an award of a tax credit in consequence of a notification of a change of circumstances may be made subject to the condition that the requirements for entitlement to the amended amount of the tax credit are satisfied at the time prescribed by paragraph (5).

(5) The time prescribed by this paragraph is the latest date which—

(a) is not more than seven days after the date on which the notification is given; and

(b) falls within the period of award in which the notification is given.

[¹(5A) In the circumstances prescribed by paragraph (2A), an amendment of an award of tax credit in consequence of a notification of a change of circumstances may be made subject to the condition that the requirements for entitlement to the amended amount of the tax credit are satisfied at the time prescribed by paragraph (5B).

(5B) The time prescribed by this paragraph is the first day of the week—

(a) in which the agreement within regulation 15(4) of the Working Tax Credit Regulations commences or the relevant change of circumstances occurs; and

(b) which is not more than seven days after the date on which notification is given and falls within the period of award in which the notification is given.

(5C) For the purposes of paragraph (5B), "week" means a period of 7 days beginning with midnight between Saturday and Sunday.]

(6) "Period of award" shall be construed in accordance with section 5 of the Act.

AMENDMENT

1. Tax Credits (Claims and Notifications and Payments by the Board) (Amendment) Regulations 2003 (SI 2003/723), reg.5 (April 6, 2003).

DEFINITIONS

"the Act"—see reg.2.
"the claim"—see para.(2).
"period of award"—see para.(6).
"tax year"—see reg.2.
"week"—see para.(5C).

Circumstances where one person may act for another in giving a notification—receivers etc.

2.323

28.—(1) In the circumstances prescribed by paragraph (2) any receiver or other person mentioned in sub-paragraph (b) of that paragraph may act for the person mentioned in sub-paragraph (a) of that paragraph in giving a notification.

(2) The circumstances prescribed by this paragraph are where—

(a) a person is unable for the time being to give a notification; and

(b) there are any of the following—

    (i) a receiver appointed by the Court of Protection with power to proceed with a claim for a tax credit on behalf of the person;

    (ii) in Scotland, a tutor, curator or other guardian acting or appointed in terms of law who is administering the estate of the person; and

    (iii) in Northern Ireland, a controller appointed by the High Court, with power to proceed with a claim for a tax credit on behalf of the person.

GENERAL NOTE

See also reg.35 in respect of receivers, etc. acting in response to final notices under TCA 2002, s.17.

2.324

Circumstances where one person may act for another in giving a notification—other appointed persons

29.—(1) In the circumstances prescribed by paragraph (2) any person mentioned in sub-paragraph (b) of that paragraph may act for the person mentioned in sub-paragraph (a) of that paragraph in giving a notification.

2.325

(2) The circumstances prescribed by this paragraph are where—

  (a) a person is unable for the time being to give a notification; and

  (b) in relation to that person, there is a person appointed under—

    (i) regulation 33(1) of the Social Security (Claims and Payments) Regulations 1987;

    (ii) regulation 33(1) of the Social Security (Claims and Payments) Regulations (Northern Ireland) 1987; or

    (iii) regulation 18(3);

and the provisions of regulation 18(3) shall apply to notifications and (under regulation 36) responses to notices under section 17 of the Act, as they apply to claims.

DEFINITION

"the Act"—see reg.2.

GENERAL NOTE

See also reg.36 in respect of appointees acting in response to final notices under TCA 2002, s.17.

2.326

[¹Form in which evidence of birth or adoption to be provided

29A. If the Board require the person, or either or both of the persons, by whom a claim is made to provide a certificate of a child's birth or adoption, the certificate so produced must be either an original certificate or a copy authenticated in such manner as would render it admissible in proceedings in any court in the jurisdiction in which the copy was made.]

2.327

AMENDMENT

1. Tax Credits (Miscellaneous Amendments No.2) Regulations 2004 (SI 2004/1241), reg.4 (May 1, 2004).

PART IV

NOTICES TO PROVIDE INFORMATION OR EVIDENCE

Employers

2.328   **30.**—(1) For the purposes of sections 14(2)(b), 15(2)(b), 16(3)(b) and 19(2)(b) of the Act the persons specified in paragraph (2) are prescribed, and, in relation to those persons, the information or evidence specified in paragraph (4) is prescribed.

(2) The persons specified in this paragraph are—

(a) any person named by a person or either of the persons by whom a claim for a tax credit is made as his employer or the employer of either of them; and

(b) any person whom the Board have reasonable grounds for believing to be an employer of a person or either of the persons by whom such a claim is made.

(3) "Employer" has the meaning given by section 25(5) of the Act.

(4) The information or evidence specified in this paragraph is information or evidence, including any documents or certificates, which relates to—

(a) the claim for the tax credit in question;

(b) the award of the tax credit in question; or

(c) any question arising out of, or under, that claim or award.

DEFINITIONS

"the Act"—see reg.2.
"the Board"—see *ibid*.
"employer"—see para.(3).

Persons by whom childcare is provided

2.329   **31.**—(1) For the purposes of sections 14(2)(b), 15(2)(b), 16(3)(b) and 19(2)(b) of the Act the persons specified in paragraph (2) are prescribed, and, in relation to those persons, the information or evidence specified in paragraph (3) is prescribed.

(2) The persons specified in this paragraph are—

(a) any person named by a person or persons by whom a claim for the childcare element of working tax credit is made as being, in relation to him or either of them, a person by whom childcare is provided; and

(b) any person whom the Board have reasonable grounds for believing to be, in relation to a person or persons by whom such a claim is made, a person by whom childcare is provided.

(3) The information or evidence specified in this paragraph is information or evidence, including any documents or certificates, which relates to—

(a) the claim for the tax credit in question;

(b) the award of the tax credit in question; or

(c) any question arising out of, or under, that claim or award.

(4) "Child care" has the meaning given by regulation 14(2) of the Working Tax Credit Regulations.

500

DEFINITIONS

"the Act"—see reg.2.
"the Board"—see *ibid*.
"childcare"—see para.(4).

Dates to be specified in notices under section 14(2), 15(2), 16(3), 18(10) or 19(2) of the Act

32. In a notice under section 14(2), 15(2), 16(3), 18(10) or 19(2) of the Act, the date which may be specified shall not be less than 30 days after the date of the notice.

2.330

DEFINITION

"the Act"—see reg.2.

PART V

FINAL DECISION

[¹Dates to be specified in notices under section 17 of the Act

33. In a notice under section 17 of the Act—
  (a) the date which may be specified for the purposes of subsection (2) or subsection (4) shall be not later than [²31st July] following the end of the tax year to which the notice relates, or 30 days after the date on which the notice is given, if later; and
  (b) the date which may be specified for the purposes of subsection (8) shall be not later than 31st January following the end of the tax year to which the notice relates, or 30 days after the date on which the notice is given, if later.]

2.331

AMENDMENTS

1. Tax Credits (Miscellaneous Amendments) Regulations 2004 (SI 2004/762), reg.3(5) (April 6, 2004).
2. Tax Credits (Miscellaneous Amendments) Regulations 2007 (SI 2007/824), reg.14(3) (April 6, 2007).

DEFINITIONS

"the Act"—see reg.2.
"tax year"—see *ibid*.

[¹Manner in which declaration or statement in response to a notice under section 17 of the Act to be made

34.—(1) This regulation prescribes the manner in which a declaration or statement in response to a notice under section 17 of the Act must be made.
  (2) A declaration or statement must be made—
  (a) in writing in a form approved by the Board for that purpose;
  (b) orally to an officer of the Board; or
  (c) in such other manner as the Board may accept as sufficient in the circumstances of any particular case.

2.332

(3) In a case falling within paragraph (2)(b) one of two joint claimants may act for both of them in response to a notice under section 17 if, at the time the declaration or statement is made, a joint claim could be made by both of them.]

AMENDMENT

1. Tax Credits (Miscellaneous Amendments) Regulations 2004 (SI 2004/762), reg.3(5) (April 6, 2004).

DEFINITIONS

"the Act"—see reg.2.
"the Board"—see *ibid.*
"joint claim"—see *ibid.*

Circumstances where one person may act for another in response to a notice under section 17 of the Act—receivers, etc.

2.333   **35.**—(1) In the circumstances prescribed by paragraph (2) any receiver or other person mentioned in sub-paragraph (b) of that paragraph may act for the person mentioned in sub-paragraph (a) of that paragraph in response to a notice under section 17 of the Act.

(2) The circumstances prescribed by this paragraph are where—
(a) a person is unable for the time being to act in response to a notice under section 17 of the Act; and
(b) there are any of the following—
　　(i) a receiver appointed by the Court of Protection with power to proceed with a claim for a tax credit on behalf of the person;
　　(ii) in Scotland, a tutor, curator or other guardian acting or appointed in terms of law who is administering the estate of the person; and
　　(iii) in Northern Ireland, a controller appointed by the High Court, with power to proceed with a claim for a tax credit and proceed with the claim on behalf of the person.

DEFINITION

"the Act"—see reg.2.

Circumstances where one person may act for another in response to a notice under section 17 of the Act

2.334   **36.**—(1) In the circumstances prescribed by paragraph (2) any person mentioned in sub-paragraph (b) of that paragraph may act for the person mentioned in sub-paragraph (a) of that paragraph in response to a notice under section 17 of the Act.

(2) The circumstances prescribed by this paragraph are where—
(a) a person is unable for the time being to act in response to a notice under section 17 of the Act; and
(b) in relation to that person, there is a person appointed under—
　　(i) regulation 33(1) of the Social Security (Claims and Payments) Regulations 1987;
　　(ii) regulation 33(1) of the Social Security (Claims and Payments) Regulations (Northern Ireland) 1987; or
　　(iii) regulation 18(3).

DEFINITION

"the Act"—see reg.2.

Tax Credits [¹(Payment by the Commissioners)] Regulations 2002

(SI 2002/2173) (AS AMENDED)

The Commissioners of Inland Revenue, in exercise of the powers conferred upon them by sections 24(2), (3), (4), (7) and (8), 65(1), (2) and (7) and 67 of the Tax Credits Act 2002, hereby make the following Regulations: **2.335**

1. Citation, commencement and effect.
2. Interpretation.
3. Child tax credit and childcare element—member of a couple prescribed for the purposes of s.24(2) of the Act.
4. Working tax credit (excluding any childcare element)—member of a couple prescribed for the purposes of s.24(2) of the Act.
5. Member of a couple prescribed for the purposes of s.24(2) of the Act where one of the members of the couple has died.
6. Person prescribed for the purposes of s.24(3) of the Act where an award of a tax credit is made on a claim which is made by one person on behalf of another.
7. Prescribed circumstances for the purposes of s.24(4) of the Act.
8. Time of payment by way of a credit to a bank account or other account.
9. Time of payment other than by way of a credit to a bank account or other account, etc.
10. Single payment of small sums of tax credit.
11. Postponement of payment.
12. Amounts of payments.
12A. Recovery of overpayments of tax credits from other payments of tax credit.
13. Manner of payment.
14. Entitlement to tax credit or element dependent on a bank account or other account having been notified to the Board.

AMENDMENT

1. Tax Credit (Payment by Employers, etc.) (Amendment) Regulations 2005 (SI 2005/2200) reg.7(2) (August 29, 2005).

GENERAL NOTE

The original policy intention of making employers responsible for payments of WTC (other than the child care element) has now been abandoned. Since April 2006 HMRC has assumed responsibility for making all payments of both CTC and WTC. Accordingly the Working Tax Credit (Payment by Employers) Regulations 2002 (SI 2002/2172) have now been revoked: see Tax Credit (Payment by Employers, etc.) (Amendment) Regulations 2005 (SI 2005/2200), reg.9. **2.336**

Citation, commencement and effect

1.—(1) These Regulations may be cited as the Tax Credits (Payments by [²the Commissioners]) Regulations 2002 and shall come into force on 6th April 2003. **2.337**

(2) These Regulations have effect in relation to payments of a tax credit, or any element of a tax credit, which must be made [¹. . .] in relation to the tax year beginning with 6th April 2003 and subsequent tax years.

[¹(3) Regulations 8 to 14 have effect only in relation to such payments as must be made by the Board.]

AMENDMENTS

1. Tax Credits (Claims and Notifications and Payments by the Board) (Amendment) Regulations 2003 (SI 2003/723), reg.7 (April 6, 2003).
2. Tax Credit (Payment by Employers, etc.) (Amendment) Regulations 2005 (SI 2005/2200), reg.7(2) (August 29, 2005).

Interpretation

2.338   **2.** In these Regulations—
"the Act" means the Tax Credits Act 2002;
[¹"the Commissioners" means Commissioners for Her Majesty's Revenue and Customs (see section 1 of the Commissioners for Revenue and Customs Act 2005);]
[²"couple" has the meaning given by section 3(5A) of the Act;]
"employee" and "employer" have the meaning given by section 25(5) of the Act;
[²...];
"period of award" shall be construed in accordance with section 5 of the Act;
"the relevant tax year" means the whole or part of the tax year for which an award of a tax credit has been made to a person or persons (referred to in section 24(4) of the Act);
"tax year" means a period beginning with 6th April in one year and ending with 5th April in the next;
[². . .].

AMENDMENTS

1. Tax Credit (Payment by Employers, etc.) (Amendment) Regulations 2005 (SI 2005/2200), reg.7(3) (August 29, 2005).
2. Civil Partnership Act 2004 (Tax Credits, etc.) (Consequential Amendments) Order 2005 (SI 2005/2919), art.6(2) (December 5, 2005).

Child tax credit and childcare element—member of a couple prescribed for the purposes of section 24(2) of the Act

2.339   **3.**—(1) This regulation has effect in relation to payments of—
(a) child tax credit; and
(b) any childcare element of working tax credit.
(2) Subject to regulation 5, the member of a [⁴couple] prescribed by paragraph (3) is prescribed for the purposes of section 24(2) of the Act.
(3) The member of a [⁴couple] [²prescribed by this paragraph is—
(a) where the [⁴couple] are for the time being resident at the same address—
   (i) the member who is identified by both members of the [⁴couple] as the main carer;
   (ii) in default of a member being so identified, the member who appears to [³ the Commissioner] to be the main carer; and
(b) where—
   (i) the members of the [⁴couple] are for the time being resident at different addresses, or

504

(ii) one member of the [⁴couple] is temporarily absent from the address at which they live together,
the member who appears to [³ the Commissioner] to be the main carer.
Here "main carer" means the member of the [⁴ couple] who is the main carer for the children and qualifying young persons for whom either or both of the members is or are responsible.]

(4) "Children" means persons who have not attained the age of 16 or who fall within the terms of regulation 4 of the Child Tax Credit Regulations 2002.

(5) "Qualifying young persons" means persons, other than children, who—

(a) have not attained the age of nineteen; and
(b) satisfy the conditions in regulation 5(3) and (4) of the Child Tax Credit Regulations 2002.

(6) Where payments are being made to the member of a [⁴couple] prescribed by virtue of paragraph (3) and the members of the [⁴couple] jointly give notice to [³ the Commissioners] that, as a result of a change of circumstances, the payments should be made to the other member as the main carer, the other member shall [², except where the notice appears to [³the Commissioners] to be unreasonable,] be treated as prescribed by virtue of paragraph (3).

[¹(7) For the purposes of this regulation, a person is responsible for a child or qualifying young person if he is treated as being responsible for that child or qualifying young person in accordance with the rules contained in regulation 3 of the Child Tax Credit Regulations 2002.]

AMENDMENTS

1. Tax Credits (Claims and Notifications and Payments by the Board) (Amendment) Regulations 2003 (SI 2003/723), reg.8 (April 6, 2003).

2. Tax Credits (Miscellaneous Amendments No.2) Regulations 2004 (SI 2004/1241), reg.5 (May 1, 2004).

3. Tax Credit (Payment by Employers, etc.) (Amendment) Regulations 2005 (SI 2005/2200), reg.7(4) (August 29, 2005).

4. Civil Partnership Act 2004 (Tax Credits, etc.) (Consequential Amendments) Order 2005 (SI 2005/2919), art.6(3) (December 5, 2005).

DEFINITIONS

"the Act"—see reg.2.
"children"—see para.(4).
"couple"—see reg.2.
"qualifying young persons"—see para.(5).

GENERAL NOTE

Section 24(2) of the TCA 2002 permits payments of tax credits, or elements within tax credits, in the case of a joint claim to whichever member of a married or unmarried couple is prescribed. This regulation deals with the payment of child tax credit and any childcare element of working tax credit by HMRC. It provides that such tax credits are payable by HMRC to the partner identified by the couple as the main carer of the children concerned or, in default, the partner identified as such by HMRC (para.(3)). The couple can ask HMRC to change the method of payment to the other partner as the main carer (para.(6)).

2.340

Working tax credit (excluding any childcare element)—member of a couple prescribed for the purposes of section 24(2) of the Act

2.341   **4.**—(1) This regulation has effect in relation to payments of working tax credit other than payments of any childcare element.

(2) Subject to regulation 5, the member of a [²couple] prescribed by para. (3) is prescribed for the purposes of section 24(2) of the Act.

(3) The member of a [²couple] prescribed by this paragraph is—

(a) if only one member of the [²couple] is engaged in remunerative work, that member;

(b) if both members of the [²couple] are engaged in remunerative work—

(i) the member elected jointly by them; or

(ii) in default of any election, such of them as appears to the Board to be appropriate.

(4) Where payments are being made to the member of [²couple] prescribed by virtue of paragraph (3)(b) and the members of the [²couple] jointly give notice to [¹the Commissioners] that, as a result of a change of circumstances, they wish payments to be made to the other member, the other member shall be treated as prescribed by virtue of paragraph (3)(b).

(5) For the purposes of paragraph (3), a member of a [²couple] is engaged in remunerative work if—

(a) he is engaged in qualifying remunerative work; or

(b) he works not less than 16 hours per week and the other member of the [²couple] is engaged in qualifying remunerative work.

(6) "Qualifying remunerative work", and being engaged in it, have the meaning given by regulation 4 of the Working Tax Credit (Entitlement and Maximum Rate) Regulations 2002.

AMENDMENTS

1. Tax Credit (Payment by Employers, etc.) (Amendment) Regulations 2005 (SI 2005/2200), reg.7(4) (August 29, 2005).
2. Civil Partnership Act 2004 (Tax Credits, etc.) (Consequential Amendments) Order 2005 (SI 2005/2919), art.6(3) (December 5, 2005).

DEFINITIONS

"the Act"—see reg.2.
"couple"—see *ibid*.
"qualifying remunerative work"—see para.(6).

GENERAL NOTE

2.342   This deals with payment of working tax credit (excluding any childcare element, on which see reg.3) by HMRC. In the case of a couple, such working tax credit should be paid by HMRC to the member of the couple who is in remunerative work for working tax credit purposes (see paras (5) and (6)) or, if they both are, to the partner nominated jointly by the couple or, in default, as HMRC sees appropriate (para.(3)). As with reg.3, the couple have the option of changing their election (para.(4)).

Member of a couple prescribed for the purposes of section 24(2) of the Act where one of the members of the couple has died

2.343   **5.**—(1) This regulation applies where one of the members of a [¹couple] has died.

(2) The member of the [¹couple] prescribed by paragraph (3) is prescribed for the purposes of section 24(2) of the Act.

(3) The member of the [¹couple] prescribed by this paragraph is the member who survives.

(4) For the purposes of this regulation, where persons have died in circumstances rendering it uncertain which of them survived the other—

(a) their deaths shall be presumed to have occurred in order of seniority; and

(b) the younger shall be treated as having survived the elder.

AMENDMENT

1. Civil Partnership Act 2004 (Tax Credits, etc.) (Consequential Amendments) Order 2005 (SI 2005/2919), art.6(3) (December 5, 2005).

DEFINITIONS

"the Act"—see reg.2.
"couple"—see *ibid*.

GENERAL NOTE

This regulation is self-explanatory. Paragraph (4) follows the general property law rule on survivorship laid down by s.184 of the Law of Property Act 1925.

2.344

Person prescribed for the purposes of section 24(3) of the Act where an award of a tax credit is made on a claim which is made by one person on behalf of another

6. For the purposes of section 24(3) of the Act, the person prescribed is—

2.345

(a) the person by whom the claim on behalf of another was made; or

(b) if at any time [¹the Commissioners] do not consider it appropriate for payments of the tax credit to be made to that person, the person on behalf of whom the claim was made.

AMENDMENT

1. Tax Credit (Payment by Employers, etc.) (Amendment) Regulations 2005 (SI 2005/2200), reg.7(4) (August 29, 2005).

DEFINITION

"the Act"—see reg.2.

GENERAL NOTE

See also regs 17, 18, 28 and 29 of the Tax Credits (Claims and Notifications) Regulations 2002 (SI 2002/2014).

2.346

Prescribed circumstances for the purposes of section 24(4) of the Act

7.—(1) Either of the circumstances prescribed by paragraphs (2) and (3) are prescribed circumstances for the purposes of section 24(4) of the Act.

2.347

(2) The circumstances prescribed by this paragraph are where—

(a) a claim for a tax credit for the next tax year has been made or treated as made by the person or persons by the date specified for the purposes of subsection (4) of section 17 of the Act in the notice given to him or them under that section in relation to the relevant tax year; and

(b) [¹the Commissioners] have not made a decision under section 14(1) of the Act in relation to that claim.

(3) The circumstances prescribed by this paragraph are where—

(a) a claim for a tax credit for the next tax year has not been made or treated as made by the person or persons; and

(b) [¹the Commissioners] have not made a decision under section 18(1) of the Act in relation to the person and persons for the relevant tax year.

AMENDMENT

1. Tax Credit (Payment by Employers, etc.) (Amendment) Regulations 2005 (SI 2005/2200), reg.7(4) (August 29, 2005).

DEFINITIONS

"the Act"—see reg.2.
"the relevant tax year"—see *ibid*.
"tax year"—see *ibid*.

GENERAL NOTE

2.348   Section 24(4) of the TCA 2002 enables payments of tax credits to continue to be paid in a following tax year in the absence of a claim and award in certain circumstances. This regulation thus allows payments to continue to be made, without interruption, at the start of each tax year while claims are being renewed in two types of circumstances. The first is where a renewal claim has been made or treated as made but has yet to be determined by HMRC (para.(2)). The second is a step further back, where no such renewal claim has been made but HMRC similarly has yet to make its final decision on the previous year (para.(3)).

Time of payment by way of a credit to a bank account or other account

2.349   8.—(1) [³. . .] This regulation applies where the tax credit or element is to be paid by way of a credit to a bank account or other account notified to [²the Commissioners].

(2) [¹Subject to paragraph (2A),] the tax credit or element shall be paid—

(a) each week; or

(b) every four weeks,

in accordance with any election given by the person to whom payment is to be made.

[¹(2A) If a person makes elections under paragraph (2) for child tax credit and any childcare element of working tax credit to be paid at differing intervals, the elections shall have no effect and [²the Commissioners] pay the child tax credit and any childcare element together either each week or every four weeks as appears to them to be appropriate.]

(3) [³ . . .]

(4) This regulation is subject to regulations 10 and 11.

AMENDMENTS

1. Tax Credits (Claims and Notifications and Payments by the Board) (Amendment) Regulations 2003 (SI 2003/723), reg.9 (April 6, 2003).

2. Tax Credit (Payment by Employers, etc.) (Amendment) Regulations 2005 (SI 2005/2200), reg.7(4) (August 29, 2005).

3. Tax Credit (Payment by Employers, etc.) (Amendment) Regulations 2005 (SI 2005/2200), reg.9(2) (April 1, 2006).

GENERAL NOTE

Employees paid tax credits by HMRC direct to their bank accounts have the option of having such payments paid weekly or four-weekly (para.(2)). However, it is not possible to have child tax credit and the childcare element of working tax credit paid at different intervals (para.(2A)). The intervals for payment via methods other than direct to a bank account are left to the discretion of HMRC (see reg.9). However, payment via bank accounts is clearly intended to be the standard method for HMRC to pay tax credits (see regs 13 and 14).

2.350

Time of payment other than by way of a credit to a bank account or other account, etc.

9.—(1) This regulation applies where—

2.351

(a) the tax credit or element is to be paid other than by way of a credit to a bank account or other account notified to [¹the Commissioners]; or

(b) [² ...].

(2) The tax credit or element shall be paid at such times as appear to [¹the Commissioners] to be appropriate.

AMENDMENTS

1. Tax Credit (Payment by Employers, etc.) (Amendment) Regulations 2005 (SI 2005/2200), reg.7(4) (August 29, 2005).

2. Tax Credit (Payment by Employers, etc.) (Amendment) Regulations 2005 (SI 2005/2200), reg.9(2) (April 1, 2006).

[¹Single payment of small sums of tax credit

10. The tax credit or element may be paid by way of a single payment, and at such time, and in such manner, as appear to [²the Commissioners] to be appropriate, in any of the following cases—

2.352

(a) where [²the Commissioners] are paying only child tax credit to a person and the weekly rate at which it is payable is less than £2;

(b) where [²the Commissioners] are paying both any childcare element (but no other element) of working tax credit and child tax credit to a person and the total weekly rate at which they are payable is less than £2;

(c) where [²the Commissioners] are paying only working tax credit (apart from any childcare element) to a person and the weekly rate at which it is payable (excluding any such childcare element) is less than £2;

(d) where [²the Commissioners] are paying both working tax credit (including elements other than, or in addition to, any childcare element) and child tax credit to a person who has elected under regulation 8(2) to have them paid at the same intervals and the total weekly rate at which they are payable is less than £2;

(e) where [²the Commissioners] are paying both working tax credit (apart from any childcare element) and child tax credit to a person who has elected under regulation 8(2) to have them paid at differing intervals and—

    (i) the total weekly rate at which any such childcare element and the child tax credit are payable is less than £2; or

    (ii) the weekly rate at which the working tax credit is payable (excluding any such childcare element) is less than £2.]

AMENDMENTS

1. Tax Credits (Claims and Notifications and Payments by the Board) (Amendment) Regulations 2003 (SI 2003/723), reg.10 (April 6, 2003).

2. Tax Credit (Payment by Employers, etc.) (Amendment) Regulations 2005 (SI 2005/2200), reg.7(4) (August 29, 2005).

GENERAL NOTE

2.353   The original version of this regulation, which was substituted by the version above before it came into force, was just one sentence long: so much for simplicity. The basic principle, however, remains the same: if tax credits are payable at an aggregate level of less than £2 a week, then HMRC will pay them in such manner as it deems appropriate (typically by way of a lump sum).

Postponement of payment

2.354   **11.**—(1) [¹The Commissioners] may postpone payment of the tax credit or element in any of the circumstances specified in paragraphs (2) and (3).

(2) The circumstances specified in this paragraph are where there is a pending determination of an appeal against a decision of [² [³ the First-tier Tribunal, the appeal tribunal, the] Upper Tribunal, the Northern Ireland] Social Security Commissioner or a court relating to—

    (a) the case in question; or

    (b) another case where it appears to [¹the Commissioners] that, if the appeal were to be determined in a particular way, an issue would arise as to whether the award in the case in question should be amended or terminated under section 16(1) of the Act.

(3) The circumstances specified in this paragraph are where confirmation is pending of—

    (a) the details of a bank account or other account by way of a credit to which payment is to be made; or

    (b) the address of the person to whom payment is to be made, where it appears to [¹the Commissioners] that such details or address as were previously notified to them are incorrect.

(4) For the purposes of paragraph (2), the circumstances where a determination of an appeal is pending include circumstances where a decision of [² [³ the First-tier Tribunal, the appeal tribunal, the] Upper Tribunal, the Northern Ireland] Social Security Commissioner or a court has been made and [¹the Commissioners]—

    (a) are awaiting receipt of the decision;

    (b) in the case of a decision by [² the [³ First-tier Tribunal or the appeal tribunal]], are considering whether to apply for a statement of reasons or have applied for, and are awaiting receipt of, a statement of reasons; or

    (c) have received the decision or statement of reasons and are considering—

      (i) whether to apply for permission to appeal; or

      (ii) where permission is not needed or has been given, whether to appeal.

  (5) "[³ Appeal tribunal]" has the meaning given by section 63(10) of the Act.

  (6) "[² Northern Ireland Social] Security Commissioner" has the meaning given by section 63(13) of the Act.

AMENDMENTS

  1. Tax Credit (Payment by Employers, etc.) (Amendment) Regulations 2005 (SI 2005/2200), reg.7(4) (August 29, 2005).

  2. Tribunals, Courts and Enforcement Act 2007 (Transitional and Consequential Provisions) Order 2008 (SI 2008/2683), art.6 and Sch.1, para.205 (November 3, 2008).

  3. Transfer of Tribunal Functions and Revenue and Customs Appeals Order 2009 (SI 2009/56), art.3(2), Sch.2, para.78 (April 1, 2009).

DEFINITIONS

  "the Act"—see reg.2.
  "Appeal tribunal"—see para.(5).
  "Social Security Commissioner"—see para.(6).

GENERAL NOTE

  This regulation sets out the two types of circumstances in which a payment of tax credits by HMRC may be postponed. The first is the straightforward situation where HMRC believes that either the bank details or recipient's address previously notified to them is incorrect (para.(3)). The second is where there is an appeal pending in relation either to the particular case or to another case in which the outcome might lead to the amendment or termination of the award in the instant case (para.(2)). This is, therefore, the tax credits equivalent of the anti-test case rule. (But note, however, that it is limited to the postponement of payment, and does not make provision for limiting the effect of test cases in terms of backdating entitlement to tax credits.) The "pending determination" must be one against a decision of an appeal tribunal, Social Security Commissioner or court (para.(2)). The notion of "pending" is defined by para.(4). There are no explicit time limits stated within this regulation on HMRC's consideration of whether or not to lodge an appeal, but there are, of course, fairly tight time constraints on the exercise of such a right in the first place.

2.355

Amounts of payments

  12.—(1) The tax credit or element shall be paid in accordance with the most recent decision by [¹the Commissioners] under section 14(1), 15(1) or 16(1) of the Act.

  (2) Where the tax credit or element is to be paid other than by way of a single payment, it shall be paid so far as possible in such amounts as will result in the person to whom payment is to be made receiving regular payments of similar amounts over the entire period of award.

  (3) Where an award of tax credit is amended, the total amount paid prior to the award being amended [²may] be taken into account by [¹the Commissioners] in determining the amount of any further payments for the remainder of the period of award.

2.356

[³ (4) Where payments under section 24(4) of the Act are to be made the Commissioners may take any or both of the following factors into account in determining the amount of those payments—

    (a) the rate at which the person or persons were entitled to the tax credit for the relevant tax year;

    (b) the estimated amount of income the person or persons referred to above may receive in the current tax year.]

AMENDMENTS

    1. Tax Credit (Payment by Employers, etc.) (Amendment) Regulations 2005 (SI 2005/2200), reg.7(4) (August 29, 2005).

    2. Tax Credits (Miscellaneous Amendments) Regulations 2007 (SI 2007/824), reg.15 (April 6, 2007).

    3. Tax Credits (Miscellaneous Amendments) Regulations 2008 (SI 2008/604), reg.5(2) (April 6, 2008).

DEFINITION

    "the Act"—see reg.2.

GENERAL NOTE

2.357   This regulation provides for the amount of tax credits payable to be determined by HMRC's most recent relevant decision (para.(1)). Such payments should, so far as possible, be apportioned equally over regular payment intervals (para. (2)). The original formulation of para.(2) was mandatory in requiring HMRC to take prior payments into account in arriving at the appropriate amount due for payment following an amended award. Paragraph (2) now gives HMRC more flexibility in deciding the amount of any further tax credits where an award of tax credits is amended. Since April 2007, HMRC have been able to exercise a discretion in such cases. So, where claimants report a fall in income during the year, their tax credit payments will be adjusted for the rest of the year but will not include a one-off payment for the earlier part of the year. Their final award will be determined at the end of the year when their actual income is known, and any underpayment will be made good at that stage. Amounts of tax credits for subsequent years can be based on a preceding year's tax credit entitlement (para.(4); see further reg.7).

[¹Recovery of overpayments of tax credit from other payments of tax credit

2.358   **12A.**—(1) This regulation applies where notice is given to a person or persons under subsection (4) of section 29 of the Act (deduction of overpayments from payments of tax credit).

(2) The maximum rate at which an overpayment may be recovered from payments of tax credit is—

    (a) where the only amount of tax credit to which the person is, or, in the case of a joint claim, the persons are, entitled, is the family element of child tax credit, 100% of that tax credit;

    (b) where the total amount of tax credit to which the person is, or, in the case of a joint claim, the persons are, entitled is not subject to reduction—

        (i) by virtue of section 7(2) of the Act; or

       (ii) because their income for the relevant year does not exceed the relevant income threshold prescribed in his or their case

in regulation 3 of the Tax Credits (Income Thresholds and Determination of Rates) Regulations 2002;
10% of that tax credit; and
(c) in any other case, 25% of the tax credit to which the person is, or in the case of a joint claim, the persons are, entitled.

(3) In paragraph (2) a reference to the amount to which a person is, or persons are, entitled is a reference to the amount to which they would be entitled but for the operation of that paragraph.]

AMENDMENT

1. Tax Credits (Miscellaneous Amendments) Regulations 2004 (SI 2004/762), reg.18 (April 6, 2004).

DEFINITION

"the Act"—see reg.2.

Manner of payment

13.—(1) Subject to paragraph (2), the tax credit or element shall be paid by way of a credit to a bank account or other account notified to [²the Commissioners] by the person to whom payment is to be made.

(2) Where [¹it does not appear to [²the Commissioners] to be appropriate] for the tax credit or element to be paid by way of a credit to a bank account or other account notified to [²the Commissioners] by the person to whom payment is to be made, the tax credit or element may be paid in such manner as appears to [²the Commissioners] to be appropriate.

(3) Subject to regulation 14, if no bank account or other account has been notified to [²the Commissioners], the tax credit or element shall be paid in such manner as appears to [²the Commissioners] to be appropriate.

2.359

AMENDMENTS

1. Tax Credits (Claims and Notifications and Payments by the Board) (Amendment) Regulations 2003 (SI 2003/723), reg.11 (April 6, 2003).
2. Tax Credit (Payment by Employers, etc.) (Amendment) Regulations 2005 (SI 2005/2200), reg.7(4) (August 29, 2005).

GENERAL NOTE

This regulation establishes the presumption in favour of payment by HMRC of tax credits to be direct to recipients' bank accounts.

2.360

Entitlement to tax credit or element dependent on a bank account or other account having been notified to the Board

14.—(1) Subject to paragraphs (2) and (3), if by the end of the relevant period no bank account or other account has been notified to [²the Commissioners] by the person to whom payment of a tax credit or element is to be made, that person shall cease to be entitled to the tax credit or element for the remainder of the period of the award until a bank account or other account is notified to [²the Commissioners].

(2) Where a person who has ceased to be entitled to a tax credit or

2.361

an element by virtue of paragraph (1) subsequently notifies to [²the Commissioners] a bank account or other account, paragraph (1)—

    (a) shall not have effect for the period of three months prior to the date on which [²the Commissioners] receive the notification; and

    (b) shall cease to have effect for the remainder of the period of award.

(3) Where there are exceptional circumstances which are expected to result in a person not being able to obtain a bank account or other account throughout the period of award, paragraph (1) shall not have effect in relation to that person's entitlement to a tax credit or element for the period of award.

(4) "The relevant period" means whichever of the following periods ends latest—

    (a) the period of eight weeks beginning on the date on which [²the Commissioners] [¹give] notice in writing for the purposes of this regulation to the person to whom payment is to be made of the requirement that a bank account or other account be notified to them;

    (b) in cases where, within the period mentioned in sub-paragraph (a), the person to whom payment is to be made—

        (i) requests from [²the Commissioners] authority to open an account for which such authority is required; and

        (ii) provides sufficient information from which [²the Commissioners] can give that authority,

    the period of three weeks beginning on the date on which [²the Commissioners] [¹give] that authority;

    (c) in cases where the person to whom payment is to be made has a reasonable excuse—

        (i) for not being able to take all necessary steps to obtain a bank account or other account within whichever of the periods set out in sub-paragraph (a) or (b) ends latest; or

        (ii) for not being able to notify to [²the Commissioners] the bank account or other account within that period,

    the period ending with the date by which the account can reasonably be expected to be notified to [²the Commissioners].

(5) "Writing" includes writing produced by electronic communications that are approved by [²the Commissioners].

AMENDMENTS

1. Tax Credits (Claims and Notifications and Payments by the Board) (Amendment) Regulations 2003 (SI 2003/723), reg.12 (April 6, 2003).

2. Tax Credit (Payment by Employers, etc.) (Amendment) Regulations 2005 (SI 2005/2200), reg.7(4) (August 29, 2005).

DEFINITIONS

"the relevant period"—see para.(4).

"writing"—see para.(5).

GENERAL NOTE

2.362   This regulation further demonstrates that entitlement to a tax credit is to be dependent on a bank account or other account having been notified to HMRC.

Tax Credits (Administrative Arrangements) Regulations 2002

(SI 2003/3036)

The Commissioners of Inland Revenue, in exercise of the powers conferred upon them by ss.58 and 65(1), (2), (7) and (9) of the Tax Credits Act 2002, hereby make the following Regulations: **2.363**

ARRANGEMENT OF ARTICLES

1. Citation and commencement.
2. Interpretation.
3. Provision of information or evidence to relevant authorities.
4. Giving of information or advice by relevant authorities.
5. Recording, verification and holding, and forwarding, of claims, etc. received by relevant authorities.

GENERAL NOTE

Section 58 of the TCA 2002 provides for regulations to make provision as to the   **2.364**
administrative arrangements to apply between a relevant authority (i.e. the Secretary of State, the equivalent Northern Ireland Department or a person providing services to either of these authorities: TCA 2002, s.58(3)) and HMRC, who have the care and management of tax credits (see TCA 2002, s.2). Section 58 applies where regulations under TCA 2002, s.4 or 6 permit or require a claim or notification relating to a tax credit to be made or given to such a relevant authority. These Regulations have therefore been made under s.58 in order to provide for administrative arrangements in relation to claims and notifications made or given to a relevant authority in accordance with the Tax Credits (Claims and Notifications) Regulations 2002 (SI 2002/2014). Regulation 5 of those Regulations requires claims to be made to "an appropriate office", which means an office of the Board, the DWP or its Northern Ireland equivalent (reg.2).

Citation and commencement

1. These Regulations may be cited as the Tax Credits (Administrative   **2.365**
Arrangements) Regulations 2002 and shall come into force on 1st January 2003.

Interpretation

2. In these Regulations—   **2.366**
"the Board" means the Commissioners of Inland Revenue;
"the principal Regulations" means the Tax Credits (Claims and Notifications) Regulations 2002;
"relevant authority" means—
  (a) the Secretary of State;
  (b) the Department for Social Development in Northern Ireland; or
  (c) a person providing services to the Secretary of State or that Department.

Provision of information or evidence to relevant authorities

3.—(1) Information or evidence relating to tax credits which is held—   **2.367**
  (a) by the Board; or

515

(b) by a person providing services to the Board, in connection with the provision of those services,

may be provided to a relevant authority for the purposes of, or for any purposes connected with, the exercise of that relevant authority's functions under the principal Regulations.

(2) Information or evidence relating to tax credits may be provided to a relevant authority by persons other than the Board (whether or not persons by whom claims or notifications relating to tax credits are or have been made or given).

DEFINITIONS

"the Board" —see reg.2.
"the principal Regulations"—see *ibid*.
"relevant authority"—see *ibid*.

Giving of information or advice by relevant authorities

2.368   **4.** A relevant authority to which a claim or notification is or has been made or given by a person in accordance with the principal Regulations may give information or advice relating to tax credits to that person.

DEFINITIONS

"the principal Regulations"—see reg.2.
"relevant authority"—see *ibid*.

Recording, verification and holding, and forwarding, of claims etc. received by relevant authorities

2.369   **5.**—(1) A relevant authority may record and hold claims and notifications received by virtue of the principal Regulations and information or evidence received by virtue of regulation 3(2).

(2) Subject to paragraphs (3) and (4), a relevant authority must forward to the Board or a person providing services to the Board such a claim or notification, or such information or evidence, as soon as reasonably practicable after being satisfied that it is complete.

(3) Before forwarding a claim in accordance with paragraph (2), a relevant authority must verify—

(a) that any national insurance number provided in respect of the person by whom the claim is made exists and has been allocated to that person;

(b) that the matters verified in accordance with sub-paragraph (a) accord with—

    (i) its own records; or

    (ii) in the case of a person providing services to the Secretary of State or the Department for Social Development in Northern Ireland, records held by the Secretary of State or that Department; and

(c) whether the details of any relevant claim for benefit that have been provided are consistent with those held by it.

(4) If a relevant authority cannot locate any national insurance number in respect of a person by whom such a claim is made, it must forward to the Board or a person providing services to the Board the claim (notwithstanding that it is not complete).

(5) "National insurance number" means the national insurance number allocated within the meaning of—
  (a) regulation 9 of the Social Security (Crediting and Treatment of Contributions, and National Insurance Numbers) Regulations 2001; or
  (b) regulation 9 of the Social Security (Crediting and Treatment of Contributions, and National Insurance Numbers) Regulations (Northern Ireland) 2001.

(6) "Claim for benefit" means a claim for—
  (a) a benefit in relation to which—
    (i) the Secretary of State has functions under the Social Security Contributions and Benefits Act 1992; or
    (ii) the Department for Social Development in Northern Ireland has functions under the Social Security Contributions and Benefits (Northern Ireland) Act 1992; or
  (b) a jobseeker's allowance under—
    (i) the Jobseekers Act 1995; or
    (ii) the Jobseekers (Northern Ireland) Order 1995.

DEFINITIONS

"the Board"—see reg.2.
"the principal Regulations"—see *ibid.*
"relevant authority"—see *ibid.*

The Tax Credits (Notice of Appeal) Regulations 2002

(SI 2002/3119)

Made   *17th December 2002*
Laid before Parliament   *17th December 2002*
Coming into force   *7th January 2003*

The Commissioners of Inland Revenue, in exercise of the powers conferred upon them by sections 39(1), 65(2) and 67 of the Tax Credits Act 2002, hereby make the following Regulations:

Citation and commencement

1. These Regulations may be cited as the Tax Credits (Notice of Appeal) Regulations 2002 and shall come into force on 7th January 2003.   2.370

Prescribed manner of notice of appeal

2.—(1) The prescribed manner of giving notice of appeal to the Board under section 39(1) of the Tax Credits Act 2002 is as follows.   2.371
  (2) The notice must—
  (a) be given in writing,
  (b) contain sufficient information to identify the appellant and the decision against which the appeal is being made, and
  (c) be signed by or on behalf of the appellant.

(3) In paragraph (2)(a) "writing" includes writing produced by electronic communications if those electronic communications are approved by the Board.

(4) In paragraph (2)(c) "signed", where the notice is in writing produced by electronic communications, means authenticated in such manner as may be approved by the Board.

(5) In this regulation "the Board" means the Commissioners of Inland Revenue.

DEFINITIONS

"the Board"—see para.(5).
"signed"—see para.(4).
"writing"—see para.(3).

GENERAL NOTE

2.372   A typed name can amount to a signature when it has been adopted by the person concerned through his or her signing another document or taking some other active step in an appeal *(R(DLA) 2/98)*. In *CIB/460/2003*, the claimant's mother, who had not been appointed to act on behalf of the claimant, signed the appeal. No-one had objected and the claimant himself had signed the form issued by the clerk asking him, among other things, whether he wanted to withdraw the appeal. He had said "no". The Commissioner rejected a submission made on behalf of the Secretary of State to the effect that the appeal was not valid.

See para.(4) for signatures on electronic documents.

The Tax Credits (Appeals) (No.2) Regulations 2002

(SI 2002/3196) (AS AMENDED)

Made   *18th December 2002*
Coming into force   *1st January 2003*

ARRANGEMENT OF REGULATIONS

PART I

General

PART II

General Appeal Matters

6.   (repealed)
7.   (repealed)
8.   Death of a party to an appeal or an application for a direction

PART III

Appeal Tribunals for Tax Credits

9-27.   repealed

Whereas a draft of this instrument was laid before Parliament in accordance with section 80(1) of the Social Security Act 1998 and approved by a resolution of each House of Parliament.

Now, therefore, the Secretary of State for Work and Pensions, in exercise of the powers conferred upon him by sections 7(6), 12(2) and (7), 14(10) and (11), 16(1), 28(1), 39(1), 79(1) and (3) to (7) and 84 of, and paragraphs 11 and 12 of Schedule 1 and Schedule 5 to the Social Security Act 1998 and all other powers enabling him in that behalf, after consultation with the Council on Tribunals in accordance with section 8 of the Tribunals and Inquiries Act 1992, hereby makes the following Regulations:

PART I

GENERAL

Citation, commencement, duration and interpretation

1.—(1) These Regulations may be cited as the Tax Credits (Appeals)   2.374
(No.2) Regulations 2002 and shall come into force on 1st January 2003.

(2) These Regulations shall cease to have effect on such day as is appointed by order made under section 63(1) of the Tax Credits Act 2002 (tax credits appeals etc.: temporary modifications).

(3) In these Regulations, unless the context otherwise requires—

"the Act" means the Social Security Act 1998;

"the 2002 Act" means the Tax Credits Act 2002;

"the Appeals Regulations" means the Tax Credits (Appeals) Regulations 2002;

"the Decisions and Appeals Regulations" means the Social Security and Child Support (Decisions and Appeals) Regulations 1999;

"the Working Tax Credit Regulations" means the Working Tax Credit (Entitlement and Maximum Rate) Regulations 2002;

"appeal" means an appeal under section 38 of the 2002 Act;

"an application for a direction" means an application for a direction to close down an enquiry made under section 19(9) of the 2002 Act;

[² . . .]
[² . . .]
[¹"couple" means—
    (a) a man and woman who are married to each other and are members of the same household;
    (b) a man and woman who are not married to each other but are living together as husband and wife;

   (c) two people of the same sex who are civil partners of each other and are members of the same household; or

   (d) two people of the same sex who are not civil partners of each other but are living together as if they were civil partners,

and for the purposes of paragraph (d), two people of the same sex are to be regarded as living together as if they were civil partners if, but only if, they would be regarded as living together as husband and wife were they instead two people of the opposite sex;]

"court" means the High Court, the Court of Appeal, the Court of Session, the High Court or Court of Appeal in Northern Ireland, the House of Lords or the Court of Justice of the European Community;

[2 . . .]
[2 . . .]
[2 . . .]

"joint claim" means a claim made under section 3(3)(a) of the 2002 Act and any reference in these Regulations to "joint claimant" shall be construed accordingly;

[2 . . .]
[2 . . .]
[2 . . .]
[2 . . .]
[2 . . .]

"partner" means, [1...], the other member of [1a] couple;

"party to the proceedings" means the Board and any other person—

   (a) who is an appellant in an appeal brought against a decision or determination set out in section 38 of the 2002 Act;

   (b) who is an applicant for a direction to close down an enquiry under section 19(9) of the 2002 Act;

   (c) who is a defendant (or defender) in penalty proceedings brought under paragraph 3 of Schedule 2 to the 2002 Act;

   (d) who is a person with a right of appeal or a right to make an application for a direction under regulation 3;

[2 . . .]
[2 . . .]
[2 . . .]

"single claim" means a claim made under section 3(3)(b) of the 2002 Act;

"tax credit" means child tax credit or working tax credit, construing those terms in accordance with section 1(1) and (2) of the 2002 Act, and any reference in these Regulations to "child tax credit" or "working tax credit" shall be construed accordingly.

AMENDMENTS

1. Civil Partnership (Pensions, Social Security and Child Support) (Consequential, etc. Provisions) Order 2005 (SI 2005/2877), para.36(2) of Sch.3 (December 5, 2005).

2. Tribunals, Courts and Enforcement Act 2007 (Transitional and Consequential Provisions) Order 2008 (SI 2008/2683), art.6 and Sch.1, para.205 (November 3, 2008).

GENERAL NOTE

"party to the proceedings"

In *CTC/2612/2005*, the Commissioner pointed out that where only one member   2.375
of a couple who should have been joint claimants had appealed, the other was not a
party to the proceedings, which was unfair as she was potentially liable to repay an
overpayment. The real problem was that it was unclear whether the Inland Revenue
had issued a decision addressed to both of them. If they had, it is suggested that an
appeal by one of member of the couple could have been treated as an appeal by both
of them unless it was clear that only one of them wished to appeal (see *R(A) 2/06*).

A more complex problem arose in *CTC/4390/2004*, where two separated parents
each claimed child tax credit. It was pointed out that the legislation made no provision for them to be parties to a single appeal even though a decision could be
binding only on the parties to it (see *CTC/2090/2004*). However, by the time the case
reached the Commissioner, there were appeals by both parents (because the award
to one parent had been terminated when the other parent won his appeal before the
tribunal) and, with the agreement of the parties, the Commissioner, when allowing
an appeal against the tribunal's decision, directed that the appeal be reheard at the
same time as the other parent's appeal against the termination of her award.

Service of notices or documents

2.—Where, by any provision of these Regulations—   2.376
(a) any notice or other document is required to be given or sent [¹ . . .] to
    the Board, that notice or document shall be treated as having been so
    given or sent on the day that it is received [¹ . . .] by the Board, and
(b) any notice or other document is required to be given or sent to any
    person other than [¹ . . .] the Board, that notice or document shall,
    if sent to that person's last known address, be treated as having been
    given or sent on the day that it was posted.

AMENDMENT

1. Tribunals, Courts and Enforcement Act 2007 (Transitional and Consequential Provisions) Order 2008 (SI 2008/2683), art.6 and Sch.1, para.206 (November 3, 2008).

DEFINITIONS

"the Board"—see s.39(1) of the Social Security Act 1998 as modified by reg.12
    of the Tax Credits (Appeals) Regulations 2002.
"clerk to the appeal tribunal"—see reg.1(3).

GENERAL NOTE

A fax is received for the purposes of reg.2(a) when it is successfully transmitted   2.377
to, and received by, a fax machine, irrespective of when it is actually collected from
the fax machine (*R(DLA) 3/05*). Furthermore, the faxed request for a statement of
reasons in that case was received by the clerk to the appeal tribunal when received
at the tribunal venue, even though the clerk did not visit that venue until some days
later. The Commissioner said that it would have been different if the venue had been
a casual venue, such as local authority premises. Here, it was a dedicated venue
and the fax number had been given to representatives precisely to enable them to
communicate with the clerk. There was nothing in any document issued with the
decision notice to indicate that the request for a statement of reasons had to be
addressed to a different place.

The "last known address" to which documents must be sent for para.(b) to
apply need not be the person's last known *residence* because the concepts are
different. Moreover, the sender must consider the address to be reliable and, if he

does not, should take reasonable steps to see whether a more reliable one exists (*CCS/2288/2005*). This approach exists to aid the innocent claimant and not the one who has failed to take reasonable steps to keep HMRC or the clerk to the tribunal aware of his whereabouts. Generally they are entitled to rely on a claimant to inform them of any move.

Deemed receipt of a document cannot cure a breach of the rules of natural justice so that, if a tribunal does not receive medical evidence submitted by the claimant in support of an application for a postponement, the decision of the tribunal can be set aside as being erroneous in point of law (*CG/2973/2004*). Decisions can also be set aside under reg.25 where documents go astray. That does not preclude an appeal, although an application for setting aside under reg.25 remains the more appropriate procedure (*CIB/303/1999*, declining to follow *R(SB) 55/83* but agreeing with *R(SB) 19/83*).

A provision similar to reg.2(b) relating to immigration appeals was held to be invalid in *R. v Secretary of State for the Home Department, ex parte Saleem* [2001] 1 W.L.R. 443, but there are sufficient remedies in these Regulations for the injustice that reg.2(b) might otherwise cause and Commissioners have distinguished *ex parte Saleem* and held the equivalent provision relating to social security and child support appeals to be valid (*CCS/6302/1999* and *CIB/303/1999*).

PART II

GENERAL APPEAL MATTERS

Other persons with a right of appeal or a right to make an application for a direction

2.378   **3.**—For the purposes of section 12(2) of the Act (as applied and modified by the Appeals Regulations), where—

   (a) a person has made a claim for a tax credit but is unable for the time being to make an appeal against a decision in respect of that tax credit; or

   (b) a person is the person in respect of whom an enquiry has been initiated under section 19(1) of the 2002 Act, but is unable for the time being to make an application for a direction,

the following other persons have a right of appeal to [² the First-tier Tribumal] or a right to make an application for a direction—

   (i) a receiver appointed by the Court of Protection with power to make a claim for a tax credit on behalf of the person;

   (ii) in Scotland, a [¹judicial factor, or guardian acting or appointed under the Adults with incapacity (Scotland) Act 2000 who has power to claim, or as the case may be, receive a tax credit on his behalf] who is administering the estate of the person;

   (iii) a person appointed under regulation 33(1) of the Social Security (Claims and Payments) Regulations 1987 (persons unable to act);

   (iv) where there is no person mentioned in sub-paragraph (iii) in relation to the person who is unable to act, a person who has applied in writing to the Board to be appointed to act on behalf of the person who is unable to act and, if a natural person, is aged 18 years or more and who has been so appointed by the Board for the purposes of this subparagraph.

AMENDMENTS

1. Social Security, Child Support and Tax Credits (Miscellaneous Amendments) Regulations 2005 (SI 2005/337), reg.4(2) (March 18, 2005).

2. Tribunals, Courts and Enforcement Act 2007 (Transitional and Consequential Provisions) Order 2008 (SI 2008/2683), art.6 and Sch.1, para.207 (November 3, 2008).

DEFINITIONS

"the Act"—see reg.1(3).
"the Appeals Regulations"—*ibid*.
"appeal"—*ibid*.
"an application for a direction"—*ibid*.
"the Board"—see s.39(1) of the Social Security Act 1998 as modified by reg.12 of the Tax Credits (Appeals) Regulations 2002.
"tax credit"—reg.1(3).

GENERAL NOTE

Section 12(2) of the Social Security Act 1998, mentioned in the opening words   2.379
of this regulation, has actually been "modified" out of existence because it and subs. (1) have been replaced by a single subsection. This regulation is made under the substituted s.12(1)(d).

It is arguable that this regulation is at least partly unnecessary as those mentioned in it could submit appeals on the basis of their general authority to act on behalf of the real appellant. Certainly it has not been thought necessary to make similar provision in respect of appeals to Commissioners.

Time within which an appeal is to be brought

4.—(1) Where a dispute arises as to whether an appeal was brought   2.380
within the time limit specified in section 39(1) of the 2002 Act, the dispute shall be referred to, and be determined by, [¹ the First-tier Tribunal].

(2) The time limit specified in section 39(1) of the 2002 Act may be extended in accordance with regulation 5.

AMENDMENT

1. Tribunals, Courts and Enforcement Act 2007 (Transitional and Consequential Provisions) Order 2008 (SI 2008/2683), art.6 and Sch.1, para.208 (November 3, 2008).

DEFINITIONS

"the 2002 Act"—see reg.1(3).
"appeal"—*ibid*.
"legally qualified panel member"—see reg.1(3).

GENERAL NOTE

The time limit specified in s.39(1) of the Tax Credits Act 2002 is the 30 days usual   2.381
in tax cases rather than the month usual in social security cases.

Late appeals

5.—(1) [¹ The Board may treat a late appeal as made in time] where the   2.382
conditions specified in paragraphs [¹(4)] to (8) are satisfied, but no appeal shall in any event be brought more than one year after the expiration of the last day for appealing under section 39(1) of the 2002 Act.

[¹ . . .]

[¹ (4) An appeal may be treated as made in time if the Board is satisfied that it is in the interests of justice.]

(5) For the purposes of paragraph (4) it is not in the interests of justice to [¹ treat the appeal as made in time unless the Board are] satisfied that—

(a) the special circumstances specified in paragraph (6) are relevant [¹ . . .]; or

(b) some other special circumstances exist which are wholly exceptional and relevant [¹ . . .],

and as a result of those special circumstances, it was not practicable for the appeal to be made within the time limit specified in section 39(1) of the 2002 Act.

(6) For the purposes of paragraph (5)(a), the special circumstances are that—

(a) the [¹ appellant] or a partner or dependant of the [¹ appellant] has died or suffered serious illness;

(b) the [¹ appellant] is not resident in the United Kingdom; or

(c) normal postal services were disrupted.

(7) In determining whether it is in the interests of justice to [¹ treat the appeal as made in time], regard shall be had to the principle that the greater the amount of time that has elapsed between the expiration of the time within which the appeal is to be brought under section 39(1) of the 2002 Act and the [¹ submission of the notice of appeal, the more compelling should be the special circumstances.]

(8) In determining whether it is in the interests of justice to [¹ treat the appeal as made in time], no account shall be taken of the following—

(a) that the applicant or any person acting for him was unaware of or misunderstood the law applicable to his case (including ignorance or misunderstanding of the time limit imposed by section 39(1) of the 2002 Act); or

(b) that [¹ the Upper Tribunal] or a court has taken a different view of the law from that previously understood and applied.

[¹ . . .]

AMENDMENT

1. Tribunals, Courts and Enforcement Act 2007 (Transitional and Consequential Provisions) Order 2008 (SI 2008/2683), art.6 and Sch.1, para.209 (November 3, 2008).

DEFINITIONS

"the 2002 Act"—see reg.1(3).
"appeal"—*ibid*.
"the Board"—see s.39(1) of the Social Security Act 1998 as modified by reg.12 of the Tax Credits (Appeals) Regulations 2002.
"court"—reg.1(3).
"legally qualified panel member"—*ibid*.
"panel member"—*ibid*.
"partner"—*ibid*.
"President"—*ibid*.

GENERAL NOTE

Para.(1)

2.383   The absolute time limit prohibiting the bringing of appeals more than a year late is not incompatible with the European Convention on Human Rights (*Denson v Secretary of State for Work and Pensions* [2004] EWCA Civ 462 (also reported as *R(CS) 4/04*). Nonetheless, it can work injustice, particularly in a case where an unrepresented claimant has been challenging the wrong decision and nobody tells him or her until it is too late which decision it is that must be challenged if he or she is to succeed in obtaining the benefit sought.

Para. (2)

HMRC may decide that a late appeal should be admitted under para.(4)(b) (but   **2.384**
not under para.(4)(a)). Presumably it is not expected that an appeal tribunal will then object, because it is not clear what it could do if it did object. Presumably it is also not expected that HMRC will use this power where it is the applicant. It may be arguable that the decision of the panel member is a decision of an appeal tribunal for the purpose of permitting an appeal to be brought against it under s.14 of the Social Security Act 1998.

Para. (4)

The amendment from 2008 means that only HMRC can consider whether the conditions in para.(4) are satisfied. It is interesting that HMRC is empowered to act "in the interests of justice".

Para. (8) (a)

If a claimant is ignorant of the time limit for appealing because HMRC failed to   **2.386**
provide the information required by s.23(2) of the Tax Credits Act 2002, it is arguable that time for appealing has not started to run. If this is correct, it is unnecessary for the would-be appellant to apply for an extension of time (which might be difficult in the light of para.8(a)) and instead he or she should apply for a ruling under reg.4(1).

Para. (8) (b)

Understood by whom? Presumably not the applicant because the view must also   **2.387**
be different from that previously applied. But is it the understanding of HMRC as a whole that matters or of a particular officer considering the application? Whatever the answer, it is not easy to see what sub-para.(b) adds to sub-para.(a).

Death of a party to an appeal or an application for a direction

8.—(1) In any proceedings relating to an appeal or an application for   **2.388**
a direction, on the death of a party to those proceedings (other than the Board) the following persons may proceed with the appeal or application for a direction in the place of such deceased party—
  (a) where the proceedings are in relation to a single claim, the personal representatives of the person who has died;
  (b) where the proceedings are in relation to a joint claim, where only one of the persons by whom the claim was made has died, the other person with whom the claim was made;
  (c) where the proceedings are in relation to a joint claim where both the persons by whom the claim was made have died, the personal representatives of the last of them to die;
  (d) for the purposes of paragraph (c), where persons have died in circumstances rendering it uncertain which of them survived the other—
    (i) their deaths shall be presumed to have occurred in order of seniority; and

(ii) the younger shall be treated as having survived the elder.

(2) Where there is no person mentioned in paragraphs (1)(a) to (1)
(c) to proceed with the appeal or application for a direction, the Board
may appoint such person as they think fit to proceed with that appeal or
that application in the place of such deceased party referred to in paragraph
(1).

(3) A grant of probate, confirmation or letters of administration to the
estate of the deceased party, whenever taken out, shall have no effect on an
appointment made under paragraph (2).

(4) Where a person appointed under paragraph (2) has, prior to the date
of such appointment, taken any action in relation to the appeal or application for a direction on behalf of the deceased party, the effective date of
appointment by the Board shall be the day immediately prior to the first day
on which such action was taken.

DEFINITIONS

"appeal"—see reg.1(3).
"an application for a direction"—*ibid*.
"the Board"—see s.39(1) of the Social Security Act 1998 as modified by reg.12
of the Tax Credits (Appeals) Regulations 2002.
"joint claimant"—reg.1(3).
"party to the proceedings"—*ibid*.
"single claimant"—*ibid*.

Tax Credits (Interest Rate) Regulations 2003

(SI 2003/123)

The Treasury, in exercise of the powers conferred upon them by ss.37(2) and
(5), 65(1) and (8) and 67 of the Tax Credits Act 2002, hereby make the following
Regulations:

ARRANGEMENT OF ARTICLES

2.389
1. Citation and commencement.
2. Interpretation.
3. Interest on overpayments of tax credit and penalties.
4. Prescribed rate of interest.

Citation and commencement

2.390
1. These Regulations may be cited as the Tax Credits (Interest Rate)
Regulations 2003 and shall come into force on 18th February 2003.

GENERAL NOTE

2.391
The tax credits regime does not adopt quite the same approach to interest on overpayments as HMRC does for late payments of income tax. Whereas interest on late
payments of income tax has long been a feature of revenue law, s.37 of the TCA 2002
adopts a compromise approach to tax credits. Thus, interest is charged on overpayments caused by fraud or neglect, but not otherwise. These regulations specify the

rate of interest to be applied on such overpayments, and also on any penalty under ss.31–33 (penalties for incorrect statements, failure to comply with requirements, etc.).

Interpretation

2.—(1) In these Regulations—

"the Board" means the Commissioners of Inland Revenue;

"established rate" means—

(a) on the coming into force of these Regulations, 6.5 per cent per annum;

(b) in relation to any date after the first reference date after the coming into force of these Regulations, the reference rate found on the immediately preceding reference date;

"operative date" means the sixth day of each month;

"reference date" means the day of each month which is the 12 working day before the sixth day of the following month;

"tax credit" means child tax credit or, as the case may be, working tax credit, provision for which is made by the Tax Credits Act 2002;

"working day" means any day other than a non-business day within the meaning of section 92 of the Bills of Exchange Act 1882.

(2) For the purposes of regulation 4(2) the reference rate found on a reference date is the percentage per annum found by averaging the base lending rates at close of business on that date of—

(a) Bank of Scotland;

(b) Barclays Bank plc;

(c) Lloyds Bank plc;

(d) HSBC Bank plc;

(e) National Westminster Bank plc;

(f) The Royal Bank of Scotland plc,

and, if the result is not a whole number, rounding the result to the nearest such number, with any result midway between two whole numbers rounded down.

DEFINITION

"reference rate"—see reg.4(2).

Interest on overpayments of tax credit and penalties

3.—(1) Where the Board decide in accordance with section 37(1) of the Tax Credits Act 2002 that the whole or part of an overpayment of a tax credit which is attributable to fraud or neglect is to carry interest, the rate of interest for the purposes of section 37(2) of that Act is that prescribed by regulation 4.

(2) The rate of interest for the purposes of section 37(5) of the Tax Credits Act 2002 (interest on a penalty under any of sections 31–33 of that Act) is that prescribed by regulation 4.

DEFINITION

"the Board"—see reg.2(1).

Prescribed rate of interest

4.—(1) The rate of interest which is prescribed is, subject to paragraph (2), 6.5 per cent per annum.

2.392

2.393

2.394

(2) Where, on a reference date after the coming into force of these Regulations, the reference rate found on that date ("RR") differs from the established rate, the rate of interest which is prescribed shall, on and after the next operative date, be the percentage per annum found by applying the formula:

$$RR + 2.5.$$

DEFINITION

"established rate"—see reg.2(1).

Tax Credits (Immigration) Regulations 2003

(SI 2003/653)

The Treasury, in exercise of the powers conferred upon them by sections 42 and 65(1), (3), (7) and (9) of the Tax Credits Act 2002, hereby make the following Regulations:

ARRANGEMENT OF ARTICLES

2.395

1. Citation and commencement
2. Interpretation
3. Exclusion of persons subject to immigration control from entitlement to tax credits
4. Modifications of Part 1 of the Act for refugees whose asylum claims have been accepted
5. Transitional relief—claimants moving from income support and incomebased Jobseeker's Allowance to child tax credit

Citation and commencement

2.396

1. These Regulations may be cited as the Tax Credits (Immigration) Regulations 2003 and shall come into force on 6th April 2003.

Interpretation

2.397

2. In these Regulations—

"the Act" means the Tax Credits Act 2002;

"the Child Tax Credit Regulations" means the Child Tax Credit Regulations 2002;

[¹"couple" has the meaning given by section 3(5A) of the Act;]

"immigration rules" has the meaning given by section 33 of the Immigration Act 1971;

"joint claim" has the meaning given by section 3(8) of the Act;

"limited leave" has the meaning given by section 33 of the Immigration Act 1971;

[¹. . .]

"person subject to immigration control" has the meaning in section 115(9) of the Immigration and Asylum Act 1999;

"refugee" means a person who has been recorded by the Secretary of State as a refugee within the definition in Article 1 of the Convention relating to the Status of Refugees done at Geneva on 28th July 1951 as extended by Article 1(2) of the Protocol relating to the Status of Refugees done at New York on 31st January 1967;

"tax credit" refers to either child tax credit or working tax credit and references to tax credits are to both of them;

"the Working Tax Credit Regulations" means the Working Tax Credit (Entitlement and Maximum Rate) Regulations 2002.

AMENDMENT

1. Civil Partnership Act 2004 (Tax Credits, etc.) (Consequential Amendments) Order 2005 (SI 2005/2919), art.7(2) (December 5, 2005).

Exclusion of persons subject to immigration control from entitlement to tax credits

3.—(1) No person is entitled to child tax credit or working tax credit while he is a person subject to immigration control, except in the following Cases, and subject to paragraphs (2) to (9).   2.398

Case 1

He is a person who—   2.399

(a) has been given leave to enter, or remain in, the United Kingdom by the Secretary of State upon the undertaking of another person or persons, pursuant to the immigration rules, to be responsible for his maintenance and accommodation; and

(b) has been resident in the United Kingdom for a period of at least five years commencing on or after the date of his entry into the United Kingdom, or the date on which the undertaking was given in respect of him, whichever is the later.

Case 2

He is a person who—   2.400

(a) falls within the terms of paragraph (a) of Case 1; and

(b) has been resident in the United Kingdom for less than the five years mentioned in para.(b) of Case 1,

but the person giving the undertaking has died or, where the undertaking was given by more than one person, they have all died.

Case 3

He is a person who satisfies the following conditions—   2.401

(a) he has limited leave to enter or remain in the United Kingdom;

(b) that leave was subject to a condition that he does not have recourse to public funds, during that period of limited leave;

(c) he has, during so much as has elapsed of that period of limited leave (including that period as extended), supported himself without recourse to public funds, other than any such recourse by reason of the previous satisfaction of these conditions;

(d) he is temporarily without funds during that period of leave because remittances to him from abroad have been disrupted;

(e) there is a reasonable expectation that his supply of funds will be resumed; and

(f) the period (or aggregate of periods) for which this Case applies does not exceed 42 days during any single period of limited leave (including any extension to that period).

Case 4

2.402   Where the claim is for working tax credit, he is—

(a) a national of a state which has ratified the European Convention on Social and Medical Assistance (done in Paris on 11th December 1953) or of a state which has ratified the Council of Europe Social Charter (signed in Turin on 18th October 1961); and

(b) lawfully present in the United Kingdom.

The Case so described also applies where—

(a) the claim is for child tax credit;

(b) the award of child tax credit would be made on or after 6th April 2004; and

(c) immediately before the award is made (and as part of the transition of claimants entitled to elements of income support and income-based Jobseeker's Allowance, to child tax credit) the person is, or will on the making of a claim be, entitled to any of the amounts in relation to income support or income-based Jobseeker's Allowance which are described in section 1(3)(d) of the Act.

Case 5

2.403   Where the claim is for child tax credit, he is—

(a) a person who is lawfully working in the United Kingdom; and

(b) a national of a State with which the Community has concluded an Agreement under Article 310 of the Treaty of Amsterdam amending the Treaty on European Union, the Treaties establishing the European Communities and certain related Acts providing, in the field of social security, for the equal treatment of workers who are nationals of the signatory State and their families.

(2) Where one member of a [¹ . . .] couple is a person subject to immigration control, and the other member is not or is within any of Cases 1 to 5 or regulation 5—

(a) the calculation of the amount of tax credit under the Act, the Child Tax Credit Regulations and the Working Tax Credit Regulations (including any second adult element or other element in respect of, or determined by reference to, that person);

(b) the method of making (or proceeding with) a joint claim by the couple; and

(c) the method of payment of the tax credit,

shall, subject to paragraph (3), be determined in the same way as if that person were not subject to such control.

(3) Where the other member is within Case 4 or 5 or regulation 5, para. (2) shall only apply to the tax credit to which he (in accordance with those provisions) is entitled.

(4) Where a person has submitted a claim for asylum as a refugee and in consequence is a person subject to immigration control, in the first instance he is not entitled to tax credits, subject to paragraphs (5) to (9).

(5) If that person—

(a) is notified that he has been recorded by the Secretary of State as a refugee; and

(b) claims tax credit within three months of receiving that notification, paragraphs (6) to (9) and regulation 4 shall apply to him.

(6) He shall be treated as having claimed tax credits—

(a) on the date when he submitted his claim for asylum; and

(b) on every 6th April (if any) intervening between the date in sub-paragraph (a) and the date of the claim referred to in paragraph (5) (b),

rather than on the date on which he makes the claim referred to in paragraph (5)(b).

(7) Regulations 7 and 8 of the Tax Credits (Claims and Notifications) Regulations 2002 shall not apply to claims treated as made by virtue of paragraph (6).

(8) He shall have his claims for tax credits determined as if he had been recorded as a refugee on the date when he submitted his claim for asylum.

(9) The amount of support provided under—

(a) section 95 or 98 of the Immigration and Asylum Act 1999;

(b) regulations made under Schedule 9 to that Act, by the Secretary of State in respect of essential living needs of the claimant and his dependants (if any); or

(c) regulations made under paragraph 3 of Schedule 8 to that Act,

(after allowing for any deduction for that amount under regulation 21ZB(3) of the Income Support (General) Regulations 1987) shall be deducted from any award of tax credits due to the claimant by virtue of paragraphs (6) and (8).

AMENDMENT

1. Civil Partnership Act 2004 (Tax Credits, etc.) (Consequential Amendments) Order 2005 (SI 2005/2919), art.7(3) (December 5, 2005).

DEFINITIONS

"the Act"—see reg.2.
"the Child Tax Credit Regulations"—see *ibid.*
"couple"—see *ibid.*
"immigration rules"—see *ibid.*
"joint claim"—see *ibid.*
"limited leave"—see *ibid.*
"person subject to immigration control"—see *ibid.*
"refugee"—see *ibid.*
"tax credit"—see *ibid.*
"the Working Tax Credit Regulations"—see *ibid.*

GENERAL NOTE

These regulations are made under s.42(1) of the Tax Credits Act 2002, which **2.404** enables regulations to make provision for the exclusion of "persons subject to immigration control" from entitlement to child tax credit or working tax credit (or both). For these purposes, a "person subject to immigration control" has the same meaning as in s.115 of the Immigration and Asylum Act 1999. Section 115(9) of the 1999 Act is the starting point for this definition, and defines a "person subject to immigration control" as a person who *either* requires leave to enter or remain in the United

Kingdom but does not have it *or* has such leave but this is (i) subject to a condition that he does not have recourse to public funds, or (ii) as a result of a maintenance undertaking, or (iii) through the continuation of leave pending certain appeals. For detailed commentary on this definition, see the annotations to reg.21(3) of the Income Support (General) Regulations 1987 (SI 1987/1967) in Vol.II in this series. It should be noted that a person who is a national of an EEA state (i.e. a national of an EU Member State or of Iceland, Liechtenstein or Norway) can *never* be a person subject to immigration control for the purposes of social security or tax credits.

The structure of reg.3 itself falls into three parts. Paragraph (1) sets out the general rule, along with certain exceptions. The position of couples, where one partner is a person subject to immigration control but the other is not, is dealt with in paras (2) and (3). Paragraphs (4)–(9) are concerned with the particular status of asylum seekers. These rules can never apply to British citizens. An individual who becomes a British citizen by naturalisation ceases to be subject to any immigration control on becoming a British citizen.

Para. (1)

2.405   The general rule is that a person subject to immigration control is not entitled to either child tax credit or working tax credit (para.(1)). This general rule is then subject to the five exceptions listed in Cases 1–5. These Cases have been adapted from the exceptions to the general rule precluding persons subject to immigration control from being entitled to the various means-tested benefits, as set out in the Schedule to the Social Security (Immigration and Asylum) Consequential Amendments Regulations 2000 (SI 2000/636: see Vol.II in this series). Thus, Case 1 in para.(1) mirrors para.3 in Pt I of the Schedule to the 2000 Regulations; Case 2 follows para.2 of Pt I of the Schedule and Case 3 is similar to para.1 in Pt I of the Schedule (but includes a 42-day limit in sub-para.(f)). These first three Cases operate as exceptions to the preclusionary rule for both child tax credit and working tax credit. The exception in Case 4 is in the same terms as para.4 in Pt I of the Schedule to the 2000 Regulations and applies to all working tax credit claims. It also applies to child tax credit claims in respect of awards made on or after April 6, 2004 where, immediately before the award the claimant was (or would have been) entitled to a child allowance or family or disabled child premium as part of an award of income support or income-based jobseeker's allowance. The exception in Case 5 is adapted from para.2 of Pt II of the Schedule to the 2000 Regulations, which deals with exceptions from the preclusionary rule in respect of certain noncontributory benefits.

There is also a special rule, applying to child tax credit only, which provides transitional relief for claimants moving from income support or income-based job-seeker's allowance to child tax credit (see reg.5).

Paras (2) and (3)

2.406   Paragraph (2) provides that where only one member of a married or unmarried couple is a person subject to immigration control, and the other is not, entitlement to tax credits is determined in the same way as if neither of them were so subject. The same applies where the other member is either within one of the excepted cases in para.(1) or covered by the transitional provisions in reg.5 below. Note also the qualification in para.(3).

Paras (4)–(9)

2.407   These provisions enable backdated claims to tax credits to be made where an asylum claim has been accepted. A claimant who has submitted a claim for asylum is a person subject to immigration control and so in the first instance is not entitled to tax credits (para.(4)). However, if such an application is accepted, the claimant may claim tax credits retrospectively (para.(5)). Any such retrospective claim must be made within three months of the notification from the IND (para.(5)(a)). This contrasts favourably with the 28 days allowed for retrospective claims for income support in similar situations (Income Support (General) Regulations 1987 (SI 1987/1967), reg.21ZB). In the event of a successful application for asylum, the claim for tax credits is treated as having been made on the date of the submission of the claim for asylum, not the post-acceptance date of the actual claim for tax credits (para.(6)(a)). The claim is also regarded as having been renewed on every intervening April 6, demonstrating an awareness of the delays which are well known in the system for determining asylum applications (para.(6)(b)). Accordingly, the normal time-limits in regs 7 and 8 of the Tax Credits (Claims and Notifications) Regulations 2002 (SI 2002/2014) for claiming tax credits are disapplied (para.(7)) and the claim treated as if the applicant had been recorded as a refugee on the date when the asylum application was actually made (para.(8)). Any arrears of tax credits which are due, following the application of these provisions, are then subject to an offset in recognition of any sums provided by way of asylum support under various statutory provisions (para.(9)).

Note that, by virtue of reg.4, the provisions of Pt I of the TCA 2002 apply to the determination of claims for tax credits made by refugees whose asylum claims have been accepted, subject to the omission of ss.14–17 and various modifications to ss.18 and 19 of the 2002 Act.

In *CTC/3692/2008* an Upper Tribunal Judge rejected a challenge to subss. (7) to (9) as discriminatory and in breach of the Human Rights Act 1998. The Commissioner decided on the facts that while the rules were not discriminatory they also had not been applied properly. After outlining what should have happened, the appeal was sent back to HMRC for it to be redetermined.

Modifications of Part I of the Act for refugees whose asylum claims have been accepted

4.—(1) For the purposes of claims falling within paragraph (2), Part I of the Act shall apply subject to the modifications set out in paras (3)–(5).

2.408

(2) A claim falls within this paragraph if it is a claim for tax credits which a person is treated as having made by virtue of regulation 3(6), other than a claim which he is treated as having made in the tax year in which he made his claim under regulation 3(5).

(3) Omit sections 14 to 17 (initial decisions, revised decisions and final notices).

(4) In section 18 (decisions after final notices)—

(a) in subsection (1) for "After giving a notice under section 17" substitute "In relation to each claim for a tax credit made by a person or persons for the whole or part of a tax year";

(b) omit subsections (2) to (9);

(c) for subsection (10) substitute—

"(10) Before making their decision the Board may by notice—

(a) require the person, or either or both of the persons, by whom the claim is made to provide any information or evidence which the Board consider they may need for making their decision; or

(b) require any person of a prescribed description to provide any information or evidence of a prescribed description which the Board consider they may need for that purpose,

by the date specified in the notice.";

(d) in subsection (11) omit—

(i) "any revision under subsection (5) or (9) and";

(ii) paragraph (a);

(iii) in paragraph (b), "in any other case,".

(5) In section 19 (enquiries)—

(a) in subsection (4), for paragraphs (a) and (b) substitute

"one year after that decision or, if—

(a) the person, or either of the persons, to whom the enquiry relates is required by section 8 of the Taxes Management Act 1970 to make a return; and

(b) the return becomes final on a day more than one year after that decision,

with that day (or, if both of the persons are so required and their returns become final on different days, with the later of those days).;"

(b) in subsection (5) omit paragraph (a) and, in paragraph (b) "in any other case,";

(c) omit subsection (6).

DEFINITIONS

"the Act"—see reg.2.
"tax credit"—see *ibid*.

GENERAL NOTE

2.409   See note to reg.3.

Transitional relief—claimants moving from income support and income-based jobseeker's allowance to child tax credit

2.410   **5.** In relation to child tax credit, a person is not treated for the purposes of these Regulations as subject to immigration control where—

(a) the award of child tax credit would be made on or after 6th April 2004;

(b) immediately before the award of child tax credit is made, he is, or will on the making of a claim be, entitled to any of the amounts in relation to income support or income-based jobseeker's allowance which are described in section 1(3)(d) of the Act; and

(c) he is a person who, immediately before the award of child tax credit is made—

(i) was receiving or entitled to income support by virtue of regulation 12(1) of the Social Security (Persons From Abroad) Miscellaneous Amendments Regulations 1996, and his claim for asylum has not been recorded by the Secretary of State as having been decided (other than on appeal) or abandoned; or

(ii) was receiving or entitled to income support or income-based jobseeker's allowance by virtue of regulation 12(3) of the Social Security (Immigration and Asylum) Consequential Amendments Regulations 2000, and his claim for asylum has not been so recorded as having been decided (other than on appeal) or abandoned.

DEFINITIONS

"the Act"—see reg.2.
"person subject to immigration control"—see *ibid*.

GENERAL NOTE

This provides for transitional relief (on or after April 6, 2004) for claimants   **2.411**
moving over from the specified elements of income support or income-based jobseeker's allowance to child tax credit.

Tax Credits (Residence) Regulations 2003

(SI 2003/654) (AS AMENDED)

The Treasury, in exercise of the powers conferred upon them by sections 3(7)
and 65(1), (7) and (9) of the Tax Credits Act 2002, hereby make the following
Regulations:

REGULATIONS

1. Citation and commencement   **2.412**
2. Interpretation
3. Circumstances in which a person is treated as not being in the United Kingdom
4. Persons temporarily absent from the United Kingdom
5. Crown servants posted overseas
6. Partners of Crown servants posted overseas
7. Transitional provision—income support and income-based Jobseeker's
Allowance

Citation and commencement

1.—These Regulations may be cited as the Tax Credits (Residence)   **2.413**
Regulations 2003 and shall come into force on 6th April 2003.

Interpretation

2.—(1) In these Regulations—   **2.414**
"the Act" means the Tax Credits Act 2002;
"child" has the same meaning as it has in the Child Tax Credit Regulations
   2002;
[¹"couple" has the meaning given by section 3(5A) of the Act];
"Crown servant posted overseas" has the meaning given in regulation
   5(2);
"partner" means where a person is a member of a [¹ . . .] couple, the other
   member of that couple;
"qualifying young person" has the meaning given in regulation 2, read
   with regulation 5, of the Child Tax Credit Regulations 2002;
"relative" means brother, sister, ancestor or lineal descendant.
(2) In these Regulations, a person is responsible for a child or qualifying
young person if he is treated as being responsible for that child or qualifying
young person in accordance with the rules contained in regulation 3 of the
Child Tax Credit Regulations 2002.

AMENDMENT

1. Civil Partnership Act 2004 (Tax Credits, etc.) (Consequential Amendments)
Order 2005 (SI 2005/2919), art.8(2) (December 5, 2005).

2.415   This regulation follows the pattern of all tax credit provisions in adopting the definitions of "child" and "qualifying young person" from the Child Tax Credit Regulations 2002 (SI 2002/2007).

Circumstances in which a person is treated as not being in the United Kingdom

2.416   **3.**—(1) A person shall be treated as not being in the United Kingdom for the purposes of Part I of the Act if he is not ordinarily resident in the United Kingdom.

(2) Paragraph (1) does not apply to a Crown servant posted overseas or his partner.

(3) A person who is in the United Kingdom as a result of his deportation, expulsion or other removal by compulsion of law from another country to the United Kingdom shall be treated as being ordinarily resident in the United Kingdom.

(4) For the purposes of working tax credit, a person shall be treated as being ordinarily resident if he is exercising in the United Kingdom his rights as a worker pursuant to Council Regulation (EEC) 1612/68 [²as amended by Council Directive No.2004/38/EC] or Commission Regulation (EEC) 1251/70 or he is a person with a right to reside in the United Kingdom pursuant to [²Council Directive No.2004/38/EC].

[¹(5) A person shall be treated as not being in the United Kingdom for the purposes of Part 1 of the Act where he—

(a)   makes a claim for child tax credit (other than being treated as making a claim under regulation 11 or 12 of the Tax Credits (Claims and Notifications) Regulations 2002 or otherwise), on or after 1st May 2004; and

(b)   does not have a right to reside in the United Kingdom.]

AMENDMENTS

1. Tax Credits (Residence) (Amendment) Regulations 2004 (SI 2004/1243), reg.3 (May 1, 2004).
2. Tax Credits (Miscellaneous Amendments) Regulations 2006 (SI 2006/766), reg.4 (April 6, 2006).

DEFINITIONS

"Crown servant posted overseas"—see reg.2.
"partner"—see reg.2.

GENERAL NOTE

2.417   Section 3(3) of the TCA 2002 makes it a requirement for entitlement to tax credits that the claimant is "in the United Kingdom". This regulation, authorised by s.3(7), imposes the income test of "ordinary residence" as an additional requirement for entitlement. Read together with the section, the regulations require that a claimant must show:

(a)   ordinary residence in the United Kingdom, and
(b)   presence in the United Kingdom or, if he or she is not present in the United Kingdom, that the absence is temporary.

The approach taken here is consistent with the general jurisdictional approach to income tax in the United Kingdom. In common with some other parts of the common law world, income tax is residence-based, rather than nationality-based (as in the United States) or source-based (as in other parts of Europe). Income tax uses two main tests: residence and ordinary residence. The Tax Credits (Definition and Calculation of Income) Regulations 2002 (SI 2002/2006), reg.3 removes the significance of both those tests for the purposes of defining the relevant income of a claimant. These Regulations impose the test at another level. Those Regulations also disapply the definitions of "residence" in the various United Kingdom double tax agreements (which, for income tax purposes, override the national legislation).

Ordinary residence

"Ordinary residence" was used as the test for WFTC (Family Credit (General) Regulations 1987 (SI 1987/1973), reg.3) where the test was worded as a requirement that the claimant be both present and ordinarily resident. In *R(M) 1/85*, the Commissioner followed *Shah* (below) for those purposes as defining the term. The new form of words appears to avoid the problem with the previous wording commented on in Vol.II of the 2002 edition of this work. One change, however, is that the test is now applied to the whole of the United Kingdom, as Northern Ireland no longer has a separate system for these purposes.

"Ordinary residence" is a question of fact, not law. For the only relevant provisions in income tax law, see the ITA 2007, ss.829–832. It is separate from the other test used for income tax, "residence". "Residence" is determined for income tax purposes by reference to each tax year. "Ordinary residence" is based on a longer view, though perhaps not so long a view as "habitual residence". It is clear from both case law and practice that a claimant can have two ordinary residences at the same time for income tax purposes, and that the status of ordinary residence can be acquired on arrival in the United Kingdom if the claimant arrives with the intention of staying. That may be compared with the approach often taken for social security purposes to "habitual residence". For the leading authorities on the approach to be taken to the test see *Levene v IRC* [1928] A.C. 217; *IRC v Lysaght* [1928] A.C. 234; and *Shah v Barnet LBC* [1983] 2 A.C. 309, HL.

HMRC has a code of practice, published as booklet IR20, which defines how HMRC treat disputed issues of ordinary residence. HMRC treat the question as partly one of intention and partly one of actual presence. The working practice is to treat someone as resident in the United Kingdom if he or she is present for more than 183 days in total in any one year (whenever that year starts), and to treat someone as ordinarily resident if present for more than an average of 91 days in each of four consecutive years. A new arrival who has a job lasting more than three years here and/or who buys a house here is likely to be treated as ordinarily resident on arrival, and the reverse will be true of those leaving. IR20 should be treated with some caution as it applies to tax credits. Commentators have taken the view on a number of occasions that the HMRC view is one that supports HMRC's own approach to the definitions, rather than necessarily takes a neutral view on the issues. Secondly, and linked with this, the HMRC code in IR20 is designed to include people who would probably prefer to be excluded from the charge to United Kingdom income tax. Will the same approach be applied where HMRC might wish to exclude the claimant, while the claimant's interest will be to be included? In other words, will HMRC apply its allegedly expansive view of its jurisdiction under IR20 in the same way when paying out tax credits as when collecting in tax? HMRC have now published a guidance leaflet that broadly follows the income tax approach: *Child and Working Tax Credits and Child Benefit: residence rules—Guidance for intermediaries*. It is on the HMRC website at *http://www.hmrc.gov.uk/taxcredits/residence-rules.htm*. The same approach is followed in the official manuals to HMRC staff.

In practice, problems will usually arise in the following situations:

(1) When someone who has been ordinarily resident in the United Kingdom goes overseas: the usual issue here will be that the claimant is no longer as a matter of fact "in" the United Kingdom to claim child tax credit for any children. Subject to the temporary absence rule in reg.4, and the rules for Crown servants in regs 5 and 6, the claimant

2.418

2.419

will cease to qualify for tax credits. However, if the person (or one of two joint claimants leaving together) returns often enough to remain "present", then it will be a question of fact whether the claimant is ordinarily resident despite the overseas link. Where one of two joint claimants goes overseas and the other does not, the claim should become a single claim.

2.420   *(2) When someone arrives in the United Kingdom:* the first practical requirement for working tax credit purposes is that the claimant has a job. If he or she has come to the United Kingdom to work and that work is likely to last at least 3 years, then current Revenue practice is to treat the person as ordinarily resident here on arrival. The position of the worker whose work here may not last that period but who has rights under EU law as a worker is protected by reg.3(4). It is suggested that if the person is accepted as ordinarily resident under either rule for working tax credit purposes then he or she should also be accepted as able to claim child tax credit as well. There will also be a practical argument in other cases that if the claimant is treated as liable to United Kingdom income tax, then he or she will expect United Kingdom tax credits. However, the liability to income tax may arise on residence alone before the individual becomes ordinarily resident in the United Kingdom.

2.421   *(3) When someone has strong links with the United Kingdom and another state:* there may be ordinary residence in both states. This will be a question of fact. Unlike regs 5 and 6 below, this regulation does not deal expressly with partners making joint claims. The position is clear from s.3 of the Act. A couple must make a joint claim if both are "in" the United Kingdom. If one of the couple is not present or ordinarily resident here, then only the other partner can make the claim. But this will have the effect of excluding the non-resident partner's income from the income calculation. It may therefore be in the interests of some claimants for child tax credit to claim, say, that the mother is present and ordinarily resident, but that the father is not. This is not now a concern for income tax purposes as all married couples are assessed to income tax separately.

   The Treasury published a consultative document with the 2003 Budget about the tests of residence, ordinary residence and domicile, entitled: *Reviewing the residence and domicile rules as they affect the taxation of individuals: a background paper.* It is available on the HM Treasury website. It contains a valuable summary of current practice and the problems it generates.

Para. (2)

2.422   Paragraph (2) relates to regs 5 and 6 below. Paragraph (3) deals with the problem that some of these individuals might not otherwise be regarded as ordinarily resident and so would be deprived of claims to either working tax credit or child tax credit. But see also the Tax Credits (Immigration) Regulations 2003 (SI 2003/653). Paragraph (4), which relates to working tax credit only, makes the necessary exception to protect the rights of movement of workers and others under EU law. See Vol.III of this work. It is not entirely clear why this is limited to working tax credit, as child tax credit would appear to be a social security family benefit for EU law purposes and therefore something to which someone with EU rights might also lay claim. Perhaps the aim is to ensure that in order to claim child tax credit in these situations the individual must first claim, or be entitled to claim, working tax credit. But that may exclude higher earners who are outside the income rules for working tax credit but not for child tax credit.

Para. (5)

2.423   It was intended to make this provision lapse on May 1, 2006 (see SI 2004/1243, reg.1), but the lapsing provision was itself revoked by SI 2006/766, reg.4, so continuing this paragraph in force without a time limit.

   The paragraph therefore now introduces for all claims after May 1, 2004 the requirement that a claimant has a "right to reside" before making any child tax credit claim. It does not apply to working tax credit claims. It therefore does not apply to in-work benefits. It applies, in particular, to those who have moved to the United Kingdom from the new member states of the European Union ("A8 and A2" citizens), and their families, if they are not economically active.

"Right to reside" has superseded the previous test of "habitual residence" for social security benefits generally. See the Social Security (Habitual Residence) (Amendment) Regulations 2004 (SI 2004/1232), discussed in Volume II of this work. The term is not defined by legislation. It does not apply to British citizens. Nor does it apply to any citizen of the European Economic Area legally working or self-employed in the United Kingdom or third country citizens with indefinite leave to remain in the United Kingdom. But it applies to any European Economic Area citizen who is economically inactive.

The test, including its application to child tax credit, was considered in a series of decisions taken by a Tribunal of Commissioners as decisions *CIS/3573/2005*, *CPC/2920/2005*, *CIS/2559/2005* and *CIS/2680/2005*. The Tribunal decided that the test of "right to reside" is a general test applying to all potentially within its scope. Further, the test is not met by reference to the other tests of lawful residence or actual habitual residence. Rather, it reflects the provisions of EU Council Directive 90/364 that Member States:

> "shall grant the right of residence to nationals of member states who do not enjoy this right under other provisions of Community Law ... provided they ... have sufficient resources to avoid becoming a burden on the social assistance system of the host member state during the period of their residence."

The Court of Appeal has dismissed an appeal against the decision of the Tribunal of Commissioners in *Abdirahman v Secrtary of State for Work and Pensions* [2007] EWCA Civ 657 *(R(IS)8/07)*; see further the commentary in Vol II.

In *Zalewska v Department for Social Development* [2008] UKHL 67 The House of Lords upheld a decision of the Northern Ireland Court of Appeal and Social Security Commissioner that the use of the derogation from European Union law under which the test of "right to reside" was adopted was itself compatible with European Union law. The House of Lords also affirmed the decision of the Commissioner that, notwithstanding that the appellant in that case, who was Polish, was a worker, the Commissioner was correct in law in holding that the law permitted refusal of income support to the appellant in the circumstances of the case. The worker registration scheme was not disproportionate to its legitimate aims. The Commissioner's decision is *C6/05-06(IS)*.

HMRC guidance about the operation of the "right to reside" rule is included in its detailed *Child and Working Tax Credits and Child Benefit: residence rules guidance for intermediaries*. See *http://www.hmrc.gov.uk/taxcredits/residence-rules.htm*. Following the approach of the Tribunal of Commissioners, this states that groups subject to the "right to reside" must have "sufficient resources not to become a burden on the social assistance system of the UK". This may be expected to exclude most of those claiming or seeking to claim income support, jobseeker's allowance, or housing benefit. But it is suggested that it cannot exclude all claimants from elsewhere in the European Economic Area for child tax credit, given that the income text for child tax credit is such that it is payable to all but the highest earning parents responsible for children. Nor does it exclude those who do have direct rights under European law.

Persons temporarily absent from the United Kingdom

4.—(1) A person who is ordinarily resident in the United Kingdom and is temporarily absent from the United Kingdom shall be treated as being in the United Kingdom during the first— 2.424

   (a) 8 weeks of any period of absence; or

   (b) 12 weeks of any period of absence where that period of absence, or any extension to that period of absence, is in connection with—

      (i) the treatment of his illness or physical or mental disability;

     (ii) the treatment of his partner's illness or physical or mental disability;

     (iii) the death of a person who, immediately prior to the date of death, was his partner;

     (iv) the death, or the treatment of the illness or physical or mental disability, of a child or qualifying young person for whom either he or his partner is, or both of them are, responsible; or

     (v) the death, or the treatment of the illness or physical or mental disability, of his or his partner's relative.

(2) A person is temporarily absent from the United Kingdom if at the beginning of the period of absence his absence is unlikely to exceed 52 weeks.

DEFINITIONS

"ordinarily resident"—see reg.3.
"partner"—see reg.2.

GENERAL NOTE

2.425   This regulation deals with the practical application of the requirement that a claimant be "in" the United Kingdom as well as ordinarily resident here. It adopts the approach long used in social security law of ignoring temporary absence. See, for comparison, Income Support (General) Regulations 1987 (SI 1987/1967), reg.4. The current rule appears reasonably generous as it ignores the first eight weeks of "any" period of absence. Presumably, a claimant could make a visit back to the United Kingdom before the end of eight (or 12) weeks to re-establish presence before starting a second period of absence, and so on. On the facts, this would also avoid the 52-week rule in para.(2). On the wording, it would seem that the 52-week rule reapplies at the beginning of each period of absence.

See reg.6 below for a modification of this regulation as it applies to the partners of Crown servants employed overseas. One problem with these provisions in practice is that they allow an individual to be treated as remaining in the United Kingdom, but they do not allow the individual to be treated as continuing to work here. One result is that although the main elements of tax credits remain payable, an individual going overseas for a short period can retain WTC but lose the childcare credit. This parallels reg.24 of the Child Benefit (General) Regulations 2006, para.3.32 which makes similar provisions.

Crown servants posted overseas

2.426   **5.**—(1) A Crown servant posted overseas shall be treated as being in the United Kingdom.

(2) A Crown servant posted overseas is a person performing overseas the duties of any office or employment under the Crown in right of the United Kingdom—

    (a) who is, or was, immediately prior to his posting or his first of consecutive postings, ordinarily resident in the United Kingdom; or

    (b) who, immediately prior to his posting or his first of consecutive postings, was in the United Kingdom in connection with that posting.

GENERAL NOTE

2.427   This regulation and reg.6 protect the position of British public servants and their partners (and therefore also their children) when working outside the United Kingdom. Section 44 of the TCA 2002 removes any doubt about the application of the tax credits scheme to Crown employees. See further reg.30 of the Child Benefit (General) Regulations 2006, para.3.41 below, which makes similar provisions.

Partners of Crown servants posted overseas

6.—(1) The partner of a Crown servant posted overseas who is accompanying the Crown servant posted overseas shall be treated as being in the United Kingdom when he is either—

(a) in the country where the Crown servant is posted; or

(b) absent from that country in accordance with regulation 4 as modified by paragraphs (3) and (4).

(2) Regulation 4 applies to the partner of a Crown servant posted overseas with the modifications set out in paragraphs (3) and (4).

(3) Omit the words "ordinarily resident in the United Kingdom and is".

(4) In relation to a partner who is accompanying the Crown servant posted overseas the references to "United Kingdom" in the phrase "temporarily absent from the United Kingdom", in both places where it occurs, shall be construed as references to the country where the Crown servant is posted.

2.428

DEFINITIONS

"Crown servant posted overseas"—see reg.5.
"partner"—see reg.2.

Transitional provision—income support and income-based jobseeker's allowance

7.—A person is exempt from the requirement to be ordinarily resident in the United Kingdom (which is set out in regulation 3(1)) in respect of child tax credit on and for three years after the date on which the award of child tax credit is made where—

(a) the award of child tax credit would be made on or after 6th April 2004;

(b) immediately before the award of child tax credit is made, he is, or will be on the making of a claim, entitled to any of the amounts in relation to income support and income-based jobseeker's allowance which are described in section 1(3)(d) of the Act; and

(c) he is a person to which one or more of the following provisions applies—

(i) paragraph (b) or (c) in the definition of "person from abroad" in regulation 21(3) of the Income Support (General) Regulations 1987;

(ii) paragraph (b) or (c) in the definition of "person from abroad" in regulation 85(4) of the Jobseeker's Allowance Regulations 1996;

(iii) paragraph (b) or (c) in the definition of "person from abroad" in regulation 21(3) of the Income Support (General) (Northern Ireland) Regulations 1987;

(iv) paragraph (b) or (c) in the definition of "person from abroad" in regulation 85(4) of the Jobseeker's Allowance Regulations (Northern Ireland)1996.

2.429

GENERAL NOTE

This is a narrow three-year transitional provision for child tax credit only. It takes effect from or after April 6, 2004—the date when CTC was planned to replace the child additions to income support and jobseeker's allowance. It is limited to:

2.430

   (a) claimants receiving either income support or income-based jobseeker's allowance including child additions immediately before the rule comes into effect; but only if

   (b) they are claiming those benefits as refugees or following a grant of exceptional leave to enter or remain in the United Kingdom under the Immigration Acts.

It should be read with the Tax Credits (Immigration) Regulations 2003 (SI 2003/653).

Tax Credits (Official Error) Regulations 2003

(SI 2003/692)

The Commissioners of Inland Revenue, in exercise of the powers conferred upon them by sections 21 and 65(2), (3), (7) and (9) of the Tax Credits Act 2002 hereby make the following Regulations:

Arrangement of Regulations

Citation and commencement

2.432   **1.** These Regulations may be cited as the Tax Credits (Official Error) Regulations 2003 and shall come into force on 6th April 2003.

Interpretation

2.433   **2.**—(1) In these Regulations—

"the Board" means the Commissioners of Inland Revenue;

"official error" means an error relating to a tax credit made by—

   (a) an officer of the Board;

   (b) an officer of the Department for Work and Pensions;

   (c) an officer of the Department for Social Development in Northern Ireland; or

   (d) a person providing services to the Board or to an authority mentioned in paragraph (b) or (c) of this definition, in connection with a tax credit or credits,

to which the claimant, or any of the claimants, or any person acting for him, or any of them, did not materially contribute, excluding any error of law which is shown to have been an error by virtue of a subsequent decision by a "Social Security Commissioner or by a court;"

"Social Security Commissioner" has the meaning given by section 63(13);

"tax year" means a period beginning with 6th April in one year and ending with April 5 in the next.

(2) In these Regulations, references to a section are to that section of the Tax Credits Act 2002.

GENERAL NOTE

The double inverted commas at the end of the very last line of the definition of "official error" are a typographical error in the HMSO version of these regulations. The lack of a heading to reg.3 is also unfortunate. **2.434**

3.—(1) A decision under section 14(1), 15(1), 16(1), 18(1), (5), (6) or (9), 19(3) or 20(1) or (4) may be revised in favour of the person or persons to whom it relates if it is incorrect by reason of official error, subject to the following paragraphs. **2.435**

(2) In revising a decision, the officer or person in question need not consider any issue that is not raised by the application for revision by the claimant or claimants or, as the case may be, did not cause him to act on his own initiative.

(3) A decision mentioned in paragraph (1) may be revised at any time not later than five years after the end of the tax year to which the decision relates.

DEFINITIONS

"official error"—see reg.2(1).
"tax year"—see *ibid*.

GENERAL NOTE

These regulations, made under s.21 of the TCA 2002, provide for decisions under the various specified sections of the Act (see reg.3(1)) to be revised in favour of the claimant(s) if they are incorrect because of "official error". The definition of "official error" in reg.2(1) is identical in all material respects to that which applies in the social security scheme under the Social Security and Child Support (Decisions and Appeals) Regulations 1999 (SI 1999/991) (see reg.1(3) and the commentary in Vol. III of this series). However, whereas a social security decision may be revised on the basis of official error and arrears of benefit paid back to the date of the original claim (SSA 1998, s.9(3) and reg.3(5)(a) of the 1999 Regulations), a claim for tax credits is subject to a time limit of five years after the end of the tax year to which the decision relates (reg.3(3)). **2.436**

Tax Credits (Provision of Information) (Functions Relating to Health) Regulations 2003

(SI 2003/731) (AS AMENDED)

The Commissioners of Inland Revenue, in exercise of the powers conferred upon them by sections 65(2) and 67 of, and paragraph 9(2) of Schedule 5 to, the Tax Credits Act 2002, hereby make the following Regulations:

ARRANGEMENT OF REGULATIONS

1. Citation and commencement **2.437**
2. Interpretation
3. Prescribed functions relating to health

Citation and commencement

2.438 **1.** These Regulations may be cited as the Tax Credits (Provision of Information) (Functions Relating to Health) Regulations 2003 and shall come into force on 6th April 2003.

GENERAL NOTE

2.439 Section 59 of and Sch.5 to the TCA 2002 make provision for the use and disclosure of information relating to claims by and between HMRC and government departments. These regulations prescribe functions for the purposes of para.9 of Sch.5 to the 2002 Act, which enables information relating to tax credits, child benefit or guardian's allowance to be provided by HMRC to the Department of Health, the National Assembly for Wales, the Scottish Ministers, or the Department of Health, Social Services and Public Safety in Northern Ireland for the purposes of such functions relating to health as may be prescribed. These functions are set out in reg.3. Information may also be provided to persons providing services to, or exercising functions on behalf of, those Departments or persons.

These regulations are supplemented by the Tax Credits (Provision of Information) (Functions Relating to Health) (No.2) Regulations 2003 (SI 2003/1650).

Interpretation

2.440 **2.** In these Regulations—
"child tax credit" shall be construed in accordance with section 8 of the Tax Credits Act 2002;
[¹"couple" has the meaning given by section 3(5A) of the Act;]
"disability element" means the disability element of working tax credit as specified in section 11(3) of the Tax Credits Act 2002;
"family" means—
(a) in the case of a joint claim for a tax credit under the Tax Credits Act 2002, the [¹. . .] couple by whom the claim is made and any child or qualifying young person for whom at least one of them is responsible, in accordance with regulation 3 of the Child Tax Credit Regulations 2002;
(b) in the case of a single claim for a tax credit under the Tax Credits Act 2002, the claimant and any child or qualifying young person for whom he is responsible in accordance with regulation 3 of the Child Tax Credit Regulations 2002;
"qualifying family" means a family—
(a) that has a relevant income of £14,200 or less; and
(b) one member of which is receiving—
(i) working tax credit and child tax credit; or
(ii) working tax credit which includes a disability element; or
(iii) child tax credit, not being eligible for working tax credit;
"qualifying young person" has the meaning given by regulation 2(1), read with regulation 5(3) and (4), of the Child Tax Credit Regulations 2002;
"relevant income" has the same meaning as in section 7(3) of the Tax Credits Act 2002;
"working tax credit" shall be construed in accordance with section 10 of the Tax Credits Act 2002.

AMENDMENT

1. Civil Partnership Act 2004 (Tax Credits, etc.) (Consequential Amendments) Order 2005 (SI 2005/2919), art.9(2) (December 5, 2005).

Prescribed functions relating to health

3. The following functions are prescribed for the purposes of paragraph 9 of Schedule 5 to the Tax Credits Act 2002 (provision of information by the Board of Inland Revenue for health purposes)—   2.441

   (a) the issue by or on behalf of the Secretary of State, the National Assembly for Wales, the Scottish Ministers or the Department of Health, Social Services, and Public Safety in Northern Ireland of a certificate confirming that the family is a qualifying family;
   (b) verification by or on behalf of the Secretary of State, the National Assembly for Wales, the Scottish Ministers or that Department at any time that a family is a qualifying family at that time;
   (c) the issue on behalf of the Secretary of State or that Department of milk tokens and free vitamins to persons entitled to receive free of charge milk (including dried milk) or vitamins in accordance with the Welfare Food Regulations 1996 or the Welfare Food Regulations (Northern Ireland) 1988;
   (d) the making on behalf of the Secretary of State or that Department of payments to such persons in accordance with those Regulations;
   (e) the giving on behalf of the Secretary of State or that Department of information relating to milk tokens and related health matters to such persons in accordance with those Regulations.

DEFINITIONS

"family"—see reg.2.
"qualifying family"—see *ibid.*

The Tax Credits (Polygamous Marriages) Regulations 2003

(SI 2003/742) (AS AMENDED)

The Treasury, in exercise of the powers conferred upon them by sections 3(7), 7(8) and (9), 8, 10 to 12, 42, 43 and 65(1), (3), (7) and (9) of the Tax Credits Act 2002, and the Commissioners of Inland Revenue, in exercise of the powers conferred on them by sections 4(1), 6, 24 and 65(2), (3), (7) and (9) of that Act, and of all other powers enabling them in that behalf, hereby make the following Regulations:

ARRANGEMENT OF REGULATIONS

Regulations 2002
35–47. Amendments to the Tax Credits (Definition and Calculation of Income) Regulations 2002
39–47A. Amendments to the Tax Credits (Claims and Notifications) Regulations 2002
48–50. Amendments to the Tax Credits (Payment by the Board) Regulations 2002
51–52. Amendments to the Tax Credits (Residence) Regulations 2003
53–56. Amendments to the Tax Credits (Immigration) Regulations 2003

Introduction and General Note

2.443
These regulations provide alternative language to that of single claims and joint claims, and the associated definitions for single and joint claims, in cases where the claimant is a party to a polygamous marriage. Part I of the TCA 2002 and all relevant regulations are altered to give consistent effect to the policy that all the members of a polygamous marriage, or "unit" as it is called, must jointly claim for and be responsible for any tax credits payable to any of them. This is a different approach from that usually taken for social security benefits purposes, under which polygamous marriages are usually ignored for benefit purposes unless they are in fact monogamous. See the Social Security and Family Allowances (Polygamous Marriages) Regulations 1975 (SI 1975/561) in Vol.I of this work.

Section 43(1) of the TCA 2002 empowers regulations to apply Pt I of that Act to persons who are parties to a polygamous marriage. "Party to a polygamous marriage" is defined by s.43(2) to include any marriage entered into under a law which permits polygamy and under which any party to the marriage has more than one spouse, that is, more than one husband or wife. The drafters have chosen to adopt different language in these Regulations and the amendments made by these Regulations to the TCA 2002 and other regulations. Instead of "polygamous marriage", the term used throughout is "polygamous unit". The significance of this is discussed in reg.2 below.

The remaining regulations give effect to those modifications as necessary within the other regulations implementing the TCA 2002. Any necessary commentary is added to the relevant amended regulation.

Citation, commencement and eVect

2.444
1.—(1) These Regulations may be cited as the Tax Credits (Polygamous Marriages) Regulations 2003 and shall come into force on 6th April 2003, immediately after the coming into force of the Child Tax Credit (Amendment) Regulations 2003.

(2) Regulations 22 to 56 only have effect in relation to members of polygamous units (and in the case of regulations 35 to 38, former members of such units).

Interpretation

2.445
2.—In these Regulations—
"the Act" means the Tax Credits Act 2002;
"polygamous couple" means a man and a woman who are married under a law which permits polygamy where—
(a) they are not separated under a court order or in circumstances in which the separation is likely to be permanent; and
(b) either of them has an additional spouse;
"polygamous unit" means—
(a) a polygamous couple; and
(b) any person who is married to either member of the polygamous couple

and who is not separated from that member under a court order or in circumstances in which the separation is likely to be permanent.

GENERAL NOTE

Section 43(2) of the TCA 2002 provides that a person is a party to a polygamous   **2.446** marriage if:

(a) he or she is a party to a marriage entered into under a law which permits polygamy; and

(b) he or she has a spouse additional to any other party to the marriage.

The effect of this definition is to limit the scope of the operation of the modifications made under these Regulations to take account also of the definition of "married couple" in s.3(5) of the TCA 2002.

Modifications to Part I of the Act for members of polygamous units

3.—Regulations 4 to 21 prescribe modifications to Part I of the Act so far   **2.447** as it applies to members of polygamous units.

4. In section 3—

(a) in subsection (3)(a) after "United Kingdom", insert "(and neither of whom are members of a polygamous unit)";

(b) after subsection (3)(a) insert—

"(aa) jointly by the members of a polygamous unit all of whom are aged at least 16 and are in the United Kingdom, or";

(c) in subsection (3)(b) after "paragraphs (a)", insert "or (aa)";

(d) after subsection (4)(a), insert—

"(aa) in the case of a joint claim under subsection (3)(a), if a member of the married or unmarried couple becomes a member of a polygamous unit; and

(ab) in the case of a joint claim under subsection (3)(aa), if there is any change in the persons who comprise the polygamous unit, and";

(e) after subsection (6), insert—

"(6A) In this Part 'polygamous unit' has the meaning given by regulation 2 of the Tax Credits (Polygamous Marriages) Regulations 2003.";

(f) in subsection (8), in the definition of "joint claim", after "para.(a)" insert "or para.(aa)".

5. In section 4(1)(g)—

(a) for "member of a married couple or an unmarried couple", substitute "or more members of a polygamous unit";

(b) for "of the married couple or unmarried couple", substitute "or members".

6. In section 7(2), for "either" substitute "any";

7. In section 8(1), for "either or both" substitute "any or all".

8. In section 9(2)(b), for "either or both" substitute "any or all".

9. In section 10—

(a) in subsection (1), for "either or both" substitute "any or all";

(b) in subsection (3), for "either" wherever it appears substitute "any".

10. In section 11—

(a) in subsection (3), for "either or both" substitute "any or all";

(b) in subsection (6)(a), for "either of the persons or the two" substitute "any of the persons or all";

(c) in subsection (6)(b), for "married couple or unmarried couple" substitute "polygamous unit";

(d) omit subsection (6)(c);

(e) in both subsection (6)(d) and (e), for "either or both" substitute "any or all".

11. In both section 12(3) and (4)(a), for "either or both" substitute "any or all".

12. In section 14(2)(a), for "either or both" substitute "any or all".

13. In section 16(3)(a), for "either or both" substitute "any or all".

14. In section 17(10)(b)—

(a) for "member of a married couple or an unmarried couple", substitute "or more members of a polygamous unit";

(b) for "married couple or unmarried couple", substitute "or members".

15. In section 18(10), for "either or both" substitute "any or all".

16. In section 19—

(a) in subsection (2)(a), for "either or both" substitute "any or all";

(b) in subsection (4)(a), for "either" substitute "any" and for "both" substitute "more than one";

(c) in subsection (9), for "either" substitute "any".

17. In section 20(4)(b), for "either" (wherever it appears) substitute "any".

18. In section 24(2)—

(a) for "married couple or an unmarried couple", substitute "polygamous unit";

(b) for "whichever of them" substitute "one or more of those persons as".

19. In section 29(4), for "either or both" substitute "any or all".

20. In section 31(2)—

(a) after "another" insert "or others";

(b) for "unless subsection (3) applies" substitute "or each of them unless subsection (3) applies to the person in question".

21. In section 37(1), for "either or both" (in each place they appear) substitute "any or all".

Amendments to the Child Tax Credit Regulations 2002

2.448 **22.**—Amend the Child Tax Credit Regulations 2002 (for members of polygamous units only) as follows.

23. In regulation 2(1)—

(a) for the definition of "joint claim", substitute the following definition—

"'joint claim' means a claim under section 3(3)(aa) of the Act, as inserted by regulation 4(b) of the Tax Credits (Polygamous Marriages) Regulations 2003;";

(b) insert at the appropriate place the following definition—"'polygamous unit' has the meaning in the Tax Credits (Polygamous Marriages) Regulations 2003;".

24. In regulation 3(1), in rule 2.1., for "married couple or unmarried couple" in each place it appears substitute "polygamous unit".

25. In regulation 7—

(a) in paragraph (1)(b), for "married couple or unmarried couple" substitute "polygamous unit";

(b) in paragraph (2)(b)(ii), for "either or both" substitute "any or all".

Amendments to the Working Tax Credit (Entitlement and Maximum Rate) Regulations 2002

26. Amend the Working Tax Credit (Entitlement and Maximum Rate)   2.449
Regulations 2002 (for members of polygamous units only) as follows.

27. In regulation 2(1)—

(a) for the definition of "joint claim", substitute the following definition—" 'joint claim' means a claim under section 3(3)(aa) of the Act (as inserted by regulation 4(b) of the Tax Credits (Polygamous Marriages) Regulations 2003);";

(b) insert at the appropriate place the following definition—" 'polygamous unit' has the meaning in the Tax Credits (Polygamous Marriages) Regulations 2003;".

28. In regulation 3(3)—

(a) for "both members of the couple satisfy", substitute "more than one member of the polygamous unit satisfies"; and

(b) for "two such elements", substitute "one such element for each of them that satisfies those conditions".

29. In regulation 4(1), in paragraph (a)(ii) of the Second Condition, for "his partner" substitute "any other member of the polygamous unit".

30. In regulation 10(2)—

(a) in sub-paragraph (c), for "couple" substitute "members of the polygamous unit";

(b) in sub-paragraph (d), for "couple" substitute "unit".

31. In regulation 11—

(a) in paragraph (1), after "element" insert "(and an additional such element for each member of the polygamous unit exceeding two in number)";

(b) in paragraph (2)(c), for "neither of the claimants" substitute "no claimant";

(c) in paragraph (4), in the words preceding sub-paragraph (a), after "adult element" insert "for any claimant";

(d) in paragraph (4)(a), for "neither claimant" substitute "none of the claimants"; and

(e) in paragraph (4)(b), for "one claimant" substitute "the claimant in question".

32. In regulation 13—

(a) omit paragraph (1)(a);

(b) in paragraph (1)(b), for "married or unmarried couple where both" substitute "polygamous unit where at least two of them";

(c) in paragraph (1)(c), for the words preceding paragraph (i) substitute "is a member or are members of a polygamous unit where at least one member is engaged in qualifying remunerative work and at least one other".

(d) in paragraph (4), for "the other member of a couple" substitute "another member of the polygamous unit";

(e) in paragraph (5), for "the other member or his partner" substitute "him or another member of the polygamous unit".

33. In regulation 14—

(a) in paragraph (1), for "either or both" substitute "any or all";

(b) in paragraph (1B), for "either or both" substitute "any or all";

(c) in paragraph (5), for "a partner or by a partner" substitute "another member of the same polygamous unit or".

34. In regulation 20—
  (a) in paragraph (1), for "single claimant or to a couple" substitute "polygamous unit";
  (b) omit paragraph (1)(c)(i);
  (c) in paragraph (1)(c)(ii), for "a couple either or both" substitute "the members of a polygamous unit, any or all of whom";
  (d) in paragraph (1)(c)(iii), for "a couple" substitute "the members of a polygamous unit";
  (e) omit paragraph (1)(e);
  (f) omit paragraph (1)(f)(i);
  (g) in paragraph (1)(f)(ii), for "couple" substitute "polygamous unit".

Amendments to the Tax Credits (Definition and Calculation of Income) Regulations 2002

2.450   **35.** Amend the Tax Credits (Definition and Calculation of Income) Regulations 2002 (for members or former members of polygamous units only) as follows.
  36. In regulation 2 (interpretation)—
  (a) in paragraph (2), in the definition of "family" for "married or unmarried couple" substitute "members of the polygamous unit";
  (b) in paragraph (2), insert at the appropriate places the following definitions—
  "'joint claim' means a claim under section 3(3)(aa) of the Act, as inserted by regulation 4(b) of the Tax Credits (Polygamous Marriages) Regulations 2003; "polygamous unit" has the meaning in the Tax Credits (Polygamous Marriages) Regulations 2003;";
  (c) in paragraph (4)(a), for the words from "a claimant's spouse" to the end substitute "another member of the same polygamous unit";
  (d) in paragraph (4)(b), for the words from "claimant's former spouse" to the end substitute "person who was formerly a member with the claimant of the same polygamous unit".
  37. In regulation 3(7), (calculation of income of claimant)—
  (a) in sub-paragraph (b), for "either or both" substitute "any or all";
  (b) in sub-paragraph (c), for "either or both" substitute "any or all".
  38. In regulation 4(1) (employment income), in the words succeeding sub-para.(k), for "either" substitute "any".

Amendments to the Tax Credits (Claims and Notifications) Regulations 2002

2.451   **39.** Amend the Tax Credits (Claims and Notifications) Regulations 2002 (for members of polygamous units only) as follows.
  40. In regulation 2 (interpretation)—
  (a) for the definition of "joint claim" substitute the following definition—
  " 'joint claim', means a claim under section 3(3)(aa) of the Act, as inserted by regulation 4(b) of the Tax Credits (Polygamous Marriages) Regulations 2003;";
  (b) insert at the appropriate place the following definition—
  "'polygamous unit' has the meaning in the Tax Credits (Polygamous Marriages) Regulations 2003;".

41. In regulation 11(2), for "both" substitute "all of the".

42. In regulation 13—

(a) in paragraph (1), for the words from "one member" to the end substitute "one or more members of a polygamous unit is to be treated as also made by the other member or members of that unit";

(b) in paragraph (2)—

   (i) for "member of a married couple or an unmarried couple", substitute "or more members of a polygamous unit";

   (ii) for "both members of the couple", substitute "all the members of the unit".

43. In regulation 15—

(a) in paragraph (3) for the words from "only one" to the end, substitute "one or more members of a polygamous unit die, the other member or members of the unit may proceed with the claim in the name or names of the person or persons who have died, as well as in their own name or names";

(b) in paragraph (4), for "both" (in each place it appears) substitute "all of".

44. In regulation 16—

(a) in paragraph (1), for the words from "member of a" to the end, substitute "or more members of a polygamous unit die and the other member or members of the unit wish to make a joint claim for a tax credit";

(b) for paragraph (2), substitute—

"(2) The survivor or survivors may make and proceed with the claim in the name of the member or members who have died as well as in his or their own names.;"

(c) in paragraph (3)(a)—

   (i) for "married couple or unmarried couple", substitute "polygamous unit";

   (ii) add at the end "(or the earliest such date if more than one)".

45. In regulation 23(2), for "either member of the married couple or unmarried couple" substitute "any member of the polygamous unit".

46. In regulation 30(2), for "either" (in each place it appears) substitute "any".

47. In regulation 31(2)(a), for "either" substitute "any".

[¹**47A.** In regulation 34(3)—

(a) for "one of two joint claimants" substitute "any member of a polygamous unit"; and

(b) for "both" (in each place where it occurs) substitute "all".]

Amendments to the Tax Credits (Payment by the Board) Regulations 2002

48. Amend the Tax Credits (Payments by the Board) Regulations 2002 (for members of polygamous units only) as follows. 2.452

49. In regulation 2 (interpretation)—

(a) omit the definitions of "married couple" and "unmarried couple";

(b) insert at the appropriate place the following definition—

" 'polygamous unit' has the meaning in the Tax Credits (Polygamous Marriages) Regulations 2003;".

50. In regulation 3—

(a) in the heading, for "couple" substitute "polygamous unit";

(b) for paragraphs (2) to (6) substitute—

"(2) There shall be established, for each particular child or qualifying young person for whom any or all of the members of the polygamous unit is or are responsible—

(a) the member of that unit who is (for the time being) identified by all the members of the unit as the main carer for that child or qualifying young person; or

(b) in default of such a member, the member of that unit who appears to the Board to be the main carer for that child or qualifying young person.

(3) The individual element of child tax credit for any child or qualifying young person shall be paid to the main carer of that child or qualifying young person.

(4) The family element of child tax credit for any polygamous unit shall be divided (pro rata) by the number of children and qualifying young persons for whom any or all of the members of that unit is or are responsible, and the proportion so attributable to each such child or qualifying young person shall be paid to the main carer of that child or qualifying young person.

(5) Any childcare element of working tax credit shall be divided (pro rata) by the number of children referred to in paragraph (2) in respect of whom relevant childcare charges are paid, and the proportion so attributable to each such child shall be paid to the main carer of that child.

(6) In this regulation—

"child" has the meaning given by the Child Tax Credit Regulations 2002;

"qualifying young person" has the meaning given by those Regulations; and

"relevant childcare charges" has the meaning given by regulation 14(1) of the Working Tax Credit (Entitlement and Maximum Rate) Regulations 2002."

Amendments to the Tax Credits (Residence) Regulations 2003

2.453

51. Amend the Tax Credits (Residence) Regulations 2003 (for members of polygamous units only) as follows.

52. In regulation 2 (Interpretation)—

(a) in the definition of "partner", for the words from "married" to the end, substitute "polygamous unit, any other member of that unit";

(b) insert at the appropriate place the following definition—" 'polygamous unit' has the meaning in the Tax Credits (Polygamous Marriages) Regulations 2003;".

Amendments to the Tax Credits (Immigration) Regulations 2003

2.454

53. Amend the Tax Credits (Immigration) Regulations 2003 (for members of polygamous units only) as follows.

54. In regulation 2 (Interpretation)—

(a) for the definition of "joint claim", substitute the following definition—

"joint claim" means a claim under section 3(3)(aa) of the Act, as inserted by regulation 4(b) of the "Tax Credits (Polygamous Marriages) Regulations 2003";

(b) insert at the appropriate place the following definition—
"polygamous unit" has the meaning in the "Tax Credits (Polygamous Marriages) Regulations 2003;".

55. In regulation 3(2)—
(a) for the words from "married couple" to "and the other", substitute "polygamous unit is a person subject to immigration control and any other";
(b) in sub-paragraph (b), for "couple" substitute "unit".

56. In regulation 4(1) (modifications to the Tax Credits Act 2002), add at the end "(which, in the case of a claim by the members of a polygamous unit, are subject to the modifications made by regulations 4 to 21 of the Tax Credits (Polygamous Marriages) Regulations 2003)".

AMENDMENT

1. Tax Credits (Miscellaneous Amendments) Regulations 2004 (SI 2004/762), reg.19 (April 6, 2004).

Tax Credits (Provision of Information) (Functions Relating to Health) (No.2) Regulations 2003

(SI 2003/1650)

The Commissioners of Inland Revenue, in exercise of the powers conferred upon them by sections 65(2) and 67 of, and paragraph 9 of Schedule 5 to the Tax Credits Act 2002 hereby make the following Regulations:

ARRANGEMENT OF REGULATIONS

GENERAL NOTE

These regulations supplement the Tax Credits (Provision of Information)   2.456
(Functions Relating to Health) Regulations 2003 (SI 2003/731).

Citation, commencement and extent

1.—(1) These Regulations may be cited as the Tax Credits (Provision of   2.457
Information) (Functions Relating to Health) (No.2) Regulations 2003 and shall come into force on 17th July 2003.

(2) These Regulations do not extend to Northern Ireland.

Prescribed functions relating to health

2.—(1) The function specified in paragraph (2) is prescribed for the pur-   2.458
poses of paragraph 9 of Schedule 5 to the Tax Credits Act 2002 (provision of information by the Board of Inland Revenue for health purposes).

(2) The function specified in this paragraph is the conduct, by a person providing services to the Secretary of State and the Scottish Ministers, of a survey of the mental health of persons in Great Britain who are under the age of 17 on 1st September 2003.

(3) Nothing in these Regulations limits the operation of the Tax Credits (Provision of Information Relating to Health) Regulations 2003.

Tax Credits (Provision of Information) (Function Relating to Employment and Training) Regulations 2003

(SI 2003/2041)

The Commissioners of Inland Revenue, in exercise of the powers conferred upon them by sections 65(2) and 67 of, and paragraph 5(2) of Schedule 5 to, the Tax Credits Act 2002, hereby make the following Regulations:

ARRANGEMENT OF REGULATIONS

2.459
1. Citation, commencement and extent
2. Prescribed function relating to employment and training

GENERAL NOTE

2.460
These regulations, made under para.5 of Sch.5 to the Tax Credits Act 2002, enable information relating to tax credits, child benefit or guardian's allowance to be provided by HMRC to the Secretary of State for the purposes of the operation of the Employment Retention and Advancement Scheme established under s.2 of the Employment and Training Act 1973.

Citation, commencement and extent

2.461
1.—(1) These Regulations may be cited as the Tax Credits (Provision of Information) (Function Relating to Employment and Training) Regulations 2003 and shall come into force on 29th August 2003.

(2) These Regulations do not extend to Northern Ireland.

Prescribed function relating to employment and training

2.462
2.—(1) The function specified in paragraph (2) is prescribed for the purposes of paragraph 5 of Schedule 5 to the Tax Credits Act 2002 (provision of information by the Board of Inland Revenue for employment and training purposes).

(2) The function specified in this paragraph is the operation of the Employment Retention and Advancement Scheme, that is to say the scheme for assisting persons to improve their job retention or career advancement, established by the Secretary of State under section 2 of the Employment and Training Act 1973.

Tax Credits Act 2002 (Child Tax Credit) (Transitional Provisions) Order 2003

(SI 2003/2170)

The Treasury, in exercise of the powers conferred upon them by section 62(2) of the Tax Credits Act 2002, make the following Order:

ARRANGEMENT OF ARTICLES

1. Citation and commencement   2.463
2. Transitional provision

GENERAL NOTE

Section 1(3)(d) of the Tax Credits Act 2002 provides for the abolition of various   2.464
component elements of the applicable amount for the purposes of income support and income-based jobseeker's allowance (namely the child allowances, family premium, disabled child premium and enhanced disability premium for a child or young person). This Order makes transitional provision in connection with the introduction of child tax credit, but only for pensioners formerly in receipt of the minimum income guarantee in income support. The Order thus applies to persons who were in receipt of income support, were aged not less than 60 and were responsible for a child, throughout the period beginning on August 22, 2003 and ending on September 28, 2003 (art.2(1)). In such a case a person is deemed to have made a claim for child tax credit (a) on August 22, 2003 for the purpose of enabling a decision to be made by HMRC on the claim and (b) on the first day of the first benefit week beginning on or after September 29, 2003 for all other purposes, e.g. as regards payment (art.2(2)). This Order is thus associated with the introduction of state pension credit as from October 2003.

Citation and commencement

1. This Order may be cited as the Tax Credits Act 2002 (Child Tax   2.465
Credit) (Transitional Provisions) Order 2003 and shall come into force on 22nd August 2003.

Transitional provision

2.—(1) This article applies in the case of a person who throughout the   2.466
period beginning on 22nd August 2003 and ending on 28th September 2003 is—
   (a) in receipt of income support;
   (b) aged not less than 60; and
   (c) responsible for a child (within the meaning of regulation 3 of the Child Tax Credit Regulations 2002).
(2) Where this article applies to a person, he shall be treated as having made a claim for child tax credit in respect of the child for whom he is responsible as mentioned in paragraph (1)(c) of this article—
   (a) on 22nd August 2003 for the purposes of enabling the Board to make an initial decision on the claim; and

(b) on the first day of the first benefit week in relation to income support beginning on or after 29th September 2003 for all other purposes.

(3) In paragraph (2) "benefit week" has the same meaning—

(a) in relation to a person in Great Britain, as it bears in regulation 2(1) of the Income Support (General) Regulations 1987; and

(b) in relation to a person in Northern Ireland, as it bears in regulation 2(1) of the Income Support (General) Regulations (Northern Ireland) 1987.

Tax Credits (Provision of Information) (Evaluation and Statistical Studies) Regulations 2003

(SI 2003/3308)

The Commissioners of Inland Revenue, in exercise of the powers conferred upon them by sections 65(2) and 67 of, and paragraph 4(2) of Schedule 5 to, the Tax Credits Act 2002 make the following Regulations:

Citation, commencement and extent

2.467

1.—(1) These Regulations may be cited as the Tax Credits (Provision of Information) (Evaluation and Statistical Studies) Regulations 2003 and shall come into force on 9th January 2004.

(2) These Regulations do not extend to Northern Ireland.

Purposes for which information may be provided

2.468

2. The purposes of conducting evaluation and statistical studies in relation to—

(a) the education of children and young people under the age of 17; and

(b) the provision and use of child care,

are prescribed under paragraph 4 of Schedule 5 to the Tax Credits Act 2002 (provision of information by the Board of Inland Revenue for evaluation and statistical studies).

Here "child care" means any care provided for a child whether or not of a description prescribed for any purpose under the Act.

Tax Credits (Provision of Information) (Evaluation and Statistical Studies) (Northern Ireland) Regulations 2004

(SI 2004/1414)

The Commissioners of Inland Revenue, in exercise of the powers conferred upon them by sections 65(2) and 67 of, and paragraph 4(2) of Schedule 5 to, the Tax Credits Act 2002 make the following Regulations:

Citation, commencement and extent

2.469

1. These Regulations may be cited as the Tax Credits (Provision of Information) (Evaluation and Statistical Studies) (Northern Ireland)

Regulations 2004, shall come into force on 14th June 2004 and extend only to Northern Ireland.

Purposes for which information may be provided

2. The purposes of conducting evaluation and statistical studies about community relations, education and employment of persons in Northern Ireland under the age of 18, are prescribed under paragraph 4 of Schedule 5 to the Tax Credits Act 2002 (provision of information by the Board of Inland Revenue for evaluation and statistical studies).

2.470

Tax Credits (Provision of Information) (Functions Relating to Health) (Scotland) Regulations 2004

(SI 2004/1895 (S.6))

The Commissioners of Inland Revenue, in exercise of the powers conferred upon them by sections 65(2) and 67 of, and paragraph 9 of Schedule 5 to, the Tax Credits Act 2002, make the following Regulations:

Citation, commencement and extent

1. These Regulations may be cited as the Tax Credits (Provision of Information) (Functions Relating to Health) (Scotland) Regulations 2004, shall come into force on 11th August 2004 and extend only to Scotland.

2.471

Purpose for which information may be provided

2.—(1) The purpose of conducting surveys of the health of children and young people under the age of 17 and their families, by the Scottish Ministers or persons providing services to them, or exercising functions on behalf of them, is prescribed under paragraph 9 of Schedule 5 to the Tax Credits Act 2002 (provision of information by the Board of Inland Revenue for health purposes).

(2) Nothing in these Regulations affects the operation of the Tax Credits (Provision of Information) (Functions Relating to Health) Regulations 2003 or the Tax Credits (Provision of Information) (Functions Relating to Health) (No.2) Regulations 2003.

2.472

Tax Credits (Provision of Information) (Function Relating to Employment and Training) Regulations 2005

(SI 2005/66)

The Commissioners of Inland Revenue, in exercise of the powers conferred upon them by sections 65(2) and 67 of, and paragraph 5(2) of Schedule 5 to, the Tax Credits Act 2002, make the following Regulations:

Citation and commencement

2.473   **1.** These Regulations may be cited as the Tax Credits (Provision of Information) (Function Relating to Employment and Training) Regulations 2005 and shall come into force on 8th February 2005.

Prescribed function relating to employment and training

2.474   **2.**—(1) The function specified in paragraph (2) is prescribed for the purposes of paragraph 5 of Schedule 5 to the Tax Credits Act 2002 (provision of information by the Board of Inland Revenue for employment and training purposes).

(2) The function specified in this paragraph is evaluation of, and research in relation to, the employment and training programmes administered—

(a) in Great Britain, by the Department for Work and Pensions; or
(b) in Northern Ireland, the Department for Employment and Learning.

The Tax Credits (Child Care Providers) (Miscellaneous Revocation and Transitional Provisions) (England) Scheme 2007

(2007/2481)

ARRANGEMENT OF SCHEME

The Secretary of State for Children, Schools and Families, being the appropriate national authority under section 12(6) of the Tax Credits Act 2002, and in exercise of the powers conferred by sections 12(5), (7) and (8) and 65(9) of that Act, makes the following Scheme:

Citation, commencement and application

2.476   **1.**—(1) This Scheme may be cited as the Tax Credits (Child Care Providers) (Miscellaneous Revocation and Transitional Provisions) (England) Scheme 2007.

(2) This Scheme comes into force—

(a) to the extent that it revokes the 2005 Scheme and the provisions of the 1999 Regulations other than regulations 11(a) and (b) and 12, on 1st October 2007; and
(b) to the extent that it revokes regulations 11(a) and (b) and 12 of the 1999 Regulations, on 1st October 2009.

(3) This Scheme applies in relation to England only.

Interpretation

2.477   **2.** In this Scheme—

"the 1999 Regulations" means the Tax Credit (New Category of Child Care Provider) Regulations 1999;

"the 2005 Scheme" means the Tax Credits (Approval of Child Care Providers) Scheme 2005;

"the inspection provisions" means regulations 11(a) and (b) and 12 of the 1999 Regulations (access to information and records by officers of the Secretary of State and Her Majesty's Revenue and Customs); and

"the transitional period" means the period beginning on 1st October 2007 and ending on 1st October 2009.

Partial revocation of the 1999 Regulations and transitional provision

3.—(1) The 1999 Regulations are revoked to the extent that they make a Scheme for determining the description of persons by whom child care is provided, and whose charges fall to be taken into account in computing the child care element of working tax credit, subject to paragraph (3) of this article.

(2) Any accreditation of an organisation by the Secretary of State pursuant to the Scheme provided for by the 1999 Regulations, and any approval granted by such an organisation, shall lapse on 1st October 2007, except for the purposes of the inspection provisions.

(3) During the transitional period the inspection provisions shall have effect as if—

(a) the reference in regulation 11 to the period for which an organisation is accredited were a reference to the transitional period; and

(b) the reference in regulation 12 to the period during which a child care provider is approved by an accredited organisation were a reference to the transitional period.

2.478

DEFINITIONS

"the 1999 Regulations"—see art. 2.
"the inspection provisions"—see *ibid.*
"the transitional period"—see *ibid.*

Revocation of the 2005 Scheme and transitional provision

4.—(1) The 2005 Scheme is revoked, subject to paragraph (2).

(2) The provisions of the 2005 Scheme continue to have effect [¹ , with the modifications in paragraph (3),] in relation to—

(a) any approval granted to a child care provider under that Scheme which is valid immediately before 1st October 2007; and

(b) any application for approval under that Scheme which has not been granted before 1st October 2007.

[¹ (3) For the purposes of paragraph (2) the 2005 Scheme is amended as follows—

(a) in article 2 omit the definitions of "the Tribunal" and "the Tribunal Regulations";

(b) in article 11—
  (i) in paragraphs (1) and (5) for "Tribunal" substitute "First-tier Tribunal";
  (ii) for paragraph (2) substitute—

"(2) Tribunal Procedure Rules shall apply to an appeal under paragraph (1) as they apply to an appeal under section 79M of the 1989 Act."; and

(c) omit paragraphs (3) and (4).]

2.479

AMENDMENT

1. Tribunals, Courts and Enforcement Act 2007 (Transitional and Consequential Provisions) Order 2008 (SI 2008/2683), art.6 and Sch.1, para.329 (November 3, 2008).

DEFINITION

"the 2005 Scheme"—see art.2.

GENERAL NOTE

2.480
This Scheme partially revokes the Tax Credit (New Category of Child Care Provider) Regulations 1999 (SI 1999/3110) and revokes the Tax Credits (Approval of Child Care Providers) Scheme 2005 (SI 2005/93), with transitional provisions (see 2007 main Volume 4 paras 2.578–2.590 for the 2005 Scheme). The new Scheme applies in relation to England only. (For Wales, see the Tax Credits (Approval of Child Care Providers) (Wales) Scheme 2007 (SI 2007/226 (W.20), as amended by the Tax Credits (Approval of Child Care Providers) (Wales) (Amendment) Scheme 2007 SI 2008/2687 (W.237)). The revocations provided for by the Scheme mostly came into force on October 1, 2007.

Article 3(1) revokes the 1999 Regulations to the extent that they make a Scheme for determining the description of persons by whom child care is provided, and whose charges fall to be taken into account in computing the child care element of working tax credit. Article 3(2) makes various transitional provision concerning the access to information and records by HMRC officers and for allied matters.

Article 4(1) revokes the 2005 Scheme. Article 4(2) makes transitional provision to ensure that approvals granted under the 2005 Scheme that were valid immediately before October 1, 2007 continue to have effect until the end of their period of validity.

The 1999 Regulations and the 2005 Scheme have been revoked following the introduction of a system of voluntary registration for certain childcare providers under the Childcare Act 2006 (see the Childcare (Voluntary Registration) Regulations 2007 (SI 2007/730)).

PART III

CHILDREN AND GUARDIANS

The Child Benefit (General) Regulations 2006

(SI 2006/223)

ARRANGEMENT OF REGULATIONS

PART 1

INTRODUCTORY

PART 2

QUALIFYING YOUNG PERSONS: PRESCRIBED CONDITIONS

PART 3

PERSON RESPONSIBLE FOR CHILD OR QUALIFYING YOUNG PERSON

PART 4

EXCLUSIONS AND PRIORITY

PART 5

ENTITLEMENT AFTER DEATH OF CHILD OR QUALIFYING YOUNG PERSON

PART 6

RESIDENCE

PART 7

GENERAL AND SUPPLEMENTARY PROVISIONS

PART 1

INTRODUCTORY

Citation, commencement and interpretation

1.—(1) These Regulations may be cited as the Child Benefit (General) **3.2**
Regulations 2006 and shall come into force on 10th April 2006 immediately after the Child Benefit Act 2005.

(2) In these Regulations—

"the 1989 Act" means the Children Act 1989;

"the 1995 Act" means the Children (Scotland) Act 1995;

"the 1995 Order" means the Children (Northern Ireland) Order 1995;

"SSCBA" means the Social Security Contributions and Benefits Act 1992;

"SSCB(NI)A" means the Social Security Contributions and Benefits (Northern Ireland) Act 1992.

(3) In these Regulations—

"advanced education" means full-time education for the purposes of—

(a) a course in preparation for a degree, a diploma of higher education, a higher national diploma, or a teaching qualification; or

(b) any other course which is of a standard above ordinary national diploma, a national diploma or national certificate of Edexcel, a general certificate of education (advanced level), or Scottish national qualifications at higher or advanced higher level;

"an appropriate office" means—

(a) in relation to child benefit under SSCBA, the Child Benefit Office, Waterview Park, Washington, Tyne and Wear;

(b) in relation to child benefit under SSCB(NI)A, the Child Benefit Office (Northern Ireland), Windsor House, Bedford Street, Belfast;

(c) in relation to child benefit under either of those Acts—

(i) Comben House, Farriers Way, Netherton, Merseyside; or

(ii) any Enquiry Centre maintained by Her Majesty's Revenue and Customs;

"approved training" means arrangements made by the Government—

(a) in relation to England, known as "Entry to Employment" or [¹ "Programme Led Apprenticeships"];

(b) in relation to Wales, known as "Skillbuild", "Skillbuild+" or "Foundation Modern Apprenticeships";

(c) in relation to Scotland, known as "Get Ready for Work", "Skillseekers" or "Modern Apprenticeships"; or

(d) in relation to Northern Ireland, known as "Access" or [¹ "Training for Success: Professional and Technical Training"];

"arrangements made by the Government" means arrangements—

(a) in relation to England and Wales, made by the Secretary of State under section 2 of the Employment and Training Act 1973;

(b) in relation to Scotland, made—

(i) by the Scottish Ministers under section 2 of the Employment and Training Act 1973;

    (ii) by Scottish Enterprise or Highlands and Islands Enterprise under section 2 of the Enterprise and New Towns (Scotland) Act 1990; or

  (c) in relation to Northern Ireland, made by the Department for Employment and Learning under section 1 of the Employment and Training Act (Northern Ireland) 1950;

"the Careers Service" means—

  (a) in England and Wales, a person with whom the Secretary of State or the National Assembly of Wales has made arrangements under section 10(1) of the Employment and Training Act 1973, and a local education authority to whom the Secretary of State or the National Assembly of Wales has given a direction under section 10(2) of that Act;

  (b) in Scotland, a person with whom the Scottish Ministers have made arrangements under section 10(1) of the Employment and Training Act 1973 and any education authority to which a direction has been given by the Scottish Ministers under section 10(2) of that Act; and

  (c) in Northern Ireland, the Careers Service of the Department for Employment and Learning;

"child benefit" has the meaning given in section 141 of SSCBA and section 137 of SSCB(NI)A (child benefit);

"civil partnership" means two people of the same sex who are civil partners of each other and are neither—

  (a) separated under a court order; nor

  (b) separated in circumstances where the separation is likely to be permanent;

"cohabiting same sex couple" means two people of the same sex who are not civil partners of each other but are living together as if they were civil partners;

"the Commissioners" means the Commissioners for Her Majesty's Revenue and Customs (see section 1 of the Commissioners for Revenue and Customs Act 2005);

"the Connexions Service" means a person of any description with whom the Secretary of State has made an arrangement under section 114(2)(a) of the Learning and Skills Act 2000 and section 10(1) of the Employment and Training Act 1973, and any person to whom he has given a direction under section 114(2)(b) of the former, or section 10(2) of the latter, Act;

"couple" means two people—

  (a) of opposite sexes who are—

    (i) spouses residing together; or

    (ii) living together as if they were married to each other; or

  (b) of the same sex who are—

    (i) civil partners in a civil partnership; or

    (ii) a cohabiting same-sex couple;

"court" means any court in the United Kingdom, the Channel Islands or the Isle of Man;

"Crown servant posted overseas" has the meaning given in regulation 30(2);

"EEA State" means—

  (a) a member State, other than the United Kingdom, or

  (b) Norway, Iceland or Liechtenstein;

"full-time education"—

(a) is education undertaken in pursuit of a course, where the average time spent during term time in receiving tuition, engaging in practical work, or supervised study, or taking examinations exceeds 12 hours per week; and

(b) in calculating the time spent in pursuit of the course, no account shall be taken of time occupied by meal breaks or spent on unsupervised study.

"hospital or similar institution" means a place in which persons suffering from mental disorders are or may be received for care or treatment but does not include a prison, a young offenders institution, Secure Training Centre, Local Authority Secure Unit, Juvenile Justice Centre, Young Offenders Centre or, if outside the United Kingdom, any comparable place;

"mental disorder" shall be construed as including references to any mental disorder within the meaning of the Mental Health Acts;

"the Mental Health Acts" means the Mental Health Act 1983, the Mental Health (Care and Treatment) (Scotland) Act 2003 or the Mental Health (Northern Ireland) Order 1986;

"partner" means, in relation to a person who is a member of a couple, the other member of that couple;

"penalty" means, in the case of any court in Great Britain or Northern Ireland—

(a) in England and Wales, a sentence of a detention and training order under section 100 of the Powers of Criminal Courts (Sentencing) Act 2000 or detention in a young offenders institution, and a sentence of detention under sections 90, 91, 92 and 93 of the Powers of Criminal Courts (Sentencing) Act 2000;

(b) in Scotland, a sentence of detention under sections 44, 205, 207, 208 or 216(7) of the Criminal Procedure (Scotland) Act 1995;

(c) in Northern Ireland, a sentence of imprisonment, or detention under Article 39, 41, 45 or 54 of, or paragraph 6 of Schedule 2 to, the Criminal Justice (Children) (Northern Ireland) Order 1998, or an order for detention in a juvenile justice centre or young offenders centre,

and in the case of any court outside the United Kingdom, any comparable sentence or order;

"relevant education" means education which is—

(a) full-time; and

(b) not advanced education;

"remunerative work" means work of not less than 24 hours a week—

(a) in respect of which payment is made; or

(b) which is done in expectation of payment;

"the Taxes Act" means the Income and Corporation Taxes Act 1988;

"writing" includes writing produced by electronic communications used in accordance with regulation 39.

(4) For the purposes of these Regulations, two people of the same sex are to be regarded as living together as if they were civil partners if, but only if, they would be regarded as living together as husband and wife were they instead two people of the opposite sex.

1. Child Benefit (General) (Amendment) Regulations 2007, (SI 2007/2150), reg.3, (August 16, 2007).

PART 2

QUALIFYING YOUNG PERSONS: PRESCRIBED CONDITIONS

Introduction

3.3   **2.**—(1) Regulations 3 to 7 prescribe—
(a) the age which a person must not have attained, and
(b) the conditions which are to be satisfied,
for a person to be a qualifying young person.

(2) Where more than one of those regulations apply to a person, he is a qualifying young person until the last of them ceases to be satisfied.

(3) Regulations 3 to 7 are subject to the following qualifications.

(4) Regulation 8 prescribes an additional condition which must be satisfied for a person to be a qualifying young person in respect of a week.

(5) No-one who had attained the age of 19 before 10th April 2006 is a qualifying young person.

DEFINITIONS

"week": SSCBA 1992, s.147.
"qualifying young person": SSCBA 1992, s.142.

Education and training condition

3.4   **3.**—(1) This regulation applies in the case of a person who has not attained the age of 20.

(2) The condition is that the person—
(a) is undertaking a course of full-time education, which is not advanced education and which is not provided by virtue of his employment or any office held by him—
   (i) which is provided at a school or college; or
   (ii) which is provided elsewhere but is approved by the Commissioners;
(b) having undertaken such a course as is mentioned in paragraph (a) [¹ has been accepted or is enrolled to undertake a further such course.]; or
(c) is undertaking approved training that is not provided by means of a contract of employment.
[¹or
(d) having undertaken a course mentioned in paragraph (a) or approved training mentioned in paragraph (c), has been accepted or is enrolled to undertake such approved training]

(3) A person is not a qualifying young person by virtue of paragraph (2) (a)(ii) unless he was receiving the education referred to in that paragraph as a child.

(4) A person who is aged 19 is only a qualifying young person by virtue of paragraph (2)(a) or (2)(c) if he began the education or training (as the case may be) referred to in that sub-paragraph [¹ or was accepted or enrolled to undertake that education or training] before attaining that age.

AMENDMENT

1. Child Benefit (General) (Amendment) Regulations 2007, (SI 2007/2150), reg.4 (August 16, 2007).

DEFINITIONS

"approved training": see reg.1.
"full-time education": see reg.1.

GENERAL NOTE

Full-time education is defined in reg.1. That definition includes time spent in "supervised study". The difference between supervised and unsupervised study was considered in *R(F) 1/93* where it was held that supervision required close attention to the pupil by a teacher, but a different conclusion, and a much wider interpretation has been held by the Court of Appeal to apply (in the context of university education), in relation to a claim for Carer's Allowance (see *Flemming v Secretary of State for Work and Pensions, R(G) 2/02*). And see the cautious approach that has been adopted to this question by Judge Hester in *AD v SSWP* [2009] UKUT 46 (AAC).

3.5

Continuation of entitlement until 31st August: 16 year olds

4.—(1) This regulation applies in the case of a person who has not attained the age of 17 and who has left relevant education or training.

3.6

(2) The condition is that the 31st August next following the person's 16th birthday has not passed.

DEFINITION

"relevant education": see reg.1.

Extension period: 16 and 17 year olds

5.—(1) This regulation applies in the case of a person who has not attained the age of 18.

3.7

(2) The condition is that—
(a) the person has ceased to be in education or training;
(b) the person is registered for work, education or for training with a qualifying body;
(c) the person is not engaged in remunerative work;
(d) the extension period which applies in the case of that person has not expired;
(e) immediately before the extension period begins, the person who is responsible for him is entitled to child benefit in respect of him without regard to this regulation; and
(f) the person who is responsible for him has made a written request to the Commissioners, within three months of his ceasing education or training, for the payment of child benefit during the extension period.
(3) For the purposes of paragraph (2) the extension period—
(a) begins on the first day of the week after that in which the person ceased to be in education or training; and

(b) ends 20 weeks after it started.

(4) In this regulation "qualifying body" means—

(a) the Careers Service or Connexions Service;

(b) the Ministry of Defence;

(c) in Northern Ireland, the Department for Employment and Learning or an Education and Library Board established under Article 3 of the Education and Libraries (Northern Ireland) Order 1986; or

(d) for the purposes of applying Council Regulation (EEC) No. 1408/71, any corresponding body in another member State.

DEFINITION

"remunerative work": see reg.1.

Interruptions

3.8 **6.**—(1) This regulation applies in the case of a person who has not attained the age of 20.

(2) If, immediately before the commencement of an interruption specified in paragraph (3)(a) or (b), a person was a qualifying young person by virtue of any other provision of these Regulations, he is such a person throughout a period of interruption during which he satisfies the condition specified in that sub-paragraph.

(3) The periods of interruption are—

(a) one of up to six months (whether beginning before or after the person concerned became 16) but only to the extent to which, in the opinion of the Commissioners, that the interruption is reasonable; and

(b) one attributable to the illness or disability of mind or body of the person concerned for such period as is reasonable in the opinion of the Commissioners.

This is subject to the following qualification.

(4) Paragraph (3) does not apply to an interruption which is, or is likely to be, followed immediately by a period during which—

(a) provision is made for training of that person which is not approved training;

(b) he is receiving advanced education;

(c) he is receiving education by virtue of his employment or of any office held by him.

DEFINITION

"advanced education": see reg.1.

GENERAL NOTE

3.9 Note that the overall test under this regulation is whether the interruption in education is, in the eyes of HMRC reasonable. Such reasonable interruptions are then disregarded for up to six months, or, if the reason for interruption is illness or disability for a longer period that is accepted as reasonable by HMRC. This provision is clearly appropriate to bridge any gap caused by school holidays and interval caused by a change of schools. In *R(F) 3/60* a gap of five months was accepted because there was difficulty in finding a suitable school for the child who suffered from a mental disability.

Qualifying young person: terminal dates

7.—(1) This regulation applies in the case of a person who has not   3.10
attained the age of 20.

(2) The condition is that the period found in accordance with Cases 1
and 2 has not expired in his case.

Case 1

1.1 The period is from the date on which he ceases to receive relevant
education or approved training, up to and including—
(a) the week including the terminal date, or
(b) if he attains the age of 20 on or before that date, the week including
the last Monday before he attains that age.
1.2 For the purposes of this Case the "terminal date" means—
(a) the last day in February,
(b) the last day in May,
(c) the last day in August,
(d) the last day in November,
whichever first occurs after the date on which the person's relevant education or approved training ceased (but subject to paragraph 1.3 of this
Case).
1.3 In the case of a person in Scotland who—
(a) undertakes the Higher Certificate or Advanced Higher Certificate
immediately before ceasing relevant education, and
(b) ceases relevant education on a date earlier than he would have done
had he undertaken the comparable examination in England and
Wales,
the terminal date shall be reckoned by reference to the date on which the
cessation would have occurred had he undertaken the comparable examination.

Case 2

2.1. Where a person's name is entered as a candidate for any external
examination in connection with relevant education which he is receiving at
that time, so long as his name continues to be so entered before ceasing to
receive such education, the prescribed period is—
(a) from the later of—
(i) date when that person ceased to receive relevant education, or
(ii) the date on which he attained the age of 16,
(b) up to and including—
(i) whichever of the dates in paragraph 1.2 (as modified by paragraph 1.3 where appropriate) first occurs after the conclusion
of the examination (or the last of the examinations if the person
is entered for more than one), or
(ii) the expiry of the week which includes the last Monday before
his 20th birthday,
whichever is the earlier.
This paragraph is subject to the following qualification.

(3) Child benefit is not payable in respect of a qualifying young person by
virtue of this regulation for any week in which he is engaged in remunerative work.

DEFINITIONS

"approved training": see reg.1.
"relevant education": see reg.1.
"remunerative work": see reg.1.
"week": see SSCBA 1992, s.147.

GENERAL NOTE

3.11   Case 1 of this regulation extends entitlement to benefit in respect of a child who has left school until the beginning of the next term following. It is a corollary of the disentitlement to Income Support that applies to the same period. Case 2 similarly covers the period between the time a child leaves school and the time he sits external examinations for which he is entered. Note the extension continues only as long as he continues to be entered for an examination so that if he withdraws this route to qualification for child benefit ceases.

Child benefit not payable in respect of qualifying young person: other financial support

3.12   **8.**—(1) This regulation applies in the case of a person who has not attained the age of 20 years.

(2) The condition is that the person is not in receipt, in a week, of—

(a) income support,

(b) income-based jobseeker's allowance within the meaning of section 1(4) of the Jobseekers Act 1995 or Article 3(4) of the Jobseekers (Northern Ireland) Order 1995,

(c) incapacity benefit by virtue of being a person to whom section 30A(1)(b) of SSCBA or section 30A(1)(b) of SSCB(NI)A applies, [1. . .]

(d) tax credit under the Tax Credits Act 2002 [1 or]

[1 (e) employment and support allowance payable under Part 1 of the Welfare Reform Act 2007 [2 or Part 1 of the Welfare Reform Act (Northern Ireland) 2007].]

AMENDMENTS

1. Employment and Support Allowance (Consequential Provisions) (No.3) Regulations 2008 (SI 2008/1897), reg.24 (October 27, 2008).

2. Employment and Support Allowance (Consequential Provisions No.2) Regulations (Northern Ireland) 2008 (SI 2008/412), reg.11 (October 27, 2008).

PART 3

PERSON RESPONSIBLE FOR CHILD OR QUALIFYING YOUNG PERSON

Child or qualifying young person in residential accommodation in prescribed circumstances

3.13   **9.**—For the purposes of section 143(3)(c) of SSCBA and section 139(3)(c) of SSCB(NI)A (absence of child or qualifying young person in residential accommodation), the prescribed circumstances are that the residential accommodation has been provided solely—

(a) because of the disability of the child or qualifying young person, or

(b) because the child or qualifying young person's health would be likely to be significantly impaired, or further impaired, unless such accommodation were provided.

Days disregarded in determining whether child or qualifying young person living with someone

10.—(1) For the purpose of section 143(4) of SSCBA and section 139(4)   **3.14** of SSCB(NI)A (number of days that may be disregarded), the prescribed number of days is 84 consecutive days, calculated in accordance with paragraph (2).

(2) Two or more distinct relevant periods separated by one or more intervals each not exceeding 28 days are treated as a continuous period equal in duration to the total of such distinct periods and ending on the last day of the latter or last of such periods.

(3) In paragraph (2) "relevant periods" means periods to which—

(a) section 143(3)(b) of SSCBA or section 139(3)(b) of SSCB(NI)A (absence of a child or qualifying young person undergoing medical or other treatment) applies;

(b) section 143(3)(c) of SSCBA or section 139(3)(c) of SSCB(NI)A (absence of a child or qualifying young person in residential accommodation) applies.

Prescribed circumstances relating to contributions and expenditure in respect of child or qualifying young person

11.—(1) For the purposes of section 143(5)(a) of SSCBA and section   **3.15** 139(5)(a) of SSCB(NI)A (contributing to the cost of providing for a child or qualifying young person) the prescribed circumstances are that—

(a) two or more persons are contributing to the cost of providing for the same child or qualifying young person;

(b) the aggregate weekly amount of their contributions equals or exceeds, but the weekly amount of each of their individual contributions is less than, the weekly rate of child benefit which would be payable in respect of that child or qualifying young person had the aggregate weekly amount of their contributions been contributed by one only of them; and

(c) they by agreement nominate in writing or, in default of such agreement, the Commissioners in their discretion determine, that the aggregate weekly amount of their contributions is to be treated as having been made by the person so nominated or determined.

This paragraph is subject to paragraph (3).

(2) The contribution subject to the nomination or determination made under paragraph (1) shall be treated as made by the person nominated or determined.

(3) Where pursuant to a nomination or determination made under paragraph (1) a person is awarded child benefit, the nomination or determination ceases to have effect in the week following that in which child benefit is awarded to that person (and accordingly thereafter the person shall be required to contribute to the maintenance of the child or qualifying young person at a rate which equals or exceeds the rate of child benefit payable in respect of that child or qualifying young person).

(4) Where spouses or civil partners are residing together a contribution made or expenditure incurred by one of them in respect of a child or qualifying young person shall if they agree, or in default of such agreement if the Commissioners in their discretion so determine, be treated as made or incurred by the other.

DEFINITIONS

"child or qualifying young person": see SSCBA 1992, s.142.
"The Commissioners": see reg.1.
"week": see SSCBA 1992, s.147.
"writing": see reg.1.

PART 4

EXCLUSIONS AND PRIORITY

Child benefit not payable: qualifying young person living with another as member of couple

3.16   **12.**—(1) Child benefit is not payable to any person ("the claimant") in respect of a qualifying young person for any week in which the qualifying young person is living with another—
  (a) as if they were spouses, or
  (b) as a member of a cohabiting same-sex couple,
unless paragraph (2) applies.
The person with whom the qualifying young person is living is referred to in paragraph (2) as "the cohabitee".
  (2) This paragraph applies if—
  (a) the cohabitee is receiving relevant education or approved training; and
  (b) the claimant is not the cohabitee.

DEFINITIONS

"approved training": see reg.1.
"cohabiting same-sex couple": see reg.1.
"relevant education": see reg.1.

GENERAL NOTE

3.17   The circumstances in which a couple are to regarded as living together are defined, in part, in reg.1(4).

Qualifying young person in a relevant relationship

3.18   **13.**—(1) A person ("the claimant") shall be entitled to child benefit in respect of a qualifying young person in a relevant relationship by virtue of paragraph 3 of Schedule 9 to SSCBA or paragraph 3 of Schedule 9 to SSCB(NI)A (entitlement: children or qualifying young persons who are married or civil partners) only if—
  (a) the claimant is not the spouse or civil partner of that qualifying young person; and

(b) the qualifying young person is not residing with his spouse or civil partner, or, if he is, the spouse or civil partner is receiving relevant education or approved training.

(2) In paragraph (1) "relevant relationship" means a marriage or a civil partnership.

DEFINITIONS

"approved training": see reg.1.
"relevant education": see reg.1.

Election under Schedule 10 to SSCBA and Schedule 10 to SSCB(NI A

14.—(1) An election under Schedule 10 to SSCBA and Schedule 10 to SSCB(NI)A (any election under that Schedule to be made in the prescribed manner) shall be made by giving notice in writing to the Commissioners at an appropriate office on a form approved by the Commissioners [¹ or by telephone to an officer of Revenue and Customs at an appropriate office] or in such other manner being in writing as the Commissioners may accept as sufficient in the circumstances of any particular case or class of cases.

(2) An election is not effective to confer entitlement to child benefit in respect of a child or qualifying young person for any week earlier than the week following that in which it is made if the earlier week is one in respect of which child benefit has been paid in respect of that child or qualifying young person and has not been required to be repaid or voluntarily repaid or recovered.

(3) An election may be superseded by a subsequent election made in accordance with this regulation.

AMENDMENT

1. Child Benefit (General) (Amendment) Regulations 2007, (SI 2007/2150), reg.5 (August 16, 2007).

DEFINITIONS

"child or qualifying young person": see SSCBA 1992, s.142.
"The Commissioners": see reg.1.
"week": see SSCBA 1992, s.147.
"writing": see reg.1.

Modification of priority between persons entitled to child benefit

15.—(1) If a person entitled to child benefit in respect of a child or qualifying young person in priority to another person gives the Commissioners notice in writing at an appropriate office [¹ or gives an officer of the Inland Revenue and Customs notice by telephone at such an office] that he does not wish to have such priority, the provisions of Schedule 10 to SSCBA and Schedule 10 to SSCB(NI)A (priority between persons entitled) have effect with the modification that that person does not have such priority.

(2) A notice under paragraph (1)—

(a) is not effective in relation to any week, before the date on which the election becomes effective, for which child benefit in respect of that child or qualifying young person is paid to the person who made the election or to another person on his behalf; and

3.19

3.20

(b) ceases to have effect if the person who gave it makes a further claim to child benefit in respect of that child or qualifying young person.

AMENDMENT

1. Child Benefit (General) (Amendment) Regulations 2007, (SI 2007/2150), reg.6 (August 16, 2007).

DEFINITIONS

"child or qualifying young person": see SSCBA 1992, s.142.
"The Commissioners": see reg.1.
"week": see SSCBA 1992, s.147.
"writing": see reg.1.

Child or qualifying young persons in detention, care etc.

3.21   **16.**—(1) Paragraph 1 of Schedule 9 to SSCBA and paragraph 1 of Schedule 9 to SSCB(NI)A do not apply to disentitle a person to child benefit in respect of a child or qualifying young person for any week—

(a) unless that week is the 9th or a subsequent week in a series of consecutive weeks in which either of those paragraphs has applied to that child or qualifying young person; or

(b) notwithstanding paragraph (a), if—

(i) that week is one in which falls the first day in a period of seven consecutive days in which the child or qualifying young person lives with that person for at least a part of the first day and throughout the following six days;

(ii) that week is one in which falls the first day in a period of seven consecutive days throughout which the child or qualifying young person lives with that person, being a period of seven consecutive days which immediately follows either a similar period of seven consecutive days or the period of seven consecutive days referred to in head (i) above;

(iii) that week is one in which falls the day, or the first day in a period of less than seven consecutive days, throughout which the child or qualifying young person lives with that person, being a day or days which immediately follow the period of seven consecutive days referred to in head (i) above or a period of seven consecutive days referred to in head (ii), or

(iv) as at that week that person establishes that he is a person with whom the child or qualifying young person ordinarily lives throughout at least one day in each week.

This paragraph is subject to the following qualifications.

(2) For the purposes of paragraph (1), a person shall not be regarded as having a child or qualifying young person living with him throughout any day or week unless he actually has that child or qualifying young person living with him throughout that day or week.

(3) Paragraph (1) does not apply for any day in any week to a person ("the carer") with whom a child or qualifying young person—

(a) is placed by a local authority in Great Britain in the carer's home in accordance with the provisions of—

(i) the Arrangements for Placements of Children (General) Regulations 1991,

      (ii) the Arrangements to Look After Children (Scotland) Regulations 1996,

      (iii) the Foster Placement (Children) Regulations 1991, or

      (iv) the Fostering of Children (Scotland) Regulations 1996,

and that authority is making a payment, in respect of either the child or qualifying young person's accommodation or maintenance or both, under section 23 of the 1989 Act or under section 26 of the 1995 Act to the carer;

    (b) is placed by an authority in Northern Ireland, in the carer's home in accordance with the provisions of the Foster Placement (Children) Regulations (Northern Ireland) 1996 where the authority has a duty to provide accommodation and maintenance for the child under the Arrangements for Placement of Children (General) Regulations (Northern Ireland) 1996.

(4) Paragraph (1) does not apply in respect of any child or qualifying young person who—

    (a) is being looked after by a local authority in Great Britain or by an authority in Northern Ireland, and

    (b) has been placed for adoption by that authority in the home of a person proposing to adopt him,

provided that the local authority or authority is making a payment in respect of either the child or qualifying young person's accommodation or maintenance or both, under section 23 of the 1989 Act, under section 26 of the 1995 Act or under Article 27 of the 1995 Order.

(5) For the purposes of paragraph (4), placing for adoption means placing for adoption in accordance with—

    (a) the Adoption Agencies Regulations 1983,

    (b) the Adoption Agencies (Scotland) Regulations 1984, or

    (c) the Adoption Agencies Regulations (Northern Ireland) 1989.

DEFINITIONS

    "child or qualifying young person": see SSCBA 1992, s.142.
    "week": see reg.19.

GENERAL NOTE

    Schedule 9 para.(1) of the Act provides that no claim can be made in respect of a child who is in prison, detention, legal custody or in certain circumstances in local authority care. But this regulation relieves from that disqualification to some extent. Disqualification does not apply to the first eight weeks of the detention etc. nor does it apply if the child actually lives with the claimant (as distinct from being maintained by the claimant) and does so for the whole week and, in effect, part weeks that commence or end a succession of whole weeks. Alternatively the claimant can retain benefit if the child ordinarily lives with him throughout at least one day each week. This means that the child must sleep at home two nights in the week. The relief outlined above does not apply if the child is placed by a local authority in a private home, is fostered, or is placed for adoption.

Child or qualifying young person undergoing imprisonment or detention in legal custody

17.—(1) For the purposes of paragraph 1(a) of Schedule 9 to SSCBA and paragraph 1(1)(a) of Schedule 9 to SSCB(NI)A, a child or qualifying

3.22

3.23

young person is not regarded as undergoing imprisonment or detention in legal custody in any week unless—

    (a) in connection with a charge brought or intended to be brought against him in criminal proceedings at the conclusion of those proceedings, or

    (b) in the case of default of payment of a sum adjudged to be paid on conviction, in respect of such default,

a court imposes a penalty upon him.

(2) Subject to paragraph (3), paragraph 1(a) of Schedule 9 to SSCBA and paragraph 1(1)(a) of Schedule 9 to SSCB(NI)A do not apply to a child or qualifying young person in respect of any week in which that child or qualifying young person is liable to be detained in a hospital or similar institution in Great Britain or Northern Ireland as a person suffering from a mental disorder.

(3) Subject to paragraph (5), paragraph (2) does not apply where subsequent to the imposition of a penalty, the child or qualifying young person was removed to the hospital or similar institution while still liable to be detained as a result of that penalty and, in the case of a person who is liable to be detained in the hospital or similar institution by virtue of any provisions of the Mental Health Acts, a direction restricting his discharge has been given under any of those Acts and is still in force.

(4) In paragraph (3) a person who is liable to be detained by virtue of any provision of the Mental Health Acts shall be treated as if a direction restricting his discharge had been given under those Acts if he is to be so treated for the purposes of any of them.

(5) Where a certificate given by or on behalf of the Secretary of State shows the earliest date on which the child or qualifying young person would have been expected to be discharged from detention pursuant to the penalty if he had not been transferred to a hospital or similar institution, paragraph (3) shall not apply from the day following that date.

DEFINITIONS

    "child or qualifying young person": see SSCBA 1992, s.142.
    "Court": see reg.1.
    "hospital or similar institution": see reg.1.
    "mental disorder": see reg.1.
    "the Mental Health Acts": see reg.1.
    "penalty": see reg.1.
    "week": see reg.19.

GENERAL NOTE

3.24   This regulation provides that the disqualification from benefit in respect of a child who is in prison, detention in legal custody applies only if the child is sentenced to be detained.

This means that if benefit has been suspended during a period that the child is in custody on remand or awaiting sentence it may become payable if the child is not sentenced to a period of detention.

The disqualification does not apply if the child is detained as a result of a mental disorder, unless the child has been transferred to a hospital or similar institution after being sentenced to a period of detention, in which case, the disqualification continues only so long as the order for detention would have continued.

Child or qualifying young person in care

18.—For the purposes of paragraph 1(c) of Schedule 9 to SSCBA and paragraph 1(c) of Schedule 9 to SSCB(NI)A (child or qualifying young person in care in such circumstances as may be prescribed), the prescribed circumstances are that—

    (a) the child or qualifying young person is provided with, or placed in, accommodation under Part 3 of the 1989 Act, under Part 2 of the 1995 Act or under Part 4 of the 1995 Order and the cost of that child or qualifying young person's accommodation or maintenance is borne wholly or partly out of local authority funds, authority funds or any other public funds, and

    (b) the child or qualifying young person is not in residential accommodation in the circumstances prescribed in regulation 9.

3.25

DEFINITIONS

    "child or qualifying young person": see SSCBA 1992, s.142.
    "the 1989 Act": see reg.1.
    "the 1995 Act": see reg.1.
    "the 1995 Order": see reg.1.

Interpretation of facts existing in a week

19.—Where paragraph 1 of Schedule 9 to SSCBA or paragraph 1 of Schedule 9 to SSCB(NI)A applies, section 147(2) of SSCBA and section 143(2) of SSCB(NI)A (references to any condition being satisfied or any facts existing in a week to be construed as references to the condition being satisfied or the facts existing at the beginning of that week) has effect as if the words "at the beginning of that week" were substituted by "throughout any day in that week".

3.26

PART 5

ENTITLEMENT AFTER DEATH OF CHILD OR QUALIFYING YOUNG PERSON

Entitlement after death of child or qualifying young person

20.—The prescribed period for the purposes of section 145A of SSCBA and section 141A of SSCB(NI)A (entitlement after death of child or qualifying young person) is—

    (a) in the case of a child, eight weeks, and

    (b) in the case of a qualifying young person the shorter of—

        (i) the period of eight weeks; and

        (ii) the period commencing the week in which his death occurred and finishing on the Monday in the week following the week in which the qualifying young person would have attained the age of 20.

3.27

PART 6

RESIDENCE

Circumstances in which a child or qualifying young person treated as being in Great Britain

3.28   **21.**—(1) For the purposes of section 146(1) of SSCBA, a child or qualifying young person who is temporarily absent from Great Britain shall be treated as being in Great Britain during—

(a) the first 12 weeks of any period of absence;

(b) any period during which that person is absent by reason only of—

(i) his receiving full-time education by attendance at a [1 school or college] in an EEA State or in Switzerland; or

(ii) his being engaged in an educational exchange or visit made with the written approval of the [1 school or college] which he normally attends;

(c) any period as is determined by the Commissioners during which the child or qualifying young person is absent for the specific purpose of being treated for an illness or physical or mental disability which commenced before his absence began; or

(d) any period when he is in Northern Ireland.

(2) For the purposes of section 146(1) of SSCBA, where a child is born while his mother is absent from Great Britain in accordance with regulation 24, he shall be treated as being in Great Britain during such period of absence after his birth as is within 12 weeks of the date on which his mother became absent from Great Britain.

AMENDMENT

1. Child Benefit (General) (Amendment) Regulations 2007, (SI 2007/2150), reg.7 (August 16, 2007).

DEFINITIONS

"child or qualifying young person": see SSCBA 1992, s.142.
"The Commissioners": see reg.1.
"EEA State": see reg.1.
"full time education": see reg.1.

Application of regulation 24 where the person is in Northern Ireland

3.29   **22.**—If a person who is in Northern Ireland is treated as being in Great Britain in accordance with regulation 24, he is treated as not being in Northern Ireland for the purposes of section 142 of SSCB(NI)A.

Circumstances in which person treated as not being in Great Britain

3.30   **23.**—(1) A person shall be treated as not being in Great Britain for the purposes of section 146(2) of SSCBA if he is not ordinarily resident in the United Kingdom.

(2) Paragraph (1) does not apply to a Crown servant posted overseas or his partner.

(3) A person who is in Great Britain as a result of his deportation, expulsion or other removal by compulsion of law from another country to Great Britain shall be treated as being ordinarily resident in the United Kingdom.

(4) A person shall be treated as not being in Great Britain for the purposes of section 146(2) of SSCBA where he [¹ makes a claim for child benefit on or after 1st May 2004 and] does not have a right to reside in the United Kingdom.

AMENDMENT

1. Child Benefit (General) (Amendment) Regulations 2007, (SI 2007/2150), reg.8 (August 16, 2007).

DEFINITIONS

"Crown servant posted overseas": see regs.1 and 30.
"partner": see regs.1 and 31.

GENERAL NOTE

Paragraph (1) of s.146 requires that both the claimant and the child in respect of whom the claim is made should be present in the UK. This regulation extends the concept of presence into that of being "ordinarily resident". This concept is considered in the note to reg.4 of the Persons Abroad Regulations in Vol. I of this work. But in brief, it requires that a person has made this country his place of abode as a voluntary and settled purpose in his life. Thus mere presence in the country is not enough. It must be legal presence, and at least for the time being, it should be his home. On cases involving EU nationals and the potential application of reg. 1408/71, see *JR v HMRC* [2009] UKUT 18 (AAC), under appeal to the Court of Appeal as *HMRC v Ruas*.

Para 2: disapplies this requirement in relation to a Crown servant who is posted overseas, his partner, and his child. These concepts are dealt with further in regulations 30, 31 and 32.

Para 3: affirms that a person who is in this country only because he has been deported from another country is, nevertheless, to be regarded as ordinarily resident here.

Persons temporarily absent from Great Britain

24.—(1) A person who is ordinarily resident in the United Kingdom and is temporarily absent from Great Britain shall be treated as being in Great Britain during the first—
  (a) 8 weeks of any period of absence; or
  (b) 12 weeks of any period of absence where that period of absence, or any extension to that period of absence, is in connection with—
    (i) the treatment of his illness or physical or mental disability;
    (ii) the treatment of his partner's illness or physical or mental disability;
    (iii) the death of a person who, immediately prior to the date of death, was his partner;
    (iv) the death, or the treatment of the illness or physical or mental disability, of a child or qualifying young person for whom either he or his partner is, or both of them are, responsible; or
    (v) the death, or the treatment of the illness or physical or mental disability, of his or his partner's relative.

3.31

3.32

Here "relative" means brother, sister, forebear or lineal descendant.

(2) A person is temporarily absent from Great Britain if at the beginning of the period of absence his absence is unlikely to exceed 52 weeks.

DEFINITIONS

"child or qualifying young person": see SSCBA 1992, s.142.
"Partner": see reg.1.

GENERAL NOTE

3.33   A person may remain ordinarily resident and so for the purposes of s.146 "present" even though he is temporarily absent from the country. The concept of "temporary" absence is considered in the notes to reg.2 of the Persons Abroad Regulations in Vol. I of this work. This regulation limits temporary absence to an absence which at its outset must be unlikely to exceed 52 weeks, and then provides that the absence is, in any case, only waived for a period of eight weeks, or, if the reason for absence (or extended absence) is illness or death of one of the parties then a maximum of 12 weeks.

Circumstances in which a child or qualifying young person treated as being in Northern Ireland

3.34   **25.**—(1) For the purposes of section 142(1) of SSCB(NI)A a child or qualifying young person who is temporarily absent from Northern Ireland shall be treated as being in Northern Ireland during—

(a) the first 12 weeks of any period of absence;

(b) any period during which the child or qualifying young person is absent by reason only of—

   (i) his receiving full-time education by attendance at a [1 school or college] in an EEA State or in Switzerland; or

   (ii) his being engaged in an educational exchange or visit made with the written approval of the [1 school or college] which he normally attends;

(c) any period as is determined by the Commissioners during which the child or qualifying young person is absent for the specific purpose of being treated for an illness or physical or mental disability which commenced before his absence began; or

(d) any period when he is in Great Britain.

(2) For the purposes of section 142(1) of SSCB(NI)A, where a child is born while his mother is absent from Northern Ireland in accordance with regulation 28, he shall be treated as being in Northern Ireland during such period of absence after his birth as is within 12 weeks of the date on which his mother became absent from Northern Ireland.

AMENDMENT

1. Child Benefit (General) (Amendment) Regulations 2007, (SI 2007/2150), reg.9 (August 16, 2007).

DEFINITIONS

"child or qualifying young person": see SSCBA 1992, s.142.
"The Commissioners": see reg.1.

"EEA State": see reg.1.
"full time education": see reg.1.

Application of regulation 28 where person in Great Britain

26.—Where a person who is in Great Britain is treated as being in   3.35
Northern Ireland in accordance with regulation 28, he is treated as not
being in Great Britain for the purposes of section 146 of SSCBA.

Circumstances in which person treated as not being in Northern Ireland

27.—(1) A person shall be treated as not being in Northern Ireland for   3.36
the purposes of section 142(2) of SSCB(NI)A if he is not ordinarily resident in the United Kingdom.

(2) A person who is in Northern Ireland as a result of his deportation,
expulsion or other removal by compulsion of law from another country to
Northern Ireland shall be treated as being ordinarily resident in the United
Kingdom.

(3) A person shall be treated as not being in Northern Ireland for the
purposes of section 142(2) of SSCB(NI)A where he does not have a right
to reside in the United Kingdom.

GENERAL NOTE

Regulation 10 of the Child Benefit (General) (Amendment) Regulations 2007,   3.37
(SI 2007/2150) appears to be intended to make the same amendment to this regulation as is made by reg.8 of those regulations to reg.23. The reference in reg.10 to
para.(4) appears to be a mistake for para.(3).

Persons temporarily absent from Northern Ireland

28.—(1) A person who is ordinarily resident in the United Kingdom and   3.38
is temporarily absent from Northern Ireland shall be treated as being in
Northern Ireland during the first—
  (a) 8 weeks of any period of absence; or
  (b) 12 weeks of any period of absence where that period of absence, or
      any extension to that period of absence, is in connection with—
      (i)   the treatment of his illness or physical or mental disability;
      (ii) the treatment of his partner's illness or physical or mental dis-
            ability;
      (iii) the death of a person who, immediately prior to the date of
            death, was his partner;
      (iv) the death, or the treatment of the illness or physical or mental
            disability, of a child for whom either he or his partner is, or both
            of them are, responsible; or
      (v)   the death, or the treatment of the illness or physical or mental
            disability, of his or his partner's relative.
Here "relative" has the same meaning as in regulation 24.

(2) A person is temporarily absent from Northern Ireland if, at the beginning of the period of absence, his absence is unlikely to exceed 52 weeks.

DEFINITION

"partner": see reg.1.

583

Overlap of entitlement to child benefit under both the legislation of Northern Ireland and Great Britain

3.39   **29.**—(1) Where by virtue of these Regulations two or more persons would be entitled to child benefit in respect of the same child or qualifying young person for the same week under both the legislation of Northern Ireland and Great Britain, one of them only shall be so entitled.

(2) Where the child is in Great Britain (except where regulation 25(1)(d) applies) or is treated as being in Great Britain, the question of which of the persons is entitled shall be determined in accordance with the legislation applying to Great Britain.

(3) Where the child is in Northern Ireland (except where regulation 21(1)(d) applies) or is treated as being in Northern Ireland, the question of which of the persons is entitled shall be determined in accordance with the legislation applying to Northern Ireland.

DEFINITIONS

"child or qualifying young person": see SSCBA 1992, s.142.
"week": see SSCBA 1992, s.147.

Crown servants posted overseas

3.40   **30.**—(1) For the purposes of section [² 146 (2)] of the Social Security and Contributions and Benefits Act, a Crown servant posted overseas shall be treated as being in Great Britain.

(2) A Crown servant posted overseas is a person performing overseas (but not in Northern Ireland) the duties of any office or employment under the Crown in right of the United Kingdom—

(a) who is, or was, immediately prior to his posting or his first of consecutive postings, ordinarily resident in the United Kingdom; or

(b) who, immediately prior to his posting or his first of consecutive postings, was in the United Kingdom in connection with that posting.

AMENDMENT

1. Child Benefit (General) (Amendment) Regulations 2007, (SI 2007/2150), reg.11 (August 16, 2007).

GENERAL NOTE

3.41   In *CF 1968/2007* Commissioner Williams held that the expression "Crown servant posted overseas" should include a consular correspondent who was appointed subsequently as an honorary consul of the UK. At all times, he said, the claimant was fulfilling functions defined in the Vienna Convention on Consular Relations. (Adopted in the UK by the Consular Relations Act 1968.) In doing so he was performing the duties of an officer under the Crown required by reg.30. It did not matter whether the duties performed were included in the Convention. Nor did it matter that the claimant had been recruited whilst he was living in the overseas country, because, in the view of the Commissioner, the words "posted overseas" were only descriptive of the place where the duties were performed and not the process by which the claimant came to be there. There remained the matter of whether the claimant could show that he was, immediately before his posting, an ordinary resident in the UK; and on that the Commissioner referred the case for rehearing. There was some evidence that he may indeed have been an ordinary resident because he was a retired army officer who was paying UK income tax on his pension. Note, too, that although it will usually be necessary for the child in respect of whom the claim is made, to be resident in the UK there is an exception provided in Regulation 32; the child will be treated as being in Great Britain where he normally lives with a parent who is a Crown servant posted overseas.

Partners of Crown servants posted overseas

31.—(1) For the purposes of section [² 146 (2)] of the Social Security and Contributions and Benefits Act the partner of a Crown servant posted overseas who is accompanying the Crown servant posted overseas shall be treated as being in Great Britain when the partner is either—

   (a) in the country where the Crown servant is posted, or

   (b) absent from that country in accordance with regulation 24 as modified by paragraphs (3) and (4).

(2) Regulations 22 and 24 apply to the partner of a Crown servant posted overseas with the modifications set out in paragraphs (3) and (4).

(3) References to "Great Britain" in the phrase "temporarily absent from Great Britain" in paragraphs (1) and (2) of regulation 24 shall be construed as references to the country where the Crown servant is posted and regulation 21(2) shall apply, where appropriate, accordingly.

(4) In regulation 24 omit the words "ordinarily resident in the United Kingdom and is".

AMENDMENT

1. Child Benefit (General) (Amendment) Regulations 2007, (SI 2007/2150), reg.11 (August 16, 2007).

Child or qualifying young persons normally living with Crown servants posted overseas

32.—(1) For the purposes of section [¹ 146(1)] of the Social Security and Contributions and Benefits Act a child or qualifying young person who normally lives with a Crown servant posted overseas shall be treated as being in Great Britain when he is either—

   (a) in the country where the Crown servant is posted, or

   (b) absent from that country in accordance with regulation 21 as modified by paragraph (2).

(2) The reference to "Great Britain" in paragraph (1) of that regulation shall be construed as a reference to the country where the Crown servant is posted.

AMENDMENT

1. Child Benefit (General) (Amendment) Regulations 2007, (SI 2007/2150), reg.11 (August 16, 2007).

DEFINITIONS

"child or qualifying young person": see SSCBA 1992, s.142.
"Crown servant posted overseas": see reg.1.

Transitional provisions for Part 6

33.—(1) In relation to a period of temporary absence which commenced before 7th April 2003, and continues after the coming into force of these Regulations, regulations 24 and 28 shall have effect subject to the modifications in paragraphs (2) and (3) respectively.

3.42

3.43

3.44

(2) For regulation 24(2) substitute—

"(2) A person is temporarily absent from Great Britain if at the beginning of the period of absence his absence was intended to be temporary and has throughout continued to be so intended.".

(3) For regulation 28(2) substitute—

"(2) A person is temporarily absent from Northern Ireland if at the beginning of the period of absence his absence was intended to be temporary and has throughout continued to be so intended.".

PART 7

GENERAL AND SUPPLEMENTARY PROVISIONS

Persons treated as residing together

3.45   **34.** For the purposes of Part 9 of SSCBA and Part 9 of SSCB(NI)A, the prescribed circumstances in which persons are treated as residing together are that spouses, two persons who are civil partners of each other, or two persons who are parents of a child [¹ or, qualifying young person] are absent from one another—

(a) where such absence is not likely to be permanent; or
(b) by reason only of the fact that either of them is, or they both are, undergoing medical or other treatment as an in-patient in a hospital or similar institution whether such absence is temporary or not.

AMENDMENT

1. Child Benefit (General) (Amendment) Regulations 2007, (SI 2007/2150) reg.12 (August 16, 2007).

DEFINITIONS

"civil partners": see reg.1.
"hospital or similar institution": see reg.1.

GENERAL NOTE

3.46   The question whether parties are residing together may be important in determining priorities, and was formerly important in relation to one parent benefit.

This regulation provides a partial definition of what is meant by "residing together" by stating two instances in which they are not to be regarded as being apart. In the first, spouses or parents of a child who are not married are to be regarded as not being absent from each other (i.e. are residing together) so long as their absence is not permanent. There is no limit on the period of absence as long as it can still be regarded as temporary. In *R(F) 4/85* this rule was applied to a couple who had never lived together. They married while the husband was serving a term of imprisonment having met through the wife's involvement as a prison visitor. Nevertheless the Commissioner held that a similarly worded regulation meant that they must be regarded as residing together.

In the second instance spouses (but only spouses) will be regarded as not absent (i.e. are residing together) if one of them is undergoing medical treatment. In this case they will be regarded as being together even if the separation is expected to be permanent. This will cover the case of a parent who is in a hospice receiving terminal care. But the concept of residing together still requires that the parties share a household rather than just a roof *(R(F)3/81)*.

Polygamous marriages

35.—(1) For the purposes of Part 9 of SSCBA and Part 9 of SSCB(NI) A, a polygamous marriage is treated as having the same consequences as a monogamous marriage for any day, but only for any day, throughout which the polygamous marriage is in fact monogamous.

(2) In paragraph (1)—

(a) "monogamous marriage" means a marriage celebrated under a law which does not permit polygamy;

(b) "polygamous marriage" means a marriage celebrated under a law which, as it applies to the particular ceremony and to the parties in question, permits polygamy;

(c) a polygamous marriage is referred to as being in fact monogamous when neither party to it has any spouse additional to the other; and

(d) the day on which a polygamous marriage is contracted, or on which it terminates for any reason, shall be treated as a day throughout which that marriage was in fact monogamous if at all times on that day after the time at which it was contracted, or as the case may be, before it terminated, it was in fact monogamous.

3.47

DEFINITION

"a polygamous marriage": see para.(2).

GENERAL NOTE

A polygamous marriage (celebrated after July 31, 1971) is void if either of the parties was at the time domiciled in the UK (Matrimonial Causes Act 1973). This regulation is therefore most likely to affect parties who have contracted a marriage in polygamous form before they settle in this country. The marriage will be recognised in relation to Child Benefit so long as it remains monogamous or, if it was once polygamous, once the extra spouse has died or been divorced.

3.48

Right to child benefit of voluntary organisations

36.—(1) Subject to paragraph (4) and (5), for the purposes of section 147(6) of SSCBA and section 143(6) of SSCB(NI)A (right to child benefit of voluntary organisations), a voluntary organisation is regarded as the only person with whom a child is living for any week in which that child is—

(a) living in premises which are provided or managed by the voluntary organisation, being premises which are required to be registered with a Government Department or local authority or which are otherwise regulated under or by virtue of any enactment relating to England and Wales, Scotland, or Northern Ireland; or

(b) placed by the voluntary organisation in the home of any person in accordance with the provisions of the Foster Placement (Children) Regulations 1991, the Fostering of Children (Scotland) Regulations

3.49

1996 or the Foster Placement (Children) Regulations (Northern Ireland) 1996.

(2) A voluntary organisation shall not be regarded as having ceased to have a child living with it by reason only of any temporary absence of that child—

(a) if the child is undergoing medical or other treatment as an in-patient in a hospital, until such absence has lasted for more than 84 days; or

(b) if the child is temporarily absent for any other reason, until such absence has lasted for more than 56 days.

(3) In calculating the period of 84 days for the purposes of paragraph (2) (a), two or more distinct periods of temporary absence separated by one or more intervals each not exceeding 28 days shall be treated as a continuous period equal in duration to the total of such distinct periods and ending on the last day of the latter or last of such periods.

(4) A voluntary organisation shall not be regarded as a person with whom a child or qualifying young person is living in any week if in that week—

(a) that individual is in residential accommodation in the circumstances prescribed in regulation 3; or

(b) paragraph 1 of Schedule 9 to SSCBA or paragraph 1 of Schedule 9 to SSCB(NI)A applies to that individual.

(5) Where immediately before the week in which paragraph (1) applies to a child or qualifying young person, that individual was living with a person who was then entitled to child benefit in respect of him, paragraph (1) shall have effect in relation to that person as if the words "the only person" were omitted for so long as the child or qualifying young person is treated as continuing to live with that person by virtue of section 143(2) of SSCBA or section 139(2) of SSCB(NI)A.

(6) Section 143(1)(b) of SSCBA and section 139(1)(b) of SSCB(NI) A (person to be treated as responsible for a child in any week if he is contributing to the cost of providing for the qualifying individual at a weekly rate not less than the weekly rate of child benefit payable in respect of the child or qualifying young person for that week) and regulation 16(1) (child or qualifying young person in detention) shall not apply to a voluntary organisation.

DEFINITIONS

"child or qualifying young person": see SSCBA 1992, s.142.
"voluntary organisation": see SSCBA 1992, s.147.
"week": see SSCBA 1992, s.147.

GENERAL NOTE

3.50 This regulation enables a voluntary organisation to claim benefit in respect of a child who is living in accommodation provided, managed or arranged by it. Living with a voluntary organisation will normally preclude a claim by any other person, except that a claim may continue to be made by a person who previously had the child living with him and subsequently has continued to maintain the child to the requisite extent. In such a case the original claimant will continue to be entitled but a claim made by the voluntary organisation would take priority under the usual rules as to priority.

No requirement to state national insurance number

37.—For the purposes of section 147(6) of SSCBA and section 143(6) of SSCB(NI)A, section 13(1A) of the Social Security Administration Act 1992 and section 11(1A) of the Social Security Administration (Northern Ireland) Act 1992 (requirement to state national insurance number) shall not apply to a claim for child benefit in respect of a child or qualifying young person who is treated as living with a voluntary organisation by virtue of regulation 36.

3.51

Exception to rules preventing duplicate payment

38.—(1) A person is not disentitled to child benefit in respect of a child or qualifying young person by virtue of section 13(2) of the Social Security Administration Act 1992 and section 11(2) of the Social Security Administration (Northern Ireland) Act 1992 (persons not entitled to benefit for any week if benefit already paid for that week to another person, whether or not that other person was entitled to it) if in respect of that week—

3.52

  (a) the determining authority has decided that the Commissioners are entitled to recover the child benefit paid in respect of that child or qualifying young person from a person in consequence of his misrepresentation of, or his failure to disclose, any material fact and, where that determining authority is one from whose decision an appeal lies, the time limit for appealing has expired and no appeal has been made; or

  (b) the child benefit paid to the other person has been voluntarily repaid to, or recovered by, the Commissioners in a case where the determining authority has decided under section 9 or 10 of the Social Security Act 1998 or under Article 10 or 11 of the Social Security (Northern Ireland) Order 1998 either—

  (i) that, while there was no entitlement to benefit, it is not recoverable, or

  (ii) that there was no entitlement to benefit but has made no decision as to its recoverability.

(2) In this regulation "determining authority" means, as the case may require—

  (a) the Commissioners;

  (b) an appeal tribunal constituted under [¹ . . .] or Article 8 of the Social Security (Northern Ireland) Act 1998;

  (c) the Chief or any other Social Security Commissioner, or a tribunal consisting of any three or more such Commissioners constituted in accordance with [¹ . . .] Article 16(7) of the Social Security (Northern Ireland) Act 1998;

[¹ (d) the First-tier Tribunal;

  (e) the Upper Tribunal.]

AMENDMENTS

1. Tribunals, Courts and Enforcement Act 2007 (Transitional and Consequential Provisions) Order 2008, art.6(1) and Sch.1, para.308 (November 3, 2008).

DEFINITIONS

"child or qualifying young person": see SSCBA 1992, s.142.

"the Commissioners": see reg.1.
"week": see SSCBA s.147.

Use of electronic communications

3.53   **39.**—Schedule 2 to the Child Benefit and Guardian's Allowance (Administration) Regulations 2003 (use of electronic communications) applies to the delivery of information to or by the Commissioners which is authorised or required by these Regulations in the same manner as it applies to the delivery of information to or by the Commissioners which is authorised or required by those Regulations.

References in this regulation to the delivery of information shall be construed in accordance with section 132(8) of the Finance Act 1999.

PART 8

REVOCATIONS

3.54   *Omitted*

Child Benefit (Residence and Persons Abroad) Regulations 1976

(SI 1976/963) (*as amended*)

3.55   These regulations were revoked with effect from April 6, 2003 by the Tax Credits Act 2002. There was a saving in respect of regs 6 and 7 until April 2, 2006. Those provisions may be found in earlier editions of this book.

The Child Benefit (Rates) Regulations 2006

(SI 2006/965) (*as amended*)

ARRANGEMENT OF REGULATIONS

3.56   1. Citation, commencement and interpretation.
2. Rate of child benefit.
3. Saving
4. *Revocations omitted.*

Citation, commencement and interpretation

3.57   **1.** —(1) These Regulations may be cited as the Child Benefit (Rates) Regulations 2006 and shall come into force on 10th April 2006 immediately after the Child Benefit (General) Regulations 2006.

(2) In these Regulations—

"SSCBA" means the Social Security Contributions and Benefits Act 1992;

"SSCB(NI)A" means the Social Security Contributions and Benefits (Northern Ireland) Act 1992;

"qualifying young person" means a person—

(a) in Great Britain, who is such a person for the purposes of Part 9 of SSCBA; and

(b) in Northern Ireland, who is such a person for the purposes of Part 9 of SSCB(NI)A.

(3) References in these Regulations to any condition being satisfied or any facts existing shall be construed as references to the condition being satisfied or the facts existing at the beginning of that week.

Rate of child benefit

2. —(1) The weekly rate of child benefit payable in respect of a child or qualifying young person shall be—   3.58

(a) subject to paragraphs (2) to (5), in a case where in any week a child or qualifying young person is the only person or, if not the only person, the elder or eldest person in respect of whom child benefit is payable to a person, [¹ £20.00] ("the enhanced rate");

(b) in any other case, [¹ £13.20].

(2) If, in any week—

(a) a person is—

  (i) living with his spouse or civil partner,

  (ii) living with another person as his spouse or civil partner, or

  (iii) a member of a polygamous marriage and is residing with other members of that marriage;

(b) child benefit would, but for this paragraph, be payable to that person in respect of a child or qualifying young person at the enhanced rate; and

(c) child benefit would, but for this paragraph, be payable at that rate to one of the other persons listed in paragraphs (i) to (iii) of sub-paragraph (a) in respect of another child or qualifying person,

the enhanced rate shall be payable in that week in respect of only the elder or eldest of the children and qualifying young persons referred to in sub-paragraphs (b) and (c).

(3) For the purposes of paragraph (2)(a) a person is a member of a polygamous marriage if—

(a) during the subsistence of the marriage any party to it is married to more than one person; and

(b) the ceremony of marriage took place under the law of a country which permits polygamy.

(4) Child benefit shall not be payable at the enhanced rate if the person to whom child benefit is payable is—

(a) a voluntary organisation; or

(b) a person residing (otherwise than as mentioned in paragraph (2)(a)) with a parent of the child or qualifying young person in respect of whom it is payable.

(5) If an allowance, or an increase of a benefit, pension or allowance, which is a specified benefit, is paid in respect of a week—

(a) to a person, and

(b) in respect of the only, elder or eldest child or qualifying young person in respect of whom that person is entitled to child benefit,

child benefit shall be payable at the enhanced rate for that week.

(6) The following are specified benefits—

(a) any benefit under SSCBA receipt of which entitles the recipient to an increase specified in column 2 of the Table in Part 4 of Schedule 4 to that Act (increases for dependants);

(b) any benefit under SSCB(NI)A receipt of which entitles the recipient to an increase specified in column 2 of the Table in Part IV of Schedule 4 to that Act (increases for dependants in Northern Ireland);

(c) an allowance for a child or a qualifying young person granted in respect of the death of a person due to service or war injury—

(i) under the Armed Forces and Reserve Forces (Compensation Scheme) Order 2005;

(ii) under the Naval, Military and Air Forces Etc. (Disablement and Death) Service Pensions Order 1983;

(iii) under the Pensions (Polish Forces) Scheme 1964;

(iv) under the War Pensions (Mercantile Marine) Scheme 1964;

(v) under the Warrant of 21st December 1964 concerning pensions and grants in respect of disablement or death due to service in the Home Guard;

(vi) under the Order of 22nd December 1964 concerning pensions and grants in respect of disablement or death due to service in the Home Guard after 27th April 1952;

(vii) under the Order by Her Majesty dated 4th January 1971 in respect of service in the Ulster Defence Regiment; or

(viii) which the Commissioners for Her Majesty's Revenue and Customs accept as being analogous to an allowance for a child granted in respect of the death of a person due to service or war injury under any of the preceding provisions of this sub-paragraph.

AMENDMENT

1. Child Benefit (Rates) (Amendment) Regulations 2008 (SI 2008/3246), reg.3 (January 5, 2009).

Saving

3.59   **3.** —(1) Despite the revocation, by regulation 4 of these Regulations, of—

(a) the Child Benefit and Social Security (Fixing and Adjustment of Rates) Regulations 1976, and

(b) the Child Benefit and Social Security (Fixing and Adjustment of Rates) Regulations (Northern Ireland) 1976,

if the amount of child benefit which would have been payable under those Regulations would, by virtue of the relevant transitional provisions and savings (had they remained in force), be greater than the amount prescribed by these Regulations, the greater amount shall be payable.

(2) In paragraph (1) "the relevant transitional provisions and savings" means—

(a) in the case of child benefit payable under SSCBA, regulations 3 and 4 of the Child Benefit and Social Security (Fixing and Adjustment of Rates) (Amendment) Regulations 1998; and

(b) in the case of child benefit payable under SSCB(NI)A, regulations 3 and 4 of the Child Benefit and Social Security (Fixing and Adjustment of Rates) (Amendment) Regulations (Northern Ireland) 1998.

REVOCATIONS

4. *Omitted*

3.60

GENERAL NOTE

These regulations specify the rate of Child Benefit. Since April 8, 1991 it has been paid at a higher rate in respect of the first or only child of the family (though not if the claimant is a voluntary organisation). Where two families are living together so that there could be two eldest children, the higher rate will be paid only in respect of one (the older) of them.

3.61

Until July 6, 1998, reg.2 of the Fixing and Adjustment of Rates Regulations 1976 provided also for the payment of a supplement where the claimant was not living with a spouse. This benefit, generally known (though never labelled in the Regulations) as One Parent Benefit (OPB) was ended for new claimants from that date. Saving provisions for existing and continuing claims were contained in the Fixing and Adjustment of Rates (Amendment) Regulations 1998.

Guardian's Allowance (General) Regulations 2003

(SI 2003/495) *(as amended)*

ARRANGEMENT OF REGULATIONS

1. Citation and commencement.
2. Interpretation.
3. Modification to section 77(2) of the Act.
4. Adopted children.
5. Illegitimate children.
6. Children of divorced parents.
7. Circumstances in which a person is to be treated as being in prison.
8. Rate of allowance and payment to the National Insurance Fund or the Northern Ireland National Insurance Fund.
9. Residence condition.
10. Prescribed manner of making an election under section 77(9) of the Act or section 77(9) of the Northern Ireland Act.
11. *Omitted.*

3.62

SCHEDULE

REVOCATIONS

Part 1—*Omitted.*
Part 2—*Omitted.*

The Treasury, in exercise of the powers conferred upon them by section 77(3), (8) and (9) of the Social Security Contributions and Benefits Act

1992, section 77(3), (8) and (9) of the Social Security Contributions and Benefits (Northern Ireland) Act 1992, and section 54(1) of the Tax Credits Act 2002 hereby make the following Regulations:

Citation and commencement

3.63   **1.**—These Regulations may be cited as the Guardian's Allowance (General) Regulations 2003 and shall come into force on 7th April 2003 immediately after the commencement of section 49 of the Tax Credits Act 2002.

Interpretation

3.64   **2.**—(1) In these Regulations—
"the Act" means the Social Security Contributions and Benefits Act 1992;
"adopted" means adopted pursuant to—
(a) an order made in the United Kingdom, the Channel Islands or the Isle of Man;
(b) an overseas adoption within the meaning of section 72(2) of the Adoption Act 1976;
(c) a Convention adoption order within the meaning of section 72(1) of the Adoption Act 1976; or
(d) a foreign adoption order within the meaning of section 4(3) of the Adoption (Hague Convention) Act (Northern Ireland) 1969.
"the Board" means the [¹ Commissioners for Her Majesty's Revenue and Customs];
"the Northern Ireland Act" means the Social Security Contributions and Benefits (Northern Ireland) Act 1992.

AMENDMENT

1. Guardian's Allowance (General) (Amendment) Regulations 2006 (SI 2006/204) (April 10, 2006).

Modification to section 77(2) of the Act

3.65   **3.** Section 77(2) of the Act and section 77(2) of the Northern Ireland Act shall be treated as modified where regulations 4 to 6 apply.

Adopted children

3.66   **4.**—(1) Where a child [¹ or qualifying young person] has been adopted by two persons jointly, a reference in section 77(2) of the Act or section 77(2) of the Northern Ireland Act to [¹ the parents of the child or qualifying young person] shall be read as a reference to those two persons.
(2) Where a child [¹ or qualifying young person] has been adopted by one person only, the circumstances to be satisfied in section 77(2) of the Act or section 77(2) of the Northern Ireland Act are that that person is dead.

AMENDMENT

1. Guardian's Allowance (General) (Amendment) Regulations 2006 (SI 2006/204) (April 10, 2006).

DEFINITIONS

"adopted": reg.2.
"child": SSCBA, s.122.

Illegitimate children

5.—Where— 3.67
(a) a child's parents are unmarried at the date of the birth; and
(b) paternity has not been established—
  (i) by a court of competent jurisdiction; or
  (ii) in the opinion of the determining authority,
    the circumstances to be satisfied in section 77(2) of the Act or
    section 77(2) of the Northern Ireland Act are that the mother
    of the child [¹ or qualifying young person] is dead.

AMENDMENT

1. Guardian's Allowance (General) (Amendment) Regulations 2006 (SI 2006/204) (April 10, 2006).

DEFINITION

"child": SSCBA, s.122.

Children of divorced parents

6.—(1) Where— 3.68
(a) [¹ the marriage or the civil partnership of a child's parents has been terminated by divorce or dissolved];
(b) at the death of one of the parents the child [² or qualifying young person] was not in the custody of or maintained by the other parent;
(c) there is no court order—
  [² (i) providing that child or qualifying young person is to reside with that other parent; or]
   (ii) imposing any liability on him for [² the maintenance of the child or qualifying young person]; and
(d) there is no maintenance assessment or maintenance calculation, as defined by section 54 of the Child Support Act 1991, or, for Northern Ireland, Article 2(2) of the Child Support (Northern Ireland) Order 1991 in force in respect of that other parent and child [² or qualifying young person],
   the circumstances to be satisfied in section 77(2) of the Act or section 77(2) of the Northern Ireland Act are that one of [² the parents of the child or qualifying young persons] is dead.

(2) Where a child [² or qualifying young person] has been adopted by two persons jointly, any reference in paragraph (1) above to [² the parents of the child or qualifying young person] shall be read as a reference to those two persons.

AMENDMENTS

1. Civil Partnership Act 2004 (Tax Credits, etc.) (Consequential Amendments) Order 2005 (SI 2005/2919) (December 5, 2005).
2. Guardian's Allowance (General) (Amendment) Regulations 2006 (SI 2006/204) (April 10, 2006).

DEFINITIONS

"adopted": reg.2.
"child": SSCBA, s.122.

Circumstances in which a person is to be treated as being in prison

3.69   **7.**—(1) The circumstances in which a person is to be treated as being in prison for the purposes of section 77 of the Act or section 77 of the Northern Ireland Act are that he is—

(a) serving a custodial sentence within the meaning of section 76 of the Powers of Criminal Courts (Sentencing) Act 2000, Article 2(2) of the Criminal Justice (Northern Ireland) Order 1996 or a sentence of detention or imprisonment within the meaning of section 307(1) of the Criminal Procedure (Scotland) Act 1995, with not less than 2 years remaining from the death of the other parent; or

(b) detained in a hospital by order of the court under—

   (i) section 37(1), 38, or 45A of the Mental Health Act 1983;

   (ii) section 5 of the Criminal Procedure (Insanity) Act 1964;

   (iii) section 6 or 14 of the Criminal Appeal Act 1968;

   (iv) section 57, section [¹ 57A] or 59A of the Criminal Procedure (Scotland) Act 1995;

   (v) Article 44, 45, 50A, or 51(2) and (3) of the Mental Health (Northern Ireland) Order 1986; or

   (vi) section 11 or 13(5A) and (6) of the Criminal Appeal (Northern Ireland) Act 1980.

(2) In calculating the length of the sentence for the purposes of paragraphs (1)(a) above and (4) below—

(a) disregard any reduction made to the length of the sentence to take account of any period spent in custody prior to sentencing; and

(b) include any period spent in custody immediately prior to sentencing, save that where he is serving a custodial sentence or sentence of detention or imprisonment with the meaning of paragraph (1)(a) above immediately prior to sentencing, include only such period of that sentence as remains following sentencing for the later sentence, but nothing in this paragraph shall permit the payment of guardian's allowance in respect of any period in custody prior to sentencing.

(3) Subject to paragraph (4) below, a person shall not cease to be treated as being in prison in accordance with paragraph (1) above by virtue of the fact that he is temporarily released, unlawfully at large, or, in the case of a person serving a sentence, transferred to a hospital.

(4) A person serving a sentence in accordance with paragraph (1)(a) above shall cease to be treated as being in prison in accordance with that paragraph where—

(a) he is released on licence, the remainder of his sentence is remitted, his sentence is reduced on appeal to a term of less than 2 years, or his conviction is quashed on appeal; or

(b) he is not in custody and has not been in custody for a period at least equal to the remaining period of his sentence,

   but that where a person to whom sub-paragraph (b) applies returns to prison to serve the remainder of the sentence, the length of the sentence for the purposes of paragraph (1)(a) above shall be the period of the remainder of the sentence.

(5) This regulation shall apply, subject to the necessary modifications, to a parent who is outside Great Britain or Northern Ireland and serving a custodial sentence with not less than 2 years remaining from the death of the other parent or detained in a hospital by a court order.

AMENDMENT

1. Mental Health (Care and Treatment) (Scotland) Act 2003 (Consequential Provisions) Order 2005 (SI 2005/2078) Sch.2 para.24 (October 5, 2005).

GENERAL NOTE

A claim for Guardian's Allowance can succeed where one parent is dead and the other is serving a sentence of imprisonment, or is custody in a hospital or youth offenders institution, but only so long as the period of the sentence remaining at the time of the death is two years or more. Calculation of the period of sentence remaining is complicated.   **3.70**

Paragraph (2) provides for disregard of any reduction of the sentence to be made if the prisoner is on remand at the time of the death, but for the inclusion of that period as part of the two years remaining to be spent in prison. Where the prisoner is sentenced on separate occasions, to consecutive but overlapping sentences the period will include the earlier sentence only to the extent that it is not subsumed by the latter.

In any case no order for payment of benefit can be made in respect of the period spent in prison prior to the sentence being imposed. Benefit remains payable until the prisoner is released from prison. Payment is not stopped if the prisoner escapes or is transferred to a hospital for medical treatment, until the remaining period of the sentence has expired. If the prisoner is subsequently returned to prison the claim may be renewed in respect of the period then remaining to be served.

Where the child or young person has only one "parent" because he has been adopted by only one person or because he is illegitimate and paternity is not established, or because his parents are divorced and no custody or maintenance order is applicable, there is no entitlement to Guardian's Allowance if that one parent is imprisoned.

Rate of allowance and payment to the National Insurance Fund or the Northern Ireland National Insurance Fund

8.—(1) Where a person treated as being in prison for the purposes of section 77 of the Act or section 77 of the Northern Ireland Act contributes to the cost of providing for a child [¹ or qualifying young person], the weekly rate of any guardian's allowance payable shall be reduced by the amount of the contribution made in the week preceding the week for which any allowance is payable.   **3.71**

(2) In a case where entitlement to guardian's allowance is established by reference to a person being in prison, that person shall, on notice being given by the Board, pay to the National Insurance Fund or the Northern Ireland National Insurance Fund an amount equal to that paid by way of guardian's allowance.

AMENDMENT

1. Guardian's Allowance (General) (Amendment) Regulations 2006 (SI 2006/204) (April 10, 2006).

DEFINITIONS

"child": SSCBA, s.122.
"week": SSCBA, s.122.

GENERAL NOTE

This regulation ensures that where a child or young person is being supported by a payment of Guardian's Allowance as a result of a person being in prison that person should, where possible, contribute towards the child's up keep and that such   **3.72** contribution should then be used to offset the cost of Guardian's Allowance. The Regulation appears to allow for this to happen in either of two ways—Paragraph (1) allows for a reduction in the benefit paid to the claimant. Paragraph (2) provides for the payment of a sum equal to the benefit, to the N.I. fund.

Residence condition

3.73   **9.**—(1) There shall be no entitlement to guardian's allowance in respect of a child [¹ or qualifying young person] unless at least one of [¹ the parents of that child or qualifying young person]—

    (a) was born in the United Kingdom; or

    (b) at the date of death of the parent whose death gives rise to the claim for guardian's allowance, has, in any two year period since the age of 16, spent at least 52 weeks of that period in Great Britain or Northern Ireland, as the case may require.

(2) For the purposes of paragraph (1)(b) above, a person shall be treated as being present in Great Britain or Northern Ireland (as the case may require) where—

    (a) his absence is by virtue of his employment—

        (i) as a serving member of the forces within the meaning of regulation 140 of the Social Security (Contributions) Regulations 2001;

        (ii) as an airman within the meaning of regulation 111 of those Regulations; or

        (iii) as a mariner within the meaning of regulation 115 of those Regulations; or

    (b) his absence is by virtue of his employment and that employment is prescribed employment within the meaning of regulation 114(1) of those Regulations (continental shelf operations).

[¹ (3) Where a child or qualifying young person has been adopted by two persons jointly references in paragraph (1) above to the parents of the child or qualifying young person are to be read as references to those two persons.

(3A) Where a child or qualifying young person has been adopted by one person only, that person must satisfy the requirements of paragraph (1) above].

(4) Where regulation 5 applies, [¹ the mother of the child or qualifying young person] must satisfy the requirement of paragraph (1) above.

AMENDMENT

1. Guardian's Allowance (General) (Amendment) Regulations 2006 (SI 2006/204) (April 10, 2006).

DEFINITIONS

"adopted": reg.2.
"child": SSCBA, s.122.
"employed": SSCBA, s.122.

Prescribed manner of making an election under section 77(9) of the Act or section 77(9) of the Northern Ireland Act

3.74   **10.**—(1) An election under section 77(9) of the Act or section 77(9) of the Northern Ireland Act (payment of guardian's allowance not to be made to a husband) must—

(a) be in writing, and
(b) be made either—
   (i) on a form approved by the Board, or
   (ii) in such other manner as the Board may accept as sufficient in the circumstances of the particular case.

[[1] (2) Notice of the election must be given at an appropriate office.

(3) In paragraph (2) "an appropriate office" means—
(a) in relation to guardian's allowance under the Act, the Child Benefit office, Waterview Park, Washington, Tyne and Wear;
(b) in relation to guardian's allowance under the Northern Ireland Act, the Child Benefit Office (Northern Ireland), Windsor House, Bedford Street, Belfast;
(c) in relation to guardian's allowance under either of these Acts—
   (i) Comben House, Farriers Way, Netherton, Merseyside' or
   (ii) Any Enquiry Centre maintained by Her Majesty's Revenue and Customs.]

(4) An election may be given by means of electronic communication in accordance with Schedule 2 to the Child Benefit and Guardian's Allowance (Administration) Regulations 2003.

AMENDMENT

1. Guardian's Allowance (General) (Amendment) Regulations 2006 (SI 2006/204) (April 10, 2006).

DEFINITION

"the Board": reg.2.

Revocations

11. *Omitted.*   3.75

Schedules omitted.   3.76

Guardian's Allowance Up-rating Order 2009

(SI 2009/797)

Citation and commencement

1. This Order may be cited as the Guardian's Allowance Up-rating Order   3.77
2009 and shall come into force on 6th April 2009.

Amendment of Schedule 4 to the Social Security Contributions and Benefits Act 1992

2. In paragraph 5 of Part 3 of Schedule 4 to the Social Security   3.78
Contributions and Benefits Act 1992 (amount of guardian's allowance) for
"£13.45" substitute "£14.10".

Guardian's Allowance Up-rating Regulations 2009

(SI 2009/810)

Citation, commencement and interpretation

3.79   **1.**—(1) These Regulations may be cited as the Guardian's Allowance Up-rating Regulations 2009 and shall come into force on 6th April 2009.

(2) In these Regulations—

"the Great Britain Up-rating Order" means the Guardian's Allowance Up-rating Order 2009);

"the Northern Ireland Up-rating Order" means the Guardian's Allowance Up-rating (Northern Ireland) Order 2009); and

"the Up-rating Orders" means the Great Britain Up-rating Order and the Northern Ireland Up-rating Order.

Exceptions relating to payment of allowance by virtue of the Up-rating Orders

3.80   **2.** Neither section 155(3) of the Social Security Administration Act 1992 nor section 135(3) of the Social Security Administration (Northern Ireland) Act 1992 shall apply if a question arises as to either—

(a) the weekly rate at which guardian's allowance is payable by virtue of either of the Up-rating Orders, or

(b) whether the conditions for receipt of that allowance at the altered rate are satisfied,

until that question has been determined in accordance with the provisions of section 8 of the Social Security Act 1998 or Article 9 of the Social Security (Northern Ireland) Order 1998 (as the case may be).

Persons not ordinarily resident in either Great Britain or Northern Ireland

3.81   **3.** Regulation 5 of the Social Security Benefit (Persons Abroad) Regulations 1975 and regulation 5 of the Social Security Benefit (Persons Abroad) (Northern Ireland) Regulations 1978 (application of disqualification in respect of up-rating of benefit) shall apply to any additional benefit payable by virtue of either of the Up-rating Orders.

PART IV

STATUTORY SICK PAY

Statutory Sick Pay (General) Regulations 1982

(SI 1982/894) (AS AMENDED)

The Secretary of State for Social Services, in exercise of the powers conferred upon him by sections 1(3) and (4), 3(5) and (7), 4(2), 5(5), 6(1), 8(1) to (3), 17(4), 18(1), 20 and 26(1) and (3) to (5) of, paragraph 1 of Schedule 1 to, and paragraphs 2(3) and 3(2) of Schedule 2 to, the Social Security and Housing Benefits Act 1982(a) and of all other powers enabling him in that behalf, hereby makes the following regulations.

ARRANGEMENT OF REGULATIONS

Citation, commencement and interpretation

1.—(1) These regulations may be cited as the Statutory Sick Pay   4.2
(General) Regulations 1982, and shall come into operation on 6th April
1983.

603

(2) In these regulations—

"the Act" means the Social Security and Housing Benefits Act 1982;

[¹"the Contributions and Benefits Act" means the Social Security Contributions and Benefits Act 1992;]

[²"income tax month" means the period beginning on the 6th day of any calendar month and ending on the 5th day of the following calendar month;]

(3) Unless the context otherwise requires, any reference—

(a) in these regulations to a numbered section or Schedule is a reference to the section or Schedule, as the case may be, of or to the Act bearing that number;

(b) in these regulations to a numbered regulation is a reference to the regulation bearing that number in these regulations; and

(c) in any of these regulations to a numbered paragraph is a reference to the paragraph bearing that number in that regulation.

AMENDMENTS

1. Social Security (Miscellaneous Provisions) Amendment (No.2) Regulations 1992 (SI 1992/2595), reg.14 (November 16, 1992).

2. Social Security Contributions, Statutory Maternity Pay and Statutory Sick Pay (Miscellaneous Amendments) Regulations 1996 (SI 1996/777), reg.2(2) (April 6, 1996).

GENERAL NOTE

4.3   The relevant provisions in Pt I of the Social Security and Housing Benefits Act 1982 have now been replaced by Pt XII of the SSCBA 1992.

Persons deemed incapable of work

4.4   **2.**—(1) A person who is not incapable of work of which he can reasonably be expected to do under a particular contract of service may be deemed to be incapable of work of such a kind by reason of some specific disease or bodily or mental disablement for any day on which either—

(a) (i) he is under medical care in respect of a disease or disablement as aforesaid,

(ii) it is stated by a registered medical practitioner that for precautionary or convalescent reasons consequential on such disease or disablement he should abstain from work, or from work of such a kind; and

(iii) he does not work under that contract of service; or

[¹(b) he is—

(i) excluded or abstains from work, or from work of such a kind, pursuant to a request or notice in writing lawfully made under an enactment; or

(ii) otherwise prevented from working pursuant to an enactment,

by reason of his being a carrier, or having been in contact with a case, of a relevant disease.]

(2) A person who at the commencement of any day is, or thereafter on that day becomes, incapable of work of such a kind by reason of some specific disease or bodily or mental disablement, and

(a) on that day, under that contract of service, does no work, or no work except during a shift which ends on that day having begun on the previous day; and

(b) does no work under that contract of service during a shift which begins on that day and ends on the next,

shall be deemed to be incapable of work of such a kind by reason of that disease or bodily or mental disablement throughout that day.

[¹(3) For the purposes of paragraph (1)(b)—

"enactment" includes an enactment comprised in, or in an instrument made under—

(a) an Act; or

(b) an Act of the Scottish Parliament; and

"relevant disease" means—

(a) in England and Wales, any disease, food poisoning, infection, infectious disease or notifiable disease—

   (i) to which section 20(1) of the Public Health (Control of Disease) Act 1984 (stopping of work to prevent spread of disease) applies; or

   (ii) to which—

      (aa) regulation 3 (public health enactments applied to certain diseases) of, and Schedule 1 to,

      (bb) regulation 9(1) (provisions for preventing the spread of typhus and relapsing fever) of, and Schedule 3 to, or

      (cc) regulation 9(2) (provisions for preventing the spread of food poisoning and food borne infections) of, and Schedule 4 to,

      the Public Health (Infectious Diseases) Regulations 1988 applies; or

   (iii) to which regulations 8 and 9 (examination, etc. of persons on aircraft and powers in respect of persons leaving aircraft) of the Public Health (Aircraft) Regulations 1979 applies; or

   (iv) to which regulations 9 and 10 (examination, etc. of persons on ships and powers in respect of certain persons on ships) of the Public Health (Ships) Regulations 1979 applies; and

(b) in Scotland, any food poisoning or infectious disease—

   (i) to which section 71(1) of the Health Services and Public Health Act 1968 (compensation for stopping employment to prevent spread of disease in Scotland) applies;

   (ii) to which—

      (aa) regulations 8 and 9 (examination, etc. of persons on aircraft and powers in respect of persons leaving aircraft) of the Public Health (Aircraft)(Scotland) Regulations 1971; or

      (bb) regulations 9 and 10 (examination, etc. of persons on ships and powers in respect of certain persons on ships) of the Public Health (Ships)(Scotland) Regulations 1971,

   applies.]

AMENDMENT

1. Statutory Sick Pay (General) Amendment Regulations 2006 (SI 2006/799), reg.2 (April 10, 2006).

DEFINITION

"contract of service"—see SSCBA 1992, s.163(1).

GENERAL NOTE

Para. (1)

4.5   Regulation 2 of the SSP (General) Regulations is in virtually identical terms to the former regs 3(1) and (2) of the old Unemployment, Sickness and Invalidity Benefit Regulations 1983 (SI 1983/1598), which covered deemed sickness for the purposes of sickness benefit (see the 1994 volume of *Bonner*, p.687). The relevant case law in that context revolved around the vexed question of whether the regulation covers a pregnant claimant who is herself fit for work but is recommended to refrain from work because of the danger of contracting a disease which would threaten the life of the foetus she is carrying. Earlier cases have involved school teachers who are pregnant when there is an outbreak of Rubella in the school.

There are two reported decisions under the old law which are worthy of note. In *R(S)24/54* it was held that a precautionary absence from work was not within sub-para.(a) of the regulation because she was not under medical care in respect of the disease during a period in which she had been advised to refrain from work simply to avoid contact with the disease. That decision was rejected by the Commissioner in *R(S)1/72* where the facts were identical, except that the claimant was awaiting the outcome of tests to determine whether she was immune to Rubella and could therefore return to work. In fact, the results of those tests were not available for about five weeks owing in part to a postal strike. The Commissioner found that during the whole of that time she was under medical care in respect of the disease and was, therefore, deemed to be incapable of work and entitled to benefit. Fortunately for her, the results showed that she was immune and she was able to return to work. No question arose as to whether she would have continued to qualify for benefit if she had not been immune and had been advised to remain off work. But, the line of the Commissioner's reasoning in that case and his rejection of *R(S)24/54* rather than any attempt to distinguish it suggest that he may well have held that the claimant would remain under medical care until the danger from the infection was past.

In *R(S)4/93* the claimant was an assistant in a veterinary practice, who was potentially in danger of infection by toxoplasmosis from handling cats. She was given certificates advising her to refrain from work over a period of about six weeks. Her claim for statutory sick pay was refused by her employer and she applied to an AO for a decision on her entitlement to statutory sick pay. The Commissioner adopted the reasoning in both of the earlier cases. Thus she found that the claimant was entitled to benefit for a period of five days while awaiting the outcome of tests, which were negative, but not entitled for a further period of five weeks for which a claim had been made. The Commissioner did not specifically address the point that there had been a change in wording to the regulation since the earlier cases. The regulation now specifically refers to absence which is recommended for "precautionary" reasons. But, given that such reasons must be "consequential on such disease", meaning one for which she is "under medical care", it is probable that the new words add nothing to the interpretation.

It is, on the face of it, a rather fine distinction to hold, as in *R(S)4/93*, that the claimant is under medical care while awaiting the outcome of the tests but not under medical care once they are known. Nor is it in point to observe, as does the Commissioner in *R(S)24/54*, that the claimant is not unfit for work, only unable to work in the particular place she was employed, because the whole point of this regulation is for a claimant to be *deemed* unfit even though she may be fit. No doubt some justice is done for a claimant whose contribution record qualifies her for contribution-based jobseeker's allowance (presumably she is not to be disqualified for voluntary leaving), but where the claimant does not have such an entitlement the loss of statutory sick pay will be hard felt.

A claimant with a contribution record could also now potentially qualify for incapacity benefit because the regulations for that benefit specifically provide for a pregnant woman who has to refrain from work because of a danger to herself or her unborn child (see Incapacity for Work (General) Regulations 1995 (SI 1995/311), reg.14—see Vol.I in this series).

The amendments made in 2006, substituting a new subs.(1)(b) and inserting a new (3), do not change the original policy intention, but merely update these provisions to reflect modern public health legislation.

[¹Linking periods of incapacity for work

2A. In subsection (3) of section 2 of the 1982 Act (linking periods of incapacity for work), 8 weeks shall be substituted for 2 weeks.]

4.6

AMENDMENT

1. Statutory Sick Pay (General) Amendment Regulations 1986 (SI 1986/477), reg.2 (April 6, 1986).

GENERAL NOTE

Section 2 of the 1982 Act, along with the other original provisions relating to statutory sick pay, was repealed by the Social Security (Consequential Provisions) Act 1992, s.3 and Sch.1. The eight-week linking rule is now to be found in SSCBA 1992, s.152(3).

4.7

Period of entitlement ending or not arising

3.—(1) In a case where an employee is detained in legal custody or sentenced to a term of imprisonment (except where the sentence is suspended) on a day which in relation to him falls within a period of entitlement, that period shall end with that day.

4.8

(2) A period of entitlement shall not arise in relation to a period of incapacity for work if the employee in question is in legal custody or sentenced to or undergoing a term of imprisonment (except where the sentence is suspended).

[⁴(2A) A period of entitlement in respect of an employee who was entitled to incapacity benefit, maternity allowance or severe disablement allowance shall not arise in relation to any day within a period of incapacity for work beginning with the first day on which paragraph 2(d) of Schedule 11 to the Contributions and Benefits Act ceases to have effect where the employee in question is a person to whom regulation 13A of the Social Security (Incapacity for Work) (General) Regulations 1995 (welfare to work beneficiary) applies.]

[⁶(2B) Paragraph (2A) shall not apply, in the case of an employee who was entitled to incapacity benefit, where paragraph 2(d)(i) of Schedule 11 to the Contributions and Benefits Act ceases to have effect by virtue of paragraph 5A of that Schedule.]

[⁷ (2C) A period of entitlement in respect of an employee who was entitled to employment and support allowance shall not arise in relation to any day within a period of limited capability for work beginning with the first day on which paragraph 2(dd) of Schedule 11 to the Contributions and Benefits Act ceases to have effect where the employee in question is a person to whom regulation 148 of the Employment and Support Allowance Regulations 2008 (work and training beneficiaries) applies.]

[¹(3) A period of entitlement as between an employee and his employer shall end after 3 years if it has not otherwise ended in accordance with [³section 153(2) of the Contributions and Benefits Act] or with regulations (other than this paragraph) made under [³section 153(6) of the Contributions and Benefits Act].]

[²[³(4) Where a period of entitlement is current as between an employee and her employer and the employee—

(a) is pregnant or has been confined; and
(b) is incapable of work wholly or partly because of pregnancy or confinement on any day which falls on or after the beginning of the [⁵4th week] before the expected week of confinement; and
(c) is not by virtue of that pregnancy or confinement entitled to statutory maternity pay under Part XII of the Contributions and Benefits Act or to maternity allowance under section 35 of that Act;

the period of entitlement shall end on that day or, if earlier, on the day she was confined.]

[³(5) Where an employee—

(a) is pregnant or has been confined; and
(b) is incapable of work wholly or partly because of pregnancy or confinement on any day which falls on or after the beginning of the [⁵4th week] before the expected week of confinement; and
(c) is not by virtue of that pregnancy or confinement entitled to statutory maternity pay under Part XII of the Contributions and Benefits Act or to maternity allowance under section 35 of that Act;

a period of entitlement as between her and her employer shall not arise in relation to a period of incapacity for work where the first day in that period falls within 18 weeks of the beginning of the week containing the day referred to at (b) above or, if earlier, of the week in which she was confined.]

(6) In paragraphs (4) and (5), "confinement" and "confined" have the same, meanings as in [³section 171 of the Contributions and Benefits Act].]

AMENDMENTS

1. Statutory Sick Pay (General) Amendment Regulations 1986 (SI 1986/477), reg.3 (April 6, 1986).
2. Statutory Sick Pay (General) Amendment (No.2) Regulations 1987 (SI 1987/868), reg.2 (June 7, 1987).
3. Social Security Maternity Benefits and Statutory Sick Pay (Amendment) Regulations 1994 (SI 1994/1367), reg.9 (June 11, 1994).
4. Social Security (Welfare to Work) Regulations 1998 (SI 1998/2231), reg.6 (October 5, 1998).
5. Social Security, Statutory Maternity Pay and Statutory Sick Pay (Miscellaneous Amendments) Regulations 2002 (SI 2002/2690), reg.13 (November 24, 2002).
6. Employment Equality (Age) (Consequential Amendments) Regulations 2007 (SI 2007/825), reg.5(2) (April 6, 2007).
7. Employment and Support Allowance (Consequential Provisions) (No.2) Regulations 2008 (SI 2008/1554), reg.45 (October 27, 2008).

DEFINITIONS

"confined"—see para.(6).
"confinement"—see *ibid*.
"employee"—see SSCBA 1992, s.163(1) and reg.16.
"employer"—see SSCBA 1992, s.163(1).
"period of entitlement"—see *ibid*.
"period of incapacity for work"—see *ibid*.
"week"—see *ibid*.

[¹Maximum entitlement to statutory sick pay in a period of entitlement

3A.—[² . . .]

AMENDMENTS

1. Statutory Sick Pay (General) Amendment Regulations 1986 (SI 1986/477), reg.4 (April 6, 1986).
2. Statutory Sick Pay (General) (Amendment) Regulations 2008 (SI 2008/1735), reg.3 (October 27, 2008).

Contract of service ended for the purpose of avoiding liability for statutory sick pay

4.—(1) The provisions of this regulation apply in any case where an employer's contract of service with an employee is brought to an end by the employer solely or mainly for the purpose of avoiding liability for statutory sick pay.

(2) Where a period of entitlement is current on the day on which the contract is brought to an end, the employer shall be liable to pay statutory sick pay to the employee until the occurrence of an event which, if the contract would have caused the period of entitlement to come to an end under section 3(2)(a), (b) or (d) or regulation 3(1) [¹of these regulations or regulation 10(2) of the Statutory Sick Pay (Mariners, Airmen and Persons Abroad) Regulations 1982], or (if earlier) until the date on which the contract would have expired.

AMENDMENT

1. Statutory Sick Pay (Mariners, Airmen and Persons Abroad) Regulations 1982 (SI 1982/1349), reg.10(3) (April 6, 1983).

DEFINITIONS

"contract of service"—see SSCBA 1992, s.163(1).
"employee"—see *ibid.* and reg.16.
"employer"—see SSCBA 1992, s.163(1).
"period of entitlement"—see *ibid.*

Qualifying days

5.—(1) In this regulation, "week" means a period of 7 consecutive days, beginning with Sunday.

(2) Where an employee and an employer of his have not agreed which day or days in any week are or were qualifying days [¹or where in any day or days are or were such as are referred to in paragraph (3)], the qualifying day or days in that week shall be—

(a) the day or days on which it is agreed between the employer and employee that the employee is or was required to work (if not incapable) for that employer or, if it is so agreed that there is or was no such day;
(b) the Wednesday, or, if there is no such agreement between and employee as mentioned in sub-paragraph (a);
(c) every day, except that or those (if any) on which it is agreed between the employer and the employee that none of that employer's

employees are or were required to work (any agreement that all day such days being ignored).

[[1](3) No effect shall be given to any agreement between an employer to treat as qualifying days—

(a) any day where the day is identified, whether expressly or reference to that or another day being a day of incapacity relation to the employee's contract of service with an employer;

(b) any day identified, whether expressly or otherwise, by period of entitlement or to a period of incapacity for work.]

AMENDMENT

1. Statutory Sick Pay (General) Amendment Regulations 1985 (SI 1985/126), reg.2 (March 5, 1985).

DEFINITIONS

"contract of service"—see SSCBA 1992, s.163(1).
"employee"—see *ibid.* and reg.16.
"employer"—see SSCBA 1992, s.163(1).
"period of entitlement"—see *ibid.*
"period of incapacity for work"—see *ibid.*
"qualifying day"—see *ibid.*
"week"—see *ibid.*

GENERAL NOTE

4.12   This prescribes the manner in which qualifying days are to be determined in the absence of any effective agreement between employer on which days are to rank as such (see also SSCBA 1992, s.154). *R(SSP)1/85* decides that "required to work" in sub-paras (a) and (c) means obliged to work under one's terms of employment, and does not embrace the situation in which the employee was merely asked to work. Thus, there the employee's normal practice of working voluntary overtime on Saturdays could not turn Saturday into a qualifying day where the contract of service merely provided for 39 hours' work on Mon–Fri. That decision (at para.10) explains how what is now SSCBA 1992, s.154 and this paragraph interrelate to set out a series of alternatives, to be applied in turn as necessary, to determine qualifying days in any particular case.

Para. (3)
4.13   This renders ineffective any agreement which, expressly or otherwise, identifies qualifying days by reference to it or another day being one of incapacity, or by reference to a period of entitlement or period of incapacity for work.

Calculation of entitlement limit

4.14   **6.**—(1) Where an employee's entitlement to statutory sick pay is calculated by reference to different weekly rates in the same period of entitlement [[2]. . .], the entitlement limit shall be calculated in the manner described in paragraphs (2) and (3), or, as the case may be, (4) and (5); and where a number referred to in paragraph (2)(b) or (d) or (4)(a)(ii) or (d)(ii) is not a whole number [[1]of thousandths, it shall be rounded up to the next thousandth].

(2) For the purpose of determining whether an employee has reached his maximum entitlement to statutory sick pay in respect of a period of entitlement there shall be calculated—

(a) the amount of statutory sick pay to which the employee became entitled during the part of the period of entitlement before the change in the weekly rate;
(b) the number by which the weekly rate (before the change) must be multiplied in order to produce the amount mentioned in subparagraph (a);
(c) the amount of statutory sick pay to which the employee has so far become entitled during the part of the period of entitlement after the change in the weekly rate; and
(d) the number by which the weekly rate (after the change) must be multiplied in order to produce the amount mentioned in subparagraph (c);
(e) the sum of the amounts mentioned in sub-paragraphs (a) and (c); and
(f) the sum of the number mentioned in sub-paragraphs (b) and (d).

(3) When the sum mentioned in paragraph (2)(f) reaches [²28], the sum mentioned in paragraph (2)(e) reaches the entitlement limit.

(4) [². . .]

(5) [². . .]

AMENDMENTS

1. Statutory Sick Pay (General) Amendment Regulations 1984 (SI 1984/385), reg.2(a) (April 16, 1984).
2. Statutory Sick Pay (General) Amendment Regulations 1986 (SI 1986/477), reg.9 (April 6, 1986).

DEFINITIONS

"employee"—see SSCBA 1992, s.163(1) and reg.16.
"period of entitlement"—see SSCBA 1992, s.163(1).

Time and manner of notification of incapacity for work

7.—(1) Subject to paragraph (2), notice of any day of incapacity for work shall be given by or on behalf of an employee to his employer—   **4.15**

(a) in a case where the employer has decided on a time limit (not being one which requires the notice to be given earlier than [¹. . .] the first qualifying day in the period of incapacity for work which includes that day of incapacity for work [¹or by a specified time during that qualifying day]) and taken reasonable steps to make it known to the employee, within that time limit; and
(b) in any other case, on or before the seventh day after that day of incapacity for work.

(2) Notice of any day of incapacity for work may be given [²one month] later than as provided by paragraph (1) where there is good cause for giving it later [², or if in the particular circumstances that is not practicable, as soon as it is reasonably practicable thereafter] so however that it shall in any event be given on or before the 91st day after that day.

(3) A notice contained in a letter which is properly addressed and sent by prepaid post shall be deemed to have been given on the day on which it was posted.

(4) Notice of any day of incapacity for work shall be given by or on behalf of an employee to his employer—

(a) in a case where the employer has decided on a manner in which it is to be given (not being a manner which imposes a requirement such as is specified in paragraph (5)) and taken reasonable steps to make it known to the employee, in that manner; and

(b) in any other case, in any manner, so however that unless otherwise agreed between the employer and employee it shall be given in writing.

(5) The requirements mentioned in paragraph (4)(a) are that notice shall be given—

(a) personally;

(b) in the form of medical evidence;

(c) more than once in every 7 days during a period of entitlement;

(d) on a document supplied by the employer; or

(e) on a printed form.

AMENDMENTS

1. Statutory Sick Pay (General) Amendment Regulations 1984 (SI 1984/385), reg.2(b) (April 16, 1984).

2. Social Security Contributions, Statutory Maternity Pay and Statutory Sick Pay (Miscellaneous Amendments) Regulations 1996 (SI 1996/777), reg.2(3) (April 6, 1996).

DEFINITIONS

"employee"—see SSCBA 1992, s.163(1) and reg.16.

"employer"—see SSCBA 1992, s.163(1).

"period of entitlement"—see *ibid.*

"period of incapacity for work"—see *ibid.*

"qualifying day"—see *ibid.*

Manner in which statutory sick pay may not be paid

4.16   **8.** Statutory sick pay may not be paid in kind or by way of the provision of board or lodging or of services or other facilities.

Time limits for paying statutory sick pay

4.17   **9.**—(1) In this regulation, "payday" means a day on which it has been agreed, or it is the normal practice, between an employer and an employee of his, that payments by way of remuneration are to be made, or, where there is no such agreement or normal practice, the last day of a calendar month.

(2) In any case where—

(a) a decision has been made by an insurance officer, local tribunal or Commissioner in proceedings under Part I that an employee is entitled to an amount of statutory sick pay; and

(b) the time for bringing an appeal against the decision has expired and either—

   (i) no such appeal has been brought; or

   (ii) such an appeal has been brought and has been finally disposed of, that amount of statutory sick pay is to be paid within the time specified in paragraph (3).

(3) Subject to paragraphs (4) and (5), the employer is required to pay the amount not later than the first pay day after—

(a) where an appeal has been brought, the day on which the employer receives notification that it has been finally disposed of;

(b) where leave to appeal has been refused and there remains no further opportunity to apply for leave, the day on which the employer receives notification of the refusal; and

(c) in any other case, the day on which the time for bringing an appeal expires.

(4) Subject to paragraph (5), where it is impracticable, in view of the employer's methods of accounting for and paying remuneration, for the requirement of payment referred to in paragraph (3) to be met by the pay day referred to in that paragraph, it shall be met not later than the next following pay day.

(5) Where the employer would not have remunerated the employee for his work on the day of incapacity for work in question (if it had not been a day of incapacity for work) as early as the pay day specified in paragraph (3) or (if it applies) paragraph (4), the requirement of payment shall be met on the first day on which the employee would have been remunerated for his work on that day.

DEFINITIONS

"employee"—see SSCBA 1992, s.163(1) and reg.16.
"employer"—see SSCBA 1992, s.163(1).

[¹Liability of the Secretary of State for payments of statutory sick pay

9A.—(1) Notwithstanding the provisions of section 1 of the Act and subject to paragraph (4), where—   4.18

(a) an adjudicating authority has determined that an employer is liable to

(b) the time for appealing against the determination has expired; and

(c) no appeal against the determination has been lodged or leave to appeal against the determination is required and has been refused,

then for any day of incapacity for work in respect of which it was determined the employer was liable to make those payments, and for any further days of incapacity for work which fall within the same spell of incapacity for work and in respect of which the employer was liable to make payments of statutory sick pay to that employee, the liability to make payments of statutory sick pay in respect of those days shall, to the extent that payment has not been made by the employer, be that of the Secretary of State and not the employer.

(2) For the purposes of this regulation a spell of incapacity for work consists of consecutive days of incapacity for work with no day of the week disregarded.

(3) In paragraph (1) above "adjudicating authority" means, as the case may be, the Chief or other adjudication officer, [² the First-tier Tribunal or the Upper Tribunal.]

(4) This regulation shall not apply to any liability of an employer to make a payment of statutory sick pay where the day of incapacity for work in respect of which the liability arose falls within a period of entitlement which commenced before 6th April 1987.]

AMENDMENTS

1. Statutory Sick Pay (General) Amendment Regulations 1987 (SI 1987/ 372), reg.2 (April 6, 1987).
2. Tribunals, Courts and Enforcement Act 2007 (Transitional and Consequential Provisions) Order 2008 (SI 2008/2683), art.6 and Sch.1, para.18 (November 3, 2008).

DEFINITIONS

"employee"—see SSCBA 1992, s.163(1) and reg.16.
"employer"—see SSCBA 1992, s.163(1).
"period of entitlement"—see *ibid.*
"week"—see *ibid.*

GENERAL NOTE

4.19   This regulation, together with regs 9B and 9C, prescribe the circumstances in which the liability to pay statutory sick pay is to be that of the Board of the Inland Revenue (now HMRC) and not the employer. (Although the regulation still refers to the Secretary of State, those functions were transferred—along with those under regs 9B and 9C—to the Board by s.1(2) of and Sch.2 to the Social Security Contributions (Transfer of Functions, etc.) Act 1999.) The relevant circumstances are where it is determined that statutory sick pay is payable but the employer neither pays the amount due nor appeals against the decision (reg.9A) and where the employer was insolvent at the time (reg.9B). Provision is also made (reg.9C) requiring HMRC to make the payments for which they are liable at weekly intervals.

[¹**Insolvency of employer**

4.20   **9B.**—(1) Notwithstanding the provisions of section 1 of the Act and subject to paragraph (3), any liability arising under Part I of the Act to make a payment of statutory sick pay in respect of a day of incapacity for work in relation to an employee's contract of service with his employer shall be that of the Secretary of State and not that of the employer where the employer is insolvent on that day.

(2) For the purposes of paragraph (1) an employer shall be taken to be insolvent if, and only if—

(a) in England and Wales—
    (i) he has been adjudged bankrupt or has made a composition or arrangement with his creditors;
    (ii) he had died and his estate falls to be administered in accordance with an order under section 421 of the Insolvency Act 1986; or
    (iii) where an employer is a company, a winding-up order [². . .] is made or a resolution for voluntary winding-up is passed with respect to it [²or it enters administration], or a receiver or manager of its undertaking is duly appointed, or possession is taken by or on behalf of the holders of any debentures secured by a floating charge, or any property of the company comprised in or subject to the charge or a voluntary arrangement proposed for the purposes of Part 1 of the Insolvency Act 1986 is approved under that Part;

(b) in Scotland—
    (i) an award of sequestration is made on his estate or he executes a trust deed for his creditors or enters into a composition contract;

(ii) he has died and a judicial factor appointed under section 11A of the Judicial Factors (Scotland) Act 1889 is required by that section to divide his insolvent estate among his creditors; or

(iii) where the employer is a company, a winding-up order [². . .] is made or a resolution for voluntary winding-up is passed with respect to it [²or it enters administration] or a receiver of its undertaking is duly appointed or a voluntary arrangement proposed for the purposes of Part 1 of the Insolvency Act 1986 is approved under that Part.

shall not apply where the employer became insolvent before 6th April 1987.]

AMENDMENTS

1. Statutory Sick Pay (General) Amendment Regulations 1987 (SI 1987/ 372), reg.2 (April 6, 1987).
2. Enterprise Act 2002 (Insolvency) Order 2003 (SI 2003/2096), art.5 and Sch.2, para.42 (September 15, 2003).

DEFINITIONS

"contract of service"—see SSCBA 1992, s.163(1).
"employee"—see *ibid.* and reg.16.
"employer"—see SSCBA 1992, s.163(1).

[¹Payments by the Secretary of State

9C. Where the Secretary of State becomes liable in accordance with regulation 9A or 9B to make payments of statutory sick pay to a person, the first payment shall be made as soon as reasonably practicable after he becomes so liable, and payments thereafter shall be made at weekly intervals, by means of an instrument of payment [², instrument for benefit payment] or by such other means as appears to the Secretary of State to be appropriate in the circumstances of the particular case.]

4.21

AMENDMENTS

1. Statutory Sick Pay (General) Amendment Regulations 1987 (SI 1987/372), reg.2 (April 6, 1987).
2. Social Security (Claims and Payments etc.) Amendment Regulations 1996 (SI 1996/672), reg.3 (April 4, 1996).

Persons unable to act

10.—(1) Where in the case of any employer— 4.22

(a) statutory sick pay is payable to him or he is alleged to be entitled to it;

(b) he is unable for the time being to act, and either—

(i) no receiver has been appointed by the Court of Protection with power to receive statutory sick pay on his behalf; or

(ii) in Scotland, his estate is not being administered by any tutor , curator or other guardian acting or appointed in terms of law,

the Secretary of State may, upon written application to him by a person who, if a natural person, is over the age of 18, appoint that person to exercise, on behalf of the employee, any right to which he may be entitled under Part I and to deal on his behalf with any sums payable to him.

(2) Where the Secretary of State has made an appointment under paragraph (1)—

(a) he may at any time in his absolute discretion revoke it;

(b) the person appointed may resign his office after having given one month's notice in writing to the Secretary of State of his intention to do so; and

(c) the appointment shall terminate when the Secretary of State is notified that a receiver or other person to whom paragraph (1)(c) applies has been appointed.

(3) Anything required by Part I to be done by or to any employee who is unable to act may be done by or to the person appointed under this regulation to act on his behalf, and the receipt of the person so appointed shall be a good discharge to the employee's employer for any sum paid.

DEFINITIONS

"employee"—see SSCBA 1992, s.163(1) and reg.16.
"employer"—see SSCBA 1992, s.163(1).

GENERAL NOTE

4.23   The Secretary of State's functions under this regulation were transferred to the Board of the Inland Revenue (now HMRC) by s.1(2) of and Sch.2 to the Social Security Contributions (Transfer of Functions, etc.) Act 1999.

Rounding to avoid fractional amounts

4.24   **11.** Where any payment of statutory sick pay is made and the statutory sick pay due for the period for which the payment purports to be made includes a fraction of a penny, the payment shall be rounded up to the next whole number of pence.

Days not to be treated as, or as parts of, periods of interruption of employment

4.25   **12.** In a case to which paragraph 3 of Schedule 2 applies, the day of incapacity for work mentioned in sub-paragraph (1)(b) of that paragraph shall not be, or form part of, a period of interruption of employment where it is a day which, by virtue of section 17(1) or (2) of the Social Security Act 1975 or any regulations made thereunder, is not to be treated as a day of incapacity for work.

Records to be maintained by employers

4.26   **13.**—[[1](1)] Every employer shall maintain for 3 years after the end of each tax year a record, in relation to each employee of his, of—

(a) any day in that tax year which was one of 4 or more consecutive days on which, according to information supplied by or on behalf of the employee, the employee was incapable by reason of some specific disease or bodily or mental disablement of doing work which he could reasonably be expected to do under any contract of service between him and the employer, whether or not he would normally have been expected to work on that day; [[2](2)]and

(b) any payment of statutory sick pay made in respect of any day recorded under sub-paragraph (a).]

[³(1A) For the purposes of paragraph (1)(b) only, the employer is not to be regarded as having made a payment of statutory sick pay where, in respect of any day recorded under paragraph (1)(a), the employee is entitled to receive, and does in fact receive, a payment or payments by way of contractual remuneration from his employer which, in aggregate, equal or exceed the amount of statutory sick pay payable in respect of that day.]

(2) [². . .]
(3) [². . .]
(4) [². . .]
(5) [². . .]

AMENDMENTS

1. Statutory Sick Pay (General) Amendment Regulations 1986 (SI 1986/477), reg.5 (April 6, 1986).

2. Social Security Contributions, Statutory Maternity Pay and Statutory Sick Pay (Miscellaneous Amendments) Regulations 1996 (SI 1996/777), reg.2(4) (April 6, 1996).

3. Statutory Sick Pay (General) Amendment Regulations 1996 (SI 1996/3042), reg.52 (April 6, 1997).

DEFINITIONS

"contract of service"—see SSCBA 1992, s.163(1).
"employee"—see *ibid.* and reg.16.
"employer"—see SSCBA 1992, s.163(1).

[¹Production of employer's records

13A.—(1) An authorised officer of the Commissioners of Inland Revenue may by notice require an employer to produce to him at the place of keeping such records as are in the employer's possession or power and as (in the officer's reasonable opinion) contain, or may contain, information relevant to satisfy him that statutory sick pay has been paid and is being paid in accordance with these regulations to employees or former employees who are entitled to it.

(2) A notice referred to in paragraph (1) shall be in writing and the employer shall produce the records referred to in that paragraph within 30 days after the date of such a notice.

(3) The production of records in pursuance of this regulation shall be without prejudice to any lien which a third party may have in respect of those records.

(4) References in this regulation to "records" means—

(a) any wage sheet or deductions working sheet; or
(b) any other document which relates to the calculation or payment of statutory sick pay to his employees or former employees,
whether kept in written form, electronically, or otherwise.

(5) In paragraph (1), "place of keeping" means such place in Great Britain that an employer and an authorised officer may agree upon, or, in the absence of such agreement—

(a) any place in Great Britain where records referred to in paragraph (1) are normally kept; or

4.27

(b) if there is no such place, the employer's principal place of business in Great Britain.]

AMENDMENT

1. Statutory Maternity Pay (General) and Statutory Sick Pay (General) (Amendment) Regulations 2005 (SI 2005/989), reg.3(2) (April 6, 2005).

DEFINITIONS

"records"—see reg.13A(4).
"place of keeping"—see reg.13A(5).

Provision of information in connection with determination of questions

4.28   **14.** Any person claiming to be entitled to statutory sick pay, or any other person who is a party to proceedings arising under Part I, shall, if he receives notification from the Secretary of State that any information is required from him for the determination of any question arising in connection therewith, furnish that information to the Secretary of State within 10 days of receiving that notification.

GENERAL NOTE

4.29   The Secretary of State's functions under this regulation were transferred to the Board of the Inland Revenue (now HMRC) by s.1(2) of and Sch.2 to the Social Security Contributions (Transfer of Functions, etc.) Act 1999.

Provision of information by employers to employees

4.30   **15.**—(1) [³Subject to paragraph (1A),] in a case which falls within paragraph (a), (b) or (c) of section 18(3) (provision of information by employers in connection with the making of claims for [²short term incapacity] and other benefits), the employer shall furnish to his employee, in writing on a form approved by the Secretary of State for the purpose [³, or in a form in which it can be processed by equipment operating automatically in response to instructions given for that purpose], the information specified in paragraphs (2), (3) or (4) below, respectively within the time specified in the appropriate one of those paragraphs.

[³(1A) For the purposes of paragraph (1), where, in the particular circumstances of a case, it is not practicable for the employer to furnish the information within the specified time mentioned in paragraph (2), (3), (4) (b)(ii) or (5), he shall, not later than the first pay day within the meaning of regulation 9(1) immediately following the relevant specified time, furnish the information to his employee.]

(2) In a case which falls within paragraph (a) (no period of entitlement arising in relation to a period of incapacity for work) of section 18(3)—

(a) the information mentioned in paragraph (1) is a statement of all the reasons why, under the provisions of paragraph 1 of Schedule 1 and regulations made thereunder, a period of entitlement does not arise; and

(b) it shall be furnished not more than 7 days after the day on which the employee's employer is notified by or on behalf of the employee of the incapacity for work on the fourth day of the period of incapacity for work.

(3) In a case which falls within paragraph (b) (period of entitlement ending but period of incapacity for work continuing) of section 18(3)—

[⁴ (a) the information mentioned in paragraph (1) above is a statement informing the employee of—
    (i) the reason why the period of entitlement ended;
    (ii) the date of the last day in respect of which the employer is or was liable to make a payment of statutory sick pay to him.]

(b) the statement shall be furnished not more than 7 days after the day on which the period of entitlement ended, or, if earlier, on the day on which it is already required to be furnished under paragraph (4).]

(4) In a case which falls within paragraph (c) (period of entitlement expected to end before period of incapacity for work ends, on certain assumptions) of section 18(3)—

[¹ [⁴ (a) the information mentioned in paragraph (1) above is a statement informing the employee of—
    (i) the reason why the period of entitlement is expected to end;
    (ii) the date of the last day in respect of which the employer is or was expected to be liable to make a payment of statutory sick pay to him.]

(b) the statement shall be furnished—
    (i) in a case where the period of entitlement is expected to end in accordance with section 3(2)(b) of the Act (maximum entitled to statutory sick pay), on or before the 42nd day before the period of entitlement is expected to end; or
    (ii) in any other case, on or before the seventh day before the period of entitlement is expected to end

[³. . .].]

(5) For the purposes of section 18(3)(c)(i) (period for which the period of incapacity for work is to be assumed to continue to run) the prescribed period shall be 14 days.

AMENDMENTS

1. Statutory Sick Pay (General) Amendment Regulations 1986 (SI 1986/477), reg.6 (April 6, 1986).

2. Social Security (Incapacity Benefit) (Consequential and Transitional Amendments and Savings) Regulations 1995 (SI 1995/829), reg.15 (April 13, 1995).

3. Social Security Contributions, Statutory Maternity Pay and Statutory Sick Pay (Miscellaneous Amendments) Regulations 1996 (SI 1996/777), reg.2(5) (April 6, 1996).

4. Statutory Sick Pay (General) (Amendment) Regulations 2008 (SI 2008/1735), reg.2 (October 27, 2008).

DEFINITIONS

"employee"—see SSCBA 1992, s.163(1) and reg.16.
"employer"—see SSCBA 1992, s.163(1).
"period of entitlement"—see *ibid.*
"period of incapacity for work"—see *ibid.*
"prescribed"—see *ibid.*
"qualifying day"—see *ibid.*
"week"—see *ibid.*

4.31   The references to ss.3(2)(b) and 18(3) of the 1982 Act should now be read as referring to SSCBA 1992, s.153(2)(b) and SSAA 1992, s.130(3), respectively.

[¹Statements relating to the payment of statutory sick pay

4.32   **15A.**—[² . . .]

AMENDMENTS

1. Statutory Sick Pay (General) Amendment Regulations 1986 (SI 1986/477), reg.7 (April 6, 1986).
2. Statutory Sick Pay (General) (Amendment) Regulations 2008 (SI 2008/1735), reg.3 (October 27, 2008).

Meaning of "employee"

4.33   **16.**—(1) [²Subject to paragraph (1ZA),] in a case where, and in so far as, a person [². . .] is treated as an employed earner by virtue of the Social Security (Categorisation of Earners) Regulations 1978, he shall be treated as an employee for the purposes of Part I and in a case where, and in so far as, such a person is treated otherwise than as an employed earner by virtue of those regulations, he shall not be treated as an employee for the purposes of Part I.

[³(1ZA) Paragraph (1) shall have effect in relation to a person who—
(a) is under the age of 16; and
(b) would or, as the case may be, would not have been treated as an employed earner by virtue of the Social Security (Categorisation of Earners) Regulations 1978 had he been over that age,
as it has effect in relation to a person who is or, as the case may be, is not so treated.]

[¹(1A) Any person who is in employed earner's employment within the meaning of the Act under a contract of apprenticeship shall be treated as an employee for the purposes of Part I.]

(2) A person who is in employed earner's employment within the meaning of the Act but whose employer—
(a) does not fulfil the conditions prescribed in regulation 119(1)(b) of the Social Security (Contributions) Regulations 1979 as to residence or presence in Great Britain, or
(b) is a person who, by reason of any international treaty to which the United Kingdom is a party or of any international convention binding the United Kingdom—
(i) is exempt from the provisions of the Act, or
(ii) is a person against whom the provisions of that Act are not enforceable,
shall not be treated as an employee for the purposes of Part I.

AMENDMENTS

1. Statutory Sick Pay (Compensation of Employers) and Miscellaneous Provisions Regulations 1983 (SI 1983/376), reg.5(2) (April 6, 1983).
2. Employment Equality (Age) Regulations 2006 (SI 2006/1031), reg.49(1) and Sch.8, Pt 2, para.50 (October 1, 2006).
3. Employment Equality (Age) (Consequential Amendments) Regulations 2007 (SI 2007/825), reg.5(3) (April 6, 2007).

DEFINITIONS

"employee"—see SSCBA 1992, s.163(1) and reg.16.
"employer"—see SSCBA 1992, s.163(1).
"prescribed"—see *ibid.*

Meaning of "earnings"

17.—(1) [³. . .]   4.34

[⁴(2) For the purposes of section 163(2) of the Contributions and Benefits Act, the expression "earnings" refers to gross earnings and includes any remuneration or profit derived from a person's employment except any payment or amount which is—

(a) excluded [⁸or disregarded in the calculation of a person's earnings under regulation 25, 27 or 123 of, or Schedule 3 to, the Social Security (Contributions) Regulations 2001] [⁷(or would have been so excluded had he not been under the age of 16)];

(b) a chargeable emolument under section 10A of the Social Security Contributions and Benefits Act 1992, except where, in consequence of such a chargeable emolument being excluded from earnings, a person would not be entitled to statutory sick pay [⁷(or where such a payment or amount would have been so excluded and in consequence he would not have been entitled to statutory sick pay had he not been under the age of 16)].]

[¹(2A) [³. . .]]

(3) For the purposes of [⁵section 163(2) of the Contributions and Benefits Act] the expression "earnings" includes also—

[⁸(za) any amount retrospectively treated as earnings by regulations made by virtue of section 4B(2) of the Contributions and Benefits Act;]

(a) any sum payable by way of maternity pay or payable by the Secretary of State in pursuance of section 40 of the Employment Protection (Consolidation) Act 1978 in respect of maternity pay;

(b) any sum which is payable by the Secretary of State by virtue of section 122(3)(a) of that Act in respect of arrears of pay and which by virtue of section 42(1) of that Act is to go towards discharging a liability to pay maternity pay;

(c) any sum payable in respect of arrears of pay in pursuance of an order for reinstatement or re-engagement under that Act;

(d) any sum payable by way of pay in pursuance of an order under that Act for the continuation of a contract of employment;

(e) any sum payable by way of remuneration in pursuance of a protective award under the Employment Protection Act 1975;

(f) any sum payable to any employee under the Temporary Short time Working Compensation Scheme administered under powers conferred by the Employment Subsidies Act 1978;

(g) any sum paid in satisfaction of any entitlement to statutory sick pay;

[²(h) any sum payable by way of statutory maternity pay under Part V of the Social Security Act 1986, including sums payable in accordance with regulations made under section 46(8)(b) of that Act.]

[⁶(i) any sum payable by way of statutory paternity pay, including any sums payable in accordance with regulations made under section 171ZD(3) of the Contributions and Benefits Act;

(j) any sum payable by way of statutory adoption pay, including any sums payable in accordance with regulations made under section 171ZM(3) of the Contributions and Benefits Act.]

(4) [³. . .]

(5) [³. . .]

AMENDMENTS

1. Statutory Sick Pay (Compensation of Employers) and Miscellaneous Provisions Regulations 1983 (SI 1983/376), reg.5(3) (April 6, 1983).

2. Statutory Sick Pay (General) Amendment (No.2) Regulations 1987 (SI 1987/868), reg.4 (June 7, 1987).

3. Social Security (Miscellaneous Provisions) Amendment (No.2) Regulations 1992 (SI 1992/2595), reg.15 (November 16, 1992).

4. Social Security Contributions, Statutory Maternity Pay and Statutory Sick Pay (Miscellaneous Amendments) Regulations 1999 (SI 1999/567), reg.13 (April 6, 1999).

5. Social Security, Statutory Maternity Pay and Statutory Sick Pay (Miscellaneous Amendments) Regulations 2002 (SI 2002/2690), reg.14(a) (November 24, 2002).

6. Social Security, Statutory Maternity Pay and Statutory Sick Pay (Miscellaneous Amendments) Regulations 2002 (SI 2002/2690), reg.14(b) (April 6, 2003).

7. Employment Equality (Age) Regulations 2006 (SI 2006/1031), reg.49(1) and Sch.8, Pt 2, para.51 (October 1, 2006).

8. Social Security, Occupational Pension Schemes and Statutory Payments (Consequential Provisions) Regulations 2007 (SI 2007/1154), reg.5(2) and (3) (April 6, 2007).

DEFINITION

"employee"—see SSCBA 1992, s.163(1) and reg.16.

Payments to be treated or not to be treated as contractual remuneration

4.35

18. For the purposes of paragraph 2(1) and (2) of Schedule 2 to the Act, those things which are included within the expression "earnings" by regulation (except paragraph (3)(g) thereof) shall be, and those things which are excluded from that expression by that regulation shall not be, treated as contractual remuneration.

Normal weekly earnings

4.36

19.—(1) For the purposes of section 26, an employee's normal weekly earnings shall be determined in accordance with the provisions of this regulation.

(2) In this regulation—

"the critical date" means the first day of the period of entitlement in relation to which a person's normal weekly earnings fall to be determined, or, in a case to which paragraph 2(c) of Schedule 1 applies, the relevant date within the meaning of Schedule 1;

"normal pay day" means a day on which the terms of an employee's contract of service require him to be paid, or the practice in his employment is for him to be paid, if any payment is due to him; and

"day of payment" means a day on which the employee was paid.

(3) Subject to paragraph (4), the relevant period (referred to in section 26(2)) is the period between—

(a) the last normal pay day to fall before the critical date; and
(b) the last normal pay day to fall at least 8 weeks earlier than the normal pay day mentioned in sub-paragraph (a), including the normal pay day mentioned in sub-paragraph (a) but excluding that first mentioned in sub-paragraph (b).

(4) In a case where an employee has no identifiable normal pay day, paragraph (3) shall have effect as if the words "day of payment" were substituted for the words "normal pay day" in each place where they occur.

(5) In a case where an employee has normal pay days at intervals of, or approximating to one or more calendar months (including intervals of or approximating to a year) his normal weekly earnings shall be calculated by dividing his earnings in the relevant period by the number of calendar months in that period (or, if it is not a whole number, the nearest whole number), multiplying the result by 12 and dividing by 52.

(6) In a case to which paragraph (5) does not apply and the relevant period is not an exact number of weeks, the employee's normal weekly earnings shall be calculated by dividing his earnings in the relevant period by the number of days in the relevant period and multiplying the result by 7.

(7) In a case where the normal pay day mentioned in sub-paragraph (a) of paragraph (3) exists but that first mentioned in sub-paragraph (b) of that paragraph does not yet exist, the employee's normal weekly earnings shall be calculated as if the period for which all the earnings under his contract of service received by him before the critical date represented payment were the relevant period.

(8) In a case where neither of the normal pay days mentioned in paragraph (3) yet exists, the employee's normal weekly earnings shall be the remuneration to which he is entitled, in accordance with the terms of his contract of service for, as the case may be—
(a) a week's work; or
(b) a number of calendar month's work, divided by that number of months multiplied by 12 and divided by 52.

DEFINITIONS

"contract of service"—see SSCBA 1992, s.163(1).
"employee"—see SSCBA 1992, s.163(1) and reg.16.
"period of entitlement"—see *ibid.*

GENERAL NOTE

For some of the difficulties in applying this regulation, see *R(SSP)1/89*. There, the relevant period for a school dinner lady extended from the end of one term until the last pay day before her period of incapacity began. This was 11 weeks, but as the relevant period began the day after the last pay day at the end of term it could not include the lump-sum payment that was made as a retainer throughout the vacation. Without that sum her average weekly earnings did not qualify her for statutory sick pay. **4.37**

Treatment of one or more employers as one

20.—(1) In a case where the earnings paid to an employee in respect of 2 more employments are aggregated and treated as a single payment of earnings under regulation 12(1) of the Social Security (Contributions) Regulations 1979, the employers of the employee in respect of those employments shall be treated as one for all purposes of Part I. **4.38**

(2) Where 2 or more employers are treated as one under the provisions of paragraph (1), liability for the statutory sick pay payable by them to the employee shall be apportioned between them in such proportions as they may agree or, in default of agreement, in the proportions which the employee's earnings from each employment bear to the amount of the aggregated earnings.

(3) [[1]Subject to paragraphs (4) and (5)] where a contract of service ("the current contract") was preceded by a contract of service entered into between the same employer and employee ("the previous contract"), and the interval between the date on which the previous contract ceased to have effect and that on which the current contract came into force was not more than 8 weeks, then, for the purposes of establishing the employee's maximum entitlement within the meaning of section 5 (limitation on entitlement to statutory sick pay in any one period of entitlement or tax year), the provisions of Part I shall not have effect as if the employer were a different employer in relation to each of those contracts of service.

[[1](4) Where a contract of service ("the current contract") was preceded by two or more contracts of service entered into between the same employer and employee ("the previous contracts") and the previous contracts—

   (a) existed concurrently for at least part of their length; and

   (b) the intervals between the dates on which each of the previous contracts ceased to have effect and that on which the current contract came into force was not more than 8 weeks,

then, for the purposes of establishing the employee's maximum entitlement within the meaning of section 5 the provisions of Part I shall not have effect as if the employer were a different employer in relation to the current contract and whichever of the previous contracts was the contract by virtue of which the employer had become liable to pay the greatest proportion of statutory sick pay in respect of any tax year or period of entitlement.

(5) If, in any case to which paragraph (4) applies, the same proportion of the employer's liability for statutory sick pay becomes due under each of the previous contracts, then, for the purpose of establishing the employee's maximum entitlement within the meaning of section 5, the provisions of Part I shall have effect in relation to only one of the previous contracts.]

AMENDMENT

1. Statutory Sick Pay (Compensation of Employers) and Miscellaneous Provisions Regulations 1983 (SI 1983/376), reg.5(4) (April 6, 1983).

DEFINITIONS

    "contract of service"—see SSCBA 1992, s.163(1).
    "employee"—see SSCBA 1992, s.163(1) and reg.16.
    "employer"—see SSCBA 1992, s.163(1).
    "period of entitlement"—see *ibid.*

GENERAL NOTE

4.39   Specific provision is made in Statutory Sick Pay (National Health Service Employees) Regulations 1991 (SI 1991/589) in the case of NHS workers with divided contracts.

Treatment of more than one contract of service as one

4.40   **21.** Where 2 or more contracts of service exist concurrently between one employer and one employee, they shall be treated as one for all purposes of Part I except where, by virtue of regulation 11 of the Social Security (Contributions) Regulations 1979, the earnings from those contracts of service are not aggregated for the purposes of earnings-related contributions.

DEFINITIONS

"contract of service"—see SSCBA 1992, s.163(1).
"employee"—see SSCBA 1992, s.163(1) and reg.16.
"employer"—see SSCBA 1992, s.163(1).

[¹Election to be treated as different employers not to apply to recovery of statutory sick pay

21A.—(1) Paragraph (2) below applies for the purposes of section 159A of the Contributions and Benefits Act (power to provide for recovery by employers of sums paid by way of statutory sick pay) and of any order made under that section.

(2) Where an employer has made 2 or more elections under regulation 3 of the Income Tax (Employments) Regulations 1993 to be treated as a different employer in respect of each of the groups of employees specified in the election, the different employers covered by each of those elections shall be treated as one employer.]

AMENDMENT

1. Statutory Sick Pay Percentage Threshold Order 1995 (Consequential) Regulations 1995 (SI 1995/513), reg.3 (April 6, 1995).

DEFINITIONS

"employee"—see SSCBA 1992, s.163(1) and reg.16.
"employer"—see SSCBA 1992, s.163(1).

[¹Offences

22. [². . .]

AMENDMENTS

1. Statutory Maternity Pay (General) and Statutory Sick Pay (General) (Amendment) Regulations 2001 (SI 2001/206), reg.2 (February 23, 2001).
2. Statutory Maternity Pay (General) and Statutory Sick Pay (General) (Amendment) Regulations 2005 (SI 2005/989), reg.3(3) (immediately before April 6, 2005).

GENERAL NOTE

The repeal of this provision was consequential upon the bringing into force of the National Insurance Contributions and Statutory Payments Act 2004.

Statutory Sick Pay (Mariners, Airmen and Persons Abroad) Regulations 1982

(SI 1982/1349) (AS AMENDED)

The Secretary of State for Social Services, in exercise of the powers conferred upon him by sections 3(5) and (7), 22(1) and 26(1) of and paragraph 1 of Schedule 1 to the Social Security and Housing Benefits Act 1982(a) and of all other powers enabling him in that behalf, hereby makes the following regulations.

4.41

4.42

4.43

ARRANGEMENT OF REGULATIONS

Citation, commencement and interpretation

4.45   **1.**—(1) These regulations may be cited as the Statutory Sick Pay (Mariners, Airmen and Persons Abroad) Regulations 1982, and shall come into operation on 6th April 1983.

(2) In these Regulations—

"the Act" means the Social Security and Housing Benefits Act 1982;

"Part I" means Part I of the Act;

[[1]"the Contributions and Benefits Act," means the Social Security Contributions and Benefits Act 1992;

"the Contributions Regulations" means the Social Security (Contributions) Regulations 1979;]

"the General Regulations" means the Statutory Sick Pay (General) Regulations 1982;

and other expressions, unless the context otherwise requires, have the same meanings as in Part I.

(3) Unless the context otherwise requires, any reference—

(a) in these regulations to a numbered regulation is a reference to the regulation bearing that number in these regulations; and

(b) in any of these regulations to a numbered paragraph is a reference to the paragraph bearing that number in that regulation.

AMENDMENT

1. Social Security Contributions, Statutory Maternity Pay and Statutory Sick Pay (Miscellaneous Amendments) Regulations 1996 (SI 1996/777), reg.3(2) (April 6, 1996).

GENERAL NOTE

4.46   These Regulations make special provision for statutory sick pay under what is now Pt XI of the SSCBA 1992 as it affects mariners, airmen, persons abroad and persons employed in operations on the Continental Shelf. Under s.163(1) of the SSCBA 1992, a person is not, as a rule, an "employee", and therefore not qualified to receive statutory sick pay, unless he or she is employed in Great Britain. Regulations 5–8 prescribe exceptions to this rule, so that certain persons who are employed in other Member States but who are subject to the legislation of the

United Kingdom, certain mariners and airmen, and certain persons employed on the Continental Shelf, are "employees", though employed outside Great Britain; and so that certain limited classes of mariners and airmen are not "employees" though employed in Great Britain. Further general provision on the meaning of "employee" is made by reg.9, while reg.10 makes general provision regarding persons from abroad. Regulations 11–13, which provided for exceptions to reg.10, were repealed in 1996.

Some of the requirements of the Act and regulations made under it impose time-limits. Regulation 14 relaxes those requirements in their application to persons who are outside the United Kingdom and for that reason cannot comply with them.

It should be noted that these regulations have never been fully updated to include appropriate references to SSCBA 1992. Accordingly, all references to Pt I of the Social Security and Housing Benefits Act 1982 in these regulations should be read as references to Pt XI of SSCBA 1992.

Mariners—interpretation

2. In regulations 6 and 11, the expressions "British ship," "foreign-going ship" "managing owner," "mariner," "owner" and "radio officer" have the same meanings as in Case C of Part VIII of the Social Security (Contributions) Regulations 1979, and the expressions "ship" and "ship or vessel," except in regulation 6(2), include hovercraft.

4.47

GENERAL NOTE

The provisions relating to Case C of Pt VIII of the Social Security (Contributions) Regulations 1979 have been re-enacted in Case C of Pt IX of the Social Security Contributions Regulations 2001 (SI 2001/1004).

4.48

Airmen—interpretation

3. In regulations 7 and 12—

4.49

"airman" means a person who is, or has been, employed under a contract of service either as a pilot, commander, navigator or other member of the crew of any aircraft, or in any other capacity on board any aircraft where—

(a) the employment in that other capacity is for the purposes of the aircraft or its crew or of any passengers or cargo or mails carried thereby; and

(b) the contract is entered into in the United Kingdom with a view to its performance (in whole or in part) while the aircraft is in flight, but does not include a person in so far as his employment is as a serving member of the forces;

"British aircraft" means any aircraft belonging to Her Majesty and any aircraft registered in the United Kingdom of which the owner (or managing owner if there is more than one owner) resides or has his principal place of business in Great Britain, and references to the owner of an aircraft shall, in relation to an aircraft which has been hired, be taken as referring to the person for the time being entitled as hirer to possession and control of the aircraft by virtue of the hiring or any subordinate hiring.

DEFINITION

"contract of service"—see SSCBA 1992, s.163(1).

Continental shelf—interpretation

4.50

4. In this regulation and regulations 8 and 13—

"designated area" means any area which may from time to time be designated by Order in Council under the Continental Shelf Act 1964 as an area within which the rights of the United Kingdom with respect to the sea-bed and subsoil and their natural resources may be exercised;

"prescribed area" means an area over which Norway or any member State (other than the United Kingdom) exercises sovereign rights for the purpose of exploring the seabed and subsoil and exploiting their natural resources, being an area outside the territorial seas of Norway or that member State [¹or any other area which is from time to time specified under section 22(5) of the Oil and Gas (Enterprise) Act 1982];

"prescribed employment" means employment in a designated area or prescribed area in connection with [¹any activity mentioned in section 23(2) of the Oil and Gas (Enterprise) Act 1982 in any designated area or in any prescribed area.]

AMENDMENT

1. Social Security and Statutory Sick Pay (Oil and Gas (Enterprise) Act 1982) (Consequential) Regulations 1982 (SI 1982/1738), reg.5 (April 6, 1983).

DEFINITION

"prescribed"—see SSCBA 1992, s.163(1).

Persons in other member States—meaning of "employee"

4.51

5. Subject to regulations 6(2), 7(2) and 9, a person who is—

(a) gainfully employed in a member State other than the United Kingdom in such circumstances that if his employment were in Great Britain he would be an employee for the purposes of Part I or a person treated as such an employee under regulation 16 of the General Regulations; and

(b) subject to the legislation of the United Kingdom under Council Regulation (EEC) No. 1408/71;

notwithstanding that he is not employed in Great Britain, shall be treated as an employee for the purposes of Part I.

DEFINITIONS

"Pt I"—see reg.1(2).
"the General Regulations"—*ibid.*

[¹Persons absent from Great Britain—meaning of "employee"

4.52

5A. Subject to regulations 5, 6(2) and 9, where a person, while absent from Great Britain for any purpose, is gainfully employed by an employer who is liable to pay in respect of him secondary Class 1 contributions under section 6 of the Contributions and Benefits Act 1992 or regulation 120 of the Contributions Regulations, he shall be treated as an employee for the purposes of Part XI of the Contributions and Benefits Act.]

AMENDMENT

1. Social Security Contributions, Statutory Maternity Pay and Statutory Sick Pay (Miscellaneous Amendments) Regulations 1996 (SI 1996/777), reg.3(3) (April 6, 1996).

DEFINITIONS

"employer"—see SSCBA 1992, s.163(1).
"the Contributions and Benefits Act"—see reg.1(2).
"the Contributions Regulations"—*ibid.*

GENERAL NOTE

The Social Security Contributions Regulations 2001 (SI 2001/1004) have nowrevoked and superseded the Social Security Contributions Regulations 1979 (SI 1979/591). Regulation 146 of the 2001 Regulations is the parallel provision to reg.120 of the 1979 Regulations.   **4.53**

Mariners—meaning of "employee"

6.—(1) Subject to regulation 9, where a mariner—   **4.54**
(a) is employed as such and—
   (i) the employment is on board a British ship; or
   (ii) the employment is on board a ship and the contract in respect of the employment is entered into the United Kingdom with a view to its performance (in whole or in part) while the ship or vessel is on her voyage; and
   (iii) in a case to which head (ii) applies, the person by whom the mariner's earnings are paid, or, in the case of employment as a master or member of the crewof a ship or vessel, either that person or the owner of the ship or vessel (or the managing owner if there is more than one owner) has a place of business in Great Britain; or
(b) is employed as a master, member of the crew or radio officer on board any ship or vessel, not being a mariner to whom the last preceding subparagraph applies; and
   (i) in the case of the employment being as a radio officer, if the contract under which the employment is performed is entered into in the United Kingdom, the employer or the person paying the radio officer his earnings for that employment has a place of business in Great Britain, or,
   (ii) in the case of the employment being as a master, member of the crew or radio officer, if the contract is not entered into in the United Kingdom, the employer or the person paying the earnings has his principal place of business in Great Britain,
then, unless he is a mariner to whom paragraph (2) applies, he shall, notwithstanding that he may not be employed in Great Britain, be treated as an employee for the purposes of Part I.
(2) A mariner who—
(a) is in employment (including any period of leave, other than leave for the purpose of study, accruing from the employment) as a master or member of the crew of a ship, where—
   (i) the employment is on a foreign-going ship; or

    (ii) the employment is partly on a foreign-going ship and partly otherwise than on such a ship, and it is a requirement of the contract of service which relates to that employment that any payment of earnings in respect of that employment is to be made during the employment on the foreign-going ship; or

(b) has been in such employment as is mentioned in sub-paragraph (a), where—

    (i) not more than thirteen weeks have elapsed since he was last in such employment;

    (ii) he continues to be employed by the employer by whom he was employed when he was last in such employment; and

    (iii) he is not employed (by that employer or any other) on terms which are inconsistent with his being able to resume such employment as is mentioned in sub-paragraph (a) after not more than thirteen weeks have elapsed since he was last in such employment;

shall, notwithstanding that he may be employed in Great Britain, not be treated as an employee for the purposes of Part I.

DEFINITIONS

    "British ship"—see reg.2.
    "contract of service"—see SSCBA 1992, s.163(1).
    "employer"—*ibid*.
    "foreign-going ship"—see reg.2.
    "managing owner"—*ibid*.
    "mariner"—*ibid*.
    "owner"—*ibid*.
    "Pt I"—see reg.1(2).
    "radio officer"—see reg.2.
    "ship"—*ibid*.
    "ship or vessel"—*ibid*.
    "week"—see SSCBA 1992, s.163(1).

Airmen—meaning of "employee"

4.55   **7.**—(1) Subject to regulation 9 and the following provisions of this regulation, where an airman is employed as such on board any aircraft, and the employer of that airman or the person paying the airman his earnings in respect of the employment (whether or not the person making the payment is acting as agent for the employer) or the person under whose directions the terms of the airman's employment and the amount of the earnings to be paid in respect thereof are determined has—

(a) in the case of the aircraft being a British aircraft, a place of business in Great Britain; or

(b) in any other case, his principal place of business in Great Britain, then, notwithstanding that he may not be employed in Great Britain, he shall be treated as an employee for the purposes of Part I.

(2) Subject to the provisions of paragraph (3), an airman shall not be treated as an employee for those purposes if he is not domiciled, and has no place of residence, in Great Britain.

(3) The provisions of paragraph (2) shall have effect subject to any

Order in Council giving effect to any reciprocal agreement made under section 143 of the Social Security Act 1975 (reciprocity with other countries).

DEFINITIONS

"airman"—see reg.3.
"British aircraft"—*ibid.*
"employee"—see SSCBA 1992, s.163(1).
"employer"—*ibid.*
"Pt I"—see reg.1(2).

GENERAL NOTE

Para. (3)
Section 143 of the Social Security Act 1975 has nowbeen replaced in similar   4.56
terms by s.179 of the SSAA 1992.

Continental shelf—meaning of "employee"

8. Subject to regulation 9, a person in prescribed employment, not-with-   4.57
standing that he may not be employed in Great Britain, shall be treated as an employee for the purposes of Part I.

DEFINITIONS

"employee"—see SSCBA 1992, s.163(1).
"Part I"—see reg.1(2).
"prescribed employment"—see reg.4.
"prescribed"—see SSCBA 1992, s.163(1).

Meaning of "employee"—general

9. No person who, by virtue of regulation 16 of the General Regulations,   4.58
would not be treated as an employee for the purposes of Part I if his employment were in Great Britain, shall be treated as an employee by virtue of any of regulations 5–8.

DEFINITIONS

"employee"—see SSCBA 1992, s.163(1).
"Part I"—see reg.1(2).
"the General Regulations"—*ibid.*

[¹Persons abroad—general

10. In a case where a mariner, an airman or a continental shelf   4.59
employee, respectively, within the meaning of regulation 6(1), 7 or 8, or a person who, is an employee or, is treated as an employee under regulation 5 or 5A, is incapable of work during a period of entitlement to statutory sick pay while absent from Great Britain, his entitlement to statutory sick pay shall cease only if he fails to satisfy the conditions of entitlement under Part XI of the Contributions and Benefits Act notwithstanding that his employer ceases, during the period of entitlement, to be liable to pay, in respect of him, secondary Class 1 contributions under section 6 of the Contributions and Benefits Act or regulation 120 of the Contributions Regulations.]

AMENDMENT

1. Social Security Contributions, Statutory Maternity Pay and Statutory Sick Pay (Miscellaneous Amendments) Regulations 1996 (SI 1996/777), reg.3(4) (April 6, 1996).

DEFINITIONS

"employee"—see SSCBA 1992, s.163(1).
"employer"—*ibid.*
"period of entitlement"—*ibid.*
"the Contributions and Benefits Act"—see reg.1(2).
"the Contributions Regulations"—*ibid.*

GENERAL NOTE

4.60 See note to reg.5A.

Mariners—exception to regulation 10

4.61 **11.** [¹. . .]

AMENDMENT

1. Social Security Contributions, Statutory Maternity Pay and Statutory Sick Pay (Miscellaneous Amendments) Regulations 1996 (SI 1996/777), reg.3(5) (April 6, 1996).

Airmen—exception to regulation 10

4.62 **12.** [¹. . .]

AMENDMENT

1. Social Security Contributions, Statutory Maternity Pay and Statutory Sick Pay (Miscellaneous Amendments) Regulations 1996 (SI 1996/777), reg.3(6) (April 6, 1996).

Continental shelf—exception to regulation 10

4.63 **13.** [¹. . .]

AMENDMENT

1. Social Security Contributions, Statutory Maternity Pay and Statutory Sick Pay (Miscellaneous Amendments) Regulations 1996 (SI 1996/777), reg.3(7) (April 6, 1996).

Time for compliance with requirements of Part I and regulations

4.64 **14.** Where—
   (a) an employee is outside the United Kingdom;
   (b) Part I or regulations made there under require any act to be done forthwith or on the happening of a certain event or within a specified time; and
   (c) because the employee is outside the United Kingdom he or his employer cannot comply with the requirement;

the employee or the employer, as the case may be, shall be deemed to have complied with it if he performs the act as soon as reasonably practicable.

DEFINITIONS

"employee"—see SSCBA 1992, s.163(1).
"employer"—*ibid.*
"Pt I"—see reg.1(2).

Statutory Sick Pay (Medical Evidence) Regulations 1985

(SI 1985/1604) (AS AMENDED)

The Secretary of State for Social Services, in exercise of the powers conferred upon him by section 17(2A) of the Social Security and Housing Benefits Act 1982, and of all other powers enabling him in that behalf, by this instrument, which contains only provisions consequential upon section 20 of the Social Security Act 1985 and regulations made under the aforesaid section 17(2A), makes the following regulations:

ARRANGEMENT OF ARTICLES

Citation, commencement and interpretation

1.—(1) These regulations may be cited as the Statutory Sick Pay (Medical Evidence) Regulations 1985 and shall come into operation on 6th April 1986.   4.66

(2) In these regulations, unless the context otherwise requires

"the 1982 Act" means the Social Security and Housing Benefits Act 1982;

"signature" means, in relation to a statement given in accordance with these regulations, the name by which the person giving that statement is usually known (any name other than the surname being either in full or otherwise indicated) written by that person in his own handwriting; and "signed" shall be construed accordingly.

(3) [¹. . .]

AMENDMENT

1. Social Security (Miscellaneous Provisions) Amendment Regulations 1992 (SI 1992/247), reg.6(2) (March 9, 1992).

GENERAL NOTE

4.67   These Regulations and the rules in Sch.1 prescribe the form of the statement to be issued by a doctor advising an employee that he or she should refrain from work (or need not refrain from work) for a period up to six months, or longer in certain circumstances. Regulation 2(2) provides that medical information cannot be required in respect of an employee's first seven days in any spell of incapacity for work.

Medical information

4.68   **2.**—[[1](1) Medical information required under section 17(2) of the 1982 Act relating to incapacity for work shall be provided either—
  (a) in the form of a statement given by a doctor in accordance with the rules set out in Part I of Schedule 1 to these Regulations on the form set out in Part II of that Schedule; or
  (b) where the doctor—
    (i) has not given a statement under sub-paragraph (a) of this paragraph since the patient was examined and wishes to give such a statement but more than one day has passed since the examination; or
    (ii) advises that the patient should refrain from work on the basis of a written report from another doctor, set out in Part I of Schedule 1A to these Regulations on the form set out in Part II of that Schedule; or
  (c) by such other means as may be sufficient in the circumstances of any particular case.]

(2) An employee shall not be required under section 17(2) of the 1982 Act to provide medical information in respect of the first 7 days in any spell of incapacity for work; and for this purpose "spell of incapacity" means a continuous period of incapacity for work which is immediately preceded by a day on which the claimant either worked or was not incapable of work.

AMENDMENT

1. Social Security (Miscellaneous Provisions) Amendment Regulations 1992 (SI 1992/247), reg.6(3) (March 9, 1992).

SCHEDULE [1]   **Regulation 1(3)**

PART I

RULES

4.69   **1.** In these rules, unless the context otherwise requires

"patient" means the person in respect of whom a statement is given in accordance with these rules;
"doctor" means a registered medical practitioner not being the patient;
"2 weeks" means any period of 14 consecutive days.

2. The doctor's statement shall be in the form set out in Part II of this Schedule.

[² **3** Where the patient—

- (a) is on the list of a person providing primary medical services under the National Health Service Act 1977 or the National Health Service (Scotland) Act 1978 and is being attended by a doctor performing such services; or
- (b) is on the list of a doctor, or list held jointly by two or more doctors performing personal medical services in connection with a pilot scheme under the National Health Service (Primary Care) Act 1997 and is being attended by such a doctor,

the doctor's statement shall be on the form provided by the Secretary of State for the purpose and shall be signed by the attending doctor.]

4. In any other case, the doctor's statement shall be on a form provided by the Secretary of State for the purpose and shall be signed by the doctor attending the patient.

5. Every doctor's statement shall be completed in ink or other indelible substance and shall contain the following particulars:—

- (a) the patient's name;
- (b) the date of the examination on which the doctor's statement is based;
- (c) the diagnosis of the patient's disorder in respect of which the doctor is advising the patient to refrain from work or, as the case may be, which has caused the patient's absence from work;
- (d) the date on which the doctor's statement is given;
- (e) the address of the doctor,

and shall bear, opposite the words "Doctor's signature", the signature of the doctor making the statement written after there have been entered the patient's name and the doctor's diagnosis.

6. Subject to rules 7 and 8 below, the diagnosis of the disorder in respect of which the doctor is advising the patient to refrain from work or, as the case may be, which has caused the patient's absence from work shall be specified as precisely as the doctor's knowledge of the patient's condition at the time of the examination permits.

7. The diagnosis may be specified less precisely where, in the doctor's opinion, a disclosure of the precise disorder would be prejudicial to the patient's well-being, or to the patient's position with his employer.

8. In the case of an initial examination by a doctor in respect of a disorder stated by the patient to have caused incapacity for work, where—

- (a) there are no clinical signs of that disorder, and
- (b) in the doctor's opinion, the patient need not refrain from work,

instead of specifying a diagnosis "unspecified" may be entered.

9. A doctor's statement must be given on a date not later than one day after the date of the examination on which it is based, and no further doctor's statement based on the same examination shall be furnished other than a doctor's statement by way of replacement of an original which has been lost or mislaid, in which case it shall be clearly marked "duplicate".

10. Where, in the doctor's opinion, the patient will become fit to resume work on a day not later than 2 weeks after the date of the examination on which the doctor's statement is based, the doctor's statement shall specify that day.

11. Subject to rules 12 and 13 below, the doctor's statement shall specify the minimum period during which, in the doctor's opinion, the patient should, by reason of his disorder, refrain from work.

12. The period specified shall begin on the date of the examination on which the doctor's statement is based and shall not exceed 6 months unless the patient has, on the advice of a doctor, refrained from work for at least 6 months immediately preceding that date.

13. Where—

- (a) the patient has, on the advice of a doctor, refrained from work for at least 6 months immediately preceding the date of the examination on which the doctor's statement is based; and
- (b) in the doctor's opinion, it will be necessary for the patient to refrain from work for the foreseeable future,

instead of specifying a period, the doctor may, having regard to the circumstances of the particular case, enter, after the word "until", the words "further notice".

14. The Notes set out in Part III of this Schedule shall accompany the form of doctor's statement provided by the Secretary of State.

PART II

FORM OF DOCTOR'S STATEMENT

DOCTOR'S STATEMENT

4.70   In confidence to

Mr/Mrs/Miss

....

I examined you today/yesterday and advised you that:

(a) you need not refrain from work   *(b)* you should refrain from work

                                                                                for ....

                                                                                OR until

Diagnosis of your disorder
causing absence from work ....

Doctor's remarks

Doctor's   Date
signature   of signing

PART III

NOTES

4.71   The following notes shall accompany the form of doctor's statement provided by the Secretary of State:

On the doctor's statement:

(1) After the words "you should refrain from work for", the period entered must not exceed 6 months unless the patient has, on the advice of a doctor, already refrained from work for a continuous period of 6 months.

(2) After the words "you should refrain from work until"—

(a) if the patient is being given a date when he can return to work, the date entered should not be more than 2 weeks after the date of the examination;

(b) if the patient has already been incapable of work for at least 6 months and recovery of capacity for work in the foreseeable future is not expected, "further notice" may be entered.

AMENDMENTS

1. Social Security (Miscellaneous Provisions) Amendment Regulations 1992 (SI 1992/247), reg.6(4) (March 9, 1992).

2. General Medical Services and Personal Medical Services Transitional and Consequential Provisions Order 2004 (SI 2004/865), art.119 and Sch.1, para.3 (April 1, 2004).

GENERAL NOTE

Paragraph 3 of Pt I to this Schedule is phrased in a slightly different form so far as Wales is concerned: see General Medical Services Transitional and Consequential Provisions (Wales) (No.2) Order 2004 (SI 2004/1016 (W.113), art.95 and Sch.1, para.3.

4.72

SCHEDULE 1A   [¹**Regulation 2(1)**

PART I

RULES

1. In these rules, unless the context otherwise requires—

4.73

"patient" means the person in respect of whom a statement is given in accordance with these rules;

"doctor" means a registered medical practitioner not being the patient;

"special statement" means the form prescribed in Part II of this Schedule.

2. Where a doctor advises a patient to refrain from work on the basis of a written report which he has received from another doctor or where a doctor has not issued a statement since the claimant was examined and he wishes to issue a statement more than a day after the examination he shall use the special statement.

3. The special statement shall be completed in the manner described in paragraph 5 of Part I to Schedule 1.

4. Subject to rules 5 and 6 below, the diagnosis of the patient's disorder in respect of which the doctor is advising the patient to refrain from work or as the case may be, which has caused the patient's absence from work shall be specified as precisely as the doctor's knowledge of the patient's condition permits.

5. The diagnosis may be specified less precisely where in the doctor's opinion, a disclosure of the precise disorder would be prejudicial to the patient's well being, or to the patient's position with his employer.

6. In a case of a disorder stated by the patient to have caused incapacity for work, where—

   (a) no clinical signs have been found of that disorder; and

   (b) in the doctor's opinion, the patient need not refrain from work, "unspecified" may be entered.

7. Part B of the special statement must only be given on a date not later than one month after the date of the written report on which the special statement is based and that part shall only be used where the patient is being advised to refrain from work for a specified period of not more than one month.

[¹PART II

4.74   FORM OF SPECIAL STATEMENT

FOR SOCIAL SECURITY AND   Special Statement
STATUTORY SICK PAY   by the Doctor
PURPOSES ONLY

In confidence to

Mr/Mrs/Miss/Ms ....

(A) I examined you on the   (B) I have not examined you but, on
                                         the basis of a recent written report from—

following dates ....

....   Doctor .... (Name if known)
                                                             of

....
and advised you that you should
refrain from work   ....
From .... To ....
                                                             .... (Address)
Diagnosis of your disorder   I have advised you that you should refrain
causing absence from work   From work for/until

....

Doctor's remarks

Doctor's   Date of signing
signature

The special circumstances in which this form may be used are described in the handbook
"Medical Evidence for Social Security and Statutory Sick Pay Purposes".

```
.............................................................
.
.
.
.
.
.
.
.
.
.
.
.
.............................................................
```

AMENDMENT

1. Social Security (Miscellaneous Provisions) Amendment Regulations 1992 (SI
1992/247), reg.6(5) and Sch.2 (March 9, 1992).

Statutory Sick Pay (National Health Service Employees) Regulations 1991

(SI 1991/589) (AS AMENDED)

The Secretary of State for Social Security in exercise of the powers conferred by sections 26(1) and (5A), 45(1) and 47 of the Social Security and Housing Benefits Act 1982 and of all other powers enabling him in that behalf, by this instrument, which contains only regulations consequential upon paragraph 16 of Schedule 6 to the Social Security Act 1990, hereby makes the following Regulations:

4.75

ARRANGEMENT OF REGULATIONS

1. Citation, commencement and interpretation
2. Treatment of more than one contract of employment as one contract
3. Notification of election
4. Provision of information by employees
5. Treatment of two or more employers as one
6. Time for which an election is to have effect

Citation, commencement and interpretation

1.—(1) These Regulations may be cited as the Statutory Sick Pay (National Health Service Employees) Regulations 1991 and shall come into force on 1st April 1991.

4.76

(2) In these Regulations, a "health authority" [²shall in relation to Wales have the same meaning it has in section 8] of the National Health Service Act 1977, and in relation to Scotland mean the health board within the meaning of section 2 of the National Health Service (Scotland) Act 1978.

[¹(3) In these Regulations, "Primary Care Trust" means a Primary Care Trust established under section 16A of the National Health Service Act 1977.]

[²(4) In these Regulations, "Strategic Health Authority" means a Strategic Health Authority established under section 8 of the National Health Service Act 1977.]

[³(5) In these Regulations, a reference to "NHS trust" shall be construed to include a reference to an NHS foundation trust within the meaning of section 1(1) of the Health and Social Care (Community Health and Standards) Act 2003 where the application for authorisation to become an NHS foundation trust was made by an NHS trust.]

AMENDMENTS

1. Health Act 1999 (Supplementary, Consequential etc. Provisions) (No.2) Order 2000 (SI 2000/694), art.3 and Sch., para.2(2) (April 1, 2000).
2. National Health Service Reform and Health Care Professions Act 2002 (Supplementary, Consequential etc. Provisions) Regulations 2002 (SI 2002/2469), reg.4 and Sch.1, Pt 2, para.50 (October 1, 2002).
3. Health and Social Care (Community Health and Standards) Act 2003 (Supplementary and Consequential Provision) (NHS Foundation Trusts) Order 2004 (SI 2004/696), art.3(17) and Sch.17 (April 1, 2004).

Treatment of more than one contract of employment as one contract

4.77   **2.** Where, in consequence of the establishment of one or more National Health Service Trusts under Part I of the National Health Service and Community Care Act 1990 or the National Health Service (Scotland) Act 1978, a person's contract of employment is treated by a scheme under that Part or Act as divided so as to constitute two or more contracts, [¹or where an order under paragraph 23(1) of Schedule 5A to the National Health Service Act 1977 provides that a woman's contract of employment is so divided,] he may elect for all those contracts to be treated as one contract for the purposes of Part I of the Social Security and Housing Benefits Act 1982.

AMENDMENT

1. Health Act 1999 (Supplementary, Consequential etc. Provisions) (No.2) Order 2000 (SI 2000/694), art.3 and Sch., para.2(3) (April 1, 2000).

Notification of election

4.78   **3.** A person who makes an election under regulation 2 above shall give written notification of that election to each of his employers under the two or more contracts of service mentioned in that regulation, before the end of the fourth day of incapacity for work in the period of incapacity for work in relation to a contract of service with the employer with whom this day first occurs.

Provision of information by employees

4.79   **4.** A person who makes an election under regulation 2 above shall, as soon as is reasonably practicable after giving notice of that election, provide each of his employers under the two or more contracts of service mentioned in that regulation with the following information—
(a) the name and address of each of his employers; and
(b) the date his employment with each of those employers commenced; and
(c) details of his earnings during the relevant period and for this purpose "earnings" and "relevant period" have the same meanings as they have for the purposes of section 26(2) of the Social Security and Housing Benefits Act 1982.

Treatment of two or more employers as one

4.80   **5.** The employer to be regarded for the purposes of statutory sick pay as the employee's employer under the one contract where 2 or more contracts of service are treated as one in accordance with regulation 2 above, shall be—
[¹(a) in the case of a person whose contract of employment is treated by a scheme under Part I of the National Health Service and Community Care Act 1990 or the National Health Service (Scotland) Act 1978 as divided—
(i) the Health Authority or Primary Care Trust from which the employee was transferred, in a case where any one of the employee's contracts of service is with that Health Authority or Primary Care Trust; or

640

    (ii) the first NHS trust to which a contract of service was transferred in a case where none of the employee's contracts of service are with the Health Authority or Primary Care Trust from which he was transferred;
    or

(b) in the case of a person whose contract of employment is divided as provided by an order under paragraph 23(1) of Schedule 5A to the National Health Service Act 1977—

    (i) the [²Strategic Health Authority], NHS trust or Primary Care Trust from which the employee was transferred, in a case where any one of the employee's contracts of service is with that body; or

    (ii) the first Primary Care Trust to which a contract of service was transferred in a case where none of the employee's contracts of service are with the body from which he was transferred.]

AMENDMENTS

1. Health Act 1999 (Supplementary, Consequential etc. Provisions) (No.2) Order 2000 (SI 2000/694), art.3 and Sch., para.2(4) (April 1, 2000).

2. National Health Service Reform and Health Care Professions Act 2002 (Supplementary, Consequential etc. Provisions) Regulations 2002 (SI 2002/2469), reg.6 and Sch.3 (October 1, 2002).

Time for which an election is to have effect

6. An election made under regulation 2 shall lapse at the end of the period of incapacity for work in relation to the contract of service with the employer mentioned in regulation 5.   4.81

Statutory Sick Pay Percentage Threshold Order 1995

(SI 1995/512)

Whereas a draft of the following Order was laid before Parliament in accordance with the provisions of section 3(3) of the Statutory Sick Pay Act 1994 and approved by resolution of each House of Parliament: 4.82

Now, therefore, the Secretary of State for Social Security, in exercise of the powers conferred by sections 159A and 175(3) and (4) of the Social Security Contributions and Benefits Act 1992 and of all other powers enabling him in that behalf, hereby makes the following Order:

Art.1. Citation, commencement and interpretation
Art.2. Right of employer to recover statutory sick pay
Art.3. Recovery by deduction from contributions payments
Art.4. Recovery from the Secretary of State
Art.5. Repeals and revocations
Art.6. Consequential amendments [*omitted*]

Citation, commencement and interpretation

1.—(1) This Order may be cited as the Statutory Sick Pay Percentage Threshold Order 1995 and shall come into force on 6th April 1995.   4.83

(2) In this Order, unless the context otherwise requires, "income tax month" means the period beginning on the 6th day of any calendar month and ending on the 5th day of the following calendar month.

(3) A reference in this Order to a payment of statutory sick pay shall not include any such payment made in respect of a day of incapacity for work before the coming into force of this Order.

(4) Unless the context otherwise requires, any reference in this Order to a numbered article is a reference to the article bearing that number in this Order and any reference in an article to a numbered paragraph is a reference to the paragraph of that article bearing that number.

GENERAL NOTE

4.84   This Order makes provision for employers to recover payments of statutory sick pay where such payments amount to more than 13 per cent of their liability for Class 1 contributions payments in any income tax month. Consequently, this facility only arises where there is widespread sickness absence in a workplace. Article 2 sets out how the amount an employer may recover is to be determined. Article 3 provides for the amount determined under art.2 to be recovered by deduction from Class 1 National Insurance contributions payments. Article 4 provides for repayment by or on behalf of HMRC to employers where the amount they are entitled to deduct exceeds their contributions payments. Article 5 repeals and revokes the former enactments which provided for recovery of statutory sick pay by small employers. Article 6 (not included here) makes amendments to various enactments which are consequential on the repeals and revocations in art.5.

Right of employer to recover statutory sick pay

4.85   **2.**—(1) Subject to paragraph (2) an employer is entitled to recover in accordance with articles 3 and 4 the amount, if any, by which the payments of statutory sick pay made by him in any income tax month exceed 13 per cent. of the amount of his liability for contributions payments in respect of that income tax month.

(2) For the purposes of calculating the amount an employer is entitled to recover under paragraph (1), there shall be excluded any payment of statutory sick pay which was not made—

    (a) in the income tax month in which he received notice, in accordance with regulation 7 of the Statutory Sick Pay (General) Regulations 1982, of the day or days of incapacity for work to which the payment related;

    (b) in a case where it would have been impracticable to make the payment in that income tax month in view of the employer's methods of accounting for and paying remuneration, in the following income tax month; or

    (c) in a case where a decision had been made by an adjudication officer, social security appeal tribunal or Commissioner that the employee was entitled to that payment, within the time-limits set out in regulation 9 of those Regulations.

DEFINITION

"income tax month"—see art.1(2).

Recovery by deduction from contributions payments

4.86   **3.**—(1) An employer may recover an amount determined in accordance with article 2 in respect of any income tax month by making one or more deductions from his contributions payments for that or any following income tax month within 6 years from the end of the tax year in which he became entitled to recover that amount, except where and insofar as—

(a) that amount has been repaid to him by or on behalf of the Secretary of State under article 4; or

(b) he has made a request in writing under article 4 that that amount be repaid to him, and he has not received notification by or on behalf of the Secretary of State that the request is refused.

(2) A deduction from contributions payments made in accordance with paragraph (1) shall be disregarded for the purposes of determining whether an employer has discharged any liability of his in respect of Class 1 contributions.

DEFINITION

"income tax month"—see art.1(2).

Recovery from the Secretary of State

4.—(1) If the amount which an employer is or would otherwise be enti-   4.87
tled to deduct under article 3 exceeds the amount of his contributions payments in respect of earnings paid in an income tax month, and the Secretary of State is satisfied that that is so, then provided that the employer has requested him in writing to do so, there shall be repaid to the employer by or on behalf of the Secretary of State such amount as the employer was unable to deduct.

(2) If an employer is not liable for any contributions payments in an income tax month but would otherwise be entitled to deduct an amount under article 3, and the Secretary of State is satisfied that that is so, then provided the employer has in writing requested him to do so, that amount shall be repaid to the employer by or on behalf of the Secretary of State.

DEFINITION

"income tax month"—see art.1(2).

GENERAL NOTE

The Secretary of State's functions under this article were transferred to the Board   4.88
of the Inland Revenue (now HMRC) by s.1(2) of, and Sch.2 to, the Social Security Contributions (Transfer of Functions, etc.) Act 1999.

Repeals and revocations

5. Subject to the savings made by regulations under section 159A(4) of   4.89
the Social Security Contributions and Benefits Act 1992—

(a) sections 158 and 159 of the Social Security Contributions and Benefits Act 1992 shall be repealed; and

(b) the Statutory Sick Pay (Compensation of Employers) and Miscellaneous Provisions Regulations 1983 and the Statutory Sick Pay (Small Employers' Relief) Regulations 1991 shall be revoked.

Consequential amendments

6. [*omitted.*]   4.90

Statutory Sick Pay and Statutory Maternity Pay (Decisions) Regulations 1999

(SI 1999/776)

The Secretary of State for Social Security, in exercise of powers conferred by section 20(3) of the Social Security Administration Act 1992, sections 8(1)(f) and 25(3) of the Social Security Contributions (Transfer of Functions, etc.) Act 1999 and of all other powers enabling him in that behalf, with the concurrence of the Commissioners of Inland Revenue, hereby makes the following Regulations:

ARRANGEMENT OF REGULATIONS

4.91 1. Citation, commencement and interpretation
2. Application for the determination of any issue arising as to, or in connection with, entitlement to statutory sick pay or statutory maternity pay
3. Applications in connection with statutory sick pay or statutory maternity pay
4. Revocation of regulation 20 of the Social Security (Adjudication) Regulations 1995

Citation, commencement and interpretation

4.92 **1.**—(1) These Regulations may be cited as the Statutory Sick Pay and Statutory Maternity Pay (Decisions) Regulations 1999 and shall come into force on 1st April 1999.
(2) In these Regulations—
(a) "the Contributions and Benefits Act" means the Social Security Contributions and Benefits Act 1992;
(b) "employee" and "employer" have, in relation to—
  (i) statutory sick pay, the meanings given by section 163(1) of the Contributions and Benefits Act;
  (ii) statutory maternity pay, the meanings given by section 171(1) of the Contributions and Benefits Act.

Application for the determination of any issue arising as to, or in connection with, entitlement to statutory sick pay or statutory maternity pay

4.93 **2.**—(1) An application for the determination of any issue arising as to, or in connection with, entitlement to statutory sick pay or statutory maternity pay may be submitted to an officer of the Board by—
(a) the Secretary of State; or
(b) the employee concerned.
(2) Such an issue shall be decided by an officer of the Board only on the basis of such an application or on his own initiative.

DEFINITION

"employee"—see reg.1(2).

Applications in connection with statutory sick pay or statutory maternity pay

3.—(1) An application for the determination of any issue referred to in regulation 2 above shall be made only in writing, in a form approved for the purpose by the Board, or in such other manner, being in writing, as an officer of the Board may accept as sufficient in the circumstances.

(2) Where such an application is made by an employee, it shall—

(a) be delivered or sent to an office of the Board within 6 months of the earliest day in respect of which entitlement to statutory sick pay or statutory maternity pay is in issue;

(b) state the period in respect of which entitlement to statutory sick pay or statutory maternity pay is in issue; and

(c) state the grounds (if any) on which the applicant's employer has denied liability for statutory sick pay or statutory maternity pay in respect of the period specified in the application.

DEFINITION

"employer"—see reg.1(2).

Revocation of regulation 20 of the Social Security (Adjudication) Regulations 1995

4. Regulation 20 of the Social Security (Adjudication) Regulations 1995 is hereby revoked.

4.94

4.95

PART V

STATUTORY MATERNITY PAY

Statutory Maternity Pay (General) Regulations 1986

(SI 1986/1960) (AS AMENDED)

The Secretary of State for Social Services, in exercise of the powers conferred by sections 46(4), (7) and (8), 47(1), (3), (6) and (7), 48(3) and (6), 50(1), (2), (4) and (5), 51(1)(g), (k), (n) and (r) and (4), 54(1), 83(1) and 84(1) of, and paragraphs 6, 8 and 12(3) of Schedule 4 to, the Social Security Act 1986(a), and of all other powers enabling him in that behalf, by this instrument, which contains only regulations made under the sections of the Social Security Act 1986 specified above and provisions consequential upon those sections and before the end of a period of 12 months from the commencement of those sections, makes the following regulations:

ARRANGEMENT OF REGULATIONS

PART I

INTRODUCTION

PART II

ENTITLEMENT

PART III

CONTINUOUS EMPLOYMENT AND NORMAL WORKING HOURS

PART I

INTRODUCTION

Citation, commencement and interpretation

1.—(1) These regulations may be cited as the Statutory Maternity Pay   5.2
(General) Regulations 1986 and shall come into operation in the case
of regulations 1, 22 and 23 on 15th March, 1987, and in the case of the
remainder of the regulations on 6th April, 1987.

(2) In these regulations, unless the context otherwise requires—
"the 1975 Act" means the Social Security Act 1975;
"the 1978 Act" means the Employment Protection (Consolidation) Act
    1978;
"the 1986 Act" means the Social Security Act 1986.
[¹"the Contributions and Benefits Act" means the Social Security
    Contributions and Benefits Act 1992.]
[²"statutory maternity leave" means ordinary maternity leave and any
    additional maternity leave under, respectively, sections 71 and 73 of
    the Employment Rights Act 1996.]

(3) Unless the context otherwise requires, any references in these regulations to—
  (a) a numbered regulation is a reference to the regulation bearing that
      number in these regulations and any reference in a regulation to a
      numbered paragraph is a reference to the paragraph of that regula-
      tion bearing that number;
  (b) any provision made by or contained in an enactment or instrument
      shall be construed as a reference to that provision as amended or
      extended by any enactment or instrument and as including a refer-
      ence to any provision which it re-enacts or replaces, or which may
      reenact or replace it, with or without modifications.

AMENDMENTS

1. Social Security (Miscellaneous Provisions) Amendment (No.2) Regulations
1992 (SI 1992/2595), reg.12 (November 16, 1992).
2. Statutory Maternity Pay (General) (Amendment) Regulations 2005 (SI
2005/729), reg.2 (April 6, 2005).

GENERAL NOTE

The text of these Regulations pre-dates SSCBA 1992 and was not amended at the   5.3
time of the SSCBA 1992 to reflect the provisions in the 1992 Act. The Regulations
remain in force, of course, by virtue of s.17(2)(b) of the Interpretation Act 1978.
As a result, regulations which survive unamended from the original text refer to
the SSA 1975 and SSA 1986, whilst post-1992 amendments refer to the parallel
provisions in SSCBA 1992. References to the 1975 Act should therefore be read as
referring to SSCBA 1992, and those to Pt V of the SSA 1986 as referring to Pt XII
of the SSCBA 1992.

PART II

ENTITLEMENT

The Maternity Pay Period

5.4

[¹ 2. —(1) Subject to paragraphs (3) to (5), where—
   (a) a woman gives notice to her employer of the date from which she expects his liability to pay her statutory maternity pay to begin; and
   (b) in conformity with that notice ceases to work for him in a week which is later than the 12th week before the expected week of confinement,

the first day of the maternity pay period shall be the day on which she expects his liability to pay her statutory maternity pay to begin in conformity with that notice provided that day is not later than the day immediately following the day on which she is confined.

(2) The maternity pay period shall be a period of 39 consecutive weeks.

(3) In a case where a woman is confined—
   (a) before the 11th week before the expected week of confinement; or
   (b) after the 12th week before the expected week of confinement and the confinement occurs on a day which precedes that mentioned in a notice given to her employer as being the day on which she expects his liability to pay her statutory maternity pay to begin,

section 165 of the Contributions and Benefits Act shall have effect so that the first day of the maternity pay period shall be the day following the day on which she is so confined.

(4) In a case where a woman is absent from work wholly or partly because of pregnancy or confinement on any day—
   (a) which falls on or after the beginning of the 4th week before the expected week of confinement; but
   (b) not later than the day immediately following the day on which she is confined,

the first day of the maternity pay period shall be the day following the day on which she is so absent.

(5) In a case where a woman leaves her employment—
   (a) at any time falling after the beginning of the 11th week before the expected week of confinement and before the start of the maternity pay period, but
   (b) not later than the day on which she is confined,

the first day of the maternity pay period shall be the day following the day on which she leaves her employment.]

AMENDMENT

1. Statutory Maternity Pay, Social Security (Maternity Allowance) and Social Security (Overlapping Benefits) (Amendment) Regulations 2006 (SI 2006/2379), reg.3(2) (October 1, 2006).

GENERAL NOTE

5.5   This regulation was substantially recast with a new version substituted with effect from October 1, 2006 which applies in relation to women whose expected week of confinement falls on or after April 1, 2007. The new version of the regulation was prompted by the enactment of the Work and Families Act 2006, which improved the SMP scheme. There are two main differences between the current and previous versions of the regulation.

First, SMP is now payable for 39 weeks as opposed to the 26 weeks that applied before October 1, 2006 (para.(2)); note that before November 24, 2002, the previous maximum period had been 18 weeks.

Secondly, before October 1, 2006 the maternity pay period for SMP purposes started from the week following the week that the woman ceased work in accordance with the requisite notice given to her employer. In practice this meant the Sunday following the day she stopped work in accordance with the notice. The new rule enables the maternity pay period to start on any day of the week as specified by the woman in her notice to the employer. This allows the start of the maternity pay period to match the start of the woman's maternity leave. Accordingly the general rule for determining the start of the maternity pay period is set out in para.(1). There are then a number of further special cases detailed in paras(3)–(5). Paragraph (3) covers those situations where the woman gives birth early. Paragraph (4) makes special provision to deal with the situation where the woman stops working because of a pregnancy-related absence in the four weeks before the expected week of confinement. Finally, para.(5) covers women who leave their employment after the start of the 11th week before the expected week of confinement, but before the maternity pay period commences and not later than day of actual confinement.

Contract of service ended for the purpose of avoiding liability for statutory maternity pay

3.—(1) A former employer shall be liable to make payments of statutory maternity pay to any woman who was employed by him for a continuous period of at least eight weeks and whose contract of service with him was brought to an end by the former employer solely or mainly for the purpose of avoiding liability for statutory maternity pay.

(2) In order to determine the amount payable by the former employer—

(a) the woman shall be deemed for the purposes of Part V of the 1986 Act to have been employed by him from the date her employment with him ended until the end of the week immediately preceding the 14th week before the expected week of confinement on the same terms and conditions of employment as those subsisting immediately before her employment ended; and

(b) her normal weekly earnings for the period of 8 weeks immediately preceding the 14th week before the expected week of confinement shall for those purposes be calculated by reference to her normal weekly earnings for the period of 8 weeks ending with the last day in respect of which she was paid under her former contract of service.

5.6

GENERAL NOTE

This regulation, made under SSCBA 1992, s.164(8), sets out the principles governing entitlement to statutory maternity pay where an employer dismisses a woman with a view to avoiding liability to pay statutory maternity pay. In order for this provision to apply, the woman must have been continuously employed for at least eight weeks (para.(1)). Such action will also constitute an automatically unfair dismissal under Employment Rights Act 1999, s.99 and an act of sex discrimination.

5.7

Modification of entitlement provisions

5.8   **4.**—(1) [¹. . .]

(2) In relation to a woman in employed earner's employment who was confined before the 14th week before the expected week of confinement [¹section 164(2)(a) and (b) of the Contributions and Benefits Act] shall have effect as if for the conditions there set out, there were substituted the conditions that—

    (a) she would but for her confinement have been in employed earner's employment with an employer for a continuous period of at least 26 weeks ending with the week immediately preceding the 14th week before the expected week of confinement; and

    (b) her normal weekly earnings for the period of 8 weeks ending with the week immediately preceding the week of her confinement are not less than the lower earnings limit in force [¹under section 5(1)(a) of the Contributions and Benefits Act] immediately before the commencement of the week of her confinement.

[¹(3) In relation to a woman to whom paragraph (2) applies, section 166 of the Contributions and Benefits Act shall be modified so that subsection (2) has effect as if the reference to the period of 8 weeks immediately preceding the 14th week before the expected week of confinement was a reference to the period of 8 weeks immediately preceding the week in which her confinement occurred.]

AMENDMENT

1. Social Security Maternity Benefits and Statutory Sick Pay (Amendment) Regulations 1994 (SI 1994/1367), reg.3 (June 11, 1994).

GENERAL NOTE

Para. (2)

5.9   If the baby is born either before or in the qualifying week, statutory maternity pay is still payable so long as the woman would have been employed for 26 weeks by the end of the qualifying week, on the assumption that the baby had not in fact been born early.

Treatment of more than one contract of service as one

5.10   **5.** Where 2 or more contracts of service exist concurrently between one employer and one employee, they shall be treated as one for the purposes of Part V of the 1986 Act, except where, by virtue of regulation 11 of the Social Security (Contributions) Regulations 1979 the earnings from those contracts of service are not aggregated for the purposes of earnings-related contributions.

[¹Prescribed rate of statutory maternity pay

5.11   **6.** The rate of statutory maternity pay prescribed under section 166(1)(b) of the Contributions and Benefits Act is a weekly rate of [²123.06.]

AMENDMENTS

1. Social Security, Statutory Maternity Pay and Statutory Sick Pay (Miscellaneous Amendments) Regulations 2002 (SI 2002/2690), reg.3 (April 6, 2003).
2. Social Security Benefits Up-rating Order 2009 (SI 2009/497), art.10 (April 5, 2009).

Liability of Secretary of State to pay Statutory Maternity Pay

7.—(1) Where— 5.12
(a) an adjudicating authority has determined that an employer is liable to make payments of statutory maternity pay to a woman; and
(b) the time for appealing against that determination has expired; and
(c) no appeal against the determination has been lodged or leave to appeal against the determination is required and has been refused,
then for any week in respect of which the employer was liable to make payments of statutory maternity pay but did not do so, and for any subsequent weeks in the maternity pay period the liability to make those payments shall, notwithstanding section 46(3) of the 1986 Act, be that of the Secretary of State and not the employer.

(2) In paragraph (1) adjudicating authority means, as the case may be, the Chief or any other adjudication officer, [² the First-tier Tribunal or the Upper Tribunal.]

(3) Liability to make payments of statutory maternity pay shall, notwithstanding section 46(3) of the 1986 Act, be a liability of the Secretary of State and not the employer as from the week in which the employer first becomes insolvent until the end of the maternity pay period.

(4) For the purposes of paragraph (3) an employer shall be taken to be insolvent if, and only if—
(a) in England and Wales—
    (i) he has been adjudged bankrupt or has made a composition or arrangement with his creditors;
    (ii) he has died and his estate falls to be administered in accordance with an order under section 421 of the Insolvency Act 1986; or
    (iii) where an employer is a company, a winding-up order [¹. . .] is made or a resolution for voluntary winding-up is passed with respect to it [¹or it enter administration], or a receiver or manager of its undertaking is duly appointed, or possession is taken by or on behalf of the holders of any debentures secured by a floating charge, of any property of the company comprised in or subject to the charge or a voluntary arrangement proposed for the purposes of Part 1 of the Insolvency Act 1986 is approved under that Part;
(b) in Scotland—
    (i) an award of sequestration is made on his estate or he executes a trust deed for his creditors or enters into a composition contract;
    (ii) he has died and a judicial factor appointed under section 1A of the Judicial Factors (Scotland) Act 1889 is required by that section to divide his insolvent estate among his creditors; or
    (iii) where the employer is a company, a winding-up order [¹. . .] is made or a resolution for voluntary winding-up is passed with respect to it [¹or it enter administration] or a receiver of its undertaking is duly appointed or a voluntary arrangement proposed for the purposes of Part 1 of the Insolvency Act 1986 is approved under that Part.

AMENDMENTS

1. Enterprise Act 2002 (Insolvency) Order 2003 (SI 2003/2096), art.5 and Sch.2, para.44 (September 15, 2003).

2. Tribunals, Courts and Enforcement Act 2007 (Transitional and Consequential Provisions) Order 2008 (SI 2008/2683), art.6 and Sch.1, para.42 (November 3, 2008).

GENERAL NOTE

5.13   The functions under this regulation were transferred from the Secretary of State for Social Security to the Board of the Inland Revenue (now HMRC) under s.1(2) of and Sch.2 to the Social Security (Transfer of Functions, etc.) Act 1999. References in this regulation to SSA 1986, s.46(3) should now be read as referring to SSCBA 1992, s.164(3).

Work after confinement

5.14   **8.**—(1) Where in the week immediately preceding the 14th week before the expected week of confinement a woman had two or more employers but one or more of them were not liable to make payments to her of statutory maternity pay ("non-liable employer"), section 47(6) of the 1986 Act shall not apply in respect of any week after the week of confinement but within the maternity pay period in which she works only for a non-liable employer.

(2) Where after her confinement a woman—

(a) works for an employer who is not liable to pay her statutory maternity pay and is not a non-liable employer, but

(b) before the end of her maternity pay period ceases to work for that employer, the person who before she commenced work was liable to make payments of statutory maternity pay to her shall, notwithstanding section 46 of the 1986 Act, not be liable to make such payments to her for any weeks in the maternity pay period after she ceases work.

GENERAL NOTE

5.15   References in this regulation to SSA 1986, ss.46 and 47(6) should now be read as referring to SSCBA 1992, ss.164 and 165(6).

No liability to pay statutory maternity pay

5.16   **9.** Notwithstanding the provisions of section 46(1) of the 1986 Act, no liability to make payments of statutory maternity pay to a woman shall arise in respect of a week within the maternity pay period for any part of which she is detained in legal custody or sentenced to a term of imprisonment (except where the sentence is suspended), or of any subsequent week within that period.

GENERAL NOTE

5.17   The reference in this regulation to SSA 1986, s.46(1) should now be read as referring to SSCBA 1992, s.164(1).

[¹ Working for not more than 10 days in the Maternity Pay Period

5.18   **9A.** In a case where a woman does any work under a contract of service with her employer on any day, but for not more than 10 days (whether consecutive or not), during her maternity pay period, statutory maternity pay shall continue to be payable to the employee by the employer.]

AMENDMENT

1. Statutory Maternity Pay, Social Security (Maternity Allowance) and Social Security (Overlapping Benefits) (Amendment) Regulations 2006 (SI 2006/2379), reg.3(3) (October 1, 2006).

GENERAL NOTE

This provision applies in relation to women whose expected week of confinement   **5.19** falls on or after April 1, 2007. It enables a woman to work for up to 10 days under her contract during the statutory maternity pay period for the employer paying her SMP and still retain her SMP for that week—previously a week's SMP was lost for any week in which such work was undertaken.

Death of woman

10. An employer shall not be liable to make payments of statutory mater-   **5.20** nity pay in respect of a woman for any week within the maternity pay period which falls after the week in which she dies.

PART III

CONTINUOUS EMPLOYMENT AND NORMAL WORKING HOURS

Continuous employment

11.—(1) Subject to the following provisions of this regulation, where in   **5.21** any week a woman is, for the whole part of the week,—
(a) incapable of work in consequence of sickness or injury; or
(b) absent from work on account of a temporary cessation of work; or
(c) absent from work in circumstances such that, by arrangement or custom, she is regarded as continuing in the employment of her employer for all or any purpose; or
(d) absent from work wholly or partly because of pregnancy or confinement, [²or
(e) absent from work in consequence of taking paternity leave, adoption leave or parental leave under Part 8 of the Employment Rights Act 1996,]
and returns to work for her employer after the incapacity for or absence from work, that week shall be treated for the purposes of Part V of the 1986 Act as part of a continuous period of employment with that employer, notwithstanding that no contract of service exists with that employer in respect of that week.

(2) Incapacity for work which lasts for more than 26 consecutive weeks shall not count for the purposes of paragraph (1)(a).

(3) Paragraph (1)(d) shall only apply to a woman who—
(a) has a contract of service with the same employer both before and after her confinement but not during any period of absence from work due to her confinement and the period between those contracts does not exceed 26 weeks; or
(b) returns to work in accordance with section 45(1) of the 1978 Act or in pursuance of an offer made in circumstances described in section

56A(2) of that Act after a period of absence from work wholly or partly occasioned by pregnancy or confinement.

[[1](3A) Where a woman who is pregnant—

(a) is an employee in an employed earner's employment in which the custom is for the employer—
  (i) to offer work for a fixed period of not more than 26 consecutive weeks;
  (ii) to offer work for such period on 2 or more occasions in a year for periods which do not overlap; and
  (iii) to offer the work available to those persons who had worked for him during the last or a recent such period, but
(b) is absent from work—
  (i) wholly or partly because of the pregnancy or her confinement; or
  (ii) because of incapacity arising from some specific disease or bodily or mental disablement,

then in her case paragraph (1) shall apply as if the words "and returns to work for an employer after the incapacity for or absence from work" were omitted and paragraph (4) shall not apply.]

(4) Where a woman is employed under a contract of service for part only of the week immediately preceding the 14th week before the expected week of confinement, the whole of that week shall count in computing any period of continuous employment for the purposes of Part V of the 1986 Act.

AMENDMENTS

1. Statutory Maternity Pay (General) Amendment Regulations 1990 (SI 1990/622), reg.2 (April 6, 1990).
2. Social Security, Statutory Maternity Pay and Statutory Sick Pay (Miscellaneous Amendments) Regulations 2002 (SI 2002/2690), reg.4 (April 6, 2003).

DEFINITIONS

"the 1978 Act"—see reg.1(2).
"the 1986 Act"—*ibid*.

Continuous employment and unfair dismissal

5.22   **12.**—(1) This regulation applies to a woman in relation to whose dismissal an action is commenced which consists—

(a) of the presentation by her of a complaint under section 67(1) of the 1978 Act; or
(b) of her making a claim in accordance with a dismissals procedure agreement designated by an order under section 65 of that Act; or
(c) of any action taken by a conciliation officer under section 134(3) of that Act; [[1]or
(d) of a decision arising out of the use of a statutory dispute resolution procedure contained in Schedule 2 to the Employment Act 2002 in a case where, in accordance with the Employment Act 2002 (Dispute Resolution) Regulations 2004, such a procedure applies.]

(2) If in consequence of an action of the kind specified in paragraph (1) a woman is reinstated or re-engaged by her employer or by a successor or associated employer of that employer the continuity of her employment shall be preserved for the purposes of Part V of the 1986 Act and any week

which falls within the interval beginning with the effective date of termination and ending with the date of reinstatement or re-engagement, as the case may be, shall count in the computation of her period of continuous employment.

(3) In this regulation—

"successor" and "dismissals procedure agreement" have the same meanings as in section 30(3) and (4) of the Trade Union and Labour Relations Act 1974; and

"associated employer" shall be construed in accordance with section 153(4) of the 1978 Act.

AMENDMENT

1. Statutory Maternity Pay (General) and the Statutory Paternity Pay and Statutory Adoption Pay (General) (Amendment) Regulations 2005 (SI 2005/358), reg.3 (April 6, 2005).

DEFINITIONS

"the 1978 Act"—see reg.1(2).
"associated employer"—see para.(3).
"dismissals procedure agreement"—*ibid.*
"successor"—*ibid.*

Continuous employment and stoppages of work

13.—(1) Where for any week or part of a week a woman does no work   5.23
because there is, within the meaning of section 19 of the 1975 Act a stoppage of work due to a trade dispute at her place of employment the continuity of her employment shall, subject to paragraph (2), be treated as continuing throughout the stoppage but, subject to paragraph (3), no such week shall count in the computation of her period of employment.

(2) Subject to paragraph (3), where during the stoppage of work a woman is dismissed from her employment, the continuity of her employment shall not be treated in accordance with paragraph (1) as continuing beyond the commencement of the day she stopped work.

(3) The provisions of paragraph (1) to the extent that they provide that a week in which a stoppage of work occurred shall not count in the computation of a period of employment, and paragraph (2) shall not apply to a woman who proves that at no time did she have a direct interest in the trade dispute in question.

GENERAL NOTE

The reference in this regulation to SSA 1975, s.19 should now be read as refer-   5.24
ring to SSCBA 1992, s.27.

Change of employer

14. A woman's employment shall, notwithstanding the change of   5.25
employer, be treated as continuous employment with the second employer where—

(a) the employer's trade or business or an undertaking (whether or not it is an undertaking established by or under an Act of Parliament) is transferred from one person to another;

659

(b) by or under an Act of Parliament, whether public or local and whenever passed, a contract of employment between any body corporate and the woman is modified and some other body corporate is substituted as her employer;

(c) on the death of her employer, the woman is taken into the employment of the personal representatives or trustees of the deceased;

(d) the woman is employed by partners, personal representatives or trustees and there is a change in the partners, or, as the case may be, personal representatives or trustees;

(e) the woman is taken into the employment of an employer who is, at the time she entered his employment, an associated employer of her previous employer, and for this purpose "associated employer" shall be construed in accordance with section 153(4) of the 1978 Act;

(f) on the termination of her employment with an employer she is taken into the employment of another employer and [¹those employers are the governors of a school maintained by a local education authority and that authority].

AMENDMENT

1. Statutory Maternity Pay (General) Amendment Regulations 1990 (SI 1990/ 622), reg.3 (April 6, 1990).

DEFINITION

"the 1978 Act"—see reg.1(2).

Reinstatement after service with the armed forces, etc.

5.26 **15.** If a woman who is entitled to apply to her former employer under the Reserve Forces (Safeguard of Employment) Act 1985 enters the employment of that employer not later than the 6 month period mentioned in section 1(4)(b) of that Act, her previous period of employment with that employer (or if there was more than one such period, the last of those periods) and the period of employment beginning in the said period of 6 months shall be treated as continuous.

Normal working weeks

5.27 **16.**—(1) For the purposes of section 48(5) of the 1986 Act, a woman's contract of service shall be treated as not normally involving or having involved employment for less than 16 hours weekly where she is normally employed for 16 hours or more weekly.

(2) Where a woman's relations with her employer were governed for a continuous period of at least 2 years by a contract of service which normally involved employment for not less than 16 hours weekly and this period was followed by a further period, ending with the week immediately preceding the 14th week before the expected week of confinement, in which her relations with that employer were governed by a contract of service which normally involved employment for less than 16 hours, but not less than 8 hours weekly, then her contract of service shall be treated for the purpose of section 48(5) of the 1986 Act as not normally involving or having involved employment for less than 16 hours weekly.

(3) Where a woman's relations with her employer are or were governed for a continuous period of at least 2 years by a contract of service which involved—

    (a) for not more than 26 weeks in that period, employment for 8 hours or more but less than 16 hours weekly; and

    (b) for the whole of the remainder of that period employment for not less than 16 hours weekly, the contract of service shall be treated for the purposes of section 48(5) of the 1986 Act as not normally involving or having involved employment for less than 16 hours weekly.

GENERAL NOTE

The references in this regulation to SSA 1986, s.48(5) should now be read as referring to SSCBA 1992, s.166(5).

    5.28

[¹Meaning of "week"

16A. Where a woman has been in employed earner's employment with the same employer in each of 26 consecutive weeks (but no more than 26 weeks) ending with the week immediately preceding the 14th week before the expected week of confinement then for the purpose of determining whether that employment amounts to a continuous period of at least 26 weeks, the first of those 26 weeks shall be a period commencing on the first day of her employment with the employer and ending at midnight on the first Saturday thereafter or on that day where her first day is a Saturday.]

    5.29

AMENDMENT

1. Statutory Maternity Pay (General) Amendment Regulations 1990 (SI 1990/622), reg.4 (April 6, 1990).

PART IV

GENERAL PROVISIONS

Meaning of "employee"

17.—(1) [¹Subject to paragraph (1A),] in a case where, and in so far as, a woman [¹. . .] is treated as an employed earner by virtue of the Social Security (Categorisation of Earners) Regulations 1978 she shall be treated as an employee for the purposes of Part V of the 1986 Act and in a case where, and in so far as, such a woman is treated otherwise than as an employed earner by virtue of those regulations, she shall not be treated as an employee for the purposes of Part V.

    5.30

[²(1A) Paragraph (1) shall have effect in relation to a woman who—

    (a) is under the age of 16; and

    (b) would or, as the case may be, would not have been treated as an employed earner by virtue of the Social Security (Categorisation of Earners) Regulations 1978 had she been over that age,

as it has effect in relation to a woman who is, or, as the case may be, is not so treated.]

(2) Any woman who is in employed earner's employment within the meaning of the 1975 Act under a contract of apprenticeship shall be treated as the employee for the purposes of Part V.

(3) A woman who is in employed earner's employment within the meaning of the 1975 Act but whose employer—

    (a) does not fulfil the conditions prescribed in regulation 119(1)(b) of the Social Security (Contributions) Regulations 1979 as to residence or presence in Great Britain, or

    (b) is a woman who, by reason of any international treaty to which the United Kingdom is a party of any international convention binding the United Kingdom—

        (i) is exempt from the provisions of the 1975 Act, or

        (ii) is a woman against whom the provisions of that Act are not enforceable, shall not be treated as an employee for the purposes of Part V of the 1986 Act.

AMENDMENTS

1. Employment Equality (Age) Regulations 2006 (SI 2006/1031), reg.49(1) and Sch.8, Part 2, para.53 (October 1, 2006).

2. Employment Equality (Age) (Consequential Amendments) Regulations 2007 (SI 2007/825), reg.6 (April 6, 2007).

Treatment of two or more employers as one

5.31   **18.**—(1) In a case where the earnings paid to a woman in respect of 2 or more employments are aggregated and treated as a single payment of earnings under regulation 12(1) of the Social Security (Contributions) Regulations 1979, the employers of the woman in respect of those employments shall be treated as one for all purposes of Part V of the 1986 Act.

(2) Where two or more employers are treated as one under the provisions of paragraph (1), liability for statutory maternity pay payable by them to a woman shall be apportioned between them in such proportions as they may agree or, in default of agreement, in the proportions which the woman's earnings from each employment bear to the amount of the aggregated earnings.

GENERAL NOTE

5.32   Specific provision is also made in the Statutory Maternity Pay (National Health Service Employees) Regulations 1991 (SI 1991/590) for NHS workers with divided contracts.

Payments to be treated as contractual remuneration

5.33   **19.** For the purposes of paragraph 12(1) and (2) of Schedule 4 to the 1986 Act, the payments which are to be treated as contractual remuneration are sums payable under the contract of service—

    (a) by way of remuneration;

    (b) for incapacity for work due to sickness or injury; and

    (c) by reason of pregnancy or confinement.

DEFINITION

"the 1986 Act"—see reg.1(2).

Meaning of "earnings"

20.—(1) [¹. . .]

5.34

[²(2) For the purposes of section 171(4) of the Contributions and Benefits Act, the expression "earnings" refers to gross earnings and includes any remuneration or profit derived from a woman's employment except any payment or amount which is—

  (a) excluded [⁶or disregarded in the calculation of a person's earnings under regulation 25, 27 or 123 of, or Schedule 3 to, the Social Security (Contributions) Regulations 2001] (payments to be disregarded and payments to directors to be disregarded respectively) [⁵(or would have been so excluded had she not been under the age of 16)];

  (b) a chargeable emolument under section 10A of the Social Security Contributions and Benefits Act 1992, except where, in consequence of such a chargeable emolument being excluded from earnings, a woman would not be entitled to statutory maternity pay. [⁵(or where such a payment or amount would have been so excluded and in consequence she would not have been entitled to statutory maternity pay had she not been under the age of 16)]]

(3) [¹. . .]

(4) For the purposes of section [³section 171(4) of the Contributions and Benefits Act] the expression "earnings" includes also—

[⁶(za) any amount retrospectively treated as earnings by regulations made by virtue of section 4B(2) of the Contributions and Benefits Act;]

  (a) any sum payable in respect of arrears of pay in pursuance of an order for reinstatement or re-engagement under the 1978 Act;

  (b) any sum payable by way of pay in pursuance of an order under the 1978 Act for the continuation of a contract of employment;

  (c) any sum payable by way of remuneration in pursuance of a protective award under the Employment Protection Act 1975;

  (d) any sum payable by way of statutory sick pay, including sums payable in accordance with regulations made under section 1(5) of the Social Security and Housing Benefits Act 1982.

[⁴(e) any sum payable by way of statutory maternity pay, including sums payable in accordance with regulations made under section 164(9)(b) of the Contributions and Benefits Act;

  (f) any sum payable by way of statutory paternity pay, including sums payable in accordance with regulations made under section 171ZD(3) of the Contributions and Benefits Act;

  (g) any sum payable by way of statutory adoption pay, including sums payable in accordance with regulations made under section 171ZM(3) of the Contributions and Benefits Act.]

(5) [¹. . .]

(6) [¹. . .]

AMENDMENTS

1. Social Security (Miscellaneous Provisions) Amendment (No.2) Regulations 1992 (SI 1992/2595), reg.13 (November 16, 1992).

2. Social Security Contributions, Statutory Maternity Pay and Statutory Sick Pay (Miscellaneous Amendments) Regulations 1999 (SI 1999/567), reg.12 (April 6, 1999).

3. Social Security, Statutory Maternity Pay and Statutory Sick Pay (Miscellaneous Amendments) Regulations 2002 (SI 2002/2690), reg.5(a) (November 24, 2002).

4. Social Security, Statutory Maternity Pay and Statutory Sick Pay (Miscellaneous Amendments) Regulations 2002 (SI 2002/2690), reg.5(b) (April 6, 2003).

5. Employment Equality (Age) Regulations 2006 (SI 2006/1031), reg.49(1) and Sch.8, Pt 2, para.53 (October 1, 2006, and in relation to any case where the expected week of confinement begins on or after January 14, 2007).

6. Social Security, Occupational Pension Schemes and Statutory Payments (Consequential Provisions) Regulations 2007 (SI 2007/1154), reg.4(2) and (3) (April 6, 2007).

Normal weekly earnings

5.35   **21.**—(1) For the purposes of [¹Part XII of the Contributions and Benefits Act], a woman's normal weekly earnings shall be calculated in accordance with the following provisions of this regulation.

(2) In this regulation—

"the appropriate date" means the first day of the 14th week before the expected week of confinement, or the first day in the week in which the woman is confined, whichever is the earlier. [¹. . .]

"normal pay day" means a day on which the terms of a woman's contract of service require her to be paid, or the practice in her employment is for her to be paid, if any payment is due to her; and "day of payment" means a day on which the woman was paid.

(3) Subject to paragraph (4), the relevant period for the purposes of [¹section 171(4) of the Contributions and Benefits Act] is the period between—

(a) the last normal pay day to fall before the appropriate date; and

(b) the last normal pay day to fall at least eight weeks earlier than the normal pay day mentioned in sub-paragraph (a), including the normal pay day mentioned in sub-paragraph (a) but excluding that first mentioned in sub-paragraph (b).

(4) In a case where a woman has no identifiable normal pay day, paragraph (3) shall have eVect as if the words "day of payment" were substituted for the words "normal pay day" in each place where they occur.

(5) In a case where a woman has normal pay days at intervals of or approximating to one or more calendar months (including intervals of or approximating to a year) her normal weekly earnings shall be calculated by dividing her earnings in the relevant period by the number of calendar months in that period (or, if it is not a whole number, the nearest whole number), multiplying the result by 12 and dividing by 52.

(6) In a case to which paragraph (5) does not apply and the relevant period is not an exact number of weeks, the woman's normal weekly earnings shall be calculated by dividing her earnings in the relevant period by the number of days in the relevant period and multiplying the result by 7.

[³(7) In any case where—

(a) a woman is awarded a pay increase (or would have been awarded such an increase had she not then been absent on statutory maternity leave); and

(b) that pay increase applies to the whole or any part of the period between the beginning of the relevant period and the end of her period of statutory maternity leave, her normal weekly earnings shall be calculated as if such an increase applied in each week of the relevant period.]

AMENDMENTS

1. Social Security Maternity Benefits and Statutory Sick Pay (Amendment) Regulations 1994 (SI 1994/1367), reg.5 (June 11, 1994).
2. Statutory Maternity Pay (General) Amendment Regulations 1996 (SI 1996/1335), reg.2 (June 12, 1996).
3. Statutory Maternity Pay (General) (Amendment) Regulations 2005 (SI 2005/729), reg.3 (April 6, 2005).

GENERAL NOTE

The new reg.21(7) is designed to give effect to the ECJ judgment in *Alabaster v Woolwich PLC and the Secretary of State for Social Security* (C-147/02), [2004] I.R.L.R. 486). It ensures that employers must recalculate a woman's entitlement (or potential entitlement) to statutory maternity pay to reflect any pay rise that the woman would have received, but for her maternity leave, and which is effective at any time between the start of the period used to calculate her entitlement and the end of her maternity leave. For the Court of Appeal judgment following the decision of the ECJ, see *Alabaster v Barclays Bank Plc and the Secretary of State for Social Security* [2005] EWCA Civ 508; [2005] I.C.R. 1246.

[1Effect of statutory maternity pay on [2incapacity benefit]

21A. [3. . .]

AMENDMENTS

1. Statutory Maternity Pay (General) Amendment Regulations 1988 (SI 1988/532), reg.3 (April 6, 1988).
2. Social Security (Incapacity Benefit) (Consequential and Transitional Amendments and Savings) Regulations 1995 (SI 1995/829), reg.18 (April 13, 1995).
3. Social Security, Statutory Maternity Pay and Statutory Sick Pay (Miscellaneous Amendments) Regulations 2002 (SI 2002/2690), reg.6 (November 24, 2002).

[1Effect of maternity allowance on statutory maternity pay

21B. Where a woman, in any week which falls within the maternity pay period, is—
  (a) in receipt of maternity allowance pursuant to the provisions of sections 35 and 35A of the Contributions and Benefits Act; and
  (b) entitled to receive statutory maternity pay in consequence of [2—
    (i) receiving a pay increase referred to in regulation 21(7), or
    (ii) being treated as having been paid retrospective earnings under regulation 20(4)(za),]
the employer shall not be liable to make payments of statutory maternity pay in respect of such a week unless, and to the extent by which, the rate of statutory maternity pay exceeds the rate of maternity allowance received by her in that week.]

AMENDMENTS

1. Statutory Maternity Pay (General) (Amendment) Regulations 2005 (SI 2005/729), reg.4 (April 6, 2005).

5.36

5.37

5.38

2. Social Security, Occupational Pension Schemes and Statutory Payments (Consequential Provisions) Regulations 2007 (SI 2007/1154), reg.4(4) (April 6, 2007).

PART V

ADMINISTRATION

Evidence of expected week of confinement

5.39   **22.**—(1) A woman shall in accordance with the following provisions of this regulation, provide the person who is liable to pay her statutory maternity pay with evidence as to—

    (a) the week in which the expected date of confinement occurs, and

    (b) where her entitlement to statutory maternity pay depends upon the fact of her confinement, the week in which she was confined.

    (2) For the purpose of paragraph (1)(b) a certificate of birth shall be sufficient evidence that the woman was confined in the week in which the birth occurred.

    (3) The evidence shall be submitted to the person who will be liable to make payments of statutory maternity pay not later than the end of the third week of the maternity pay period so however that where the woman has good cause the evidence may be submitted later than that date but not later than the end of the 13th week of the maternity pay period.

    (4) For the purposes of paragraph (3) evidence contained in an envelope which is properly addressed and sent by prepaid post shall be deemed to have been submitted on the day on which it was posted.

Notice of absence from work

5.40   **23.**—(1) Where a woman is confined before the beginning of the 14th week before the expected week of confinement, she shall be entitled to payments of statutory maternity pay only if—

    (a) she gives notice to the person who will be liable to pay it [²of the date on which she was confined], and

    (b) that notice is given within [²28 days] of the date she was confined or if in the particular circumstances that is not practicable, as soon as is reasonably practicable thereafter; and

    (c) where the person so requests, the notice in writing.

    (2) Where a woman is confined before the date stated in a notice provided in accordance with [¹section 164(4) of the Contributions and Benefits Act] as being the date her absence from work is due to begin, she shall be entitled to payments of statutory maternity pay only if—

    (a) she gives a further notice to the person who will be liable to pay it specifying the date she was confined and the date her absence from work [². . .] began, and

    (b) that further notice is given within [²28 days] of the date she was confined or if in the particular circumstances that is not practicable, as soon as is reasonably practicable thereafter; and

    (c) where the person so requests, the notice is in writing.

(3) For the purposes of this regulation, a notice contained in an envelope which is properly addressed and sent by prepaid post shall be deemed to be given on the date on which it is posted.

[¹[²(4) Subject to paragraph (5), section 164(4) of the Contributions and Benefits Act (statutory maternity pay entitlement and liability to pay) shall not have effect in the case of a woman who leaves her employment with the person who will be liable to pay her statutory maternity pay after the beginning of the week immediately preceding the 14th week before the expected week of confinement.]

(5) A woman who is exempted from section 164(4) of the Contributions and Benefits Act by paragraph (4) but who is confined before the 11th week before the expected week of confinement shall only be entitled to statutory maternity pay if she gives the person who will be liable to pay it notice specifying the date she was confined.]

AMENDMENTS

1. Social Security Maternity Benefits and Statutory Sick Pay (Amendment) Regulations 1994 (SI 1994/1367), reg.6 (June 11, 1994).

2. Social Security, Statutory Maternity Pay and Statutory Sick Pay (Miscellaneous Amendments) Regulations 2002 (SI 2002/2690), reg.7 (November 24, 2002).

Notification of employment after confinement

24. A woman who after the date of confinement but within the maternity pay period commences work in employed earner's employment with a person who is not liable to make payments of statutory maternity pay to her and is not a non-liable employer for the purposes of regulation 8(1), shall within seven days of the day she commenced work inform any person who is so liable of the date she commenced work.

5.41

Provision of information in connection with determination of questions

25. Any woman claiming to be entitled to statutory maternity pay, or any other person who is a party to proceedings arising under the 1986 Act relating to statutory maternity pay, shall, if she receives notification from the Secretary of State that any information is required from her for the determination of any question arising in connection therewith, furnish that information to the Secretary of State within 10 days of receiving that notification.

5.42

DEFINITION

"the 1986 Act"—see reg.1(2).

GENERAL NOTE

The functions under this regulation were transferred from the Secretary of State for Social Security to the Board of the Inland Revenue (now HMRC) under s.1(2) of and Sch.2 to the Social Security (Transfer of Functions, etc.) Act 1999.

5.43

[¹Provision of information relating to claims for certain other benefits

25A.—(1) Where an employer who has been given notice in accordance with [³section 164(4)(a) or (9)(ea) of the Contributions and Benefits Act] or regulation 23 by a woman who is or has been an employee—

5.44

(a) decides that he has no liability to make payments of statutory maternity pay to her; or

(b) has made one or more payments of statutory maternity pay to her but decides, before the end of the maternity pay period and for a reason specified in paragraph (3), that he has no liability to make further payments to her,

then, in connection with the making of a claim by the woman for a maternity allowance [⁴, incapacity benefit or an employment and support allowance], he shall furnish her with the information specified in the following provisions of this regulation.

(2) Where the employer decides he has no liability to make payments of statutory maternity pay to the woman, he shall furnish her with details of the decision and the reasons for it.

(3) Where the employer decides he has no liability to make further payments of statutory maternity pay to the woman because [³ . . .] she has within the maternity pay period been detained in legal custody or sentenced to a term of imprisonment which was not suspended, [³ . . .], he shall furnish her with—

(a) details of his decision and the reasons for it; and

(b) details of the last week in respect of which a liability to pay statutory maternity pay arose and the total number of weeks within the maternity pay period in which such a liability arose.

(4) The employer shall—

(a) return to the woman any maternity certificate provided by her in support of the notice referred to in paragraph (1); and

(b) comply with any requirements imposed by the preceding provisions of this regulation—

   (i) in a case to which paragraph (2) applies, within 7 days of the decision being made, or, if earlier, within [³ 28 days] of the day the woman gave notice of her intended absence or of her confinement if that had occurred; or

   (ii) in a case to which paragraph (3) refers, within 7 days of being notified of the woman's detention or sentence [³ . . .].

(5) In this regulation, 'incapacity benefit' means [²incapacity benefit] or a severe disablement allowance.]

AMENDMENTS

1. Statutory Maternity Pay (General) Amendment Regulations 1990 (SI 1990/622), reg.7 (April 6, 1990).

2. Social Security (Incapacity Benefit) (Consequential and Transitional Amendments and Savings) Regulations 1995 (SI 1995/829), reg.18 (April 13, 1995).

3. Social Security, Statutory Maternity Pay and Statutory Sick Pay (Miscellaneous Amendments) Regulations 2002 (SI 2002/2690), reg.8 (November 24, 2002).

4. Employment and Support Allowance (Consequential Provisions) (No.2) Regulations 2008 (SI 2008/1554), reg.46 (October 27, 2008).

Records to be maintained by employers

5.45   **26.**—(1) Every employer shall maintain for 3 years after the end of the tax year in which the maternity pay period ends a record in relation to any woman who is or was an employee of his of—

(a) the date of the first day of absence from work wholly or partly because of pregnancy or confinement as notified by her and, if different, the date of the first day when such absence commenced;

(b) the weeks in that tax year in which statutory maternity pay was paid and the amount paid in each week; and

(c) any week in that tax year which was within her maternity pay period but for which no payment of statutory maternity pay was made to her and the reasons no payment was made.

(2) Except where he was not liable to make a payment of statutory maternity pay and subject to paragraphs (3) and (4), every employer shall retain for 3 years after the end of the tax year in which the maternity pay period ends any medical certificate or other evidence relating to the expected week of confinement, or as the case may be, the confinement which was provided to him by a woman who is or was an employee of his.

(3) Where an employer returns a medical certificate to an employee of his for the purpose of enabling her to make a claim for benefit under the 1975 Act, it shall be sufficient for the purposes of paragraph (2) if he retains a copy of that certificate.

(4) An employer shall not retain any certificate of birth provided to him as evidence of confinement by a woman who is or was an employee of his but shall retain a record of the date of birth.

DEFINITION

"the 1975 Act"—see reg.1(2).

[¹Production of employer's records

26A.—(1) An authorised officer of the Commissioners of Inland Revenue may by notice require an employer to produce to him at the place of keeping such records as are in the employer's possession or power and as (in the officer's reasonable opinion) contain, or may contain, information relevant to satisfy him that statutory maternity pay has been paid and is being paid in accordance with these regulations to employees or former employees who are entitled to it.

(2) A notice referred to in paragraph (1) shall be in writing and the employer shall produce the records referred to in that paragraph within 30 days after the date of such a notice.

(3) The production of records in pursuance of this regulation shall be without prejudice to any lien which a third party may have in respect of those records.

(4) References in this regulation to "records" means—

(a) any wage sheet or deductions working sheet; or

(b) any other document which relates to the calculation or payment of statutory maternity pay to his employees or former employees,

whether kept in written form, electronically, or otherwise.

(5) In paragraph (1), "place of keeping" means such place in Great Britain that an employer and an authorised officer may agree upon, or, in the absence of such agreement—

(a) any place in Great Britain where records referred to in paragraph (1) are normally kept; or

(b) if there is no such place, the employer's principal place of business in Great Britain.]

5.46

669

AMENDMENT

1. Statutory Maternity Pay (General) and Statutory Sick Pay (General) (Amendment) Regulations 2005 (SI 2005/989), reg.2(2) (April 6, 2005).

PART VI

PAYMENT

Payment of statutory maternity pay

5.47   **27.** Payment of statutory maternity pay may be made in a like manner to payments of remuneration but shall not include payments in kind or by way of the provision of board or lodgings or of services or other facilities.

Rounding to avoid fractional amounts

5.48   [¹**28.** Where any payment of statutory maternity pay is paid for any week or part of a week and the amount due includes a fraction of a penny, the payment shall be rounded up to the next whole number of pence.]

AMENDMENT

1. Statutory Maternity Pay, Social Security (Maternity Allowance) and Social Security (Overlapping Benefits) (Amendment) Regulations 2006 (SI 2006/2379), reg.3(4) (October 1, 2006, and in relation to women whose expected week of confinement falls on or after April 1, 2007).

Time when statutory maternity pay is to be paid

5.49   **29.**—(1) In this regulation, "payday" means a day on which it has been agreed, or it is the normal practice between an employer or former employer and a woman who is or was an employee of his, that payments by way of remuneration are to be made, or, where there is no such agreement or normal practice, the last day of a calendar month.

(2) In any case where—

(a) a decision has been made by an adjudication officer, appeal tribunal or Commissioner in proceedings under [Social Security Administration Act 1992] as a result of which a woman is entitled to an amount of statutory maternity pay; and

(b) the time for bringing an appeal against the decision has expired and either—

  (i) no such appeal has been brought; or

  (ii) such an appeal has been brought and has been finally disposed of that amount of statutory maternity pay shall be paid within the time specified in paragraph (3).

(3) Subject to paragraphs (4) and (5), the employer or former employer shall pay the amount not later than the first pay day after—

(a) where an appeal has been brought, the day on which the employer or former employer receives notification that it has been finally disposed of,

(b) where leave to appeal has been refused and there remains no further opportunity to apply for leave, the day on which the employer or former employer receives notification of the refusal; and

(c) in any other case, the day on which the time for bringing an appeal expires.

(4) Subject to paragraph (5), where it is impracticable, in view of the employer's or former employer's methods of accounting for and paying remuneration, for the requirement of payment referred to in paragraph (3) to be met by the pay day referred to in that paragraph, it shall be met not later than the next following pay day.

(5) Where the employer or former employer would not have remunerated the woman for her work in the week in question as early as the pay day specified in paragraph (3) or (if it applies) paragraph (4), the requirement of payment shall be met on the first day on which the woman would have been remunerated for her work in that week.

Payments by the Secretary of State

30. Where the Secretary of State becomes liable in accordance with regulation 7 to make payments of statutory maternity pay to a woman, the first payment shall be made as soon as reasonably practicable after he becomes so liable, and payments thereafter shall be made at weekly intervals, by means of an instrument of payment or by such other means as appears to the Secretary of State to be appropriate in the circumstances of any particular case.

5.50

GENERAL NOTE

The functions under this regulation were transferred from the Secretary of State for Social Security to the Board of the Inland Revenue (now HMRC) under s.1(2) of and Sch.2 to the Social Security (Transfer of Functions, etc.) Act 1999.

5.51

Persons unable to act

31.—(1) Where in the case of any woman—

5.52

(a) statutory maternity pay is payable to her or she is alleged to be entitled to it;

(b) she is unable for the time being to act;

(c) either—

(i) no receiver has been appointed by the Court of Protection with power to receive statutory maternity pay on her behalf, or

(ii) in Scotland, her estate is not being administrated by any tutor, curator or other guardian acting or appointed in terms of law,

the Secretary of State may, upon written application to him by a person who, if a natural person, is over the age of 18, appoint that person to exercise, on behalf of the woman any right to which she may be entitled under Part V of the 1986 Act and to deal on her behalf with any sums payable to her.

(2) Where the Secretary of State has made an appointment under paragraph (1)—

(a) he may at any time in his absolute discretion revoke it;

(b) the person appointed may resign his office after having given one month's notice in writing to the Secretary of State of his intention to do so; and

(c) the appointment shall terminate when the Secretary of State is notified that a receiver or other person to whom paragraph (1)(c) applies has been appointed.

(3) Anything required by Part V of the 1986 Act to be done by or to any woman who is unable to act may be done by or to the person appointed under this regulation to act on her behalf, and the receipt of the person so appointed shall be a good discharge to the woman's employer or former employer for any sum paid.

GENERAL NOTE

5.53   The functions under this regulation were transferred from the Secretary of State for Social Security to the Board of the Inland Revenue (now HMRC) under s.1(2) of and Sch.2 to the Social Security (Transfer of Functions, etc.) Act 1999.

PART VII

OFFENCES

[¹**Offences**

5.54   **32.** [². . .]

GENERAL NOTE

5.55   See now ss.113A and 113B of the Social Security Administration Act 1992.

Statutory Maternity Pay (Medical Evidence) Regulations 1987

(SI 1987/235) (AS AMENDED)

5.56   The Secretary of State for Social Services, in exercise of the powers conferred by sections 49 and 84(1) of and paragraph 6 of Schedule 4 to the Social Security Act 1986, and of all other powers enabling him in that behalf, by this instrument, which is made before the end of the period of 12 months from the commencement of the enactments contained in the 1986 Act under which it is made, makes the following regulations:

ARRANGEMENT OF REGULATIONS

1. Citation, commencement and interpretation
2. Evidence of pregnancy and confinement

SCHEDULE—Part I—Rules
            Part II—Form of certificate

Citation, commencement and interpretation

5.57   **1.**—(1) These regulations may be cited as the Statutory Maternity Pay (Medical Evidence) Regulations 1987 and shall come into force on 15th March 1987.

(2) In these regulations, unless the context otherwise requires—

"the Act" means the Social Security Act 1986;

[¹"registered midwife" means a midwife who is registered as a midwife with the Nursing and Midwifery Council under the Nursing and Midwifery Order 2001;]

"doctor" means a registered medical practitioner;

"signature" means, in relation to any statement or certificate given in accordance with these regulations, the name by which the person giving that statement or certificate, as the case may be, is usually known (any name other than the surname being either in full or otherwise indicated) written by that person in his own handwriting; and "signed" shall be construed accordingly.

[²"Primary Care Trust" means a Primary Care Trust established under section 16A of the National Health Service Act 1977.]

AMENDMENTS

1. Nursing and Midwifery Order 2001 (Consequential Amendments) Order 2002 (SI 2002/881), art.2 and Sch., para.2 (April 17, 2002).

2. National Health Service Reform and Health Care Professions Act 2002 (Supplementary, Consequential etc. Provisions) Regulations 2002 (SI 2002/2469), reg.11 and Sch.8 (October 1, 2002).

Evidence of pregnancy and confinement

2. The evidence as to pregnancy and the expected date of confinement which a woman is required to provide to a person who is liable to pay her statutory maternity pay shall be furnished in the form of a maternity certificate given by a doctor or by a registered midwife, not earlier than the beginning of the [¹20th week] before the expected week of confinement, in accordance with the rules set out in Part I of the Schedule to these regulations—   5.58

(a) in the appropriate form as set out in Part II of that Schedule; or

(b) in a form substantially to the like effect with such variations as the circumstances may require.

AMENDMENT

1. Social Security (Medical Evidence) and Statutory Maternity Pay (Medical Evidence) (Amendment) Regulations 2001 (SI 2001/2931), reg.3(2) (September 28, 2001).

DEFINITIONS

"doctor"—see reg.1(2).
"registered midwife"—see *ibid*.

PART I

RULES

5.59   **1.** In these rules any reference to a woman is a reference to the woman in respect of whom a maternity certificate is given in accordance with these rules.

2. A maternity certificate shall be given by a doctor or registered midwife attending the woman and shall not be given by the woman herself.

3. The maternity certificate shall be on a form provided by the Secretary of State for the purpose and the wording shall be that set out in the appropriate part of the form specified in Part II of this Schedule.

4. Every maternity certificate shall be completed in ink or other indelible substance and shall contain the following particulars—

(a) the woman's name;

(b) the week in which the woman is expected to be confined or, if the maternity certificate is given after confinement, the date of that confinement and the date the confinement was expected to take place [1. . .];

(c) the date of the examination on which the maternity certificate is based;

(d) the date on which the maternity certificate is signed; and

[4(e) the address of the doctor or where the maternity certificate is signed by a registered midwife the personal identification number given to her on her registration in [6. . .] the register maintained by the Nursing and Midwifery Council [6("NMC") under article 5 of] the Nursing and Midwifery Order 2001 and the expiry date of that registration,]

and shall bear opposite the word "Signature", the signature of the person giving the maternity certificate written after there has been entered on the maternity certificate the woman's name and the expected date or, as the case may be, the date of the confinement.

5. After a maternity certificate has been given, no further maternity certificate based on the same examination shall be furnished other than a maternity certificate by way of replacement of an original which has been lost or mislaid, in which case it shall be clearly marked "duplicate".

[²PART II

FORM OF CERTIFICATE

MATERNITY CERTIFICATE   5.60

Please fill in this form in ink

Name of patient

Fill in this part if you are giving the certificate before the confinement.

Do not fill this in more [³than 20 weeks] before the week the baby is expected.

I certify that I examined you on the date given below. In my opinion you can expect to have your baby in the week that includes

.... / .... / ....

Week means period of 7 days starting on a Sunday and ending on a Saturday. Fill in this part if you are giving the certificate after the confinement.

I certify that I attended you in connection with the birth which took place on
.... / .... / ....   when you were delivered of a child [ ] children.

In my opinion your baby was expected in the week that includes ..../ .... / ....

Date of examination ..... / ..... / ......

Date of signing .... / .... / ....

Signature

Registered midwives

Please give your [⁶NMC] Personal Identification Number and the expiry date of your registration with the [⁶NMC].

Doctors
Please stamp your name and address here if the form has not been stamped by the [⁵ᵃ"Primary Care Trust or Local Health Board in whose medical performers list you are included (or, in Scotland, by the Health Board in whose primary medical services performers list you are included)].

AMENDMENTS

1. Social Security (Miscellaneous Provisions) Amendment Regulations 1991 (SI 1991/2284) reg.23 (November 1, 1991).
2. Social Security (Miscellaneous Provisions) Amendment Regulations 1991 (SI 1991/2284) reg.24 (November 1, 1991).

3. Social Security (Medical Evidence) and Statutory Maternity Pay (Medical Evidence) (Amendment) Regulations 2001 (SI 2001/2931), reg.3(3) (September 28, 2001).

4. Nursing and Midwifery Order 2001 (Consequential Amendments) Order 2002 (SI 2002/881), art.2 and Sch., para.3 (April 17, 2002).

5. General Medical Services and Personal Medical Services Transitional and Consequential Provisions Order 2004 (SI 2004/865), art.119 and Sch.1, para.5 (April 1, 2004).

6. Health Act 1999 (Consequential Amendments) (Nursing and Midwifery) Order 2004 (SI 2004/1771), art.3 and Sch., para.51 (August 1, 2004).

Definitions

"doctor"—see reg.1(2).
"registered midwife"—see *ibid*.
"signature"—see *ibid*.
"signed"—see *ibid*.

Statutory Maternity Pay (Persons Abroad and Mariners) Regulations 1987

(SI 1987/418) (as amended)

The Secretary of State for Social Services, in exercise of the powers conferred upon him by sections 80 and 84(1) of the Social Security Act 1986 and of all other powers enabling him in that behalf, by this instrument, which is made before the end of the period of 12 months from the commencement of the enactments under which it is made, makes the following Regulations:

Arrangement of Regulations

5.61
1. Citation, commencement and interpretation
2. Persons in other member States—meaning of "employee"
2A. Persons absent from Great Britain—meaning of "employee"
3. Meaning of "employee"—general
4. (*repealed*)
5. Women who worked in the European Community
6. Time for compliance with Part V of the 1986 Act and Regulations
7. Mariners
8. Continental shelf
9. (*repealed*)

Citation, commencement and interpretation

5.62
1.—(1) These Regulations may be cited as the Statutory Maternity Pay (Persons Abroad and Mariners) Regulations 1987 and shall come into force on 6th April 1987.

(2) In these Regulations, the "1986 Act" means the Social Security Act 1986;

[¹"the Contributions and Benefits Act" means the Social Security Contributions and Benefits Act 1992, "the Contributions Regulations" means the Social Security (Contributions) Regulations 1979"], and the "General Regulations" means the Statutory Maternity Pay (General) Regulations 1986.

(3) Unless the context otherwise requires, any reference in these Regulations to a numbered regulation is a reference to the regulation bearing that number in these Regulations and any reference in a regulation to a numbered paragraph is a reference to the paragraph of that regulation bearing that number.

AMENDMENT

1. Social Security Contributions, Statutory Maternity Pay and Statutory Sick Pay (Miscellaneous Amendments) Regulations 1996 (SI 1996/777), reg.4(2) (April 6, 1996).

GENERAL NOTE

These Regulations were made under the authority of what is now SSCBA 1992,   **5.63**
s.170 and make special provision for statutory maternity pay as regards persons who are abroad or who are mariners. See also SMP (General) Regulations 1986 (SI 1986/1960), reg.17(3).

Persons in other member States—meaning of "employee"

2. Subject to regulation 3, a woman who is—   **5.64**
   (a) gainfully employed in a member State other than the United Kingdom in such circumstances that if her employment were in Great Britain she would be an employee for the purposes of Part V of the 1986 Act or a woman treated as such an employee under regulation 17 of the General Regulations; and
   (b) subject to the legislation of the United Kingdom under Council Regulation (EEC) No. 1408/71; notwithstanding that she is not employed in Great Britain, shall be treated as an employee for the purposes of Part V of the 1986 Act.

DEFINITIONS

"the 1986 Act"—see reg.1(2).
"the General Regulations"—see *ibid*.

[¹Persons absent from Great Britain—meaning of "employee"

2A. Subject to regulations 2, 3 and 7(3), where a woman, while absent   **5.65**
from Great Britain for any purpose, is gainfully employed by an employer who is liable to pay in respect of her secondary Class 1 contributions under section 6 of the Contributions and Benefits Act or regulation 120 of the Contributions Regulations, she shall be treated as an employee for the purposes of Part XII of the Contributions and Benefits Act.]

AMENDMENT

1. Social Security Contributions, Statutory Maternity Pay and Statutory Sick Pay (Miscellaneous Amendments) Regulations 1996 (SI 1996/777), reg.4(3) (April 6, 1996).

DEFINITIONS

"the Contributions and Benefits Act"—see reg.1(2).
"the Contributions Regulations"—see *ibid*.

Meaning of "employee"—general

5.66   **3.** No woman who, by virtue of regulation 17 of the General Regulations, would be treated as not being an employee for the purposes of Part V of the 1986 Act if her employment were in Great Britain, shall be treated as an employee by virtue of these Regulations.

DEFINITIONS

"the 1986 Act"—see reg.1(2).
"the General Regulations"—see *ibid*.

Women outside the European Community

5.67   **4.** [[1]. . .]

AMENDMENT

1. Social Security Contributions, Statutory Maternity Pay and Statutory Sick Pay (Miscellaneous Amendments) Regulations 1996 (SI 1996/777), reg.4(4) (April 6, 1996).

Women who worked in the European Community

5.68   **5.**—(1) A woman who is an employee or treated as an employee under regulation 2 and who—
    (a) in the week immediately preceding the 14th week before the expected week of confinement was in employed earner's employment with an employer in Great Britain, and
    (b) had in any week within the period of [[1]26 weeks] immediately preceding that week been employed by the same employer in another member State,
shall be treated for the purposes of sections 46(2) and 48 of the 1986 Act as having been employed in employed earner's employment in those weeks in which she was so employed in the other member State.
    (2) [[1]. . .]

AMENDMENT

1. Social Security Contributions, Statutory Maternity Pay and Statutory Sick Pay (Miscellaneous Amendments) Regulations 1996 (SI 1996/777), reg.4(5) (April 6, 1996).

DEFINITION

"the 1986 Act"—see reg.1(2).

Time for compliance with Part V of the 1986 Act and Regulations

5.69   **6.** Where—
    (a) a woman is outside the United Kingdom;
    (b) Part V of the 1986 Act or Regulations made under that Act or under Part III of the Social Security Act 1975 require any act to be done

forthwith or on the happening of a certain event or within a specified
time; and

(c) because the woman is outside the United Kingdom she or her
employer cannot comply with the requirement;

the woman or the employer, as the case may be, shall be deemed to have
complied with it if the act is performed as soon as reasonably practicable.

DEFINITION

"the 1986 Act"—see reg.1(2).

Mariners

7.—(1) In this regulation, "foreign-going ship", "home-trade ship" and   **5.70**
"mariner" have the same meanings as in Case C of Part VIII of the Social
Security (Contributions) Regulations 1979 and the expressions "ship" and
"ship or vessel", except in paragraph (3), include hovercraft.

(2) Subject to regulation 3, a mariner engaged in employment on board
a home-trade ship with an employer who has a place of business within the
United Kingdom shall be treated as an employee for the purposes of Part
V of the 1986 Act, notwithstanding that she may not be employed in Great
Britain.

(3) A mariner who is engaged in employment—

(a) on a foreign-going ship; or

(b) on a home-trade ship with an employer who does not have a place
of business within the United Kingdom, shall not be treated as an
employee for the purposes of Part V of the 1986 Act, notwithstanding that she may have been employed in Great Britain.

DEFINITIONS

"foreign-going ship"—see para.(1).
"home-trade ship"—see *ibid.*
"mariner"—see *ibid.*
"ship"—see *ibid.*
"ship or vessel"—see *ibid.*

Continental shelf

8.—(1) In this regulation—   **5.71**

"designated area" means any area which may from time to time be designated by Order in Council under the Continental Shelf Act 1964 as an
area within which the rights of the United Kingdom with respect to the
seabed and subsoil and their natural resources may be exercised;

"prescribed area" means an area over which Norway or any member
State (other than the United Kingdom) exercises sovereign rights
for the purpose of exploring the seabed and subsoil and exploiting their
natural resources, being an area outside the territorial seas of Norway
or that member State or any other area which is from time to time specified under section 22(5) of the Oil and Gas (Enterprise) Act 1982;

"prescribed employment" means employment in a designated area or
prescribed area in connection with any activity mentioned in section
23(2) of the Oil and Gas (Enterprise) Act 1982 in any designated area
or in any prescribed area.

(2) Subject to regulation 3, a woman in prescribed employment shall be treated as an employee for the purposes of Part V of the 1986 Act notwithstanding that she may not be employed in Great Britain.

DEFINITIONS

"the 1986 Act"—see reg.1(2).
"designated area"—see para.(2).
"prescribed area"—see *ibid.*
"prescribed employment"—see *ibid.*

Persons Abroad—maternity pay period not commencing or ending

5.72   **9.** [¹ . . .]

AMENDMENT

1. Social Security Contributions, Statutory Maternity Pay and Statutory Sick Pay (Miscellaneous Amendments) Regulations 1996 (SI 1996/777), reg.4(6) (April 6, 1996).

Statutory Maternity Pay (National Health Service Employees) Regulations 1991

(SI 1991/590)

5.73   The Secretary of State for Social Security, in exercise of the powers conferred by sections 49, 50(2A), 84(1) of, and paragraph 6 of Schedule 4 to the Social Security Act 1986 and of all other powers enabling him in that behalf, by this instrument, which contains only Regulations consequential upon paragraph 22 of Schedule 6 to the Social Security Act 1990, makes the following Regulations:

ARRANGEMENT OF REGULATIONS

1. Citation, commencement and interpretation
2. Treatment of more than one contract of employment as one contract
3. Notification of election
4. Provision of information
5. Treatment of two or more employers as one
6. Time for which an election is to have effect

Citation, commencement and interpretation

5.74   **1.**—(1) These Regulations may be cited as the Statutory, Maternity Pay (National Health Service Employees) Regulations 1991 and shall come into force on 1st April 1991.

(2) In these Regulations, a "health authority" [²shall in relation to Wales have the same meaning it has in section 8] of the National Health Service Act 1977, and in relation to Scotland mean the health board within the meaning of section 2 of the National Health Service (Scotland) Act 1978.

[¹(3) In these Regulations, "Primary Care Trust" means a Primary Care Trust established under section 16A of the National Health Service Act 1977.]

[²(4) In these Regulations, "Strategic Health Authority" means a Strategic Health Authority established under section 8 of the National Health Service Act 1977.]

[³(5) In these Regulations, a reference to "NHS trust" shall be construed to include a reference to an NHS foundation trust within the meaning of section 1(1) of the Health and Social Care (Community Health and Standards) Act 2003 where the application for authorisation to become an NHS foundation trust was made by an NHS trust.]

AMENDMENTS

1. Health Act 1999 (Supplementary, Consequential etc. Provisions) (No.2) Order 2000 (SI 2000/694), art.3 and Sch., para.3(2) (April 1, 2000).

2. National Health Service Reform and Health Care Professions Act 2002 (Supplementary, Consequential etc. Provisions) Regulations 2002 (SI 2002/2469), reg.4 and Sch.1, Pt 2, para.51 (October 1, 2002).

3. Health and Social Care (Community Health and Standards) Act 2003 (Supplementary and Consequential Provision) (NHS Foundation Trusts) Order 2004 (SI 2004/696), art.3(17) and Sch.17 (April 1, 2004).

Treatment of more than one contract of employment as one contract

2. Where, in consequence of the establishment of one or more National Health Service Trusts under Part I of the National Health Service and Community Care Act 1990, or the National Health Service (Scotland) Act 1978, a woman's contract of employment is treated by a scheme under that Part or Act as divided so as to constitute two or more contracts, [¹or where an order under paragraph 23(1) of Schedule 5A to the National Health Service Act 1977 provides that a woman's contract of employment is so divided,] she may elect for all those contracts to be treated as one contract for the purposes of Part V of the Social Security Act 1986.

5.75

AMENDMENT

1. Health Act 1999 (Supplementary, Consequential etc. Provisions) (No.2) Order 2000 (SI 2000/694), art.3 and Sch., para.3(3) (April 1, 2000).

Notification of election

3. A woman who makes an election under regulation 2 above shall give written notification of that election to each of her employers under the two or more contracts of service mentioned in that regulation at least [¹28 days] before the first day she is going to be absent from work with any of her employers, wholly or partly because of pregnancy, or if in the particular circumstances that is not practicable, as soon as is reasonably practicable.

5.76

AMENDMENT

1. Social Security, Statutory Maternity Pay and Statutory Sick Pay (Miscellaneous Amendments) Regulations 2002 (SI 23002/2690), reg.11 (November 24, 2002).

Provision of information

5.77   **4.** A woman who makes an election under regulation 2 above shall, within [¹28 days] of giving notice of that election or if in the particular circumstances that is not practicable, as soon as is reasonably practicable thereafter, provide each of her employers under the two or more contracts of service mentioned under that regulation with the following information—

   (a) the name and address of each of those employers; and
   (b) the date her employment with each of those employers commenced; and
   (c) details of her earnings during the relevant period from each employer and for this purpose the expressions "earnings" and "relevant period" have the same meanings as they have for the purposes of section 50(3) of the Social Security Act 1986.

AMENDMENT

1. Social Security, Statutory Maternity Pay and Statutory Sick Pay (Miscellaneous Amendments) Regulations 2002 (SI 2002/2690), reg.12 (November 24, 2002).

Treatment of two or more employers as one

5.78   **5.** The employer to be regarded for the purposes of statutory maternity pay as the employer under the one contract where 2 or more contracts of service are treated as one in accordance with regulation 2 above shall be—

   [¹(a) in the case of a woman whose contract of employment is treated by a scheme under Part I of the National Health Service and Community Care Act 1990 or the National Health Service (Scotland) Act 1978 as divided—
      (i) the Health Authority or Primary Care Trust from which the woman was transferred, in a case where any one of the contracts of service is with that Health Authority or Primary Care Trust; or
      (ii) the first NHS trust to which a contract of service was transferred in a case where none of the contracts of service are with the Health Authority or Primary Care Trust from which she was transferred;
   or
   (b) in the case of a woman whose contract of employment is divided as provided by an order under paragraph 23(1) of Schedule 5A to the National Health Service Act 1977—
      (i) the [²Strategic Health Authority], NHS trust or Primary Care Trust from which the woman was transferred, in a case where any one of the contracts of service is with that body; or
      (ii) the first Primary Care Trust to which a contract of service was transferred in a case where none of the contracts of service are with the body from which she was transferred.]

AMENDMENTS

1. Health Act 1999 (Supplementary, Consequential etc. Provisions) (No.2) Order 2000 (SI 2000/694), art.3 and Sch., para.3(4) (April 1, 2000).
2. National Health Service Reform and Health Care Professions Act 2002 (Supplementary, Consequential etc. Provisions) Regulations 2002 (SI 2002/2469), reg.6 and Sch.3 (October 1, 2002).

Time for which an election is to have effect

6. An election made under regulation 2 shall lapse at the end of the   5.79
maternity pay period.

Statutory Maternity Pay (Compensation of Employers) and Miscellaneous Amendment Regulations 1994

(SI 1994/1882) (AS AMENDED)

The Secretary of State for Social Security, in exercise of powers conferred on him by sections 35(3), 167(1), (1A), (1B) and (4), 171(1) and 175(1) to (4) of the Social Security Contributions and Benefits Act 1992 and of all other powers enabling him in that behalf after agreement by the Social Security Advisory Committee that proposals in respect of regulation 9 should not be referred to it, hereby makes the following Regulations:

ARRANGEMENT OF REGULATIONS

1. Citation, commencement and interpretation   5.80
2. Meaning of "small employer"
3. Determination of the amount of additional payment to which a small employer shall be entitled
4. Right of employers to prescribed amount
5. Application for advance funding from the Board
6. Deductions from payments to the Board
6A. Payments to employers by the Board
7. Date when certain contributions are to be treated as paid
7A. Overpayments
8. Revocation
9. *Omitted*

Citation, commencement and interpretation

1.—(1) These Regulations may be cited as the Statutory Maternity Pay   5.81
(Compensation of Employers) and Miscellaneous Amendment Regulations
1994 and regulations 2–7 shall have effect in relation to payments of statutory maternity pay due on or after 4th September 1994.

(2) This regulation and regulation 9 shall come into force on July 31, 1994.

(3) Regulations 2 to 8 shall come into force on 4th September 1994.

(4) In these Regulations—

[1"the Board" means the Commissioners of Inland Revenue;]

"the Contributions and Benefits Act" means the Social Security Contributions and Benefits Act 1992;

"the Maternity Allowance Regulations" means the Social Security (Maternity Allowance) Regulations 1987;

[1. . .];

[1"contributions payments" has the same meaning as in section 167(8) of the Contributions and Benefits Act;]

683

[1"the Contributions Regulations" means the Social Security (Contributions) Regulations 2001;]

"employer" shall include a person who was previously an employer of a woman to whom a payment of statutory maternity pay was made, whether or not that person remains her employer at the date any deduction from contributions payments is made by him in accordance with regulation 5 or, as the case may be, any payment is received by him in accordance with regulation 6;

[1"the Employment Act" means the Employment Act 2002;]

"income tax month" means the period beginning on the 6th day of any calendar month and ending on the 5th day of the following calendar month;

[1. . .];

[1"income tax quarter" means, in any tax year, the period beginning on 6th April and ending on 5th July the period beginning on 6th July and ending on 5th October the period beginning on 6th October and ending on 5th January or the period beginning on 6th January and ending on 5th April;]

"qualifying day" means the first day in the week immediately preceding the 14th week before the expected week of confinement in which a woman who is or has been an employee first satisfies the conditions of entitlement to statutory maternity pay for which a deduction from a contributions payment is made by her employer in respect of a payment of statutory maternity pay made by him;

"qualifying tax year" means the tax year preceding the tax year in which the qualifying day in question falls.

[1"statutory adoption pay" means any payment under section 171ZL of the Contributions and Benefits Act;

"statutory paternity pay" means any payment under section 171ZA or 171ZB of the Contributions and Benefits Act;

"tax year" means the period of 12 months beginning on 6th April in any year;

"writing" includes writing delivered by means of electronic communications approved by directions issued by the Board pursuant to regulations made under section 132 of the Finance Act 1999;]

[1(5) Any reference in these Regulations to the employees of any employer includes, where the context permits, a reference to his former employees.]

(6) [1. . .].

AMENDMENT

1. Statutory Maternity Pay (Compensation of Employers) Amendment Regulations 2003 (SI 2003/672), reg.2 (April 6, 2003).

GENERAL NOTE

5.82   These Regulations make provision for employers to be reimbursed for the cost of paying statutory maternity pay. The basic rule is that employers can recover 92 per cent of the total gross statutory maternity pay payments they make in any tax month (reg.4(a)). This is done by deducting such costs from tax payments, National Insurance contributions and other sums due to HMRC (reg.6). In certain circumstances employers may apply for advance funding from HMRC in order to meet their statutory maternity pay liabilities (reg.5; but see reg.7A regarding overpayments of such sums). Small employers—currently defined as those whose total National Insurance contributions do not exceed £45,000 in the previous tax year (reg.2(1))—are entitled to 100 per cent of the cost of their statutory maternity pay payments (reg.4(b)) together with a further 4.5 per cent of the total statutory maternity pay paid (reg.3). This additional amount is intended to compensate small employers for the cost of employers' National Insurance contributions on statutory maternity pay.

Regulation 9 of these Regulations contained a miscellaneous amendment to reg.3(4) of the Social Security (Maternity Allowance) Regulations 1987 (SI 1987/416), which has itself subsequently been revoked, and so is not included in this volume (see Vol.I).

Meaning of "small employer"

2.—(1) Subject to the following provisions of this regulation, a small employer is an employer whose contributions payments for the qualifying tax year do not exceed [¹£45,000].

5.83

(2) For the purposes of this regulation, the amount of an employer's contributions payments shall be determined without regard to any deductions that may be made from them under any enactment or instrument.

(3) Where in the qualifying tax year an employer has made contributions payments in one or more, but less than 12, of the income tax months, the amount of his contributions payments for that tax year shall be estimated by adding together all of those payments, dividing the total amount by the number of those months in which he has made those payments and multiplying the resulting figure by 12.

(4) Where in the qualifying tax year an employer has made no contributions payments, but does have such payments in one or more income tax months which fall both—

(a) in the tax year in which the qualifying day falls; and
(b) before the qualifying day or, where there is more than one such day in that tax year, before the first of those days,

then the amount of his contributions payments for the qualifying tax year shall be estimated in accordance with paragraph (3) but as if the amount of the contributions payments falling in those months had fallen instead in the corresponding tax months in the qualifying tax year.

AMENDMENT

1. Statutory Maternity Pay (Compensation of Employers) Amendment Regulations 2004 (SI 2004/698), reg.2 (April 6, 2004).

DEFINITIONS

"contributions payments"—see reg.1(4).
"employer"—see *ibid.*
"qualifying day"—see *ibid.*
"qualifying tax year"—see *ibid.*

Determination of the amount of additional payment to which a small employer shall be entitled

3. In respect of any payment of statutory maternity pay [¹made in the tax year commencing [²6th April 2002], or in any subsequent tax year,] a

5.84

small employer shall be [³entitled to recover an additional amount] being an amount equal to [²4.5 per cent.] of such payment, that percentage being the total amount of secondary Class 1 contributions estimated by the Secretary of State as to be paid in respect of statutory maternity pay by all employers in that year, expressed as a percentage of the total amount of statutory maternity pay estimated by him to be paid by all employers in that year.

AMENDMENTS

1. Statutory Maternity Pay (Compensation of Employers) Amendment Regulations 1995 (SI 1995/566), reg.2 (April 6, 1995).
2. Statutory Maternity Pay (Compensation of Employers) Amendment Regulations 2002 (SI 2002/225), reg.2 (April 6, 2002).
3. Statutory Maternity Pay (Compensation of Employers) Amendment Regulations 2003 (SI 2003/672), reg.3 (April 6, 2003).

DEFINITIONS

"employer"—see reg.1(4).
"payment of statutory maternity pay"—see *ibid*.
"small employer"—see reg.2(1).

[¹Right of employers to prescribed amount

5.85   **4.** An employer who has made, or is liable to make, any payment of statutory maternity pay shall be entitled to recover—
(a) an amount equal to 92 per cent of such payment; or
(b) if he is a small employer—
(i)   an amount equal to such payment; and
(ii) an additional amount under regulation 3, in accordance with the provisions of these Regulations.]

AMENDMENT

1. Statutory Maternity Pay (Compensation of Employers) Amendment Regulations 2003 (SI 2003/672), reg.4 (April 6, 2003).

DEFINITIONS

"employer"—see reg.1(4).
"payment of statutory maternity pay"—see *ibid*.
"small employer"—see reg.2(1).

[¹Application for advance funding from the Board

5.86   **5.**—(1) If an employer is entitled to recover an amount determined in accordance with regulation 4 in respect of statutory maternity pay which he is required to pay to an employee or employees in any income tax month or income tax quarter and the amount exceeds the aggregate of—
(a) the total amount of tax which the employer is required to pay to the collector of taxes in respect of deductions from the emoluments of his employees in accordance with the Income Tax (Employments) Regulations 1993 for that income tax month or income tax quarter;
(b) the total amount of deductions made by the employer from the emoluments of his employees for that income tax month or income tax quarter in accordance with regulations made under section 22(5)

of the Teaching and Higher Education Act 1998 or section 73B of the Education (Scotland) Act 1980 or in accordance with Article 3(5) of the Education (Student Support) (Northern Ireland) Order 1988;

(c) the total amount of contributions payments which the employer is required to pay to the collector of taxes in respect of the emoluments of his employees (whether by means of deduction or otherwise) in accordance with the Contributions Regulations for that income tax month or income tax quarter;

(d) the total amount of payments which the employer is required to pay to the collector of taxes in respect of deductions made on account of tax from payments to sub-contractors in accordance with section 559 of the Income and Corporation Taxes Act 1988 for that income tax month or income tax quarter; and

(e) the statutory paternity pay, statutory adoption pay and statutory maternity pay which the employer is required to pay to his employees in that income tax month or income tax quarter,

the employer may apply to the Board in accordance with paragraph (2) for funds ("advance funding") to pay that excess (or so much of it as remains outstanding) to the employee or employees.

(2) Where—

(a) the conditions in paragraph (1) are satisfied; or

(b) the employer considers that the conditions in paragraph (1) will be satisfied on the date of any subsequent payment of emoluments to one or more employees who are entitled to a payment of statutory maternity pay,

the employer may apply to the Board for advance funding on a form approved for that purpose by the Board.

(3) An application by an employer under paragraph (2) shall be for an amount not exceeding the amount of statutory maternity pay which the employer is entitled to recover in accordance with regulation 4 and which he is required to pay to an employee or employees for the income tax month or income tax quarter to which the payment of emoluments relates.]

AMENDMENT

1. Statutory Maternity Pay (Compensation of Employers) Amendment Regulations 2003 (SI 2003/672), reg.4 (April 6, 2003).

DEFINITIONS

"advance funding"—see para.(1).
"the Board"—see reg.1(4).
"the Contributions Regulations"—see *ibid.*
"contributions payments"—see *ibid.*
"employer"—see *ibid.*
"income tax month"—see *ibid.*
"income tax quarter"—see *ibid.*
"statutory adoption pay"—see *ibid.*
"statutory paternity pay"—see *ibid.*

[¹Deductions from payments to the Board

6. An employer who is entitled to recover an amount under regulation 4 may do so by making one or more deductions from the aggregate of the

5.87

amounts specified in sub-paragraphs (a) to (e) of regulation 5(1), except where and insofar as—

(a) those amounts relate to earnings paid before the beginning of the income tax month or income tax quarter in which the payment of statutory maternity pay was made;

(b) those amounts are paid by him later than six years after the tax year in which the payment of statutory maternity pay was made;

(c) the employer has received advance funding from the Board in accordance with an application under regulation 5; or

(d) the employer has made a request in writing under regulation 5 that the amount which he is entitled to recover under regulation 4 be paid to him and he has not received notification by the Board that such request is refused.]

AMENDMENT

1. Statutory Maternity Pay (Compensation of Employers) Amendment Regulations 2003 (SI 2003/672), reg.4 (April 6, 2003).

DEFINITIONS

"advance funding"—reg.5(1).
"the Board"—see reg.1(4).
"employer"—see *ibid*.
"income tax month"—see *ibid*.
"income tax quarter"—see *ibid*.
"writing"—see *ibid*.

[¹Payments to employers by the Board

5.88   **6A.** If, in an income tax month or an income tax quarter—

(a) the total amount that the employer is entitled to deduct under regulation 6 is less than the amount which the employer is entitled to recover under regulation 4;

(b) the Board is satisfied that this is so; and

(c) the employer has so requested in writing, the Board shall pay to the employer the sum that the employer is unable to deduct under regulation 6.]

AMENDMENT

1. Statutory Maternity Pay (Compensation of Employers) Amendment Regulations 2003 (SI 2003/672), reg.4 (April 6, 2003).

DEFINITIONS

"the Board"—see reg.1(4).
"income tax month"—see *ibid*.
"income tax quarter"—see *ibid*.
"writing"—see *ibid*.

Date when certain contributions are to be treated as paid

5.89   **7.** Where an employer has made a deduction from a contributions payment under [¹regulation 6], the date on which it is to be treated as having been paid for the purposes of [¹section 167(6)] of the Contributions and Benefits Act (amount deducted to be treated as paid and received towards discharging liability in respect of Class 1 contributions) is—

(a) in a case where the deduction did not extinguish the contributions payment, the date on which the remainder of the contributions payment or, as the case may be, the first date on which any part of the remainder of the contributions payment was paid; and

(b) in a case where the deduction extinguished the contributions payment, the 14th day after the end of the income tax month during which there were paid the earnings in respect of which the contributions payment was payable.

AMENDMENT

1. Statutory Maternity Pay (Compensation of Employers) Amendment Regulations 2003 (SI 2003/672), reg.5 (April 6, 2003).

DEFINITIONS

"the Contributions and Benefits Act"—see reg.1(4).
"contributions payments"—see *ibid.*
"employer"—see *ibid.*
"income tax month"—see *ibid.*

[¹Overpayments

7A.—(1) Where advance funding has been provided to an employer in accordance with an application under regulation 5, the Board may recover any part of it not used to pay statutory maternity pay ("the overpayment").   5.90

(2) An officer of the Board shall decide to the best of his judgement the amount of the overpayment and shall give notice in writing of his decision to the employer.

(3) A decision under paragraph (2) may be in respect of funding provided in accordance with regulation 5 for one or more income tax months or income tax quarters in a tax year—

(a) in respect of one or more classes of employees specified in a decision notice (where a notice does not name any individual employee); or

(b) in respect of one or more individual employees named in a decision notice.

(4) Subject to paragraphs (5), (6) or (7), Part 6 of the Taxes Management Act 1970 (collection and recovery) shall apply with any necessary modifications to a decision under this regulation as if the amount specified were an assessment and as if the amount set out in the notice were income tax charged on the employer.

(5) Where a decision under paragraph (2) relates to more than one employee, proceedings may be brought to recover the amount overpaid without distinguishing the sum to be repaid in respect of each employee and without specifying the employee in question.

(6) A decision to recover an amount made in accordance with this regulation shall give rise to one cause of action or matter of complaint for the purpose of proceedings under sections 65, 66 or 67 of the Taxes Management Act 1970.

(7) Nothing in paragraph (5) shall prevent separate proceedings being brought for the recovery of any amount which the employer is liable to repay in respect of each employee to whom the decision relates.]

DEFINITIONS

"the Board"—see reg.1(4).
"the overpayment"—see para.(1).
"advance funding"—see reg.5(1).
"employee"—see reg.1(5).
"employer"—see reg.1(4).
"income tax month"—see *ibid.*
"income tax quarter"—see *ibid.*
"tax year"—see *ibid.*
"writing"—see *ibid.*

Revocation

5.91   **8.** The Statutory Maternity Pay (Compensation of Employers) Regulations 1987 are hereby revoked.

Statutory Maternity Pay (General) (Modification and Amendment) Regulations 2000

(SI 2000/2883)

The Secretary of State for Social Security, in exercise of the powers conferred on him by sections 164(4), (9)(e) and (10), 165(1) and (3), 171(1) and 175(1) to (4) of the Social Security Contributions and Benefits Act 1992 and of all other powers enabling him in that behalf, after agreement by the Social Security Advisory Committee that proposals to make these Regulations should not be referred to it, hereby makes the following Regulations:

ARRANGEMENT OF REGULATIONS

5.92   1. Citation, commencement and interpretation
2. Modification of s.164(2)(a) of the Contributions and Benefits Act
3. Amendment of the Statutory Maternity Pay Regulations
4. Transitional provision

Citation, commencement and interpretation

5.93   **1.**—(1) These Regulations may be cited as the Statutory Maternity Pay (General) (Modification and Amendment) Regulations 2000 and shall come into force on 17th November 2000.

(2) In these Regulations—

"the Contributions and Benefits Act" means the Social Security Contributions and Benefits Act 1992;

"the Statutory Maternity Pay Regulations" means the Statutory Maternity Pay (General) Regulations 1986.

Modification of s.164(2)(a) of the Contributions and Benefits Act

5.94   **2.** Subject to regulation 4, in relation to a woman who is dismissed, or whose employment is otherwise terminated without her consent, after the beginning of the week immediately preceding the 14th week before the expected week of confinement, section 164(2)(a) of the Contributions and Benefits Act (conditions of entitlement to statutory maternity pay) shall be modified and have effect so that the words, "wholly or partly because of pregnancy or confinement" shall not apply.

DEFINITION

"Contributions and Benefits Act"—see reg.1(2).

GENERAL NOTE

In order to qualify for statutory maternity pay, the general rule under SSCBA 1992, s.164(2)(a) is that the claimant must have been continuously employed in an employed earner's employment for 26 weeks up to the 15th week before the expected week of confinement but has then ceased to work for the employer "wholly or partly because of pregnancy or confinement". This latter requirement caused problems for women who were dismissed for some other reason (e.g. redundancy). These Regulations were therefore enacted in 2000 (but with effect from 4th March 2001: reg.4) so as to extend the right to statutory maternity pay to all women, unless they left their job voluntarily.

5.95

Amendment of the Statutory Maternity Pay Regulations

3. . . .

5.96

GENERAL NOTE

The amendments made by reg.3 have been incorporated into the text of the Statutory Maternity Pay (General) Regulations 1986 (SI 1986/1960) in this volume.

5.97

Transitional provision

4. In relation to a woman whose expected week of confinement begins before 4th March 2001, the Contributions and Benefits Act and the Statutory Maternity Pay Regulations shall have effect as if these Regulations were not in force.

5.98

DEFINITIONS

"Contributions and Benefits Act"—see reg.1(2).
"Statutory Maternity Pay Regulations"—see *ibid.*

PART VI

STATUTORY PATERNITY PAY AND
STATUTORY ADOPTION PAY

Statutory Paternity Pay and Statutory Adoption Pay (Weekly Rates) Regulations 2002

(SI 2002/2818) (AS AMENDED)

Whereas a draft of the following Regulations was laid before Parliament in accordance with section 176(1)(a) of the Social Security Contributions and Benefits Act 1992 and approved by a resolution of each House of Parliament:

Now, therefore, the Secretary of State, in exercise of the powers conferred on her by sections 171ZE(1) and 171ZN(1) of the Social Security Contributions and Benefits Act 1992 and section 5(1)(l) of the Social Security Administration Act 1992, by this instrument, which contains only provision made by virtue of sections 2, 4 and 53 of and paragraphs 8 and 11 of Schedule 7 to the Employment Act 2002 and is made before the end of the period of 6 months from the coming into force of those enactments, hereby makes the following Regulations—

ARRANGEMENT OF REGULATIONS

1. Citation and commencement.   6.1
2. Weekly rate of payment of statutory paternity pay.
3. Weekly rate of payment of statutory adoption pay.
4. Rounding of fractional amounts.

Citation and commencement

1.—These Regulations may be cited as the Statutory Paternity Pay and   6.2
Statutory Adoption Pay (Weekly Rates) Regulations and shall come into
force on 8th December 2002.

GENERAL NOTE

These Regulations specify the weekly rate of statutory paternity pay and statutory   6.3
adoption pay. In the current year, statutory paternity pay is the lower of £112.75
per week or 90 per cent of the employee's normal weekly earnings where the paternity pay period starts after that date (reg.2). Statutory adoption pay is set at the
lower of £112.75 per week or 90 per cent of the employee's normal weekly earnings
(reg.3). Fractional amounts are rounded in accordance with reg.4.

[¹Weekly rate of payment of statutory paternity pay

2. The weekly rate of payment of statutory paternity pay shall be the   6.4
smaller of the following two amounts—
  (a) [²£123.06];
  (b) 90 per cent. of the normal weekly earnings of the person claiming
      statutory paternity pay, determined in accordance with regulations
      39 and 40 of the Statutory Paternity Pay and Statutory Adoption Pay
      (General) Regulations 2002.]

AMENDMENTS

1. Statutory Paternity Pay and Statutory Adoption Pay (Weekly Rates) (Amendment) Regulations 2004 (SI 2004/925), reg.2 (April 4, 2004).
2. Social Security Benefits Up-rating Order 2009 (SI 2009/497), art.11(a) (April 5, 2009).

Weekly rate of payment of statutory adoption pay

6.5   **3.** The weekly rate of payment of statutory adoption pay shall be the smaller of the following two amounts—
    (a) [¹£123.06];
    (b) 90 per cent of the normal weekly earnings of the person claiming statutory adoption pay, determined in accordance with regulations 39 and 40 of the Statutory Paternity Pay and Statutory Adoption Pay (General) Regulations 2002.

AMENDMENT

1. Social Security Benefits Up-rating Order 2009 (SI 2009/497), art.11(a) (April 5, 2009).

Rounding of fractional amounts

6.6   [¹**4.** Where any payment of—
    (a) statutory paternity pay is made on the basis of a calculation at—
        (i) the weekly rate specified in regulation 2(b); or
        (ii) the daily rate of one-seventh of the weekly rate specified in regulation 2(a) or (b); or
    (b) statutory adoption pay is made on the basis of a calculation at—
        (i) the weekly rate specified in regulation 3(b); or
        (ii) the daily rate of one-seventh of the weekly rate specified in regulation 3(a) or (b),
and that amount includes a fraction of a penny, the payment shall be rounded up to the next whole number of pence.]

AMENDMENT

1. Statutory Paternity Pay and Statutory Adoption Pay (General) and the Statutory Paternity Pay and Statutory Adoption Pay (Weekly Rates) (Amendment) Regulations 2006 (SI 2006/2236), reg.4 (October 1, 2006).

GENERAL NOTE

6.7   The amended version of reg.4 applies in relation to an entitlement to SPP (birth) in respect of children whose expected week of birth begins on or after April 1, 2007 and to SPP (adoption) and SAP in respect of children expected to be placed for adoption, where the placement is expected to occur on or after April 1, 2007 (see reg.2 of SI 2006/2236).

Statutory Paternity Pay and Statutory Adoption Pay (National Health Service Employees) Regulations 2002

(SI 2002/2819) (AS AMENDED)

The Secretary of State, in exercise of the powers conferred on her by virtue of sections 171ZJ(9) and (10) and 171ZS(9) and (10) of the Social Security Contributions and Benefits Act 1992 and with the concurrence of the Commissioners of Inland Revenue by this instrument, which contains only provision made by virtue of sections 2 and 4 of the Employment Act 2002 and is made before the end of the period of 6 months from the coming into force of those enactments hereby makes the following Regulations—

ARRANGEMENT OF SECTIONS

6.8

Citation, commencement and interpretation

1.—(1) These Regulations may be cited as the Statutory Paternity Pay and Statutory Adoption Pay (National Health Service Employees) Regulations 2002 and shall come into force on 8th December 2002.

6.9

(2) In these Regulations—

"the Act" means the Social Security Contributions and Benefits Act 1992;

"the 1977 Act" means the National Health Service Act 1977;

"the 1978 Act" means the National Health Service (Scotland) Act 1978;

"the 1990 Act" means the National Health Service and Community Care Act 1990;

"the 2002 Act" means the National Health Service Reform and Health Care Professions Act 2002;

"Health Authority" means, in relation to Wales, a Health Authority established under section 8 of the 1977 Act and in relation to Scotland means a Health Board established under section 2 of the 1978 Act;

["NHS trust" shall be construed to include a reference to an NHS foundation trust within the meaning of section 1(1) of the Health and Social Care (Community Health and Standards) Act 2003 where the application for authorisation to become an NHS foundation trust was made by an NHS trust.]

"Primary Care Trust" means a Primary Care Trust established under section 16A of the 1977 Act;

"statutory adoption pay period" means the period prescribed under section 171ZN(2) of the Act as the period in respect of which statutory adoption pay is payable to a person;

"statutory paternity pay period" means the period determined in accordance with section 171ZE(2) of the Act as the period in respect of which statutory paternity pay is payable to a person;

"Strategic Health Authority" means a Strategic Health Authority established under section 8 of the 1977 Act.

AMENDMENT

1. Health and Social Care (Community Health and Standards) Act 2003 (Supplementary and Consequential Provision) (NHS Foundation Trusts) Order 2004 (SI 2004/696), art.3(1) and Sch.1, para.42 (April 1, 2004).

GENERAL NOTE

6.10   These Regulations, made under the authority of SSCBA 1992, ss.171ZJ(9) and (10) and 171ZS(9) and (10), make special provision for those NHS workers who are employed under two or more separate contracts of employment with different NHS Trusts. The regulations enable them to elect to have such contracts treated as one contract for the purposes of entitlement to statutory paternity pay and statutory adoption pay.

Treatment of more than one contract of employment as one contract

6.11   **2.** Where, in consequence of the establishment of one or more National Health Service Trusts under section 5 of the 1990 Act or section 12A of the 1978 Act, a person's contract of employment is treated by a scheme under section 6 of the 1990 Act or section 12B of the 1978 Act as divided so as to constitute two or more contracts, or where an order under paragraph 23(1) of Schedule 5A to the 1977 Act provides that a person's contract is so divided, he may elect for all those contracts to be treated as one contract for the purposes of Parts 12ZA and 12ZB of the Act.

DEFINITIONS

"the Act"—see reg.1(2).
"the 1977 Act"—see *ibid.*
"the 1978 Act"—see *ibid.*
"the 1990 Act"—see *ibid.*

Notification of election

6.12   **3.** A person who makes an election under regulation 2 above shall give written notification of that election to each of his employers under the two or more contracts of employment mentioned in that regulation at least 28 days before the beginning of the statutory paternity pay period or adoption pay period or, if in the particular circumstances that is not practicable, as soon as is reasonably practicable.

DEFINITIONS

"statutory adoption pay period"—see reg.1(2).
"statutory paternity pay period"—see *ibid.*

Provision of information

6.13   **4.** A person who makes an election under regulation 2 above shall, within 28 days of giving notification of that election or, if in the particular circumstances that is not practicable, as soon as is reasonably practicable thereafter, provide each of his employers under the two or more contracts of employment mentioned in that regulation with the following information—

(a) the name and address of each of those employers;

(b) the date his employment with each of those employers commenced; and

(c) details of his normal weekly earnings during the relevant period from each employer, and for this purpose the expressions "normal weekly earnings" and "relevant period" have the same meanings as they have for the purposes of Parts 12ZA and 12ZB of the Act.

DEFINITIONS

"normal weekly earnings"—para.(c) and SSCBA 1992, ss.171ZJ(6) and 171ZS(6) and Statutory Paternity Pay and Statutory Adoption Pay (General) Regulations 2002 (SI 2002/2822), reg.40.

"relevant period"—para.(c) and SSCBA 1992, ss.171ZJ(7) and 171ZS(7) and Statutory Paternity Pay and Statutory Adoption Pay (General) Regulations 2002 (SI 2002/2822), reg.40(3).

Treatment of two or more employers as one

5. The employer to be regarded for the purposes of statutory paternity pay or statutory adoption pay as the employer under the one contract where two or more contracts are treated as one in accordance with regulation 2 above shall be—

6.14

(a) in the case of a person whose contract of employment is treated by a scheme under section 6 of the 1990 Act or section 12B of the 1978 Act as divided—

  (i) the Health Authority or Primary Care Trust from which the person was transferred in a case where any one of the contracts of employment is with that Health Authority or Primary Care Trust; or

  (ii) the first NHS trust to which a contract of employment was transferred in a case where none of the contracts of employment is with the Health Authority or Primary Care Trust; or

(b) in the case of a person whose contract of employment is divided as provided by an order under paragraph 23(1) of Schedule 5A to the 1977 Act—

  (i) the Strategic Health Authority, NHS trust or Primary Care Trust from which the person was transferred, in a case where any one of the contracts of employment is with that body; or

  (ii) the first Primary Care Trust to which a contract of employment was transferred in a case where none of the contracts of employment is with the body from which he was transferred.

DEFINITIONS

"the 1977 Act"—see reg.1(2).

"the 1978 Act"—see *ibid.*

"Health Authority"—see *ibid.*

"Primary Care Trust"—see *ibid.*

"Strategic Health Authority"—see *ibid.*

Time for which an election is to have effect

6.15   **6.** An election made under regulation 2 shall lapse at the end of the statutory paternity pay period or, as the case may be, the adoption pay period.

DEFINITIONS

"statutory adoption pay period"—see reg.1(2).
"statutory paternity pay period"—see *ibid.*

Statutory Paternity Pay and Statutory Adoption Pay (Administration) Regulations 2002

(SI 2002/2820)

The Secretary of State, in exercise of the powers conferred on her by sections 7(1), (2)(a) and (b), (4)(a), (b) and (c) and (5), 8(1) and (2)(a), (b) and (c), 10(1) and (2) and 51(1) of the Employment Act 2002 and sections 8(1)(f) and (ga) and 25 of the Social Security Contributions (Transfer of Functions, etc.) Act 1999 and with the concurrence of the Commissioners of Inland Revenue, hereby makes the following Regulations—

ARRANGEMENT OF SECTIONS

6.16   1. Citation and commencement.
2. Interpretation.
3. Funding of employers' liabilities to make payments of statutory paternity or statutory adoption pay.
4. Application for funding from the Board.
5. Deductions from payments to the Board.
6. Payments to employers by the Board.
7. Date when certain contributions are to be treated as paid.
8. Overpayments.
9. Records to be maintained by employers.
10. Inspection of employers' records.
11. Provision of information relating to entitlement to statutory paternity pay or statutory adoption pay.
12. Application for the determination of any issue arising as to, or in connection with, entitlement to statutory paternity pay or statutory adoption pay.
13. Applications in connection with statutory paternity pay or statutory adoption pay.
14. Provision of information.

Citation and commencement

6.17   **1.** These Regulations may be cited as the Statutory Paternity Pay and Statutory Adoption Pay (Administration) Regulations 2002 and shall come into force on 8th December 2002.

GENERAL NOTE

6.18   These Regulations provide for employers to be reimbursed for the cost of making payments of statutory paternity pay and statutory adoption pay. They are therefore modelled in part on the Statutory Maternity Pay (Compensation of Employers) and Miscellaneous Amendment Regulations 1994 (SI 1994/1882). As with the regulations governing statutory maternity pay, they provide for employers to claim back 92 per cent of the total costs of their statutory paternity pay and statutory adoption pay payments, or 100 per cent in the case of small employers, with a small additional element in the latter instance (reg.3). Employers receive such monies by making deductions from income tax, National Insurance contributions and other payments that would otherwise be due to HMRC (reg.4). There is provision for HMRC to make a direct payment to an employer where such deductions would otherwise be insufficient (reg.6). HMRC also has the power to recover overpayments from employers (reg.8).

These Regulations also require employers to maintain relevant records (reg.9) and to permit HMRC officers to inspect such records (reg.10). Furthermore, employers who decide that they have no liability to pay statutory paternity pay or statutory adoption pay to an employee or ex-employee must give any such person details of that decision and the reasons for it (reg.11). Any question relating to entitlement to statutory paternity pay or statutory adoption pay may be submitted by the employee concerned to HMRC for decision (regs 12 and 13). HMRC has information-gathering powers as set out in reg.14.

Regulations 2 and 11 of these regulations are amended for the purposes of adoptions from overseas by the Statutory Paternity Pay (Adoption) and Statutory Adoption Pay (Adoptions from Overseas) (Administration) Regulations 2003 (SI 2003/1192).

Interpretation

2.—(1) In these Regulations—   **6.19**

"adopter", in relation to a child, means a person with whom the child is matched for adoption;

"adoption leave" means leave under section 75A of the Employment Rights Act 1996;

"adoption pay period" means the period prescribed under section 171ZN(2) of the Contributions and Benefits Act as the period in respect of which statutory adoption pay is payable to a person;

"the Board" means the Commissioners of Inland Revenue;

"the Contributions and Benefits Act" means the Social Security Contributions and Benefits Act 1992;

"contributions payments" has the same meaning as in section 7 of the Employment Act;

"the Contributions Regulations" means the Social Security (Contributions) Regulations 2001;

"the Employment Act" means the Employment Act 2002;

"income tax month" means the period beginning on the 6th day of any calendar month and ending on the 5th day of the following calendar month;

"income tax quarter" means the period beginning on the 6th day of April and ending on the 5th day of July, the period beginning on the 6th day of July and ending on the 5th day of October, the period beginning on the 6th day of October and ending on the 5th day of January or the period beginning on the sixth day of January and ending on the 5th day of April;

"paternity leave" means leave under section 80A or section 80B of the Employment Rights Act 1996;

"paternity pay period" means the period determined in accordance with section 171ZE(2) of the Contributions and Benefits Act as the period in respect of which statutory paternity pay is payable to a person;

"statutory adoption pay" means any payment under section 171ZL of the Contributions and Benefits Act;

"statutory paternity pay" means any payment under section 171ZA or section 171ZB of the Contributions and Benefits Act;

"tax year" means the 12 months beginning with 6th April in any year;

"writing" includes writing delivered by means of electronic communications approved by directions issued by the Board pursuant to regulations under section 132 of the Finance Act 1999;

(2) Any reference in these Regulations to the employees of an employer includes former employees of his.

Funding of employers' liabilities to make payments of statutory paternity or statutory adoption pay

6.20   **3.**—(1) An employer who has made any payment of statutory paternity pay or statutory adoption pay shall be entitled—

(a) to an amount equal to 92 per cent of such payment; or

(b) if the payment qualifies for small employer's relief by virtue of section 7(3) of the Employment Act—

  (i) to an amount equal to such payment; and

  (ii) to an additional payment equal to the amount to which the employer would have been entitled under section 167(2)(b) of the Contributions and Benefits Act had the payment been a payment of statutory maternity pay.

(2) The employer shall be entitled in either case (a) or case (b) to apply for advance funding in respect of such payment in accordance with regulation 4, or to deduct it in accordance with regulation 5 from amounts otherwise payable by him.

DEFINITIONS

"Contributions and Benefits Act"—see reg.2(1).
"Employment Act"—see *ibid*.
"statutory adoption pay"—see *ibid*.
"statutory paternity pay"—see *ibid*.

Application for funding from the Board

6.21   **4.**—(1) If an employer is entitled to a payment determined in accordance with regulation 3 in respect of statutory paternity pay or statutory adoption pay which he is required to pay to an employee or employees for an income tax month or income tax quarter, and the payment exceeds the aggregate of—

(a) the total amount of tax which the employer is required to pay to the collector of taxes in respect of the deductions from the emoluments of his employees in accordance with the Income Tax (Employments) Regulations 1993 for the same income tax month or income tax quarter;

(b) the total amount of the deductions made by the employer from the emoluments of his employees for the same income tax month or income tax quarter in accordance with regulations under section 22(5) of the Teaching and Higher Education Act 1998 or section

73B of the Education (Scotland) Act 1980 or in accordance with article 3(5) of the Education (Student Support) (Northern Ireland) Order 1998;

(c) the total amount of contributions payments which the employer is required to pay to the collector of taxes in respect of the emoluments of his employees (whether by means of deduction or otherwise) in accordance with the Contributions Regulations for the same income tax month or income tax quarter; and

(d) the total amount of payments which the employer is required to pay to the collector of taxes in respect of the deductions made on account of tax from payments to sub-contractors in accordance with section 559 of the Income and Corporation Taxes Act 1988 for the same income tax month or income tax quarter,

the employer may apply to the Board in accordance with paragraph (2) for funds to pay the statutory paternity pay or statutory adoption pay (or so much of it as remains outstanding) to the employee or employees.

(2) Where—

(a) the condition in paragraph (1) is satisfied; or

(b) the employer considers that the condition in paragraph (1) will be satisfied on the date of any subsequent payment of emoluments to one or more employees who are entitled to payment of statutory paternity pay or statutory adoption pay,

the employer may apply to the Board for funding in a form approved for that purpose by the Board.

(3) An application by an employer under paragraph (2) shall be for an amount up to, but not exceeding, the amount of the payment to which the employer is entitled in accordance with regulation 3 in respect of statutory paternity pay and statutory adoption pay which he is required to pay to an employee or employees for the income tax month or income tax quarter to which the payment of emoluments relates.

DEFINITIONS

"the Board"—see reg.2(1).
"contributions payments"—see *ibid.*
"the Contributions Regulations"—see *ibid.*
"income tax month"—see *ibid.*
"income tax quarter"—see *ibid.*
"statutory adoption pay"—see *ibid.*
"statutory paternity pay"—see *ibid.*

Deductions from payments to the Board

5. An employer who is entitled to a payment determined in accordance with regulation 3 may recover such payment by making one or more deductions from the aggregate of the amounts specified in subparagraphs (a) to (d) of regulation 4(1) except where and in so far as—

6.22

(a) those amounts relate to earnings paid before the beginning of the income tax month or income tax quarter in which the payment of statutory paternity pay or statutory adoption pay was made;

(b) those amounts are paid by him later than six years after the end of the tax year in which the payment of statutory paternity pay or statutory adoption pay was made;

    (c) the employer has received payment from the Board under regulation 4; or

    (d) the employer has made a request in writing under regulation 4 that the payment to which he is entitled in accordance with regulation 3 be paid to him and he has not received notification by the Board that the request is refused.

DEFINITIONS

"the Board"—see reg.2(1).
"income tax month"—see *ibid*.
"income tax quarter"—see *ibid*.
"statutory adoption pay"—see *ibid*.
"statutory paternity pay"—see *ibid*.
"tax year"—see *ibid*.
"writing"—see *ibid*.

Payments to employers by the Board

6.23   **6.** If the total amount which an employer is or would otherwise be entitled to deduct under regulation 5 is less than the payment to which the employer is entitled in accordance with regulation 3 in an income tax month or income tax quarter, and the Board are satisfied that this is so, then provided that the employer has in writing requested them to do so, the Board shall pay the employer such amount as the employer was unable to deduct.

DEFINITIONS

"the Board"—see reg.2(1).
"income tax month"—see *ibid*.
"income tax quarter"—see *ibid*.
"writing"—see *ibid*.

Date when certain contributions are to be treated as paid

6.24   **7.** Where an employer has made a deduction from a contributions payment under regulation 5, the date on which it is to be treated as having been paid for the purposes of section 7(5) of the Employment Act (when amount deducted from contributions payment to be treated as paid and received by the Board) is—

    (a) in a case where the deduction did not extinguish the contributions payment, the date on which the remainder of the contributions payment or, as the case may be, the first date on which any part of the remainder of the contributions payment was paid; and

    (b) in a case where the deduction extinguished the contributions payment, the 14th day after the end of the income tax month or income tax quarter during which there were paid the earnings in respect of which the contributions payment was payable.

DEFINITIONS

"the Board"—see reg.2(1).
"contributions payments"—see *ibid*.
"Employment Act"—see *ibid*.
"income tax month"—see *ibid*.
"income tax quarter"—see *ibid*.

Overpayments

8.—(1) This regulation applies where unds have been provided to the   6.25
employer pursuant to regulation 4 in respect of one or more employees
and it appears to an officer of the Board that the employer has not used
the whole or part of those funds to pay statutory paternity pay or statutory
adoption pay.

(2) An officer of the Board shall decide to the best of his judgement the
amount of funds provided pursuant to regulation 4 and not used to pay
statutory paternity pay or statutory adoption pay and shall serve notice in
writing of his decision on the employer.

(3) A decision under this regulation may cover funds provided pursuant
to regulation 4—

- (a) for any one income tax month or income tax quarter, or more than
one income tax month or income tax quarter, in a tax year; and
- (b) in respect of a class or classes of employees specified in the decision
notice (without naming the individual employees), or in respect of
one or more employees named in the decision notice.

(4) Subject to the following provisions of this regulation, Part 6 of the
Taxes Management Act 1970 (collection and recovery) shall apply with
any necessary modifications to a decision under this regulation as if it were
an assessment and as if the amount of funds determined were income tax
charged on the employer.

(5) Where an amount of funds determined under this regulation relates
to more than one employee, proceedings may be brought for the recovery of
that amount without distinguishing the amounts making up that sum which
the employer is liable to repay in respect of each employee and without
specifying the employee in question, and the amount determined under
this regulation shall be one cause of action or one matter of complaint
for the purposes of proceedings under sections 65, 66 or 67 of the Taxes
Management Act 1970.

(6) Nothing in paragraph (5) prevents the bringing of separate proceedings for the recovery of any amount which the employer is liable to repay in
respect of each employee.

DEFINITIONS

"the Board"—see reg.2(1).
"income tax month"—see *ibid.*
"income tax quarter"—see *ibid.*
"statutory adoption pay"—see *ibid.*
"statutory paternity pay"—see *ibid.*
"tax year"—see *ibid.*
"writing"—see *ibid.*

Records to be maintained by employers

9. Every employer shall maintain for three years after the end of a tax year   6.26
in which he made payments of statutory paternity pay or statutory adoption
pay to any employee of his a record of—

- (a) if the employee's paternity pay period or adoption pay period began
in that year—
  - (i) the date on which that period began; and

    (ii) the evidence of entitlement to statutory paternity pay or statutory adoption pay provided by the employee pursuant to regulations made under section 171ZC(3)(c) or section 171ZL(8)(c) of the Contributions and Benefits Act;

(b) the weeks in that tax year in which statutory paternity pay or statutory adoption pay was paid to the employee and the amount paid in each week; and

(c) any week in that tax year which was within the employee's paternity pay period or adoption pay period but for which no payment of statutory paternity pay or statutory adoption pay was made to him and the reason no payment was made.

DEFINITIONS

"adoption pay period"—see reg.2(1).
"the Contributions and Benefits Act"—see *ibid.*
"paternity pay period"—see *ibid.*
"statutory adoption pay"—see *ibid.*
"statutory paternity pay"—see *ibid.*
"tax year"—see *ibid.*

Inspection of employers' records

6.27   **10.**—(1) Every employer, whenever called upon to do so by any authorised officer of the Board, shall produce the documents and records specified in paragraph (2) to that officer for inspection, at such time as that officer may reasonably require, at the prescribed place.

(2) The documents and records specified in this paragraph are—

(a) all wages sheets, deductions working sheets, records kept in accordance with regulation 9 and other documents and records whatsoever relating to the calculation or payment of statutory paternity pay or statutory adoption pay to his employees in respect of the years specified by such officer; or

(b) such of those wages sheets, deductions working sheets, or other documents and records as may be specified by the authorised officer.

(3) The "prescribed place" mentioned in paragraph (1) means—

(a) such place in Great Britain as the employer and the authorised officer may agree upon; or

(b) in default of such agreement, the place in Great Britain at which the documents and records referred to in paragraph (2)(a) are normally kept; or

(c) in default of such agreement and if there is no such place as is referred to in sub-paragraph (b) above, the employer's principal place of business in Great Britain.

(4) The authorised officer may—

(a) take copies of, or make extracts from, any document or record produced to him for inspection in accordance with paragraph (1);

(b) remove any document or record so produced if it appears to him to be necessary to do so, at a reasonable time and for a reasonable period.

(5) Where any document or record is removed in accordance with paragraph (4)(b), the authorised officer shall provide—

(a) a receipt for the document or record so removed; and

(b) a copy of the document or record, free of charge, within seven days, to the person by whom it was produced or caused to be produced where the document or record is reasonably required for the proper conduct of a business.

(6) Where a lien is claimed on a document produced in accordance with paragraph (1), the removal of the document under paragraph (4)(b) shall not be regarded as breaking the lien.

(7) Where records are maintained by computer, the person required to make them available for inspection shall provide the authorised officer with all facilities necessary for obtaining information from them.

DEFINITIONS

"the Board"—see reg.2(1).
"prescribed place"—see para.(3).
"statutory adoption pay"—see reg.2(1).
"statutory paternity pay"—see *ibid*.

Provision of information relating to entitlement to statutory paternity pay or statutory adoption pay

11.—(1) Where an employer who has been given evidence of entitlement to statutory paternity pay or statutory adoption pay pursuant to regulations made under section 171ZC(3)(c) or section 171ZL(8)(c) of the Contributions and Benefits Act by a person who is or has been an employee decides that he has no liability to make payments of statutory paternity pay or statutory adoption pay to the employee, the employer shall furnish the employee with details of the decision and the reasons for it. **6.28**

(2) Where an employer who has been given such evidence of entitlement to statutory adoption pay has made one or more payments of statutory adoption pay to the employee but decides, before the end of the adoption pay period, that he has no liability to make further payments to the employee because he has been detained in legal custody or sentenced to a term of imprisonment which was not suspended, the employer shall furnish the employee with—

(a) details of his decision and the reasons for it; and
(b) details of the last week in respect of which a liability to pay statutory adoption pay arose and the total number of weeks within the adoption pay period in which such a liability arose.

(3) The employer shall—

(a) return to the employee any evidence provided by him as referred to in paragraph (1) or (2); and
(b) comply with the requirements imposed by paragraph (1) within 28 days of—
  (i) in the case of entitlement to statutory paternity pay under section 171ZA(1) of the Contributions and Benefits Act, the day the employee gave notice of his intended absence or the end of the fifteenth week before the expected week of birth, whichever is the later; or
  (ii) in the case of entitlement to statutory paternity pay under section 171ZB(1) or of statutory adoption pay under section 171ZL(1) of the Contributions and Benefits Act, the end of the seven-day period that starts on the date on which the adopter is notified of having been matched with the child;

(c) comply with the requirements imposed by paragraph (2) within seven days of being notified of the employee's detention or sentence.

(4) For the purposes of paragraph (3)(b)(ii), an adopter is notified of having been matched with a child on the date on which he receives notification, under regulation 11(2) of the Adoption Agencies Regulations 1983 or regulation 12(3) of the Adoption Agencies (Scotland) Regulations 1996 that an adoption agency has decided that he would be a suitable adoptive parent for the child.

DEFINITIONS

"adopter"—see reg.2(1).
"adoption pay period"—see *ibid.*
"the Contributions and Benefits Act"—see *ibid.*
"statutory adoption pay"—see *ibid.*
"statutory paternity pay"—see *ibid.*

GENERAL NOTE

6.29   This regulation is modified for the purposes of adoptions from overseas by the Statutory Paternity Pay (Adoption) and Statutory Adoption Pay (Adoptions from Overseas) (Administration) Regulations 2003 (SI 2003/1192).

Application for the determination of any issue arising as to, or in connection with, entitlement to statutory paternity pay or statutory adoption pay

6.30   **12.**—(1) An application for the determination of any issue arising as to, or in connection with, entitlement to statutory paternity pay or statutory adoption pay may be submitted to an officer of the Board by the employee concerned.

(2) Such an issue shall be decided by an officer of the Board only on the basis of such an application or on his own initiative.

DEFINITIONS

"the Board"—see reg.2(1).
"statutory adoption pay"—see *ibid.*
"statutory paternity pay"—see *ibid.*

Applications in connection with statutory paternity pay or statutory adoption pay

6.31   **13.**—(1) An application for the determination of any issue referred to in regulation 12 shall be made in a form approved for the purpose by the Board.

(2) Where such an application is made by an employee, it shall—

(a) be made to an officer of the Board within six months of the earliest day in respect of which entitlement to statutory paternity pay or statutory adoption pay is in issue;

(b) state the period in respect of which entitlement to statutory paternity pay or statutory adoption pay is in issue; and

(c) state the grounds (if any) on which the applicant's employer had denied liability for statutory paternity pay or statutory adoption pay in respect of the period specified in the application.

Provision of information

14.—(1) Any person specified in paragraph (2) shall, where informa- 6.32
tion or documents are reasonably required from him to ascertain whether
statutory paternity pay or statutory adoption pay is or was payable,
furnish that information or those documents within 30 days of receiving
a notification from an officer of the Board requesting such information or
documents.

(2) The requirement to provide such information or documents applies
to—

(a) any person claiming to be entitled to statutory paternity pay or statutory adoption pay;

(b) any person who is, or has been, the spouse [¹, the civil partner] or
partner of such a person as is specified in paragraph (a);

(c) any person who is, or has been, an employer of such a person as is
specified in paragraph (a);

(d) any person carrying on an agency or other business for the introduction or supply to persons requiring them of persons available to do
work or to perform services; and

(e) any person who is a servant or agent of any such person as is specified in paragraphs (a) to (d).

AMENDMENT

1. Civil Partnership Act 2004 (Amendments to Subordinate Legislation) Order
2005 (SI 2005/2114), art.2(17) and Sch.17, para.2 (December 5, 2005).

Statutory Paternity Pay and Statutory Adoption Pay (Persons Abroad and Mariners) Regulations 2002

(SI 2002/2821)

The Secretary of State, in exercise of the powers conferred upon her by
virtue of sections 171ZI, 171ZJ(1), 171ZR and 171ZS(1) of the Social Security
Contributions and Benefits Act 1992 and with the concurrence of the Treasury,
by this instrument, which contains only provision made by virtue of sections 2
and 4 of the Employment Act 2002 and is made before the end of the period of 6
months from the coming into force of those enactments, hereby makes the following Regulations:

6.33

Citation, commencement and interpretation

6.34

1.—(1) These Regulations may be cited as the Statutory Paternity Pay and Statutory Adoption Pay (Persons Abroad and Mariners) Regulations 2002 and shall come into force on 8th December 2002.

(2) In these Regulations—

"the Act" means the Social Security Contributions and Benefits Act 1992;

"adopter", in relation to a child, has the same meaning as it has in the General Regulations;

"the Contributions Regulations" means the Social Security Contributions Regulations 2001;

"EEA" means European Economic Area;

"EEA Agreement" means the Agreement on the European Economic Area signed at Oporto on 2nd May 1992 as adjusted by Protocol signed at Brussels on 17th March 1993;

"EEA State" means a State which is a contracting party to the EEA Agreement;

"the General Regulations" means the Statutory Paternity Pay and Statutory Adoption Pay (General) Regulations 2002;

"statutory paternity pay (birth)" and "statutory paternity pay (adoption)" have the same meaning as they have in the General Regulations;

"week" means a period of 7 days beginning with Sunday.

(3) For the purposes of these Regulations, a person is notified of having been matched with a child for the purposes of adoption on the date on which he receives notification, under regulation 11(2) of the Adoption Agencies Regulations 1983 or regulation 12(3) of the Adoption Agencies (Scotland) Regulations 1996, that an adoption agency has decided that the person would be a suitable adoptive parent for the child, either individually or jointly with another person.

GENERAL NOTE

6.35

These Regulations modify Pts XIIZA and XIIZB of the SSCBA 1992, which govern statutory paternity pay and statutory adoption pay respectively, in relation to persons abroad, those who work as mariners and persons who work on the Continental Shelf. They are modified in relation to adoptions from overseas by the Statutory Paternity Pay (Adoption) and Statutory Adoption Pay

(Adoptions from Overseas) (Persons Abroad and Mariners) Regulations 2003 (SI 2003/1193).

Restriction on scope

2. A person who would not be treated under regulation 32 of the General Regulations as an employee for the purposes of Parts 12ZA (statutory paternity pay) and 12ZB (statutory adoption pay) of the Act if his employment were in Great Britain shall not be treated as an employee under these Regulations.

6.36

DEFINITIONS

"the Act"—see reg.1(2).
"the General Regulations"—see *ibid.*

Treatment of persons in other EEA States as employees

3. A person who is—

(a) gainfully employed in an EEA State other than the United Kingdom in such circumstances that, if his employment were in Great Britain, he would be an employee for the purposes of Parts 12ZA and 12ZB of the Act, or a person treated as such an employee under regulation 32 of the General Regulations; and

(b) subject to the legislation of the United Kingdom under Council Regulation (EEC) No.1408/71,

notwithstanding that he is not employed in Great Britain, shall be treated as an employee for the purposes of Parts 12ZA and 12ZB of the Act.

6.37

DEFINITIONS

"the Act"—see reg.1(2).
"EEA"—see *ibid.*
"EEA State"—see *ibid.*
"the General Regulations"—see *ibid.*

Treatment of certain persons absent from Great Britain as employees

4. Subject to regulation 8(3), where a person, while absent from Great Britain for any purpose, is gainfully employed by an employer who is liable to pay secondary Class 1 contributions in respect of his employment under section 6 of the Act or regulation 146 of the Contributions Regulations, he shall be treated as an employee for the purposes of Parts 12ZA and 12ZB of the Act.

6.38

DEFINITIONS

"the Act"—see reg.1(2).
"the Contributions Regulations"—see *ibid.*

Entitlement to statutory paternity pay where person has worked in an EEA State

5.—(1) A person who is an employee or treated as an employee under regulation 3 and who—

6.39

   (a) in the week immediately preceding the 14th week before the expected week of the child's birth was in employed earner's employment with an employer in Great Britain; and

   (b) had in any week within the period of 26 weeks immediately preceding that week been employed by the same employer in another EEA State,

shall be treated for the purposes of section 171ZA of the Act (entitlement to statutory paternity pay (birth)) as having been employed in employed earner's employment in those weeks in which he was so employed in the other EEA State.

(2) A person who is an employee or treated as an employee under regulation 3 and who—

   (a) in the week in which the adopter is notified of being matched with the child for purposes of adoption was in employed earner's employment with an employer in Great Britain; and

   (b) had in any week within the period of 26 weeks immediately preceding that week been employed by the same employer in another EEA State,

shall be treated for the purposes of section 171ZB of the Act (entitlement to statutory paternity pay (adoption)) as having been employed in employed earner's employment in those weeks in which he was so employed in the other EEA State.

DEFINITIONS

> "the Act"—see reg.1(2).
> "adopter"—see *ibid.*
> "EEA"—see *ibid.*
> "EEA State"—see *ibid.*
> "statutory paternity pay (adoption)"—see *ibid.*
> "statutory paternity pay (birth)"—see *ibid.*
> "week"—see *ibid.*

Entitlement to statutory adoption pay where person has worked in an EEA State

6.40   **6.** A person who is an employee or treated as an employee under regulation 3 and who—

   (a) in the week in which he is notified that he has been matched with the child for the purposes of adoption was in employed earner's employment with an employer in Great Britain; and

   (b) had in any week within the period of 26 weeks immediately preceding that week been employed by the same employer in another EEA State,

shall be treated for the purposes of section 171ZL of the Act (entitlement to statutory adoption pay) as having been employed in employed earner's employment in those weeks in which he was so employed in the other EEA State.

DEFINITIONS

> "the Act"—see reg.1(2).
> "EEA"—see *ibid.*

"EEA State"—see *ibid.*
"week"—see *ibid.*

Time for compliance with Parts 12ZA and 12ZB of the Act or regulations made under them

7. Where—

(a) a person is outside the United Kingdom;

(b) Parts 12ZA or 12ZB of the Act or regulations made under them require any act to be done forthwith or on the happening of a certain event or within a specified time; and

(c) because the person is outside the United Kingdom he or his employer cannot comply with the requirement,

the person or the employer, as the case may be, shall be deemed to have complied with it if the act is performed as soon as reasonably practicable.

6.41

DEFINITION

"the Act"—see reg.1(2).

Mariners

8.—(1) In this regulation, "foreign-going ship", "home-trade ship" and "mariner" have the same meanings as in Case C of Part 9 of the Contributions Regulations (mariners) and the expressions "ship" and "ship or vessel", except in paragraph (3), include hovercraft.

(2) A mariner engaged in employment on board a home-trade ship with an employer who has a place of business within the United Kingdom shall be treated as an employee for the purposes of Parts 12ZA and 12ZB of the Act, notwithstanding that he may not be employed in Great Britain.

(3) A mariner who is engaged in employment—

(a) on a foreign-going ship; or

(b) on a home-trade ship with an employer who does not have a place of business within the United Kingdom,

shall not be treated as an employee for the purposes of Parts 12ZA and 12ZB of the Act, notwithstanding that he may have been employed in Great Britain.

6.42

DEFINITIONS

"the Act"—see reg.1(2).
"the Contributions Regulations"—see *ibid.*
"foreign-going ship"—see para.(1).
"home-trade ship"—see *ibid.*
"mariner"—see *ibid.*
"ship"—see *ibid.*
"ship or vessel"—see *ibid.*

Continental shelf

9.—(1) In this regulation—

"designated area" means any area which may from time to time be designated by Order in Council under section 1(7) of the Continental Shelf Act 1964 as an area within which the rights of the United Kingdom with respect to the seabed and subsoil and their natural resources may be exercised;

6.43

"prescribed employment" means any employment (whether under a contract of service or not) in a designated area in connection with continental shelf operations, as defined in section 120(2) of the Act.

(2) A person in prescribed employment shall be treated as an employee for the purposes of Parts 12ZA and 12ZB of the Act notwithstanding that he may not be employed in Great Britain.

DEFINITIONS

"the Act"—see reg.1(2).
"designated area"—see para.(1).
"prescribed employment"—see *ibid*.

Statutory Paternity Pay and Statutory Adoption Pay (General) Regulations 2002

(SI 2002/2822) (AS AMENDED)

The Secretary of State, in exercise of the powers conferred on her by sections 171ZA(2)(a), 171ZB(2)(a), 171ZC(3)(a), (c), (d), (f) and (g), 171ZD(2) and (3), 171ZE(2)(a), (b)(i), (3), (7) and (8), 171ZG(3), 171ZJ(1), (3), (4), (7) and (8), 171ZL(8)(b) to (d), (f) and (g), 171ZM(2) and (3), 171ZN(2), (5) and (6), 171ZP(6), 171ZS(1), (3), (4), (7) and (8), and 175(4) of the Social Security Contributions and Benefits Act 1992 and section 5(1)(g), (i) and (p) of the Social Security Administration Act 1992 and with the concurrence of the Commissioners of Inland Revenue in so far as such concurrence is required, by this instrument, which contains only provision made by virtue of sections 2, 4 and 53 of and paragraphs 8 and 11 of Schedule 7 to the Employment Act 2002 and is made before the end of the period of 6 months from the coming into force of those enactments, hereby makes the following Regulations—

ARRANGEMENT OF REGULATIONS

PART 1

Introduction

6.44

1. Citation and commencement.
2. Interpretation.
3. Application.

PART 2

Statutory paternity pay (birth)

4. Conditions of entitlement to statutory paternity pay (birth): relationship with newborn child and child's mother.

PART 3

Statutory paternity pay (adoption)

PART 4

Statutory paternity pay: provisions applicable to both statutory paternity pay (birth) and statutory paternity pay (adoption)

PART 5

Statutory adoption pay

PART 6

Statutory paternity pay and statutory adoption pay: provisions applicable to both statutory paternity pay and statutory adoption pay

PART 1

INTRODUCTION

Citation and commencement

6.45   **1.** These Regulations may be cited as the Statutory Paternity Pay and Statutory Adoption Pay (General) Regulations 2002 and shall come into force on 8th December 2002.

Interpretation

6.46   **2.**—(1) In these Regulations—
"the Act" means the Social Security Contributions and Benefits Act 1992;
"adopter", in relation to a child, means a person who has been matched with the child for adoption;
"adoption agency" has the meaning given, in relation to England and Wales, by section 1(4) of the Adoption Act 1976 and in relation to Scotland, by section 1(4) of the Adoption (Scotland) Act 1978;
"the Board" means the Commissioners of Inland Revenue;
"the Contributions Regulations" means the Social Security (Contributions) Regulations 2001;
"expected week", in relation to the birth of a child, means the week, beginning with midnight between Saturday and Sunday, in which it is expected that the child will be born;

"statutory paternity pay (adoption)" means statutory paternity pay payable in accordance with the provisions of Part 12ZA of the Act where the conditions specified in section 171ZB(2) of the Act are satisfied;

"statutory paternity pay (birth)" means statutory paternity pay payable in accordance with the provisions of Part 12ZA of the Act where the conditions specified in section 171ZA(2) of the Act are satisfied.

(2) For the purposes of these Regulations—

(a) a person is matched with a child for adoption when an adoption agency decides that that person would be a suitable adoptive parent for the child, either individually or jointly with another person; and

(b) a person is notified of having been matched with a child on the date on which he receives notification of the agency's decision, under regulation 11(2) of the Adoption Agencies Regulations 1983 or regulation 12(3) of the Adoption Agencies (Scotland) Regulations 1996.

Application

3.(1) Subject to the provisions of Part 12ZA of the Act (statutory paternity pay) and of these Regulations, there is entitlement to—   **6.47**

(a) statutory paternity pay (birth) in respect of children—

    (i) born on or after 6th April 2003; or

    (ii) whose expected week of birth begins on or after that date;

(b) statutory paternity pay (adoption) in respect of children—

    (i) matched with a person who is notified of having been matched on or after 6th April 2003; or

    (ii) placed for adoption on or after that date.

(2) Subject to the provisions of Part 12ZB of the Act (statutory adoption pay) and of these Regulations, there is entitlement to statutory adoption pay in respect of children—

(a) matched with a person who is notified of having been matched on or after 6th April 2003; or

(b) placed for adoption on or after that date.

DEFINITIONS

"the Act"—see reg.2(1).

"expected week"—see *ibid.*

"statutory paternity pay (adoption)"—see *ibid.*

"statutory paternity pay (birth)"—see *ibid.*

PART 2

STATUTORY PATERNITY PAY (BIRTH)

Conditions of entitlement to statutory paternity pay (birth): relationship with newborn child and child's mother

4. The conditions prescribed under section 171ZA(2)(a) of the Act are   **6.48**
those prescribed in regulation 4(2)(b) and (c) of the Paternity and Adoption Leave Regulations 2002.

"the Act"—see reg.2(1).

GENERAL NOTE

6.49   See the annotation to SSCBA 1992, s.171ZA.

Modification of entitlement conditions: early birth

6.50   **5.** Where a person does not meet the conditions specified in section 171ZA(2)(b) to (d) of the Act because the child's birth occurred earlier than the 14th week before the expected week of the birth, it shall have effect as if, for the conditions there set out, there were substituted the conditions that—

(a) the person would, but for the date on which the birth occurred, have been in employed earner's employment with an employer for a continuous period of at least 26 weeks ending with the week immediately preceding the 14th week before the expected week of the child's birth;

(b) his normal weekly earnings for the period of 8 weeks ending with the week immediately preceding the week in which the child is born are not less than the lower earnings limit in force under section 5(1)(a) of the Act immediately before the commencement of the week in which the child is born.

DEFINITIONS

"the Act"—see reg.2(1).
"expected week"—see *ibid.*

Period of payment of statutory paternity pay (birth)

6.51   **6.**—(1) Subject to paragraph (2) and regulation 8, a person entitled to statutory paternity pay (birth) may choose the statutory paternity pay period to begin on—

(a) the date on which the child is born or, where he is at work on that day, the following day;

(b) the date falling such number of days after the date on which the child is born as the person may specify;

(c) a predetermined date, specified by the person, which is later than the first day of the expected week of the child's birth.

(2) In a case where statutory paternity pay (birth) is payable in respect of a child whose expected week of birth begins before 6th April 2003, the statutory paternity pay period shall begin on a predetermined date, specified by the person entitled to such pay in a notice under section 171ZC(1) of the Act, which is at least 28 days after the date on which that notice was given, unless the person liable to pay statutory paternity pay (birth) agrees to the period beginning earlier.

(3) A person may choose for statutory paternity pay (birth) to be paid in respect of a period of a week.

(4) A choice made in accordance with paragraph (1) or (2) is not irrevocable, but where a person subsequently makes a different choice in rela-

tion to the beginning of the statutory pay period, section 171ZC(1) of the Act shall apply to it.

DEFINITIONS

"the Act"—see reg.2(1).
"expected week"—see *ibid.*
"statutory paternity pay (birth)"—see *ibid.*

Additional notice requirements for statutory paternity pay (birth)

7.—(1) Where the choice made by a person in accordance with para- 6.52
graph (1) of regulation 6 and notified in accordance with section 171ZC(1) of the Act is that mentioned in sub-paragraph (a) or (b) of that paragraph, the person shall give further notice to the person liable to pay him statutory paternity pay, as soon as is reasonably practicable after the child's birth, of the date the child was born.

(2) Where the choice made by a person in accordance with paragraph (1) of regulation 6 and notified in accordance with section 171ZC(1) of the Act is that specified in sub-paragraph (c) of that paragraph, and the date of the child's birth is later than the date so specified, the person shall, if he wishes to claim statutory paternity pay (birth), give notice to the person liable to pay it, as soon as is reasonably practicable, that the period in respect of which statutory paternity pay is to be paid shall begin on a date different fromthat originally chosen by him.

(3) That date may be any date chosen in accordance with paragraph (1) of regulation 6.

DEFINITIONS

"the Act"—see reg.2(1).
"statutory paternity pay (birth)"—see *ibid.*

Qualifying period for statutory paternity pay (birth)

8. The qualifying period for the purposes of section 171ZE(2) of the Act 6.53
(period within which the statutory paternity pay period must occur) is a period which begins on the date of the child's birth and ends—
  (a) except in the case referred to in paragraph (b), 56 days after that date;
  (b) in a case where the child is born before the first day of the expected week of its birth, 56 days after that day.

DEFINITIONS

"the Act"—see reg.2(1).
"expected week"—see *ibid.*

Evidence of entitlement to statutory paternity pay (birth)

9.—(1) A person shall provide evidence of his entitlement to statutory 6.54
paternity pay (birth) by providing in writing to the person who will be liable to pay him statutory paternity pay (birth)—
  (a) the information specified in paragraph (2);

(b) a declaration that he meets the conditions prescribed under section 171ZA(2)(a) of the Act and that it is not the case that statutory paternity pay (birth) is not payable to him by virtue of the provisions of section 171ZE(4) of the Act.

(2) The information referred to in paragraph (1)(a) is as follows—

(a) the name of the person claiming statutory paternity pay (birth);

(b) the expected week of the child's birth and, where the birth has already occurred, the date of birth;

(c) the date from which it is expected that the liability to pay statutory paternity pay (birth) will begin;

(d) whether the period chosen in respect of which statutory paternity pay (birth) is to be payable is a week.

(3) The information and declaration referred to in paragraph (1) shall be provided at least 28 days before the date mentioned in sub-paragraph (c) of paragraph (2) or, if that is not reasonably practicable, as soon as is reasonably practicable thereafter.

(4) Where the person who will be liable to pay statutory paternity pay (birth) so requests, the person entitled to it shall inform him of the date of the child's birth within 28 days, or as soon as is reasonably practicable thereafter.

DEFINITIONS

"the Act"—see reg.2(1).
"expected week"—see *ibid*.
"statutory paternity pay (birth)"—see *ibid*.

GENERAL NOTE

6.55   The evidence of entitlement to statutory paternity pay (birth) is essentially a form of self-certification by the father or prospective father. This contrasts with the requirement to produce a medical certificate for statutory maternity pay purposes. The justification for the self-certification approach here is that it "balances the need for a light-touch procedure with the desire employers have expressed for some form of evidence to justify their payment of Statutory Paternity Pay" (*Government's Response on Simplification of Maternity leave, Paternity Leave and Adoption Leave* (DTI, 2001), para.41).

Entitlement to statutory paternity pay (birth) where there is more than one employer

6.56   **10.** Statutory paternity pay (birth) shall be payable to a person in respect of a statutory pay week during any part of which he works only for an employer—

(a) who is not liable to pay him statutory paternity pay (birth); and

(b) for whom he has worked in the week immediately preceding the 14th week before the expected week of the child's birth.

DEFINITIONS

"expected week"—see *ibid*.
"statutory paternity pay (birth)"—see *ibid*.

PART 3

STATUTORY PATERNITY PAY (ADOPTION)

Conditions of entitlement to statutory paternity pay (adoption): relationship with child and with person with whom the child is placed for adoption

11.—(1) The conditions prescribed under section 171ZB(2)(a) of the Act are that a person—

(a) is married to [², the civil partner] or the partner of a child's adopter (or in a case where there are two adopters, married to [², the civil partner] or the partner of the other adopter); and

(b) has, or expects to have, the main responsibility (apart from the responsibility of the child's adopter, or in a case where there two adopters, together with the other adopter) for the upbringing of the child.

(2) For the purposes of paragraph (1), "partner" means a person (whether of a different sex or the same sex) who lives with the adopter and the child in an enduring family relationship but is not a relative of the adopter of a kind specified in paragraph [¹(2A)].

[¹(2A) The relatives of the adopter referred to in paragraph (2) are the adopter's parent, grandparent, sister, brother, aunt or uncle.]

(3) References to relationships in paragraph [¹(2A)]—

(a) are to relationships of the full blood or half blood, or, in the case of an adopted person, such of those relationships as would exist but for the adoption; and

(b) include the relationship of a child with his adoptive, or former adoptive parents but do not include any other adoptive relationships.

6.57

AMENDMENTS

1. Statutory Paternity Pay and Statutory Adoption Pay (Amendment) Regulations 2004 (SI 2004/488), reg.2 (April 6, 2004).

2. Civil Partnership Act 2004 (Amendments to Subordinate Legislation) Order 2005 (SI 2005/2114), art.2(17) and Sch.17, para.3 (December 5, 2005).

DEFINITIONS

"the Act"—see reg.2(1).
"adopter"—see *ibid.*
"partner"—see para.(2).

GENERAL NOTE

This regulation sets out the prescribed conditions for the purposes of SSCBA 1992, s.171ZB(2)(a), i.e. for the payment of statutory paternity pay in the case of adoption. The claimant must either be the adoptive parent's spouse or partner and expect to have the main responsibility (other than the adopter) for the child's upbringing. The definition of "partner" in para.(2) is innovative, in that it recognises that partners may be in a heterosexual or same sex relationship. The only qualifications are that the partner lives with the adopter and the child in "an enduring family relationship" and is not a relative of the adopter as defined in paras (2A) and

6.58

(3). Guidance on the notion of "an enduring family relationship" in the context of a same-sex relationship might be sought in the decisions in *Fitzpatrick v Sterling Housing Association* [2001] A.C. 27 and *Ghaidan v Godin-Mendoza* [2004] UKHL 30; [2004] 3 W.L.R. 113. This explicit statutory recognition in English law of parity of treatment for heterosexual and same-sex couples pre-dated the Civil Partnership Act 2004.

Period of payment of statutory paternity pay (adoption)

6.59 **12.**—(1) Subject to paragraph (2) and regulation 14, a person entitled to statutory paternity pay (adoption) may choose the statutory paternity pay period to begin on—

(a) the date on which the child is placed with the adopter or, where the person is at work on that day, the following day;

(b) the date falling such number of days after the date on which the child is placed with the adopter as the person may specify;

(c) a predetermined date, specified by the person, which is later than the date on which the child is expected to be placed with the adopter.

(2) In a case where statutory paternity pay (adoption) is payable in respect of a child matched with an adopter who is notified of having been matched before 6th April 2003, the statutory paternity pay period shall begin on a predetermined date, specified by the person entitled to such pay in a notice under section 171ZC(1) of the Act, which is at least 28 days after the date on which that notice was given, unless the person liable to pay statutory paternity pay (birth) agrees to the period beginning earlier.

(3) A person may choose for statutory paternity pay (adoption) to be paid in respect of a period of a week.

(4) A choice made in accordance with paragraph (1) is not irrevocable, but where a person subsequently makes a different choice in relation to the beginning of the statutory paternity pay period, section 171ZC(1) of the Act shall apply to it.

DEFINITIONS

"the Act"—see reg.2(1).
"adopter"—see *ibid.*
"statutory paternity pay (adoption)"—see *ibid.*
"statutory paternity pay (birth)"—see *ibid.*

Additional notice requirements for statutory paternity pay (adoption)

6.60 **13.**—(1) Where the choice made by a person in accordance with paragraph (1) of regulation 12 and notified in accordance with section 171ZC(1) of the Act is that mentioned in sub-paragraph (a) or (b) of that paragraph, the person shall give further notice to the person liable to pay him statutory paternity pay as soon as is reasonably practicable of the date on which the placement occurred.

(2) Where the choice made by a person in accordance with paragraph (1) of regulation 12 and notified in accordance with section 171ZC(1) of the Act is that mentioned in sub-paragraph (c) of that paragraph, or a date is specified under paragraph (2) of that regulation, and the child is placed for adoption later than the date so specified, the person shall, if he wishes

to claim statutory paternity pay (adoption), give notice to the person liable to pay it, as soon as is reasonably practicable, that the period in respect of which statutory paternity pay is to be paid shall begin on a date different from that originally chosen by him.

(3) That date may be any date chosen in accordance with paragraph (1) of regulation 12.

DEFINITIONS

"the Act"—see reg.2(1).
"statutory paternity pay (adoption)"—see *ibid.*

Qualifying period for statutory paternity pay (adoption)

14. The qualifying period for the purposes of section 171ZE(2) of the Act (period within which the statutory pay period must occur) is a period of 56 days beginning with the date of the child's placement for adoption.

6.61

DEFINITION

"the Act"—see reg.2(1).

Evidence of entitlement for statutory paternity pay (adoption)

15.—(1) A person shall provide evidence of his entitlement to statutory paternity pay (adoption) by providing in writing to the person who will be liable to pay him statutory paternity pay (adoption)—

6.62

(a) the information specified in paragraph (2);
(b) a declaration that he meets the conditions prescribed under section 171ZB(2)(a) of the Act and that it is not the case that statutory paternity pay (adoption) is not payable to him by virtue of the provisions of section 171ZE(4) of the Act;
(c) a declaration that he has elected to receive statutory paternity pay (adoption), and not statutory adoption pay under Part 12ZB of the Act.

(2) The information referred to in paragraph (1) is as follows—
(a) the name of the person claiming statutory paternity pay (adoption);
(b) the date on which the child is expected to be placed for adoption or, where the child has already been placed for adoption, the date of placement of the child;
(c) the date from which it is expected that the liability to pay statutory paternity pay (adoption) will begin;
(d) whether the period chosen in respect of which statutory paternity pay (adoption) is to be payable is a week;
(e) the date the adopter was notified he had been matched with the child for the purposes of adoption.

(3) The information and declarations referred to in paragraph (1) shall be provided to the person liable to pay statutory paternity pay at least 28 days before the date mentioned in sub-paragraph (c) of paragraph (2) or, if that is not reasonably practicable, as soon as is reasonably practicable thereafter.

(4) Where the person who will be liable to pay statutory paternity pay (adoption) so requests, the person entitled to it shall inform him of the date of the child's placement within 28 days, or as soon as is reasonably practicable thereafter.

"the Act"—see reg.2(1).
"statutory paternity pay (adoption)"—see *ibid.*

Entitlement to statutory paternity pay (adoption) where there is more than one employer

6.63   **16.** Statutory paternity pay (adoption) shall be payable to a person in respect of a statutory pay week during any part of which he works only for an employer—

(a) who is not liable to pay him statutory paternity pay (adoption); and

(b) for whom he has worked in the week in which the adopter is notified of being matched with the child.

DEFINITIONS

"adopter"—see *ibid.*
"statutory paternity pay (adoption)"—see *ibid.*

PART 4

STATUTORY PATERNITY PAY: PROVISIONS APPLICABLE TO BOTH
STATUTORY PATERNITY PAY (BIRTH) AND STATUTORY PATERNITY PAY
(ADOPTION)

Work during a statutory paternity pay period

6.64   **17.**—(1) Where, in a case where statutory paternity pay is being paid to a person who works during the statutory paternity pay period for an employer who is not liable to pay him statutory paternity pay and who does not fall within paragraph (b) of regulation 10 or, as the case may be, paragraph (b) of regulation 16, there shall be no liability to pay statutory paternity pay in respect of any remaining part of the statutory paternity pay period.

(2) In a case falling within paragraph (1), the person shall notify the person liable to pay statutory paternity pay within seven days of the first day during which he works during the statutory pay period.

(3) The notification mentioned in paragraph (2) shall be in writing, if the person who has been liable to pay statutory paternity pay so requests.

Cases where there is no liability to pay statutory paternity pay

6.65   **18.** There shall be no liability to pay statutory paternity pay in respect of any week—

(a) during any part of which the person entitled to it is entitled to statutory sick pay under Part 11 of the Act;

(b) following that in which the person claiming it has died; or

(c) during any part of which the person entitled to it is detained in legal custody or sentenced to a term of imprisonment (except where the sentence is suspended), or which is a subsequent week within the same statutory paternity pay period.

Statutory paternity pay and contractual remuneration

19. For the purposes of section 171ZG(1) and (2) of the Act, the pay-   **6.66**
ments which are to be treated as contractual remuneration are sums payable
under a contract of service—
  (a) by way of remuneration;
  (b) for incapacity for work due to sickness or injury;
  (c) by reason of the birth or adoption of a child.

Avoidance of liability for statutory paternity pay

20.—(1) A former employer shall be liable to make payments of statutory   **6.67**
paternity pay to a former employee in any case where the employee had
been employed for a continuous period of at least 8 weeks and his contract
of service was brought to an end by the former employer solely, or mainly,
for the purpose of avoiding liability for statutory paternity pay.
  (2) In a case falling within paragraph (1)—
  (a) the employee shall be treated as if he had been employed for a con-
       tinuous period ending with the child's birth or, as the case may be,
       the placement of the child for adoption;
  (b) his normal weekly earnings shall be calculated by reference to his
       normal weekly earnings for the period of 8 weeks ending with the
       last day in respect of which he was paid under his former contract of
       service.

PART 5

Statutory adoption pay

Adoption pay period

21.—(1) Subject to paragraph (2), a person entitled to statutory adoption   **6.68**
pay may choose the adoption pay period to begin—
  (a) on the date on which the child is placed with him for adoption or,
       where he is at work on that day, on the following day;
  (b) subject to paragraph (2), on a predetermined date, specified by him,
       which is no more than 14 days before the date on which the child is
       expected to be placed with him and no later than that date.
  (2) In a case where statutory adoption pay is payable in respect of a child
matched with an adopter who is notified of having been matched before
6th April 2003, the statutory adoption pay period shall begin on a predetermined date which is—
  (a) on or after 6th April 2003; and

(b) no more than 14 days before the date on which the child is expected to be placed with the adopter.

(3) Subject to paragraph (4), where the choice made is that mentioned in sub-paragraph (b) of paragraph (1) or in a case where paragraph (2) applies, the adoption pay period shall, unless the employer agrees to the adoption pay period beginning earlier, begin no earlier than 28 days after notice under section 171ZL(6) of the Act has been given.

(4) Where the beginning of the adoption pay period determined in accordance with paragraph (3) is later than the date of placement, it shall be the date of placement.

(5) Subject to regulation 22, the duration of any adoption pay period shall be a continuous period of [¹39] weeks.

(6) A choice made under paragraph (1), or a date specified under paragraph (2), is not irrevocable, but where a person subsequently makes a different choice, section 171ZL(6) of the Act shall apply to it.

AMENDMENT

1. Statutory Paternity Pay and Statutory Adoption Pay (General) and the Statutory Paternity Pay and Statutory Adoption Pay (Weekly Rates) (Amendment) Regulations 2006 (SI 2006/2236), reg.4 (October 1, 2006).

DEFINITIONS

"the Act"—see reg.2(1).
"adopter"—see *ibid*.

Adoption pay period in cases where adoption is disrupted

6.69

22.—(1) Where—
   (a) after a child has been placed for adoption—
       (i) the child dies;
       (ii) the child is returned to the adoption agency under section 30(3) of the Adoption Act 1976 or section 30(3) of the Adoption (Scotland) Act 1978; or
   (b) the adoption pay period has begun prior to the date the child has been placed for adoption, but the placement does not take place, the adoption pay period shall terminate in accordance with the provisions of paragraph (2).

(2) The adoption pay period shall, in a case falling within paragraph (1), terminate 8 weeks after the end of the week specified in paragraph (3).

(3) The week referred to in paragraph (2) is—
   (a) in a case falling within paragraph (1)(a)(i), the week during which the child dies;
   (b) in a case falling within paragraph (1)(a)(ii), the week during which the child is returned;
   (c) in a case falling within paragraph (1)(b), the week during which the person with whom the child was to be placed for adoption is notified that the placement will not be made.

(4) For the purposes of paragraph (3), "week" means a period of 7 days beginning with Sunday.

DEFINITION

"week"—see para.(4).

Additional notice requirements for statutory adoption pay

23.—(1) Where a person gives notice under section 171ZL(6) of the   6.70
Act he shall at the same time give notice of the date on which the child is
expected to be placed for adoption.

(2) Where the choice made in accordance with paragraph (1) of regulation 21 and notified in accordance with section 171ZL(6) of the Act is that
mentioned in sub-paragraph (a) of that paragraph, the person shall give
further notice to the person liable to pay him statutory adoption pay as soon
as is reasonably practicable of the date the child is placed for adoption.

DEFINITION

"the Act"—see reg.2(1).

Evidence of entitlement to statutory adoption pay

24.—(1) A person shall provide evidence of his entitlement to statutory   6.71
adoption pay by providing to the person who will be liable to pay it—
  (a) the information specified in paragraph (2), in the form of one or
      more documents provided to him by an adoption agency, containing
      that information;
  (b) a declaration that he has elected to receive statutory adoption pay,
      and not statutory paternity pay (adoption) under Part 12ZA of the
      Act.
(2) The information referred to in paragraph (1) is—
  (a) the name and address of the adoption agency and of the person
      claiming payment of statutory adoption pay;
  (b) the date on which the child is expected to be placed for adoption
      or, where the child has already been placed for adoption, the date of
      placement; and
  (c) the date on which the person claiming payment of statutory adoption
      pay was informed by the adoption agency that the child would be
      placed for adoption with him.
(3) The information and declaration referred to in paragraph (1) shall
be provided to the person liable to pay statutory adoption pay at least 28
days before the date chosen as the beginning of the adoption pay period in
accordance with paragraph (1) of regulation 21, or, if that is not reasonably
practicable, as soon as is reasonably practicable thereafter.

DEFINITIONS

"the Act"—see reg.2(1).
"adoption agency"—see *ibid.*
"statutory paternity pay (adoption)"—see *ibid.*

Entitlement to statutory adoption pay where there is more than one employer

25. Statutory adoption pay shall be payable to a person in respect of a   6.72
week during any part of which he works only for an employer—
  (a) who is not liable to pay him statutory adoption pay; and
  (b) for whom he has worked in the week in which he is notified of being
      matched with the child.

Work during an adoption pay period

6.73   **26.**—(1) Where, in a case where statutory adoption pay is being paid to a person who works during the adoption pay period for an employer who is not liable to pay him statutory adoption pay and who does not fall within paragraph (b) of regulation 25, there shall be no liability to pay statutory adoption pay in respect of any remaining part of the adoption pay period.

(2) In a case falling within paragraph (1), the person shall notify the person liable to pay statutory adoption pay within 7 days of the first day during which he works during the adoption pay period.

(3) The notification contained in paragraph (2) shall be in writing if the person who has been liable to pay statutory adoption pay so requests.

Cases where there is no liability to pay statutory adoption pay

6.74   **27.**—(1) There shall be no liability to pay statutory adoption pay in respect of any week—
> (a) during any part of which the person entitled to it is entitled to statutory sick pay under Part 9 of the Act;
> (b) following that in which the person claiming it has died; or
> (c) subject to paragraph (2), during any part of which the person entitled to it is detained in legal custody or sentenced to a term of imprisonment (except where the sentence is suspended).

(2) There shall be liability to pay statutory adoption pay in respect of any week during any part of which the person entitled to it is detained in legal custody where that person—
> (a) is released subsequently without charge;
> (b) is subsequently found not guilty of any offence and is released; or
> (c) is convicted of an offence but does not receive a custodial sentence.

DEFINITION
"the Act"—see reg.2(1).

[¹ Working for not more than 10 days during an adoption pay period

6.75   **27A.** In the case where an employee does any work under a contract of service with his employer on any day for not more than 10 such days during his adoption pay period, whether consecutive or not, statutory adoption pay shall continue to be payable to the employee by the employer.]

AMENDMENT

1. Statutory Paternity Pay and Statutory Adoption Pay (General) and the Statutory Paternity Pay and Statutory Adoption Pay (Weekly Rates) (Amendment) Regulations 2006 (SI 2006/2236), reg.5 (October 1, 2006).

Statutory adoption pay and contractual remuneration

6.76   **28.** For the purposes of section 171ZP(4) and (5) of the Act, the payments which are to be treated as contractual remuneration are sums payable under a contract of service—
> (a) by way of remuneration;

(b) for incapacity for work due to sickness or injury;

(c) by reason of the adoption of a child.

DEFINITION

"the Act"—see reg.2(1).

Termination of employment before start of adoption pay period

29.—(1) Where the employment of a person who satisfies the conditions of entitlement to statutory adoption pay terminates for whatever reason (including dismissal) before the adoption pay period chosen in accordance with regulation 21 has begun, the period shall begin 14 days before the expected date of placement or, where the termination occurs on, or within 14 days before, the expected date of placement, on the day immediately following the last day of his employment.

6.77

(2) In a case falling within paragraph (1), the notice requirements set out in section 171ZL(6) of the Act and these Regulations shall not apply.

DEFINITION

"the Act"—see reg.2(1).

Avoidance of liability for statutory adoption pay

30.—(1) A former employer shall be liable to make payments of statutory adoption pay to a former employee in any case where the employee had been employed for a continuous period of at least 8 weeks and his contract of service was brought to an end by the former employer solely, or mainly, for the purpose of avoiding liability for statutory adoption pay.

6.78

(2) In a case falling within paragraph (1)—

(a) the employee shall be treated as if he had been employed for a continuous period ending with the week in which he was notified of having been matched with the child for adoption; and

(b) his normal weekly earnings shall be calculated by reference to his normal weekly earnings for the period of 8 weeks ending with the last day in respect of which he was paid under his former contract of service.

PART 6

STATUTORY PATERNITY PAY AND STATUTORY ADOPTION PAY: PROVISIONS
APPLICABLE TO BOTH STATUTORY PATERNITY PAY AND STATUTORY
ADOPTION PAY

Introductory

31.—(1) Subject to paragraph (2), the provisions of regulations 32–47 below apply to statutory paternity pay payable under Part 12ZA of the Act and to statutory adoption pay payable under Part 12ZB of the Act.

6.79

(2) The provisions of regulation 44 only apply to statutory adoption pay.

"the Act"—see reg.2(1).

Treatment of persons as employees

6.80   **32.**—(1) [¹Subject to paragraph (1A),] in a case where, and in so far as, a person [¹. . .] is treated as an employed earner by virtue of the Social Security (Categorisation of Earners) Regulations 1978 he shall be treated as an employee for the purposes of Parts 12ZA and 12ZB of the Act, and in a case where, and in so far as, such a person is treated otherwise than as an employed earner by virtue of those Regulations, he shall not be treated as an employee for the purposes of Parts 12ZA and 12ZB of the Act.

[²(1A) Paragraph (1) shall have effect in relation to a person who—
  (a) is under the age of 16; and
  (b) would or, as the case may be, would not have been treated as an employed earner by virtue of the Social Security (Categorisation of Earners) Regulations 1978 had he been over that age,
as it has effect in relation to a person who is or, as the case may be, is not so treated.]

(2) A person who is in employed earner's employment within the meaning of the Act under a contract of apprenticeship shall be treated as an employee for the purposes of Parts 12ZA and 12ZB of the Act.

(3) A person who is in employed earner's employment within the meaning of the Act but whose employer—
  (a) does not fulfil the conditions prescribed in regulation 145(1) of the Contributions Regulations in so far as that provision relates to residence or presence in Great Britain; or
  (b) is a person who, by reason of any international treaty to which the United Kingdom is a party or of any international convention binding the United Kingdom—
     (i) is exempt from the provisions of the Act; or
     (ii) is a person against whom the provisions of the Act are not enforceable,
shall not be treated as an employee for the purposes of Parts 12ZA and 12ZB of the Act.

AMENDMENTS

1. Employment Equality (Age) Regulations 2006 (SI 2006/1031), reg.49(1) and Sch.8, Pt 2, para.60 (October 1, 2006).
2. Employment Equality (Age) (Consequential Amendments) Regulations 2007 (SI 2007/825), reg.7 (April 6, 2007).

DEFINITIONS

"the Act"—see reg.2(1).
"Contributions Regulations"—see *ibid*.

Continuous employment

6.81   **33.**—(1) Subject to the following provisions of this regulation, where in any week a person is, for the whole or part of the week—
  (a) incapable of work in consequence of sickness or injury;

(b) absent from work on account of a temporary cessation of work;
(c) absent from work in circumstances such that, by arrangement or custom, he is regarded as continuing in the employment of his employer for all or any purposes,

and returns to work for his employer after the incapacity for or absence from work, that week shall be treated for the purposes of sections 171ZA, 171ZB and 171ZL of the Act as part of a continuous period of employment with that employer, notwithstanding that no contract of service exists with that employer in respect of that week.

(2) Incapacity for work which lasts for more than 26 consecutive weeks shall not count for the purposes of paragraph (1)(a).

(3) Where a person—

(a) is an employee in an employed earner's employment in which the custom is for the employer—
  (i) to offer work for a fixed period of not more than 26 consecutive weeks;
  (ii) to offer work for such period on two or more occasions in a year for periods which do not overlap; and
  (iii) to offer the work available to those persons who had worked for him during the last or a recent such period, but
(b) is absent from work because of incapacity arising from some specific disease or bodily or mental disablement,

then in that case paragraph (1) shall apply as if the words "and returns to work for his employer after the incapacity for or absence from work," were omitted and paragraph (4) shall not apply.

(4) Where a person is employed under a contract of service for part only of the relevant week within the meaning of subsection (3) of section 171ZL of the Act (entitlement to statutory adoption pay), the whole of that week shall count in computing a period of continuous employment for the purposes of that section.

DEFINITION

"the Act"—see reg.2(1).

Continuous employment and unfair dismissal

34.—(1) This regulation applies to a person in relation to whose dismissal an action is commenced which consists— 6.82

(a) of the presentation by him of a complaint under section 111(1) of the Employment Rights Act 1996;
(b) of his making a claim in accordance with a dismissals procedure agreement designated by an order under section 110 of that Act; [[1]. . .]
(c) of any action taken by a conciliation officer under section 18 of the Employment Tribunals Act 1996; [[1]or
(d) of a decision arising out of the use of a statutory dispute resolution procedure contained in Schedule 2 to the Employment Act 2002 in a case where, in accordance with the Employment Act 2002 (Dispute Resolution) Regulations 2004, such a procedure applies.]

(2) If, in consequence of an action of the kind specified in paragraph (1), a person is reinstated or re-engaged by his employer or by a successor or associated employer of that employer, the continuity of his employment

shall be preserved for the purposes of Part 12ZA or, as the case may be, Part 12ZB of the Act, and any week which falls within the interval beginning with the effective date of termination and ending with the date of reinstatement or re-engagement, as the case may be, shall count in the computation of his period of continuous employment.

(3) In this regulation—

"successor" and "dismissal procedures agreement" have the same meanings as in section 235 of the Employment Rights Act 1996; and

"associated employer" shall be construed in accordance with section 231 of the Employment Rights Act 1996.

AMENDMENT

1. Statutory Maternity Pay (General) and the Statutory Paternity Pay and Statutory Adoption Pay (General) (Amendment) Regulations 2005 (SI 2005/358), reg.4 (April 56, 2005).

DEFINITIONS

"the Act"—see reg.2(1).
"associated employer"—see para.(3).
"dismissal procedures agreement"—see *ibid.*
"successor"—see *ibid.*

Continuous employment and stoppages of work

6.83   **35.**—(1) Where, for any week or part of a week a person does not work because there is a stoppage of work due to a trade dispute within the meaning of section 35(1) of the Jobseekers Act 1995 at his place of employment, the continuity of his employment shall, subject to paragraph (2), be treated as continuing throughout the stoppage but, subject to paragraph (3), no such week shall count in the computation of his period of employment.

(2) Subject to paragraph (3), where during the stoppage of work a person is dismissed from his employment, the continuity of his employment shall not be treated in accordance with paragraph (1) as continuing beyond the commencement of the day he stopped work.

(3) The provisions of paragraph (1), to the extent that they provide that a week in which the stoppage of work occurred shall not count in the computation of a period of employment, and paragraph (2) shall not apply to a person who proves that at no time did he have a direct interest in the trade dispute in question.

Change of employer

6.84   **36.** A person's employment shall, notwithstanding a change of employer, be treated as continuous employment with the second employer where—

(a) the employer's trade or business or an undertaking (whether or not it is an undertaking established by or under an Act of Parliament) is transferred from one person to another;

(b) by or under an Act of Parliament, whether public or local and whenever passed, a contract of employment between any body corporate and the person is modified and some other body corporate is substituted as his employer;

(c) on the death of his employer, the person is taken into employment of the personal representatives or trustees of the deceased;

(d) the person is employed by partners, personal representatives or trustees and there is a change in the partners, or, as the case may be, personal representatives or trustees;

(e) the person is taken into the employment of an employer who is, at the time he entered his employment, an associated employer of his previous employer, and for this purpose "associated employer" shall be construed in accordance with section 231 of the Employment Rights Act 1996;

(f) on the termination of his employment with an employer he is taken into the employment of another employer and those employers are governors of a school maintained by a local education authority and that authority.

Reinstatement after service with the armed forces etc.

37. If a person who is entitled to apply to his employer under the Reserve 6.85
Forces (Safeguard of Employment) Act 1985 enters the employment of that employer within the 6-month period mentioned in section 1(4)(b) of that Act, his previous period of employment with that employer (or if there was more than one such period, the last of those periods) and the period of employment beginning in that 6-month period shall be treated as continuous.

DEFINITION

"the Act"—see reg.2(1).

Treatment of two or more employers or two or more contracts of service as one

38.—(1) In a case where the earnings paid to a person in respect of two or 6.86
more employments are aggregated and treated as a single payment of earnings under regulation 15(1) of the Contributions Regulations, the employers of that person in respect of those employments shall be treated as one for the purposes of Part 12ZA or, as the case may be, Part 12ZB of the Act.

(2) Where two or more employers are treated as one under the provisions of paragraph (1), liability for statutory paternity pay or, as the case may be, statutory adoption pay, shall be apportioned between them in such proportions as they may agree or, in default of agreement, in the proportions which the person's earnings from each employment bear to the amount of the aggregated earnings.

(3) Where two or more contracts of service exist concurrently between one employer and one employee, they shall be treated as one for the purposes of Part 12ZA or, as the case may be, Part 12ZB of the Act, except where, by virtue of regulation 14 of the Contributions Regulations, the earnings from those contracts of service are not aggregated for the purposes of earnings-related contributions.

DEFINITIONS

"the Act"—see reg.2(1).
"Contributions Regulations"—see *ibid*.

Meaning of "earnings"

6.87   **39.**—(1) For the purposes of section 171ZJ(6) (normal weekly earnings for the purposes of Part 12ZA of the Act) and of section 171ZS(6) of the Act (normal weekly earnings for the purposes of Part 12ZB of the Act), the expression "earnings" shall be construed in accordance with the following provisions of this regulation.

(2) The expression "earnings" refers to gross earnings and includes any remuneration or profit derived from a person's employment except any payment or amount which is—

   (a) excluded from the computation of a person's earnings under regulation 25 of and Schedule 3 to, and regulation 123 of, the Contributions Regulations (payments to be disregarded) and regulation 27 of those Regulations (payments to directors to be disregarded) [[1](or would have been so excluded had he not been under the age of 16)];

   (b) a chargeable emolument under section 10A of the Act, except where, in consequence of such a chargeable emolument being excluded from earnings, a person would not be entitled to statutory paternity pay or, as the case may be, statutory adoption pay [[1](or where such a payment or amount would have been so excluded and in consequence he would not have been entitled to statutory paternity pay and statutory adoption pay had he not been under the age of 16)].

(3) For the avoidance of doubt, "earnings" includes—

[[2](za) any amount retrospectively treated as earnings by regulations made by virtue of section 4B(2) of the Act;]

   (a) any sum payable in respect of arrears of pay in pursuance of an order for reinstatement or re-engagement under the Employment Rights Act 1996;

   (b) any sum payable by way of pay in pursuance of an order made under the Employment Rights Act 1996 for the continuation of a contract of employment;

   (c) any sum payable by way of remuneration in pursuance of a protective award under section 189 of the Trade Union and Labour Relations (Consolidation) Act 1992;

   (d) any sum payable by way of statutory sick pay, including sums payable in accordance with regulations made under section 151(6) of the Act;

   (e) any sum payable by way of statutory maternity pay;

   (f) any sum payable by way of statutory paternity pay;

   (g) any sum payable by way of statutory adoption pay.

AMENDMENTS

1. Employment Equality (Age) Regulations 2006 (SI 2006/1031), reg.49(1) and Sch.8, Pt 2, para.61 (October 1, 2006).

2. Social Security, Occupational Pension Schemes and Statutory Payments (Consequential Provisions) Regulations 2007 (SI 2007/1154), reg.6 (April 6, 2007).

DEFINITIONS

"the Act"—see reg.2(1).
"Contributions Regulations"—see *ibid.*

Normal weekly earnings

40.—(1) For the purposes of Part 12ZA and Part 12ZB of the Act, a   **6.88**
person's normal weekly earnings shall be calculated in accordance with the
following provisions of this regulation.

(2) In this regulation—

"the appropriate date" means—

(a) in relation to statutory paternity pay (birth), the first day of the 14th
week before the expected week of the child's birth or the first day in
the week in which the child is born, whichever is the earlier;

(b) in relation to statutory paternity pay (adoption) and statutory adoption pay, the first day of the week after the week in which the adopter
is notified of being matched with the child for the purposes of adoption;

"normal pay day" means a day on which the terms of a person's contract
of service require him to be paid, or the practice in his employment is
for him to be paid, if any payment is due to him; and

"day of payment" means a day on which the person was paid.

(3) Subject to paragraph (4), the relevant period for the purposes of sections 171ZJ(6) and 171ZS(6) is the period between—

(a) the last normal pay day to fall before the appropriate date; and

(b) the last normal pay day to fall at least 8 weeks earlier than the normal
pay day mentioned in sub-paragraph (a),

including the normal pay day mentioned in sub-paragraph (a) but excluding that first mentioned in sub-paragraph (b).

(4) In a case where a person has no identifiable normal pay day, paragraph (3) shall have effect as if the words "day of payment" were substituted for the words "normal pay day" in each place where they occur.

(5) In a case where a person has normal pay days at intervals of or
approximating to one or more calendar months (including intervals of or
approximating to a year) his normal weekly earnings shall be calculated
by dividing his earnings in the relevant period by the number of calendar
months in that period (or, if it is not a whole number, the nearest whole
number), multiplying the result by 12 and dividing by 52.

(6) In a case to which paragraph (5) does not apply and the relevant
period is not an exact number of weeks, the person's normal weekly earnings shall be calculated by dividing his earnings in the relevant period by the
number of days in the relevant period and multiplying the result by 7.

(7) In any case where a person receives a back-dated pay increase which
includes a sum in respect of a relevant period, normal weekly earnings shall
be calculated as if such a sum was paid in that relevant period even though
received after that period.

DEFINITIONS

"the Act"—see reg.2(1).
"adopter"—see *ibid.*
"the appropriate date"—see para.(2).
"day of payment"—— see *ibid.*
"expected week"—see reg.2(1).
"normal pay day"—see para.(2).
"statutory paternity pay (adoption)"—see reg.2(1).
"statutory paternity pay (birth)"—see *ibid.*

Payment of statutory paternity pay and statutory adoption pay

6.89   **41.** Payments of statutory paternity pay and statutory adoption pay may be made in a like manner to payments of remuneration but shall not include payment in kind or by way of the provision of board or lodgings or of services or other facilities.

Time when statutory paternity pay and statutory adoption pay are to be paid

6.90   **42.**—(1) In this regulation, "pay day" means a day on which it has been agreed, or it is the normal practice between an employer or former employer and a person who is or was an employee of his, that payments by way of remuneration are to be made, or, where there is no such agreement or normal practice, the last day of a calendar month.

(2) In any case where—

(a) a decision has been made by an officer of the Board under section 8(1) of the Social Security Contributions (Transfer of Functions, etc.) Act 1999 as a result of which a person is entitled to an amount of statutory paternity pay or statutory adoption pay; and

(b) the time for bringing an appeal against the decision has expired and either—

   (i) no such appeal has been brought; or

   (ii) such an appeal has been brought and has been finally disposed of,

that amount of statutory paternity pay or statutory adoption pay shall be paid within the time specified in paragraph (3).

(3) Subject to paragraphs (4) and (5), the employer or former employer shall pay the amount not later than the first pay day after—

(a) where an appeal has been brought, the day on which the employer or former employer receives notification that it has been finally disposed of;

(b) where leave to appeal has been refused and there remains no further opportunity to apply for leave, the day on which the employer or former employer receives notification of the refusal; and

(c) in any other case, the day on which the time for bringing an appeal expires.

(4) Subject to paragraph (5), where it is impracticable, in view of the employer's or former employer's methods of accounting for and paying remuneration, for the requirement of payment referred to in paragraph (3) to be met by the pay day referred to in that paragraph, it shall be met not later than the next following pay day.

(5) Where the employer or former employer would not have remunerated the employee for his work in the week in question as early as the pay day specified in paragraph (3) or (if it applies) paragraph (4), the requirement of payment shall be met on the first day on which the employee would have been remunerated for his work in that week.

DEFINITIONS

"the Board"—see reg.2(1).
"pay day"—see para.(1).

Liability of the Board to pay statutory paternity pay or statutory adoption pay

43.—(1) Where—

6.91

(a) an officer of the Board has decided that an employer is liable to make payments of statutory paternity pay or, as the case may be, statutory adoption pay to a person;

(b) the time for appealing against the decision has expired; and

(c) no appeal against the decision has been lodged or leave to appeal against the decision is required and has been refused,

then for any week in respect of which the employer was liable to make payments of statutory paternity pay or, as the case may be, statutory adoption pay but did not do so, and for any subsequent weeks in the paternity pay period or, as the case may be, adoption pay period, the liability to make those payments shall, notwithstanding sections 171ZD and 171ZM of the Act, be that of the Board and not the employer.

(2) Liability to make payments of statutory paternity pay or, as the case may be, statutory adoption pay shall, notwithstanding sections 171ZD and 171ZM of the Act, be a liability of the Board and not the employer as from the week in which the employer first becomes insolvent until the end of the paternity pay or adoption pay period.

(3) For the purposes of paragraph (2), an employer shall be taken to be insolvent if, and only if—

(a) in England and Wales—

(i) he has been adjudged bankrupt or has made a composition or arrangement with his creditors;

(ii) he has died and his estate falls to be administered in accordance with an order made under section 421 of the Insolvency Act 1986; or

(iii) where an employer is a company or a limited liability partnership, a winding-up order [1. . .] is made or a resolution for a voluntary winding-up is passed (or, in the case of a limited liability partnership, a determination for a voluntary winding-up has been made) with respect to it [1or it enters administration], or a receiver or a manager of its undertaking is duly appointed, or possession is taken, by or on behalf of the holders of any debentures secured by a floating charge, of any property of the company or limited liability partnership comprised in or subject to the charge, or a voluntary arrangement proposed for the purposes of Part 1 of the Insolvency Act 1986 is approved under that Part of that Act;

(b) in Scotland—

(i) an award of sequestration is made on his estate or he executes a trust deed for his creditors or enters into a composition contract;

(ii) he has died and a judicial factor appointed under section 11A of the Judicial Factors (Scotland) Act 1889 is required by that section to divide his insolvent estate among his creditors; or

(iii) where the employer is a company or a limited liability partnership, a winding-up order [1. . .] is made or a resolution for voluntary winding-up is passed (or, in the case of a limited liability partnership, a determination for a voluntary winding-up is made) with respect to it [¹or it enters administration], or a receiver of its undertaking is duly appointed, or a voluntary arrangement proposed for the purposes of Part 1 of the Insolvency Act 1986 is approved under that Part.

AMENDMENT

1. Enterprise Act 2002 (Insolvency) Order 2003 (SI 2003/2096), art.5 and Sch.2, para.79 (September 15, 2003).

DEFINITIONS

"the Act"—see reg.2(1).
"the Board"—see reg.2(1).

Liability of the Board to pay statutory adoption pay in cases of legal custody or imprisonment

6.92
44. Where—
(a) there is liability to pay statutory adoption pay in respect of a period which is subsequent to the last week falling within paragraph (1)(c) of regulation 27; or
(b) there is liability to pay statutory adoption pay during a period of detention in legal custody by virtue of the provisions of paragraph (2) of that regulation,

that liability shall, notwithstanding section 171ZM of the Act, be that of the Board and not the employer.

DEFINITIONS

"the Act"—see reg.2(1).
"the Board"—see reg.2(1).

Payments by the Board

6.93
45. Where the Board become liable in accordance with regulation 43 or 44 to make payments of statutory paternity pay or, as the case may be, statutory adoption pay to a person, the first payment shall be made as soon as reasonably practicable after they become so liable, and payments thereafter shall be made at weekly intervals, by means of an instrument of payment or by such other means as appears to the Board to be appropriate in the circumstance of any particular case.

DEFINITION

"the Board"—see reg.2(1).

Persons unable to act

6.94
46.—(1) Where in the case of any person—
(a) statutory paternity pay or, as the case may be, statutory adoption pay is payable to him or he is alleged to be entitled to it;
(b) he is unable for the time being to act; and
(c) either—
(i) no receiver has been appointed by the Court of Protection with power to receive statutory paternity pay or, as the case may be, statutory adoption pay on his behalf; or

(ii) in Scotland, his estate is not being administered by any tutor, curator or other guardian acting or appointed in terms of law,

the Board may, upon written application to them by a person who, if a natural person, is over the age of 18, appoint that person to exercise, on behalf of the person unable to act, any right to which he may be entitled under Part 12ZA or, as the case may be, Part 12ZB of the Act and to deal on his behalf with any sums payable to him.

(2) Where the Board have made an appointment under paragraph (1)—

(a) they may at any time in their absolute discretion revoke it;

(b) the person appointed may resign his office after having given one month's notice in writing to the Board of his intention to do so; and

(c) the appointment shall terminate when the Board are notified that a receiver or other person to whom paragraph (1)(c) applies has been appointed.

(3) Anything required by Part 12ZA or 12ZB of the Act to be done by or to any person who is unable to act may be done by or to the person appointed under this regulation to act on his behalf, and the receipt of the person so appointed shall be a good discharge to the person's employer or former employer for any sum paid.

DEFINITIONS

"the Act"—see reg.2(1).
"the Board"—see reg.2(1).

Service of notices by post

47. A notice given in accordance with the provisions of these Regulations in writing contained in an envelope which is properly addressed and sent by prepaid post shall be treated as having been given on the day on which it is posted.

6.95

Social Security Contributions and Benefits Act 1992 (Application of Parts 12ZA and 12ZB to Adoptions from Overseas) Regulations 2003

(SI 2003/499) (AS AMENDED)

The Secretary of State, in exercise of the powers conferred on her by sections 171ZK and 171ZT of the Social Security Contributions and Benefits Act 1992 by this instrument, which contains only provision made by virtue of sections 2 and 4 of the Employment Act 2002 and is made before the end of the period of 6 months from the coming into force of those enactments, hereby makes the following Regulations—

ARRANGEMENT OF REGULATIONS

6.96

Schedule 1—Application of Part 12ZA of the Act to adoptions from overseas.
Schedule 2—Application of Part 12ZB of the Act to adoptions from overseas.

Citation, commencement and interpretation

6.97   **1.**—(1) These Regulations may be cited as the Social Security Contributions and Benefits Act 1992 (Application of Parts 12ZA and 12ZB to Adoptions from Overseas) Regulations 2003 and shall come into force, in so far as they apply powers to make regulations, on 10th March 2003, and for all other purposes on 6th April 2003.

(2) In these Regulations—

"adoption from overseas" means the adoption of a child who enters Great Britain from outside the United Kingdom in connection with or for the purposes of adoption which does not involve the placement of the child for adoption under the law of any part of the United Kingdom;

"the Act" means the Social Security Contributions and Benefits Act 1992.

GENERAL NOTE

6.98   These Regulations, made under provisions inserted into the SSCBA 1992 by the Employment Act 2002, apply Pts XIIZA and XIIZB of the 1992 Act, as modified by these Regulations, to adoptions from overseas. These are adoptions of children who enter Great Britain from outside the United Kingdom in connection with or for the purposes of adoption which does not involve the placement of a child for adoption under the law of any part of the United Kingdom. The relevant adoption law requirements are set out in the Adoption (Bringing Children into the United Kingdom) Regulations 2003 (SI 2003/1173). The regulations relating to statutory paternity pay and statutory adoption pay in connection with such overseas adoptions are the Statutory Paternity Pay (Adoption) and Statutory Adoption Pay (Adoptions from Overseas) Regulations 2003 (SI 2003/500).

Application of Part 12ZA of the Act to adoptions from overseas

6.99   **2.** Part 12ZA of the Act shall apply in relation to adoptions from overseas, with the modifications of sections 171ZB, 171ZE and 171ZJ of the Act specified in the second column of Schedule 1.

Application of Part 12ZB of the Act to adoptions from overseas

6.100   **3.** Part 12ZB of the Act shall apply in relation to adoptions from overseas, with the modifications of sections 171ZL and 171ZS of the Act specified in the second column of Schedule 2.

SCHEDULE 1   **Regulation 2**

APPLICATION OF PART 12ZA OF THE ACT TO ADOPTIONS FROM OVERSEAS

6.101

Provision	Modification
Section 171ZB(2)	[1. . .] In paragraph (a)(i), for "who is placed for adoption under the law of any part of the United Kingdom" substitute "who is adopted from overseas".

Provision	Modification	6.101
	In paragraph (a)(ii), for "a person with whom the child is so placed for adoption" substitute "an adopter of the child". [¹In paragraph (b), omit "ending with the relevant week".] In paragraph (d), for "the day on which the child is placed for adoption" substitute "the day on which the child enters Great Britain". In paragraph (e), for "a person with whom the child is placed for adoption" substitute "an adopter of the child".	
Section 171ZB(3)	[¹For subsection (3) substitute— "(3) The references in subsection (2)(c) and (d) to the relevant week are to— (a) the week in which official notification is sent to the adopter, or (b) the week at the end of which the person satisfies the condition in subsection (2)(b), whichever is the later."]	
Section 171ZB(6)	For "the placement for adoption of more than one child as part of the same arrangement" substitute "the adoption from overseas of more than one child as part of the same arrangement".	
Section 171ZB(7)	Omit subsection (7).	
Section 171ZE(3)	In paragraph (b), for "with the date of the child's placement for adoption" substitute "with the date of the child's entry into Great Britain".	
Section 171ZE(10)	For subsection (10) substitute— "(10) Where more than one child is the subject of adoption from overseas as part of the same arrangement, and the date of entry of each child is different, the reference in subsection (3)(b) to the date of the child's entry into Great Britain shall be interpreted as a reference to the date of the entry of the first child to enter Great Britain".	
Section 171ZJ(1)	In the appropriate places in the alphabetical order, insert— "adopter", in relation to a child, means a person by whom the child has been or is to be adopted;" "adoption from overseas" means the adoption of a child who enters Great Britain from outside the United Kingdom in connection with or for the purposes of adoption which does not involve the placement of the child for adoption under the law of any part of the United Kingdom, and the references to a child adopted from overseas shall be construed accordingly;" "official notification" means written notification, issued by or on behalf of the relevant domestic authority, that it is prepared to issue a certificate to the overseas authority concerned with the adoption of the child, or has issued a certificate and sent it to that authority, confirming, in either case, that the adopter is eligible to adopt and has been assessed and approved as being a suitable adoptive parent;" "relevant domestic authority" means— (a) in the case of an adopter to whom the Intercountry Adoption (Hague Convention) Regulations 2003 apply and who is habitually resident in Wales, the National Assembly of Wales; (b) in the case of an adopter to whom the Intercountry Adoption (Hague Convention) (Scotland) Regulations 2003 apply and who is habitually resident in Scotland, the Scottish Ministers; (c) in any other case, the Secretary of State".	

AMENDMENT

1. Statutory Paternity Pay and Statutory Adoption Pay (Amendment) Regulations 2004 (SI 2004/488), reg.3(2) (April 6, 2004).

SCHEDULE 2   **Regulation 3**

APPLICATION OF PART 12ZB OF THE ACT TO ADOPTIONS FROM OVERSEAS

6.102

Provision	Modification
Section 171ZL(2)	[¹. . .] In paragraph (a), for "with whom a child is, or is expected to be, placed for adoption under the law of any part of the United Kingdom" substitute "who is, or is expected to be, an adopter of a child from overseas". [¹In paragraph (b), omit "ending with the relevant week".]

Section 171ZL(3)	[¹For subsection (3) substitute—
	"(3) The reference in subsection (2)(d) to the relevant week is to—
	   (a) the week in which official notification is sent to the adopter, or
	   (b) the week at the end of which the person satisfies the condition in subsection (2)(b), whichever is the later."]

	[¹. . .]
Section 171ZL(4)	In paragraph (b), for "placed for adoption with him" substitute "adopted by him".
Section 171ZL(5)	For "the placement, or expected placement, for adoption of more than one child" substitute "the adoption, or expected adoption, from overseas of more than one child".

Section 171ZS(1)	In the appropriate places in the alphabetical order, insert—
	""adopter", in relation to a child, means a person by whom a child has been or is to be adopted;"
	"adoption from overseas" means the adoption of a child who enters Great Britain from outside the United Kingdom in connection with or for the purposes of adoption which does not involve the placement of the child for adoption under the law of any part of the United Kingdom, and the reference to an adopter from overseas shall be construed accordingly;"
	"official notification" means written notification, issued by or on behalf of the relevant domestic authority, that it is prepared to issue a certificate to the overseas authority concerned with the adoption of the child, or has issued a certificate and sent it to that authority, confirming, in either case, that the adopter is eligible to adopt and has been assessed and approved as being a suitable adoptive parent;"
	"relevant domestic authority" means—
	   (a) in the case of an adopter to whom the Intercountry Adoption (Hague Convention) Regulations 2003 apply and who is habitually resident in Wales, the National Assembly of Wales;
	   (b) in the case of an adopter to whom the Intercountry Adoption (Hague Convention) (Scotland) Regulations 2003 apply and who is habitually resident in Scotland, the Scottish Ministers;
	   (c) in any other case, the Secretary of State".

AMENDMENT

1. Statutory Paternity Pay and Statutory Adoption Pay (Amendment) Regulations 2004 (SI 2004/488), reg.3(3) (April 6, 2004).

Statutory Paternity Pay (Adoption) and Statutory Adoption Pay (Adoptions from Overseas) (Administration) Regulations 2003

(SI 2003/1192)

The Secretary of State, in exercise of the powers conferred on her by sections 7(1), 2(a) and (b), (4)(a), (b) and (c) and (5), 8(1) and (2)(a), (b) and (c), 10(1) and (2) and 51(1) of the Employment Act 2002 and sections 8(1)(f) and 25 of the Social Security Contributions (Transfer of Functions, etc.) Act 1999 and with the concurrence of the Commissioners of Inland Revenue, hereby makes the following Regulations:

ARRANGEMENT OF REGULATIONS

1. Citation and commencement.   6.103
2. Interpretation.
3. Application of the Statutory Paternity Pay and Statutory Adoption Pay (Administration) Regulations 2002 to adoptions from overseas.

Citation and commencement

1. These Regulations may be cited as the Statutory Paternity Pay (Adoption)   6.104
and Statutory Adoption Pay (Adoptions from Overseas) (Administration) Regulations 2003 and shall come into force on 23rd May 2003.

GENERAL NOTE

These Regulations apply the Statutory Paternity Pay and Statutory Adoption Pay   6.105
(Administration) Regulations 2002 (SI 2002/2820) to adoptions from overseas with the necessary modifications.

Interpretation

2. In these Regulations, "adoption from overseas" means the adoption   6.106
of a child who enters Great Britain from outside the United Kingdom in connection with or for the purposes of adoption which does not involve the placement of the child for adoption under the law of any part of the United Kingdom.

Application of the Statutory Paternity Pay and Statutory Adoption Pay (Administration) Regulations 2002 to adoptions from overseas

3.—(1) The Statutory Paternity Pay and Statutory Adoption Pay   6.107
(Administration) Regulations 2002 shall apply in the case of adoptions from overseas with the modifications set out in the following paragraphs of this regulation.

743

(2) In regulation 2(1) (interpretation)—

(a) in the definition of "adopter", for the words "with whom the child is matched for adoption" substitute "by whom the child has been or is to be adopted";

(b) after the definition of "income tax quarter", insert—

"official notification" means written notification, issued by or on behalf of the relevant domestic authority, that it is prepared to issue a certificate to the overseas authority concerned with the adoption of the child, or has issued a certificate and sent it to that authority, confirming, in either case, that the adopter is eligible to adopt and has been assessed and approved as being a suitable adoptive parent";

(c) in the definition of "paternity leave", insert at the end "as modified in its application to adoptions from overseas by the Employment Rights Act 1996 (Application of Section 80B to Adoptions from Overseas) Regulations 2003"; and

(d) after the definition of "paternity pay period" insert—

"relevant domestic authority means:—

(a) in the case of an adopter to whom the Intercountry Adoption (Hague Convention) Regulations 2003 apply and who is habitually resident in Wales, the National Assembly for Wales;

(b) in the case of an adopter to whom the Intercountry Adoption (Hague Convention) (Scotland) Regulations 2003 apply and who is habitually resident in Scotland, the Scottish Ministers; and

(c) in any other case, the Secretary of State;".

(3) After regulation 2(2), insert—

"(3) References in these Regulations to provisions of Parts 12ZA and 12ZB of the Contributions and Benefits Act are to be construed as references to those provisions as modified by the Social Security Contributions and Benefits Act 1992 (Application of Parts 12ZA and 12ZB to Adoptions from Overseas) Regulations 2003."

(4) In regulation 11(3)(b)(ii) (time within which an employer is required to give decision that he has no liability to make payments), for "the end of the seven-day period that starts on the date on which the adopter is notified of having been matched with the child" substitute "the date on which the employer's evidence was provided, or, where not all of the evidence referred to in paragraph (1) was provided on one date, the date on which the last of the evidence was provided".

(5) Omit regulation 11(4).

Statutory Paternity Pay (Adoption) and Statutory Adoption Pay (Adoptions from Overseas) (Persons Abroad and Mariners) Regulations 2003

(SI 2003/1193)

The Secretary of State, in exercise of the powers conferred upon her by virtue of sections 171ZI, 171ZJ(1), 171ZR and 171ZS(1) of the Social Security Contributions and Benefits Act 1992 and with the concurrence of the Treasury, by this instrument, which contains only provision made by virtue of sections 2 and 4 of the Employment Act 2002 and is made before the end of the period of 6 months from the coming into force of those enactments, hereby makes the following Regulations:

ARRANGEMENT OF REGULATIONS

1. Citation and commencement.
2. Interpretation.
3. Application of the Statutory Paternity Pay and Statutory Adoption Pay (Persons Abroad and Mariners) Regulations 2002 to adoptions from overseas.

6.108

Citation and commencement

1. These Regulations may be cited as the Statutory Paternity Pay (Adoption) and Statutory Adoption Pay (Adoptions from Overseas) (Persons Abroad and Mariners) Regulations 2003 and shall come into force on 23rd May 2003.

6.109

GENERAL NOTE

These Regulations modify the application of the Statutory Paternity Pay and Statutory Adoption Pay (Persons Abroad and Mariners) Regulations 2002 (SI 2002 /2821) as regards adoptions from overseas.

6.110

Interpretation

2. In these Regulations, "adoption from overseas" means the adoption of a child who enters Great Britain from outside the United Kingdom in connection with or for the purposes of adoption which does not involve the placement of the child for adoption under the law of any part of the United Kingdom.

6.111

Application of the Statutory Paternity Pay and Statutory Adoption Pay (Persons Abroad and Mariners) Regulations 2002 to adoptions from overseas

3.—(1) The Statutory Paternity Pay and Statutory Adoption Pay (Persons Abroad and Mariners) Regulations 2002 shall have effect in relation to adoptions from overseas with the modifications set out in the following paragraphs of this regulation.

6.112

(2) In regulation 1(2) (interpretation)—

(a) in the definition of "adopter", for "has the same meaning as it has in the General Regulations" substitute "means a person by whom the child has been or is to be adopted";

(b) after the definition of "the General Regulations", insert—

"official notification" means written notification, issued by or on behalf of the relevant domestic authority, that it is prepared to issue a certificate to the overseas authority concerned with the adoption of the child, or has issued a certificate and sent it to that authority, confirming, in either case, that the adopter is eligible to adopt and has been assessed and approved as being a suitable adoptive parent;

"relevant domestic authority" means—

(a) in the case of an adopter to whom the Intercountry Adoption (Hague Convention) Regulations 2003 apply and who is habitually resident in Wales, the National Assembly for Wales;

(b) in the case of an adopter to whom the Intercountry Adoption (Hague Convention) (Scotland) Regulations 2003 apply and who is habitually resident in Scotland, the Scottish Ministers; and

(c) in any other case, the Secretary of State;".

(c) for the definition of "statutory paternity pay (birth)" and "statutory paternity pay (adoption)" substitute—

"statutory paternity pay (adoption)" means statutory paternity pay payable in accordance with the provisions of Part 12ZA of the Act, where the conditions specified in section 171ZB(2) of the Act are satisfied;".

(3) For regulation (3), substitute—

"(3) References in these Regulations to provisions of Parts 12ZA and 12ZB of the Act are to be construed as references to those provisions as modified by the Social Security Contributions and Benefits Act 1992 (Application of Parts 12ZA and 12ZB to Adoptions from Overseas) Regulations 2003."

(4) In regulation 5(2) (entitlement to statutory paternity pay adoption))—

(a) in the first line, after "and who" insert ", in the week in which the adopter receives an official notification or completes 26 weeks' continuous employment with his employer, whichever is the later"; and

(b) in sub-paragraph (a), omit the words "in the week in which the adopter is notified of being matched with the child for the purposes of adoption".

(5) In regulation 6 (entitlement to statutory adoption pay)—

(a) in the first line, after "and who" insert ", in the week in which he receives an official notification or completes 26 weeks' continuous employment with his employer, whichever is the later"; and

(b) in paragraph (a), omit the words "in the week in which he is notified that he has been matched with the child for the purposes of adoption".

Statutory Paternity Pay (Adoption) and Statutory Adoption Pay (Adoptions from Overseas) (No.2) Regulations 2003

(SI 2003/1194) (AS AMENDED)

The Secretary of State, in exercise of the powers conferred on her by sections 171ZB(2)(a), 171ZC(3)(a) to (d), (f) and (g), 171ZD(2) and (3), 171ZE(2)(a) and (b)(i), (3)(b), (7) and (8), 171ZG(3), 171ZJ(1), (3), (4), (7) and (8), 171ZL(8)(b) to (d), (f) and (g), 171ZM(2) and (3), 171ZN(2), (5) and (6), 171ZP(6), 171ZS(1), (3), (4), (7) and (8), and 175(4) of the Social Security Contributions and Benefits Act 1992, section 5(1)(g), (i) and (p) of the Social Security Administration Act 1992 and with the concurrence of the Commissioners of Inland Revenue in so far as such concurrence is required, by this instrument, which contains only provision made by virtue of sections 2, 4 and 53 and paragraphs 8 and 11 of Schedule 7 to the Employment Act 2002 and is made before the end of the period of 6 months from the coming into force of these enactments, hereby makes the following Regulations:

6.113

General

Citation and commencement

6.114   **1.** These Regulations may be cited as the Statutory Paternity Pay (Adoption) and Statutory Adoption Pay (Adoptions from Overseas) (No.2) Regulations 2003 and shall come into force on 30th May 2003.

GENERAL NOTE

6.115   These Regulations, made under provisions inserted into the SSCBA 1992 by the Employment Act 2002, make provision relating to statutory paternity pay and statutory adoption pay in respect of adoptions from overseas. They should be read together with the Social Security Contributions and Benefits Act 1992 (Application of Pts XIIZA and XIIZB to Adoptions from Overseas) Regulations 2003 (SI 2003/499), which provide for Pts XIIZA and XIIZB of the 1992 Act to have effect, with the modification prescribed in those Regulations, in relation to cases which involve adoption, but not the placement of a child for adoption under the law of any part of the United Kingdom. Regulation 19 of these (No.2) Regulations revokes the Statutory Pay (Adoption) and Statutory Adoption Pay (Adoptions from Overseas) Regulations 2003 (SI 2003/500), which came into force on April 6, 2003 and originally made provision for paternity and adoption pay in the case of adoptions from overseas. The (No.2) Regulations are virtually in identical form to the original set. The main difference is the correction of "employee" to read "employer" in reg.11 where it first appears, but a number of other minor drafting amendments have also been made.

Interpretation and scope

6.116   **2.**—(1) In these Regulations—
"the Act" means the Social Security Contributions and Benefits Act 1992;
"adopter", in relation to a child, means a person by whom the child has been or is to be adopted;
"adoption from overseas" means the adoption of a child who enters Great Britain from outside the United Kingdom in connection with or for the purposes of adoption which does not involve the placement of the child for adoption under the law of any part of the United Kingdom;
"the Application Regulations" means the Social Security Contributions and Benefits Act 1992 (Application of Parts 12ZA and 12ZB to Adoptions from Overseas) Regulations 2003;
"the Board" means the Commissioners of Inland Revenue;
"enter Great Britain" means enter Great Britain from outside the United Kingdom in connection with or for the purposes of adoption, and cognate expressions shall be construed accordingly;
"the General Regulations" means the Statutory Paternity Pay and Statutory Adoption Pay (General) Regulations 2002;
"official notification" means written notification, issued by or on behalf of the relevant domestic authority, that it is prepared to issue a certificate to the overseas authority concerned with the adoption of the child, or has issued a certificate and sent it to that authority, confirming, in either case, that the adopter is eligible to adopt, and has been assessed and approved as being a suitable adoptive parent;
"relevant domestic authority" means—

(a) in the case of an adopter to whom the Intercountry Adoption (Hague Convention) Regulations 2003 apply and who is habitually resident in Wales, the National Assembly for Wales;

(b) in the case of an adopter to whom the Intercountry Adoption (Hague Convention) (Scotland) Regulations apply and who is habitually resident in Scotland, the Scottish Ministers;

(c) in any other case, the Secretary of State;

"statutory paternity pay (adoption)" means statutory paternity pay payable in accordance with the provisions of Part 12ZA of the Act, as modified by the Application Regulations, where the conditions specified in section 171ZB(2) of the Act, as modified by the Application Regulations, are satisfied.

(2) References in these Regulations to the provisions of Parts 12ZA and 12ZB of the Act are to be construed as references to those provisions as modified by the Application Regulations.

(3) These Regulations apply to statutory paternity pay (adoption) and statutory adoption pay in respect of adoptions from overseas.

Application of the General Regulations to these Regulations

3.—(1) Subject to paragraph (2), the provisions of the General Regulations mentioned in paragraph (3) shall, in so far as they apply to statutory paternity pay (adoption) and statutory adoption pay, apply to adoptions from overseas.

6.117

(2) Any references to the provisions of Parts 12ZA or 12ZB of the Act in the regulations of the General Regulations mentioned in paragraph (3) shall be construed as references to those provisions as modified by the Application Regulations.

(3) The provisions of the General Regulations referred to in paragraph (1) are regulations 17 to 19, 26 to 28, 31 to 39, 41 to 47 and, subject to paragraph (4), regulation 40.

(4) In the General Regulations, the provisions of regulation 40 shall apply as if—

[[1](a) in paragraph (2)(b), for "the week in which the adopter is notified of being matched with the child for the purposes of adoption" there were substituted—

"the week in which—

(i) official notification is sent to the adopter or

(ii) the person satisfies the condition in section 171ZB(2)(b) or 171ZL(2)(b) of the Act (26 weeks' continuous employment), whichever is the later;"]

(b) at the end of paragraph (2), there were added " 'official notification' has the same meaning in the Statutory Paternity Pay (Adoption) and Statutory Adoption Pay (Adoptions from Overseas) (No.2) Regulations 2003".

AMENDMENT

1. Statutory Paternity Pay and Statutory Adoption Pay (Amendment) Regulations 2004 (SI 2004/488), reg.4 (April 6, 2004).

DEFINITIONS

"the Act—see reg.2(1).
"adopter"—see *ibid.*

"adoption from overseas"—see *ibid.*
"the Application Regulation"—see *ibid.*
"the General Regulations"—see *ibid.*
"official notification"—see *ibid.*
"statutory paternity pay (adoption)"—see *ibid.*

Application

6.118   **4.**—(1) Subject to the provisions of Part 12ZA of the Act (statutory paternity pay), the provisions of the General Regulations mentioned in paragraph (3) of regulation 3 and these Regulations, there is entitlement to statutory paternity pay (adoption) in respect of children who enter Great Britain on or after 6th April 2003.

(2) Subject to the provisions of Part 12ZB of the Act (statutory adoption pay), the provisions of the General Regulations mentioned in paragraph (3) of regulation 3 and these Regulations, there is entitlement to statutory adoption pay in respect of children who enter Great Britain on or after 6th April, 2003.

DEFINITIONS

"the Act"—see reg.2(1).
"enter Great Britain"—see *ibid.*
"the General Regulation"—see *ibid.*
"Part XIIZA"—see reg.(2).
"Pt XIIZB"—see *ibid.*
"statutory paternity pay (adoption)"—see reg.2(1).

Statutory paternity pay (adoption)

Conditions of entitlement to statutory paternity pay (adoption) in respect of adoptions from overseas: relationship with child and with adopter

6.119   **5.**—(1) The conditions prescribed under section 171ZB(2)(a) of the Act are that a person—
(a) is married to [¹, the civil partner] or the partner of a child's adopter (or in a case where there are two adopters, married to [¹, the civil partner] or the partner of the other adopter); and
(b) has, or expects to have, the main responsibility (apart from the responsibility of the child's adopter or, in a case where there are two adopters, together with the other adopter) for the upbringing of the child.

(2) For the purpose of paragraph (1), "partner" means a person (whether of a different sex or the same sex) who lives with the adopter and the child in an enduring family relationship but is not a relative of the adopter of a kind specified in paragraph (3).

(3) The relatives of a child's adopter referred to in the definition of "partner" in paragraph (2) are the adopter's parent, grandparent, sister, brother, aunt or uncle.

(4) References to relationships in paragraph (3)—
(a) are to relationships of the full blood or half blood or, in the case of

an adopted person, such of those relationships as would exist but for the adoption; and

(b) include the relationship of a child with his adoptive, or former adoptive parents but do not include any other adoptive relationships.

AMENDMENT

1. Civil Partnership Act 2004 (Amendments to Subordinate Legislation) Order 2005 (SI 2005/2114), art.2(17) and Sch.17, para.6 (December 5, 2005).

DEFINITIONS

"the Act"—see reg.2(1).
"adopter"—see *ibid.*
"partner"—see para.(2).

Period of payment of statutory paternity pay (adoption) in respect of adoptions from overseas

6.—(1) Subject to notice under section 171ZC(1) of the Act, paragraph (92) and reg.8, a person entitled to statutory paternity pay (adoption) may choose the statutory paternity pay period to begin on—

(a) the date on which the child enters Great Britain or, where the person is at work on that day, the following day; or

(b) a pre-determined date, specified by the person, which is later than the date on which the child enters Great Britain.

6.120

(2) In a case where statutory paternity pay (adoption) is payable in respect of a child where the adopter has received official notification before 6th April 2003, the statutory paternity pay period shall begin on a predetermined date, later than the date of entry, specified by the person entitled to such pay in a notice under section 171ZC(1) of the Act, which is at least 28 days after the date on which that notice was given, unless the person liable to pay statutory paternity pay (adoption) agrees to the period beginning earlier.

(3) A person may choose for statutory paternity pay (adoption) to be paid in respect of a period of a week.

(4) A choice made in accordance with paragraph (1) is not irrevocable, but where a person subsequently makes a different choice in relation to the beginning of the statutory paternity pay period, section 171ZC(1) of the Act shall apply to it.

DEFINITIONS

"the Act"—see reg.2(1).
"adopter"—see *ibid.*
"enter Great Britain"—see *ibid.*
"official notification"—see *ibid.*
"statutory paternity pay (adoption)"—see *ibid.*

Additional notice requirements for statutory paternity pay (adoption) in respect of adoptions from overseas

7.—(1) Where a person gives notice under section 171ZC(1) of the Act he shall give further notice of the following matters to the person liable to pay him statutory paternity pay (adoption)—

(a) the date on which official notification was received, within 28 days of

6.121

that date, or within 28 days of his completion of 26 weeks of continuous employment with that person, whichever is the later;

(b) the date on which the child enters Great Britain, within 28 days of entry.

(2) Where the child has not entered Great Britain on the expected date, the person shall, if he wishes to claim statutory paternity pay (adoption), give notice to the person liable to pay it, as soon as is reasonably practicable, that the period in respect of which statutory paternity pay is to be paid shall begin on a date different from that originally chosen by him.

(3) That date may be any date chosen in accordance with paragraph (1) of regulation 6 or specified in accordance with paragraph (2) of that regulation.

(4) Where it becomes known to that person that the child will not enter Great Britain, he shall notify the person who would have been liable to pay statutory pay (adoption), as soon as is reasonably practicable.

DEFINITIONS

"the Act"—see reg.2(1).
"enter Great Britain"—see *ibid*.
"official notification"—see *ibid*.
"statutory paternity pay (adoption)"—see *ibid*.

Qualifying period for statutory paternity pay (adoption) in respect of adoptions from overseas

6.122   **8.** The qualifying period for the purposes of section 171ZE(2) of the Act (period within which the statutory pay period must occur) is a period of 56 days beginning with the date the child enters Great Britain.

DEFINITIONS

"the Act"—see reg.2(1).
"enter Great Britain"—see *ibid*.

Evidence of entitlement for statutory paternity pay (adoption) in respect of adoptions from overseas

6.123   **9.**—(1) A person shall produce evidence of his entitlement to statutory paternity pay (adoption) in respect of adoptions from overseas by providing in writing to the person who will be liable to pay him statutory paternity pay (adoption) the declarations specified in paragraph (2) and the information specified in paragraph (3).

(2) The declarations referred to in para.(1) are as follows—

(a) that he meets the conditions prescribed under section 171ZB(2) (a) of the Act and that it is not the case that statutory paternity pay (adoption) is not payable to him by virtue of the provisions of section 171ZE(4) of the Act;

(b) that he has elected to receive statutory paternity pay (adoption), and not statutory adoption pay under Part 12ZB of the Act;

(c) that official notification has been received.

(3) The information referred to in paragraph (1) is as follows—

(a) the name of the person claiming statutory paternity pay (adoption);

(b) the date on which it is expected that the child will enter Great Britain or, where the child has already entered Great Britain, that date;

(c) the date from which it is expected that the liability to pay statutory paternity pay (adoption) will begin;

(d) whether the period chosen in respect of which statutory paternity pay (adoption) is to be payable is a week.

(4) The declarations mentioned in paragraph (2) and information mentioned in paragraph (3) shall be provided to the person liable to pay statutory paternity pay (adoption) at least 28 days before the date mentioned in sub-paragraph (c) of paragraph (3) or, if that is not reasonably practicable, as soon as is reasonably practicable thereafter.

DEFINITIONS

"the Act"—see reg.2(1).
"adoption from overseas"—see *ibid.*
"enter Great Britain"—see *ibid.*
"official notification"—see *ibid.*
"Pt XIIZB"—see reg.2(2).
"statutory paternity pay (adoption)"—see reg.2(1).

Entitlement to statutory paternity pay (adoption) where there is more than one employer in respect of adoptions from overseas

10. Statutory paternity pay (adoption) shall be payable to a person in respect of a statutory pay week during any part of which he works only for an employer—   6.124

(a) who is not liable to pay him statutory paternity pay (adoption); and

(b) for whom he has worked in the week in which the adopter receives official notification.

DEFINITIONS

"adopter"—see reg.2(1).
"official notification"—see *ibid.*
"statutory paternity pay (adoption)"—see *ibid.*

Avoidance of liability for statutory paternity pay (adoption) in respect of adoptions from overseas

11.—(1) A former employer shall be liable to make payments of statutory paternity pay (adoption) to a former employee in any case where the employee has been employed for a continuous period of at least 8 weeks and his contract of service was brought to an end by the former employer solely, or mainly, for the purpose of avoiding liability for statutory paternity pay (adoption).   6.125

(2) In a case falling within paragraph (1)—

(a) the employee shall be treated as if he had been employed for a continuous period ending with the day the child enters Great Britain;

(b) his normal weekly earnings shall be calculated by reference to his normal weekly earnings for the period of 8 weeks ending with the last day in respect of which he was paid under his former contract of service.

DEFINITIONS

"enter Great Britain"—see reg.2(1).
"statutory paternity pay (adoption)"—see *ibid.*

Statutory adoption pay

Adoption pay period in respect of adoptions from overseas

6.126   **12.**—(1) Subject to paragraph (2), a person entitled to statutory adoption pay may choose the adoption pay period to begin—

(a) on the date on which the child enters Great Britain or, where the person is at work on that day, on the following day;

(b) on the pre-determined date, specified by him, which is no later than 28 days after the date the child enters Great Britain.

(2) In a case where statutory adoption pay is payable in respect of a child where the adopter has received official notification before 6th April 2003, the statutory adoption pay period shall begin on a predetermined date, later than the date of entry, specified by the person entitled to such pay in a notice under section 171ZL(6) of the Act, which is at least 28 days after the date on which that notice was given, unless the person liable to pay statutory adoption pay agrees to the period commencing earlier.

(3) Where the choice made is that mentioned in sub-paragraph (b) of paragraph (1) or in a case where paragraph (2) applies, the adoption pay period shall, unless the employer agrees to the adoption pay period beginning earlier, begin no earlier than 28 days after notice under section 171ZL(6) of the Act has been given.

(4) Subject to regulation 13, the duration of any adoption pay period shall be a continuous period of 26 weeks.

(5) A choice made under paragraph (1), or a date specified under paragraph (2), is not irrevocable, but where a person subsequently makes a different choice or specifies a different date in relation to the beginning of the statutory adoption pay period, section 171ZL(6) of the Act shall apply to it.

DEFINITIONS

"the Act"—see reg.2(1).
"adopter"—see *ibid.*
"enter Great Britain"—see *ibid.*
"official notification"—see *ibid.*

Adoption pay period in respect of adoptions from overseas where adoption is disrupted

6.127   **13.**—(1) Where after a child enters Great Britain the child—

(a) dies; or

(b) ceases to live with the adopter,

the adoption pay period shall terminate in accordance with the provisions of paragraph (2).

(2) The adoption pay period shall, in a case falling within paragraph (1), terminate 8 weeks after the end of the week specified in paragraph (3).

(3) The week referred to in paragraph (2) is—

(a) in a case falling within paragraph (1)(a), the week during which the child dies;

(b) in a case falling within paragraph (1)(b), the week during which the child ceases to live with the adopter.

(4) For the purposes of paragraph (3), "week" means a period of 7 days beginning with Sunday.

DEFINITIONS

"adopter"—see reg.2(1).
"enter Great Britain"—see *ibid*.
"week"—see para.(4).

Additional notice requirements for statutory adoption pay in respect of adoptions from overseas

14.—(1) Where a person gives notice under section 171ZL(6) of the Act he shall give further notice of the following matters to the person liable to pay statutory adoption pay—

(a) the date on which official notification was received, within 28 days of that date, or within 28 days of his completion of 26 weeks of continuous employment, whichever is the later;

(b) the date on which the child enters Great Britain, within 28 days of entry.

(2) Where the child has not entered Great Britain on the expected date, the person shall, if he wishes to claim statutory adoption pay, give notice to the person liable to pay it, as soon as is reasonably practicable, that the period in respect of which statutory adoption pay is to be paid shall begin on a date different fromthat originally chosen by him.

(3) That date may be any date chosen in accordance with paragraph (1) of regulation 12 or specified in accordance with paragraph (2) of that regulation.

(4) Where it becomes known to the adopter that the child will not enter Great Britain, he shall notify the person who would have been liable to pay statutory adoption pay as soon as is reasonably practicable.

6.128

DEFINITIONS

"the act"—see reg.2(1).
"adopter"—see *ibid*.
"enter Great Britain"—see *ibid*.
"official notification"—see *ibid*.

Evidence of entitlement to statutory adoption pay in respect of adoptions from overseas

15.—(1) A person shall provide evidence of his entitlement to statutory adoption pay by providing, to the person who will be liable to pay it, a copy of the official notification and, in writing—

(a) the information specified in paragraph (2);

(b) a declaration that he has elected to receive statutory adoption pay, and not statutory paternity pay (adoption) under Part 12ZA of the Act;

(c) evidence, to be provided within 28 days of the child's entry into Great Britain, as to that date.

(2) The information referred to in paragraph (1) is—

(a) the name and address of the person claiming statutory adoption pay;

(b) the date on which it is expected that the child will enter Great Britain or, where he has already done so, the date of entry.

6.129

(3) The information and declaration referred to in paragraph (1) shall be provided to the person liable to pay statutory adoption pay at least 28 days before the date chosen as the beginning of the adoption pay period in accordance with paragraph (1) of regulation 12 or specified in accordance with paragraph (2) of that regulation or, if that is not reasonably practicable, as soon as is reasonably practicable thereafter.

DEFINITIONS

"the Act"—see reg.2(1).
"enter Great Britain"—see *ibid.*
"official notification"—see *ibid.*
"Pt XIIZA"—see reg.2(2).
"statutory paternity pay (adoption)"—see reg.2(1).

Entitlement to statutory adoption pay in respect of adoptions from overseas where there is more than one employer

6.130   **16.** Statutory adoption pay shall be payable to a person in respect of a week during any part of which he works for an employer—
(a) who is not liable to pay him statutory adoption pay; and
(b) for whom he has worked in the week in which he receives official notification.

DEFINITION

"official notification"—see reg.2(1).

Termination of employment and liability to pay statutory adoption pay in respect of adoptions from overseas

6.131   **17.**—(1) Where the employment of a person who satisfies the conditions of entitlement to statutory adoption pay in respect of adoptions from overseas terminates for whatever reason (including dismissal) before the adoption pay period chosen or specified by that person in accordance with regulation 12 has begun, the period shall begin on a date chosen by that person which is at least 28 days after notice has been given and within 28 days of the date of the child's entry into Great Britain.

(2) Where the statutory adoption pay period has not commenced within a period of 6 months of the adopter's leaving his employer, liability to pay statutory adoption pay shall, notwithstanding section 171ZM(1) of the Act, pass to the Board.

(3) Where liability to pay statutory adoption pay has passed to the Board in accordance with paragraph (2) and the adopter, having started employment as an employed earner, becomes entitled to statutory adoption pay by virtue of that employment, the liability of the Board shall cease and section 171ZM(1) of the Act shall apply.

DEFINITIONS

"the Act"—see reg.2(1).
"adopter"—see *ibid.*
"adoption from overseas"—see *ibid.*
"the Board"—see *ibid.*

Avoidance of liability for statutory adoption pay in respect of adoptions from overseas

18.—(1) A former employer shall be liable to make payments of statutory adoption pay to a former employee in any case where the employee had been employed for a continuous period of at least 8 weeks and his contract of service was brought to an end by the former employer solely, or mainly, for the purpose of avoiding liability for statutory adoption pay.

(2) In a case falling within paragraph (1)—

(a) the employee shall be treated as if he had been employed for a continuous period ending with the week in which he received official notification; and

(b) his normal weekly earnings shall be calculated by reference to his normal weekly earnings for the period of 8 weeks ending with the last day in respect of which he was paid under his former contract of service.

6.132

DEFINITION

"official notification"—see reg.2(1).

Revocation

19. The Statutory Paternity Pay (Adoption) and Statutory Adoption Pay (Adoptions from Overseas) Regulations 2003 are hereby revoked.

6.133

PART VII

CHILD TRUST FUNDS

Child Trust Funds Act 2004 (Commencement No.1) Order 2004

(SI 2004/2422 (C.103))

The Treasury, in exercise of the powers conferred upon them by section 27 of the Child Trust Funds Act 2004, make the following Order:

Citation and interpretation

1.—(1) This Order may be cited as the Child Trust Funds Act 2004 (Commencement No.1) Order 2004.

(2) In this Order—

"account" means an account which (from the appointed day) is capable of being a child trust fund (within the meaning in the Act);

"the Act" means the Child Trust Funds Act 2004;

"the appointed day" means the day appointed under section 27 of the Act for the purposes of sections 8 and 9 of the Act.

7.1

Commencement of certain provisions of the Act

2. The following provisions of the Act shall come into force on 1st January 2005 for the purposes mentioned in relation to each provision:

7.2

Provision	Purposes
Section 1(3) of the Act	All purposes
Section 3(1) and (3) of the Act	All purposes (save that an account may only be a child trust fund from the appointed day)
Section 3(2), (4) to (9) and (12) of the Act	To allow accounts to be opened, and contracts with an account provider for their management to be signed, save that the account is only to be: (a) a child trust fund, or (b) subscribed to and operated, from the appointed day.
Section 5(1) and (2) of the Act	To ensure an orderly introduction of accounts, by issuing some vouchers before the appointed day.
Section 5(3) to (5) of the Act	Where a voucher has been issued before the appointed day under section 5(1) of the Act, to allow

Provision	Purposes
	accounts to be opened, save that the account is only to be: (a) a child trust fund, or (b) subscribed to and operated, from that day.
Section 15(1), (2)(a) and (3) of the Act	So far as those provisions relate to the persons referred to in section 15(2)(a) of the Act
Section 17 of the Act	All purposes
Section 18 of the Act	All purposes
Section 20(1) (except paragraphs (b) and (c)), (2) to (6), (7) (except paragraph (c)), (8) and (9) of the Act	All purposes (except for the purposes of sections 6, 7, 9, 10 or 13 of the Act)
Section 21 of the Act	For the purposes of the provisions of section 20 of the Act which are commenced by this Order
Section 22(1) and (6) of the Act	All purposes
Section 23(1) to (3) of the Act	For the purposes of section 22(1) and (6) of the Act
Section 24(1) (except paragraph (c)), (2) and (3) of the Act	For the purposes of section 22(1) and (6) of the Act
Section 24(5) to (7) of the Act	All purposes

Child Trust Funds Act 2004 (Commencement No. 2) Order 2004

(SI 2004/3369 (C.158))

The Treasury, in exercise of the powers conferred upon them by section 27 of the Child Trust Funds Act 2004, make the following Order:

ARRANGEMENT OF ARTICLES

1. Citation and interpretation
2. Commencement of provisions of the Act

Citation and interpretation

7.3   **1.**—(1) This Order may be cited as the Child Trust Funds Act 2004 (Commencement No.2) Order 2004.

(2) In this Order—

"the Act" means the Child Trust Funds Act 2004;

"the earlier Order" means the Child Trust Funds Act 2004 (Commencement No. 1) Order 2004.

Commencement of provisions of the Act

2.—(1) Sections 1 to 24 of the Act shall come into force on 6th April 2005, subject to the following paragraphs.

(2) Paragraph (1) does not apply to provisions brought into force for all purposes by the earlier Order.

(3) Section 23(1) of the Act shall come into force for all purposes on 1st January 2005.

(4) Where a provision of the Act (other than section 23(1)) was partially brought into force by the earlier Order, that provision shall come into force for all other purposes on 6th April 2005.

7.4

Child Trust Funds Regulations 2004

(SI 2004/1450) (AS AMENDED)

ARRANGEMENT OF REGULATIONS

PART 1

Introductory

7.5

PART 2

Other requirements to be satisfied in relation to accounts

PART 3

Tax and administration of accounts

The Treasury, in exercise of the powers conferred upon them by sections 3(1) to (5) and (7), 5(1), (4) and (5), 6, 7, 8(1), 9(2) and (10)(b), 11(1), 12(2), 13, 15, 16, 23(1) and 28(1) to (4) of the Child Trust Funds Act 2004, hereby make the following Regulations:

PART 1

INTRODUCTORY

Citation and commencement

1. These Regulations may be cited as the Child Trust Funds Regulations 2004 and shall come into force for the purposes of—

(a) issuing vouchers (see regulation 3),

(b) completing account-opening formalities (see regulation 5),

(c) applications under regulation 13 to open an account with effect from the appointed day,

(d) applications under regulation 14 to be approved as an account provider to manage accounts from the appointed day,

(e) regulation 17, so far as it relates to applications referred to in paragraph (d), and

(f) making a fortnightly claim and financial return (see regulation 30),

on 1st January 2005, and for all other purposes on the appointed day.

7.6

Interpretation

2.—(1) In these Regulations—

(a) the following expressions have the meanings given in the Child Trust Funds Act 2004 ("the Act")—

"child"

"child trust fund"

"eligible child"

[5 "the income threshold" (see section 9(6) of the Act)]

"Inland Revenue"

"Inland Revenue contributions" (see section 11(2) of the Act),

"parental responsibility" (see section 3(9) of the Act);

[5 "the relevant income" (see section 9(6) of the Act)]

"relevant person" (see section 15(2) of the Act),

[5 "relevant social security benefit" (see section 9(6) of the Act)]

"responsible person", in relation to a child under 16 (see section 3(8) of the Act),

[5 "tax year" (see section 9(6) of the Act)]

"the person entitled to child benefit in respect of the child" (see section 2(1)(a), (4) and (6) of the Act);

(b) except where the context otherwise requires—

"account" means a scheme of investment which (except in regulation 22(1)) qualifies as a child trust fund, other than in the cases of—

(i) an account with a deposit-taker,

(ii) a share or deposit account with a building society, or

(iii) a deposit account with a person falling within section 840A(1)(b) of the Taxes Act, or a relevant European institution;

an "account investment" is an investment under the account which is a qualifying investment for an account within the meaning of regulation 12;

7.7

an "account provider" is a person who fulfils the conditions of these Regulations and is approved by the Board for the purpose of these Regulations as an account provider;

"appointed day" means the day appointed, under section 27 of the Act, for the purposes of sections 8 and 9 of the Act;

"assurance undertaking" has the meaning in Article 2 of the Council Directive of 5th November 2002 concerning life assurance (2002/83/EC);

[¹"Bank of England base rate" means the rate announced from time to time by the Monetary Policy Committee of the Bank of England as the official dealing rate, being the rate at which the Bank is willing to enter into transactions for providing short-term liquidity in the money markets;]

[³"the Board" means the Commissioners for Her Majesty's Revenue and Customs;]

"building society" means a building society within the meaning of the Building Societies Act 1986, or the Irish Building Societies Act 1989;

[⁴"building society bonus", except in regulation 24(a)(i), excludes any bonus, distribution of funds or the conferring of rights in relation to shares—

(a) in connection with an amalgamation, transfer of engagements or transfer of business of a building society, and

(b) mentioned in section 96 or 100 of the Building Societies Act 1986,

and "payment under a building society bonus scheme" shall be construed accordingly;]

"company", except in regulation 12(4)(a), means any body corporate having a share capital other than—

  (i) an open-ended investment company, within the meaning given by section 236 of the Financial Services and Markets Act 2000,

 (ii) a UCITS,

(iii) an industrial and provident society, or

(iv) a body corporate which is a 51 per cent. subsidiary of any industrial and provident society;

[²"credit union" means a society registered as a credit union under the Industrial and Provident Societies Act 1965 or the Credit Unions (Northern Ireland) Order 1985;]

"deposit-taker" has the meaning given by section 481(2) of the Taxes Act;

"the Director of Savings" has the same meaning as in the National Debt Act 1972;

"the Distance Marketing Directive" means Directive 2002/65/EC of the European Parliament and of the Council of 23rd September 2002, and includes any provisions by which an EEA State or the United Kingdom has transposed the Directive or has corresponding obligations in its domestic law, and "distance contract" has the meaning in that Directive;

"electronic communications" includes any communications by means of a telecommunication system (within the meaning in the Telecommunications Act 1984);

"EEA Agreement" means the Agreement on the European Economic Area signed at Oporto on 2nd May 1992, as adjusted by the Protocol signed at Brussels on 17th March 1993;

"EEA State" means a State, other than the United Kingdom, which is a Contracting Party to the EEA Agreement;

"European institution" means an EEA firm of the kind mentioned in paragraph 5(a), (b) or (c) of Schedule 3 to the Financial Services and Markets Act 2000 which is an authorised person for the purposes of that Act as a result of qualifying for authorisation under paragraph 12 of that Schedule;

"51 per cent. subsidiary" and "75 per cent. subsidiary" have the meanings given by section 838 of the Taxes Act;

"gains", except in regulations 22(1) to (3), 24(a)(ii), (iii) and (v), 37(5) and 38, means "chargeable gains" within the meaning in the 1992 Act;

"gilt-edged securities" has the meaning given by paragraphs 1 and 1A of Schedule 9 to the 1992 Act;

"incorporated friendly society" means a society incorporated under the Friendly Societies Act 1992;

"industrial and provident society" means a society registered or deemed to be registered under the Industrial and Provident Societies Act 1965 or under the Industrial and Provident Societies (Northern Ireland) Act 1969;

"investments under the account" has the same meaning as investments under a child trust fund in the Act;

investment trust" has the meaning given by section 842 of the Taxes Act, and references to the "eligible rental income" of an investment trust have the same meaning as in that section;

"the Management Act" means the Taxes Management Act 1970;

"market value" shall be construed in accordance with section 272 of the 1992 Act;

[³"the New Collective Investment Schemes Sourcebook" means the Sourcebook of that name made by the Financial Services Authority under the Financial Services and Markets Act 2000;

"non-UCITS retail scheme"—

(a) has the meaning in the New Collective Investment Schemes Sourcebook (that is, a scheme to which, or to whose authorised fund manager and depositary, Sections 5.1, 5.4 and 5.6 of that Sourcebook apply),

(b) includes a "recognised scheme" by virtue of section 270 or 272 of the Financial Services and Markets Act 2000, which would fall within paragraph (a) of this definition if it were an authorised fund, and

(c) includes a sub-fund of an umbrella which the terms of the scheme identify as a sub-fund which would fall within paragraph (a) or (b) of this definition if it were itself an authorised fund or a recognised scheme.

In this definition, expressions defined in the Glossary forming part of the Financial Services Authority Handbook have those defined meanings;]

"the 1992 Act" means the Taxation of Chargeable Gains Act 1992;

"notice" except in regulations 12(12) and 37(6)(a), means notice in writing;

[³"qualifying units in or shares of a non-UCITS retail scheme" means that—

(a) the instrument constituting the scheme secures that redemption of the units or shares in question shall take place no less frequently than bi-monthly (see Rule 6.2.16(6) of the New Collective Investment Schemes Sourcebook omitting the words "Except where (7) applies, and", read with Rule 6.3.4(1), whether or not those Rules apply to the scheme), and

(b) a provision for suspension of dealings in exceptional conditions in accordance with Rule 7.2 of that Sourcebook (or any foreign procedure which is a direct foreign equivalent of that Rule) shall not be treated as a provision contrary to paragraph (a) of this definition;]

"recognised stock exchange" has the same meaning as in section 841 of the Taxes Act;

"registered friendly society" has the meaning given by the Friendly Societies Act 1992 and includes any society that by virtue of section 96(2) of that Act is to be treated as a registered friendly society;

"relevant authorised person" has the same meaning as in section 333A(12) of the Taxes Act;

"relevant European institution" has the meaning given by section 326A(10) of the Taxes Act;

"security" means any loan stock or similar security of a company whether secured or unsecured;

"subscriptions" has the meaning in section 12(1) of the Act (but excluding Inland Revenue contributions and income or gains arising from investments under the account);

"tax" where neither income tax nor capital gains tax is specified means either of those taxes;

"the Taxes Act" means the Income and Corporation Taxes Act 1988;

"year", except in the expression "subscription year" in regulations 9, 21(5)(b) and 32(2)(b)(iv), means a year of assessment (within the meaning in section 832(1) of the Taxes Act, or section 288(1) of the 1992 Act, as the case may be);

(c) "authorised fund" means—

(i) an authorised unit trust, or

(ii) an open-ended investment company with variable capital incorporated in the United Kingdom in the case of which an authorisation order made by the Financial Services Authority under regulation 14 of the Open-Ended Investment Companies Regulations 2001 is in force;

"authorised unit trust" means a unit trust scheme in the case of which an authorisation order made by the Financial Services Authority under section 243 of the Financial Services and Markets Act 2000 is in force;

"the Collective Investment Schemes Sourcebook" means the sourcebook of that name made by the Financial Services Authority under the Financial Services and Markets Act 2000;

"depositary interest" means the rights of the person mentioned in paragraph (ii), under a certificate or other record (whether or not in the form of a document) acknowledging—

(i) that a person holds relevant investments or evidence of the right to them, and

(ii) that another person is entitled to rights in or in relation to those or identical relevant investments, including the right to receive such investments, or evidence of the right to them or the proceeds from such investments, from the person mentioned in paragraph (i),

where "relevant investments" means investments which are exclusively qualifying investments for an account falling within regulation 12(2)(a) to (i), and the rights mentioned in paragraph (ii) are exclusively rights in or in relation to relevant investments;

"fund of funds scheme" means—

(i) an authorised fund which according to the terms of the scheme is a fund of funds scheme belonging to the category under that name established by the Financial Services Authority, and

(ii) a part of an umbrella scheme which the terms of the scheme identify as a part that would belong to that category if it were itself an authorised fund;

"money market scheme" means—

(i) an authorised fund which according to terms of the scheme is a money market scheme belonging to the category under that name established by the Financial Services Authority, and

(ii) a part of an umbrella scheme which the terms of the scheme identify as a part that would belong to that category if it were itself an authorised fund;

"open-ended investment company", except in sub-paragraph (a), has the meaning given by subsection (10) of section 468 of the Taxes Act as that subsection is added in relation to open-ended investment companies by regulation 10(4) of the 1997 Regulations, and "shares" in relation to an open-ended investment company, includes shares of any class and of any denomination of a given class and, in relation to a part of an umbrella company, means shares in the company which confer for the time being rights in that part;

"securities scheme" means—

(i) an authorised fund which according to the terms of the scheme is a securities scheme belonging to the category under that name established by the Financial Services Authority, and

(ii) a part of an umbrella scheme which the terms of the scheme identify as a part which would belong to that category if it were itself an authorised fund;

"the 1997 Regulations" means the Open-ended Investment Companies (Tax) Regulations 1997;

"UCITS" means undertakings for collective investment in transferable securities within the meaning of Article 1 of Council Directive 85/611;

"umbrella scheme" means an authorised fund which according to the terms of the scheme is an umbrella scheme belonging to the category under that name established by the Financial Services Authority, and—

(i) in the case of an authorised fund which is an authorised unit trust, references to a part of an umbrella scheme shall be construed in accordance with subsection (8) of section 468 of the Taxes Act, and, in relation to a part of an umbrella scheme, references to investments subject to the trusts of an authorised unit trust and to a unit holder shall be construed in accordance with subsection (9) of that section, and

(ii) in the case of an authorised fund which is an open-ended investment company, references to a part of an umbrella scheme shall be construed in accordance with subsection (18) of section 468 of the Taxes Act as that subsection is added in relation to open-ended investment companies by regulation 10(4) of the 1997 Regulations, and, in relation to a part of an umbrella scheme, references to investments of the company shall be construed in accordance with subsection (12) of that section as so added;

"unit holder", except in relation to a part of an umbrella scheme, has the meaning given by subsection (6) of section 468 of the Taxes Act;

"unit trust scheme" has the meaning given by subsection (6) of section 468 of the Taxes Act;

"units", in relation to an authorised unit trust, means the rights or interests (however described) of the unit holders in that unit trust and, in relation to a part of an umbrella scheme, means the rights or interests for the time being of the unit holders in that part;

"warrant scheme" means—

(i) an authorised fund which according to the terms of the scheme is a warrant scheme belonging to the category under that name established by the Financial Services Authority, and

(ii) a part of an umbrella scheme which the terms of the scheme identify as a part that would belong to that category if it were itself an authorised fund.

(2) The table below indexes other definitions in these Regulations—

7.8	Term defined	Regulation
	"the applicant"	5
	"the commencement date"	7(8)
	"description" of an account	4
	"the disqualifying circumstances"	16
	"first return period"	30(1)
	"fortnightly period"	30(1)
	"initial contribution"	7(1)
	"interim tax claim"	26(2)
	"local authority"	33(1)
	"looked after child"	33(1)
	"management agreement"	5
	"the named child"	5 and 8(1)
	"qualifying circumstances"	14
	"qualifying investments for an account"	12
	"registered contact"	8(1)(d)
	"second return period"	30(1)
	"special contribution"	7(1)

Term defined	Regulation
"subscription year"	9(2)
"supplementary contribution"	7(5)
"the termination event"	12(12)
"the transfer instructions"	8(2)(h)
"the internal transfer instructions"	8(2)(i)

AMENDMENTS

1. Child Trust Funds (Amendment) Regulations 2004 (SI 2004/2676), reg.3 (April 6, 2005).

2. Child Trust Funds (Amendment No.2) Regulations 2005 (SI 2005/909), reg.3 (April 6, 2005).

3. Child Trust Funds (Amendment No.3) Regulations 2005 (SI 2005/3349), reg.3 (December 27, 2005).

4. Child Trust Funds (Amendment No.3) Regulations 2006 (SI 2006/3195), reg.3 (January 1, 2007).

5. Child Trust Funds (Amendment) Regulations 2009 (SI 2009/475), reg.3 (April 6, 2009, but have effect where the Child Benefit commencement date for the child (first day for which child benefit was paid in respect of the child) is on or after April 6, 2008).

Vouchers

3.—(1) The voucher to be issued under section 5(1) of the Act shall contain the following particulars—   7.9
   (a) the full name of the child,
   (b) his date of birth,
   (c) his unique reference number,
   (d) the expiry date of the voucher, and
   (e) the amount of the initial contribution (see regulation 7(1)),
and a statement that the voucher cannot be exchanged for money.

(2) The voucher shall be sent to the person who is entitled to child benefit in respect of the child (or, in the case of a child who is an eligible child because of section 2(3) of the Act, to a responsible person in relation to the child) by post.

(3) The expiry date [¹. . .] shall be whichever is the earlier of—
   (a) the date 12 months from the date of issue of the voucher, or
   (b) where the child is over 17 years of age, the date on which he will attain the age of 18 years.

AMENDMENT

1. Child Trust Funds (Amendment) Regulations 2006 (SI 2006/199), reg.3 (February 7, 2006).

DEFINITIONS

"child"—see reg.2(1)(a).
"eligible child"—see *ibid*.
"responsible person"—see *ibid*.

Descriptions of accounts

4.—(1) An account may be of either of the following descriptions—   7.10

Stakeholder account

Where the account meets the characteristics and conditions in the Schedule to these Regulations.

Non-stakeholder account

Where any of those characteristics or conditions is not met.

(2) Accounts opened by the Inland Revenue (see regulation 6) must be stakeholder accounts.

DEFINITION

"account"—see reg.2(1)(b).

Opening of account by responsible person or the child

7.11   **5.**—(1) For the purposes of these Regulations, subject to [¹paragraphs (1A) and (2)], an account is opened for a child ("the named child") with an account provider on the date the last of the following conditions is satisfied (in any order), where "the applicant" means—

(a) if the named child is 16 or over, the child; and

(b) in any other case, a responsible person in relation to the named child.

Condition 1

The applicant gives the voucher relating to the named child to the account provider [¹not later than 7 days after its expiry date] [² or, where the account provider has chosen to open accounts without sight of the relevant voucher, the applicant gives the following information to the account provider:

(a) the expiry date of the voucher,

(b) the amount of the initial contribution as specified on the voucher, and

(c) where the date of birth shown on the voucher differs from the actual date of birth of the child (see regulation 13(5)(c)), the date of birth shown on the voucher]

Condition 2

The applicant enters into an agreement with the account provider (the "management agreement") for the management of the account (see regulation 8(1) and (2)), which includes the application and declaration required by regulation 13.

Condition 3

Where that application is not in writing the applicant has agreed, or is treated as having agreed, the contents of the copy of the declaration required by regulation 13(3).

Condition 4

(a) In any case where the management agreement is a distance contract, the agreement must be an initial service agreement for the purposes of the Distance Marketing Directive, and contain the instructions required by regulation 8(1)(f), and

772

(b) in every case where there is any right to cancel (or automatic cancellation of) the management agreement, the period during which it may be exercised or occur has expired without that right being exercised or cancellation occurring.

(2) An account must satisfy the requirements that—

(a) no subscription to the account is accepted by the account provider until the account has been opened in accordance with paragraph (1); and

(b) where the account is so opened before the appointed day, it shall not be treated as open for the purpose of accepting subscriptions until the appointed day.

[¹(1A) The application to open the account must be made, and Condition 2 satisfied, not later than the expiry date of the voucher.]

AMENDMENTS

1. Child Trust Funds (Amendment) Regulations 2006 (SI 2006/199), reg.4 (February 7, 2006).

2. Child Trust Funds (Amendment No.2) Regulations 2009 (SI 2009/694), reg.3 (April 6, 2009).

DEFINITIONS

"account"—see reg.2(1)(b).
"account provider"—see *ibid.*
"appointed day"—see *ibid.*
"child"—see reg.2(1)(a).
"the Distance Marketing Directive"—see reg.2(1)(b).
"responsible person"—see reg.2(1)(a).
"subscriptions"—see reg.2(1)(b).

Opening of account by Inland Revenue—(Revenue allocated accounts)

6.—(1) The Board shall apply to open an account for a child to whom section 6 of the Act applies, by forwarding to an account provider the particulars which would be required for a voucher (see regulation 3), but omitting paragraph (1)(d) of that regulation.

(2) The account provider shall immediately open a stakeholder account in the name of the child, which shall have the same effect as if a responsible person for the child (or the child if aged 16 or over) had entered into the account provider's standard management agreement for the stakeholder account in question, including the terms mentioned in Condition 2 of regulation 5(1) (but treating the reference to the application and declaration required by regulation 13 as a reference to the authorisation required by regulation 13(4)) and regulation 8(1)(f).

(3) The Inland Revenue shall maintain (and update from time to time) a list of account providers who have agreed to accept Revenue allocated accounts under this regulation, in the order of the date of their agreement, and the account provider shall be selected in rotation from the current list.

(4) Where the account provider offers two or more types of stakeholder account [²—

(a) the account provider shall select the type or types to be used for the purposes of this regulation (subject to sub-paragraph (b)),

(b) any type selected must be offered to the general public at the time of opening a Revenue allocated account of that type, and

7.12

(c) if more than one type has been selected, the account to be opened shall be chosen by the account provider in rotation between the selected types of accounts.]

[[1](5) The Inland Revenue shall write to the person who is entitled to child benefit in respect of the child (or, in the case of a child who is an eligible child because of section 2(3) of the Act, to a responsible person in relation to the child) to inform them of the opening of the account and particulars of it.]

AMENDMENTS

1. Child Trust Funds (Amendment) Regulations 2004 (SI 2004/2676), reg.4 (April 6, 2005).
2. Child Trust Funds (Amendment No.3) Regulations 2005 (SI 2005/3349), reg.4 (December 27, 2005).

DEFINITIONS

"account"—see reg.2(1)(b).
"account provider"—see *ibid.*
"child"—see reg.2(1)(a).
"eligible child"—see *ibid.*
"responsible person"—see *ibid.*

Government contributions

7.13   7.—(1) The amounts of the contribution for the purposes of section 8(1) of the Act are set out in paragraphs (2) to (4), (the amounts set out in paragraphs (2) and (4)(a) to be known as the "initial contribution", and the amounts set out in paragraphs (3) and (4)(b) as the "special contribution").

(2) Where the child is an eligible child on the appointed day by virtue of section 2(1)(a) of the Act (by reason of a child benefit award), and—
  (i) was born after 31st August 2002 but before 6th April 2003, the amount is £277,
  (ii) was born between 6th April 2003 and 5th April 2004, the amount is £268, and
  (iii) was born between 6th April 2004 and the day preceding the appointed day, the amount is £256.

(3) Where the child is an eligible child on the appointed day by virtue of section 2(1)(b) of the Act (by reason of being a child in the care of a local authority at that date) and—
  (i) was born after 31st August 2002 but before 6th April 2003, the amount is £554,
  (ii) was born between 6th April 2003 and 5th April 2004, the amount is £536, and
  (iii) was born between 6th April 2004 and the day preceding the appointed day, the amount is £512.

(4) Where the child [[1]becomes an eligible child] on or after the appointed day and—
  (a) is first an eligible child by virtue of section 2(1)(a) of the Act, the amount is £250, and
  (b) is first an eligible child by virtue of section 2(1)(b) of the Act, the amount is £500.

(5) The amounts of the supplementary contribution for the purposes of section 9(2) of the Act (to be known as the "supplementary contribution") are set out in paragraphs (6) and (7).

(6) Where the child is an eligible child on the appointed day (and is a child to whom section 9 of the Act applies), the amount—

(a) if the commencement date was after 31st August 2002 but before 6th April 2003, is £266,

(b) if the commencement date was between 6th April 2003 and 5th April 2004, is £258,

(c) if the commencement date was between 6th April 2004 and the appointed day, is £250.

(7) Where the child becomes an eligible child after the appointed day (and is a child to whom section 9 of the Act applies), the amount is £250.

(8) The "commencement date", in relation to a child, means the first day for which child benefit was paid (under a decision mentioned in section 2(6) of the Act) in respect of the child, except that—

(a) where entitlement to child benefit is wholly excluded by a directly applicable Community provision, it means the date on which that exclusion took effect, and

(b) where the child was prevented from being an eligible child by virtue of section 2(5) of the Act, it means the date on which the child became an eligible child.

[¹(9) The Inland Revenue shall, following final determination of entitlement to child tax credit, write to the person who is entitled to child benefit in respect of the child (or, in the case of a child who is an eligible child because of section 2(3) of the Act, to a responsible person in relation to the child) to inform them that the supplementary contribution is being paid into the child's account.]

[²(10) A further contribution under section 10 of the Act of £250 is due for any child where—

(a) the commencement date (for child benefit: see paragraph (8)) in relation to that child is after 5th April 2005, and

(b) income support or income-based jobseeker's allowance was paid for that commencement date to a person whose applicable amount included an amount in respect of the child.

[³ (10A) A further contribution under section 10 of the Act of £250 is due for any child if—

(a) an account is held by the child,

(b) the child was first an eligible child by virtue of section 2(1)(a) of the Act,

(c) section 9 of the Act does not apply to the child,

(d) a contribution is not, and has not been, due for the child under paragraph (10),

(e) the child is an eligible child on the day identified under the provisions of paragraph (10B) or (10C) as the case may be, and

(f) the condition in paragraph (10B) or (10C) is satisfied in relation to the child.

(10B) The condition in this paragraph is that it has been determined in accordance with the provision made by and by virtue of sections 18 to 21 of the Tax Credits Act 2002—

(a) that a person was, or persons were, entitled to child tax credit in respect of the child for any day falling—

(i) after the commencement date, but

(ii) not later than three months immediately preceding the expiry date of the voucher for the child (see regulation 3), and

(b) that either the relevant income of the person or persons for the tax year in which that day fell does not exceed the income threshold or the person, or either of those persons, was entitled to a relevant social security benefit for that day,

and that determination has not been overturned.

(10C) The condition in this paragraph is that income support, or income-based jobseeker's allowance, was paid for any day falling—

(a) after the commencement date, but

(b) not later than one month immediately preceding the expiry date of the voucher for the child (see regulation 3),

to a person whose applicable amount included an amount in respect of the child.]

(11) On receipt of the further contribution [³ mentioned in paragraph (10) or (10A)] from the Inland Revenue the account provider must credit the account held by the child with the amount of the payment.]

AMENDMENTS

1. Child Trust Funds (Amendment) Regulations 2004 (SI 2004/2676), reg.5 (April 6, 2005).
2. Child Trust Funds (Amendment) Regulations 2005 (SI 2005/383), reg.3 (April 6, 2005).
3. Child Trust Funds (Amendment) Regulations 2009 (SI 2009/475), reg.4 (April 6, 2009, but have effect where the Child Benefit commencement date for the child (first day for which child benefit was paid in respect of the child) is on or after April 6, 2008).

DEFINITIONS

"account"—see reg.2(1)(b).
"account provider"—see *ibid.*
"appointed day"—see *ibid.*
"child"—see reg.2(1)(a).
"eligible child"—see *ibid.*
"responsible person"—see *ibid.*

[¹ **Age 7 payments**

7.14   **7A.**—(1) A further contribution under section 10 of the Act is due for any child who is an eligible child on his or her seventh birthday, in accordance with paragraphs (2) to (5).

(2) Where the child is an eligible child on his or her seventh birthday by virtue of—

(a) section 2(1)(b) of the Act (child benefit entitlement excluded by reason of being a child in care on that date), or

(b) section 2(1)(a) of the Act (child benefit entitlement), but is also a looked after child or looked after and accommodated child within the meanings of those expressions in regulation 33, on that date, the amount is £500.

(3) Where the child is an eligible child on his or her seventh birthday by virtue of section 2(1)(a) of the Act (by reason of a person being entitled to child benefit in respect of the child on that date) and does not fall within

776

the terms of paragraph (2), the amount is £250 and, if the condition in paragraph (4) or (5) is satisfied in relation to the child, the further amount of £250.

(4) The condition in this paragraph is that it has been determined in accordance with the provision made by and by virtue of sections 18 to 21 of the Tax Credits Act 2002—

(a) that a person was, or persons were, entitled to child tax credit in respect of the child for any date ("the CTC date") falling within the same tax year as the child's seventh birthday, and

(b) that either the relevant income of the person or persons for the tax year in which the CTC date fell does not exceed the income threshold or the person, or either of those persons, was entitled to a relevant social security benefit for the CTC date,

and that determination has not been overturned.

(5)) The condition in this paragraph is that income support, or income-based jobseeker's allowance, was paid for any date falling within the same tax year as the child's seventh birthday to a person whose applicable amount included an amount in respect of the child.

(6) On receipt of the further contribution from Her Majesty's Revenue and Customs the account provider must credit the account held by the child with the amount of the payment.]

AMENDMENT

1. Child Trust Funds (Amendment) Regulations 2009 (SI 2009/475), reg.5 (April 6, 2009).

GENERAL NOTE

This regulation provides for the top-up child trust fund Government payment to all eligible children when they reach the age of 7. The amount is a universal payment of £250 (para. (3)) with a further £250 for children in low income families (paras. (3), (4) and (5)). Children who are looked after by local authorities will automatically receive the higher £500 top-up payment (para. (2)).

7.15

PART 2

OTHER REQUIREMENTS TO BE SATISFIED IN RELATION TO ACCOUNTS

General requirements for accounts

8.—(1) An account must satisfy the requirements that—

(a) it is the account for a single child ("the named child");

(b) the named child is or has been an eligible child;

(c) no child may hold more than one account;

(d) at any time—

(i) where the named child is under 16, only a single responsible person in relation to the named child, or

(ii) where the named child is 16 or over, only the child,

("the registered contact") may give instructions to the account provider with respect to its management;

7.16

(e) the account must at all times be managed in accordance with these Regulations by an account provider and, subject to regulation 6(2), under terms agreed and recorded in a management agreement made between the account provider and the registered contact (on behalf of the named child where appropriate); and

(f) the management agreement must include instructions to the provider as to the manner in which Inland Revenue contributions and any subscriptions made are to be invested under the account.

(2) Apart from other requirements of these Regulations the terms so agreed shall include the conditions that—

(a) the account investments shall be in the beneficial ownership of the named child;

(b) the title to all account investments, except those falling within regulation 12(2)(k), (l) or (m), shall be vested in the account provider or his nominee, subject to sub-paragraph (f);

(c) where a share certificate or other document evidencing title to an account investment is issued, it shall be held by the account provider or as he may direct, subject to sub-paragraph (f);

(d) in relation to qualifying investments falling within regulation 12(2) (a), (b) and (f) to (j), the account provider shall, if the registered contact so elects (and subject to any charge for the arrangement), arrange for the registered contact to receive a copy of the annual report and accounts issued to investors by every company, unit trust, open-ended investment company or other entity in which account investments are held;

(e) in relation to qualifying investments falling within regulation 12(2) (a), (b) and (f) to (j), the account provider shall, if the registered contact so elects (subject to any charge for the arrangement, and to any provisions made under any enactment), be under an obligation to arrange for the registered contact to be able—

   (i) to attend any meetings of investors in companies, unit trusts, open-ended investment companies and other entities in which account investments are held,

   (ii) to vote, and

   (iii) to receive, in addition to the documents referred to in sub-paragraph (d), any other information issued to investors in such companies, unit trusts, open-ended investment companies and other entities;

(f) if and so long as a person falling within regulation 14(2)(d)(iv) acts as account provider of an account, and the account investments include a policy of life insurance—

   (i) the title to all such policies shall be vested in the registered contact, and

   (ii) where a policy document or other document evidencing title to such policies of life insurance is issued, it shall be held by the registered contact;

(g) the account provider shall satisfy himself that any person to whom he delegates any of his functions or responsibilities under the management agreement is competent to carry out those functions or responsibilities;

(h) on the instructions of the registered contact ("the transfer instructions") and within such time as is stipulated by the registered contact in the transfer instructions, the whole of an account, with all rights and obligations of the parties to it, shall be transferred free of expense (except any incidental expenses) to another account provider subject to and in accordance with regulation 21;

[[1](ha) where the account is or has been transferred to the account provider by a transfer under regulation 21, that no charges or expenses are due in respect of that transfer, except in accordance with sub-paragraph (h);]

(i) where the account provider offers accounts of another description or type, on the instructions of the registered contact ("the internal transfer instructions") and within such time as is stipulated by the registered contact in the internal transfer instructions, the account shall become (free of expense, except any incidental expenses) an account of that other description or type (any necessary change in the investments being made accordingly); and

(j) the account provider shall notify the registered contact if by reason of any failure to satisfy the provisions of these Regulations an account is or will become no longer exempt from tax by virtue of regulation 24.

(3) Where the transfer instructions or internal transfer instructions, or any new management agreement entered into by the registered contact with the account provider (or a new account provider) under regulation 8(1)(e), is a distance contract, the transfer or internal transfer shall only take effect once those contracts satisfy Condition 4 in regulation 5(1).

(4) The time stipulated in transfer instructions or internal transfer instructions shall be subject to any reasonable business period (not exceeding 30 days) of the account provider required for the practical implementation of the instructions.

(5) In this regulation, "incidental expenses" means stamp duty and other dealing costs of disposing of or acquiring investments.

AMENDMENT

1. Child Trust Funds (Amendment) Regulations 2004 (SI 2004/2676), reg.6 (April 6, 2005).

DEFINITIONS

"account"—see reg.2(1)(b).
"account investment"—see *ibid*.
"account provider"—see *ibid*.
"child"—see reg.2(1)(a).
"company"—see reg.2(1)(b).
"incidental expenses"—see reg.8(5).
"open-ended investment company"—see reg.2(1)(c).
"responsible person"—see reg.2(1)(a).
"subscriptions"—see reg.2(1)(b).
"tax"—see *ibid*.

Annual limit on subscriptions

9.—(1) Any person (including the child) may make subscriptions to a child's account, subject to paragraphs (2) and (3).

(2) Subscriptions to an account made during any subscription year, that is—

7.17

779

(a) the period beginning with the day on which the account is opened (or if opened before the appointed day, opened for the purpose of accepting subscriptions under regulation 5(2)(b)), and ending immediately before the child's next birthday, and

(b) any succeeding period of twelve months,

shall not in aggregate exceed the sum of £1,200.

(3) Where the aggregate of subscriptions in any year falls short of £1,200 or is nil, there shall be no addition to the amount for any succeeding year.

DEFINITIONS

"account"—see reg.2(1)(b).
"appointed day"—see *ibid.*
"child"—see reg.2(1)(a).
"subscriptions"—see reg.2(1)(b).

Statements for an account

7.18

10.—(1) The account provider must issue a statement for the account—

(a) annually, and

(b) where an account is transferred to another account provider under regulation 21, as at the transfer date.

(2) The statement date in the case of an annual statement must be—

(a) any date not more than [¹61] days before or after the named child's birthday, and

(b) not more than 12 months from the previous statement date.

(3) The statement shall be sent—

(a) where the named child is the registered contact, to the child,

(b) where a responsible person is the registered contact, to the named child care of the registered contact,

(c) where the Official Solicitor or Accountant of Court has been appointed under section 3(10) of the Act, to the Official Solicitor or Accountant of Court, on behalf of the child, and

(d) in any other case, to the named child,

within 30 days of the statement date.

(4) Statements shall include the following information—

(a) the full name of the child;

(b) his address;

(c) his date of birth;

(d) his unique reference number;

(e) the description of the account (see regulation 4);

(f) the name of the registered contact (if any);

(g) the statement date;

(h) the total market value of the investments under the account at the previous statement date (where the account provider held the account at the named child's previous birthday);

(i) the amount of any Government contributions [¹"(see regulation 7) received by the account provider], during the period between—

(i) the previous statement date referred to in paragraph (1)(a) or (b), or the opening of the account (whichever is the later), and

(ii) the statement date;

(j) the aggregate amount of subscriptions (if any) received during the period in sub-paragraph (i);

(k) the total amount of deductions (including management charges) made during the period in sub-paragraph (i);

(l) the total market value of the investments under the account at the statement date;

(m) the number or amount, description and market value of each of the investments under the account at the statement date;

(n) the basis used in calculating the market value of each investment under the account (together with a statement of any change from a basis used in the previous statement); and

(o) the exchange rate used where any investment is, or is denominated in, a currency other than sterling.

[[1](5) As an alternative to the information in paragraph (4)(k), the statement may include, in relation to any management charges or other incidental expenses deducted from the account during the period in paragraph (4)(i)—

(a) the rate, expressed as an annual percentage rate, at which, and the period in relation to which, such deductions were made, or

(b) where such deductions were made in relation to different periods at different rates—

    (i) each rate, expressed as an annual percentage rate, at which those deductions were made; and

    (ii) the period in relation to which they were made at that rate.]

AMENDMENT

1. Child Trust Funds (Amendment) Regulations 2004 (SI 2004/2676), reg.7 (April 6, 2005).

DEFINITIONS

"account"—see reg.2(1)(b).
"account provider"—see *ibid*.
"child"—see reg.2(1)(a).
"investments under the account"—see reg.2(1)(b).
"market value"—see *ibid*.
"responsible person"—see reg.2(1)(a).
"subscriptions"—see reg.2(1)(b).

General investment rules

11.—(1) All transactions by way of purchase by an account provider of investments under an account shall be made—

(a) in the case of an authorised fund which is a dual priced unit trust, at the manager's price for the sale of the relevant class of units within the meaning of, and complying with the requirements of, rule 15.4.4 of the Collective Investment Schemes Sourcebook;

(b) in the case of an authorised fund which is a single priced unit trust or an open-ended investment company, at the price of a unit or share within the meaning of, and complying with the requirements of, rule 4.3.11 of the Collective Investment Schemes Sourcebook; and

(c) in the case of all other account investments, at the price for which those investments might reasonably be expected to be purchased in the open market.

(2) In paragraph (1)—

7.19

"a dual priced unit trust" means an authorised unit trust in respect of which the manager gives different prices for buying and selling units at the same time;

"a single priced unit trust" means an authorised unit trust in respect of which the manager gives the same price for buying and selling units at the same time.

(3) All other transactions by way of sale or otherwise by an account provider in investments under an account shall be made at the price for which those investments might reasonably be expected to be sold or otherwise transacted, as the case may be, in the open market.

(4) Investments, or rights in respect of investments, may not at any time—

(a) be purchased or made otherwise than out of cash which an account provider holds under an account at that time; or

(b) be purchased from—

    (i) the named child, or

    (ii) the spouse [3or civil partner] of the named child,

so as to become account investments under the account.

(5) Subject to paragraph (6), contributions, subscriptions and any other cash held by an account provider under an account shall be held only in sterling and be deposited in an account with a deposit-taker [1(including for this purpose a credit union)], or a deposit account or a share account with a building society, which is designated as a CTF account for the purposes of these Regulations only.

(6) An account provider who is a European institution, a relevant authorised person or an assurance undertaking may hold an account investor's cash subscription and other cash held under an account in the currency of the EEA State in which he has his principal place of business and may deposit such cash in an account, which is designated as mentioned in paragraph (5), with any person authorised under the law of that State to accept deposits.

AMENDMENTS

1. Child Trust Funds (Amendment No.2) Regulations 2005 (SI 2005/909), reg.4 (April 6, 2005).

2. Civil Partnership Act 2004 (Tax Credits, etc.) (Consequential Amendments) Order 2005 (SI 2005/2919), art.15 (December 5, 2006).

DEFINITIONS

"account"—see reg.2(1)(b).

"account investment"—see *ibid*.

"account provider"—see *ibid*.

"assurance undertaking"—see *ibid*.

"authorised fund"—see reg.2(1)(c).

"building society"—see reg.2(1)(b).

"child"—see reg.2(1)(a).

"Collective Investment Schemes Sourcebook"—see reg.2(1)(c).

"credit union"—see reg.2(1)(b).

"deposit taker"—see *ibid*.

"dual priced unit trust"—see reg.11(2).

"EEA State"—see reg.2(1)(b).

"European institution"—see *ibid*.

"investments under the account"—see *ibid*.

"open-ended investment company"—see reg.2(1)(c).
"relevant authorised person"—see reg.2(1)(b).
"single priced unit trust"—see reg.11(2).
"subscriptions"—see reg.2(1)(b).
"units"—see reg.2(1)(c).

Qualifying investments for an account

12.—(1) This regulation specifies the kind of investments ("qualifying   7.20
investments for an account") which may be purchased, made or held under
an account.

(2) Qualifying investments for an account to which paragraph (1) refers
are—

(a) shares, not being shares in an investment trust, issued by a company
wherever incorporated and officially listed on a recognised stock
exchange (see paragraph (3));

(b) securities—
(i) issued by a company wherever incorporated,
(ii) which satisfy at least one of the conditions specified in paragraph (5), and
(iii) in the case of securities of an investment trust, purchased or
acquired by the account provider in circumstances where the
investment trust satisfies the condition specified in paragraph
(6);

(c) gilt-edged securities;

(d) any securities issued by or on behalf of a government of any EEA
State;

(e) any securities which, in relation to a security mentioned in
sub-paragraph (d), would be a strip of that security if "strip" had
the same meaning as in section 47 of the Finance Act 1942, with the
omission of the words "issued under the National Loans Act 1968";

(f) shares in an investment trust, listed in the Official List of the Stock
Exchange (see paragraph (3)), in circumstances where the trust satisfies the condition specified in paragraph (6);

(g) units in, or shares of, a securities scheme, warrant scheme or fund of
funds scheme;

(h) units in, or shares of, a money market scheme;

(i) units in, or shares of, a UCITS;

(j) a depositary interest;

(k) cash deposited in a deposit account with a building society, or a
person falling within section 840A(1)(b) of the Taxes Act [²(including
for this purpose a credit union)] or a relevant European institution,
subject to paragraph (8);

(l) cash deposited in a share account with a building society, subject to
paragraph (8);

(m) policies of life insurance which satisfy the conditions specified in
paragraphs (9) and (10);

(n) any securities issued under the National Loans Act 1968—
(i) for the purpose of or in connection with raising money under
the auspices of the Director of Savings within the meaning of
section 11(1)(a) of the National Debt Act 1972, and
(ii) other than national savings certificates, premium savings bonds,
national savings stamps and national savings gift tokens,

which, according to the terms and conditions subject to which they are issued and purchased, are expressly permitted to be held under an account.

[³(o) arrangements falling within section 47 of the Finance Act 2005 (alternative finance arrangements) under which the person referred to in that section as Y is a financial institution;

(p) arrangements falling within section 49 of that Act;

(q) qualifying units in or shares of a non-UCITS retail scheme.]

(3) An investment in shares fulfils the condition as to official listing in paragraph (2)(a) or (f) if—

(a) in pursuance of a public offer, the account provider applies for the allotment or allocation to him of shares in a company or investment trust which are due to be admitted to such listing within 30 days of the allocation or allotment, and which, when admitted to such listing, would be qualifying investments for an account, and

(b) the shares are not allotted or allocated to the account provider in the circumstances specified in paragraph (4).

(4) The circumstances specified in this paragraph are where—

(a) the allotment or allocation of the shares was connected with the allotment or allocation of—

   (i) shares in the company or investment trust of a different class, or

   (ii) rights to shares in the company or investment trust of a different class, or

   (iii) shares or rights to shares in another company or investment trust, or

   (iv) units in or shares in, or rights to units in or shares in, an authorised fund or a part of an umbrella scheme, or

   (v) securities or rights to securities of the company or investment trust, or of another company or investment trust,

to the account provider, the registered contact or any other person; and

(b) the terms on which the first-mentioned shares in this paragraph were offered were significantly more favourable to the account provider or the named child than they would have been if their allotment or allocation had not been connected as described in sub-paragraph (a).

(5) The conditions specified in this paragraph are—

(a) that the shares in the company issuing the securities are listed on the official list of a recognised stock exchange;

(b) that the securities are so listed;

(c) that the company issuing the securities is a 75 per cent subsidiary of a company whose shares are so listed.

(6) The condition specified in this paragraph is that the investment trust has no eligible rental income, in its most recent accounting period to end before the date on which the shares in, or securities of, the investment trust first become investments under the account, provided that the shares or securities shall cease to be qualifying investments for an account if the investment trust has any eligible rental income, in subsequent accounting periods, during which the shares or securities are held.

(7) In paragraph (4)(a), "company" means any body corporate having a share capital.

(8) A deposit account or share account which is a qualifying investment for an account falling within paragraph (2)(k) or (l) must not be

connected with any other investment, held by the named child or any other person, and for this purpose such an account is connected with an investment if—

    (a) either was opened or acquired with reference to the other, or with a view to enabling the other to be opened or acquired on particular terms, or with a view to facilitating the opening or acquisition of the other on particular terms, and

    (b) the terms on which the account was opened would have been significantly less favourable to the holder if the investment had not been acquired.

(9) The conditions specified in this paragraph are that—

    (a) the insurance is on the life of the named child only;

    (b) the terms and conditions of the policy provide—

        (i) that the policy may only be owned or held as a qualifying investment for an account which satisfies the provisions of these Regulations;

        (ii) that the policy shall automatically terminate if it comes to the notice of the account provider, in any manner, that the event specified in paragraph (11) has occurred in relation to the policy;

        (iii) for an express prohibition of any payment of the proceeds from the termination of the policy or a partial surrender of the rights conferred by the policy, to the named child (while he is still a child) [[1]except in accordance with regulation 18A (terminal illness)]; and

        (iv) that the policy, the rights conferred by the policy and any share or interest in the policy or rights respectively, shall not be capable of assignment or (in Scotland) assignation, other than that they may be vested in the named child's personal representatives, and that the title to the policy may be transferred to a new account provider subject to and in accordance with regulations 8(2)(f) and 21;

    (c) the policy evidences or secures a contract of insurance which—

        (i) falls within paragraph 1 or 3 of Part 2 of Schedule 1 to the Financial Services and Markets Act 2000 (Regulated Activities) Order 2001, or

        (ii) would fall within either of those paragraphs if the insurer were a company with permission under Part 4 of the Financial Services and Markets Act 2000 to effect or carry out contracts of insurance;

    (d) the policy is not—

        (i) a contract to pay an annuity on human life,

        (ii) a personal portfolio bond within the meaning given by regulation 2(1) of the Personal Portfolio Bonds (Tax) Regulations 1999, or

        (iii) a contract, the effecting and carrying out of which constitutes "pension business" within the meaning given by section 431B(1) of the Taxes Act; and

    (e) after the first payment in respect of a premium in relation to the policy has been made, there is no contractual obligation on any person to make any other such payment.

(10) The condition specified in this paragraph is that no sum may at any time, at or after the making of the insurance, be lent to or at the direction of

the named child or registered contact by or by arrangement with the insurer for the time being responsible for the obligations under the policy.

(11) The event specified in this paragraph is that—

(a) there has been a breach of any of the conditions in paragraph (9) or (10), or any of those conditions was not satisfied at the date on which the insurance was made; and

(b) the breach or non-compliance cannot be remedied in accordance with regulation 23, or (in any other case), has not been remedied within a reasonable time.

(12) Where the event specified in paragraph (11) occurs in relation to a policy, the policy shall nevertheless be treated, for the purposes of these Regulations, excepting paragraphs (9)(b)(ii) and (11), and regulations 37(6) and 38, as if it had satisfied the conditions in paragraphs (9) and (10) during the period—

(a) commencing at the time when that specified event occurred, and

(b) ending immediately before—

(i) the end of the final year in relation to the policy, within the meaning in section 546(4) of the Taxes Act, or

(ii) the time at which that specified event came to the notice of the account provider,

whichever first occurs (the "termination event").

AMENDMENTS

1. Child Trust Funds (Amendment) Regulations 2004 (SI 2004/2676), reg.8 (April 6, 2005).

2. Child Trust Funds (Amendment No.2) Regulations 2005 (SI 2005/909), reg.5 (April 6, 2005).

3. Child Trust Funds (Amendment No.3) Regulations 2005 (SI 2005/3349), reg.5 (December 27, 2005).

DEFINITIONS

"account"—see reg.2(1)(b).
"account provider"—see *ibid.*
"authorised fund"—see reg.2(1)(c).
"building society"—see reg.2(1)(b).
"child"—see reg.2(1)(a).
"company"—see regs.2(1)(b) and 12(7).
"credit union"—see reg.2(1)(b).
"depositary interest"—see reg.2(1)(c).
"EEA State"—see reg.2(1)(b).
"European institution"—see *ibid.*
"fund of funds scheme"—see reg.2(1)(c).
"gilt-edged securities"—see reg.2(1)(b).
"investments under the account"—see *ibid.*
"investment trust"—see *ibid.*
"money market scheme"—see reg.2(1)(c).
"recognised stock exchange"—see reg.2(1)(b).
"relevant European institution"—see *ibid.*
"securities scheme"—see reg.2(1)(c).
"security"—see reg.2(1)(b).
"the Taxes Act"—see *ibid.*
"UCITS"—see reg.2(1)(c).
"umbrella scheme"—see *ibid.*

"units"—see *ibid.*
"warrant scheme"—see *ibid.*
"year"—see reg.2(1)(b).

Conditions for application by responsible person or the child to open an account (and changes to an account)

13.—(1) An application by a responsible person in relation to a child   7.21
or the child if 16 or over, as the case may be, ("the applicant") to open an
account for the child with an account provider must be made to the account
provider in a statement which must satisfy the conditions specified in paragraphs (2) to (6).

(2) An application must specify the description of account applied for.

(3) An application must incorporate a declaration by the applicant
that he—

(a) is aged 16 years of age or over,

(b) is—

    (i) (where the child is under 16) a responsible person in relation
to the named child (that is, that he has parental responsibility
[¹or, in Scotland, parental responsibilities] in relation to the
child), or

    (ii) the child if 16 or over, and

(c) is to be the registered contact for the account;

and where the application is not in writing, must authorise the account provider to record the terms of the declaration in a written declaration made
on behalf of the applicant.

(4) The applicant must authorise the account provider (on behalf of the
named child where appropriate)—

(a) to hold the child's Inland Revenue contributions, subscriptions,
account investments, interest, dividends and any other rights or proceeds in respect of those investments and cash, and

(b) to make on his behalf any claims to relief from tax in respect of
account investments,

and the authority must continue until a further application and declaration
is made in accordance with paragraph (10).

(5) An application must contain—

(a) the applicant's full name,

(b) his address, including postcode,

(c) the named child's full name [¹and date of birth],

(d) his address, including postcode, and

(e) the child's unique reference number on the voucher.

(6) There may be only one declaration and authorisation under
paragraphs (3) to (5) in force for an account at any time.

(7) Except in the case—

(a) of the death or incapacity of the registered contact,

(b) where the registered contact cannot be contacted,

(c) of the bringing to an end of a Court order, under which he is a
responsible person for the named child,

(d) of the named child attaining the age of 16 years,

(e) where the Official Solicitor or Accountant of Court is appointed
under section 3(10) of the Act, or

(f) where a Court so orders,

any change in the identity of the registered contact shall require confirmation by the current registered contact that his declaration and authorisation under paragraphs (3)(c) and (4) is cancelled.

(8) An account provider must decline to accept an application if he has reason to believe that—

    (a) the voucher has expired, or is not or might not be genuine, or

    (b) the applicant has given untrue information in his application.

(9) Where the application is not in writing, the account provider shall make the written declaration referred to in paragraph (3), and notify the applicant of its contents, and such declaration shall take effect from the date on which the applicant agrees the contents (subject to any corrections), and if he neither agrees or disagrees with the contents within 30 days, he shall be treated as having agreed them.

(10) Where—

    (a) there is a change in the identity of the registered contact, the new registered contact, or

    (b) an account has been opened by the Inland Revenue under regulation 6 (Revenue allocated accounts) and a responsible person in relation to the child (or the child, if 16 or over) subsequently applies to the account provider to be the registered contact for the account, he,

shall make the application and declaration required by paragraphs (3) to (5).

[[1](11) Where the new registered contact is the Official Solicitor or the Accountant of Court, he shall make the declaration and authorisation required by paragraphs (3)(c) and (4) [[2]and shall be treated as a party to the existing management agreement for the account in question].]

AMENDMENTS

1. Child Trust Funds (Amendment) Regulations 2004 (SI 2004/2676), reg.9 (April 6, 2005).

2. Child Trust Funds (Amendment No.2) Regulations 2004 (SI 2004/3382), reg.3 (April 6, 2005).

DEFINITIONS

"account"—see reg.2(1)(b).
"account investment"—see *ibid*.
"account provider"—see *ibid*.
"child"—see reg.2(1)(a).
"parental responsibility"—see *ibid*.
"responsible person"—see *ibid*.
"subscriptions"—see reg.2(1)(b).
"tax"—see *ibid*.

Account provider—qualifications and Board's approval

7.22   **14.**—(1) This regulation specifies the circumstances ("qualifying circumstances") in which a person may be approved by the Board as an account provider.

(2) The qualifying circumstances are the following—

    (a) the person must make an application to the Board for approval in a form specified by the Board;

    (b) the person must undertake with the Board—

    (i) to either offer stakeholder accounts to the general public (whether or not accounts of another description are offered), or to fulfil the requirements in paragraph (3),

    (ii) to accept vouchers from any responsible person or the child if 16 or over (subject to [²paragraph (iia) and] regulation 13(8)),

[³(iia) in the case of a credit union, to accept vouchers from any responsible person or the child if 16 or over, if the child to which the voucher relates is a member, or fulfils or is treated as fulfilling a qualification for admission to membership, of the credit union (subject to regulation 13(8))]

    (iii) where the person accepts Revenue allocated accounts, to allow instructions for their management to be made or given by post (whether or not other methods are allowed),

    (iv) to publicise (and up-date where appropriate) statements of the minimum amount which may be subscribed to an account on a single occasion, and the permitted means of payment of subscriptions,

    (v) to inform persons proposing to make subscriptions to an account (other than the named child) that the subscription is a gift to the child,

    (vi) to publicise (and up-date where appropriate) statements of the extent to which social, environmental or ethical decisions are taken into account in selecting, retaining or realising investments,

    (vii) that a child's unique reference number shall only be used for the purposes of the child's account (and of fulfilling the requirements of these Regulations with regard to that account), and

    (viii) that whether there is an initial contribution or special contribution to an account, whether there is a supplementary contribution to the account, and whether the account is a Revenue allocated account is information held for the purposes mentioned in paragraph (vii) only, and shall not be used for other purposes (including marketing other products);

(c) the person must demonstrate to the satisfaction of the Board that the person can correctly operate the procedures in regulation 30;

(d) an account provider must be—

    (i) an authorised person within the meaning of section 31(1)(a) or (c) of, or Schedule 5 to, the Financial Services and Markets Act 2000, who has permission to carry on one or more of the activities specified in Articles 14, 21, 25, 37, 40, 45, 51, 53 and (in so far as it applies to any of those activities) 64 of the Financial Services and Markets Act 2000 (Regulated Activities) Order 2001, but excluding any person falling within paragraph (iv) below;

[⁴[⁵(iia) in the case of a credit union, an authorised person within the meaning of section 31(1)(a) of the Financial Services and Markets Act 2000, who has permission to carry on one or more of the activities specified in Article 5 of the Financial Services and Markets Act 2000 (Regulated Activities) Order 2001;]

    (ii) a European institution which carries on one or more of those activities;

    (iii) a building society, a person falling within section 840A(1)(b) of the Taxes Act or a relevant European institution; or

(iv) an insurance company within the meaning given by section 431(2) of the Taxes Act, an incorporated friendly society or a registered friendly society, or any other assurance undertaking;

(e) an account provider must not be prevented from acting as such by any requirement imposed under section 43 of the Financial Services and Markets Act 2000, or by any prohibition imposed by or under any rules made by the Financial Services Authority under that Act; and

(f) an account provider who—

(i) is a European institution or a relevant authorised person and who does not have a branch or business establishment in the United Kingdom, or has such a branch or business establishment but does not intend to carry out all his functions as an account provider at that branch or business establishment, or

(ii) falls within the expression "any other assurance undertaking" in sub-paragraph (d)(iv),

must fulfil one of the three requirements specified in regulation 15.

(3) The requirements in this paragraph are that the person provides to any potential applicant for a child trust fund ([¹before commencement of completion of] any application under regulation 13)—

(a) a statement that a stakeholder account is available from a named alternative account provider who offers it on the terms in paragraph (2)(b)(i) (omitting the words from ", or to" to the end);

(b) a detailed description of that stakeholder account; and

(c) sufficient information (according to the method of communication used, and including documentation where appropriate) to put the potential applicant in the position to make an application to that alternative account provider, complying with regulation 13.

(4) The terms of the Board's approval may include conditions designed to ensure that the provisions of these Regulations are satisfied.

AMENDMENTS

1. Child Trust Funds (Amendment) Regulations 2004 (SI 2004/2676), reg.10 (April 6, 2005).

2. Child Trust Funds (Amendment No.2) Regulations 2005 (SI 2005/909), reg.6 (April 6, 2005).

3. Child Trust Funds (Amendment No.2) Regulations 2005 (SI 2005/909), reg.7 (April 6, 2005).

4. Child Trust Funds (Amendment No.2) Regulations 2005 (SI 2005/909), reg.8 (April 6, 2005).

5. Child Trust Funds (Amendment No.3) Regulations 2005 (SI 2005/3349), reg.6 (December 27, 2005).

DEFINITIONS

"account"—see reg.2(1)(b).
"account provider"—see *ibid.*
"applicant"—see reg.5.
"assurance undertaking"—see reg.2(1)(b).
"building society"—see *ibid.*
"child"—see reg.2(1)(a).
"child trust fund"—see *ibid.*
"company"—see reg.2(1)(b).
"credit union"—see *ibid.*

"European institution"—see *ibid.*
"incorporated friendly society"—see *ibid.*
"registered friendly society"—see *ibid.*
"relevant authorised person"—see *ibid.*
"relevant European institution"—see *ibid.*
"responsible person"—see reg.2(1)(a).
"subscriptions"—see reg.2(1)(b).
"the Taxes Act"—see *ibid.*

Account provider—appointment of tax representative

15.—(1) This regulation specifies the requirements mentioned in regulation 14(2)(f).

7.23

(2) The first requirement specified in this regulation is that—

(a) a person who falls within subsection (5) of section 333A of the Taxes Act is for the time being appointed by the account provider to be responsible for securing the discharge of the duties prescribed by paragraph (5) which fall to be discharged by the account provider, and

(b) his identity and the fact of his appointment have been notified to the Board by the account provider.

(3) The second requirement specified in this regulation is that there are for the time being other arrangements with the Board for a person other than the account provider to secure the discharge of such duties.

(4) The third requirement specified in this regulation is that there are for the time being other arrangements with the Board designed to secure the discharge of such duties.

(5) The duties prescribed by this paragraph are those that fall to be discharged by an account provider under these Regulations.

(6) The appointment of a person in pursuance of the first requirement shall be treated as terminated in circumstances where—

(a) the Board have reason to believe that the person concerned—

   (i) has failed to secure the discharge of any of the duties prescribed by paragraph (5), or

   (ii) does not have adequate resources to discharge those duties, and

(b) the Board have notified the account provider and that person that they propose to treat his appointment as having terminated with effect from the date specified in the notice.

(7) Where, in accordance with the first requirement, a person is at any time responsible for securing the discharge of duties, the person concerned—

(a) shall be entitled to act on the account provider's behalf for any of the purposes of the provisions relating to the duties;

(b) shall secure (where appropriate by acting on the account provider's behalf) the account provider's compliance with and discharge of the duties; and

(c) shall be personally liable in respect of any failure of the account provider to comply with or discharge any such duty as if the duties imposed on the account provider were imposed jointly and severally on the account provider and the person concerned.

DEFINITIONS

"account provider"—see reg.2(1)(b).
"notice"—see *ibid.*
"the Taxes Act"—see *ibid.*

Account provider—withdrawal by Board of approval

7.24   **16.**—(1) This regulation specifies the circumstances ("the disqualifying circumstances") in which the Board may by notice withdraw their approval of a person as an account provider in relation to an account.

(2) The disqualifying circumstances are that the Board have reason to believe—

(a) that any provision of the Act or these Regulations, or any term of an undertaking given in accordance with regulation 14(2)(b) or condition under regulation 14(4), is not or at any time has not been satisfied, either in respect of account managed by the account provider or otherwise; or

(b) that a person to whom they have given approval to act as an account provider is not qualified so to act.

(3) The notice to which paragraph (1) refers shall specify—

(a) the date from which the Board's approval is withdrawn; and

(b) the disqualifying circumstances.

DEFINITIONS

"account"—see reg.2(1)(b).
"account provider"—see *ibid.*
"notice"—see *ibid.*

Account provider—appeal against non-approval or withdrawal of Board's approval

7.25   **17.** A person who has been notified of a decision by the Board not to approve that person as an account provider, or an account provider to whom notice of withdrawal of approval has been given under regulation 16, may appeal against the decision by notice given to the Board within 30 days after the date of the notification or notice.

DEFINITIONS

"account provider"—see reg.2(1)(b).
"notice"—see *ibid.*

Permitted withdrawals from an account

7.26   **18.** Withdrawals from an account before the date on which the named child attains the age of 18 years may only be made—

(a) by the account provider, to settle any management charges and other incidental expenses, which are due by or under the management agreement, or

[¹(ab) in accordance with regulation 18A, or]

(b) where the account provider is satisfied that the named child has died under that age.

AMENDMENT

1. Child Trust Funds (Amendment) Regulations 2004 (SI 2004/2676), reg.11 (April 6, 2005).

DEFINITIONS

"account"—see reg.2(1)(b).
"account provider"—see *ibid.*
"child"—see reg.2(1)(a).

[¹Permitted withdrawals from an account where the child is terminally ill

18A.—(1) A person with parental responsibility (or, in Scotland, parental responsibilities) for the named child (including a local authority, but excluding a person under 16), or the named child if 16 or over, may make a claim to the Board, for withdrawals from an account to be permitted in accordance with this regulation.

7.27

(2) The claim shall be—

(a) made in a manner prescribed by the Board, which shall include the giving of any consent necessary for the verification or consideration of the claim, and

(b) accepted in either of the following cases:

Case 1

The child has been, or is, accepted by the Department for Work and Pensions as falling within section 72(5) of the Social Security Contributions and Benefits Act 1992 (special rules for terminally ill person's entitlement to care component of disability living allowance).

Case 2

Evidence that the named child is terminally ill has been supplied to the satisfaction of the Board.

(3) The Board shall issue a letter to the claimant authorising withdrawals from the account under this regulation, and shall also notify the account provider.

(4) Once a claim has been accepted, withdrawals may be made by the registered contact (on behalf of the named child, where he is not the child) at any time—

(a) provided that, immediately following any withdrawal, a balance sufficient to keep the account open is maintained in the account, and

(b) excepting any transfer of a policy of life insurance (as opposed to the proceeds from such a policy).

(5) Where account investments are withdrawn in a form other than sterling currency, regulation 36(1)(b) shall apply (with any necessary modifications) to any such investment immediately before it is withdrawn.

(6) In this regulation, "terminally ill" has the meaning in section 66(2)(a) of the Social Security Contributions and Benefits Act 1992.]

AMENDMENT

1. Child Trust Funds (Amendment) Regulations 2004 (SI 2004/2676), reg.12 (April 6, 2005).

DEFINITIONS

"account"—see reg.2(1)(b).
"account investment"—see *ibid.*
"account provider"—see *ibid.*
"child"—see reg.2(1)(a).
"parental responsibility"—see *ibid.*

Account provider ceasing to act (or ceasing to accept Revenue allocated accounts)

7.28   **19.**—(1) A person shall give notice to the Board and to the registered contact of the account which he manages (or, if there is no registered contact, the named child) of his intention to cease to act as the account provider not less than 30 days before he so ceases so that his obligations to the Board under the account can be conveniently discharged at or about the time he ceases so to act, and the notice to the registered contact or the named child shall inform him of the right to transfer the account under regulation 21, and of his rights under regulation 20(3).

(2) A person shall also give notice to the Board of his intention to cease to accept further Revenue allocated accounts under regulation 6, not less than 30 days before he so ceases.

DEFINITIONS

"account"—see reg.2(1)(b).
"account provider"—see *ibid*.
"child"—see reg.2(1)(a).
"notice"—see reg.2(1)(b).

Account provider ceasing to qualify

7.29   **20.**—(1) A person shall cease to qualify as an account provider and shall notify the Board within 30 days of the relevant event in sub-paragraphs (a) to (f), of that relevant event, where—
   (a) the person no longer fulfils the conditions of regulation 14;
   (b) in the case of an individual, he becomes bankrupt, or the subject of a bankruptcy restrictions order or an interim bankruptcy restrictions order or, in Scotland, his estate is sequestrated;
   (c) he makes any arrangement or composition with his creditors generally;
   (d) in the case of a company, a resolution has been passed or a petition has been presented to wind it up;
   (e) in the case of a building society, a person falling within section 840A(1)(b) of the Taxes Act or a relevant European institution—
       (i) it ceases to be a building society or to fall within section 840A(1)(b) of the Taxes Act or to be a relevant European institution, as the case may be;
       (ii) its directors have made a proposal under Part 1 of the Insolvency Act 1986 for a composition in satisfaction of its debts or a scheme of arrangement of its affairs; or
       (iii) a receiver or manager of its property has been appointed; or
   (f) in the case of a European institution, a relevant authorised person or an assurance undertaking which falls within regulation 14(2)(d)(iv), action corresponding to any described in sub-paragraph (b) to (e) has been taken by or in relation to the institution, person or undertaking under the law of an EEA State.

(2) On giving the notice referred to in paragraph (1), the person shall also notify the registered contact (or, if there is no registered contact, the named child) of the right to transfer the account under regulation 21, and the notice shall inform the recipient of the rights under paragraph (3).

(3) Where a registered contact—

(a) receives a notice under paragraph (2), or regulation 19(1), and

(b) within 30 days of the sending of the notice, transfers the account to another account provider pursuant to regulation 21,

the period between the transferor ceasing to act or qualify as an account provider, and the transfer to the transferee, shall be ignored in determining whether the account has at all times been managed by an account provider.

DEFINITIONS

"account"—see reg.2(1)(b).
"account provider"—see *ibid*.
"assurance undertaking"—see *ibid*.
"building society"—see *ibid*.
"child"—see reg.2(1)(a).
"company"—see reg.2(1)(b).
"EEA State"—see *ibid*.
"European institution"—see *ibid*.
"notice"—see *ibid*.
"relevant authorised person"—see *ibid*.
"relevant European institution"—see *ibid*.
"the Taxes Act"—see *ibid*.

Transfer of accounts to other account providers

21.—(1) Where—   7.30

(a) arrangements are made by a registered contact to transfer the whole of the investments under an account from one account provider ("the transferor") to another account provider ("the transferee"), or

(b) the whole of the investments under an account are so transferred in consequence of an account provider ("the transferor") ceasing to act or to qualify as an account provider,

the transfer shall be treated as a transfer of the account.

(2) The account and its description under regulation 4 shall not be affected for the purposes of these Regulations by reason of the transfer, save that, where the registered contact specifies in accordance with paragraph (3)(a) an account of a different description, the account shall, on the transfer, become an account of that other description.

(3) The registered contact shall make—

(a) the application required by regulation 13(2) (modified as if the words "applied for" were replaced with [¹ following the transfer]), and

(b) the application and declaration required by regulation 13(3) to (5), to the transferee.

[¹(3A) Where a registered contact applies in accordance with paragraph (3) to a potential transferee for a transfer under this regulation, specifying a stakeholder account offered by the transferee, the transferee shall not decline to accept that application (or the transfer in consequence of it) except where—

(a) the transferee has reason to believe that the registered contact has given untrue information in his application;

(b) the transferee demonstrates to the satisfaction of the Board that acceptance of transfers, or a class of transfers, during a particular period would jeopardise his ability to prevent any of the matters mentioned in regulation 16(2)(a); or

(c) the transferor does not give the transferee the notice in accordance with paragraph (4).]

(4) The transferor shall on the date of the transfer give the transferee a notice containing the information specified in paragraph (5) and the declaration specified in paragraph (6).

(5) The information specified in this paragraph is—

(a) as regards the named child—
    (i) his full name,
    (ii) his date of birth,
    (iii) his unique reference number;

(b) as regards the account—
    (i) the description of the account,
    (ii) the date of the transfer,
    (iii) the total amount subscribed to the account during the period from the beginning of the subscription year in which the transfer takes place to the date of the transfer,
    (iv) any amount which has been claimed from the Board under regulations 26, 27 or 30 and which has not been paid at the date of the transfer;

(c) the full name and address, including postcode, of the registered contact who has made the transfer arrangements.

(6) The declaration specified in this paragraph is a declaration by the transferor that—

(a) he has fulfilled all his obligations to the named child, the Board or otherwise, which are imposed by these Regulations;

(b) he has transferred to the transferee or his nominee all the account investments and that, where registration of any such transfer is required, he has taken the necessary steps to ensure that those account investments can be registered in the name of the transferee or nominee;

(c) he will forward any further payment received in respect of those account investments to the transferee, on receipt of the payment, and

(d) the information contained in the notice is correct.

AMENDMENT

1. Child Trust Funds (Amendment) Regulations 2004 (SI 2004/2676), reg.13 (April 6, 2005).

DEFINITIONS

"account"—see reg.2(1)(b).
"account investment"—see *ibid*.
"account provider"—see *ibid*.
"child"—see reg.2(1)(a).
"eligible child"—see *ibid*.
"notice"—see reg.2(1)(b).

Recoupment of Inland Revenue contributions to void accounts (and other accounts)

7.31   **22.**—(1) Where—

(a) the named child has never been an eligible child (see regulation 8(1)(b)), or

(b) there is a breach of regulation 8(1)(c) in relation to an account, the account is void, and the persons mentioned in paragraph (3) shall account to the Inland Revenue for Inland Revenue contributions paid in respect of the account, together with income and gains which have arisen in consequence of the crediting of any of those payments to the account.

(2) Where—

(a) the condition in section 9(5) of the Act [² or regulation 7(10B) or 7A(4)] was satisfied in relation to a child, but the determination under sections 18 to 21 of the Tax Credits Act 2002 has been over-turned, or

(b) the condition in section 9(8) of the Act was satisfied in relation to a child, but it has subsequently been determined that payment of the relevant benefit or tax credit mentioned in that subsection should not have been made, or that the applicable amount or tax credit should not have included an amount or credit in respect of the child, [¹or

(c) the requirements of regulation 7(10) [², or the condition in regulation 7(10C) or 7A(5) was,] were satisfied in relation to a child, but it has subsequently been determined that payment of the relevant benefit mentioned in [² the relevant provision] should not have been made, or that the applicable amount should not have included an amount in respect of that child,]

the persons mentioned in paragraph (3) shall account to the Inland Revenue for any supplementary contribution [¹, or further contribution, as the case may be,] paid in respect of the account, together with income and gains which have arisen in consequence of the crediting of any such payment to the account.

(3) The persons mentioned in paragraphs (1) and (2) are—

(a) the account provider (to the extent that he has assets in his posses-sion or control),

(b) the registered contact,

(c) the named child, and

(d) any person in whom the Inland Revenue contributions, income or gains, or any property directly or indirectly representing any of them, is vested (whether beneficially or otherwise)

and they shall be jointly and severally liable.

(4) Where a person accountable under this regulation is notified by the Inland Revenue that an amount is due from him under it, that amount shall be treated for the purposes of Part 6 of the Management Act (collection and recovery) as if it were tax charged in an assessment on that person, and due and payable.

AMENDMENTS

1. Child Trust Funds (Amendment) Regulations 2005 (SI 2005/383), reg.4 (April 6, 2005).
2. Child Trust Funds (Amendment) Regulations 2009 (SI 2009/475), reg.6 (April 6, 2009).

DEFINITIONS

"account"—see reg.2(1)(b).
"account provider"—see *ibid*.
"child"—see reg.2(1)(a).
"eligible child"—see *ibid*.

"the Management Act"—see reg.2(1)(b).
"tax"—see *ibid.*

"Repair" of invalid accounts

7.32   **23.**—(1) Except in the case of a breach of regulation 8(1)(b) or (c) (where no repair of an account is possible), it is an overriding requirement to be satisfied in relation to an account that the account provider and registered contact, as the case may be, take any steps necessary to remedy any breach of these Regulations.

(2) Where a breach is remedied as mentioned in paragraph (1), the account shall, to the extent of that breach, be treated as having been a valid account at all times, except for determining whether there has been a breach of these Regulations for the purposes of section 20 of the Act (penalties).

DEFINITIONS

"account"—see reg.2(1)(b).
"account provider"—see *ibid.*

PART 3

TAX AND ADMINISTRATION OF ACCOUNTS

Exemption from tax of account income and gains

7.33   **24.** Subject to compliance with these Regulations (and in particular regulation 9)—

(a) no tax shall be chargeable on the account provider or his nominee, or on the named child or registered contact (on his behalf)—

    (i) in respect of interest, dividends, distributions or gains in respect of account investments [²(excluding any building society bonus)],

    [¹(ia) in respect of alternative finance return or profit share return paid by a financial institution (within the meanings in Chapter 5 of Part 2 of the Finance Act 2005);]

    [²(ib) in respect of a payment under a building society bonus scheme, so far as the payment is calculated by reference to account investments (and if paid directly by the society into the account, the payment shall not count towards the subscription limit in regulation 9);]

    (ii) on any annual profits or gains treated by section 714(2) of the Taxes Act as having been received by any of them in respect of account investments,

    (iii) on an offshore income gain to which a disposal made by any of them of an account investment gives rise, which is treated by section 761(1) of the Taxes Act as constituting profits or gains,

    (iv) on a profit realised by any of them from the discount on a relevant discounted security within the meaning of Schedule 13 to the Finance Act 1996, which is held as an account investment, or

      (v) in respect of gains treated by section 541 of the Taxes Act as arising in connection with a policy of life insurance which is an account investment;

  (b) losses accruing on any disposal of account investments shall be disregarded for the purposes of capital gains tax;

[³(ba) any gain or loss accruing on and attributable to a payment within paragraph (ib) of sub-paragraph (a) shall not be a chargeable gain or allowable loss for capital gains tax purposes;]

  (c) section 349B(4) of the Taxes Act shall apply with the following modifications—

      (i) for references to a plan manager, substitute references to an account provider,

      (ii) for references to a plan, substitute references to an account, and

      (iii) for the reference to [¹Chapter 3 of Part 6 of ITTOIA 2005], substitute a reference to the Act;

  (d) a corresponding deficiency occurring at the end of the final year, within the meaning of section 549(1) of the Taxes Act, so far as it relates to a policy of life insurance which is an account investment, shall not be allowable as a deduction from the total income of the named child;

  (e) relief in respect of tax shall be given in the manner and to the extent provided by these Regulations; and

  (f) income arising from account investments shall not be regarded as income for any income tax purposes (including [¹section 629 of ITTOIA 2005]).

AMENDMENTS

1. Child Trust Funds (Amendment No.3) Regulations 2005 (SI 2005/3349), reg.7 (December 27, 2005).

2. Child Trust Funds (Amendment No.3) Regulations 2006 (SI 2006/3195), reg.4 (January 1, 2007).

3. Child Trust Funds (Amendment No.3) Regulations 2006 (SI 2006/3195), reg.5 (January 1, 2007).

DEFINITIONS

"account"—see reg.2(1)(b).
"account investment"—see *ibid.*
"account provider"—see *ibid.*
"child"—see reg.2(1)(a).
"gains"—see reg.2(1)(b).
"security"—see *ibid.*
"tax"—see *ibid.*
"the Taxes Act"—see *ibid.*
"year"—see *ibid.*

Tax liabilities and reliefs—account provider to act on behalf of the named child

25.—(1) An account provider may under these Regulations make tax claims, conduct appeals and agree on behalf of the named child (or of the registered contact in respect of the child) liabilities for and reliefs from tax in respect of an account.

7.34

(2) Tax claims shall be made to the Board in accordance with the provisions of regulations 26 and 27.

(3) Where any relief or exemption from tax previously given in respect of an account has by virtue of these Regulations become excessive, in computing the relief due on any claim there shall be deducted (so that amounts equal to that excess are set-off or repaid to the Board, as the case may be) notwithstanding that those amounts have been invested, any other amount of tax due to the Board by the account provider in respect of any tax liability in respect of account investments under an account including (but without prejudice to the making of an assessment under that Schedule) any amount falling due in respect of a liability under paragraph 3 or 4 of Schedule 23A to the Taxes Act.

DEFINITIONS

"account"—see reg.2(1)(b).
"account investment"—see *ibid.*
"account provider"—see *ibid.*
"child"—see reg.2(1)(a).
"tax"—see *ibid.*
"the Taxes Act"—see *ibid.*

Repayments in respect of tax to account provider—interim tax claims

7.35   **26.**—(1) Notwithstanding the provisions of any other enactment, the Board shall not be under an obligation to make any repayment in respect of tax under these Regulations earlier than the end of the month following the month in which the claim for the repayment is received.

(2) A claim for repayment in respect of tax which is not an annual claim ("interim tax claim") may be made only for a period of a month (or a number of months not exceeding six) beginning on the 6th day of the month and ending on the 5th day of the relevant following month.

(3) No claim for repayment may be made for the month ending 5th October or any subsequent month in a year until the annual claim due under regulation 27(2) in respect of an account for the preceding year has been duly made by the account provider and received by the Board.

(4) Where, on the occasion of a claim, there is due to the Board an amount in respect of tax, that amount shall be recoverable by the Board in the same manner as tax charged by an assessment on the account provider which has become final and conclusive.

(5) This regulation and regulation 27 shall not apply to any repayment in respect of tax on account investments falling within regulation 12(2)(m) (life insurance), or on distributions and other rights or proceeds in respect of those investments.

DEFINITIONS

"account"—see reg.2(1)(b).
"account investment"—see *ibid.*
"account provider"—see *ibid.*
"tax"—see *ibid.*
"year"—see *ibid.*

Repayments in respect of tax to account provider—annual tax claims

27.—(1) An annual tax claim is a claim for repayment in respect of tax   7.36
for a year and may not be made at any time more than six years after the
end of the year.

(2) Where the account provider—

(a) has made at least one interim tax claim during a year, or

(b) wishes to reclaim tax, or there is due to the Board an amount in
    respect of tax, following the end of the year,

the account provider shall within six months after the end of the year make
an annual tax claim to establish the total of tax repayments due under an
account for that year.

(3) Where the aggregate of the repayments in respect of interim tax
claims for the year shown by an annual tax claim exceeds the amount of tax
repayable for the year shown on the claim, the account provider shall repay
the amount of the excess to the Board with the claim.

(4) If an account provider fails to make the annual tax claim required
under paragraph (2)(a) within the time limited, the Board may issue a
notice to the account provider showing the aggregate of payments in respect
of the interim tax claims for the year, and stating that the Board are not
satisfied that the amount due to the account provider for that year exceeds
the lower amount stated in the notice.

(5) If an annual tax claim is not delivered to the Board within 14 days
after the issue of a notice under paragraph (4) the amount of the difference
between the aggregate and the lower amount stated in the notice shall
immediately become recoverable by the Board in the same manner as tax
charged by an assessment on the account provider which has become final
and conclusive.

(6) Where an annual tax claim has been made and the account provider
subsequently discovers that an error or mistake has been made in the claim
the account provider may make a supplementary annual claim within the
time allowed in paragraph (1).

DEFINITIONS

"account"—see reg.2(1)(b).
"account provider"—see *ibid.*
"notice"—see *ibid.*
"tax"—see *ibid.*
"year"—see *ibid.*

Account provider's tax claims—supplementary provisions

28.—(1) Section 42 of the Management Act shall not apply to tax claims   7.37
under these Regulations.

(2) No appeal shall lie from the Board's decision on an interim tax
claim.

(3) An appeal [¹ . . .] from the Board's decision on an annual tax claim,
[¹. . .] shall be brought by giving notice to the Board within 30 days of
receipt of notice of the decision.

(4) No payment or repayment made or other thing done on or in relation
to an interim tax claim or a notice under regulation 27(4) shall prejudice
the decision on an annual tax claim.

(5) The provisions contained in Part 5 of the Management Act (appeals and other proceedings) shall apply to an appeal under paragraph (3) above, [¹ and, on an appeal that is notified to the tribunal, the tribunal] may vary the decision appealed against whether or not the variation is to the advantage of the appellant.

(6) All such assessments, payments and repayments shall be made as necessary to give effect to the Board's decision on an annual tax claim or to any variation of that decision on appeal.

(7) Claims under these Regulations shall be in such form and contain such particulars as the Board prescribe and, subject to regulation 32(1), shall be signed by the account provider, and forms prescribed for annual claims may require a report to be given by a person qualified for appointment as auditor of a company.

AMENDMENT

1. Transfer of Tribunal Functions and Revenue and Customs Appeals Order 2009 (SI 2009/56), art.3(2), Sch.2, para.127 (April 1, 2009).

DEFINITIONS

"account provider"—see reg.2(1)(b).
"company"—see *ibid*.
"the Management Act"—see *ibid*.
"notice"—see *ibid*.
"tax"—see *ibid*.

Assessments for withdrawing relief and recovering tax

7.38   **29.**—(1) Where—
   (a) any relief or exemption from tax given in respect of income or gains under an account is found not to be due or to be excessive, or
   (b) the full amount of tax in respect of the income or gains under an account has not otherwise been fully accounted for and paid to the Board on behalf of the named child,
an assessment to tax may be made by the Board in the amount or further amount which in their opinion ought to be charged.

(2) An assessment to which paragraph (1) refers may be made on the account provider or on the registered contact (in respect of the child where the child is under the age of 16).

(3) If the assessment is made to recover tax in respect of income under an account it shall be made under Case VI of Schedule D.

(4) Sections 72 and 73 of the Management Act shall be modified in relation to accounts, so that—
   (a) references to a parent or guardian include a reference to the registered contact for an account held by the named child, and
   (b) references to an incapacitated person, in relation to Scotland, are to a person under the age of 16 years.

DEFINITIONS

"account"—see reg.2(1)(b).
"account provider"—see *ibid*.
"child"—see reg.2(1)(a).
"gains"—see reg.2(1)(b).

"the Management Act"—see *ibid.*
"tax"—see *ibid.*

Fortnightly claim and financial returns

30.—(1) In this regulation— 7.39
"fortnightly period" means a period—
(a) beginning on the 1st, and ending on the 15th, day of a calendar month, or
(b) beginning on the 16th, and ending on the last, day of a calendar month;
"first return period", in relation to account providers approved with effect from a date between 1st January 2005 and 28th February 2005, means the period beginning on the date on which the approval takes effect and ending on 28th February 2005;
"second return period", in relation to account providers approved with effect from a date between 1st January 2005 and 31st March 2005, means the period beginning on the later of 1st March 2005 and the date on which the approval takes effect, and ending on 31st March 2005;
"initial return period", in relation to account providers approved later, means the period—
(a) beginning on the date on which the approval takes effect, or the appointed day (whichever is the later), and
(b) ending simultaneously with the end of the current fortnightly period.
(2) The following provisions of this regulation apply to an account provider in relation to—
(a) that provider's first, second or initial return period, and
(b) each succeeding fortnightly period (other than succeeding a first return period),
during which, or during any part of which, he acted as an account provider.
(3) Within—
(a) ten days of the end of a provider's first return period (if any), and
(b) five days of the end of any other period mentioned in paragraph (2),
the account provider shall deliver by means of electronic communications to the Board, a return for that period, in a form specified by the Board.
(4) The return shall include a declaration of the information in paragraph (5), and a claim as mentioned in paragraph (6) (in each case, stated separately for each account, quoting the named child's unique reference number and date of birth).
(5) The information is that, during that period—
(a) the account provider has opened an account in accordance with regulation 5 [2 . . .];
(b) the account provider has opened a Revenue allocated account in accordance with regulation 6;
(c) an account has been transferred to the account provider in accordance with regulation 21, and is held with the account provider at the end of the period; or
(d) an account has been closed, due to the named child dying under the age of 18 (and the date of death).
(6) The claim is—

   (a) where paragraph (5)(a) or (b) applies, a claim for the initial contribution or special contribution due to the account in accordance with
regulation 7(1) to (4); [¹. . .]

   (b) where the Inland Revenue have informed the account provider that
section 9 of the Act applies to the named child, a claim for the supplementary contribution due to the account in accordance with
regulation 7(5) to (7) [¹; and

   (c) where the Inland Revenue have informed the account provider that
[³ a further contribution is due for] the named child [³ in accordance
with regulation 7(10) or (10A) or regulation 7A], a claim for the
further contribution due to the account in accordance with [³ the
relevant provision]].

(7) Paragraphs (5)(a) and (b) and (6)(a) and (b) shall apply notwithstanding any transfer of the account to another account provider under
regulation 21, before the end of the period in question.

AMENDMENTS

   1. Child Trust Funds (Amendment) Regulations 2005 (SI 2005/383), reg.5
(April 6, 2005).
   2. Child Trust Funds (Amendment) Regulations 2006 (SI 2006/199), reg.4
(February 7, 2006).
   3. Child Trust Funds (Amendment) Regulations 2009 (SI 2009/475), reg.7
(April 6, 2009).

DEFINITIONS

   "account"—see reg.2(1)(b).
   "account provider"—see *ibid.*
   "appointed day"—see *ibid.*
   "child"—see reg.2(1)(a).
   "electronic communications"—see reg.2(1)(b).
   "first return period"—see reg.30(1).
   "fortnightly period"—see *ibid.*
   "initial return period"—see *ibid.*
   "second return period"—see *ibid.*

Records to be kept by account provider

7.40   **31.**—(1) An account provider shall at all times keep sufficient records in
respect of an account to enable the requirements of these Regulations to be
satisfied.

(2) In particular, an account provider shall produce (when required to do
so by an officer of the Board) any—

   (a) application made under regulation 13(1) or (10),
   (b) voucher given to him,
   (c) annual statement issued by him, and
   (d) transfer notice given to him under regulation 21(4),

or electronic copies, within the period of 3 years from when it was made,
issued or given (notwithstanding any transfer of the account under regulation 21).

DEFINITIONS

   "account"—see reg.2(1)(b).
   "account provider"—see *ibid.*

"notice"—see *ibid.*
"year"—see *ibid.*

Returns of information by account provider

32.—(1) An account provider shall within 60 days after the end of each   7.41
year in which he acts as an account provider, and after ceasing to act or to
qualify as an account provider, deliver by means of electronic communications to the Board a return for that year, or for the part of that year in which
he so acted or qualified, in a form specified by the Board, which contains
the information specified in paragraph (2).

(2) The information specified in this paragraph is information relating to
each account in respect of which he acted as account provider, in the year
or the part of the year for which the return is made, other than accounts
transferred to another account provider under regulation 21 in that year or
part of a year, as to—

  (a) as regards the named child—
      (i) [¹. . .]
     (ii) [¹. . .]
    (iii) his unique reference number;
  (b) as regards each such account—
      (i) whether or not the account is a stakeholder account,
     (ii) whether or not there is a registered contact for the account,
    (iii) the aggregate market value of the account investments held
          under the account, subject to paragraph (3), the value of each
          account investment being determined either as at 5th April in
          that year, or any other valuation date not falling earlier than 5th
          October in that year, and
     (iv) the total amount of cash subscribed to the account, in the sub-
          scription year ending during the year or the part of the year for
          which the return is made.

(3) The reference in paragraph (2)(b)(iii) to market value shall be
construed—

  (a) in the case of policies of life insurance, as a reference to their surren-
      der value, and
  (b) as referring to separate values for—
      (i) cash falling within regulation 12(2)(k) or (l), and
     (ii) policies of life insurance and all other account investments.

(4) No claim for repayment, or repayment, may be made under regulations 26 and 27 until the returns which have become due under this regulation have been duly made by the account provider and received by the
Board.

AMENDMENT

  1. Child Trust Funds (Amendment No.2) Regulations 2005 (SI 2005/909), reg.9
(April 6, 2005).

DEFINITIONS

  "account"—see reg.2(1)(b).
  "account investment"—see *ibid.*
  "account provider"—see *ibid.*
  "child"—see reg.2(1)(a).

"electronic communications"—see reg.2(1)(b).
"market value"—see *ibid*.
"year"—see *ibid*.

Information about "looked after children" from Local Authorities

7.42   **33.**—(1) In this regulation—
"local authority" includes an authority within the meaning of the Children (Northern Ireland) Order 1995;
"looked after and accommodated child", in Scotland, means a child who is—

(a) both looked after, and provided with or placed in accommodation, by a local authority within the meaning of those expressions in Part 2 of the Children (Scotland) Act 1995, or

(b) accommodated by a local authority under section 22 of that Act, and related expressions shall be construed accordingly;
"looked after child"—

(a) in England and Wales, has the meaning in section 22(1) of the Children Act 1989, extended to include a child accommodated by a local authority under section 17 of that Act, and

(b) in Northern Ireland, means a child accommodated under Part 4 of the Children (Northern Ireland) Order 1995,
and related expressions shall be construed accordingly;
"return period" means a period—

(a) beginning on the day immediately succeeding the appointed day, and ending one month after the appointed day, and

(b) each succeeding period of one month.

(2) Within one month of the appointed day, every local authority shall deliver by means of electronic communications to the Board, a return in a form specified by the Board, which contains the information in paragraph (3) for every child who was—

(a) looked after (in Scotland, looked after and accommodated) by the authority on the appointed day, and

(b) born after 31st August 2002,
or a return stating that there were no such children.

(3) The information in this paragraph is a statement (prepared separately for each child) of—

(a) the name of the local authority,

(b) its address,

(c) the unique identifier for the local authority,

(d) the name of the local authority officer responsible for the return,

(e) the child's full name, sex and date of birth,

[3(ea) the full name and address of the child's mother, if known (or failing that, the same information for the child's father, if known), unless the local authority considers the child's situation to be particularly sensitive;]

(f) the Home Office reference number, if any, of the child, and

(g) either—

(i) the full name and address of an individual who has parental responsibility (in Scotland, parental responsibilities) in relation to the child, or

(ii) if paragraph (i) is considered inappropriate, a correspondence address for the child.

(4) Within [⁴ten] days of the end of each return period, every local authority shall deliver by means of electronic communications to the Board a return for that period in a form specified by the Board, covering every child—

(a) born after 31st August 2002, and

(b) who during that period has become a child looked after (in Scotland, looked after and accommodated) by that authority, for the first time since the appointed day,

or a return stating that there were no such children.

(5) After 31st August 2009, the return in paragraph (4) shall in addition cover every child who was looked after (in Scotland, looked after and accommodated) on his 7th birthday.

(6) The return in paragraph (4) shall consist of a statement (prepared separately for each child) of—

(a) the information in paragraph (3),

(b) the date on which the child first became a child looked after (in Scotland, looked after and accommodated) by that authority,

(c) where the child has also died during that period, the name and address of his personal representatives [¹,

and where sub-paragraph (c) applies, the local authority shall also send a copy of the death certificate (or other documentary evidence of death) to the Board by post.]

[¹(7) As an alternative to delivering the return required by paragraph (2) by means of electronic communications, the local authority may (until this paragraph is revoked) send the return to the Board by registered post.]

[²(8) Regulations 34 and 35 shall apply to local authorities, as if, in those regulations, for—

(a) "relevant person" there were substituted "local authority"; and

(b) references to an account or account investments there were substituted references to returns, forms or children mentioned in this regulation and regulation 33A,

so far as the Board may reasonably require information to be provided or records to be made available for the purposes of this regulation and regulation 33A.]

AMENDMENTS

1. Child Trust Funds (Amendment) Regulations 2004 (SI 2004/2676), reg.14 (April 6, 2005).

2. Child Trust Funds (Amendment No.2) Regulations 2004 (SI 2004/3382), reg.4 (April 6, 2005).

3. Child Trust Funds (Amendment No.2) Regulations 2006 (SI 2006/2684), reg.3 (October 31, 2006).

4. Child Trust Funds (Amendment No.2) Regulations 2006 (SI 2006/2684), reg.4 (October 31, 2006).

DEFINITIONS

"account"—see reg.2(1)(b).
"account investment"—see *ibid*.
"appointed day"—see *ibid*.
"child"—see reg.2(1)(a).
"electronic communications"—see reg.2(1)(b).
"local authority"—see reg.33(1).

"looked after and accommodated child"—see *ibid.*
"looked after child"—see *ibid.*
"parental responsibility"—see reg.2(1)(a).
"relevant person"—see *ibid.*
"return period"—see reg.33(1).

[¹ The Official Solicitor or Accountant of Court to be the person who has the authority to manage an account

7.43   **33A.**—(1) Every local authority shall be under a duty to—
(a) identify any child born after 31st August 2002 and under 16, who falls within the circumstances specified in paragraph (2) and, for each such child,
(b) deliver a form (as part of the return required by regulation 33(2) or (4), as the case may be) in accordance with paragraph (3)(a).
(2) The circumstances specified are where—
(a) the child is looked after (in Scotland, looked after and accommodated) by the local authority, and
(b) at least one of the following conditions is satisfied.

Condition 1

There is no person, or no person other than the local authority, who has parental responsibility (in Scotland, parental responsibilities) for the child.

Condition 2

It is part of the care plan for the child that—
(a) the child will live indefinitely away from home (or his former home), and
(b) the child will not have face to face contact with any parent having parental responsibility (in Scotland, parental responsibilities) for the child.

Condition 3

An order has been made under section 34(4) of the Children Act 1989 or Article 53(4) of the Children (Northern Ireland) Order 1995, authorising the local authority to refuse to allow contact between the child and any person with parental responsibility (or, in Scotland, a supervision requirement made with a condition regulating contact under section 70(5)(b) of the Children (Scotland) Act 1995 that the child shall have no contact with a person with parental responsibilities), and there is no other individual with parental responsibility (in Scotland, parental responsibilities) for the child to act as registered contact.

Condition 4

The Court of Protection has—
(a) appointed a [³ deputy] for a person with parental responsibility for the child, or
[³ (b) determined that such a person lacks capacity within the meaning of the Mental Capacity Act 2005 (c.9) to manage the child's property and affairs]

and there is no other individual with parental responsibility for the child to act as registered contact.

In Scotland, in this Condition for—

(a) "Court of Protection" substitute "Sheriff",

(b) [³ "deputy"] substitute "guardian appointed under section 58 of the Adults with Incapacity (Scotland) Act 2000",

(c) the reference to a [³ person lacking capacity], substitute "incapable for the purposes of the Adults with Incapacity (Scotland) Act 2000," and

(d) "parental responsibility" substitute "parental responsibilities".

Condition 5

The child has been lost or abandoned, and there is no prospect for the foreseeable future of reunification of the child with a parent having parental responsibility (in Scotland, parental responsibilities) for the child.

In this Condition, "lost or abandoned"—

(a) in England and Wales, has the meaning in section 20(1)(b) of the Children Act 1989;

(b) in Northern Ireland, has the meaning in Article 21(1)(b) of the Children (Northern Ireland) Order 1995; and

(c) in Scotland, has the meaning in section 25(1)(b) of the Children (Scotland) Act 1995.

[²Condition 6

In England and Wales, an adoption agency or local authority has been authorised to place the child for adoption under section 19, or by a placement order under section 21, of the Adoption and Children Act 2002, or in Northern Ireland, an Order has been made under Article 17 or 18 of the Adoption (Northern Ireland) Order 1987 to free the child for adoption.]

(3) Where—

(a) the local authority (by a means authorised by regulation 33) delivers to the Board a form specified by the Board, giving particulars of the child and of the circumstances specified in paragraph (2) relevant to the child, and

(b) the Board (subject to checking and if necessary correcting the contents of the form) delivers it to the Official Solicitor (where the child is in England and Wales or Northern Ireland) or the Accountant of Court (where the child is in Scotland),

the Official Solicitor or Accountant of Court, as the case may be, shall be the person who has the authority to manage the child's account for the purposes of section 3(6)(b) of the Act.

(4) The Official Solicitor or Accountant of Court shall cease to be the person who has the authority to manage the child's account (and shall be discharged from the duties of registered contact) where—

(a) the child attains the age of 16,

(b) in any case where the child is under 16 and still looked after (in Scotland, looked after and accommodated) by a local authority—

(i) the local authority confirms to the Official Solicitor or Accountant of Court that there is a named responsible person in relation to the child, who is able to be the registered contact for the child's account, and that none of the Conditions in paragraph (2) applies, and

    (ii) the Official Solicitor or Accountant of Court cancels his declaration and authorisation in accordance with regulation 13(7) and is replaced as registered contact by that responsible person, in accordance with regulation 13(10), or

(c) in any case where the child is under 16 and is not looked after (in Scotland, looked after and accommodated) by a local authority—

    (i) a responsible person for the child provides evidence to the satisfaction of the Official Solicitor or Accountant of Court, as the case may be, that he has parental responsibility for the child, and

    (ii) the Official Solicitor or Accountant of Court cancels his declaration and authorisation in accordance with regulation 13(7) and is replaced as registered contact by that responsible person, in accordance with regulation 13(10).

(5) A local authority shall, for the purposes of paragraph (4), confirm to the Official Solicitor or Accountant of Court, as the case may be—

(a) whether the child is still looked after (in Scotland, looked after and accommodated) by the authority, and

(b) the identity of the person or persons who had parental responsibility for the child at the date when he ceased to be looked after (in Scotland, looked after and accommodated) by the authority (or, at the option of the authority, any later date).

(6) Expressions defined in regulation 33 shall bear the same meanings in this regulation.]

AMENDMENTS

1. Child Trust Funds (Amendment No.2) Regulations 2004 (SI 2004/3382), reg.5 (April 6, 2005).
2. Child Trust Funds (Amendment No.2) Regulations 2006 (SI 2006/2684), reg.5 (October 31, 2006).
3. Mental Capacity Act 2005 (Transitional and Consequential Provisions) Order 2007 (SI 2007/1898), art.6 and Sch.1, para.33 (October 1, 2007).

DEFINITIONS

"account"—see reg.2(1)(b).
"child"—see reg.2(1)(a).
"parental responsibility"—see *ibid.*
"responsible person"—see *ibid.*

Information to be provided to the Board

7.44   **34.** The Board may by notice require any relevant person to furnish them, within such time (not being less than 14 days) as may be provided in the notice, such information about any account or about any account investment (including copies of or extracts from any books or other records) as they may reasonably require for the purposes of these Regulations.

DEFINITIONS

"account"—see reg.2(1)(b).
"account investment"—see *ibid.*
"notice"—see *ibid.*
"relevant person"—see reg.2(1)(a).

Inspection of records by officer of the Board

35.—(1) The Board may by notice require any relevant person, within   7.45
such time (not being less than 14 days) as may be provided in the notice, to
make available for inspection at a place within the United Kingdom by an
officer of the Board authorised for that purpose all documents (including
books and other records) in his possession or under his control relating to
any account or to any account investment.

(2) Where records are maintained by computer the person required to
make them available for inspection shall provide the officer making the
inspection with all the facilities necessary for obtaining information from
them.

DEFINITIONS

"account"—see reg.2(1)(b).
"account investment"—see *ibid*.
"notice"—see *ibid*.
"relevant person"—see reg.2(1)(a).

Capital gains tax—adaptation of enactments

36.—(1) For the purposes of capital gains tax—   7.46
  (a) any assets held by a named child as account investments shall be
      regarded as held by the child in a separate capacity from that in
      which he holds any other assets of the same description; and
  (b) the named child shall be treated as having sold all the account invest-
      ments, and as having reacquired them in his personal capacity, for
      a consideration equal to their market value, immediately before he
      attains the age of 18 years (and ceases to be a child).

(2) Sections 127 to 131 of the 1992 Act shall not apply in relation to
qualifying investments falling within any of sub-paragraphs (a), (b), and
(f) to (i) of regulation 12(2) which are held under an account if there is by
virtue of any allotment for payment as is mentioned in section 126(2) of
that Act a reorganisation affecting those assets.

DEFINITIONS

"account"—see reg.2(1)(b).
"account investment"—see *ibid*.
"child"—see reg.2(1)(a).
"market value"—see reg.2(1)(b).
"the 1992 Act"—see *ibid*.

Administration of tax in relation to accounts—supplementary

37.—(1) Nothing in these Regulations shall be taken to prejudice any   7.47
powers conferred or duties imposed by or under any enactment in relation
to the making of returns of income or gains, or for the recovery of tax, penalties or interest by means of an assessment or otherwise.

(2) Notwithstanding the provisions of these Regulations an account
provider shall not be released from obligations under these Regulations in
relation to an account except under conditions agreed in writing with and
notified to that person by the Board.

(3) The provisions contained in the Management Act shall apply to any assessment under these Regulations as if it were an assessment to tax for the year in which, apart from these Regulations, the named child would have been liable (by reason of his ownership of the investments).

(4) No obligation as to secrecy imposed by statute or otherwise shall preclude the Board from disclosing to an account provider or registered contact that any provision of these Regulations has not been satisfied or that relief has been given or claimed in respect of investments under an account.

(5) If—
(a) a chargeable event, within the meaning given by Chapter 2 of Part 13 of the Taxes Act, has happened in relation to a policy of life insurance which is an account investment, and
(b) the body by whom the policy was issued is satisfied that no gain is to be treated as chargeable to tax on the happening of the event by virtue of regulation 24(a)(v),

the body shall not be obliged to deliver the certificates mentioned in section 552(1) of that Act.

This paragraph does not prevent the operation of section 552(1) in a case to which regulation 38(1) applies.

(6) Where—
(a) it comes to the notice of the account provider, in any manner, that the event specified in regulation 12(11) has occurred in relation to a policy, and
(b) the account provider is not the insurer for the time being responsible for the obligations under the policy or, where the policy is not still in existence, the person who was the last such insurer,

the account provider shall, within 30 days of the event coming to his notice give notice to that insurer, specifying the event mentioned in sub-paragraph (a) and the termination event.

DEFINITIONS

"account"—see reg.2(1)(b).
"account investment"—see *ibid*.
"account provider"—see *ibid*.
"child"—see reg.2(1)(a).
"gains"—see reg.2(1)(b).
"the Management Act"—see *ibid*.
"notice"—see *ibid*.
"tax"—see *ibid*.
"the Taxes Act"—see *ibid*.
"year"—see *ibid*.

Application of the provisions of Chapter 2 of Part 13 of the Taxes Act to policies

7.48   **38.**—(1) This paragraph applies to a case where—
(a) the event specified in regulation 12(11) has occurred in relation to a policy of life insurance, and
(b) a termination event within the meaning in regulation 12(12) occurs in relation to that policy.
(2) Where—
(a) there is a case to which paragraph (1) applies, and

(b) a chargeable event in relation to the policy, within the meaning given by section 540 of the Taxes Act, has occurred prior to the time at which the termination event mentioned in paragraph (1)(b) occurs,

the named child shall cease to be, and shall be treated as not having been, entitled to relief from tax under regulation 24(a)(v), in respect of gains treated as arising on the occurrence of any chargeable event mentioned in sub-paragraph (b).

(3) The provisions of Chapter 2 of Part 13 of the Taxes Act shall apply, in a case to which paragraph (1) applies, to—

(a) the termination event mentioned in paragraph (1)(b), and

(b) any chargeable event mentioned in paragraph (2)(b),

with the modifications provided for in paragraphs (4) to (8) of this regulation, and the registered contact and the account provider shall account to the Board in accordance with this regulation for tax from which relief under regulation 24 has been given on the basis that the named child was so entitled, or in circumstances such that the named child was not so entitled.

(4) A termination of a policy of insurance pursuant to regulation 12(9) (b)(ii) shall be treated as the surrender in whole of the rights conferred by the policy, for the purposes of section 540(1)(a)(iii) of the Taxes Act.

(5) In section 547(5) of the Taxes Act, for the words after "total income" (where that expression first appears) substitute "that gain shall be chargeable to tax under Case VI of Schedule D".

(6) Relief under section 550 of the Taxes Act shall be computed as if paragraph (5) had not been enacted.

(7) In section 552 of the Taxes Act—

(a) in subsection (1)(b) for "policy holder" substitute "named child";

(b) in subsection (3)—

(i) omit "(or, where the appropriate policy holder is a company, the corresponding financial year)";

(ii) for "the name and address of the appropriate policy holder" substitute "the name and address of the named child";

(iii) omit "and the corresponding financial year,";

(c) in subsection (5)—

(i) for "the appropriate policy holder" substitute "the named child";

(ii) omit sub-paragraph (b)(ii);

(iii) omit paragraph (c);

(iv) in paragraph (d) omit "except where paragraph (c) above applies,";

(v) omit paragraph (f);

(d) in subsection (6)—

(i) omit paragraph (b);

(ii) for paragraph (c) substitute—

"(c) if the event is a death, the period of three months beginning with the receipt of written notification of the death;";

(iii) after paragraph (c) insert—

"(d) if the event is—

(i) a termination event, or

(ii) a chargeable event preceding a termination event (as mentioned in regulation 38(2) of the Child Trust Funds Regulations 2004),

813

the period of three months beginning with the date on which the insurer received notice under regulation 37(6) of those Regulations or, if earlier, actual notice of the termination event.";

(e) in subsection (7)—
(i) in paragraph (a) omit ", or, where the policy holder is a company, the financial year,";
(ii) omit paragraph (b);
(iii) for paragraph (c) substitute—
"(c) if the event is a death, the period of three months beginning with the receipt of written notification of the death;";
(iv) after paragraph (c) insert—
"(ca) if the event is—
(i) a termination event, or
(ii) a chargeable event preceding such a termination event (as mentioned in regulation 38(2) of the Child Trust Funds Regulations 2004,
the period of three months beginning with the date on which the insurer received notice under regulation 37(6) of those Regulations or, if earlier, actual notice of the termination event."; and
(v) in paragraph (d) after "paragraph (c)" insert "or (ca)";
(f) in subsection (8)—
(i) in paragraph (b) for "policy holder" substitute "named child in respect";
(ii) in paragraph (c) omit the words from "or" to the end;
(g) in subsection (9) omit "or financial year" in each place where they occur;
(h) in subsection (10)—
(i) before the definition of "amount" insert—
"'named child' has the same meaning as in the Child Trust Funds Regulations 2004;";
(ii) omit the definitions of "appropriate policy holder" and "financial year";
(iii) for the definition of "the relevant year of assessment" substitute—
"'the relevant year of assessment', in the case of any gain, means the year of assessment to which the gain is attributable;"; and
(iv) after the definition of "section 546 excess" insert—
"'termination event' has the same meaning as in the Child Trust Funds Regulations 2004;"; and
(v) omit subsection (11).
(8) In section 552ZA of the Taxes Act—
(a) in subsection (2)(b) omit the words "or an assignment"; and
(b) omit subsections (3) and (4).
(9) The account provider shall account for and pay income tax at the lower rate in force for the year in which the termination event, or the chargeable event mentioned in paragraph (2)(b) occurred, as the case may be, and any amount so payable—
(a) may be set off against any repayment in respect of tax due under regulation 26 or 27 and subject thereto,

(b) shall be treated as an amount of tax due not later than 6 months after the end of the year in which the event specified in regulation 12(11) came to the notice of the account provider, and

(c) shall be payable without the making of an assessment.

(10) Where tax is charged in accordance with paragraph (3)(a) or (b)—

(a) an assessment to income tax at the lower rate in force for the relevant year may be made on the account provider or on the registered contact (on behalf of the named child), and

(b) an assessment to income tax at the higher rate within the meaning of section 832(1) of the Taxes Act, for that year, may be made on the registered contact (on behalf of the named child) within five years after the 31st January next following that year, and regulation 29 shall not apply.

DEFINITIONS

"account provider"—see *ibid.*
"child"—see reg.2(1)(a).
"company"—see reg.2(1)(b).
"notice"—see *ibid.*
"tax"—see *ibid.*
"the Taxes Act"—see *ibid.*
"year"—see *ibid.*

SCHEDULE

STAKEHOLDER ACCOUNTS

Description of stakeholder account

1. An account is a stakeholder account where it has the characteristics and complies with the conditions set out in paragraph 2.

7.49

Characteristics of stakeholder account etc

2.—(1) A stakeholder account must have the characteristics set out in sub-paragraph (2) and must comply with the conditions set out in sub-paragraphs (3) to (5).

7.50

(2) The characteristics of a stakeholder account are—

(a) the account does not directly hold investments of any of the following kinds—

   (i) those referred to in regulation 12(2)(f) (shares in an investment trust);

   (ii) securities of an investment trust;

   (iii) rights in with-profits endowment policies;

   (iv) rights, under a contract of insurance, in a with-profits fund;

   (v) units or shares in a relevant collective investment scheme unless it is a requirement of that scheme that the purchase and sale price of those units or shares shall, at any given time, not differ from each other and that the price must be made available to the public on a daily basis;

   (vi) rights under a contract of insurance which are expressed as shares in funds held by the insurer unless it is a requirement of the contract of insurance that the purchase and sale price of those shares shall, at any given time, not differ from each other and that the price must be made available to the public on a daily basis;

   [1(via) shares referred to in regulation 12(2)(a) (shares issued by a company wherever incorporated and officially listed on a recognised stock exchange)]

   (vii) depositary interests, where the investments concerned are investments of any of the kinds listed above in this paragraph;

(b) [1the requirement is fulfilled that] the account provider, and any relevant person, [1. . .] ensure that, subject to the other provisions of this paragraph, the account has exposure to equities [1. . .];

815

[¹(ba) interest accrues on investments referred to in regulation 12(2)(k) and (l) (cash deposited in a deposit account or in a share account) on a daily basis at a rate that is not less than the Bank of England base rate minus 1 per cent per annum [³, except where cash is held temporarily on deposit in the course of dealing in investments under the account];

[²(baa) when the Bank of England base rate increases, the interest rate on investments referred to in regulation 12(2)(k) and (l) (cash deposited in a deposit account or in a share account) must be raised within one month of the date of that increase;]

(bb) in relation to qualifying investments which are securities (other than in an investment trust) or a depositary interest where the relevant investments (within the meaning in that definition) are such securities, the requirement is fulfilled that—

(i) the securities fall within regulation 12(2)(c) [², (d) or (e)], or

(ii) where the securities fall within regulation 12(2)(b) [². . .] or (n), the contract under which the securities are or have been acquired, or any other transaction entered into by the registered contact or any other person, has the effect that the named child is not exposed, or not exposed to a significant extent, to the risk of loss from fluctuations in the value of the securities exceeding 20% of the capital consideration paid or payable for the acquisition of those securities, during the period when the securities in question are held in the account.]

(c) [¹the requirement is fulfilled that] the account provider and any relevant person [¹. . .] have regard to—

(i) the need for diversification of investments of the account, in so far as is appropriate to the circumstances of the account; and

(ii) the suitability for the purposes of the account of any investment, investment strategy or investment option proposed; and

(d) except where otherwise instructed by the registered contact, the account is subject to lifestyling.

(3) The account provider must permit payment of subscriptions to the account by—

(a) cheque;

(b) direct debit;

(c) standing order;

(d) direct credit (other than standing order).

[¹For the purposes of this sub-paragraph, those means of payment do not include payments by cash, credit card or debit card or any combination including a payment by cash, credit card or debit card.]

(4) The minimum amount which may be subscribed to the account on a single occasion is £10 except where the account provider permits a smaller amount.

(5) Deductions from the account may only be made in the circumstances, and to the extent, set out in paragraph 3.

(6) In this paragraph—

"equities" means shares issued by a company wherever incorporated and officially listed on a recognised stock exchange;

"insurer" means—

(a) a person who has permission under Part 4 of the Financial Services and Markets Act 2000 to effect or carry out contracts of insurance, or

(b) an EEA firm of the kind mentioned in paragraph 5(d) of Schedule 3 to that Act, which has permission under paragraph 15 of that Schedule (as a result of qualifying for authorisation under paragraph 12 of that Schedule) to effect or carry out contracts of insurance;

"lifestyling" means the process beginning from a date on or before the child is 13 years of age, or from when the account is opened, whichever is later, and continuing until the child is 18 years of age, by which the account provider, and any relevant person, adopts an investment strategy which aims progressively to minimise the variation or potential variation in capital value of the account caused by market conditions from time to time;

"relevant collective investment scheme" means an authorised unit trust scheme, an authorised open-ended investment company or a recognised scheme, as the case may be, as defined in section 237(3) of the Financial Services and Markets Act 2000;

"relevant person" means any person to whom the account provider has delegated any of his functions or responsibilities under the management agreement; and

"with-profits fund" means a fund maintained by an insurer in respect of a particular part of its long-term business for which—

    (a) separate accounting records are maintained by the insurer in respect of all income and expenditure relating to that part of its business; and

    (b) the benefits payable in respect of policies allocated to that fund are determined partly by reference to a discretion exercisable by any person.

(7) In this paragraph, the definitions of "contract of insurance" and "insurer" must be read with—

    (a) section 22 of the Financial Services and Markets Act 2000,

    (b) any relevant order made under that section, and

    (c) Schedule 2 to that Act.

Stakeholder accounts—charges etc

3.—(1) Deductions from a stakeholder account may only be made to the extent set out in this paragraph.   **7.51**

(2) Subject to sub-paragraph (5), charges for the management of, and other expenses in connection with, a stakeholder account may be recovered from the account to the extent that they do not exceed whichever is the greater of—

    (a) 3/730 per cent of the value of the child's rights in the account for each day on which the account is held; or

    (b) 3/730 per cent of the value of the investments under the account for each day on which the account is held.

(3) For the purposes of sub-paragraph (2)—

    (a) the frequency, which must be daily, weekly or monthly, with which rights or investments are to be valued; and

    (b) where valuation is to take place weekly or monthly, the day of the week or, as the case may be, the date in the month on which it is to take place,

must be specified in advance in writing by the account provider to the registered contact, and the specification may not be amended during the period of 12 months after the date on which it is made.

(4) When calculating the value of a child's rights or of investments for the purposes of sub-paragraph (2), where the account provider has specified under sub-paragraph (3) that they are to be valued weekly or monthly—

    (a) where they are to be valued weekly, they are to be valued on such day of the week ("the specified day") as has been so specified by the account provider (except that, where that day is not a working day, the rights are to be valued on the next working day), and the value of the rights on each subsequent day prior to the next specified day is to be taken to be the value of the rights on the previous specified day; and

    (b) where they are to be valued monthly, they are to be so valued on such date in each month ("the specified date") as has been so specified by the account provider (except that, where that date is not a working day, the rights are to be valued on the next working day), and the value of the rights on each subsequent day prior to the next specified date is to be taken to be the value of the rights on the previous specified date.

(5) The following charges and expenses may be deducted in full from the account and are not subject to and do not count towards the limit provided for in sub-paragraph (2)—

    (a) any stamp duty, stamp duty reserve tax [¹, value added tax] or other charges [¹(including any dilution levy)] incurred by the account provider directly or indirectly in the sale or purchase of investments held under the account;

[¹(aa) where any amount of tax is paid or anticipated to be payable in respect of income received or capital gains realised by the account provider in respect of investments held for the purposes of the account, the amount so deducted or anticipated;]

    (b) any charges or expenses incurred by the account provider directly or indirectly in complying with an order of the court or any other requirements imposed by law; and

    (c) expenses incurred by the account provider in complying with its obligations under regulation 8(2)(d) and (e).

(6) Valuations for the purpose of sub-paragraph (2) shall be after the deduction of any charges or expenses properly deducted from the account under sub-paragraph (5).

AMENDMENTS

1. Child Trust Funds (Amendment) Regulations 2004 (SI 2004/2676), reg.15 (April 6, 2005).

2. Child Trust Funds (Amendment No.2) Regulations 2004 (SI 2004/3382), reg.6 (April 6, 2005).

3. Child Trust Funds (Amendment No.2) Regulations 2006 (SI 2006/2684), reg.6 (October 31, 2006).

DEFINITIONS

"account"—see reg.2(1)(b).
"account provider"—see *ibid*.
"Bank of England base rate"—see *ibid*.
"child"—see reg.2(1)(a).
"company"—see reg.2(1)(b).
"contract of insurance"—see para.2(7).
"depositary interest"—see reg.2(1)(c).
"equities"—see para.2(6).
"insurer"—see *ibid*., and para.2(7).
"investments under the account"—see reg.2(1)(b).
"investment trust"—see *ibid*.
"lifestyling"—see para.2(6).
"open-ended investment company"—see reg.2(1)(c).
"recognised stock exchange"—see reg.2(1)(b).
"relevant collective investment scheme"—see para.2(6).
"relevant person"—see reg.2(1)(a) and para.2(6).
"subscriptions"—see reg.2(1)(b).
"tax"—see *ibid*.
"units"—see reg.2(1)(c).
"with-profits fund"—see para.2(6).

Child Trust Funds (Insurance Companies) Regulations 2004

(SI 2004/2680)

7.52   The Treasury, in exercise of the powers conferred upon them by section 333B of the Income and Corporation Taxes Act 1988 as extended by section 14(1) of the Child Trust Funds Act 2004, hereby make the following Regulations:

ARRANGEMENT OF REGULATIONS

1. Citation and commencement
2. Interpretation
3. Child trust fund business
4.–17. Modifications of the Taxes Act
18.–19. Modification of the Taxation of Chargeable Gains Act 1992
20.–21. Modification of the Capital Allowances Act 2001
22. Amendments to the Insurance Companies Regulations

Citation and commencement

7.53   **1.** These Regulations may be cited as the Child Trust Funds (Insurance Companies) Regulations 2004 and shall come into force on the day appointed under section 27 of the Child Trust Funds Act 2004, for the purposes of sections 8 and 9 of that Act.

Interpretation

2. In these Regulations—

"child trust fund business" has the meaning given by regulation 3;
"individual savings account business" has the meaning given in the Insurance Companies Regulations;
"the Insurance Companies Regulations" means the Individual Savings Account (Insurance Companies) Regulations 1998;
"the principal Regulations" means the Child Trust Funds Regulations 2004;
"the Taxes Act" means the Income and Corporation Taxes Act 1988.

Child trust fund business

3. For the purposes of these Regulations "child trust fund business", in relation to an insurance company, means so much of that company's life assurance business as is referable to any policy of life insurance, or to the reinsurance of liabilities under any such policy, where the policy is, on the date on which the insurance is made, a qualifying investment for an account within the meaning of regulation 12 of the principal Regulations.

Modifications of the Taxes Act

4. Regulations 5 to 17 specify modifications of provisions of the Taxes Act so far as concerns the child trust fund business (and, in the case of regulations 11(b) and (c), 13 and 14, the individual savings account business) of insurance companies.

5. In section 431(2) insert at the appropriate place the following definition—

"'child trust fund business' has the meaning given by regulation 3 of the Child Trust Funds (Insurance Companies) Regulations 2004;".

6. In both of sections 431C(1) and 431D(1) after "pension business" insert ", child trust fund business".

7. In section 431F after "pension business," insert "child trust fund business,".

8. In section 432A(2) (as modified by the Insurance Companies Regulations) after paragraph (aa) insert—

"(ab) child trust fund business;".

9. In section 432AA(4) (as modified by the Insurance Companies Regulations) after paragraph (aa) insert—

"(ab) child trust fund business;".

10. In both of sections 432C(1) and 432D(1) after "pension business," insert "child trust fund business,".

11. In section 436—

(a) after the words "pension business", in each place where they occur, insert "or child trust fund business";
(b) in subsection (1)(a) for "that business" substitute "the business of each such category".
(c) after subsection (3)(c) insert—
  "(ca) there may be set off (so far as it has not been set off under paragraph (c)), against the profits of child trust fund business any loss, to be computed on the same basis as the profits, which has arisen from

819

7.54

7.55

7.56

individual savings account business, in the same or any previous accounting period;

(cb) there may be set off (so far as it has not been set off under paragraph (c)), against the profits of individual savings account business any loss, to be computed on the same basis as the profits, which has arisen from child trust fund business, in the same or any previous accounting period;".

12. In section 438(1) add at the end "or child trust fund business".

13. In section 440(4)(a) add at the end, "individual savings account business or child trust fund business, or assets linked to any of those categories but not to any other category of business".

14. In section 440A(2)(a)(i) after "pension business" insert ", individual savings account business or child trust fund business or any of those categories of business".

15. In section 466(2) insert at the appropriate place the following definition—

"'child trust fund business' shall be construed in accordance with section 431(2);".

16. In section 755A (as modified by the Insurance Companies Regulations) after paragraph (aa) in each of subsections (4) and (13) insert—

"(ab) child trust fund business,".

17. In paragraph 5(5) of Schedule 19AA after "pension business," insert "child trust fund business,".

Modification of the Taxation of Chargeable Gains Act 1992

7.57   **18.** Regulation 19 specifies a modification of section 212 of the Taxation of Chargeable Gains Act 1992 so far as concerns child trust fund business of insurance companies.

19. In section 212(2) after "pension business" insert, "child trust fund business".

Modification of the Capital Allowances Act 2001

7.58   **20.** Regulation 21 specifies a modification of section 256 of the Capital Allowances Act 2001 so far as concerns child trust fund business of insurance companies.

21. In section 256(3)(a) after "pension business" insert, "child trust fund business".

Amendments to the Insurance Companies Regulations

7.59   **22.** Regulations 13(b), 15 and 16 of the Insurance Companies Regulations (which are superseded by regulations 11(b), 13 and 14 of these Regulations) shall cease to have effect.

GENERAL NOTE

7.60   These Regulations make various technical modifications to revenue law provisions. They provide for the exemption from corporation tax of income and gains made by an insurance company providing child trust funds, so far as they relate to the company's child trust fund business. They also provide for the profit from operating child trust fund business to be taxed in the same way as profits from the company's Individual Savings Account (ISA) business, and for losses arising one category to be set off against profits from the other.

The Child Trust Funds (Non-tax Appeals) Regulations 2005

(SI 2005/191)

Made	*3 February 2005*
Laid before Parliament	*4 February 2005*
Coming into force	*25 February 2005*

The Treasury, in exercise of the powers conferred upon them by sections 23(1), 24(5) and 28(1) to (4) of the Child Trust Funds Act 2004, make the following Regulations:

7.61

Citation, commencement and duration

1.—(1) These Regulations may be cited as the Child Trust Funds (Non-tax Appeals) Regulations 2005 and shall come into force on 25 February 2005.

7.62

(2) [¹ . . .]

AMENDMENT

1. Transfer of Tribunal Functions and Revenue and Customs Appeals Order 2009 (SI 2009/56), art.3(2), Sch.2, para.132 (April 1, 2009).

Interpretation

2. *Omitted.*

7.63

Prescribed manner of notice of appeal

3.—(1) The prescribed manner of giving notice of appeal [¹, in respect of an appeal to an appeal tribunal,] to the Inland Revenue under section 23(1) of the Child Trust Funds Act 2004 is as follows.

7.64

(2) The notice must—

(a) be given in writing,

(b) contain sufficient information to identify the appellant and the decision against which the appeal is being made, and

(c) be signed by or on behalf of the appellant.

(3) In paragraph (2)(a) "writing" includes writing produced by electronic communications if those electronic communications are approved by the Commissioners of Inland Revenue.

(4) In paragraph (2)(c) "signed", where the notice is in writing produced by electronic communications, means authenticated in any manner approved by those Commissioners.

AMENDMENT

1. Tribunals, Courts and Enforcement Act 2007 (Transitional and Consequential Provisions) Order 2008 (SI 2008/2683), art. 6(1) and Sch. 1, para. 262 (November 3, 2008).

DEFINITIONS

"Inland Revenue"—see Child Trust Funds Act 2004, s.29, but see the note below.
"signed"—see para.(4).
"writing"—see para.(3).

GENERAL NOTE

7.65   For what amounts to a signature, see the annotation to reg.2 of the Tax Credits (Notice of Appeal) Regulations 2002. Also, see para.(4) for signatures on electronic documents.
     The functions of the Commissioners of Inland Revenue have been transferred to the Commissioners for Her Majesty's Revenue and Customs (Commissioners for Revenue and Customs Act 2005, s.5(2)(a)).

7.66   **4.–15.** *Omitted.*

The Child Trust Funds (Appeals) Regulations 2005

(SI 2005/990)

Made   *24th March 2005*
Coming into force in accordance with regulation 1(1)

7.67   Whereas a draft of this instrument was laid before Parliament in accordance with section 80(1) of the Social Security Act 1998 and approved by resolution of each House of Parliament.
     Now therefore, the Secretary of State for Work and Pensions, in exercise of the powers conferred upon him by sections 7(6) and (7), 12(7), 14(10) (a) and (11), 16(1) and (3)(a), 28(1), 79(1) and (4) to (7) and 84 of, and paragraphs 7, 11 and 12 of Schedule 1 to, and paragraphs 1 to 6 of Schedule 5 to, the Social Security Act 1998, after consultation with the Council on Tribunals in accordance with section 8 of the Tribunals and Inquiries Act 1992, hereby makes the following Regulations:

Citation, commencement, duration and interpretation

7.68   **1.**—(1) These Regulations may be cited as the Child Trust Funds (Appeals) Regulations 2005 and shall come into force on the day after they are made.
     (2) [² . . .]
     (3) In these Regulations, unless the context otherwise requires—
     "the Act" means the Social Security Act 1998;
     "the 2004 Act" means the Child Trust Funds Act 2004;
     "appeal" means an appeal under section 22 of the 2004 Act to [¹ the First-tier Tribunal];
     "the Board" means the Commissioners of Inland Revenue;
     [¹ . . .]
     [¹ . . .]
     [¹ . . .]
     [¹ . . .]

"notification period" has the meaning given in regulation 3;
"party to the proceedings" means the Board and any person who brings
   an appeal;
[¹ . . .]
(4) [¹ . . .]

AMENDMENTS

1. Tribunals, Courts and Enforcement Act 2007 (Transitional and Consequential
Provisions) Order 2008 (SI 2008/2683), art.6(1) and Sch.1, para.291 (November
3, 2008).
2. Transfer of Tribunal Functions and Revenue and Customs Appeals Order 2009
(SI 2009/56), art.3(2), Sch.2, para.136 (April 1, 2009).

GENERAL NOTE

Para. (3)—"the Board"
   The functions of the Commissioners of Inland Revenue have been transferred to   **7.69**
the Commissioners for Her Majesty's Revenue and Customs (Commissioners for
Revenue and Customs Act 2005, s.5(2)(a)).

Service of notices or documents

2. Where by any provision of these Regulations—   **7.70**
   (a) any notice or other document is required to be given or sent to [¹ . . .]
       the Board, that notice or document shall be treated as having been
       so given or sent on the day that it is received by [¹ . . .] by the Board,
       and
   (b) any notice or other document is required to be given or sent to any
       person other than [¹ . . .] the Board, that notice or document shall,
       if sent to that person's last known address, be treated as having been
       given or sent on the day that it was posted.

AMENDMENTS

1. Tribunals, Courts and Enforcement Act 2007 (Transitional and Consequential
Provisions) Order 2008 (SI 2008/2683), art.6(1) and Sch.1, para.292 (November
3, 2008).

DEFINITION

   "the Board"—see reg.1(3), but see also the note below.

GENERAL NOTE

   The functions of the Commissioners of Inland Revenue ("the Board") have   **7.71**
been transferred to the Commissioners for Her Majesty's Revenue and Customs
(Commissioners for Revenue and Customs Act 2005, s.5(2)(a)).

Disputes about notices of appeal

3. Where a dispute arises as to whether notice of an appeal was given to   **7.72**
the Board within the period of thirty days specified in section 23(1) of the
2004 Act ("the notification period") the dispute shall be referred to, and be
determined by, [¹ the First-tier Tribunal].

1. Tribunals, Courts and Enforcement Act 2007 (Transitional and Consequential Provisions) Order 2008 (SI 2008/2683), art.6(1) and Sch.1, para.293 (November 3, 2008).

DEFINITIONS

"the 2004 Act"—see reg.1(3).
"the Board"—*ibid.*, but see also the note below.

GENERAL NOTE

7.73   The functions of the Commissioners of Inland Revenue ("the Board") have been transferred to the Commissioners for Her Majesty's Revenue and Customs (Commissioners for Revenue and Customs Act 2005, s.5(2)(a)).

Late appeals

7.74   **4.**—(1) Where the conditions specified in paragraphs [¹ (4) to (8) are satisfied, the Board may treat an appeal as made in time where an appeal is] brought within a period of one year after the expiration of the notification period.

(2) [¹ . . .]

(3) [¹ . . .]

[¹ (4) The Board must not treat the appeal as made in time unless the Board is satisfied that it is in the interests of justice.]

(5) For the purposes of paragraph (4) it is not in the interests of justice to [¹ treat the appeal as made in time unless the Board are] satisfied that—

(a) the special circumstances specified in paragraph (6) are relevant [¹ . . .]; or

(b) some other special circumstances exist which are wholly exceptional and relevant [¹ . . .],

and as a result of those special circumstances, it was not practicable for the appeal to be brought within the notification period.

(6) For the purposes of paragraph (5)(a), the special circumstances are that—

(a) the [¹ appellant] or a partner or dependant of the [¹ appellant] has died or suffered serious illness;

(b) the [¹ appellant] is not resident in the United Kingdom; or

(c) normal postal services were disrupted.

(7) In determining whether it is in the interests of justice to [¹ treat the appeal as made in time], regard shall be had to the principle that the greater the amount of time that has elapsed between the expiration of the notification period and the [¹ submission of the notice of appeal, the more compelling should be the special circumstances.]

(8) In determining whether it is in the interests of justice to [¹ treat the appeal as made in time] no account shall be taken of the following—

(a) that the [¹ appellant] or any person acting for him was unaware of or misunderstood the law applicable to his case (including ignorance or misunderstanding of the notification period); or

(b) that [¹the Upper Tribunal] or a court has taken a different view of the law from that previously understood and applied.

(9) [¹ . . .]

(10) [¹ . . .]

(11) As soon as practicable after the decision is made a copy of the decision shall be sent or given to every party to the proceedings.

AMENDMENTS

1. Tribunals, Courts and Enforcement Act 2007 (Transitional and Consequential Provisions) Order 2008 (SI 2008/2683), art.6(1) and Sch.1, para.294 (November 3, 2008).

DEFINITIONS

"the 2004 Act"—see reg.1(3).
"appeal"—*ibid*.
"the Board"—*ibid*., but see also the note below.
"notification period"—*ibid*.
"party to the proceedings"—*ibid*.

GENERAL NOTE

See the note to reg.5 of the Tax Credit (Appeals) (No.2) Regulations 2002.   7.75
The functions of the Commissioners of Inland Revenue ("the Board") have been transferred to the Commissioners for Her Majesty's Revenue and Customs (Commissioners for Revenue and Customs Act 2005, s.5(2)(a)).

Death of a party to an appeal

5. In any proceedings relating to an appeal under section 22(2), (4), (5)   7.76
or (6) of the 2004 Act, on the death of a party to the proceedings (other than the Board) the personal representative of the person who has died may represent him at any hearing.

DEFINITIONS

"the 2004 Act"—see reg.1(3).
"appeal"—*ibid*.
"the Board"—*ibid*., but see also the note below.
"party to the proceedings"—*ibid*.

GENERAL NOTE

The functions of the Commissioners of Inland Revenue ("the Board") have   7.77
been transferred to the Commissioners for Her Majesty's Revenue and Customs (Commissioners for Revenue and Customs Act 2005, s.5(2)(a)).

PART VIII

HEALTH IN PREGNANCY GRANTS

Health in Pregnancy Grant (Entitlement and Amount) Regulations 2008

(SI 2008/3108)

ARRANGEMENT OF REGULATIONS

The Treasury, in exercise of the powers conferred by sections 140A(1),(2), (4) to (6), 140B(1) and 175 of the Social Security Contributions and Benefits Act 1992, sections 136A(1),(2),(4) to (6), 136B(1) and 171 of the Social Security Contributions and Benefits (Northern Ireland) Act 1992 and section 115(3) and (5) of the Immigration and Asylum Act 1999 make the following regulations:

Citation, commencement and interpretation

1.—(1) These Regulations may be cited as the Health in Pregnancy   8.2
Grant (Entitlement and Amount) Regulations 2008 and shall come into force on the 1st January 2009.

(2) In these Regulations—

"SSCBA" means the Social Security Contributions and Benefits Act 1992;

"SSCB(NI)A" means the Social Security Contributions and Benefits (Northern Ireland) Act 1992;

"health professional" has the meaning given to it by regulation 3.

Conditions in relation to entitlement

2. — In order for a woman to be entitled to health in pregnancy grant,   8.3
she must, at the time of her claim,—

(a) be pregnant;

(b) have reached the 25th week of her pregnancy;

(c) have received advice from a health professional on matters relating to her maternal health; and

(d) have a due date on or after 6th April 2009.

Meaning of "health professional"

8.4   **3.** — "Health professional" in section 140A(5) SSCBA and section 136A of SSCB(NI)A means a person who provides maternity care to the woman and who is either—

(a) a practicing midwife, who is registered with the Nursing and Midwifery Council; or

(b) an obstetrician or General Practitioner, who is registered with the General Medical Council.

Circumstances in which a woman is to be treated as not being in Great Britain or Northern Ireland - general

8.5   **4.**—(1) For the purposes of section 140A(3)(b) of SSCBA, a woman is to be treated as not being in Great Britain if —

(a) she is not ordinarily resident in the United Kingdom, or

(b) she does not have a right to reside in the United Kingdom.

(2) For the purposes of section 136A of SSCB(NI)A, a woman is to be treated as not being in Northern Ireland if—

(a) she is not ordinarily resident in the United Kingdom, or

(b) she does not have a right to reside in the United Kingdom.

(3) A woman who is in the United Kingdom as a result of deportation, expulsion or other removal by compulsion of law from another country to the United Kingdom shall be treated as being ordinarily resident in the United Kingdom.

Crown servants posted overseas

8.6   **5.**—(1) For the purposes of section 140A(3)(b) of SSCBA, a woman is to be treated as being in Great Britain if she is a Crown servant posted overseas.

(2) A Crown servant posted overseas is a person performing overseas (but not in Northern Ireland) the duties of any office or employment under the Crown who—

(a) immediately prior to her posting or her first of consecutive postings, was ordinarily resident in the United Kingdom; or

(b) immediately prior to her posting or her first of consecutive postings, was in the United Kingdom in connection with that posting.

Partners of Crown servants posted overseas

8.7   **6.**—(1) The partner of a Crown servant posted overseas will be treated as being in Great Britain if, at the time of her claim—

(a) she is in the country where the Crown servant is posted; and

(b) she is accompanying the Crown servant.

(2) In paragraph (1) "partner" has the meaning in the Health in Pregnancy (Administration) Regulations 2008.

Daughters of Crown servants posted overseas

8.8   **7.** A daughter of a Crown servant posted overseas will be treated as being in Great Britain if, at the time of her claim—

(a) she is in the country where the Crown servant is posted;

(b) she is accompanying the Crown servant; and

(c) child benefit is being paid in respect of her.

Regulations 8 and 9 omitted.   **8.9**

Amount of Health in Pregnancy Grant

10. The amount of health in pregnancy grant shall be £190.   **8.10**

GENERAL NOTE

See commentary on ss.140A and 140B of the Social Security Contributions and   **8.11**
Benefits Act 1992 as inserted by Part 4 of the Health and Social Care Act 2008.

PART IX

HMRC CODES OF PRACTICE AND GUIDANCE

NOTE

HMRC publishes manuals, guides and forms dealing with all parts of the law under its management. HMRC policy is to publish a full series of leaflets about tax credits, together with all the forms of use to claimants and those representing them, on the HMRC website. See: http://www.hmrc. gov.uk/taxcredits/forms-and-leaflets/leaflets.htm.

All the guides are official publications. But none in this field carry the force of law. Nonetheless some of them are particularly important as they set out the terms on which HMRC exercises discretions (for example as to overpayments and penalties). They also detail the administrative procedures and standards that HMRC sets itself. The key guides to the way in which HMRC deals with overpayments and penalties are set out in this volume. They are marked in bold in the following list of leaflets:

WTC1	Child Tax Credit and Working Tax Credit. An introduction (reissued June 2008)
WTC2	Child Tax Credit and Working Tax Credit—a guide (reissued April 2009)
WTC5	Help with the costs of childcare—information for parents and childcare providers (reissued October 2008)
WTC6	Child Tax Credit and Working Tax Credit Other types of help you may be able to get (reissued April 2008)
WTC7	**Tax Credits penalties** **What happens at the end of a check** **(reissued April 2009)**
WTC/AP	Child Tax Credit and Working Tax Credit: how to appeal against a tax credit decision or award (October 2004)
WTC/FS1	Tax credits enquiry (reissued April 2009)
WTC/FS2	Tax credits examinations (reissued March 2009)
WTC/FS3	Tax credits formal request for information (May 2006)
WTC/FS4	Tax credits meetings (May 2006)
COP26	**Code of Practice 26: What happens if we have paid you too much tax credit?** (reissued April 2008)

The following leaflets have been withdrawn from current use and are archived on the HMRC site: WTC3, WTC4, COP23 (Child Tax Credit and Working Tax Credit local office examination), COP27 (Child Tax Credit and Working Tax Credit local office enquiries).

The key standard forms are available to download from the site above. They are:

TC600	Tax Credits claim form
TC602	Checking a tax credits award
TC603R	Tax Credits renewal pack
TC603RD	Tax Credits renewal and annual declaration
TC689	Authority for intermediary to act
TC846	Request to reconsider recovery of overpaid tax credits

The standard manuals issued to staff are:

CCM	New Tax Credits Claimant Compliance Manual
NTC Manual	Clerical procedures
TCTM	Tax Credits Technical Manual

All are available on the site above (although some paragraphs are withheld under the Freedom of Information Act exemptions).

LEAFLET WTC 7

TAX CREDITS PENALTIES

WHAT HAPPENS AT THE END OF A CHECK
(REISSUED APRIL 2009)

This leaflet tells you about the penalties you may get if your claim for tax credits is not correct. It also explains how to appeal against those penalties.

Introduction

When you make a claim for Child Tax Credit or Working Tax Credit you are responsible for making sure that the information on your claim form is correct.   9.1

This leaflet is for anyone who we may charge a penalty after we have carried out a check on their tax credits claim. It does not tell you everything about penalties, but it does tell you what is likely to happen and what you can do if we charge you a penalty.

Information about how and why we carry out tax credits checks is in factsheets WTC/FS1 and WTC/FS2. We normally give these to customers when we start a check. They are also available at
www.hmrc.gov.uk/leaflets/credit.htm

Why do we charge penalties?

We charge penalties to: 9.2

- encourage people to be careful and make sure their

- claims are correct

- stop customers from giving us incorrect information, and

- penalise people who try to defraud the system.

Your penalty

You may have to pay a penalty if: 9.3

- we find that you have not told us about a change in your circumstances that you are required to tell us about, or

- you have given us incorrect information about your tax credits claim and you did not take reasonable care to give us correct information.

Not telling us about a change in circumstances

If you do not tell us about the following changes in your circumstances we can charge you a maximum penalty of up to £300.   9.4

Your relationship changes:

837

- you marry or become a civil partner or part of a couple who live together as husband and wife or as civil partners

- you stop being part of a married couple, civil partnership or a couple living together as husband and wife or as civil partners.

Your childcare changes:

- your average weekly childcare costs go down by £10 a week or more for four weeks in a row

- you stop paying childcare costs.

Your work changes:

- your usual working hours change so that you now work

  — less than 16 hours a week, or – less than 30 hours a week (for couples with

  — children it is your joint working hours that count towards the 30 hours)

- you have been laid off (see page 5)

- you have been on strike for more than 10 days

- you stop work.

Your family changes:

- a child or young person you are responsible for leaves the family and moves to live with someone else. This includes a child who has been

  — taken into care or fostered to another family

  — found guilty by a court and sentenced to custody or detention for a period of four months or more

- a child or young person you are responsible for stops qualifying for support, for example they

  — leave full-time non-advanced education or approved training before they reach 20

  — start to have their training provided under a contract of employment

  — stop being registered with a careers service, the Connexions Service or equivalent

  — start to claim Income Support, Incapacity Benefit, Jobseeker's Allowance, Employment and Support Allowance or tax credits in their own right

- a child or young person you are responsible for dies

- you or your partner leave the country for more than eight weeks. This is extended to 12 weeks if you go, or stay abroad because you, or a member of your family, is ill or has died.

Usually it will be obvious when there has been a change, and you must tell us **within one month** of the date the change happened.

For example, you change your job on 8 May 2009 and instead of working 35 hours a week you now work 25 hours a week. You must tell us about this by 8 June 2009.

Sometimes it might not be clear exactly when there has been a change, so you must tell us **within one month** of the date when you realised a change has happened.

Example: change in circumstances

For example, the exact number of hours you work each week varies as you often work overtime as well as your standard hours of 26 hours a week. Most weeks you work more than four hours overtime so your usual hours are more than 30 hours a week. However, the amount of overtime available varies and you do not always work all the overtime available. On 7 September 2009 when looking back you realise that your usual hours are now less than 30 hours a week and have been since 18 August 2009. You must tell us about this by 7 October 2009.   **9.5**

Week starting Monday	Overtime offered	Overtime worked	Actual hours worked	Usual hours
16/6	14	14	40	30+
23/6	10	10	36	30+
30/6	6	4	30	30+
7/7	1	1	27	30+
14/7	10	10	36	30+
21/7	3	3	29	30+
28/7	14	14	40	30+
4/8	0	0	26	30+
11/8	4	4	30	30+
18/8	2	2	28	16–30
25/8	0	0	20.8*	16–30
1/9	1	1	27	16–30

* Didn't work the bank holiday

If you are laid off

You must tell us within one month if your employer lays you off. You will still get Working Tax Credit for four weeks after the date this happens.   **9.6**

If your employer lays you off but expects you to go back to work

For Working Tax Credit you are still working for up to four weeks from the date your employer lays you off. After that, you are treated as if you have stopped work. This means that you can get Working Tax Credit for four more weeks – eight weeks in total.   **9.7**

Example 1

John Smith is laid off on 8 January 2009. He will still get Working Tax Credit up to 5 March 2009.

If your employer lays you off but cannot tell you if you will go back to work or lose your job

9.8   If during the first four weeks you are laid off your employer tells you that you are now laid off indefinitely or you have lost your job, you will be treated as if you have stopped work from the date your employer tells you. You will still get Working Tax Credit for four more weeks from that date.

Example 2

Anne Jones is laid off on 8 January 2009 and her employer tells her that she can expect to go back to work on 1 February 2009. On 26 January, her employer tells her that they don't know if she will be able to go back to work at all. Anne will still get Working Tax Credit up to 23 February 2009 (four weeks from 26 January 2009).

Reasonable excuse

9.9   We will not charge you a penalty if you have a reasonable excuse for not telling us about a change in your circumstances.

What is a reasonable excuse?

9.10   A reasonable excuse might be that:

- you had a serious illness that stopped you giving us the information
- we received your notification late because of an unexpected postal dispute.

A reasonable excuse is not that you:

- have been too busy to tell us about a change in circumstances
- did not know you had to tell us about a change in circumstances.

Please tell us if you think you have a reasonable excuse and we will consider what you say.

Whether your excuse is reasonable or not is a matter of law. If we do not agree that your excuse is reasonable you can ask the Tribunal Service to decide (see 'Your rights' on page 11).

Giving us incorrect information

9.11   We can charge you a penalty of up to £3,000 if you:

- have not taken reasonable care to make sure any information you gave us was correct, or
- have given us information which you knew was incorrect.

This includes the information you give:

- in your claim
- on any notification of a change in circumstances
- in response to a particular request for information during our checks.

We calculate penalties as a percentage of the tax credits you have over-claimed as a result of the incorrect claim. The percentage increases depending on the behaviour which led to the error.

We will explain why we believe that you have not taken reasonable care or have deliberately given us incorrect information. If you do not accept our explanation you can ask the Tribunal Service to decide (see 'Your rights' on page 11).

What is 'taking reasonable care'?

We will not charge a penalty if you have taken reasonable care to give us the correct information, even if you make a mistake which results in you claiming too much tax credits.

A careful person would:

- make a complete and correct claim to the best of their knowledge and belief

- read the notes supplied with the claim that relate to their own circumstances

- ask for help if they are unable to cope with the claim or declaration themselves.

'Taking reasonable care' can be different for different people depending on their individual circumstances. We will consider how a careful person would act in **your** circumstances. We will consider your ability to give us correct information, taking into account factors such as your:

- experience in dealing with tax credits or financial matters

- access to support, guidance or advice

- health and well-being, including the impact of a disability.

The Claimant Compliance Manual contains examples of what is taking reasonable care. You can find it online at
www.hmrc.gov.uk/manuals/ccmmanual/index.htm

If you are careless in the way you deal with your claim for tax credits then you are likely to be charged a penalty.

We accept that you have taken reasonable care if you have followed advice from the Tax Credit Helpline or an Enquiry Centre, or from another reliable source such as Jobcentre Plus or the Citizens Advice.

Couples

If you have made a joint claim with your partner, you are both responsible for the information you provide in your claim.

We will charge you a penalty as a couple where:

- either of you could have told us about any change in circumstances, or

- you were both responsible for giving us incorrect information.

If the incorrect information relates to one partner – and the other person could not have reasonably known that it was not correct – we will only charge the penalty on that partner.

The maximum penalty for a joint claim is no more than the maximum penalty for an individual claim.

9.12

9.13

The amount of your penalty

9.14   When working out the amount of your penalty, we will take into account:

- the amount of tax credits over-claimed
- the behaviour that led to the over-claim
- if you have told us of any errors you think you have made before we begin a tax credits check.

The level of the penalty depends on the behaviour that led to you claiming too much tax credits – such as how careful you were in making your claim or whether it was a deliberate attempt to get money you were not entitled to. The penalty levels are:

- mistake or misunderstanding – no penalty
- failure to take reasonable care – penalty of 15% of over-claimed tax credits
- serious or deliberate errors – penalty of 25% of over-claimed tax credits
- deliberate and systematic over-claims – penalty of 50% of over-claimed tax credits.

If you repeat errors you have made before, or continue to make a number of errors, we may charge you a higher penalty.

Your penalty will be reduced if you tell us about any errors you think you have made **before** we begin a tax credits check. We will:

- not charge you a penalty for 'failure to take reasonable care'
- halve your penalty for 'serious or deliberate errors' and 'deliberate and systematic over-claims'.

If you do not understand our explanation of the penalty, you can ask us to put it in writing so that you can seek independent advice.

Interest

9.15   We may charge you interest if we have overpaid tax credits because you failed to take reasonable care. We also charge interest on any penalties that you pay late.

Paying your penalty

9.16   We will contact you if we think that you have become liable to a penalty. We can do this:

- by phone
- in a meeting, or
- in writing.

We will explain why we are charging you a penalty and tell you both the maximum amount chargeable and the amount of the penalty we propose to charge. We are always willing to discuss with you the amount of the penalty and the reasons for it.

If you accept the amount of the penalty

We will discuss the arrangements for payment covering: 9.17

- any overpaid tax credits
- any interest due, and
- the penalty.

We will ask you to enter into an agreement to pay either in a lump sum or by instalments.

Arranging payment

Once we have agreed the arrangements we will ask you to sign a letter 9.18
that sets out the:

- total amount you have to pay
- final date for payment, or the number of instalments and when they are due.

We will send you a final letter accepting the arrangement. This exchange of letters is a legally binding contract. If you refuse to pay, we will take legal action to recover any money you owe.

If you disagree with the penalty or how it should be paid

You should tell us. We will listen to what you have to say. If we cannot 9.19
agree, we will send you a penalty notice so that you can appeal or appoint a representative to appeal for you.

Co-operation

The extent to which you co-operate and give us information is entirely 9.20
up to you. You should remember that if you tell us of errors you think you have made before we start a tax credits check you will be charged no penalty or a reduced penalty.

If you are not sure whether to give us the information, or if you are reluctant to co-operate, we suggest you get independent advice before deciding what to do. We may decide to reduce or stop your current tax credits payments based on the information we hold.

A number of independent organisations offer help with tax credits, such as the Citizens Advice. You will find them in *The Phone Book*.

Your rights

You have the right to appeal if we: 9.21

- ask you to pay penalties or interest, or
- change your award.

You can get more information about how to appeal by going online at www.hmrc.gov.uk/leaflets/wtc_ap.htm or by visiting any Enquiry Centre.

We will not treat your right of appeal as non co-operation.

Tribunals Service

9.22   If we do not agree with your appeal we will send your claim to the independent Tribunals Service. They will listen to both of us and decide whether you will have to pay the penalty and how much you will have to pay.

Further information

9.23   You may find useful the Frequently Asked Questions on our website at www.hmrc.gov.uk/taxcredits/exams-enqs.htm
The Claimant Compliance Manual contains more details about our work in this area. You can find it online at
www.hmrc.gov.uk/manuals/ccmmanual/index.htm

Customer Service

HM Revenue & Customs commitment

9.24   We aim to provide a high quality service with guidance that is simple, clear and accurate.
We will:

• be professional and helpful

• act with integrity and fairness, and

• treat your affairs in strict confidence within the law.

We aim to handle your affairs promptly and accurately so that you receive or pay only the right amount due.

Putting things right

9.25   If you are not satisfied with our service, please let the person dealing with your affairs know what is wrong. We will work as quickly as possible to put things right and settle your complaint.
If you are still unhappy, ask for your complaint to be referred to the Complaints Manager.

Customers with particular needs

9.26   We offer a range of facilities for customers with particular needs, including:

• wheelchair access to nearly all HMRC Enquiry Centres

• help with filling in forms

• for people with hearing difficulties

— RNID Typetalk

— Induction loops.

We can also arrange additional support, such as:

• home visits, if you have limited mobility or caring responsibilities and cannot get to one of our Enquiry Centres

• services of an interpreter

- sign language interpretation
- leaflets in large print, Braille and audio.

For complete details please:

- go online at www.hmrc.gov.uk/enq, or

- contact us. You will find us in *The Phone Book* under HM Revenue & Customs.

WHAT HAPPENS IF WE HAVE PAID YOU TOO MUCH TAX CREDIT?

Note from editors:
This is the text of COP 26 published in April 2008 after extensive consultation. It differs in several ways from the previous version of the COP. HMRC has indicated that this version applies to any new dispute after January 2008. The previous version (see previous editions of this work) continues to apply to disputes started before then.

Introduction

9.27   An overpayment means we've paid you more money than you're entitled to. Please phone the Tax Credits Helpline if you:

- aren't sure whether we are right when we say you've been overpaid

- have a query about your tax credit claim or whether you can claim

- don't know what to do about any letter, or award notice we've sent you.

Tax credits depend on your income and your family circumstances. When your income or family circumstances change then your entitlement or the amount we pay you may change.

We pay you tax credits for a year—from 6 April to 5 April. Initially we work out how much to pay you from what you tell us about your previous year's income and your family's circumstances now.

After 5 April each year, we send you a renewal pack which asks you to:

- check the information we hold about you

- tell us how much income you had in the year.

You should try to complete and return your renewal form as quickly as possible. We'll then work out the actual amount due to you for the year that has just ended and also the amount for the year that started on 6 April.

An overpayment happens if:

- you don't give us the right information either when you claim or when you renew your claim at the end of the year

- you're late telling us about a change in your circumstances

- your income is £25,000 more than it was in the previous year

- you give us wrong information when you tell us about a change in your circumstances or income

- we make a mistake when we record the information you give us

- we don't act on information you give us.

You should keep us up-to-date with any changes in your income and your family circumstances. The law says that you must tell us about certain changes **within one month** of them happening.

You should use the checklist that we sent with your award notice to check what changes you need to tell us about, a copy of the checklist is included with this leaflet, and if you're still not sure please phone our Helpline.

After you tell us about a change we'll work out the new amount of tax credit payments you're due and send you a new award notice.

Our responsibilities and yours

To help get your award right and avoid an overpayment it's important that we meet our responsibilities and you meet yours.

9.28

Our responsibilities are:

- **When you contact us for information we should** give you the correct advice based on the information you give us. We'll offer you support, for example, if you want us to explain your award notice to you, we'll talk you through it in detail.

- **When you make or renew your claim we should** accurately record and use the information you give us to work out your tax credits and pay you the correct amount.

- **When we send you an award notice we should** include information you've given us about your family and your income. If you tell us that there is a mistake or something missing on your award notice, we'll put it right and send you a corrected award notice.

- **When you contact us to tell us about a change of circumstance we should** accurately record what you've told us and send you a new award notice within 30 days. The 30 days doesn't start until we get all of the information we need from you to make the change. It is therefore important that you give us all of the information when you tell us about a change.

Your responsibilities:

- **When you make or renew your claim you should** give us accurate, complete and up-to-date information.

- **You should tell us about any change of circumstance throughout the year** so we have accurate and up-to-date information. The law says you must tell us about certain changes **within one month** of them happening—you should use the checklist we sent with your award notice to check what the changes are, a copy of the checklist is included with this leaflet. To reduce the chance of getting an overpayment, we recommend that you tell us about any changes in income as soon as possible.

- **Each time you get an award notice you should** use the checklist we sent with it, a copy of the checklist is included with this leaflet. You should check all the items listed and tell us if anything is wrong, missing or incomplete. You must tell us about some changes **within one month** of them happening—these are listed on the back of the checklist. The main details we expect you to check are:

  — whether the award is for you as an individual or as part of a couple

  — the hours you work

— whether you get Income Support or income-based Jobseeker's Allowance or Pension Credit

— whether you, or anyone in your household, has a disability element

— the number and age of any children in your household

— childcare costs

— your total household income for the period shown on the award notice.

We'll send you a corrected award notice when you tell us if anything is wrong, missing or incomplete. **If you don't get an award notice within one month of telling us about a change in circumstance please phone our Helpline as soon as possible**.

- **After you get any award notice you should** check that the payments you get from us every week or every four weeks match the amount we said you should get on the award notice. We expect you to tell us if you got any payments that didn't match what was shown on the award notices during the period an overpayment arose.

- **If you spot a mistake on your award notice you should** tell us **within one month** of getting your award notice. Please make a note of when you got your award notice and when you told us about the mistake. We may ask you for this information to show that you acted **within one month**.

If you don't understand any award notice please phone our Helpline.

If we fail to meet our responsibilities, but you meet **all** of yours, we won't ask you to pay back all of an overpayment caused by our failure.

However—you must tell us about any mistakes on your award notice within one month of getting your award notice. If you do, then you won't be responsible for an overpayment caused by our mistake. If you tell us about a mistake **more than one month** after getting your award notice we may ask you to pay back an overpayment until the time you contact us.

Example 1
On 1 September you tell us about a change in your circumstances but we don't change your award until 16 October. We won't collect back any overpayment that arises **after** 30 September.

Example 2
On 12 August you tell us about a change in your income. We send you a new award notice which you get on 19 August, but we haven't correctly recorded the information you gave us. If you spot and tell us about the mistake by 18 September (30 days from 19 August) we won't collect any overpayment caused by our mistake.

Example 3
On 12 August you tell us about a change in your income. We send you a new award notice which you get on 19 August but we haven't correctly recorded the information you gave us. If you spot this and don't tell us

about the mistake until 27 September (38 days from 19 August) you may be responsible for the overpayment up until the date you contacted us. **Whenever you tell us about a mistake we won't collect an overpayment that may build up if we fail to correct our mistake from this time.**

If you fail to meet your responsibilities, but we meet **all** of ours, we'll normally ask you to pay back all of an overpayment. For example if you tell us about a mistake on your award notice **more than one month** after getting it, then you may have to pay back an overpayment which has built up until the time you contact us.

If we both fail to meet one or more of our responsibilities, we'll look at the circumstances of your case and may write off parts of an overpayment.

We ask you to tell us about any mistakes we've made **within one month** of you getting your award notice. If you don't tell us **within one month**, we'll ask you to pay back an overpayment up to the date you told us. **We won't ask you to pay back an overpayment, which is caused by our mistake, after the date you told us**.

However, we understand that exceptional circumstances may mean that it wasn't possible for you to meet your responsibilities on time. For example, you or a close family member may have been seriously ill when you got your award notice and you couldn't tell us about our mistake **within one month** of getting your award notice. Please phone our Helpline, if you think this applies to you, or if you're not sure whether we've made a mistake.

If you don't understand why there is an overpayment If you don't understand why there is an overpayment, please phone our Helpline. We can give you an explanation over the phone or in writing.

Challenging the recovery of an overpayment

There are two main ways of challenging an overpayment. You can dispute the recovery of an overpayment, or you can appeal if you don't think the level of your award was correct.

9.29

If you don't agree that we should ask you to pay back an overpayment you can ask us to look at this again. We call this **disputing** an overpayment. To do this, we recommend you fill in form *Tax credits overpayments* (TC846), available from our Helpline. You may write to us instead, but you'll need to give us all your details, and tell us why you think you shouldn't have to pay back an overpayment.

When we get your dispute we'll write to you telling you that we've stopped collecting an overpayment while we consider whether you must pay it back.

If you dispute an overpayment, we'll check whether you met your responsibilities and we met ours.

We'll check:

- that we accurately recorded and acted on any information you gave us **within one month** of you telling us about a change of circumstance

- that we accurately calculated and paid you your correct entitlement

- that the information we included on your award notice was accurate at the date of the notice

- what you told us if you contacted us, and whether the advice we gave you based on that information was correct. We'll also check whether you contacted us to discuss any queries on your award notice, and whether we answered them.

We'll also check:

- that you gave us accurate and up-to-date information when you claimed tax credits
- that you told us about any changes of circumstance at the right time (in the timescales listed on the checklist)
- that you checked your award notice **within one month** of getting it and checked that the payments you got matched the amounts on the award notice
- that you checked your award notice **within one month** of getting it, and if and when you told us about any mistakes
- whether you told us of any exceptional circumstances that meant you couldn't tell us about a change of circumstance or about our mistake **within one month**.

Once we've checked whether we've met our responsibilities and you've met yours we'll decide whether an overpayment should be paid back.

We'll decide whether you must pay back all or only part of an over-payment. We'll give you our decision, along with our reasons, usually in writing.

We may not ask you to pay back an overpayment if you contacted us to tell us your difficult personal circumstances meant you couldn't check your award notice or bank payments. For example, a member of your family may be seriously injured in a car crash. If this is the case please phone our Helpline as soon as possible.

If you're still unhappy that we've decided to continue collecting an over-payment and this is because you've **new** information to give us, please write to us as soon as possible, see page 12. We'll stop collecting an overpayment while we review the **new** information.

We may also review your case if you feel we haven't considered information you've previously given us. However we won't stop collecting an over-payment whilst we do this.

If you don't have any new information to give us, but you're still unhappy with our decision, you may wish to contact a professional adviser or an organization like Citizens Advice to consider what options are open to you, including any through the courts.

If you're not happy with our service please see "Putting things right" on page 12.

Whilst you can't appeal against our decision to recover an overpayment, you can appeal against your tax credit award if you're not happy with our decision about the **amount** of an overpayment.

You can also appeal against any penalty we've imposed in connection with your tax credits claim.

We'll always tell you if you've a right of appeal on the notice that sets out our decision.

For more information about making an appeal, please see our leaflet *How to appeal against a tax credits decision or award (WTC/AP)*. You can get a copy:

- online at **www.hmrc.gov.uk**

- from any HMRC office or Enquiry Centre.

Paying back an overpayment

We can collect back an overpayment from you in two ways. We can reduce the payments you get from an ongoing award, or ask you to make direct payments to us. In some cases we may ask you to do both.

9.30

If you're still getting tax credit payments as the same household for which an overpayment arose, we'll automatically reduce your payments to recover an overpayment from an ongoing award. How much we reduce your payments by will depend on how much you're getting. We reduce awards at different levels, please see the table below.

Your tax credit award	The most we'll take back
If you're getting the maximum tax credits with no reduction due to income	10%
If you're only getting the family element of Child Tax Credit	100%
All other awards—for example, those entitled to Child Tax Credit above the family element, or Working Tax Credit below the maximum	25%

If you want help understanding which recovery rate applies to you, please phone our Helpline.

If you feel that you can't meet your essential living expenses because we've reduced your payments please see 'If you can't pay your essential living expenses' on page 10.

If you're no longer entitled to tax credits, we'll ask you to make a direct payment to us. Or, if your tax credit award has ended (this might happen if there is a change in your household for example, you were single and now you're in a couple) then we'll ask you to make a direct payment to us. We'll do this even if you're getting another award of tax credits for a new household you're part of.

This may happen if you've an overpayment from an old award which ended and you've an overpayment from a current award. For example, you and your partner separate and you then made another claim as a single person or in a new couple. We could ask you to pay back an overpayment from your current award as well as a direct payment from your previous award.

If we've asked you to pay back an overpayment directly from a previous award but you need more time to pay it back, please phone our Payment Helpline on **0845 302 1429** as soon as possible. We can arrange for you to pay it back in equal installments over 12 months.

If you need more than 12 months, please tell us when you phone. We'll want to know:

- your family circumstances, in particular anyone chronically ill or disabled
- your income now and in the future
- your living expenses (for example, rent, council tax, gas or electricity bills)
- your savings, investments and other assets
- your other debts (for example, mortgage repayments)
- how long it will take you to pay back an overpayment
- whether you're paying backing a previous overpayment or have recently repaid one.

If you need to discuss financial hardship with us, but exceptional circumstances such as a family crisis, mean that you don't have time to give us the full details, please try and give us a quick call to explain this. We'll put the recovery on hold until you can discuss your situation in detail.

When you phone we may ask you about any family circumstances that may lead to extra living costs. For example if you're looking after someone who is chronically ill or disabled. In some exceptional circumstances, we may write off an overpayment altogether.

We can tell you more about the different direct payment options if you phone our Helpline.

If

- you're paying back an overpayment directly, or
- we've reduced your ongoing payments so you can pay back an overpayment, or
- we've asked you to pay back an overpayment, and
- you can't pay for your essential living expenses such as your rent, gas, or electricity please phone our Helpline.

We'll ask you about your circumstances in detail. Please see "Asking for more time to pay back a direct payment" on page 9.

Whether you are repaying your overpayment from a reduction in your tax credit payments or through a direct payment, we may offer you an option for extending the period over which you pay back the overpayment by reducing the amount being recovered each month or stop recovery in exceptional circumstances. If we do reduce the amount, it will take you longer to pay off an overpayment.

In exceptional circumstances, we may write off an overpayment altogether.

If you and your partner separate, your joint claim will end. We'll work out if you've been overpaid. If you have, we'll write to you both, usually at the end of the tax year to:

- tell you how much we've overpaid you by
- ask you to contact us to arrange to pay back the money.

We'll usually ask each of you to pay 50% by direct payment, within 30 days. Or, you can both agree to pay different amounts. For example, one of you can agree to pay 30% and the other 70%. However, if your agreement fails we'll ask you to pay 50%.

We'll make every effort to contact you both, but if we cannot contact one of you, we may ask the person we can contact to pay the whole amount. This is because by law we are able to recover the whole overpayment from both of you or one of you alone. However, we will only ask you to pay the whole amount after making every possible attempt to contact your ex-partner and failing to do so.

If you feel that you can't pay back the full amount please phone our Helpline. We may be able to arrange for you to pay less, or in exceptional circumstances write off the overpayment.

You can make a new claim as a single person or with a new partner. To make a claim please phone our Helpline. However, we can't reduce your payments from your new claim to collect back an overpayment from an earlier claim. You must pay for a previous overpayment directly.

Contact us

When you contact us please tell us:

9.31

- your full name
- your National Insurance number
- a daytime telephone number.

By phone:

- Tax Credits Helpline on **0845 300 3900**. Open from 8.00am to 8.00pm seven days a week. Textphone **0845 300 3909**
- if you prefer to speak in Welsh **0845 302 1489**
- from abroad if you can't get through on the Helpline, please phone **00 44 289 0808 316**

In person:

- visit any HMRC office or Enquiry Centre—you may need to make an appointment to see an adviser.

In writing: Write to us at the

- address shown on your award notice, or
- Tax Credit Office

  Preston

  PR1 0SB.

Customer Service

We aim to provide a high quality service with guidance that is simple, clear and accurate.

9.32

We'll:

- be professional and helpful

853

- act with integrity and fairness, and

- treat your affairs in strict confidence within the law.

We aim to handle your affairs promptly and accurately so that you get or pay only the right amount due.

If you're not satisfied with our service, please let the person dealing with your affairs know what is wrong. We'll work as quickly as possible to put things right and settle your complaint.

If you're still unhappy, ask for your complaint to be referred to the Complaints Manager.

If you've exhausted HM Revenue & Customs complaints procedures and are still unhappy, you may wish to take your case to the Adjudicator or Parliamentary Ombudsman. For more information please see our factsheet *Complaints and putting things right* (C/FS). You can get a copy

- online at **www.hmrc.gov.uk**

- from any Enquiry Centre.

We offer a range of facilities for customers with particular needs, including:

- wheelchair access to nearly all HMRC Enquiry Centres

- help with filling in forms

- for people with hearing difficulties

  — BT Typetalk

  — Induction loops.

We can also arrange additional support, such as:

- home visits, if you've limited mobility or caring responsibilities and cannot get to one of our Enquiry Centres

- services of an interpreter

- sign language interpretation

- leaflets in large print, Braille and audio.

For complete details please:

- contact your nearest Enquiry Centre

- contact us. You'll find us in *The Phone Book* under HM Revenue & Customs.

INDEX

LEGAL TAXONOMY
FROM SWEET & MAXWELL

This index has been prepared using Sweet and Maxwell's Legal Taxonomy. Main index entries conform to keywords provided by the Legal Taxonomy except where references to specific documents or non-standard terms (denoted by quotation marks) have been included. These keywords provide a means of identifying similar concepts in other Sweet & Maxwell publications and online services to which keywords from the Legal Taxonomy have been applied. Readers may find some minor differences between terms used in the text and those which appear in the index. Suggestions to *sweetandmaxwell.taxonomy@thomson.com*.

(All references are to paragraph number)

50-plus element
working tax credit, 2.83–2.84
Accounting date
trading income, 1.637
Administration
See **Administrative requirements**
Administrative requirements (statutory
  adoption pay)
adoption from overseas, 6.103–6.107
determination of entitlement issues
  application, 6.30
  form of application, 6.31
employers' records
  generally, 6.26
  inspection, 6.27
funding of liabilities
  application to Revenue, 6.21
  date of payment of contributions, 6.24
  generally, 6.20
  method, 6.22–6.23
  overpayments, 6.25
  provision of information, 6.32
**Administrative requirements (statutory
  maternity pay)**
employer's records
  maintenance, 5.45
  production, 5.46
expected week of confinement, 5.39
notice of absence from work, 5.40
notification of employment after
  confinement, 5.41
provision of information
  claims for other benefits, 5.44
  determination of questions, 5.42–5.43
**Administrative requirements (statutory
  paternity pay)**
adoption from overseas, 6.103–6.107
determination of entitlement issues
  application, 6.30
  form of application, 6.31
employers' records
  generally, 6.26

inspection, 6.27
funding of liabilities
  application to Revenue, 6.21
  date of payment of contributions, 6.24
  generally, 6.20
  method, 6.22–6.23
  overpayments, 6.25
  provision of information, 6.32
**Administrative requirements (tax
  credits)**
definitions, 2.366
general note, 2.364
forwarding of claims, 2.369
holding of claims, 2.369
provision of information
  by authorities, 2.368
  to authorities, 2.367
recording of claims, 2.369
statutory provision, 1.338–1.339
Adopted children
child benefit
  Regulations, 3.21
  statutory basis, 1.149–1.150
guardian's allowance, 3.66
Adopters
annual payments, 1.691
Adoption
statutory paternity pay
  See also **Statutory paternity pay**
  conditions of entitlement, 6.57–6.58
  evidence of entitlement, 6.62
  notice requirements, 6.60
  payment period, 6.59
  qualifying period, 6.61
  statutory provisions, 1.108–1.109
  treatment of more than one employer,
    6.63
working tax credit, 2.40–2.43
Adoption from overseas
and **Overseas adoption**
Adoption pay
See **Statutory adoption pay**

855

Index

897

general note, 2.443
modification of Regulations,
 2.448–2.454
modification of TCA 2002, 2.447
statutory provision, 1.326–1.327
provision of information
 authorities, by, 2.368
 authorities, to, 2.367
 functions relating to employment,
  2.462, 2.474
 functions relating to health,
  2.439–2.441, 2.458, 2.472
 functions relating to training, 2.462,
  2.474
qualifying remunerative work
 excepted activities, 2.38
 generally, 2.28–2.34
 hours worked, 2.39
 minimum level of continuity, 2.36
 remunerative work, 2.37
 routes to entitlement, 2.35
qualifying young persons
 childcare element, 2.76
 death, 2.85–2.86
rate, 1.265–1.266
recording of claims, 2.369
remunerative work, 2.37
residence requirements
 Crown servants posted overseas,
  2.426–2.428
 definitions, 2.414–2.415
 ordinary residence, 2.419–2.422
 person treated as not being in UK,
  2.416–2.423
 temporary absence from UK,
  2.424–2.425
routes to entitlement, 2.35
seasonal work, 2.46–2.47
second-adult element, 2.68–2.69
severe disability element, 2.81–2.82
sickness, 2.44–2.45
sports award, 2.42
statutory provisions
 See also **Tax credits**
 appeals, 1.314–1.319
 child tax credit, 1.249–1.254
 decisions, 1.267–1.289
 fraud, 1.308–1.311
 generally, 1.217–1.248
 interest, 1.312–1.313
 payment, 1.290–1.299
 penalties, 1.300–1.308
 rate, 1.265–1.266
 supplementary, 1.320–1.337
 working tax credit, 1.255–1.264

strike periods, 2.48–2.49
suspension from work, 2.50–2.51
term-time work, 2.46–2.47
30-hour element, 2.66–2.67
training allowance, 2.61
underpayments, 1.298–1.299
use of information, 1.340–1.341
verification of claims, 2.369
voluntary work, 2.38
working less than 16 hours a week,
 2.54–2.55
**Working Tax Credit (Entitlement and
 Maximum Rate) Regulations 2002**
arrangement of Regulations, 2.22
citation, 2.23
commencement, 2.23
definitions, 2.25
effect, 2.23–2.24
general note, 2.24
general provisions
 conditions of entitlement, 2.28–2.86
 elements of credit, 2.26–2.27
 maximum rate, 2.87–2.88
modifications to, 2.449
schedules
 disabilities, 2.89–2.101
 maximum rates, 2.102
**Working Tax Credit (Payment by
 Employers) Regulations 2002**
general note, 2.336
"Wounds pension"
pension income, 2.135
Young persons (child benefit)
care, in
 generally, 3.25
 statutory basis, 1.149–1.150
continuation of entitlement, 3.6
definition, 1.45
detention, in
 generally, 3.21–3.24
 statutory basis, 1.149–1.150
education and training condition, 3.4–3.5
extension period, 3.7
interruptions, 3.8–3.9
introduction, 3.3
living with another as a couple, where,
 3.16–3.17
other financial support, 3.12
person responsible for child, 3.13–3.15
prescribed conditions, 3.3–3.12
relevant relationship, in, 3.18
terminal dates, 3.10–3.11
youth training, in, 3.21–3.24
"Youth training schemes"
child benefit, 3.20–3.21